Fifth Workshop on Noisy User-generated Text (W-NUT 2019)

Hong Kong, China
4 November 2019

ISBN: 978-1-7138-0088-0

W-NUT 2019

The Fifth Workshop on
Noisy User-generated Text
(W-NUT 2019)

Proceedings of the Workshop

Nov 4, 2019
Hong Kong, China

Introduction

The W-NUT 2019 workshop focuses on a core set of natural language processing tasks on top of noisy user-generated text, such as that found on social media, web forums and online reviews. Recent years have seen a significant increase of interest in these areas. The internet has democratized content creation leading to an explosion of informal user-generated text, publicly available in electronic format, motivating the need for NLP on noisy text to enable new data analytics applications.

We received 89 long and short paper submissions this year. There are two invited speakers, Isabelle Augenstein (University of Copenhagen) and Jing Jiang (Singapore Management University) with each of their talks covering a different aspect of NLP for user-generated text. We have the best paper award(s) sponsored by Google this year, for which we are thankful. We would like to thank the Program Committee members who reviewed the papers this year. We would also like to thank the workshop participants.

Wei Xu, Alan Ritter, Tim Baldwin and Afshin Rahimi
Co-Organizers

Organizers:

Wei Xu, Ohio State University
Alan Ritter, Ohio State University
Tim Baldwin, University of Melbourne
Afshin Rahimi, University of Melbourne

Program Committee:

Mostafa Abdou (University of Copenhagen)
Muhammad Abdul-Mageed (University of British Columbia)
Željko Agić (Corti)
Gustavo Aguilar (University of Houston)
Hadi Amiri (Harvard University)
Rahul Aralikatte (University of Copenhagen)
Eiji Aramaki (NAIST)
Roy Bar-Haim (IBM)
Francesco Barbieri (UPF Barcelona)
Cosmin Bejan (Vanderbilt University)
Eric Bell (PNNL)
Adrian Benton (JHU)
Eduardo Blanco (University of North Texas)
Su Lin Blodgett (UMass Amherst)
Matko Bošnjak (University College London)
Julian Brooke (University of British Columbia)
Annabelle Carrell (JHU)
Xilun Chen (Cornell University)
Anne Cocos (University of Pennsylvania)
Arman Cohan (AI2)
Nigel Collier (University of Cambridge)
Paul Cook (University of New Brunswick)
Marina Danilevsky (IBM Research)
Leon Derczynski (IT University of Copenhagen)
Seza Doğruöz (Tilburg University)
Jay DeYoung (Northeastern University)
Eduard Dragut (Temple University)
Xinya Du (Cornell University)
Heba Elfardy (Amazon)
Micha Elsner (Ohio State University)
Sindhu Kiranmai Ernala (Georgia Tech)
Manaal Faruqui (Google Research)
Lisheng Fu (New York University)
Yoshinari Fujinuma (University of Colorado, Boulder)
Dan Garrette (Google Research)
Kevin Gimpel (TTIC)
Dan Goldwasser (Purdue University)
Amit Goyal (Criteo)
Nizar Habash (NYU Abu Dhabi)
Masato Hagiwara (Duolingo)

Bo Han (Kaplan)
Abe Handler (University of Massachusetts Amherst)
Shudong Hao (University of Colorado, Boulder)
Devamanyu Hazarika (National University of Singapore)
Jack Hessel (Cornell University)
Dirk Hovy (Bocconi University)
Xiaolei Huang (University of Colorado, Boulder)
Sarthak Jain (Northeastern University)
Kenny Joseph (University at Buffalo)
David Jurgens (University of Michigan)
Nobuhiro Kaji (Yahoo! Research)
Pallika Kanani (Oracle)
Dongyeop Kang (Carnegie Mellon University)
Emre Kiciman (Microsoft Research)
Svetlana Kiritchenko (National Research Council Canada)
Roman Klinger (University of Stuttgart)
Ekaterina Kochmar (University of Cambridge)
Vivek Kulkarni (University of California Santa Barbara)
Jonathan Kummerfeld (University of Michigan)
Ophélie Lacroix (Siteimprove)
Wuwei Lan (Ohio State University)
Chen Li (Tencent)
Jing Li (Tencent AI)
Jessy Junyi Li (University of Texas Austin)
Yitong Li (University of Melbourne)
Nut Limsopatham (University of Glasgow)
Patrick Littell (National Research Council Canada)
Zhiyuan Liu (Tsinghua University)
Fei Liu (University of Melbourne)
Nikola Ljubešić (University of Zagreb)
Wei-Yun Ma (Academia Sinica)
Mounica Maddela (Ohio State University)
Suraj Maharjan (University of Houston)
Aaron Masino (The Children's Hospital of Philadelphia)
Paul Michel (CMU)
Shachar Mirkin (Xerox Research)
Saif M. Mohammad (National Research Council Canada)
Ahmed Mourad (RMIT University)
Günter Neumann (DFKI)
Vincent Ng (University of Texas at Dallas)
Eric Nichols (Honda Research Institute)
Xing Niu (University of Maryland, College Park)
Benjamin Nye (Northeastern University)
Alice Oh (KAIST)
Naoki Otani (CMU)
Patrick Pantel (Microsoft Research)
Umashanthi Pavalanathan (Georgia Tech)
Yuval Pinter (Georgia Tech)
Barbara Plank (IT University of Copenhagen)
Christopher Potts (Stanford University)
Daniel Preoţiuc-Pietro (Bloomberg)

Chris Quirk (Microsoft Research)
Ella Rabinovich (University of Toronto)
Dianna Radpour (University of Colorado Boulder)
Preethi Raghavan (IBM Research)
Revanth Rameshkumar (Microsoft)
Sudha Rao (Microsoft Research)
Marek Rei (University of Cambridge)
Roi Reichart (Technion)
Adithya Renduchintala (JHU)
Carolyn Penstein Rose (CMU)
Alla Rozovskaya (City University of New York)
Koustuv Saha (Georgia Tech)
Keisuke Sakaguchi (Allen Institute for Artificial Intelligence)
Maarten Sap (University of Washington)
Natalie Schluter (IT University of Copenhagen)
Andrew Schwartz (Stony Brook University)
Djamé Seddah (University Paris-Sorbonne)
Amirreza Shirani (University of Houston)
Dan Simonson (BlackBoiler)
Evangelia Spiliopoulou (Carnegie Mellon University)
Jan Šnajder (University of Zagreb)
Gabriel Stanovsky (Allen Institute for Artificial Intelligence)
Ian Stewart (Georgia Tech)
Jeniya Tabassum (Ohio State University)
Joel Tetreault (Grammarly)
Sara Tonelli (FBK)
Rob van der Goot (University of Groningen)
Rob Voigt (Stanford University)
Byron Wallace (Northeastern University)
Xiaojun Wan (Peking University)
Zeerak Waseem (University of Sheffield)
Zhongyu Wei (Fudan University)
Diyi Yang (Georgia Tech)
Yi Yang (ASAPP)
Guido Zarrella (MITRE)
Justine Zhang (Cornell University)
Jason Shuo Zhang (University of Colorado, Boulder)
Shi Zong (Ohio State University)

Invited Speakers:

Isabelle Augenstein (University of Copenhagen)
Jing Jiang (Singapore Management University)

Table of Contents

xi

Conference Program

Monday, November, 4, 2019

9:00–9:05   **Opening**

9:05–9:50   **Invited Talk: Isabelle Augenstein**

9:50–10:35   **Oral Session I**

9:50–10:05   *Weakly Supervised Attention Networks for Fine-Grained Opinion Mining and Public Health*
Giannis Karamanolakis, Daniel Hsu and Luis Gravano

10:05–10:20   *Formality Style Transfer for Noisy, User-generated Conversations: Extracting Labeled, Parallel Data from Unlabeled Corpora*
Isak Czeresnia Etinger and Alan W Black

10:20–10:35   *Multilingual Whispers: Generating Paraphrases with Translation*
Christian Federmann, Oussama Elachqar and Chris Quirk

10:35–11:00   **Coffee Break**

11:00–12:15   **Oral Session II**

11:00–11:15   *Personalizing Grammatical Error Correction: Adaptation to Proficiency Level and L1*
Maria Nadejde and Joel Tetreault

11:15–11:30   *Exploiting BERT for End-to-End Aspect-based Sentiment Analysis*
Xin Li, Lidong Bing, Wenxuan Zhang and Wai Lam

11:30–11:45   *Training on Synthetic Noise Improves Robustness to Natural Noise in Machine Translation*
vladimir karpukhin, Omer Levy, Jacob Eisenstein and Marjan Ghazvininejad

11:45–12:00   *Character-Based Models for Adversarial Phone Extraction: Preventing Human Sex Trafficking*
Nathanael Chambers, Timothy Forman, Catherine Griswold, Kevin Lu, Yogaish Khastgir and Stephen Steckler

12:00–12:15   *Tkol, Httt, and r/radiohead: High Affinity Terms in Reddit Communities*
Abhinav Bhandari and Caitrin Armstrong

12:30–2:00   **Lunch**

2:00–3:00   **Lightning Talks**

Large Scale Question Paraphrase Retrieval with Smoothed Deep Metric Learning
Daniele Bonadiman, Anjishnu Kumar and Arpit Mittal

Hey Siri. Ok Google. Alexa: A topic modeling of user reviews for smart speakers
Hanh Nguyen and Dirk Hovy

Predicting Algorithm Classes for Programming Word Problems
vinayak athavale, aayush naik, rajas vanjape and Manish Shrivastava

Automatic identification of writers' intentions: Comparing different methods for predicting relationship goals in online dating profile texts
Chris van der Lee, Tess van der Zanden, Emiel Krahmer, Maria Mos and Alexander Schouten

Contextualized Word Representations from Distant Supervision with and for NER
Abbas Ghaddar and Phillippe Langlais

Extract, Transform and Filling: A Pipeline Model for Question Paraphrasing based on Template
Yunfan Gu, yang yuqiao and Zhongyu Wei

An In-depth Analysis of the Effect of Lexical Normalization on the Dependency Parsing of Social Media
Rob van der Goot

Who wrote this book? A challenge for e-commerce
Béranger Dumont, Simona Maggio, Ghiles Sidi Said and Quoc-Tien Au

Mining Tweets that refer to TV programs with Deep Neural Networks
Takeshi Kobayakawa, Taro Miyazaki, Hiroki Okamoto and Simon Clippingdale

3:00–4:30   **Poster Session (all papers above)**

4:30–4:55   **Coffee Break**

Monday, November, 4, 2019 (continued)

5:00–5:45   Invited Talk: Jing Jiang

5:45–6:00   **Closing and Best Paper Awards**

Weakly Supervised Attention Networks
for Fine-Grained Opinion Mining and Public Health

Giannis Karamanolakis, Daniel Hsu, Luis Gravano
Columbia University, New York, NY 10027, USA
{gkaraman, djhsu, gravano}@cs.columbia.edu

Abstract

In many review classification applications, a fine-grained analysis of the reviews is desirable, because different segments (e.g., sentences) of a review may focus on different aspects of the entity in question. However, training supervised models for segment-level classification requires segment labels, which may be more difficult or expensive to obtain than review labels. In this paper, we employ Multiple Instance Learning (MIL) and use only weak supervision in the form of a single label per review. First, we show that when inappropriate MIL aggregation functions are used, then MIL-based networks are outperformed by simpler baselines. Second, we propose a new aggregation function based on the sigmoid attention mechanism and show that our proposed model outperforms the state-of-the-art models for segment-level sentiment classification (by up to 9.8% in F1). Finally, we highlight the importance of fine-grained predictions in an important public-health application: finding actionable reports of foodborne illness. We show that our model achieves 48.6% higher recall compared to previous models, thus increasing the chance of identifying previously unknown foodborne outbreaks.

1 Introduction

Many applications of text review classification, such as sentiment analysis, can benefit from a fine-grained understanding of the reviews. Consider the Yelp restaurant review in Figure 1. Some segments (e.g., sentences or clauses) of the review express positive sentiment towards some of the items consumed, service, and ambience, but other segments express a negative sentiment towards the price and food. To capture the nuances expressed in such reviews, analyzing the reviews at the segment level is desirable.

In this paper, we focus on segment classification when only review labels—but not segment

Figure 1: A Yelp review discussing both positive and negative aspects of a restaurant, as well as food poisoning.

labels—are available. The lack of segment labels prevents the use of standard supervised learning approaches. While review labels, such as user-provided ratings, are often available, they are not directly relevant for segment classification, thus presenting a challenge for supervised learning.

Existing weakly supervised learning frameworks have been proposed for training models such as support vector machines (Andrews et al., 2003; Yessenalina et al., 2010; Gartner et al., 2002), logistic regression (Kotzias et al., 2015), and hidden conditional random fields (Täckström and McDonald, 2011). The most recent state-of-the-art approaches employ the Multiple Instance Learning (MIL) framework (Section 2.2) in hierarchical neural networks (Pappas and Popescu-Belis, 2014; Kotzias et al., 2015; Angelidis and Lapata, 2018; Pappas and Popescu-Belis, 2017; Ilse et al., 2018). MIL-based hierarchical networks combine the (unknown) segment labels through an aggregation function to form a single review label. This enables the use of ground-truth review labels as a weak form of supervision for training segment level classifiers. However, it remains unanswered whether performance gains in current models stem from the hierarchical structure of the models or from the representational power of their deep learning components. Also, as we will see, the current modeling choices for the MIL aggregation function might be problematic for some applications and, in turn, might hurt the performance of the resulting classifiers.

As a first contribution of this paper, we show that non-hierarchical, deep learning approaches for segment-level sentiment classification —with only review-level labels— are strong, and they equal or exceed in performance hierarchical networks with various MIL aggregation functions.

As a second contribution of this paper, we substantially improve previous hierarchical approaches for segment-level sentiment classification and propose the use of a new MIL aggregation function based on the sigmoid attention mechanism to jointly model the relative importance of each segment as a product of Bernoulli distributions. This modeling choice allows multiple segments to contribute with different weights to the review label, which is desirable in many applications, including segment-level sentiment classification. We demonstrate that our MIL approach outperforms all of the alternative techniques.

As a third contribution, we experiment beyond sentiment classification and apply our approach to a critical public health application: the discovery of foodborne illness incidents in online restaurant reviews. Restaurant patrons increasingly turn to social media—rather than official public health channels—to discuss food poisoning incidents (see Figure 1). As a result, public health authorities need to identify such rare incidents among the vast volumes of content on social media platforms. We experimentally show that our MIL-based network effectively detects segments discussing food poisoning and has a higher chance than all previous models to identify unknown foodborne outbreaks.

2 Background and Problem Definition

We now summarize relevant work on fully supervised (Section 2.1) and weakly supervised models (Section 2.2) for segment classification. We also describe a public health application for our model evaluation (Section 2.3). Finally, we define our problem of focus (Section 2.4).

2.1 Fully Supervised Models

State-of-the-art supervised learning methods for segment classification use segment embedding techniques followed by a classification model. During segment encoding, a segment $s_i = (x_{i1}, x_{i2}, \ldots, x_{iN_i})$ composed of N_i words is encoded as a fixed-size real vector $h_i \in \mathbb{R}^{\ell}$ using transformations such as the average of word embeddings (Wieting et al., 2015; Arora et al., 2017), Recurrent Neural Networks (RNNs) (Wieting and Gimpel, 2017; Yang et al., 2016), Convolutional Neural Networks (CNNs) (Kim, 2014), or self-attention blocks (Devlin et al., 2019; Radford et al., 2018). We refer to the whole segment encoding procedure as $h_i = \text{ENC}(s_i)$. During segment classification, the segment s_i is assigned to one of C predefined classes $[C] := \{1, 2, \ldots, C\}$. To provide a probability distribution $p_i = \langle p_i^1, \ldots, p_i^C \rangle$ over the C classes, the segment encoding h_i is fed to a classification model: $p_i = \text{CLF}(h_i)$. Supervised approaches require ground-truth *segment labels* for training.

2.2 Weakly Supervised Models

State-of-the-art weakly supervised approaches for segment and review classification employ the Multiple Instance Learning (MIL) framework (Zhou et al., 2009; Pappas and Popescu-Belis, 2014; Kotzias et al., 2015; Pappas and Popescu-Belis, 2017; Angelidis and Lapata, 2018). In contrast to traditional supervised learning, where *segment labels* are required to train segment classifiers, MIL-based models can be trained using *review labels* as a weak source of supervision, as we describe next.

MIL is employed for problems where data are arranged in groups (bags) of instances. In our setting, each review is a group of segments: $r = (s_1, s_2, \ldots, s_M)$. The key assumption followed by MIL is that the observed review label is an aggregation function of the unobserved segment labels: $p = \text{AGG}(p_1, \ldots, p_M)$. Hierarchical MIL-based models (Figure 2) work in three main steps: (1) encode the review segments into fixed-size vectors $h_i = \text{ENC}(s_i)$, (2) provide segment predictions $p_i = \text{CLF}(h_i)$, and (3) aggregate the predictions to get a review-level probability estimate $p = \text{AGG}(p_1, \ldots, p_M)$. Supervision during training is provided in the form of review labels.

Different modeling choices have been taken for each part of the MIL hierarchical architecture. Kotzias et al. (2015) encoded sentences as the in-

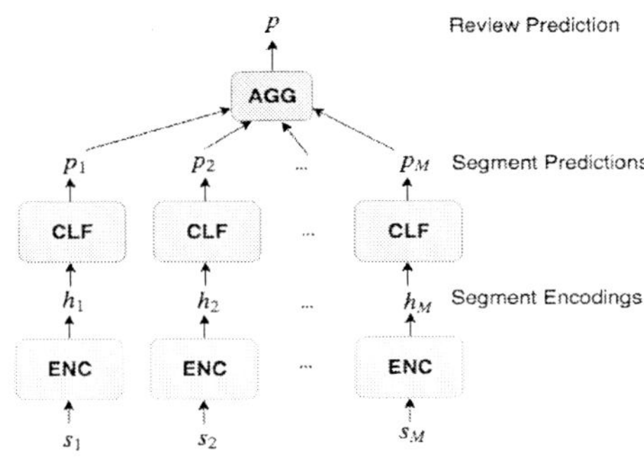

Figure 2: MIL-based hierarchical models.

ternal representations of a hierarchical CNN that was pre-trained for document-level sentiment classification (Denil et al., 2014). For sentence-level classification, they used logistic regression, while the aggregation function was the uniform average. Pappas and Popescu-Belis (2014, 2017) employed Multiple Instance Regression, evaluated various models for segment encoding, including feed forward neural networks and Gated Recurrent Units (GRUs) (Bahdanau et al., 2015), and used the weighted average for the aggregation function, where the weights were computed by linear regression or a one-layer neural network. Angelidis and Lapata (2018) proposed an end-to-end Multiple Instance Learning Network (MILNET), which outperformed previous models for sentiment classification using CNNs for segment encoding, a softmax layer for segment classification, and GRUs with attention (Bahdanau et al., 2015) to aggregate segment predictions as a weighted average. Our proposed model (Section 4) also follows the MIL hierarchical structure of Figure 2 for both sentiment classification and an important public health application, which we discuss next.

2.3 Foodborne Illness Discovery in Online Restaurant Reviews

Health departments nationwide have started to analyze social media content (e.g., Yelp reviews, Twitter messages) to identify foodborne illness outbreaks originating in restaurants. In Chicago (Harris et al., 2014), New York City (Effland et al., 2018), Nevada (Sadilek et al., 2016), and St. Louis (Harris et al., 2018), text classification systems have been successfully deployed for the detection of social media documents mentioning foodborne illness. (Figure 1 shows a Yelp review discussing a food poisoning incident.) After such social media documents are flagged by the classifiers, they are typically examined manually by epidemiologists, who decide if further investigation (e.g., interviewing the restaurant patrons who became ill, inspecting the restaurant) is warranted. This manual examination is time-consuming, and hence it is critically important to (1) produce accurate review-level classifiers, to identify foodborne illness cases while not showing epidemiologists large numbers of false-positive cases; and (2) annotate the flagged reviews to help the epidemiologists in their decision-making.

We propose to apply our segment classification approach to this important public health application. By identifying which review segments discuss food poisoning, epidemiologists could focus on the relevant portions of the review and safely ignore the rest. As we will see, our evaluation will focus on Yelp restaurant reviews. Discovering foodborne illness is fundamentally different from sentiment classification, because the mentions of food poisoning incidents in Yelp are rare. Furthermore, even reviews mentioning foodborne illness often include multiple sentences unrelated to foodborne illness (see Figure 1).

2.4 Problem Definition

Consider a text review for an entity, with M contiguous segments $r = (s_1, \ldots, s_M)$. Segments may have a variable number of words and different reviews may have a different number of segments. A discrete label $y_r \in [C]$ is provided for each review but the individual segment labels are not provided. Our goal is to train a segment-level classifier that, given an unseen test review $r^t = (s_1^t, s_2^t, \ldots, s_{M_t}^t)$, predicts a label $p_i \in [C]$ for each segment and then aggregates the segment labels to infer the review label $y_r^t \in [C]$ for r^t.

3 Non-Hierarchical Baselines

We can address the problem described in Section 2.4 without using hierarchical approaches such as MIL. In fact, the hierarchical structure of Figure 2 for the MIL-based deep networks adds a level of complexity that has not been empirically justified, giving rise to the following question: do performance gains in current MIL-based models stem from their hierarchical structure or just from the representational power of their deep learning components?

We explore this question by evaluating a class of simpler non-hierarchical baselines: deep neural networks trained at the *review level* (without encoding and classifying individual segments) and applied at the *segment level* by treating each test segment as if it were a short "review." While the distribution of input length is different during training and testing, we will show that this class of non-hierarchical models is quite competitive and sometime outperforms MIL-based networks with inappropriate modeling choices.

4 Hierarchical Sigmoid Attention Networks

We now describe the details of our MIL-based hierarchical approach, which we call Hierarchical Sigmoid Attention Network (HSAN). HSAN works in three steps to process a review, following the general architecture in Figure 2: (1) each segment s_i in the review is encoded as a fixed-size vector using word embeddings and CNNs (Kim, 2014): $h_i = \text{CNN}(s_i) \in \mathbb{R}^\ell$; (2) each segment encoding h_i is classified using a softmax classifier with parameters $W \in \mathbb{R}^\ell$ and $b \in \mathbb{R}$: $p_i = \text{softmax}(Wh_i + b)$; and (3) a review prediction p is computed as an aggregation function of the segment predictions $p_1, \ldots, p_M$ from the previous step. A key contribution of our work is the motivation, definition, and evaluation of a suitable aggregation function for HSAN, a critical design issue for MIL-based models.

The choice of aggregation function has a substantial impact on the performance of MIL-based models and should depend on the specific assumptions about the relationship between bags and instances (Carbonneau et al., 2018). Importantly, the performance of MIL algorithms depends on the witness rate (WR), which is defined as the proportion of positive instances in positive bags. For example, when WR is very low (which is the case in our public health application), using the uniform average as an aggregation function in MIL is not an appropriate modeling choice, because the contribution of the few positive instances to the bag label is outweighed by that of the negative instances.

The choice of the uniform average of segment predictions (Kotzias et al., 2015) is also problematic because particular segments of reviews might be more informative than other segments for the task at hand and thus should contribute with higher weights to the computation of the review label.

For this reason, we opt for the weighted average (Pappas and Popescu-Belis, 2014; Angelidis and Lapata, 2018):

$$p = \frac{\sum_{i=1}^{M} \alpha_i \cdot p_i}{\sum_{i=1}^{M} \alpha_i}. \tag{1}$$

The weights $\alpha_1, \ldots, \alpha_M \in [0, 1]$ define the relative contribution of the corresponding segments $s_1, \ldots, s_M$ to the review label. To estimate the segment weights, we adopt the attention mechanism (Bahdanau et al., 2015). In contrast to MIL-NET (Angelidis and Lapata, 2018), which uses the traditional softmax attention, we propose to use the sigmoid attention. Sigmoid attention is both functionally and semantically different from softmax attention and is more suitable for our problem, as we show next.

The probabilistic interpretation of softmax attention is that of a categorical latent variable $z \in \{1, \ldots, M\}$ that represents the index of the segment to be selected from the M segments (Kim et al., 2017). The attention probability distribution is:

$$p(z = i \mid e_1, \ldots, e_M) = \frac{\exp(e_i)}{\sum_{i=1}^{M} \exp(e_i)}, \tag{2}$$

where:

$$e_i = u_a^T \tanh(W_a h_i' + b_a), \tag{3}$$

where h_i' are context-dependent segment vectors computed using bi-directional GRUs (Bi-GRUs), $W_a \in \mathbb{R}^{m \times n}$ and $b_a \in \mathbb{R}^n$ are the attention model's weight and bias parameter, respectively, and $u_a \in \mathbb{R}^m$ is the "attention query" vector parameter. The probabilistic interpretation of Equation 2 suggests that, when using the softmax attention, exactly one segment should be considered important under the constraint that the weights of all segments sum to one. This property of the softmax attention to prioritize one instance explains the successful application of the mechanism for problems such as machine translation (Bahdanau et al., 2015), where the role of attention is to align each target word to (usually) one of the M words from the source language. However, softmax attention is not well suited for estimating the aggregation function weights for our problem, where multiple segments usually affect the review-level prediction.

We hence propose using the sigmoid attention mechanism to compute the weights $\alpha_1, \ldots, \alpha_M$.

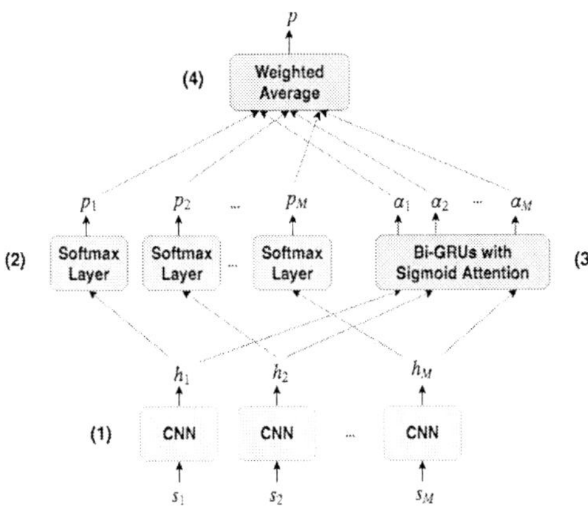

Figure 3: Our Hierarchical Sigmoid Attention Network.

In particular, we replace softmax in Equation (2) with the sigmoid (logistic) function:

$$\alpha_i = \sigma(e_i) = \frac{1}{1 + \exp(-e_i)}. \qquad (4)$$

With sigmoid attention, the computation of the attention weight α_i does not depend on scores e_j for $j \neq i$. Indeed, the probabilistic interpretation of sigmoid attention is a vector z of discrete latent variables $z = [z_1, \ldots, z_M]$, where $z_i \in \{0, 1\}$ (Kim et al., 2017). In other words, the relative importance of each segment is modeled as a Bernoulli distribution. The sigmoid attention probability distribution is:

$$p(z_i = 1 \mid e_1, \ldots, e_M) = \sigma(e_i). \qquad (5)$$

This probabilistic model indicates that $z_1, \ldots, z_M$ are conditionally independent given $e_1, \ldots, e_M$. Therefore, sigmoid attention allows multiple segments, or even no segments, to be selected. This property of sigmoid attention explains why it is more appropriate for our problem. Also, as we will see in the next sections, using the sigmoid attention is the key modeling change needed in MIL-based hierarchical networks to outperform non-hierarchical baselines for segment-level classification. Attention mechanisms using sigmoid activation have also been recently applied for tasks different than segment-level classification of reviews (Shen and Lee, 2016; Kim et al., 2017; Rei and Søgaard, 2018). Our work differs from these approaches in that we use the sigmoid attention

mechanism for the MIL aggregation function of Equation 1, i.e., we aggregate segment labels p_i (instead of segment vectors h_i) into a single review label p (instead of review vectors h).

We summarize our HSAN architecture in Figure 3. HSAN follows the MIL framework and thus it does not require segment labels for training. Instead, we only use ground-truth review labels and jointly learn the model parameters by minimizing the negative log-likelihood of the model parameters. Even though a single label is available for each review, our model allows different segments of the review to receive different labels. Thus, we can appropriately handle reviews such as that in Figure 1 and assign a mix of positive and negative segment labels, even when the review as a whole has a negative (2-star) rating.

5 Experiments

We now turn to another key contribution of our paper, namely, the evaluation of critical aspects of hierarchical approaches and also our HSAN approach. For this, we focus on two important and fundamentally different, real-world applications: segment-level sentiment classification and the discovery of foodborne illness in restaurant reviews.

5.1 Experimental Settings

For segment-level sentiment classification, we use the Yelp'13 corpus with 5-star ratings (Tang et al., 2015) and the IMDB corpora with 10-star ratings (Diao et al., 2014). We do not use segment labels for training any models except the fully supervised Seg-* baselines (see below). For evaluating the segment-level classification performance on Yelp'13 and IMDB, we use the SPOT-Yelp and SPOT-IMDB datasets, respectively (Angelidis and Lapata, 2018), annotated at two levels of granularity, namely, sentences (SENT) and Elementary Discourse Units (EDUs)[1] (see Table 1). For dataset statistics and implementation details, see the supplementary material.

For the discovery of foodborne illness, we use a dataset of Yelp restaurant reviews, manually labeled by epidemiologists in the New York City Department of Health and Mental Hygiene. Each review is assigned a binary label ("Sick" vs. "Not Sick"). To test the models at the sentence level, epidemiologists have manually annotated each

---

[1] The use of EDUs for sentiment classification is motivated in (Angelidis and Lapata, 2018).

Statistic	SPOT-Yelp		SPOT-IMDB	
	SENT	EDU	SENT	EDU
# Segments	1,065	2,110	1,029	2,398
Positive segments (%)	39.9	32.9	37.9	25.6
Neutral segments (%)	21.7	34.3	29.2	47.7
Negative segments (%)	38.4	32.8	32.9	26.7
Witness positive (# segs)	7.9	12.1	6.0	8.5
Witness negative (# segs)	7.3	11.6	6.6	11.2
Witness salient (# segs)	8.5	14.0	7.6	12.6
WR positive	0.74	0.58	0.55	0.36
WR negative	0.68	0.53	0.63	0.43
WR salient	0.80	0.65	0.76	0.55

Table 1: Label statistics for the SPOT datasets. "WR (x)" is the witness rate, meaning the proportion of segments with label x in a review with label x. "Witness (x)" is the average number of segments with label x in a review with label x. "Salient" is the union of the "positive" and "negative" classes.

sentence for a subset of the test reviews (see the supplementary material). In this sentence-level dataset, the WR of the "Sick" class is 0.25, which is significantly lower than the WR on sentiment classification datasets (Table 1). In other words, the proportion of "Sick" segments in "Sick" reviews is relatively low; in contrast, in sentiment classification the proportion of positive (or negative) segments is relatively high in positive (or negative) reviews.

For a robust evaluation of our approach (HSAN), we compare against state-of-the-art models and baselines:

- **Rev-*:** non-hierarchical models, trained at the review level and applied at the segment level (see Section 3); this family includes a logistic regression classifier trained on review embeddings, computed as the element-wise average of word embeddings ("Rev-LR-EMB"), a CNN ("Rev-CNN") (Kim, 2014), and a Bi-GRU with attention ("Rev-RNN") (Bahdanau et al., 2015). For foodborne classification we also report a logistic regression classifier trained on bag-of-words review vectors ("Rev-LR-BoW"), because it is the best performing model in previous work (Effland et al., 2018).

- **MIL-*:** MIL-based hierarchical deep learning models with different aggregation functions. "MIL-avg" computes the review label as the average of the segment-level predictions (Kotzias et al., 2015). "MIL-softmax" uses the softmax attention mechanism –this is

the best performing MILNET model reported in (Angelidis and Lapata, 2018) ("MIL-NETgt"). "MIL-sigmoid" uses the sigmoid attention mechanism as we propose in Section 4 (HSAN model). All MIL-* models have the hierarchical structure of Figure 2 and for comparison reasons we use the same functions for segment encoding (ENC) and segment classification (CLF), namely, a CNN and a softmax classifier, respectively.

For the evaluation of hierarchical non-MIL networks such as the hierarchical classifier of Yang et al. (2016), see Angelidis and Lapata (2018). Here, we ignore this class of models as they have been outperformed by MILNET.

The above models require only review-level labels for training, which is the scenario of focus of this paper. For comparison purposes, we also evaluate a family of fully supervised baselines trained at the *segment* level:

- **Seg-*:** fully supervised baselines using SPOT segment labels for training. "Seg-LR" is a logistic regression classifier trained on segment embeddings, which are computed as the element-wise average of the corresponding word embeddings. We also report the CNN baseline ("Seg-CNN"), which was evaluated in Angelidis and Lapata (2018). Seg-* baselines are evaluated using 10-fold cross-validation on the SPOT dataset.

For sentiment classification, we evaluate the models using the macro-averaged F1 score. For foodborne classification, we report both macro-averaged F1 and recall scores (for more metrics, see the supplementary material).

5.2 Experimental Results

Sentiment Classification: Table 2 reports the evaluation results on SPOT datasets for both sentence- and EDU-level classification.

The Seg-* baselines are not directly comparable with other models, as they are trained at the segment level on the (relatively small) SPOT datasets with segment labels. The more complex Seg-CNN model does not significantly improve over the simpler Seg-LR, perhaps due to the small training set available at the segment level.

Rev-CNN outperforms Seg-CNN in three out of the four datasets. Although Rev-CNN is trained at the review level (but is applied at the segment

Method	SPOT-Yelp		SPOT-IMDB	
	SENT	**EDU**	**SENT**	**EDU**
Seg-LR	55.6	59.2	60.5	62.8
Seg-CNN	56.2	60.0	58.3	63.0
Rev-LR-EMB	51.2	49.3	52.7	48.6
Rev-CNN	60.6	61.5	60.8	60.1
Rev-RNN	58.5	53.9	55.3	50.8
MIL-avg	51.8	46.8	45.7	38.4
MIL-softmax	63.4	59.9	64.0	59.9
MIL-sigmoid	**64.6**	**63.3**	**66.2**	**65.7**

Table 2: F1 score for segment-level sentiment classification.

level), it is trained with 10 times as many examples as Seg-CNN. This suggests that, for the non-hierarchical CNN models, review-level training may be advantageous with more training examples. In addition, Rev-CNN outperforms Rev-LR-EMB, indicating that the fine-tuned features extracted by the CNN are an improvement over the pre-trained embeddings used by Rev-LR-EMB.

Rev-CNN outperforms MIL-avg and has comparable performance to MILNET: non-hierarchical deep learning models trained at the review level and applied at the segment level are strong baselines, because of their representational power. Thus, the Rev-* model class should be evaluated and compared with MIL-based hierarchical models for applications where segment labels are not available.

Interestingly, MIL-sigmoid (HSAN) consistently outperforms all models, including MIL-avg, MIL-softmax (MILNET), and the Rev-* baselines. This shows that:

1. the choice of aggregation function of MIL-based classifiers heavily impacts classification performance; and

2. MIL-based hierarchical networks can indeed outperform non-hierarchical networks when the appropriate aggregation function is used.

We emphasize that we use the same ENC and CLF functions across all MIL-based models to show that performance gains stem solely from the choice of aggregation function. Given that HSAN consistently outperforms MILNET in all datasets for segment-level sentiment classification, we conclude that the choice of sigmoid attention for aggregation is a better fit than softmax for this task.

The difference in performance between HSAN and MILNET is especially pronounced on the *-EDU datasets. We explain this behavior with the statistics of Table 1: "Witness (Salient)" is higher in *-EDU datasets compared to *-SENT datasets. In other words, *-EDU datasets contain more segments that should be considered important than *-SENT datasets. This implies that the attention model needs to "attend" to more segments in the case of *-EDU datasets: as we argued in Section 4, this is best modeled by sigmoid attention.

Foodborne Illness Discovery: Table 3 reports the evaluation results for both review- and sentence-level foodborne classification.[2] For more detailed results, see the supplementary material. Rev-LR-EMB has significantly lower F1 score than Rev-CNN and Rev-RNN: representing a review as the uniform average of the word embeddings is not an appropriate modeling choice for this task, where only a few segments in each review are relevant to the positive class.

MIL-sigmoid (HSAN) achieves the highest F1 score among all models for review-level classification. MIL-avg has lower F1 score compared to other models: as discussed in Section 2.2, in applications where the value of WR is very low (here WR=0.25), the uniform average is not an appropriate aggregation function for MIL.

Applying the best classifier reported in Effland et al. (2018) (Rev-LR-BoW) for sentence-level classification leads to high precision but very low recall. On the other hand, the MIL-* models outperform the Rev-* models in F1 score (with the exception of MIL-avg, which has lower F1 score than Rev-RNN): the MIL framework is appropriate for this task, especially when the weighted average is used for the aggregation function. The significant difference in recall and F1 score between different MIL-based models highlights once again the importance of choosing the appropriate aggregation function. MIL-sigmoid consistently outperforms MIL-softmax in all metrics, showing that the sigmoid attention properly encodes the hierarchical structure of reviews. MIL-sigmoid also outperforms all other models in all metrics. Also, MIL-sigmoid's recall is 48.6% higher than that of Rev-LR-BoW. In other words, MIL-sigmoid detects more sentences relevant to foodborne illness than Rev-LR-BoW, which is especially desirable

---

[2]We report review-level classification results because epidemiologists rely on the *review-level* predictions to decide whether to investigate restaurants; in turn, *segment-level* predictions help epidemiologists focus on the relevant portions of positively labeled reviews.

	REV	**SENT**			
Method	**F1**	**Prec**	**Rec**	**F1**	**AUPR**
Rev-LR-BoW	86.7	**82.1**	58.8	68.6	80.9
Rev-LR-EMB	63.3	50.0	84.3	62.8	48.9
Rev-CNN	84.8	79.3	59.4	67.9	24.7
Rev-RNN	86.7	81.0	74.5	77.6	11.3
MIL-avg	59.8	75.0	78.0	76.5	73.6
MIL-softmax	87.6	75.5	83.3	79.2	81.6
MIL-sigmoid	**89.6**	76.4	**87.4**	81.5	**84.0**

Table 3: Review-level (left) and sentence-level (right) evaluation results for discovering foodborne illness.

Pred	Att	Text
✓	0.00	I wish I could give it zero stars.
✓	0.00	I actually created a yelp account to write this review!
✓	0.00	At first I thought it was great that we got a table for 5 morning of on a Saturday.
✓	0.00	The food was okay- the poached eggs on the Benedict were a little over cooked, but nothing to complain about.
✓	0.00	The service was good, it was overall fine.
✓	0.00	That is- until I got home and me and boy friend spent the rest of the day/night and into the morning hunched over or sitting on the toilet!
☢	0.18	I have never experienced such violent food poisoning in my life!
✓	0.00	That was the only place we ate or drank anything at that day, so I know it was from this restaurant.
☢	0.82	By far the most miserable I've been- chills and crippling abdominal pain along with uncontrollable vomiting and something worse out the other end for my boyfriend!
☢	0.00	Whatever you do, do not eat here, it is not worth the risk of ending up so unwell.
✓	0.00	To clarify what I believe caused this- we both had carrot juice randomly.
☢	0.00	I know more than one person who has gotten food poisoning recently from carrot juice- especially if its raw or cold pressed

☢ : Sick   ✓ : Not Sick

Figure 4: HSAN's fine-grained predictions for a Yelp review: for each sentence, HSAN provides one binary label (Pred) and one attention score (Att). A sentence is highlighted if its attention score is greater than 0.1.

for this application, as discussed next.

Important Segment Highlighting Fine-grained predictions could potentially help epidemiologists to quickly focus on the relevant portions of the reviews and safely ignore the rest. Figure 4 shows how the segment predictions and attention scores predicted by HSAN —with the highest recall and F1 score among all models that we evaluated— could be used to highlight important sentences of a review. We highlight sentences in red if the corresponding attention scores exceed a pre-defined threshold. In this example, high attention scores are assigned by HSAN to sentences that mention food poisoning or symptoms related to food poisoning. (For more examples, see the supplementary material.) This is particularly important because reviews on Yelp and other platforms can be long, with many irrelevant sentences surrounding the truly important ones for the task at hand. The fine-grained predictions produced by our model could inform a graphical user interface in health departments for the inspection of candidate reviews. Such an interface would allow epidemiologists to examine reviews more efficiently and, ultimately, more effectively.

6 Conclusions and Future Work

We presented a Multiple Instance Learning-based model for fine-grained text classification that requires only review-level labels for training but produces both review- and segment-level labels. Our first contribution is the observation that non-hierarchical deep networks trained at the review level and applied at the segment level (by treating each test segment as if it were a short "review") are surprisingly strong and perform comparably or better than MIL-based hierarchical networks with a variety of aggregation functions. Our second contribution is a new MIL aggregation function based on the sigmoid attention mechanism, which explicitly allows multiple segments to contribute to the review-level classification decision with different weights. We experimentally showed that the sigmoid attention is the key modeling change needed for MIL-based hierarchical networks to outperform the non-hierarchical baselines for segment-level sentiment classification. Our third contribution is the application of our weakly supervised approach to the important public health application of foodborne illness discovery in online restaurant reviews. We showed that our MIL-based approach has a higher chance than all previous models to identify unknown foodborne outbreaks, and demonstrated how its fine-grained segment annotations can be used to highlight the segments that were considered important for the computation of the review-level label.

In future work, we plan to consider alternative techniques for segment encoding (ENC), such as pre-trained transformer-based language models (Devlin et al., 2019; Radford et al., 2018), which we expect to further boost our method's performance. We also plan to quantitatively evaluate the extent to which the fine-grained predictions of our model help epidemiologists to efficiently examine candidate reviews and to interpret classification decisions. Indeed, choosing segments of the review text that explain the review-level decisions can help interpretability (Lei et al., 2016; Yessenalina et al., 2010; Biran and Cotton, 2017). Another important direction for future work is to study if minimal supervision at the fine-grain level, either in the form of expert labels or rationales (Bao et al., 2018), could effectively guide the weakly supervised models. This kind of supervision is especially desirable to satisfy prior beliefs about the intended role of fine-grained predictions in downstream applications. We believe that building this kind of fine-grained models is particularly desirable when model predictions are used by humans to take concrete actions in the real world.

Acknowledgments

We thank the anonymous reviewers for their constructive feedback. This material is based upon work supported by the National Science Foundation under Grant No. IIS-15-63785.

References

Stuart Andrews, Ioannis Tsochantaridis, and Thomas Hofmann. 2003. Support vector machines for multiple-instance learning. In *Advances in Neural Information Processing Systems*, pages 577–584.

Stefanos Angelidis and Mirella Lapata. 2018. Multiple instance learning networks for fine-grained sentiment analysis. *Transactions of the Association for Computational Linguistics*, 6:17–31.

Sanjeev Arora, Yingyu Liang, and Tengyu Ma. 2017. A simple but tough-to-beat baseline for sentence embeddings. In *Proceedings of the 5th International Conference on Learning Representations*.

Dzmitry Bahdanau, Kyunghyun Cho, and Yoshua Bengio. 2015. Neural machine translation by jointly learning to align and translate. In *Proceedings of the 3rd International Conference on Learning Representations*.

Yujia Bao, Shiyu Chang, Mo Yu, and Regina Barzilay. 2018. Deriving machine attention from human rationales. In *Proceedings of the 2018 Conference on Empirical Methods in Natural Language Processing*.

Or Biran and Courtenay Cotton. 2017. Explanation and justification in machine learning: A survey. In *IJCAI-17 Workshop on Explainable AI (XAI)*.

Marc-André Carbonneau, Veronika Cheplygina, Eric Granger, and Ghyslain Gagnon. 2018. Multiple instance learning: A survey of problem characteristics and applications. *Pattern Recognition*, 77:329–353.

Misha Denil, Alban Demiraj, and Nando de Freitas. 2014. Extraction of salient sentences from labelled documents. *Technical report, University of Oxford*.

Jacob Devlin, Ming-Wei Chang, Kenton Lee, and Kristina Toutanova. 2019. Bert: Pre-training of deep bidirectional transformers for language understanding. In *Proceedings of the 2019 Conference of the North American Chapter of the Association for Computational Linguistics: Human Language Technologies*.

Qiming Diao, Minghui Qiu, Chao-Yuan Wu, Alexander J Smola, Jing Jiang, and Chong Wang. 2014. Jointly modeling aspects, ratings and sentiments for movie recommendation (JMARS). In *Proceedings of the 20th ACM SIGKDD International Conference on Knowledge Discovery and Data Mining*, pages 193–202.

Thomas Effland, Anna Lawson, Sharon Balter, Katelynn Devinney, Vasudha Reddy, HaeNa Waechter, Luis Gravano, and Daniel Hsu. 2018. Discovering foodborne illness in online restaurant reviews. *Journal of the American Medical Informatics Association*.

Thomas Gärtner, Peter A Flach, Adam Kowalczyk, and Alexander J Smola. 2002. Multi-instance kernels. In *Proceedings of the International Conference on Machine Learning*, volume 2, pages 179–186.

Jenine K Harris, Leslie Hinyard, Kate Beatty, Jared B Hawkins, Elaine O Nsoesie, Raed Mansour, and John S Brownstein. 2018. Evaluating the implementation of a Twitter-based foodborne illness reporting tool in the City of St. Louis Department of Health. *International Journal of Environmental Research and Public Health*, 15(5).

Jenine K Harris, Raed Mansour, Bechara Choucair, Joe Olson, Cory Nissen, and Jay Bhatt. 2014. Health department use of social media to identify foodborne illness-Chicago, Illinois, 2013-2014. *Morbidity and Mortality Weekly Report*, 63(32):681–685.

Maximilian Ilse, Jakub M Tomczak, and Max Welling. 2018. Attention-based deep multiple instance learning. In *Proceedings of the 36th International Conference on Machine Learning*.

Yoon Kim. 2014. Convolutional neural networks for sentence classification. In *Proceedings of the 2014 Conference on Empirical Methods in Natural Language Processing*, pages 1746–1751.

Yoon Kim, Carl Denton, Luong Hoang, and Alexander M Rush. 2017. Structured attention networks. In *Proceedings of the 5th International Conference on Learning Representations*.

Dimitrios Kotzias, Misha Denil, Nando De Freitas, and Padhraic Smyth. 2015. From group to individual labels using deep features. In *Proceedings of the 21st ACM SIGKDD International Conference on Knowledge Discovery and Data Mining*, pages 597–606.

Tao Lei, Regina Barzilay, and Tommi Jaakkola. 2016. Rationalizing neural predictions. In *Proceedings of the 2016 Conference on Empirical Methods in Natural Language Processing*, pages 107–117.

Nikolaos Pappas and Andrei Popescu-Belis. 2014. Explaining the stars: Weighted multiple-instance learning for aspect-based sentiment analysis. In *Proceedings of the 2014 Conference on Empirical Methods in Natural Language processing*, pages 455–466.

Nikolaos Pappas and Andrei Popescu-Belis. 2017. Explicit document modeling through weighted multiple-instance learning. *Journal of Artificial Intelligence Research*, 58:591–626.

Alec Radford, Karthik Narasimhan, Tim Salimans, and Ilya Sutskever. 2018. Improving language understanding by generative pre-training. *https://blog.openai.com/language-unsupervised*.

Marek Rei and Anders Søgaard. 2018. Zero-shot sequence labeling: transferring knowledge from sentences to tokens. In *Proceedings of the 2018 Conference of the North American Chapter of the Association for Computational Linguistics: Human Language Technologies*, volume 1, pages 293–302.

Adam Sadilek, Henry A Kautz, Lauren DiPrete, Brian Labus, Eric Portman, Jack Teitel, and Vincent Silenzio. 2016. Deploying nEmesis: Preventing foodborne illness by data mining social media. In *Proceedings of the AAAI Conference on Artificial Intelligence*, pages 3982–3990.

Sheng-syun Shen and Hung-yi Lee. 2016. Neural attention models for sequence classification: Analysis and application to key term extraction and dialogue act detection. In *Proceedings of INTERSPEECH*, pages 2716–2720.

Oscar Täckström and Ryan McDonald. 2011. Discovering fine-grained sentiment with latent variable structured prediction models. In *European Conference on Information Retrieval*, pages 368–374.

Duyu Tang, Bing Qin, and Ting Liu. 2015. Document modeling with gated recurrent neural network for sentiment classification. In *Proceedings of the 2015 Conference on Empirical Methods in Natural Language Processing*, pages 1422–1432.

John Wieting, Mohit Bansal, Kevin Gimpel, and Karen Livescu. 2015. Towards universal paraphrastic sentence embeddings. *In Proceedings of the 3rd International Conference on Learning Representations*.

John Wieting and Kevin Gimpel. 2017. Revisiting recurrent networks for paraphrastic sentence embeddings. In *Proceedings of the 55th Annual Meeting of the Association for Computational Linguistics*, volume 1, pages 2078–2088.

Zichao Yang, Diyi Yang, Chris Dyer, Xiaodong He, Alex Smola, and Eduard Hovy. 2016. Hierarchical attention networks for document classification. In *Proceedings of the 2016 Conference of the North American Chapter of the Association for Computational Linguistics: Human Language Technologies*, pages 1480–1489.

Ainur Yessenalina, Yisong Yue, and Claire Cardie. 2010. Multi-level structured models for document-level sentiment classification. In *Proceedings of the 2010 Conference on Empirical Methods in Natural Language Processing*, pages 1046–1056.

Zhi-Hua Zhou, Yu-Yin Sun, and Yu-Feng Li. 2009. Multi-instance learning by treating instances as non-IID samples. In *Proceedings of the 26th International Conference on Machine Learning*, pages 1249–1256.

Formality Style Transfer for Noisy Text: Leveraging Out-of-Domain Parallel Data for In-Domain Training via POS Masking

Isak Czeresnia Etinger   Alan W. Black
Language Technologies Institute
Carnegie Mellon University
{ice,awb}@cs.cmu.edu

Abstract

Typical datasets used for style transfer in NLP contain aligned pairs of two opposite extremes of a style. As each existing dataset is sourced from a specific domain and context, most use cases will have a sizable mismatch from the vocabulary and sentence structures of any dataset available. This reduces the performance of the style transfer, and is particularly significant for noisy, user-generated text. To solve this problem, we show a technique to derive a dataset of aligned pairs (style-agnostic vs stylistic sentences) from an unlabeled corpus by using an auxiliary dataset, allowing for in-domain training. We test the technique with the Yahoo Formality Dataset and 6 novel datasets we produced, which consist of scripts from 5 popular TV-shows (*Friends, Futurama, Seinfeld, Southpark, Stargate SG-1*) and the *Slate Star Codex* online forum. We gather 1080 human evaluations, which show that our method produces a sizable change in formality while maintaining fluency and context; and that it considerably outperforms OpenNMT's Seq2Seq model directly trained on the Yahoo Formality Dataset. Additionally, we publish the full pipeline code and our novel datasets [1].

1 Introduction

Typical datasets used for style transfer in NLP contain aligned pairs of two opposite extremes of a style (Hughes et al., 2012; Xu et al., 2012; Jhamtani et al., 2017; Carlson et al., 2017; Xu, 2017; Rao and Tetreault, 2018). Those datasets are useful for training neural networks that perform style transfer on text that is similar (both in vocabulary and structure) to the text in the datasets. However, as each of those datasets is sourced from a specific domain and context, in most use cases there is not

an available dataset of parallel data with vocabulary and structure similar to the one requested.

This is especially significant for style transfer with noisy/user-generated text, where a mismatch is common even when the training dataset is also noisy/user-generated. We explore formality transfer specifically for noisy/user-generated text. To the best of our knowledge, the best dataset for this is currently the Yahoo Formality Dataset (Rao and Tetreault, 2018). However, this dataset is limited to few domains and to the context of Yahoo answers instead of other websites or in-person chat.

To overcome this problem, we propose a technique to derive a dataset of aligned pairs from an unlabeled corpus by using an auxiliary dataset; and we apply this technique to the task of formality transfer on noisy/user-generated conversations.

2 Related Work

Textual style transfer has been a large topic of research in NLP. Early research directly fed labeled, parallel data to train generic Seq2Seq models. Jhamtani et al. (2017) employed this technique on Shakespeare and modern literature. Carlson et al. (2017) employed it on bible translations.

More recent methods have tackled the problem of training models with unlabeled corpora. They seek to obtain latent representations that would correspond to stylistics and semantics separately, then change the stylistic representation while maintaining the semantic one. This can be done by one of 3 ways (Tikhonov and Yamshchikov, 2018): employing back-translation; training a stylistic discriminator; or embedding words or sentences and segmenting embedding state-space into semantic and stylistic sections. Our method differs from those works in many aspects.

Artetxe et al. (2017) worked on unsupervised machine translation. It differs from our objective

---

[1] https://github.com/ICEtinger/StyleTransfer

Proceedings of the 2019 EMNLP Workshop W-NUT: The 5th Workshop on Noisy User-generated Text, pages 11–16
Hong Kong, Nov 4, 2019. ©2019 Association for Computational Linguistics

because it is translation instead of style transfer. Our work employs POS tags as a latent shared representation of syntactic structures and style-free semantics across sentences of different styles. This is not possible (or much less direct) across different languages.

Han et al. (2017) presented a Seq2Seq model that uses two switches with tensor product to control the style transfer in the encoding and decoding processes. Fu et al. (2018) proposed adversarial networks for the task of textual style transfer. Yang et al. (2018) presented a new technique that uses a target domain language model as the discriminator to improve training. Our method is modular with respect to the main Seq2Seq neural model, so it can more easily leverage state-of-the-art (Merity et al., 2017) new models, e.g. most recent versions of OpenNMT (Klein et al., 2017).

Shen et al. (2017) proposed a model that assumes a shared latent content distribution across different text corpora, and leverages refined alignment of latent representations to perform style transfer. Our method does not assume such shared latent content distribution across different corpora. We instead leverage shared latent content distribution across different styles of a same corpus.

Zhang et al. (2018) presented a Seq2Seq model architecture using shared and private model parameters to better train a model from multiple corpora of different domains. Our method is modular with respect to the main Seq2Seq neural model, and is trained with a single corpus each time.

Li et al. (2018) proposed a method that uses retrieval of training sentences (after a deletion operation) during inference time to improve sentence generation. Our method uses a similar inspiration of selecting the "deleted" terms, but instead of being deleted, they are replaced by a latent shared representation of syntactic structures and style-free semantics in the form of POS tags. Additionally, we employ a modular Seq2Seq neural model with the replaced representation instead of retrieving training sentences.

Prabhumoye et al. (2018) presented a method that uses back-translation in French to obtain a latent representation of sentences with less stylistic characteristics. That technique requires that the French translation be trained on a dataset with similar vocabulary and structure as the data on which style transfer is applied. Our work does not have this requirement. Additionally, that work

fixes the encoder and decoder in order to employ the back-translation, while our work employs a modular Seq2Seq neural model to leverage state-of-the-art Seq2Seq neural models.

3 Technique for Dataset Generation

Consider an unlabeled corpus A and a labeled, parallel dataset B. We show a technique that uses B to derive a dataset A' of aligned pairs from A.

If B contains aligned pairs of sentences with styles s_1 and s_2, then one technique to generate A' is to train a classifier between s_1 and s_2 on B, then to use the classifier to select subsets A_1 and A_2 from A following each style, i.e:

$$A_i = \{x \in A | P(class(x) = s_i) > t\}, \quad t \text{ constant}$$

Then, to create parallel data from $\{A_1, A_2\}$, use the classifier to select the terms that have the most weight in determining the style of sentences (e.g.: if Logistic Regression, use term coefficients, select term with coefficients above a certain threshold). Call the set of those terms T. For each sentence $x \in A_1 \cup A_2$, map x with an altered sentence x' which is equal to x when all terms in x that are in T are replaced by their POS tags in x. The set of pairs $\{(x, x')\} = A'$ is now parallel data.

POS tags are employed as a latent shared representation of syntactic structures and style-free semantics across sentences of different styles.

4 Neural Network Models

After obtaining the dataset in the format $\{(x, x')\}$ as described in Section 3, we train a typical Seq2Seq model to predict x from x'. Then, on inference time, we apply the same transformation described in Section 3 to the test set (that may have different styles from the training set), and apply the model on that transformed test set.

For example, consider we have a classifier of two styles: `formal` and `informal`. We use the classifier to produce datasets A_{formal} and $A_{informal}$ from an unlabeled corpus A. From A_{formal}, we produce $\{(x, x')\}$, and use it to train a model that predicts $\{x\}$ from $\{x'\}$. Recall that x' is equal to x when all terms in x that are the most characteristic of formality are replaced by their POS tags in x. During inference time, we want to transform a neutral or an informal sentence y to formal. We derive a y' from y at the same way we did for x', but now we replace the terms most characteristic of informality by their POS tags. We

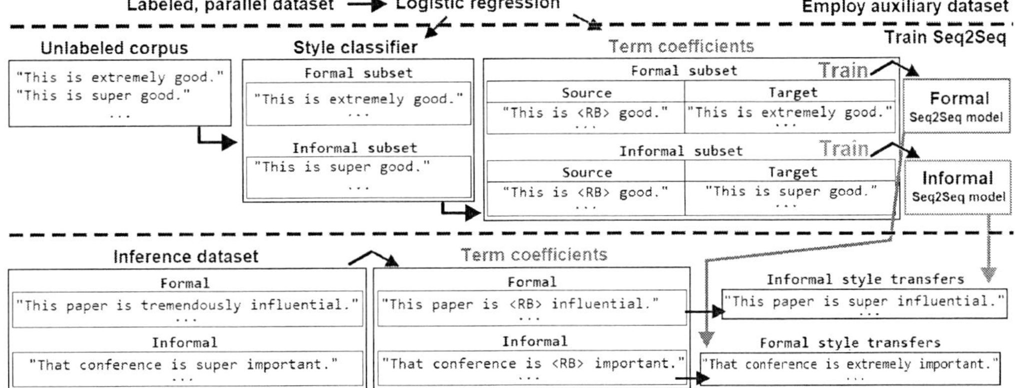

Figure 1: Pipeline for generating data, training Seq2Seq models, and applying style transfer.

feed this transformed y' to the model, and it predicts $\hat{y}$, which should be formal because the model learned to replace POS tags by words that are formal and are suited to the other words in the sentence. The full pipeline is shown in Figure 1.

5 Datasets

We used multiple datasets, existing and novel.

The **Yahoo Formality Dataset** was obtained from (Rao and Tetreault, 2018), and it contains 106k formal-informal pairs of sentences. Informal sentences were extracted from Yahoo Answers ("Entertainment & Music" and "Family & Relationships" categories). Formal (parallel) sentences were produced with mechanical turks.

The **TV-Shows Datasets** are the scripts of 5 popular TV-shows from the 1990's and 2000's (*Friends, Futurama, Seinfeld, Southpark, Stargate SG 1*), with 120k sentences in total. The datasets are novel: we produced them by crawling a website that contains scripts of TV-shows and movies (IMS); except for *Friends*, obtained from (Fri).

The **Slate Star Codex** is a novel dataset we produced in this work. It is comprised of 3.2 million sentences from comments in the online forum *Slate Star Codex*(SSC), which contains very formal language in the areas of science and philosophy. It was obtained by crawling the website, and contains posts from 2013 to 2019.

6 Experimental Setup

We applied the techniques explained in Sections 3 and 4. We used the Yahoo Formality Dataset as labeled dataset B and either a TV-show dataset, all TV-shows together, or the Slate Star Codex

dataset as unlabeled corpus A. A Logistic Regression model was employed as the classifier [2], and OpenNMT as the Seq2Seq models [3].

The hyperparameters of the Seq2Seq models are shown in Table 1.

Hyper-parameter	Value
Encoder	
type	LSTM
rnn hidden size	100
layers	1
Decoder	
type	LSTM
rnn hidden size	100
layers	1
General	
word vec size	200
optimizer	Adam
learning rate	$1e^{-3}$
train/validation split	90/10
vocabulary size	30k for SSC, TV merged 10k for single TV-shows

Table 1: Hyperparameters.

---

[2] Scikit-learn's model was used. Terms were stemmed with Porter Stemming before being fed to the model, and only terms with frequency ≥ 2 in the dataset were fed.

[3] To derive formal and informal datasets from each of our original unlabeled corpora, we applied our logistic regression model on each sentence in each corpus. Sentences with informality scores ≤ 0.6 were considered formal, scores ≥ 0.65 were considered informal, and others were ignored for being neutral. Terms were replaced by POS tags in the following manner: the N terms in each sentence with the highest absolute weight (from the Log-Reg model) are replaced by POS tags, provided they pass a certain threshold (-0.001 for formal terms, and 0.2 for informal terms). N is the floor of the number of terms in the sentence divided by 5.

Dataset	Target formality	Avg. formality score (1–5)	Avg. suitability score (1–5)	Total # of sentences
Friends	formal	$2.25 \to 3.43\ (+1.2)$	$3.44 \to 3.43\ (-0.0)$	105k
	informal	$3.91 \to 1.63\ (-2.3)$	$3.18 \to 3.53\ (+0.4)$	
Futurama	formal	$2.04 \to 3.43\ (+1.4)$	$3.39 \to 2.29\ (-1.1)$	27k
	informal	$4.41 \to 1.85\ (-2.6)$	$3.71 \to 3.00\ (-0.7)$	
Seinfeld	formal	$1.84 \to 3.18\ (+1.3)$	$3.58 \to 2.82\ (-0.8)$	94k
	informal	$3.62 \to 1.71\ (-1.9)$	$4.00 \to 3.41\ (-0.6)$	
Southpark	formal	$1.92 \to 3.47\ (+1.6)$	$3.00 \to 3.18\ (+0.2)$	77k
	informal	$3.92 \to 1.59\ (-2.3)$	$3.69 \to 3.06\ (-0.6)$	
Stargate-SG1	formal	$2.17 \to 4.06\ (+1.9)$	$3.50 \to 3.17\ (-0.3)$	117k
	informal	$4.59 \to 1.77\ (-2.8)$	$3.41 \to 3.30\ (-0.1)$	
All TV-Shows	formal	$2.38 \to 4.18\ (+1.8)$	$3.77 \to 3.76\ (-0.0)$	420k
	informal	$3.94 \to 1.92\ (-2.0)$	$4.24 \to 3.92\ (-0.3)$	
Slate Star Codex	formal	$3.53 \to 4.40\ (+0.9)$	$3.67 \to 3.93\ (+0.3)$	3.2M
	informal	$4.75 \to 2.86\ (-1.9)$	$4.19 \to 3.93\ (-0.3)$	
Yahoo (baseline)	formal	$2.45 \to 2.80\ (+0.4)$	$3.85 \to 3.05\ (-0.8)$	218k
	informal	$3.89 \to 3.33\ (-0.6)$	$4.33 \to 2.79\ (-1.5)$	

Table 2: Results of experiments on formality and sentence suitability.

Numbers and proper names were replaced by symbols <NUMBER> and <NAME> respectively, in order to greatly reduce data sparcity.

After splitting each corpus in formal and informal sentences (according to our logistic regression model), we randomly selected 60 sentences from each corpus (30 formal and 30 informal) as held-out test sets, and transformed them to opposite styles. Sentences were assigned evenly split to 3 human evaluators. To avoid bias, each sentence was randomly shown either original or transformed with equal probabilities (without evaluators' knowledge). Each sentence was shown accompanied with a *context*: preceding sentence in the TV-show (or SSC post), character speaking and TV-show name. Evaluators rated each sentence formality and *suitability* (how fluent and appropriate it is for the context) in a 1–5 scale[4].

Additionally, to serve as baseline, we trained two Seq2Seq models (formal-to-informal and informal-to-formal) on OpenNMT directly on the pairs of parallel sentences of the Yahoo Formality Dataset. We used the same hyper-parameters as the other experiments. Then we applied the model on the All TV-Shows corpus and performed the same human evaluation as described above, but we doubled the number of sentences analyzed to 120.

7 Results

Results are presented in Table 2. The average scores show the differences between the scores of the original and transformed sentences.

The technique produced a sizable change in formality while maintaining fluency and context. When transforming informal sentences to formal, the average formality score increased by ~ 1.5 points (in a 5-point scale) for TV shows, and 0.9 point for SSC. In the formal-to-informal transformation, the formality score decreased by ~ 2.2. The absolute changes in formality seem to correlate with the formality scores of the original sentences. They do not seem to correlate with the total number of sentences in each dataset.

Average suitability scores suffered a small decrease for corpora with a low number of sentences. The biggest decrease was for Futurama, whose training datasets contained only ~ 10k sentences (after splitting the 27k total in the corpus). Other datasets contained smaller decreases in suitability, or even small improvements over the original sen-

<hr>

[4] **1:** The sentence does not form any grammatical structure, or the evaluator cannot understand its meaning. **2:** The sentence forms segments of grammatical structures, and the evaluator can barely understand the intended meaning. **3:** The sentence is a few words away from perfect English, and the evaluator probably understands its meaning; or meaning is clear, but not appropriate for the context. **4:** The sentence is in almost perfect English (usually only missing a word or a comma, which is common in informal oral speech) and the meaning is clear; or the English is perfect but the meaning or words used are not perfectly appropriate for the context. **5:** The sentence is in perfect English and perfectly appropriate for the context.

tences. The largest corpora (All TV-Shows and SSC) maintained suitability scores approximately unchanged ($\in [-0.3, +0.3]$).

In general, all datasets showed sizable differences of formality when the formal or informal transformation was applied, and showed small decreases in suitability for small datasets (e.g. 10k training sentences for Futurama) and approximately no changes in suitability for larger datasets. Note that the suitability scores for the original sentences were not 5, because many sentences in the conversations employed in the datasets are in oral ("wrong") English, had small typos, or do not seem appropriate for the context.

The baseline (directly training the OpenNMT model with the Yahoo Formality Dataset) only showed small absolute changes in formality ($\sim$0.5) and lost a sizable amount of average suitability score (-0.8 or -1.5). We suspect the main reason for the loss of average suitability is the mismatch of the data used to train the model with the data on which the style transfer was applied, both in terms of vocabulary and in structure. The main reason for the smaller absolute change in formality scores, we suspect, is the model being conservative on making changes when it encountered sentences with many new terms. For many sentences generated by the model, the generated sentence was equal to the original sentence, which did not occurred as frequently in the other models (probably because of a greater match between training data and inference data).

On the All TV-Shows dataset, our method outperforms the baseline by 1.4 points in absolute formality change (both formal and informal transfers), and by 0.8 and 1.2 in average suitability.

8 Conclusion

In this work we presented a technique to derive a dataset of aligned pairs from an unlabeled corpus by using an auxiliary dataset. The technique is particularly important for noisy/user-generated text, which often lack datasets of matching vocabulary and structure. We tested the technique with the Yahoo Formality Dataset and 7 novel datasets we produced by web-crawling, which consists of scripts from 5 TV-shows, all TV-shows together, and the SSC online forum. We gathered 1080 human evaluations on the formality and suitability of sentences, and showed that our method produced a sizable change in formality while maintaining fluency and context; and that it considerably outperformed OpenNMT's Seq2Seq model trained directly on the Yahoo Formality Dataset.

A possible application of this technique in industry is to use large standard datasets as auxiliary to build style transformers based on specific corpora relevant to the industry. For example, a company wishing to change the formality of comments in its website could use the Yahoo Formality Dataset as the auxiliary dataset and use the logs of comments in its own website as the main corpus. This would enable them to create style transfers that are suited to the vocabulary and structures they use, improving style-transfer and fluency.

For future work, we plan to research different models for selecting the words most characteristic of formality instead of the logistic regression model used, such as neural models.

We make available the full pipeline code (ready-to-run) and our novel datasets: `https://github.com/ICEtinger/StyleTransfer`

References

Friends dataset. `https://github.com/npow/friends-chatbot/tree/master/data`.

IMSDB. `https://www.imsdb.com/`.

Slate Star Codex online forum. `https://slatestarcodex.com/`.

Mikel Artetxe, Gorka Labaka, Eneko Agirre, and Kyunghyun Cho. 2017. Unsupervised neural machine translation. *arXiv preprint arXiv:1710.11041*.

Keith Carlson, Allen Riddell, and Daniel Rockmore. 2017. Zero-shot style transfer in text using recurrent neural networks. *arXiv preprint arXiv:1711.04731*.

Zhenxin Fu, Xiaoye Tan, Nanyun Peng, Dongyan Zhao, and Rui Yan. 2018. Style transfer in text: Exploration and evaluation. In *Thirty-Second AAAI Conference on Artificial Intelligence*.

Mengqiao Han, Ou Wu, and Zhendong Niu. 2017. Unsupervised automatic text style transfer using lstm. In *National CCF Conference on Natural Language Processing and Chinese Computing*, pages 281–292. Springer.

James M Hughes, Nicholas J Foti, David C Krakauer, and Daniel N Rockmore. 2012. Quantitative patterns of stylistic influence in the evolution of literature. *Proceedings of the National Academy of Sciences*, 109(20):7682–7686.

Harsh Jhamtani, Varun Gangal, Eduard Hovy, and Eric Nyberg. 2017. Shakespearizing modern language using copy-enriched sequence-to-sequence models. *arXiv preprint arXiv:1707.01161*.

Guillaume Klein, Yoon Kim, Yuntian Deng, Jean Senellart, and Alexander M Rush. 2017. Opennmt: Open-source toolkit for neural machine translation. *arXiv preprint arXiv:1701.02810*.

Juncen Li, Robin Jia, He He, and Percy Liang. 2018. Delete, retrieve, generate: A simple approach to sentiment and style transfer. *CoRR*, abs/1804.06437.

Stephen Merity, Nitish Shirish Keskar, and Richard Socher. 2017. Regularizing and optimizing lstm language models. *arXiv preprint arXiv:1708.02182*.

Shrimai Prabhumoye, Yulia Tsvetkov, Ruslan Salakhutdinov, and Alan W. Black. 2018. Style transfer through back-translation. *CoRR*, abs/1804.09000.

Sudha Rao and Joel R. Tetreault. 2018. Dear sir or madam, may I introduce the YAFC corpus: Corpus, benchmarks and metrics for formality style transfer. *CoRR*, abs/1803.06535.

Tianxiao Shen, Tao Lei, Regina Barzilay, and Tommi Jaakkola. 2017. Style transfer from non-parallel text by cross-alignment. In *Advances in neural information processing systems*, pages 6830–6841.

Alexey Tikhonov and Ivan P Yamshchikov. 2018. What is wrong with style transfer for texts? *arXiv preprint arXiv:1808.04365*.

Wei Xu. 2017. From shakespeare to twitter: What are language styles all about? In *Proceedings of the Workshop on Stylistic Variation*, pages 1–9.

Wei Xu, Alan Ritter, Bill Dolan, Ralph Grishman, and Colin Cherry. 2012. Paraphrasing for style. *Proceedings of COLING 2012*, pages 2899–2914.

Zichao Yang, Zhiting Hu, Chris Dyer, Eric P Xing, and Taylor Berg-Kirkpatrick. 2018. Unsupervised text style transfer using language models as discriminators. In *Advances in Neural Information Processing Systems*, pages 7287–7298.

Ye Zhang, Nan Ding, and Radu Soricut. 2018. Shaped: Shared-private encoder-decoder for text style adaptation. *arXiv preprint arXiv:1804.04093*.

Multilingual Whispers: Generating Paraphrases with Translation

Christian Federmann, Oussama Elachqar, Chris Quirk
Microsoft
One Microsoft Way
Redmond, WA 98052 USA
{chrife,ouelachq,chrisq}@microsoft.com

Abstract

Naturally occurring paraphrase data, such as multiple news stories about the same event, is a useful but rare resource. This paper compares translation-based paraphrase gathering using human, automatic, or hybrid techniques to monolingual paraphrasing by experts and non-experts. We gather translations, paraphrases, and empirical human quality assessments of these approaches. Neural machine translation techniques, especially when pivoting through related languages, provide a relatively robust source of paraphrases with diversity comparable to expert human paraphrases. Surprisingly, human translators do not reliably outperform neural systems. The resulting data release will not only be a useful test set, but will also allow additional explorations in translation and paraphrase quality assessments and relationships.

1 Introduction

Humans naturally paraphrase. These paraphrases are often a byproduct: when we can't recall the exact words, we can often generate approximately the same meaning with a different surface realization. Recognizing and generating paraphrases are key challenges in many tasks, including translation, information retrieval, question answering, and semantic parsing. Large collections of sentential paraphrase corpora could benefit such systems.[1]

Yet when we ask humans to generate paraphrases of a given task, they are often a bit stuck. How much should be changed? Annotators tend to preserve the reference expression: a safe choice, as the only truly equivalent representation is to leave the text unchanged. Each time we replace a word with a synonym, some shades of meaning change, some connotations or even denotations shift.

---

[1]Expanding beyond the sentence boundary is also very important, though we do not explore cross-sentence phenomena in this paper.

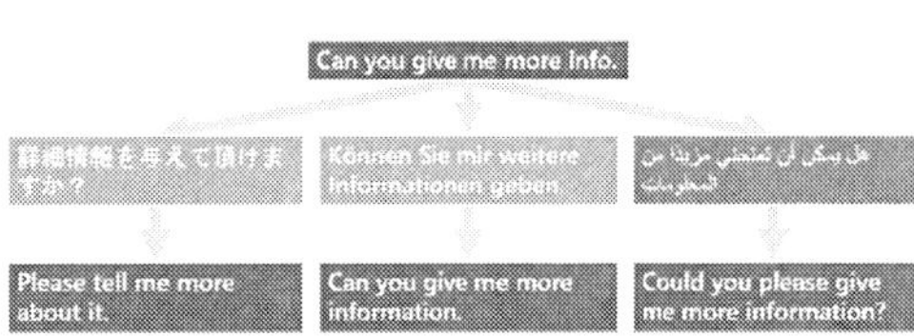

Figure 1: Generating broad-coverage paraphrases through pivot translation.

One path around the obstacle of reference bias is to provide a non-linguistic input, then ask humans to describe this input in language. For instance, crowd-sourced descriptions of videos provide a rich source of paraphrase data that is grounded in visual phenomena (Chen and Dolan, 2011). Such visual grounding helps users focus on a clear and specific activity without imparting a bias toward particular lexical realizations. Unfortunately, these paraphrases are limited to phenomena that can be realized visually. Another path is to find multiple news stories describing the same event (Dolan et al., 2004), or multiple commentaries about the same news story (Lan et al., 2017). Although this provides a rich and growing set of paraphrases, the language is again biased, this time toward events commonly reported in the news.

An alternative is to provide input in a foreign language. Nearly anything expressible in one human language can be written in another language. When users translate content, some variation in lexical realization occurs. To gather monolingual paraphrases, we can first translate a source sentence into a variety of target languages, then translate back into the source language, using either humans or machines. This provides naturalistic variation in language, centered around a common yet relatively unconstrained starting point. Although several research threads have explored this possibility (e.g., (Wieting and Gimpel, 2018)), we have seen few if any comparative evaluations of the quality of this approach.

Proceedings of the 2019 EMNLP Workshop W-NUT: The 5th Workshop on Noisy User-generated Text, pages 17–26
Hong Kong, Nov 4, 2019. ©2019 Association for Computational Linguistics

Our primary contribution is to evaluate various methods of constructing paraphrase corpora, including monolingual methods with experts and non-experts as well as automated, semi-automated, and manual translation-based approaches. Each paraphrasing method is evaluated for fluency (*"does the resulting paraphrase sound not only grammatical but natural?"*) and adequacy (*"does the paraphrase accurately convey the original meaning of the source?"*) using human direct assessment, inspired by effective techniques in machine translation evaluation (Federmann, 2018).

In addition, we measure the degree of change between the original and rewritten sentence using both edit distance and BLEU (Papineni et al., 2002). Somewhat surprisingly, fully automatic neural machine translation actually outperforms manual human translation in terms of adequacy. The semi-automatic method of post-editing neural machine translation output with human editors leads to fluency improvements while retaining diversity and adequacy. Although none of the translation-based approaches outperform monolingual rewrites in terms of adequacy or fluency, they do produce greater diversity. Human editors, particularly non-experts, tend toward small edits rather than substantial rewrites. We conclude that round-tripping with neural machine translation is a cheap and effective means of gathering diverse paraphrases.

Our second contribution is a unique data release. As a byproduct of this evaluation, we have compiled a data set consisting of paraphrases gathered using monolingual rewrites and translation paraphrases generated through human translation, neural machine translation, and human post-edited neural machine translation. These 500 source sentences—together with all rewrites and intermediate translations—comprise a rare and interesting multilingual data set, useful for both monolingual and translation tasks. We include all human quality assessments for adequacy (semantic equivalence) and fluency of paraphrases, as well as translation adequacy assessments. Data is publicly available at `https://aka.ms/MultilingualWhispers`.

2   Related Work

Translation as a means of generating paraphrases has been explored for decades. Paraphrase corpora can be extracted from multiple translations of the same source material (Barzilay and McKeown, 2001). Sub-sentential paraphrases (mostly phrasal replacements) can be gathered from these multiple translations. Alternatively, one can create a large body of phrasal replacements from by pivoting on the phrase-tables used by phrase-based statistical machine translation (Bannard and Callison-Burch, 2005; Ganitkevitch et al., 2013; Pavlick et al., 2015).

Recent work has also explored using neural machine translation to generate paraphrases via pivoting (Prakash et al., 2016; Mallinson et al., 2017). One can also use neural MT systems to generate large monolingual paraphrase corpora. Another line of work has translated the Czech side of a Czech-English parallel corpus into English, thus producing 50 million words of English paraphrase data (Wieting and Gimpel, 2018). Not only can the system generate interesting paraphrases, but embeddings trained on the resulting data set prove useful in sentence similarity tasks. When added to a paraphrase system, constraints obtained from a semantic parser can reduce the semantic drift encountered during rewrites (Wang et al., 2018). Adding lexical constraints to the output can also increase diversity (Hu et al., 2019).

Past research has also explored effective methods for gathering paraphrases from the crowd (Jiang et al., 2017). However, to the best of our knowledge, no prior work has compared the efficacy of human experts, crowd-workers, human post-editing approaches and machine translation systems on gathering paraphrase quality.

3   Methodology

To run a comprehensive evaluation of paraphrase techniques, we create many paraphrases of a common data set using multiple methods, then evaluate using human direct assessment as well as automatic diversity measurements.

3.1   Data

Input data was sampled from two sources: Reddit provides volumes of casual online conversations; the Enron email corpus represents communication in the professional world.[2] Both are noisier than usual NMT training data; traditionally, such noise has been challenging for NMT systems (Michel and Neubig, 2018) and should provide a lower-bound on their performance. It would definitely be valuable, albeit expensive, to rerun our experiments on a cleaner data source.

---

[2]However, the Enron emails often contain conversations about casual and personal matters.

			Tokens per segment			
Segments	Types	Tokens	median	mean	min	max
500	2,370	9,835	19	19.67	4	46

Table 1: Key characteristics of the source sentences.

			Tokens per segment			
Segments	Types	Tokens	median	mean	min	max
14,500	7,196	285,833	19	19.72	1	68

Table 2: Key characteristics of collected paraphrases.

As an initial filtering step, we ran automatic grammar and spell-checking, in order to select sentences that exhibit some disfluency or clear error. Additionally, we asked crowd workers to discard sentences that contain any personally identifiable information, URLs, code, XML, Markdown, and non-English sentences. The crowd workers were also encouraged to select noisy sentences containing slang, run-ons, contractions, and other behavior observed in informal communications.

3.2 Paraphrase techniques

Expert human monolingual paraphrase. We hired trained linguists (who are native speakers of English) to provide paraphrases of the given source sentences, targeting highest quality rewrites. These linguists were also encouraged to fix any misspellings, grammatical errors, or disfluencies.

Crowd-worker monolingual paraphrase. As a less expensive and more realistic setting, we asked English native speaking crowd workers who passed a qualification test to perform the same task.

Human round-trip translation. For the first set of translation-based paraphrases, we employed human translators who translated the source text from English into some pivot language and back again. The translations were provided by a human translation service, potentially using multiple different translators (though the exact number was not visible to us). In our experiments we focused on a diverse set of pivot languages, namely: Arabic, Chinese, French, German, Japanese, and Russian.

While French and German seem like a better choice for translation from and back into English, due to the close proximity of English as part of the Germanic language family and its shared vocabulary with French, we hypothesize that the use of more distant pivot languages may result in a greater diversity of the back translation output.

We employed professional translators—native in the chosen target language—who were instructed to generate translations from scratch, without the use of any online translation tools. Translation from English into the pivot languages and back into English were conducted in separate phases, by different translators.

Post-edited round-trip translation. Second, we created round-trip translation output based on human post-editing of neural machine translation output. Given the much lower post-editing cost, we hypothesize that results contain only minimal edits, mostly improving fluency but not necessarily fixing problems with translation adequacy.

Neural machine translation. We kept the NMT output used to generate post-editing-based paraphrases, without further human modification. Given the unsupervized nature of machine translation, we hypothesize that resulting output may be closer to the source syntactically (and hopefully more diverse lexically), especially those source sentences which a human editor would consider incomplete or low quality.

Crowd-worker monolingual paraphrase grounded by translation. Finally, we also use a variant of the Crowd-worker monolingual paraphrase technique where the crowd worker is *grounded* by a translation-based paraphrase output. The crowd worker is then asked to modify the translation-based paraphrase to make it more fluent than the source, and as adequate.

Intuitively, one assumes that human translation output should achieve both highest adequacy and fluency scores, while post-editing should result in higher adequacy than raw neural machine translation output.

Considering translation fluency scores, NMT output should be closer to both post-editing and human translation output, as neural MT models usually achieve high levels of fluency (Bojar et al., 2016; Castilho et al., 2017; Läubli et al., 2018).

We hypothesize that translation helps to increase diversity of the resulting back translation output, irrespective of the specific method.

3.3 Assessments

We measure four dimensions of quality:

1. Paraphrase adequacy;
2. Paraphrase relative fluency;
3. Translation adequacy;
4. Paraphrase diversity.

Eval mode	Priming question used
Par_A	How accurately does candidate text B convey the original semantics of candidate text A? Slider ranges from *Not at all* (left) to *Perfectly* (right).
Par_F	Which of the two candidate texts is more fluent? Slider marks preference for *Candidate A* (left), no difference (middle) or preference for *Candidate B* (right).
NMT_A	How accurately does the above candidate text convey the original semantics of the source text? Slider ranges from *Not at all* (left) to *Perfectly* (right).

Table 3: Priming questions used for human evaluation of paraphrase adequacy (Par_A), paraphrase fluency (Par_F), and translation adequacy (NMT_A). Paraphrase evaluation campaigns referred to source and candidate text as "candidate A" and "B", respectively. Translation evaluation campaigns used "source" and "candidate text" instead.

Paraphrase adequacy For adequacy, we ask annotators to assess semantic similarity between source and candidate text, labeled as "candidate A" and "B", respectively. The annotation interface implements a slider widget to encode perceived similarity as a value $x \in [0, 100]$. Note that the exact value is hidden from the human, and can only be guessed based on the positioning of the slider. Candidates are displayed in random order, preventing bias.

Paraphrase fluency For fluency, we use a different priming question, implicitly asking the human annotators to assess fluency for candidate "B" relative to that of candidate "A". We collect scores $x \in [-50, 50]$, with -50 encoding that candidate "A" is much more fluent than "B", while a value of 50 denotes the polar opposite. Intuitively, the middle value 0 encodes that the annotator could not determine a meaningful difference in fluency between both candidates. Note that this may mean two things:

1. candidates are semantically equivalent but similarly fluent or non-fluent; or
2. candidates have different semantics.

We observe that annotators have a tendency to fall back to "neutral" $x = 0$ scoring whenever they are confused, e.g., when semantic similarity of both candidates is considered low.

Translation Adequacy We measure translation adequacy using our own implementation of source-based direct assessment. Annotators do not know that the source text shown might be translated content, and they do not know about the actual goal of using back-translated output for paraphrase generation. Except for the labels for source and candidate text, the priming question is identical to the one used for paraphrase adequacy evaluation. Notably, we have to employ bilingual annotators to collect these assessments. Scores for translation adequacy again are collected as $x \in [0, 100]$.

Paraphrase diversity Additionally, we measure diversity of all paraphrases (both monolingual and based on translation) by computing the average number of token edits between source and candidate texts. To focus our attention on meaningful changes as opposed to minor function word rewrites, we normalize both source and candidate by lower-casing and excluding any punctuation and stop words using NLTK (Bird et al., 2009).

We adopt *source-based direct assessment* (src-DA) for human evaluation of adequacy and fluency. The original DA approach (Graham et al., 2013, 2014) is reference-based and, thus, needs to be adapted for use in our paraphrase assessment and translation scoring scenarios. In both cases, we can use the source sentence to guide annotators in their assessment. Of course, this makes translation evaluation more difficult, as we require bilingual annotators. Src-DA has previously been used, e.g., in (Cettolo et al., 2017; Bojar et al., 2018).

Direct assessment initializes mental context for annotators by asking a priming question. The user interface shows two sentences:

- the source (src-DA, reference otherwise); and
- the candidate output.

Annotators read the priming question and both sentences and then assign a score $x \in [0, 100]$ to the candidate shown. The interpretation of this score considers the context defined by the priming question, effectively allowing us to use the same annotation method to collect human assessments with respect to the different dimensions of quality a defined above. Our priming questions are shown above in Table 3.

3.4 Profanity handling

Some source segments from Reddit contain profanities, which may have affected results reported in this paper. While a detailed investigation of such effects is outside the scope of this work, we want

Method	Par$_A$ ↑	Par$_F$ ↑	Par$_D$ ↑	NMT$_A$ ↑
Expert	83.20	**11.80**	3.48	–
HT	63.13	-7.13	5.98	88.8
NMT	64.62	-8.60	3.58	85.1
Non-Expert	**87.10**	9.40	1.11	–
Post-Edited NMT	67.57	-4.20	4.43	**90.0**
Multi-Hop NMT	42.05	-20.65	**6.18**	50.7

Table 4: Results by paraphrasing method. Adequacy (Par$_A$) and fluency (Par$_F$) are human assessments of paraphrases; paraphrase diversity (Par$_D$) is measured by the average string-edit-distance between source and paraphrase (higher means greater diversity); NMT$_A$ is a human assessment of translation quality.

Language	Par$_A$ ↑	Par$_F$ ↑	Par$_D$ ↑	NMT$_A$ ↑
Arabic	58.33	-12.57	4.96	81.6
Chinese	61.57	-7.67	5.70	71.3
Chinese-Japanese	40.60	-22.30	**6.42**	53.9
French	**71.50**	**-1.80**	3.68	84.2
German	70.90	-2.77	3.80	**87.5**
Japanese	59.67	-9.33	5.38	69.5
Japanese-Chinese	43.50	-19.00	5.95	47.4
Russian	68.67	-5.73	4.47	81.4

Table 5: Results by pivot language.

to highlight two potential issues which could be introduced by profanity in the source text:

1. Profanity may have caused additional monolingual rewrites (in an attempt to clean the resulting paraphrase), possibly inflating diversity scores;
2. Human translators may have performed similar cleanup, increasing the likelihood of back translations having a lower adequacy score.

4 Results

In total, we collect 14,500 paraphrases from 29 different systems, as described below:

- Expert paraphrase;
- Non-Expert paraphrase;
- Human translation (HT), for 6 languages;
- Human Post-editing (PE), for 6 languages;
- Neural MT (NMT), for 6 languages;
- Neural "multi-hop" NMT, for 2 languages;
- Grounded Non-Expert (GNE), with grounding from 7 translation methods.

All data collected in this work is publicly released. This includes paraphrases as well as assessments of adequacy, fluency, and translation adequacy. Human scores are based on two evaluation campaigns—one for adequacy, the other for fluency—with $t = 27$ annotation tasks, $a = 54$ human annotators, $r = 4$ redundancy, and $tpa = 2$ tasks per annotator, resulting in a total of $t * r = a * tpa = 108$ annotated tasks—equivalent to at least $9,504$ assessments per campaign (more in case of duplicates in the set of paraphrases to be evaluated), based on the alternate HIT structure with $88 : 12$ candidates-vs-controls setting as described in (Bojar et al., 2018).

Table 4 presents empirical results organized by paraphrasing method, while Table 5 organizes by pivot languages used. "Multi-Hop NMT" refers to an experiment in which we created paraphrases translating via two non-English pivot languages, namely Chinese and Japanese. French and German perform best as pivot languages, while Chinese-Japanese achieves best diversity.

Table 6 shows results from our grounded paraphrasing experiment in which we compared how different translation methods affect monolingual rewriting quality. Based on results in Tables 5, we focus on French and German as our pivot languages. We also keep Chinese-Japanese "Two-Pivot NMT" to see how additional pivot languages may affect resulting paraphrase diversity.

Figure 2 shows convergence of adequacy scores for the grounded paraphrasing experiment, over time. Figure 3 shows convergence of relative fluency scores. Note how clustering reported in Table 6 appears after a few hundred annotations only. The clusters denote sets of systems that are not statistically significantly different.

4.1 Error Analysis

While neural machine translation based paraphrases achieve surprising results in terms of diversity compared to paraphrases generated by human Non-Experts, NMT does not reach the adequacy or fluency level provided by Expert paraphrases. The examples in Table 7 provides a flavor of the outputs from each method and demonstrates some of the error cases.

Partially paraphrasing entities and common expressions. NMT systems often mangle multi-word units, rewriting parts of non-compositional phrases that change meaning ("Material Design" → "hardware design") or decrease fluency.

Informal language. Inadequate or disfluent paraphrases are also caused by typos, slang and

Method	Par_A ↑	Par_F ↑	Par_D ↑	BLEU ↓	Labelling Time [seconds]						
					Min	P_{25}	Median	Mean	P_{75}	Max	StdDev
Non-Expert	91.7	13.3	1.106	78.8	7.47	21.52	30.84	40.35	48.07	120.0	28.34
GNE-PE French	88.2	11.9	2.222	59.9	4.73	10.26	18.64	33.16	43.39	120.0	32.30
Expert	88.2	14.6	3.482	39.0	–	–	–	–	–	–	–
GNE-PE German	88.1	11.7	2.214	60.5	4.50	9.58	15.05	35.36	52.05	120.0	35.91
GNE-NMT German	87.9	10.5	2.068	62.2	2.28	10.72	19.74	30.98	39.62	120.0	29.73
GNE-HT French	85.4	12.4	3.160	47.3	4.50	17.07	39.90	52.21	81.65	120.0	39.37
GNE-NMT French	83.1	5.1	2.374	54.9	1.75	2.80	7.29	22.48	28.64	120.0	30.92
GNE-HT German	82.8	9.9	3.914	36.8	6.02	14.48	41.47	50.53	76.67	120.0	38.66
GNE-NMT Chinese-Japanese	74.3	4.3	4.608	32.8	3.84	24.08	45.83	54.11	79.17	120.0	35.45

Table 6: Results for translation-based rewriting, ordered by decreasing average adequacy (Par_A). Horizontal lines between methods denote significance cluster boundaries. Edits measures average number of edits needed to create rewrite (higher means greater diversity). BLEU score measures overlap with original sentence (lower means greater diversity). Labelling time measured in seconds, with a maximum timeout set to two minutes. P_{25} and P_{75} refer to the 25th and 75th percentiles of observed labelling time, respectively; StdDev to standard deviation.

other informal patterns. As prior work has mentioned (Michel and Neubig, 2018), NMT models often corrupt these inputs, leading to bad paraphrases.

Negation handling. One classic struggle for machine translation approaches is negation – losing or adding negation is a common error type. Paraphrases generated through NMT are no exception.

4.2 Key findings

Given our experimental results, we formulate the following empirical conclusions:

"Monolingual is better" Human rewriting achieves higher adequacy and fluency scores compared to all tested translation methods. This comes at a relatively high cost, though.

"Non-experts more adequate..." Human experts appear worse than non-experts in adequacy. We have empirically identified a way to either save or produce more paraphrases for the same budget.

"...but less diverse" Non-expert paraphrases are not as diverse as those created by experts. Expert rewrites also fix source text issues such as profanity.

"MT is not bad" Neural machine translation performs surprisingly well, creating more diverse output than human experts.

"Post-editing is better" Paraphrase adequacy, paraphrase fluency and translation adequacy benefit from human post-editing. In our experiments, this method achieved best performance of all tested translation methods.

"Human translations are expensive and less adequate" While humans achieve high translation adequacy scores and good paraphrase diversity, the corresponding paraphrase adequacy values are worst among all tested methods (except two-pivot NMT, which solves a harder problem).

"Related languages are better..." Generating paraphrases by translation works better when pivot languages are closely related.

"...but less diverse" Unrelated pivot languages create more diverse paraphrases.

"Use neural MT for cheap, large data!" Seems good enough to work for constrained budgets, can be improved with post-editing as needed. Specifically, we have empirically proven that you can increase paraphrase diversity by using NMT pivot translation, combined with non-expert rewriting.

5 Conclusions

Somewhat surprisingly, strong neural machine translation is more effective at paraphrase generation than humans: it is cheap, adequate, and diverse. In contrast, crowd workers required more money, producing more adequate translations but with trivial edits. Although neural MT also produced less fluent outputs, post-editing could improve the quality with little additional expenditure. Expert linguists produced the highest quality paraphrases, but at substantially greater cost. Translation-based paraphrases are more diverse.

One limitation of this survey is the input data selection: generally all input sentences contained some kind of error. This may benefit some techniques – humans in particular can navigate these errors easily. Also, the casual data used often included profanity and idiomatic expressions. Translators often rewrote profane expressions, perhaps decreasing adequacy. Future work on different data sets could further quantify such data effects.

Method	Text
ORIGINAL	Rick, It was really great visiting with you the other day.
EXPERT	Rick, it was ~~really~~ great visiting ~~with~~ you the other day.
NMT CHINESE-JAPANESE	Rick, the visit with you a few days ago was great.
PE GERMAN	Rick, it was ~~really~~ great visiting with you the other day.
PE FRENCH	Rick, It was really fantastic visiting with you the other day.
HT FRENCH	Rick, it was really good to visit you the other day.
HT GERMAN	Rick, it was really great to visit you recently.
NON-EXPERT	Rick, it was really great visiting with you the other day.
NMT FRENCH	Rick, it was really great to visit with you the other day.
NMT GERMAN	Rick, It was really great to visit with you the other day.
ORIGINAL	Yeah exactly, btw how did u manage to update ur nvidia driver ?
EXPERT	Yes, exactly. How did you update your Nvidia driver?
NMT CHINESE-JAPANESE	Yes, exactly. By the way, how were you able to update your NVIDIA drivers?
PE GERMAN	Yes, exactly - how did you update your Nvidia driver?
PE FRENCH	Yes exactly, by the way how did you manage to update your Nvidia driver ?
HT FRENCH	Yeah, exactly, by the way, how did you manage to update your NVIDIA driver?
HT GERMAN	Yes exactly, moreover, how did you manage to update your NVIDIA driver?
NON-EXPERT	Yes, exactly. By the way, did you manage to update your Nvidia driver?
NMT FRENCH	Yes exactly, BTW How did you manage to update your NVIDIA driver?
NMT GERMAN	Yes, exactly, ~~btw~~ how did you manage to update your nvidia driver?
ORIGINAL	Is it actually more benefitial/safe to do this many exercises a day?
EXPERT	Is it ~~actually~~ more beneficial and safe to do so many exercises in a day?
NMT CHINESE-JAPANESE	Tell me if daily practice is good?
PE GERMAN	Is it actually more safe and important to do this many exercises a day?
PE FRENCH	Is it actually more benefitial/safe to do as many exercises a day?
HT FRENCH	Is it really more beneficial/safe to do so much exercise per day?
HT GERMAN	Is it really more beneficial / safer to do so many exercises per day?
NON-EXPERT	Is it actually more beneficial and safe to do this many exercises a day?
NMT FRENCH	Is it actually more benefitial/safe to do ~~this~~ many exercises per day?
NMT GERMAN	Is it actually beneditialat/sure to do these many exercises a day?
ORIGINAL	The cold and rain couldn't effect my enjoyment.
EXPERT	The cold and rain could not affect my enjoyment.
NMT CHINESE-JAPANESE	Cold and rain can not detract from my enjoyment.
PE GERMAN	The cold and rain will not affect my enjoyment.
PE FRENCH	The cold and rain could not effect my enjoyment.
HT FRENCH	Cold and rain dont satisfy me.
HT GERMAN	The cold and rain couldnt spoil my enjoyment.
NON-EXPERT	The cold and the rain couldn't affect my happiness.
NMT FRENCH	The cold and the rain could not affect my pleasure.
NMT GERMAN	The cold and rain couldn't affect my enjoyment.

Table 7: Example paraphrases generated by several monolingual and bilingual methods. Changed regions are highlighted – insertions are presented in green, and deleted phrases from the original sentence are highlighted in ~~red and strikethrough~~. Note how Non-Expert translations tend to be the most conservative, except when clearly informal language is rewritten or corrected.

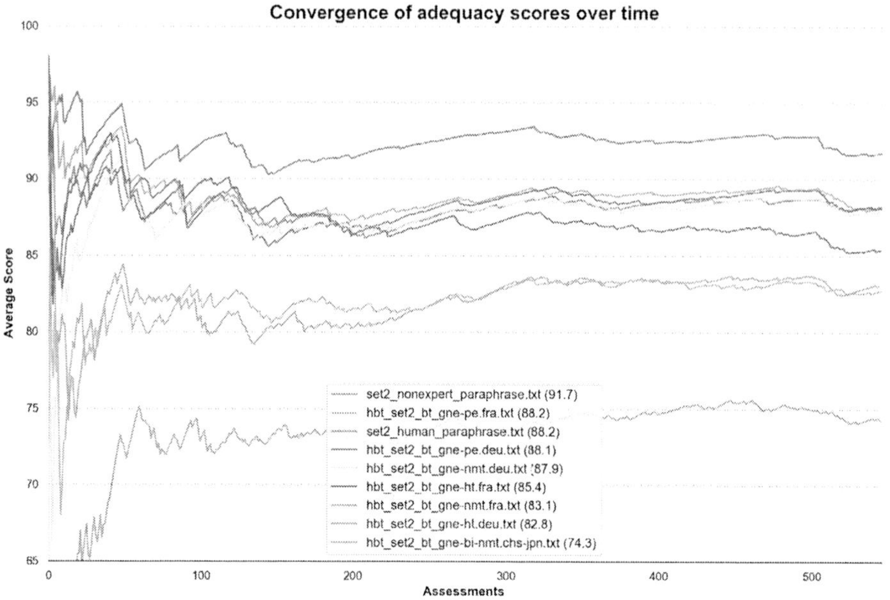

Figure 2: Convergence of adequacy scores over time. Despite the lack of an absolute standard of system assessment, a diverse set of judges rapidly converge to a consistent ranking of system quality. Within a 100 to 200 judgements, the rating has basically stabilized, though we continue to assess the whole set for greatest stability and confidence in ranking. We note, however, that readers should take caution in an absolute reading of these ratings – instead, it should reflect a relative quality assessment among the approaches under consideration.

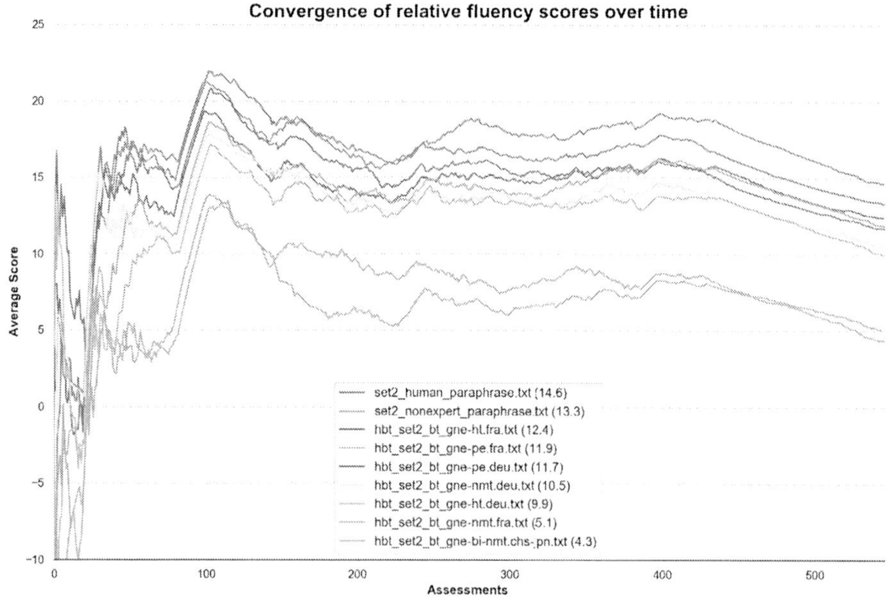

Figure 3: Convergence of relative fluency scores over time. These assessments reflect the same trends as adequacy – raters rapidly converge on a relative assessment of distinct systems.

Acknowledgments

The authors thank the three anonymous reviewers for their feedback and valuable suggestions, which we have addressed in the final version of this paper.

References

Colin Bannard and Chris Callison-Burch. 2005. Paraphrasing with Bilingual Parallel Corpora. In *Proceedings of the 43rd Annual Meeting of the Association for Computational Linguistics (ACL'05)*, pages 597–604, Ann Arbor, Michigan. Association for Computational Linguistics.

Regina Barzilay and Kathleen R. McKeown. 2001. Extracting Paraphrases from a Parallel Corpus. In *Proceedings of 39th Annual Meeting of the Association for Computational Linguistics*, pages 50–57, Toulouse, France. Association for Computational Linguistics.

Steven Bird, Ewan Klein, and Edward Loper. 2009. *Natural Language Processing with Python*. O'Reilly Media.

Ondřej Bojar, Rajen Chatterjee, Christian Federmann, Yvette Graham, Barry Haddow, Matthias Huck, Antonio Jimeno Yepes, Philipp Koehn, Varvara Logacheva, Christof Monz, Matteo Negri, Aurelie Neveol, Mariana Neves, Martin Popel, Matt Post, Raphael Rubino, Carolina Scarton, Lucia Specia, Marco Turchi, Karin Verspoor, and Marcos Zampieri. 2016. Findings of the 2016 Conference on Machine Translation. In *Proceedings of the First Conference on Machine Translation*, pages 131–198, Berlin, Germany. Association for Computational Linguistics.

Ondřej Bojar, Christian Federmann, Mark Fishel, Yvette Graham, Barry Haddow, Matthias Huck, Philipp Koehn, and Christof Monz. 2018. Findings of the 2018 Conference on Machine Translation (WMT18). In *Proceedings of the Third Conference on Machine Translation, Volume 2: Shared Task Papers*, pages 272–307, Belgium, Brussels. Association for Computational Linguistics.

Sheila Castilho, Joss Moorkens, Federico Gaspari, Iacer Calixto, John Tinsley, and Andy Way. 2017. Is Neural Machine Translation the New State of the Art? *The Prague Bulletin of Mathematical Linguistics*, 108:109–120.

Mauro Cettolo, Marcello Federico, Luisa Bentivogli, Jan Niehues, Sebastian Stüker, Katsuhito Sudoh, Koichiro Yoshino, and Christian Federmann. 2017. Overview of the IWSLT 2017 Evaluation Campaign. In *International Workshop on Spoken Language Translation*, pages 2–14, Tokyo, Japan.

David Chen and William Dolan. 2011. Collecting Highly Parallel Data for Paraphrase Evaluation. In *Proceedings of the 49th Annual Meeting of the Association for Computational Linguistics: Human Language Technologies*, pages 190–200. Association for Computational Linguistics.

Bill Dolan, Chris Quirk, and Chris Brockett. 2004. Unsupervised Construction of Large Paraphrase Corpora: Exploiting Massively Parallel News Sources. In *Proceedings of the 20th International Conference on Computational Linguistics*, COLING '04, Stroudsburg, PA, USA. Association for Computational Linguistics.

Christian Federmann. 2018. Appraise Evaluation Framework for Machine Translation. In *Proceedings of the 27th International Conference on Computational Linguistics: System Demonstrations*, pages 86–88, Santa Fe, New Mexico. Association for Computational Linguistics.

Juri Ganitkevitch, Benjamin Van Durme, and Chris Callison-Burch. 2013. PPDB: The Paraphrase Database. In *Proceedings of the 2013 Conference of the North American Chapter of the Association for Computational Linguistics: Human Language Technologies*, pages 758–764, Atlanta, Georgia. Association for Computational Linguistics.

Yvette Graham, Timothy Baldwin, Alistair Moffat, and Justin Zobel. 2013. Continuous Measurement Scales in Human Evaluation of Machine Translation. In *Proceedings of the 7th Linguistic Annotation Workshop and Interoperability with Discourse*, pages 33–41. Association for Computational Linguistics.

Yvette Graham, Timothy Baldwin, Alistair Moffat, and Justin Zobel. 2014. Is Machine Translation Getting Better over Time? In *Proceedings of the 14th Conference of the European Chapter of the Association for Computational Linguistics*, pages 443–451. Association for Computational Linguistics.

J. Edward Hu, Rachel Rudinger, Matt Post, and Benjamin Van Durme. 2019. ParaBank: Monolingual bitext generation and sentential paraphrasing via lexically-constrained neural machine translation. In *Proceedings of AAAI*.

Youxuan Jiang, Jonathan K. Kummerfeld, and Walter S. Lasecki. 2017. Understanding Task Design Tradeoffs in Crowdsourced Paraphrase Collection. In *Proceedings of the 55th Annual Meeting of the Association for Computational Linguistics (Volume 2: Short Papers)*, pages 103–109, Vancouver, Canada. Association for Computational Linguistics.

Wuwei Lan, Siyu Qiu, Hua He, and Wei Xu. 2017. A Continuously Growing Dataset of Sentential Paraphrases. In *Proceedings of The 2017 Conference on Empirical Methods on Natural Language Processing (EMNLP)*, pages 1224–1234, Copenhagen, Denmark. Association for Computational Linguistics.

Samuel Läubli, Rico Sennrich, and Martin Volk. 2018. Has Machine Translation Achieved Human Parity? A Case for Document-level Evaluation. In *Proceedings of the 2018 Conference on Empirical Methods in Natural Language Processing*, pages 4791–4796. Association for Computational Linguistics.

Jonathan Mallinson, Rico Sennrich, and Mirella Lapata. 2017. Paraphrasing Revisited with Neural Machine Translation. In *Proceedings of the 15th Conference of the European Chapter of the Association for Computational Linguistics: Volume 1, Long Papers*, pages 881–893, Valencia, Spain. Association for Computational Linguistics.

Paul Michel and Graham Neubig. 2018. MTNT: A Testbed for Machine Translation of Noisy Text. In *Proceedings of the 2018 Conference on Empirical Methods in Natural Language Processing*, pages 543–553, Brussels, Belgium. Association for Computational Linguistics.

Kishore Papineni, Salim Roukos, Todd Ward, and Wei-Jing Zhu. 2002. Bleu: a Method for Automatic Evaluation of Machine Translation. In *Proceedings of the 40th Annual Meeting of the Association for Computational Linguistics*, pages 311–318, Philadelphia, Pennsylvania, USA. Association for Computational Linguistics.

Ellie Pavlick, Pushpendre Rastogi, Juri Ganitkevich, Benjamin Van Durme, and Chris Callison-Burch. 2015. PPDB 2.0: Better Paraphrase Ranking, fine-grained Entailment Relations, Word Embeddings, and Style Classification. In *Proceedings of the 53rd Annual Meeting of the Association for Computational Linguistics and the 7th International Joint Conference on Natural Language Processing (Volume 2: Short Papers)*, pages 425–430, Beijing, China. Association for Computational Linguistics.

Aaditya Prakash, Sadid A. Hasan, Kathy Lee, Vivek Datla, Ashequl Qadir, Joey Liu, and Oladimeji Farri. 2016. Neural Paraphrase Generation with Stacked Residual LSTM Networks. In *Proceedings of COLING 2016, the 26th International Conference on Computational Linguistics: Technical Papers*, pages 2923–2934, Osaka, Japan. The COLING 2016 Organizing Committee.

Su Wang, Rahul Gupta, Nancy Chang, and Jason Baldridge. 2018. A task in a suit and a tie: paraphrase generation with semantic augmentation. *CoRR*, abs/1811.00119.

John Wieting and Kevin Gimpel. 2018. ParaNMT-50M: Pushing the Limits of Paraphrastic Sentence Embeddings with Millions of Machine Translations. In *Proceedings of the 56th Annual Meeting of the Association for Computational Linguistics (Volume 1: Long Papers)*, pages 451–462. Association for Computational Linguistics.

Personalizing Grammatical Error Correction:
Adaptation to Proficiency Level and L1

Maria Nădejde
Grammarly
maria.nadejde@grammarly.com

Joel Tetreault*
Dataminr
jtetreault@dataminr.com

Abstract

Grammar error correction (GEC) systems have become ubiquitous in a variety of software applications, and have started to approach human-level performance for some datasets. However, very little is known about how to efficiently personalize these systems to the user's characteristics, such as their proficiency level and first language, or to emerging domains of text. We present the first results on adapting a general purpose neural GEC system to both the proficiency level and the first language of a writer, using only a few thousand annotated sentences. Our study is the broadest of its kind, covering five proficiency levels and twelve different languages, and comparing three different adaptation scenarios: adapting to the proficiency level only, to the first language only, or to both aspects simultaneously. We show that tailoring to both scenarios achieves the largest performance improvement (3.6 $F_{0.5}$) relative to a strong baseline.

1 Introduction

Guides for English teachers have extensively documented how grammatical errors made by learners are influenced by their native language (L1). Swan and Smith (2001) attribute some of the errors to "transfer" or "interference" between languages. For example, German native speakers are more likely to incorrectly use a definite article with general purpose nouns or omit the indefinite article when defining people's professions. Other errors are attributed to the absence of a certain linguistic feature in the native language. For example, Chinese and Russian speakers make more errors involving articles, since these languages do not have articles.

A few grammatical error correction (GEC) systems have incorporated knowledge about L1. Ro-

zovskaya and Roth (2011) use a different prior for each of five L1s to adapt a Naive Bayes classifier for preposition correction. Rozovskaya et al. (2017) expand on this work to eleven L1s and three error types. Mizumoto et al. (2011) showed for the first time that a statistical machine translation (SMT) system applied to GEC performs better when the training and test data have the same L1. Chollampatt et al. (2016) extend this work by adapting a neural language model to three different L1s and use it as a feature in SMT-based GEC system. However, we are not aware of prior work addressing the impact of both proficiency level and native language on the performance of GEC systems. Furthermore, neural GEC systems, which have become state-of-the-art (Gehring et al., 2017; Junczys-Dowmunt et al., 2018; Grundkiewicz and Junczys-Dowmunt, 2018), are general purpose and domain agnostic.

We believe the future of GEC lies in providing users with feedback that is personalized to their proficiency level and native language (L1). In this work, we present the first results on adapting a general purpose neural GEC system for English to both of these characteristics by using fine-tuning, a transfer learning method for neural networks, which has been extensively explored for domain adaptation of machine translation systems (Luong and Manning, 2015; Freitag and Al-Onaizan, 2016; Chu et al., 2017; Miceli Barone et al., 2017; Thompson et al., 2018). We show that a model adapted to both L1 and proficiency level outperforms models adapted to only one of these characteristics. Our contributions also include the first results on adapting GEC systems to proficiency levels and the broadest study of adapting GEC to L1 which includes twelve different languages.

---

*This research was conducted while the author was at Grammarly.

Proceedings of the 2019 EMNLP Workshop W-NUT: The 5th Workshop on Noisy User-generated Text, pages 27–33
Hong Kong, Nov 4, 2019. ©2019 Association for Computational Linguistics

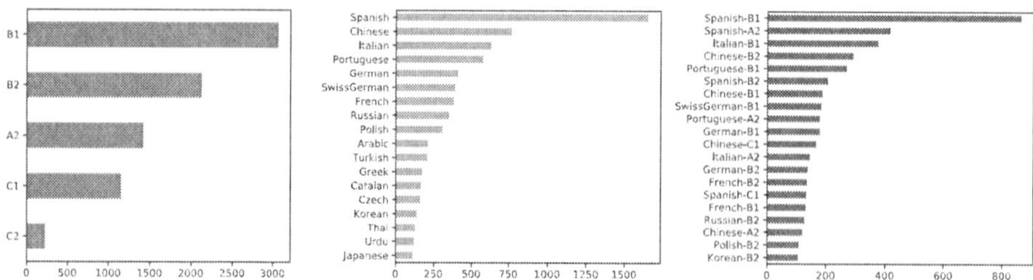

Figure 1: Corpus Distributions for CEFR Level, L1 and L1-Level.

2 Personalizing GEC

Data In this work, we adapt a general purpose neural GEC system, initially trained on two million sentences written by both native and non-native speakers and covering a variety of topics and styles. All the sentences have been corrected for grammatical errors by professional editors.[1]

Adaptation of the model to proficiency level and L1 requires a corpus annotated with these features. We use the Cambridge Learner Corpus (CLC) (Nicholls, 2003) comprising examination essays written by English learners with six proficiency levels[2] and more than 100 different native languages. Each essay is corrected by one annotator, who also identifies the minimal error spans and labels them using about 80 error types. From this annotated corpus we extract a parallel corpus comprising of source sentences with grammatical errors and the corresponding corrected target sentences.

We do note the proprietary nature of the CLC which makes reproducibility difficult, though it has been used in prior research, such as Rei and Yannakoudakis (2016). It was necessary for this study as the other GEC corpora available are not annotated for both L1 and level. The Lang-8 Learner Corpora (Mizumoto et al., 2011) also provides information about L1, but it has no information about proficiency levels. The FCE dataset (Yannakoudakis et al., 2011) is a subset of the CLC, however, it only covers one proficiency level and there are not enough sentences for each L1 for our experiments. Previous work on adapting GEC classifiers to L1 (Rozovskaya et al., 2017) used the FCE corpus, and thus did not address adaptation to different proficiency levels. One of our future goals is to create a public corpus for this type of work.

Experimental Setup Our baseline neural GEC system is an RNN-based encoder-decoder neural network with attention and LSTM units (Bahdanau et al., 2015). The system takes as input an English sentence which may contain grammatical errors and decodes the corrected sentence. We train the system on the parallel corpus extracted from the CLC with the OpenNMT-py toolkit (Klein et al., 2018) using the hyperparameters listed in the Appendix. To increase the coverage of the neural network's vocabulary, without hurting efficiency, we break source and target words into sub-word units. The segmentation into sub-word units is learned from unlabeled data using the Byte Pair Encoding (BPE) algorithm (Sennrich et al., 2016). The vocabulary, consisting of 20,000 BPE sub-units, is shared between the encoder and decoder.[3] We truncate sentences longer than 60 BPE sub-units and train the baseline system with early stopping on a development set sampled from the base dataset.[4]

To train and evaluate the adapted models, we extract subsets of sentences from the CLC that have been written by learners having a particular Level, L1, or L1-Level combination. We consider all subsets having at least 11,000 sentences, such that we can allocate 8,000 sentences for training, 1,000 for tuning and 2,000 for testing. We compare adapted models trained and evaluated on the same subset of the data. For example, we adapt a model using the Chinese training data and then evaluate it on the Chinese test set.

Since our base dataset and CLC are different domains, we wanted to make sure that improve-

---

ments by fine-tuning by Level or L1 were not due to simply being in-domain with the test data, which is also from the CLC. To control for this, we construct another baseline system ("Random") by adapting the general purpose GEC system to a random sample of learner data drawn from the CLC. In Figure 1 we show the distribution of Level, L1 and L1-Level sentences in a random CLC sample, for the subsets having at least 100 sentences. B1 is the most frequent level, while A2, the lowest proficiency level included in this study, is half as frequent in the random sample. The L1 distribution is dominated by Spanish, with Chinese second with half as many sentences. Among the L1-Level subsets, Spanish-B2 is the most frequent with Spanish-A2 covering half as many sentences.

Fine-tuning We build adapted GEC models using fine-tuning, a transfer learning method for neural networks. We continue training the parameters of the general purpose model on the "in-domain" subset of the data covering a particular Level, L1, or L1-Level. Thompson et al. (2018) showed that adapting only a single component of the encoder-decoder network is almost as effective as adapting the entire set of parameters. In this work, we fine-tune the parameters of the source embeddings and encoder, while keeping the other parameters fixed.

To avoid quickly over-fitting to the smaller "in-domain" training data, we reduce the batch size (Thompson et al., 2018) and continue using the dropout regularization (Miceli Barone et al., 2017). We apply dropout to all the layers and to the source words, as well as variational dropout (Gal and Ghahramani, 2016) on each step, all with probability 0.1. We also reduce the learning rate by four times and use the `start_decay_at` option which halves the learning rate after each epoch. Consequently, the updates become small after a few epochs. To enable the comparison between different adaptation scenarios, all fine-tuned models are trained for 10 epochs on 8,000 sentences of "in-domain" data.

3   Results

We report the results for the three adaptation scenarios: adapting to Level only, adapting to L1 only, and adapting to both L1 and Level. We summarize the results by showing the average M^2 $F_{0.5}$ score (Dahlmeier and Ng, 2012) across all the test sets included in the respective scenario.

We first note that the strong baseline ("Random"), which is a model adapted to a random sample of CLC , achieves improvements between 11 to 13 $F_{0.5}$ points on average on all scenarios. While not the focus of the paper, this large improvement shows the performance gains by simply adapting to a new domain (in this case CLC data). Second, we note that the models adapted only by Level or by L1 are on average better than the "Random" model by 2.1 and 2.3 $F_{0.5}$ points respectively. Finally, the models adapted to both Level and L1 outperform all others, beating the "Random" baseline on average by 3.6 $F_{0.5}$ points.

On all adaptation scenarios we report the performance of the single best model released by Junczys-Dowmunt et al. (2018). Their model, which we call *JD single*, was trained on English learner data of comparable size to our base dataset and optimized using the CoNLL14 training and test data.

Adaptation by Proficiency Level We adapt GEC models to five of the CEFR proficiency levels: A2, B1, B2, C1, C2. The results in Table 1 show that performance improves for all levels compared to the "Random" baseline. The largest improvement, 5.2 $F_{0.5}$ points, is achieved for A2, the lowest proficiency level. We attribute the large improvement to this level having a higher error rate, a lower lexical diversity and being less represented in the random sample on which the baseline is trained on. In contrast, for the B1 and B2 levels, the most frequent in the random sample, improvements are more modest: 0.7 and 0.2 $F_{0.5}$ points respectively. Our adapted models are better than the *JD single* model on all levels, and with a large margin on the A2 and C1 levels.

Adapt	A2	B1	B2	C1	C2	Avg.
No	30.4	34.9	33.1	32.5	33.0	32.8
Rand.	48.4	47.9	42.5	41.4	39.2	43.8
Level	**53.6**	**48.6**	**42.7**	**43.3**	**41.1**	**45.9**
JD single	44.1	47.1	41.7	37.8	35.0	44.1

Table 1: Adaptation to Proficiency Level in $F_{0.5}$

Adaptation by L1 We adapt GEC models to twelve L1s: Arabic, Chinese, French, German, Greek, Italian, Polish, Portuguese, Russian, Spanish, Swiss-German and Turkish. The results in Table 2 (top) show that all L1-adapted models are better than the baseline, with improvements ranging from 1.2 $F_{0.5}$ for Chinese and French, up

Adapt	AR	CN	FR	DE	GR	IT	PL	PT	RU	ES	CH	TR	Avg
No	37.5	36.2	32.7	31.4	32.7	29.3	36.0	31.7	35.8	32.1	31.1	35.4	33.5
Random	46.3	45.0	44.9	44.7	46.4	44.9	46.2	45.2	45.3	47.6	44.2	47.0	45.6
L1	**48.3**	**46.2**	**46.1**	**47.1**	**49.0**	**46.8**	**48.4**	**47.6**	**47.8**	**49.8**	**47.1**	**50.6**	**47.9**
JD single	47.0	44.7	44.2	41.4	44.1	40.7	46.0	44.6	43.7	44.8	40.7	47.5	44.1

Adapt	CN-B2	CN-C1	FR-B1	DE-B1	IT-B1	PT-B1	ES-A2	ES-B1	ES-B2	Avg.
No	36.1	32.5	31.8	31.2	28.1	31.4	28.9	31.9	33.7	31.8
Random	42.7	39.1	45.3	46.1	43.5	45.2	50.2	46.4	44.1	44.7
Level	43.4	41.0	46.5	46.9	45.3	46.1	56.6	47.5	43.7	46.3
L1	44.1	40.9	46.5	48.1	46.5	46.2	53.8	47.6	44.4	46.5
L1 & Level	**45.5**	**43.1**	**48.1**	**50.2**	**47.3**	**47.9**	**58.2**	**48.8**	**45.6**	**48.3**
JD single	43.0	35.8	46.9	43.8	41.6	46.7	43.4	45.0	41.0	43.0

Table 2: Top: Adaptation to L1 Only. Bottom: Adaptation to Level and L1. Eval metric: $F_{0.5}$

to 3.6 $F_{0.5}$ for Turkish. For the languages that are less frequent in the random sample of CLC (Greek, Turkish, Arabic, Polish and Russian) we see consistent improvements of over 2 $F_{0.5}$ points. Our adapted models are better than the *JD single* model on all L1s, and with a margin larger than 5 $F_{0.5}$ points on German, Swiss-German, Italian, Greek and Spanish.

Adaptation by L1 and Proficiency Level Finally, we adapt GEC models to the following nine L1 – Level subsets: Chinese-B2, Chinese-C1, French-B1, German-B1, Italian-B1, Portuguese-B1, Spanish-A2, Spanish-B1 and Spanish-B2. We include these subsets in our study because they meet the requirement of having at least 8,000 sentences for training. All the models adapted to both Level and L1 outperform the models adapted to only one of these features, as shown in Table 2 (bottom). Focusing on the two levels for Chinese native speakers, we see the model adapted to C1 achieves a larger improvement over the baseline, 4.1 $F_{0.5}$ points, compared to 2.7 $F_{0.5}$ points for the B2 level. Again, this is explained by the lower frequency of the C1 level in the random sample of CLC, which is also reflected by the lowest $F_{0.5}$ score for the baseline model. Similarly, among the models adapted to different levels of Spanish native speakers, the one adapted to Spanish-A2 achieves the largest gains of 8 $F_{0.5}$ points. The Spanish-A2 testset has the highest number of errors per 100 words among all the L1-Level testsets, as shown in Table 1 in the Appendix. Furthermore, the A2 level is only half as frequent as the B1 level in the random sample of CLC. Finally, our adapted models are better than the *JD single* model on all L1–Level subsets, with a margin of 5

$F_{0.5}$ points on average.

Adapted	P	R	F0.5
Random	61.9	35.6	54.0
CN-C1	61.1	37.0	54.1
CN-B2	62.4	37.5	55.1
+ spellcheck	63.6	40.3	57.0
JD single	59.1	40.4	54.1
JD ensemble	63.1	42.6	57.5

Table 3: Results on the CoNLL14 testsets for Chinese models.

CoNLL14 Evaluation We compare our adapted models on the CoNLL14 testset (Ng et al., 2014) in Table 3. The model adapted to Chinese-B2 improves the most over the baseline, achieving 55.1 $F_{0.5}$. This result aligns with how the test set was constructed: it consists of essays written by university students, mostly Chinese native speakers. When we pre-process the evaluation set before decoding with a commercial spellchecker[5], our adapted model scores 57.0 which places it near other leading models, trained on a similar amount of data, such as Chollampatt and Ng (2018) (56.52) and Junczys-Dowmunt et al. (2018)[6] (57.53) even though we do not use the CoNLL14 in-domain training data. We note that the most recent state-of-the-art models (Zhao et al., 2019; Grundkiewicz et al., 2019), are trained on up to one hundred million additional synthetic parallel sentences, while we adapt models with only eight thousand parallel sentences.

---

[5] Details removed for anonymity.

[6] We call their ensemble of four models with language model re-scoring *JD ensemble* and their single best model without language model re-scoring *JD single*

Adapt	Det	Prep	Verb	Tense	NNum	Noun	Pron
CN-C1	3.53	5.90	2.99	1.77	8.28	8.02	22.78
FR-B1	2.34	1.99	12.54	5.16	9.16	3.48	1.13
DE-B1	8.85	1.77	2.04	2.37	3.86	7.18	22.75
IT-B1	2.37	5.32	12.48	6.74	4.40	3.29	8.99
ES-A2	6.06	12.52	7.51	8.54	8.73	12.39	10.57

Table 4: L1-Level breakdown by error type in relative improvements in $F_{0.5}$ over the "Random" baseline.

Error-type Analysis We conclude our study by reporting improvements on the most frequent error types, excluding punctuation, spelling and orthography errors. We identify the error types in each evaluation set with Errant, a rule-based classifier (Bryant et al., 2017). Table 4 shows the results for the systems adapted to both L1 and Level that improved the most in overall $F_{0.5}$. The adapted systems consistently outperform the "Random" baseline on most error types. For Chinese-C1, the adapted model achieves the largest gains on pronoun (Pron) and noun number agreement errors (NNum). The Spanish-A2 adapted model achieves notable gains on preposition (Prep), noun and pronoun errors. Both the French-B1 and Italian-B1 adapted models gain the most on verb errors. For German-B1, the adapted model improves the most on pronoun (Pron) and determiner (Det) errors. The large improvement of 22.75 $F_{0.5}$ points for the pronoun category is in part an artefact of the small error counts. The adapted model corrects 35 pronouns (P=67.3) while the baseline corrects only 15 pronouns (P=46.9). We leave an in depth analysis by error type to future work.

Below, we give an example of a confused auxiliary verb that the French-B1 adapted model corrects. The verb phrase corresponding to "go shopping" in French is "faire des achats", where the verb "faire" would translate to "make/do".

Orig	He told me that celebrity can be bad because he can't *do* shopping normally.
Rand	He told me that *the* celebrity can be bad because he can't *do* shopping normally.
FR-B1	He told me that celebrity can be bad because he can't *go* shopping normally.
Ref	He told me that celebrity can be bad because he can't *go* shopping normally.

4 Conclusions

We present the first results on adapting a neural GEC system to proficiency level and L1 of language learners. This is the broadest study of its kind, covering five proficiency levels and twelve different languages. While models adapted to either proficiency level or L1 are on average better than the baseline by over 2 $F_{0.5}$ points and the largest improvement (3.6 $F_{0.5}$) is achieved when adapting to both characteristics simultaneously.

We envision building a single model that combines knowledge across L1s and proficiency levels using a mixture-of-experts approach. Adapted models could also be improved by using the *mixed fine tuning* approach which uses a mix of in-domain and out-of-domain data (Chu et al., 2017).

Acknowledgements

The authors would like to thank the anonymous reviewers for their feedback. We are also grateful to our colleagues for their assistance and insights: Dimitrios Alikaniotis, Claudia Leacock, Dmitry Lider, Courtney Napoles, Jimmy Nguyen, Vipul Raheja and Igor Tytyk.

References

Dzmitry Bahdanau, Kyunghyun Cho, and Yoshua Bengio. 2015. Neural machine translation by jointly learning to align and translate. In *Proceedings of the International Conference on Learning Representations (ICLR)*.

Christopher Bryant, Mariano Felice, and Ted Briscoe. 2017. Automatic annotation and evaluation of error types for grammatical error correction. In *Proceedings of the 55th Annual Meeting of the Association for Computational Linguistics (Volume 1: Long Papers)*, pages 793–805, Vancouver, Canada. Association for Computational Linguistics.

Shamil Chollampatt, Duc Tam Hoang, and Hwee Tou Ng. 2016. Adapting grammatical error correction based on the native language of writers with neural network joint models. In *Proceedings of the*

2016 Conference on Empirical Methods in Natural Language Processing, pages 1901–1911. Association for Computational Linguistics.

Shamil Chollampatt and Hwee Tou Ng. 2018. Neural quality estimation of grammatical error correction. In *Proceedings of the 2018 Conference on Empirical Methods in Natural Language Processing*, pages 2528–2539, Brussels, Belgium. Association for Computational Linguistics.

Chenhui Chu, Raj Dabre, and Sadao Kurohashi. 2017. An empirical comparison of domain adaptation methods for neural machine translation. In *Proceedings of the 55th Annual Meeting of the Association for Computational Linguistics (Volume 2: Short Papers)*, pages 385–391. Association for Computational Linguistics.

Daniel Dahlmeier and Hwee Tou Ng. 2012. Better evaluation for grammatical error correction. In *Proceedings of the 2012 Conference of the North American Chapter of the Association for Computational Linguistics: Human Language Technologies*, pages 568–572, Montréal, Canada. Association for Computational Linguistics.

Markus Freitag and Yaser Al-Onaizan. 2016. Fast domain adaptation for neural machine translation. *CoRR*, abs/1612.06897.

Yarin Gal and Zoubin Ghahramani. 2016. A theoretically grounded application of dropout in recurrent neural networks. In *Proceedings of the 30th International Conference on Neural Information Processing Systems*, NIPS'16, pages 1027–1035, USA. Curran Associates Inc.

Jonas Gehring, Michael Auli, David Grangier, Denis Yarats, and Yann N. Dauphin. 2017. Convolutional sequence to sequence learning. In *Proceedings of the 34th International Conference on Machine Learning*, volume 70 of *Proceedings of Machine Learning Research*, pages 1243–1252, International Convention Centre, Sydney, Australia. PMLR.

Roman Grundkiewicz and Marcin Junczys-Dowmunt. 2018. Near human-level performance in grammatical error correction with hybrid machine translation. In *Proceedings of the 2018 Conference of the North American Chapter of the Association for Computational Linguistics: Human Language Technologies, Volume 2 (Short Papers)*, pages 284–290. Association for Computational Linguistics.

Roman Grundkiewicz, Marcin Junczys-Dowmunt, and Kenneth Heafield. 2019. Neural grammatical error correction systems with unsupervised pre-training on synthetic data. In *Proceedings of the Fourteenth Workshop on Innovative Use of NLP for Building Educational Applications*, pages 252–263, Florence, Italy. Association for Computational Linguistics.

Marcin Junczys-Dowmunt, Roman Grundkiewicz, Shubha Guha, and Kenneth Heafield. 2018. Approaching neural grammatical error correction as a low-resource machine translation task. In *Proceedings of the 2018 Conference of the North American Chapter of the Association for Computational Linguistics: Human Language Technologies, Volume 1 (Long Papers)*, pages 595–606. Association for Computational Linguistics.

Guillaume Klein, Yoon Kim, Yuntian Deng, Vincent Nguyen, Jean Senellart, and Alexander Rush. 2018. Opennmt: Neural machine translation toolkit. In *Proceedings of the 13th Conference of the Association for Machine Translation in the Americas (Volume 1: Research Papers)*, pages 177–184. Association for Machine Translation in the Americas.

Minh-Thang Luong and Christopher D. Manning. 2015. Stanford neural machine translation systems for spoken language domain. In *International Workshop on Spoken Language Translation*.

Antonio Valerio Miceli Barone, Barry Haddow, Ulrich Germann, and Rico Sennrich. 2017. Regularization techniques for fine-tuning in neural machine translation. In *Proceedings of the 2017 Conference on Empirical Methods in Natural Language Processing*, pages 1489–1494. Association for Computational Linguistics.

Tomoya Mizumoto, Mamoru Komachi, Masaaki Nagata, and Yuji Matsumoto. 2011. Mining revision log of language learning sns for automated japanese error correction of second language learners. In *Proceedings of 5th International Joint Conference on Natural Language Processing*, pages 147–155. Asian Federation of Natural Language Processing.

Hwee Tou Ng, Siew Mei Wu, Ted Briscoe, Christian Hadiwinoto, Raymond Hendy Susanto, and Christopher Bryant. 2014. The CoNLL-2014 shared task on grammatical error correction. In *Proceedings of the Eighteenth Conference on Computational Natural Language Learning: Shared Task*, pages 1–14, Baltimore, Maryland. Association for Computational Linguistics.

Diane Nicholls. 2003. The Cambridge Learner Corpus: Error coding and analysis for lexicography and ELT. In *Proceedings of the Corpus Linguistics 2003 conference*, volume 16, pages 572–581.

Marek Rei and Helen Yannakoudakis. 2016. Compositional sequence labeling models for error detection in learner writing. In *Proceedings of the 54th Annual Meeting of the Association for Computational Linguistics (Volume 1: Long Papers)*, pages 1181–1191, Berlin, Germany. Association for Computational Linguistics.

Alla Rozovskaya and Dan Roth. 2011. Algorithm selection and model adaptation for esl correction tasks. In *Proceedings of the 49th Annual Meeting of the Association for Computational Linguistics: Human Language Technologies - Volume 1*, HLT '11, pages 924–933, Stroudsburg, PA, USA. Association for Computational Linguistics.

Alla Rozovskaya, Dan Roth, and Mark Sammons. 2017. Adapting to learner errors with minimal supervision. *Computational Linguistics*, 43(4):723–760.

Rico Sennrich, Barry Haddow, and Alexandra Birch. 2016. Neural machine translation of rare words with subword units. In *Proceedings of the 54th Annual Meeting of the Association for Computational Linguistics (Volume 1: Long Papers)*, Berlin, Germany. Association for Computational Linguistics.

Michael Swan and Bernard Smith. 2001. *Learner English: A Teacher's Guide to Interference and other Problems. Second Edition.* Cambridge University Press.

Brian Thompson, Huda Khayrallah, Antonios Anastasopoulos, Arya D. McCarthy, Kevin Duh, Rebecca Marvin, Paul McNamee, Jeremy Gwinnup, Tim Anderson, and Philipp Koehn. 2018. Freezing subnetworks to analyze domain adaptation in neural machine translation. In *Proceedings of the Third Conference on Machine Translation, Volume 1: Research Papers*, pages 124–132, Belgium, Brussels. Association for Computational Linguistics.

Helen Yannakoudakis, Ted Briscoe, and Ben Medlock. 2011. A new dataset and method for automatically grading ESOL texts. In *Proceedings of the 49th Annual Meeting of the Association for Computational Linguistics: Human Language Technologies*, pages 180–189, Portland, Oregon, USA. Association for Computational Linguistics.

Wei Zhao, Liang Wang, Kewei Shen, Jia Ruoyu, and Jingming Liu. 2019. Better evaluation for grammatical error correctionimproving grammatical error correction via pre-training a copy-augmented architecture with unlabeled data. In *Proceedings of the 2019 Conference of the North American Chapter of the Association for Computational Linguistics: Human Language Technologies*, Minneapolis, MN, USA. Association for Computational Linguistics.

Exploiting BERT for End-to-End Aspect-based Sentiment Analysis[*]

Xin Li[1], Lidong Bing[2], Wenxuan Zhang[1] and Wai Lam[1]
[1]Department of Systems Engineering and Engineering Management
The Chinese University of Hong Kong, Hong Kong
[2]R&D Center Singapore, Machine Intelligence Technology, Alibaba DAMO Academy
{lixin,wxzhang,wlam}@se.cuhk.edu.hk
l.bing@alibaba-inc.com

Abstract

In this paper, we investigate the modeling power of contextualized embeddings from pre-trained language models, e.g. BERT, on the E2E-ABSA task. Specifically, we build a series of simple yet insightful neural baselines to deal with E2E-ABSA. The experimental results show that even with a simple linear classification layer, our BERT-based architecture can outperform state-of-the-art works. Besides, we also standardize the comparative study by consistently utilizing a hold-out development dataset for model selection, which is largely ignored by previous works. Therefore, our work can serve as a BERT-based benchmark for E2E-ABSA.[1]

1 Introduction

Aspect-based sentiment analysis (ABSA) is to discover the users' sentiment or opinion towards an aspect, usually in the form of explicitly mentioned aspect terms (Mitchell et al., 2013; Zhang et al., 2015) or implicit aspect categories (Wang et al., 2016), from user-generated natural language texts (Liu, 2012). The most popular ABSA benchmark datasets are from SemEval ABSA challenges (Pontiki et al., 2014, 2015, 2016) where a few thousand review sentences with gold standard aspect sentiment annotations are provided.

Table 1 summarizes three existing research problems related to ABSA. The first one is the original ABSA, aiming at predicting the sentiment polarity of the sentence towards the given aspect. Compared to this classification problem, the second one and the third one, namely, Aspect-oriented Opinion Words Extraction (AOWE) (Fan

et al., 2019) and End-to-End Aspect-based Sentiment Analysis (E2E-ABSA) (Ma et al., 2018a; Schmitt et al., 2018; Li et al., 2019a; Li and Lu, 2017, 2019), are related to a sequence tagging problem. Precisely, the goal of AOWE is to extract the aspect-specific opinion words from the sentence given the aspect. The goal of E2E-ABSA is to jointly detect aspect terms/categories and the corresponding aspect sentiments.

Many neural models composed of a task-agnostic pre-trained word embedding layer and task-specific neural architecture have been proposed for the original ABSA task (i.e. the aspect-level sentiment classification) (Tang et al., 2016; Wang et al., 2016; Chen et al., 2017; Liu and Zhang, 2017; Ma et al., 2017, 2018b; Majumder et al., 2018; Li et al., 2018; He et al., 2018; Xue and Li, 2018; Wang et al., 2018; Fan et al., 2018; Huang and Carley, 2018; Lei et al., 2019; Li et al., 2019b)[2], but the improvement of these models measured by the accuracy or F1 score has reached a bottleneck. One reason is that the task-agnostic embedding layer, usually a linear layer initialized with Word2Vec (Mikolov et al., 2013) or GloVe (Pennington et al., 2014), only provides context-independent word-level features, which is insufficient for capturing the complex semantic dependencies in the sentence. Meanwhile, the size of existing datasets is too small to train sophisticated task-specific architectures. Thus, introducing a context-aware word embedding[3] layer pre-trained on large-scale datasets with deep LSTM (McCann et al., 2017; Peters et al., 2018; Howard and Ruder, 2018) or Transformer (Radford et al., 2018, 2019; Devlin et al., 2019; Lample

---

[*]The work described in this paper is substantially supported by a grant from the Research Grant Council of the Hong Kong Special Administrative Region, China (Project Code: 14204418).

[1]Our code is open-source and available at: https://github.com/lixin4ever/BERT-E2E-ABSA

[2]Due to the limited space, we can not list all of the existing works here, please refer to the survey (Zhou et al., 2019) for more related papers.

[3]In this paper, we generalize the concept of "word embedding" as a mapping between the word and the low-dimensional word representations.

Proceedings of the 2019 EMNLP Workshop W-NUT: The 5th Workshop on Noisy User-generated Text, pages 34–41
Hong Kong, Nov 4, 2019. ©2019 Association for Computational Linguistics

Sentence:	<Great> [food]$_P$ but the [service]$_N$ is <dreadful>.	
Settings	Input	Output
1. ABSA	sentence, aspect	aspect sentiment
2. AOWE	sentence, aspect	opinion words
3. E2E-ABSA	sentence	aspect, aspect sentiment

Table 1: Different problem settings in ABSA. Gold standard aspects and opinions are wrapped in [] and <> respectively. The subscripts N and P refer to aspect sentiment. Underline $\sim$ or $*$ indicates the association between the aspect and the opinion.

and Conneau, 2019; Yang et al., 2019; Dong et al., 2019) for fine-tuning a lightweight task-specific network using the labeled data has good potential for further enhancing the performance.

Xu et al. (2019); Sun et al. (2019); Song et al. (2019); Yu and Jiang (2019); Rietzler et al. (2019); Huang and Carley (2019) have conducted some initial attempts to couple the deep contextualized word embedding layer with downstream neural models for the original ABSA task and establish the new state-of-the-art results. It encourages us to explore the potential of using such contextualized embeddings to the more difficult but practical task, i.e. E2E-ABSA (the third setting in Table 1).[4] Note that we are not aiming at developing a task-specific architecture, instead, our focus is to examine the potential of contextualized embedding for E2E-ABSA, coupled with various simple layers for prediction of E2E-ABSA labels.[5]

In this paper, we investigate the modeling power of BERT (Devlin et al., 2019), one of the most popular pre-trained language model armed with Transformer (Vaswani et al., 2017), on the task of E2E ABSA. Concretely, inspired by the investigation of E2E-ABSA in Li et al. (2019a), which predicts aspect boundaries as well as aspect sentiments using a single sequence tagger, we build a series of simple yet insightful neural baselines for the sequence labeling problem and fine-tune the task-specific components with BERT or deem BERT as feature extractor. Besides, we standardize the comparative study by consistently utilizing the hold-out development dataset for model selection, which is ignored in most of the existing

---

[4]Both of ABSA and AOWE assume that the aspects in a sentence are given. Such setting makes them less practical in real-world scenarios since manual annotation of the fine-grained aspect mentions/categories is quite expensive

[5]Hu et al. (2019) introduce BERT to handle the E2E-ABSA problem but their focus is to design a task-specific architecture rather than exploring the potential of BERT.

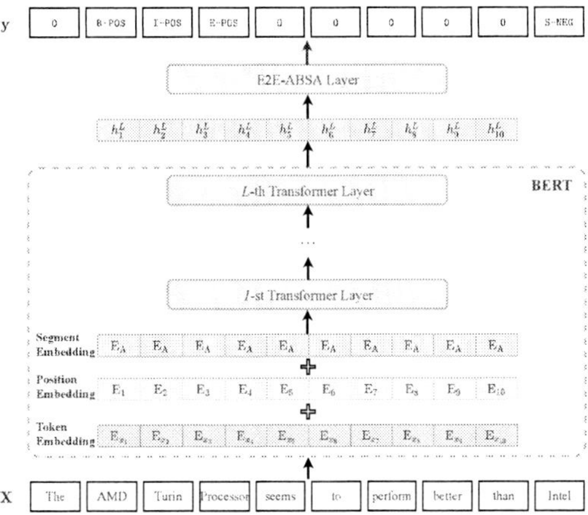

Figure 1: Overview of the designed model.

ABSA works (Tay et al., 2018).

2 Model

In this paper, we focus on the aspect term-level End-to-End Aspect-Based Sentiment Analysis (E2E-ABSA) problem setting. This task can be formulated as a sequence labeling problem. The overall architecture of our model is depicted in Figure 1. Given the input token sequence $\mathbf{x} = \{x_1, \cdots, x_T\}$ of length T, we firstly employ BERT component with L transformer layers to calculate the corresponding contextualized representations $H^L = \{h_1^L, \cdots, h_T^L\} \in \mathbb{R}^{T \times \dim_h}$ for the input tokens where $\dim_h$ denotes the dimension of the representation vector. Then, the contextualized representations are fed to the task-specific layers to predict the tag sequence $\mathbf{y} = \{y_1, \cdots, y_T\}$. The possible values of the tag y_t are B-{POS, NEG, NEU}, I-{POS, NEG, NEU}, E-{POS, NEG, NEU}, S-{POS, NEG, NEU} or O, denoting the beginning of aspect, inside of aspect, end of aspect, single-word aspect, with positive, negative or neutral sentiment respectively, as well as outside of aspect.

2.1 BERT as Embedding Layer

Compared to the traditional Word2Vec- or GloVe-based embedding layer which only provides a single context-independent representation for each token, the BERT embedding layer takes the sentence as input and calculates the token-level representations using the information from the entire sentence. First of all, we pack the input features as $H^0 = \{e_1, \cdots, e_T\}$, where e_t ($t \in [1, T]$) is the combination of the token embedding, position embedding and segment embedding corresponding to the input token x_t. Then L transformer layers are introduced to refine the token-level features layer by layer. Specifically, the representations $H^l = \{h_1^l, \cdots, h_T^l\}$ at the l-th ($l \in [1, L]$) layer are calculated below:

$$H^l = \text{Transformer}_l(H^{l-1}) \tag{1}$$

We regard H^L as the contextualized representations of the input tokens and use them to perform the predictions for the downstream task.

2.2 Design of Downstream Model

After obtaining the BERT representations, we design a neural layer, called E2E-ABSA layer in Figure 1, on top of BERT embedding layer for solving the task of E2E-ABSA. We investigate several different design for the E2E-ABSA layer, namely, linear layer, recurrent neural networks, self-attention networks, and conditional random fields layer.

Linear Layer The obtained token representations can be directly fed to linear layer with softmax activation function to calculate the token-level predictions:

$$P(y_t|x_t) = \text{softmax}(W_o h_t^L + b_o) \tag{2}$$

where $W_o \in \mathbb{R}^{\dim_h \times |\mathcal{Y}|}$ is the learnable parameters of the linear layer.

Recurrent Neural Networks Considering its sequence labeling formulation, Recurrent Neural Networks (RNN) (Elman, 1990) is a natural solution for the task of E2E-ABSA. In this paper, we adopt GRU (Cho et al., 2014), whose superiority compared to LSTM (Hochreiter and Schmidhuber, 1997) and basic RNN has been verified in Jozefowicz et al. (2015). The computational formula of the task-specific hidden representation $h_t^T \in \mathbb{R}^{\dim_h}$ at the t-th time step is shown below:

$$\begin{aligned} \begin{bmatrix} r_t \\ z_t \end{bmatrix} &= \sigma(\text{LN}(W_x h_t^L) + \text{LN}(W_h h_{t-1}^T)) \\ n_t &= \tanh(\text{LN}(W_{xn} h_t^L) + r_t * \text{LN}(W_{hn} h_{t-1}^T)) \\ h_t^T &= (1 - z_t) * n_t + z_t * h_{t-1}^T \end{aligned} \tag{3}$$

where σ is the sigmoid activation function and r_t, z_t, n_t respectively denote the reset gate, update gate and new gate. $W_x, W_h \in \mathbb{R}^{2\dim_h \times \dim_h}$, $W_{xn}, W_{hn} \in \mathbb{R}^{\dim_h \times \dim_h}$ are the parameters of

GRU. Since directly applying RNN on the output of transformer, namely, the BERT representation h_t^L, may lead to unstable training (Chen et al., 2018; Liu, 2019), we add additional layer-normalization (Ba et al., 2016), denoted as LN, when calculating the gates. Then, the predictions are obtained by introducing a softmax layer:

$$p(y_t|x_t) = \text{softmax}(W_o h_t^T + b_o) \tag{4}$$

Self-Attention Networks With the help of self attention (Cheng et al., 2016; Lin et al., 2017), Self-Attention Network (Vaswani et al., 2017; Shen et al., 2018) is another effective feature extractor apart from RNN and CNN. In this paper, we introduce two SAN variants to build the task-specific token representations $H^T = \{h_1^T, \cdots, h_T^T\}$. One variant is composed of a simple self-attention layer and residual connection (He et al., 2016), dubbed as "SAN". The computational process of SAN is below:

$$\begin{aligned} H^T &= \text{LN}(H^L + \text{SLF-ATT}(Q, K, V)) \\ Q, K, V &= H^L W^Q, H^L W^K, H^L W^V \end{aligned} \tag{5}$$

where SLF-ATT is identical to the self-attentive scaled dot-product attention (Vaswani et al., 2017). Another variant is a transformer layer (dubbed as "TFM"), which has the same architecture with the transformer encoder layer in the BERT. The computational process of TFM is as follows:

$$\begin{aligned} \hat{H}^L &= \text{LN}(H^L + \text{SLF-ATT}(Q, K, V)) \\ H^T &= \text{LN}(\hat{H}^L + \text{FFN}(\hat{H}^L)) \end{aligned} \tag{6}$$

where FFN refers to the point-wise feed-forward networks (Vaswani et al., 2017). Again, a linear layer with softmax activation is stacked on the designed SAN/TFM layer to output the predictions (same with that in Eq(4)).

Conditional Random Fields Conditional Random Fields (CRF) (Lafferty et al., 2001) is effective in sequence modeling and has been widely adopted for solving the sequence labeling tasks together with neural models (Huang et al., 2015; Lample et al., 2016; Ma and Hovy, 2016). In this paper, we introduce a linear-chain CRF layer on top of the BERT embedding layer. Different from the above mentioned neural models maximizing the token-level likelihood $p(y_t|x_t)$, the CRF-based model aims to find the globally most

	Model	LAPTOP			REST		
		P	R	F1	P	R	F1
Existing Models	(Li et al., 2019a)[♮]	61.27	54.89	57.90	68.64	71.01	69.80
	(Luo et al., 2019)[♮]	-	-	60.35	-	-	72.78
	(He et al., 2019)[♭]	-	-	58.37	-	-	-
LSTM-CRF	(Lample et al., 2016)[♭]	58.61	50.47	54.24	66.10	66.30	66.20
	(Ma and Hovy, 2016)[♭]	58.66	51.26	54.71	61.56	67.26	64.29
	(Liu et al., 2018)[♮]	53.31	59.40	56.19	68.46	64.43	66.38
BERT Models	BERT+Linear	62.16	58.90	60.43	71.42	75.25	73.22
	BERT+GRU	61.88	60.47	**61.12**	70.61	76.20	73.24
	BERT+SAN	62.42	58.71	60.49	72.92	76.72	**74.72**
	BERT+TFM	63.23	58.64	60.80	72.39	76.64	74.41
	BERT+CRF	62.22	59.49	60.78	71.88	76.48	74.06

Table 2: Main results. The symbol ♮ denotes the numbers are officially reported ones. The results with ♭ are retrieved from Li et al. (2019a).

Dataset		Train	Dev	Test	Total
LAPTOP	# sent	2741	304	800	4245
	# aspect	2041	256	634	2931
REST	# sent	3490	387	2158	6035
	# aspect	3893	413	2287	6593

Table 3: Statistics of datasets.

probable tag sequence. Specifically, the sequence-level scores $s(\mathbf{x}, \mathbf{y})$ and likelihood $p(\mathbf{y}|\mathbf{x})$ of $\mathbf{y} = \{y_1, \cdots, y_T\}$ are calculated as follows:

$$s(\mathbf{x}, \mathbf{y}) = \sum_{t=0}^{T} M^A_{y_t, y_{t+1}} + \sum_{t=1}^{T} M^P_{t, y_t} \quad (7)$$
$$p(\mathbf{y}|\mathbf{x}) = \mathrm{softmax}(s(\mathbf{x}, \mathbf{y}))$$

where $M^A \in \mathbb{R}^{|\mathcal{Y}| \times |\mathcal{Y}|}$ is the randomly initialized transition matrix for modeling the dependency between the adjacent predictions and $M^P \in \mathbb{R}^{T \times |\mathcal{Y}|}$ denote the emission matrix linearly transformed from the BERT representations H^L. The softmax here is conducted over all of the possible tag sequences. As for the decoding, we regard the tag sequence with the highest scores as output:

$$\mathbf{y}^* = \arg\max_{\mathbf{y}} s(\mathbf{x}, \mathbf{y}) \quad (8)$$

where the solution is obtained via Viterbi search.

3 Experiment

3.1 Dataset and Settings

We conduct experiments on two review datasets originating from SemEval (Pontiki et al., 2014, 2015, 2016) but re-prepared in Li et al. (2019a). The statistics are summarized in Table 3. We use the pre-trained "bert-base-uncased" model[6],

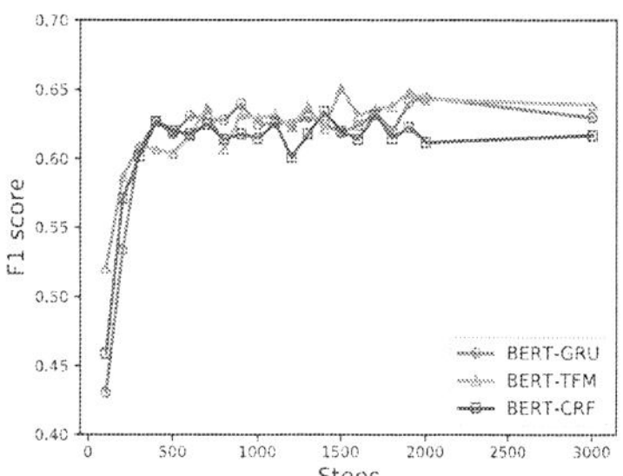

Figure 2: Performances on the Dev set of REST.

where the number of transformer layers $L = 12$ and the hidden size $\dim_h$ is 768. For the downstream E2E-ABSA component, we consistently use the single-layer architecture and set the dimension of task-specific representation as $\dim_h$. The learning rate is 2e-5. The batch size is set as 25 for LAPTOP and 16 for REST. We train the model up to 1500 steps. After training 1000 steps, we conduct model selection on the development set for very 100 steps according to the micro-averaged F1 score. Following these settings, we train 5 models with different random seeds and report the average results.

We compare with **Existing Models**, including tailor-made E2E-ABSA models (Li et al., 2019a; Luo et al., 2019; He et al., 2019), and competitive **LSTM-CRF** sequence labeling models (Lample et al., 2016; Ma and Hovy, 2016; Liu et al., 2018).

3.2 Main Results

From Table 2, we surprisingly find that only introducing a simple token-level classifier, namely, BERT-Linear, already outperforms the existing

---

[6]https://github.com/huggingface/transformers

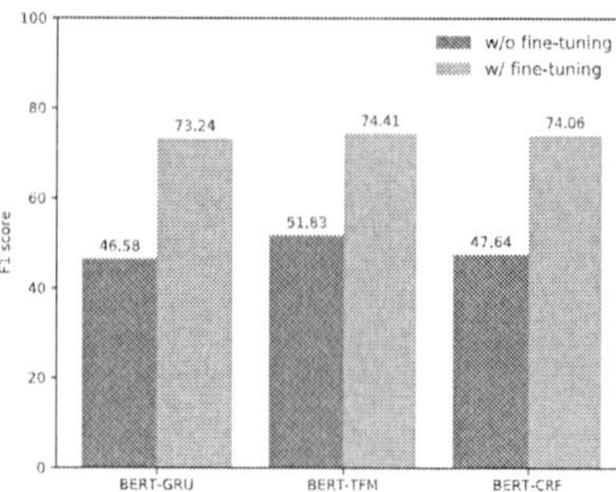

Figure 3: Effect of fine-tuning BERT.

works without using BERT, suggesting that BERT representations encoding the associations between arbitrary two tokens largely alleviate the issue of context independence in the linear E2E-ABSA layer. It is also observed that slightly more powerful E2E-ABSA layers lead to much better performance, verifying the postulation that incorporating context helps to sequence modeling.

3.3 Over-parameterization Issue

Although we employ the smallest pre-trained BERT model, it is still over-parameterized for the E2E-ABSA task (110M parameters), which naturally raises a question: does BERT-based model tend to overfit the small training set? Following this question, we train BERT-GRU, BERT-TFM and BERT-CRF up to 3000 steps on REST and observe the fluctuation of the F1 measures on the development set. As shown in Figure 2, F1 scores on the development set are quite stable and do not decrease much as the training proceeds, which shows that the BERT-based model is exceptionally robust to overfitting.

3.4 Finetuning BERT or Not

We also study the impact of fine-tuning on the final performances. Specifically, we employ BERT to calculate the contextualized token-level representations but kept the parameters of BERT component unchanged in the training phase. Figure 3 illustrate the comparative results between the BERT-based models and those keeping BERT component fixed. Obviously, the general purpose BERT representation is far from satisfactory for the downstream tasks and task-specific fine-tuning is essential for exploiting the strengths of BERT to improve the performance.

4 Conclusion

In this paper, we investigate the effectiveness of BERT embedding component on the task of End-to-End Aspect-Based Sentiment Analysis (E2E-ABSA). Specifically, we explore to couple the BERT embedding component with various neural models and conduct extensive experiments on two benchmark datasets. The experimental results demonstrate the superiority of BERT-based models on capturing aspect-based sentiment and their robustness to overfitting.

References

Jimmy Lei Ba, Jamie Ryan Kiros, and Geoffrey E Hinton. 2016. Layer normalization. *arXiv preprint arXiv:1607.06450*.

Mia Xu Chen, Orhan Firat, Ankur Bapna, Melvin Johnson, Wolfgang Macherey, George Foster, Llion Jones, Mike Schuster, Noam Shazeer, Niki Parmar, Ashish Vaswani, Jakob Uszkoreit, Lukasz Kaiser, Zhifeng Chen, Yonghui Wu, and Macduff Hughes. 2018. The best of both worlds: Combining recent advances in neural machine translation. In *ACL*, pages 76–86.

Peng Chen, Zhongqian Sun, Lidong Bing, and Wei Yang. 2017. Recurrent attention network on memory for aspect sentiment analysis. In *EMNLP*, pages 452–461.

Jianpeng Cheng, Li Dong, and Mirella Lapata. 2016. Long short-term memory-networks for machine reading. In *EMNLP*, pages 551–561.

Kyunghyun Cho, Bart van Merriënboer, Caglar Gulcehre, Dzmitry Bahdanau, Fethi Bougares, Holger Schwenk, and Yoshua Bengio. 2014. Learning phrase representations using RNN encoder–decoder for statistical machine translation. In *EMNLP*, pages 1724–1734.

Jacob Devlin, Ming-Wei Chang, Kenton Lee, and Kristina Toutanova. 2019. BERT: Pre-training of deep bidirectional transformers for language understanding. In *NAACL*, pages 4171–4186.

Li Dong, Nan Yang, Wenhui Wang, Furu Wei, Xiaodong Liu, Yu Wang, Jianfeng Gao, Ming Zhou, and Hsiao-Wuen Hon. 2019. Unified language model pre-training for natural language understanding and generation. *arXiv preprint arXiv:1905.03197*.

Jeffrey L Elman. 1990. Finding structure in time. *Cognitive science*, 14(2):179–211.

Feifan Fan, Yansong Feng, and Dongyan Zhao. 2018. Multi-grained attention network for aspect-level sentiment classification. In *EMNLP*, pages 3433–3442.

Zhifang Fan, Zhen Wu, Xin-Yu Dai, Shujian Huang, and Jiajun Chen. 2019. Target-oriented opinion words extraction with target-fused neural sequence labeling. In *NAACL*, pages 2509–2518.

Kaiming He, Xiangyu Zhang, Shaoqing Ren, and Jian Sun. 2016. Deep residual learning for image recognition. In *CVPR*, pages 770–778.

Ruidan He, Wee Sun Lee, Hwee Tou Ng, and Daniel Dahlmeier. 2018. Exploiting document knowledge for aspect-level sentiment classification. In *ACL*, pages 579–585.

Ruidan He, Wee Sun Lee, Hwee Tou Ng, and Daniel Dahlmeier. 2019. An interactive multi-task learning network for end-to-end aspect-based sentiment analysis. In *ACL*, pages 504–515.

Sepp Hochreiter and Jürgen Schmidhuber. 1997. Long short-term memory. *Neural computation*, 9(8):1735–1780.

Jeremy Howard and Sebastian Ruder. 2018. Universal language model fine-tuning for text classification. In *ACL*, pages 328–339.

Minghao Hu, Yuxing Peng, Zhen Huang, Dongsheng Li, and Yiwei Lv. 2019. Open-domain targeted sentiment analysis via span-based extraction and classification. In *ACL*, pages 537–546.

Binxuan Huang and Kathleen Carley. 2018. Parameterized convolutional neural networks for aspect level sentiment classification. In *EMNLP*, pages 1091–1096.

Binxuan Huang and Kathleen M Carley. 2019. Syntax-aware aspect level sentiment classification with graph attention networks. *arXiv preprint arXiv:1909.02606*.

Zhiheng Huang, Wei Xu, and Kai Yu. 2015. Bidirectional lstm-crf models for sequence tagging. *arXiv preprint arXiv:1508.01991*.

Rafal Jozefowicz, Wojciech Zaremba, and Ilya Sutskever. 2015. An empirical exploration of recurrent network architectures. In *ICML*, pages 2342–2350.

John D Lafferty, Andrew McCallum, and Fernando CN Pereira. 2001. Conditional random fields: Probabilistic models for segmenting and labeling sequence data. In *ICML*, pages 282–289.

Guillaume Lample, Miguel Ballesteros, Sandeep Subramanian, Kazuya Kawakami, and Chris Dyer. 2016. Neural architectures for named entity recognition. In *NAACL*, pages 260–270.

Guillaume Lample and Alexis Conneau. 2019. Cross-lingual language model pretraining. *arXiv preprint arXiv:1901.07291*.

Zeyang Lei, Yujiu Yang, Min Yang, Wei Zhao, Jun Guo, and Yi Liu. 2019. A human-like semantic cognition network for aspect-level sentiment classification. In *AAAI*, pages 6650–6657.

Hao Li and Wei Lu. 2017. Learning latent sentiment scopes for entity-level sentiment analysis. In *AAAI*, pages 3482–3489.

Hao Li and Wei Lu. 2019. Learning explicit and implicit structures for targeted sentiment analysis. *arXiv preprint arXiv:1909.07593*.

Xin Li, Lidong Bing, Wai Lam, and Bei Shi. 2018. Transformation networks for target-oriented sentiment classification. In *ACL*, pages 946–956.

Xin Li, Lidong Bing, Piji Li, and Wai Lam. 2019a. A unified model for opinion target extraction and target sentiment prediction. In *AAAI*, pages 6714–6721.

Zheng Li, Ying Wei, Yu Zhang, Xiang Zhang, and Xin Li. 2019b. Exploiting coarse-to-fine task transfer for aspect-level sentiment classification. In *AAAI*, pages 4253–4260.

Zhouhan Lin, Minwei Feng, Cicero Nogueira dos Santos, Mo Yu, Bing Xiang, Bowen Zhou, and Yoshua Bengio. 2017. A structured self-attentive sentence embedding. In *ICLR*.

Bing Liu. 2012. Sentiment analysis and opinion mining. *Synthesis lectures on human language technologies*, 5(1):1–167.

Jiangming Liu and Yue Zhang. 2017. Attention modeling for targeted sentiment. In *EACL*, pages 572–577.

Liyuan Liu, Jingbo Shang, Xiang Ren, Frank F Xu, Huan Gui, Jian Peng, and Jiawei Han. 2018. Empower sequence labeling with task-aware neural language model. In *AAAI*, pages 5253–5260.

Yang Liu. 2019. Fine-tune bert for extractive summarization. *arXiv preprint arXiv:1903.10318*.

Huaishao Luo, Tianrui Li, Bing Liu, and Junbo Zhang. 2019. DOER: Dual cross-shared RNN for aspect term-polarity co-extraction. In *ACL*, pages 591–601.

Dehong Ma, Sujian Li, and Houfeng Wang. 2018a. Joint learning for targeted sentiment analysis. In *EMNLP*, pages 4737–4742.

Dehong Ma, Sujian Li, Xiaodong Zhang, and Houfeng Wang. 2017. Interactive attention networks for aspect-level sentiment classification. In *IJCAI*, pages 4068–4074.

Xuezhe Ma and Eduard Hovy. 2016. End-to-end sequence labeling via bi-directional LSTM-CNNs-CRF. In *ACL*, pages 1064–1074.

Yukun Ma, Haiyun Peng, and Erik Cambria. 2018b. Targeted aspect-based sentiment analysis via embedding commonsense knowledge into an attentive lstm. In *AAAI*.

Navonil Majumder, Soujanya Poria, Alexander Gelbukh, Md. Shad Akhtar, Erik Cambria, and Asif Ekbal. 2018. IARM: Inter-aspect relation modeling with memory networks in aspect-based sentiment analysis. In *EMNLP*, pages 3402–3411.

Bryan McCann, James Bradbury, Caiming Xiong, and Richard Socher. 2017. Learned in translation: Contextualized word vectors. In *NeurIPS*, pages 6294–6305.

Tomas Mikolov, Ilya Sutskever, Kai Chen, Greg S Corrado, and Jeff Dean. 2013. Distributed representations of words and phrases and their compositionality. In *NeurIPS*, pages 3111–3119.

Margaret Mitchell, Jacqui Aguilar, Theresa Wilson, and Benjamin Van Durme. 2013. Open domain targeted sentiment. In *EMNLP*, pages 1643–1654.

Jeffrey Pennington, Richard Socher, and Christopher Manning. 2014. Glove: Global vectors for word representation. In *EMNLP*, pages 1532–1543.

Matthew Peters, Mark Neumann, Mohit Iyyer, Matt Gardner, Christopher Clark, Kenton Lee, and Luke Zettlemoyer. 2018. Deep contextualized word representations. In *NAACL*, pages 2227–2237.

Maria Pontiki, Dimitris Galanis, Haris Papageorgiou, Ion Androutsopoulos, Suresh Manandhar, Mohammad AL-Smadi, Mahmoud Al-Ayyoub, Yanyan Zhao, Bing Qin, Orphée De Clercq, Véronique Hoste, Marianna Apidianaki, Xavier Tannier, Natalia Loukachevitch, Evgeniy Kotelnikov, Nuria Bel, Salud María Jiménez-Zafra, and Gülşen Eryiğit. 2016. SemEval-2016 task 5: Aspect based sentiment analysis. In *SemEval*, pages 19–30.

Maria Pontiki, Dimitris Galanis, Haris Papageorgiou, Suresh Manandhar, and Ion Androutsopoulos. 2015. SemEval-2015 task 12: Aspect based sentiment analysis. In *SemEval*, pages 486–495.

Maria Pontiki, Dimitris Galanis, John Pavlopoulos, Harris Papageorgiou, Ion Androutsopoulos, and Suresh Manandhar. 2014. SemEval-2014 task 4: Aspect based sentiment analysis. In *SemEval*, pages 27–35.

Alec Radford, Karthik Narasimhan, Tim Salimans, and Ilya Sutskever. 2018. Improving language understanding by generative pre-training.

Alec Radford, Jeffrey Wu, Rewon Child, David Luan, Dario Amodei, and Ilya Sutskever. 2019. Language models are unsupervised multitask learners. *OpenAI Blog*, 1(8).

Alexander Rietzler, Sebastian Stabinger, Paul Opitz, and Stefan Engl. 2019. Adapt or get left behind: Domain adaptation through bert language model finetuning for aspect-target sentiment classification. *arXiv preprint arXiv:1908.11860*.

Martin Schmitt, Simon Steinheber, Konrad Schreiber, and Benjamin Roth. 2018. Joint aspect and polarity classification for aspect-based sentiment analysis with end-to-end neural networks. In *EMNLP*, pages 1109–1114.

Tao Shen, Tianyi Zhou, Guodong Long, Jing Jiang, Shirui Pan, and Chengqi Zhang. 2018. Disan: Directional self-attention network for rnn/cnn-free language understanding. In *AAAI*.

Youwei Song, Jiahai Wang, Tao Jiang, Zhiyue Liu, and Yanghui Rao. 2019. Attentional encoder network for targeted sentiment classification. *arXiv preprint arXiv:1902.09314*.

Chi Sun, Luyao Huang, and Xipeng Qiu. 2019. Utilizing BERT for aspect-based sentiment analysis via constructing auxiliary sentence. In *NAACL*, pages 380–385.

Duyu Tang, Bing Qin, and Ting Liu. 2016. Aspect level sentiment classification with deep memory network. In *EMNLP*, pages 214–224.

Yi Tay, Luu Anh Tuan, and Siu Cheung Hui. 2018. Learning to attend via word-aspect associative fusion for aspect-based sentiment analysis. In *Thirty-Second AAAI Conference on Artificial Intelligence*.

Ashish Vaswani, Noam Shazeer, Niki Parmar, Jakob Uszkoreit, Llion Jones, Aidan N Gomez, Łukasz Kaiser, and Illia Polosukhin. 2017. Attention is all you need. In *NeurIPS*, pages 5998–6008.

Shuai Wang, Sahisnu Mazumder, Bing Liu, Mianwei Zhou, and Yi Chang. 2018. Target-sensitive memory networks for aspect sentiment classification. In *ACL*, pages 957–967.

Yequan Wang, Minlie Huang, Xiaoyan Zhu, and Li Zhao. 2016. Attention-based LSTM for aspect-level sentiment classification. In *EMNLP*, pages 606–615.

Hu Xu, Bing Liu, Lei Shu, and Philip Yu. 2019. BERT post-training for review reading comprehension and aspect-based sentiment analysis. In *NAACL*, pages 2324–2335.

Wei Xue and Tao Li. 2018. Aspect based sentiment analysis with gated convolutional networks. In *ACL*, pages 2514–2523.

Zhilin Yang, Zihang Dai, Yiming Yang, Jaime Carbonell, Ruslan Salakhutdinov, and Quoc V Le. 2019. Xlnet: Generalized autoregressive pretraining for language understanding. *arXiv preprint arXiv:1906.08237*.

Jianfei Yu and Jing Jiang. 2019. Adapting bert for target-oriented multimodal sentiment classification. In *IJCAI*, pages 5408–5414.

Meishan Zhang, Yue Zhang, and Duy-Tin Vo. 2015. Neural networks for open domain targeted sentiment. In *EMNLP*, pages 612–621.

Jie Zhou, Jimmy Xiangji Huang, Qin Chen, Qinmin Vivian Hu, Tingting Wang, and Liang He. 2019. Deep learning for aspect-level sentiment classification: Survey, vision and challenges. *IEEE Access*.

Training on Synthetic Noise
Improves Robustness to Natural Noise in Machine Translation

Vladimir Karpukhin   Omer Levy   Jacob Eisenstein[*]   Marjan Ghazvininejad

Facebook Artificial Intelligence Research
Seattle, WA

Abstract

Contemporary machine translation systems achieve greater coverage by applying sub-word models such as BPE and character-level CNNs, but these methods are highly sensitive to orthographical variations such as spelling mistakes. We show how training on a mild amount of random synthetic noise can dramatically improve robustness to these variations, without diminishing performance on clean text. We focus on translation performance on natural typos, and show that robustness to such noise can be achieved using a balanced diet of simple synthetic noises at training time, without access to the natural noise data or distribution.

1 Introduction

Machine translation systems are generally trained on clean data, without spelling errors. Yet many translation scenarios require robustness to such errors: for example, social media text in which there is little emphasis on standard spelling (Michel and Neubig, 2018), and interactive settings in which users must enter text on a mobile device. Systems trained on clean data generally perform poorly when faced with such errors at test time (Heigold et al., 2017; Belinkov and Bisk, 2018).

One potential solution is to introduce noise at training time, similar in spirit to the use of adversarial examples (Goodfellow et al., 2014; Ebrahimi et al., 2018). So far, using synthetic noise at training time has been found to improve performance only on test data with exactly the same kind of synthetic noise, while at the same time impairing performance on *clean* test data (Heigold et al., 2017; Belinkov and Bisk, 2018). We desire methods that perform well on both clean text and naturally-occurring noise, but this is beyond the current state of the art.

Drawing inspiration from dropout and noise-based regularization methods, we explore the space of random noising methods at training time, and evaluate performance on both clean text and text corrupted by "natural noise" found in real spelling errors. We find that by feeding our translation models a balanced diet of several types of synthetic noise at training time (random character deletions, insertions, substitutions, and swaps), it is possible to obtain substantial improvements on such naturally noisy data, with minimal impact on the performance on clean data, and without accessing the test noise data or even its distribution.

Our method substantially improves the robustness of a transformer-based machine translation model with CNN character encoders to spelling errors across multiple input languages (German, French, and Czech). Of the different noise types we use at training, we find that random character deletions are particularly useful, followed by character insertions. However, noisy training does not improve translations of social media text, as indicated by performance on the MTNT dataset of Reddit posts (Michel and Neubig, 2018). This finding aligns with previous work arguing that the distinctive feature of social media text is not noise or orthographical errors, but rather, variation in writing style and vocabulary (Eisenstein, 2013).

2 Noise Models

We focus on *orthographical noise*: character-level noise that affects the spelling of individual terms. Orthographical noise is problematic for machine translation systems that operate on token-level embeddings because noised terms are usually out-of-vocabulary, even when divided into subwords using techniques such as byte pair encoding (BPE; Sennrich et al., 2015). Interestingly, orthographical noise can also pose problems for *character-*

---

[*] Jacob Eisenstein is now at Google Research.

Proceedings of the 2019 EMNLP Workshop W-NUT: The 5th Workshop on Noisy User-generated Text, pages 42–47
Hong Kong, Nov 4, 2019. ©2019 Association for Computational Linguistics

Deletion	A character is deleted.	whale → whle
Insertion	A character is inserted into a random position.	whale → wxhale
Substitution	A character is replaced with a random character.	whale → whalz
Swap	Two adjacent characters change position.	whale → wahle

Table 1: The synthetic noise types applied during training. Noise is applied on a random character, selected from a uniform distribution. The right column illustrates the application of each noise type on the word "whale."

level encoding models, which are based on models such as convolutional neural networks (CNNs; Kim et al., 2016). These models learn to match filters against specific character n-grams, so when n-grams are disrupted by orthographical noise, the resulting encoding may radically differ from the encoding of a "clean" version of the same text. Belinkov and Bisk (2018) report significant degradations in performance after applying noise to only a small fraction of input tokens.

Synthetic Noise Table 1 describes the four types of synthetic noise we used during training. Substitutions and swaps were experimented with extensively in previous work (Heigold et al., 2017; Belinkov and Bisk, 2018), but deletion and insertion were not. Deletion and insertion pose a different challenge to character encoders, because they alter the distances between character sequences in the word, as well as the overall word length.

During training, we noised each token by sampling from a multinomial distribution of 60% clean (no noise) and 10% probability for each of the four noise types. The noise was added dynamically, allowing for different mutations of the same example over different epochs.

Natural Noise We evaluate our models on *natural* noise from edit histories of Wikipedia (for French and German; Max and Wisniewski, 2010; Zesch, 2012) and manually-corrected essays (for Czech; Šebesta et al., 2017). These authors have obtained a set of likely spelling error pairs, each involving a clean spelling and a candidate error. We used that set to replace correct words with their misspelled versions for each evaluation sample text in the source language. When there are multiple error forms for a single word, an error is selected randomly. Not all words have errors, and so even with maximal noise, only 20-50% of the tokens are noised.

Natural noise is more representative of what might actually be encountered by a deployed machine translation system, so we reserve it for test data. While it is possible, in theory, to use nat-

ural noise for training, it is not always realistic. Significant engineering effort is required to obtain such noise examples, making it difficult to build naturally-noised training sets for any source language. Furthermore, orthography varies across demographics and periods, so it is unrealistic to anticipate the exact distribution of noise at test time.

3 Experiment

Data Following Belinkov and Bisk (2018), we evaluated our method on the IWSLT 2016 machine translation benchmark (Cettolo et al., 2016). We translated from three source languages (German, French, Czech) to English, each with a training set of approximately 200K sentence pairs. Synthetic noise was added only to the training data, and natural noise was added only to the test data; the validation data remained untouched.

Model We used a transformer-based translation model (Vaswani et al., 2017) with a CNN-based character encoder (Kim et al., 2016).

Hyperparameters We followed the base configuration of the transformer (Vaswani et al., 2017) with 6 encoder and decoder layers of 512/2048 model/hidden dimensions and 8 attention heads. Character embeddings had 256 dimensions and the character CNN followed the specifications of Kim et al. (2016). We optimized the model with Adam and used the inverse square-root learning rate schedule typically used for transformers, but with a peek learning rate of 0.001. Each batch contained a maximum of 8,000 tokens. We used a dropout rate of 0.2. We generated the translations with beam search (5 beams), and computed BLEU scores to measure test set performance.

Results Table 2 shows the model's performance on data with varying amounts of natural errors. As observed in prior art (Heigold et al., 2017; Belinkov and Bisk, 2018), when there are significant amounts of natural noise, the model's performance drops significantly. However, training on our synthetic noise cocktail greatly improves performance, regaining between 19% and 54% of the

Dataset	Noise Probability	Noised Tokens	BLEU			
			Clean Training Data	+ Synthetic Noise	Δ	%Recovered
de-en	0.00%	0.00%	34.20	33.53	−0.67	–
de-en	25.00%	9.72%	27.93	31.32	3.39	54.1%
de-en	100.00%	39.36%	12.49	23.34	10.85	50.0%
fr-en	0.00%	0.00%	39.61	39.94	0.33	–
fr-en	25.00%	13.47%	30.48	34.07	3.59	39.3%
fr-en	100.00%	53.74%	11.48	19.43	7.95	28.3%
cs-en	0.00%	0.00%	27.48	27.09	−0.39	–
cs-en	25.00%	6.14%	24.31	24.91	0.60	18.9%
cs-en	100.00%	24.53%	16.64	18.91	2.27	20.9%

Table 2: Performance on the IWSLT 2016 translation task with varying rates of natural noise in the test set. **Noise Probability** is the probability of attempting to apply natural noise to a test token, while **Noised Tokens** is the fraction of tokens that were noised in practice; not every word in the vocabulary has a corresponding misspelling.

Training Noise	BLEU	Δ
No Training Noise	12.49	
+ Deletion	17.39	4.90
+ Insertion	15.00	2.51
+ Substitution	11.99	−0.50
+ Swap	14.04	1.55
All Training Noise	23.34	
− Deletion	14.96	-8.38
− Insertion	18.81	-4.53
− Substitution	20.23	-3.11
− Swap	23.07	-0.27

Table 3: Performance on IWSLT 2016 de-en test with maximal natural noise when training with one noise type (top) and three noise types (bottom).

Dataset	Del	Ins	Sub	Swap
de-en	16.6%	26.5%	17.0%	6.0%
fr-en	11.8%	11.4%	9.7%	2.6%
cs-en	6.6%	6.1%	41.7%	0.4%

Table 4: The proportion of natural errors caused by deleting/inserting/substituting a single character or swapping two adjacent characters.

BLEU score that was lost to natural noise. Moreover, this training regime has minimal impact on clean text translations, with negative and positive fluctuations that are smaller than 1 BLEU point.

To determine the ceiling performance of noise-based training, we split the set of natural typos and used one part for training and the other for test. However, we observed that training on natural noise behaves very similarly to training without noise at all (not shown), perhaps because the natural typos did not have enough variance to encourage the model to generalize well.

Ablation Analysis To determine the individual contribution of each type of synthetic noise, we conduct an ablation study. We first add only one type of synthetic noise at 10% (i.e. 90% of the training data is clean), and measure performance. We then take the full set of noise types, and remove a single type at each time to see how important it is given the other noises.

Table 3 shows the model's performance on the German dataset when training with various mixtures of noise. We find that deletion is by far the most effective synthetic noise in preparing our model for natural errors, followed by insertion. We observe the same trend for French and Czech. This result could explain why our experiments show a significant improvement when training on synthetic noise, while previous work, which trained only on synthetic substitutions and swaps, did not observe similar improvements.

Natural Noise Analysis Finally, we analyze how well our synthetic noise covers the distribution of natural noise. Table 4 shows the percentage of noised tokens that can be covered by a single noising operation. With the exception of substitutions in Czech, higher overlap between synthetic and natural noise appears to correlate with higher recovery rate in Table 2. One possible explanation for this outlier is that random synthetic substitutions might be less effective at imitating real substitutions, and that perhaps a more informed model is needed for simulating synthetic substitutions.

4 Translating Social Media Text

We also apply our synthetic noise training procedure to social media, using the recently-released MTNT dataset of Reddit posts (Michel and Neubig, 2018), focusing on the English-French translation pair. Note that no noise was inserted into the test data in this case; the only source of noise is the

Dataset	Clean Train	+ Synthetic Noise
en-fr	21.1	20.6
fr-en	23.6	24.1

Table 5: The performance of a machine translation model on the MTNT task.

non-standard spellings inherent to the dataset.

As shown in Table 5, noised training has minimal impact on performance. We did not exhaustively explore the space of possible noising strategies, and so these negative results should be taken only as a preliminary finding. Nonetheless, there are reasons to believe that synthetic training noise may not help in this case. Michel and Neubig (2018) note that the rate of spelling errors, as reported by a spell check system, is not especially high in MTNT; other differences from standard corpora include the use of entirely new words and names, terms from other languages (especially English), grammar differences, and paralinguistic phenomena such as emoticons. These findings align with prior work showing that social media does not feature high rates of misspellings (Rello and Baeza-Yates, 2012). Furthermore, many of the spelling variants in MTNT have very high edit distance (e.g., *catholique* → *catho* [Fr]). It is unlikely that training with mild synthetic noise would yield robustness to these variants, which reflect well-understood stylistic patterns rather than random variation at the character level.[1]

5   Related work

The use of noise to improve robustness in machine learning has a long history (e.g., Holmstrom and Koistinen, 1992; Wager et al., 2013), with early work by Bishop (1995) demonstrating a connection between additive noise and regularization. To achieve robustness to orthographical errors, we require noise that operates at the character level. Heigold et al. (2017) demonstrated that synthetic noising operations such as random swaps and replacements can degrade performance when inserted at test time; they also show that some robustness can be obtained by inserting the same noise at training time. Similarly, Sperber et al. (2017) explore the impact of speech-like noise.

Most relevant for us is the work of Belinkov and Bisk (2018), who evaluated on natural noise obtained from Wikipedia edit histories (e.g., Max and Wisniewski, 2010). They find that robustness to natural noise can be obtained by training on the same noise model, but that (a) training on synthetic noise does *not* yield robustness to natural noise at test time, and (b) training on natural noise significantly impairs performance on clean text. In contrast, we show that training on the right blend of synthetic noise can yield substantial improvements on natural noise at test time, without significantly impairing performance on clean data. Our ablation results suggest that deletion and insertion noise (not included by Belinkov and Bisk) are essential to achieving robustness to natural noise.

An alternative to noise infusion is to build character-level encoders that are robust to noise by design. Belinkov and Bisk (2018) experiment with a bag of characters, while Sakaguchi et al. (2017) use character-level recurrent neural networks combined with special representations for the first and last characters of each token. These models are particularly suited for specific types of swapping and scrambling noises, but are not robust to natural noise. We conducted preliminary experiments with noise-invariant encoders, but obtained better results by adding noise at training time. A related idea is to optimize an adversarial objective, in which a discriminator tries to distinguish noised and clean examples from their encoded representations (Cheng et al., 2018). This improves performance on clean data, but it makes optimization unstable, which is a well-known defect of adversarial learning (Arjovsky et al., 2017). Cheng et al. (2018) do not evaluate on natural noise.

6   Conclusion

This work takes a step towards making machine translation robust to character-level noise. We show how training on synthetic character-level noise, similar in spirit to dropout, can significantly improve a translation model's robustness to natural spelling mistakes. In particular, we find that deleting and inserting random characters play a key role in preparing the model for test-time typos. While our method works well on misspellings, it does not appear to generalize to non-standard text in social media. We conjecture that spelling mistakes constitute a small part of the deviations from standard text, and that the main challenges in this

---

[1] Contemporaneous work shows that MTNT performance can be improved by a domain-specific noising distribution that includes character insertions and deletions, as well as the random insertion of emoticons, stopwords, and profanity (Vaibhav et al., 2019). The specific impact of spelling noise is not evaluated, nor is the impact on clean text.

domain stem from other linguistic phenomena.

Acknowledgments Thanks to the anonymous reviewers for their feedback. We also thank Luke Zettlemoyer and our colleagues at FAIR for valuable feedback. Specifically, we thank Abdelrahman Mohamed for sharing his expertise on non-autoregressive models.

References

Martin Arjovsky, Soumith Chintala, and Léon Bottou. 2017. Wasserstein generative adversarial networks. In *International Conference on Machine Learning*, pages 214–223.

Yonatan Belinkov and Yonatan Bisk. 2018. Synthetic and natural noise both break neural machine translation. In *ICLR*.

Chris M Bishop. 1995. Training with noise is equivalent to tikhonov regularization. *Neural computation*, 7(1):108–116.

Mauro Cettolo, Niehues Jan, Stüker Sebastian, Luisa Bentivogli, Roldano Cattoni, and Marcello Federico. 2016. The IWSLT 2016 evaluation campaign. In *International Workshop on Spoken Language Translation*.

Yong Cheng, Zhaopeng Tu, Fandong Meng, Junjie Zhai, and Yang Liu. 2018. Towards robust neural machine translation. In *Proceedings of the 56th Annual Meeting of the Association for Computational Linguistics (Volume 1: Long Papers)*, pages 1756–1766, Melbourne, Australia. Association for Computational Linguistics.

Javid Ebrahimi, Anyi Rao, Daniel Lowd, and Dejing Dou. 2018. Hotflip: White-box adversarial examples for text classification. In *Proceedings of the 56th Annual Meeting of the Association for Computational Linguistics (Volume 2: Short Papers)*, pages 31–36, Melbourne, Australia. Association for Computational Linguistics.

Jacob Eisenstein. 2013. What to do about bad language on the internet. In *Proceedings of the 2013 conference of the North American Chapter of the association for computational linguistics: Human language technologies*, pages 359–369.

Ian J Goodfellow, Jonathon Shlens, and Christian Szegedy. 2014. Explaining and harnessing adversarial examples. *arXiv preprint arXiv:1412.6572*.

Georg Heigold, Günter Neumann, and Josef van Genabith. 2017. How robust are character-based word embeddings in tagging and mt against wrod scramlbing or randdm nouse? *arXiv preprint arXiv:1704.04441*.

Lasse Holmstrom and Petri Koistinen. 1992. Using additive noise in back-propagation training. *IEEE Transactions on Neural Networks*, 3(1):24–38.

Yoon Kim, Yacine Jernite, David Sontag, and Alexander M Rush. 2016. Character-aware neural language models. In *AAAI*, pages 2741–2749.

Aurélien Max and Guillaume Wisniewski. 2010. Mining naturally-occurring corrections and paraphrases from wikipedia's revision history. In *LREC*.

Paul Michel and Graham Neubig. 2018. Mtnt: A testbed for machine translation of noisy text. In *EMNLP*.

Luz Rello and Ricardo A Baeza-Yates. 2012. Social media is not that bad! the lexical quality of social media. In *ICWSM*.

Keisuke Sakaguchi, Kevin Duh, Matt Post, and Benjamin Van Durme. 2017. Robsut wrod reocginiton via semi-character recurrent neural network. In *AAAI*, pages 3281–3287.

Karel Šebesta, Zuzanna Bedřichová, Kateřina Šormová, Barbora Štindlová, Milan Hrdlička, Tereza Hrdličková, Jiří Hana, Vladimír Petkevič, Tomáš Jelínek, Svatava Škodová, Petr Janeš, Kateřina Lundáková, Hana Skoumalová, Šimon Sládek, Piotr Pierscieniak, Dagmar Toufarová, Milan Straka, Alexandr Rosen, Jakub Náplava, and Marie Poláčková. 2017. CzeSL grammatical error correction dataset (CzeSL-GEC). LINDAT/CLARIN digital library at the Institute of Formal and Applied Linguistics (ÚFAL), Faculty of Mathematics and Physics, Charles University.

Rico Sennrich, Barry Haddow, and Alexandra Birch. 2015. Neural machine translation of rare words with subword units. *arXiv preprint arXiv:1508.07909*.

Matthias Sperber, Jan Niehues, and Alex Waibel. 2017. Toward robust neural machine translation for noisy input sequences. In *International Workshop on Spoken Language Translation (IWSLT), Tokyo, Japan*.

Vaibhav, Sumeet Singh, Craig Stewart, and Graham Neubig. 2019. Improving robustness of machine translation with synthetic noise. *arXiv preprint arXiv:1902.09508*.

Ashish Vaswani, Noam Shazeer, Niki Parmar, Jakob Uszkoreit, Llion Jones, Aidan N Gomez, Łukasz Kaiser, and Illia Polosukhin. 2017. Attention is all you need. In *Advances in Neural Information Processing Systems*, pages 5998–6008.

Stefan Wager, Sida Wang, and Percy S Liang. 2013. Dropout training as adaptive regularization. In *Advances in neural information processing systems*, pages 351–359.

Torsten Zesch. 2012. Measuring contextual fitness using error contexts extracted from the wikipedia revision history. In *Proceedings of the 13th Conference of the European Chapter of the Association for Computational Linguistics*, pages 529–538. Association for Computational Linguistics.

Character-Based Models for Adversarial Phone Number Extraction: Preventing Human Sex Trafficking

Nathanael Chambers   **Timothy Forman**   **Catherine Griswold**
Yogaish Khastgir   **Kevin Lu**   **Stephen Steckler**
Department of Computer Science
United States Naval Academy
nchamber@usna.edu

Abstract

Illicit activity on the Web often uses noisy text to obscure information between client and seller, such as the seller's phone number. This presents an interesting challenge to language understanding systems; how do we model adversarial noise in a text extraction system? This paper addresses the sex trafficking domain, and proposes some of the first neural network architectures to learn and extract phone numbers from noisy text. We create a new adversarial advertisement dataset, propose several RNN-based models to solve the problem, and most notably propose a *visual* character language model to interpret unseen unicode characters. We train a CRF jointly with a CNN to improve number recognition by 89% over just a CRF. Through data augmentation in this unique model, we present the first results on characters never seen in training.

1   Introduction

One reason people intentionally obscure textual content is to evade automatic extraction systems. There are good reasons for wanting to do this, privacy being at the forefront. However, illicit activity is another reason, and human sex trafficking is one of the most egregious uses. We draw inspiration from this domain, but extracting information from *adversarial* noisy text is a more general challenge for the NLP community. It is a language understanding task that humans can easily do, but which presents difficulty for automated methods. This paper presents the first deep learning models for adversarial phone number extraction, and releases new datasets for future experimentation.

An obscured example number is shown here:

(9I4) Too.46-callme-ÖÖ1/4

The true phone number is 914-246-0014, but this breaks even the most comprehensive rule-based extractors. It contains examples of visual substitution (I for 1 and unicode for 0), word substitution ("Too" for 2), and character confounders (separators '.', '-', '/' and other words). Any one challenge might be solvable in isolation, but they often combine together:

n1ne0one 7n1ne3 n1ne351

Rather than swapping letters for digits (I for 1), this example swaps digits for letters (1 for i) which are also part of a word swap ('nine' for 9). There are four '1' characters in the string, but only one of them maps to one of the two 1 digits in the number 901-793-9351. Beyond this, the most challenging noise occurs when unicode is injected, thus rendering finite character models ineffective since they've never seen these characters in training. This paper proposes to model all of this noise with several neural network architectures.

The domain of focus for our study is human sex trafficking, although our proposed models apply to any domain with obscured information (social media, for instance, often mixes unusual characters, confounding normal language models). This topic is important in terms of global need, but it also has attractive language properties for research. Since our datasets come from people who need to post contact information, they can't obscure the text *too much*, or nobody could call them. This results in an interesting cognitive challenge that humans can solve, but state-of-the-art extraction struggles.

The main contributions in this paper are (1) the first neural models for noisy phone number extraction, (2) a visual language model over images of characters, (3) a combined CRF with CNN input, (4) a data augmentation technique for training that helps recognize unseen unicode, and (5) state-of-the-art extraction results on new datasets.

Proceedings of the 2019 EMNLP Workshop W-NUT: The 5th Workshop on Noisy User-generated Text, pages 48–56
Hong Kong, Nov 4, 2019. ©2019 Association for Computational Linguistics

2   Previous Work

A number of papers have looked into the sex trafficking domain. Some focus on classifying entire ads as trafficking or not (Alvari et al., 2016, 2017), while others build knowledge graphs of mentioned entities (Szekely et al., 2015) or focus on normalizing attributes like geolocations (Kapoor et al., 2017; Kejriwal and Szekely, 2017; Kejriwal et al., 2017). Most of these use phone numbers as features, and several found them to be among the most important input (Dubrawski et al., 2015; Nagpal et al., 2017; Li et al., 2018). In fact, phone numbers are used as gold truth to connect similar ads or link traffickers (Rabbany et al., 2018; Li et al., 2018). Phone numbers have also been shown to be some of the most stable links to entities (Costin et al., 2013), so are important for entity linking tasks. Almost all of these threads assume correct phone extraction and ignore the difficulty of ads with obscured numbers. Although sometimes unspecified, they all appear to use rule-based extractors.

Most relevant to this paper is TJBatchExtractor, a rule-based regular expression system (Dubrawski et al., 2015) which is still state-of-the-art for extraction, and is used by other work on trafficking ID (Nagpal et al., 2017). We employ TJBatchExtractor to identify the ads with obscured text from which it *fails* to extract a number. Our paper thus focuses on only the difficult ads with noisy phone numbers.

Most language models use words or characters as their base inputs. One of our contributions is a visual model of characters. We use an image database of 65k unicode characters developed by BBVA Next Security Lab[1] for phishing prevention. Most similar is Liu et al. (2017) who use CNNs for Asian-language classification. They aren't addressing noise like our paper, but rather the semantics inherent to their visual characters.

Finally, we employ data augmentation (Ding et al., 2016; Xu et al., 2016) during training of our visual character model. This is commonly used in the visual community (Salamon and Bello, 2017; Zhong et al., 2017) and we adopt their overall idea to randomly perturb our character images to learn a robust character recognizer.

---

[1] https://github.com/next-security-lab

3   Data and Attributes

3.1   Noisy and Obscured Data

We begin by highlighting the main methods people use for adversarial noise in written text. This is not an exhaustive list, but it covers the vast majority of cases observed in this paper's datasets.

1. **Digits as Lexemes**. The most basic approach to obscuring numbers is to substitute lexemes (words) for digits. These are often easy to identify, and regular expressions with a dictionary are usually sufficient for detection. Words might be capitalized (FOUR) or camel case (foUr), such as in the text, "**threeoh2FOUR070six22**".

2. **Homophones**. This method replaces digits with homophones or near-rhymes, thereby confusing dictionary approaches as in "**337 9twennyfo 06juan9**". Tokens "twenny" and "juan" share phonological similarities with the digit pronunciation. Regular expressions cannot capture these without complex phoneme modeling.

3. **Letters as Digits**. This method substitutes ASCII letters for their digit lookalikes (e.g., *615 093 93B6*). The 'I' and 'B' are representing 1 and 8 respectively. These substitutions can grow more complicated with things like '()' for 0 and what was popularized as leetspeak in the 1980's with 'E' for '3' and other such inversions.

4. **Visual Deception and Unicode**. This is a variant of 'Letters as Digits' above, but goes beyond ASCII substitution to use Unicode characters. Unicode presents a huge challenge to extraction as these rely entirely on visual similarities in the character images. Below are just *some* unicode options that resemble the ASCII character '8':

8 8 8 8 8 8 8 8 8 8 8 8

A rule-based approach would have to manually map all possible characters to their digits, an impossible task for 138k current unicode characters (with future room for 1mil). This would also fail on the larger problem of capturing visually ambiguous close-matches. For instance, an emoticon smiley face can be used for the ASCII letter 'o':

(4 ☺ n e 2) 456 9412

We are the first to our knowledge to model visual noise with a language model architecture.

5. **Confounding Separators**. Another common noise tactic is to insert arbitrary characters as separators. For example: *–270**1tree&&822==31–*. The noise in this obscured text is meant to confuse a pattern matcher as to when a digit's substring begins and ends. Other difficult versions of this method uses digit characters themselves as the separators: **111 410 111 897 111 3245 111**

6. **Human Reasoning**. The most difficult class of obscured text is that which requires reasoning to solve. For instance, including arithmetic (3+1) or instructions to invert digits. This type is a small minority in obscured phone numbers, but they prove most challenging.

Some of these challenges have rule-based solutions in isolation, but combined together, they overlap and build on each other for an exponential number of noisy combinations. This paper addresses all of these challenges except for homophones and human reasoning. We leave phoneme modeling to future work, and reasoning requires a different approach than discriminative classifiers. The most significant challenge this paper addresses is that of the visual deceptions (letters as digits, unicode, and visual sim). We propose the first neural model for visual similarity detection with a unique visual model based on a CNN.

4 Corpora

4.1 Real-World Noisy Advertisements

Our initial corpus started from a 250k advertisement crawl of Backpage and Craigslist escort sections, shared with us by the Global Emancipation Network. The majority of these ads (180k) are one line with a standard phone number and no actual text. We filtered these out to focus on ads with written descriptions.

After removing one-liners, we ran the state-of-the-art extractor (Dubrawski et al., 2015) to identify all ads where the extractor failed to extract anything. This remaining subset contains ads that either don't have a phone number, or they contain an obscured number that fooled the rule-based extractor. Figure 1 shows one such explicit ad.

Undergraduate volunteers manually inspected the remaining ads, removed those without numbers, and identified minimal text spans that encompassed any obscured phone numbers. These annotations resulted in approximately 200 real-world obscured ads with their obscured text spans.

Ad for Phone 555-584-4630

Sexy Slim 555 Ready for fun let me 584 satisfy your 4630 every desire no disappointments..!! **IF YOUR NOT SERIOUS PLEASE DON'T CALL ME..!!Kik Me-*censored* ___****CAR PLAY ONLY****

Figure 1: An example advertisement from the escort section of Backpage. Phone and username changed for anonymity. This ad illustrates an obscured number with normal digits, but text is interspersed in between.

Desiring a larger test set for evaluation, we created an adversarial data collection environment for undergrads to try and "beat" the TJBatchExtractor. This small-scale collection resulted in about 200 more obscured phone examples.

Merging the crawl with these adversarial obscured numbers, we had 390 real-world examples. We split into 250 test numbers and 140 for development (dev). The dev set was used for model improvement and parameter tuning, and the test set only for final results. Two examples from the dev set are given here:

Gold Phone	Ad Text
3189481720	tree1ate_nein 48-one7 twenty
4177015067	4!7 70! fifty6svn

Due to the nature of this domain, training data is difficult to obtain so neural models are stymied. We instead chose to "fake" the training data, creating our own computer-based adversarial dataset. Though training data is artificial, all experiments use the above *real-world* data annotations.

4.2 Artificial Noisy Adversarial Data

A core research question is now whether artificial training data can train this real-world task. This section describes our approach.

The generation algorithm starts with a 10 digit number string (randomly selected[2]), and then transforms the string with a sequence of obfuscation operations. Space prevents a full description of this process and its details, but we will release the code upon publication. Example transformations are as follows:

1. Insert separator ASCII chars between digits.
2. Replace a digit with an ASCII lookalike.

---

[2] We used a US area code dictionary, and followed the constraint that the 4th digit must be [2-9] whereas the 5th to 10th digits are [0-9]. Numbers were then chosen randomly.

Artificial Obscured Phone Numbers

2 1tree\6-zero0###33\~15
778cinco7five688 PaRtyGiRL 6
*forejuan*for 55!826ate
5 1290 si&te4 ‾‾‾‾‾‾‾135
ate0 5 ***2 08–88 8nine

Figure 2: Examples from the artificial phone number training set.

3. Replace a digit with its English, Spanish, or homonym (2 to 'two')
4. Capitalize letters or replace with an ASCII lookalike (C to '(')
5. Replace two digits with its English word ('18' to 'eighteen')
6. Insert random English words as separators

These occur in sequence, each with random chance, so the original digit '2' might become 'too' which then becomes 'To0' after character conversion. The output of this process is arguably more difficult than many real-world examples. See Figure 2 for generated examples. We ultimately trained on 100k of these.

5 Models for Obscured Extraction

5.1 Baseline Models

We use two baselines: one from prior work and another with a basic RNN model.

5.1.1 Rule-Based Baseline

The state-of-the-art for phone number extraction is the TJBatchExtractor from Debrawski et al. (2015). This is a large set of regular expressions designed to capture phone numbers even with variation and noise, mostly focused on what we've named "Digits as Lexemes" and "Letters as Digits". Their previous results showed 99% extraction accuracy, however, we found that 72% of ads are one line with just unobscured digits, so their result masks a more challenging subset.

5.1.2 RNN Baseline

Our baseline neural architecture is a character-based bi-directional LSTM. Input is a 70 character span of obscured text, and each character is mapped to its embedding vector. The embeddings are randomly initialized and learned during training. Each embedding is fed into the biLSTM, and the final hidden state of the biLSTM is treated as the representation of the obscured text. The hidden state is then passed to 10 independent dense layers, one for each of the 10 digits in the phone number. A softmax is then used on the output of each dense layer to predict the digit in that position of the 10-digit phone number.

We also tested GRUs instead of LSTMs, but performance did not significantly change.

5.2 Obscured Models

5.2.1 RNN with Positional Attention

The RNN baseline transforms the input text to a single vector from the biLSTM, and then predicts the digits in the phone number from this vector. We found that the model quickly learns to predict the first digits and the last digits, but learning for the middle digits is hindered. This intuitively makes sense because the vector represents the entire text without directed guidance on identifying *where* in the text the digits exist. How does the final dense layer know where the 4th and 5th digits begin? The initial digit, in contrast, is easier to identify because it leads the string.

Our solution to this deficiency was to add *positional attention* to the LSTM. Instead of using its final LSTM state, the vector is a weighted sum of *all* hidden states. The weight vector α is the learned positional attention. Formally, the ith digit in the 10 digit phone number is predicted by a dense layer over context vector input W_i:

$$W_i = \sum_{j=0}^{N} \alpha_{ij} * V_j \qquad (1)$$

where N is the length of the LSTM, V_j is the jth LSTM hidden state, i is the ith digit in the phone, and α_i is the ith digit's positional attention vector. This allows the network to learn which part of the text is relevant for each digit. The first digit in the number should learn a weight vector α_0 that weights the front of the LSTM more than the end, and vice versa for α_9. Figure 3 shows this model.

We experimented with individual attention (each digit i has its own learned α_i) and a single shared attention (all digits use the same learned α). We only report on individual attention since it outperformed shared attention.

We also tested multiple stacked LSTM layers. Stacking showed no further improvement.

5.2.2 RNN with Conditioned Prediction

One characteristic of our task is that each digit prediction is *mostly* independent from the previous digit. Unlike many domains in NLP, this is

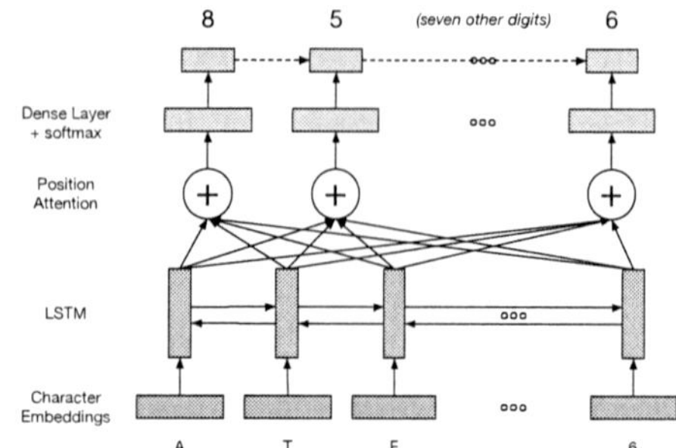

Figure 3: LSTM with position attention. Dotted lines included with conditioned prediction (Sec 5.2.2).

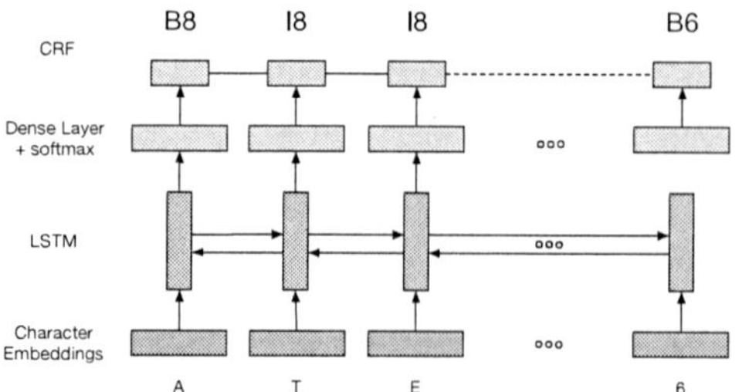

Figure 4: Neural architecture with a CRF top layer.

not a sequence modeling problem where knowing the previous digit semantically assists in guessing the next. For instance, a 5 is not more likely to be followed by a 4.[3] Despite position attention, the model still had difficulty distinguishing which portion of the context vector was relevant to a middle digit. It sometimes repeats an inner digit because the 4th and 5th positions were too nearby in the obscured text. Observe these 2 examples:

41093four 2830
4109threeefour tooo830

The seventh digit is a 2, but it starts five characters later in the second string. We observed repeated digit predictions like: 4109344830. It would predict the same number twice, and then skip over the next due to the shifting positions.

Our quick solution to avoiding repeats was to pass the predictions forward. We added a simple conditional dependency that feeds the softmax output of the previous digit to the current digit. The dotted lines in Figure 3 illustrate this new link. This removed many of our repeated digits, and also increased accuracy in other examples that weren't even repeated but just made mistakes.

5.2.3 Conditional Random Field Model

Given that providing the previous digit prediction showed slight improvements on the development set, we wanted to formalize the sequence predictions with proper transition probabilities. If a digit prediction leads to an unlikely next prediction (according to the model), then perhaps the previous digit should switch to its 2nd most likely in order to maximize the joint prediction.

The other RNN problem is that input varies in length and noise. Some input is only about digits:

4treeTOO564ateSVN33

Others contain varying complex separators:

–4**tree**TOO sms 564ate+SVN+33

RNNs must learn to ignore separators in ways that don't confuse the subsequent dense layers. The network is remarkably adept at this, but we hypothesized that a better model should make a prediction *on each and every input character* rather than merging all into the same hidden state.

Conditional Random Fields (Lafferty et al., 2001) are a natural way of modeling the above. A CRF tags each character as it goes, and performs both training and inference, using viterbi search to find the most likely output prediction sequence. Figure 4 shows this model. We used the CRF implementation in Keras inspired by (Huang et al., 2015) to overlay a CRF on top of the RNN-based models (see also Ma and Hovy (2016)).

The output of a CRF is different since it must output a label for every character (rather than just 10 phone digits). We use the standard CRF labels to mark the beginning (B) and included (I) characters. This means that instead of a single label for each possible phone digit (e.g., 8), we now have two labels which represent a character that begins a digit (B8) and a character in the middle or end of a digit (I8). We additionally use an Other label 'O' to label the noisy separator characters that aren't part of any digit's substring. The following is an example:

B2 I2 I2 B4 B7 O B6 I6 I6 B9 B9
T O O 4 7 - s i x 9 9

The mapping from CRF labels (B2,I2,I2) to actual digits (2) is deterministic. Evaluation metrics for the previous RNNs also apply to the CRF output after it is mapped. However, training for the CRF is done entirely on the CRF label loss.

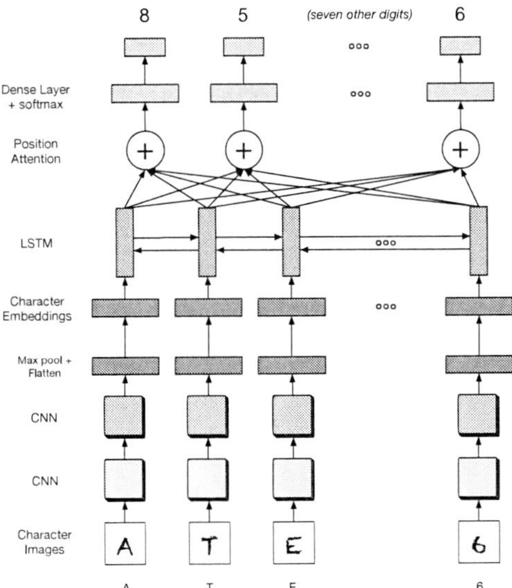

Figure 5: CNN architecture for visual image input to the LSTM model.

5.2.4 Visual Characters with CNNs

As with most NLP tasks, out of vocabulary (OOV) input is an issue. Our adversarial task is even more severe because visual substitutions are intentional, and often OOV as there are 138k current unicode options. If the character is unseen in training, only context can try to guess the digit. Below are examples of such replacement:

Digits	ASCII	Unicode
410	41o	41◌

Why are these easy for humans to decipher? It's purely due to visual similarity. In a "normal" NLP neural model, each character (or token) is mapped to an embedding, so unseen characters have no representation. We might use the default approach of mapping all unknowns to a shared 'UNK' embedding, but this loses the different visual characteristics of each character.

All of this motivates our new *Visual-Based Character RNN*. Our model does not learn a dictionary of character embeddings, but instead uses a series of CNN layers that transform 34x34 images of the characters. The transformations then feed into our above models. This is now a model that can interpret *unseen* (in training) characters.

Figure 5 shows the CNN combined with our positional attention RNN. We use two 3x3 convolution layers with 4 and 8 filters respectively. Each layer is followed by a relu layer and a batch nor-

malization layer (not shown in the figure). The convolutions are followed by a max pooling layer and then flattened. A dense layer with softmax then reduces the flattened vector. We experimented with up to 3 convolution layers, up to 32 filters, and varied the size of the dense layer.

Visual input changes the model significantly. It is no longer learning an NLP-style character *embedding*, but rather learning CNN parameters to transform an image input into that embedding. Our first models ran into problems because they simply memorized each 34x34 image. Since all ASCII '3' characters map to the same flattened representation, the model memorizes it, and unicode variations fail no matter how similar. We thus introduced *data augmentation* during training. Each 34x34 input is 'jiggled' with random transformations: (1) translation of the image up/down or right/left, (2) darken/lighten the image, (3) stretch or widen, and (4) rotate up to 20 degrees. This provided different inputs for the same ASCII chars, so the CNN was encouraged to learn key visual features across all variants. Data augmentation led to our most significant improvements on unseen unicode character input.

6 Experiments

All models were trained on the 100k artificial obscured phone dataset (Section 4.2). 90k was used for training and 10k to determine convergence. The RNNs were set to $N = 70$ in length, and inputs were padded to that length. The rare input text longer than 70 is cropped. Embedding size $N=100$ and LSTM internal dimensions $M=200$ were chosen for all RNNs based on dev set performance. The CRFs performed best at $N=200$. We also applied dropout of 0.2 for the LSTMs and 0.5 CRF.

We report results with three metrics: digit accuracy, Levenshtein edit distance, and perfect accuracy. Digit accuracy is the simple alignment of predicted digit with gold digit (# correct / 10). If a predicted phone number is longer than 10 digits (CRFs are not bound to strictly 10 predictions), digit accuracy is computed only over the first 10 predicted digits.

Digit accuracy is flawed because a model might insert one extra digit, but still guess correct for the remainder. For example:

> Gold: 4109342309
> Guess: 41109342309

The CRF inserted an extra 1 digit, just one mistake, but digit accuracy is now a very low 0.2.

Model	Development Set			Test Set		
	Digit	Lev	Perfect	Digit	Lev	Perfect
TJBatch Rules	0.0	0.0	0.0	0.0	0.0	0.0
LSTM (5.1.2)	77.0	79.7	48.1	74.4	78.2	40.3
LSTM-2	77.5	79.4	49.7	74.8	77.6	40.6
LSTM +att (5.2.1)	78.5	80.5	48.6	76.6	78.9	43.5
LSTM +cond (5.2.2)	**79.7**	81.6	48.5	76.5	79.5	39.8
LSTM +att +cond	79.1	81.2	48.3	**77.2**	79.8	42.3
CRF with LSTM (5.2.3)	72.9	**84.0**	**58.1**	67.7	**83.4**	**48.2**

Table 1: Results on dev and test. Though flawed, digit accuracy is included for completeness. The +att and +cond options are not compatible with the CRF which does not need attention since it predicts at every input character.

We thus use the Levenshtein edit distance to better evaluate performance. Levenshtein's measure judges string similarity based on the minimum number of "edits" required to transform the prediction into the gold: $(1.0 - edits/10)$. In the above case, one deletion is required to make the strings the same, so the score is $(1 - 1/10) = 0.9$.

Finally, perfect accuracy is the number of perfect phone numbers (all 10 digits) that were correctly guessed, divided by the size of the test set.

Real-world Test: We report results only on the *real-world* test set from Section 4.1. The artificial data was solely used for training. We did not run models on the test set until the very end after choosing our best settings (on the dev set).

Real-world Challenge Test: To further illustrate the challenge of noisy text, we enhanced the real-world test set with *unicode injections*. Using a hand-created character lookup of visually similar unicode characters, we replaced 10% of the characters with randomly chosen unicode lookalikes not in the training data. This results in a very challenging test set to further benchmark the models.

Finally, all results in the next section are the average of 4 train/test runs of the same model.

7 Results

Table 1 contains results *without CNNs* for the baselines, RNNs, and CRF. The models listed are those that showed consistent improvement on development, and the test set columns were run only at the end for publication results. Adding position attention and conditional dependence each showed improvements of 1-2% Levenshtein. Stacking two LSTMs showed little gain. The CRF excelled with a 11% relative gain (on test) for perfect prediction over best LSTM setup.

CNN Comparison (Perfect Acc)

	Test		Challenge	
	Lev	Perf	Lev	Perf
Best LSTM (no CNN)	**81.2**	**48.3**	72.9	22.1
CNN-LSTM	77.3	42.1	65.5	15.6
CNN-LSTM +aug	79.7	39.8	**75.2**	**27.3**
Best CRF (no CNN)	**84.0**	**58.1**	74.9	17.6
CNN-CRF	82.8	54.2	73.4	14.6
CNN-CRF +aug	83.3	56.1	**79.7**	**33.3**

Table 2: Results of the CNN models. Challenge has 10% unseen unicode injected. +aug used visual data augmentation during training.

For CNN results, Table 2 shows test set performance. Adding just the CNNs does not improve recognition, but in fact are slightly worse. However, more compelling is the challenge set with injected unicode confounders. Recall the importance of *data augmentation* during training so the models learn real visual features. These "+aug" results show why it is needed with a 89% relative improvement in perfect phone accuracy (from 17.6% to 33.3%). The non-CNN LSTM and CRF struggle at 17-22%. They simply cannnot represent unseen characters.

Our new CRF model (no CNN) outperforms the RNNs on the test set by 10% absolute. When comparing challenge test performance, the best CRF-CNN outperforms the best non-CNN LSTM by 11% absolute. To further illustrate the effect of unicode confounders, we varied how much we injected and graphed performance in Figure 3. The CNN models consistently outperform.

8 Full Ad Extraction

We wrapup with a pilot for full ad extraction. The models presented so far extract from one span of text (it assumes a phone number exists). This for-

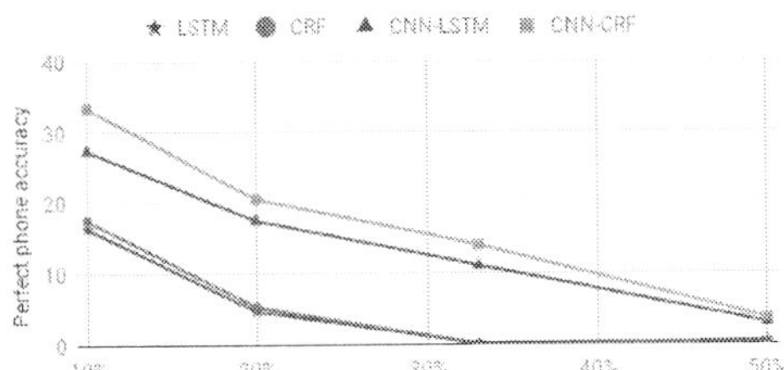

Table 3: Phone accuracy as a higher % of unicode substitutions are made for lookalike ASCII characters.

mulation is a well-defined task for research, but we also propose how one might apply these extractors to the more difficult task of full document extraction when the location of the phone number is unknown. We briefly describe initial tests.

The most straightforward way to extract from a document is to split it into text windows (spans) and try all possible extractions. Since these are probabilistic models, we can compute $P(phone|span)$, and find the window span that maximizes the probability.

$$best = max_{span} P(phone|span) \qquad (2)$$

$$P(phone|span) = \prod_{i=0}^{9} max_j P(d_i = j|span) \qquad (3)$$

The phone number extracted from the best span is the phone number in the text.

We collected a set of real advertisements that don't have phone numbers, and artificially inserted an obscured number from our artificial dataset. This allows us to track which span contains the phone number, and then evaluate an extractor.

The difficulty with this task is that our models are trained on precise text spans, whereas this full document dataset contains lots of non-phone-related text. To address this difference, we stopped padding our snippet input with null values (up to the length of the RNN), and instead pad with randomly selected text snippets from real ads. The models are exactly the same, we just change how padding works when the training text is shorter than length 70. We refer to this as the "ad pad".

Datum: 6I5 093 93B6
Null-Pad: 6I5 093 93B6____________________
Ad-Pad: 6I5 093 93B6always in town call

To be clear, no models were changed, just how training input is padded. Can the models identify the correct text span that contains a phone number? Table 4 shows these results for standard

Text Span ID of Phone Numbers

	Full	Full+Partial
Zero pad	70.3%	92.1%
Craigslist ad pad	99.3%	99.7%
Backpage ad pad	98.0%	99.6%

Table 4: Results of choosing text spans with the full phone number, or a partial match. Partial matches contained on average 7-8 of the 10 digits.

null-padding versus ad-padding, as well as cross-domain tests. We trained on Craigslist and Backpage separately, then tested on only Backpage ads.

Window identification works very well as long as training padded its input with real ad text. This is encouraging in that it seems these models can reliably identify *where* a phone number is present.

Finally, we tested how the models also extract from these spans after identifying them. Extraction showed 80% accuracy on full numbers, compared to 98% when train/test only on artificial phone snippets. We attribute the drop to the difficult task - window spans contain more noise than a precise text span. Future work will focus on this full document task with real-world numbers.

9   Discussion

This is the first work to model noisy phone number extraction with neural models. Most notably, our CNNs explore how to use visual characteristics of the characters, rather than standard NLP-style models with trained embeddings. To the best of our knowledge, this is the first proposal for a visual language model in an extraction architecture.

We showed results on new challenge datasets with injected unicode. These results illustrate the challenge for extractors, but also the usefulness of CNN recognizers. In fact, current rule-based extractors cannot extract any of the numbers in our test sets. Our CRF outperformed an LSTM-only model by 10% absolute, and data augmentation improved on unicode tests by a relative 89% gain.

Possible future work could investigate a Generative Adversarial Network (GAN) (Goodfellow et al., 2014). GANs have become popular in vision tasks, but the normal GAN setup requires training data to start from, and this sparse domain prohibits its straightforward use.

Data from this work's training and evaluation are available online[4], and we hope this spurs further work on this important societal challenge.

---

[4] www.usna.edu/Users/cs/nchamber/data/phone/

10 Acknowledgments

This work would not be possible without the help of the Global Emancipation Network. Many thanks also to Jeff Kosseff for bringing this issue to our attention in the first place. We recognize and appreciate the support of the DoD HPC Modernization Office for enhancing our undergraduate education and research. Finally, thanks to Rebecca Hwa for helpful conversations early on in this work.

References

Hamidreza Alvari, Paulo Shakarian, and J. E. Kelly Snyder. 2017. Semi-supervised learning for detecting human trafficking. In *Semi-supervised learning for detecting human trafficking*.

Hamidreza Alvari, Paulo Shakarian, and J.E. Kelly Snyder. 2016. A non-parametric learning approach to identify online human trafficking. In *IEEE Conference on Intelligence and Security Informatics (ISI)*.

Andrei Costin, Jelena Isacenkova, Marco Balduzzi, Aurélien Francillon, and Davide Balzarotti. 2013. The role of phone numbers in understanding cybercrime schemes. In *2013 Eleventh Annual Conference on Privacy, Security and Trust*, pages 213–220. IEEE.

Jun Ding, Bo Chen, Hongwei Liu, and Mengyuan Huang. 2016. Convolutional neural network with data augmentation for sar target recognition. *IEEE Geoscience and remote sensing letters*, 13(3):364–368.

Artur Dubrawski, Kyle Miller, Matthew Barnes, Benedikt Boecking, and Emily Kennedy. 2015. Leveraging publicly available data to discern patterns of human-trafficking activity. *Journal of Human Trafficking*, 1.

Ian Goodfellow, Jean Pouget-Abadie, Mehdi Mirza, Bing Xu, David Warde-Farley, Sherjil Ozair, Aaron Courville, and Yoshua Bengio. 2014. Generative adversarial nets. In *Advances in neural information processing systems*, pages 2672–2680.

Zhiheng Huang, Wei Xu, and Kai Yu. 2015. Bidirectional lstm-crf models for sequence tagging. *arXiv preprint arXiv:1508.01991*.

Rahul Kapoor, Mayank Kejriwal, and Pedro Szekely. 2017. Using contexts and constraints for improved geotagging of human trafficking webpages. In *Proceedings of the Fourth International ACM Workshop on Managing and Mining Enriched Geo-Spatial Data*.

Mayank Kejriwal, Jiayuan Ding, Runqi Shao, Anoop Kumar, and Pedro Szekely. 2017. Flagit: A system for minimally supervised human trafficking indicator mining.

Mayank Kejriwal and Pedro Szekely. 2017. Information extraction in illicit web domains. In *WWW*.

John Lafferty, Andrew McCallum, and Fernando CN Pereira. 2001. Conditional random fields: Probabilistic models for segmenting and labeling sequence data.

Lin Li, Olga Simek, Angela Lai, Matthew P. Daggett, Charlie K. Dagli, and Cara Jones. 2018. Detection and characterization of human trafficking networks using unsupervised scalable text template matching. In *IEEE International Conference on Big Data (Big Data)*.

Frederick Liu, Han Lu, Chieh Lo, and Graham Neubig. 2017. Learning character-level compositionality with visual features. In *ACL*.

Xuezhe Ma and Eduard Hovy. 2016. End-to-end sequence labeling via bi-directional lstm-cnns-crf. *arXiv preprint arXiv:1603.01354*.

C. Nagpal, K. Miller, B. Boecking, and A. Dubrawski. 2017. An entity resolution approach to isolate instances of human trafficking online.

Reihaneh Rabbany, David Bayani, and Artur Dubrawski. 2018. Active search of connections for case building and combating human trafficking. In *KDD*.

Justin Salamon and Juan Pablo Bello. 2017. Deep convolutional neural networks and data augmentation for environmental sound classification. *IEEE Signal Processing Letters*, 24(3):279–283.

Pedro Szekely, Craig Knoblock, Jason Slepickz, Andrew Philpot, et al. 2015. Building and using a knowledge graph to combat human trafficking. In *International Conference on Semantic Web (ICSW)*.

Yan Xu, Ran Jia, Lili Mou, Ge Li, Yunchuan Chen, Yangyang Lu, and Zhi Jin. 2016. Improved relation classification by deep recurrent neural networks with data augmentation. *arXiv preprint arXiv:1601.03651*.

Zhun Zhong, Liang Zheng, Guoliang Kang, Shaozi Li, and Yi Yang. 2017. Random erasing data augmentation. *arXiv preprint arXiv:1708.04896*.

Community Characteristics and Semantic Shift of
High Affinity Terms on Reddit

Abhinav Bhandari[†‡]   **Caitrin Armstrong**[†]

[†]School of Computer Science, McGill University
[‡]Agoop Corp, 3-35-8 Jingumae, Shibuya City, Tokyo
`abhinav.bhandari,caitrin.armstrong{@mail.mcgill.ca}`

Abstract

Language is an important marker of a cultural
group, large or small. One aspect of language
variation between communities is the employment of highly specialized terms with unique
significance to the group. We study these high
affinity terms across a wide variety of communities by leveraging the rich diversity of Red-
dit.com. We provide a systematic exploration
of high affinity terms, the often rapid semantic
shifts they undergo, and their relationship to
subreddit characteristics across 2600 diverse
subreddits. Our results show that high affinity terms are effective signals of loyal communities, they undergo more semantic shift than
low affinity terms, and that they are partial
barrier to entry for new users. We conclude
that Reddit is a robust and valuable data source
for testing further theories about high affinity
terms across communities.

1 Introduction

The evolution and semantic change of human language has been studied extensively, both in a historical context (Garg et al., 2017) and, increasingly, in the online context (Jaidka et al., 2018).
However, few studies have explored the evolution
of words across different online communities that
allow a comparison between community characteristics and terms that have high affinity to a community.

The banning of r/CoonTown and r/fatpeoplehate
in 2015, as analyzed by Saleem et al., provides
good motivation for our work. r/CoonTown was
a racist subreddit with a short life span of 8
months (November 2014 - June 2015)(Saleem
et al., 2017). During this time, as shown
by Saleem (2017), these subreddits underwent
rapid semantic development through which new
words, such as "dindu", "tbi" and "nuffin" were
not only created, but increasingly became more

context-specific (accumulated in meaning). In
r/fatpeoplehate existing words such as "moo",
"xxl" and "whale" underwent localized semantic shift such that their meanings transformed to
derogatory terms (Saleem et al., 2017).

These two cases demonstrate that not only are
new words conceived within subreddits, existing
words undergo localized transition. They also suggest that this phenomenon likely takes place in a
short time period for high affinity words. In order to evaluate whether such trends are consistent
across subreddits, we study semantic shift and the
roles high affinity terms play in 2600 different subreddits between November 2014 to June 2015.

Our aim is to provide a characterization of high
affinity terms by mapping their relationship to different types of online communities and the semantic shifts they undergo in comparison to generalized terms (low affinity terms). We leverage data
curated from the multi-community social network
Reddit and the types of subreddit characteristics
we study are loyalty, dedication, number of users
and number of comments. Our paper explores the
following research questions:

1. Do certain community characteristics correlate with the presence of high affinity terms?

2. Do high affinity terms undergo greater semantic shift than low affinity terms?

3. Do high affinity terms and community characteristics function as a barriers to entry for
   new users to participate?

Some key findings include:

1. Loyalty is strongly correlated to the presence
   of high affinity terms in a community.

2. High affinity terms undergo greater semantic shift than generalized terms (low affinity
   terms) in a short interval of time.

Proceedings of the 2019 EMNLP Workshop W-NUT: The 5th Workshop on Noisy User-generated Text, pages 57–67
Hong Kong, Nov 4, 2019. ©2019 Association for Computational Linguistics

3. High affinity terms, and dedication values of a subreddit strongly correlate to the number of new users that participate, indicating that the degree of high affinity terms establishes a lexical barrier to entry to a community.

2 Related Work and Concepts

2.1 Understanding Community Specific Terms

Before defining high affinity terms, we examine the traits observed in community specific terms from past literature.

Studies have shown that words specific to a community have qualities of cultural carriers (Goddard, 2015). While culture is "something learned, transmitted, passed down from one generation to the next, through human actions," (Duranti et al., 1997) these transmissions through language affect a culture's system of "classifications, specialized lexicons, metaphors, and reference forms" in communities (Cuza, 2011). Pierre Bourdieu argues that language is not only grammar and systematic arrangemennt of words, but it is symbolic of cultural ideas for each community. To speak a certain language, is to view the world in a particular way. To Bourdieu, through language people are members of a community of unique ideas and practices (Bourdieu et al., 1991). As such, community specific terms are usually not easily translatable across different communities. For example, in Hungarian "life" is metaphorically described as "life is a war" and "life is a compromise", whereas in American English "life" is metaphorically represented as "life is a precious posesssion", or "life is a game" (KÃ, 2010). These definitions of similar entities vary due to different cultural outlooks in communities.

Besides words that are cultural carriers, slang is also a form of terminology specific to a community. While there is no standard operational definition of slang, many philosophical linguists define slang as terms that are vulgar (Green, 2016; Allens, 1993), encapsulate local cultural value and a type of insider speech that roots from subcultures (Partridge and Beale, 2002). Morphological properties of slang are defined as "extra-grammatical", and these morphological properties in slang are shown to be distinguishable from morphological properties of standard words in English (Mattiello, 2013). There has been an increase of slang in online spaces (Eble, 2012), with many terms falling under the extra-grammatical classifications of abbreviation ('DIY', 'hmu', 'lol'), blends ('brangelina', 'brunch'), and clippings ('doc (doctor)', 'fam (family)') (Mattiello, 2013; Kulkarni and Wang, 2018).

By extracting terms that have a high affinity to a community, we approximate words that are either cultural carriers or slang.

2.2 Measuring Affinity of Terms

Measurements for affinity of terms to a community have been explored in research, where the frequency of a word is compared to some background distribution to extract linguistic variations that are more likely in one setting (Monroe et al.; Zhang et al., 2018). Most helpful to our approach is a past study that computed a term's specificity sp_c to a subreddit through the pointwise mutual information (PMI) of a word w in one community c relative to all other communities C in Reddit (Zhang et al., 2017).

$$sp_c(w) = \log \frac{P_c(w)}{P_C(w)}$$

An issue with this metric is that terms with equal specificity can differ in their frequency. Specificity does not show which term is more dominant within a community by frequency, as show in Table 1. Due to this, we compute the affinity value of a term by measuring its *locality* and *dominance* to a community. Locality is the likelihood of a term belonging to some community, and dominance captures the presence of the term in the said community by its frequency.

We therefore calculate the locality l of a word w_j in subreddit s_i through the conditional probability of a word occurring in s_i, relative to it occurring in all other subreddits S.

$$l_{s_i}(w_j) = \frac{P_{s_i}(w_j)}{P_S(w_j)}$$

We then calculate dominance d in two steps. First we calculate an intermediate value r, which is the difference between the count of word w_j in s_i subtracted by the sum of all terms W in s_i multiplied by constant ϵ, which in our work was sufficient as 0.0001. If the value of r is negative, we disregard it, as it is likely to be an infrequent word of little semantic significance, such as a typo.

$$r_{s_i}(w_j) = \text{Count}_{s_i}(w_j) - \text{Count}_{s_i}(W) \times \epsilon$$

	mccoy	slowmo	ducati	bleacher	takahashi	motogp
sp_c	0.000	0.000	-0.004	0.000	0.000	-0.004
a_{s_i}	0.942	0.666	0.987	0.500	0.833	0.987

Table 1: Affinity and Specificity of terms found in r/motogp calculated on the word distributions of 10 sample subreddits. This shows that less frequently occurring words and frequently occurring words can have the same specificity value, however the affinity value takes into account the degree of frequency of each term in a community.

where

$$r_{s_i}(w_j) = \begin{cases} r_{s_i}(w_j) & r_{s_i}(w_j) > 1 \\ 1 & r_{s_i}(w_j) \leq 1 \end{cases}$$

Then, we calculate the dominance d as a negative hyperbolic function of each word's occurrence:

$$d_{s_i}(w_j) = 1 - \frac{1}{r_{s_i}(w_j)}$$

Finally, we compute the affinity value of a word to a subreddit as a product of a word's dominance and locality:

$$a_{s_i}(w_j) = d_{s_i}(w_j) \times l_{s_i}(w_j)$$

After extracting affinity values of each word relative to a subreddit, we partition the sets of words into high affinity terms and low affinity terms.

High Affinity Terms: For each subreddit, we extract 50 terms with the highest affinity values, and we categorize them as *high affinity terms*. The average of high affinity terms is denoted as *high affinity average*.

Low Affinity Terms: For each subreddit, we extract 50 terms with the lowest affinity values, and we categorize them as *low affinity terms*. The average of low affinity terms is denoted as *low affinity average*.

2.3 How Semantic Shift Can Capture Cultural Shifts

As previously stated, high affinity terms are approximations for words that are either cultural carriers or slang.

Research has shown that shifts of local neighborhoods across embeddings are more effective in capturing cultural shifts than to calculate distances of a word across aligned embeddings, which is used to measure structural shifts (Hamilton et al., 2016; Eger and Mehler, 2016). Studies have represented k-nearest neighbors n of a word w through second-order vectors $V^{|n|}$ that are made of the cosine similarities between n and w, then calculate the difference between these second-order vectors to identify shifts (Hamilton et al., 2016; Eger and Mehler, 2016). Recent works have also modeled shifts in words through the change in common neighbors across different embeddings (Wendlandt et al., 2018; Eger and Mehler, 2016).

2.4 Measuring Semantic Change

Our measurement of semantic shift is based on the concepts of semantic *narrowing* of words, a process in which words become more specialized to a context, and semantic *broadening* of words, a process in which words become more generalized from a context (Bloomfield, 1933; Blank and Koch, 1999). We capture this contextual information by constructing 300 dimensional word embeddings (word2vec) for each subreddit using skip-gram with negative sampling algorithms, where a distributional model is trained on words predicting their context words (Mikolov et al., 2013). For each word, we measure narrowing as an increase in co-occurrence of a word's nearest neighbors, and broadening as a decrease in co-occurrence of a word's nearest neighbors (Crowley and Bowern, 2010).

To measure semantic shift, we extract common vocabulary $V = (w_1, ..., w_m)$ across all time intervals $t \in T$. Then, for some t and $t + n$, we take a word w_j's set of k nearest-neighbors (according to cosine similarity). These neighbor sets are denoted as $A_k^t(w_j)$ and $A_k^{t+n}(w_j)$. We then calculate the neighbours co-occurrence value CO as the Jaccard similarity of neighbours sets (Hamilton et al., 2016), in subreddit s_i.

$$A_k^t(w_j) = \text{cos-sim}(w_j^t, k)$$

$$A_k^{t+n}(w_j) = \text{cos-sim}(w_j^{t+n}, k)$$

$$CO_{s_i}(w_j^t, w_j^{t+n}) = \frac{|A_k^t(w_j) \cap A_k^{t+n}(w_j)|}{|A_k^t(w_j) \cup A_k^{t+n}(w_j)|}$$

Then, we calculate the difference of CO across successive embeddings in T. We label, chronologically, the first time interval (t_1) as *initial point* and the last time interval (t_p) as *terminal point*, across which narrowing and broadening are measured. We used $k = 10$ for all computations.

Broadening Measurement: We measure broadening as the sum of the difference of CO_{s_i}

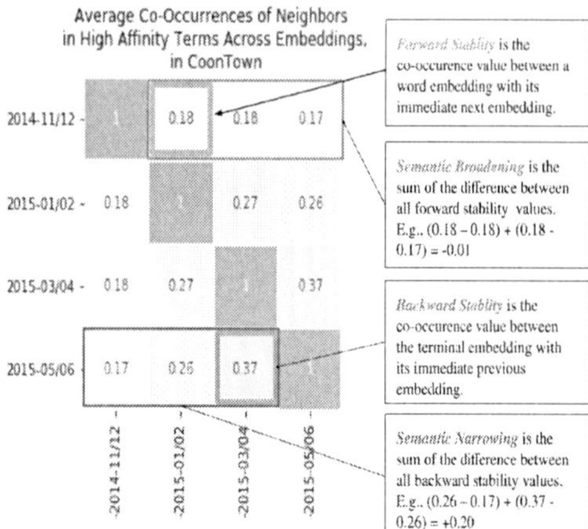

Figure 1: This figure provides a visual representation of our methodology of semantic shift measurement. The initial point embedding is trained on 2014-11/12 dataset. The terminal point embedding is trained on 2015-05/06. All semantic shift measurements follow a chronological order of comparison, such that narrowing and broadening are both measurements of embedding$_{t+1}$ - embedding$_t$.

between initial point embedding and all successive embeddings. This is defined as:

$$b_{s_i}(w_j) = \sum_{t=2}^{p-1}(CO_{s_i}(w_j^1, w_j^{t+1}) - CO_{s_i}(w_j^1, w_j^t))$$

By comparing an embedding to its future embeddings, we are able to see which contexts are lost as a word's meaning becomes more broad.

Narrowing Measurement: Similarly, we measure narrowing by calculating the sum of the difference of CO between terminal point embedding and all previous embeddings.

$$n_{s_i}(w_j) = \sum_{t=1}^{p-2}(CO_{s_i}(w_j^p, w_j^{t+1}) - CO_{s_i}(w_j^p, w_j^t))$$

By comparing an embedding to its previous embeddings, we are able to see which contexts associated with a word have increased in specificity over time.

A visual representation of the metrics are provided in Figure 1.

2.5 Extracting Rate of Change of Frequency

Many past works have also modelled relationships between frequency and semantic shift (Lancia, 2007; Hilpert and Gries, 2016; Lijffijt et al., 2014).

One study shows that an increase in frequency of a term across decades results in a semantic broadening, while a decrease in frequency causes it to narrow (Feltgen et al., 2017). For example an increase in frequency of the word "dog" evolved its meaning from a breed to an entire species, and the decrease in frequency of "deer" localized its meaning from "animal" to a specific animal (undergoing narrowing) (Hilpert and Gries, 2016).

Very few studies have modelled narrowing and broadening of terms in the short term. As such, we are interested in the frequency patterns of terms that go through short-term cultural shifts. One study showed the effect of frequency on learning new words, and how it affects the use of new words in their correct context. They conducted their experiments in a physical capacity on children of five years old who were made familiar with new words (Abbot-Smith and Tomasello, 2010) in a short time period. Their results demonstrate that familiarizing children with new words allowed them to use the word in correct grammatical contexts, and greater frequency of exposure to new words resulted in *more* narrowed and correct use of the word to a context. This pattern of teaching is categorized as *lexically-based learning*.

Due to this, we assess whether in the short-term in subreddits, narrowing and broadening of terms correlates to the rate of change of frequencies.

We calculate rate of change of frequency across time periods T for a subreddit s_i as such, where n is the size of T:

$$\Delta f_{s_i}(w_j) = \sum_{t=1}^{n-1} \frac{f_{t+1}(w_j) - f_t(w_j)}{f_{t+1}(w_j)}$$

A positive value shows an increasing rate of frequency, and a negative value shows a decreasing rate of frequency.

2.6 Characteristics of Subreddits

We introduce four quantifiers that describe subreddit networks based on existing typology. Using these quantitative chararacteristics we can evaluate and identify systemic patterns that exist between types of subreddits and high affinity terms. The four quantifiers are loyalty, dedication, number of comments, and number of users.

Loyalty: Previous work on subreddit characteristics has defined community loyalty as a percentage of users that demonstrate both *preference* and *commitment*, over other communities in multiple

	Subreddits	High Aff. Avg.	High Aff. Terms	Low Aff. Avg.	Low Aff. Terms
Top 1%	bravefrontier	0.999	'sbb', 'zelnite', 'darvanshel', 'tridon', 'ulkina'	0.000	'food', 'drive', 'park', 'episode', 'photo'
	chess	0.999	'pgn', 'bxc', 'nxe', 'nxd', 'bxf'	0.000	'character', 'compose', 'pack', 'message', 'damage'
Arbitrary	radiohead	0.732	'cuttooth', 'backdrifts', 'tkol', 'crushd', 'htdc'	0.000	'willing', 'phone', 'gain', 'sell', 'provide'
	fatpeoplehate	0.357	'pco', 'tubblr', 'fatshion', 'fatkini', 'feedee'	0.000	'application', 'network', 'engine', 'element', 'cable'
Bottom 1%	Wellthatsucks	0.002	'helmet', 'shoe', 'brake', 'truck', 'tire'	0.000	'help', 'team', 'love', 'include', 'question'
	gif	0.002	'gif', 'prank', 'repost', 'swim', 'ftfy'	0.000	'subreddit', 'order', 'account', 'game', 'issue'

Table 2: A sample presentation of high affinity terms and low affinity terms from subreddits with high *high affinity averages* (top 1%), and low *high affinity averages* (bottom 1%).

time periods (Hamilton et al., 2017). Preference is demonstrated by more than half of a user's comments contributing to subreddit $s_i \in S$, and commitment is measured by a user commenting in s_i in multiple time periods $t \in T$. It has been shown that community wide loyalty impacts usage of linguistic features such as singular ("I") and plural ("We") pronoun (Hamilton et al., 2017). Communities with greater loyalty have a higher usage of plural pronouns than communities with low loyalty which have a heavier usage of singular pronouns. Following this finding, we investigate relationships between loyal communities and high affinity terms, to gauge whether loyal communities are also strongly correlated to use of other types of terms.

Dedication: Other studies have also shown that user retention correlates to increased use of subreddit specific terms (similar to high affinity terms) (Zhang et al., 2017). We calculate user retention to measure a community characteristic similar to commitment as defined in a past study (Hamilton et al., 2017), by extracting users that comment in subreddit $s_i \in S$ a minimum of n number of times across all time periods $t \in T$ and label this retention value as *dedication*. A key difference between dedication and loyalty is that a user does not have to contribute more than 50% of their comments to a particular subreddit to be dedicated, which is a requirement for loyalty. This means that a user can be dedicated to multiple subreddits, while a user is loyal to only one group at a particular time. The comparison between loyalty and dedication allows us to explore whether preference is a strong factor in the linguistic evolution of high affinity terms in online communities.

Number of Comments and Number of Users: Lastly, we measure raw metadata of subreddits which are the number of comments made, and the number of users that participated in a subreddit.

Existing work has shown that areas with large populations experience a larger introduction of new words, whereas areas with small populations experience a greater rate of word loss (Bromham et al., 2015). Furthermore, words in larger populations are suspect to greater language evolution. While this is a correlation found in physical communities, we assess whether this remains consistent in online communities. As a proxy for population we consider both the number of users and the number of comments.

3 Description of Data

Our dataset consists of all subreddits between November 2014 to June 2015 with more than 10000 comments in that period. We performed our measures on the curated data in time intervals of 2 months. We manually removed communities that are mostly in non-ascii or run by bots. This resulted in a dataset of 2626 subreddits.

4 Qualitative Overview of High Affinity and Low Affinity Terms

We examine high and low affinity terms across subreddits. Our results, as shown in Table 2, demonstrate that high affinity terms have different characteristics across communities.

Certain high affinity terms exist independent of online communications. For example in r/chess, the high affinity terms "bxc", "bxf", "nxc" are all numerical representations used to communicate game moves. Similarly in r/bravefrontier,

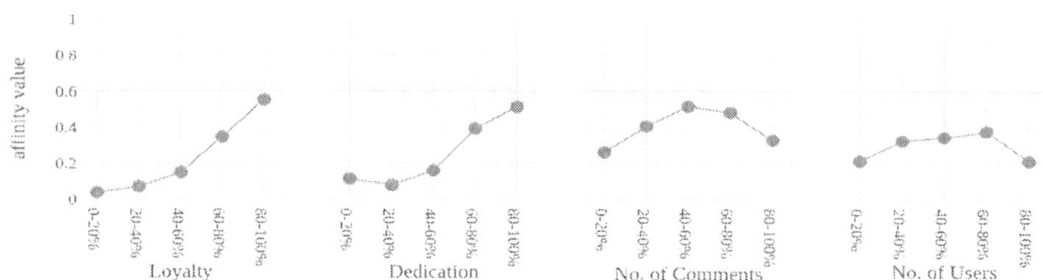

Figure 2: This figure shows the relationship between community characteristics and high affinity averages. Each community characteristics is binned into intervals of 20% by percentile. Loyalty most strongly correlates with high affinity averages.

the terms "zelnite" and "darvanshel" are game characters. However in r/fatpeoplehate, there are high affinity terms that originate online. Terms in r/fatpeoplehate demonstrate extra-grammatical qualities of slang, such as "fatkini", which is a blend of "fat" + "bikini", and "feedee", which is clipping of "feeder", signalling word development through online communication (Kulkarni and Wang, 2018).

Interestingly, across the topically different subreddits, abbreviations are common form of high affinity terms. For instance, "pgn" in r/chess stands for "portable game notation", "tkol" in r/radiohead stand for "The king of Limbs", "ftfy" in r/gif stands for "fixed that for you". The use of abbreviations illustrates the transformation of "gibberish" into collective meaning within a community. It is only with the context of domain and culture, that one can attribute meaning to these terms.

Named Entity Recognition (NER) of Top 100 and Bottom 100 subreddits by high affinity averages: We performed NER using bablefy on the names of the top 100 and bottom 100 subreddits by high affinity averages. Through this analysis, we observe that 82 of the top 100 are named entities, whereas only 18 of bottom 100 are named entities. Of the 82, 33 subreddits are videogames, 19 are regional subreddits and 11 are sports subreddits. This shows that communities with high affinity averages are likely to be strongly linked with a physical counterpart. Whereas the bottom 100 subreddits consisted of discussion and generalized subreddits such as r/TrueReddit, r/Showerthoughts, r/blackpeoplegifs whose creation and culture can directly be attributed to online communities rather than physical counterparts. This provides an explanation for subreddits with low high affinity averages having extremely generalized high affinity terms, such as "helmet" and "shoe" in r/Wellthatsucks.

5 Impact of Community Characteristics on Affinity of Terms

We conducted prediction tasks using community characteristics to demonstrate meaningful relationships between high affinity terms. We treated each of the community characteristics as features (log-transformed), and perform linear regressions, with five cross-validation, to predict the high affinity average (log-transformed) of a subreddit.

5.1 Prediction of High Affinity Terms from Community Characteristics

We find that loyalty of a subreddit is remarkably correlated to the high affinity average of subreddits. A linear model trained on loyalty to predict high affinity average of a subreddit achieves an R^2 of 0.364 (p-value $<$ 0.001). Compared to this, a linear model trained on dedication results in an R^2 value of 0.274 (p-value $<$ 0.001). This implies that *preference* is a strong factor in the likelihood of high affinity terms in communities.

In contrast, models trained on number of comments and number of users resulted in an R^2 of 0.071 and 0.004. Loyalty is therefore a much more effective measure than most standard community measures at least when measured on a linear scale. This finding supports existing work, which shows that distinctiveness of a community is strongly related to its rate of user retention (Zhang et al., 2017).

Community Type	R^2	p-value	Community Type	R^2	p-value
loyalty	0.038	< 0.001	loyalty	0.005	< 0.001
dedication	0.036	< 0.001	dedication	0.002	0.032
no. comments	**0.048**	$\mathbf{< 0.001}$	**no. comments**	**0.016**	$\mathbf{< 0.001}$
no. users	0.004	0.001	no. users	0.001	0.062

Table 3: Coefficient of determination values for linear models trained on community characteristics that predict semantic narrowing (left) and semantic broadening (right) of high affinity terms.

5.2 Prediction of Low Affinity Terms from Community Characteristics

Although low affinity terms for almost all subreddits have values that are very close to 0, we find that raw subreddit meta data (log-transformed) is an effective predictor of low average affinity term value (log-transformed). A linear model trained on number of comments results in a R^2 of 0.456 (p-value < 0.001). This makes sense intuitively, because as the number of comments increases, low affinity terms have more likelihood of being generalized.

A similar model trained on number of users attains an R^2 of 0.180, with a model trained on loyalty performing the worst with an R^2 of 0.055.

Finally, as we might expect a multivariate regression model trained on both loyalty and number of comments performs the best out of all models, scoring an R^2 of 0.391 (p-value < 0.001) when predicting high affinity averages and scoring an R^2 of 0.470 (p-value < 0.001) when predicting low affinity averages, which are significant improvements.

6 Assessing Semantic Shift of High Affinity Terms

Calculating semantic shifts of high affinity terms enables us to test whether high affinity terms are subject to cultural shifts and whether linguistic developments in online spaces are consistent with trends in physical communities.

6.1 Evaluating Semantic Shift to Community Characteristics

We perform linear regression between community characteristics and semantic shifts to assess their relationships. Our results show that all community characteristics are weak predictors of semantic shifts. This is surprising as they are effective predictors of affinity values.

Semantic Narrowing and Semantic Broadening: Table 3 shows that number of comments has the strongest correlation to semantic narrowing and semantic broadening of high affinity terms, achieving R^2 values of 0.037 and 0.019 (p-value < 0.001). In contrast, while loyalty and dedication have similarly high R^2 values when used for modeling semantic narrowing of high affinity terms as shown in Table 3, it is more weakly linked to the semantic broadening of high affinity terms.

Perhaps the most surprising finding is that number of users is a poor predictor of both semantic narrowing and semantic broadening (R^2 of 0.004 and 0.001) in online spaces. This is surprising because number of users and number of comments are highly correlated features (Pearson coefficient of 0.726, p-value < 0.001), but their performance in approximation of semantic shifts are broadly different.

These results provide insight into how the concept of "population" works in online spaces in contrast to physical communities. Previous works show a weak correlation between population of a geographic area and the occurrence of language evolution (Bromham et al., 2015; Greenhill et al., 2018). A limitation of these studies was their inability to account for language output that was not written (i.e, oral communications). This limitation is not present in online communities because all language output is recorded via online comments. As such, the number of comments having a stronger correlation to semantic shift than number of users, indicates that the amount of oral communication may have contributed to language evolution.

6.2 Comparing Semantic Shift in High Affinity and Low Affinity Terms

First we compute a metric that shows the overall semantic shift a subreddit has experienced. This is measured by computing the difference between semantic narrowing and semantic broadening, where a positive value indicates overall narrowing and a negative value indicates overall broadening. We label this result as net semantic shift. Then we compute net semantic shift for high affinity terms and low affinity terms for all subreddits.

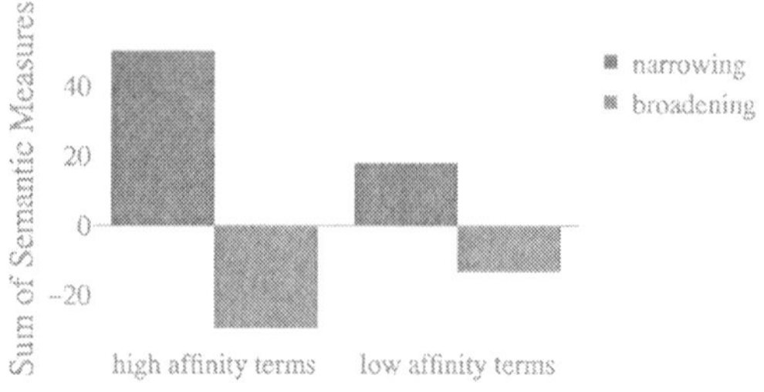

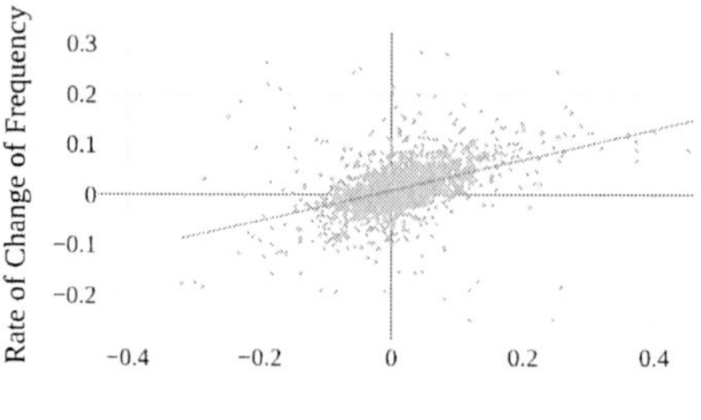

Figure 3: The sum of semantic narrowing and semantic broadening from all subreddits by high affinity and low affinity terms. High affinity terms are more volatile and sensitive to cultural shifts.

Figure 4: This figure illustrates the relationship between net semantic shift of subreddits and their average rate of change of frequency for high-affinity terms.

We find that out of 2626 subreddits, 1638 (62%) subreddits demonstrate a positive net semantic shift in high affinity terms, whereas, 1529 (58%) subreddits demonstrate a positive net semantic shift in low affinity terms.

In Figure 3, we show that across all subreddits, the sum of net semantic shift in high affinity terms is 20.462 (50.253-29.791), whereas the sum of net semantic shift in low affinity terms is 4.402 (17.878-13.476). This implies that high affinity terms in general are more likely to attain qualities that are defining of neologisms, and are more likely to be narrowed in communities across Reddit.

This is explained by our results which show that the rate of decrease of semantic broadening is slower than the rate of increase of semantic narrowing (Pearson coefficient of -0.192, p-value < 0.001), as demonstrated by a regression coefficient of -0.148. This trend is consistent when modeling semantic narrowing and semantic broadening with other community characteristics.

Interestingly, in communities with very high affinity averages, we observe several cases where the semantic narrowing and semantic broadening are close to 0. Examples of such subreddits are r/kpop, r/chess, and r/Cricket. We notice that these groups contain terms that are essential and almost exclusive to the domain of that community. However, these terms do not undergo extraordinary cultural impetus that causes a shift in meaning. For instance in r/chess there is little motivation to use "bxe", "cdf" outside of the context of game moves.

Additionally, we observe highest semantic shifts in groups that are mostly video games, tv-shows and sports communities, with high affinity averages being less than 0.5 in most cases - the average high affinity score of top 100 semantic narrowing groups is 0.367. These lower scores that tend away from the possible extremes, show that niche terms that shift the most are also slightly distributed in few other communities, but clearly dominant in one. Terms that are likely to undergo high levels of semantic shift have potential of being cross-cultural and adopted by a different group of people. Study of external influence of high affinity terms in other communities is an area of future research, and may reveal factors that make some high affinity terms more likely to evolve in a short period of time.

6.3 Mapping of Frequency

Past studies show that in the long term words that narrow decrease in frequency (Feltgen et al., 2017; Hilpert and Gries, 2016). However, our results, as shown in Figure 4, indicate that in the short term net semantic shift is strongly correlated with increase in frequency.

By testing the relationship between Δf_{s_i} and net semantic shift, we discovered a strong linear relationship (Pearson coefficient of 0.429, p-value < 0.001).

Language adoption studies have shown that increased familiarization with a word in the short term - measured through frequency - actually enables a person to use the word more accurately and precisely. This is achieved, in both adults and children through lexically-based learning (Abbot-Smith and Tomasello, 2010). Our results indicate that online communities also employ lexically-

Community Characteristic	R^2	p-value
loyalty	0.340	< 0.001
dedication	**0.518**	< 0.001
High Aff. Avg.	0.201	< 0.001

Community Characteristic	R^2	p-value
loyalty + dedication	0.503	< 0.001
loyalty + High Aff.	0.377	< 0.001
dedication + High Aff.	**0.539**	< 0.001

Table 4: Coefficient of determination values for linear and multivariate models trained on community characteristics that predict rate of new users ($\delta u(s_i)$).

based learning in the short term, and may factor into linguistic culture adoption and development. We derive this finding from the fact that increase in frequency is strongly correlated with semantic narrowing.

7 Barriers to Entry

In this section, we evaluate the impact high affinity values have on the rate of new users participating in each time period.

We calculate the rate of new users $\delta u(s_i)$ as:

$$\delta u(s_i) = \sum_{t=1}^{n-1} \frac{U_{t+1}(s_i) - U_t(s_i)}{U_{t+1}(s_i)}$$

where U is the set of users in subreddit s_i at time period t.

In Table 4 we present our results of regression and correlation testing. We find that dedication shows the strongest correlation to the rate of new users in a community. This insinuates that absolute *preference* is an unlikely indicator of $\delta u(s_i)$.

Although weaker, high affinity terms also show a correlation to $\delta u(s_i)$. However, as shown in Table 4, it is remarkable that dedication and high affinity averages outperform the combination of loyalty and dedication in predicting the value of $\delta u(s_i)$. This is because loyalty has a stronger correlation with $\delta u(s_i)$ than high affinity averages. Due to this, a model trained on loyalty and dedication should perform better. However not only does it not perform better than a model trained on dedication and high affinity averages, it performs worse than a model trained only on dedication. This suggests that loyalty likely captures barriers to entry similar to dedication but more poorly. It also suggests that high affinity terms and dedication capture different types of barriers to entry.

Furthermore, we observe that communities which show the least $\delta u(s_i)$, are mostly topics that originate outside of Reddit, such as r/NASCAR (sports) and r/SburbRP (sexual roleplay).

These results indicate that there are linguistic and non-linguistic barriers that prevent people from engaging in certain online communities. While this may not be concerning for innocuous topics such as r/Chess, issues may arise for ideologically-themed subreddits. In the age of political polarization, hate groups and infamous echo chambers, further research could be conducted into barriers to entry and the role high affinity terms play.

8 Conclusion and Future Work

Through several analyses we have shown there to be a strong relationship between online community behaviour and several aspects of high affinity terms. We found correlations with subreddit characteristics related to collective user behaviour, especially loyalty. The high affinity terms underwent semantic shift at a high rate given our very condensed timescale. Finally, we showed a relationship between user retention and the presence of these terms.

All three conclusions, and the secondary analyses conducted alongside them, show that high affinity terms have strong potential for further elucidating online community behaviour, and likely are correlated with further characteristics more difficult to measure than subreddit loyalty such as community cohesion (the strength and salience of group identity (Rogers and Lea, 2004)) or behaviour leading to the formation of extremist hate groups. Finally, our results and further investigation can contribute to the literature surrounding the relationship between vocabulary and social mobility between groups.

References

Kirsten Abbot-Smith and Michael Tomasello. 2010. The influence of frequency and semantic similarity on how children learn grammar. *First Language*, 30(1):79–101.

Irving Lewis Allens. 1993. *The city in slang : New York life and popular speech*, 1 edition, volume 1 of *1*. Oxford University Press. An optional note.

A. Blank and P. Koch. 1999. *Historical Semantics and Cognition*. Cognitive linguistics research. Mouton de Gruyter.

Leonard Bloomfield. 1933. *Language*. Holt, New York.

P. Bourdieu, J.B. Thompson, G. Raymond, and M. Adamson. 1991. *Language and Symbolic Power*. Social theory. Harvard University Press.

Lindell Bromham, Xia Hua, Thomas Fitzpatrick, and Simon Greenhill. 2015. Rate of language evolution is affected by population size. *Proceedings of the National Academy of Sciences of the United States of America*, 112.

T. Crowley and C. Bowern. 2010. *An Introduction to Historical Linguistics*. Oxford University Press USA - OSO.

Alexandru Ioan Cuza. 2011. Translation of cultural terms : Possible or impossible ?

A. Duranti, Cambridge University Press, S.R. Anderson, J. Bresnan, B. Comrie, W. Dressler, and C.J. Ewen. 1997. *Linguistic Anthropology*. Cambridge Textbooks in Linguistics. Cambridge University Press.

C. Eble. 2012. *Slang and Sociability: In-Group Language Among College Students*. University of North Carolina Press.

Steffen Eger and Alexander Mehler. 2016. On the linearity of semantic change: Investigating meaning variation via dynamic graph models. In *Proceedings of the 54th Annual Meeting of the Association for Computational Linguistics (Volume 2: Short Papers)*, pages 52–58, Berlin, Germany. Association for Computational Linguistics.

Quentin Feltgen, Benjamin Fagard, and Jean-Pierre Nadal. 2017. Frequency patterns of semantic change: Corpus-based evidence of a near-critical dynamics in language change. *Royal Society Open Science*, 4.

Nikhil Garg, Londa Schiebinger, Dan Jurafsky, and James Zou. 2017. Word embeddings quantify 100 years of gender and ethnic stereotypes. *CoRR*, abs/1711.08412.

Cliff Goddard. 2015. *Words as Carriers of Cultural Meaning*, pages 380–400.

J. Green. 2016. *Slang: A Very Short Introduction*. Very short introductions. Oxford University Press.

Simon J. Greenhill, Xia Hua, Caela F. Welsh, Hilde Schneemann, and Lindell Bromham. 2018. Population size and the rate of language evolution: A test across indo-european, austronesian, and bantu languages. *Frontiers in Psychology*, 9:576.

William L. Hamilton, Jure Leskovec, and Dan Jurafsky. 2016. Cultural shift or linguistic drift? comparing two computational measures of semantic change. *CoRR*, abs/1606.02821.

William L. Hamilton, Justine Zhang, Cristian Danescu-Niculescu-Mizil, Dan Jurafsky, and Jure Leskovec. 2017. Loyalty in online communities. *CoRR*, abs/1703.03386.

Martin Hilpert and Stefan Th. Gries. 2016. *Quantitative approaches to diachronic corpus linguistics*, Cambridge Handbooks in Language and Linguistics, page 36–53. Cambridge University Press.

Kokil Jaidka, Niyati Chhaya, and Lyle Ungar. 2018. Diachronic degradation of language models: Insights from social media. In *Proceedings of the 56th Annual Meeting of the Association for Computational Linguistics (Volume 2: Short Papers)*, pages 195–200. Association for Computational Linguistics.

ZoltÃ¡n KÃ. 2010. Metaphor, language, and culture. *DELTA: DocumentaÃ§Ãde Estudos em LingÃÃstica TeÃe Aplicada*, 26:739 – 757.

Vivek Kulkarni and William Yang Wang. 2018. Simple models for word formation in english slang. *CoRR*, abs/1804.02596.

Franco Lancia. 2007. Word co-occurrence and similarity in meaning.

Jefrey Lijffijt, Terttu Nevalainen, Tanja Säily, Panagiotis Papapetrou, Kai Puolamäki, and Heikki Mannila. 2014. Significance testing of word frequencies in corpora. *Digital Scholarship in the Humanities*, 31(2):374–397.

E. Mattiello. 2013. *Extra-grammatical Morphology in English: Abbreviations, Blends, Reduplicatives, and Related Phenomena*. Topics in English Linguistics [TiEL]. De Gruyter.

Tomas Mikolov, Ilya Sutskever, Kai Chen, Greg Corrado, and Jeffrey Dean. 2013. Distributed representations of words and phrases and their compositionality. In *Proceedings of the 26th International Conference on Neural Information Processing Systems - Volume 2*, NIPS'13, pages 3111–3119, USA. Curran Associates Inc.

Burt L. Monroe, Michael P. Colaresi, and Kevin M. Quinn. Fightin' words: Lexical feature selection and evaluation for identifying the content of political conflict. *Political Analysis*, 16(4):372–403.

E. Partridge and P. Beale. 2002. *A Dictionary of Slang and Unconventional English: Colloquialisms and Catch Phrases, Fossilised Jokes and Puns, General Nicknames, Vulgarisms and Such Americanisms as Have Been Naturalised*. Dictionary of Slang and Unconvetional English. Routledge.

P Rogers and M Lea. 2004. Cohesion in online groups. *WIT Transactions on Information and Communication Technologies*, 31.

Haji Mohammad Saleem, Kelly P. Dillon, Susan Benesch, and Derek Ruths. 2017. A web of hate: Tackling hateful speech in online social spaces. *CoRR*, abs/1709.10159.

Laura Wendlandt, Jonathan K. Kummerfeld, and Rada Mihalcea. 2018. Factors influencing the surprising instability of word embeddings. *CoRR*, abs/1804.09692.

Jason Shuo Zhang, Chenhao Tan, and Qin Lv. 2018. "this is why we play": Characterizing online fan communities of the NBA teams. *CoRR*, abs/1809.01170.

Justine Zhang, William L. Hamilton, Cristian Danescu-Niculescu-Mizil, Dan Jurafsky, and Jure Leskovec. 2017. Community identity and user engagement in a multi-community landscape. *CoRR*, abs/1705.09665.

Large Scale Question Paraphrase Retrieval with Smoothed Deep Metric Learning

Daniele Bonadiman
University of Trento
Trento, Italy
d.bonadiman@unitn.it

Anjishnu Kumar
Amazon Alexa
Seattle, USA
anjikum@amazon.com

Arpit Mittal
Amazon Alexa
Cambridge, UK
mitarpit@amazon.com

Abstract

The goal of a Question Paraphrase Retrieval (QPR) system is to retrieve similar questions that result in the same answer as the original question. Such a system can be used to understand and answer rare and noisy reformulations of common questions by mapping them to a set of canonical forms. This task has large-scale applications for community Question Answering (cQA) and open-domain spoken language question-answering systems. In this paper, we describe a new QPR system implemented as a Neural Information Retrieval (NIR) system consisting of a neural network sentence encoder and an approximate k-Nearest Neighbour index for efficient vector retrieval. We also describe our mechanism to generate an annotated dataset for question paraphrase retrieval experiments automatically from question-answer logs via distant supervision. We show that the standard loss function in NIR, triplet loss, does not perform well with noisy labels. We propose the smoothed deep metric loss (SDML), and with our experiments on two QPR datasets we show that it significantly outperforms triplet loss in the noisy label setting.

1 Introduction

In this paper, we propose a Question Paraphrase Retrieval (QPR) (Bernhard and Gurevych, 2008) system that can operate at industrial scale when trained on noisy training data that contains some number of false-negative samples. A QPR system retrieves a set of paraphrase questions for a given input, enabling existing question answering systems to answer rare formulations present in incoming questions. QPR finds natural applications in open-domain question answering systems, and is especially relevant to the community Question Answering (cQA) systems.

Open-domain QA systems provide answers to a user's questions with or without human intervention. These systems are employed by virtual assistants such as Alexa, Siri, Cortana and Google Assistant. Most virtual assistants use noisy channels, such as speech, to interact with users. Questions that are the output of an Automated Speech Recognition (ASR) system could contain errors such as truncations and misinterpretations. Transcription errors are more likely to occur for rarer or grammatically non-standard formulations of a question. For example 'Where Michael Jordan at?' could be a reformulation for 'Where is Michael Jordan?'. QPR systems mitigate the impact of this noise by identifying an answerable paraphrase of the noisy query and hence improves the overall performance of the system.

Another use of QPR is with cQA websites such as Quora or Yahoo Answers. These websites are platforms in which users interact by asking questions to the community and answering questions that have been posted by other users. The community-driven nature of these platforms leads to problems such as question duplication. Therefore, having a way to identify paraphrases can reduce clutter and improve the user experience. Question duplication can be prevented by presenting users a set of candidate paraphrase questions by retrieving them from the set of questions that have been already answered.

Despite some similarities, QPR task differs from the better known Paraphrase Identification (PI) task. In order to retrieve the most similar question to a new question, QPR system needs to compare the new question with all other questions in the dataset. Paraphrase Identification (Mihalcea et al., 2006; Islam and Inkpen, 2009; He et al., 2015) is a related task where the objective is to recognize whether a pair of sentences are paraphrases. The largest dataset for this task

Proceedings of the 2019 EMNLP Workshop W-NUT: The 5th Workshop on Noisy User-generated Text, pages 68–75
Hong Kong, Nov 4, 2019. ©2019 Association for Computational Linguistics

was released by Quora.com[1]. State-of-the-art approaches on this dataset use neural architectures with attention mechanisms across both the query and candidate questions. (Parikh et al., 2016; Wang et al., 2017; Devlin et al., 2019). However, these systems are increasingly impractical when scaled to millions of candidates as in the QPR setting, since they involve a quadratic number of vector comparisons per question pair, which are nontrivial to parallelize efficiently.

Information Retrieval (IR) systems have been very successful to operate at scale for such tasks. However, standard IR systems, such as BM25 (Robertson et al., 2004), are based on lexical overlap rather than on a deep semantic understanding of the questions (Robertson et al., 2009), making them unable to recognize paraphrases that lack significant lexical overlap. In recent years, the focus of the IR community has moved towards neural network-based systems that can provide a better representation of the object to be retrieved while maintaining the performance of the standard model. Neural representations can capture latent syntactic and semantic information from the text, overcoming the shortcomings of systems based purely on lexical information. Moreover, representations trained using a neural network can be task-specific, allowing them to encode domain-specific information that helps them outperform generic systems. The major components of a Neural Information Retrieval (NIR) system are a neural encoder and a k-Nearest Neighbour (kNN) index (Mitra and Craswell, 2017). The encoder is a neural network capable of transforming an input example, in our case a question, to a fixed size vector representation. In a standard setting, the encoder is trained via triplet loss (Schroff et al., 2015; Rao et al., 2016) to reduce the distance between a paraphrase vector when compared to a paraphrase vector with respect to a non-paraphrase vector. After being trained for this task, the encoder is used to embed the questions that can be later retrieved at inference time. The encoded questions are added to the kNN index for efficient retrieval. The input question is encoded and used as a query to the index, returning the top k most similar questions

Public datasets, such as Quora Question Pairs, are built to train and evaluate classifiers to iden-

tify paraphrases rather than evaluating retrieval systems. Additionally, the Quora dataset is not manually curated, thus resulting in a dataset that contains false-negative question paraphrases. This problem introduces noise in the training procedure when minimizing the triplet loss, since each question is compared with a positive and a negative example, that could be a false negative, at each training step. This noise is further exacerbated in approaches for training that exploit the concept of hard negatives, i.e., mining the non-paraphrase samples that are close to paraphrase samples in the vector space (Manmatha et al., 2017; Rao et al., 2016). Rather than treating these false negatives as a quirk of our data generation process, we recognize that false negatives are unavoidable in all large scale information retrieval scenarios with orders of millions or billions of documents - it is not feasible to get complete annotations as that would be of quadratic complexity in the number of documents. Usually, in these settings, randomly selected documents are treated as negative examples - thus the presence of noisy annotations with a bias towards false negatives is a recurring phenomenon in machine-learning based information retrieval.

In this work, we propose a loss function that minimizes the effect of false negatives in the training data. The proposed loss function trains the model to identify the valid paraphrase in a set of randomly sampled questions and uses label smoothing to assign some probability mass to negative examples, thus mitigating the impact of false negatives.

The proposed technique is evaluated on two datasets: a distantly supervised dataset of questions collected from a popular virtual assistant system, and a modified version of the Quora dataset that allows models to be evaluated in a retrieval setting. The effect of our proposed loss and the impact of the smoothing parameters are analyzed in Section 4.

2 Question Paraphrase Retrieval

In QPR the task is to retrieve a set of candidate paraphrases for a given query. Formally, given a new query q_{new}, the task is to retrieve k-questions, Q_k ($|Q_k| = k$), that are more likely to be paraphrases of the original question. The questions need to be retrieved from a given set of questions Q_{all} such that $Q_k \subseteq Q_{all}$, e.g., questions already answered in a cQA website.

---

[1] https://data.quora.com/First-Quora-Dataset-Release-Question-Pairs

2.1 System overview

The QPR system described in this paper is made of two core components: a neural encoder and an index. The encoder ϕ is a function ($\phi : Q \to \mathbb{R}^n$) that takes as input a question $q \in Q$ and maps it to a dense n-dimensional vector representation. The index is defined as the encoded set of all the questions that can be retrieved $\{\phi(q')|q' \in Q_{all}\}$ using the standard kNN search mechanism.

2.1.1 Encoder

The encoder ϕ used by our system is a neural network that transforms the input question to a fixed size vector representation. To this end, we use a convolutional encoder since it scales better (is easily parallelizable) compared to a recurrent neural network encoder and transformers (Vaswani et al., 2017), that have quadratic comparisons while maintaining good performance on sentence matching tasks (Yin et al., 2017). Additionally, convolutional encoders are less sensitive to the global structure of the sentence then recurrent neural network thus being more resilient to noisy nature of user-generated text The encoder uses a three-step process:

1. An embedding layer maps each word w_i in the question q to its corresponding word embedding $x_i \in \mathbb{R}^{e_{dim}}$ and thereby generating a sentence matrix $X_q \in \mathbb{R}^{l \times e_{dim}}$, where l is number of words in the question. We also use the hashing trick of (Weinberger et al., 2009) to map rare words to m bins via random projection to reduce the number of false matches at the retrieval time.

2. A convolutional layer (Kim, 2014) takes the question embedding matrix X_q as input and applies a trained convolutional filter $W \in \mathbb{R}^{e_{dim}win}$ iteratively by taking at each timestep i a set of win word embeddings. This results in the output:

$$h_i^{win} = \sigma(W x_{i-\frac{win}{2}:i+\frac{win}{2}} + b) \quad (1)$$

, where σ is a non linearity function, $tanh$ in our case, and $b \in \mathbb{R}$ is the bias parameter. By iterating over the whole sentence it produces a feature map $\mathbf{h}^{win} = [h_1^{win}, .., h_l^{win}]$.

3. A global max pooling operation is applied over the feature map ($\hat{h}^{win} = max(\mathbf{h}^{win})$) to reduce it into a single feature value. The convolutional and global max pooling steps described above are applied multiple times (c_{dim} times) with varying window size with resultant $\hat{h}$ values concatenated to get a feature vector $h \in \mathbb{R}^{c_{dim}}$ which is then linearly projected to an n-dimensional output vector using a learned weight matrix $W_p \in \mathbb{R}^{n \times c_{dim}}$.

2.1.2 kNN Index

Despite there is no restriction on the type of kNN index that can be used, for performance reasons, we use FAISS[2] (Johnson et al., 2017) as an approximate kNN index[3]. All the questions (Q_{all}) are encoded *offline* using the encoder ϕ and added to the index. At retrieval time a new question is encoded and used as a query to the index. The kNN index uses a predefined distance function (e.g. Euclidean distance) to retrieve the nearest questions in the vector space.

3 Training

Typical approaches for training the encoder use triplet loss (Schroff et al., 2015; Rao et al., 2016). This loss attempts to minimize the distance between positive examples while maximizing the distance between positive and negative examples.

The loss is formalized as follows:

$$\sum_i^N [\|\phi(q_i^a) - \phi(q_i^p)\|_2^2 - \|\phi(q_i^a) - \phi(q_i^n)\|_2^2 + \alpha]_+ \quad (2)$$

where q_i^a is a positive (anchor) question, q_i^p is a positive match to the anchor (a valid paraphrase), q_i^n is a negative match (i.e. a non-paraphrase), α is a margin parameter and N is the batch size.

In a recent work by Manmatha et al. 2017 the authors found that better results could be obtained by training the above objective with hard negative samples. These hard negatives are samples from the negative class that are the closest in vector space to the positive samples, hence most likely to be misclassified.

However, in our case, and in other cases with noisy training data, this technique negatively impacts the performance of the model since it starts focusing disproportionately on any false-negative samples in the data (i.e. positive examples labelled

---

[2] https://github.com/facebookresearch/faiss

[3] FAISS provides efficient implementations of various approximated kNN search algorithms for both CPU and GPU

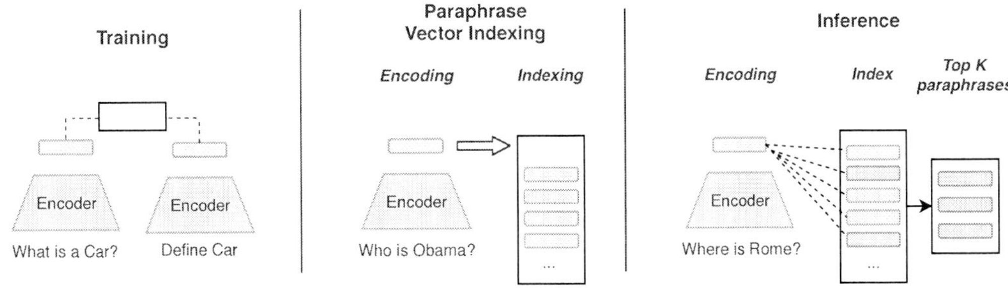

Figure 1: System

as negative due to noise) making the learning process faulty. For example in the Quora dataset positive examples are marked as paraphrase, duplicate, by users using the website however there is no manual check for the negative examples, thus leading to a number of false negatives that happens to be close in the vector space.

3.1 Smoothed Deep Metric Learning

In this paper, we propose a new loss function that overcomes the limitation of triplet loss in the noisy setting. Instead of minimizing the distance between positive examples with respect to negative examples, we view the problem as a classification problem. Ideally, we would like to classify the paraphrases of the original question amongst all other questions in the dataset. This process is infeasible due to time and memory constraints. We can, however, approximate this general loss by identifying a valid paraphrase in a set of randomly sampled questions (Kannan et al., 2016). We map vector distances into probabilities similar to Goldberger et al. 2005 by applying a softmax operation over the negative squared euclidean distance:

$$\hat{p}(a, i) = \frac{e^{-\|\phi(q^a)-\phi(q^i)\|_2^2}}{\sum_j^N e^{-\|\phi(q^a)-\phi(q^j)\|_2^2}} \tag{3}$$

where q^a is an anchor question and q^j and q^i are questions belonging in a batch of size N containing one paraphrase and $N-1$ randomly sampled non-paraphrases. The network is then trained to assign a higher probability, hence a shorter distance, to pair of questions that are paraphrases.

Additionally, we apply the label smoothing regularization technique (Szegedy et al., 2016) to reduce impact of false negatives. This technique reduces the probability of the ground truth by a

smoothing factor ϵ and redistributes it uniformly across all other values, i.e.,

$$p'(k|a) = (1 - \epsilon)p(k|a) + \frac{\epsilon}{N} \tag{4}$$

where $p(k|a)$ is the probability for the gold label. The new smoothed labels computed in this way are used to train the network using Cross-Entropy (CE) or Kullback-Leibler (KL) divergence loss[4]. In our setting, the standard cross-entropy loss tries to enforce the euclidean distance between all random points to become infinity, which may not be feasible and could lead to noisy training and slow convergence. Instead, assigning a constant probability to random interactions tries to position random points onto the surface of a hypersphere around the anchor which simplifies the learning problem.

The sampling required for this formulation can be easily implemented in frameworks like PyTorch (Paszke et al., 2017) or MxNet (Chen et al., 2015) using a batch of positive pairs $< q_{1,j}, q_{2,j} >$ derived from a shuffled dataset, as depicted in Figure 2. In this setting, each question $q_{1,i}$ would have exactly one paraphrase, i.e., $q_{2,i}$ and $N-1$ all other questions $q_{2,j}$ when $j \neq i$ would serve as counter-examples. This batched implementation reduces training time and makes sampling tractable by avoiding sampling N questions for each example, reducing the number of forward passes required to encode the questions in a batch from $\mathcal{O}(N^2)$ in a naive implementation to $\mathcal{O}(2N)$.

---

[4] In this setting, CE loss and KL divergence loss are equivalent in expected values. However, we use the KL divergence loss for performance reasons.

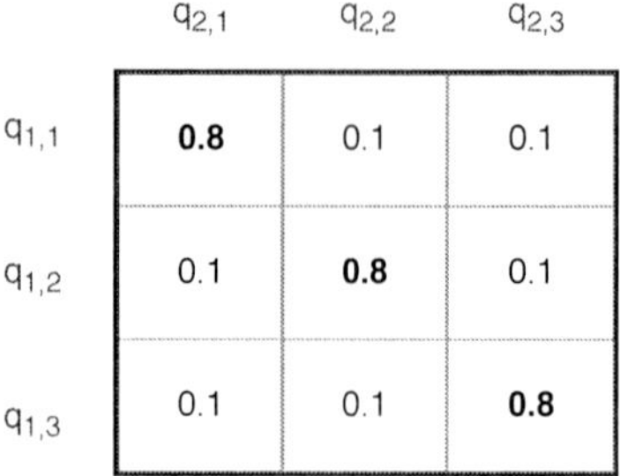

Figure 2: Batched implementation of the loss with smoothing parameter $\epsilon = 0.3$ and batch size $N = 3$. Each paraphrase pair $< q_{1,j}, q_{2,j} >$ in the batch is compared with all the others questions in the batch.

4 Experiments

In this section, we present the experimental setup used to validate our approach for QPR using the Smoothed Deep Metric Learning (SDML) technique.

4.1 Datasets

In order to generate a dataset for question paraphrase retrieval, we propose a technique that uses distant supervision to create it automatically from high-precision question-answer (QA) logs. Additionally, due to the proprietary nature of our internal dataset, we tested our approach on a modified version of the Quora paraphrase identification dataset that has been adapted for the paraphrase retrieval task.

4.1.1 Open Domain QA dataset

Our open domain Q&A dataset is created by weak supervision method using high precision QA logs of a large scale industrial virtual assistant. From the logs, we retrieve 'clusters' of questions that are mapped to the same answer. However, we notice that this may generate clusters where unrelated questions are mapped to a generic answer. For instance, many different math questions may map to the same answer; e.g. a given number. To further refine these clusters, the data is filtered using a heuristic based on an intra-cluster similarity metric that we call cluster *coherence*, denoted as c. We define this metric as the mean Jaccard similarity (Levandowsky and Winter, 1971) of each question in a cluster to the cluster taken as the whole.

Mathematically, for a given cluster $\mathbb{A} = \{q_1, q_2...q_n\}$ and defining $\mathbb{T}_{q_i} = \{w_{i_1}, w_{i_2}, ...w_{i_k}\}$ as shorthand for the set of unique tokens present in a given question, the coherence of the cluster is defined as:

$$\mathbb{S} = \bigcup_{i=1}^{n} \mathbb{T}_{q_i} \tag{5}$$

$$c = \frac{1}{n}\Sigma_{i=1}^{n} \frac{|\mathbb{T}_{q_i} \cap \mathbb{S}|}{|\mathbb{S}|} \tag{6}$$

In practice, we found that even a small coherence filter ($c < 0.1$) can eliminate all incoherent question clusters. Our approach to weak supervision can be considered as a generalized instance of the candidate-generation noise-removal pipeline paradigm used by Kim et al. 2018. Once the incoherent clusters are removed from the dataset, the remaining clusters are randomly split in an 80:10:10 ratio into training, validation and test sets and question pairs are generated from them[5]. A second filter is applied to remove questions in the validation and test sets that overlap with questions in the training set. The final output of the weak supervision process is a set of silver labelled clusters with $> 99\%$ accuracy based on spot-checking, a random sample of 200 clusters.

4.1.2 Quora dataset

We introduce a variant of the Quora dataset for QPR task. The original dataset consists of pairs of questions with a positive label if they are paraphrases, and a negative label if they are not. Similarly to Haponchyk et al. (2018), we identify question clusters in the dataset by exploiting the transitive property of the paraphrase relation in the original pairs, i.e., if q_1 and q_2 are paraphrases, and q_2 and q_3 are paraphrases then q_1 and q_3 are also paraphrases, hence q_1, q_2, and q_3 belong to the same cluster. After iterating over the entire dataset, we identified $60,312$ question clusters. The question clusters are split into the training, validation and test sets such that the resulting validation and test set contains roughly $5,000$ question pairs each, and the training set contains $219,369$ question pairs[6]. The kNN index is composed of all the questions in the original Quora datasets (including questions that appear only as negative, thus not being part of any cluster) for a total of $556,107$ questions.

---

[5]The open-domain QA dataset contains on order of 100k - 1M training clusters, 10k - 100k clusters each for validation and testing, and a search index of size $\approx 10M$.

[6]The code to generate the splits will be released upon acceptance.

4.2 Experimental setup

We described the architecture of our encoder previously in section 2.1.1. For experimentation, we randomly initialized word embeddings. The size of vocabulary for Quora dataset is fixed at 50,000 whereas for the bigger open-domain QA dataset we used a vocabulary of size 100,000. To map rare words we use the hashing trick (Weinberger et al., 2009) with 5,000 bins for the Quora dataset and 10,000 bins for the QA dataset.

We set the dimensionality of word embeddings at 300 (i.e., $e_{dim} = 300$); the convolutional layer uses a window size of 5 (i.e., $win = 5$) and the encoder outputs a vector of size $n = 300$. For triplet loss the network is trained with margin $\alpha = 0.5$. The default batch size for all the experiments is 512 (i.e., $N = 512$) and the smoothing factor for SDML, ϵ, is 0.3. For all experiments training is performed using the Adam optimizer with learning rate $\lambda = 0.001$ until the model stops improving on the validation test, using early stopping (Prechelt, 1998) on the ROC AUC metric (Bradley, 1997).

4.3 Evaluation

We use *IVF2000, Flat* configuration of the FAISS library as our index, which is a hierarchical index consisting of an index of k-means centroids as the top-level index. For evaluation, we retrieve 20 questions with 10 probes into the index each returning a pair of paraphrase questions, with an average query time of < 10 ms. These questions are used to measure the system performance via standard information retrieval metrics, Hits@N ($H@N$) and Mean Reciprocal Rank (MRR). $H@N$ measures if at least one question in the first N that are retrieved is a paraphrase and MRR is the mean reciprocal rank (position) at which the first retrieved paraphrase is encountered.

4.4 Results

In the first set of experiments, we measured the impact of varying the smoothing factor ϵ. The results for the Quora validation set are presented in Table 1. We observe that the presence of smoothing leads to a significant increase over the baseline (simple cross-entropy loss) and increasing this parameter has a positive impact up to $\epsilon = 0.3$.

In our second experiment, we hold the ϵ constant at 0.3 and experiment with varying the num-

ϵ	H@1	H@10	MRR
0	0.5568	0.7381	0.6217
0.1	0.5901	0.7841	0.6591
0.2	0.6030	0.8090	0.6762
0.3	**0.6133**	0.8113	**0.6837**
0.4	0.6107	**0.8144**	0.6815

Table 1: Impact of smoothing factor ϵ on the Quora validation set.

N	H@1	H@10	MRR
32	0.5389	0.7444	0.6103
64	0.5710	0.7726	0.6410
128	0.6093	0.8085	0.6777
256	0.6112	**0.8141**	0.6833
512	**0.6133**	0.8113	**0.6837**
1024	0.6081	0.8008	0.6764

Table 2: Impact of the batch size N on the Quora validation set. For computing SDML a batch consists of a paraphrase and $N - 1$ negative examples.

ber of negative samples. Table 2 shows the effect of an increase in the number of negative examples in a batch. The model's performance reaches its maximum value at $N = 512$, i.e., with 511 negative samples for each positive sample. We want to point out that we limited our exploration to 1024 due to memory constraints. However, better performance may be achieved by further increasing the number of examples, since the batch becomes a better approximation of the real distribution.

Table 3 and 4 compare the proposed loss with the triplet loss with random sampling, TL(Rand). We compared the proposed approach with two variants of triplet loss that uses different distance functions Euclidean Distance (EUC) and Sum of Squared Differences (SSD). The Euclidean distance is the standard distance function for triplet loss implementation present in popular deep learning frameworks, PyTorch and Mxnet, whereas SSD is the distance function used in the original paper of Schroff et al. 2015. Our approach improves over the original triplet loss considerably on both datasets. The SSD distance also outperforms the EUC implementation of the loss.

Tables 5 and 6 show the results on the open domain QA dataset validation and test set. TL(Rand) is the triplet loss with random sampling of negative examples, whereas TL(Hard) is a variant with hard negative mining. In both cases, the SDML outperforms triplet loss by a considerable mar-

Loss	Dist	H@1	H@10	MRR
TL (Rand)	EUC	0.4742	0.6509	0.5359
TL (Rand)	SSD	0.5763	0.7640	0.6421
SDML	SSD	**0.6133**	**0.8113**	**0.6837**

Table 3: Comparison of different loss functions on Quora validation set.

Loss	Dist	H@1	H@10	MRR
TL (Rand)	EUC	0.4641	0.6523	0.5297
TL (Rand)	SSD	0.5507	0.7641	0.6265
SDML	SSD	**0.6043**	**0.8179**	**0.6789**

Table 4: Comparison of different loss functions on Quora test set.

Loss	Dist	H@1	H@10	MRR
TL (Rand)	EUC	0.5738	0.7684	0.6428
TL (Rand)	SSD	0.6506	0.8579	0.7252
TL (Hard)	EUC	0.5549	0.7534	0.6256
TL (Hard)	SSD	0.5233	0.7077	0.5870
SDML	EUC	0.6526	**0.8832**	0.7361
SDML	SSD	**0.6745**	0.8817	**0.7491**

Table 5: Comparison of different loss functions on open domain QA dataset validation set.

Loss	Dist	H@1	H@10	MRR
TL (Rand)	EUC	0.5721	0.7695	0.6431
TL (Rand)	SSD	0.6538	0.8610	0.7271
TL (Hard)	EUC	0.5593	0.7593	0.6304
TL (Hard)	SSD	0.5201	0.7095	0.5863
SDML	EUC	0.6545	**0.8846**	0.7382
SDML	SSD	**0.6718**	0.8830	**0.7480**

Table 6: Comparison of different loss functions on open domain QA dataset test set.

gin. It is important to note that, since our dataset contains noisy examples, triplet loss with random sampling outperforms hard sampling setting, in contrast with the results presented in Manmatha et al. 2017.

The results presented in this section are consistent with our expectations based on the design of the loss function.

5 Conclusion

We investigated a variant of the paraphrase identification task - large scale question paraphrase retrieval, which is of particular importance in industrial question answering applications. We devised a weak supervision algorithm to generate training data from the logs of an existing high precision question-answering system and introduced a variant of the popular Quora dataset for this task. In order to solve this task efficiently, we developed a neural information retrieval system consisting of a convolutional neural encoder and a fast approximate nearest neighbour search index.

Triplet loss, a standard baseline for learning-to-rank setting, tends to overfit to noisy examples in training. To deal with this issue, we designed a new loss function inspired by label smoothing, which assigns a small constant probability to randomly paired question utterances in a training mini-batch resulting in a model that demonstrates superior performance. We believe that our batch-wise smoothed loss formulation will be applicable to a variety of metric learning and information retrieval problems for which triplet loss is currently widespread. The loss function framework we describe is also flexible enough to experiment with different priors - for e.g. allocating probability masses based on the distances between the points.

References

Delphine Bernhard and Iryna Gurevych. 2008. Answering learners' questions by retrieving question paraphrases from social q&a sites. In *Proceedings of the third workshop on innovative use of NLP for building educational applications*, pages 44–52. Association for Computational Linguistics.

Andrew P Bradley. 1997. The use of the area under the roc curve in the evaluation of machine learning algorithms. *Pattern recognition*, 30(7):1145–1159.

Tianqi Chen, Mu Li, Yutian Li, Min Lin, Naiyan Wang, Minjie Wang, Tianjun Xiao, Bing Xu, Chiyuan Zhang, and Zheng Zhang. 2015. Mxnet: A flexible and efficient machine learning library for heterogeneous distributed systems. *arXiv preprint arXiv:1512.01274*.

Jacob Devlin, Ming-Wei Chang, Kenton Lee, and Kristina Toutanova. 2019. Bert: Pre-training of deep bidirectional transformers for language understanding. In *Proceedings of the 2019 Conference of the North American Chapter of the Association for Computational Linguistics: Human Language Technologies, Volume 1 (Long and Short Papers)*, pages 4171–4186.

Jacob Goldberger, Geoffrey E Hinton, Sam T Roweis, and Ruslan R Salakhutdinov. 2005. Neighbourhood components analysis. In *Advances in neural information processing systems*, pages 513–520.

Iryna Haponchyk, Antonio Uva, Seunghak Yu, Olga Uryupina, and Alessandro Moschitti. 2018. Supervised clustering of questions into intents for dialog system applications. In *Proceedings of the 2018 Conference on Empirical Methods in Natural Language Processing*, pages 2310–2321.

Hua He, Kevin Gimpel, and Jimmy Lin. 2015. Multiperspective sentence similarity modeling with convolutional neural networks. In *Proceedings of the 2015 Conference on Empirical Methods in Natural Language Processing*, pages 1576–1586.

Aminul Islam and Diana Inkpen. 2009. Semantic similarity of short texts. *Recent Advances in Natural Language Processing V*, 309:227–236.

Jeff Johnson, Matthijs Douze, and Hervé Jégou. 2017. Billion-scale similarity search with gpus. *arXiv preprint arXiv:1702.08734*.

Anjuli Kannan, Karol Kurach, Sujith Ravi, Tobias Kaufmann, Andrew Tomkins, Balint Miklos, Greg Corrado, Laszlo Lukacs, Marina Ganea, Peter Young, et al. 2016. Smart reply: Automated response suggestion for email. In *Proceedings of the 22nd ACM SIGKDD International Conference on Knowledge Discovery and Data Mining*, pages 955–964. ACM.

Yoon Kim. 2014. Convolutional neural networks for sentence classification. In *Proceedings of the 2014 Conference on Empirical Methods in Natural Language Processing (EMNLP)*, pages 1746–1751.

Young-Bum Kim, Dongchan Kim, Anjishnu Kumar, and Ruhi Sarikaya. 2018. Efficient large-scale neural domain classification with personalized attention. In *Proceedings of the 56th Annual Meeting of the Association for Computational Linguistics (Volume 1: Long Papers)*, volume 1, pages 2214–2224.

Michael Levandowsky and David Winter. 1971. Distance between sets. *Nature*, 234(5323):34.

R Manmatha, Chao-Yuan Wu, Alexander J Smola, and Philipp Krähenbühl. 2017. Sampling matters in deep embedding learning. In *Computer Vision (ICCV), 2017 IEEE International Conference on*, pages 2859–2867. IEEE.

Rada Mihalcea, Courtney Corley, Carlo Strapparava, et al. 2006. Corpus-based and knowledge-based measures of text semantic similarity.

Bhaskar Mitra and Nick Craswell. 2017. Neural models for information retrieval. *arXiv preprint arXiv:1705.01509*.

Ankur P Parikh, Oscar Täckström, Dipanjan Das, and Jakob Uszkoreit. 2016. A decomposable attention model for natural language inference. *arXiv preprint arXiv:1606.01933*.

Adam Paszke, Sam Gross, Soumith Chintala, Gregory Chanan, Edward Yang, Zachary DeVito, Zeming Lin, Alban Desmaison, Luca Antiga, and Adam Lerer. 2017. Automatic differentiation in pytorch. In *NIPS-W*.

Lutz Prechelt. 1998. Early stopping-but when? In *Neural Networks: Tricks of the trade*, pages 55–69. Springer.

Jinfeng Rao, Hua He, and Jimmy Lin. 2016. Noise-contrastive estimation for answer selection with deep neural networks. In *Proceedings of the 25th ACM International on Conference on Information and Knowledge Management*, pages 1913–1916. ACM.

Stephen Robertson, Hugo Zaragoza, and Michael Taylor. 2004. Simple bm25 extension to multiple weighted fields. In *Proceedings of the Thirteenth ACM International Conference on Information and Knowledge Management*, CIKM '04.

Stephen Robertson, Hugo Zaragoza, et al. 2009. The probabilistic relevance framework: Bm25 and beyond. *Foundations and Trends® in Information Retrieval*, 3(4):333–389.

Florian Schroff, Dmitry Kalenichenko, and James Philbin. 2015. Facenet: A unified embedding for face recognition and clustering. In *Proceedings of the IEEE conference on computer vision and pattern recognition*, pages 815–823.

Christian Szegedy, Vincent Vanhoucke, Sergey Ioffe, Jon Shlens, and Zbigniew Wojna. 2016. Rethinking the inception architecture for computer vision. In *Proceedings of the IEEE conference on computer vision and pattern recognition*, pages 2818–2826.

Ashish Vaswani, Noam Shazeer, Niki Parmar, Jakob Uszkoreit, Llion Jones, Aidan N Gomez, Łukasz Kaiser, and Illia Polosukhin. 2017. Attention is all you need. In *Advances in neural information processing systems*, pages 5998–6008.

Zhiguo Wang, Wael Hamza, and Radu Florian. 2017. Bilateral multi-perspective matching for natural language sentences. In *Proceedings of the 26th International Joint Conference on Artificial Intelligence*, pages 4144–4150. AAAI Press.

Kilian Weinberger, Anirban Dasgupta, Josh Attenberg, John Langford, and Alex Smola. 2009. Feature hashing for large scale multitask learning. *arXiv preprint arXiv:0902.2206*.

Wenpeng Yin, Katharina Kann, Mo Yu, and Hinrich Schütze. 2017. Comparative study of cnn and rnn for natural language processing. *arXiv preprint arXiv:1702.01923*.

Hey Siri. Ok Google. Alexa:
A topic modeling of user reviews for smart speakers

Hanh Nguyen
Bocconi University
hn@hanhng.com

Dirk Hovy
Bocconi University
dirk.hovy@unibocconi.it

Abstract

User reviews provide a significant source of information for companies to understand their market and audience. In order to discover broad trends in this source, researchers have typically used topic models such as Latent Dirichlet Allocation (LDA). However, while there are metrics to choose the "best" number of topics, it is not clear whether the resulting topics can also provide in-depth, actionable product analysis. Our paper examines this issue by analyzing user reviews from the Best Buy US website for smart speakers. Using coherence scores to choose topics, we test whether the results help us to understand user interests and concerns. We find that while coherence scores are a good starting point to identify a number of topics, it still requires manual adaptation based on domain knowledge to provide market insights. We show that the resulting dimensions capture brand performance and differences, and differentiate the market into two distinct groups with different properties.

1 Introduction

The Internet has provided a platform for people to express their opinions on a wide range of issues, including reviews for products they buy. Listening to what users say is critical to understanding the product usage, helpfulness, and opportunities for further product development to deliver better user experience. User reviews – despite some potentially inherent biases[1] – have quickly become an invaluable (and cheap) form of information for product managers and analysts (Dellarocas, 2006). However, the speed, amount, and varying format of user feedback also creates a need to effectively extract the most important insights.

Topic models, especially LDA (Blei et al., 2003), are one of the most widely used tools for these purposes. However, due to their stochastic nature, they can present a challenge for interpretability (McAuliffe and Blei, 2008; Chang et al., 2009). This is less problematic when the analysis is exploratory, but proves difficult if it is to result in actionable changes, for example product development. The main dimension of freedom in LDA is the number of topics: while there are metrics to assess the optimal number according to a criterion, it is unclear whether the resulting topics provide us with a useful discrimination for product and market analysis. The question is *"Can we derive market-relevant information from topic modeling of reviews?"*

We use smart speakers as a test case to study LDA topic models for both high-level and in-depth analyses. We are interested in to answer the following research questions:

- What are the main dimensions of concerns when people talk about smart speakers?

- Can the LDA topic mixtures be used to directly compare smart speakers by Amazon, Google, Apple, and Sonos?

Smart speakers are a type of wireless speaker that provides a voice interface for people to use spoken input to control household devices and appliances. While still relatively new, smart speakers are rapidly growing in popularity. As the Economist (2017) put it: "voice has the power to transform computing, by providing a natural means of interaction." We use a dataset of smart speaker reviews and coherence scores as a metric to choose the number of topics, and evaluate the resulting model both in terms of human judgement and in its ability to meaningfully discriminate brands in the market.

---

[1] People tend to over-report negative experiences, while some positive reviews are bought (Hovy, 2016).

Proceedings of the 2019 EMNLP Workshop W-NUT: The 5th Workshop on Noisy User-generated Text, pages 76–83
Hong Kong, Nov 4, 2019. ©2019 Association for Computational Linguistics

	Raw data	After pre-processing
# reviews		53,273
# words	1,724,842	529,035
# unique words	25,007	10,102

Table 1: Summary of dataset.

Contributions We show that LDA can be a valuable tool for user insights: 1) basic user concerns can be distinguished with LDA by using coherence scores (Röder et al., 2015) to determine the best number of topics, but an additional step is still needed for consolidation; 2) human judgement correlates strongly with the model findings; 3) the extracted topic mixture distributions accurately reflect the qualitative dimensions to compare products and distinguish brands.

2 Dataset

2.1 Data collection

From the Best Buy US website, we collect a dataset of 53,273 reviews for nine products from four brands: **Amazon** (Echo, Echo Dot, Echo Spot), **Google** (Home, Home Mini, Home Max), **Apple** (HomePod) and **Sonos** (One, Beam). Each review includes a review text and the brand associated with it. Our collection took place in November 2018. Due to their later market entries and significantly smaller market sizes, the number of available Apple and Sonos reviews is limited. Amazon, Google, Apple, and Sonos reviews account for 53.9%, 41.1%, 3.5% and 1.5% of the dataset, respectively.

2.2 Review text pre-processing

We pre-process the review text as follows: First, we convert all text to lowercase and tokenize it. We then remove punctuation and stop words. We build bigrams and remove any remaining words with 2 or fewer characters. Finally, we lemmatize the data. The statistics of the resulting bag-of-words representation are described in Table 1.

3 Methodology

3.1 Topic extraction

The main issue in LDA is choosing the optimal number of topics. To address this issue, we use the coherence score (Röder et al., 2015) of the resulting topics. This metric is more useful for interpretability than choosing the number of topics on held-out data likelihood, which is a proxy and can still result in semantically meaningless topics (Chang et al., 2009).

The question is: what is coherent? A set of topic descriptors are said to be coherent if they support each other and refer to the same topic or concept. For example, "music, subscription, streaming, spotify, pandora" are more coherent than "music, machine, nlp, yelp, love." While this difference is obvious to human observers, we need a way to quantify it algorithmically.

Coherence scores are a way to do this. Several versions exist, but the one used here has the highest correlation with human ratings (Röder et al., 2015). It takes the topic descriptors and combines four measures of them that capture different aspects of "coherence": 1) a segmentationn S_{set}^{one}, 2) a boolean sliding window $P_{sw(110)}$, 3) the indirect cosine measure with normalized pointwise mutual information (NPMI) $\tilde{m}_{cos(nlr)}$, and 4) the arithmetic mean of the cosine similarities σ_a.

The input to the scoring function is a set W of the N top words describing a topic, derived from the fitted model. The first step is their segmentation S_{set}^{one}. It measures how strongly W^* supports W' by quantifying the similarity of W^* and W' in relation to all the words in W:

$$\{(W', W^*)|W' = \{w_i\}; w_i \in W; W^* = W\}$$

In order to so do, W' and W^* are represented as context vectors $\vec{v}(W')$ and $\vec{v}(W^*)$ by pairing them with all words in W:

$$\vec{v}(W') = \left\{ \sum_{w_i \in W'} \text{NPMI}(w_i, w_j)^\gamma \right\}_{j=1,\dots,|W|}$$

The same applies for $\vec{v}(W^*)$. In addition:

$$\text{NPMI}(w_i, w_j)^\gamma = \left(\frac{\log \frac{P(w_i, w_j) + \varepsilon}{P(w_i) \cdot P(w_j)}}{-\log(P(w_i, w_j) + \varepsilon)} \right)^\gamma$$

An increase of γ gives higher NPMI values more weight. ε is set to a small value to prevent logarithm of zero. We choose $\gamma = 1$ and $\varepsilon = 10^{-12}$.

Second, the probability $P_{sw(110)}$ captures proximity between word tokens. It is the boolean sliding window probability, i.e., the number of doc-

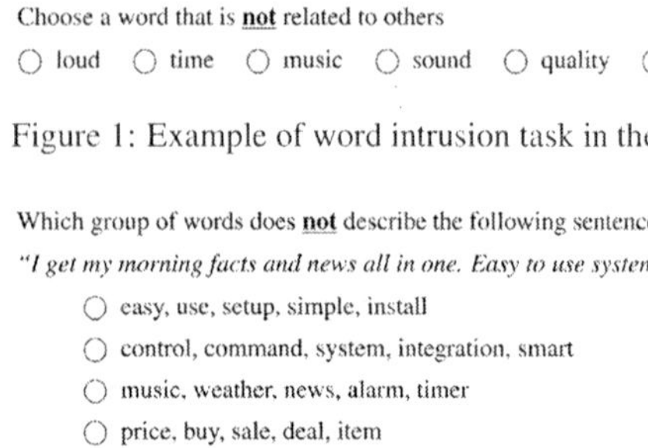

Figure 1: Example of word intrusion task in the survey

Figure 2: Example of topic intrusion task in the survey

uments in which the word occurs, divided by the number of sliding windows of size $s = 110$.

Third, given context vectors $\vec{u} = \vec{v}(W')$ and $\vec{w} = \vec{v}(W^*)$ for the word sets of a pair $S_i = (W', W^*)$, the similarity of W' and W^* is the cosine vector similarity between all context vectors.

$$s_{\cos}(\vec{u}, \vec{w}) = \frac{\sum_{i=1}^{|W|} u_i \cdot w_i}{\|\vec{u}\|_2 \cdot \|\vec{w}\|_2}$$

Finally, the cosine similarity measures are averaged, giving us a single coherence score for each model (each model has a different number of topics).

We fit LDA models, using Gensim library in Python, with the number of topics ranging from 2 to 20 to calculate the coherence score. For each model, we choose the top 20 words of each topic as inputs to calculate the model's coherence score. We move forward with the model with the highest coherence score (13 topics) for validation, and use the document-topic distributions and topic-word distributions from that model in the subsequent steps.

3.2 LDA validation

To evaluate the semantic interpretability of the resulting LDA model from the coherence score selection, we run a human judgment survey using word intrusion and topic intrusion. We used 125 human judges. Each of 125 human subjects responds to 10 questions (5 questions for word intrusion, and 5 questions for topic intrusion), which are randomly selected from a collection of 20 questions.

For the **word intrusion** task, each subject is asked to choose which word they think does not belong to the topic (Fig. 1). Each question is comprised of the 5 words with the highest probabili-

ties in that topic, and one random word with low probability in that topic but high probability (top 5 most frequent words) in another topic. The word that does *not* belong to the topic is called the *true intruder word*. The hypothesis of word intrusion is that if the topics are interpretable, they are coherent, and subjects will consistently choose the true intruder words.

For topic k, let w_k be the true intruder word, $i_{k,s}$ be the intruder selected by the subject s. S is the number of subjects. The model precision for topic k is defined as the fraction of subjects agreeing with the model:

$$MP_k = \frac{\sum_s |(i_{k,s} = w_k)|}{S}$$

The model precision ranges from 0 to 1, with higher value indicating a better model.

For the **topic intrusion** task, each survey subject is shown a short review text and is asked to choose a group of words which they think do *not* describe the review (Fig. 2). Each group of words represents a topic. Each question is comprised of 3 topics with the highest probabilities LDA assigned to that review, and 1 random topic with low probability. The topic with low probability is called the *true intruder topic*. The hypothesis of topic intrusion is that if the association of topics to a document is interpretable, subjects will consistently choose the true intruder topic.

For review r, let j_r be the true intruder topic, $j_{r,s}$ be the intruding topic selected by subject s. θ_r is the probability that the review r belongs to each topic. The topic log odds for a review r are defined as the log ratio of a) the probability mass assigned to the true intruder to b) the probability mass assigned to the intruder selected by the subject:

$$TLO_r = \frac{\sum_s \left(\log \theta_{r,j_r} - \log \theta_{r,j_{r,s}}\right)}{S}$$

The topic log odds have an upper bound of 0, which indicates the perfect match between judgments of the model and the subjects. This metric is preferred for the topic intrusion task rather than the model precision, which only takes into account right or wrong answers, because each topic has a probability of generating the review. Thus, the topic log odds serve as an error function (Lukasiewicz et al., 2018).

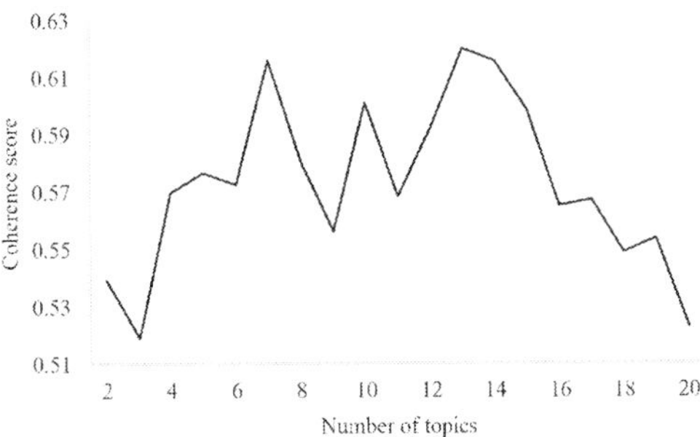 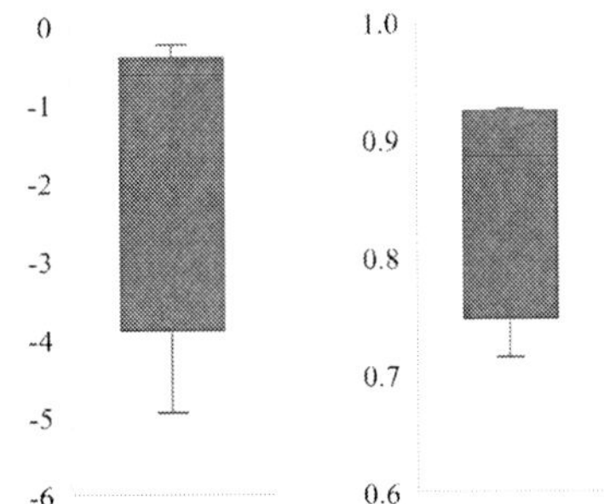

Figure 3: Coherence score for each model. Models with 7, 13, and 14 topics have highest coherence score.

Figure 4: Model precision with word intrusion (left) and topic log odds with topic intrusion (right).

4 Results and discussion

4.1 Topic extraction

For each model, we compute topic coherence based on the top 20 words in each topic. The topic coherence plot (Fig. 3) shows three candidates for the best number of topics, 7, 13, and 14, all with a score of 0.62. We manually examine the top 20 words for each. The 7-topic model has some mixed and chained topics e.g., *"easy, use, great, setup, gift, christmas."* The 14-topic model does not provide any more meaningful topics compared to 13 topics. Thus, we choose the 13-topic model.

4.2 LDA validation and consolidation

We extract document-topic and topic-word distributions for 13 topics and evaluate them in a human judgment survey on word and topic intrusion. The mean of the word intrusion precision is 0.85 (standard deviation 0.086), and the mean of the topic log odds is -1.66 (standard deviation 1.58). Fig. 4 shows the box plots for the results of both tasks. Model precision and topic log odds are on different scales, see section 3.2. Model precision is sufficiently good, while topic log odds are acceptable, but with higher variance. They are on a par with the best models in (Chang et al., 2009; Arnold et al., 2016).

Reviews dominated by few topics show more agreement between model and human judges, reviews with many topics show a greater divergence. For example, for the review with the lowest level of agreement (lowest topic log odds): *"Once I managed to get all the apps synced with this speaker, I was blown away by the sound quality. Using Alexa's voice recognition is great, even from the other side of the room."*, LDA assigns fairly equal proportions to the top 3 topics (23%, 25%, and 32%). For the review with the highest level of agreement (highest topic log odds): *"I get my morning facts and news all in one easy to use system."*, LDA assigns 48% to a dominant topic, and 15% and 26% to the next two topics.

After running the intrusion tests with the 13-topic model, we manually merge some topics that were similar to each other. This process results in 8 dimensions (we call them "dimensions" to differentiate them from the 13-topic model of the previous steps). We use these 8 dimensions to measure brand performance.

As (Boyd-Graber et al., 2014) pointed out, different researchers might combine topics differently. Here, the merging step is based on our domain knowledge in the smart speaker market. We group topics with similar top words into one dimension. For topics that we cannot label, we group them to the most similar topics based on the top words. Doing so, we aim to make the topics maximally distinguished from each other, and to be able to label the topics appropriately.

Table 2 shows the respective top keywords. The following describes the resulting 8 dimensions.

1. **Price**: price and worthiness, especially as gifts. Example: *"Love my Echo Dot, great purchase! Made a great Christmas gift."* (Amazon)

2. **Integration**: ability to connect, and control devices/household appliances (e.g., lighting, thermostat) in a smart home. Bedroom and kitchen are the two rooms in which people put their smart speakers most often. Example: *"I use these in several rooms in my home to control lights and my AV system. They integrate with my Samsung Smart Things Hub*

Label	Top keywords
Price	price, buy, gift, christmas, worth, black_friday, money, sale, deal, item
Integration	light, control, command, system, integration, thermostat, room, ecosystem, connect
Sound quality	speaker, sound, quality, small, music, loud, great, room, bluetooth, volume
Accuracy	question, answer, time, response, quick, issue, problem, work, search, good
Skills	music, weather, news, alarm, timer, kitchen, morning, reminder, shopping_list
Fun	fun, family, kid, useful, helpful, great, friend, game, information, question
Ease of use	easy, use, set, setup, simple, install, recommend, connect, quick, work
Playing music	music, play, song, playlist, favorite, pandora, prime, stream, subscription, beam

Table 2: 8 merged dimensions and the keywords reveal how people use smart speakers and their perceptions.

and Harmony Hub." (Amazon)

3. **Sound quality**: ability to provide high-quality sound. Example: *"Can't believe this little device has such great sound quality"* (Apple). *"This is a great speaker! The sound is just WOW! And the speaker doesn't take up much space."* (Sonos)

4. **Accuracy**: ability to respond accurately to the users voice commands, provide answers to questions, and to issues they might encounter. Example: *"It is amazing how many simple questions stump Alexa. Too frequently the response I hear is "I don't understand" or "Sorry, I can't find the answer.""* (Amazon)

5. **Skills**: variety of applications that the smart speaker provides. They are referred to as "skills" in Amazon Alexa, and as "actions" in Google Assistant. I.e., music, weather forecast, news, alarms, setting kitchen timers, reminders, and shopping lists. Example: *"You can ask Alexa anything. Find information about the weather, sports, or the news. Also, ask her to play your favorite music. All you have to do is ask."* (Amazon)

6. **Fun**: pleasure to interact with smart speakers, especially with/for kids and family. Example: *"Lots of fun and lots of great information. It was fun to ask it all kinds of questions."* (Google)

7. **Ease of use**: ease of setup and connecting to an existing internet connection via the mobile app to use voice commands. Example: *"Fun and easy to operate. Connects to your Wi-Fi in a simple and quick manner."* (Amazon)

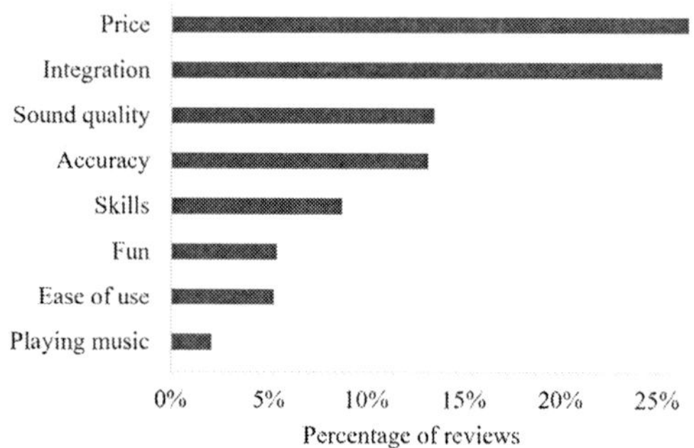

Figure 5: % of reviews based on dominant dimensions.

8. **Playing music**: ability to play music, connect with music services, like Amazon Music and Pandora. Example: *"Upload all of your music for free to Google Play Music and then tell the Mini what to play from your music and it will!"* (Google)

Since the LDA model can assign a review to multiple topics, it is more difficult to see the proportion of reviews for each. We define the *dominant dimension* for each review as the topic with the highest probability for the review. The most frequently mentioned dominant dimensions (Fig. 5) are *price* (27% of total reviews), *integration* (25%), *sound quality* (14%), and *accuracy* (13%).

4.3 Brand performance along dimensions

Brand performance measures how frequently each dimension was mentioned in user reviews.

As described in section 2.1, the amount of available data across companies is highly imbalanced. Thus, in order to compare the relative performance of brands along the 8 dimensions, we normalize the amount of data for each company. We define a relative dimension score for a brand b (Ama-

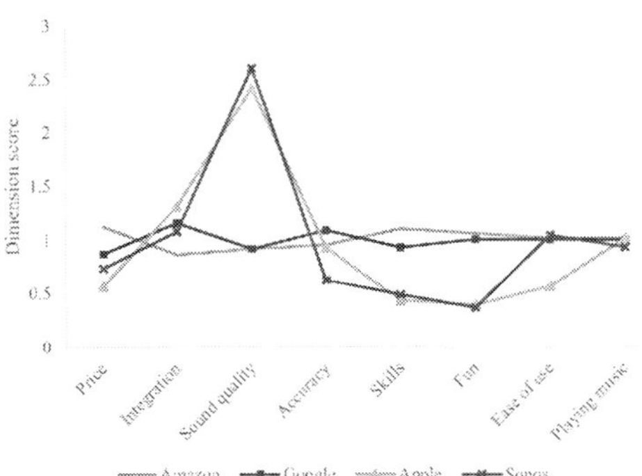

Figure 6: Company profiles along 8 dimensions form 2 groups with similar positioning.

zon, Google, Apple Sonos) along a dimension d_k ($k \in [1,8]$) as the normalized topic probability:

$$DS_{b,d_k} = \frac{{}^1/_{N_b} \sum_{r=1}^{N_b} p_{r,d_k}}{{}^1/_{N} \sum_{r=1}^{N} p_{r,d_k}}$$

p_{r,d_k} is the probability that review r belongs to dimension d_k. N_b is the number of reviews for brand b. N is the total number of reviews for all brands.

The line plot in Fig. 6 reveals some interesting differences between the brands' relative strengths and weaknesses.

Amazon and Google speakers are similar to each other, with a balanced performance on all dimensions. On the other hand, Apple and Sonos speakers are also similar to each other, but with a focus on sound quality. This suggests a segmentation of the smart speaker market into two groups along those lines.

Apple and Sonos clearly outperform Amazon and Google speakers in terms of sound quality. Indeed, both Apple and Sonos speakers are high-end products, arguably the best sounding smart speakers on the market, using, e.g., adaptive audio (beamforming) to determine the position of a user and adjust its microphones accordingly. Sonos has digital amplifiers, a tweeter, a woofer, and a 6-microphone array, and an adaptive noise suppression algorithm.

Interestingly, Amazon and Google users mention using their speakers to listen to music as much as Apple and Sonos users do. This is most likely due to the fact that playing music is the most popular task on every smart speaker. However, it does suggest that only a few people are willing to pay extra for better sound quality, and that they do greatly appreciate sound quality and mention it often.

Amazon performs best in term of price, followed by Google. Users mention that prices are reasonable, and many people buy it as a gift for Christmas or during sales such as Black Friday. Amazon speakers do have the lowest prices among the 4 brands (Amazon: $49.99, Echo 2nd Gen: $99.99, Echo Spot: $129.99). Google's high-end speaker, the HomeMax ($399.00) is much less popular than its Home Mini ($49.00) and Home ($129.00). The main competition in terms of price and gift is between Amazon Echo Dot ($49.99) and Google Home Mini ($49).

For skills, Amazon/Google perform better than Apple/Sonos. Siri is strictly limited to Apple's ecosystem (e.g., users can only stream music from Apple Music, not from Spotify). This is potentially interesting for Sonos to distinguish themselves, as the speakers are Alexa-enabled (as of November 2018 when the reviews were collected), so users could exploit its skills just like Amazon users. One possible explanation could be that Sonos users focus more on music and sound quality, and that other skills become less important to them so they mention other skills less often.

5   Related work

Several topic models have been proposed, such as Latent Semantic Indexing (LSI) (Deerwester et al., 1990), Probabilistic LSI (pLSI) (Hofmann, 1999), and the most commonly used, Latent Dirichlet Allocation (Blei et al., 2003). LDA assumes that a document is comprised of mixtures over latent topics, and each topic is a distribution over words.

LDA has some limitations. The main limitations are the assumption that the number of topics is known and fixed, together with the validity of the assignments, and the interpretability of topics. LDA evaluation schemes can be categorized into *intrinsic evaluation* (holdout-log likelihood/ perplexity (Blei et al., 2003; Wallach et al., 2009), *topic coherence* (Newman et al., 2010; Röder et al., 2015), *human-in-the-loop* (word or topic intrusion (Chang et al., 2009; Lau et al., 2014)), and *extrinsic evaluation* (e.g., document clustering (Jagarlamudi et al., 2012), information retrieval (Wei and Croft, 2006)). Those work mainly focus on extracting meaningful high-level topic descriptors.

In this paper, we show that those techniques, when combined appropriately together, are useful in not only high-level topics but also in-depth insights from data. In order to do so, we address LDA limitations with topic coherence, human-in-the-loop, and incorporating human knowledge to merge topics for better quality (Boyd-Graber et al., 2014).

6 Conclusion

In this paper, we use the coherence score by Röder et al. (2015) as a guide to choose the optimal number of topics, and evaluate this choice with respect to human judgement and its ability to provide market insights. While coherence scores are judged meaningful (in word intrusion and topic intrusion) and provide a good starting point, they require and additional merging step based on domain knowledge to provide market insights. We merge the optimal choice of 13 topics into 8 dimensions for easier interpretation. We show that the topic mixture proportions are useful to give more insights about brand performance and market structure, separating the brands into two distinct camps with similar properties. Further research directions could assess the generalizability of the methodology on other datasets and tasks.

Acknowledgments

Hanh Nguyen is grateful to Raffaella Piccarreta for the inspiration that led to this work. The authors would like to thank Barbara Plank for useful feedback, as well as the reviewers for their helpful comments to make the paper clearer. Dirk Hovy is a member of the Bocconi Institute for Data Science and Analytics (BIDSA) and the Data and Marketing Insights (DMI) unit.

References

Corey W. Arnold, Andrea Oh, Shawn Chen, and William Speier. 2016. Evaluating topic model interpretability from a primary care physician perspective. *Computer Methods and Programs in Biomedicine*, 124:67–75.

David M Blei, Andrew Y Ng, and Michael I Jordan. 2003. Latent dirichlet allocation. *Journal of Machine Learning Research*, 3(Jan):993–1022.

Jordan Boyd-Graber, David Mimno, and David Newman. 2014. Care and feeding of topic models: Problems, diagnostics, and improvements. *Handbook of Mixed Membership Models and Their Applications*, 225255.

Jonathan Chang, Sean Gerrish, Chong Wang, Jordan L Boyd-Graber, and David M Blei. 2009. Reading tea leaves: How humans interpret topic models. In *Advances in Neural Information Processing Systems*, pages 288–296.

Scott Deerwester, Susan T Dumais, George W Furnas, Thomas K Landauer, and Richard Harshman. 1990. Indexing by latent semantic analysis. *Journal of the American Ssociety for Information Science*, 41(6):391–407.

Chrysanthos Dellarocas. 2006. Strategic manipulation of internet opinion forums: Implications for consumers and firms. *Management Science*, 52(10):1577–1593.

Economist. 2017. How voice technology is transforming computing - now we are talking. *The Economist*, 422(Jan):7.

Thomas Hofmann. 1999. Probabilistic latent semantic analysis. In *Proceedings of the 15th Conference Conference on Uncertainty in Artificial Intelligence*, pages 289–296. Morgan Kaufmann Publishers Inc.

Dirk Hovy. 2016. The enemy in your own camp: How well can we detect statistically-generated fake reviews – an adversarial study. In *Proceedings of the 54th Annual Meeting of the Association for Computational Linguistics (Volume 2: Short Papers)*, pages 351–356, Berlin, Germany. Association for Computational Linguistics.

Jagadeesh Jagarlamudi, Hal Daume III, and Raghavendra Udupa. 2012. Incorporating lexical priors into topic models. In *Proceedings of the 13th Conference of the European Chapter of the Association for Computational Linguistics*, pages 204–213. Association for Computational Linguistics.

Jey Han Lau, David Newman, and Timothy Baldwin. 2014. Machine reading tea leaves: Automatically evaluating topic coherence and topic model quality. In *Proceedings of the 14th Conference of the European Chapter of the Association for Computational Linguistics*. Association for Computational Linguistics.

Wojciech Lukasiewicz, Alexandru Todor, and Adrian Paschke. 2018. Human perception of enriched topic models. In *Business Information Systems*, pages 15–29. Springer International Publishing.

Jon D. McAuliffe and David M. Blei. 2008. Supervised topic models. In J. C. Platt, D. Koller, Y. Singer, and S. T. Roweis, editors, *Advances in Neural Information Processing Systems*, pages 121–128. Curran Associates, Inc.

David Newman, Jey Han Lau, Karl Grieser, and Timothy Baldwin. 2010. Automatic evaluation of topic coherence. In *Human Language Technologies: The 2010 Annual Conference of the North American Chapter of the Association for Computational Linguistics*, pages 100–108. Association for Computational Linguistics.

Michael Röder, Andreas Both, and Alexander Hinneburg. 2015. Exploring the space of topic coherence measures. In *Proceedings of the 8th ACM International Conference on Web Search and Data Mining*. ACM Press.

Hanna M. Wallach, Iain Murray, Ruslan Salakhutdinov, and David Mimno. 2009. Evaluation methods for topic models. In *Proceedings of the 26th Annual International Conference on Machine Learning*. ACM Press.

Xing Wei and W. Bruce Croft. 2006. LDA-based document models for ad-hoc retrieval. In *Proceedings of the 29th Annual International ACM SIGIR Conference on Research and Development in Information Retrieval*. ACM Press.

Predicting Algorithm Classes for Programming Word Problems

Vinayak Athavale *[1]   **Aayush Naik** *[2]   **Rajas Vanjape** [1]   **Manish Shrivastava** [1]
(vinayak.athavale, rajas.vanjape)@research.iiit.ac.in, aayushnaik17@gmail.com, m.shrivastava@iiit.ac.in
[1] Language Technologies Research Center, IIIT Hyderabad
[2] IIIT Hyderabad

Abstract

We introduce the task of algorithm class prediction for programming word problems. A programming word problem is a problem written in natural language, which can be solved using an algorithm or a program. We define classes of various programming word problems which correspond to the class of algorithms required to solve the problem. We present four new datasets for this task, two multiclass datasets with 550 and 1159 problems each and two multilabel datasets having 3737 and 3960 problems each. We pose the problem as a text classification problem and train neural network and non-neural network based models on this task. Our best performing classifier gets an accuracy of 62.7 percent for the multiclass case on the five class classification dataset, Codeforces Multiclass-5 (CFMC5). We also do some human-level analysis and compare human performance with that of our text classification models. Our best classifier has an accuracy only 9 percent lower than that of a human on this task. To the best of our knowledge, these are the first reported results on such a task. We make our code and datasets publicly available.

1 Introduction

In this paper we introduce and work on the problem of predicting algorithms classes for programming word problems (PWPs). A PWP is a problem written in natural language which can be solved using a computer program. These problems generally map to one or more classes of algorithms, which are used to solve them. Binary search, disjoint-set union, and dynamic programming are some examples. In this paper, our aim is to automatically map programming word problems to the relevant classes of algorithms. We ap-

---

* denotes equal contribution

Figure 1: An example programming word problem. Note that the example shown here is one of the easy Codeforces problems – most problems are much harder.

proach this problem by treating it as a classification task.

Programming word problems A programming word problem (PWP) requires the solver to design correct and efficient programs. The correctness and efficiency is checked by various testcases provided by the problem writer. A PWP usually consists of three parts – the problem statement, a well-defined input and output format, and time and memory constraints. An example PWP can be seen in Figure 1.

Solving PWPs is difficult for several reasons. One reason is, the problems are often embedded in a narrative, that is, they are described as quasi real-world situations in the form of short stories or riddles. The solver must first decode the intent of the problem, or understand *what* the problem is. Then the solver needs to apply their knowledge of algorithms to write a solution program. Another reason is that, the solution programs must be effi-

Proceedings of the 2019 EMNLP Workshop W-NUT: The 5th Workshop on Noisy User-generated Text, pages 84–93
Hong Kong, Nov 4, 2019. ©2019 Association for Computational Linguistics

"""

cient with respect to the given time and memory constraints. An outgrowth of this is that, the algorithm required to solve a particular problem not only depends on the problem statement, but also the constraints. Consider that there may be two different algorithms which will generate the correct output, for example, linear search, and binary search, but only one of those will abide by the time and memory constraints.

With the growing popularity of these problems, various competitions like ACM-ICPC, and Google CodeJam have emerged. Additionally, several companies including Google, Facebook, and Amazon evaluate problem-solving skills of candidates for software-related jobs (McDowell, 2016) using PWPs. Consequently, as noted by Forišek (2010), programming problems have been becoming more difficult over time. To solve a PWP, humans get information from all its parts, not just the the problem statement. Thus, we predict algorithms from the entire text of a PWP. We also try to identify which parts of a PWP contribute the most towards predicting algorithms.

Significance of the Problem Many interesting real-world problems can be solved and optimised using standard algorithms. Time spent grocery shopping can be optimised by posing it as a graph traversal problem (Gertin, 2012). Arranging and retrieving items like mail, or books in a library can be done more efficiently using sorting and searching algorithms. Solving problems using algorithms can be scaled by using computers, transforming the algorithms into programs. A program is an algorithm that has been customised to solve a specific task under a specific set of circumstances using a specific language. Converting textual descriptions of such real-world problems into algorithms, and then into programs has largely been a human endeavour. An AI agent that could automatically generate programs from natural language problem descriptions could greatly increase the rate of technological advancement by quickly providing efficient solutions to the said real-world problems. A subsystem that could identify algorithm classes from natural language would significantly narrow down the search space of possible programs. Consequently, such a subsystem would be a useful feature for, or likely be even part of, such an agent. Therefore, building a system to predict algorithms from programming word problems is potentially an important first step toward

an automatic program generating AI. More immediately, such a system could serve as an application to help people in improving their algorithmic problem-solving skills for software job interviews, competitive programming, and other uses.

As per our knowledge, this task has not been addressed in the literature before. Hence, there is no standard dataset available for this task. We generate and introduce new datasets by extracting problems from Codeforces[1], a sport programming platform. We release the datasets and our experiment code at [2].

Contribution The major contributions of this paper are: **Four datasets** on programming word problems - two multiclass[3] datasets having 5 and 10 classes and two multilabel[4] datasets having 10 and 20 classes. **Evaluation of Classifiers** on various multiclass and multilabel classifiers that can predict classes for programming word problems on our datasets along with the human baseline. We define our problem more clearly in section 2. Then we explain our datasets – their generation and format along with human evaluation in section 3. We describe the models we use for multiclass and multilabel classification in section 4. We delineate our experiments, models, and evaluation metrics in section 5. We report our classification results in section 6. We analyse some dataset nuances in section 7. Finally, we discuss related work and the conclusion in sections 8 and 9 respectively.

2 Problem Definition

The focus of this paper is the problem of mapping a PWP to one or more classes of algorithms. A *class* of algorithms is a set containing more specific algorithms. For example, breadth-first search, and Dijkstra's algorithm belong to the class of graph algorithms. A PWP can be solved using one of the algorithms in the class it is mapped to. Problems on the Codeforces platform have *tags* that correspond to the class of algorithms.

Thus, our aim is to find a tagging function, f^* : $\mathcal{S} \rightarrow \mathcal{P}(\mathcal{T})$ which maps a PWP string, $s \in \mathcal{S}$, to a set of tags, $\{t_1, t_2, ...\} \in \mathcal{P}(\mathcal{T})$. We also consider another variant of the problem. For the PWPs that only have one tag, we focus on finding a tagging

---

[1] codeforces.com

[2] https://github.com/aayn/codeforces-clean

[3] each problem belongs to only one class

[4] each problem belongs to one or more classes

Dataset	Size	Vocab	classes	Avg. words	Class percentage
CFMC5	550	9326	5	504	greedy: 20%, implementation:20%, data structures: 20%, dp: 20%, math: 20%
CFMC10	1159	14691	10	485	implementation: 34.94%, dp: 12.42%, math: 11.38%, greedy: 10.44%, data structures: 9.49%, brute force: 5.60%, geometry: 4.22%, constructive algorithms: 5.52%, dfs and similar: 3.10%, strings: 2.84%

Table 1: Dataset statistics for multiclass datasets. CFMC5 has 550 problems with a balanced class distribution. CFMC10 has 1159 problems and has a class imbalance. CFMC5 is a subset of CFMC10. Red classes belong to the solution category; blue classes belong to the problem category.

Dataset	Size	Vocab	N classes	Avg. len	Label card	Label den	Label subsets
CFML10	3737	28178	10	494	1.69	0.169	231
CFML20	3960	29433	20	495	2.1	0.105	808

Table 2: Dataset statistics for multilabel datasets. The problems of the CFML10 dataset are a subset of those in the CFML20 dataset.

function, $f_1^* : \mathcal{S} \to \mathcal{T}$, which maps a PWP string, $s \in \mathcal{S}$, to a tag, $t \in \mathcal{T}$. We approximate f^* and f_1^* by training models on data.

3 Dataset

3.1 Data Collection

We collected the data from a popular sport programming platform called Codeforces. Codeforces was founded in 2010, and now has over 43000 active registered participants[5]. We first collected a total of 4300 problems from this platform. Each problem has associated tags, with most of the problems having more than one tag. These tags correspond to the algorithm or class of algorithms that can be used to solve that particular problem. The tags for a problem are given by the problem writer and they can only be edited only by high-rated (expert) contestants who have solved the problem. Next, we performed basic filtering on the data – removing the problems which had non-algorithmic tags, problems with no tags assigned to them, and also the problems wherein the problem statement was not extracted completely. After this filtering, we got 4019 problems with 35 different tags. This forms the Codeforces dataset. The label (tag) cardinality (average number of labels/tags per problem) was 2.24. Since the Codeforces dataset is the first dataset generated for a new problem, we select different subsets of this

[5]http://codeforces.com/ratings/page/219

dataset with differing properties. This is to check if classification models are robust to different variations of the problem.

3.2 Multilabel Datasets

We found that a large number of tags had a very low frequency. Hence, we removed those problems and tags from the Codeforces dataset as follows. First, we got the list of 20 most frequently occurring tags, ordered by decreasing frequency. We observed that the 20th tag in this list had a frequency of 98, in other words, 98 problems had this tag. Next, for each problem, we removed the tags that are not in this list. After that, all problems that did not have any tags left were removed.

This led to the formation of the Codeforces Multilabel-20 (CFML20) dataset, which has 20 tags. We used the same procedure for the 10 most frequently occurring tags to get the Codeforces Multilabel-10 (CFML10) dataset. The CFML20 has 98.53 (3960 problems) percent of the problems of the original dataset and the label (tag) cardinality only reduces from 2.24 to 2.21. CFML10 on the other hand has 92.9 percent of the problems with label (tag) cardinality 1.69. Statistics about both these multilabel datasets are given in Table 2.

3.3 Multiclass Datasets

To generate the multiclass datasets, first, we extracted the problems from the CFML20 dataset that only had one tag. There were about 1300 such problems. From those, we selected the problems whose tags occur in the list of 10 most common tags. These problems formed the Codeforces Multiclass-10 (CFMC10) dataset which contains 1159 examples. We found that the CFMC10 dataset has a class (tag) imbalance. We also make a balanced dataset, Codeforces Multiclass-5 (CFMC5), in which the prior class (tag) distribution is uniform. The CFMC5 dataset has five tags, each having 110 problems. To make CFMC5, first we extracted the problems whose tags are among the five most common tags. The fifth most common tag occurs 110 times. We sampled 110 random problems corresponding to the other four tags to give a total of 550 problems. Statistics about both the multiclass datasets are given in Table 1.

3.4 Dataset Format

Each problem in the datasets follows the same format (refer to Figure 1 for an example problem). The header contains the problem title, and the time and memory constraints for a program running on the problem testcases. The problem statement is the natural language description of the problem framed as a real world scenario. The input and output format describe the input to, and the output from a valid solution program. It also contains constraints that will be put on the size of inputs (for example, max size of input array, max size of 2 input values). The tags associated with the problem are the algorithm classes that we are trying to predict using the above information.

3.5 Class Categories in the Dataset

The classes for PWPs can be divided into two categories: **Problem category** classes tell us what kind of broad class of problem the PWP belongs to. For instance, *math*, and *string* are two such classes. **Solution category** classes tell us what kind of algorithm can solve a particular PWP. For example, a PWP of class *dp* or *binary search* would need a dynamic programming or binary search based algorithm to solve it.

Problem category PWPs are easier to classify because, in some cases, simple keyword mapping may lead to the classification (an equation in the problem is a strong indicator that a problem is of math type). Whereas, for solution category PWPs, a deeper understanding of the problem is required.

The classes belong to problem and solution categories for CFML20 are mentioned in the supplementary material.

3.6 Human Evaluation

In this section, we evaluate and analyze the performance of an average competitor on the task of predicting an algorithm for a PWP. The tags for a given PWP are added by its problem setter or other high-rated contestants who have solved it. Our test participants were recent computer science graduates with some experience in algorithms and competitive programming. We gave 5 participants the problem text along with all the constraints, and the input and output format. We also provided them with a list of all the tags and a few example problems for each tag. We randomly sample 120 problems from the CFML20 dataset and split them into two parts – containing 20 and 100 problems respectively. The 20 problems were given along with their tags to familiarize the participants with the task. For the remaining 100 problems, the participants were asked to predict the tags (one or more) for each problem. We chose to sample the problems from the CFML20 dataset as it is the closest to a real-world scenario of predicting algorithms for solving problems. We find that there is some variation in the accuracy reported by different humans with the highest F1 micro score being 11 percent greater than that of the the lowest. (see supplementary material for more details). The F1 micro score averaged over all 5 participants was 51.8 while the averaged F1 Macro was 42.7. The results are not surprising since this task is like any other problem solving task, and people based on their proficiency would get different results. This shows us that the problem is hard even for humans with a computer science education.

4 Classification Models

To test the compatibility of our problem with text classification paradigm, we apply to it some standard text classification models from recent literature.

4.1 Multiclass Classification

To approximate the optimal tagging function f_1^* (see section 2) we use the following models.

Multinomial Naive Bayes (MNB) and Support Vector Machine (SVM) Wang and Manning (2012) proposed several simple and effective baselines for text classification. An MNB is a naive Bayes classifier for multinomial models. An SVM is a discriminative hyperplane-based classifier (Hearst et al., 1998). These baselines use unigrams and bigrams as features. We also try applying TF-IDF to these features.

Multi-layer Perceptron (MLP) An MLP is a class of artificial neural network that uses back-propagation for training in a supervised setting (Rumelhart et al., 1986). MLP-based models are standard for text classification baselines (Glorot et al., 2011).

Convolutional Neural Network (CNN) We also train a Convolutional Neural Network (CNN) based model, similar to the one used by Kim (2014) in their paper, to classify the problems. We use the model both with and without pre-trained GloVe word-embeddings (Pennington et al., 2014).

CNN ensemble Hansen and Salamon (1990) introduce neural network ensemble learning, in which many neural networks are trained and their predictions combined. These neural network systems show greater generalization ability and predictive power. We train five CNN networks and combine their predictions using the majority voting system.

4.2 Multilabel Classifiers

To approximate, f^* (see section 2), we apply the following augmentations to the models described above.

Multinomial Naive Bayes (MNB) and Support Vector Machine (SVM) For applying these models to the multilabel case, we use the one-vs-rest (or, one-vs-all) strategy. This strategy involves training a single classifier for each class, with the samples of that class as positive samples and all other samples as negatives (Bishop, 2006).

Multi-layer Perceptron (MLP) Nam et al. (2014) use MLP-based models for multilabel text classification. We use similar models, but use the MSE loss instead of the cross-entropy loss.

Convolutional Neural Network (CNN) For multilabel classification we use a CNN based feature extractor similar to the one used in (Kim, 2014). The output is passed through a sigmoid activation function, $\sigma(x) = \frac{1}{1+e^{-x}}$. The labels which have a corresponding activation greater than 0.5 are considered (Liu et al., 2017). Similar to the multiclass case, we train the model both with and without pre-trained GloVe (Pennington et al., 2014) word-embeddings.

CNN ensemble We train five CNNs and add their output linear activation values. We pass this sum through a sigmoid function and consider the labels (tags) with activation greater than 0.5.

5 Experiment setup

All hyperparameter tuning experiments were performed with 10-fold cross validation. For the non-neural network-based methods, we first vectorize each problem using a bag-of-words vectorizer, scikit-learn's (Pedregosa et al., 2011) CountVectorizer. We also experiment with TF-IDF features for each problem. In the multiclass case, we use the LIBSVM (chung Chang and Lin, 2001) implementation of the SVM classifier and we grid search over different kernels. However, the LIBSVM implementation is not compatible with the one-vs-rest strategy (complexity $\mathcal{O}(n)$ where n is the number of classes), but only the one-vs-one (complexity $\mathcal{O}(n^2)$). This becomes prohibitively slow and thus, we use the LIBLINEAR (Fan et al., 2008) implementation for the multilabel case. For hyperparameter tuning, we applied a grid search over the parameters of the vectorizers, classifiers, and other components. The exact parameters tuned can be seen in our code repository. For the neural network-based methods, we tokenize each problem using the spaCy tokenizer (Honnibal and Montani, 2017). We only use words appearing 2 or more times in building the vocabulary and replace the words that appear fewer times with a special UNK token. Our CNN network architecture is similar to that used by Kim (2014). The batch size used is 32. We apply 512 one-dimensional convolution filters of size 3, 4, and 5 on each problem. The rectifier, $R(x) = max(x, 0)$, is used as the activation function. We concatenate these filters, apply a global max-pooling followed by a fully-connected layer with output size equal to the number of classes. We use the PyTorch framework (Paszke et al., 2017) to build this model. For the word embedding we use two approaches - a vanilla PyTorch trainable embedding layer and a 300-dimensional GloVe embedding (Pennington et al., 2014). The networks were initialized using the Xavier method (Glorot and Bengio, 2010) at the beginning of each fold. We use the Adam optimization algorithm (Kingma and Ba, 2014) as we observe that it converges faster than vanilla stochastic gradient descent.

Classifier	CFMC5		CFMC10	
	Acc	F1 W	Acc	F1 W
CNN Random	25.0	22.1	35.2	19.2
MNB	47.6	47.5	43.9	37.4
SVM BoW	49.3	49.1	47.9	43.2
SVM TFIDF	47.8	47.6	45.7	41.2
MLP	47.8	47.6	49.3	46.2
CNN	61.7	61.3	**54.7**	51.3
CNN Ensemble	**62.7**	**62.2**	53.5	50.5
CNN GloVe	62.2	61.3	54.5	**51.4**

Table 3: Classification Accuracy for single label classification. Note that all results were obtained on 10-fold cross validation. CNN Random refers to a CNN trained on a random labelling of the dataset. F1 W stands for weighted macro F1-score.

6 Results

6.1 Multiclass Results

We see that the classification accuracy of the best performing classifier, CNN ensemble, for the CFMC5 dataset is 62.7 %. The highest accuracy for the CFMC10 dataset was achieved by the CNN classifer which does not use any pretrained embeddings. For all the multiclass classification results refer to table 3. We observe that CNN-based classifiers perform better than other classifiers – MLP, MNB, and SVM for both CFMC5 and CFMC10 datasets. Since these are the first learning results on the task of algorithm prediction for PWPs, we train a CNN classifier on a random labelling of the dataset. The results are given in the row called CNN random. To obtain this random labelling we shuffle the current mapping from problem to tag randomly. This ensures that the class distribution of the datasets remain the same. We see that all the classifiers significantly outperform the performance on the random dataset. We also observe that the classification accuracy is not the same for every class. We get the highest accuracy (see Fig. 2) for the class, *data structures*, at 90%, while, the lowest accuracy is for the class, *greedy*, at 40%. These results are on the CFMC5 dataset.

6.2 Multilabel Results

We see that CNN-based classifiers give the best results for the CFML10 and CFML20 datasets. The best F1 micro and macro scores for the CFML10 dataset were 45.32, 38.9 respectively. These were obtained by the CNN Ensemble model. For com-

plete results see table 4. The best performing model on the CFML20 dataset was also the CNN ensemble. As we did in the multiclass case, we train a CNN model on the randomly shuffled labelling for both CFML10, CFML20 datasets. We find that all the classifers significantly outperform the model trained on a shuffled labelling. The human-level F1 micro and macro scores on a subset of the CFML20 dataset were 51.2 and 40.5. In comparison, our best performing classifier on the CMFL20 dataset, CNN Ensemble, got F1 macro and micro scores of 42.75, 37.29 respectively. We see that the performance of our best classifiers trail average human performance by about 8.45% and 3.21% on F1 micro and F1 macro scores respectively.

7 Analysis

7.1 Experiments with various subsets of the problem

As described in section 1, a PWP consists of three components – the problem statement, input and output format, and time and memory constraints. We seek to answer the following questions. Does one component contribute to the accuracy more than any other? Does the contribution of different components vary over the problem class? We performed some experiments to address these questions. We split the problem into two parts – 1) the problem statement, and 2) the input and output format, and time and memory constraints. We train an SVM, and a CNN on these two components independently.

Multiclass PWP component analysis We find classifier accuracies on the CFMC5 dataset. We choose the CFMC5 dataset out of the two multiclass datasets because it has a balanced class distribution. We find that the classifiers perform quite well on only the input and output format, and time and memory constraints – the best classifier getting an accuracy of 56.4 percent (only 5.3 percent lower than the accuracy of CNN with the whole problem). Classification using only the problem statement gives worse results than using the format and constraints, with a classification accuracy of 45.2 percent for the best classifier CNN (16.5 percent lower than the accuracy of a CNN trained on the whole problem). Complete results are given in table 5. We also see that the performance across different classes varies when trained on different inputs. We find that the class *dp* performs better

Classifier	CFML10			CFML20		
	hamming loss	F1 micro	F1 macro	hamming loss	F1 micro	F1 macro
CNN Random TWE	0.2158	15.98	9.39	0.1207	12.07	4.02
MNB BoW	0.1706	30.57	25.73	0.1067	29.67	23.41
SVM BoW	0.1713	36.08	31.09	0.1056	34.93	30.70
SVM BoW + TF-IDF	0.1723	38.20	33.68	0.1059	38.55	34.70
MLP BoW	0.1879	39.13	34.92	0.1167	38.12	31.37
CNN TWE	**0.1671**	39.20	32.59	**0.1023**	38.44	30.38
CNN Ensemble TWE	0.1703	**45.32**	**38.93**	0.1093	**42.75**	**37.29**
CNN GloVe	0.1676	39.22	33.77	0.1052	37.56	30.29
Human	-	-	-	-	**51.8**	**42.7**

Table 4: Classification Accuracy for multi-label classification. TWE stands for trainable word embeddings initialized with a normal distribution. Note that all results were obtained on 10-fold cross validation. CNN Random refers to a CNN trained on a random labelling of the dataset.

when trained on the problem statement, whereas the other classes perform much better on the format and constraints. For each class except *greedy*, we see an additive trend – the accuracy is improved by combining both these features. Refer to figure 2 for more details.

Multilabel partial problem results We also tabulate the classifier accuracies on the CFML20 dataset by training it only on the format and constraints, and the problem statement. Even here, we observe similar trends as the multiclass partial problem experiments. We find that classifiers are more accurate when trained only on the format and constraints than only on the problem statement. Again, the accuracy is improved by combining both these features. Refer to table 5 for more details.

7.2 Problem category and Solution category results

We find that correctly classifying PWPs of the solution category is harder than correctly classifying PWPs of the problem category (table 5). For instance, take a look at the row corresponding to CFMC5 dataset and "all prob" feature. The accuracy for solution category is 54.24% as compared to 71.36% for the problem category. This trend is followed for both CFMC5 and CFML20 datasets and also when using different features of the PWPs. In spite of the difficulty, the classification scores for the solution category are significantly better than random.

8 Related Work

Our work is related to three major topics of research, math word problem solving, text document classification and program synthesis.

Math word problem solving In the recent years, many models have been built to solve different kinds of math word problems. Some models solve only arithmetic problems (Hosseini et al., 2014), while others solve algebra word problems (Kushman et al., 2014). There are some recent solvers which solve a wide range preuniversity level math word problems (Matsuzaki et al., 2017), (Hopkins et al., 2017). Wang et al. (2017), and Mehta et al. (2017) have built deep neural network based solvers for math word problems. **Program synthesis** Work related to the task of converting natural language description to code comes under the research areas of program synthesis and natural language understanding. This work is still in its nascent stage. Zhong et al. (2017) worked on generating SQL queries automatically from natural language descriptions. Lin et al. (2017) worked on automatically generating bash commands from natural language descriptions. Iyer et al. (2016) worked on summarizing source code. Sudha et al. (2017) use a CNN based model to classify the algorithm used in a programming problem using the C++ code. Our model tries to accomplish this task by using the natural language problem description. Gulwani et al. (2017) is a comprehensive treatise on program synthesis. **Document classification** The problem of classifying a programming word problem in natural language is similar to the task of document classification. The state-of-the-art approach currently for single label classification is to use a hierarchical attention network based model (Yang et al., 2016). This model is improved by using transfer learning (Howard and Ruder, 2018).

Dataset	Features	Classifier	Soln. category		Prob. category		all	
			F1 Mi	F1 Ma	F1 Mi	F1 Ma	F1 Mi	F1 Ma
CFMC5	only statement	cnn	42.73	46.14	51.32	64.35	46.13	45.20
CFMC5	only i/o	cnn	44.24	51.73	74.73	81.31	56.42	55.41
CFMC5	all prob	cnn	54.24	59.91	71.36	78.32	61.71	61.32
CFML20	only statement	cnn	30.83	17.32	38.64	41.82	33.59	28.34
CFML20	only i/o	cnn	34.63	19.59	44.49	44.34	38.44	30.38
CFML20	all prob	cnn	34.39	19.23	45.36	44.02	39.20	32.59

Table 5: Performance on different categories of PWPs for different parts of the PWPs. The rows with "only statement" features use only the problem description part of the PWP, the rows with "only i/o" use only the I/O and constraint information, and "all prob" use the entire PWP. The results under the "Soln category", "Prob category" columns are for the problems which have the label under problem, solution category respectively. "All" is for the entire dataset. So, for example, the F1 Micro score using only I/O and constraint for solution category problems of CFML20 is 34.63. Note that for CFMC5, F1 Mi (F1 Micro) is the same as accuracy, and F1 Ma (F1 Macro) score is a weighted Macro F1-score.

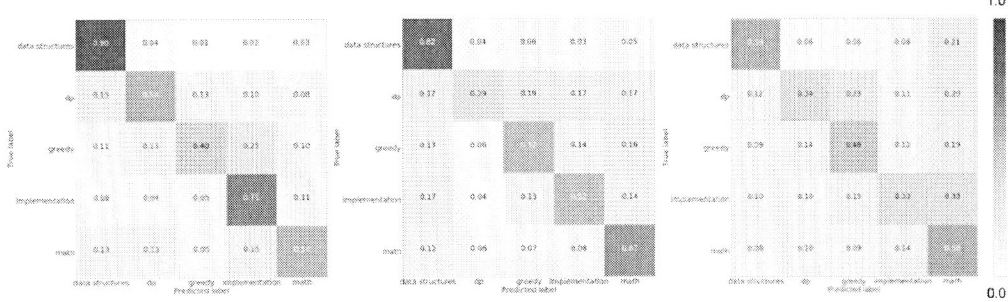

Figure 2: Confusion matrices for different parts of the problem on CFMC5. Whole problem text (left), only format and constraints information (center), and only problem statement (right). Perfomance on the whole problem is the highest, followed by only format and constraints information. Performance across different classes (except *greedy*) is additive, which shows that features extracted from both the parts are of importance

Other approaches include a Recurrent Convolutional Neural Network based approach (Lai et al., 2015) or the fasttext model (Joulin et al., 2016) which uses bag-of-words features and a hierarchical softmax. Nam et al. (2014) use a feed-forward neural network with binary cross entropy per label to perform multilabel document classification. Kurata et al. (2016) leverage label co-occurrence to improve multilabel classification. Liu et al. (2017) use a CNN based architecture to perform extreme multilabel classification.

9   Conclusion

We introduced a new problem of predicting the algorithm classes for programming word problems. For this task we generated four datasets – two multiclass (CFMC5 and CFMC10), having five and 10 classes respectively, and two multilabel (CFML10 and CFML20), having 10 and 20 classes respec-

tively. Our classifiers are falling short only by about 9 percent of the human score. We also did some experiments which show that increasing the size of the train dataset improves the accuracy (see supplementary material). These problems are much harder than high school math word problems as they require a good knowledge of various computer science algorithms and an ability to reduce a problem to these known algorithms. Even our human analysis shows that trained computer science graduates only get an F1 of 51.8. Based on these results, we see that algorithm class prediction is compatible with and can be solved using text classification.

References

Christopher M. Bishop. 2006. *Pattern Recognition and Machine Learning (Information Science and Statistics)*. Springer-Verlag, Berlin, Heidelberg.

Chih chung Chang and Chih-Jen Lin. 2001. Libsvm: a library for support vector machines.

Rong-En Fan, Kai-Wei Chang, Cho-Jui Hsieh, Xiang-Rui Wang, and Chih-Jen Lin. 2008. LIBLINEAR: A library for large linear classification. *Journal of Machine Learning Research*, 9:1871–1874.

Michal Forišek. 2010. The difficulty of programming contests increases. In *International Conference on Informatics in Secondary Schools-Evolution and Perspectives*, pages 72–85. Springer.

Thomas Gertin. 2012. *Maximizing the cost of shortest paths between facilities through optimal product category locations*. Ph.D. thesis.

Xavier Glorot and Yoshua Bengio. 2010. Understanding the difficulty of training deep feedforward neural networks. In *In Proceedings of the International Conference on Artificial Intelligence and Statistics (AISTATS10). Society for Artificial Intelligence and Statistics*.

Xavier Glorot, Antoine Bordes, and Yoshua Bengio. 2011. Domain adaptation for large-scale sentiment classification: A deep learning approach. In *Proceedings of the 28th international conference on machine learning (ICML-11)*, pages 513–520.

Sumit Gulwani, Oleksandr Polozov, Rishabh Singh, et al. 2017. Program synthesis. *Foundations and Trends® in Programming Languages*, 4(1-2):1–119.

L. K. Hansen and P. Salamon. 1990. Neural network ensembles. *IEEE Transactions on Pattern Analysis and Machine Intelligence*, 12(10):993–1001.

Marti A. Hearst, Susan T Dumais, Edgar Osuna, John Platt, and Bernhard Scholkopf. 1998. Support vector machines. *IEEE Intelligent Systems and their applications*, 13(4):18–28.

Matthew Honnibal and Ines Montani. 2017. spacy 2: Natural language understanding with bloom embeddings, convolutional neural networks and incremental parsing. *To appear*.

Mark Hopkins, Cristian Petrescu-Prahova, Roie Levin, Ronan Le Bras, Alvaro Herrasti, and Vidur Joshi. 2017. Beyond sentential semantic parsing: Tackling the math sat with a cascade of tree transducers. In *Proceedings of the 2017 Conference on Empirical Methods in Natural Language Processing*, pages 795–804.

Mohammad Javad Hosseini, Hannaneh Hajishirzi, Oren Etzioni, and Nate Kushman. 2014. Learning to solve arithmetic word problems with verb categorization. In *Proceedings of the 2014 Conference on Empirical Methods in Natural Language Processing (EMNLP)*, pages 523–533.

Jeremy Howard and Sebastian Ruder. 2018. Universal language model fine-tuning for text classification. In *Proceedings of the 56th Annual Meeting of the Association for Computational Linguistics (Volume 1: Long Papers)*, volume 1, pages 328–339.

Srinivasan Iyer, Ioannis Konstas, Alvin Cheung, and Luke Zettlemoyer. 2016. Summarizing source code using a neural attention model. In *Proceedings of the 54th Annual Meeting of the Association for Computational Linguistics (Volume 1: Long Papers)*, volume 1, pages 2073–2083.

Armand Joulin, Edouard Grave, Piotr Bojanowski, and Tomas Mikolov. 2016. Bag of tricks for efficient text classification. *arXiv preprint arXiv:1607.01759*.

Yoon Kim. 2014. Convolutional neural networks for sentence classification. *arXiv preprint arXiv:1408.5882*.

Diederik P Kingma and Jimmy Ba. 2014. Adam: A method for stochastic optimization. *arXiv preprint arXiv:1412.6980*.

Gakuto Kurata, Bing Xiang, and Bowen Zhou. 2016. Improved neural network-based multi-label classification with better initialization leveraging label co-occurrence. In *Proceedings of the 2016 Conference of the North American Chapter of the Association for Computational Linguistics: Human Language Technologies*, pages 521–526.

Nate Kushman, Yoav Artzi, Luke Zettlemoyer, and Regina Barzilay. 2014. Learning to automatically solve algebra word problems. In *Proceedings of the 52nd Annual Meeting of the Association for Computational Linguistics (Volume 1: Long Papers)*, volume 1, pages 271–281.

Siwei Lai, Liheng Xu, Kang Liu, and Jun Zhao. 2015. Recurrent convolutional neural networks for text classification. In *AAAI*, volume 333, pages 2267–2273.

Xi Victoria Lin, Chenglong Wang, Deric Pang, Kevin Vu, Luke Zettlemoyer, and Michael D Ernst. 2017. Program synthesis from natural language using recurrent neural networks. *University of Washington Department of Computer Science and Engineering, Seattle, WA, USA, Tech. Rep. UW-CSE-17-03-01*.

Jingzhou Liu, Wei-Cheng Chang, Yuexin Wu, and Yiming Yang. 2017. Deep learning for extreme multi-label text classification. In *Proceedings of the 40th International ACM SIGIR Conference on Research and Development in Information Retrieval*, pages 115–124. ACM.

Takuya Matsuzaki, Takumi Ito, Hidenao Iwane, Hirokazu Anai, and Noriko H Arai. 2017. Semantic parsing of pre-university math problems. In *Proceedings of the 55th Annual Meeting of the Association for Computational Linguistics (Volume 1: Long Papers)*, volume 1, pages 2131–2141.

Gayle Laakmann McDowell. 2016. *Cracking the Coding Interview: 189 Programming Questions and Solutions*. CareerCup, LLC.

Purvanshi Mehta, Pruthwik Mishra, Vinayak Athavale, Manish Shrivastava, and Dipti Sharma. 2017. Deep neural network based system for solving arithmetic word problems. *Proceedings of the IJCNLP 2017, System Demonstrations*, pages 65–68.

Jinseok Nam, Jungi Kim, Eneldo Loza Mencía, Iryna Gurevych, and Johannes Fürnkranz. 2014. Large-scale multi-label text classificationrevisiting neural networks. In *Joint european conference on machine learning and knowledge discovery in databases*, pages 437–452. Springer.

Adam Paszke, Sam Gross, Soumith Chintala, Gregory Chanan, Edward Yang, Zachary DeVito, Zeming Lin, Alban Desmaison, Luca Antiga, and Adam Lerer. 2017. Automatic differentiation in pytorch. In *NIPS-W*.

F. Pedregosa, G. Varoquaux, A. Gramfort, V. Michel, B. Thirion, O. Grisel, M. Blondel, P. Prettenhofer, R. Weiss, V. Dubourg, J. Vanderplas, A. Passos, D. Cournapeau, M. Brucher, M. Perrot, and E. Duchesnay. 2011. Scikit-learn: Machine learning in Python. *Journal of Machine Learning Research*, 12:2825–2830.

Jeffrey Pennington, Richard Socher, and Christopher D. Manning. 2014. Glove: Global vectors for word representation. In *In EMNLP*.

David E. Rumelhart, Geoffrey E. Hinton, and Ronald J. Williams. 1986. Learning internal representations by error propagation. In David E. Rumelhart and James L. Mcclelland, editors, *Parallel Distributed Processing: Explorations in the Microstructure of Cognition, Volume 1: Foundations*, pages 318–362. MIT Press, Cambridge, MA.

S Sudha, A Arun Kumar, M Muthu Nagappan, and R Suresh. 2017. Classification and recommendation of competitive programming problems using cnn. In *International Conference on Intelligent Information Technologies*, pages 262–272. Springer.

Sida Wang and Christopher D. Manning. 2012. Baselines and bigrams: Simple, good sentiment and topic classification. In *Proceedings of the 50th Annual Meeting of the Association for Computational Linguistics: Short Papers - Volume 2*, ACL '12, pages 90–94, Stroudsburg, PA, USA. Association for Computational Linguistics.

Yan Wang, Xiaojiang Liu, and Shuming Shi. 2017. Deep neural solver for math word problems. In *Proceedings of the 2017 Conference on Empirical Methods in Natural Language Processing*, pages 845–854.

Zichao Yang, Diyi Yang, Chris Dyer, Xiaodong He, Alex Smola, and Eduard Hovy. 2016. Hierarchical attention networks for document classification. In *Proceedings of the 2016 Conference of the North American Chapter of the Association for Computational Linguistics: Human Language Technologies*, pages 1480–1489.

Victor Zhong, Caiming Xiong, and Richard Socher. 2017. Seq2sql: Generating structured queries from natural language using reinforcement learning. *arXiv preprint arXiv:1709.00103*.

Automatic identification of writers' intentions: Comparing different methods for predicting relationship goals in online dating profile texts

Chris van der Lee, Tess van der Zanden, Emiel Krahmer, Maria Mos, and **Alexander Schouten**

Tilburg center for Cognition and Communication (TiCC),
School of Humanities and Digital Sciences, Tilburg University
`{c.vdrlee,t.vdrzanden}@tilburguniversity.edu`
`{maria.mos,a.p.schouten,e.j.krahmer}@tilburguniversity.edu`

Abstract

Psychologically motivated, lexicon-based text analysis methods such as LIWC (Pennebaker et al., 2015) have been criticized by computational linguists for their lack of adaptability, but they have not often been systematically compared with either human evaluations or machine learning approaches. The goal of the current study was to assess the effectiveness and predictive ability of LIWC on a relationship goal classification task. In this paper, we compared the outcomes of (1) LIWC, (2) machine learning, and (3) a human baseline. A newly collected corpus of online dating profile texts (a genre not explored before in the ACL anthology) was used, accompanied by the profile writers' self-selected relationship goal (long-term versus date). These three approaches were tested by comparing their performance on identifying both the intended relationship goal and content-related text labels. Results show that LIWC and machine learning models both correlate with humans in terms of content-related label assignment. Furthermore, LIWC's content-related labels corresponded more strongly to humans than those of the machine learning model. Moreover, all approaches were similarly accurate in predicting the relationship goal.

1 Introduction

When investigating large textual datasets, it is oftentimes necessary to use (automated) tools in order to make sense of the texts. Such tools can help expose properties of texts or of the texts' author (Riffe et al., 2014). A distinction in these tools can be made between predefined lexicon-based approaches and more content-specific machine learning approaches. One commonly used lexicon-based approach is the Linguistic Inquiry and Word Count program (LIWC; Pennebaker et al., 2015). This approach assigns words to one or more (psychologically validated) labels associated with the word. These labels might reveal more about a writer's thought processes, emotional states, and intentions (Tausczik and Pennebaker, 2010).

Text analysis tools such as LIWC have become more popular with the surge of social media: researchers want to assess, for instance, the sentiment of social media users on various matters, and lexicon-based text analysis tools can provide help with that. At the same time, these tools have also garnered criticism, for example, because they do not differentiate between domains and cannot deal with non-literal language use (e.g., irony), or out-of-vocabulary terms frequently seen within noisy text (e.g., typos or (internet) slang) (Panger, 2016; Franklin, 2015; Schwartz et al., 2013). This is something that machine learning methods might be better suited for as they can be trained on specific content, thus are able to analyze more complex language. Yet, not much is known about the effectiveness of lexicon-based compared to machine learning methods or a ground truth: comparative research is scarce, with few exceptions like Hartmann et al. (2019). Thus, outcomes of lexicon-based approaches are often taken at face value, without knowing how they compare to human attributions. While some researchers dispute the effectiveness of lexicon-based approaches (Kross et al., 2019; Johnson and Goldwasser, 2018), there are others who found that such approaches are helpful on their own (Do and Choi, 2015), or that classification performance increases with the addition of features from such approaches (Sawhney et al., 2018; Pamungkas and Patti, 2018). Additionally, most work on writer's intentions focuses on basic emotions only (Yang et al., 2018; Chen et al., 2018; Yu et al., 2018). Thus, LIWC's wide range of psychology-related label detection is presently not matched by others.

Proceedings of the 2019 EMNLP Workshop W-NUT: The 5th Workshop on Noisy User-generated Text, pages 94–100
Hong Kong, Nov 4, 2019. ©2019 Association for Computational Linguistics

The social media domain, which the online dating domain (hereafter: dating profiles) is part of, might be challenging for LIWC, since these texts often contain non-standard language and noise. LIWC may nevertheless be a viable tool for analyzing dating profiles. Previous research has found that intended relationship goals are related to psychological traits (Feeney and Noller, 1990; Peter and Valkenburg, 2007), and that dating profiles can contain information about a writer's psychological and mental states (Ellison et al., 2006). This underlying psychological layer is something that may be exploited by LIWC, since previous research found that the tool can expose such psychological and mental states from linguistic behavior (Tausczik and Pennebaker, 2010; Van der Zanden et al., 2019).

The goal of the current study was to assess the effectiveness and predictive ability of LIWC on a relationship goal classification task. For this, LIWC was compared to human judgment and machine learning approaches in three steps. First, the quality of LIWC's content-related labels was assessed by comparing the values given to content-related labels to those of humans and a regression model. Second, the meaningfulness of LIWC's dictionary was investigated by using the label values as features for a classification model that predicts relationship type, contrasting these results with the predictions of humans and a classification model using word features. Third, a qualitative evaluation based on topic models, Gini Importance scores, and log-likelihood ratios was conducted to find limitations of LIWC's lexicon.

2 Method

2.1 Corpus

Corpus	Long-term			Date		
	Texts	Tokens	Types	Texts	Tokens	Types
Full	10,696	863,227	32,020	1,634	127,644	11,274
Train+val	1,464	117,947	9,973	1,464	115,227	10,540
Test	150	11,886	2,383	150	11,738	2,592

Table 1: Descriptives of the dating profile corpus

A total sample of 12,310 dating profiles together with the indicated desired relationship goal was collected from a popular Dutch dating site (see Table 1). These profiles were anonymized after collection, and were between 50 and 100 words, written in Dutch ($M = 80.36$ words, $SD = 14.56$).

Ethical clearance was obtained from the university for the collection of the dating profiles and the use for further text analysis. The (anonymized) corpus itself and the results from the human evaluation are available upon request.

2.2 LIWC

LIWC 2015 (Pennebaker et al., 2015) was used for the experiments, with the Dutch lexicon by Van Wissen and Boot (2017). This Dutch version of LIWC is of similar size as the English version and the scores have been found to correlate well with those of its English counterpart when tested on parallel corpora (Van Wissen and Boot, 2017). LIWC works by iterating over all words and multi-word phrases in a text and checking whether the word or phrase is in the predefined lexicon of one or more labels. There are 70 labels in total. LIWC outputs percentage scores. For example, if 8% of words are an I-reference, the I-reference score would be 8.

2.3 Human Evaluation

In this study, 152 university students participated (68% female, mean age = 21.8 years). For their voluntary participation they received course credit. Altogether, these participants rated a random sample of 300 profile texts (test set in Table 1). Each participant judged six texts in total: 3 texts where the indicated goal was a long-term relationship, and 3 texts where this goal was a date. Approximately three judgments for each of the 300 profile texts were obtained.

Participants rated the degree to which the profile writer discussed six topics which were deemed important for dating profiles based on previous research (status, physical appearance, positive emotion, I-references, you-references, we-references; see Appendix A) (Davis and Fingerman, 2016; Groom and Pennebaker, 2005; Van der Zanden et al., 2019). These ratings were done on six items, all 7-point Likert scales ("To what degree is the writer of the text talking about: status related qualities (e.g., job, achievements), physical qualities (e.g., height, build), positive emotions, themself (use of 'I'), the reader (use of 'you'), a group the writer belongs to (use of 'we')", ranging from "low degree" to "high degree"). The judgments were used as a baseline for the label assignment task. Furthermore, participants indicated whether they thought the profile text writer sought for a long-term relationship or a date (Krippendorff's α

Method	Status	Physical appearance	Positive emotion	I	You	We
LIWC	.42**	.20**	**.30****	**.45****	.44**	.36**
Regression	.51**	.13*	**.13***	**.31****	.37**	.29**

Table 2: Pearson's r compared to humans. Vertically aligned bold values differ significantly. *$p < .05$, ** $p < .001$.

Metric	Human	LIWC	Word	Meta
Precision	0.55	0.54	**0.61**	**0.61**
Recall	0.67	**0.87**	0.65	0.65
F1	0.60	**0.67**	0.63	0.63
Accuracy	0.57	0.56	**0.62**	**0.62**

Table 3: Accuracy scores by humans and classification models. Bold indicates highest score on metric.

= 0.24). These predictions were used as a baseline for the relationship goal classification task. Additionally, participants were asked to highlight the words in the text on which they based their long-term or date prediction. All marked words were then collected and counted for the qualitative analysis.

2.4 Label Assignment Task

The goal of this task was to evaluate the similarity of labels from lexicon-based and machine learning approaches compared to a human baseline. The output of LIWC was limited to the six labels discussed in Section 2.3. The 300 dating profiles evaluated in the human evaluation task were rated by LIWC for fair comparison.

The same 300 texts were also used (with random ten-fold cross-validation) for the regression model. This model was trained to give continuous scores on the six text labels. Word features were chosen for fair comparison, since LIWC is word-based and humans also tend to analyze texts at word, phrase, or sentence level (Marsi and Krahmer, 2005). TheilSenRegressor was the regression algorithm used (see Appendix B for details).

2.5 Relationship Goal Identification Task

With this task, the meaningfulness of the lexicons used by LIWC to capture writers' relationship goals was investigated and compared to the feature sets that humans and machine learning approaches use. To do so, three classification models were used. One classification model used LIWC's label scores on the aforementioned six labels as features. The second classification model used word features. Furthermore, a meta-classifier was trained on the probability scores of the classification model with LIWC features and the model with word features. This was done to investigate if LIWC and word features use different facets of a text to distinguish between relationship goals. If so, pooling them together could achieve some kind of synergy, resulting in higher accuracy scores.

A total of 3,228 texts (1,614 texts for each relationship group; see Table 1) was used for training and testing. This sample was randomly stratified on gender, age and education level based on the distribution of the group of date seekers. For the classification models, the text was trained using 2,635 texts and validated on 293 texts. Finally, to enable fair comparison between methods, the model was tested on the 300 texts rated by humans. While this test dataset is relatively small, only minor differences were found between accuracy scores when trained on the full dataset using ten-fold cross-validation (approximately 1-2%). Thus, the test set was sufficiently large to obtain relatively stable results. Furthermore, a test was done using Dutch word2vec word-embeddings pre-trained on the COW corpus (Řehůřek and Sojka, 2010; Tulkens et al., 2016) for the classification model with word features, but this did not lead to an increase of accuracy scores. For all classification models, an LSTM network with eight layers was used (see Appendix B for details).

2.6 Qualitative analysis

A qualitative analysis of the output on the relationship goal identification task was performed to analyze possible shortcomings of LIWC's lexicon. Indicative words for identification according to Gini Importance scores obtained with XGBoost were compared to LIWC's lexicon (Breiman et al., 1984). Furthermore, LIWC's lexicon was compared to indicative words according to humans and according to log-likelihood ratio scores (Dunning, 1993). Labels from LIWC were also compared with topics obtained by topic modeling (see Appendix B).

3 Results

3.1 Label Assignment Task

For the label assignment task, the performance of LIWC and the regression model were measured using (two-tailed) Pearson's r. Results show that

Topic name	Words
Person characteristics	I, humor, good, man, honest, sportive, like, social, sometimes, sweet, spontaneous, woman, positive, little bit, open, stubborn, especially, reliable, human, happy
Self-disclosure	I, you, none, much, say, come, good, something, myself, human, find, become, we, think, sit, always, see, sometime, other
Being together	I, you, want, woman, someone, together, man, sweet, find, know, with, you, good, each other, relationship, spontaneous, cozy, go, where, come
Family and occupation	I, LOCATION, PERSON, reside, year, name, visit, ORGANISATION, work, child, you, come, MISCELLANEOUS, go, time, since, like, old
Named entities, English, and Misc.	*pro*, MISCELLANEOUS, LOCATION, PERSON, *you*, *the*, ORGANIZATION, *to*, *a*, none, *and*, *à*, *what*, *I*, *one*, *life*, rather, music, EVENT, *my*
Nature and hobbies	I, like, find, nice, go, friend, eat, movie, cozy, time, watch, couch, delightful, walk, evening, day, good, make, enjoy, music

Table 4: Translated topic models with assigned topic names.

both LIWC and the regression model correlate significantly with human behavior for all six investigated labels. This suggests that LIWC and a regression model can obtain label scores similar to humans. However, it should be noted that the correlation coefficients are relatively low (ranging from .13 to .51), which indicates a weak to moderate relationship between the regression models and human judgments.

Fishers r to z transformation was employed to investigate whether the strength of the correlation with humans differed significantly between LIWC scores and word-based regression scores. Overall, LIWC performed better on this task: the correlation for LIWC on positive emotions ($p = .03$) as well as I-references ($p = .05$) was significantly stronger than the correlation scores for the regression model on these labels (see Table 2). This indicates that LIWC scores are more similar to the label scores of human annotators (at least for positive emotions and I-references) than the scores of the regression model.

3.2 Relationship Goal Identification Task

For the intended relationship goal identification task, chi-square tests were performed on the predictions for all different methods, to compare them to chance and to each other. All methods turned out to perform better than chance (humans: $\chi^2(1) = 17.58$, $p < .001$; word-based classifier: $\chi^2(1) = 17.28$, $p < .001$; classifier with LIWC features: $\chi^2(1) = 5.33$, $p = .02$; meta-classifier: $\chi^2(1) = 17.28$, $p < .001$). These results suggest that humans, LIWC, and a word-based regression model are similarly accurate in identifying a writer's relationship goal. This was further corroborated by a 4 (text analysis method) x 2 (correct vs. incorrect judgments) not significant chi-square test ($\chi^2(3) = 4.22$, $p = .24$), meaning that there was no method that performed significantly better than any other

method (see Table 3).

Accuracy for the meta-classifiers did not increase for the relationship goal identification task. The accuracy score of the meta-classifier was the same as the word-based classifier, which suggests that LIWC features and word features pick up on the same aspects of the text. Since the classification model with word features performed slightly better, the meta-classifier likely learns to focus on the probability scores of that model.

3.3 Qualitative Analysis

With all 70 labels, LIWC manages to capture only 15% of the types in the dating profile texts, which suggests that a substantial amount of information is not captured by the approach. Information that is missing are words such as 'date', 'profile', 'click', and 'friendship' (all $\chi^2(1) >= 5.39$, and $p <= .02$): important relationship-related words, and good discriminators according to the word-based classification model, humans, and log-likelihood ratio. This illustrates that LIWC was not necessarily built with dating profiles in mind.

Distinctive words like 'spontaneous' ($\chi^2(1) = 0.13$, $p = .72$, but distinctive according to humans and Gini Importances), 'caring', 'quiet', 'honest', and 'sweet' (all $\chi^2(1) >= 7.18$, and $p <= .007$) show that LIWC is missing a person characteristics category. Topic modeling also found a personality traits topic, further emphasizing the importance of this label. Similarly, words like 'sea' and 'nature' (both $\chi^2(1) >= 5.99$ and $p = .01$), and a nature-related topic model shows that a nature-focused label is important to distinguish relationship goals, which LIWC is currently lacking (see Table 4 and Table 5).

However, while there are some systematic patterns to be found regarding what LIWC is not capturing, do note that LIWC's scores on the two tasks were similar to machine learning and to humans. This suggests that the relatively small percentage of word types that LIWC is processing is meaningful. The top 100 most important features according to log likelihood ratios, humans, and Gini Importances corroborates this suggestion. 62% of the top 100 most important words according to log likelihood ratios are found in LIWC, 81% of the top 100 most important words according to humans, and 90% of the top 100 most important words according to Gini Importances.

Method	Important features
Human	seek, date, nice, know, people, undertake, spontaneous, sweet, terrace, pretty, enjoy, child wish, family person
Classifier	date, spontaneous, let, live, nature, sociable, send, build, exercise, nice, independent, again, friendship, sea, girl, terrace
LLR	quiet, sweet, nothing, nature, fetch, again, profile, click, feel free, weekend, sea, people, visit, caring

Table 5: Translated words not in LIWC's lexicon ordered by importance for relationship goal identification. Blue is indicative of long-term, red is indicative of date

4 Discussion

In this study, a lexicon-based text analysis method (LIWC) was compared to machine learning approaches (regression, classification model), with human judgment scores as a baseline. Lexicon-based methods are criticized because they may not capture complex elements of language and do not discriminate between domains. Still, research often takes the outcomes of these approaches at face value without assessing whether they accurately reflect reality. This study aimed to address these issues using three tasks: (1) assigning content-related labels to texts, (2) predicting intended relationship goals, and (3) comparing the output of the different approaches with a qualitative study. While (1) was used to investigate if LIWC's labels reflect reality, (2) and (3) aimed to elucidate if LIWC's labels are sufficient to highlight differences in intended relationship goals. The three tasks were conducted on a newly collected corpus of online dating profiles.

The results of this study show that LIWC is a viable text analysis method for these tasks. Despite the fact that it uses a fixed word list and therefore might miss context and out-of-vocabulary words, it performed similarly to machine learning methods and humans. The label assignment task showed that the labels of LIWC and the regression model both correlated with the labels assigned by humans. Furthermore, for some labels, LIWC's scores corresponded more to human judgments than those of the regression model. This suggests that LIWC's lexicon was chosen meaningfully and that despite its limitations, it seems to be good at exposing textual themes. This is corroborated by the fact that most of the important words according to Gini Importances, log likelihood ratio, and humans were in LIWC's lexicon.

However, it should be noted that the sample size for this task was small (300 texts), and that results could be different if there was more training data. Relationship goal prediction turned out to be a difficult task (low accuracy scores overall, and low inter-rater agreement). Thus, future research should look into extending the human evaluation dataset with more texts and judgments per text. Nevertheless, humans and all classification models scored similarly on accuracy and performed above chance, suggesting that LIWC does cover categorical differences between long-term relationship and date seekers, although LIWC seems to pick up on the same signal as the word-based classification model. Results from the qualitative analysis show that the categories in LIWC might not be sufficient to cover the full range of categorical linguistic differences between the two groups. These shortcomings might be addressed by novel approaches that aim to combine dictionaries with neural text analysis methods, such as Empath (Fast et al., 2016). Or by extending neural Emotion Classification and Emotion Cause Detection systems like (Yang et al., 2018; Chen et al., 2018; Yu et al., 2018) to cover more psychology-relevant categories. Using novel pre-trained word-embeddings such as BERT (Devlin et al., 2019) could also boost the results for the current approach, as this has improved results for many tasks.

The focus of this study on the intended relationship goals of online daters was a challenge that had not been investigated in previous computational linguistics research. We must note that this is just one example of a task for which LIWC could be used. Studies have shown that LIWC may be less suited for some tasks, such as sentiment analysis (Hartmann et al., 2019). However, the current results indicate that it can be a viable method for tasks that tend to look at other, deeper, psychological constructs.

Acknowledgements

We received support from RAAK-PRO SIA (2014-01-51PRO) and The Netherlands Organization for Scientific Research (NWO 360-89-050), which is gratefully acknowledged. We would also like to thank the anonymous reviewers for their valuable and insightful comments.

References

Bing Bai. 2017. LSTM with word2vec embeddings.

L. Breiman, J. H. Friedman, R. A. Olshen, and C. J. Stone. 1984. *Classification and Regression Trees*. Wadsworth and Brooks, Monterey, CA.

Ying Chen, Wenjun Hou, Xiyao Cheng, and Shoushan Li. 2018. Joint learning for emotion classification and emotion cause detection. In *Proceedings of the 2018 Conference on Empirical Methods in Natural Language Processing*, pages 646–651.

François Chollet et al. 2015. Keras.

Xin Dang, Hanxiang Peng, Xueqin Wang, and Heping Zhang. 2008. Theil-sen estimators in a multiple linear regression model. *Olemiss Edu*.

Eden M Davis and Karen L Fingerman. 2016. Digital dating: Online profile content of older and younger adults. *Journals of Gerontology Series B: Psychological Sciences and Social Sciences*, 71(6):959–967.

Jacob Devlin, Ming-Wei Chang, Kenton Lee, and Kristina Toutanova. 2019. BERT: Pre-training of deep bidirectional transformers for language understanding. In *Proceedings of the 2019 Conference of the North American Chapter of the Association for Computational Linguistics: Human Language Technologies, Volume 1 (Long and Short Papers)*, pages 4171–4186, Minneapolis, Minnesota. Association for Computational Linguistics.

Hyo Jin Do and Ho-Jin Choi. 2015. Korean Twitter emotion classification using automatically built emotion lexicons and fine-grained features. In *Proceedings of the 29th Pacific Asia Conference on Language, Information and Computation: Posters*, pages 142–150.

Ted Dunning. 1993. Accurate methods for the statistics of surprise and coincidence. *Computational Linguistics*, 19(1):61–74.

Nicole Ellison, Rebecca Heino, and Jennifer Gibbs. 2006. Managing impressions online: Self-presentation processes in the online dating environment. *Journal of Computer-Mediated Communication*, 11(2):415–441.

Ethan Fast, Binbin Chen, and Michael S Bernstein. 2016. Empath: Understanding topic signals in large-scale text. In *Proceedings of the 2016 CHI Conference on Human Factors in Computing Systems*, pages 4647–4657. ACM.

Judith A Feeney and Patricia Noller. 1990. Attachment style as a predictor of adult romantic relationships. *Journal of Personality and Social Psychology*, 58(2):281–291.

Emma Franklin. 2015. Some theoretical considerations in off-the-shelf text analysis software. In *Proceedings of the Student Research Workshop associated with RANLP 2015*, pages 8–15.

Carla J Groom and James W Pennebaker. 2005. The language of love: Sex, sexual orientation, and language use in online personal advertisements. *Sex Roles*, 52(7-8):447–461.

Jochen Hartmann, Juliana Huppertz, Christina Schamp, and Mark Heitmann. 2019. Comparing automated text classification methods. *International Journal of Research in Marketing*, 36(1):20–38.

Sepp Hochreiter and Jürgen Schmidhuber. 1997. Long short-term memory. *Neural Computation*, 9(8):1735–1780.

Kristen Johnson and Dan Goldwasser. 2018. Classification of moral foundations in microblog political discourse. In *Proceedings of the 56th Annual Meeting of the Association for Computational Linguistics (Volume 1: Long Papers)*, pages 720–730.

Ethan Kross, Philippe Verduyn, Margaret Boyer, Brittany Drake, Izzy Gainsburg, Brian Vickers, Oscar Ybarra, and John Jonides. 2019. Does counting emotion words on online social networks provide a window into peoples subjective experience of emotion? A case study on Facebook. *Emotion*, 19(1):97–107.

Erwin Marsi and Emiel Krahmer. 2005. Classification of semantic relations by humans and machines. In *Proceedings of the ACL workshop on Empirical Modeling of Semantic Equivalence and Entailment*, pages 1–6. Association for Computational Linguistics.

Andrew K McCallum. 2002. *MALLET: A machine learning for language toolkit*. http://mallet.cs.umass.edu.

Endang Wahyu Pamungkas and Viviana Patti. 2018. Exploiting emojis and affective content for irony detection in English tweets. In *International Workshop on Semantic Evaluation*, pages 649–654. Association for Computational Linguistics.

Galen Panger. 2016. Reassessing the Facebook experiment: Critical thinking about the validity of Big Data research. *Information, Communication & Society*, 19(8):1108–1126.

James W Pennebaker, Roger J Booth, and Martha E Francis. 2015. *Linguistic Inquiry and Word Count: LIWC2015*. http://www.liwc.net Pennebaker Conglomerates, Austin, TX.

Jochen Peter and Patti M Valkenburg. 2007. Who looks for casual dates on the internet? A test of the compensation and the recreation hypotheses. *New Media & Society*, 9(3):455–474.

Radim Řehůřek and Petr Sojka. 2010. Software Framework for Topic Modelling with Large Corpora. In *Proceedings of the LREC 2010 Workshop on New Challenges for NLP Frameworks*, pages 45–50, Valletta, Malta. ELRA.

Daniel Riffe, Stephen Lacy, and Frederick Fico. 2014. *Analyzing media messages: Using quantitative content analysis in research*. Routledge.

Ramit Sawhney, Prachi Manchanda, Raj Singh, and Swati Aggarwal. 2018. A computational approach to feature extraction for identification of suicidal ideation in tweets. In *Proceedings of ACL 2018, Student Research Workshop*, pages 91–98.

Hansen Andrew Schwartz, Johannes Eichstaedt, Eduardo Blanco, Lukasz Dziurzyński, Margaret L Kern, Stephanie Ramones, Martin Seligman, and Lyle Ungar. 2013. Choosing the right words: Characterizing and reducing error of the word count approach. In *Proceedings of the Second Joint Conference on Lexical and Computational Semantics*, volume 1, pages 296–305.

Jasper Snoek, Hugo Larochelle, and Ryan P Adams. 2012. Practical bayesian optimization of machine learning algorithms. In *Advances in neural information processing systems*, pages 2951–2959.

Yla R Tausczik and James W Pennebaker. 2010. The psychological meaning of words: LIWC and computerized text analysis methods. *Journal of Language and Social Psychology*, 29(1):24–54.

Laure Thompson and David Mimno. 2018. Authorless topic models: Biasing models away from known structure. In *Proceedings of the 27th International Conference on Computational Linguistics*, pages 3903–3914.

Stephan Tulkens, Chris Emmery, and Walter Daelemans. 2016. Evaluating unsupervised Dutch word embeddings as a linguistic resource. In *Proceedings of the 10th International Conference on Language Resources and Evaluation*, Paris, France. European Language Resources Association.

Leon Van Wissen and Peter Boot. 2017. An electronic translation of the LIWC dictionary into Dutch. In *Proceedings of eLex 2017 conference*, pages 703–715.

Yang Yang, Zhou Deyu, and Yulan He. 2018. An interpretable neural network with topical information for relevant emotion ranking. In *Proceedings of the 2018 Conference on Empirical Methods in Natural Language Processing*, pages 3423–3432.

Jianfei Yu, Luis Marujo, Jing Jiang, Pradeep Karuturi, and William Brendel. 2018. Improving multi-label emotion classification via sentiment classification with dual attention transfer network. In *Proceedings of the 2018 Conference on Empirical Methods in Natural Language Processing*, pages 1097–1102.

Tess Van der Zanden, Alexander P Schouten, Maria Mos, Chris Van der Lee, and Emiel Krahmer. 2019. Effects of relationship goal on linguistic behavior in online dating profiles: A multi-method approach. *Frontiers in Communication*, pages 1–30.

Contextualized Word Representations from Distant Supervision with and for NER

Abbas Ghaddar
RALI-DIRO
Université de Montréal
Montréal, Canada
abbas.ghaddar@umontreal.ca

Philippe Langlais
RALI-DIRO
Université de Montréal
Montréal, Canada
felipe@iro.umontreal.ca

Abstract

We describe a special type of deep contextualized word representation that is *learned from* distant supervision annotations and *dedicated to* named entity recognition. Our extensive experiments on 7 datasets show systematic gains across all domains over strong baselines, and demonstrate that our representation is complementary to previously proposed embeddings. We report new state-of-the-art results on CoNLL and ONTONOTES datasets.

1 Introduction

Contextualized word representations are nowadays a resource of choice for most NLP tasks (Peters et al., 2018). These representations are trained with unsupervised language modelling (Jozefowicz et al., 2016), masked-word prediction (Devlin et al., 2018), or supervised objectives like machine translation (McCann et al., 2017). Despite their strength, best performances on downstream tasks (Akbik et al., 2018; Lee et al., 2018; He et al., 2018) are always obtained when these representations are stacked with traditional (classic) word embeddings (Mikolov et al., 2013; Pennington et al., 2014).

Our main contribution in this work is to revisit the work of Ghaddar and Langlais (2018a) that explores distant supervision for learning *classic* word representations, used later as features for Named Entity Recognition (NER). Motivated by the recent success of pre-trained language model embeddings, we propose a contextualized word representation trained on the distant supervision material made available by the authors. We do so by training a model to predict the entity type of each word in a given sequence (e.g. paragraph).

We run extensive experiments feeding our representation, along side with previously proposed traditional and contextualized ones, as features to a vanilla Bi-LSTM-CRF (Ma and Hovy, 2016). Results shows that our contextualized representation leads to significant boost in performances on 7 NER datasets of various sizes and domains. The proposed representation surpasses the one of Ghaddar and Langlais (2018a) and is complementary to popular contextualized embeddings like ELMo (Peters et al., 2018).

By simply stacking various representations, we report new state-of the-art performances on CoNLL-2003 (Tjong Kim Sang and De Meulder, 2003) and ONTONOTES 5.0 (Pradhan et al., 2013) with a F1 score of 93.22 and 89.95 respectively.

2 Related Work

Pre-trained contextualized word-embeddings have shown great success in NLP due to their ability to capture both syntactic and semantic properties. ELMo representations (Peters et al., 2018) are built from internal states of forward and backward word-level language models. Akbik et al. (2018) showed that pure character-level language models can also be used. Also, McCann et al. (2017) used the encoder of a machine translation model to compute contextualized representations. Recently, (Devlin et al., 2018) proposed BERT, an encoder based on the Transformer architecture (Vaswani et al., 2017). To overcome the unidirectionality of the language model objective, the authors propose two novel tasks for unsupervised learning: masked words and next sentence prediction.

Ghaddar and Langlais (2018a) applied distant supervision (Mintz et al., 2009) in order to induce traditional word representations. They used WiFiNE[1] (Ghaddar and Langlais, 2018b, 2017), a Wikipedia dump with massive amount of automatically annotated entities, using the fine-grained

---

[1] http://rali.iro.umontreal.ca/rali/en/ wikipedia-lex-sim

Proceedings of the 2019 EMNLP Workshop W-NUT: The 5th Workshop on Noisy User-generated Text, pages 101–108
Hong Kong, Nov 4, 2019. ©2019 Association for Computational Linguistics

tagset proposed in (Ling and Weld, 2012). Making use of Fasttext (Bojanowski et al., 2016), they embedded words and (noisy) entity types in this resource into the same space from which they induced a 120-dimensional word-representation, where each dimension encodes the similarity of a word with one of the 120 types they considered. While the authors claim the resulting representation captures contextual information, they do not specifically train it to do so. Our work revisits precisely this.

3   Data and Preprocessing

We leverage the entity type annotations in WiFiNE which consists of 1.3B tokens annotated with 159.4M mentions, which cover 15% of the tokens. A significant amount of named entities such as person names and countries can actually be resolved via their mention tokens only (Ghaddar and Langlais, 2016a,b). With the hope to enforce context, we use the fine-grained type annotation available in the resource (e.g. /person/politician). Also, inspired by the recent success of masked-word prediction (Devlin et al., 2018), we further apply preprocessing to the original annotations by (a) replacing an entity by a special token [MASK] with a probability of 0.2, and (b) replacing primary entity mentions, e.g. all mentions of *Barack Obama* within its dedicated article, by the special mask token with a probability of 0.5. In WiFiNE, named-entities that do not have a Wikipedia article (e.g. *Malia Ann* in Figure 2) are left unannotated, which introduces false negatives. Therefore, we mask non-entity words when we calculate the loss.

Although contextualized representation learning has access to arbitrary large contexts (e.g. the document), in practice representations mainly depend on sentence level context (Chang et al., 2019). To overcome this limitation to some extent, we use the Wikipedia layout provided in WiFiNE to concatenate sentences of the same paragraphs, sections and document up to a maximum size of 512 tokens.

An illustration of the preprocessing is depicted in Figure 2 where for the sake of space, a single sentence is being showed. Masked entities encourage the model to learn good representations for non-entity words even if they do not participate in the final loss. Because our examples are sections and paragraphs, the model will be forced to encode sentence- as well as document-based context. In addition, training on (longer) paragraphs is much faster and memory efficient than batching sentences.

4   Learning our Representation

We use a model (Figure 1) composed of a multi-layer bidirectional encoder that produces hidden states for each token in the input sequence. At the output layer, the last hidden states are fed into a softmax layer for predicting entity types. Following (Strubell et al., 2017), we used as our encoder the Dilated Convolutional Neural Network (DCNN) with an exponential increasing dilated width. DCNN was first proposed by (Yu and Koltun, 2015) for image segmentation, and was successfully deployed for NER by (Strubell et al., 2017). The authors show that stacked layers of DCNN that incorporate document context have comparable performance to Bi-LSTM while being 8 times faster. DCNN with a size 3 convolution window needs 8 stacked layers to incorporate the entire input context of a sequence of 512 tokens, compared to 255 layers using a regular CNN. This greatly reduces the number of parameters and makes training more scalable and efficient. Because our examples are paragraphs rather than sentences, we employ a self-attention mechanism on top of DCNN output with the aim to encourage the model to focus on salient global information. In this paper, we adopt the multi-head self-attention formulation by Vaswani et al. (2017). Comparatively, Transformer-based architectures (Devlin et al., 2018) require a much larger[2] amount of resources and computations. To improve the handling of rare and unknown words, our input sequence consists of WordPiece embeddings (Wu et al., 2016) as used by Devlin et al. (2018); Radford et al. (2018). We use the same vocabulary distributed by the authors, as it was originally learned on Wikipedia. Model parameters and training details are provided in Appendix A.1.

5   Experiments on NER

5.1   Datasets

To compare with state-of-the-art models, we consider two well-established NER benchmarks: CoNLL-2003 (Tjong Kim Sang and De Meulder, 2003) and ONTONOTES 5.0 (Pradhan et al., 2012).

---

[2]Actually prohibitive with our single GPU computer.

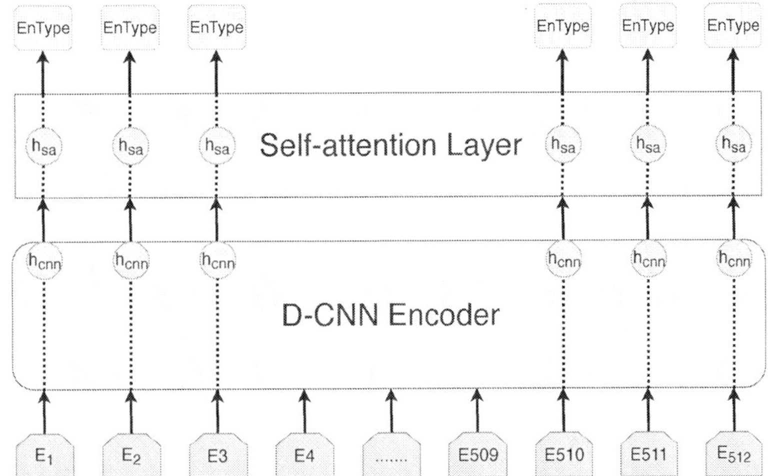

Figure 1: Illustration of the architecture of the model used for learning our representation. It consists of stacked layers of dilated convolutional neural network followed by a self-attention layer. The input is a sequence of tokens with a maximum length of 512, where the output is the associated entity type sequence. We use the hidden state of the last DCNN layer and the self-attention layer as our representation.

before	*[Obama]* first daughter, Malia Ann, was born in *[July 1998]* at *[Chicago]*, *[Illinois]*.
after	*[MASK]* first daughter, Malia Ann, was born in *[July 1998]* at *[Chicago]*, *[Illinois]*.
tags	`/person/politician X X X X X X X X /date /date X /location/city X /location/province X`

Figure 2: Sequence before and after masking, along with output tags. X indicates that no prediction is made for the corresponding token.

To further determine how useful our learned representation is on other domains, we also considered three additional datasets: WNUT17 (Derczynski et al., 2017) (social media), I2B2 (Stubbs and Uzuner, 2015) (biomedical), and FIN (Alvarado et al., 2015) (financial). In addition, we perform an out-domain evaluation for models trained on CoNLL-2003 and tested on WIKIGOLD (Balasuriya et al., 2009) (wikipedia) and WEB-PAGES (Ratinov and Roth, 2009) (web pages). Statistics of the datasets are provided in Appendix A.2.

5.2 Input Representations

Our NER model is a vanilla Bi-LSTM-CRF (Ma and Hovy, 2016) that we feed with various representations (hereafter described) at the input layer. Model parameters and training details are provided in Appendix A.3.

5.2.1 Word-Shape Features

We use 7 word-shape features: `allUpper`, `allLower`, `upperFirst`, `upperNotFirst`, `numeric`, `punctuation` or `noAlphaNum`. We randomly allocate a 25-dimensional vector for each feature, and learn them during training.

5.2.2 Traditional Word Embeddings

We use the 100-dimensional case sensitive SSKIP (Ling et al., 2015) word embeddings. We also compare with the previously described 120-dimensional vector representation of (Ghaddar and Langlais, 2018a), they call it LS.

5.2.3 Contextualized Word Embeddings

We tested 3 publicly available contextualized word representations: ELMo (Peters et al., 2018): $dim = 1024$, $layers = 3$; FLAIR (Akbik et al., 2018): $d = 2048$, $l = 1$; and BERT (Devlin et al., 2018): $d = 1024$, $l = 4$. For the latter, we use the hidden state of the 4 last layers of the `Large` model. For the proposed representation, we use the hidden state of the last DCNN layer and the self-attention layer as feature input ($d = 384$, $l = 2$). Following Peters et al. (2018), each representation (including ours) is the weighted sum of the hidden layers, where weights are learned

	Conll			Ontonotes		
	$\mathcal{X}$	LS	ours	$\mathcal{X}$	LS	ours
ws+sskip	90.37	91.23 (+0.9)	91.76 (+1.4)	86.44	87.95 (+0.9)	88.13 (+0.9)
ws+sskip+elmo	92.47	92.49 (+0.0)	92.82 (+0.4)	89.37	89.44 (+0.1)	89.68 (+0.3)
ws+sskip+elmo+flair	92.69	92.75 (+0.1)	**93.22 (+0.5)**	89.55	89.59 (+0.0)	89.73 (+0.2)
ws+sskip+elmo+flair+bert	92.91	92.87 (+0.0)	93.01 (+0.1)	89.66	89.70 (+0.0)	**89.95 (+0.3)**
(Peters et al., 2018)	92.20			-		
(Clark et al., 2018)	92.61			88.81		
(Devlin et al., 2018)	92.80			-		

Table 1: F1 scores over five runs on CoNLL and OntoNotes test set of ablation experiments. We evaluate 4 baselines without additional embeddings (column $\mathcal{X}$) and with LS embeddings (Ghaddar and Langlais, 2018a) or ours. Figures in parenthesis indicate the gain over the baselines.

during training. We use concatenation to stack the resulting representations in the input layer of our vanilla Bi-LSTM-CRF model, since Coates and Bollegala (2018) show that concatenation performs reasonably well in many NLP tasks.

6 Experiments

6.1 Comparison to LS embeddings

Since we used the very same distant supervision material for training our contextual representation, we compare it to the one of Ghaddar and Langlais (2018a). We concentrate on CoNLL-2003 and OntoNotes 5.0, the datasets most often used for benchmarking NER systems.

Table 1 reports results of 4 strong baselines that use popular embeddings (column $\mathcal{X}$), further adding either the LS representation (Ghaddar and Langlais, 2018a) or ours. In all experiments, we report the results on the test portion of models performing the best on the official development set of each dataset. As a point of comparison, we also report 2018 state-of-the-art systems.

First we observe that adding our representation to all baseline models leads to systematic improvements, even for the very strong baseline which exploits all three contextual representations (fourth line). The LS representation does not deliver such gains, which demonstrates that our way of exploiting the very same distant supervision material is more efficient. Second, we see that adding our representation to the weakest baseline (line 1), while giving a significant boost, does not deliver as good performance as when adding other contextual embeddings. Nevertheless, combining all embeddings yields state-of-the-art on both CoNLL and OntoNotes.

6.2 Comparing Contextualized Embeddings

Table 2 reports F1 scores on the test portion of the 7 datasets we considered, for models trained with different embedding combinations. Our baseline is composed of word-shape and traditional (SSKIP) embeddings. Then, contextualized word representations are added greedily, that is, the representation that yields the largest gain when considered is added first and so forth.

Expectedly, ELMo is the best representation to add to the baseline configuration, with significant F1 gains for all test sets. We are pleased to observe that the next best representation to consider is ours, significantly outperforming FLAIR. This is likely due to the fact that both FLAIR and ELMo embeddings are obtained by training a language model, therefore encoding similar information.

Continuously aggregating other contextual embeddings (FLAIR and BERT) leads to some improvements on some datasets, and degradations on others. In particular, stacking all representations leads to the best performance on 2 datasets only: OntoNotes and I2B2. Those datasets are large, domain diversified, and have more tags than other ones. In any case, stacking word-shapes, SSKIP, ELMo and our representation leads to a strong configuration across all datasets. Adding our representation to ELMo, actually brings noticeable gains (over 2 absolute F1 points) in out-domain settings, a very positive outcome.

Surprisingly, BERT did not perform as we expected, since they bring minor (OntoNotes) or no (CoNLL) improvement. We tried to reproduce the results of fine-tuned and feature-based approaches reported by the authors on CoNLL,

	In Domain					Out Domain	
	Conll	**Onto**	**WNUT**	**Fin**	**I2B2**	**WikiGold**	**WebPage**
WS+SSKIP	90.73	86.44	32.30	81.82	86.41	66.03	45.13
+ELMo	92.47	89.37	44.15	82.03	94.47	76.34	54.45
+Ours	92.96	89.68	**47.40**	83.00	94.75	**78.51**	**57.23**
+Flair	**93.22**	89.73	46.80	**83.11**	94.79	77.77	56.20
+Bert	93.02	**89.97**	46.47	81.94	**94.92**	78.06	56.84

Table 2: Mention-level F1 scores. The baseline (first line) uses word shape and traditional (classic) embeddings. Variants stacking various representations are presented in decreasing order of F1 return. So for instance, ELMo is the best representation to add to the baseline one.

but as many others,[3] our results were disappointing.

6.3 Analysis

We suspect one reason for the success of our representation is that it captures document wise context. We inspected the words the most attended according to the the self-attention layer of some documents, an excerpt of which is reported in Figure 3. We observe that attended words in the document are often related to the topic of the document.

84	economic	*Stock, mark, Wall, Treasury, bond*
148	sport	*World, team, record, game, win*
201	news	*truck, Fire, store, hospital, arms*

Figure 3: top 5 attended words for some randomly picked documents in the dev set of CoNLL. Column 1 indicate document number, while column 2 is our appreciation of the document topic.

We further checked whether the gain could be imputable to the fact that WiFiNE contains the mentions that appear in the test sets we considered. While this of course happens (for instance 38% of the test mentions in OntoNotes are in the resource), the performance on those mentions with our representation is no better than the performance on other mentions.

7 Conclusion and Future Work

We have explored the idea of generating a contextualized word representation from distant supervision annotations coming from Wikipedia, improving over the static representation of Ghaddar and Langlais (2018a). When combined with popular contextual ones, our representation leads to state-of-the-art performance on both CoNLL and OntoNotes. We are currently analyzing the complementarity of our representation to others.

We plan to investigate tasks such as coreference resolution and non-extractive machine reading comprehension, where document level context and entity type information is crucial. The source code and the pre-trained models we used in this work are publicly available at `http://rali.iro.umontreal.ca/rali/en/wikipedia-ds-cont-emb`

Acknowledgments

We gratefully acknowledge the support of NVIDIA Corporation with the donation of the Titan Xp and Titan V GPUs used for this research. We thank the anonymous reviewers for their insightful comments.

References

Martín Abadi, Ashish Agarwal, Paul Barham, Eugene Brevdo, Zhifeng Chen, Craig Citro, Greg S Corrado, Andy Davis, Jeffrey Dean, Matthieu Devin, et al. 2016. Tensorflow: Large-scale machine learning on heterogeneous distributed systems. *arXiv preprint arXiv:1603.04467*.

Alan Akbik, Duncan Blythe, and Roland Vollgraf. 2018. Contextual string embeddings for sequence labeling. In *Proceedings of the 27th International Conference on Computational Linguistics*, pages 1638–1649.

Julio Cesar Salinas Alvarado, Karin Verspoor, and Timothy Baldwin. 2015. Domain adaption of named entity recognition to support credit risk assessment. In *Proceedings of the Australasian Language Technology Association Workshop 2015*, pages 84–90.

Dominic Balasuriya, Nicky Ringland, Joel Nothman, Tara Murphy, and James R Curran. 2009. Named

---

[3] `https://github.com/google-research/bert/issues?utf8=%E2%9C%93&q=NER`

Entity Recognition in Wikipedia. In *Proceedings of the 2009 Workshop on The People's Web Meets NLP: Collaboratively Constructed Semantic Resources*, pages 10–18. Association for Computational Linguistics.

Piotr Bojanowski, Edouard Grave, Armand Joulin, and Tomas Mikolov. 2016. Enriching Word Vectors with Subword Information. *arXiv preprint arXiv:1607.04606*.

Ming-Wei Chang, Kristina Toutanova, Kenton Lee, and Jacob Devlin. 2019. Language Model Pre-training for Hierarchical Document Representations. *arXiv preprint arXiv:1901.09128*.

Kevin Clark, Minh-Thang Luong, Christopher D Manning, and Quoc V Le. 2018. Semi-supervised sequence modeling with cross-view training. *arXiv preprint arXiv:1809.08370*.

Joshua Coates and Danushka Bollegala. 2018. Frustratingly easy meta-embedding–computing meta-embeddings by averaging source word embeddings. *arXiv preprint arXiv:1804.05262*.

Leon Derczynski, Eric Nichols, Marieke van Erp, and Nut Limsopatham. 2017. Results of the WNUT2017 shared task on novel and emerging entity recognition. In *Proceedings of the 3rd Workshop on Noisy User-generated Text*, pages 140–147.

Jacob Devlin, Ming-Wei Chang, Kenton Lee, and Kristina Toutanova. 2018. Bert: Pre-training of deep bidirectional transformers for language understanding. *arXiv preprint arXiv:1810.04805*.

Abbas Ghaddar and Philippe Langlais. 2016a. Wiki-Coref: An English Coreference-annotated Corpus of Wikipedia Articles. In *Proceedings of the Tenth International Conference on Language Resources and Evaluation (LREC 2016)*, Portorož, Slovenia.

Abbas Ghaddar and Phillippe Langlais. 2016b. Coreference in Wikipedia: Main concept resolution. In *Proceedings of The 20th SIGNLL Conference on Computational Natural Language Learning*, pages 229–238.

Abbas Ghaddar and Phillippe Langlais. 2017. WiNER: A Wikipedia Annotated Corpus for Named Entity Recognition. In *Proceedings of the Eighth International Joint Conference on Natural Language Processing (Volume 1: Long Papers)*, volume 1, pages 413–422.

Abbas Ghaddar and Phillippe Langlais. 2018a. Robust Lexical Features for Improved Neural Network Named-Entity Recognition. In *COLING 2018, 27th International Conference on Computational Linguistics*, pages 1896–1907.

Abbas Ghaddar and Phillippe Langlais. 2018b. Transforming Wikipedia into a Large-Scale Fine-Grained Entity Type Corpus. In *Proceedings of the Eleventh International Conference on Language Resources and Evaluation (LREC-2018)*.

Luheng He, Kenton Lee, Omer Levy, and Luke Zettlemoyer. 2018. Jointly predicting predicates and arguments in neural semantic role labeling. *arXiv preprint arXiv:1805.04787*.

Rafal Jozefowicz, Oriol Vinyals, Mike Schuster, Noam Shazeer, and Yonghui Wu. 2016. Exploring the limits of language modeling. *arXiv preprint arXiv:1602.02410*.

Diederik Kingma and Jimmy Ba. 2014. Adam: A method for stochastic optimization. *arXiv preprint arXiv:1412.6980*.

Kenton Lee, Luheng He, and Luke Zettlemoyer. 2018. Higher-order coreference resolution with coarse-to-fine inference. *arXiv preprint arXiv:1804.05392*.

Wang Ling, Yulia Tsvetkov, Silvio Amir, Ramon Fermandez, Chris Dyer, Alan W Black, Isabel Trancoso, and Chu-Cheng Lin. 2015. Not all contexts are created equal: Better word representations with variable attention. In *Proceedings of the 2015 Conference on Empirical Methods in Natural Language Processing*, pages 1367–1372.

Xiao Ling and Daniel S Weld. 2012. Fine-Grained Entity Recognition. In *AAAI*.

Xuezhe Ma and Eduard Hovy. 2016. End-to-end sequence labeling via bi-directional lstm-cnns-crf. *arXiv preprint arXiv:1603.01354*.

Bryan McCann, James Bradbury, Caiming Xiong, and Richard Socher. 2017. Learned in translation: Contextualized word vectors. In *Advances in Neural Information Processing Systems*, pages 6297–6308.

Tomas Mikolov, Ilya Sutskever, Kai Chen, Greg S Corrado, and Jeff Dean. 2013. Distributed representations of words and phrases and their compositionality. In *Advances in neural information processing systems*, pages 3111–3119.

Mike Mintz, Steven Bills, Rion Snow, and Dan Jurafsky. 2009. Distant supervision for relation extraction without labeled data. In *Proceedings of the Joint Conference of the 47th Annual Meeting of the ACL and the 4th International Joint Conference on Natural Language Processing of the AFNLP: Volume 2-Volume 2*, pages 1003–1011. Association for Computational Linguistics.

Jeffrey Pennington, Richard Socher, and Christopher D Manning. 2014. Glove: Global Vectors for Word Representation. In *EMNLP*, volume 14, pages 1532–1543.

Matthew E Peters, Mark Neumann, Mohit Iyyer, Matt Gardner, Christopher Clark, Kenton Lee, and Luke Zettlemoyer. 2018. Deep contextualized word representations. *arXiv preprint arXiv:1802.05365*.

Sameer Pradhan, Alessandro Moschitti, Nianwen Xue, Hwee Tou Ng, Anders Björkelund, Olga Uryupina, Yuchen Zhang, and Zhi Zhong. 2013. Towards

Robust Linguistic Analysis using OntoNotes. In *CoNLL*, pages 143–152.

Sameer Pradhan, Alessandro Moschitti, Nianwen Xue, Olga Uryupina, and Yuchen Zhang. 2012. CoNLL-2012 shared task: Modeling multilingual unrestricted coreference in OntoNotes. In *Joint Conference on EMNLP and CoNLL-Shared Task*, pages 1–40.

Alec Radford, Karthik Narasimhan, Tim Salimans, and Ilya Sutskever. 2018. Improving language understanding by generative pre-training. *URL https://s3-us-west-2. amazonaws. com/openai-assets/research-covers/languageunsupervised/language understanding paper. pdf.*

Lev Ratinov and Dan Roth. 2009. Design challenges and misconceptions in named entity recognition. In *Proceedings of the Thirteenth Conference on Computational Natural Language Learning*, pages 147–155. Association for Computational Linguistics.

Nitish Srivastava, Geoffrey E Hinton, Alex Krizhevsky, Ilya Sutskever, and Ruslan Salakhutdinov. 2014. Dropout: a simple way to prevent neural networks from overfitting. *Journal of machine learning research*, 15(1):1929–1958.

Emma Strubell, Patrick Verga, David Belanger, and Andrew McCallum. 2017. Fast and Accurate Entity Recognition with Iterated Dilated Convolutions. In *Proceedings of the 2017 Conference on Empirical Methods in Natural Language Processing*, pages 2660–2670.

Amber Stubbs and Özlem Uzuner. 2015. Annotating longitudinal clinical narratives for de-identification: The 2014 i2b2/UTHealth corpus. *Journal of biomedical informatics*, 58:S20–S29.

Erik F Tjong Kim Sang and Fien De Meulder. 2003. Introduction to the CoNLL-2003 shared task: Language-independent named entity recognition. In *Proceedings of the seventh conference on Natural language learning at HLT-NAACL 2003-Volume 4*, pages 142–147. Association for Computational Linguistics.

Ashish Vaswani, Noam Shazeer, Niki Parmar, Jakob Uszkoreit, Llion Jones, Aidan N Gomez, Łukasz Kaiser, and Illia Polosukhin. 2017. Attention is all you need. In *Advances in Neural Information Processing Systems*, pages 5998–6008.

Yonghui Wu, Mike Schuster, Zhifeng Chen, Quoc V Le, Mohammad Norouzi, Wolfgang Macherey, Maxim Krikun, Yuan Cao, Qin Gao, Klaus Macherey, et al. 2016. Google's neural machine translation system: Bridging the gap between human and machine translation. *arXiv preprint arXiv:1609.08144.*

Fisher Yu and Vladlen Koltun. 2015. Multi-scale context aggregation by dilated convolutions. *arXiv preprint arXiv:1511.07122.*

A Appendices

A.1 Training Representation

We use 8 stacked layers of DCNN to encode input sequences of maximum length of 512. WordPiece and position embeddings, number of filters in each dilated layer and self-attention hidden units were all set to 384. For self-attention, we use 6 attention heads and set intermediate hidden unit to 512. We apply a dropout mask (Srivastava et al., 2014) with a probability of 0.3 at the end of each DCNN layer, and at the input and output of the self-attention layer. We adopt the Adam (Kingma and Ba, 2014) optimization algorithm, set the initial learning rate to $1e^{-4}$, and use an exponential decay. We train our model up to 1.5 millions steps with mini-batch size of 64. We implemented our system using the Tensorflow (Abadi et al., 2016) library, and training requires about 5 days on a single TITAN XP GPU.

A.2 Dataset

Table 3 list the dataset used in this study domain, label size, and number of mentions in train/dev/test portions.

Dataset	Domain	Types	# entities		
			train	dev	test
CoNLL	news	4	23499	5942	5648
OntoNotes	news	18	81828	11066	11257
WNUT17	tweet	6	1975	836	1079
I2B2	bio	23	11791	5453	11360
Fin	finance	4	460	-	120
WikiGold	wikipedia	4	-	-	3558
WebPages	web	4	-	-	783

Table 3: Statistics on the datasets used in our experiments.

We used the last 2 datasets to perform an out-of-domain evaluation of CoNLL models. Those are small datasets extracted from Wikipedia articles and web pages respectively, and manually annotated following CoNLL-2003 annotation scheme.

A.3 NER Model Training

Our system is a single Bi-LSTM layer with a CRF decoder, with 128 hidden units for all datasets except for OntoNotes and I2B2 where we use 256 hidden units. For each learned representations (ours, ELMo, Flair, Bert), we use the weighted sum of all layers as input, where weights are learned during training. For each word, we stack the embeddings by concatenating them to form the input feature of the encoder.

Training is carried out by mini-batch of stochastic gradient descent (SGD) with a momentum of 0.9 and a gradient clipping of 5.0. To mitigate over-fitting, we apply a dropout mask with a probability of 0.7 on the input and output vectors of the Bi-LSTM layer. The mini-batch is 10 and learning rate is 0.011 for all datasets. We trained the models up to 63 epochs and use early stopping based on the official development set. For Fin, we randomly sampled 10% of the train set for development.

Extract, Transform and Fill: A Pipeline Model for Question Paraphrasing Based on Templates

Yufan Gu[12], Yuqiao Yang[13], Zhongyu Wei[1*]

[1]School of Data Science, Fudan University
[2]Alibaba Group, China
[3]Department of Information and Communication, School of Engineering, Tokyo institute of Technology
aleck16@163.com, yyqfaust@gmail.com, zywei@fudan.edu.cn

Abstract

Question paraphrasing aims to restate a given question with different expressions but keep the original meaning. Recent approaches are mostly based on neural networks following a sequence-to-sequence fashion, however, these models tend to generate unpredictable results. To overcome this drawback, we propose a pipeline model based on templates. It follows three steps, a) identifies template from the input question, b) retrieves candidate templates, c) fills candidate templates with original topic words. Experiment results on two self-constructed datasets show that our model outperforms the sequence-to-sequence model in a large margin and the advantage is more promising when the size of training sample is small.

1 Introduction

Paraphrase means sentences or phrases that convey the same meaning with different expressions. Popular tasks about paraphrases are paraphrase identification (Yin and Schütze, 2015), paraphrase generation (Li et al., 2018; Gupta et al., 2018), sentence rewriting (Barzilay and Lee, 2003), etc. As a special case of paraphrase generation, question paraphrasing (McKeown, 1983) aims to restate an input question. It can be applied in a question answering system for the expansion of question set to enhance the coverage of candidate answers. Besides, it is able to probe the need of users within an interactive system by rephrasing questions.

Traditional approaches for paraphrase generation are mostly based on external knowledge, including manually constructed templates (McKeown, 1983), or external thesaurus (Hassan et al.,

Original Question
请帮我查一下卡片的开户行
Please help me check the card's bank.
Paraphrase Questions
我想知道卡片的开户行
I would like to know the card's bank
您好,请帮我查询一下卡片的开户行
Hi, please help me check the card's bank
卡片的开户行请帮我查询一下
The card's bank, please help me check it
卡片的开户行能帮我查询一下吗?
The card's bank, can you help me check it?

Table 1: Example of an question and its paraphrases. Underlined phrases are topic words and others are templates.

2007). The generated paraphrases are usually fluent and informative. However, it is very time-consuming to construct templates by human and external thesaurus are always absent for some languages. Recently, researchers start to use neural network based approaches by formulating the generation task in a fashion of sequence-to-sequence (Sutskever et al., 2014; Bahdanau et al., 2014; Prakash et al., 2016). However, these models tend to "lose control" generating some unpredictable results.

In order to alleviate the uncertainty in sequence-to-sequence model, Cao et al. (2018) propose to search for similar sentences as soft template to back up the neural generation model in the scenario of text summarization. With this inspiration, we also try to bridge neural-based models and template-based approaches for question paraphrasing. An example of question paraphrasing can be seen in Table 1. We have two observations. First, words in a question can be easily divided into two types, namely, topic words and template words. Template words define the information need of the question while topic words are related to some specific entities or events. Second, for a pair of paraphrase questions, they tend to share the

---

* Corresponding author

Proceedings of the 2019 EMNLP Workshop W-NUT: The 5th Workshop on Noisy User-generated Text, pages 109–114
Hong Kong, Nov 4, 2019. ©2019 Association for Computational Linguistics

same topic words while template words are different. Motivated by these two observations, we try to identify template and topic words in the original question and construct paraphrase questions by considering these two parts separately.

In this paper, we propose a template-based framework to generate question paraphrase in a pipeline. The framework mainly includes three components, namely template extraction, template transforming and template filling. The contribution of our paper is three-fold.

- First, we propose a pipeline model to identify template and topic words from a question and generate the question paraphrases via template transforming and filling.

- Second, we construct two datasets for question paraphrasing collected from two domains, namely financial domain and automotive domain. All topic words are labeled in questions. The dataset is available here [1]

- Third, extensive experiments are performed on the self-constructed dataset to evaluate the effectiveness of our pipeline model. Results show that our model outperforms the state-of-the-art approach in a large margin.

2 Datasets Description

Two datasets are collected and annotated for question paraphrasing, including banking service questions from the financial domain and sales service questions from the automotive domain. The annotation consists of two parts. First, we classify questions into different clusters so that questions in each cluster share the same meaning. Second, we label template and topic words in each question. The number of question clusters for the financial domain and automotive domain are 2,589 and 526 respectively. Note that, for each cluster in financial dataset, we have 5 paraphrasing questions and for each cluster in automotive dataset, we have 4 paraphrasing questions.

The annotation of question cluster is performed by experts in the two domains, while two student annotators are hired for the labeling of the templates. For the template identification, annotators are instructed that the template part should be generalized, which means that the question will be

readable if we replace the topic words with other similar content.

The agreement between annotators for template identification is 0.558 and 0.568 for the domain of finance and automotive respectively. Further observations on the annotation results of template identification show that even if templates identified by the two annotators are different, both templates can be reasonable. We therefore construct two versions of datasets for experiments. One keeps both annotations (union) and the other includes questions with same labels from annotators (intersection). The statistics of our datasets can be seen in Table 2.

Statistics	financial		automotive	
	inter.	union	inter.	union
# of questions	7,218	12,938	1,195	2,103
# of templates	6,574	17,300	1,184	2,998
# of vocab.	908	1,100	656	907
# of template vocab.	325	528	144	303
# of topic vocab.	869	1,063	620	873

Table 2: Statistics of annotated datasets for question paraphrasing. *inter.* is short for intersection; *vocab.* is short for vocabulary; vocabulary here means unique tokens.

3 Proposed Model

Given the input question q, question paraphrasing system aims to generate questions with the same meaning but different expressions. Our proposed template-based model follows a pipeline fashion. It includes three main components, namely, template extraction, template transforming and template filling. The template extraction module classifies words in the input question into template part and topic part. Template transforming module searches for candidate templates for paraphrasing. Finally template filling module fills in the slots of the retrieved templates with topic words. And we take two training approaches, one is separate training and the other is joint training. A running example can be seen in Figure 1.

3.1 Template Extraction

Take a question as input, template extraction module classifies words into template and topic ones. We treat the problem as a supervised sequence labeling task and modify the classical *BIO* tagging strategy to fit our scenario. Specifically, we use "O" to specify the template part, and treat "B" and "I" as the topic part. As Bi-LSTM has been

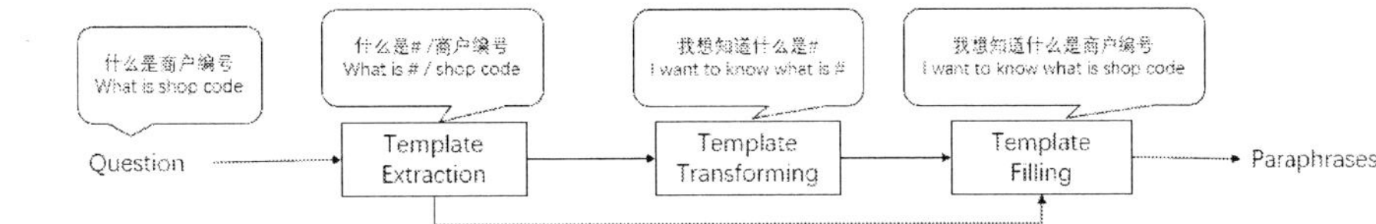

Figure 1: The overview of the proposed framework.

proved to be effective for the task of sequence labeling (Ma and Hovy, 2016), we also utilize such structure for template extraction. Cross-entropy (CE) is used for training and the loss is J_{TE}.

3.2 Template Transforming

Take the extracted template from previous module as input, template transforming module searches for candidate templates for paraphrasing. We utilize a retrieval-based approach to search for candidate templates. We first build an index for all the templates in our dataset. Then we use a score function (e.g. cosine similarity) to evaluate the similarity between original template and candidate templates to find out the most similar template.

To better represent our template, we train a sequence-to-sequence model with attention for template transforming. For each template, the hidden state resulted from the encoder is used as its representation. Note that, we also tried the generation results directly, however, preliminary experiment results showed the model performs poor. The loss for training seq-to-seq model is J_{TT}.

3.3 Template Filling

Take a candidate template and topic words as input, template filling module fills each slot in the template with topic words to form a new question. In practice, we use two encoders to encode subsequence of topic part and candidate template separately. Then we concatenate topic representation and candidate representation, and put them into a classifier to predict the position of the slot for the particular topic word. Cross-entropy is used here for training and loss is denoted by J_{TF}.

3.4 Training

We study two different approaches for the training of our pipeline model, namely *separate training* and *joint training*. For separate training, we train three modules (template extraction, template transforming and template filling) separately and combine them together for the whole framework.

We can also train them together to ease the error propagation problem resulted from separate training. The loss function here is the sum of each module.

$$J(\theta) = J_{TE}(\theta) + J_{TT}(\theta) + J_{TF}(\theta) \quad (1)$$

4 Experiments

4.1 Experimental Setup

We test our model on datasets described in Section 2. Both datasets are divided into training, validation and test with split ratio of 7:2:1. We use Adam as our optimization method and set the learning rate as 0.0001. We set the dimension of hidden state as 128. For padding, we set the max length as 64. We use BERT-Chinese tokenizer(Devlin et al., 2018) to separate characters.

For the general evaluation, we evaluate the quality of the generated paraphrase questions. BLEU-1, BLEU-2, BLEU-3, BLEU-4((Papineni et al., 2002)) are used as evaluation measures. Three models are compared.

seq2seq (Bahdanau et al., 2014) uses an encoder-decoder structure with attention for generation.

ours (separate) this is our pipeline model consisting of three modules. Each module is trained separately.

ours (joint) this is our pipeline model consisting of three modules and joint training is used.

4.2 Overall Evaluation

The overall experiment results can be seen in Table 3. Both of our pipeline models based on template outperform sequence-to-sequence model in a large margin on all the four datasets in terms of all the four metrics. The performance of *ours (joint)* is better than that of *ours (separate)* which indicates that joint training is effective for the pipeline model. The performances of all three models on the *union* set are better than their counter-part on

Dataset	Model	BLEU-1		BLEU-2		BLEU-3		BLEU-4	
		intersection	union	intersection	union	intersection	union	intersection	union
Financial	seq2seq	0.658	0.803	0.577	0.741	0.504	0.683	0.444	0.630
	ours (separate)	0.863	0.892	0.808	0.832	0.753	0.772	0.698	0.716
	ours (joint)	**0.873**	**0.902**	**0.827**	**0.857**	**0.782**	**0.812**	**0.739**	**0.770**
Automotive	seq2seq	0.581	0.771	0.526	0.723	0.482	0.684	0.441	0.648
	ours (separate)	0.826	**0.850**	0.757	0.777	0.701	0.713	0.650	0.654
	ours (joint)	**0.859**	0.849	**0.808**	**0.790**	**0.763**	**0.738**	**0.720**	**0.690**

Table 3: The overall performance of different models on four datasets from two domains (**bold** number in each column is the best performance on that dataset).

the *intersection* set. This is probably because the size of training samples are larger in the *union* set. Moreover, the sequence-to-sequence model is more sensitive to the size of training set, while our template-based model can achieve comparable performance on both sets.

4.3 Further Analysis for Transfer Learning

In addition to the overall performance of our pipeline model, we also analyze its performance for transfer learning. Since we have datasets from two domains, and the financial one is much bigger than the one from automotive domain. It is natural to train the model in the bigger dataset and transfer it to the domain with less training data. We thus report the experiment results for transfer learning from financial domain to the automotive one. Here, we compare three settings for the training of our model.

f2a: Model is trained on the financial dataset.

a2a: Model is trained on the automotive dataset only. It is the same joint model as we used in the previous section.

f+a2a: Model is pre-trained on the financial dataset and then fine-tuned on the automotive dataset.

Model	BLEU-1	BLEU-2	BLEU-3	BLEU-4
Seq2Seq(f2a)	0.251	0.167	0.110	0.085
Seq2Seq(a2a)	0.581	0.526	0.482	0.441
Seq2Seq(f+a2a)	0.715	0.661	0.619	0.580
ours (f2a)	0.796	0.722	0.656	0.598
ours (a2a)	0.859	0.808	0.763	0.720
ours (f+a2a)	**0.881**	**0.835**	**0.791**	**0.747**

Table 4: Transfer learning performance of our pipeline model on the intersection datasets (**bold** number in each column is the best performance on that dataset).

Performance for transfer learning can be seen in Table 4. The performance of *ours (f2a)* that directly applies the model trained on financial domain to automotive domain is better than the performance of *Seq2Seq*. This indicates that template-based model is easier to be transferred

from one domain to the other. *ours (f2a)* is worse than *our (a2a)*, this is reasonable because there is a gap between dataset, such as different vocabularies and different templates. The performance of *ours (f+a2a)* is better than *ours (a2a)*. This shows that fine-tuning on the target domain can further improve the model. The results on *Seq2Seq (f2a)*, *Seq2Seq (a2a)* and *Seq2Seq (f+a2a)* show the same trend. The experiment we have done in this part also gives us a new way to improve the performance of our model when the size of target dataset is limited.

5 Related Work

There are two lines of research for paraphrase generation including knowledge based ones and neural network based ones. Some researchers provide rules (Bhagat and Hovy, 2013) or corpus including knowledge (Fader et al., 2013; Ganitkevitch et al., 2013; Pavlick et al., 2015). Other researchers try to make use of templates (Berant and Liang, 2014), semantic information (Kozlowski et al., 2003) and thesaurus (Hassan et al., 2007) for paraphrase generation.

Rush (2015) have applied Seq2Seq model with attention mechanism for text summarization. Prakash (2016) employ a residual net in Seq2Seq model to generate paraphrases. Cao (2017) combine a copying decoder and a generative decoder for paraphrase generation. Cao(2018) try to utilize template information to help text summarization, however, the template is vague in that paper. We hope to utilize the special structure of question and extract the template explicitly from questions.

6 Conclusion

In this paper, we proposed a template-based framework for paraphrase question generation including three components, template extraction, template transforming and template filling. We identify template and topic words via template extraction and generate paraphrase questions via template transforming and filling. Experiment results on two self-constructed datasets from two domains showed that our pipeline model outperforms seq2seq model in a large margin.

Acknowledgments

Thanks for the constructive comments from anonymous reviewers. This work is partially funded by National Natural Science Foundation of China (No. 61751201), National Natural Science Foundation of China (No. 61702106) and Shanghai Science and Technology Commission (No. 17JC1420200, No. 17YF1427600 and No. 16JC1420401).

References

Dzmitry Bahdanau, Kyunghyun Cho, and Yoshua Bengio. 2014. Neural machine translation by jointly learning to align and translate. *arXiv preprint arXiv:1409.0473*.

Regina Barzilay and Lillian Lee. 2003. Learning to paraphrase: an unsupervised approach using multiple-sequence alignment. In *Proceedings of the 2003 Conference of the North American Chapter of the Association for Computational Linguistics on Human Language Technology-Volume 1*, pages 16–23. Association for Computational Linguistics.

Jonathan Berant and Percy Liang. 2014. Semantic parsing via paraphrasing. In *Proceedings of the 52nd Annual Meeting of the Association for Computational Linguistics (Volume 1: Long Papers)*, volume 1, pages 1415–1425.

Rahul Bhagat and Eduard Hovy. 2013. What is a paraphrase? *Computational Linguistics*, 39(3):463–472.

Ziqiang Cao, Wenjie Li, Sujian Li, and Furu Wei. 2018. Retrieve, rerank and rewrite: Soft template based neural summarization. In *Proceedings of the 56th Annual Meeting of the Association for Computational Linguistics (Volume 1: Long Papers)*, volume 1, pages 152–161.

Ziqiang Cao, Chuwei Luo, Wenjie Li, and Sujian Li. 2017. Joint copying and restricted generation for paraphrase. In *Thirty-First AAAI Conference on Artificial Intelligence*.

Jacob Devlin, Ming-Wei Chang, Kenton Lee, and Kristina Toutanova. 2018. Bert: Pre-training of deep bidirectional transformers for language understanding. *arXiv preprint arXiv:1810.04805*.

Anthony Fader, Luke Zettlemoyer, and Oren Etzioni. 2013. Paraphrase-driven learning for open question answering. In *Proceedings of the 51st Annual Meeting of the Association for Computational Linguistics (Volume 1: Long Papers)*, volume 1, pages 1608–1618.

Juri Ganitkevitch, Benjamin Van Durme, and Chris Callison-Burch. 2013. Ppdb: The paraphrase database. In *Proceedings of the 2013 Conference of the North American Chapter of the Association for Computational Linguistics: Human Language Technologies*, pages 758–764.

Ankush Gupta, Arvind Agarwal, Prawaan Singh, and Piyush Rai. 2018. A deep generative framework for paraphrase generation. In *Thirty-Second AAAI Conference on Artificial Intelligence*.

Samer Hassan, Andras Csomai, Carmen Banea, Ravi Sinha, and Rada Mihalcea. 2007. Unt: Subfinder: Combining knowledge sources for automatic lexical substitution. In *Proceedings of the Fourth International Workshop on Semantic Evaluations (SemEval-2007)*, pages 410–413.

Raymond Kozlowski, Kathleen F McCoy, and K Vijay-Shanker. 2003. Generation of single-sentence paraphrases from predicate/argument structure using lexico-grammatical resources. In *Proceedings of the second international workshop on Paraphrasing-Volume 16*, pages 1–8. Association for Computational Linguistics.

Zichao Li, Xin Jiang, Lifeng Shang, and Hang Li. 2018. Paraphrase generation with deep reinforcement learning. In *Proceedings of the 2018 Conference on Empirical Methods in Natural Language Processing*, pages 3865–3878. Association for Computational Linguistics.

Xuezhe Ma and Eduard Hovy. 2016. End-to-end sequence labeling via bi-directional lstm-cnns-crf. *arXiv preprint arXiv:1603.01354*.

Kathleen R McKeown. 1983. Paraphrasing questions using given and new information. *Computational Linguistics*, 9(1):1–10.

Kishore Papineni, Salim Roukos, Todd Ward, and Wei-Jing Zhu. 2002. Bleu: a method for automatic evaluation of machine translation. In *Proceedings of the 40th annual meeting on association for computational linguistics*, pages 311–318. Association for Computational Linguistics.

Ellie Pavlick, Pushpendre Rastogi, Juri Ganitkevitch, Benjamin Van Durme, and Chris Callison-Burch. 2015. Ppdb 2.0: Better paraphrase ranking, fine-grained entailment relations, word embeddings, and style classification. In *Proceedings of the 53rd Annual Meeting of the Association for Computational Linguistics and the 7th International Joint Conference on Natural Language Processing (Volume 2: Short Papers)*, volume 2, pages 425–430.

Aaditya Prakash, Sadid A Hasan, Kathy Lee, Vivek Datla, Ashequl Qadir, Joey Liu, and Oladimeji Farri. 2016. Neural paraphrase generation with stacked residual lstm networks. *arXiv preprint arXiv:1610.03098*.

Alexander M Rush, Sumit Chopra, and Jason Weston. 2015. A neural attention model for abstractive sentence summarization. *arXiv preprint arXiv:1509.00685*.

Ilya Sutskever, Oriol Vinyals, and Quoc V Le. 2014. Sequence to sequence learning with neural networks. In *Advances in neural information processing systems*, pages 3104–3112.

Wenpeng Yin and Hinrich Schütze. 2015. Convolutional neural network for paraphrase identification. In *Proceedings of the 2015 Conference of the North American Chapter of the Association for Computational Linguistics: Human Language Technologies*, pages 901–911.

An In-depth Analysis of the Effect of Lexical Normalization on the Dependency Parsing of Social Media

Rob van der Goot

Center for Language and Cognition
University of Groningen

Department of Computer Science
IT University of Copenhagen

robv@itu.dk

Abstract

Existing natural language processing systems have often been designed with standard texts in mind. However, when these tools are used on the substantially different texts from social media, their performance drops dramatically. One solution is to translate social media data to standard language before processing, this is also called normalization. It is well-known that this improves performance for many natural language processing tasks on social media data. However, little is known about which types of normalization replacements have the most effect. Furthermore, it is unknown what the weaknesses of existing lexical normalization systems are in an extrinsic setting. In this paper, we analyze the effect of manual as well as automatic lexical normalization for dependency parsing. After our analysis, we conclude that for most categories, automatic normalization scores close to manually annotated normalization and that small annotation differences are important to take into consideration when exploiting normalization in a pipeline setup.

1 Introduction

It is well known that many traditional natural language processing systems are focused on standard texts, and their performance drops when used on another domain. This is also called the problem of domain adaptation. Recently, much focus has been on the notoriously noisy domain of social media. The hasty and informal nature of communication on social media results in highly nonstandard texts, including a variety of phenomena not seen in standard texts, like phrasal abbreviations, slang, typos, lengthening, etc. One approach to adapt natural language processing tools to the social media domain is to 'translate' input to standard text before processing it, this is also referred to as normalization. In this ap-

proach, the input data is made more similar to the type of data the tool is expecting. Previous work has shown that normalization improves performance on social media data for tasks like POS tagging, parsing, lemmatization and named entity tagging (Baldwin and Li, 2015; Schulz et al., 2016; Zhang et al., 2013), however, it often remains unknown which types of replacements are most influential and which type of replacements still have potential to improve the usefulness of an automatic normalization system.

Baldwin and Li (2015) already investigated this effect in detail. They evaluate the effect of manual normalization beyond the word-level (including insertion and deletion of words). To the best of our knowledge, no automatic systems are available to obtain such a normalization, which is why Baldwin and Li (2015) focused only on the theoretical effect (i.e. manually annotated normalization). In this work, we will instead focus on lexical normalization, which is normalization on the word level. For this task, publicly available datasets and automatic systems are available (Han and Baldwin, 2011; Baldwin et al., 2015).

Recently, multiple English social media treebanks were released (Blodgett et al., 2018; Liu et al., 2018; van der Goot and van Noord, 2018) in Universal Depencies format (Nivre et al., 2017), as well as novel categorizations of phenomena occurring in lexical normalization (van der Goot et al., 2018). In this work, we combine both of these tasks into one dataset, which allows us not only to evaluate the theoretical effect of lexical normalization for dependency parsing, but also a real-world situation with automatic normalization.

The main contributions of this paper are:

- We add a layer of annotation to a social media treebank to also include normalization categories.

Proceedings of the 2019 EMNLP Workshop W-NUT: The 5th Workshop on Noisy User-generated Text, pages 115–120
Hong Kong, Nov 4, 2019. ©2019 Association for Computational Linguistics

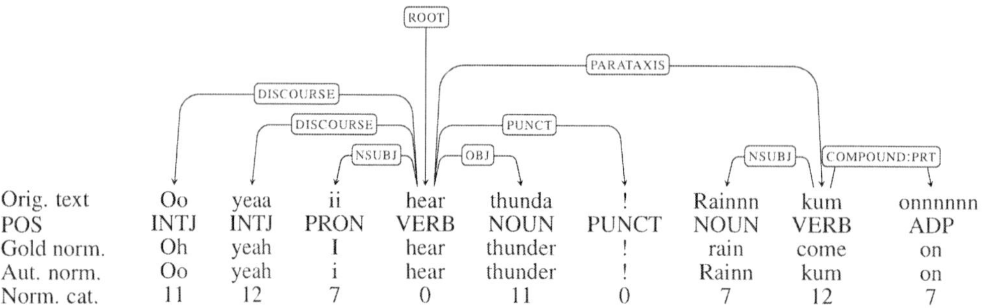

Figure 1: Example annotation for the sentence "Oo yeaa ii hear thunda ! Rainnn kum onnnnnn"

- We analyze the theoretical effect of lexical normalization for dependency parsing by using manually annotated normalization.

- We analyze the effect of an automatic lexical normalization model for dependency parsing, thereby showing which type of replacements still require attention.

2 Data

In this section we shortly discuss our choices for datasets and annotation formats, starting with the treebank data, followed by the lexical normalization categories annotation and automatic normalization. See Figure 1 for a fully annotated example instance from our development data.

2.1 Treebank

In 2018, three research groups simultaneously annotated dependency trees in the Universal Dependencies format on tweets: Liu et al. (2018) focussed on training a better parser by using an ensemble strategy, Blodgett et al. (2018) improved a dependency parser by using several adaptation methods, whereas van der Goot and van Noord (2018) focused on the use of normalization. Because the treebank created by van der Goot and van Noord (2018) is already annotated for lexical normalization, we will use this treebank.

The data from the treebank is taken from Li and Liu (2015), where van der Goot and van Noord (2018) only kept the tweets that were still available at the time of writing. The data from Li and Liu (2015) was in turn taken from two different sources: the LexNorm dataset (Han and Baldwin, 2011), originally annotated with lexical normalization and the dataset by Owoputi et al. (2013), originally annotated with POS tags. Li and Liu

(2015) complemented this annotation so that both sets contain normalization as well as POS tags, to which van der Goot and van Noord (2018) added Universal Dependency structures. Similar to van der Goot and van Noord (2018) we use the English Web Treebank treebank (Silveira et al., 2014) for training, and Owoputi (development data) for the analysis. The test split is not used in this work, since our aim is not to improve the parser.

2.2 Normalization Categories

We choose to use the taxonomy of van der Goot et al. (2018) for three main reasons: 1) to the best of our knowledge, this is the most detailed categorization for lexical normalization 2) annotation for the same source data as the treebanks is available from Reijngoud (2019) 3) systems are available to automatically perform this type of normalization, as opposed to the taxonomy used by Baldwin and Li (2015). The existing annotation is edited to fit the treebank tokenization; if a word is split in the treebank, the normalization is split accordingly, and both resulting words are annotated in the same category. (Reijngoud, 2019) added one category to the taxonomy: informal contractions, which includes splitting of words like 'gonna' and 'wanna'. The frequencies of the categories in the development data are shown in Table 1. The 'split', 'merge' and 'phrasal abbreviations' categories are very infrequent, because the original annotation only included 1-1 replacements, these categories have been added when transforming the annotation to treebank tokenization.

2.3 Automatic Lexical Normalization

We use the state-of-the-art model for lexical normalization: MoNoise (van der Goot, 2019), which

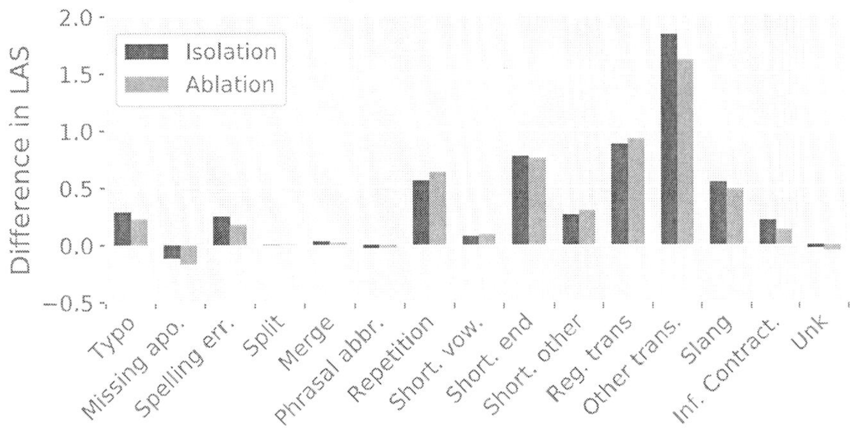

Figure 2: The effect of the categories when using manually annotated normalization. Isolation is the increase in performance when using only one category compared to using no normalization. Ablation is the loss when disabling only one category (higher is better).

Category	Freq.	%	Category	Freq.	%
No norm.	3,743	81.76	Short. vow.	22	0.48
Typo	30	0.66	Short. end	64	1.40
Missing apo.	176	3.84	Short. other	35	0.76
Spelling err.	44	0.96	Reg. trans.	66	1.44
Split	0	0.0	Other trans.	18	4.06
Merge	10	0.22	Slang	42	0.92
Phrasal abbr.	2	0.04	Inf. Contr.	56	1.22
Repetition	90	1.97	Unk	12	0.26

Table 1: Distribution of the replacement categories in the development data, 'No norm.' refers to words which are not normalized. For a detailed description of the categories we refer to (van der Goot et al., 2018).

is a modular normalization model, consisting of two steps; candidate generation and candidate ranking. For the generation, the most important modules are a lookup list based on the training data, the Aspell spell-checker[1] and word embeddings. For the ranking of candidates, features from the generation are complemented with n-gram probabilities and used as input to a random forest classifier, which predicts the confidence that a candidate is the correct replacement.

We train MoNoise on data from (Li and Liu, 2014), because it is most similar in annotation style to our development and test sets. Performance on the normalization task is slightly lower compared to the reported results (Error reduction rate (van der Goot, 2019) on the word level dropped from 60.61 to 45.38), because of differ-

ences in tokenization required for Universal Dependencies annotation. Also, the model clearly has issues with capitalization (see for example Figure 1) because capitalization is not corrected in the normalization training data.

3 Effect of Manual Normalization

We use the UUparser(de Lhoneux et al., 2017) for our experiments, with similar settings as van der Goot and van Noord (2018), including a heuristic to correctly parse a sentence starting with a retweet token or a username. All results reported in this paper are obtained with the official UD evaluation script[2] and are the average of 10 runs with different random seeds for the parser. For both settings (manual/automatic) we inspected the LAS graphs as well as the UAS graphs, but because the UAS scores showed very similar trends they are not reported here. The parser scores 52.56 LAS on the original input data, which improves to 57.83 when using the full gold normalization.

To evaluate the effect of each category, we measure performance twofold: in isolation, and in an ablation setting. For the isolation, we look at the difference between the baseline parser (without normalization) and a parser which only has access to normalization replacements of one category. For the ablation setting, we look at the loss when removing one category from the full model.

---

[1]http://aspell.net/

[2]http://universaldependencies.org/
conll18/conll18_ud_eval.py

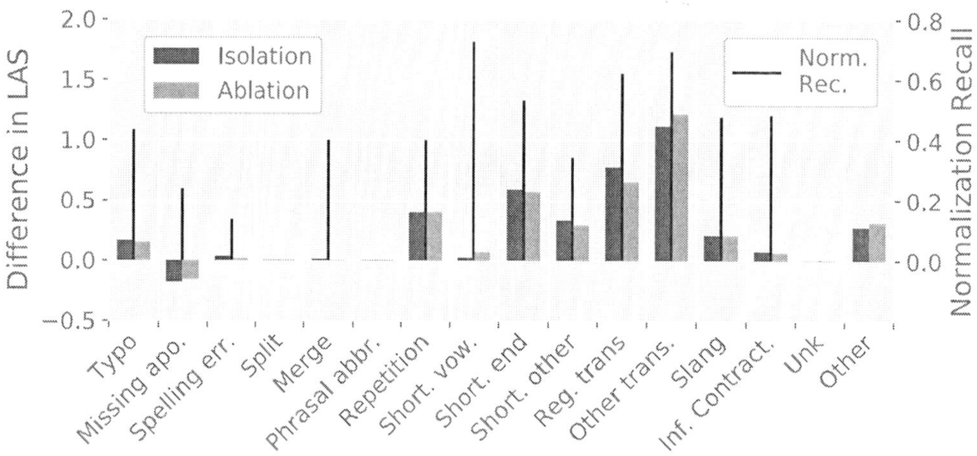

Figure 3: The effect of the categories when using automatic normalization. On the right y-axis the performance of the normalization model on this category is plotted (recall). The 'Other' category shows the effect of normalization replacements that were not annotated (but are still replaced by MoNoise).

The results for each category with gold normalization are shown in Figure 2. From these results, it becomes clear that some categories have a much larger effect compared to other categories. Not surprisingly, there is a correlation visible with the frequencies (Table 1). The categories going beyond the 1-1 normalization have only very little effect since they are very rare in this dataset[3]. The most important category is 'other transformation', this is mainly due to very frequent short words (e.g. 2↦to, u↦you). Other important categories are 'shortening end' and 'regular transformations'. This can be explained by the fact that they repair the suffixes, which often contain important syntactic clues.

It also becomes clear that differences in tokenization guidelines play a large role; one of the most frequent categories 'missing apostrophe' seems to be not useful for parsing; a manual inspection showed that this is because these also occur in the training data in their not-normalized form (e.g. 'll↦ will), thereby normalizing them creates more diversity. For the same reason, informal contractions (e.g. wanna, gonna) also have a relatively small effect.

4 Effect of Automatic Normalization

When using the full normalization model, the parser achieves a LAS of 56.32 when using all

normalization categories, which is 72% of the gain that can be achieved with gold normalization compared to the baseline setting (52.56). Similar to the previous section, we run an isolation as well as an ablation experiment. In this setting, we only allow the normalization to replace words that are annotated as the category under evaluation (for the ablation experiments the inverse).

The parser performance as well as the recall of the normalization model on each category are plotted in Figure 3. Results show that the 'other transformations' and 'slang' category have the most room for improvement in LAS compared to gold normalization, even though they are not the worst categories with respect to the normalization performance. Furthermore, trends are rather similar compared to the gold normalization, even though there are differences in normalization performance. As expected from the gold normalization, the 'missing apostrophe' category is not helpful.

Interestingly, the 'other' category, which includes normalization replacements that were not annotated in the gold normalization, shows a small increase in performance. This category includes replacements like 'supp'↦'support' and 'da'↦'the', which were overlooked by the annotator. This could also be due to differences in the scope of annotation between the training data and development data.

---

[3]they were not annotated in their original releases, but were added when used in the treebank

5 Conclusion

We have introduced a novel annotation layer for an existing treebank with normalization annotation, which indicates which types of replacements are made. This allowed us to evaluate the effect of lexical normalization on the dependency parsing of tweets, both with manual normalization annotation and automatically predicted normalization. The automatic normalization obtained over 70% of the performance increase that could be obtained with gold normalization. The most influential categories were 'other transformation', which includes many replacements for very short words, and the categories with a high frequency that repair a words' suffix: 'shortening end' and 'regular transformation'. The categories which have the most potential for improvement in parser performance are the 'other transformation' and 'slang' categories. Furthermore, we saw that some predicted normalization replacements which were not annotated in the gold data also led to an increase in performance. Our results suggest that care should be taken when taking out-of-the-box annotation, because differences in annotation and the scope of the normalization task (i.e. tokenization, missed normalization) could lead to sub-optimal performance.

The dataset and code for the analysis is available on: `https://bitbucket.org/robvanderg/taxeval/`.

6 Acknowledgments

I would like to thank Wessel Reijngoud for providing the annotation of the normalization categories and Gertjan van Noord and the anonymous reviewers for their feedback.

References

Timothy Baldwin, Marie-Catherine de Marneffe, Bo Han, Young-Bum Kim, Alan Ritter, and Wei Xu. 2015. Shared tasks of the 2015 workshop on noisy user-generated text: Twitter lexical normalization and named entity recognition. In *Proceedings of the Workshop on Noisy User-generated Text*, pages 126–135, Beijing, China. Association for Computational Linguistics.

Tyler Baldwin and Yunyao Li. 2015. An in-depth analysis of the effect of text normalization in social media. In *Proceedings of the 2015 Conference of the North American Chapter of the Association for Computational Linguistics: Human Language Tech-*
nologies, pages 420–429, Denver, Colorado. Association for Computational Linguistics.

Su Lin Blodgett, Johnny Wei, and Brendan O'Connor. 2018. Twitter universal dependency parsing for African-American and mainstream American English. In *Proceedings of the 56th Annual Meeting of the Association for Computational Linguistics (Volume 1: Long Papers)*, pages 1415–1425, Melbourne, Australia. Association for Computational Linguistics.

Rob van der Goot. 2019. MoNoise: A multi-lingual and easy-to-use lexical normalization tool. In *Proceedings of the 57th Annual Meeting of the Association for Computational Linguistics: System Demonstrations*, pages 201–206, Florence, Italy. Association for Computational Linguistics.

Rob van der Goot and Gertjan van Noord. 2018. Modeling input uncertainty in neural network dependency parsing. In *Proceedings of the 2018 Conference on Empirical Methods in Natural Language Processing*, pages 4984–4991, Brussels, Belgium. Association for Computational Linguistics.

Rob van der Goot, Rik van Noord, and Gertjan van Noord. 2018. A taxonomy for in-depth evaluation of normalization for user generated content. In *Proceedings of the Eleventh International Conference on Language Resources and Evaluation (LREC-2018)*, Miyazaki, Japan. European Languages Resources Association (ELRA).

Bo Han and Timothy Baldwin. 2011. Lexical normalisation of short text messages: Makn sens a #twitter. In *Proceedings of the 49th Annual Meeting of the Association for Computational Linguistics: Human Language Technologies*, pages 368–378, Portland, Oregon, USA. Association for Computational Linguistics.

Miryam de Lhoneux, Sara Stymne, and Joakim Nivre. 2017. Arc-hybrid non-projective dependency parsing with a static-dynamic oracle. In *Proceedings of the The 15th International Conference on Parsing Technologies (IWPT).*, Pisa, Italy.

Chen Li and Yang Liu. 2014. Improving text normalization via unsupervised model and discriminative reranking. In *Proceedings of the ACL 2014 Student Research Workshop*, pages 86–93, Baltimore, Maryland, USA. Association for Computational Linguistics.

Chen Li and Yang Liu. 2015. Joint POS tagging and text normalization for informal text. In *Proceedings of the Twenty-Fourth International Joint Conference on Artificial Intelligence, IJCAI 2015, Buenos Aires, Argentina, July 25-31, 2015*, pages 1263–1269.

Yijia Liu, Yi Zhu, Wanxiang Che, Bing Qin, Nathan Schneider, and Noah A. Smith. 2018. Parsing tweets into universal dependencies. In *Proceedings of the 2018 Conference of the North American Chapter of the Association for Computational Linguistics: Human Language Technologies, Volume 1 (Long Papers)*, pages 965–975, New Orleans, Louisiana. Association for Computational Linguistics.

Joakim Nivre, Željko Agić, Lars Ahrenberg, Maria Jesus Aranzabe, Masayuki Asahara, Aitziber Atutxa, Miguel Ballesteros, John Bauer, Kepa Bengoetxea, Riyaz Ahmad Bhat, Eckhard Bick, Cristina Bosco, Gosse Bouma, Sam Bowman, Marie Candito, Gülşen Cebiroğlu Eryiğit, Giuseppe G. A. Celano, Fabricio Chalub, Jinho Choi, Çağrı Çöltekin, Miriam Connor, Elizabeth Davidson, Marie-Catherine de Marneffe, Valeria de Paiva, Arantza Diaz de Ilarraza, Kaja Dobrovoljc, Timothy Dozat, Kira Droganova, Puneet Dwivedi, Marhaba Eli, Tomaž Erjavec, Richárd Farkas, Jennifer Foster, Cláudia Freitas, Katarína Gajdošová, Daniel Galbraith, Marcos Garcia, Filip Ginter, Iakes Goenaga, Koldo Gojenola, Memduh Gökırmak, Yoav Goldberg, Xavier Gómez Guinovart, Berta Gonzáles Saavedra, Matias Grioni, Normunds Grūzītis, Bruno Guillaume, Nizar Habash, Jan Hajič, Linh Hà Mỹ, Dag Haug, Barbora Hladká, Petter Hohle, Radu Ion, Elena Irimia, Anders Johannsen, Fredrik Jörgensen, Hüner Kaşıkara, Hiroshi Kanayama, Jenna Kanerva, Natalia Kotsyba, Simon Krek, Veronika Laippala, Phuong Lê H`ông, Alessandro Lenci, Nikola Ljubešić, Olga Lyashevskaya, Teresa Lynn, Aibek Makazhanov, Christopher Manning, Cătălina Mărănduc, David Mareček, Héctor Martínez Alonso, André Martins, Jan Mašek, Yuji Matsumoto, Ryan McDonald, Anna Missilä, Verginica Mititelu, Yusuke Miyao, Simonetta Montemagni, Amir More, Shunsuke Mori, Bohdan Moskalevskyi, Kadri Muischnek, Nina Mustafina, Kaili Müürisep, Luong Nguy˜ên Thị, Huy`ên Nguy˜ên Thị Minh, Vitaly Nikolaev, Hanna Nurmi, Stina Ojala, Petya Osenova, Lilja Øvrelid, Elena Pascual, Marco Passarotti, Cenel-Augusto Perez, Guy Perrier, Slav Petrov, Jussi Piitulainen, Barbara Plank, Martin Popel, Lauma Pretkalniņa, Prokopis Prokopidis, Tiina Puolakainen, Sampo Pyysalo, Alexandre Rademaker, Loganathan Ramasamy, Livy Real, Laura Rituma, Rudolf Rosa, Shadi Saleh, Manuela Sanguinetti, Baiba Saulīte, Sebastian Schuster, Djamé Seddah, Wolfgang Seeker, Mojgan Seraji, Lena Shakurova, Mo Shen, Dmitry Sichinava, Natalia Silveira, Maria Simi, Radu Simionescu, Katalin Simkó, Mária Šimková, Kiril Simov, Aaron Smith, Alane Suhr, Umut Sulubacak, Zsolt Szántó, Dima Taji, Takaaki Tanaka, Reut Tsarfaty, Francis Tyers, Sumire Uematsu, Larraitz Uria, Gertjan van Noord, Viktor Varga, Veronika Vincze, Jonathan North Washington, Zdeněk Žabokrtský, Amir Zeldes, Daniel Zeman, and Hanzhi Zhu. 2017. Universal dependencies 2.0. LINDAT/CLARIN digital library at the Institute of Formal and Applied Linguistics (ÚFAL), Faculty of Mathematics and Physics, Charles University.

Olutobi Owoputi, Brendan O'Connor, Chris Dyer, Kevin Gimpel, Nathan Schneider, and Noah A. Smith. 2013. Improved part-of-speech tagging for online conversational text with word clusters. In *Proceedings of the 2013 Conference of the North American Chapter of the Association for Computational Linguistics: Human Language Technologies*, pages 380–390, Atlanta, Georgia. Association for Computational Linguistics.

Wessel Reijngoud. 2019. Automatic classification of normalisation replacement categories: within corpus and cross corpora. Master's thesis, University of Groningen.

Sarah Schulz, Guy De Pauw, Orphée De Clercq, Bart Desmet, Véronique Hoste, Walter Daelemans, and Lieve Macken. 2016. Multimodular text normalization of Dutch user-generated content. *ACM Transactions on Intelligent Systems Technology*, 7(4):1–22.

Natalia Silveira, Timothy Dozat, Marie-Catherine de Marneffe, Samuel Bowman, Miriam Connor, John Bauer, and Christopher D. Manning. 2014. A gold standard dependency corpus for English. In *Proceedings of the Ninth International Conference on Language Resources and Evaluation (LREC-2014)*.

Congle Zhang, Tyler Baldwin, Howard Ho, Benny Kimelfeld, and Yunyao Li. 2013. Adaptive parser-centric text normalization. In *Proceedings of the 51st Annual Meeting of the Association for Computational Linguistics (Volume 1: Long Papers)*, pages 1159–1168, Sofia, Bulgaria. Association for Computational Linguistics.

Who wrote this book? A challenge for e-commerce

Béranger Dumont, Simona Maggio, Ghiles Sidi Said & Quoc-Tien Au
Rakuten Institute of Technology Paris
{beranger.dumont,simona.maggio}@rakuten.com,
{ts-ghiles.sidisaid,quoctien.au}@rakuten.com

Abstract

Modern e-commerce catalogs contain millions of references, associated with textual and visual information that is of paramount importance for the products to be found via search or browsing. Of particular significance is the book category, where the author name(s) field poses a significant challenge. Indeed, books written by a given author might be listed with different authors' names due to abbreviations, spelling variants and mistakes, among others. To solve this problem at scale, we design a composite system involving open data sources for books, as well as deep learning components, such as approximate match with Siamese networks and name correction with sequence-to-sequence networks. We evaluate this approach on product data from the e-commerce website Rakuten France, and find that the top proposal of the system is the normalized author name with 72% accuracy.

1 Introduction

Unlike brick-and-mortar stores, e-commerce websites can list hundreds of millions of products, with thousands of new products entering their catalogs every day. The availability and the reliability of the information on the products, or *product data*, is crucial for the products to be found by the users via textual or visual search, or using faceted navigation.

Books constitute a prominent part of many large e-commerce catalogs. Relevant book properties include: title, author(s), format, edition, and publication date, among others. In this work, we focus on the names of book authors, as they are found to be extremely relevant to the user and are commonly used in search queries on e-commerce websites, but suffer from considerable variability and noise. To the best of our knowledge, there is no large-scale public dataset for books that captures the variability arising on e-commerce marketplaces from user-generated input. Thus, in this work we use product data from Rakuten France (RFR).[1]

The variability and noise is evident in the RFR dataset. For example, books written by F. Scott Fitzgerald are also listed with the following author's names: "Francis Scott Fitzgerald" (full name), "Fitzgerald, F. Scott" (inversion of the first and last name), "Fitzgerald" (last name only), "F. Scott Fitgerald" (misspelling of the last name), "F SCOTT FITZGERALD" (capitalization and different typological conventions), as well as several combinations of those variations. The variability of the possible spellings for an author's name is very hard to capture using rules, even more so for names which are not primarily written in latin alphabet (such as arabic or asian names), for names containing titles (such as "Dr." or "Pr."), and for pen names which may not follow the usual conventions. This motivated us to explore automated techniques for normalizing the authors' names to their best known ("canonical") spellings.

Fortunately, a wealth of open databases exist for books, making it possible to match a significant fraction of the books listed in e-commerce catalogs. While not always clean and unambiguous, this information is extremely valuable and enables us to build datasets of name variants, used to train machine learning systems to normalize authors' names. To this end, in addition to the match with open databases, we will explore two different approaches: approximate match with known authors' names using Siamese neural networks, and direct correction of the provided author's name using sequence-to-sequence learning with neural networks. Then, an additional machine learning component is used to rank the results.

The rest of the paper is organized as follows: we present the data from RFR and from the open databases in Section 2, before turning to the experimental setup for the overall system and for each of its components in Section 3. Finally, we give results in Section 4, we present related works in Section 5, and conclude in Section 6.

2 Book data

2.1 Rakuten France data

The RFR dataset contains 12 million book references[2]. The most relevant product data for normalization is:

---

[1] https://fr.shopping.rakuten.com

[2] The RFR dataset is publicly available at https://rit.rakuten.co.jp/data_release.

Proceedings of the 2019 EMNLP Workshop W-NUT: The 5th Workshop on Noisy User-generated Text, pages 121–125
Hong Kong, Nov 4, 2019. ©2019 Association for Computational Linguistics

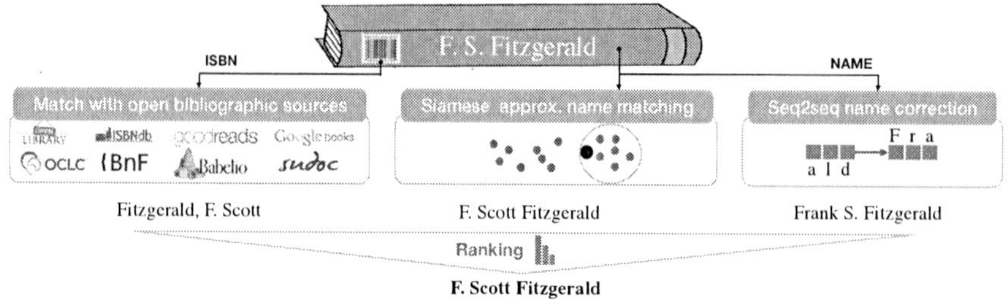

Figure 1: Overview of the system for normalizing author names. Each component is detailed in Section 3.

Table 1: Performances of the external bibliographic resources used for matching books on RFR via ISBN.

Source	URL	% of ISBNs
Open Library	openlibrary.org	24.9%
ISBNdb	isbndb.com	36.3%
Goodreads	www.goodreads.com	64.7%
Google Books	books.google.com	51.2%
OCLC	www.oclc.org	52.2%
BnF	www.bnf.fr	7.4%
Sudoc	www.sudoc.abes.fr	29.0%
Babelio	www.babelio.com	7.9%

- **ISBN**[3] in 10 digit or 13 digit format;

- **product title**, which includes the book title, often supplemented with extra information in free text;

- **author(s)** of the book as the input catalog name provided by the seller.

In particular, the ISBN is a worldwide unique identifier for books, which makes it a prime candidate for unambiguous matching with external sources. In this dataset, an ISBN is present for about 70% of the books. Among the books with no ISBN, 30% are ancient books which are not expected to be associated an ISBN.

2.2 External bibliographic resources

There is no central authority providing consistent information on books associated with an ISBN. However, there is a wealth of bibliographic resources and open databases for books. In order to retrieve the author's name(s) associated with the books in the RFR dataset, we perform ISBN matching using public APIs on eight of them, listed in Table 1 along with the fraction of found ISBNs from this dataset. We find the sources to be highly complementary and that 75% of the books with an ISBN are matched with at least one source. The match via ISBN on external bibliographic resources is the first component of the system depicted in Fig. 1.

2.3 Dataset of name entities

In order to train and evaluate machine learning systems to match or correct authors' names, a dataset of name entities containing the different surface forms (or variants) of authors' names is required. The entities should reflect as well as possible the variability that can be found in the RFR dataset, as was illustrated in the case of F. Scott Fitzgerald in Section 1.

For each entity, a canonical name should be elected and correspond to the name that should be preferred for the purpose of e-commerce. Instead of setting these gold spellings by following some predefined rules (i.e. family name in the first position, initial of first name, etc.), for e-commerce applications it is more appropriate that the displayed authors names have the most popular spellings among readers. In agreement with Rakuten catalog analysts we set the most popular spelling of an author name as the one found on Wikipedia[4] or DBpedia (Lehmann et al., 2015).

While Wikipedia seems more pertinent to select canonical names matching the e-commerce user expectations, specialized librarian data services, such as the Library of Congress Name Authority[5], could be used in future research to enrich the dataset of name entities.

Name entities are collected in three distinct ways:

1. **ISBN matching**: for each book the different author names found via ISBN search on external sources and the RFR author name field build up an entity. The canonical form is the one that is matched with Wikipedia or DBpedia; else the one provided by the greatest number of sources.

2. **Matching of Rakuten authors**: we build entities using fuzzy search on the author name field on DBpedia and consider the DBpedia value to be canonical. We limit the number of false positives in fuzzy search by tokenizing both names, and keeping only the names where at least one token from the name on RFR is approximately found in the external resource (Levenshtein distance < 2).

3. **Name variants**: DBpedia, BnF, and JRC-names (Steinberger et al., 2011; Maud et al., 2016) directly provide data about people (not limited to book authors) and their name variants.

---

[3]International Standard Book Number, see https://www.isbn-international.org

[4]https://www.wikipedia.org
[5]id.loc.gov/authorities/names.html

As an example, by using the wikiPageRedirects field in DBpedia we can build a large entity for the canonical name "Anton Tchekhov", containing "Anton Tchechov", "Antòn Pàvlovič Chéchov", "Checkhov", "Anton Chekov", and many more.

After creating the name entity dataset, we normalize all names to latin-1. We obtain about 750,000 entities, for a total of 2.1 million names.

2.4 Annotated Rakuten France data

In order to evaluate the overall system, we need product data from RFR for which the canonical author name has been carefully annotated and can be considered as the ground truth. To this end, we have considered a subset of 1000 books from the RFR dataset, discarding books written by more than one author for simplicity.[6] We find that 467 books have a canonical author name that differs from RFR's original (unnormalized) author name. Also, 310 do not have an ISBN or do not match on any of the bibliographic resources listed in Section 2.2. Among them, 208 books have a canonical name that differs from the input catalog name provided by the seller.

3 Experimental setup

The overview of the system can be found in Fig. 1. Its first component, the matching via ISBN against external databases, has already been presented in Section 2.2. In the rest of this section, we will shed light on the three machine learning components of the system.

3.1 Siamese approximate name matching

We want to learn a mapping that assigns a similarity score to a pair of author names such that name variants of the same entity will have high similarity, and names that belong to different entities will have low similarity. Once learned, this mapping will enable us to assign an entity to any given name.

To this end, we might use a classical string metric such as the Levenshtein distance or the n-gram distance (Kondrak, 2005). However, those are not specific to people's names, and might return a large distance (low similarity) in cases such as the inversion between first name and last name or the abbreviation of the first name to an initial. Thus, we want to use the dataset of name entities to learn a specialized notion of similarity—this is known as distance metric learning (Kulis et al., 2013).

To this purpose, we use a pair of neural networks with shared weights, or Siamese neural network (Bromley et al., 1994). Each network is a recurrent neural network (RNN) composed of a character-level embedding layer with 256 units, a bidirectional long short-term memory (LSTM) (Hochreiter and Schmidhuber, 1997) with 2×128 units, and a dense layer with 256 units. Each network takes a name as input and outputs a representation—the two representations are then compared using cosine similarity with a target value equal to

1 for name variants of the same entity, and to 0 otherwise. We preprocess the input by representing all characters in ASCII and lowercase. We consider a sequence length of 32 using zero padding.

The Siamese network is trained with contrastive loss (Hadsell et al., 2006) in order to push the similarity towards 1 for similar pairs, and below a certain margin (that we set to 0) for dissimilar pairs. The optimization is done using Adam (Kingma and Ba, 2014), with a learning rate of 10^{-3} and a gradient clipping value of 5. We use batches of 512 samples, consider a negative to positive pairs ratio of $4 : 1$, and randomly generate new negative pairs at every epoch.

At test time, we search for the canonical name whose representation is closest to that of the query, using only the high-quality name entities from DBpedia, BnF, and JRC-names. To this end, we do approximate nearest neighbor search using Annoy[7].

3.2 Name correction with seq2seq networks

We use a generative model to correct and normalize authors' names directly. The dataset of name entities is again employed to train a sequence-to-sequence (seq2seq) model (Sutskever et al., 2014) to produce the canonical form of a name from one of its variants. The dataset is further augmented by including additional variants where the first name is abbreviated to an initial.

The seq2seq model is an encoder-decoder using RNNs, with a character embedding layer, as in the case of the Siamese network. The encoder is a bi-directional LSTM with 2×256 units, while the decoder is a plain LSTM with 512 units connected to a softmax layer that computes a probability distribution over the characters.

The training is performed by minimizing the categorical cross-entropy loss, using teacher forcing (Williams and Zipser, 1989). The optimization setting is identical to that of the Siamese nework, with batches of 1024 samples. For inference, we collect the 10 output sequences with highest probability using beam search.

3.3 Ranking of the proposals

For any given book with an ISBN and an author's name, all three techniques shown in Fig. 1 provide one or several candidate canonical names. As we aim at providing an automated tool to enhance the quality of the book products, the final system should provide a ranked list of candidates with a calibrated confidence level. For this purpose we train a logistic regression to estimate the probability that a proposal is the canonical form for an author's name. This information is then used as a confidence score to rank the different candidate names returned by the three normalization approaches.

Specifically, we represent a proposal with a set of 12 features: 11 indicating whether it is found in the bibliographic sources, generated from the seq2seq model, matched with the Siamese network or equal to the input name, and one last feature corresponding to the cosine

---

[6]The annotated RFR dataset is publicly available at https://rit.rakuten.co.jp/data_release.

[7]https://github.com/spotify/annoy

distance between the representation of the proposal and that of the input name. The selected features reflect that the confidence of the global system should increase with *(i)* the consensus among the different sources, and *(ii)* the similarity of the candidate to the input name.

For this component we use the annotated dataset introduced in Section 2.4, splitting the books between training and test sets, with a ratio of $50\% : 50\%$, generating a total of 11185 proposals.

4 Results

The three machine learning components discussed in the previous section have been individually evaluated on their specific task. Furthermore the final system has been evaluated in terms of correctly normalized book authors in a real case scenario.

Siamese approximate name matching We evaluate the Siamese network on a held out test set, and compare it to an n-gram distance, by checking that the nearest neighbor of a name variant is the canonical name of the entity to which it belongs. We find an accuracy of 79.8% for the Siamese network, against 71.1% for the n-gram baseline with $n = 3$. We have also checked metrics when introducing a threshold distance above which we consider that no matching entity is found, and found systematic improvement over the baseline. In the final system, we set the threshold to infinity.

Siamese networks are more effective than simpler rule-based approaches and more specifically they perform better than the n-gram baseline on the following cases:

- Vittorio Hugo $\rightarrow$ Victor Hugo: capturing name variants in different languages;

- Bill Shakespeare $\rightarrow$ William Shakespeare: capturing common nicknames

Name correction with seq2seq networks Similarly to the previous approach, the seq2seq network is evaluated on a held out test set by checking that one of the generated name variants is the canonical name of the entity to which it belongs. As expected, name normalization using seq2seq network gives poorer performances than approximate matching within a dataset of known authors, but constitutes a complementary approach that is useful in case of formatting issues or incomplete names. This approach alone reaches a top-10 accuracy of 42% on the entire test set, 26% on a test set containing only names with initials, and 53% on a test set containing only minor spelling mistakes.

Some examples where seq2seq performs better than the other methods are as follows:

- V. Hugo $\rightarrow$ Victor Hugo: first name prediction for authors we don't have in the canonical database;

- Vicor Hugo $\rightarrow$ Victor Hugo: misspelling correction for authors we don't have in the canonical database.

Table 2: Global system top-k accuracy at the book level.

Type of books	#samples	acc@1	acc@3
all	500	72%	85%
unnorm. input author	235	49%	67%
no ISBN match	151	50%	64%
unnorm. + no ISBN	109	35%	49%

Ranking of the proposals With a decision threshold of $p = 0.5$, the trained classifier has an accuracy of 93% for both positive and negative candidates in the test set. The coefficients of the estimator reveal the importance of the features and, thus, of the related components. The three most important contributions are the match with the Siamese network, the match via ISBN in Babelio, and the similarity with the input catalog name, confirming the relevance of a multi-approach design choice.

Global system In order to reflect the actual use of the global system on e-commerce catalog data, the final evaluation is performed at the book level, by considering all the proposals provided by the different components for a given book. The metric used is the top-k accuracy on the ranked list of proposals for each book; results are summarized in Table 2. We find that 72% of the books have the author's name normalized by the highest ranked proposal. Excluding from the evaluation books where the ground truth for the author's name equals the catalog value, this accuracy drops to 49%. In the case of books without ISBN or that do not match on any of the bibliographic resources, thus relying on machine learning-based components only, we find that 50% of the books are normalized by the top proposal. Finally, for the combination of the above two restrictions, we find a top-1 accuracy of 35%.

5 Related works

There is a long line of work on author name disambiguation for the case of bibliographic citation records (Hussain and Asghar, 2017). While related, this problem differs from the one of book authors. Indeed, unlike most books, research publications usually have several authors, each of them having published papers with other researchers. The relationships among authors, which can be represented as a graph, may be used to help disambiguate the bibliographic citations.

Named entity linking (Shen et al., 2015), where one aims at determining the identity of entities (such as a person's name) mentioned in text, is another related problem. The crucial difference with the disambiguation of book authors is that entity linking systems leverage the context of the named entity mention to link unambiguously to an entity in a pre-populated knowledge base.

The conformity of truth in web resources is also a related problem, addressed in the literature by TruthFinder (Yin et al., 2008) algorithms. Similarly, the proposed global model in which we combine sources learns to some extent the level of trust of the different sources. Unlike our technique, the TruthFinder approach needs to start from a book we can unambiguously identify in several sources and, thus, needs its ISBN.

Distance metric learning with neural networks has been used for merging datasets on names (Srinivas et al., 2018), for normalizing job titles (Neculoiu et al., 2016), and for the disambiguation of researchers (Zhang et al., 2018). Sequence-to-sequence learning has been used for the more general task of text normalization (Sproat and Jaitly, 2016), and for sentence-level grammar error identification (Schmaltz et al., 2016).

To the best of our knowledge, the problem of normalization of book authors name has not been tackled in the previous literature, except for a work on named entity linking for French writers (Frontini et al., 2015).

6 Conclusions

We provided a first attempt at solving the problem of author name normalization in the context of books sold on e-commerce websites. To this end, we used a composite system involving open data sources for books, approximate match with Siamese networks, name correction with sequence-to-sequence networks, and ranking of the proposals. We find that 72% of the books have the author's name normalized by the highest ranked proposal.

In order to facilitate future research, we are releasing data from Rakuten France: a large dataset containing product information, and a subset of it with expert human annotation for the authors' names. They are accessible at `rit.rakuten.co.jp/data_release`.

Multiple challenges remain and are left for future research. First, the system should be extended to handle the case of books with multiple authors. In addition, the book title could be used to help disambiguate between authors and to query external bibliographic resources. This work can also be seen as an intermediate step towards a knowledge base for book author names with name variants, extending public ones such as BnF, using the ISNI[8] for easier record linkage whenever available.

Acknowledgments

We thank Raphaël Ligier-Tirilly for his help with the deployment of the system as microservices, and Laurent Ach for his support.

References

J. Bromley et al. 1994. Signature verification using a "siamese" time delay neural network. pages 737–744.

F. Frontini et al. 2015. Semantic web based named entity linking for digital humanities and heritage texts.

R. Hadsell, S. Chopra, and Y. LeCun. 2006. Dimensionality reduction by learning an invariant mapping.

S. Hochreiter and J. Schmidhuber. 1997. Long short-term memory. *Neural computation* 9(8):1735–1780.

I. Hussain and S. Asghar. 2017. A survey of author name disambiguation techniques: 2010 to 2016. *The Knowledge Engineering Review* 32.

D. P. Kingma and J. Ba. 2014. Adam: A method for stochastic optimization .

G. Kondrak. 2005. N-gram similarity and distance. Springer, pages 115–126.

B. Kulis et al. 2013. Metric learning: A survey. *Foundations and Trends in Machine Learning* 5(4):287–364.

J. Lehmann et al. 2015. DBpedia - a large-scale, multilingual knowledge base extracted from wikipedia. *Semantic Web Journal* 6(2):167–195.

E. Maud et al. 2016. Jrc-names: Multilingual entity name variants and titles as linked data. *Semantic Web Journal* 8(2):283–295.

P. Neculoiu et al. 2016. Learning text similarity with siamese recurrent networks.

A. Schmaltz et al. 2016. Sentence-level grammatical error identification as sequence-to-sequence correction.

W. Shen, J. Wang, and J. Han. 2015. Entity linking with a knowledge base: Issues, techniques, and solutions. *IEEE TKDE* .

R. Sproat and N. Jaitly. 2016. Rnn approaches to text normalization: A challenge .

K. Srinivas, A. Gale, and J. Dolby. 2018. Merging datasets through deep learning .

R. Steinberger et al. 2011. Jrc-names: A freely available, highly multilingual named entity resource.

I. Sutskever, O. Vinyals, and Q. V. Le. 2014. Sequence to sequence learning with neural networks.

R. J. Williams and D. Zipser. 1989. A learning algorithm for continually running fully recurrent neural networks. *Neural computation* 1(2):270–280.

X. Yin et al. 2008. Truth discovery with multiple conflicting information providers on the web. *IEEE Transactions on Knowledge and Data Engineering* .

Y. Zhang et al. 2018. Name disambiguation in aminer: Clustering, maintenance, and human in the loop.

---

[8]International Standard Name Identifier, `isni.org`

Mining Tweets that refer to TV programs with Deep Neural Networks

Takeshi S. Kobayakawa   **Taro Miyazaki**   **Hiroki Okamoto**   **Simon Clippingdale**
{kobayakawa.t-ko,miyazaki.t-jw,okamoto.h-iw,simon.c-fe}@nhk.or.jp

NHK (Japan Broadcasting Corporation)
1-10-11 Kinuta, Setagaya-ku, Tokyo 157-8510, JAPAN

Abstract

The automatic analysis of expressions of opinion has been well studied in the opinion mining area, but a remaining problem is robustness for user-generated texts. Although consumer-generated texts are valuable since they contain a great number and wide variety of user evaluations, spelling inconsistency and the variety of expressions make analysis difficult. In order to tackle such situations, we applied a model that is reported to handle context in many natural language processing areas, to the problem of extracting references to the opinion target from text. Experiments on tweets that refer to television programs show that the model can extract such references with more than 90% accuracy.

1 Introduction

For some decades, opinion mining has been among the more extensively studied natural language applications, as plenty of consumer-generated texts have become widely available on the Internet. Consumer-generated texts in the real world are not always "clean" in the sense that vocabulary not in dictionaries is frequently used, so some measures for handling out-of-vocabulary (OOV) words are required. (Turney, 2002) gave a solution to this problem in the form of a semantic orientation measure, defined by pointwise mutual information, to automatically calculate the polarity of words.

However, these kinds of measures, usually called sentiment analysis, are only one aspect of opinion mining; another big problem to be tackled is the detection of the target of the opinion. Unlike analyzing opinions about, say, a well-known product that is referred to by name without many variations, analyzing opinions about an inconcrete object such as media content requires the extraction of the opinion target. Real tweets that refer to television (TV) programs frequently do not explicitly mention the proper full name of the program. Although official hashtags supplied by broadcasters are sometimes used, unofficial hashtags may also appear, and on occasion, paraphrased versions of the content may be used without either hashtags or the program name. Thus some method for finding paraphrases in that context is required in order to extract the target of such tweets.

Following the advent of Deep Neural Networks (DNNs), many context processing models have been proposed. One of the most successful models is Long Short-term Memory (LSTM) (Hochreiter and Schmidhuber, 1997), which we adopt as the basis for context processing. The recurrent architecture of LSTM is thought to handle long-term dependencies.

Our task is to detect references to TV programs as described in section 3. Viewers of TV programs generate many tweets, and broadcasters pay much attention to what viewers say, including what specific part of a program is being discussed. Producers and directors want to know as specifically as possible what viewers talk about, in order to assess in detail the impact that their programs have on audiences.

Formally, our task is to extract relevant parts from a sentence, which is similar to named entity recognition (NER) in the sense that it is a sequence detection problem, but rather more semantic. Our motivation is to clarify how well various NER models work on our task. The contribution of this paper is the performance comparison, on our task, of three NER methods that are reported to perform at state-of-the-art levels. We also conducted the same experiment on the CoNLL 2003 NER task, to allow comparison against our task.

2 Related Work

Related to our task in this study is the extraction of opinion targets in sentiment analysis that was conducted as a shared task in SemEval 2016,

Proceedings of the 2019 EMNLP Workshop W-NUT: The 5th Workshop on Noisy User-generated Text, pages 126–130
Hong Kong, Nov 4, 2019. ©2019 Association for Computational Linguistics

called aspect-based sentiment analysis (Pontiki et al., 2016), where opinion target extraction was one measure of performance for a sentence-level subtask. Unlike other sentiment analysis tasks, such a task requires the extraction of entity types including the opinion target and attribute labels as aspects of the opinion. However, entities to be extracted remain at the word level, and the candidates are given, such as "RESTAURANT", "FOOD", etc. Aspects to be extracted are similar in that one word can be chosen among given candidates, such as "PRICE", "QUALITY" and so on. In our task, the opinion target to be extracted is not restricted to a word but rather can be a phrase, and is not in general specified in advance. There have been many studies related to paraphrases, one of which was a shared task in SemEval 2015, known as paraphrase identification (Xu et al., 2015).

As regards phrase extraction, NER has a long history from (Tjong Kim Sang and De Meulder, 2003). The state-of-the-art models are thought to be (Huang et al., 2015; Lample et al., 2016; Ma and Hovy, 2016).

3 Task and Data

The task is to extract references to TV programs in the text part of tweets. We call such expressions "referers". Figure 1 shows these notions with an example. The referer part is not always the proper name of the program or an officially-defined hashtag, but can be a paraphrased reference to the program content.

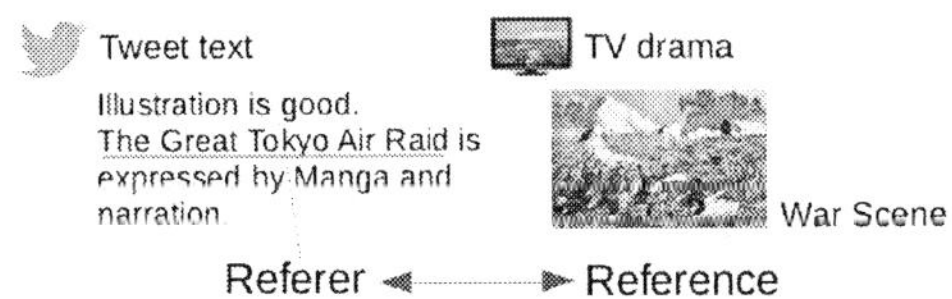

Figure 1: Terminology with an example

The targeted TV program is a Japanese TV drama, described in Table 1. We prepared a population of tweets that refer to TV programs by selecting tweets manually in a best-effort manner: tweets that contain wider general terms are likely to contain some portion of targeted data (including the broadcaster name NHK, for this study) if transmitted during the broadcast time of the program. Tweets were then selected manually to prepare research data.

The referer parts in the text are annotated manually as a region, using the brat rapid annotation tool by (Stenetorp et al., 2012). Since such anno-

tations are performed at the character level before the tokenization process, labels for the sequence tagging problem are converted to the positions of tokens during the tokenization process. The coding scheme for the region of the reference is IOB tags (Ramshaw and Marcus, 1995).

The tweets and targeted program names are both in Japanese, and since Japanese has no spaces between words, a Japanese tokenizer is used to separate words. We used SentencePiece (Kudo, 2018), a kind of subword tokenizer that handles OOVs and de-tokenization well. SentencePiece is trained with the same training data as the main task. Raw data are as described in Table 2. Sequence lengths in terms of words and characters are given as averages and standard deviations. Table 3 shows the characteristics of annotated tags. The referer part is annotated more finely, i.e. subcategorized by type of reference such as people, scene, music, etc., but for this study, we gather them into a single type of reference. Almost one third of the tokens has some kind of reference to the targeted program, and many chunks consist of more than one token, since there are many I-REFERENCE tags in the corpus. The data thus prepared are used for both training and evaluation.

Broadcast time	2019.4.1 8:00-8:15
Broadcaster	NHK (GTV channel)
Program title	Natsuzora[1]
Genre	television drama series
Synopsis	The story of an animator who decides to go to Tokyo.

Table 1: Targeted TV program

# tweets	3,745	
# chars per. tweet	30.1(ave.)	19.5(SD.)
# words per. tweet	11.6(ave.)	9.4(SD.)
# vocab of chars	1,693	
# vocab of words	7,727	

Table 2: Statistics of Raw Data

# B-REFERENCE	7,871
# I-REFERENCE	5,558
# O	29,829

Table 3: Statistics of Reference Tags

---

[1] https://en.wikipedia.org/wiki/Natsuzora

4 Model and Training Procedure

We treat the extraction of referer sections as a sequence tagging problem, and the state-of-the-art model for such a sequence tagging problem is a LSTM model combined with CRF, as reported in (Huang et al., 2015). We used a modified version of LSTM-CRF [2], implemented by TensorFlow [3].

The models used have three types of layers. Inputs for the model are a sequence of tokenized words, and to deal with large vocabulary tasks, distributed representations are used. The first layer is a trainable embedding layer that inputs sequences of words. The second layer is a recurrent layer, LSTM, where contexts are handled. The third layer is a CRF layer. The Viterbi decoding becomes the model output. For robustness purposes, a dropout (Hinton et al., 2012) layer is inserted at each layer, and can be thought of as a kind of regularizer.

Models are trained to maximize the f1 score (harmonic mean of precision and recall), and training is stopped when there is no further improvement. We tried three variants of these models, details of which are described as follows.

4.1 Bidirectional LSTM-CRF

The basic type of LSTM-CRF model was discussed in (Huang et al., 2015). The model consists generally of three layers: embedding, recurrent, and CRF.

Although several pre-trained models are available for the embedding layer, such as GLoVE (Pennington et al., 2014) or Word2Vec (Mikolov et al., 2013), we elected to train the embedding itself during the training procedure.

For the recurrent layer, contexts are handled by the LSTM type cell, whose input is whole sequence of words (distributed reps.) of a text, and whose output is a sequence of the same length as the input. The input is treated bi-directionally, so that a reversed word order is equivalent, in order to handle both forward and backward context dependencies. Forward and backward computations are performed separately, and they are concatenated just before the next CRF layer.

At the CRF layer, the concatenated outputs from the preceding recurrent layer are input to a linear-chain CRF. Like the original CRF (Lafferty et al., 2001), output labels are also used in the estimation of subsequent outputs.

[2] https://github.com/guillaumegenthial/tf_ner
[3] TensorFlow: Large-Scale Machine Learning on Heterogeneous Systems. http://tensorflow.org/

4.2 Character Embeddings

Given the sparsity problem with vocabularies, characters (the components of words) are used and combined with words. Like (Lample et al., 2016), characters are fed into the embedding layer and their parameters are also trained like the word input layer. The embeddings of both words and characters are concatenated, for input to the following recurrent layer.

4.3 Character Convolutions

There is also a model that uses convolutions for character inputs. (Ma and Hovy, 2016) used a convolutional neural network for characters, which then performed max-pooling. We also evaluated this model.

5 Experiments

5.1 Data allocation

Data with referer tags, as described in section 3, were divided into sets for training, validation, and evaluation, in the proportions 90%, 5%, and 5%, respectively.

The three models described in the previous section were compared on two tasks. One task is the original CoNLL 2003 Named Entity Recognition task (Tjong Kim Sang and De Meulder, 2003) in English. Named entities here are persons, locations, organizations, and names of miscellaneous entities, found in the Reuters news corpus. The second task is the task for this study, described in section 3.

We used texts without part-of-speech tags. Details of the training parameters are given in Table 4. Character type parameters are only used for those models that include character-level modeling. The training took 10 to 20 minutes on a laptop computer. Training was stopped at around 4,000 iterations.

Mini-batch size	20
Char. embedding dims.	100
Word embedding dims.	100
Char LSTM size	25
Word LSTM size	100
Dims. of context representations	300
Dropout rate	0.5

Table 4: Training Parameters

5.2 Results

The results are shown in Table 5. Figures for accuracy, precision, and recall have the same meanings

Task	Model	Accuracy(%)	Precision(%)	Recall(%)
CoNLL 2003	Majority Voting	82.54	**100.00**	0.05
	LSTM-CRF	94.15	75.61	69.97
	With char-emb.	95.92	80.35	77.90
	With conv. of char-emb.	**96.19**	81.00	**79.76**
Extraction of referer part for TV program extraction from tweets	Majority Voting	78.12	7.73	5.11
	LSTM-CRF	90.27	76.53	**82.95**
	With char-emb.	**91.23**	**77.38**	82.70
	With conv. of char-emb.	91.06	76.71	**82.95**

Table 5: Results

as in CoNLL 2003. Accuracy is an overall correct ratio including O tags (which means containing no kind of tags of interest). Precision is a measure for extracted instances, while recall relates to relevant instances, as usual in information retrieval parlance. The three models described in section 4 are compared together with majority voting as a trivial baseline model. The trivial model chooses the most frequent output seen in the training data as the trained output. Bold-faced figures are the best results among the four models compared.

Figures for the CoNLL 2003 NER task are almost the same as those given for the state-of-the-art models, so the implementation seems correct. On the CoNLL 2003 NER task, models that use convolution of character embeddings were the best performing, as reported in (Ma and Hovy, 2016). The 100% precision attained by majority voting comes at the price of extremely low recall, so it is not of much use; majority voting works very conservatively, only working when confident of the occurrence.

Figures for our task are original, and first reported here as far as we know. Unlike the NER task, the best performing model except for recall is LSTM-CRF with simple character embeddings, while simple word-level LSTM-CRF with convolutional character embeddings performed best for recall. Convolution of character embeddings performed a little worse than the model without convolutions. This may be due to over-modeling of characters, when in fact they are not so important for this task, while character level modeling remains effective.

6 Discussions

The experiments showed that referer sections for TV programs were well extracted using the state-of-the-art models for sequence tagging. However, the performance on this task was somewhat different than that on the NER task. This is be-cause the extracted parts are longer than named entities, and tend to form explanatory phrase expressions. These expressions can be thought of as phrase-level coreferences, or paraphrases, which are thought to relate linguistically to the high-level understanding of natural languages, such as rhetorical structures.

One possibility is to improve the embedding layer. Several phrase-level embeddings have been studied, and they may be useful for this kind of task. As words and characters are combined, phrases can also be combined to represent input sequences, and such models are probably worth trying.

A second possibility is to improve the recurrent layer. For deeper context handling, simply stacking LSTM layers is proposed. Techniques from semantic parsers may also help in capturing semantic chunks from the whole sentence. Whether further handling of contexts is possible is of much interest.

7 Conclusions and Future Work

We applied sequence tagging models to study the performance of extracting referer sections from relevant tweets for a targeted TV program. The extraction accuracy achieved by LSTM-CRF was significantly better than that attained by majority voting. Further treatment of deep contexts is suggested by comparisons of the experimental results on NER tasks, which remains a topic for future work. We suspect that some variations of deep neural networks may be able to solve this problem, especially for this kind of domain, because although noisy, large amounts of data addressing the same topic are available.

Acknowledgment

The authors would like to acknowledge the significant contribution to this work made by the late Dr. Atsushi Matsui.

References

Geoffrey E. Hinton, Nitish Srivastava, Alex Krizhevsky, Ilya Sutskever, and Ruslan Salakhutdinov. 2012. Improving neural networks by preventing co-adaptation of feature detectors. *CoRR*, abs/1207.0580.

Sepp Hochreiter and Jürgen Schmidhuber. 1997. Long short-term memory. *Neural computation*, 9:1735–80.

Zhiheng Huang, Wei Xu, and Kai Yu. 2015. Bidirectional LSTM-CRF models for sequence tagging. *CoRR*, abs/1508.01991.

Taku Kudo. 2018. Subword regularization: Improving neural network translation models with multiple subword candidates. In *Proceedings of the 56th Annual Meeting of the Association for Computational Linguistics (Volume 1: Long Papers)*, pages 66–75, Melbourne, Australia. Association for Computational Linguistics.

John D. Lafferty, Andrew McCallum, and Fernando C. N. Pereira. 2001. Conditional random fields: Probabilistic models for segmenting and labeling sequence data. In *Proceedings of the Eighteenth International Conference on Machine Learning*, ICML '01, pages 282–289, San Francisco, CA, USA. Morgan Kaufmann Publishers Inc.

Guillaume Lample, Miguel Ballesteros, Sandeep Subramanian, Kazuya Kawakami, and Chris Dyer. 2016. Neural architectures for named entity recognition. In *Proceedings of the 2016 Conference of the North American Chapter of the Association for Computational Linguistics: Human Language Technologies*, pages 260–270, San Diego, California. Association for Computational Linguistics.

Xuezhe Ma and Eduard Hovy. 2016. End-to-end sequence labeling via bi-directional LSTM-CNNs-CRF. In *Proceedings of the 54th Annual Meeting of the Association for Computational Linguistics (Volume 1: Long Papers)*, pages 1064–1074, Berlin, Germany. Association for Computational Linguistics.

Tomas Mikolov, Wen-tau Yih, and Geoffrey Zweig. 2013. Linguistic regularities in continuous space word representations. In *HLT-NAACL*, pages 746–751.

Jeffrey Pennington, Richard Socher, and Christopher D. Manning. 2014. Glove: Global vectors for word representation. In *Empirical Methods in Natural Language Processing (EMNLP)*, pages 1532–1543.

Maria Pontiki, Dimitris Galanis, Haris Papageorgiou, Ion Androutsopoulos, Suresh Manandhar, Mohammad AL-Smadi, Mahmoud Al-Ayyoub, Yanyan Zhao, Bing Qin, Orphée De Clercq, Véronique Hoste, Marianna Apidianaki, Xavier Tannier, Natalia Loukachevitch, Evgeniy Kotelnikov, Nuria Bel,

Salud María Jiménez-Zafra, and Gülşen Eryiğit. 2016. SemEval-2016 task 5: Aspect based sentiment analysis. In *Proceedings of the 10th International Workshop on Semantic Evaluation (SemEval-2016)*, pages 19–30, San Diego, California. Association for Computational Linguistics.

Lance Ramshaw and Mitch Marcus. 1995. Text chunking using transformation-based learning. In *Third Workshop on Very Large Corpora*.

Pontus Stenetorp, Sampo Pyysalo, Goran Topić, Tomoko Ohta, Sophia Ananiadou, and Jun'ichi Tsujii. 2012. brat: a web-based tool for NLP-assisted text annotation. In *Proceedings of the Demonstrations Session at EACL 2012*, Avignon, France. Association for Computational Linguistics. Available from http://brat.nlplab.org.

Erik F. Tjong Kim Sang and Fien De Meulder. 2003. Introduction to the conll-2003 shared task: Language-independent named entity recognition. In *Proceedings of CoNLL-2003*, pages 142–147. Edmonton, Canada.

Peter Turney. 2002. Thumbs up or thumbs down? semantic orientation applied to unsupervised classification of reviews. In *Proceedings of the 40th Annual Meeting of the Association for Computational Linguistics*, pages 417–424, Philadelphia, Pennsylvania, USA. Association for Computational Linguistics.

Wei Xu, Chris Callison-Burch, and Bill Dolan. 2015. SemEval-2015 task 1: Paraphrase and semantic similarity in twitter (PIT). In *Proceedings of the 9th International Workshop on Semantic Evaluation (SemEval 2015)*, pages 1–11, Denver, Colorado. Association for Computational Linguistics.

Normalising Non-standardised Orthography in Algerian Code-switched User-generated Data

Wafia Adouane, Jean-Philippe Bernardy and Simon Dobnik
Department of Philosophy, Linguistics and Theory of Science (FLoV),
Centre for Linguistic Theory and Studies in Probability (CLASP), University of Gothenburg
`firstname.lastname@gu.se`

Abstract

We work with Algerian, an under-resourced non-standardised Arabic variety, for which we compile a new parallel corpus consisting of user-generated textual data matched with normalised and corrected human annotations following data-driven and our linguistically motivated standard. We use an end-to-end deep neural model designed to deal with context-dependent spelling correction and normalisation. Results indicate that a model with two CNN sub-network encoders and an LSTM decoder performs the best, and that word context matters. Additionally, pre-processing data token-by-token with an edit-distance based aligner significantly improves the performance. We get promising results for the spelling correction and normalisation, as a pre-processing step for downstream tasks, on detecting binary Semantic Textual Similarity.

1 Introduction

Natural language processing (NLP) research has achieved impressive results, notably thanks to the use of deep neural networks (DNNs) which has pushed the field forward, achieving unprecedented performance for various tasks. However, research is often focused on large, standardised, monolingual and well-edited corpora that exist for a few well-resourced languages. We believe that such corpora will not generalise to all languages and domains, particularly regarding the colloquial varieties used in new communication channels. In fact, the large unstructured data coming from such channels is not only unedited, it also poses serious challenges to the current NLP processing pipelines and approaches as a whole.

Traditionally, the *standard language ideology* has dominated linguistic studies: it has been frequently assumed that languages are naturally uniform and monolingual. Nevertheless, the new

online data reveals that standardisation is neither natural nor universal, it is rather a *human invention* (Milroy, 2001), and variation is the norm. This variation presents several challenges to studying and processing dialects in social media (Jørgensen et al., 2015). These challenges are even more pronounced in multilingual societies where people use more than one language or language variety at the same time. We consider the case of the colloquial language used in Algeria (hereafter referred to as ALG) which combines both linguistic challenges mentioned above: (i) it is non-standardised, and (ii) it is a mixture of languages which involves code-switching between Modern Standard Arabic (MSA) and local Arabic, French, Berber, and English. (We refer the interested reader to the work of Adouane et al. (2018), who provides an overview of the linguistic landscape in Algeria.)

In interactive scenarios, people usually use spoken-like language and spontaneous orthography which reflects local variations. Our observations confirm those of Eisenstein (2013), namely that speakers have some-kind of tacit knowledge of spelling which is not completely arbitrary. However, it is hard to distinguish between local varieties and draw a clear borderline between them due to the free mobility of people, their ability to interact online, and the fact that these varieties are closely related and therefore hard to describe formally. Therefore, we find that using location to map dialectal variation (Doyle, 2014) is not useful. In many cases, the spelling is not consistent even by a single person within the same conversation. There is nothing intrinsically wrong with this inconsistency for there is no standard form to take as a reference. Besides, spelling variation does not hinder mutual understanding.

Current NLP approaches based on learning underlying regularities from data is not suitable to

Proceedings of the 2019 EMNLP Workshop W-NUT: The 5th Workshop on Noisy User-generated Text, pages 131–140
Hong Kong, Nov 4, 2019. ©2019 Association for Computational Linguistics

sparse noisy data. Furthermore, the data written in Arabic script is already rich in orthographic ambiguity because vowels are not written, except in very specific settings. Our focus is to process such user-generated textual data, reflecting the real use of a language. Therefore, for computational purposes, we want to automatically reduce the data sparsity caused by spelling inconsistency by normalising it based on spelling decisions that we designed, and build a tool that can be used for pre-processing such texts for other NLP tasks.

This paper is an attempt to take advantage of DNNs to reduce spelling inconsistency by performing several transformations (normalisation, disambiguation, etc.) detailed in Section 3 as a single machine-learning task. It is significantly different from the well-established spelling error correction mainly because we have to deal with a non-standardised code-switched language. In addition to the fact that ALG is an under-resourced language with respect to the size, quality and the diversity of the available labelled data, it suffers from the absence of other tools and linguistic resources required by current NLP techniques such as tokenisers, syntactic parsers, morphological taggers, lexicons, etc.

As contributions, (i) we introduce a new user-generated corpus for ALG with its parallel spelling normalised and corrected version produced by human annotators. (ii) We describe our spelling decisions aiming to reduce orthographic ambiguity and inconsistency for NLP tasks. These decisions are not the only possible ones, and can be debated and further refined. (iii) We propose a general end-to-end model for context sensitive text normalisation of non-standardised languages. We opt for end-to-end deep learning approach (with only a simple automatic pre-processing) because it is not only expensive and time consuming to build equivalent rule-based tools from bottom up, but it is also hard to exhaustively define spelling norms given the high linguistic variation.

The paper is organised as follows. In Section 2 we survey related work. In Section 3, we present our newly compiled parallel corpus and explain our data processing decisions. In Section 4, we give information about data statistics and data alignment. In Section 5, we describe our models. In Section 6, we describe our experiments and discuss the results. We conclude in Section 7 with potential future improvements.

2   Related Work

The task of normalising user-generated non-standardised data is closely related to the one of historical text normalisation (Pettersson, 2016), namely they present similar challenges for the current NLP – little sparse data. While the latter has a standardised spelling as a reference, the former does not because many colloquial languages have not undergone the standardisation process. Bollmann (2019) surveys the approaches used for historical text normalization for a set of languages. Both tasks are mainly framed as (statistical/neural) machine translation mostly at a token level where the source and the target language are the same or a standardised version of one another.

Similarly to the previous work, we formulate our task as a sequence-to-sequence (seq2seq) learning problem, but in contrast we take word context into account. A large body of work has been done to address the problem of seq2seq prediction and has achieved impressive results for diverse NLP tasks. Encoder-decoder models are most frequently used for seq2seq prediction with varying the architectures of the encoder like Recurrent Neural Network (RNN) in (Cho et al., 2014; Sutskever et al., 2014), bidirectional Long Short-Term Memory (LSTM) (Hochreiter and Schmidhuber, 1997) in (Bahdanau et al., 2014), Convolutional Neural Networks (CNN) in (Vinyals et al., 2015).

Our CNN-based architecture (see Section 5) is reminiscent of what has been proposed for machine translation by Gehring et al. (2017) but instead they use CNN for both encoder and decoder with multi-step attention. A difference with our model is that we use two sub-networks (LSTM/CNN and CNN/CNN) as an encoder, jointly trained to learn contextual representations of words. Then we use an LSTM as decoder instead of a CNN. Compared to the model of Bahdanau et al. (2014), an important difference is that we do not jointly train alignment and seq2seq prediction. Instead we perform alignment separately as a pre-processing step using edit-distance.

None of the mentioned models have been tested on the same prediction task as ours or on a related language. As the most closely related work for spell checking, Ghosh and Kristensson (2017) propose a seq2seq neural attention network system for automatic text correction and completion. They combine a character-based CNN and a Gated Recurrent Unit (GRU) (Cho et al., 2014) as encoder and a word-based GRU as decoder using a 12 million word English corpus. Recently, Sooraj et al. (2018) employed a character-based LSTM language model to detect and correct spelling errors for Malayalam. In the same line of research, Etoori et al. (2018) propose an attention model with a bidirectional character-based LSTM encoder-decoder trained end-to-end for Hindi and Telugu spelling correction using synthetic datasets.

Contrary to the task we are trying to address in this paper, the mentioned work deals either with spelling correction for monolingual standardised languages or historical text normalisation for standardised languages. This makes our task linguistically more challenging because our data includes more languages hence the model has to find the correct spelling of a word not only based on its context but also based on its language.

There has been work done for Arabic automatic error correction mainly for MSA including the work of Shaalan et al. (2012) and others included in the Arabic shared task (Mohit et al., 2014). Still they are inadequate to process non-standardised Arabic varieties given the significant phonological, morphological and lexicon differences between MSA and Arabic dialects (Watson, 2007). To the best of our knowledge, this is the first effort to process user-generated non-standardised dialectal Arabic textual data end-to-end.

3 Data Preparation

3.1 Corpus creation

As a basis we take the extended version of the unlabelled dataset of Adouane et al. (2018). Our extended version of it consists of 408,832 automatically pre-processed user-generated short texts from social media, such as forum discussions, and contains more than 6 million words. The automatic pre-processing involves removal of punctuation, emoticons and reduction of repeated letters to a maximum of two. Indeed, Arabic orthography does not use more than two adjacent occurrences of the same letter, and repeats in social media texts are mainly typos or emphasis. For this work, we further pre-processed this dataset by removing any existing diacritics representing short vowels because they are used rarely and inconsistently, even in the texts generated by the same user. We assume that such idiosyncratic variation will not affect our task in terms of semantics and bring about more robustness to language processing, especially because diacritics are not commonly used outside of the formal register. We also normalised many commonly used (often french-based) Latin script abbreviations to their full versions using the most frequent spelling in Arabic script including psk/because, r7/recipe, bnj/good morning, b1/well, 2m1/see you tomorrow, dsl/sorry, on+/moreover, tj/always, etc.

All texts are written in Arabic script and display spelling variations, typos and misspellings wrt. MSA, diglossic code-switching between MSA and local colloquial Arabic varieties, bilingual code-switching between Arabic varieties; French; Berber and English. From this further pre-processed unlabelled dataset, we created a parallel corpus of manually normalised texts. For this purpose, we randomly selected 185,219 texts and had 5 human annotators, who are native speakers with (computational) linguistics background, to edit and process them. The process took 6 months mainly working on lexical and syntactic ambiguities which require linguistically informative decisions, and all annotators checked the annotations of each other. We give here a few examples of spelling variation, but the corpus contains 50,456 words and 26,199 types to be normalised or corrected. Note that we will use word to refer to lexical words and tokens to refer to lexical words plus digits and interjections.

3.2 Annotation standard

In order to guide the annotators in producing parallel normalised text, we designed the following annotation standard which involves (i) spelling correction and (ii) spelling normalisation tasks.

3.2.1 Spelling correction for MSA

Misspelled MSA words are corrected using MSA orthography based on their context. نضيف، غذاءيه، جزاءر، مناقشه (clean, nutritional, Algeria, discussion) are corrected as نظيف، غذائية، جزائر، مناقشة.

3.2.2 Typographical error correction

The texts have been written on different kinds of keyboards resulting in lot of typos which mainly include missing spaces like in ومخلوهاشتخرجو or additional spaces like in لعا يلة which have been respectively corrected as وماخلوهاش تخرج و (and they did not let her to go out and) and لعايلة (the family). There are also keyboard related typos like reversing the order of letters or substituting one letter by another like in وليدي where ب should be replaced by ي to get the correct intended word وليدي (my son).

These typos can be detected from their context by manual checking. Usually they are not valid words and tend to be consistently generated by the same user which suggests that they may be related to their typing style and conditions. In فغيها خيها the user used the same wrong letter ي twice instead of ر and the correct form is خيرها فغيرها (the better is in something else).

3.2.3 Spelling normalisation

Non-MSA words including local Arabic varieties, French, Berber, English and neologisms are spelled spontaneously in Arabic script where users use improvised phonetically-based orthography.

A. Local Arabic varieties To deal with the spelling variation in colloquial varieties, a conventional orthography for dialectal Arabic (CODA) has been proposed for Egyptian (Eskander et al., 2013) and has been extended for Algerian (Saadane and Habash, 2015) and recently for several other Arabic varieties (Habash et al., 2018). We share the overall goals with the authors of CODA that a conventional orthography for developing NLP tools should preserve phonological, morphological and syntactic information of dialectal texts, should not diverge substantially from the existing forms, and should be easy to learn and write by the annotators.

However, CODA is primarily a recommendation of guidelines with several open questions related to how these guidelines could be implemented in new scenarios. In our case the most relevant open question is how to deal with multilingual code-switched data found in ALG. Using the existing recommendations from CODA would be in several cases impractical because several phonological distinctions required by the varieties in ALG could not be encoded and would have to be listed as exceptions. In other cases, the application of CODA would also require a substantial rewriting of the original user-generated text. Instead we use data statistics as heuristics to find the canonical forms.

We first train word embeddings using FastText (Joulin et al., 2016) on the entire unlabelled data. We collect a list of all words in the corpus and for each word we use FastText to predict the 10 most similar words and their frequencies. This normally returns the spelling variations of that word. A human annotator then decides whether the returned cluster should be considered as a spelling variation and assigns the most frequent spelling as the canonical form for all word occurrences in this cluster.

This is not a trivial task to be performed fully automatically because the model often returns unrelated words for less frequent words (case of the majority of words in the dataset). Hence a human expertise is needed. Contrary to CODA where every word has a single orthographic rendering, if a word has more than one frequently occurring spelling we keep such variations because they reflect local lexical or phonological differences which may be useful for sociolinguistic studies. For example, we keep both spelling variations of question words علاش، وعلاه and قداش، قداه (when and why) because they occurred very frequently and could be mapped to the same form if needed.

In cases where the difference between MSA and local Arabic spelling of a word is based on phonetically close sounds such as the sounds س [s] and ص [sˤ] as in صمعة، سمعة (reputation) or between ت [t] and ط [tˤ] as in تريق، طريق (road), and the meaning is preserved, MSA spelling is used. These cases are hard to identify automatically and require human expertise. Making spelling MSA-like as practically as possible will facilitate the reuse of existing MSA resources. Nevertheless, in cases where a word does not exist in MSA and has several different spellings, the most frequent one is used provided that it is not homonymous with another existing word. Such words include frequent local Arabic words like علاجال، ضك، امالا (so, now, for) with 27, 59 and 39 spellings respectively, along with the newly created words like نريض (I practise sports) and نرمضن (I fast).

B. Non-Arabic words The dataset includes French, Berber and English words, and the limitation of the Arabic script creates more ambiguity regrading how to spell non-existing sounds like /g, p, v/. The most frequent spelling with long vowels is used. For example, the French word "journal"

(newspaper) occurs with 6 spellings all mapped to
جورنال which is the most frequent spelling.

3.2.4 Word sense disambiguation

Using various languages with spelling variation
at the same time creates considerable ambiguity,
especially when all the varieties are written in
the Arabic script. One particular frequent source
of lexical ambiguity concerns the spelling of the
French definite articles (le, la, les) spelled as لي ،
لو ، لا ، either separated or concatenated to the
word they associate with. However, the Arabic
spelling is ambiguous because each of the above
words means something else in MSA or local Arabic. For instance, لي when written as a separate
word could either be a prepositional phrase (for
me) in MSA or a relative pronoun (who / that /
which) in local Arabic. For this reason we decided
to spell French definite articles attached as prefixes
like the Arabic definite article ال . This allows
disambiguation of cases like: لي ماش (hair strand
dyeing) in French and (who is not) in local Arabic.

The Berber word for "window" is spelt as طاقة
which means energy in MSA. Since Berber does
not have a standardised spelling in Arabic script[1],
we decided to change the spelling to تاقة which
is another spelling found in the dataset. Furthermore, lexical ambiguity is caused by the absence
of sounds (and corresponding graphemes) in Arabic like /g,v,p/. "Group" is spelled : قرووب ،
غروب and قرووب where جروب ، قروب ، قغوب ، غروب ،
قروب mean "sunset" and "closeness" in MSA. To
disambiguate these senses قـغـوب is used for
"group".

3.2.5 Negation particle

The various spellings of the word ما cause significant lexical and syntactic ambiguity. When
written separately, it could be a relative pronoun
or an interjection in MSA, a feminine possessive
pronoun in French, 'mother', 'water' or a negative particle in local Arabic. We decided to spell
this negation particle as a proclitic with a long Alif
when used with verbs (ما instead of م). This removes ambiguity for cases like the local Arabic
negated verb ماكان (there was not) from the MSA
noun مكان (place) and the local Arabic هذا ما كان
(that's it). All negated verbs in local Arabic are

spelled with ما as proclitic and ش as enclitic. As
a result it is easier to get the non-negated form by
stripping off the negation clitics. By removing the
initial ما and the final ش from ماعيطش (he did not
call) we get عيط (he called).

3.2.6 Word segmentation and tokenisation

Users tend to spell prepositions, reduced question
words and conjunctions as proclitics. This creates
an unnecessary sparse and large vocabulary. To
reduce the size of the vocabulary, we write such
proclitics as separate full forms, among others: وش
، ح ، م ، في ، كي ، او ، ف ، واش ، شا ، غ ، ك،
بلا، تع ، ع ، عل ، ه ، ولا. We split لي and ما when
they occur as relative pronouns attached to a verb.
وشيكون (who is him) is tokenised to واش يكون,
I will) حنديرلو (from the crisis) as من الازمة مالازمة
make him) راح نديرلو, and split relative pronouns
in ليكان and ما تمناي (what you wish) as ماتتمناي in
(who was) as لي كان. Other ambiguous cases include ورانا which could be either وين رانا (where are
we) or و رانا (and we are) or وراءنا (behind us)
depending on the context.

3.2.7 Abbreviations and acronyms

We collapse acronyms written as several tokens
to a single token and extend abbreviated words to
their full form based on their context. For instance,
م اس (SMS), and لاساماس is collapsed to لاس أم اس
is extended to مغرف كبيرة (tablespoon).

4 Data Statistics and Alignment

4.1 Data statistics

The final processed parallel corpus, described in
Section 3 consists of 185,219 unique (input, output) text pairs where the input is from the automatically pre-processed data and the output is from
the manually corrected and normalised data. The
input corpus has 3,175,788 words, and 272,421
types (unique words) where 90.20% of them occurred less than 10 times and 59.60% occurred
only once in the entire corpus. These figures serve
to give an idea about how sparse the data is. The

---

[1]Berber has its own script called Tifinagh and a standardised Latin spelling.

longest text has 112 words. The output corpus has 3,125,332 words and 246,222 types (unique words). The longest text has 112 words. The difference in the vocabulary size between the two corpora (50,456 words and 26,199 types) is primarily because of the introduced transformations.

4.2 Data alignment

Another difference between the two corpora is that the lengths of the input and the output may vary as a result of different tokenisation. This is not a problem in terms of machine learning, because the models described in Section 5 are designed to deal with variable length input and output sequences. However, because our two sequences are from the same language with the same meaning (the only difference is in spelling) we expect that alignment at the token level will lead to improved performance (see Section 6.1).

To this end, we have developed an aligner whose task is to make sure that every single unit (token) in the input (with potential misspelling) matches a unit (token) in the output. This may seem trivial until one remembers that misspellings may include added or deleted spaces. Our aligner works by computing the minimal edits to transform the input into the output (using the standard Levenshtein distance algorithm).

These minimal edits are not the basis for training (they will be discarded) *unless* they concern spaces. If a space is added, then to preserve word alignment we replace the corresponding space in the output by a special symbol (#). In inference mode (see Section 5.4), this symbol will be replaced by a space. If on the contrary a space is deleted, then it is added back (and words are aligned again). A special extra symbol ($) is added to mark that a spurious space was added and should be eventually deleted again when the model is used in inference mode. This alignment algorithm provides correct results whenever the Levenshtein distance at the sequence level is the sum of the Levenshtein distances for each unit (token) that is misspellings are not so large as to make deleting/inserting whole words a shorter operation than changing characters within words; and this condition is satisfied in our corpus.

5 Models

We frame the task of spelling correction and normalisation as a sequence-to-sequence (seq2seq) prediction problem, i.e., given an input sequence what is the best predicted output sequence. Note that sequence refers to user texts of any length including one token or more. We use an encoder-decoder architecture which consists of two neural networks where the first one reads an input sequence and transforms it into a vector representation, and the second one, representing a language model, conditions the generation of output symbols on the input sequence representation and generates an output sequence (Cho et al., 2014).

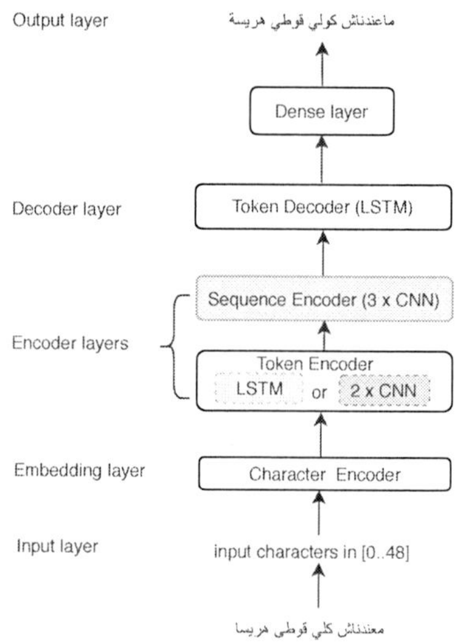

Figure 1: Model architecture.

As shown in Figure 1, the encoder consists of two sub-neural networks, namely token encoder and sequence encoder.

5.1 Token encoder

It reads the input sequence character by character and outputs a vector representation for each token in the sequence. Two configurations are used: either an LSTM encoder or a CNN encoder.

- **LSTM encoder:** represented in yellow and takes as input character embeddings with vocabulary size of 49, 100 dimensions, token representation size of 50 and a dropout rate of 30%.

- **CNN encoder:** represented in red and takes as input character embeddings. It is composed of 2 CNN layers with 50 filters of size 5, a RELU activation, a dropout rate of 20% followed by max pooling in the temporal dimension.

5.2 Sequence encoder

Represented in blue and consists of 3 CNN layers with 200 filters for the two first layers and 100 for the third layer, all filters have size 3, a RELU activation and dropout rate of 5%.

5.3 Token decoder

It is composed of one character-based LSTM layer with the same hyper-parameters as the LSTM encoder, followed by a dense layer.

5.4 Training and inference

All models are trained end-to-end to maximise the likelihood of the output sequence conditioned on the input sequence for 150 epochs using a batch size of 64 and Adam optimiser. Gradients with a norm greater than 5 are clipped.

For inference (generating an output character sequence), we use beam-search with a size of 20. Note that beam-search is used only to generate an output sequence and does not influence neither model training nor validation. The models generate characters starting from the start symbol ($<$) and stop at the end symbol ($>$) or at a predefined sequence length given as a hyper-parameter, whichever comes first.

6 Experiments and Results

In order to test our models and the gain from the aligner (see Section 4.2), we experiment with both versions of data: the non-aligned and the aligned data. It is worth mentioning that the only difference between them is that the aligned one contains extra symbols (# and $) marking missing or extra spaces. An extra space — thus word — is also added for every dollar sign. Moreover, to measure the effect of the context, we feed the data either token-by-token or sentence by sentence.

We split both the datasets into 75% (138,917 samples) for training, 5% (9,261 samples) for development, and 20% (37,041 samples) for validation. The reported hyper-parameters in Section 5 were fine-tuned on the development set.

We conduct two evaluations: (i) how well the suggested models perform on the seq2seq task, and (ii) how good is the best performing model for spelling correction and normalisation task, and what is its effect as a pre-processing step on downstream tasks like Semantic Textual Similarity (STS). We evaluate (i) using character-level accuracy, and we evaluate (ii) by calculating Precision, Recall and the F-score for the class of tokens that should be changed. Hence, Recall is the ratio of the correctly changed tokens to the number of tokens that should be changed, and Precision is the ratio of the correctly changed tokens to the number of tokens that are changed. F-score is the harmonic average of both.

6.1 Comparing models on Seq2seq task

In Table 1 we report the overall character level accuracy of the 4 best performing models for each configuration and experiment: (1) LSTM-Token-seq: the model with the Token LSTM + Sequence encoder (yellow and blue parts of Figure 1) and Token decoder, (2) CNN-Token-seq: the model with the Token CNN + Sequence encoder (red and blue parts of Figure 1) and Token decoder. Both (1) and (2) are trained and evaluated on non-aligned data with a sequence of tokens as input. (3) CNN-Token-seq-alig the same as model (2) but trained and evaluated on aligned data. (4) CNN-Token-token-alig: the same as (3) but with one token as input (token-by-token).

Results indicate that the LSTM encoder in (1) does not suit our task / data and fails to learn the sequential representations with an overall character accuracy of only 23.90%. This could be because of the high sparsity of the data which makes it hard to learn regularities. In contrast, the CNN encoder in (2) performs much better, with an overall character accuracy of 89.20%, suggesting that learning sequences of patterns through convolutions suits better our task / data than sequence modelling with LSTM. This is in line with what has been reported for machine translation in (Gehring et al., 2017).

The CNN encoder performs even better with the aligned data in (3). The difference can be attributed to the positive effect of the aligner which boosts the accuracy by 7%. The 9.1% drop in the accuracy in (4) compared to (3) is due to the lack of word context. This indicates that word context is essential, especially for word sense disambiguation in such highly varied data.

6.2 Quality and effect

- **Quality** We use the best performing model (3) and run the inference mode, (see Section 5.4), on the validation set which contains 567,308 words of which 507,429 words are already correctly spelled and 59,880 words must be changed, either corrected or normalised. We

	Models	Input	Data	Validation
1	LSTM-Token-seq	sequence of tokens	non-aligned	23.90
2	CNN-Token-seq	sequence of tokens	non-aligned	89.20
3	CNN-Token-seq-alig	sequence of tokens	aligned	**96.20**
4	CNN-Token-token-alig	one token	aligned	87.10

Table 1: Accuracy of models (%) on Seq2seq task.

perform quantitative and qualitative analysis of the generated sequences in terms of the changed spellings at a word level. Model (3) achieves an overall F-score of 64.74%, Recall of 88.58% and Precision of 51.02% on the words to change. It correctly spells 53,041 words from the total words to change and fails to correctly change 6,839 words. However, it introduces 50,914 incorrect changes (newly misspelled words or infelicitous corrections).

- **Error analysis** Examining the generated sequences shows that most errors are at the level of one character (duplicating or substituting one character) and the generated words are very similar to the reference. This is similar to the conclusion of Tiedemann (2009) that many errors of a character level phrase-based statistical machine translation for Norwegian and Swedish are of small length. Furthermore, we find that most of the not properly corrected words actually do not have enough representative instances, i.e., most of them occurred only once in the validation data and were not seen during the training. The high sparsity of the data is an interesting challenge for the current neural networks for which more research is needed.

With the settings of our experiments, the high Recall of the model at a word level indicates that it can be used for detecting errors and words to normalise but not for *automatically* fixing them because of its low Precision. Actually the reported low Precision is not that dramatic as it might seem because it is aggressive, i.e., a single wrong character means the entire word is wrong. Besides improving our inference settings, a better metric for evaluating such cases is needed.

- **Effect** We evaluate the effect of spelling correction and normalisation, as a pre-processing step for downstream tasks, on detecting binary Semantic Textual Similarity. We chose this task because it is one of the few available tasks for ALG we are aware of. We apply our spelling correction and normalisation on the ALG data reported by (Adouane et al., 2019). We replicate the best performing model for which the authors report an accuracy of 92.76%, and we get an accuracy of 94.40% with the same settings. The gain indicates that the spelling correction and normalisation is potentially a useful pre-processing step for downstream tasks.

7   Conclusion and Future Work

We compiled a new parallel corpus for ALG with linguistically motivated decisions for spelling correction and normalisation. Considerations such as being practical to implement and suitability for our goals are taken into account. We designed, implemented and tested 2 deep neural network architectures trained end-to-end to capture the knowledge encoded in the corrected and normalised corpus. The results showed that a CNN token-sequence encoder and an LSTM decoder performed the best when including context information. Additionally, applying a token aligner on the input data yielded better performance compared to the non-aligned data. Even though, with the current inference settings, the model generated some errors at a character level mainly due to the data sparsity, it is general and does not require extra resources except a parallel corpus. Hence it could be applied to other languages with the same settings.

In future work, we plan to improve the current inference mode by investigating other settings, improve the decoder by pre-training on the corrected and normalised data and a large MSA corpus to avoid generating incorrect character sequences. Moreover, we will evaluate the model extrinsically by using it to pre-process data for tasks such as code-switch detection, and topic detection to see how much it helps or hinders attempts to tackle these tasks.

Acknowledgement

The research reported in this paper was supported by a grant from the Swedish Research Council (VR project 2014-39) for the establishment of the Centre for Linguistic Theory and Studies in Probability (CLASP) at the University of Gothenburg. We are grateful to the annotators and all people who helped collecting the data. We also thank the anonymous reviewers for their useful comments.

References

Wafia Adouane, Jean-Philippe Bernardy, and Simon Dobnik. 2018. Improving Neural Network Performance by Injecting Background Knowledge: Detecting Code-switching and Borrowing in Algerian Texts. In *Proceedings of the Third Workshop on Computational Approaches to Linguistic Code-Switching*, pages 20–28. Association for Computational Linguistics (ACL).

Wafia Adouane, Jean-Philippe Bernardy, and Simon Dobnik. 2019. Neural Models for Detecting Binary Semantic Textual Similarity for Algerian and MSA. In *Proceedings of the Fourth Arabic Natural Language Processing Workshop*, pages 78–87, Florence, Italy. Association for Computational Linguistics (ACL).

Dzmitry Bahdanau, Kyunghyun Cho, and Yoshua Bengio. 2014. Neural Machine Translation by Jointly Learning to Align and Translate. *arXiv*, arXiv:1409.0473.

Marcel Bollmann. 2019. A Large-scale Comparison of Historical Text Normalization Systems. In *Proceedings of the 2019 Conference of the North American Chapter of the Association for Computational Linguistics: Human Language Technologies, Volume 1 (Long and Short Papers)*, pages 3885–3898. Association for Computational Linguistics (ACL).

Kyunghyun Cho, Bart Van Merriënboer, Caglar Gulcehre, Dzmitry Bahdanau, Fethi Bougares, Holger Schwenk, and Yoshua Bengio. 2014. Learning Phrase Representations using RNN Encoder–Decoder for Statistical Machine Translation. In *Proceedings of the 2014 Conference on Empirical Methods in Natural Language Processing (EMNLP)*, pages 1724–1734, Doha, Qatar. Association for Computational Linguistics (ACL).

Gabriel Doyle. 2014. Mapping Dialectal Variation by Querying Social Media. In *Proceedings of the 14th Conference of the European Chapter of the Association for Computational Linguistics*, pages 98–106. Association for Computational Linguistics (ACL).

Jacob Eisenstein. 2013. Phonological Factors in Social Media Writing. In *Proceedings of the Workshop on Language Analysis in Social Media*, pages 11–19, Atlanta.

Ramy Eskander, Nizar Habash, Owen Rambow, and Nadi Tomeh. 2013. Processing Spontaneous Orthography. In *Proceedings of the 2013 Conference of the North American Chapter of the Association for Computational Linguistics: Human Language Technologies*, pages 585–595. Association for Computational Linguistics (ACL).

Pravallika Etoori, Manoj Chinnakotla, and Radhika Mamidi. 2018. Automatic Spelling Correction for Resource-scarce Languages Using Deep Learning. In *Proceedings of Association for Computational Linguistics 2018, Student Research Workshop*, pages 146–152. Association for Computational Linguistics (ACL).

Jonas Gehring, Michael Auli, David Grangier, Denis Yarats, and Yann N. Dauphin. 2017. Convolutional Sequence to Sequence Learning. In *Proceedings of the 34th International Conference on Machine Learning*, volume 70 of *Proceedings of Machine Learning Research*, pages 1243–1252, International Convention Centre, Sydney, Australia. PMLR.

Shaona Ghosh and Per Ola Kristensson. 2017. Neural Networks for Text Correction and Completion in Keyboard Decoding. *arXiv*, arXiv: 1709.06429.

Nizar Habash, Fadhl Eryani, Salam Khalifa, Owen Rambow, Dana Abdulrahim, Alexander Erdmann, Reem Faraj, Wajdi Zaghouani, Houda Bouamor, Nasser Zalmout, Sara Hassan, Faisal Al shargi, Sakhar Alkhereyf, Basma Abdulkareem, Ramy Eskander, Mohammad Salameh, and Hind Saddiki. 2018. Unified Guidelines and Resources for Arabic Dialect Orthography. In *Proceedings of the Eleventh International Conference on Language Resources and Evaluation (LREC 2018)*, Miyazaki, Japan. European Language Resources Association (ELRA).

Sepp Hochreiter and Jürgen Schmidhuber. 1997. Long Short-Term Memory. *Neural Computation*, 9(8):1735–1780.

Anna Jørgensen, Dirk Hovy, and Anders Søgaard. 2015. Challenges of Studying and Processing Dialects in Social Media. In *Proceedings of the Workshop on Noisy User-generated Text*, pages 9–18. Association for Computational Linguistics (ACL).

Armand Joulin, Edouard Grave, Piotr Bojanowski, and Tomas Mikolov. 2016. Bag of Tricks for Efficient Text Classification. *arXiv*, arXiv:1607.01759.

James Milroy. 2001. Language Ideologies and the Consequence of Standardization. *Journal of Sociolinguistics*, 5:530 – 555.

Behrang Mohit, Alla Rozovskaya, Nizar Habash, Wajdi Zaghouani, and Ossama Obeid. 2014. The First QALB Shared Task on Automatic Text Correction for Arabic. In *Proceedings of the EMNLP 2014 Workshop on Arabic Natural Langauge Processing (ANLP)*, pages 39–47, Doha, Qatar.

Eva Pettersson. 2016. Spelling Normalisation and Linguistic Analysis of Historical Text for Information Extraction. *PhD thesis*, Studia Liguistica Upsaliensia 17, Uppsala: Acta Universitatis Upsaliensis.

Houda Saadane and Nizar Habash. 2015. A Conventional Orthography for Algerian Arabic. In *Proceedings of the Second Workshop on Arabic Natural Language Processing, ANLP, ACL 2015, Beijing, China, July 30, 2015*, pages 69–79. Association for Computational Linguistics (ACL).

Khaled Shaalan, Mohammed Attia, Pavel Pecina, Younes Samih, and Josef van Genabith. 2012. Arabic Word Generation and Modelling for Spell Checking. In *Proceedings of the Eight International Conference on Language Resources and Evaluation (LREC'12)*, Istanbul, Turkey. European Language Resources Association (ELRA).

S. Sooraj, K. Manjusha, M. Kumar, and K.P. Soman. 2018. Deep Learning Based Spell Checker for Malayalam Language. *Journal of Intelligent & Fuzzy Systems*, 34:1427–1434.

Ilya Sutskever, Oriol Vinyals, and Quoc V. Le. 2014. Sequence to Sequence Learning with Neural Networks. In *Advances in Neural Information Processing Systems 27: Annual Conference on Neural Information Processing Systems 2014, December 8-13 2014, Montreal, Quebec, Canada*, pages 3104–3112.

Jörg Tiedemann. 2009. Character-based PSMT for Closely Related Languages. In *Proceedings of 13th Annual Conference of the European Association for Machine Translation*, pages 12–19, Barcelona, Spain.

Oriol Vinyals, Alexander Toshev, Samy Bengio, and Dumitru Erhan. 2015. Show and Tell: A Neural Image Caption Generator. In *Computer Vision and Pattern Recognition*.

Janet C. E. Watson. 2007. *The Phonology and Morphology of Arabic*. The Phonology of the World's Languages. OUP Oxford.

Dialect Text Normalization to Normative Standard Finnish

Niko Partanen
Department of Finnish,
Finno-Ugrian
and Scandinavian Studies
University of Helsinki

Mika Hämäläinen
Department of Digital
Humanities
University of Helsinki

Khalid Alnajjar
Department of Computer Science
University of Helsinki

`firstname.lastname@helsinki.fi`

Abstract

We compare different LSTMs and transformer models in terms of their effectiveness in normalizing dialectal Finnish into the normative standard Finnish. As dialect is the common way of communication for people online in Finnish, such a normalization is a necessary step to improve the accuracy of the existing Finnish NLP tools that are tailored for normative Finnish text. We work on a corpus consisting of dialectal data from 23 distinct Finnish dialect varieties. The best functioning BRNN approach lowers the initial word error rate of the corpus from 52.89 to 5.73.

1 Introduction

Normalization is one of the possible pre-processing steps that can be applied to various text types in order to increase their compatibility with tools designed for the standard language. This approach can be taken in an essentially similar manner with dialectal texts, historical texts or colloquial written genres, and can be beneficial also as one processing step with many types of spoken language materials.

Our study focuses to the normalization of dialect texts, especially within the format of transcribed dialectal audio recordings, published primarily for linguistic research use. However, the dialectal correspondences in this kind of material are comparable to phenomena in other texts where dialectal features occur, the results are expected to be generally applicable.

This paper introduces a method for dialect transcript normalization, which enables the possibility to use existing NLP tools targeted for normative Finnish on these materials. Previous work conducted in English data indicates that normalization is a viable way of improving the accuracy of NLP methods such as POS tagging (van der Goot et al., 2017). This is an important motivation as the non-standard colloquial Finnish is the de facto language of communication on a multitude of internet platforms ranging from social media to forums and blogs. In its linguistic form, the colloquial dialectal Finnish deviates greatly from the standard normative Finnish, a fact that lowers the performance of the existing NLP tools for processing Finnish on such text.

2 Related work

Automated normalization has been tackled in the past many times especially in the case of historical text normalization. A recent meta-analysis on the topic (Bollmann, 2019) divides the contemporary approaches into five categories: substitution lists like VARD (Rayson et al., 2005) and Norma (Bollmann, 2012), rule-based methods (Baron and Rayson, 2008; Porta et al., 2013), edit distance based approaches (Hauser and Schulz, 2007; Amoia and Martinez, 2013), statistical methods and most recently neural methods.

For statistical methods, the most prominent recent ones have been different statistical machine translation (SMT) based methods. These methods often assimilate the normalization process with a regular translation process by training an SMT model on a character level. Such methods have been used for historical text (Pettersson et al., 2013; Hämäläinen et al., 2018) and contemporary dialect normalization (Samardzic et al., 2015).

Recently, many normalization methods utilized neural machine translation (NMT) analogously to the previous SMT based approaches on a character level due to its considerable ability in addressing the task. Bollmann and Søgaard (2016) have used a bidirectional long short-term memory (bi-LSTM) deep neural network to normalize historical German on a character level. The authors have also tested the efficiency of the model

Proceedings of the 2019 EMNLP Workshop W-NUT: The 5th Workshop on Noisy User-generated Text, pages 141–146
Hong Kong, Nov 4, 2019. ©2019 Association for Computational Linguistics

when additional auxiliary data is used during the training phase (i.e. multi-task learning). Based on their benchmarks, normalizations using the neural network approach outperformed the ones by conditional random fields (CRF) and Norma, where models trained with the auxiliary data generally had the best accuracy.

Tursun and Cakici (2017) test out LSTM and noisy channel model (NCM), a method commonly used for spell-checking text, to normalize Uyghur text. In addition to the base dataset ($\approx$ 200 sentences obtained from social networks, automatically and manually normalized), the authors have generated synthetic data by crawling news websites and introducing noise in it by substituting characters with their corresponding corrupted characters at random. Both of the methods have normalized the text with high accuracy which illustrates the their effectiveness. Similarly, Mandal and Nanmaran (2018) had employed an LSTM network and successfully normalized code-mixed data with an accuracy of 90.27%.

A recent study on historical English letters (Hämäläinen et al., 2019) compares different LSTM architectures finding that bi-directional recurrent neural networks (BRNN) work better than one-directional RNNs, however different attention models or deeper architecture do not have a positive effect on the results. Also providing additional data such as social metadata or century information makes the accuracy worse. Their findings suggest that post-processing is the most effective way of improving a character level NMT normalization model. The same method has been successfully applied in OCR post-correction as well (Hämäläinen and Hengchen, 2019).

3 Data

Finnish dialect materials have been collected systematically since late 1950s. These materials are currently stored in the Finnish Dialect Archive within Institute for the Languages of Finland, and they amount all in all 24,000 hours. The initial goal was to record 30 hours of speech from each pre-war Finnish municipality. This goal was reached in the 70s, and the work evolved toward making parts of the materials available as published text collections. Another approach that was initiated in the 80s was to start follow-up recordings in the same municipalities that were the targets of earlier recording activity.

Later the work on these published materials has resulted in multiple electronic corpora that are currently available. Although they represent only a tiny fraction of the entire recorded material, they reach remarkable coverage of different dialects and varieties of spoken Finnish. Some of these corpora contain various levels of manual annotation, while others are mainly plain text with associated metadata. Materials of this type can be characterized by an explicit attempt to represent dialects in linguistically accurate manner, having been created primarily by linguists with formal training in the field. These transcriptions are usually written with a transcription systems specific for each research tradition. The result of this type of work is not simply a text containing some dialectal features, but a systematic and scientific transcription of the dialectal speech.

The corpus we have used in training and testing is the Samples of Spoken Finnish corpus (Institute for the Languages of Finland, 2014). It is one of the primary traditional Finnish dialect collections, and one that is accompanied with hand-annotated normalization into standard Finnish. The size of corpus is 696,376 transcribed words, of which 684,977 have been normalized. The corpus covers 50 municipalities, and each municipality has two dialect samples. The materials were originally published in a series between 1978-2000. The goal was to include various dialects systematically and equally into the collection. The modern digital corpus is released under CC-BY license, and is available with its accompanying materials and documentation in the Language Bank of Finland.[1]

The data has been tokenized and the normative spellings have been aligned with the dialectal transcriptions on a token level. This makes our task with normalization model easier as no preprocessing is required. We randomly sort the sentences in the data and split them into a training (70% of the sentences), validation (15% of the sentences) and test (15% of the sentences) sets.

4 Dialect normalization

Our approach consists of a character level NMT model that learns to translate the dialectal Finnish to normative spelling. We experiment with two different model types, one being an LSTM based BRNN (bi-directional recurrent neural network) approach as taken by many in the past, and the

---

[1] http://urn.fi/urn:nbn:fi:lb-201407141

other is a transformer model as it has been reported to outperform LSTMs in many other sequence-to-sequence tasks.

For the BRNN model, we use mainly the Open-NMT (Klein et al., 2017) defaults. This means that there are two layers both in the encoder and the decoder and the attention model is the general global attention presented by Luong et al. (2015). The transformer model is that of Vaswani et al. (2017). Both models are trained for the default 100,000 training steps.

We experiment with three different ways of training the models. We train a set of models on a word level normalization, which means that the source and target consist of single words split into characters by white spaces. In order to make the models more aware of the context, we also train a set of models on chunked data. This means that we train the models by feeding in 3 words at a time; the words are split into characters and the word boundaries are indicated with an underscore character (_). Lastly we train one set of models on a sentence level. In this case the models are trained to normalize full sentences of words split into characters and separated by underscores.

In terms of the size of the training data, the word level data consists of 590k, the chunk level of 208k and the sentence level of 35k parallel rows. All of the models use the same split of training, testing and validation datasets as described earlier. The only difference is in how the data is fed into the models.

5 Results & Evaluation

We evaluate the methods by counting the word error rate[2] (WER) of their output in comparison with the test dataset. WER is a commonly used metric to assess the accuracy of text normalization.

Table 1 shows the WERs of the different methods. The initial WER of the non normalized dialectal text in comparison with the normalized text is shown in the column *No normalization*. As we can see from this number, the dialectal text is very different from the standardized spelling. Both the word level and chunk level normalization methods reach to a very high drop in the WER meaning that they manage to normalize the text rather well. Out of these, the chunk level BRNN achieves the best results. The performance is the worst in the sen-

tence level models, even to a degree that the transformer model manages to make the WER higher than the original.

5.1 Error analysis

Table 2 illustrates the general performance of the model, with errors marked in bold. The example sentence fragments are chosen by individual features they exhibit, as well as by how well they represent the corpus data.

Since the model accuracy is rather high, the errors are not very common in the output. We can also see clearly that the chunk model is able to predict the right form even when form is reduced to one character, as on line 5.

Since the dialectal variants often match the standard Finnish, over half of the forms need no changes. The model learns this well. Vast majority of needed changes are individual insertions, replacements or deletions in the word end, as illustrated in Table 2 at lines 2, 4, 6, 7, 15, 16, 17 and 18. However, also word-internal changes are common, as shown at lines 11 and 12. Some distinct types of common errors can be detected, and they are discussed below.

In some cases the errors are clearly connected to the vowel lengthening that does not mark ordinary phonological contrast. Line 3 shows how the dialectal pronoun variant of *he* 'he / she', *het*, is occasionally present in dialect material as *heet*, possibly being simply emphasized in a way that surfaces with an unexpected long vowel. This kind of sporadic vowel lengthening is rare, but seems to lead regularly to a wrong prediction, as these processes are highly irregular. This example also illustrates that when the model is presented a rare or unusual form, it seems to have a tendency to return prediction that has overgone no changes at all.

The model seems to learn relatively well the phonotactics of literary Finnish words. However, especially with compounds it shows a trait to classify word boundaries incorrectly. A good example of this is *ratapölökyntervaaus""kon* 'railroad tie treatment machine', for which the correct analysis would be 'rata#pölkyn#tervaus#kone'[3], but the model proposes 'rata#pölkyn#terva#uskoinen' which roughly translates as 'railroad tie creosote believer'. The latter variant is semantically quite awkward, but morphologically possible. This

---

	No normalization	Words		Chunks of 3		Sentences	
		BRNN	Transformer	BRNN	Transformer	BRNN	Transformer
WER	52.89	6.44	6.34	**5.73**	6.1	46.52	53.23

Table 1: The word error rates of the different models in relation to the test set

	source	correct target	prediction
1	joo	joo	joo
2	ettε	että	että
3	heet	he	**heet**
4	uskovah	uskovat	uskovat
5	n	niin	niin
6	ette	että	että
7	sinn	sinne	sinne
8	ei	ei	ei
9	ole	ole	ole
10	,	,	,
11	kukhaan	kukaan	kukaan
12	ymmärtänny	ymmärtänyt	ymmärtänyt
13	mennä	mennä	mennä
14	.	.	.
15	Artjärveŋ	Artjärven	Artjärven
16	kirkolt	kirkolta	kirkolta
17	mennäh	mennään	mennään
18	sinneh	sinne	sinne
19	Hiiteläh	Hiitelään	**Hiitelässä**

Table 2: Examples from input, output and prediction

phonotactic accuracy makes selection of correct analysis from multiple predicted variants more difficult, as it is not possible to easily detect morphologically valid and invalid forms. The longer words such as this also have more environments where normalization related changes have to be done, which likely makes their correct prediction increasingly difficult.

In word level model there are various errors related to morphology that has eroded from the dialectal realizations of the words, or correspond to a more complicated sequences. Long vowel sequences in standard Finnish often correspond to diphthongs or word internal -h- characters, and these multiple correspondence patterns may be challenging for the model to learn. Chunk model performs few percentages better than word model in predictions where long vowel sequences are present, which could hint that the model benefits from wider syntactic window the neighbouring words can provide. On line 19 a case of wrongly selected spatial case is illustrated.

There are cases where dialectal wordforms are ambiguous without context, i.e. standard Finnish cases adessive (-lla) and allative (-lle) are both marked with single character (-l). Various sandhi-phenomena at the word boundary also blurren the picture by introducing even more possible interpretations, such as *vuoristol laitaa*, where the correct underlying form of the first element would be *vuoriston* 'mountain-GEN'. The decision about correct form cannot be done with information provided only by single forms in isolation. The chunk level model shows small but consistent improvements in these cases. This is expected, as the word level model simply has no context to make the correct prediction.

It is important to note that since the model is trained on linguistic transcriptions, its performance is also limited to this context. For example, in the transcriptions all numbers, such as years and dates, are always written out as words. Thereby the model has never seen a number, and is doesn't process them either. Improving the model with additional training data that accounts this phenomena should, on the other hand, be relatively straightforward. Similarly the model has had only very limited exposure to upper case characters and some of the punctuation characters used in ordinary literary language, which should all be taken into account when attempting to use the model with novel datasets.

6 Conclusion & Future work

The normalization method we have proposed reaches remarkable accuracy with this dialectal transcription dataset of spoken Finnish. The error rate is so low that even if manual normalization would be the ultimate target, doing this in combination with our approach would make the work manifold faster. We have tested the results with large enough material that we assume similar method would work in other conditions where same preliminary conditions are met. These are sufficiently large amount of training data and systematic transcription system used to represent the dialectal speech.

Future work needs to be carried out to evaluate the results on different dialectal Finnish datasets, many of which have been created largely within the activities described earlier, but which are also continuously increasing as research on Finnish is a very vibrant topic in Finland and elsewhere. This method could also be a very efficient in increasing the possibilities for natural language processing of other contemporary spoken Finnish texts. Our method could also be easily used within OCR correction workflows, for example, as a step after automatic error correction.

Situation is essentially similar, to our knowledge, also in other countries with comparable history of dialectal text collection. Already within Finnish archives there are large collections of dialectal transcriptions in Swedish, as well as in the endangered Karelian and Sami languages. Applying our method into these resources would also directly improve their usability. However, it has to be kept in mind that our work has been carried out in a situation where the manually annotated training data is exceptionally large. In order to understand how widely applicable our method is for an endangered language setting, it would be important to test further how well the model performs with less data.

The performance with less data is especially crucial with low-resource languages. Many endangered languages around the world have text collections published in the last centuries, which, however, customarily use a linguistic transcription system that deviates systematically from the current standard orthography. Such a legacy data can be highly useful in language documentation work and enrich modern corpora, but there are challenges in normalization and further processing of this data (Blokland et al., 2019). The approach presented in our paper could be applicable into such data in various language documentation situations, and the recent interest the field has displayed toward language technology creates good conditions for further integration of these methods (Gerstenberger et al., 2016).

We have released the chunk-level BRNN normalization model openly on GitHub as a part of an open-source library called Murre[4]. We hope that the normalization models developed in this paper are useful for other researchers dealing with a variety of downstream Finnish NLP tasks.

____

[4]https://github.com/mikahama/murre

7   Acknowledgements

Niko Partanen's work has been conducted within the project Language Documentation meets Language Technology: The Next Step in the Description of Komi, funded by the Kone Foundation.

References

Marilisa Amoia and Jose Manuel Martinez. 2013. Using comparable collections of historical texts for building a diachronic dictionary for spelling normalization. In *Proceedings of the 7th workshop on language technology for cultural heritage, social sciences, and humanities*, pages 84–89.

Alistair Baron and Paul Rayson. 2008. VARD2: A tool for dealing with spelling variation in historical corpora. In *Postgraduate conference in corpus linguistics*.

Rogier Blokland, Niko Partanen, Michael Rießler, and Joshua Wilbur. 2019. Using computational approaches to integrate endangered language legacy data into documentation corpora: Past experiences and challenges ahead. In *Workshop on Computational Methods for Endangered Languages, Honolulu, Hawai'i, USA, February 26–27, 2019*, volume 2, pages 24–30. University of Colorado.

Marcel Bollmann. 2012. (Semi-)automatic normalization of historical texts using distance measures and the Norma tool. In *Proceedings of the Second Workshop on Annotation of Corpora for Research in the Humanities (ACRH-2)*, Lisbon, Portugal.

Marcel Bollmann. 2019. A large-scale comparison of historical text normalization systems. In *Proceedings of the 2019 Conference of the North American Chapter of the Association for Computational Linguistics: Human Language Technologies, Volume 1 (Long and Short Papers)*, pages 3885–3898, Minneapolis, Minnesota. Association for Computational Linguistics.

Marcel Bollmann and Anders Søgaard. 2016. Improving historical spelling normalization with bidirectional LSTMs and multi-task learning. In *Proceedings of COLING 2016, the 26th International Conference on Computational Linguistics: Technical Papers*, pages 131–139, Osaka, Japan. The COLING 2016 Organizing Committee.

Ciprian Gerstenberger, Niko Partanen, Michael Rießler, and Joshua Wilbur. 2016. Utilizing language technology in the documentation of endangered Uralic languages. *Northern European Journal of Language Technology*, 4:29–47.

Rob van der Goot, Barbara Plank, and Malvina Nissim. 2017. To normalize, or not to normalize: The impact of normalization on Part-of-Speech tagging. In *Proceedings of the 3rd Workshop on Noisy User-generated Text*, pages 31–39.

Mika Hämäläinen and Simon Hengchen. 2019. From the Paft to the Fiiture: a fully automatic NMT and Word Embeddings Method for OCR Post-Correction. In *Recent Advances in Natural Language Processing*, pages 432–437. INCOMA.

Mika Hämäläinen, Tanja Säily, Jack Rueter, Jörg Tiedemann, and Eetu Mäkelä. 2018. Normalizing early English letters to present-day English spelling. In *Proceedings of the Second Joint SIGHUM Workshop on Computational Linguistics for Cultural Heritage, Social Sciences, Humanities and Literature*, pages 87–96.

Mika Hämäläinen, Tanja Säily, Jack Rueter, Jörg Tiedemann, and Eetu Mäkelä. 2019. Revisiting NMT for normalization of early English letters. In *Proceedings of the 3rd Joint SIGHUM Workshop on Computational Linguistics for Cultural Heritage, Social Sciences, Humanities and Literature*, pages 71–75, Minneapolis, USA. Association for Computational Linguistics.

Andreas W Hauser and Klaus U Schulz. 2007. Unsupervised learning of edit distance weights for retrieving historical spelling variations. In *Proceedings of the First Workshop on Finite-State Techniques and Approximate Search*, pages 1–6.

Institute for the Languages of Finland. 2014. Suomen kielen näytteitä - Samples of Spoken Finnish [online-corpus], version 1.0. http://urn.fi/urn:nbn:fi:lb-201407141.

Guillaume Klein, Yoon Kim, Yuntian Deng, Jean Senellart, and Alexander M. Rush. 2017. OpenNMT: Open-Source Toolkit for Neural Machine Translation. In *Proc. ACL*.

Minh-Thang Luong, Hieu Pham, and Christopher D Manning. 2015. Effective approaches to attention-based neural machine translation. *arXiv preprint arXiv:1508.04025*.

Soumil Mandal and Karthick Nanmaran. 2018. Normalization of transliterated words in code-mixed data using Seq2Seq model & Levenshtein distance. In *Proceedings of the 2018 EMNLP Workshop W-NUT: The 4th Workshop on Noisy User-generated Text*, pages 49–53, Brussels, Belgium. Association for Computational Linguistics.

Eva Pettersson, Beáta Megyesi, and Jörg Tiedemann. 2013. An SMT approach to automatic annotation of historical text. In *Proceedings of the workshop on computational historical linguistics at NODALIDA 2013; May 22-24; 2013; Oslo; Norway. NEALT Proceedings Series 18*, 087, pages 54–69. Linköping University Electronic Press.

Jordi Porta, José-Luis Sancho, and Javier Gómez. 2013. Edit transducers for spelling variation in Old Spanish. In *Proceedings of the workshop on computational historical linguistics at NODALIDA 2013; May 22-24; 2013; Oslo; Norway. NEALT Proceedings Series 18*, 087, pages 70–79. Linköping University Electronic Press.

Paul Rayson, Dawn Archer, and Nicholas Smith. 2005. VARD versus WORD: a comparison of the UCREL variant detector and modern spellcheckers on english historical corpora. *Corpus Linguistics 2005*.

Tanja Samardzic, Yves Scherrer, and Elvira Glaser. 2015. Normalising orthographic and dialectal variants for the automatic processing of Swiss German. In *Proceedings of the 7th Language and Technology Conference*. ID: unige:82397.

Osman Tursun and Ruket Cakici. 2017. Noisy Uyghur text normalization. In *Proceedings of the 3rd Workshop on Noisy User-generated Text*, pages 85–93, Copenhagen, Denmark. Association for Computational Linguistics.

Ashish Vaswani, Noam Shazeer, Niki Parmar, Jakob Uszkoreit, Llion Jones, Aidan N Gomez, Łukasz Kaiser, and Illia Polosukhin. 2017. Attention is all you need. In *Advances in neural information processing systems*, pages 5998–6008.

A Cross-Topic Method for Supervised Relevance Classification

Jiawei Yong
kai.yuu@jp.ricoh.com
Ricoh Company, Ltd.

Abstract

In relevance classification, we hope to judge whether some utterances expressed on a topic are relevant or not. A usual method is to train a specific classifier respectively for each topic. However, in that way, it easily causes an underfitting problem in supervised learning model, since annotated data can be insufficient for every single topic. In this paper, we explore the common features beyond different topics and propose our cross-topic relevance embedding aggregation methodology (CREAM) that can expand the range of training data and apply what has been learned from source topics to a target topic. In our experiment, we show that our proposal could capture common features within a small amount of annotated data and improve the performance of relevance classification compared with other baselines.

1 Introduction

Relevance classification is a task of automatically distinguishing relevant information for a specific topic (Kimura et al., 2019). It can be regarded as a preprocessing task of stance detection, since potential stances should be refined into relevant

Topic: we should move Tsukiji Market to Toyosu.
Utterance1: I do not agree to move Tsukiji Market because of its long history. **Relevance**: relevant
Utterance2: The number of foreign tourists to Japan has been on the rise.   **Relevance**: irrelevant

Table 1: An example of relevance classification.

ones to improve accuracy and efficiency. In Table 1, we show a simple example of relevance classification task in NTCIR-14.

Here utterance1 is relevant to the topic not only for the contained topic words but also for its related

semantics, and then we could leverage its features available for further stance detection. On the contrary, utterance2 is irrelevant to the topic, and its further calculation of stance detection is meaningless. Previously, the relevance task could be approached in an unsupervised way by calculating pairwise semantic distances between topic and utterance (Achananuparp et al., 2008; Kusner et al., 2015). However, in most instances, their performance is not as good as a supervised approach. As to the supervised method, traditionally, a specific topic-oriented classifier could be trained for prediction on a single topic (Hasan and Ng, 2013; Y Wang et al., 2017), but this method actually builds up an isolation among different topics and wastes existing annotated data for new predictions.

Cross-topic classification, which enables the classifier to adapt different topics even in different domains, is an alternative to a supervised approach (Augenstein et al., 2016; Xu et al., 2018). It allows the model to assimilate the common features from existing topics and make inferences for a new topic. For example, in the NTCIR-14 relevance classification task, we could start with an existing classifier containing a well-prepared set of ground-truth data from some other Tsukiji Market history or economic topics, to give a prediction about Tsukiji Market relocation topic.

In this paper, aiming to alleviate insufficient annotated data problems for a specific topic, we have concentrated on cross-topic relevance classification by our novel CREAM proposal. The basic idea of the CREAM method is to capture the common pairwise features between existing topic and utterance, and then apply them to relevance prediction on a target topic. By analyzing F1-scores in experiment results, we have known that CREAM has shown its better performance on a known topic's relevance classification compared with baselines. In addition, an associated value to

Proceedings of the 2019 EMNLP Workshop W-NUT: The 5th Workshop on Noisy User-generated Text, pages 147–152
Hong Kong, Nov 4, 2019. ©2019 Association for Computational Linguistics

the unknown topic relevance has also been evaluated.

2 Related Work

To establish a cross-topic relevance classification model for supervised learning, here we regard it as a two-step procedure including pairwise text embedding and binary text classifier. Besides, the literatures around stance detection bright us inspiration as well.

2.1 Text Embedding

There are 3 well-known embedding methods named Word2Vec (Mikolov et al., 2013), GloVe (Pennington et al., 2014) and fastText (Joulin et al., 2016) for word-level representation. Although GloVe and fastText show higher performance on some specific aspects, there's no escaping the fact that Word2Vec (CBOW, Skip-Gram) is most popular and widely used among different languages.

As to sentence-level embeddings, the Word2Vec inventor Mikolov proposed doc2vec (Quoc et al., 2014), as its name implies, to learn sentence or document embeddings. What's more, averaged word embeddings (Han and Baldwin, 2016) is also a common sentence-level embedding method.

2.2 Text Classifier

There are several classical ML/DL models utilized for text classification such as Support Vector Machine (SVM) (Vapnik, 1998; Vapnik, 2013), and an RNN variant Long Short-term Memory (LSTM) (Hochreiter and Schmidhuber, 1997). It is noteworthy that SVM has an advantage in processing low-resource data.

Besides, nowadays we also could utilize a pre-trained model such as BERT (Devlin et al., 2018) or ELMO (Matthew et al., 2018) as a contextual text classifier. However, note that they are always pre-trained by a tremendous amount of open data (E.X. Wikipedia), we still need fine-tuning data on a large scale for root domain recognition.

2.3 Stance Detection

Stance detection, which is the task of classifying the attitude expressed in text towards a target, also provides us with valuable inspiration on text classification. For example, Augenstein (Augenstein et al., 2016) tried to utilize conditional LSTM encoding to build a representation for

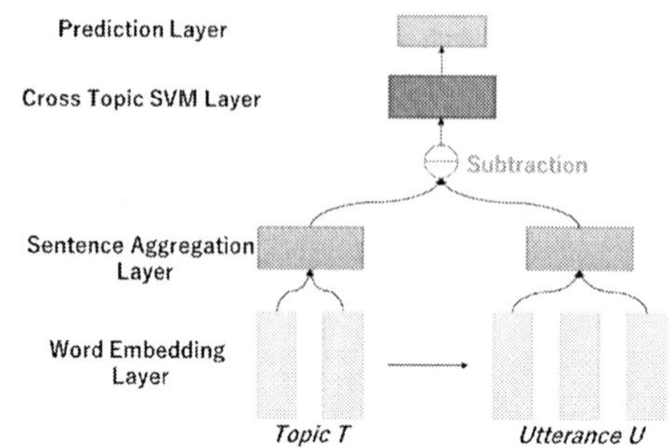

Figure 1: The overall architecture of CREAM.

stance and target independently, and an end-to-end memory network (Mohtarami et al., 2018), which integrates CNN with LSTM, has also been presented to solve this classification task. What's more, a simple but tough-to-beat baseline (Riedel et al., 2017) shows the potential of TF-IDF and cosine similarity on this pairwise classification task. Note that relevance classification can be regarded as a preprocessing of stance detection, since irrelevant stances should be excluded before being classified into support, against or even a neutral stance.

3 Methodology

In this section, we would like to give a comprehensive introduction about our proposed cross-topic method CREAM, for supervised relevance classification. The overall architecture of CREAM is depicted in Figure 1. As described in the previous section, we briefly divide the whole model into 2 parts including text embedding and text classifier. In the text embedding part, we have implemented Word Embedding Layer and Sentence Aggregation Layer, and as to the text classifier, the SVM Layer and Prediction Layer would achieve their functions. The expected input includes a pair of topic text and topic-oriented utterance in the same domain, and the output would be predicted binary relevance label. In the following, we would illustrate the implementation details of each layer in CREAM.

3.1 Word Embedding Layer

Here we adopt pre-trained Word2Vec embeddings to represent each word of two inputs (a topic text T containing n words and a topic-oriented utterance U, e.g., topic and utterance1 in Table 1). Note that utterance could be much longer than topic text, so here we select the same number of words as topic T from utterance U. For each selected word of T, we select one word with the highest Word2Vec similarity from U. The outputs of this layer are two sequences of word vectors with the same length $T = \{\vec{t}_1,...,\vec{t}_n\}$ and $U = \{\vec{u}_1,...,\vec{u}_n\}$.

3.2 Sentence Aggregation Layer

The sentence aggregation layer is the key to our cross-topic method CREAM. Here we manage to aggregate topic and utterance vectors by two steps to represent common features.

Separated Aggregation: In this step, we aim to provide a sentence-level embedding for T and U respectively. Here we separately aggregate $|T|$ word vectors for topic and utterance by averaged word embeddings:

$$\vec{T} = \frac{\sum_i^n \vec{t}_i}{n} \quad \vec{U} = \frac{\sum_i^n \vec{u}_i}{n} \tag{1}$$

Topic-Utterance Aggregation: Here we further concentrate on applying an aggregation between topic and utterance to represent the common features of relevance. As we have known there exists a classical conclusion from Word2Vec: $\vec{king} - \vec{man} + \vec{woman} = \vec{queen}$, we could get an inference that there exist some common features between word pairs (king, man) and (queen, woman) since $\vec{king} - \vec{man} = \vec{queen} - \vec{woman}$ is still workable.

As to sentence-level relevance classification, here we also conduct a vector subtraction between topic $\vec{T}$ and utterance $\vec{U}$ to represent relevance vector $\vec{R}$ as below.

$$\vec{R} = \frac{\vec{T} - \vec{U}}{|T|} \tag{2}$$

It is noteworthy that here we normalize each dimension value of relevance vector $\vec{R}$ by dividing $|T|$ to limit the subtraction result in the same range. Therefore, assuming that we have a relevance vector $\vec{R}_1$ (topic1) and $\vec{R}_2$ (topic2), they would be treated equally for the same cross-topic training if they all denote the same relevant relationship (e.g., $\vec{R}_1$ represents a utterance is relevant to topic1, $\vec{R}_2$ represents another utterance is relevant to topic2).

3.3 Cross-Topic SVM Layer

In this layer, we decide to adopt a supervised learning model SVM for cross-topic binary classification. The reason is because of low-resource data we have stated in chapter 2.2. In our case, SVM can efficiently perform a non-linear classification using kernel function (Mark et al., 1964) to fit the maximum-margin hyperplane in a transformed feature space. Here the following

sigmoid kernel function for relevance vectors $\vec{R}_1$ and $\vec{R}_2$ makes SVM acted as multi-layer neural networks even they are different topics.

$$K(\vec{R}_1, \vec{R}_2) = \tanh(a\,\vec{R}_1^{\mathrm{T}}\,\vec{R}_2 - b) \tag{3}$$

After applying the kernel function, the target function of maximum-margin hyperplane could be written in:

$$y = sign(\sum_{i \in S} \alpha_i^* t_i K(\vec{R}_i, x) - h^*) \tag{4}$$

Here h^*, α^* are optimal parameters to distinguish binary hyperplane, and t is the correct class label for training.

3.4 Prediction Layer

We predict the relevance label of each topic-utterance pair via sigmoid-fitting method:

$$p_i = \frac{1}{1 + \exp(Ay_i + B)} \tag{5}$$

Where we apply the sigmoid operation to get the predicted probability for relevant and irrelevant classes with parameters A and B.

4 Experiments

In this section, we would introduce the evaluation results of our proposed methodology. We have evaluated our CREAM on the NTCIR-14 QALab dataset (Kimura et al., 2019). Note that NTCIR-14 QALab dataset maybe is the first dataset focusing on relevance classification besides fact-check and stance detection. Besides our own method, we have also taken three baseline approaches to cross-topic relevance classification.

Word Mover's Distance (WMD): this classical unsupervised learning method is often utilized to calculate a word travel cost between two documents. Here we predict the relevance label based on switch cost boundary from utterance to its topic.

Bidirectional LSTM (BiLSTM): this approach receives encoded-word sequences (topic and utterance) and makes a concatenation to merge them into one sequence. Finally, the concatenated vector would be fed into its prediction layer to give a relevance label prediction.

BERT: There is no doubt that BERT is the state-of-the-art model to solve NLP issues such as text classification. It is well-known that BERT could receive pairwise texts as inputs and output the label between them. Therefore, BERT is also applicable to this relevance classification theoretically. Here

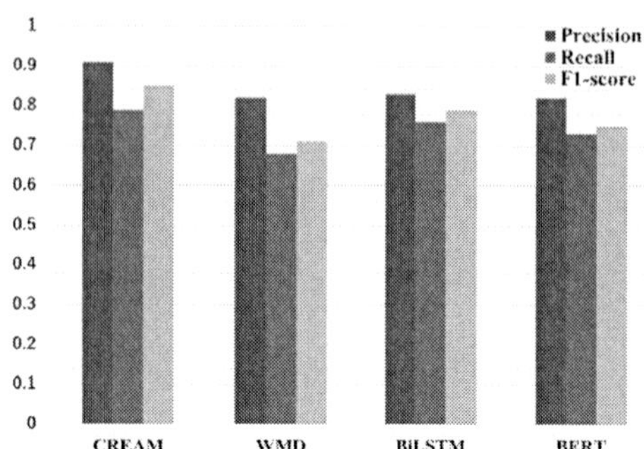

Figure 2: The averaged precision recall and F1-score of CREAM and baselines in experiment 1.

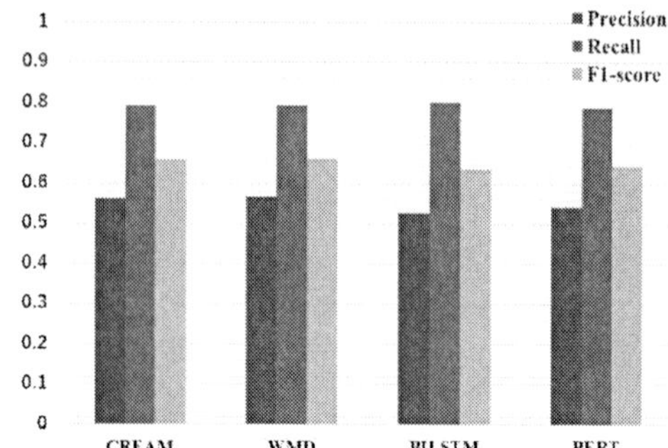

Figure 3: The averaged precision recall and F1-score of CREAM and baselines in experiment 2.

we beforehand input labelled topic and utterance separately into pre-trained BERT for fine-tuning.

4.1 Experiment dataset

NTCIR-14 QALab: This dataset is a Japanese collection for the relevance classification task, which contains around 10000 topic-oriented utterances on 14 different topics. Although task organizers do manual labeling by crowdsourcing, it is still difficult to provide an even larger amount of labeled dataset for each topic. Therefore, the traditional method with low-resource data would easily cause an underfitting problem.

4.2 Experiment Setup

Our initial word embeddings are obtained from the pre-trained Wikipedia word vectors (Suzuki et al., 2016).

In experiment 1, we divide our dataset into training data (1620) and test data (180) with the proportion 9:1. Note that there is no new topic in test data of experiment 1 since all topics have been included for training in the learning phase.

In experiment 2, we hope to verify the performance of our method compared with others on unknown topic relevance prediction. Therefore, we extract 13 topics' data for training to predict the last one topic in cross-validation.

4.3 Experiment Results

We mainly use F1-score to evaluate classification performance. Figure 2 illustrates the F1-score and averaged precision/recall as well among four methods in experiment 1, and the averaged evaluation results of cross-validation in experiment 2 have been summarized in Figure 3.

Furthermore, the relationship between the threshold of word mover's distance and F1 score is

shown as an example in Figure 4. We just go through all the potential thresholds to find out the optimal one on the peak point to give a prediction for test data.

5 Discussion

As shown in Figure 2, we have known our CREAM has improved performance of relevance classification through experiment 1 since its F1-score is higher than others. The potential reasons of improvement are listed in the below.

- The sentence aggregation layer could extract common features between topic-utterance pairs and demonstrate the pairwise relevance degree by sentence aggregation processing.
- The cross-topic SVM layer shows high performance especially in low-resource data even compared with BiLSTM and BERT model. The BERT model pre-trained with open data perhaps is limited by the fine-

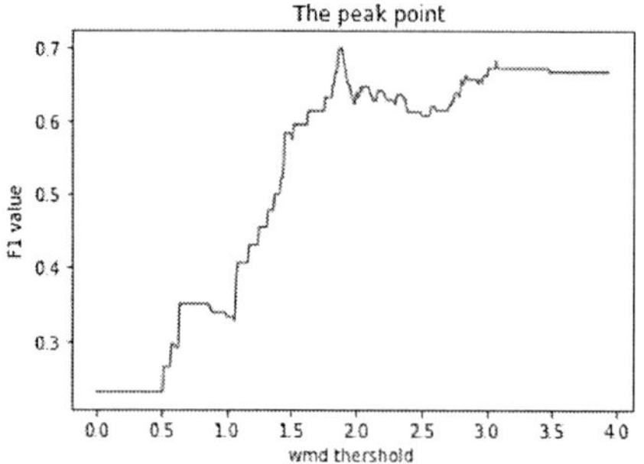

Figure 4: The relationship between the threshold of word mover's distance and F1 score.

tuning need for larger-scale data.

As to the unknown topic's relevance prediction in experiment 2, the result of our method is close to the unsupervised WMD method which shows a powerful predictive power to new data. We believe our CREAM method has an associated value on relevance prediction for unknown topics since the impact of a specific topic has been deducted by topic-utterance aggregation across different topics.

6 Conclusion and Future Work

In this paper, we have proposed a novel cross-topic aggregation model named CREAM to generalize the common features for solving low-resource data problems in relevance classification. Experiment results show its excellent performance on a known topic's relevance classification by F1-score over baselines. Meanwhile, we have also known that CREAM has an associated value to the unknown topic relevance prediction.

In the future, CREAM for relevance classification deserves more experiments with different datasets. For example, we could evaluate our methodology on multilingual datasets, in order to make it more impressive. Moreover, we could also input extern synonyms from the domain-based thesaurus to expand topic texts. Finally, self-attention mechanisms can be a promising improvement for imbalance length problems between topic and utterance instead of Word2Vec-style extraction.

Acknowledgments

Thanks to all relevant members of Ricoh System research center and NLU research group for their advices. Also, we would like to thank the anonymous reviewers and chairs for valuable feedback and discussions.

References

Isabelle Augenstein, Tim Rocktaschel, Andreas Vla-̈ chos, and Kalina Bontcheva. 2016. Stance detection with bidirectional conditional encoding. In *Proceedings of the Conference on Empirical Methods in Natural Language Processing (EMNLP)*. pages 876–885.

Xu Chang et al. *Cross-Target Stance Classification with Self-Attention Networks*. arXiv preprint arXiv: 1805.06593 (2018).

Sepp Hochreiter and J̈urgen Schmidhuber. 1997. *Long Short-term Memory*. Neural computation, 9(8): pages 1735–1780.

Devlin Jacob et al. *Bert: Pre-training of deep bidirectional transformers for language understanding*. arXiv preprint arXiv:1810.04805 (2018).

Lau Jey Han and Baldwin Timothy. 2016. *An empirical evaluation of doc2vec with practical insights into document embedding generation*. Computing Research Repository, arXiv preprint arXiv:1607.05368.

Armand Joulin, Edouard Grave, Piotr Bojanowski and Tomas Mikolov. 2016. *Bag of Tricks for Efficient Text Classification*. Computing Research Repository, arXiv:1607.01759.

Aizerman Mark A, Braverman, Emmanuel M, and Rozonoer, Lev I. 1964. *Theoretical foundations of the potential function method in pattern recognition learning*. Automation and Remote Control. 25: pages 821–837.

Peters Matthew E et al. *Deep contextualized word representations*. arXiv preprint arXiv:1802.05365 (2018).

Kusner Matt, Sun Yu, Kolkin Nicholas, and Weinberger Kilian. 2015. From word embeddings to document distances. In *Proceedings of International Conference on Machine Learning*, pages 957-966.

Tomas Mikolov, Ilya Sutskever, Kai Chen, Greg S Corrado and Jeff Dean. 2013. *Distributed Representations of Words and Phrases and Their Compositionality*. Advances in Neural Information Processing Systems, pages 3111-3119.

Mohtarami Mitra et al. *Automatic stance detection using end-to-end memory networks*. arXiv preprint arXiv:1804.07581 (2018).

Achananuparp Palakorn, Hu Xiaohua and Shen Xiajiong. 2008. The Evaluation of Sentence Similarity Measures. In *Proceedings of Data Warehousing and Knowledge Discovery*, pages 305-316.

Jeffrey Pennington, Richard Socher and Christopher Manning. 2014. Glove: Global vectors for word representation. In *Proceedings of the 2014 conference on empirical methods in natural language processing (EMNLP)*, pages 1532-1543.

Le Quoc and Tomas Mikolov. 2014. Distributed representations of sentences and documents. In *proceedings of International conference on machine learning*. pages 1188-1196.

Benjamin Riedel et al. *A simple but tough-to-beat baseline for the Fake News Challenge stance detection task*. arXiv preprint arXiv:1707.03264 (2017).

Kazi Saidul Hasan and Vincent Ng. 2013. Stance classification of ideological debates: Data, models, features, and constraints. In *Proceedings of the 6th*

International Joint Conference on Natural Language Processing. pages 1348–1356.

Masatoshi Suzuki, Koji Matsuda, Satoshi Sekine, Naoaki Okazaki and Kentaro Inui. 2016. Neural Joint Learning for Classifying Wikipedia Articles into Fine-grained Named Entity Types. In *Proceedings of the 30th Pacific Asia Conference on Language, Information and Computation*, pages 535-544.

Vapnik Vladimir. 1998. *Statistical learning theory.* Wiley, New York.

Vapnik Vladimir. 2013. *The Nature of Statistical Learning theory.* Springer Science & Business Media.

Yue Wang, Jidong Ge, Yemao Zhou, Yi Feng, Chuanyi Li, Zhongjin Li, Xiaoyu Zhou and Bin Luo. 2017. Topic Model Based Text Similarity Measure for Chinese Judgment Document. In *Proceedings of ICPCSEE*, vol 728.

Kimura Yasumoto et al. 2019. Overview of the NTCIR-14 QA Lab-PoliInfo task. In *Proceedings of the 14th NTCIR Conference*.

Exploring Multilingual Syntactic Sentence Representations

Chen Liu, Anderson de Andrade, Muhammad Osama
Wattpad
Toronto, ON, Canada
`cecilia, anderson, muhammad.osama@wattpad.com`

Abstract

We study methods for learning sentence embeddings with syntactic structure. We focus on methods of learning syntactic sentence-embeddings by using a multilingual parallel-corpus augmented by Universal Parts-of-Speech tags. We evaluate the quality of the learned embeddings by examining sentence-level nearest neighbours and functional dissimilarity in the embedding space. We also evaluate the ability of the method to learn syntactic sentence-embeddings for low-resource languages and demonstrate strong evidence for transfer learning. Our results show that syntactic sentence-embeddings can be learned while using less training data, fewer model parameters, and resulting in better evaluation metrics than state-of-the-art language models.

1 Introduction

Recent success in language modelling and representation learning have largely focused on learning the semantic structures of language (Devlin et al., 2018). Syntactic information, such as part-of-speech (POS) sequences, is an essential part of language and can be important for tasks such as authorship identification, writing-style analysis, translation, etc. Methods that learn syntactic representations have received relatively less attention, with focus mostly on evaluating the semantic information contained in representations produced by language models.

Multilingual embeddings have been shown to achieve top performance in many downstream tasks (Conneau et al., 2017; Artetxe and Schwenk, 2018). By training over large corpora, these models have shown to generalize to similar but unseen contexts. However, words contain multiple types of information: semantic, syntactic, and morphologic. Therefore, it is possible that syntactically different passages have similar embeddings due to their semantic properties. On tasks like the ones mentioned above, discriminating using patterns that include semantic information may result in poor generalization, specially when datasets are not sufficiently representative.

In this work, we study methods that learn sentence-level embeddings that explicitly capture syntactic information. We focus on variations of sequence-to-sequence models (Sutskever et al., 2014), trained using a multilingual corpus with universal part-of-speech (UPOS) tags for the target languages only. By using target-language UPOS tags in the training process, we are able to learn sentence-level embeddings for source languages that lack UPOS tagging data. This property can be leveraged to learn syntactic embeddings for low-resource languages.

Our main contributions are: to study whether sentence-level syntactic embeddings can be learned efficiently, to evaluate the structure of the learned embedding space, and to explore the potential of learning syntactic embeddings for low-resource languages.

We evaluate the syntactic structure of sentence-level embeddings by performing nearest-neighbour (NN) search in the embedding space. We show that these embeddings exhibit properties that correlate with similarities between UPOS sequences of the original sentences. We also evaluate the embeddings produced by language models such as BERT (Devlin et al., 2018) and show that they contain some syntactic information.

We further explore our method in the few-shot setting for low-resource source languages without large, high quality treebank datasets. We show its transfer-learning capabilities on artificial and real low-resource languages.

Lastly, we show that training on multilingual parallel corpora significantly improves the learned

Proceedings of the 2019 EMNLP Workshop W-NUT: The 5th Workshop on Noisy User-generated Text, pages 153–159
Hong Kong, Nov 4, 2019. ©2019 Association for Computational Linguistics

syntactic embeddings. This is similar to existing results for models trained (or pre-trained) on multiple languages (Schwenk, 2018; Artetxe and Schwenk, 2018) for downstream tasks (Lample and Conneau, 2019).

2 Related Work

Training semantic embeddings based on multilingual data was studied by MUSE (Conneau et al., 2017) and LASER (Artetxe and Schwenk, 2018) at the word and sentence levels respectively. Multitask training for disentangling semantic and syntactic information was studied in (Chen et al., 2019). This work also used a nearest neighbour method to evaluate the syntactic properties of models, though their focus was on disentanglement rather than embedding quality.

The syntactic content of language models was studied by examining syntax trees (Hewitt and Manning, 2019), subject-object agreement (Goldberg, 2019), and evaluation on syntactically altered datasets (Linzen et al., 2016; Marvin and Linzen, 2018). These works did not examine multilingual models.

Distant supervision (Fang and Cohn, 2016; Plank and Agic, 2018) has been used to learn POS taggers for low-resource languages using crosslingual corpora. The goal of these works is to learn word-level POS tags, rather than sentence-level syntactic embeddings. Furthermore, our method does not require explicit POS sequences for the low-resource language, which results in a simpler training process than distant supervision.

3 Method

3.1 Architecture

We iterated upon the model architecture proposed in LASER (Artetxe and Schwenk, 2018). The model consists of a two-layer Bi-directional LSTM (BiLSTM) encoder and a single-layer LSTM decoder. The encoder is language agnostic as no language context is provided as input. In contrast to LASER, we use the concatenation of last hidden and cell states of the encoder to initialize the decoder through a linear projection.

At each time-step, the decoder takes an embedding of the previous POS target concatenated with an embedding representing the language context, as well as a max-pooling over encoder outputs. Figure 1 shows the architecture of the proposed model.

Table 1: Hyperparameters

Parameter	Value
Number of encoder layers	2
Encoder forward cell size	128
Encoder backward cell size	128
Number of decoder layers	1
Decoder cell size	512
Input BPE vocab size	40000
BPE embedding size	100
UPOS embedding size	100
Language embedding size	20
Dropout rate	0.2
Learning rate	1e-4
Batch size	32

The input embeddings for the encoder were created using a jointly learned Byte-Pair-Encoding (BPE) vocabulary (Sennrich et al., 2016) for all languages by using sentencepiece[1].

3.2 Training

Training was performed using an aligned parallel corpus. Given a source-target aligned sentence pair (as in machine translation), we:

1. Convert the sentence in the source language into BPE
2. Look up embeddings for BPE as the input to the encoder
3. Convert the sentence in a target language into UPOS tags, in the tagset of the target language.
4. Use the UPOS tags in step 3 as the targets for a cross-entropy loss.

Hence, the task is to predict the UPOS sequence computed from the translated input sentence.

The UPOS targets were obtained using StandfordNLP (Qi et al., 2018) [2]. Dropout with a drop probability of 0.2 was applied to the encoder. The Adam optimizer (Kingma and Ba, 2015) was used with a constant learning rate of 0.0001. Table 1 shows a full list of the hyperparameters used in the training procedure.

3.3 Dataset

To create our training dataset, we followed an approach similar to LASER. The dataset contains 6

---

[1]https://github.com/google/sentencepiece
[2]https://stanfordnlp.github.io/stanfordnlp/index.html

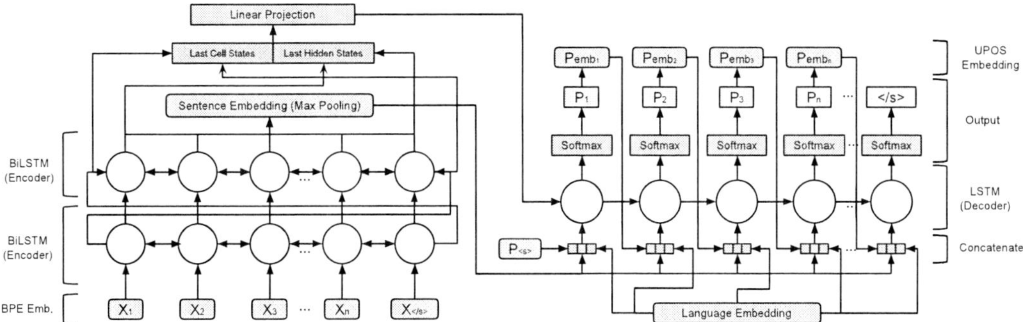

Figure 1: Proposed architecture.

languages: English, Spanish, German, Dutch, Korean and Chinese Mandarin. These languages use 3 different scripts, 2 different language orderings, and belong to 4 language families.

English, Spanish, German, and Dutch use a Latin-based script. However, Spanish is a Romantic language while the others are Germanic languages. Chinese Mandarin and Korean are included because they use non-latin based scripts and originate from language families distinct from the other languages. Although the grammatical rules vary between the selected languages, they share a number of key characteristics such as the *Subject-Verb-Object* ordering, except Korean (which mainly follows the *Subject-Object-Verb* order). We hope to extend our work to other languages with different scripts and sentence structures, such as Arabic, Japanese, Hindi, etc. in the future.

The dataset was created by using translations provided by Tatoeba[3] and OpenSubtitles[4] (Lison and Tiedemann, 2016). They were chosen for their high availability in multiple languages.

Statistics of the final training dataset are shown in Table 2. Rows and columns correspond to source and target languages respectively.

3.3.1 Tatoeba

Tatoeba is a freely available crowd-annotated dataset for language learning. We selected all sentences in English, Spanish, German, Dutch, and Korean. We pruned the dataset to contain only sentences with at least one translation to any of the other languages. The final training set contains 1.36M translation sentence pairs from this source.

3.3.2 OpenSubtitles

We augmented our training data by using the 2018 OpenSubtitles dataset. OpenSubtitles is a publicly available dataset based on movie subtitles (Lison and Tiedemann, 2016). We created our training dataset from selected aligned subtitles by taking the unique translations among the first million sentences, for each aligned parallel corpus. We further processed the data by pruning to remove samples with less than 3 words, multiple sentences, or incomplete sentences. The resulting dataset contains 1.9M translation sentence pairs from this source.

4 Experiments

We aim to address the following questions:

1. Can syntactic structures be embedded? For multiple languages?
2. Can parallel corpora be used to learn syntactic structure for low-resource languages?
3. Does multilingual pre-training improve syntactic embeddings?

We address question 1 in Secs. 4.1 and 4.2 by evaluating the quality of syntactic and semantic embeddings in several ways. Questions 2 and 3 are addressed in Sec. 4.3 by studying the transfer-learning performance of syntactic embeddings.

4.1 Quality of Syntactic Embeddings

We studied the quality of the learned syntactic embeddings by using a nearest-neighbour (NN) method.

First, we calculated the UPOS sequence of all sentences in the Tatoeba dataset by using a tagger. Sentences were then assigned to distinct groups according to their UPOS sequence, i.e., all sentences belonging to the same group had the same

[3]https://tatoeba.org/eng/
[4]http://opus.nlpl.eu/OpenSubtitles-v2018.php

Table 2: Training Dataset Statistics

	English	German	Spanish	Chinese	Korean	Dutch
English	-	521.87k	194.51k	41.33k	31.81k	190.86k
German	520.64k	-	217.96k	5.67k	0.21k	12.20k
Spanish	193.01k	217.46k	-	159.67k	28.68k	144.82k
Chinese	40.79k	5.62k	159.73k	-	0.05k	0.32k
Korean	31.05k	1.37k	28.89k	0.07k	-	56.93k
Dutch	215.18k	25.75k	155.35k	0.66k	56.92k	-

UPOS sequence.

For all languages except Korean, a held-out test set was created by randomly sampling groups that contained at least 6 sentences. For Korean, all groups containing at least 6 sentences were kept as the test set since the dataset is small.

During evaluation, we applied max-pooling to the outputs of the encoder to obtain the syntactic embeddings of the held-out sentences[5].

For each syntactic embedding, we find its top nearest neighbour (1-NN) and top-5 nearest neighbours (5-NN) in the embedding space for the held-out sentences, based on their UPOS group.

Given n sentences $S = \{s_0, \ldots, s_{n-1}\}$ and their embeddings $E = \{e_0, \ldots, e_{n-1}\}$, for each s_i there is a set of k gold nearest neighbours $G(i,k) = \{g_0, \ldots, g_{k-1}\}$, $G(i,k) \subseteq S$ such that $d(s_i, g) \leq d(s_i, s)$ for all $g \in G(i,k)$ and $s \in S \setminus G(i,k)$, where $d(\cdot, \cdot)$ is the cosine distance.

Given embedding e_i, we calculate cosine distances $\{d(e_i, e_j)$ for $e_j \in E, e_j \neq e_i\}$ and sort them into non-decreasing order $d_{j_0} \leq d_{j_1} \leq \cdots \leq d_{j_{n-2}}$. We consider the ordering to be unique as the probability of embedding cosine distances being equal is very small.

The set of embedded k-nearest neighbours of s_i is defined as

$$N(i,k) = \{s_j \text{ for } j \in \{j_0, \ldots, j_{k-1}\}\}.$$

Finally, the k-nearest neighbours accuracy for s_i is given by

$$\frac{|N(i,k) \cap G(i,k)|}{k}.$$

A good embedding model should cluster the embeddings for similar inputs in the embedding space. Hence, the 5-NN test can be seen as an indicator of how cohesive the embedding space is.

Table 3: Syntactic Nearest-Neighbour Accuracy (%)

	ISO	1-NN/5-NN	Total/Groups
English	en	97.27/93.36	2784/160
German	de	93.45/86.77	1282/91
Spanish	es	93.81/86.24	1503/81
Chinese	zh	71.26/61.44	167/22
Korean	ko	28.27/18.40	527/40
Dutch	nl	74.17/51.71	3171/452

The results are shown in Table 3. The differences in the number of groups in each language are due to different availabilities of sentences and sentence-types in the Tatoeba dataset.

The high nearest neighbours accuracy indicates that syntax information was successfully captured by the embeddings. Table 3 also shows that the syntactic information of multiple languages was captured by a single embedding model.

4.1.1 Language Model

A number of recent works (Hewitt and Manning, 2019; Goldberg, 2019) have probed language models to determine if they contain syntactic information. We applied the same nearest neighbours experiment (with the same test sets) on a number of existing language models: Universal Sentence Encoder (USE) (Cer et al., 2018), LASER, and BERT. For USE we used models available from TensorHub[6]. For LASER we used models and created embeddings from the official repository [7].

For BERT, we report the results using max (BERT_{max}) and average-pooling (BERT_{avg}), obtained from the BERT embedding toolkit[8] with the multilingual cased model (104 languages, 12-layers, 768-hidden units, 12-heads), and 'pooled-output' (BERT_{output}) from the TensorHub version

---

[5]Evaluation data will be hosted at https://github.com/ccliu2/syn-emb

[6]https://www.tensorflow.org/hub

[7]https://github.com/facebookresearch/LASER

[8]https://github.com/imgarylai/bert-embedding

of the model with the same parameters.

We computed the nearest neighbours experiment for all languages in the training data for the above models. The results are shown in Table 4. The results show that general purpose language models do capture syntax information, which varies greatly across languages and models.

The nearest neighbours accuracy of our syntactic embeddings in Table 3 significantly outperforms the general purpose language models. Arguably these language models were trained using different training data. However, this is a reasonable comparison because many real-world applications rely on released pre-trained language models for syntactically related information. Hence, we want to show that we can use much smaller models trained with direct supervision, to obtain syntactic embeddings with similar or better quality. Nonetheless, the training method used in this work can certainly be extended to architectures similar to BERT or USE.

4.2 Functional Dissimilarity

The experiments in the previous section showed that the proposed syntactic embeddings formed cohesive clusters in the embedding space, based on UPOS sequence similarities. We further studied the spatial relationships within the embeddings.

Word2Vec (Mikolov et al., 2013) examined spatial relationships between embeddings and compared them to the semantic relationships between words. Operations on vectors in the embedding space such as $King - Man + Woman = Queen$ created vectors that also correlated with similar operations in semantics. Such semantic comparisons do not directly translate to syntactic embeddings. However, syntax information shifts with edits on POS sequences. Hence, we examined the spatial relationships between syntactic embeddings by comparing their cosine similarities with the edit distances between UPOS sequence pairs.

Given n UPOS sequences $U = \{u_0, ..., u_{n-1}\}$, we compute the matrix $L \in \mathbb{R}^{n \times n}$, where $l_{ij} = l(u_i, u_j)$, the complement of the normalized Levenshtein distance between u_i and u_j.

Given the set of embedding vectors $\{e_0, ..., e_{n-1}\}$ where e_i is the embedding for sentence s_i, we also compute $D \in \mathbb{R}^{n \times n}$, where $d_{ij} = d(e_i, e_j)$. We further normalize d_{ij} to be within $[0, 1]$ by min-max normalization to obtain

$$\hat{D} = \text{minMax}(D).$$

Following (Yin and Shen, 2018), we define the *functional dissimilarity score* by

$$\frac{\|L - \hat{D}\|_\text{F}}{n}.$$

Intuitively, UPOS sequences that are similar (smaller edit distance) should be embedded close to each other in the embedding space, and embeddings that are further away should have dissimilar UPOS sequences. Hence, the functional dissimilarity score is low if the relative changes in UPOS sequences are reflected in the embedding space. The score is high if such changes are not reflected.

The functional dissimilarity score was computed using sentences from the test set in CoNLL 2017 Universal Dependencies task (Nivre et al., 2017) for the relevant languages with the provided UPOS sequences. Furthermore, none of the evaluated models, including the proposed method, were trained with CoNLL2017 data.

We compared the functional dissimilarity scores of our syntactic representations against embeddings obtained from BERT and LASER, to further demonstrate that simple network structures with explicit supervision may be sufficient to capture syntactic structure. All the results are shown in Table 5. We only show the best (lowest) results from BERT.

4.3 Transfer Performance of Syntactic Embeddings

Many NLP tasks utilize POS as features, but human annotated POS sequences are difficult and expensive to obtain. Thus, it is important to know if we can learn sentences-level syntactic embeddings for low-sources languages without treebanks.

We performed zero-shot transfer of the syntactic embeddings for French, Portuguese and Indonesian. French and Portuguese are simulated low-resource languages, while Indonesian is a true low-resource language. We reported the 1-NN and 5-NN accuracies for all languages using the same evaluation setting as described in the previous section. The results are shown in Table 6 (top).

We also fine-tuned the learned syntactic embeddings on the low-resource language for a varying number of training data and languages. The results are shown in Table 6 (bottom). In this table, the low-resource language is denoted as the 'source', while the high-resource language(s) is denoted as the 'target'. With this training method, no UPOS

Table 4: Syntactic Nearest-Neighbour for Language Models (%)

Model	English 1-NN/5-NN	German 1-NN/5-NN	Spanish 1-NN/5-NN	Chinese 1-NN/5-NN	Korean 1-NN/5-NN	Dutch 1-NN/5-NN
USE	71.83/55.68	59.87/44.26	53.05/38.06	39.23/30.18	21.22/12.43	28.66/12.77
BERT_{max}	**90.19/86.36**	**83.66/77.63**	**83.89/79.92**	**67.96/68.40**	20.30/11.92	37.67/19.51
BERT_{avg}	89.06/84.70	79.54/74.82	78.24/75.61	65.75/67.07	20.30/11.47	37.04/19.46
BERT_{output}	77.75/63.44	66.20/51.89	65.21/50.41	52.49/46.34	16.39/10.98	24.27/10.67
LASER	86.33/76.66	76.56/62.88	72.49/59.72	56.89/45.15	**26.63/15.90**	**50.75/31.00**

Table 5: Functional Dissimilarity Scores (Lower is Better)

Model	English	German	Spanish	Chinese	Korean	Dutch
BERT_{avg}	0.3463	0.3131	0.2955	0.2935	0.3001	0.3131
LASER	0.1602	0.1654	0.2074	0.3099	0.2829	0.1654
Proposed Work	0.1527	0.1588	0.1588	0.2267	0.2533	0.1588

tag information was provided to the model for the 'source' languages, where supervising information comes solely from parallel sentences and UPOS tags in high-resource languages.

The results show that for a new language (French and Portuguese) that is similar to the family of pre-training languages, there are two ways to achieve higher 1-NN accuracy. If the number of unique sentences in the new language is small, accuracy can be improved by increasing the size of the parallel corpora used to fine-tune. If only one parallel corpus is available, accuracy can be improved by increasing the number of unique sentence-pairs used to fine-tune.

For a new language that is dissimilar to the family of pre-training languages, e.g. Indonesian in Table 6, the above methods only improved nearest neighbours accuracy slightly. This may be caused by differing data distribution or by tagger inaccuracies. The results for Indonesian do indicate that some syntactic structure can be learned by using our method, even for a dissimilar language.

A future direction is to conduct a rigorous analysis of transfer learning between languages from the same versus different language families.

5 Conclusion

We examined the possibility of creating syntactic embeddings by using a multilingual method based on sequence-to-sequence models. In contrast to prior work, our method only requires parallel corpora and UPOS tags in the target language.

We studied the quality of learned embeddings by examining nearest neighbours in the embed-

Table 6: Syntactic Nearest-Neighbour on New languages (%)

Lang (ISO)	1-NN/5-NN	Total/Group
French (fr)	35.86/22.11	6816/435
Protuguese (pt)	48.29/23.15	4608/922
Indonesian (id)	21.00/35.92	657/59

	Number of Parallel Sentence Pairs	
Source -Target(s)	2k	10k
ISO	1-NN/5-NN	1-NN/5-NN
fr-en	47.37/32.18	58.41/42.87
fr-(en,es)	46.82/31.92	58.01/42.65
pt-en	56.75/30.14	64.52/36.94
pt-(en,es)	57.94/30.63	65.00/37.06
id-en	27.09/47.64	31.35/56.01

ding space and investigating their functional dissimilarity. These results were compared against recent state-of-the-art language models. We also showed that pre-training with a parallel corpus allowed the syntactic embeddings to be transferred to low-resource languages via few-shot fine-tuning.

Our evaluations indicated that syntactic structure can be learnt by using simple network architectures and explicit supervision. Future directions include improving the transfer performance for low-resource languages, disentangling semantic and syntactic embeddings, and analyzing the effect of transfer learning between languages belong to the same versus different language families.

References

Mikel Artetxe and Holger Schwenk. 2018. Massively multilingual sentence embeddings for zeroshot cross-lingual transfer and beyond. *arXiv preprint arXiv:1812.10464.*

Daniel Cer, Yinfei Yang, Sheng yi Kong, Nan Hua, Nicole Limtiaco, Rhomni St. John, Noah Constant, Mario Guajardo-Cespedes, Steve Yuan, Chris Tar, Yun-Hsuan Sung, Brian Strope, and Ray Kurzweil. 2018. Universal sentence encoder. *CoRR,* abs/1803.11175.

Mingda Chen, Qingming Tang, Sam Wiseman, and Kevin Gimpel. 2019. A multi-task approach for disentangling syntax and semantics in sentence representations. In *NAACL2019.*

Alexis Conneau, Guillaume Lample, Marc'Aurelio Ranzato, Ludovic Denoyer, and Hervé Jégou. 2017. Word translation without parallel data. *arXiv preprint arXiv:1710.04087.*

Jacob Devlin, Ming-Wei Chang, Kenton Lee, and Kristina Toutanova. 2018. Bert: Pre-training of deep bidirectional transformers for language understanding. *arXiv preprint arXiv:1810.04805.*

Meng Fang and Trevor Cohn. 2016. Learning when to trust distant supervision: An application to low-resource POS tagging using cross-lingual projection. In *Proceedings of the 20th SIGNLL Conference on Computational Natural Language Learning.*

Yoav Goldberg. 2019. Assessing bert's syntactic abilities. *arXiv preprint arXiv:1901.05287.*

John Hewitt and Christopher D. Manning. 2019. A structural probe for finding syntax in word representations. In *NAACL2019.*

Diederik P. Kingma and Jimmy Ba. 2015. Adam: A method for stochastic optimization. *CoRR,* abs/1412.6980.

Guillaume Lample and Alexis Conneau. 2019. Cross-lingual language model pretraining. *CoRR,* abs/1901.07291.

Tal Linzen, Emmanuel Dupoux, and Yoav Goldberg. 2016. Assessing the ability of lstms to learn syntax-sensitive dependencies. *Transactions of the Association for Computational Linguistics.*

Pierre Lison and Jörg Tiedemann. 2016. Opensubtitles2016: Extracting large parallel corpora from movie and tv subtitles.

Rebecca Marvin and Tal Linzen. 2018. Targeted syntactic evaluation of language models. In *EMNLP2018.*

Tomas Mikolov, Ilya Sutskever, Kai Chen, Gregory S. Corrado, and James A. Dean. 2013. Distributed representations of words and phrases and their compositionality. In *NIPS.*

Joakim Nivre, Željko Agić, Lars Ahrenberg, et al. 2017. Universal dependencies 2.0. lindat/clarin digital library at the institute of formal and applied linguistics, charles university, prague.

Barbara Plank and Zeljko Agic. 2018. Distant supervision from disparate sources for low-resource part-of-speech tagging. In *EMNLP2018.*

Peng Qi, Timothy Dozat, Yuhao Zhang, and Christopher D. Manning. 2018. Universal dependency parsing from scratch. In *Proceedings of the CoNLL 2018 Shared Task: Multilingual Parsing from Raw Text to Universal Dependencies,* pages 160–170, Brussels, Belgium. Association for Computational Linguistics.

Holger Schwenk. 2018. Filtering and mining parallel data in a joint multilingual space. In *ACL.*

Rico Sennrich, Barry Haddow, and Alexandra Birch. 2016. Neural machine translation of rare words with subword units. In *Proceedings of the 54th Annual Meeting of the Association for Computational Linguistics (Volume 1: Long Papers),* pages 1715–1725, Berlin, Germany. Association for Computational Linguistics.

Ilya Sutskever, Oriol Vinyals, and Quoc V. Le. 2014. Sequence to sequence learning with neural networks. In *NIPS.*

Zi Yin and Yuanyuan Shen. 2018. On the dimensionality of word embedding. In *Advances in Neural Information Processing Systems,* pages 887–898.

FASPell: A Fast, Adaptable, Simple, Powerful Chinese Spell Checker Based On DAE-Decoder Paradigm

Yuzhong Hong, Xianguo Yu, Neng He, Nan Liu, Junhui Liu

Intelligent Platform Division, iQIYI, Inc.

{hongyuzhong, yuxianguo, heneng, liunan, liujunhui}@qiyi.com

Abstract

We propose a Chinese spell checker – **FAS**Pell based on a new paradigm which consists of a denoising autoencoder (DAE) and a decoder. In comparison with previous state-of-the-art models, the new paradigm allows our spell checker to be **F**aster in computation, readily **A**daptable to both simplified and traditional Chinese texts produced by either humans or machines, and to require much **S**impler structure to be as much **P**owerful in both error detection and correction. These four achievements are made possible because the new paradigm circumvents two bottlenecks. First, the DAE **curtails the amount of Chinese spell checking data needed for supervised learning (to <10k sentences)** by leveraging the power of unsupervisedly pre-trained masked language model as in BERT, XLNet, MASS etc. Second, the decoder helps to **eliminate the use of confusion set** that is deficient in flexibility and sufficiency of utilizing the salient feature of Chinese character similarity.

1 Introduction

There has been a long line of research on detecting and correcting spelling errors in Chinese texts since some trailblazing work in the early 1990s (Shih et al., 1992; Chang, 1995). However, despite the spelling errors being reduced to substitution errors in most researches[1] and efforts of multiple recent shared tasks (Wu et al., 2013; Yu et al., 2014; Tseng et al., 2015; Fung et al., 2017), Chinese spell checking remains a difficult task. Moreover, the methods for languages like English can hardly be directly used for the Chinese language because there are no delimiters between words, whose lack of morphological variations makes the syntactic and semantic interpretations of any Chinese character highly dependent on its context.

1.1 Related work and bottlenecks

Almost all previous Chinese spell checking models deploy a common paradigm where a fixed set of similar characters of each Chinese character (called *confusion set*) is used as candidates, and a filter selects the best candidates as substitutions for a given sentence. This naive design is subjected to two major bottlenecks, whose negative impact has been unsuccessfully mitigated:

- **overfitting to under-resourced Chinese spell checking data**. Since Chinese spell checking data require tedious professional manual work, they have always been under-resourced. To prevent the filter from overfitting, Wang et al. (2018) propose an automatic method to generate pseudo spell checking data. However, the precision of their spell checking model ceases to improve when the generated data reaches 40k sentences. Zhao et al. (2017) use an extensive amount of ad hoc linguistic rules to filter candidates, only to achieve worse performance than ours even though our model does not leverage any linguistic knowledge.

- **inflexibility and insufficiency of confusion set in utilizing character similarity**. The feature of Chinese character similarity is very salient as it is related to the main cause of spelling errors (see subsection 2.2). However, the idea of confusion set is troublesome in utilizing it:

  1. *inflexibility* to address the issue that confusing characters in one scenario may not be confusing in another. The difference between simplified and traditional Chinese shown in Table 1 is an example. Wang et al. (2018) also suggest that confusing characters for ma-

---

[1] Likewise, this paper only covers substitution errors.

Proceedings of the 2019 EMNLP Workshop W-NUT: The 5th Workshop on Noisy User-generated Text, pages 160–169
Hong Kong, Nov 4, 2019. ©2019 Association for Computational Linguistics

chines are different from those for humans. Therefore, in practice, it is very likely that the correct candidates for substitution do not exist in a given confusion set, which harms recall. Also, considering more similar characters to preserve recall will risk lowering precision.

2. *insufficiency* in utilizing character similarity. Since a cut-off threshold of quantified character similarity (Liu et al., 2010; Wang et al., 2018) is used to produce the confusion set, similar characters are actually treated indiscriminately in terms of their similarity. This means the information of character similarity is not sufficiently utilized. To compensate this, Zhang et al. (2015) propose a spell checker that has to consider many less salient features such as word segmentation, which add more unnecessary noises to their model.

1.2 Motivation and contributions

The motivation of this paper is to circumvent the two bottlenecks in subsection 1.1 by changing the paradigm for Chinese spell checking.

As a major contribution and as exemplified by our proposed Chinese spell checking model in Figure 1, the most general form of the new paradigm consists of a denoising autoencoder[2] (DAE) and a decoder. To prove that it is indeed a novel contribution, we compare it with two similar paradigms and show their differences as follows:

1. Similar to the old paradigm used in previous Chinese spell checking models, a model under the DAE-decoder paradigm also produces candidates (by DAE) and then filters the candidates (by the decoder). However, candidates are produced on the fly based on contexts. If the DAE is powerful enough, we should expect that all contextually suitable candidates are recalled, which prevent the inflexibility issue caused by using confusion set. The DAE will also prevent the overfitting issue because it can be trained unsupervisedly using a large number of natural texts. Moreover, character similarity can be used by the decoder without losing any information.

2. The DAE-decoder paradigm is *sequence-to-sequence*, which makes it resemble the encoder-decoder paradigm in tasks like machine translation, grammar checking, etc. However, in the encoder-decoder paradigm, the encoder extracts semantic information, and the decoder generates texts that embody the information. In contrast, in the DAE-decoder paradigm, the DAE provides candidates to reconstruct texts from the corrupted ones based on contextual feature, and the decoder[3] selects the best candidates by incorporating other features.

Besides the new paradigm per se, there are two additional contributions in our proposed Chinese spell checking model:

- we propose a more precise quantification method of character similarity than the ones proposed by Liu et al. (2010) and Wang et al. (2018) (see subsection 2.2);

- we propose an empirically effective decoder to filter candidates under the principle of getting the highest possible precision with minimal harm to recall (see subsection 2.3).

1.3 Achievements

Thanks to our contributions mentioned in subsection 1.2, our model can be characterized by the following achievements relative to previous state-of-the-art models, and thus is named **FASPell**.

- Our model is **F**ast. It is shown (subsection 3.3) to be faster in filtering than previous state-of-the-art models either in terms of absolute time consumption or time complexity.

- Our model is **A**daptable. To demonstrate this, we test it on texts from different scenarios – texts by humans, such as learners of Chinese as a Foreign Language (CFL), and by machines, such as Optical Character Recognition (OCR). It can also be applied to both simplified Chinese and traditional Chinese, despite the challenging issue that some erroneous usages of characters in traditional texts are considered valid usages in simplified texts (see Table 1). To the best of our knowledge, all previous state-of-the-art models only focus on human errors in traditional Chinese texts.

---

[2]the term *denoising autoencoder* follows the same sense used by Yang et al. (2019), which is arguably more general than the one used by Vincent et al. (2008).

[3]The term *decoder* here is analogous as in *Viterbi decoder* in the sense of finding the best path along candidates.

Table 1: Examples on the left are considered valid usages in simplified Chinese (SC). Notes on the right are about how they are erroneous in traditional Chinese (TC) and suggested corrections. This inconsistency is because multiple traditional characters were merged into identical characters in the simplification process. Our model makes corrections for this type of errors only in traditional texts. In simplified texts, they are not detected as errors.

SC Examples	Notes on TC usage	
周末 (weekend)	周 → 週	周 only in 周到, etc.
旅游 (trip)	游 → 遊	游 only in 游泳, etc.
制造 (make)	制 → 製	制 only in 制度, etc.

- Our model is **S**imple. As shown in Figure 1, it has only a masked language model and a filter as opposed to multiple feature-producing models and filters being used in previous state-of-the-art proposals. Moreover, only a small training set and a set of visual and phonological features of characters are required in our model. No extra data are necessary, including confusion set. This makes our model even simpler.

- Our model is **P**owerful. On benchmark data sets, it achieves similar F1 performances (subsection 3.2) to those of previous state-of-the-art models on both detection and correction level. It also achieves arguably high precision (78.5% in detection and 73.4% in correction) on our OCR data set.

2 FASPell

As shown in Figure 1, our model uses masked language model (see subsection 2.1) as the DAE to produce candidates and confidence-similarity decoder (see subsection 2.2 and 2.3) to filter candidates. In practice, doing several rounds of the whole process is also proven to be helpful (subsection 3.4).

2.1 Masked language model

Masked language model (MLM) guesses the tokens that are masked in a tokenized sentence. It is intuitive to use MLM as the DAE to detect and correct Chinese spelling errors because it is in line with the task of Chinese spell checking. In the original training process of MLM in BERT (Devlin et al., 2018), the errors are the random masks, which are the special token [MASK] 80% of the

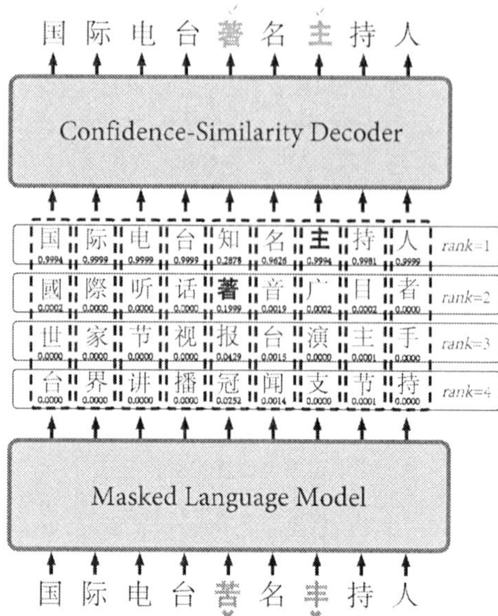

Figure 1: A real example of how an erroneous sentence which is supposed to have the meaning of "*A famous international radio broadcaster*" is successfully spell-checked with two erroneous characters 苦 and 丰 being detected and corrected using FASPell. Note that with our proposed confidence-similarity decoder, the final choice for substitution is not necessarily the candidate ranked the first.

time, a random token in the vocabulary 10% of the time and the original token 10% of the time. In cases where a random token is used as the mask, the model actually learns how to correct an erroneous character; in cases where the original tokens are kept, the model actually learns how to detect if a character is erroneous or not. For simplicity purposes, FASPell adopts the architecture of MLM as in BERT (Devlin et al., 2018). Recent variants – XLNet (Yang et al., 2019), MASS (Song et al., 2019) have more complex architectures of MLM, but they are also suitable.

However, just using a pre-trained MLM raises the issue that the errors introduced by random masks may be very different from the actual errors in spell checking data. Therefore, we propose the following method to fine-tune the MLM on spell checking training sets:

- For texts that have no errors, we follow the original training process as in BERT;

- For texts that have errors, we create two types of training examples by:

1. given a sentence, we mask the erroneous tokens with themselves and set their target labels as their corresponding correct characters;

2. to prevent overfitting, we also mask tokens that are not erroneous with themselves and set their target labels as themselves, too.

The two types of training examples are balanced to have roughly similar quantity.

Fine-tuning a pre-trained MLM is proven to be very effective in many downstream tasks (Devlin et al., 2018; Yang et al., 2019; Song et al., 2019), so one would argue that this is where the power of FASPell mainly comes from. However, we would like to emphasize that the power of FASPell should not be biasedly attributed to MLM. In fact, we show in our ablation studies (subsection 3.2) that MLM itself can only serve as a very *weak* Chinese spell checker (its performance can be as poor as F1 being only 28.9%), and the decoder that utilizes character similarity (see subsection 2.2 and 2.3) is also significantly indispensable to producing a *strong* Chinese spell checker.

2.2 Character similarity

Erroneous characters in Chinese texts by humans are usually either visually (subsection 2.2.1) or phonologically similar (subsection 2.2.2) to corresponding correct characters, or both (Chang, 1995; Liu et al., 2010; Yu and Li, 2014). It is also true that erroneous characters produced by OCR possess visual similarity (Tong and Evans, 1996).

We base our similarity computation on two open databases: *Kanji Database Project*[4] and *Unihan Database*[5] because they provide shape and pronunciation representations for all CJK Unified Ideographs in all CJK languages.

2.2.1 Visual similarity

The *Kanji Database Project* uses the Unicode standard – Ideographic Description Sequence (IDS) to represent the shape of a character.

As illustrated by examples in Figure 2, the IDS of a character is formally a string, but it is essentially the preorder traversal path of an ordered tree.

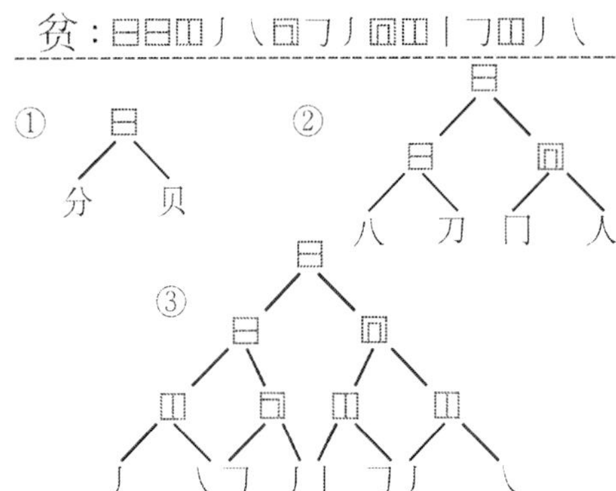

Figure 2: The IDS of a character can be given in different granularity levels as shown in the tree forms in ①-③ for the simplified character 贫 (meaning *poor*). In FASPell, we only use stroke-level IDS in the form of a string, like the one above the dashed ruling line. Unlike using only actual strokes (Wang et al., 2018), the Unicode standard Ideographic Description Characters (e.g., the non-leaf nodes in the trees) describe the layout of a character. They help us to model the subtle nuances in different characters that are composed of identical strokes (see examples in Table 2). Therefore, IDS gives us a more precise shape representation of a character.

In our model, we only adopt the string-form IDS. We define the visual similarity between two characters as one minus normalized[6] Levenshtein edit distance between their IDS representations. The reason for normalization is twofold. Firstly, we want the similarity to range from 0 to 1 for the convenience of later filtering. Secondly, if a pair of more complex characters have the same edit distance as a pair of less complex characters, we want the similarity of the more complex characters to be slightly higher than that of the less complex characters (see examples in Table 2).

We do not use the tree-form IDS for two reasons even as it seems to make more sense intuitively. Firstly, even with the most efficient algorithm (Pawlik and Augsten, 2015, 2016) so far, tree edit distance (TED) has far greater time complexity than edit distance of strings ($O(mn(m + n))$ vs. $O(mn)$). Secondly, we did try TED in preliminary experiments, but there was no significant difference from using edit distance of strings in terms of spell checking performance.

---

[6]Since the maximal value of Levenshtein edit distance is the maximum of the lengths of the two strings in question, we normalize it simply by dividing it by the maximum length.

Table 2: Examples of the computation of character similarities. IDS is used to compute visual similarity (V-sim) and pronunciation representations in Mandarin Chinese (MC), Cantonese Chinese (CC), Japanese On'yomi (JO), Korean (K) and Vietnamese (V) are used to compute phonological similarity (P-sim). Note that the normalization of edit distance gives us the desired fact that less complex character pair (午, 牛) has smaller visual similarity than more complex character pair (田, 由) even though both of their IDS edit distances are 1. Also, note that 午 and 牛 have more similar pronunciations in some languages than in others; the combination of the pronunciations in multiple languages gives us a more continuous phonological similarity.

	IDS	MC	CC	JO	K	V	V-sim	P-sim
午 (noon)	⊟⊡丿一⊕一丨	wu3	ng5	go	o	ngọ	0.857	0.280
牛 (cow)	⊕⊡丿一⊕一丨	niu2	ngau4	gyuu	wu	ngưu		
田 (field)	⊡⊡丨𠃌⊟⊕一丨一	tian2	tin4	den	cen	diền	0.889	0.090
由 (from)	⊕⊡丨𠃌⊟⊕一丨一	you2	jau4	yuu	yu	do		

2.2.2 Phonological similarity

Different Chinese characters sharing identical pronunciation is very common (Yang et al., 2012), which is the case for any CJK language. Thus, If we were to use character pronunciations in only one CJK language, the phonological similarity of character pairs would be limited to a few *discrete* values. However, a more *continuous* phonological similarity is preferred because it can make the curve used for filtering candidates smoother (see subsection 2.3).

Therefore, we utilize character pronunciations of all CJK languages (see examples in Table 2), which are provided by the *Unihan Database*. To compute the phonological similarity of two characters, we first calculate one minus normalized Levenshtein edit distance between their pronunciation representations in all CJK languages (if applicable). Then, we take the mean of the results. Hence, the similarity should range from 0 to 1.

2.3 Confidence-Similarity Decoder

Candidate filters in many previous models are based on setting various thresholds and weights for multiple features of candidate characters. Instead of this naive approach, we propose a method that is empirically effective under the principle of getting the highest possible precision with minimal harm to recall. Since the decoder utilizes contextual confidence and character similarity, we refer to it as the confidence-similarity decoder (CSD). The mechanism of CSD is explained, and its effectiveness is justified as follows:

First, consider the simplest case where only one candidate character is provided for each original character. For those candidates that are the same as their original characters, we do not substitute the original characters. For those that are different, we can draw a confidence-similarity scatter graph. If we compare the candidates with the ground truths, the graph will resemble the plot ① of Figure 3. We can observe that the true-detection-and-correction candidates are denser toward the upper-right corner; false-detection candidates toward the lower-left corner; true-detection-and-false-correction candidates in the middle area. If we draw a curve to filter out false-detection candidates (plot ② of Figure 3) and use the rest as substitutions, we can optimize character-level precision with minimal harm to character-level recall for detection; if true-detection-and-false-correction candidates are also filtered out (plot ③ of Figure 3), we can get the same effect for correction. In FASPell, we optimize correction performance and manually find the filtering curve using a training set, assuming its consistency with its corresponding testing set. But in practice, we have to find two curves – one for each type of similarity, and then take the union of the filtering results.

Now, consider the case where there are $c > 1$ candidates. To reduce it into the previously described simplest case, we rank the candidates for each original character according to their contextual confidence and put candidates that have the same rank into the same group (i.e., c groups in total). Thus, we can find a filter as previously described for each group of candidates. All c filters combined further alleviate the harm to recall because more candidates are taken into account.

In the example of Figure 1, there are $c = 4$ groups of candidates. We get a correct substitution 丰 → 主 from the group whose rank $= 1$, another one 苦 → 著 from the group whose rank $= 2$, and no more from the other two groups.

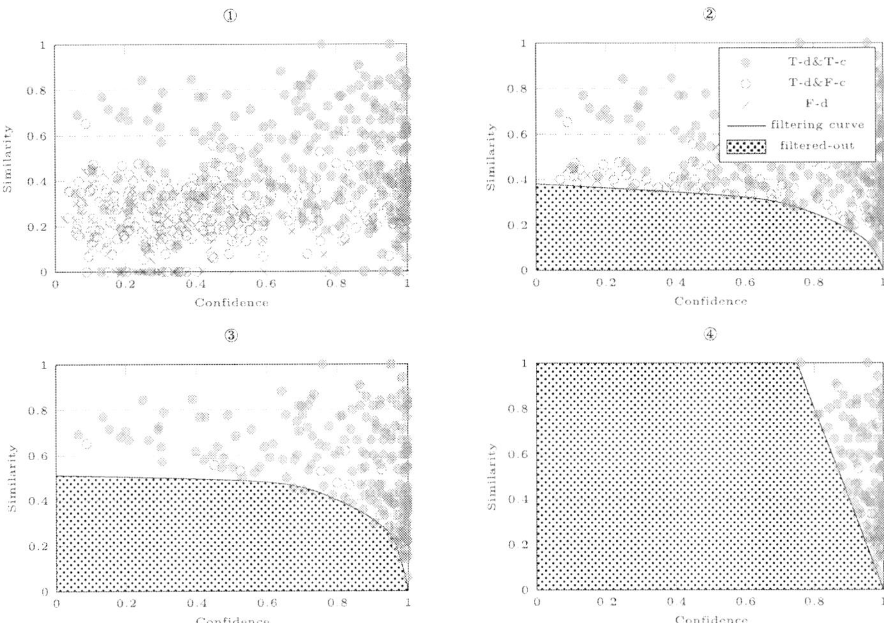

Figure 3: All four plots show the same confidence-similarity graph of candidates categorized by being true-detection-and-true-correction (T-d&T-c), true-detection-and-false-correction (T-d&F-c) and false-detection (F-d). But, each plot shows a different way of filtering candidates: in plot ①, no candidates are filtered; in plot ②, the filtering optimizes detection performance; in plot ③, as adopted in FASPell, the filtering optimizes correction performance; in plot ④, as adopted by previous models, candidates are filtered out by setting a threshold for weighted confidence and similarity ($0.8 \times confidence + 0.2 \times similarity < 0.8$ as an example in the plot). Note that the four plots use the actual first-rank candidates (using visual similarity) for our **OCR data** (Trn_{ocr}) except that we randomly sampled only 30% of the candidates to make the plots more viewable on paper.

3 Experiments and results

We first describe the data, metrics and model configurations adopted in our experiments in subsection 3.1. Then, in subsection 3.2, we show the performance on spell checking texts written by humans to compare FASPell with previous state-of-the-art models; we also show the performance on data that are harvested from OCR results to prove the adaptability of the model. In subsection 3.3, we compare the speed of FASPell and three state-of-the-art models. In subsection 3.4, we investigate how hyper-parameters affect the performance of FASPell.

3.1 Data, metrics and configurations

We adopt the benchmark datasets (all in traditional Chinese) and sentence-level[7] accuracy, precision,

Table 3: Statistics of datasets.

Dataset	# erroneous sent	# sent	Avg. length
Trn_{13}	350	700	41.8
Trn_{14}	3432	3435	49.6
Trn_{15}	2339	2339	31.3
Tst_{13}	996	1000	74.3
Tst_{14}	529	1062	50.0
Tst_{15}	550	1100	30.6
Trn_{ocr}	3575	3575	10.1
Tst_{ocr}	1000	1000	10.2

recall and F1 given by SIGHAN13 - 15 shared tasks on Chinese spell checking (Wu et al., 2013; Yu et al., 2014; Tseng et al., 2015). We also harvested 4575 sentences (4516 are simplified Chinese) from OCR results of Chinese subtitles in videos. We used the OCR method by Shi et al. (2017). Detailed data statistics are in Table 3.

We use the pre-trained masked language

---

[7] Note that although we do not use character-level metrics (Fung et al., 2017) in evaluation, they are actually important in the justification of the effectiveness of the CSD as in subsection 2.3

Table 4: Configurations of FASPell. FT means the training set for fine-tuning; CSD means the training set for CSD; r means the number of rounds and c means the number of candidates for each character. U is the union of all the spell checking data from SIGHAN13 - 15.

FT	CSD	Test set	r	c	FT steps
$U - Tst_{13}$	Trn_{13}	Tst_{13}	1	4	10k
$U - Tst_{14}$	Trn_{14}	Tst_{14}	3	4	10k
$U - Tst_{15}$	Trn_{15}	Tst_{15}	3	4	10k
(-)	Trn_{ocr}	Tst_{ocr}	2	4	(-)

Table 5: Speed comparison (ms/sent). Note that the speed of FASPell is the average in several rounds.

Test set	FASPell	Wang et al. (2018)
Tst_{13}	**446**	680
Tst_{14}	**284**	745
Tst_{15}	**177**	566

model[8] provided by Devlin et al. (2018). Settings of its hyper-parameters and pre-training are available at `https://github.com/google-research/bert`. Other configurations of FASPell used in our major experiments (subsection 3.2 - 3.3) are given in Table 4. For ablation experiments, the same configurations are used except when CSD is removed, we take the candidates ranked the first as default outputs. Note that we do not fine-tune the mask language model for OCR data because we learned in preliminary experiments that fine-tuning worsens performance for this type of data[9].

3.2 Performance

As shown in Table 6, FASPell achieves state-of-the-art F1 performance on both detection level and correction level. It is better in precision than the model by Wang et al. (2018) and better in recall than the model by Zhang et al. (2015). In comparison with Zhao et al. (2017), It is better by any metric. It also reaches comparable precision on OCR data. The lower recall on OCR data is partially because many OCR errors are harder to correct even for humans (Wang et al., 2018).

Table 6 also shows that all the components of FASPell contribute effectively to its good performance. FASPell without both fine-tuning and CSD is essentially the pre-trained mask language model. Fine-tuning it improves recall because FASPell can learn about common errors and how they are corrected. CSD improves its precision with minimal harm to recall because this is the un-

derlying principle of the design of CSD.

3.3 Filtering Speed[10]

First, we measure the filtering speed of Chinese spell checking in terms of absolute time consumption per sentence (see Table 5). We compare the speed of FASPell with the model by Wang et al. (2018) in this manner because they have reported their absolute time consumption[11]. Table 5 clearly shows that FASPell is much faster.

Second, to compare FASPell with models (Zhang et al., 2015; Zhao et al., 2017) whose absolute time consumption has not been reported, we analyze the time complexity. The time complexity of FASPell is $O(scmn + sc \log c)$, where s is the sentence length, c is the number of candidates, mn accounts for computing edit distance and $c \log c$ for ranking candidates. Zhang et al. (2015) use more features than just edit distance, so the time complexity of their model has additional factors. Moreover, since we do not use confusion set, the number of candidates for each character of their model is practically larger than ours: $x \times 10$ vs. 4. Thus, FASPell is faster than their model. Zhao et al. (2017) filter candidates by finding the single-source shortest path (SSSP) in a directed graph consisting of all candidates for every token in a sentence. The algorithm they used has a time complexity of $O(|V| + |E|)$ where $|V|$ is the number of vertices and $|E|$ is the number of edges in the graph (Eppstein, 1998). Translating it in terms of s and c, the time complexity of their model is $O(sc + c^s)$. This implies that their model is exponentially slower than FASPell for long sentences.

---

[8] `https://storage.googleapis.com/bert_models/2018_11_03/chinese_L-12_H-768_A-12.zip`

[9] It is probably because OCR errors are subject to random noise in source pictures rather than learnable patterns as in human errors. However, since the paper is not about OCR, we do not elaborate on this here.

[10] Considering only the filtering speed is because the Transformer, the Bi-LSTM and language models used by previous state-of-the-art models or us before filtering are already well studied in the literature.

[11] We have no access to the 4-core Intel Core i5-7500 CPU used by Wang et al. (2018). To minimize the difference of speed caused by hardware, we only use 4 cores of a 12-core Intel(R) Xeon(R) CPU E5-2650 in the experiments.

Table 6: This table shows spell checking performances on both detection and correction level. Our model – FASPell achieves similar performance to that of previous state-of-the-art models. Note that fine-tuning and CSD both contribute effectively to its performance according to the results of ablation experiments. ($-$ FT means removing fine-tuning; $-$ CSD means removing CSD.)

Test set	Models	Detection Level				Correction Level			
		Acc. (%)	Prec. (%)	Rec. (%)	F1 (%)	Acc. (%)	Prec. (%)	Rec. (%)	F1 (%)
Tst_{13}	Wang et al. (2018)	(-)	54.0	**69.3**	60.7	(-)	(-)	(-)	52.1
	Yeh et al. (2013)	(-)	(-)	(-)	(-)	62.5	70.3	62.5	66.2
	FASPell	63.1	**76.2**	63.2	**69.1**	60.5	73.1	60.5	**66.2**
	FASPell $-$ FT	40.9	75.5	40.9	53.0	39.6	**73.2**	39.6	51.4
	FASPell $-$ CSD	41.0	42.3	41.1	41.6	31.3	32.2	31.3	31.8
	FASPell $-$ FT $-$ CSD	47.9	65.2	47.8	55.2	35.6	48.4	35.4	40.9
Tst_{14}	Zhao et al. (2017)	(-)	(-)	(-)	(-)	(-)	55.5	39.1	45.9
	Wang et al. (2018)	(-)	51.9	**66.2**	**58.2**	(-)	(-)	(-)	**56.1**
	FASPell	70.0	**61.0**	53.5	57.0	69.3	**59.4**	52.0	55.4
	FASPell $-$ FT	57.8	54.5	18.1	27.2	57.7	53.7	17.8	26.7
	FASPell $-$ CSD	49.0	31.0	42.3	35.8	44.9	25.0	34.2	28.9
	FASPell $-$ FT $-$ CSD	56.3	38.4	26.8	31.6	52.1	26.0	18.0	21.3
Tst_{15}	Zhang et al. (2015)	70.1	**80.3**	53.3	**64.0**	69.2	**79.7**	51.5	62.5
	Wang et al. (2018)	(-)	56.6	**69.4**	62.3	(-)	(-)	(-)	57.1
	FASPell	74.2	67.6	60.0	63.5	73.7	66.6	59.1	**62.6**
	FASPell $-$ FT	61.5	74.1	25.5	37.9	61.3	72.5	24.9	37.1
	FASPell $-$ CSD	65.5	49.3	59.1	53.8	60.0	40.2	48.2	43.8
	FASPell $-$ FT $-$ CSD	63.7	59.1	35.3	44.2	57.6	38.3	22.7	28.5
Tst_{ocr}	FASPell	18.6	**78.5**	18.6	30.1	17.4	**73.4**	17.4	**28.1**
	FASPell $-$ CSD	**34.5**	65.8	**34.5**	**45.3**	**18.9**	36.1	**18.9**	24.8

3.4 Exploring hyper-parameters

First, we only change the number of candidates in Table 4 to see its effect on spell checking performance. As illustrated in Figure 4, when more candidates are taken into account, additional detections and corrections are recalled while maximizing precision. Thus, increase in the number of candidates always results in the improvement of F1. The reason we set the number of candidates $c = 4$ in Table 4 and no larger is because there is a trade-off with time consumption.

Second, we do the same thing to the number of rounds of spell checking in Table 4. We can observe in Figure 4 that the correction performance on Tst_{14} and Tst_{15} reaches its peak when the number of rounds is 3. For Tst_{13} and Tst_{ocr}, that number is 1 and 2, respectively. A larger number of rounds sometimes helps because FASPell can achieve high precision in detection in each round, so undiscovered errors in last round may be detected and corrected in the next round without falsely detecting too many non-errors.

4 Conclusion

We propose a Chinese spell checker – FASPell that reaches state-of-the-art performance. It is based on DAE-decoder paradigm that requires only a small amount of spell checking data and gives up the troublesome notion of confusion set. With FASPell as an example, each component of the paradigm is shown to be effective. We make our code and data publically available at `https://github.com/iqiyi/FASPell`.

Future work may include studying if the DAE-decoder paradigm can be used to detect and correct grammatical errors or other less frequently studied types of Chinese spelling errors such as dialectical colloquialism (Fung et al., 2017) and insertion/deletion errors.

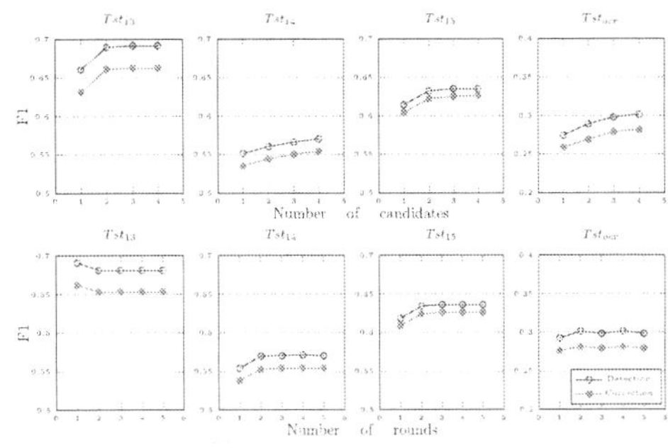

Figure 4: The four plots in the first row show how the number of candidates for each character affects F1 performances. The four in the second row show the impact of the number of rounds of spell checking.

Acknowledgments

The authors would like to thank the anonymous reviewers for their comments. We also thank our colleagues from the IT Infrastructure team of iQIYI, Inc. for the hardware support. Special thanks go to Prof. Yves Lepage from Graduate School of IPS, Waseda University for his insightful advice about the paper.

References

Chao-Huang Chang. 1995. A new approach for automatic chinese spelling correction. In *Proceedings of Natural Language Processing Pacific Rim Symposium*, volume 95, pages 278–283. Citeseer.

Jacob Devlin, Ming-Wei Chang, Kenton Lee, and Kristina Toutanova. 2018. BERT: pre-training of deep bidirectional transformers for language understanding. *CoRR*, abs/1810.04805.

David Eppstein. 1998. Finding the k shortest paths. *SIAM Journal on computing*, 28(2):652–673.

Gabriel Fung, Maxime Debosschere, Dingmin Wang, Bo Li, Jia Zhu, and Kam-Fai Wong. 2017. Nlptea 2017 shared task – Chinese spelling check. In *Proceedings of the 4th Workshop on Natural Language Processing Techniques for Educational Applications (NLPTEA 2017)*, pages 29–34, Taipei, Taiwan. Asian Federation of Natural Language Processing.

Chao-Lin Liu, Min-Hua Lai, Yi-Hsuan Chuang, and Chia-Ying Lee. 2010. Visually and phonologically similar characters in incorrect simplified chinese words. In *Proceedings of the 23rd International Conference on Computational Linguistics: Posters*, pages 739–747, Beijing, China. Association for Computational Linguistics.

Mateusz Pawlik and Nikolaus Augsten. 2015. Efficient computation of the tree edit distance. *ACM Trans. Database Syst.*, 40(1):3:1–3:40.

Mateusz Pawlik and Nikolaus Augsten. 2016. Tree edit distance: Robust and memory-efficient. *Information Systems*, 56:157 – 173.

Baoguang Shi, Xiang Bai, and Cong Yao. 2017. An end-to-end trainable neural network for image-based sequence recognition and its application to scene text recognition. *IEEE transactions on pattern analysis and machine intelligence*, 39(11):2298–2304.

DS Shih et al. 1992. A statistical method for locating typo in Chinese sentences. *CCL Research Journal*, pages 19–26.

Kaitao Song, Xu Tan, Tao Qin, Jianfeng Lu, and Tie-Yan Liu. 2019. Mass: Masked sequence to sequence pre-training for language generation. *arXiv preprint arXiv:1905.02450*.

Xiang Tong and David A. Evans. 1996. A statistical approach to automatic OCR error correction in context. In *Fourth Workshop on Very Large Corpora*.

Yuen-Hsien Tseng, Lung-Hao Lee, Li-Ping Chang, and Hsin-Hsi Chen. 2015. Introduction to SIGHAN 2015 bake-off for Chinese spelling check. In *Proceedings of the Eighth SIGHAN Workshop on Chinese Language Processing*, pages 32–37.

Pascal Vincent, Hugo Larochelle, Yoshua Bengio, and Pierre-Antoine Manzagol. 2008. Extracting and composing robust features with denoising autoencoders. In *Proceedings of the 25th international conference on Machine learning*, pages 1096–1103. ACM.

Dingmin Wang, Yan Song, Jing Li, Jialong Han, and Haisong Zhang. 2018. A hybrid approach to automatic corpus generation for Chinese spelling check. In *Proceedings of the 2018 Conference on Empirical Methods in Natural Language Processing*, pages 2517–2527, Brussels, Belgium. Association for Computational Linguistics.

Shih-Hung Wu, Chao-Lin Liu, and Lung-Hao Lee. 2013. Chinese spelling check evaluation at SIGHAN bake-off 2013. In *Proceedings of the Seventh SIGHAN Workshop on Chinese Language Processing*, pages 35–42, Nagoya, Japan. Asian Federation of Natural Language Processing.

Shaohua Yang, Hai Zhao, Xiaolin Wang, and Bao liang Lu. 2012. Spell checking for Chinese. In *Proceedings of the Eight International Conference on Language Resources and Evaluation (LREC'12)*, Istanbul, Turkey. European Language Resources Association (ELRA).

Zhilin Yang, Zihang Dai, Yiming Yang, Jaime Carbonell, Ruslan Salakhutdinov, and Quoc V Le. 2019. Xlnet: Generalized autoregressive pretraining for language understanding. *arXiv preprint arXiv:1906.08237*.

Jui-Feng Yeh, Sheng-Feng Li, Mei-Rong Wu, Wen-Yi Chen, and Mao-Chuan Su. 2013. Chinese word spelling correction based on n-gram ranked inverted index list. In *Proceedings of the Seventh SIGHAN Workshop on Chinese Language Processing*, pages 43–48, Nagoya, Japan. Asian Federation of Natural Language Processing.

Junjie Yu and Zhenghua Li. 2014. Chinese spelling error detection and correction based on language model, pronunciation, and shape. In *Proceedings of The Third CIPS-SIGHAN Joint Conference on Chinese Language Processing*, pages 220–223.

Liang-Chih Yu, Lung-Hao Lee, Yuen-Hsien Tseng, and
Hsin-Hsi Chen. 2014. Overview of SIGHAN 2014
bake-off for Chinese spelling check. In *Proceedings of The Third CIPS-SIGHAN Joint Conference
on Chinese Language Processing*, pages 126–132,
Wuhan, China. Association for Computational Linguistics.

Shuiyuan Zhang, Jinhua Xiong, Jianpeng Hou, Qiao
Zhang, and Xueqi Cheng. 2015. HANSpeller++: A
unified framework for Chinese spelling correction.
In *Proceedings of the Eighth SIGHAN Workshop on
Chinese Language Processing*, pages 38–45, Beijing, China. Association for Computational Linguistics.

Hai Zhao, Deng Cai, Yang Xin, Yuzhu Wang, and
Zhongye Jia. 2017. A hybrid model for Chinese
spelling check. *ACM Trans. Asian Low-Resour.
Lang. Inf. Process.*, 16(3):21:1–21:22.

Latent semantic network induction in the context of linked example senses

Hunter Scott Heidenreich
Department of Computer Science
College of Computing and Informatics
hsh28@drexel.edu

Jake Ryland Williams
Department of Information Science
College of Computing and Informatics
jw3477@drexel.edu

Abstract

The Princeton WordNet is a powerful tool for studying language and developing natural language processing algorithms. With significant work developing it further, one line considers its extension through aligning its expert-annotated structure with other lexical resources. In contrast, this work explores a completely data-driven approach to network construction, forming a wordnet using the entirety of the open-source, noisy, user-annotated dictionary, Wiktionary. Comparing baselines to WordNet, we find compelling evidence that our network induction process constructs a network with useful semantic structure. With thousands of semantically-linked examples that demonstrate sense usage from basic lemmas to multiword expressions (MWEs), we believe this work motivates future research.

1 Introduction

Wiktionary is a free and open-source collaborative dictionary[1] (Wikimedia). With the ability for anyone to add or edit lemmas, definitions, relations, and examples, Wiktionary has the potential to be larger and more diverse than any printable dictionary. Wiktionary features a rich set of examples of sense usage for many of its lemmas which, when converted to a usable format, supports language processing tasks such as sense disambiguation (Meyer and Gurevych, 2010a; Matuschek and Gurevych, 2013; Miller and Gurevych, 2014) and MWE identification (Muzny and Zettlemoyer, 2013; Salehi et al., 2014; Hosseini et al., 2016). With natural alignment to other languages, Wiktionary can likewise be used as a resource for machine translation tasks (Matuschek et al., 2013; Borin et al., 2014; Göhring, 2014). With these uses in mind, this work introduces the creation

of a network—much like the Princeton WordNet (Miller, 1995; Fellbaum, 1998)—that is constructed solely from the semi-structured data of Wiktionary. This relies on the noisy annotations of the editors of Wiktionary to naturally induce a network over the entirety of the English portion of Wiktionary. In doing so, the development of this work produces:

- an induced network over Wiktionary, enriched with semantically linked examples, forming a directed acyclic graph (DAG);

- an exploration of the task of relationship disambiguation as a means to induce network construction; and

- an outline for directions of expansion, including increasing precision in disambiguation, cross-linking example usages, and aligning English Wiktionary with other languages.

We make our code freely available[2], which includes code to download data, to disambiguate relationships between lemmas, to construct networks from disambiguation output, and to interact with networks produced through this work.

2 Related work

2.1 WordNet

The Princeton WordNet, or WordNet as it's more commonly referred to, is a lexical database originally created for the English language (Miller, 1995; Fellbaum, 1998). It consists of expert-annotated data, and has been more or less continually updated since its creation (Harabagiu et al., 1999; Miller and Hristea, 2006). WordNet is built up of *synsets*, collections of lexical items that all

---

[1] https://www.wiktionary.org/

[2] Code will be available at https://github.com/hunter-heidenreich/lsni-paper

Proceedings of the 2019 EMNLP Workshop W-NUT: The 5th Workshop on Noisy User-generated Text, pages 170–180
Hong Kong, Nov 4, 2019. ©2019 Association for Computational Linguistics

have the same meaning. For each synset, a definition is provided, and for *some* synsets, usage examples are also presented. If extracted and attributed properly, the example usages present on Wiktionary could critically enhance WordNet by filling gaps. While significant other work has been done in utilizing Wiktionary to enhance WordNet for purposes like this (discussed in the next sections), this work takes a novel step by constructing a wordnet through entirely computational means, i.e. under the framing of a machine learning task based on Wiktionary's data.

2.2 Wiktionary

Wiktionary is an open-source, Wiki-based, open content dictionary organized by the WikiMedia Foundation (Wikimedia). It has a large and active volunteer editorial community, and from its noisy, crowd-sourced nature, includes *many* MWEs, colloquial terms, and their example usages, which could ultimately fill difficult-to-resolve gaps left in other linguistic resources, such as WordNet.

Thus, Wiktionary has a significant history of exploration for the enhancement of WordNet, including efforts that extend WordNet for better domain coverage of word senses (Meyer and Gurevych, 2011; Gurevych et al., 2012; Miller and Gurevych, 2014), automatically derive new lemmas (Jurgens and Pilehvar, 2015; Rusert and Pedersen, 2016), and develop the creation of multilingual wordnets (de Melo and Weikum, 2009; Gurevych et al., 2012; Bond and Foster, 2013). While these works constitute important steps in the usage of *extracted* Wiktionary contents for the development of WordNet, none before this effort has attempted to utilize the *entirety* of Wiktionary alone for the construction of such a network.

Most similarly, Wiktionary has been used in a sense-disambiguated fashion (Meyer and Gurevych, 2012b) and to construct an ontology (Meyer and Gurevych, 2012a). Our work does not create an ontology, but instead attempts to create a semantic wordnet. In this context, our work can be viewed as building on notions of sense-disambiguating Wiktionary to construct a WordNet-like resource.

2.3 Relation Disambiguation

The task of taking definitions, a semantic relationship, and sub selecting the definitions that belong to that relationship is one of critical importance to our work. Sometimes called sense linking or relationship anchoring, this task has been previously explored in the creation of machine-readable dictionaries (Krovetz, 1992), ontology learning (Pantel and Pennacchiotti, 2006, 2008), and German Wiktionary (Meyer and Gurevych, 2010b).

As mentioned above, Meyer and Gurevych explore relationship disambiguation in the context of Wiktionary, motivating a sense-disambiguated Wiktionary as a powerful resource (Meyer and Gurevych, 2012a,b). This task is frequently viewed as a binary classification: Given two linked lemmas, do these pairs of definitions belong to the relationship? While easier to model, this framing can suffer from a combinatorial explosion as all pairs of definitions must be compared. This work attempts to model the task differently, disambiguating all definitions in the context of a relationship and its lemmas.

3 Model

3.1 Framework

This work starts by identifying a set of lemmas, W, and a set of senses, S. It then proceeds, assuming that S forms the vertex set of a Directed Acyclic Graph (DAG) with edge set E, organizing S by refinement of specificity. That is, if senses $s, t \in S$ have a link $(t, s) \in E$—to s—then s is one degree of refinement more specific than t.

Next, we suppose a lemma $u \in W$ has relation $\sim$ (e.g., synonymy) indicated to another lemma $v \in W$. Assuming $\sim$ is recorded from u to v (e.g., from u's page), we call u the source and v the sink. Working along these lines, the model then assumes a given indicated relation $\sim$ is qualified by a sense s; this semantic equivalence is denoted $u \overset{s}{\sim} v$.

Like others (Landauer and Dumais, 1997; Blei et al., 2003; Bengio et al., 2003), this work assumes senses exist in a latent semantic space. Processing a dictionary, one can empirically discover relationships like $u \overset{s}{\sim} v$ and $v \overset{t}{\sim} w$. But for a larger network structure one must know if $s = t$—that is, do s and t refer to the same relationship—and often neither s nor t are known, explicitly. Hence, this work sets up approximations of s and t for comparison. Given a lemma, $u \in W$, suppose a set of definitions, D_u, exists and form the basis for disambiguation of a lemma's senses. We then assume that for any $d \subset D_u$ there exists one or more senses, $s \in S$, such that $d \implies s$, that is, the definition d conveys the sense s.

Having assumed a DAG structure for S, this work denotes specificity of sense by using the formalism of a partial order, $\preceq$, which, for senses $s, t \in S$ having $s \preceq t$, indicates that the sense s is comparable to t and more specific. Note that—as with any partial order—senses can be, and are often non-comparable.

Intuitively, a given definition d might convey multiple senses $d \implies s, t$ of differing specificities, $s \preceq t$. So for a given definition d, the model's goal is to find the sense t that is least specific in being conveyed. Satisfying this goal implies resolving the sense identification function, $f : D \to S$, for which any lemma $u \in W$ and definition $d \in D_u$ with $d \implies s \in S$, it is assured that $s \preceq f(d)$. Since no direct knowledge of any $s \in S$ is assumed known for any annotated relationship between lemmas, systems must approximate senses according to the available resources, e.g., definitions or example usages.

3.2 Task development

On Wiktionary, every lemma has its own page. Each page is commonly broken down into sections such as languages, etymologies, and parts-of-speech (POS). Under each POS, a lemma features a set of definitions that can be automatically extracted. An example of the word *induce* on English Wiktionary can be seen in Figure 1.

A significant benefit of using Wiktionary as a resource to build a wordnet lies in the wealth of examples it offers. Examples come in two flavors: basic usage and usage from reference material. Currently, each example is linked to its origination definition and lemma, however, in future works, these examples could be segmented and sense disambiguated, offering new network links and densely connected example usages.

For each lemma, Wiktionary may offer relationship annotations between lemmas. These relationships span many categories including acronyms, alternative forms, anagrams, antonyms, compounds, conjugations, derived terms, descendants, holonyms, hypernyms, hyponyms, meronyms, related terms, and synonyms. For this work's purposes, only antonyms and synonyms are considered, exploiting their more typical structure on Wiktionary and clear theoretical basis in semantic equivalence to induce a network. Exploring more of these relationships is of interest in future work.

Additionally, a minority of annotations present 'gloss' labels, which indicate the definitions that apply to relationships. So from the data there is some knowledge of exact matching, but due to their limited, noisy, and crowd-sourced nature, the labelings may not cover all definitions that belong.

We assume annotations exhibit relationships between lemmas. Finding one: $u \overset{s}{\sim} v$, if u is the source, we assume there exists some definition $d \in D_u$ that implies the appropriate sense: $d \implies s$. This good practice assumption models editor behavior as a response to exposure to a particular definition on the source page. Provided this, an editor won't necessarily annotate the relationship on the sink page—even if the sink page has a definition that implies the sense s. Thus, our task doesn't *require* identification of a definition on the sink's page. More precisely, no $d \in D_v$ might exist that implies s ($d \implies s$) for an annotated relationship, $u \overset{s}{\sim} v$.

Altogether, for an annotated relationship the task aims to identify the sense-conveying subset:

$$D_{u \overset{s}{\sim} v} = \{d \in D_u \cup D_v \mid d \implies s\}$$

for which at least one definition must be drawn from D_u. Note that the model *does not* assume that arbitrary $d, \tilde{d} \in D_{u \overset{s}{\sim} v}$ map through the sense identification function to the same most general sense. Presently, these details are resolved by a separate algorithm (developed below), leaving direct modeling of the sense identification function to future work.[3]

3.3 Semantic hierarchy induction

This section outlines preliminary work inferring a semantic hierarchy from pairwise relationships. If A is the set of relationships, a model's output, C, will be a collection of sense-conveying subsets, $D_{u \overset{s}{\sim} v}$, in one-to-one correspondence: $A \leftrightarrow C$. So, for all $\mathbb{D} \in \mathcal{P}(C)$, one has a covering of (some) senses by pairwise relationships, $D_{u \overset{s}{\sim} v} \in \mathbb{D}$.

Under our assumptions, any collection of sense conveying subsets $\mathbb{D} \in \mathcal{P}(C)$ with non-empty intersection restricts to a set of definitions that must convey at least one common sense, s'. Notably, s' must be at least as general as any qualifying a particular annotated relationship, i.e., $s \preceq s'$ for any s (implicitly) defining any $D_{u \overset{s}{\sim} v} \in \mathbb{D}$.

---

[3] A major challenge to this approach is the increased complexity required for the development of evaluation data.

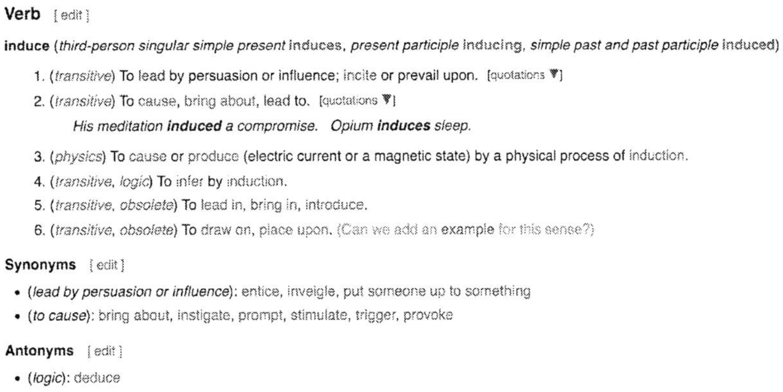

Figure 1: The Verb section of the induce page on English Wiktionary. Definitions are enumerated, with example usages as sub-elements or drop-down quotations. Relationships for this page are well annotated, with gloss labels to indicate the definition that prompted annotation.

So this work induces the sense-identification function, f, through pre-images: for $\mathbb{D} \in \mathcal{P}(C)$, an implicit sense, s, is assumed such that that $f^{-1}(s) \subseteq \bigcap_{\mathbb{D}} D_{u \overset{s}{\sim} v}$. Now, if a covering $\mathbb{D}' \supset \mathbb{D}$ exists with non-empty intersection, then its (smaller) intersection comprises definitions that convey a sense, s' which is more-general than s. So to precisely resolve f through pre-images the model must 'hole punch' the more-general definitions, constructing the hierarchy by allocating the more general definitions in the intersection of $\mathbb{D}'$ to the more general senses:

$$f^{-1}(t) = \left(\bigcap_{\mathbb{D}} D_{u \overset{s}{\sim} v} \right) \setminus \left(\bigcap_{\mathbb{D}' \supset \mathbb{D}} \bigcap_{\mathbb{D}'} D_{u' \overset{s'}{\sim} v'} \right).$$

This allocates each definition to exactly one implicit sense approximation, t, which is the most general sense indicated by the definition. Additionally, all senses then fall under a DAG hierarchy (excepting the singletons, addressed below) as set inclusion, $\mathbb{D}' \supset \mathbb{D}$ defines a partial order. This deterministic algorithm for hierarchy induction is presented in Algorithm 1.

Considering the output of a model, C, if d is not covered by C the model assumes a singleton sense. These include definitions not selected during relationship disambiguation as well as the definitions of lemmas that feature no relationship annotations. Singletons are then placed in the DAG at the lowest level, disconnected from all other senses. Figure 2 visually represents this full semantic hierarchy.

Algorithm 1 Construction of semantic hierarchy through pairwise collection.

Require: C: Collection of $D_{u \overset{s}{\sim} v}$

  $levels \leftarrow List()$
  $prev \leftarrow C$
  while $prev \neq \emptyset$ **do**
    $next \leftarrow List()$
    $defs \leftarrow \emptyset$
    for $p, p' \in prev$ **do**
      if $p \neq p'$ and $p \cap p' \neq \emptyset$ **then**
        $Append(next, p \cap p')$
        $Union(defs, p \cap p')$
      end if
    end for
    $filtered \leftarrow List()$
    for $p \in prev$ **do**
      $Append(filtered, p \setminus defs)$
    end for
    $Append(levels, filtered)$
    $prev \leftarrow next$
  end while
  return $levels$

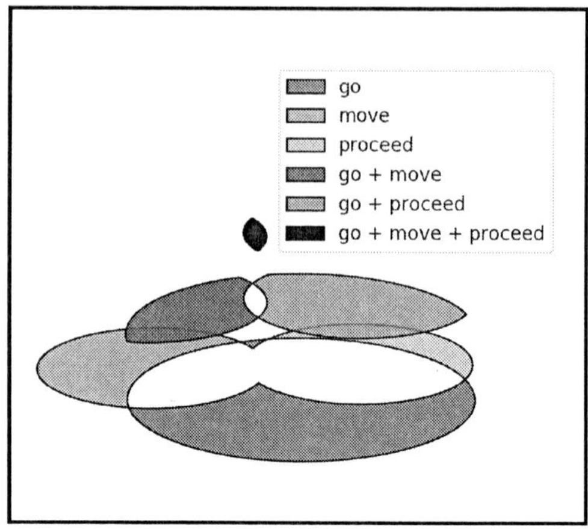

Figure 2: A visualization of 3 lemmas intersecting to create a semantic hierarchy.

4 Evaluation

4.1 Characteristics of Wiktionary data

Data was downloaded from Wiktionary on 1/23/19 using the Wikimedia Rest API[4]. To evaluate performance, a 'gold' dataset was created to compare modeling strategies. In totality, 298,377 synonym and 44,758 antonym links were generated from Wiktionary. 'Gold' links were randomly sampled, selecting 400 synonym and 100 antonym links. For each link, source and sink lemmas were considered independently. Definitions were included if they could plausibly refer to the other lemma. This process is supported by the available examples, testing if one lemma can replace the other lemma in the example usages. This dataset was constructed in contrast to other Wiktionary relationship disambiguation tasks due to the modeling differences and desire for more synonym- and antonym-specific evaluations (Meyer and Gurevych, 2012a,b).

4.2 Evaluation strategy

This work's evaluation considers precision, recall, and variants of the F_β score (biasing averages of precision and recall). As there is selection on both source and sink sides, we consider several averaging schemes. For a final evaluation, each sample is averaged at the side-level and averaged across all relationships. Macro-averages compute an unweighted average, while micro-averages weight performance based on the number of definitions involved in the selection process. Intuitively, micro metrics weight based on size, while macro metrics ignore size (treating all potential links and sides as equal).

4.3 Setting up baselines

For baselines, we present two types of models, which we refer to as *return all* and *vector similarity*. The return all baseline model assumes that for a given relationship link, all definitions belong. This is not intended as a model that could produce a useful network as many definitions and lemmas would be linked that clearly do not belong together. This achieves maximum recall at the expense of precision, demonstrating a base level of precision that must be exceeded.

The vector similarity baseline model takes advantage of semantic vector representations for computing similarity (Bengio et al., 2003; Mikolov et al., 2013; Pennington et al., 2014; Joulin et al., 2017). It computes the similarity between lemmas and definitions, utilizing thresholds that flag to either retain similarities above (max), below (min), or with magnitude above the threshold (abs).

Wiktionary features many MWEs and uncommon lemmas requiring use of a vectorization strategy that allows for handling of lemmas not observed in the representation's training. Thus, Fast-Text was selected for its ability to represent out-of-vocabulary lemmas through its bag-of-character n-gram modeling (Bojanowski et al., 2017). To compute similarity between lemmas and definitions, this model aggregates word vectors of the individual tokens present in a definition. Following other work (Lilleberg et al., 2015; Wu et al., 2018), TF-IDF weighted averages of word vectors were utilized in a very simple averaging scheme.

Initial results indicated that a simple cosine similarity with a linear kernel performed marginally above the return all baseline[5]. Thus, kernel tricks (Cristianini and Shawe-Taylor, 2000) were explored (to positive effect). The Gaussian kernel is often recommended as a good initial kernel to try as a baseline (Schölkopf et al., 1995; Joachims,

---

[5] This is interesting to note, since previous work has found that word embeddings like GloVe and word2vec contain a surprising amount of word frequency effects that pollute simple cosine similarity (Schnabel et al., 2015). This may explain why vanilla cosine similarity performed poorly with FastText vectors here and provides more evidence against using it as the default similarity measure.

1998). It is formulated using a radial basis function (RBF), only dependent on a measure of distance. The Laplacian kernel is a slight variation of the Gaussian kernel, measuring distance as the L1 distance where the Gaussian measures distance as L2 distance. Both kernels fall in the RBF category with a single regularization parameter, γ, and were used in comparison to cosine similarity.

For these kernels, a grid search over γ was conducted from 10^{-3} to 10^3 at steps of powers of 10. Similarly, similarity comparison thresholds were considered from -1.0 to 1.0 at steps of 0.05 for all 3 thresholding schemes (min, max, abs).

When selecting a final model, F_1 scores were not considered as recall scores outweighed precision under a simple harmonic mean. This resulted in models with identical performance to the return all model or worse. Instead, models were considered against full-precision and $F_{0.1}$ scores.

4.4 Semantic Structure Correlation

Creating a wordnet solely from Wiktionary's noisy, crowd-sourced data begs the question: Does the generated network structure resemble the structure present in Princeton's WordNet? To get a sense of this, we compare the capacities of each of these resources as a basis for semantic similarity modeling (using Pearson correlation (Pearson, 1895)). This work considers three notions of graph-based semantic similarity that are present in WordNet: path similarity (PS), Leacock Chodorow similarity (LCH) (Leacock and Chodorow, 1998), and Wu Palmer similarity (WP) (Wu and Palmer, 1994).

The point of this experiment is *not* to enforce a notion that this network should mirror the structure of WordNet. Given Wiktionary's size, it likely possesses a great deal of information not represented by WordNet (resolved our other experiment on word similarity, Sec. 5.3). But if there is some association between the semantic representation capacities of these two networks we may possibly draw some insight into a more basic question: "has this model produced *some* relevant semantic structure?"

For this experiment, only nouns and verbs are considered as they are the only POS for which WordNet defines these metrics. Additionally, these metrics are defined at the synset level. There is no direct mapping between synsets in our network and WordNet, therefore, scores are considered at a lemma level. By computing values of all pairs of synsets between lemmas, three values per metric are generated: minimum, maximum, and average. Additionally, only lemmas that differ in minimum and maximum similarity are retained, restricting the experiment to the most polysemous portions of the networks.

5 Results

5.1 Baseline model performance

Table 1 shows baseline model performance on the relationship disambiguation task and highlights model parameters. During evaluation, the Laplacian kernel was found to consistently outperform the Gaussian kernel. For this reason, this work presents the scores from the return all baseline and two variants of the Laplacian kernel model—one optimized for precision and the other for $F_{0.1}$.

Note that in the synonym case, max-threshold selection performed best, while in the antonym case min- and abs-threshold fared better. This aligns well with the notion that while synonyms are semantically similar, antonyms are semantically anti-similar—an interesting consideration for future model development.

Overall, from the scores in Table 1 one can see that the vector similarity models improve over the return all, but that there is much work to be done to further improve precision and recall.

5.2 Comparison against WordNet

WordNet publishes several statistics[6] that one can use for quantitative comparison with the network constructed herein. Reviewing the count statistics shows that Wiktionary is an order of magnitude larger than WordNet and that Wiktionary features 344,789 linked example usages to WordNet's 68,411.

Polysemy. Table 2 report polysemy statistics. Despite the difference in creation processes, the induced networks do not have polysemy averages drastically different from WordNet.

In comparing the three networks induced, there is a common theme of increase in polysemy when shifting from recall to precision. This makes sense due to the fact that the return all model will merge all possible lemmas that overlap in relationship annotations resulting in lower polysemy statistics,

---

[6] Statistics are taken from WordNet's website for WordNet 3.0, last accessed on 8/11/2019: `https://wordnet.princeton.edu/documentation/wnstats7wn`

| Model | Thresh. | Synonyms | | | | Thresh. | Antonyms | | | |
| | | Recall | | Precision | | | Recall | | Precision | |
		Macro	Micro	Macro	Micro		Macro	Micro	Macro	Micro
Ret. All		1.000	1.000	0.602	0.268		1.000	1.000	0.527	0.280
Precision	$max_{0.35}$	0.433	0.258	0.847	0.541	$min_{-0.35}$	0.266	0.196	0.820	0.600
$F_{0.1}$	$max_{0.30}$	0.535	0.404	0.814	0.532	$abs_{0.25}$	0.730	0.763	0.619	0.397

Table 1: Model performance with threshold selection. All $\gamma = 0.1$, except for antonym precision where $\gamma = 100$.

whereas a precision-based model will result in pair-wise clusters that do not overlap as broadly, resulting in more complex hierarchies.

Structural differences. Intentionally, the presented notion of a semantic hierarchy functions similarly to the hypernym connections within WordNet. Moving up the semantic hierarchy produces sense approximations from definitions that are more general, and moving down the hierarchy produces more specific senses. However, in the induced networks, this is a notion applied to every POS—WordNet only produces these connections for nouns and verbs. An example taken from the $F_{0.1}$ network is that of the adjective *good* (referring to Holy) being subsumed by a synset featuring the adjective *proper* (referring to suitable, acceptable, and following the established standards).

5.3 Word Similarity

In previous works, WordNet and Wiktionary have been used to create vector representations of words. A common method for evaluating the quality of word vectors is performance on word similarity tasks. Performance on these tasks is evaluated through Spearman's rank correlation (Spearman, 2010) between cosine similarity of vector representations and human annotations.

Using Explicit Semantic Analysis (ESA), a technique based on concept vectors, our network constructs vectors using a word's tf-idf scores over concepts, as has been done in prior works (Gabrilovich and Markovitch, 2007; Zesch et al., 2008; Meyer and Gurevych, 2012b). We define our concepts as senses of the $F_{0.1}$ network and compute cosine similarity in this representation.

We compare performance against other ESA methods (Zesch et al., 2008; Meyer and Gurevych, 2012b) on common datasets: Rubenstein and Goodenough's 65 noun pairs (1965, RG-65), Miller and Charles's 30 noun pairs (1991, MC-30), Finklestein et. al's 353 word similarity pairs (2002, WS-353, split into Fin-153 and Fin-200 due to different annotators), and Yang and Powers's 130 verb pairs (2006, YP-130). Our results are summarized in Table 3.

We also compare $F_{0.1}$ against latent word vector representations like word2vec's continuous bag-of-words (CBOW) and skip-grams (SG) (Mikolov et al., 2013), GloVe (Pennington et al., 2014), and FastText (Bojanowski et al., 2017). These results are presented in Table 4.

In analyzing these results, the $F_{0.1}$ network performs well. Against other ESA methods, it is highly competitive, achieving the highest performance in two datasets. When strictly comparing performance against ESA with WordNet as the source, it has approximately equal or better performance in all datasets except YP-130. We hypothesize that this is due to a lack of precision in verb disambiguation, reinforced by the low polysemy seen above. Additionally, the work from Zesch et al. (2008) evaluated on subsets of the data in which all three resources had coverage. In their work, YP-130 performance is computed for only 80 of the 130 pairs.

Comparing $F_{0.1}$ to latent word vectors, it has the highest performance on noun datasets and is competitive on WS-353. While not directly comparable, it achieves this through 26 million tokens of structured text in contrast to billions of tokens of unstructured text that train latent vectors.

5.4 Network Correlation Results

Table 5 displays correlation values between graph-based semantic similarity metrics of $F_{0.1}$ and WordNet. Pairs of 1,009 verb and 1,303 noun lemmas were considered. In generating similarities, disconnected lemma pairs were discarded, producing 31,373 verb and 16,530 noun pairs. The table shows that for nouns, the two networks produce similarity values that are weakly to moderately correlated, however, verbs produce values that are, at most, very weakly correlated, if at all.

Due to the fact that $F_{0.1}$ produced better results

POS	With Monosemous Words				Without Monosemous Words			
	WordNet	$F_{0.01}$	Precision	Return All	WordNet	$F_{0.01}$	Precision	Return All
Noun	1.24	1.17	1.18	1.10	2.79	2.94	2.99	2.66
Verb	2.17	1.20	1.22	1.10	3.57	3.18	3.33	2.78
Adjective	1.18	1.18	1.18	1.10	2.71	2.59	2.62	2.33
Adverb	1.25	1.11	1.12	1.08	2.50	2.34	2.36	2.25

Table 2: Average polysemy statistics.

Dataset	RG-65	MC-30	Fin-153	Fin-200	YP-130
$F_{0.1}$	0.831	**0.849**	**0.723**	0.557	0.687
WordNet* (Zesch et al., 2008)	0.82	0.78	0.61	0.56	0.71
Wikipedia* (Zesch et al., 2008)	0.76	0.68	0.70	0.50	0.29
Wiktionary* (Zesch et al., 2008)	**0.84**	0.84	0.70	**0.60**	0.65
Wiktionary (Meyer and Gurevych, 2012b)	-	-	-	-	**0.73**

Table 3: Spearman's rank correlation coefficients on word similarity tasks. Best values are in bold.

Dataset	RG-65	MC-30	WS-353
$F_{0.1}$	**0.831**	**0.849**	0.669
FastText	-	-	0.73
CBOW (6B)	0.682	0.656	0.572
SG (6B)	0.697	0.652	0.628
GloVe (6B)	0.778	0.727	0.658
GloVe (42B)	0.829	0.836	**0.759**
CBOW (100B)	0.754	0.796	0.684

Table 4: Spearman's correlation on word similarity tasks. Best values are in bold. Number of tokens in training data is featured in parentheses, if reported. FastText is reported from (Bojanowski et al., 2017), and all others are from (Pennington et al., 2014).

	Noun	Verb
PS min	0.266	0.132
PS max	0.495	0.189
PS avg	0.448	0.082
LCH min	0.207	0.120
LCH max	0.384	0.056
LCH avg	0.359	-0.013
WP min	0.116	0.090
WP max	0.219	0.005
WP avg	0.226	-0.025

Table 5: Correlations between $F_{0.1}$ and WordNet similarity metrics: path similarity (PS), Leacock Chodorow similarity (LCH), and Wu Palmer similarity (WP).

on noun similarity tasks, we hypothesize that this indicates better semantic structure for nouns than for verbs, further emphasizing that a possible limitation of the current baseline produced is its lack of precision when it comes to polysemous verbs. However, the positive correlation values seen for nouns, coupled with noun similarity performance, offer strong indications that the $F_{0.1}$ does provide useful semantic structure that can be further increased through better modeling.

6 Future work

Here, several directions are highlighted along which we see this work being extended.

Better models. The development of more accurate models for predicting definitions involved in the pair-wise relations will produce more interesting and useful networks, especially with the magnitude of examples of sense usage. Precision of verb relations seems to be a critical component of a better model.

Supervision. Relationship prediction is currently unsupervised. While it is an interesting task to model in this fashion, crowd sourcing the annotation of this data would be possible through services like Amazon Mechanical Turk. This would allow for the potential of exploring supervised models for predicting relationship links, particularly for relationships like synonymy and antonymy which are familiar concepts for a broad community of potential annotators.

WordNet semi-supervision. Another logical transformation of this task would be to use Word-Net to inform the induction of a network in a semi-supervised fashion. There are many ways to go about this such as using statistics from WordNet to create a loss function, or using the structure of

WordNet as a base. As this work aimed to create a network solely from the data of Wiktionary, these ideas were not explored. However, using WordNet in this fashion is one of the directions of greatest interest for exploration in the future.

Sense usage examples. The examples present in Wiktionary have only begun to be used in this work. When examples are pulled, the source definition and lemma are linked. However, these examples have the potential to be linked to other senses and lemmas. This would an immense amount of structured, sense-usage data that could be used for many machine learning tasks.

Multilingual networks Wiktionary has been explored as a multilingual resource in previous works (de Melo and Weikum, 2009; Gurevych et al., 2012; Meyer and Gurevych, 2012b; Bond and Foster, 2013) largely due to the natural alignment across languages. Extending this approach to a multilingual setting could prove to be extremely useful for machine translation, and could allow low resource languages to benefit from alignment with other languages that have more annotations.

7 Conclusion

This paper introduced the idea of constructing a wordnet solely using the data from Wiktionary. Wiktionary is a powerful resource, featuring millions of pages that describe lemmas, their senses, example usages, and the relationships between them. Previous work has explored aligning resources like this with other networks like the Princeton WordNet. However, no work has fully explored the idea of building an entire network from the ground up using just Wiktionary.

This work explores simple baselines for constructing a network from Wiktionary through antonym and synonym relationships and compares induced networks with WordNet to find similar structures and statistics that appear to highlight strong future directions of particular interest, including but not limited to improving network modeling, linking more semantic examples, and reinforcing network construction using expert-annotated networks, like WordNet.

As conducted, this work is an initial step in transforming Wikitionary from an open-source dictionary into a powerful tool, dataset, and framework, with the hope of driving and motivating further work at endeavors studying languages and developing language processing systems.

References

Yoshua Bengio, Rjean Ducharme, Pascal Vincent, and Christian Jauvin. 2003. A neural probabilistic language model. *Journal of machine learning research*, 3:1137–1155.

David M. Blei, Andrew Y. Ng, and Michael I. Jordan. 2003. Latent dirichlet allocation. *Journal of machine learning research*, 3:993–1022.

Piotr Bojanowski, Edouard Grave, Armand Joulin, and Tomas Mikolov. 2017. Enriching word vectors with subword information. *Transactions of the Association for Computational Linguistics*, 5:135–146.

Francis Bond and Ryan Foster. 2013. Linking and extending an open multilingual wordnet. In *Proceedings of the 51st Annual Meeting of the Association for Computational Linguistics (Volume 1: Long Papers)*, pages 1352–1362, Sofia, Bulgaria. Association for Computational Linguistics.

Lars Borin, Jens Allwood, and Gerard de Melo. 2014. Bring vs. mtroget: Evaluating automatic thesaurus translation. In *Proceedings of the Ninth International Conference on Language Resources and Evaluation (LREC'14)*, pages 2115–2121, Reykjavik, Iceland. European Language Resources Association (ELRA).

Nello Cristianini and John Shawe-Taylor. 2000. *An introduction to Support Vector Machines: and other kernel-based learning methods*. Cambridge University Press, New York, NY, USA.

Christiane Fellbaum. 1998. *WordNet: An Electronic Lexical Database*. MIT Press, Cambridge, MA, USA.

Lev Finkelstein, Evgeniy Gabrilovich, Yossi Matias, Ehud Rivlin, Zach Solan, Gadi Wolfman, and Eytan Ruppin. 2002. Placing search in context: The concept revisited. *ACM Trans. Inf. Syst.*, 20:116–131.

Evgeniy Gabrilovich and Shaul Markovitch. 2007. Computing semantic relatedness using wikipedia-based explicit semantic analysis. In *Proceedings of the 20th International Joint Conference on Artifical Intelligence*, IJCAI'07, pages 1606–1611, San Francisco, CA, USA. Morgan Kaufmann Publishers Inc.

Anne Göhring. 2014. Building a spanish-german dictionary for hybrid mt. In *Proceedings of the 3rd Workshop on Hybrid Approaches to Machine Translation (HyTra)*, pages 30–35, Gothenburg, Sweden. Association for Computational Linguistics.

Iryna Gurevych, Judith Eckle-Kohler, Silvana Hartmann, Michael Matuschek, Christian M. Meyer, and Christian Wirth. 2012. Uby - a large-scale unified lexical-semantic resource based on lmf. In *Proceedings of the 13th Conference of the European Chapter of the Association for Computational Linguistics*, pages 580–590, Avignon, France. Association for Computational Linguistics.

Sanda M. Harabagiu, George A. Miller, and Dan I. Moldovan. 1999. Wordnet 2 - a morphologically and semantically enhanced resource. In *SIGLEX99: Standardizing Lexical Resources*.

Mohammad Javad Hosseini, Noah A. Smith, and Su-In Lee. 2016. Uw-cse at semeval-2016 task 10: Detecting multiword expressions and supersenses using double-chained conditional random fields. In *Proceedings of the 10th International Workshop on Semantic Evaluation (SemEval-2016)*, pages 931–936, San Diego, California. Association for Computational Linguistics.

Thorsten Joachims. 1998. Text categorization with support vector machines: Learning with many relevant features. In *Machine Learning: ECML-98*, pages 137–142, Berlin, Heidelberg. Springer Berlin Heidelberg.

Armand Joulin, Edouard Grave, Piotr Bojanowski, and Tomas Mikolov. 2017. Bag of tricks for efficient text classification. In *Proceedings of the 15th Conference of the European Chapter of the Association for Computational Linguistics: Volume 2, Short Papers*, pages 427–431, Valencia, Spain. Association for Computational Linguistics.

David Jurgens and Mohammad Taher Pilehvar. 2015. Reserating the awesometastic: An automatic extension of the wordnet taxonomy for novel terms. In *Proceedings of the 2015 Conference of the North American Chapter of the Association for Computational Linguistics: Human Language Technologies*, pages 1459–1465, Denver, Colorado. Association for Computational Linguistics.

Robert Krovetz. 1992. Sense-linking in a machine readable dictionary. In *30th Annual Meeting of the Association for Computational Linguistics*, pages 330–332, Newark, Delaware, USA. Association for Computational Linguistics.

Thomas K. Landauer and Susan T. Dumais. 1997. A solution to plato's problem: The latent semantic analysis theory of acquisition, induction, and representation of knowledge. *Psychological Review*, 104(2):211–240.

C. Leacock and M. Chodorow. 1998. Combining local context and WordNet similarity for word sense identification. *WordNet: An Electronic Lexical Database*, pages 265–283.

J. Lilleberg, Y. Zhu, and Y. Zhang. 2015. Support vector machines and word2vec for text classification with semantic features. In *2015 IEEE 14th International Conference on Cognitive Informatics Cognitive Computing (ICCI*CC)*, pages 136–140.

Michael Matuschek and Iryna Gurevych. 2013. Dijkstra-wsa: A graph-based approach to word sense alignment. *Transactions of the Association for Computational Linguistics*, 1:151–164.

Michael Matuschek, Christian M. Meyer, and Iryna Gurevych. 2013. Multilingual knowledge in aligned wiktionary and omegawiki for translation applications. *Translation: Computation, Corpora, Cognition*, 3(1).

Gerard de Melo and Gerhard Weikum. 2009. Towards a universal wordnet by learning from combined evidence. In *Proceedings of the 18th ACM Conference on Information and Knowledge Management*, CIKM '09, pages 513–522, New York, NY, USA. ACM.

Christian M. Meyer and Iryna Gurevych. 2010a. How web communities analyze human language: Word senses in wiktionary. *Proceedings of the 2nd Web Science Conference*.

Christian M. Meyer and Iryna Gurevych. 2010b. Worth its weight in gold or yet another resource–a comparative study of wiktionary, openthesaurus and germanet. In *Computational Linguistics and Intelligent Text Processing*, pages 38–49, Berlin, Heidelberg. Springer Berlin Heidelberg.

Christian M. Meyer and Iryna Gurevych. 2011. What psycholinguists know about chemistry: Aligning wiktionary and wordnet for increased domain coverage. In *Proceedings of 5th International Joint Conference on Natural Language Processing*, pages 883–892, Chiang Mai, Thailand. Asian Federation of Natural Language Processing.

Christian M. Meyer and Iryna Gurevych. 2012a. Ontowiktionary — constructing an ontology from the collaborative online dictionary wiktionary. In M. T. Pazienza and A. Stellato, editors, *Semi-Automatic Ontology Development: Processes and Resources*, pages 131—161. IGI Global, Hershey, PA.

Christian M. Meyer and Iryna Gurevych. 2012b. To exhibit is not to loiter: A multilingual, sense-disambiguated Wiktionary for measuring verb similarity. In *Proceedings of COLING 2012*, pages 1763–1780, Mumbai, India. The COLING 2012 Organizing Committee.

Tomas Mikolov, Ilya Sutskever, Kai Chen, Greg S Corrado, and Jeff Dean. 2013. Distributed representations of words and phrases and their compositionality. In C. J. C. Burges, L. Bottou, M. Welling, Z. Ghahramani, and K. Q. Weinberger, editors, *Advances in Neural Information Processing Systems 26*, pages 3111–3119. Curran Associates, Inc.

George A. Miller. 1995. Wordnet: A lexical database for english. *Communications of the ACM*, 38(11):39–31.

George A. Miller and Walter G. Charles. 1991. Contextual correlates of semantic similarity. *Language and Cognitive Processes*, 6(1):1–28.

George A. Miller and Florentina Hristea. 2006. Squibs and discussions: Wordnet nouns: Classes and instances. *Computational Linguistics*, 32(1):1–3.

Tristan Miller and Iryna Gurevych. 2014. Wordnet—wikipedia—wiktionary: Construction of a three-way alignment. In *Proceedings of the Ninth International Conference on Language Resources and Evaluation (LREC'14)*, pages 2094–2100, Reykjavik, Iceland. European Language Resources Association (ELRA).

Grace Muzny and Luke Zettlemoyer. 2013. Automatic idiom identification in Wiktionary. In *Proceedings of the 2013 Conference on Empirical Methods in Natural Language Processing*, pages 1417–1421, Seattle, Washington, USA. Association for Computational Linguistics.

Patrick Pantel and Marco Pennacchiotti. 2006. Espresso: Leveraging generic patterns for automatically harvesting semantic relations. In *Proceedings of the 21st International Conference on Computational Linguistics and 44th Annual Meeting of the Association for Computational Linguistics*, pages 113–120, Sydney, Australia. Association for Computational Linguistics.

Patrick Pantel and Marco Pennacchiotti. 2008. Automatically harvesting and ontologizing semantic relations. In *Ontology Learning and Population: Bridging the Gap between Text and Knowledge*, pages 171–198, Amsterdam, Netherlands. IOS Press.

Karl Pearson. 1895. Notes on regression and inheritance in the case of two parents. In *Proceedings of the Royal Society of London*, volume 58, pages 240–242. The Royal Society of London.

Jeffrey Pennington, Richard Socher, and Christopher Manning. 2014. Glove: Global vectors for word representation. In *Proceedings of the 2014 Conference on Empirical Methods in Natural Language Processing (EMNLP)*, pages 1532–1543, Doha, Qatar. Association for Computational Linguistics.

Herbert Rubenstein and John Goodenough. 1965. Contextual correlates of synonymy. *Communications of the ACM*, 8:627–633.

Jon Rusert and Ted Pedersen. 2016. Umnduluth at semeval-2016 task 14: Wordnet's missing lemmas. In *Proceedings of the 10th International Workshop on Semantic Evaluation (SemEval-2016)*, pages 1346–1350, San Diego, California. Association for Computational Linguistics.

Bahar Salehi, Paul Cook, and Timothy Baldwin. 2014. Detecting non-compositional mwe components using wiktionary. In *Proceedings of the 2014 Conference on Empirical Methods in Natural Language Processing (EMNLP)*, pages 1792–1797, Doha, Qatar. Association for Computational Linguistics.

Tobias Schnabel, Igor Labutov, David Mimno, and Thorsten Joachims. 2015. Evaluation methods for unsupervised word embeddings. pages 298–307.

Bernhard Schölkopf, Chris Burges, and Vladimir Vapnik. 1995. Extracting support data for a given task. In *Proceedings of the First International Conference on Knowledge Discovery and Data Mining*, KDD'95, pages 252–257. AAAI Press.

C Spearman. 2010. The proof and measurement of association between two things. *International Journal of Epidemiology*, 39(5):1137–1150.

Wikimedia. Wiktionary, the free dictionary.

Lingfei Wu, Ian En-Hsu Yen, Kun Xu, Fangli Xu, Avinash Balakrishnan, Pin-Yu Chen, Pradeep Ravikumar, and Michael J. Witbrock. 2018. Word mover's embedding: From word2vec to document embedding. In *Proceedings of the 2018 Conference on Empirical Methods in Natural Language Processing*, pages 4524–4534, Brussels, Belgium. Association for Computational Linguistics.

Z. Wu and M. Palmer. 1994. Verbs semantics and lexical selection. *Proceedings of the 32nd conference on Association for Computational Linguistics*, pages 133–138.

Dongqiang Yang and David Powers. 2006. Verb similarity on the taxonomy of wordnet. *Proceedings of the 3rd International WordNet Conference (GWC)*, pages 121–128.

Torsten Zesch, Christof Muller, and Iryna Gurevych. 2008. Using wiktionary for computing semantic relatedness. In *In Proceedings of AAAI*, pages 861–867.

SmokEng: Towards Fine-grained Classification of Tobacco-related Social Media Text

Kartikey Pant, Venkata Himakar Yanamandra, Alok Debnath and Radhika Mamidi
International Institute of Information Technology
Hyderabad, Telangana, India
{kartikey.pant, himakar.y, alok.debnath}@research.iiit.ac.in
radhika.mamidi@iiit.ac.in

Abstract

Contemporary datasets on tobacco consumption focus on one of two topics, either public health mentions and disease surveillance, or sentiment analysis on topical tobacco products and services. However, two primary considerations are not accounted for, the language of the demographic affected and a combination of the topics mentioned above in a fine-grained classification mechanism. In this paper, we create a dataset of 3144 tweets, which are selected based on the presence of colloquial slang related to smoking and analyze it based on the semantics of the tweet. Each class is created and annotated based on the content of the tweets such that further hierarchical methods can be easily applied.

Further, we prove the efficacy of standard text classification methods on this dataset, by designing experiments which do both binary as well as multi-class classification. Our experiments tackle the identification of either a specific topic (such as tobacco product promotion), a general mention (cigarettes and related products) or a more fine-grained classification. This methodology paves the way for further analysis, such as understanding sentiment or style, which makes this dataset a vital contribution to both disease surveillance and tobacco use research.

1 Introduction

As Twitter has grown in popularity to 330 million monthly active users, researchers have increasingly been using it as a source of data for tobacco surveillance (Lienemann et al., 2017). Tobacco-related advertisements, tweets, awareness posts, and related information is most actively viewed by young adults (aged 18 to 29), who are extensive users of social media and also represent the largest population of smokers in the US and

Canada [1]. Furthermore, it allows us to understand patterns in ethnically diverse and vulnerable audiences (Lienemann et al., 2017). Social media provides an active and useful platform for spreading awareness, especially dialog platforms, which have untapped potential for disease surveillance (Platt et al., 2016). These platforms are useful in stimulating the discussion on societal roles in the domain of public health (Platt et al., 2016). Sharpe et al. (2016) has shown the utility of social media by highlighting that the number of people using social media channels for information about their illnesses before seeking medical care.

Correlation studies have shown that the most probable leading cause of preventable death globally is the consumption of tobacco and tobacco products (Prochaska et al., 2012). The disease most commonly associated with tobacco consumption is lung cancer, with two million cases reported in 2018 alone [2]. While cigarettes are condemned on social media, this has been rivaled by the rising popularity and analysis of the supposed benefits of e-cigarettes (Dai and Hao, 2017). Information pertaining to new flavors and inno vations in the industry and surrounding culture have generated sizable traffic on social media as well (Hilton et al., 2016). Studies show that social acceptance is a leading factor to the use and proliferation of e-cigarettes, with some reports claiming as many as 2.39 million high school and 0.63 million middle school students having used an e-cigarette at least once (Malik et al., 2019; Mantey et al., 2019). However, there are strong claims suggesting the use of e-cigarettes as a 'gateway' drug for other illicit substances (Unger et al.,

---

[1] https://www.cdc.gov/tobacco/data_statistics/fact_sheets/adult_data/cig_smoking/

[2] https://www.wcrf.org/dietandcancer/cancer-trends/lung-cancer-statistics

Proceedings of the 2019 EMNLP Workshop W-NUT: The 5th Workshop on Noisy User-generated Text, pages 181–190
Hong Kong, Nov 4, 2019. ©2019 Association for Computational Linguistics

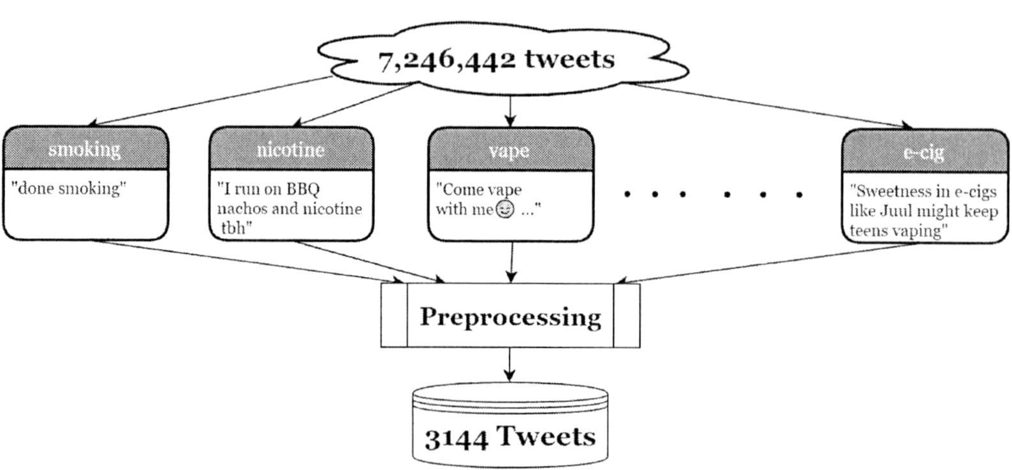

Figure 1: Procedure for Data Collection. We started out with approximately 7 million Tweets which were mined based on 24 slang terms. These were pre-processed to select relevant tweets with decent traction on Twitter. A final cleaned dataset of 3144 tweets is presented.

2016).

In this paper, we aim at classifying tweets relating to cigarettes, e-cigarettes, and other tobacco-related products into distinct classes. This classification is fine-grained in order to assist in the analysis of the type of tweets which affect the users the most for each product or category. The extensive, manually annotated dataset of 3144 tweets pertains to tobacco use classification into advertisement, general information, personal information, and non-tobacco drug classes. Such classification provides insight into the type of tweet and associated target audience. For example, present cessation programs target users who are ready to quit rather than people who use it regularly, which can be solved using twitter and other online social media (Prochaska et al., 2012). Unlike many previous studies, we also include common slang terms into the classification scheme so as to be able to work with the social media discourse of the target audience.

Finally, we present several text-classification models for the fine-grained classification tasks pertaining to tobacco-related tweets on the released dataset[3]. In doing so, we extend the work in topical Twitter content analysis as well as the study of public health mentions on Twitter.

2 Related Work

Myslín et al. (2013) explored content and senti-

ment analysis of Tobacco-related Twitter posts and performed analysis using machine learning classifiers for the detection of tobacco-relevant posts with a particular focus on emerging products like e-cigarettes and hookah. Their work depends on a triaxial classification along and uses basic statistical classifiers. However, their feature-engineered keyword-based systems do not account for slang associated with tobacco consumption.

Vandewater et al. (2018) performs a classification study based on identifying brand associated with a post using basic text analytics using keywords and image-based classifiers to determine the brands that were most responsible to posting about their brands on social media. Cortese et al. (2018) does a similar analysis on the consumer side, for female smokers on Instagram, targeting the same age group, but based entirely on feature extraction on images, particularly selfies.

More recently, Malik et al. (2019) explored patterns of communication of e-cigarette company Juul use on Twitter. They categorized 1008 randomly selected tweets across four dimensions, namely, user type, sentiment, genre, theme. However, they explore the effects of only Juul, and not other cigarettes or e-cigarettes, further limiting their experiment to only Juul-based analysis and inferences.

In the domain of Disease Surveillance, Aramaki et al. (2011) explored the problem of identifying influenza epidemics using machine-learning based tweet classifiers along with search engine trends

[3]https://github.com/kartikeypant/smokeng-tobacco-classification

Name	Label	Annotation Class
Mention of Non-Tobacco Drugs	OD	-1
Unrelated or Ambiguous Mention	UM	0
Personal or Anecdotal Mention	PM	1
Informative or Advisory Mention	IM	2
Advertisements	AD	3

Table 1: Label and ID associated with each class.

for medical keywords and medical records for the disease in a local environment. For doing so, they use SVM based classifiers for extracting tweets that mention actual influenza patients. However, since they use only SVM based classifiers, they are limited in their accuracy in classification.

Dai et al. (2017) also focuses on public health surveillance, and uses word embeddings on a topic classifier in order to identify and capture semantic similarities between medical tweets by disease and tweet type for a more robust yet very filtered classification, not accounting for the variety of linguistic features in tweets such as slang, abbreviations and the like in the keyword-based classification mechanism. Jiang et al. (2018) works on a similar problem using machine learning solutions such as an LSTM classifier.

3 Dataset Creation

In this section, we explain the development of the dataset that we present along with this paper. We summarize the methods for collecting and filtering through the tweets to arrive at the final dataset and provide some examples of the types of tweets and features we focused on. We also provide the dataset annotation schema and guidelines.

3.1 Data Collection

Using the Twitter Application Programming Interface (API[4]), we collected a sample of tweets between 1st October 2018 and 7th October 2018 that represented 1% of the entire Twitter feed. This 1% sample consisted of an average 1,035,206 million tweets per day. Out of the 7,246,442 tweets, only tweets written in English and written by users with more than 100 followers have selected for the next step in order to clear spam written by bots.

In order to extract tobacco related tweets from this dataset, we constructed a list of keywords relevant to general tobacco usage, including hookah

---

[4]https://developer.twitter.com/en/products/tweets/sample.html

and e-cigarettes. Our initial list consisted of 32 such terms compiled from online slang dictionaries, but we pruned this list to 24 terms. These were *smoking, cigarette, e-cig*, cigar, tobacco, hookah, shisha, e-juice, e-liquid, vape, vaping, cheroot, cigarillo, roll-up, ashtray, baccy, rollies, claro, chain-smok*, vaper, ciggie, nicotine, non-smoker, non-smoking.*

By taking the dataset for a full week, we thus avoided potential bias based on the day of the week, which has been observed for alcohol related tweets, which spike in positive sentiment on Fridays and Saturdays (Cavazos-Rehg et al., 2015). For each of the 7 days, all tweets matching any of the listed keywords were included. Tweets matching these tobacco related keywords reflected 0.00043% of all tweets in the Twitter API 1% sample. The resulting final dataset thus contained 3144 tweets, with a mean of 449 tweets per day.

3.2 Data Annotation

The collected data was then annotated based on the categories mentioned in Table 1. These categories were chosen on the basis of frequency of occurrence, motivated by the general perception of tobacco and non-tobacco drug related tweets. These included advertisements as well anecdotes, information and cautionary tweets. We further noticed that a similar pattern was seen for e-cigarettes and also pertained to some other drugs. While we have explored e-cigarettes in this classification, we have marked the mention of other drugs that were tagged with the same keywords.

A formal definition of each of the categories is given below.

- **Unrelated or Ambiguous Mention**: This category of tweets contain tweets containing information unrelated to tobacco or any other drug, or pertaining to ambiguity in the intent of the tweet, such as sarcasm.

Label	Examples
UM	*"What are you smoking bruh ?"* *"The smoking gun on Kavanaugh! URL "*
PM	*"im smoking and doing whats best for me"* *"I haven't had a cigarette in $NUMBER$ months why do I want one so bad now??"*
IM	*"Obama puffed. Clinton did cigar feel.Churchill won major wars on whisky."* *"The FDA's claim of a teen vaping addiction epidemic doesn't add up. #ecigarette #health"*
AD	*"Which ACID Kuba Kuba are you aiming for? #De4L #ExperienceAcid #cigar #cigars URL"* *"Spookah Lounge: A concept - a year round Halloween-themed hookah lounge"*
OD	*"Making my money and smoking my weed"* *"Mobbin in da Bentley smoking moonrocks."*

Table 2: Examples for each category represented by its label.

- **Personal or Anecdotal Mention**: Tweets are classified as containing a personal or anecdotal mention if they imply either personal use of tobacco products or e-cigarettes, or provide instances of use of the products by themselves or others.

- **Informative or Advisory Mention**: This class of tweets consist of a broad range of topics such as:

  - mention or discussion on statistics of tobacco and e-cigarette use or consumption
  - mention associated health risks or benefits
  - portray the use of tobacco products or e-cigarettes by a public figure
  - emphasize social campaigns for anti-smoking, smoking cessation and related products such as patches

- **Advertisements**: All tweets written with the intent of the sale of tobacco products, e-cigarettes and associated products or services are marked advertisements. In this classification, intent is considered using the mention of price as an objective measure.

- **Mention of Non-Tobacco Drugs**: Tweets which mention the use, sale, anecdotes and information about drugs other than e-cigarettes or tobacco products are annotated in this category.

3.3 Inter-annotator Agreement

Annotation of the dataset to detect the presence of tobacco substance use was carried out by two human annotators having linguistic background and proficiency in English. A sample annotation set consisting of 10 tweets per class was selected randomly from all across the corpus. Both annotators were given the selected sample annotation set. These sample annotation set served as a reference baseline of each category of the text.

In order to validate the quality of annotation, we calculated the Inter-Annotator Agreement (IAA) for the fine-grain classification between the two annotation sets of 3,144 tobacco-related tweets using Cohen's Kappa coefficient (Fleiss and Cohen, 1973). The Kappa score of **0.791** indicates that the quality of the annotation and presented schema is productive.

4 Methodology

In this section we describe the classifiers designed for this task of fine grained classification. The classifier architecture is based upon a combination of choosing word representations, along with a discriminator that is compatible with that representation. We use the TF-IDF for the suport vector machines and GloVe embeddings (Pennington et al., 2014) with our convolutional neural network architecture and recurrent architectures (LSTM and Bi-LSTM). We also used FastText and BERT embeddings (both base and large) with their native classifiers to note the change in the accuracies.

4.1 Support Vector Machines (SVM)

The first learning model used for classification in our experiment was Support Vector Machines (SVM) (Cortes and Vapnik, 1995). We used term frequency-inverse document frequency (TF-IDF) as a feature to classify the annotated tweets in our data set (Salton and Buckley, 1988). TF-IDF captures the importance of the given the word in a document, defined in Equation 1.

$$tfidf(t, d, D) = f(t, d) \times \log \frac{N}{|\{d \epsilon D : t \epsilon d\}|} \quad (1)$$

where $f(t, d)$ indicates the number of times term t appears in context, d and N is the total number of documents $|d \epsilon D : t \epsilon d|$ represents the total number of documents where t occurs.

The SVM classifier finds the decision boundary that maximizes the margin by minimizing $\|\mathbf{w}\|$ to find the optimal hyperplane for all the classification tasks:

$$\min f : \tfrac{1}{2}\|\mathbf{w}\|^2$$

$$\text{s.t.} \quad y^{(i)}\left(\mathbf{w}^T\mathbf{x}^{(i)} + b\right) \geq 1, \quad i = 1, \ldots, m \quad (2)$$

where $\mathbf{w}$ is the weight vector, $\mathbf{x}$ is the input vector and b is the bias.

4.2 Convolutional Neural Networks (CNN)

In this subsection, we outline the Convolutional Neural Networks (Fukushima, 1988) for classification and also provide the process description for text classification in particular. Convolutional neural networks are multistage trainable neural networks architectures developed for classification tasks (Lecun et al., 1998). Each of these stages consist of the types of layers described below:

- **Embedding Layer**: The purpose of an embedding layer is to transform the text inputs into a form which can be used by the CNN model. Here, each word of a text document is transformed into a dense vector of fixed size.

- **Convolutional Layers**: A Convolutional layer consists of multiple kernel matrices that perform the convolution mathematical operation on their input and produce an output matrix of features upon the addition of a bias value.

- **Pooling Layers**: The purpose of a pooling layer is to perform dimensionality reduction of the input feature vectors. Pooling layers use sub-sampling to the output of the convolutional layer matrices combing neighbouring elements. We have used the commonly used max-pooling function for the pooling.

- **Fully-Connected Layer**: It is a classic fully connected neural network layer. It is connected to the Pooling layers via a Dropout layer in order to prevent overfitting. Softmax activation function is used for defining the final output of this layer.

The following objective function is commonly used in the task:

$$E_w = \frac{1}{n} \sum_{p=1}^{P} \sum_{j=1}^{N_L} (o_{j,p}^{L} - y_{j,p})^2 \quad (3)$$

where P is the number of patterns, $o_{j,p}^{L}$ is the output of jth neuron that belongs to L^{th} layer, N_L is the number of neurons in output of Lth layer, $y_{j,p}$ is the desirable target of jth neuron of pattern p and y_i is the output associated with an input vector x_i to the CNN.

We use Adam Optimizer (Kingma and Ba, 2014) to minimize the cost function E_w.

4.3 Recurrent Neural Architectures

Recurrent neural networks (RNN) have been employed to produce promising results on a variety of tasks, including language model and speech recognition (Mikolov et al., 2010, 2011; Graves and Schmidhuber, 2005). An RNN predicts the current output conditioned on long-distance features by maintaining a memory based on history information.

An input layer represents features at time t. One-hot vectors for words, dense vector features such as word embeddings, or sparse features usually represent an input layer. An input layer has the same dimensionality as feature size. An output layer represents a probability distribution over labels at time t and has the same dimensionality as the size of the labels. Compared to the feedforward network, an RNN contains a connection between the previous hidden state and current hidden state. This connection is made through the recurrent layer, which is designed to store history information. The following equation is used to compute the values in the hidden, and output layers:

$$\mathbf{h}(t) = f(\mathbf{U}\mathbf{x}(t) + \mathbf{W}\mathbf{h}(t-1)). \quad (4)$$

$$\mathbf{y}(t) = g(\mathbf{V}\mathbf{h}(t)), \quad (5)$$

where U, W, and V are the connection weights to be computed during training, and $f(z)$ and $g(z)$

Model/Experiment	Personal Health Mentions	Tobacco-related Mentions
SVM	82.17%	83.44%
CNN	84.08%	82.48%
$LSTM$	84.39%	83.32%
$BiLSTM$	83.92%	82.97%
$FastText$	83.76%	81.05%
$BERT_{Base}$	85.19%	85.50%
$BERT_{Large}$	**87.26%**	**85.67%**

Table 3: Binary Classification accuracies for specific topic (Personal Health Mention) or general theme (Tobacco-related Mentions).

are sigmoid and softmax activation functions as follows.

$$f(z) = \frac{1}{1 + e^{-z}}, \qquad (6)$$

$$g(z_m) = \frac{e^{z_m}}{\sum_k e_k^z} \qquad (7)$$

In this paper, we apply Long Short Term Memory (LSTM) and Bidirectional Long Short Term Memory(Bi-LSTM) to sequence tagging (Hochreiter and Schmidhuber, 1997; Graves and Schmidhuber, 2005; Graves et al., 2013).

LSTM networks use purpose-built memory cells to update the hidden layer values. As a result, they may be better at finding and exploiting long-range dependencies in the data than a standard RNN. The following equation implements the LSTM model:

$$i_t = \sigma(W_{xi}x_t + W_{hi}h_{t-1} + W_{ci}c_{t-1} + b_i) \quad (8)$$

$$f_t = \sigma(W_{xf}x_t + W_{hf}h_{t-1} + W_{cf}c_{t-1} + b_f) \quad (9)$$

$$o_t = \sigma(W_{xo}x_t + W_{ho}h_{t-1} + W_{co}c_t + b_o) \quad (10)$$

$$h_t = o_t tanh(c_t) \qquad (11)$$

In sequence tagging task, we have access to both past and future input features for a given time. Thus, we can utilize a bidirectional LSTM network (Bi-LSTM) as proposed in (Graves et al., 2013).

4.4 FastText

FastText classifier has proven to be efficient for text classification (Joulin et al., 2016). It is often at par with deep learning classifiers in terms of accuracy, and much faster for training and evaluation. FastText uses bag of words and bag of n-grams as features for text classification. Bag of n-grams feature captures partial information about the local word order. FastText allows updating word vectors through back-propagation during training allowing the model to fine-tune word representations according to the task at hand (Bojanowski et al., 2016). The model is trained using stochastic gradient descent and a linearly decaying learning rate.

4.5 BERT

While previous studies on word representations focused on learning context-independent representations, recent works have focused on learning contextualized word representations. One of the more recent contextualized word representation is BERT (Devlin et al., 2019).

BERT is a contextualized word representation model, pre-trained using bidirectional transformers(Vaswani et al., 2017). It uses a masked language model that predicts randomly masked in a sequence. It uses the task of *next sentence prediction* for learning the embeddings with a broader context. It outperforms many existing techniques on most NLP tasks with minimal task-specific architectural changes. It is pretrained on 3.3B words from various sources including BooksCorpus and the English Wikipedia.

Based on the transformer architecture used, BERT is classified into two types: $BERT_{Base}$ and $BERT_{Large}$. $BERT_{Base}$ uses a 12-layered transformer with 110M parameters. $BERT_{Large}$ uses a 24-layered transformer with 340M parameters. We use the cased variant of both models.

Methods	Accuracy	F1 Score	Recall
SVM	65.45%	0.678	0.657
CNN	66.72%	0.668	0.599
$LSTM$	64.97%	0.641	0.583
$BiLSTM$	65.29%	0.643	0.597
$FastText$	69.43%	0.696	0.669
$BERT_{Base}$	70.86%	0.708	0.709
$BERT_{Large}$	**71.34%**	**0.714**	**0.713**

Table 4: Evaluation scores for the Fine-grained classification experiment.

5 Experiments

In this section, we describe three experiments on the dataset created in the section above. The experiments are designed to show how well existing models perform on the naive binary classification based on this dataset as well as the fine-grained five-class classification system. The first experiment is based on detecting just personal or anecdotal mentions. The second is based on identifying whether a tweet is about tobacco or not. The last experiment is a full fine-grained classification experiment.

The following experiments were conducted keeping an 80-20 split between training and test data, with 2517 tweets in the training dataset and 629 tweets in the test dataset. All tweets were shuffled randomly before the train-test split.

$BERT_{Large}$ was observed to perform the best in all three experiments, followed closely by $BERT_{Base}$ in all the experiments that were conducted.

5.1 Experiment 1: Detecting Personal Mentions of Tobacco Use

The first experiment in the study was to detect tweets containing personal mentions of tobacco use. Tweets containing personal mentions of tobacco use are the ones marking implicit or explicit use of a tobacco substance by the poster. The objective of this experiment is to analyze the best method to identify tweets which talk about tobacco in an anecdotal manner, which can be used to understand the semantic similarity between such tweets. Table 3 illustrates the results for this experiment.

5.2 Experiment 2: Identifying Tobacco-related Mentions

The next experiment in the study was to detect all tobacco-related tweets related. These include the

following categories of tweets: personal mentions of tobacco-use, general information about tobacco or its use, advertisements. Thus, the experiment was to determine whether the tweet belonged to one of the above categories or not. The objective here is also to gauge semantic information in tweets with mentions of tobacco, suggesting that tweets using the similar slang might be talking about other drugs or ambiguous or unrelated information. Table 3 illustrates the results for this experiment.

5.3 Experiment 3: Performing Fine-grained Classification of Tobacco-related Mentions

The last experiment conducted in the study was to classify the tweets into all five categories: UM, PM, IM, AD, OD. Table 4 illustrates the results of the experiment. This is essentially the fine grained classification experiment which relies on semantic information as well as lexical choice. We see that models from all the three experiments perform differently given the type of task. Table 4 illustrates the results for this experiment.

6 Discussion

In this section, we analyze our contributions from the perspective of advancing work in the fields of topical content analysis as well as the study of public health mentions in tweets, with regards to tobacco products, as well as e-cigarettes and related products. Given the effects of both as well as the significant overlap in the demographic of consumers of tobacco products and Twitter users, we found it necessary to understand the nature of the tweets produced and consumed by them.

Our dataset, a collection of 3144 tweets, accumulated and filtered over the period of just a week, implies that tobacco and related drugs are tweeted about and spoken of quite frequently, but

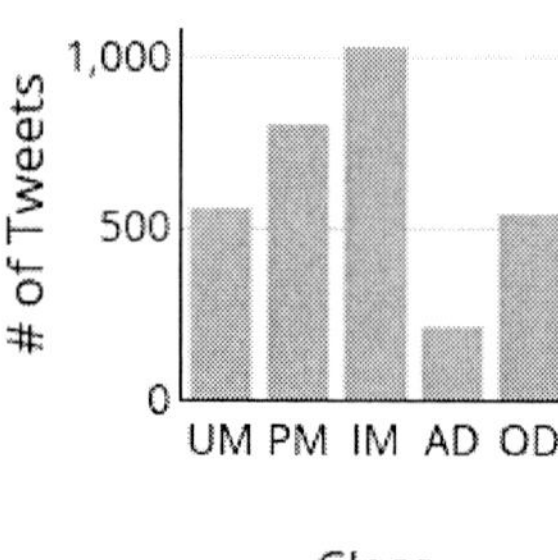

Figure 2: Distribution of tweets among different categories

Category	Retweets	Favorites
UM	1079.05	0.794
PM	12171.60	0.904
IM	680.24	3.918
AD	140.81	4.586
OD	873.08	0.868

Table 5: Average retweets and favorites across classes

the linguistic cues common among these tweets was not considered until now. The inclusion of tweets into the corpus based on slang terminology is an attempt to analyze the Twitter landscape in the language of the audience which most highly correlates with the demographic of consumers for the aforementioned products. To the best of our knowledge, using common slang as a basis of dataset creation and filtration for this task has not been attempted before.

Contemporary methods in the field focus on two basic characterizations, user based and sentiment based. User based classification such as Malik et al. (2019) and Jo et al. (2016) are based on the analyzing activity from a particular user or set of users, while sentiment based analyses such as Paul and Dredze (2011); Allem et al. (2018) and Myslín et al. (2013) are based on understanding the sentiment of the users on the basis of a new product, category or a more generalized perception of smoking in general. On the other hand, public health mention research such as Jawad et al. (2015) focuses on effect of a particular type of tweet, generally health campaigns. Fundamen-

tally, the classes we have chosen for the collected data are based on the same principle as the data collection mechanism, with the aim to bridge the gap between the classification studies and the public health surveillance research. This is because our categories cover the breadth of the tweets evenly, directed towards semantically understanding the nature of the tweets. This information is vital for addressing the validity and reach of campaigns, advertisements and other efforts.

Figure 2 shows the distribution of the number of tweets in each class. We see that in the span of a week, informative or advisory and personal mentions are the most widely posted. The tweets that provide general information about smokers or the habits of smoking tobacco or e-cigarettes are generated the most, implying that a larger section of the population tweets of smoking in an anecdotal manner. Similarly, Table 5 shows an interesting trends for the favorites. Advertisements have a higher average favorite count than most other classes, while anecdotal and advisory tweets are the most retweeted on average. This difference is an interesting observation, primarily because on further work such as sentiment analysis and doing short text style transfer (Luo et al., 2019) for these categories may provide an effective strategy for advertisers and campaigners alike.

7 Conclusion and Future Work

In this paper, we created a dataset of tweets and classified them in order to understand the social media atmosphere around tobacco, e-cigarettes and other related products. Our schema for categorization targets posts on public health as much as tobacco related products, therefore allowing us to know the number and type of tweets used in public health surveillance for the above mentioned products. Most importantly, we consider slang as a very important aspect of our data collection mechanism, which has allowed us to factor in the content which is circulated and exposed to the majority of the consumers of social media and the aforementioned products both.

This contribution can be further extended by working with other social media platforms, where the methods introduced above can be easily replicated. Social media specific slang can be taken into account to make a more robust dataset for this task. Furthermore, on the public health surveillance aspect, more metadata using the tweets can be extracted, which gives an idea of the type of tweets or posts needed to grab the attention of a wider audience on topics of public health and awareness for the grave topic of tobacco products and e-cigarettes.

References

Jon-Patrick Allem, Likhit Dharmapuri, Adam Leventhal, Jennifer Unger, and Tess Cruz. 2018. Hookah-related posts to twitter from 2017 to 2018: Thematic analysis. *Journal of Medical Internet Research*, 20:e11669.

Eiji Aramaki, Sachiko Maskawa, and Mizuki Morita. 2011. Twitter catches the flu: detecting influenza epidemics using twitter. In *Proceedings of the conference on empirical methods in natural language processing*, pages 1568–1576. Association for Computational Linguistics.

Piotr Bojanowski, Edouard Grave, Armand Joulin, and Tomas Mikolov. 2016. Enriching word vectors with subword information. *Transactions of the Association for Computational Linguistics*, 5:135–146.

Patricia A. Cavazos-Rehg, Melissa J. Krauss, Shaina Sowles, and Laura J. Bierut. 2015. "hey everyone, i'm drunk." an evaluation of drinking-related twitter chatter. *Journal of studies on alcohol and drugs*, 76 4:635–43.

Corinna Cortes and Vladimir Vapnik. 1995. Support-vector networks. *Mach. Learn.*, 20(3):273–297.

Daniel K Cortese, Glen Szczypka, Sherry Emery, Shuai Wang, Elizabeth Hair, and Donna Vallone. 2018. Smoking selfies: using instagram to explore young women's smoking behaviors. *Social Media+ Society*, 4(3):2056305118790762.

Hongying Dai and Jianqiang Hao. 2017. Mining social media data for opinion polarities about electronic cigarettes. *Tobacco control*, 26(2):175–180.

Xiangfeng Dai, Marwan Bikdash, and Bradley Meyer. 2017. From social media to public health surveillance: Word embedding based clustering method for twitter classification. In *SoutheastCon 2017*, pages 1–7. IEEE.

Jacob Devlin, Ming-Wei Chang, Kenton Lee, and Kristina Toutanova. 2019. BERT: pre-training of deep bidirectional transformers for language understanding. In *Proceedings of the 2019 Conference of the North American Chapter of the Association for Computational Linguistics: Human Language Technologies, NAACL-HLT 2019, Minneapolis, MN, USA, June 2-7, 2019, Volume 1 (Long and Short Papers)*, pages 4171–4186.

Joseph L. Fleiss and Jacob Cohen. 1973. The equivalence of weighted kappa and the intraclass correlation coefficient as measures of reliability. *Educational and Psychological Measurement*, 33(3):613–619.

Kunihiko Fukushima. 1988. Neocognitron: A hierarchical neural network capable of visual pattern recognition. *Neural Networks*, 1(2):119–130.

Alex Graves, Abdel rahman Mohamed, and Geoffrey E. Hinton. 2013. Speech recognition with deep recurrent neural networks. *2013 IEEE International Conference on Acoustics, Speech and Signal Processing*, pages 6645–6649.

Alex Graves and Jürgen Schmidhuber. 2005. Framewise phoneme classification with bidirectional lstm and other neural network architectures. *Neural networks : the official journal of the International Neural Network Society*, 18 5-6:602–10.

Shona Hilton, Heide Weishaar, Helen Sweeting, Filippo Trevisan, and Srinivasa Vittal Katikireddi. 2016. E-cigarettes, a safer alternative for teenagers? a uk focus group study of teenagers' views. *BMJ Open*, 6(11).

Sepp Hochreiter and Jürgen Schmidhuber. 1997. Long short-term memory. *Neural Computation*, 9:1735–1780.

Mohammed Jawad, Jooman Abass, Ahmad Hariri, and Elie A Akl. 2015. Social media use for public health campaigning in a low resource setting: the case of waterpipe tobacco smoking. *BioMed research international*, 2015.

Keyuan Jiang, Shichao Feng, Qunhao Song, Ricardo A Calix, Matrika Gupta, and Gordon R Bernard. 2018. Identifying tweets of personal health experience through word embedding and lstm neural network. *BMC bioinformatics*, 19(8):210.

Catherine L Jo, Rachel Kornfield, Yoonsang Kim, Sherry Emery, and Kurt M Ribisl. 2016. Price-related promotions for tobacco products on twitter. *Tobacco control*, 25(4):476–479.

Armand Joulin, Edouard Grave, Piotr Bojanowski, and Tomas Mikolov. 2016. Bag of tricks for efficient text classification. In *EACL*.

Diederik P. Kingma and Jimmy Ba. 2014. Adam: A method for stochastic optimization. Cite arxiv:1412.6980Comment: Published as a conference paper at the 3rd International Conference for Learning Representations, San Diego, 2015.

Yann Lecun, Léon Bottou, Yoshua Bengio, and Patrick Haffner. 1998. Gradient-based learning applied to document recognition. In *Proceedings of the IEEE*, pages 2278–2324.

Brianna Lienemann, Jennifer Unger, Tess Cruz, and Kar-Hai Chu. 2017. Methods for coding tobacco-related twitter data: A systematic review. *Journal of Medical Internet Research*, 19:e91.

Fuli Luo, Peng Li, Pengcheng Yang, Jie Zhou, Yutong Tan, Baobao Chang, Zhifang Sui, and Xu Sun. 2019. Towards fine-grained text sentiment transfer. In *Proceedings of the 57th Conference of the Association for Computational Linguistics*, pages 2013–2022.

Aqdas Malik, Yisheng Li, Habib Karbasian, Juho Hamari, and Aditya Johri. 2019. Live, love, juul: User and content analysis of twitter posts about juul. *American Journal of Health Behavior*, 43:326–336.

Dale S Mantey, Cristina S Barroso, Ben T Kelder, and Steven H Kelder. 2019. Retail access to e-cigarettes and frequency of e-cigarette use in high school students. *Tobacco Regulatory Science*, 5(3):280–290.

Tomas Mikolov, Anoop Deoras, Daniel Povey, Lukás Burget, and Jan ernocký. 2011. Strategies for training large scale neural network language models. *2011 IEEE Workshop on Automatic Speech Recognition Understanding*, pages 196–201.

Tomas Mikolov, Martin Karafiát, Lukás Burget, Jan ernocký, and Sanjeev Khudanpur. 2010. Recurrent neural network based language model. In *INTER-SPEECH*.

Mark Myslín, Shu-Hong Zhu, Wendy Chapman, and Mike Conway. 2013. Using twitter to examine smoking behavior and perceptions of emerging tobacco products. *Journal of medical Internet research*, 15:e174.

Michael J. Paul and Mark Dredze. 2011. You are what you tweet: Analyzing twitter for public health. In *ICWSM*. The AAAI Press.

Jeffrey Pennington, Richard Socher, and Christopher Manning. 2014. Glove: Global vectors for word representation. In *Proceedings of the 2014 conference on empirical methods in natural language processing (EMNLP)*, pages 1532–1543.

Tevah Platt, Jodyn Platt, Daniel Thiel, and Sharon L. R Kardia. 2016. Facebook advertising across an engagement spectrum: A case example for public health communication. *JMIR Public Health and Surveillance*, 2:e27.

Judith Prochaska, Cornelia Pechmann, Romina Kim, and James Leonhardt. 2012. Twitter = quitter? an analysis of twitter quit smoking social networks. *Tobacco Control*, 21:447–449.

Gerard Salton and Christopher Buckley. 1988. Term-weighting approaches in automatic text retrieval. *Inf. Process. Manage.*, 24(5):513–523.

Danielle Sharpe, Richard S Hopkins, Robert Cook, and Catherine Striley. 2016. Evaluating google, twitter, and wikipedia as tools for influenza surveillance using bayesian change point analysis: A comparative analysis. *JMIR Public Health and Surveillance*, 2:e161.

Jennifer Unger, Daniel Soto, and Adam Leventhal. 2016. E-cigarette use and subsequent cigarette and marijuana use among hispanic young adults. *Drug and Alcohol Dependence*, 163.

Elizabeth A Vandewater, Stephanie L Clendennen, Emily T Hébert, Galya Bigman, Christian D Jackson, Anna V Wilkinson, and Cheryl L Perry. 2018. Whose post is it? predicting e-cigarette brand from social media posts. *Tobacco regulatory science*, 4(2):30–43.

Ashish Vaswani, Noam Shazeer, Niki Parmar, Jakob Uszkoreit, Llion Jones, Aidan N Gomez, Łukasz Kaiser, and Illia Polosukhin. 2017. Attention is all you need. In *Advances in Neural Information Processing Systems*, pages 5998–6008.

Modelling Uncertainty in Collaborative Document Quality Assessment

Aili Shen   Daniel Beck   Bahar Salehi   Jianzhong Qi   Timothy Baldwin

School of Computing and Information Systems
The University of Melbourne
Victoria, Australia

`ailis@student.unimelb.edu.au`
`d.beck@unimelb.edu.au  baharsalehi@gmail.com`
`jianzhong.qi@unimelb.edu.au    tb@ldwin.net`

Abstract

In the context of document quality assessment, previous work has mainly focused on predicting the quality of a document relative to a putative gold standard, without paying attention to the subjectivity of this task. To imitate people's disagreement over inherently subjective tasks such as rating the quality of a Wikipedia article, a document quality assessment system should provide not only a prediction of the article quality but also the uncertainty over its predictions. This motivates us to measure the uncertainty in document quality predictions, in addition to making the label prediction. Experimental results show that both *Gaussian processes* (GPs) and *random forests* (RFs) can yield competitive results in predicting the quality of Wikipedia articles, while providing an estimate of uncertainty when there is inconsistency in the quality labels from the Wikipedia contributors. We additionally evaluate our methods in the context of a semi-automated document quality class assignment decision-making process, where there is asymmetric risk associated with overestimates and underestimates of document quality. Our experiments suggest that GPs provide more reliable estimates in this context.

1   Introduction

The volume of textual web content generated collaboratively — through sites such as Wikipedia, or community question answering platforms such as Stack Overflow — has been growing progressively. Such collaborative paradigms give rise to a problem in quality assessment: how to ensure documents are reliable and useful to end users.

Given the volume of such documents, and velocity with which they are being produced, there has been recent interest in *automatic* quality assessment using machine learning techniques (Dang and Ignat, 2016a; Dalip et al., 2017; Shen

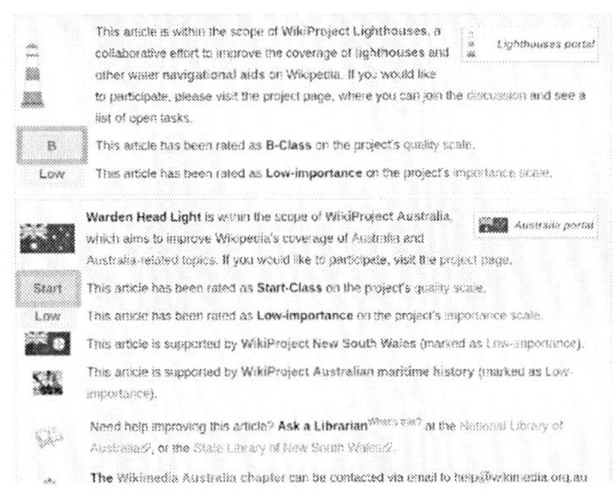

Figure 1: A screenshot of the "Warden Head Light" Talk page. Wikipedia Project *Lighthouses* assigns a B-class quality label to this article, while Wikipedia Project *Australia* assigns a Start-class quality label.

et al., 2017). However, previous work has treated this problem using off-the-shelf predictors, which fail to take into account two key aspects. First, any quality rating is inherently *subjective*: different end users can heavily disagree on the quality of a document. For example, as shown in Figure 1, the Wikipedia article *Warden Head Light*[1] is assigned to different labels from different Wikipedia Projects:[2] B (in the green block) by Wikipedia Project *Lighthouses*, and Start (in the orange block) by Wikipedia Project *Australia*;[3] among a 30K datatset we collected, there are 7% such articles (even including high-quality articles), where contributors disagree over the article quality. Second, previous work has ignored *decision-making*

---

[1] `https://en.wikipedia.org/w/index.php?title=Warden_Head_Light&oldid=759074867`

[2] A Wikipedia Project is a group of Wikipedia contributors who work together to improve Wikipedia articles that they are interested in.

[3] We return to describe the full label set in Section 2.

Proceedings of the 2019 EMNLP Workshop W-NUT: The 5th Workshop on Noisy User-generated Text, pages 191–201
Hong Kong, Nov 4, 2019. ©2019 Association for Computational Linguistics

procedures (such as expert reviewing, and featuring articles on the Wikipedia main page) that are impacted by the results of the prediction, which can vary in non-trivial ways.

In this work, we address these two gaps by modelling the *uncertainty* in the quality labels by treating predictions as probability distributions. In order to obtain these distributions, we experiment with both Bayesian models (Gaussian Processes, GPs, Rasmussen and Williams, 2006) and frequentist, ensemble-based methods (Random Forests, RFs, Breiman, 2001), applying them to English Wikipedia articles. Our results show that these approaches are competitive with the state-of-the-art in terms of predictive performance, while also providing estimates of uncertainty in the form of predictive distributions.

As a case study on the utility of uncertainty estimates, we analyse a typical Wikipedia scenario, where articles with predicted high quality are sent to expert reviewers to confirm their status. Such reviewing procedures are costly: if a low-quality article is predicted to be a featured article (the highest quality in Wikipedia), the triggered manual review can substantially waste time and human effort. Conversely, if a high-quality article is predicted to be of a lower-quality class, there is no cost to the editor community.[4] This is an example of asymmetric risk, where underestimates and overestimates have different penalties. In this paper, we show how to use uncertainty estimates from predictions in order to make a quality prediction that minimises this asymmetric risk.

In summary, this paper makes the following contributions:

(i) We are the first to propose to measure the uncertainty of article quality assessment systems. We find that both GPs and RFs can achieve performance competitive with the state-of-the-art, while providing uncertainty estimates over their predictions in the form of predictive distributions.

(ii) To model asymmetric risk scenarios in Wikipedia, we propose to combine the predictive distributions provided by our methods with asymmetric cost functions. Experimental results show that GPs are superior to RFs under such scenarios.

(iii) We constructed a 30K Wikipedia article

dataset containing both gold-standard labels and Wikipedia Project labels, which we release for public use along with all code associated with this paper at https://github.com/AiliAili/ measure_uncertainty.

2   Preliminaries

In this section, we detail the specific scenario addressed in this study: quality assessment of Wikipedia articles. We also describe the procedure to construct our dataset.

2.1   Problem Definition

In line with previous work (Warncke-Wang et al., 2015; Dang and Ignat, 2016a,b, 2017), we consider six quality classes of Wikipedia articles, ordered from highest to lowest: Featured Article ("FA"), Good Article ("GA"), B-class Article ("B"), C-class Article ("C"), Start Article ("Start"), and Stub Article ("Stub"). A description of the quality grading criteria can be found in the Wikipedia grading scheme page.[5]

The quality assessment process over a Wikipedia article is done in a collaborative way, through discussions on the corresponding article's Talk page.[6] Wikipedia contributors also carefully review articles that are GA and FA candidates. In particular, FA articles are eligible to appear on the main page of the website. A reliable automatic quality assessment model should take these decision making aspects into account.

Problem statement.   In this paper, our aim is to predict the quality of unseen Wikipedia articles, paired with an estimate of uncertainty over each prediction, which we evaluate in a risk-aware decision making scenario. Figure 2 summarises model application and actions depending on the uncertainty: (1) quality-indicative features are first extracted from a Wikipedia article; (2) a model predicts the article quality and provides an indication of how confident it is of its prediction; and (3) different actions are taken based on the predicted quality and confidence value, such as expert review and featuring on the Wikipedia main page if an article is predicted to be FA/GA with high confidence.

---

[4] Although there may be an opportunity cost (in terms of not showcasing high-quality articles), and the potential demotivation of the associated editors.

[5] https://en.wikipedia.org/wiki/ Template:Grading_scheme

[6] Such as the Talk page for the "Warden Head Light" article: https://en.wikipedia.org/wiki/Talk: Warden_Head_Light

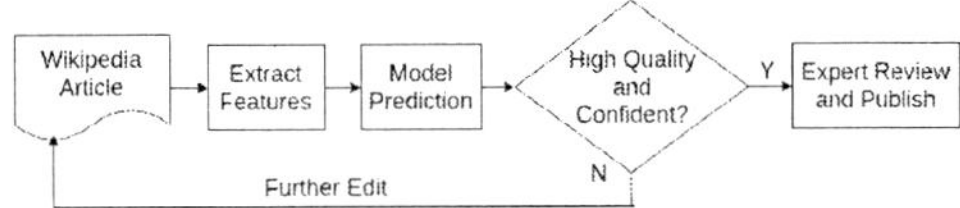

Figure 2: Model application and decision-making procedure.

2.2 Data Collection

We constructed an evaluation dataset by collecting articles from Wikipedia in a balanced way. From each quality class, we crawled 5K articles from its corresponding repository.[7] As mentioned in Section 1, quality assessment is subjective and multiple editors/Wikipedia Projects may disagree when assigning a quality label to an article. We can observe this behaviour by inspecting an article's corresponding Talk page, which records quality labels from different Wikipedia Projects.[8] For roughly 7% of the articles, there is a disagreement between editors/Wikipedia Projects. Take Figure 1 in Section 1 as an example, although the *primary* label of the Wikipedia article *Warden Head Light* is B, two other quality labels are assigned to it: B class (in the green block) by Wikipedia Project *Lighthouses*, and Start class (in the orange block) by Wikipedia Project *Australia*. Since we are interested in investigating how an automatic quality assessment system performs when there is a disagreement, we also crawl these *secondary* labels when building our dataset. Finally, we remove markup that relates to the document quality classes, such as {*Featured Article*} or {*geo-start*}, to alleviate any overt indication of the quality label in the text of the article.

The resulting dataset contains 29,097 Wikipedia articles, which we partition into two subsets for separate evaluation in Section 4: (1) *consistent* articles, where *primary* and *secondary* labels fully agree; and (2) *inconsistent* articles, where there is disagreement among *secondary* labels, with at least one of them agreeing with the *primary* label. We emphasise that we keep *all secondary* labels for the latter, without performing any label aggregation (e.g., voting). Our aim is to make qual-

---

		Train	Dev	Test	Total
FA	consistent	3956	470	538	4998
	inconsistent	28	4	2	
GA	consistent	3887	468	495	4878
	inconsistent	16	6	6	
B	consistent	3138	400	416	4843
	inconsistent	702	85	102	
C	consistent	3036	382	381	4523
	inconsistent	570	69	85	
Start	consistent	3725	451	472	4924
	inconsistent	223	28	25	
Stub	consistent	3863	470	492	4931
	inconsistent	83	12	11	
Total	—	23227	2845	3025	29097

Table 1: A breakdown of our Wikipedia dataset.

ity predictions as close as possible to the *primary* labels while also providing uncertainty estimates of such predictions: lower uncertainty over *consistent* articles and higher uncertainty over *inconsistent* articles. The dataset is then stratified into training, development, and test sets, as detailed in Table 1.

3 Methods

A key aspect of the task is the ordinal nature of the quality labels, e.g., a Start article is close in quality to a C, but much worse than an FA. Surprisingly though, most previous studies (Dang and Ignat, 2016a,b, 2017; Shen et al., 2017) formulate the problem as multi-class classification and use accuracy as the evaluation metric. Such modelling and evaluation procedures completely disregard the ordinal nature of the labels, which in turn does not correspond to real world scenarios: the cost of mispredicting a Start article as C is different to mispredicting it as an FA (standard classification metrics such as accuracy assume equal cost for all mispredictions).

To better address the scenarios we are interested in, we treat quality assessment as a regression problem, in terms of both modelling and evaluation. In order to do this, we encode the quality class labels as real values by mapping them to the interval $[-2.5, 2.5]$ with increments of 1. These labels are -2.5, -1.5, -0.5, 0.5, 1.5, and 2.5, respectively, where higher values indicate higher quality.[9] We perform this step to be able to use off-the-shelf regression models, while also center-

---

ing the labels. The remainder of this section details the regression methods we use, as well as two types of features we employ to represent each article. Both methods provide uncertainty estimates through *predictive distributions* (Gaussian distributions in our case).

3.1 Gaussian Processes

A principled approach to obtain predictive distributions is to use GPs (Rasmussen and Williams, 2006), a Bayesian non-parametric framework widely considered the state-of-the-art for regression (Hensman et al., 2013). Given a latent function f, which explains the relationship between an input vector x and its corresponding output value y, the model assumes that f is distributed according to a GP, i.e.,

$$f(x) \sim \mathcal{GP}(m(x), k(x, x')),$$

where $m(x)$ is a mean function, and $k(x, x')$ is a covariance or *kernel* function.

Following common practice, we fix the mean function to zero, as our output values are centered. Most of the information obtained from the training data can be encoded in the kernel function, of which the most common one is the Radial Basis Function (RBF), defined as

$$k(x, x') = \sigma_v \exp\left(-\frac{1}{2} \sum_{j=1}^{d} \frac{1}{\ell_j^2} (x_j - x_j')^2 \right),$$

where σ_v is the variance hyperparameter controlling the scale of the labels, and ℓ_j is the lengthscale for the jth dimension of the input. The lengthscales are learned by maximising the marginal likelihood (Rasmussen and Williams, 2006), resulting in a feature selection procedure known as *Automatic Relevance Determination* (ARD): lower lengthscales indicate features with higher discriminative power. We use this procedure to perform a feature analysis in Section 4.1. Besides the RBF, we also experiment with a range of other kernels used in GP models: see Rasmussen and Williams (2006, Chap. 4) for details.

Standard GP inference takes $\mathcal{O}(n^3)$ time, where n is the number of instances in the training data. As this is prohibitively expensive given the size of our dataset, we employ Sparse GPs (Titsias, 2009; Gal et al., 2014), a scalable extension that approximates an exact GP by using a small set of latent *inducing points*. These are learned by maximising

a variational lower bound on the marginal likelihood: see Titsias (2009) for details.

3.2 Random Forests

As an alternative method to obtain predictive distributions, we use RFs (Breiman, 2001), which are ensembles of decision trees (regression trees in our case). Each tree is trained on a bootstrapped sample of the training set and within each tree, a random subset of features is used when splitting nodes. To obtain predictive distributions, we assume that the individual tree predictions follow an "empirical" Gaussian distribution. The mean and the variance are computed from the full set of predictions obtained by the RF. While this approach is less principled — since there is no reason to believe the distribution over individual predicted values is Gaussian — it can work well in practice. For instance, RFs have been used before to obtain uncertainty estimates in the context of Bayesian Optimisation (Hutter et al., 2011).

3.3 Features and Preprocessing

Following Dang and Ignat (2016a), we use hand-crafted features, in the form of 11 structural features and 10 readability scores, which are listed in Dang and Ignat (2016a) and Shen et al. (2017).[10] Structural features can reflect the quality of Wikipedia articles in different ways. For example, *References*, *Pagelinks*, and *Citation* show how the article content is supported by information from different sources, indicating whether the article is reliable and thus indicating higher/lower quality, while features *Level2*, and *Level3+* indicate how the content is organised, which is another quality indicator of Wikipedia articles. Readability scores reflect the usage of language and comprehension difficulty of a Wikipedia article. For example, *Difficult Words* (Chall and Dale, 1995), *Dale-Chall* (Dale and Chall, 1948), and *Gunning-Fog* (Gunning, 1969) use the number or percentage of difficult words to measure the comprehension difficulty of a text, where a difficult word is a word not in a list of predefined words that fourth-grade American students can reliably understand. These hand-crafted features are extracted from Wikipedia articles using the open-source packages

---

[10]Dang and Ignat (2016a) explore nine readability scores, to which we add an extra readability score denoted *Consensus*. This score represents the estimated school grade level required to understand the content.

wikiclass[11] and *textstat*.[12]

As features from the revision history, such as the number of revisions and the article–editor network, are indirect quality indicators, we only focus on direct quality indicators from the content itself.

4 Experimental Study

In this section, we detail four sets of experiments: (1) intrinsic comparison of our methods with respect to their predictive distributions; (2) comparative experiments with the state-of-the-art with respect to point estimates only; (3) experiments measuring the performance of our methods in a transfer setting, where the goal is to predict *secondary* labels; and (4) a case study where automatic labels are used to filter articles for manual revisions and we use distributions to incorporate risk in the quality predictions. All our models are trained on the *primary* labels but we explicitly report our results on two different test sets: one with *consistent* and one with *inconsistent* labels, as explained in Section 2.2.

4.1 Intrinsic Evaluation

Our first set of experiments evaluates the performance of methods intrinsically, with respect to their predictive distributions.

GP settings. We use GP models from the *GPflow* toolkit (Matthews et al., 2017). In particular, we use a Sparse GP with 300 inducing points, which are initialised with k-means clusters learned on the training set and we explore different kernels (RBF, Arccosine (Cho and Saul, 2009), Matérn 32, Matérn 52, Rational Quadratic (RQ)).

RF settings. We use the RF implementation in *scikit-learn* (Pedregosa et al., 2011), with 300 trees and a maximum depth of 40, fine-tuning over the development set. All other hyperparameters are set to default values.

Evaluation metrics. Standard metrics to evaluate regression models such as Root Mean Squared Error (RMSE) and Pearson's correlation (r) are only based on *point estimate* predictions. These are not ideal for our setting since we aim to assess predictive *distributions* instead. For such settings, Candela et al. (2005) proposed the Negative

	NLPD *(consistent)*	NLPD *(inconsistent)*
RF	**0.978**[†]	1.642
GP$_{\text{RBF}}$	1.224	**1.364**[†]
GP$_{\text{arc0}}$	1.280	1.460
GP$_{\text{arc1}}$	1.266	1.428
GP$_{\text{arc2}}$	1.286	1.426
GP$_{\text{Matérn32}}$	1.275	1.427
GP$_{\text{Matérn52}}$	1.275	1.425
GP$_{\text{RQ}}$	1.271	1.442

Table 2: Intrinsic evaluation results. GP$_{\text{arc0}}$, GP$_{\text{arc1}}$, and GP$_{\text{arc2}}$ denote GP using an Arccosine kernel with orders of 0, 1, and 2. GP$_{\text{Matérn32}}$, GP$_{\text{Matérn52}}$, and GP$_{\text{RQ}}$ denote GP using Matérn32, Matérn52, and RQ, respectively. The best result is indicated in **bold**, and marked with "†" if the improvement is statistically significant (based on a one-tailed Wilcoxon signed-rank test; $p < 0.05$).

Log Predictive Density ("NLPD") as an alternative metric, which is commonly used in the literature (Chalupka et al., 2013; Hernández-Lobato and Adams, 2015; Beck et al., 2016) to evaluate probabilistic regression models.

Given a test set containing the input and its reference score (x_i, y_i), NLPD is defined as

$$\text{NLPD} = -\frac{1}{n} \sum_{i=1}^{n} \log p(\hat{y}_i = y_i | x_i),$$

where n is the number of test samples and $p(\hat{y}_i | x_i)$ is the predictive distribution for input x_i. For Gaussian distributions, NLPD penalises both overconfident wrong predictions and underconfident correct predictions.

Results. Table 2 shows the average NLPD over 10 runs on both test sets. Clearly, RFs outperform GPs on the consistent set while the opposite happens on the inconsistent set. In general, this shows that GPs tend to give more conservative predictive distributions compared to RFs. This is beneficial when there is label disagreement, and therefore, high uncertainty over the labels. However, it also translates into worse performance when labels are consistent, where the higher confidence obtained by RFs give better results. In terms of kernels, we obtained the best results using RBF for both test sets.

Feature Analysis. To find out which features contribute most to the performance of our models, we analyse the lengthscales from GP and the feature weigths from RF. Figure 3 shows the top

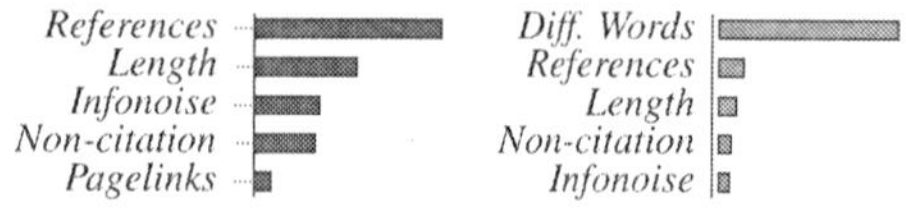

Figure 3: Feature importance values in the GP model (left) and RF model (right) . A full description of all features can be found in Dang and Ignat (2016a) and Shen et al. (2017).

| | consistent | | inconsistent | |
	RMSE	r	RMSE	r
BiLSTM[+]	**0.795**[†]	**0.897**[†]	0.951	0.522
BiLSTM[−]	0.810	0.891	0.936	**0.548**[†]
RF	0.805	0.892	0.942	0.527
GP$_{RBF}$	0.822	0.887	**0.932**	0.545

Table 3: Point estimate comparison results.

five features in each model: four of those shared by both GP and RF, indicating their importance as quality indicators in both methods. In particular, the length of an article is a consistently good indicator: a possible explanation is that short articles lack enough content to be considered high quality articles. The presence of structured indicators such as number of references and non-citation templates is also interesting, as it is evidence of the contribution of non-textual information in the quality assessment process.

4.2 Point Estimate Comparison

In terms of point estimates, the state-of-the-art in our task is a neural model based on a BiLSTM architecture (Shen et al., 2017). As we model quality prediction of Wikipedia articles as a regression problem, where a linear transformation is used as the final layer instead of a softmax, the neural network model does not provide predictive distributions, limiting their applicability in the scenarios which we focus on in this work. However, to put our proposed methods into perspective, we compare their performance with these neural models in terms of point estimates. Specifically, we use the mean of the distributions for both GP and RF as predictions and use standard regression metrics (RMSE and Pearson's r correlation) to assess the performance of our models against BiLSTM.

For the GP model, we restrict our evaluation in this section (and in the remainder of this paper) to the one with an RBF kernel, as it performed significantly better in Section 4.1. We compare with two BiLSTM models: (1) with pre-trained word embeddings, using GloVe (Pennington et al., 2014) ("BiLSTM[+]" hereafter); and with randomly initialised word embeddings ("BiLSTM[−]" hereafter). See Shen et al. (2017) for a detailed description of all hyperparameters.

Results. From Table 3, we see that while BiLSTM[+] outperform our methods in the *consis-*

tent set, the difference is small and we obtain good results nevertheless. In particular, correlation is close to 0.9 for all methods. Therefore, we can see that GPs and RFs obtain comparable results with the state-of-the-art while providing additional information through the predictive distributions.

The importance of having distributions as predictions becomes clear when we see the results for the *inconsistent* set, in Table 3. Here, not only do GPs perform on par with the BiLSTM models, but the overall correlation is much lower (between 0.52 and 0.55). This highlights the harder task of predicting quality labels under disagreement, which further motivates the additional uncertainty information coming from predictive distributions.

4.3 Prediction of Secondary Labels

As explained in Section 2.2, the *inconsistent* articles are ones where the *primary* label is in disagreement with the *secondary* ones, from different Wikipedia Projects. In this section, we assess how our models fare under a transfer scenario, where the goal is to predict these secondary labels. Such a scenario can be useful, for instance, if we want to incorporate information from Projects to decide the quality of a document.

To measure the performance with *secondary* labels as references, one option is to aggregate the labels of an article into a single one (through voting or averaging, for instance) and use that value as the reference. Instead, we opt to embrace the disagreement, and propose a *weighted* extension of NLPD, namely wNLPD, which we define as

$$\text{wNLPD} = -\frac{1}{n} \sum_{i=1}^{n} \log \sum_{j=1}^{m_i} w_j p(\hat{y}_i = y_j | \boldsymbol{x_i}),$$

where m_i is the number of *secondary* labels for article $\boldsymbol{x_i}$, and w_j is the weight for label j. If we have prior information about the reliability of some label sources (for instance, different

	wNLPD	wRMSE
RF	1.460	1.158
GP$_\text{RBF}$	**1.412**†	**1.152**†

Table 4: Results for prediction of secondary labels.

Wikipedia Projects), one can plug this information into the weights. Here we assume equal reliability and use uniform weights $w_j = \text{freq}(j)/m_i$, where freq is the count of label j among *secondary* labels. The metric degrades to standard NLPD when labels are consistent. We also evaluate point estimate performance using a similar weighting scheme for RMSE (which we denote as wRMSE).

Results. Table 4 summarises the results. Notice that in this setting we only report results for the *inconsistent* test set, as the *consistent* one has no disagreement (and therefore, numbers would match the ones in Section 4.1). Here we also see that GPs achieve significantly better performance than RFs, although by a much lower margin compared to the results on the *primary* labels (Table 2). This reflects the harder aspect of this setting. We hypothesize we can obtain better performance in this scenario by incorporating the *secondary* labels at training time, which we leave for future work.

4.4 Case Study: Quality Prediction as Filtering for Manual Revision

As mentioned in Section 1, one use for a quality prediction system is to filter documents for manual revision. In the case of Wikipedia, such revisions are mandatory for articles to be assigned as a Good Article or a Featured Article. This incurs in an *asymmetric risk*: the cost of mispredicting an article as GA and FA is higher than other labels, as these trigger expensive, manual labour. Such a scenario can be modelled through *asymmetric loss functions* (Varian, 1975).

If a quality model provides predictive distributions, one can obtain *optimal* quality decisions under an asymmetric loss function through the framework of Minimum Bayes Risk (MBR). This setting has been studied before by Christoffersen and Diebold (1997) and more recently applied by Beck et al. (2016) in the context of machine translation post-editing. However, these assume a regression scenario. While we employ regression models in our work for ease of modelling reasons, the final decisions in the pipeline are discrete (although still ordinal).

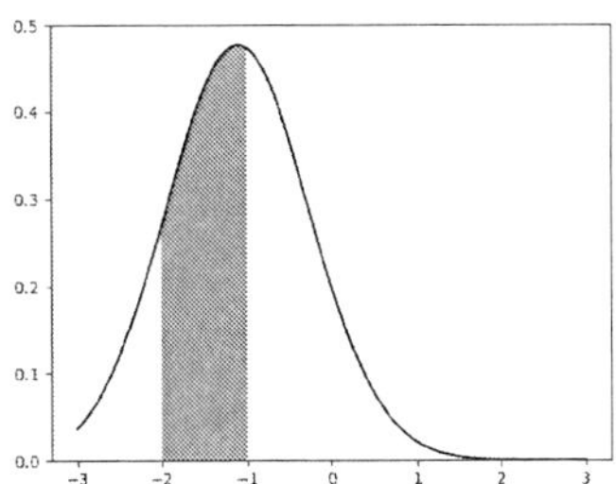

Figure 4: Discretisation of a continuous predictive distribution. The shaded area shows the probability of quality label Start (-1.5).

To adapt the MBR framework into our case, we first define the risk $\delta(q)$ of predicting the quality label q as

$$\delta(q) = \sum_{\hat{q}} \mathcal{L}(\hat{q}, q) p(\hat{q}|\boldsymbol{x}),$$

where $\mathcal{L}(\hat{q}, q)$ is an (asymmetric) loss function over the discrete quality labels and $p(\hat{q}|\boldsymbol{x})$ is the *discretised* probability of quality label $\hat{q}$ for document $\boldsymbol{x}$ under one of our proposed models. We detail these two terms below.

Discretised distribution Given a predictive distribution obtained by a regression model we can discretise it by using the cumulative density function (cdf). Define $\ell(\hat{q})$ as the real value which we encode quality label $\hat{q}$, as described in Section 3. With this, we obtain the discretised probability mass function

$$p(\hat{q}|\boldsymbol{x}) = \begin{cases} 1 - \text{cdf}(\ell(\hat{q}) - 0.5) & \text{if } \hat{q} = \text{FA} \\ \text{cdf}(\ell(\hat{q}) + 0.5) & \text{if } \hat{q} = \text{Stub} \\ \text{cdf}(\ell(\hat{q}) + 0.5) - \text{cdf}(\ell(\hat{q}) - 0.5) & \text{otherwise,} \end{cases}$$

where the cdf is obtained from the predictive distribution. As we only consider Gaussian distributions for predictions, we can easily use off-the-shelf implementations to obtain the cdf. Figure 4 gives an example of how to obtain the probability of an instance being predicted to be Start (-1.5).

Asymmetric loss function To incorporate asymmetry into the quality label prediction, we define it as

$$\mathcal{L}(\hat{q}, q) = \begin{cases} 0 & \text{if } \hat{q} = q \\ \alpha & \text{if } \hat{q} \neq q, \hat{q} \notin S, q \in S \\ 1 & \text{otherwise} \end{cases},$$

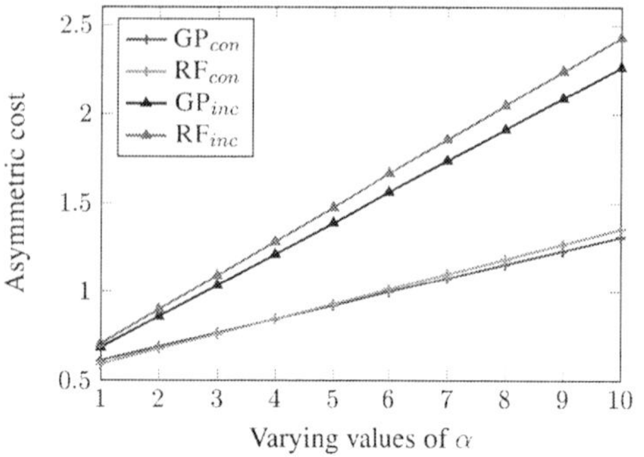

Figure 5: Asymmetric risk vs. α (best viewed in color). Here, GP_{con}/RF_{con} denote risk values achieved by GP/RF over *consistent* articles, respectively; GP_{inc}/RF_{inc} denote risk values achieved by GP/RF over *inconsistent* articles.

where S is a high-risk label set and $\alpha > 1$ is the penalty associated with a higher risk prediction. In our scenario, we set $S = \{\mathsf{GA}, \mathsf{FA}\}$, as these are the labels we want to give larger penalties when there is a misprediction. Notice that this loss is only an example tailored to our specific setting: other scenarios might warrant different definitions.

Evaluation Under a deployment scenario, one would evaluate $\delta(q)$ for all possible 6 labels and choose the one with minimum risk. However, since in our case we have access to true test set labels, we can just average all $\delta(q)$ for the *gold* labels q in order to assess the models we are interested in (GPs and RFs). As in the previous sections, we report average results over 10 runs for both *consistent* and *inconsistent* test sets.

Results. In Figure 5 we plot the average risk while varying the penalty cost α. As in the intrinsic evaluation result, we see that GPs tend to perform better in the *inconsistent* set. On the other hand, the results in the *consistent* set are very similar, and no conclusions can be made about which method performs best. Overall, the results are favourable towards GPs but the inconclusive results for *consistent* labels shows that there is room for improvements in uncertainty modelling, which we leave for future work.

5 Related Work

The quality assessment of Wikipedia articles is a task that assigns a quality label to a Wikipedia article, reflecting the quality assessment process carried out by the Wikipedia community.

Hand-crafted feature-based approaches use features from the article itself (e.g., article length), meta-data features (the number of revisions of an article), and a combination of these two. Various features derived from Wikipedia articles have been used for assessing the quality of Wikipedia articles (Blumenstock, 2008; Lipka and Stein, 2010; Warncke-Wang et al., 2013, 2015; Dang and Ignat, 2016a). For example, Blumenstock (2008) and Lipka and Stein (2010) use article length and writing styles (represented by binarised character trigram features) to differentiate FA articles from non-featured articles, respectively. Warncke-Wang et al. (2015) proposed 11 structural features (such as the number of references and whether there is an infobox or not) to assess the quality of Wikipedia articles. Dang and Ignat (2016a) further proposed nine readability scores (such as the Flesch reading-ease score (Kincaid et al., 1975)) to assess the quality of Wikipedia articles. Based on these last two studies, an online Objective Revision Evaluation Service has been built to measure the quality of Wikipedia articles (Halfaker and Taraborelli, 2015). Features derived from the meta-data of Wikipedia articles — e.g., the number of revisions a Wikipedia article has received — have been proposed to assess the quality of Wikipedia articles (Stvilia et al., 2005; Stein and Hess, 2007; Adler et al., 2008; Dalip et al., 2009, 2017, 2014). For example, Stein and Hess (2007) and Adler et al. (2008) use the authority of editors to measure the quality of Wikipedia articles, as determined by the quality of articles they edited.

Different neural network architectures have been exploited to learn high-level representations of Wikipedia articles. For example, Dang and Ignat (2016b) use a distributed memory version of Paragraph Vector (Le and Mikolov, 2014) to learn Wikipedia article representations, which are used to predict the quality of Wikipedia articles. Dang and Ignat (2017) and Shen et al. (2017) exploit LSTMs (Hochreiter and Schmidhuber, 1997) to learn document-level representations to train a classifier and predict the quality label of an unseen Wikipedia article. Observing that the visual rendering of a Wikipedia article can capture implicit quality indicators (such as images and tables), Shen et al. (2019) use Inception V3 (Szegedy et al., 2016) to capture visual representations, which are used to classify Wikipedia articles based on their quality. They further propose a joint model, which combines textual representations from bidirectional LSTM with visual representations from Inception V3, to predict the quality of Wikipedia articles.

Beck et al. (2016) explore prediction uncertainty in machine translation quality estimation (QE), where post-editing rate is the dependent variable. In QE, the post-editing rate — which is computed by dividing the post-editing time by the length of the translation hypothesis — is a positive real value. The performance of a GP model was studied in both underestimate and overestimate scenarios. Beck and Cohn (2017); Beck (2017) employ GPs to model text representation noise in emotion analysis, where Pearson's correlation and NLPD are used as the evaluation metrics. Our work is different from these two studies as we model the subjectivity of quality assessment explicitly, which can mimic people's different opinions over the quality of a document.

There is also a rich body of work on identifying trustworthy annotators and predicting the correct underlying labels from multiple annotations (Hovy et al., 2013; Cohn and Specia, 2013; Passonneau and Carpenter, 2014; Graham et al., 2017; Paun et al., 2018). For example, Hovy et al. (2013) propose an item-response model to identify trustworthy annotators and predict the true labels of instances in an unsupervised way. However, our task is to measure the uncertainty of a model over its predictions (as distinct from attempting to learn the "true" label for an instance from potentially biased/noisy annotations), in addition to correctly predicting the gold label, in the context of assessing the quality of Wikipedia articles. Additionally, we have a rich representation of the data point (i.e. document) that we are attempting to label, whereas in work on interpreting multiply-annotated data, there is little or no representation of each data point that has been annotated. Finally, we do not have access to the IDs of annotators across documents, and thus cannot model annotator reliability or bias.

6   Conclusion and Future Work

In this paper, we proposed to measure the uncertainty of Wikipedia article quality assessment systems using Gaussian processes and random forests, utilising the NLPD evaluation metric to measure performance over *consistent* and *inconsistent* articles. Experimental results show that both GPs and RFs are less certain over *inconsistent* articles, where people tend to disagree over their quality, and GPs are more conservative in their predictions over such articles. To imitate a real world scenario where decision-making processes based on model predictions can lead to different costs, we proposed an asymmetric cost, which takes the prediction uncertainty into consideration. Empirical results show that GPs are a better option if overestimates are heavily penalised.

In the future, we are interested in conducting a user study to find out how Wikipedians respond to the utility of uncertainty information provided to them. On the modelling side, having equal intervals between adjacent quality classes is a heuristic, which is potentially inappropriate in the case of Wikipedia. Thus we are also planning to model the quality assessment of Wikipedia articles as an ordinal regression problem, where the gap between adjacent quality labels can vary.

References

B. Thomas Adler, Krishnendu Chatterjee, Luca De Alfaro, Marco Faella, Ian Pye, and Vishwanath Raman. 2008. Assigning trust to Wikipedia content. In *Proceedings of the 4th International Symposium on Wikis*, pages 26:1–26:12.

Daniel Beck. 2017. Modelling representation noise in emotion analysis using Gaussian processes. In *IJC-NLP*, volume 2, pages 140–145.

Daniel Beck and Trevor Cohn. 2017. Learning kernels over strings using Gaussian processes. In *IJCNLP*, pages 67–73.

Daniel Beck, Lucia Specia, and Trevor Cohn. 2016. Exploring prediction uncertainty in machine translation quality estimation. In *CoNLL*, pages 208–218.

Joshua E. Blumenstock. 2008. Size matters: Word count as a measure of quality on Wikipedia. In *WWW*, pages 1095–1096.

Leo Breiman. 2001. Random forests. *Mach. Learn.*, 45(1):5–32.

Joaquin Quiñonero Candela, Carl Edward Rasmussen, Fabian H. Sinz, Olivier Bousquet, and Bernhard Schölkopf. 2005. Evaluating predictive uncertainty challenge. In *Machine Learning Challenges*, volume 3944, pages 1–27.

Jeanne Sternlicht Chall and Edgar Dale. 1995. *Readability Revisited: The New Dale-Chall Readability Formula*. Brookline Books.

Krzysztof Chalupka, Christopher K. I. Williams, and Iain Murray. 2013. A framework for evaluating approximation methods for Gaussian process regression. *Journal of Machine Learning Research*, 14(1):333–350.

Youngmin Cho and Lawrence K. Saul. 2009. Kernel methods for deep learning. In *NIPS*, pages 342–350.

Peter F. Christoffersen and Francis X. Diebold. 1997. Optimal Prediction Under Asymmetric Loss. *Econometric Theory*, 13(06):808–817.

Trevor Cohn and Lucia Specia. 2013. Modelling annotator bias with multi-task gaussian processes: An application to machine translation quality estimation. In *ACL*, pages 32–42.

Edgar Dale and Jeanne S. Chall. 1948. A formula for predicting readability: Instructions. *Educational Research Bulletin*, 27(2):37–54.

Daniel H. Dalip, Marcos A. Gonçalves, Marco Cristo, and Pável Calado. 2009. Automatic quality assessment of content created collaboratively by web communities: A case study of Wikipedia. In *JCDL*, pages 295–304.

Daniel Hasan Dalip, Marcos André Gonçalves, Marco Cristo, and Pável Calado. 2017. A general multi-view framework for assessing the quality of collaboratively created content on web 2.0. *Journal of the Association for Information Science and Technology*, 68(2):286–308.

Daniel Hasan Dalip, Harlley Lima, Marcos André Gonçalves, Marco Cristo, and Pável Calado. 2014. Quality assessment of collaborative content with minimal information. In *JCDL*, pages 201–210.

Quang-Vinh Dang and Claudia-Lavinia Ignat. 2016a. Measuring quality of collaboratively edited documents: The case of Wikipedia. In *The 2nd IEEE International Conference on Collaboration and Internet Computing*, pages 266–275.

Quang-Vinh Dang and Claudia-Lavinia Ignat. 2016b. Quality assessment of Wikipedia articles without feature engineering. In *JCDL*, pages 27–30.

Quang-Vinh Dang and Claudia-Lavinia Ignat. 2017. An end-to-end learning solution for assessing the quality of Wikipedia articles. In *The 13th International Symposium on Open Collaboration*, pages 4:1–4:10.

Yarin Gal, Mark van der Wilk, and Carl E. Rasmussen. 2014. Distributed variational inference in sparse Gaussian process regression and latent variable models. In *NIPS*, pages 3257–3265.

Yvette Graham, Timothy Baldwin, Alistair Moffat, and Justin Zobel. 2017. Can machine translation systems be evaluated by the crowd alone? *Natural Language Engineering*, 23(1):3–30.

Robert Gunning. 1969. The fog index after twenty years. *International Journal of Business Communication*, 6(2):3–13.

Aaron Halfaker and Dario Taraborelli. 2015. Artificial intelligence service "ore" gives Wikipedians x-ray specs to see through bad edits. *[online] Available: https://blog.wikimedia.org/2015/11/30/artificial-intelligence-x-ray-specs*.

James Hensman, Nicoló Fusi, and Neil D. Lawrence. 2013. Gaussian processes for big data. In *Proceedings of the Twenty-Ninth Conference on Uncertainty in Artificial Intelligence*.

José Miguel Hernández-Lobato and Ryan P. Adams. 2015. Probabilistic backpropagation for scalable learning of Bayesian neural networks. In *ICML*, pages 1861–1869.

Sepp Hochreiter and Jürgen Schmidhuber. 1997. Long short-term memory. *Neural Computation*, 9(8):1735–1780.

Dirk Hovy, Taylor Berg-Kirkpatrick, Ashish Vaswani, and Eduard H. Hovy. 2013. Learning whom to trust with MACE. In *NACCL-HLT*, pages 1120–1130.

Frank Hutter, Holger H. Hoos, and Kevin Leyton-Brown. 2011. Sequential model-based optimization for general algorithm configuration. In *5th International Conference on Learning and Intelligent Optimization*, pages 507–523.

J. Peter Kincaid, Robert P. Fishburne Jr., Richard L. Rogers, and Brad S. Chissom. 1975. Derivation of new readability formulas (automated readability index, Fog count and Flesch reading ease formula) for navy enlisted personnel. Technical report, Institute for Simulation and Training, University of Central Florida.

Quoc Le and Tomas Mikolov. 2014. Distributed representations of sentences and documents. In *ICML*, pages 1188–1196.

Nedim Lipka and Benno Stein. 2010. Identifying featured articles in Wikipedia: Writing style matters. In *WWW*, pages 1147–1148.

Alexander G. de G. Matthews, Mark van der Wilk, Tom Nickson, Keisuke. Fujii, Alexis Boukouvalas, Pablo León-Villagrá, Zoubin Ghahramani, and James Hensman. 2017. GPflow: A Gaussian process library using TensorFlow. *Journal of Machine Learning Research*, 18(40):1–6.

Rebecca J. Passonneau and Bob Carpenter. 2014. The benefits of a model of annotation. *TACL*, 2:311–326.

Silviu Paun, Bob Carpenter, Jon Chamberlain, Dirk Hovy, Udo Kruschwitz, and Massimo Poesio. 2018. Comparing bayesian models of annotation. *TACL*, 6:571–585.

Fabian Pedregosa, Gaël Varoquaux, Alexandre Gramfort, Vincent Michel, Bertrand Thirion, Olivier Grisel, Mathieu Blondel, Peter Prettenhofer, Ron Weiss, Vincent Dubourg, Jake Vanderplas, Alexandre Passos, David Cournapeau, Matthieu Brucher,

Matthieu Perrot, and Édouard Duchesnay. 2011. Scikit-learn: Machine learning in Python. *Journal of Machine Learning Research*, 12:2825–2830.

Jeffrey Pennington, Richard Socher, and Christopher D. Manning. 2014. GloVe: Global vectors for word representation. In *EMNLP*, volume 14, pages 1532–1543.

Carl Edward Rasmussen and Christopher KI Williams. 2006. *Gaussian Process for Machine Learning*. MIT press.

Aili Shen, Jianzhong Qi, and Timothy Baldwin. 2017. A hybrid model for quality assessment of Wikipedia articles. In *Australasian Language Technology Association Workshop*, pages 43–52.

Aili Shen, Bahar Salehi, Timothy Baldwin, and Jianzhong Qi. 2019. A joint model for multimodal document quality assessment. In *JCDL*.

Klaus Stein and Claudia Hess. 2007. Does it matter who contributes: A study on featured articles in the German Wikipedia. In *Hypertext*, pages 171–174.

Besiki Stvilia, Michael B. Twidale, Linda C. Smith, and Les Gasser. 2005. Assessing information quality of a community-based encyclopedia. In *The 2005 International Conference on Information Quality*, pages 442–454.

Christian Szegedy, Vincent Vanhoucke, Sergey Ioffe, Jonathon Shlens, and Zbigniew Wojna. 2016. Rethinking the Inception architecture for computer vision. In *CVPR*, pages 2818–2826.

Michalis K. Titsias. 2009. Variational learning of inducing variables in sparse Gaussian processes. In *International Conference on Artificial Intelligence and Statistics*, pages 567–574.

Hal Varian. 1975. A Bayesian Approach to Real Estate Assessment. *Studies in Bayesian Econometrics and Statistics in Honor of Leonard J. Savage*, pages 195–208.

Morten Warncke-Wang, Vladislav R. Ayukaev, Brent Hecht, and Loren Terveen. 2015. The success and failure of quality improvement projects in peer production communities. In *The 18th ACM Conference on Computer-Supported Cooperative Work and Social Computing*, pages 743–756.

Morten Warncke-Wang, Dan Cosley, and John Riedl. 2013. Tell me more: An actionable quality model for Wikipedia. In *The 9th International Symposium on Open Collaboration*, pages 8:1–8:10.

Conceptualisation and Annotation of Drug Nonadherence Information for Knowledge Extraction from Patient-Generated Texts

Anja Belz
University of Brighton, UK
a.s.belz@brighton.ac.uk

Elizabeth Ford
Brighton and Sussex Medical School, UK
e.m.ford@bsms.ac.uk

Richard Hoile
Sussex Partnership NHS Foundation Trust, UK
Richard.Hoile@sussexpartnership.nhs.uk

Azam Mullick
University of Brighton, UK
a.mullick@brighton.ac.uk

Abstract

Approaches to knowledge extraction (KE) in the health domain often start by annotating text to indicate the knowledge to be extracted, and then use the annotated text to train systems to perform the KE. This may work for annotating named entities or other contiguous noun phrases (drugs, some drug effects), but becomes increasingly difficult when items tend to be expressed across multiple, possibly non-contiguous, syntactic constituents (e.g. most descriptions of drug effects in user-generated text). Other issues include that it is not always clear how annotations map to actionable insights, or how they scale up to, or can form part of, more complex KE tasks. This paper reports our efforts in developing an approach to extracting knowledge about drug nonadherence from health forums which led us to conclude that development cannot proceed in separate steps but that all aspects—from conceptualisation to annotation scheme development, annotation, KE system training and knowledge graph instantiation—are interdependent and need to be co-developed. Our aim in this paper is two-fold: we describe a generally applicable framework for developing a KE approach, and present a specific KE approach, developed with the framework, for the task of gathering information about antidepressant drug nonadherence. We report the conceptualisation, the annotation scheme, the annotated corpus, and an analysis of annotated texts.

1 Introduction

Depression is experienced by 1 in 4 people in the UK. More than two thirds of patients are mostly managed with antidepressant medication, yet nonadherence rates are very high. One study found that 4.2% of patients who were prescribed antidepressants did not take them at all, and 23.7% filled only a single prescription (van Geffen et al., 2009). Nonadherence is a major obstacle in the effective treatment of depression, but cannot currently be predicted or explained adequately (van Dulmen et al., 2007). An influential WHO report (Sabaté et al., 2003) concluded: "[i]ncreasing the effectiveness of adherence interventions may have a far greater impact on the health of the population than any improvement in specific medical treatments". Nonadherence is hard to investigate via controlled studies meaning alternative sources of information are needed. Recent results indicate a strong signal relating to usage of psychiatric medications on health forums and social media (Tregunno, 2017), and that social media users report nonadherence and reasons for it (Onishi et al., 2018).

The work reported in this paper aimed (i) to develop a conceptualisation of the information space around drug nonadherence, defining the relevant concepts, properties and relations; (ii) to develop an annotation scheme based on the conceptualisation; (iii) to annotate a corpus of depression health forum posts with the scheme; and (iv) to use the annotated data to examine the prevalence, and co-occurrence, of different kinds of nonadherence information (testing signal strength). We examine the interdependent and mutually constraining relationship between conceptualisation, annotation scheme and knowledge extraction processes.

The ultimate goal is to perform automatic knowledge extraction (KE) in order to provide valuable non-adherence information from a large sample about why and how non-adherence occurs. We hope this will in turn lead to better prescribing, better adherence and more informed discussions between patient and prescriber around medication.

2 Nonadherence and Health Forums

Different terms have been used to describe the "suboptimal taking of medicine by patients" (Hugtenburg et al., 2013). Among these, non-compliance and nonadherence both mean *not tak-*

Proceedings of the 2019 EMNLP Workshop W-NUT: The 5th Workshop on Noisy User-generated Text, pages 202–211
Hong Kong, Nov 4, 2019. ©2019 Association for Computational Linguistics

Quitting your meds can be awful, for sure. I started trying to get off Zoloft by myself 5 years ago. I went cold turkey which was a complete disaster. Next I tried cutting down by large amounts which was slightly less of a disaster. Finally I tapered off very slowly. ONE WHOLE YEAR to get from 200mg to zero. With the tapering off the brain zaps were much less severe. Simply takes a long time to wean yourself off these drugs.

I reduced my mirtazapine from 45mg first to 30mg, and then to 15mg, then stopped it altogether. After two weeks I was feeling awful so I decided to restart it at 15mg.

So I stopped Fluoxetine about a month ago sort of by accident. After I missed a few doses I just decided to keep going. So far I've only had rather minor symptoms. One of my symptoms has been an electric shock sensation from my brain down my spine/body. This happens especially when I get up, sit down or move suddenly.

Last week my doctor increased my Lamictol dosage to 200 MG. I am beginning to notice serious cognitive deficits. For example constantly losing/misplacing things.. Has anyone else experienced this situation?

Figure 1: Four example depression forum posts created to closely resemble real posts.

ing a drug as instructed (the intended meaning in the present context), but nonadherence is the term now preferred as reflecting a more equal prescriber-patient relationship (Hugtenburg et al., 2013). Two types of nonadherence are distinguished, *intentional*, where a patient "actively decides" not to follow instructions, and *unintentional* nonadherence, including forgetting and not knowing how to take a drug (Hugtenburg et al., 2013).

Consider the four example posts from health forums for specific antidepressants in Figure 1. Some of the sentences contain explicit statements that the modifications described were instigated by the patient ("I started trying to get off Zoloft by myself 5 years ago"; "After two weeks I was feeling awful so I decided to restart it at 15mg"; "So I stopped Fluoxetine about a month ago sort of by accident"). Other modifications described in the first three posts (unlike in the fourth) are likely to also have been instigated by the patient, but clinician involvement cannot be ruled out.

These are typical examples of how patients talk about nonadherence in health forums: explicit statements ('my doctor told me to do one thing, but I did another') are rare (7% of posts on the depression forums we have been looking at, see also Section 5). More typically, a drug modification is described along with the side effect and/or other reason(s) that gave rise to it, but the extent to which the prescribing physician was involved in deciding to make the modification can only be inferred, with varying degrees of certainty, from the language, or on the basis of medical knowledge (e.g. a modification is known to be dangerous).

3 Conceptualisation and KE Task

Posts like the ones in Figure 1 clearly contain information about the *why* and *how* of drug nonad-

herence, but how can it be automatically extracted and rendered useful? In this section we discuss the main issues in developing a knowledge extraction (KE) approach for a specific domain and a specific KE task, nonadherence event extraction in our case. To introduce the different components in developing an approach to KE (overview see Figure 2, we use as an illustrative running example the simpler task of drug effect extraction which is—in contrast to the far more complex task of nonadherent event extraction we are addressing here— already a well established research task[1] (Leaman et al., 2010; Nikfarjam et al., 2015). Drug effect detection is an important subtask of nonadherence event extraction, because drug effects as perceived by the patient play an important role in nonadherence and are often the reason for it. The last post in Figure 1 is a typical example, containing a claim that a drug referred to as "Lamictol", is causing an effect described as "cognitive deficits".

3.1 From Text to Meaning

Suppose that we have a method capable of identifying drug and effect mentions in text and determining which ones are linked (i.e. which drug causes which effect), and that we extract a linked drug and effect pair from the fourth post in Figure 1 for which we could choose the following notation: *cause("Lamictol", "cognitive deficits")*. Suppose from this and other posts we extract five such linked pairs as follows:

$$
\begin{aligned}
&cause(\textit{"Lamictol", "serious cognitive deficits"}) \\
&cause(\textit{"Lamictol", "constantly losing/misplacing} \\
&\quad \textit{things"}) \\
&cause(\textit{"Lamictal", "uncoordinated"}) \\
&cause(\textit{"lamotrigine", "so forgetful"}) \\
&cause(\textit{"Lamotrigene", "keep losing my phone and} \\
&\quad \textit{going upstairs and forgetting what for"})
\end{aligned} \tag{1}
$$

---

[1]See e.g. Task 2 at this year's SMM4H Shared Task event: https://healthlanguageprocessing.org/smm4h/challenge/

If this was the actual output of our method, it would be nothing more than a list of drug-effect mentions in a given set of texts, possibly with counts of multiple occurrences of identical mentions (none in Example 1 above). One important type of knowledge would be entirely inaccessible, namely that the above five pairs in fact all claim the same side effect for the same drug (lamotrigine, a mood-stabilising medication sometimes prescribed for depression).[2] In order to extract that knowledge (crucial to be able e.g. to act upon side effect reports depending on novelty or report frequency), the identified word strings need to be mapped to a more abstract level of representation where knowledge is encoded in terms of concepts, rather than word strings. It is only once this process, known as entity linking[3] (Han et al., 2011; Hachey et al., 2013; Rao et al., 2013; Smith et al., 2018), has been performed that the five linked pairs above can be interpreted as five mentions of the same drug effect. In this crucial step, we move from extracting word strings (surface representations) to extracting concept structures (meaning representations); from something that can be compared in terms of string similarity and counted, to something that can be incorporated into a knowledge graph and reasoned about.

3.2 Concept Model and KE Template

In the case of drug effect extraction it is clear what we want to extract, and how it is structured. A very simple conceptualisation suffices to express that understanding: a single parent concept, *drug_effect*, consisting of a *drug*, an *effect* and a causal relation, possibly implicit. Depending on application context, further concepts, such as duration or severity, could also be added (these would be required e.g. if the application task was automatic completion of Yellow Card reports). One of many possible notations for this conceptualisation is the following (for a complete concept model the range of possible values of the component concepts would also have to specified):

DRUG_EFFECT [*DRUG; EFFECT; SEVERITY; DURATION*]   (2)

The above can be seen as providing both a concept model representing a piece of domain knowledge,

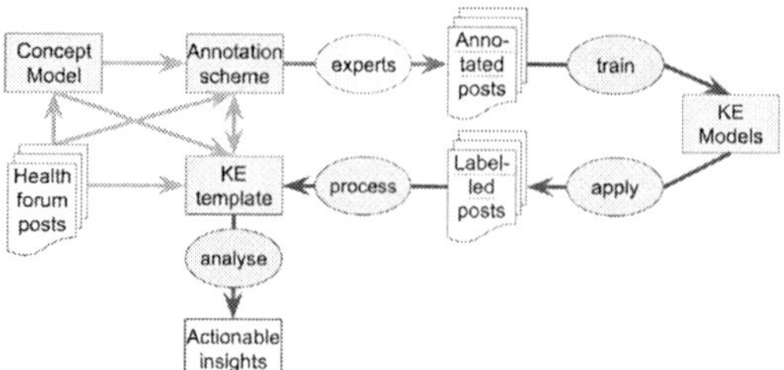

Figure 2: Components in developing KE approach.

and a template to be instantiated by a specific KE tool (depending on the application task, only subsets of concepts might be used for KE). A possible instantiation produced by a KE tool via entity detection and linking for the last post in Figure 1 is the following (initial underscores indicating terminal concepts as opposed to word strings):

DRUG_EFFECT [
    DRUG= _lamotrigine;
    EFFECT= _confusional_state;   (3)
    SEVERITY= _moderate;
    DURATION= _continuous;   ]

In order to produce the above we have to have created a suitable conceptualisation (concept model), a KE template, a KE task construal and methods for implementing it, here detecting word spans corresponding to the above concepts and for mapping the word spans to concepts. In order to be able to do the latter, we also need texts which have been labelled for entities such as drugs and effects and the links between them. All these aspects are shown to the left of Figure 2 which provides an overview of elements and steps involved in developing a KE approach. In the next sections we look at how conceptualisation and annotation scheme interact with possible KE tasks (Section 3.3), followed by issues in determining the details of the annotation scheme (Section 3.4).

3.3 Text Annotation and KE Task

Useful one-off analysis can be conducted on the basis of manual mark-up of text, but for knowledge extraction from *large* quantities of *new* texts, automatic processes are needed. Two common types of KE model are word sequence (post, sentence, phrase, etc.) classifiers and labellers. These tend to be supervised models, i.e. they require labelled training data the creation of which, especially initially, requires human annotation effort.

How the data is annotated limits what kind of KE tasks and models it can be used for. Con-

---

[2]Whether they are considered the same depends on the concept set linked to, in our case SIDER (Kuhn et al., 2015).

[3]A.k.a. normalisation, e.g. for adverse effect normalisation see Task 3 at this year's SMM4H Shared Task event: https://healthlanguageprocessing.org/sm m4h/challenge/

versely, aiming for a particular KE task has implications for the kinds of annotations that are needed. For the KE task described above, i.e. mapping from health forum posts (Figure 1) to instantiated KE templates (Example 3), the most straightforward way to interpret the annotation task would be to annotate each post (as a whole) with an instantiated KE template for every mention of a drug effect contained in the post. However, this would make the annotators' task cognitively extremely challenging (requiring multiple judgments to be made in conjunction), and very time-intensive (involving look up of concepts in databases and inventories). Moreover, it is not obvious how to define a corresponding KE modelling task and training regime. It is also not feasible to define one output class for each possible instantiated template, because that would lead to an unmanageable combinatorial explosion of classes.

In the relatively simple case of adverse drug effect extraction, the divide-and-conquer approach that tends to be used instead (Nikfarjam et al., 2015; Metke-Jimenez and Karimi, 2016) construes the task, as mentioned above, as a sequence of subtasks, first identifying all mentions of drugs and effects in the text, then linking them to concepts and to each other. For the first step to be possible, drug mentions and effect mentions need to be identified in the text, for which corresponding mark-up needs to be available in the training data. Similarly, any links between the marked up entities also need to be present in the annotations. The identified text strings can then be mapped (linked) in a separate step to drug (e.g. _lamictol) and effect (e.g. _confusional state) concepts, potentially with separately retrained off-the-shelf tools.

The above discussion points to an annotation scheme involving a DRUG concept (but not concepts for individual drugs), and an EFFECT concept (but not concepts for specific effects), and for corresponding labels to be inserted into texts as mark up. However, more issues arise when mapping these conclusions to an annotation scheme.

3.4 Towards an Annotation Scheme

Some of the questions that arise in text annotation are (1) whether conceptually grounded annotations should attach to word strings (a) with the meaning 'these words together express the given concept', or (b) with the meaning 'somewhere in this text there is an occurrence of the concept';

(2) whether labels should be (a) terminal concepts (e.g. _lamictol) or (b) classes of terminal concepts (e.g. *Drug*); (3) how to treat instances where an entity or event is mentioned, but is not asserted to have occurred or have been observed, which happens e.g. with negation, questions or hypothetical considerations; and (4) how to present the task to annotators in such a way that the cognitive load is within manageable limits and annotations can be replicated with sufficient consistency.

Not all concepts can clearly and easily be associated with specific words in the text. While mentions of a drug or effect entity always have corresponding words in the text (entity annotations fall under (1a) above), this is not necessarily the case of concepts naturally seen as relations between other concepts. Consider again the last post in Figure 1: there are no substrings that can be associated with Lamictol *causing* cognitive deficits. Rather, it is the first two sentences in their entirety that imply (but do not state explicitly) the causal link. It tends to be considered not appropriate to mark up such relations in text, and they attach instead to one or more already marked up word strings (meaning they fall under (1b) above).

Regarding (2) above, aside from the issues raised in Section 3.3, available resources are a deciding factor: e.g. it would take annotators far longer to determine the specific drug concept label for a drug mention than it would to simply label each such mention with a generic drug label.

Regarding (3), while KE would typically aim to extract information with factual status from text (e.g. all drug effects patients claim to have experienced), far from all mentions of such information have factual status (drug effect mentions an be negated, part of a question, etc.). Simply treating e.g. a negated drug effect as not a drug effect is unlikely to be helpful in a machine learning context, because negated and non-negated versions will look identical except for a negation marker elsewhere in the text, potentially resulting in a large number of spurious negative examples. It is more likely to help generalisation to treat all drug effect mentions identically, and to additionally mark up in annotations, and subsequently learn, the characteristics of negation. The same holds for generalisations, questions and similar phenomena.

Regarding (4), it is virtually impossible to achieve perfect consistency between annotators, or even self-consistency, with mark-up annotation

```
DRUG_NONADHERENCE [
    +DRUG_MODIFICATION [ instigated_by = _patient_
                intentional || _patient_unintentional ]  ]

DRUG_MODIFICATION [
    drug : Drugs
    change : DOSE_CHANGE || FORM_CHANGE || PROD
            UCT_CHANGE
    +reason : DRUG_EFFECT || DRUG_PROPERTY ||
            Other_Reason
    instigated_by : Instigator
    +mod_effect : EFFECT || Other_Outcome   ]

DOSE_CHANGE [
    ?from_dose : ( Numbers, Units, Time_Span )
    ?to_dose : ( Numbers, Units, Time_Span )
    dose_mod_type : DoseModTypes   ]

FORM_CHANGE [
    ?from_form : Form_Types
    ?to_form : Form_Types   ]

PRODUCT_CHANGE [
    ?from_product : Drug_Products
    ?to_product : Drug_Products   ]

DRUG_EFFECT [
    drug : Drugs
    medDRA_preferred_term : MPTs
    duration : ( Numbers, Units )
    severity : Severity_Levels   ]

DRUG_PROPERTY [
    drug : Drugs
    property : Drug_Properties   ]

Drugs = {x|x is a drug entry in SIDER}
Drug_Products = {x|x is a drug product entry in SIDER}
MPTs = {x|x is an MPT entry in SIDER}
Drug_Properties = { _effective, _ineffective, _like, _dis-
            like, _cheap, _expensive, ...}
Numbers = {x|x ∈ ℝ}
Units = { _ml, _mg, ...}
Time_Span = { _halfday, _day, _week, ...}
Form_Types = { _tablet, _powder, _solution, _cream, ...}
DoseModTypes = { _start, _stop, _increase, _decrease}
Other_Reason = { _life_event, _insurance_financial,
            _view_belief, ...}
Instigator = { _patient_intentional, _patient_unintentional,
            _clinician, _both_together, _other}
Other_Outcome = { _negative, _positive, _neutral}
Severity_Levels = { _mild, _moderate, _severe}
```

Figure 3: Nonadherence concept model (UML-like notation). + = 1 or more; || = xor; ? = at least 1 of two.

schemes. For simpler concepts corresponding to fewer possible word strings, such as named entities of type drug, issues are comparatively simple, and inter-annotator agreement (IAA, the extent to which annotators agree where drug mentions begin/end) would be high. As is apparent even in the simple example word strings in Example 1, there is comparatively higher variation in word strings describing side effects: if the last two examples were extracted from the longer strings *I'm being so forgetful* and *I just keep losing my phone...*, respectively, in our experience there tends to be considerable variation among annotators about where to place the start of the effect mention.

One way to address this is to ensure that the concepts underlying annotation labels are highly coherent and crisply defined, so that there is high concurrence among annotators in how to interpret and apply them. This underlines the need to co-develop conceptualisation and annotation scheme, because they provide the formal grounding that can help ensure coherence and crispness. For high IAA, the tasks annotators are asked to perform need to be focused and homogeneous, and the visual interfaces as uncluttered as possible. If this is not the case it can make the task too difficult, and also quickly lead to frustration among annotators.

4   An Approach to Nonadherence KE

In this section, we scale up the insights from Section 3 to an approach to knowledge extraction (KE) in the nonadherence domain, a substantially more complex task than drug effect detection. We adopt the definition of nonadherence as *not taking a drug as instructed* (Section 2), and assume that the relationship between a patient and a drug starts with a prescription and instructions issued by a clinician. We see nonadherence as one or more modifications to the original prescription regimen, or to a previous modification, made without the approval of the prescribing clinician. Our first task then is to model the concept of modification, after which we can define nonadherence as modifications instigated by the patient. Our goal is to design a concept model, KE template and annotation scheme for nonadherence that support KE methods that extract information about the *how* and *why* of drug nonadherence.

4.1   Concept Model

Information about *how* and *why* nonadherent drug modifications occur will necessarily involve a specific **drug**. To address the *how* part, we need to know what **type of modification** was carried out. Nonadherent modifications in all examples we have encountered involve some change to the **dose** that is taken, if stopping, starting and forgetting to take a drug are considered dose modifications. Other types of modifications also apply to drug **form** (tablet, capsule, etc.), or drug **brand** (e.g. generic vs. branded). To address the *why* part, we also need to know the **reason** for the modification and its **effect**, because it often becomes the reason for a further modification. Our nonadherence concept model is shown in Figure 3. Starting from the top, it defines drug nonadherence as one or more drug modifications instigated by the patient either intentially or unintentionally. A drug modification is composed of a drug, a change, optionally a reason and an effect, plus a specification of instigation. A reason is either a drug effect, drug property or another reason. A drug effect is as defined in Section 3; a drug property identifies the drug it relates to and covers non-effect properties such as cost, how well it works and whether the patient likes it. Other reasons include reasons relating to life events, insurance issues and beliefs held by the patient. Others are possible, and as indicated in the model, we have not defined a final set of terminal concepts for some of the preterminals (preterminal concepts are indicated by italics). In order to define the possible terminal concepts for the preterminal drugs, drug products and effects concepts, we use the SIDER knowledge base (Kuhn et al., 2015).

4.2 KE Template and Task

The concept model in Figure 3 is task-agnostic. For the specific task of nonadherence event extraction from health forum posts it needs to be mapped to a KE template, task specification and annotation scheme that are necessarily task-specific. Following inspection of about 200 random texts from our corpus of 150K posts (Section 5), and based on the concept model above, we construe the nonadherence KE task as follows:

1. Binary classification of posts into first person narration vs. others.

2. Binary classification of posts into containing modification mentions vs. others.

3. Anaphora resolution: replace drug, drug form and drug dose anaphora with full references.

4. Entity detection: drug, dose, effect, modification.

5. Entity linking: drug, effect, modification (yielding modification type); text normalisation: dose.

6. Topic segmentation: drug related, other.

7. NE relation detection via binary classification (applied to drug-related topic fields only):

   - drug, dose, context → dose_of?
   - drug, effect, context → drug_effect?
   - dose, effect, context → dose_effect?
   - modification, drug, context → drug_modification?
   - modification, dose, context → drug_modification?

   - drug_modification, effect, context → mod_reason?
   - drug_modification, context → clinician, patient_in tentional, patient_unintentional, both_together, not_stated?
   - drug_modification, context → stop, start, increase, decrease, unclear?

Note that we do not currently include product or form changes in the task construal. Moreover, we are leaving identification of drug properties, and modification reasons other than effects to future work. While the first six tasks above would need to be implemented, in this order, in a pipeline, there is no intention to imply that the subtasks under (7) would be implemented separately and in a specific order. Rather, there is likely to be benefit from jointly modelling some or even all of them.

The above KE process is aimed at filling KE templates derived from the concept model in Figure 3 (and the annotation scheme in the next section). Initially, we are using the following template for each drug_modification identified by the KE process, here instantiated for the second and third sentences in the first post in Figure 1:

$$\text{DRUG\_MODIFICATION } [\\ \quad \text{DRUG= \_sertraline;} \\ \quad \text{DOSE= \_unknown;} \\ \quad \text{MOD\_REASON= \_unknown;} \quad\quad (4) \\ \quad \text{MOD\_TYPE= \_stop;} \\ \quad \text{INSTIGATED\_BY= \_patient\_intentional; } \quad]$$

Ideally we would also like to extract information about the severity and duration of drug effects, and the order in which they occur, but have had to exclude those for the time being as infeasibly hard from health forum posts.

4.3 Nonadherence Annotation Scheme

The annotation scheme we have devised to match the concept model, KE task and KE template above, consists of 8 entities and 3 events, as shown in Figure 4. The entities are annotated as labels attached to identified word strings in the text, with the meaning of (1a) in Section 3.4. Events are not associated with word spans, but link two or more entities; events also have sets of attributes.

In order to minimise cognitive load for our annotators, we made several implementational choices that are not reflected in Figure 4, partly influenced by the brat evaluation tool we are using for annotating texts.[4] E.g. we annotated DRUG_EFFECT and DRUG_PROPERTY events in one round, and DRUG_MODIFICATION events in another,

---

[4]brat.nlplab.org

Entities:
Drug, Drugs, Drug_Dose, Drug_Form, Drug_Brand, Drug_Effect, Drug_Property, Other_Reason.
Events:
DRUG_EFFECT:
Argument 1: (Drug|Drugs|Drug_Form|Drug_Dose|Drug_Brand)+
Argument 2: Drug_Effect.
Attributes (binary, optional): Question, Negation, Generalisation, Speculation, ReducedCertainty.
DRUG_PROPERTY:
Argument 1: (Drug|Drugs|Drug_Form|Drug_Dose|Drug_Brand)+
Argument 2: Drug_Property
Attributes (binary, optional): Question, Negation, Generalisation, Speculation, ReducedCertainty.
DRUG_MODIFICATION:
Argument 1: Drug|Drug_Form|Drug_Dose|Drug_Brand
Argument 2 (reason(s) for modification): (DRUG_EFFECT|DRUG_PROPERTY|Other_Reason)*
Attributes (binary, optional): Question, Negation, Generalisation, Speculation, ReducedCertainty.
Attributes (multiple valued, obligatory):
Instigated_By = {not_stated, clinician, patient_intentional, patient_unintentional, both_together}.
Mod_Type = {increase, decrease, start, stop, unclear}.
Relations:
antecedent: links pronouns and common noun references to their most recent antecedent (named reference).
dose_of, form_of, brand_of: link dose, form and brand mentions to the drugs they relate to.

Figure 4: Nonadherence annotation scheme.

separate round; we annotated antecedent links as chains of antecedent relations to the nearest full reference, using all intervening anaphoric references, in order to minimise clutter in the interface.

4.4 Agreement among annotators

The scheme was developed in several iterations of development /testing, each time improving concept model, scheme and Inter-Annotator Agreement (InterAA). For annotations with the final version of the scheme we allowed four hours per 50 posts (average post length is 83 words). InterAA for entities, as measured by averaged brateval scores (F1 on combined label/span matches) computed on 50 random posts, between our two main annotators, ranges from 0.74 for Drug_Effect, and 0.64 for Drug, to 0.39 for Drug_Property. The corresponding IntraAA scores are 0.85, 0.8 and 0.75 for one annotator, and 0.75, 0.73, and 0.81 for the other (numbers for Drug_Property indicate annotators are interpreting the guidance differently).

5 Data Collection and Analysis

We opted for arms-length data scraping and de-identification where a trusted third party scraped health forum posts, and de-identified the texts, making available to us the masked version of the dataset only. The partner accessed and downloaded all posts on the 11 drug-specific forums on www.depressionforums.org at the end of 20 Dec 2018, yielding 148,575 posts. The posts were processed and converted to text-only form, forum post IDs were removed and replaced with new dataset-specific post IDs, and personally identifiable information (PII) was masked, e.g. usernames were replaced by the token [USER] and person names by [NAME]. In addition, the partner performed adverse event (AE) (Nielsen, 2011) and sentiment scoring (Xu and Painter, 2016) for each post. AE scores express the probability p that the post contains mention of an adverse event (AE), thresholded at p=0.7. Sentiment scores range from -5 to 5, with negative sentiment thresholded at -1, and positive sentiment at 1, with scores from -1 to 1 indicating neutral sentiment.

Post were distributed over the 11 forums as shown in Table 1 in terms of number of posts and percentage of total (columns 2 and 3); also shown are median post length, percentage of posts with AEs, and percentages of posts with positive/negative/neutral sentiment. Some trends can be observed in Table 1. Post length tends to go up as forum size increases. Some forums contain substantially higher rates of AE mentions than others: prevalence ranges from 47.6% of posts for Abilify, to 63.9% for Citalopram. These correlate to some extent with sentiment scores: e.g. 22.5% of Abilify posts were classified as negative in sentiment, compared to 28.1% for Citalopram. There is no correlation (Pearsons r=0.17) between % AE mention and % positive sentiment; there is a strong inverse correlation (r=-0.74) between % AE and % neutral sentiment, and some correlation (r=0.3) between % AE and % negative sentiment.

We have so far annotated 2,000 posts in Phase 1. In the annotated posts, there are 3,882 individual

Forum	Posts	%-age	Median tokens	% AE mention	% pos sentim.	% neg sentim.	% neut sentim.
55-citalopram-celexa-lexapro-escitalopram	31,286	21.1%	87	63.9%	50.2%	21.7%	28.1%
46-other-depression-and-anxiety-medications	21,408	14.4%	80	56.3%	47.7%	24.7%	27.6%
56-wellbutrin-bupropion	20,098	13.5%	93.5	62.6%	51.0%	21.8%	27.2%
53-zoloftlustral-sertraline	19,597	13.2%	87	64.4%	50.2%	21.2%	28.5%
54-effexor-venlafaxine-pristiq-desvenlafaxine	15,014	10.1%	82	63.8%	46.5%	23.1%	30.4%
50-cymbalta-duloxetine	12,439	8.4%	85	62.1%	49.0%	22.0%	28.9%
52-prozac-fluoxetine	11,166	7.5%	80	54.3%	47.7%	23.2%	29.0%
51-remeron-mirtazapine	8,142	5.5%	80	61.4%	51.7%	22.6%	25.7%
57-paxilseroxat-paroxetine	4,476	3.0%	68	52.2%	45.9%	23.4%	30.7%
103-abilify-aripiprazole	3,223	2.2%	56	47.6%	52.2%	25.3%	22.5%
102-viibryd-vilazodone	1,726	1.2%	59	55.7%	42.9%	26.4%	30.7%
Total	*148,575*	*100.0%*	*83*	*60.9%*	*49.2%*	*22.6%*	*28.2%*

Table 1: Data set statistics, adverse drug event (AE) and sentiment scores.

Drug	Drugs	Drug_Dose	Drug_Form	Drug_Effect	Drug_Property	Que.	Neg.	Gen.	Spec.	Red.
2,320	216	615	51	2,845	1,037	137	360	313	169	308

Table 2: Occurrence counts for Phase 1 annotations (Que=Question, Neg=Negation, Gen=Generalisation, Spe= Speculation, Red=ReducedCertainty; see Section 4.3).

Drug_Effect and Drug_Property annotations altogether. 999 posts have at least one such annotation; 258 posts have exactly 1, 197 have 2, 151 have 3, 108 have 4, and 285 have 5 or more (up to 28). Table 2 presents occurrence counts for entities and events from Phase 1.

6 Related Research

Structured information resources in health informatics range from ordered lists of terms, glossaries and medical thesauri (MeSH[5], UMLS (Bodenreider, 2004)), to ontologies like SNOMED CT (Donnelly, 2006) and BioPax (Demir et al., 2010). Such resources have underlying concept models, from the very simple (e.g. in a drug list each entry is a member of the class drug) to the much more complex, e.g. ontologies incorporating complex relations, properties and structures.

KE work in health informatics involves implicit or explicit underlying concept models. Examples include adverse drug effect detection (Karimi et al., 2015; Yates et al., 2015), usually involving two main stages—entity identification and entity linking—although some simply classify posts as containing a drug-effect mention or not (Bollegala et al., 2018). Others have applied further layers of interpretation such as sentiment extraction, e.g. headache is negative (Cameron et al., 2013).

Conceptualisations have been developed for more complex health domains. Mowery et al. classify posts as containing evidence of depression to yield a first layer of information which is then instantiated by either a specific symptom or psychosocial stressor (Mowery et al., 2015). Other studies have addressed suicide (Desmet and Hoste, 2014; Huang et al., 2017), flu avoidance (Collier et al., 2011), cyber-bullying (Van Hee et al., 2015), and rumours (Zubiaga et al., 2016).

7 Conclusion

In this paper our aim has been to pin down and clarify the interdependent and mutually constraining elements involved in developing an approach to knowledge extraction, encompassing the underlying concept model, KE task construal and corresponding KE template, as well as the annotation scheme. We have discussed the issues that arise when addressing each of the elements, the choices that need to be made and the trade-offs involved.

All this reflects our experience of developing an annotation scheme for drug nonadherence. While we have discussed the steps involved in developing a KE approach in the context of the nonadherence domain, we found that many of the steps and issues are not domain-specific, and are also applicable to KE in other domains.

Acknowledgments

The research reported here was carried out as part of the CoQuaND project funded by the EPSRC UK Healthcare Text Analytics Research Network (Healtex, EP/N027280).

---

[5]http://www.nlm.nih.gov/mesh/meshhome.html

References

Olivier Bodenreider. 2004. The unified medical language system (umls): integrating biomedical terminology. *Nucleic acids research*, 32(suppl_1):D267–D270.

Danushka Bollegala, Simon Maskell, Richard Sloane, Joanna Hajne, and Munir Pirmohamed. 2018. Causality patterns for detecting adverse drug reactions from social media: Text mining approach. *JMIR public health and surveillance*, 4(2):e51.

Delroy Cameron, Gary A Smith, Raminta Daniulaityte, Amit P Sheth, Drashti Dave, Lu Chen, Gaurish Anand, Robert Carlson, Kera Z Watkins, and Russel Falck. 2013. Predose: a semantic web platform for drug abuse epidemiology using social media. *Journal of biomedical informatics*, 46(6):985–997.

Nigel Collier, Nguyen Truong Son, and Ngoc Mai Nguyen. 2011. Omg u got flu? analysis of shared health messages for bio-surveillance. *Journal of biomedical semantics*, 2(5):S9.

Emek Demir, Michael P Cary, Suzanne Paley, Ken Fukuda, Christian Lemer, Imre Vastrik, Guanming Wu, Peter D'eustachio, Carl Schaefer, Joanne Luciano, et al. 2010. The biopax community standard for pathway data sharing. *Nature biotechnology*, 28(9):935.

Bart Desmet and Véronique Hoste. 2014. Recognising suicidal messages in dutch social media. In *9th international conference on language resources and evaluation (LREC)*, pages 830–835.

Kevin Donnelly. 2006. Snomed-ct: The advanced terminology and coding system for ehealth. *Studies in health technology and informatics*, 121:279.

Sandra van Dulmen, Emmy Sluijs, Liset Van Dijk, Denise de Ridder, Rob Heerdink, and Jozien Bensing. 2007. Patient adherence to medical treatment: A review of reviews. *BMC health services research*, 7(1):55.

Erica CG van Geffen, Helga Gardarsdottir, Rolf van Hulten, Liset van Dijk, Antoine CG Egberts, and Eibert R Heerdink. 2009. Initiation of antidepressant therapy: Do patients follow the gp's prescription? *Br J Gen Pract*, 59(559):81–87.

Ben Hachey, Will Radford, Joel Nothman, Matthew Honnibal, and James R Curran. 2013. Evaluating entity linking with wikipedia. *Artificial intelligence*, 194:130–150.

Xianpei Han, Le Sun, and Jun Zhao. 2011. Collective entity linking in web text: a graph-based method. In *Proceedings of the 34th international ACM SIGIR conference on Research and development in Information Retrieval*, pages 765–774. ACM.

Xiaolei Huang, Linzi Xing, Jed R Brubaker, and Michael J Paul. 2017. Exploring timelines of confirmed suicide incidents through social media. In *2017 IEEE International Conference on Healthcare Informatics (ICHI)*, pages 470–477. IEEE.

Jacqueline G Hugtenburg, Lonneke Timmers, Petra JM Elders, Marcia Vervloet, and Liset van Dijk. 2013. Definitions, variants, and causes of nonadherence with medication: A challenge for tailored interventions. *Patient preference and adherence*, 7:675.

Sarvnaz Karimi, Alejandro Metke-Jimenez, Madonna Kemp, and Chen Wang. 2015. Cadec: A corpus of adverse drug event annotations. *Journal of Biomedical Informatics*, 55:73 – 81.

Michael Kuhn, Ivica Letunic, Lars Juhl Jensen, and Peer Bork. 2015. The sider database of drugs and side effects. *Nucleic acids research*, 44(D1):D1075–D1079.

Robert Leaman, Laura Wojtulewicz, Ryan Sullivan, Annie Skariah, Jian Yang, and Graciela Gonzalez. 2010. Towards internet-age pharmacovigilance: extracting adverse drug reactions from user posts to health-related social networks. In *Proceedings of the 2010 workshop on biomedical natural language processing*, pages 117–125. Association for Computational Linguistics.

Alejandro Metke-Jimenez and Sarvnaz Karimi. 2016. Concept identification and normalisation for adverse drug event discovery in medical forums. In *BMDID@ ISWC*.

Danielle Mowery, Craig Bryan, and Mike Conway. 2015. Towards developing an annotation scheme for depressive disorder symptoms: A preliminary study using twitter data. In *Proceedings of the 2nd Workshop on Computational Linguistics and Clinical Psychology: From Linguistic Signal to Clinical Reality*, pages 89–98.

Finn Årup Nielsen. 2011. A new anew: Evaluation of a word list for sentiment analysis in microblogs. *arXiv preprint arXiv:1103.2903*.

Azadeh Nikfarjam, Abeed Sarker, Karen Oconnor, Rachel Ginn, and Graciela Gonzalez. 2015. Pharmacovigilance from social media: mining adverse drug reaction mentions using sequence labeling with word embedding cluster features. *Journal of the American Medical Informatics Association*, 22(3):671–681.

Takeshi Onishi, Davy Weissenbacher, Ari Klein, Karen O'Connor, and Graciela Gonzalez-Hernandez. 2018. Dealing with medication non-adherence expressions in twitter. In *Proceedings of the 2018 EMNLP Workshop SMM4H: The 3rd Social Media Mining for Health Applications Workshop and Shared Task*, pages 32–33, Brussels, Belgium. Association for Computational Linguistics.

Delip Rao, Paul McNamee, and Mark Dredze. 2013. Entity linking: Finding extracted entities in a knowledge base. In *Multi-source, multilingual information extraction and summarization*, pages 93–115. Springer.

Eduardo Sabaté et al. 2003. *Adherence to long-term therapies: evidence for action*. World Health Organization.

Karen Smith, Su Golder, Abeed Sarker, Yoon Loke, Karen OConnor, and Graciela Gonzalez-Hernandez. 2018. Methods to compare adverse events in twitter to faers, drug information databases, and systematic reviews: Proof of concept with adalimumab. *Drug safety*, 41(12):1397–1410.

Phil Tregunno. 2017. Use of social media in pharmacovigilance. Report on WEB-RADR results to 2017 Yellow Card Centre Conference, Wales.

Cynthia Van Hee, Ben Verhoeven, Els Lefever, Guy De Pauw, Véronique Hoste, and Walter Daelemans. 2015. Guidelines for the fine-grained analysis of cyberbullying.

Yingzi Xu and Jeffery L Painter. 2016. Application of classification and clustering methods on mvoc (medical voice of customer) data for scientific engagement.

Andrew Yates, Nazli Goharian, and Ophir Frieder. 2015. Extracting adverse drug reactions from social media. In *Twenty-Ninth AAAI Conference on Artificial Intelligence*.

Arkaitz Zubiaga, Maria Liakata, Rob Procter, Geraldine Wong Sak Hoi, and Peter Tolmie. 2016. Analysing how people orient to and spread rumours in social media by looking at conversational threads. *PloS one*, 11(3):e0150989.

What A Sunny Day 🌂:
Toward Emoji-Sensitive Irony Detection

Aditi Chaudhary*   Shirley Anugrah Hayati*   Naoki Otani*   Alan W Black
Language Technologies Institute
Carnegie Mellon University
{aschaudh, shayati, notani, awb}@cs.cmu.edu

Abstract

Irony detection is an important task with applications in identification of online abuse and harassment. With the ubiquitous use of nonverbal cues such as emojis in social media, in this work we study the role of these structures in irony detection. Since the existing irony detection datasets have <10% ironic tweets with emoji, classifiers trained on them are insensitive to emojis. We propose an automated pipeline for creating a more balanced dataset.

1   Introduction

Social media text often contains non-verbal cues, such as emojis, for users to convey their intention. Statistics have shown that more than 45% of internet users in the United States have used an emoji in social media[1]. Due to this prevalent usage of emoji, some works attempt to exploit the occurences of emoji for tackling NLP tasks, such as sentiment analysis (Chen et al., 2019), emotion detection, and sarcasm detection (Felbo et al., 2017), as the presence of emoji can change the meaning a text as an emoji can have positive or negative tone.

We are interested in analyzing the role of emoji in irony since this specific linguistic phenomenon is related to sentiment analysis and opinion mining (Pang et al., 2008). Irony can also relate to more serious issues, such as criticism (Hee et al., 2018) or online harassment (Van Hee et al., 2018). Based on our analysis on existing irony dataset from SemEval 2018 (Van Hee et al., 2018), only 9.2% of the ironic tweets contain an emoji. Furthermore, they crawled tweets using irony-related hashtags (i.e. #irony, #sarcasm, #not). This does not capture all variations of ironic occurrences, especially those caused by emojis.

How an emoji changes the meaning of irony tweets is illustrated by the following example. If we have this tweet: "What a sunny day ☀️", it does not sound ironic. However, "What a sunny day 🌂" is ironic. From these examples, we can see that we cannot ignore the importance of emoji to identify irony.

Due to the sparcity of ironic tweets containing emoji, our goal is to augment the existing dataset such that the model requires both textual and emoji cues for irony detection.

We first analyze the behavior of emojis in ironic and non-ironic expressions. We find that the presence of emojis can convert a non-ironic text to an ironic text by causing sentiment polarity contrasts. We develop heuristics for data augmentation and evaluate the results. Then, we propose a simple method for generating ironic/non-ironic texts using sentiment polarities and emojis.

2   Related Work

A common definition of verbal irony is saying things opposite to what is meant (McQuarrie and Mick, 1996; Curcó, 2007). Many studies have diverse opinions regarding sarcasm and irony being different phenomenon (Sperber and Wilson, 1981; Grice, 1978, 1975) or being the same (Reyes et al., 2013; Attardo et al., 2003). In this work, we do not make a distinction between sarcasm and irony.

Previous work on irony detection relied on hand-crafted features such as punctuation and smiles (Veale and Hao, 2010) or lexical features, such as gap between rare and common words, intensity of adverbs and adjectives, sentiments, and sentence structure (Barbieri and Saggion, 2014).

More recently, Van Hee et al. (2016) explore constructions of verbal irony in social media texts, reporting that detection of contrasting polarities is a strong indicator and use sentiment analysis

---

* equal contributions

[1] https://expandedramblings.com/index.php/interesting-emoji-statistics/

Proceedings of the 2019 EMNLP Workshop W-NUT: The 5th Workshop on Noisy User-generated Text, pages 212–216
Hong Kong, Nov 4, 2019. ©2019 Association for Computational Linguistics

Train	All	Ironic				Non-Ironic
		Irony	1	2	3	
# Tweets	3817	1901	1383 (73%)	316 (17%)	202 (10%)	1916
# Tweets containing emoji	406	175	162 (93%)	7 (4%)	6 (3%)	231
# Unique emojis	158	104				122
Test						
# Tweets	784	311	164 (53%)	85 (27%)	62 (20%)	473
# Tweets containing emoji	88	33	27 (82%)	3 (9%)	3 (9%)	55
# Unique emojis	81	23				70

Table 1: Dataset statistics

Ironic		Non-ironic	
Emoji	**Count**	**Emoji**	**Count**
	42 (29.0%)		49 (31.2%)
	26 (17.9%)		22 (14.0%)
	12 (8.3%)		16 (10.2%)
	11 (7.6%)		14 (8.9%)
	10 (6.9%)		14 (8.9%)
	9 (6.2%)		11 (7.0%)
	9 (6.2%)		11 (7.0%)
	9 (6.2%)		11 (7.0%)
	9 (6.2%)		9 (5.5%)
	8 (5.5%)		8 (4.8%)

Table 2: Top 10 most frequent emojis in ironic tweets and non-ironic tweets along with the count and percentage of each emoji.

for the same. Machine learning algorithms such as SVMs informed with sentiment features have shown good performance gains in irony detection (Van Hee, 2017, 2018).

Some neural network-based methods have been conducted. LSTM has proven to be successful for predicting irony. Wu et al. (2018), that ranks first for SemEval 2018: Shared Task on Irony in English Tweets Task A, utilizes multitask-learning dense LSTM network. The second-ranked participants, Baziotis et al. (2017), uses bidirectional LSTM (biLSTM) and self-attention mechanism layer. Ilić et al. (2018)'s architecture is based on Embeddings from Language Model (ELMo) (Peters et al., 2018) and passes the contextualized embeddings to a biLSTM. Ilić et al. (2018)'s model becomes the state of the art for sarcasm and irony detection in 6 out of 7 datasets from 3 different data sources (Twitter, dialog, Reddit).

3 Proposed Approach

3.1 Dataset Analysis

We analyze the SemEval 2018: Irony Detection in English Tweets dataset (Van Hee et al., 2018). Table 1 shows the data statistics for both ironic and non-ironic tweets. Row 2 shows the tweet distri-bution with respect to the presence of emojis. We can see that only 11% of the all tweets contain an emoji, out of which 46% are ironic. In order to study the robustness of current irony detection model to ironic text containing emoji, it is necessary to augment the existing dataset with additional tweets containing emojis due to the limited amount of ironic tweets with emojis.

We hypothesize that the emojis used for ironic tweets may be different from the emojis used for non-ironic tweets. Table 2 shows ten emojis that most frequently appear in ironic tweets and non-ironic tweets in the English dataset. appears most often in both ironic (42 times) tweets and non-ironic (49 times) tweets. For other frequent emojis, except for , the emojis in ironic tweets are different from the emojis in non-ironic tweets. Emojis in the ironic tweets mostly does not have positive sentiment, if we do not want to say negative, such as , , , , and while the most frequent emojis in the non-ironic tweets are dominated by positive emojis, such as , , , , and . Moreover, some tweets may contain multiple emojis. We found that out of 175 ironic tweets that contain emoji, 45% of them contain multiple emojis. We consider to follow this distribution when we are building our ironic tweet generation pipeline.

3.2 Manual Data Augmentation

To further analyze the role of emoji in ironic expressions, we conduct qualitative analysis while controlling the effect of the text content. Concretely, we generate ironic and non-ironic texts by manipulating emoji without changing the texts. The resulting texts give us an insight about emoji use and can also be used as an evaluation resource for developing emoji-sensitive irony detection.

Our manual inspection focuses on the three cases of emoji manupulation below.

1. **Case 1 - Irony with emoji $\rightarrow$ non-irony:** We randomly sample 50 ironic tweets containing

	Original Example	Transformed Example
Case 1	My year is ending perfectly 😂 (Ironic)	My year is ending perfectly 😊 💜 (Non-Ironic)
Case 2	Finally went to the doctor and feeling so much better. (Non-Ironic)	Finally went to the doctor and feeling so much better 🖤 . (Ironic)
Case 3	Another day in paradise haha (Ironic)	Another day in paradise haha 😕 💜 (Non-Ironic)

Table 3: Examples of annotated tweets with respect to the different cases.

emojis from the original dataset and inspect whether replacing/removing the emojis converts these ironic tweets to non-ironic tweets.

2. **Case 2 - Non-irony without emoji $\rightarrow$ irony:** We randomly sample 50 non-ironic tweets without containing emojis and inspect whether adding emoji turns these non-ironic tweets to ironic tweets.

3. **Case 3 - Irony without emoji $\rightarrow$ non-irony:** For another set of randomly sampled 50 ironic tweets not containing any emojis originally, we inspect whether addition of any emojis converts these ironic tweets to non-ironic tweets.

For each original tweet in each case, three annotators assign a label '1' in case a conversion is possible and '0' otherwise. Additionally, for tweets that can be converted, each of the annotators provides one transformed tweet. Table 3 shows some example tweets. After this annotation step, we obtained 171 transformed tweets in total.

We calculate the inter-annotator agreement for each case in Table 4. Case 2 has the worst agreement. This is possibly because it is difficult to convert non-ironic tweets to ironic tweets only by adding emoji.

For instance, two out of the three annotators felt the following non-ironic tweet "*@MiriamMockbill must b in the #blood lol x*" can be transformed into an ironic tweet "*@MiriamMockbill must b in the #blood lol x* 😋" by adding emojis, however the irony in the transformed tweet is not very evident.

Next, we validate the quality of the generated texts. Each example of the generated texts is given to the two annotators. The annotators must rate the given example as 'ironic' or 'non-ironic'. The agreement was moderately high. We achieved 100% agreement on 100 out of 171 tweets (58.4%). We call this dataset consisting of the generated 100 tweets plus their 60 original tweets **Imoji** dataset and use it in a subsequent analysis. To the best of our knowledge, this is the first dataset which contain multiple ironic/non-

	Fleiss' κ	% Agreement
Case 1	0.49	62%
Case 2	0.02	30%
Case 3	0.23	52%

Table 4: Fleiss' κ and percent agreement scores for calculating inter-annotator agreement.

ironic expressions with the same text body and different emojis.

3.3 Automatic Data Augmentation

Analysis of Imoji dataset suggests that emojis tend to be used for causing "irony by clash" in most cases. Positive emoji is likely to be paired with negative texts in ironic expressions, and vice versa.

3.3.1 Method

Following the insight drawn from Imoji dataset, we propose a simple data augmentation using sentiment analysis dataset so that we can build an ironic detector more robust to emoji.

1. We collected emoji-sentiment lexicon from Emoji Sentiment Ranking (Kralj Novak et al., 2015). This resource contains the emojis' frequency and sentiment polarity. Then, we preprocessed the emojis in from this Emoji Sentiment Ranking, resulting in 48 strongly positive 48 emojis and 48 strongly negative emojis. We filter out low-frequency emoji (bottom 50% frequency), ignore non-emotional symbols (e.g. arrows), and extract top 10% emoji in terms of normalized sentiment scores for each of positive and negative sentiments.

2. Collect tweets with positive and negative sentiments from SemEval 2018 Affect in Tweets Task 3 dataset (Mohammad et al., 2018). This dataset contains total of 2,600 tweets with negative emotions, such as sadness, anger and fear, joy tweets, and sarcastic tweets. Crowdsourcers were asked to annotate them as positive or negative tweets.

3. Generate ironic/non-ironic tweets by adding emoji at the end of texts.

Text	Tweet	Emoji	Label
now that I have my future planned out, I feel so much happier #goals #life #igotthis #yay	+	-	Ironic (Yes)
Never let me see you frown	-	+	Ironic (?)
MC: what are you listen to these days?Bogum: these days I feel gloomy, I listen to ccm (spiritual song) often. Church oppa mode. :)	-	+	Ironic (No)
Love your new show @driverminnie	+	+	Non-ironic (Yes)

Table 5: Generated ironic examples. Tweet refers to tweet sentiment and emoji refers to emoji sentiment

3.3.2 Evaluation of Automatic Generation

We conduct manual analysis of the generated tweets. Table 5 displays the generated ironic and non-ironic tweets.

The first example is generated by combining positive sentiment tweet with negative sentiment emoji, and we agree that it is an ironic text. For the second example, it is quite unclear whether the text is ironic or not. ♥ may not make the text ironic if the writer's purpose is really not to see the other person frown even though the sentiment of the text without emoji itself is slightly negative. The third example is not ironic although it is generated by combining negative tweet with positive emoji. "Bogum" is a Korean actor and "oppa" is commonly used by fangirls to call older Korean male. Thus, using ♥ in the text makes sense and does not make it ironic. The last example is a generated non-ironic text by adding positive emoji to positive tweet. Based on this analysis, we decided to use only tweets with positive sentiments as seeds to generate accurate ironic/non-ironic tweets.

4 Experiments

4.1 Preprocessing

To normalize special strings in tweets like URLs, mentions and hashtags, we run ekphrasis[2] (Baziotis et al., 2017) to normalize texts. We also correct non-standard spellings. We collect sentiment analysis datasets for automatic data augmentation from SemEval 2018 Shared Task (Mohammad et al., 2018). Then we obtained 768 additional irony detection instances.

4.2 Baseline Model

We use the NTUA-SLP system (Baziotis et al., 2018) from SemEval 2018. It uses standard two-layer biLSTMs and a self-attention mechanism to encode a tweet into a fixed-sized vector and makes a prediction by a logistic regression classifier taking the encoded tweet as input. Embedding layers

[2]https://github.com/cbaziotis/ekphrasis

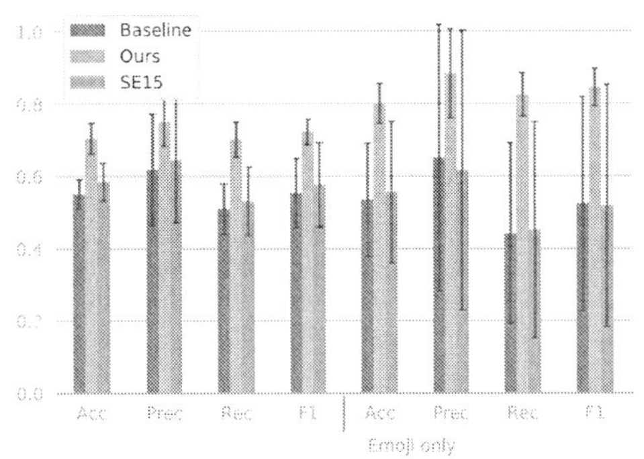

Figure 1: Result on irony detection in Imoji dataset. Baseline referes to SemEval 2018 train set, ours is baseline and our generated data (+767 instances), SE15 is baseline and SemEval 2015 dataset (+767 instances). Performances are mean averages over 10 trials, and error bars denote standard deviations.

are initialized with 300D pre-trained word embeddings, word2vec model trained on tweets for English ((Baziotis et al., 2017)).

4.3 Result

We train the model on our augmented data and test it on the Imoji dataset as shown in Figure 1. To make sure that the performance change by our augmented data (Ours) is not only from the increased number of training instances, we also collect the same number of ironic detection instances as the generated instances from another dataset containing irony annotations (Ghosh et al., 2015). Interestingly, the classifier trained on our augmented dataset achieve much higher recall.

5 Conclusion

In this work, we presented an automatic pipeline for generating ironic data using sentiment analysis. We observe that our method works well for the irony based on polarity contrast. In summary, the experimental results show our augmented data helped classifiers improve their sensitivity to emojis in irony detection tasks without damaging the overall performance of irony detection on the whole datasets. An interesting future direction is to apply our method to multilingual irony dataset.

References

Salvatore Attardo, Jodi Eisterhold, Jennifer Hay, and Isabella Poggi. 2003. Multimodal markers of irony and sarcasm. *Humor*, 16(2):243–260.

Francesco Barbieri and Horacio Saggion. 2014. Modelling irony in twitter. In *Proceedings of the Student Research Workshop at EACL*, pages 56–64.

Christos Baziotis, Athanasiou Nikolaos, Pinelopi Papalampidi, Athanasia Kolovou, Georgios Paraskevopoulos, Nikolaos Ellinas, and Alexandros Potamianos. 2018. Ntua-slp at semeval-2018 task 3: Tracking ironic tweets using ensembles of word and character level attentive rnns. In *Proceedings of SemEval*, pages 613–621.

Christos Baziotis, Nikos Pelekis, and Christos Doulkeridis. 2017. Datastories at semeval-2017 task 4: Deep lstm with attention for message-level and topic-based sentiment analysis. In *Proceedings of SemEval*, pages 747–754.

Zhenpeng Chen, Sheng Shen, Ziniu Hu, Xuan Lu, Qiaozhu Mei, and Xuanzhe Liu. 2019. Emoji-powered representation learning for cross-lingual sentiment classification. In *The World Wide Web Conference*, pages 251–262. ACM.

Carmen Curcó. 2007. Irony: Negation, Echo, and Metarepresentation. *Irony in Language and Thought*, pages 269–296.

Bjarke Felbo, Alan Mislove, Anders Søgaard, Iyad Rahwan, and Sune Lehmann. 2017. Using millions of emoji occurrences to learn any-domain representations for detecting sentiment, emotion and sarcasm. In *Conference on Empirical Methods in Natural Language Processing (EMNLP)*.

Aniruddha Ghosh, Guofu Li, Tony Veale, Paolo Rosso, Ekaterina Shutova, John Barnden, and Antonio Reyes. 2015. SemEval-2015 Task 11: Sentiment Analysis of Figurative Language in Twitter. In *Proceedings of SemEval*, pages 470–478.

H Paul Grice. 1975. Logic and conversation. speech acts, ed. by peter cole and jerry morgan, 41-58.

H Paul Grice. 1978. Further notes on logic and conversation. *1978*, 1:13–128.

Cynthia Van Hee, Els Lefever, and Véronique Hoste. 2018. Exploring the fine-grained analysis and automatic detection of irony on twitter. *Language Resources and Evaluation*, 52(3):707–731.

Suzana Ilić, Edison Marrese-Taylor, Jorge A Balazs, and Yutaka Matsuo. 2018. Deep contextualized word representations for detecting sarcasm and irony. *arXiv preprint arXiv:1809.09795*.

Petra Kralj Novak, Jasmina Smailović, Borut Sluban, and Igor Mozetič. 2015. Sentiment of emojis. *PLoS ONE*, 10(12):e0144296.

Edward F McQuarrie and David Glen Mick. 1996. Figures of rhetoric in advertising language. *Journal of Consumer Research*, 22(4):424–438.

Saif Mohammad, Felipe Bravo-Marquez, Mohammad Salameh, and Svetlana Kiritchenko. 2018. SemEval-2018 Task 1: Affect in Tweets. In *Proceedings of SemEval*, pages 1–17.

Bo Pang, Lillian Lee, et al. 2008. Opinion mining and sentiment analysis. *Foundations and Trends® in Information Retrieval*, 2(1–2):1–135.

Matthew E Peters, Mark Neumann, Mohit Iyyer, Matt Gardner, Christopher Clark, Kenton Lee, and Luke Zettlemoyer. 2018. Deep contextualized word representations. *arXiv preprint arXiv:1802.05365*.

Antonio Reyes, Paolo Rosso, and Tony Veale. 2013. A multidimensional approach for detecting irony in twitter. *Language Resources and Evaluation*, 47(1):239–268.

Dan Sperber and Deirdre Wilson. 1981. Irony and the use-mention distinction. *Philosophy*, 3:143–184.

Cynthia Van Hee. 2017. Can machines sense irony?

Cynthia Van Hee. 2018. Exploring the fine-grained analysis and automatic detection of irony on twitter. In *Proceedings of LREC*.

Cynthia Van Hee, Els Lefever, and Véronique Hoste. 2016. Exploring the realization of irony in twitter data. In *Proceedings of LREC*.

Cynthia Van Hee, Els Lefever, and Véronique Hoste. 2018. Semeval-2018 task 3: Irony detection in english tweets. In *Proceedings of SemEval*, pages 39–50.

Tony Veale and Yanfen Hao. 2010. Detecting Ironic Intent in Creative Comparisons. In *Proceedings of ECAI*, pages 765–770.

Chuhan Wu, Fangzhao Wu, Sixing Wu, Junxin Liu, Zhigang Yuan, and Yongfeng Huang. 2018. Thu_ngn at semeval-2018 task 3: Tweet irony detection with densely connected lstm and multi-task learning. In *Proceedings of SemEval*, pages 51–56.

Geolocation with Attention-Based Multitask Learning Models

Tommaso Fornaciari, Dirk Hovy
Bocconi University, Milan, Italy
`{fornaciari|dirk.hovy}@unibocconi.it`

Abstract

Geolocation, predicting the location of a post based on text and other information, has a huge potential for several social media applications. Typically, the problem is modeled as either multi-class classification or regression. In the first case, the classes are geographic areas previously identified; in the second, the models directly predict geographic coordinates. The former requires discretization of the coordinates, but yields better performance. The latter is potentially more precise and true to the nature of the problem, but often results in worse performance. We propose to combine the two approaches in an attention-based multitask convolutional neural network that jointly predicts both discrete locations and continuous geographic coordinates. We evaluate the multi-task (MTL) model against single-task models and prior work. We find that MTL significantly improves performance, reporting large gains on one data set, but also note that the correlation between labels and coordinates has a marked impact on the effectiveness of including a regression task.

1 Introduction

Knowing the location of a social media post is useful for a variety of applications: from improving content relevance for the socio-cultural environment of a geographic area (Rakesh et al., 2013), to the understanding of demographic distributions for disaster relief (Lingad et al., 2013).

However, most social media posts do not include location. On Twitter, one of the most studied social media, geotagging is enabled for at most 5% of the posts (Sloan and Morgan, 2015; Cebeillac and Rault, 2016). In order to address this issue, samples of geolocated data have been used to create corpora of geo-tagged texts. Those corpora allow us to train supervised models to predict the geographic location for a post, relying on the post's text and, possibly, users' interaction information and other meta-data provided by the social media. While a lot of work has gone into this problem, it is still far from solved.

The task is usually framed as a multi-class *classification* problem, but actual location information is normally given as a pair of continuous-valued latitude/longitude coordinates (e.g.: 51.5074° N, 0.1278° W). Using these coordinates in classification requires translation into labels corresponding to a geographic area (e.g., cities, states, countries). This translation is another non-trivial task (Wing and Baldridge, 2014), and necessarily loses information. Much less frequently, geolocation is framed as *regression*, i.e., direct prediction of the coordinates. While potentially more accurate, regression over geographic coordinates presents a host of challenges (values are continuous but bounded, can be negative, and distances are non-Euclidean, due to the Earth's curvature). It is therefore usually less effective than classification.

Ideally, we would like to combine the advantages of both approaches, i.e., let the regression over continuous-valued coordinates guide the discrete location classification. So far, however, no work has tried to combine the two approaches. With recent advances in multi-task learning (MTL), we have the opportunity to combine them. In this paper, we do exactly that.

We combine classification and regression in a multi-task attention-based convolutional neural network (MTL-Att-CNN), which jointly learns to predict the geographic labels *and* the relative coordinates. We evaluate on two data sets widely used in the geolocation literature, TWITTER-US and TWITTER-WORLD (Section 3). In line with prior research on MTL (Alonso and Plank, 2017; Bingel and Søgaard, 2017), we do find that auxiliary regression can indeed help classification performance, but under a somewhat surprising con-

Proceedings of the 2019 EMNLP Workshop W-NUT: The 5th Workshop on Noisy User-generated Text, pages 217–223
Hong Kong, Nov 4, 2019. ©2019 Association for Computational Linguistics

dition: when there are enough classification labels. We show this by evaluating on two different schemes for discretizing coordinates into labels. The first (Rahimi et al., 2017b) identifies irregular areas via k-d trees, and is the most common in the literature. The second (Fornaciari and Hovy, 2019b) directly identifies towns of at least 15K inhabitants and allows the evaluation of the method in a more realistic scenario, but results in 3–6 times more labels.

Contributions 1) We propose a novel multi-task CNN model, which learns geographic label prediction and coordinate regression together. 2) Based on Fornaciari and Hovy (2019b), we propose an alternative coordinate discretization, which correlates more with geocoordinates (Section 3). We find that label granularity impacts the effectiveness of MTL.

2 Related Work

Most successful recent approaches to geolocation use Deep Learning architectures for the task (Liu and Inkpen, 2015; Iso et al., 2017; Han et al., 2016). Many authors (Miura et al., 2016; Bakerman et al., 2018; Rahimi et al., 2018; Ebrahimi et al., 2018; Do et al., 2018; Fornaciari and Hovy, 2019a) follow a hybrid approach, combining the text representation with network information and further meta-data. However, recent works explore the effectiveness of purely textual data for geolocation (Tang et al., 2019).

Other researchers have directly predicted the geographic coordinates associated with the texts. Eisenstein et al. (2010) was the first to formulate the problem as a regression task predicting the coordinate values as numerical values. Lourentzou et al. (2017) use very simple labels, but create a neural model which separately performs both the classification task and the prediction of the geographic coordinates. They evaluate the relative performance of each approach.

Rahimi et al. (2017a) created a dense representation of bi-dimensional points using Mixture Density Networks (Bishop, 1994). They motivate the higher complexity of such multi-dimensional representations with the limits of the loss minimization in uni-modal distributions for multi-target scenarios. In particular, they underline that minimizing the squared loss is equivalent to positioning the predicted point in the middle of the possible outputs, when more flexible representa-

tions would be useful for geographic prediction: "a user who mentions content in both NYC and LA is predicted to be in the centre of the U.S.".

We address this point with a model which jointly solves the classification and regression problem, similar to the approach by Subramanian et al. (2018), who combine regression with a classification-like "ordinal regression" in order to predict both the number of votes for a petition as well as the voting threshold it reaches.

There is a rich literature on the use of multitask learning (Caruana, 1996; Caruana et al., 1996; Caruana, 1997) in NLP, highlighting the importance of choosing the right auxiliary tasks (Alonso and Plank, 2017; Bingel and Søgaard, 2017; Benton et al., 2017; Lamprinidis et al., 2018).

3 Data

Corpora We use two publicly available data sets commonly used for geolocation, known as TWITTER-US and TWITTER-WORLD. They were released by Roller et al. (2012) and Han et al. (2012) respectively. Both data sets consist of geolocated tweets written in English, coming from North America and from everywhere in the World. Each instance consists of a set of tweets from a single user, associated with a pair of geographic coordinates (latitude and longitude). TWITTER-US has 449 694 instances, TWITTER-WORLD 1 386 766. Both corpora have predefined development and test sets of 10 000 records each. These corpora were used in the shared task of W-NUT 2016, providing the basis for comparison with other models in the literature.

Labels Since the location is represented as coordinates, there is no single best solution for translating them into meaningful labels (i.e., geographic areas). We follow two distinct discretizing approaches, resulting in different label sets. First, to allow comparison with prior work, we implement the coordinate clustering method proposed by Rahimi et al. (2017b). It relies on the k-d tree procedure (Maneewongvatana and Mount, 1999) and led to the identification of 256 geographic areas for TWITTER-US and 930 for TWITTER-WORLD. These areas, however, are quite large and do not always correspond to any meaningful territorial division (e.g., city, county, state, etc).

In order to create labels sets corresponding more closely to existing geographic distinctions, we follow the Point2City - P2C, another algorithm based on k-d tree with additional steps, proposed by Fornaciari and Hovy (2019b). This results in more fine-grained geographic labels.

P2C clusters all points closer than 11 km (which correspond to the first decimal point on the longitude axis), then iteratively merges the centroids until no centroids are closer than 11 km to each other. Finally, these points are labeled with the name of the closest city of at least 15 000 inhabitants, according to the information provided by the free database GeoNames. We refer the reader to Fornaciari and Hovy (2019b) for more details of the method.

The mean distance between P2C labels and the respective actual city centers is less than 3.5 km. P2C results in 1 593 labels for TWITTER-US and 2 975 for TWITTER-WORLD, a factor of respectively 6 and 3 greater than the method used by Rahimi et al. (2017b). We provide our labels and our models on GitHub Bocconi-NLPLab.

Pre-processing and feature selection We pre-process the text by converting it to lowercase, removing URLs and stop-words. We reduce numbers to 0, except for those appearing in mentions (e.g., @abc123). In order to make the vocabulary size computationally tractable, we restrict the allowed words to those with a minimum frequency of 5 for each corpus. Since this removes about 80% of the vocabulary, losing possibly relevant information, we convert a part of the low-frequency words into replacement tokens. In particular, considering the training set only, we selected all those appearing uniquely in the same place according to the P2C labels. We discarded the low frequency terms found in more than one geographic area. In this way, the resulting vocabulary size is 1.470M words for TWITTER-US and 470K for TWITTER-WORLD.

We follow Han et al. (2014) and Forman (2003) in limiting both vocabularies to the same number of tokens, i.e., 470K tokens, by filtering the terms according to their Information Gain Ratio (IGR). This is a measure of the degree of informativeness for each term, according to its distribution among a set of labels – geographic areas in our case.

4 Methods

We train embeddings for both corpora, and use them as input to the multi-task learning model.

Embeddings Since tweets are natively short texts further reduced by removing stop words,
we use a small context window size of 5 words. We trained our embeddings on the training sets of each corpus. As we are interested in potentially rare geographically informative words, we use the skip-gram model, which is more sensitive to low-frequency terms than CBOW (Mikolov et al., 2013) and train for 50 epochs. We use an embedding size of 512, choosing a power of 2 for memory efficiency, and the size as a compromise between a rich representation and the computational tractability of the embeddings matrix. For the same reason, we limit the length of each instance to 800 words for TWITTER-US and 400 words for TWITTER-WORLD, which preserves the entire text for 99.5% of the instances in each corpus.

MTL-Att-CNN We implement a CNN with the following structure. The input layer has the word indices of the text, converted via the embedding matrix into a matrix of shape $words \times embeddings$. We convolve two parallel channels with max-pooling layers and convolutional window sizes 4 and 8 over the input. The two window sizes account for both short and relatively long patterns in the texts. In both channels, the initial number of filters is 128 for the first convolution, and 256 in the second one. We join the output of the convolutional channels and pass it through an attention mechanism (Bahdanau et al., 2014; Vaswani et al., 2017) to emphasize the weight of any meaningful pattern recognized by the convolutions. We use the implementation of Yang et al. (2016). The output consists of two independent, fully-connected layers for the predictions, respectively in the form of discrete labels for classification and of continuous latitude and longitude values for regression.

Gradient Normalization Multi-task networks are quite sensitive to the choice of auxiliary tasks and the associated loss (Benton et al., 2017). If the loss function outputs of different tasks differ in scale, backpropagation also involves errors at different scales. This can imbalance the relative contributions of each task on the overall results: the "lighter" task can therefore be disadvantaged up to the point to become untrainable, since the backpropagation becomes dominated by the task with the larger error scale. To prevent this problem, we first normalize the coordinates to the range $0 - 1$. Since coordinates include negative values, we transform them by adding 180 and dividing by

TWITTER-US						
method	model	# labels	Acc	Acc@161	mean	median
Han et al. (2014)	NB + IGR	378	26%	45%	-	260
Rahimi et al. (2017b)	MLP + k-means	256	-	**55%**	**581**	**91**
k-d labels	STL-Att-CNN	256	21.06%	44.51%	845.23[†]	272.15
	MTL-Att-CNN	256	20.75%	44.35%	856.60	276.99
P2C labels	STL-Att-CNN	1,593	31.22%	44.48%	944.89	304.99
	MTL-Att-CNN	1,593	**31.36%**	44.64%	889.98[**]	293.26

TWITTER-WORLD						
Han et al. (2014)	NB + IGR	3135	13%	26%	-	913
Rahimi et al. (2017b)	MLP + k-means	930	-	36%	1417	373
k-d labels	STL-Att-CNN	930	30.67%	48.13%	1656.06	202.68
	MTL-Att-CNN	930	30.70%	48.46%	1640.16	**195.18**
P2C labels	STL-Att-CNN	2,975	35.67%	47.95%	1695.85	203.50
	MTL-Att-CNN	2,975	**36.07%**	**48.48%**[*]	1643.29[**]	195.54

Table 1: Performance of prior work and proposed model. NB= Naive Bayes, MLP=Multi-Layer Perceptron, CNN=Convolutional Neural Net, STL=Single Task, MTL=Multi Task. Significance on MTL vs. STL: $^*: p \leq 0.05$, $^{**}: p \leq 0.01$, $^{†}: p \leq 0.005$

360. As loss function, we compute the Euclidean distance between the predicted and the target coordinates.[1] We rescale all distances to within $0-1$ as well, i.e., to the same scale as the softmax output of the classification task.

For the main task (i.e., classification), we use the Adam optimizer (Kingma and Ba, 2014). This gradient descent optimizer is widely used as it uses moving averages of the parameters (i.e., the momentum), in practice adjusting the step size during the training (Bengio, 2012). The Adam optimizer, though, requires a high number of parameter. For the auxiliary task (i.e., regression), we simply used standard gradient descent.

5 Experiments

We carry out 8 experiments, 4 on TWITTER-US and 4 on TWITTER-WORLD. For each data set, we compare the performance of multi-task (MTL) and single-task (i.e., classification) models (STL), both with the labels of Rahimi et al. (2017b) and our own label set. For each of the 8 conditions, we report results averaged over three runs to reduce the impact of the random initializations. For each condition, we compute significance between STL and MTL via bootstrap sampling (Berg-Kirkpatrick et al., 2012; Søgaard et al., 2014).

TWITTER-US and TWITTER-WORLD are two remarkably different data sets. Not only they address areas of different size, with different geographic density of the entities to locate, they also differ in vocabulary size (larger in TWITTER-US), even considering different pre-processing procedures. Therefore, the performance difference many studies report is not surprising.

The outcomes are shown in Table 1. On both data sets, MTL yields the best results for exact accuracy. On TWITTER-US, we outperform Han et al. (2014) in exact accuracy, but cannot compare to Rahimi et al. (2017b), and do not reach their acc@161 or distance measures. For TWITTER-WORLD, we report the best results for both types of accuracy and median distance. Interestingly, mean distance is higher, suggesting a very long tail of far-away predictions.

The effectiveness of MTL increases with label granularity. This makes sense, since under a more fine-grained label scheme, the correlation between coordinates and labels is higher, which is exactly what we learn in the auxiliary task. Under the broader labeling scheme by Rahimi et al. (2017b), label areas are of irregular size, and so the correlation with the coordinates varies. With the k-d tree labels, the mean distance between the coordinates and the cluster centroids is 50 Km for TWITTER-US and 40 km for TWITTER-WORLD, while with our labels the mean distance is 16 and 7 km, re-

---

[1] We also experimented with incorporating radians into the distance measure, but did not find any particular improvement, since it is learned directly during the training process.

spectively. With highly granular P2C labels, MTL consistently outperforms STL; in contrast, with wider areas, STL mean distance beats MTL in TWITTER-US. The auxiliary regression adds valuable information to the classification task: MTL improves significantly over STL.

6 Ablation study

In order to verify the impact of the network components on the overall performance, we carry out a brief ablation study. In particular, we are interested in the attention mechanism, implemented following Yang et al. (2016). To this end, we train a MTL model *without* attention mechanism. We note that they are not directly comparable to those shown in table 1, since they used different, randomly initialized embeddings, and should be interpreted with caution. The results do suggest, though, that we can expect the attention mechanism to increase performance by about 10 points percent (both for accuracy and for acc@161), and to increase median distance by about 150 km. This effect holds for both multi-task and single-task models.

7 Conclusion

IN this paper, we propose a novel multi-task learning framework with attention for geolocation, combining label classification with regression over geo-coordinates.

We find that the granularity of the labels (and their correlation with the coordinates) has a direct impact on the effectiveness of MTL, with more labels counter-intuitively resulting in higher exact accuracy. Besides the labels commonly adopted in the literature, we also evaluate with a greater number and more specific locations (arguably a more realistic way to evaluate the geolocation for many real life applications). This effect holds independent of whether the model is trained with attention or not.

The auxiliary regression task is helpful for classification when using more fine-grained labels, which address specific rather than broad areas. Our models are optimized for exact accuracy, rather than to Acc@161, and we report some of the best accuracy measures for TWITTER-WORLD, and competitive results for TWITTER-US.

Acknowledgments

The authors would like to thank the reviewers of the various drafts for their comments. Both authors are members of the Bocconi Institute for Data Science and Analytics (BIDSA) and the Data and Marketing Insights (DMI) unit. This research was supported by a GPU donation from Nvidia, as well as a research grant from CERMES to set up a GPU server, which enabled us to run these experiments.

References

Héctor Martínez Alonso and Barbara Plank. 2017. When is multitask learning effective? Semantic sequence prediction under varying data conditions. In *Proceedings of the 15th Conference of the European Chapter of the Association for Computational Linguistics: Volume 1, Long Papers*, volume 1, pages 44–53.

Dzmitry Bahdanau, Kyunghyun Cho, and Yoshua Bengio. 2014. Neural machine translation by jointly learning to align and translate. *arXiv preprint arXiv:1409.0473*.

Jordan Bakerman, Karl Pazdernik, Alyson Wilson, Geoffrey Fairchild, and Rian Bahran. 2018. Twitter geolocation: A hybrid approach. *ACM Transactions on Knowledge Discovery from Data (TKDD)*, 12(3):34.

Yoshua Bengio. 2012. Practical recommendations for gradient-based training of deep architectures. In *Neural networks: Tricks of the trade*, pages 437–478. Springer.

Adrian Benton, Margaret Mitchell, and Dirk Hovy. 2017. Multitask learning for mental health conditions with limited social media data. In *Proceedings of the 15th Conference of the European Chapter of the Association for Computational Linguistics: Volume 1, Long Papers*, volume 1, pages 152–162.

Taylor Berg-Kirkpatrick, David Burkett, and Dan Klein. 2012. An empirical investigation of statistical significance in NLP. In *Proceedings of the 2012 Joint Conference on Empirical Methods in Natural Language Processing and Computational Natural Language Learning*, pages 995–1005. Association for Computational Linguistics.

Joachim Bingel and Anders Søgaard. 2017. Identifying beneficial task relations for multi-task learning in deep neural networks. In *Proceedings of the 15th Conference of the European Chapter of the Association for Computational Linguistics: Volume 2, Short Papers*, volume 2, pages 164–169.

Christopher M Bishop. 1994. Mixture density networks. Technical report, Citeseer.

Rich Caruana. 1996. Algorithms and applications for multitask learning. In *ICML*, pages 87–95.

Rich Caruana. 1997. Multitask learning. *Machine learning*, 28(1):41–75.

Rich Caruana, Shumeet Baluja, and Tom Mitchell. 1996. Using the future to "sort out" the present: Rankprop and multitask learning for medical risk evaluation. In *Advances in neural information processing systems*, pages 959–965.

Alexandre Cebeillac and Yves-Marie Rault. 2016. Contribution of geotagged twitter data in the study of a social group's activity space. the case of the upper middle class in delhi, india. *Netcom. Réseaux, communication et territoires*, 30(3/4):231–248.

Tien Huu Do, Duc Minh Nguyen, Evaggelia Tsiligianni, Bruno Cornelis, and Nikos Deligiannis. 2018. Twitter user geolocation using deep multi-view learning. In *2018 IEEE International Conference on Acoustics, Speech and Signal Processing (ICASSP)*, pages 6304–6308. IEEE.

Mohammad Ebrahimi, Elaheh ShafieiBavani, Raymond Wong, and Fang Chen. 2018. A unified neural network model for geolocating twitter users. In *Proceedings of the 22nd Conference on Computational Natural Language Learning*, pages 42–53.

Jacob Eisenstein, Brendan O'Connor, Noah A Smith, and Eric P Xing. 2010. A latent variable model for geographic lexical variation. In *Proceedings of the 2010 conference on empirical methods in natural language processing*, pages 1277–1287. Association for Computational Linguistics.

George Forman. 2003. An extensive empirical study of feature selection metrics for text classification. *Journal of machine learning research*, 3(Mar):1289–1305.

Tommaso Fornaciari and Dirk Hovy. 2019a. Dense Node Representation for Geolocation. In *Proceedings of the 5th Workshop on Noisy User-generated Text (WNUT)*.

Tommaso Fornaciari and Dirk Hovy. 2019b. Identifying Linguistic Areas for Geolocation. In *Proceedings of the 5th Workshop on Noisy User-generated Text (WNUT)*.

Bo Han, Paul Cook, and Timothy Baldwin. 2012. Geolocation prediction in social media data by finding location indicative words. *Proceedings of COLING 2012*, pages 1045–1062.

Bo Han, Paul Cook, and Timothy Baldwin. 2014. Text-based twitter user geolocation prediction. *Journal of Artificial Intelligence Research*, 49:451–500.

Bo Han, Afshin Rahimi, Leon Derczynski, and Timothy Baldwin. 2016. Twitter Geolocation Prediction Shared Task of the 2016 Workshop on Noisy User-generated Text. In *Proceedings of the 2nd Workshop on Noisy User-generated Text (WNUT)*, pages 213–217.

Hayate Iso, Shoko Wakamiya, and Eiji Aramaki. 2017. Density estimation for geolocation via convolutional mixture density network. *arXiv preprint arXiv:1705.02750*.

Diederik P Kingma and Jimmy Ba. 2014. Adam: A method for stochastic optimization. *arXiv preprint arXiv:1412.6980*.

Sotiris Lamprinidis, Daniel Hardt, and Dirk Hovy. 2018. Predicting news headline popularity with syntactic and semantic knowledge using multi-task learning. In *Proceedings of the 2018 Conference on Empirical Methods in Natural Language Processing*, pages 659–664.

John Lingad, Sarvnaz Karimi, and Jie Yin. 2013. Location extraction from disaster-related microblogs. In *Proceedings of the 22nd international conference on world wide web*, pages 1017–1020. ACM.

Ji Liu and Diana Inkpen. 2015. Estimating user location in social media with stacked denoising auto-encoders. In *Proceedings of the 1st Workshop on Vector Space Modeling for Natural Language Processing*, pages 201–210.

Ismini Lourentzou, Alex Morales, and ChengXiang Zhai. 2017. Text-based geolocation prediction of social media users with neural networks. In *2017 IEEE International Conference on Big Data (Big Data)*, pages 696–705. IEEE.

Songrit Maneewongvatana and David M Mount. 1999. It's okay to be skinny, if your friends are fat. In *Center for Geometric Computing 4th Annual Workshop on Computational Geometry*, volume 2, pages 1–8.

Tomas Mikolov, Wen-tau Yih, and Geoffrey Zweig. 2013. Linguistic regularities in continuous space word representations. In *Proceedings of the 2013 Conference of the North American Chapter of the Association for Computational Linguistics: Human Language Technologies*, pages 746–751.

Yasuhide Miura, Motoki Taniguchi, Tomoki Taniguchi, and Tomoko Ohkuma. 2016. A simple scalable neural networks based model for geolocation prediction in twitter. In *Proceedings of the 2nd Workshop on Noisy User-generated Text (WNUT)*, pages 235–239.

Afshin Rahimi, Timothy Baldwin, and Trevor Cohn. 2017a. Continuous representation of location for geolocation and lexical dialectology using mixture density networks. In *Empirical Methods in Natural Language Processing*. Association for Computational Linguistics.

Afshin Rahimi, Trevor Cohn, and Tim Baldwin. 2018. Semi-supervised user geolocation via graph convolutional networks. *arXiv preprint arXiv:1804.08049*, pages 2009–2019.

Afshin Rahimi, Trevor Cohn, and Timothy Baldwin. 2017b. A neural model for user geolocation and lexical dialectology. *arXiv preprint arXiv:1704.04008*, pages 209–216.

Vineeth Rakesh, Chandan K Reddy, and Dilpreet Singh. 2013. Location-specific tweet detection and topic summarization in twitter. In *Proceedings of the 2013 IEEE/ACM International Conference on Advances in Social Networks Analysis and Mining*, pages 1441–1444. ACM.

Stephen Roller, Michael Speriosu, Sarat Rallapalli, Benjamin Wing, and Jason Baldridge. 2012. Supervised text-based geolocation using language models on an adaptive grid. In *Proceedings of the 2012 Joint Conference on Empirical Methods in Natural Language Processing and Computational Natural Language Learning*, pages 1500–1510. Association for Computational Linguistics.

Luke Sloan and Jeffrey Morgan. 2015. Who tweets with their location? understanding the relationship between demographic characteristics and the use of geoservices and geotagging on twitter. *PloS one*, 10(11):e0142209.

Anders Søgaard, Anders Johannsen, Barbara Plank, Dirk Hovy, and Héctor Martínez Alonso. 2014. What's in a p-value in nlp? In *Proceedings of the eighteenth conference on computational natural language learning*, pages 1–10.

Shivashankar Subramanian, Timothy Baldwin, and Trevor Cohn. 2018. Content-based Popularity Prediction of Online Petitions Using a Deep Regression Model. In *Proceedings of the 56th Annual Meeting of the Association for Computational Linguistics (Volume 2: Short Papers)*, pages 182–188. Association for Computational Linguistics.

Haina Tang, Xiangpeng Zhao, and Yongmao Ren. 2019. A multilayer recognition model for twitter user geolocation. *Wireless Networks*, pages 1–6.

Ashish Vaswani, Noam Shazeer, Niki Parmar, Jakob Uszkoreit, Llion Jones, Aidan N Gomez, Łukasz Kaiser, and Illia Polosukhin. 2017. Attention is all you need. In *Advances in Neural Information Processing Systems*, pages 5998–6008.

Benjamin Wing and Jason Baldridge. 2014. Hierarchical discriminative classification for text-based geolocation. In *Proceedings of the 2014 Conference on Empirical Methods in Natural Language Processing (EMNLP)*, pages 336–348.

Zichao Yang, Diyi Yang, Chris Dyer, Xiaodong He, Alex Smola, and Eduard Hovy. 2016. Hierarchical attention networks for document classification. In *Proceedings of the 2016 Conference of the North American Chapter of the Association for Computational Linguistics: Human Language Technologies*, pages 1480–1489.

Dense Node Representation for Geolocation

Tommaso Fornaciari, Dirk Hovy
Bocconi University, Milan, Italy
`{fornaciari|dirk.hovy}@unibocconi.it`

Abstract

Prior research has shown that geolocation can be substantially improved by including user network information. While effective, it suffers from the curse of dimensionality, since networks are usually represented as sparse adjacency matrices of connections, which grow exponentially with the number of users. In order to incorporate this information, we therefore need to limit the network size, in turn limiting performance and risking sample bias. In this paper, we address these limitations by instead using dense network representations. We explore two methods to learn continuous node representations from either 1) the network structure with `node2vec` (Grover and Leskovec, 2016), or 2) *textual* user mentions via `doc2vec` (Le and Mikolov, 2014). We combine both methods with input from social media posts in an attention-based convolutional neural network and evaluate the contribution of each component on geolocation performance. Our method enables us to incorporate arbitrarily large networks in a fixed-length vector, without limiting the network size. Our models achieve competitive results with similar state-of-the-art methods, but with much fewer model parameters, while being applicable to networks of virtually any size.

1 Introduction

Current state-of-the-art methods for user geolocation in social media rely on a number of data sources. Text is the main source, since people use location-specific terms (Salehi et al., 2017). However, research has shown that text should be augmented with network information, since people interact with other from their local social circles. Even though social media allows for worldwide connections, most people have a larger number of connections with people who live close-by (from their school, workplace, or friend network). The most successful predictive models are therefore architectures that combine these different kinds of inputs (Rahimi et al., 2018; Ebrahimi et al., 2018).

However, incorporating network information is the computational bottleneck of these hybrid approaches: we want to represent the whole network, but we have to do so efficiently. We show that both are possible with dense representations, and indeed improve performance over previous sparse graph network representations. Following graph theory (Bondy et al., 1976), networks are typically represented as connections between entities in a square adjacency matrix, whose size corresponds to the number of users in the network. This means, though, that the matrix grows quadratically with the number of nodes/users. For large-scale social media analysis, where the number of users is often in the millions, this property creates a computational bottleneck: Incorporating such a matrix in a neural architecture, for example through graph-convolution (Kipf and Welling, 2017), easily increases the parameters by orders of magnitude, making training more expensive and increasing the risk of overfitting.

Previous work has therefore usually resorted to sampling methods. While sampling addresses the space issue, it necessarily loses a large amount of information, especially in complex networks, and introduces the risk of sampling biases.

Compounding the problem is the fact that adjacency matrices, despite their size, are very sparse, and do not represent information efficiently. This problem is analogous to sparse word and text representations, which were successfully replaced by dense embeddings (Mikolov et al., 2013a).

We show how to incorporate dense network representations in two ways: 1) with an existing word2vec-based method based on network structure, node2vec (Grover and Leskovec, 2016), and 2) with a new, doc2vec-based method of document

Proceedings of the 2019 EMNLP Workshop W-NUT: The 5th Workshop on Noisy User-generated Text, pages 224–230
Hong Kong, Nov 4, 2019. ©2019 Association for Computational Linguistics

representations (Le and Mikolov, 2014) over the set of user mentions in the text of posts (M2V). Both allow us to represent mentions as dense vectors that encode the network interactions so that similar users will have similar representations. However, they capture different aspects of interactions: people we are connected with vs. people we mention.

We compare the geolocation performance of models that combine a text view with the network views of both node2vec *and* the doc2vec-based method. We measure the contribution of each component to performance. Our results show that dense network representations significantly improve over sparse network representations, but that mention representations (M2V) are more important than structure representations (node2vec).

Contributions The contributions of the study are the following:

- We propose a document embeddings application that builds effective network representations through dense vectors, with no need of sampling procedures even in large networks;

- We show that the node representations can be tuned via two parameters which model the width and strength of their interactions.

2 Related work

Different kinds of data sources and methods can be used for the geolocation of users in Social Media. The the most straightforward approach is to exploit the geographic information conveyed by the linguistic behavior of the user. The first studies relied on the idea of exploiting *Location Indicative Words* (LIW) (Han et al., 2012, 2014). More recently, neural models have been applied to the same strategy (Rahimi et al., 2017; Tang et al., 2019), improving performance.

The problem, however, can be modeled in different ways, including the different designs of the geographic areas to predict, such as grids (Wing and Baldridge, 2011), hierarchical grids (Wing and Baldridge, 2014), or different kinds of clusters (Han et al., 2012, 2014). In this paper, we test our models both on the set of geographic areas - i.e., labels - used in the shared task of the Workshop on Noisy User-generated Text - W-NUT (Han et al., 2016), and the more fine-grained clusters obtained through the method of Fornaciari and Hovy (2019b). Geographic coordinates themselves can

also be exploited, as Fornaciari and Hovy (2019a) showed in a multi-task model that jointly predicts continuous geocoordinates and discrete labels.

In general, geolocation with multi-source models is becoming more popular, as indicated by their increased use in state-of-the-art performances. Miura et al. (2016, 2017) considered text, metadata and network information, modeling the last as a combination user and city embeddings. Similarly to our study, Rahimi et al. (2015) exploited the mentions, even though they used them to build undirected graphs. Ebrahimi et al. (2017, 2018) also used mentions to create an undirected graph, that they pruned and fed into an embedding layer followed by an attention mechanism, in order to create a network representation.

The study of Rahimi et al. (2018) is an example of network segmentation for use in a neural model. They propose a Graph Convolutional Neural Network (GCN), where network and text data are vertically concatenated in a single channel, rather than employed as parallel channels into the same model. Do et al. (2017, 2018) present the Multi-Entry Neural Network (MENET), a model which, similarly to our study, employs node2vec and, separately, includes doc2vec as methods for extraction of document features.

These works represent the state-of-the-art benchmark with respect to the implementation of network views in the models. Other models (Ebrahimi et al., 2017, 2018; Do et al., 2018) also include metadata or other source of information.

3 Methods

3.1 The data sets

We test our methods on three data sets: GEOTEXT (Eisenstein et al., 2010), TWITTER-US (Roller et al., 2012) and TWITTER-WORLD (Han et al., 2012). They contain English tweets, concatenated by author, with geographic coordinates associated with each author. GEOTEXT contains 10K texts, TWITTER-US 450K and TWITTER-WORLD 1.390M. The corpora are each split into training, development and test sets.

3.2 Learning network representations

3.2.1 *node2vec*

Grover and Leskovec (2016) presented node2vec, a method to obtain dense node representations through a skip-gram model. Those representations, however, are obtained through a tiered sampling procedure. While that allows node2vec to explore large networks, by balancing the breadth and depth of the search for the neighbours' identification, it does introduce a random factor. In addition, since node2vec uses the word2vec skip-gram model (Mikolov et al., 2013c), the sequence of the nodes does not carry any meaning, essentially functioning as a further random neighbors selection. In the geolocation scenario, though, network breadth is more important than depth, as similarity between entities grows with their proximity: we would like to preserve this is information entirely, even and especially in large networks. For this reason, we follow the authors settings for the detection of nodes' homophily, rather than their structural similarity in the network, and set the *node2vec* parameters $p = 1$ and $q = 0.5$ (Grover and Leskovec, 2016, p. 11).

3.2.2 *mentions2vec* - M2V

We introduce a novel network representation method which does not depend on graph theory. We bypass the adjacency matrices and directly learn the social interactions from the *content* of social media messages. In many social media this is straightforward, as the users' mentions are introduced by the at sign '@', but in general other forms of Named Entity Recognition (NER) might be considered for the same purpose.

Concretely, we filter from the text everything but the user mentions and apply *doc2vec* to the resulting "texts" (Mikolov et al., 2013b). Basically, we are representing the users according to their communicative behavior directed at other users, in the temporal order these mentions appear in. Therefore, similarly to node2vec, M2V creates a dense representation of the user interactions.

As pointed out earlier, node2vec is applied to a sequence of nodes sampled form the whole network that does not account for temporal ordering. In contrast, M2V does not address nodes, but mentions, which are themselves an evidence of personal connection. The consequence of this choice is two-fold. First, there is no need for a sampling procedure: the whole set of interactions can be considered, even for wide networks. Second, the order of the mentions in the texts reflects the time sequence of the interactions, possibly encoding patterns of social behaviors.

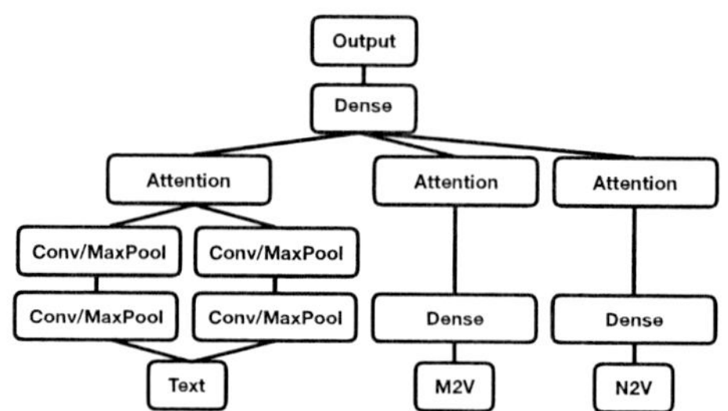

Figure 1: The Multiview Attention-based Convolutional Model. The inputs are the texts, mentions2vec (M2V) and *node2vec* (N2V)

3.3 Labels

For our experiments we use two different sets of labels: those used in the W-NUT 2016 task (Han et al., 2016), and our own labels (Fornaciari and Hovy, 2019b). Our label identification method, called point2city (P2C), clusters all points closer than 25 km and associates each cluster with the closest town of at least 15K people. For further details, see Fornaciari and Hovy (2019b). The resulting labels are highly granular and precise in the identification of meaningful administrative regions.

3.4 Feature selection

The label sets were involved in the preprocessing as follows. Using only the training data, we first select the terms with frequency greater or equal to 10 and 5 for TWITTER-US and TWITTER-WORLD, respectively. This choice is motivated by the different vocabulary size of the two data sets. Any term with frequency greater than 2, but below these thresholds, which is associated with only one label, we replace with label-representative tokens. Low-frequency terms found in more than one place are considered geographically ambiguous and discarded. This allows us to reduce remarkably the vocabulary size, maintaining the useful geographic information of the huge amount of low frequency terms. Considering the terms' Zipf distribution (Powers, 1998), this procedure allows us to replace a small number of types, but a great number of tokens.

Following Han et al. (2012), we further filter the vocabulary by applying Information Gain Ratio (IGR), selecting the terms with the highest values until we reach a manageable vocabulary size: 750K and 470K for TWITTER-US and TWITTER-WORLD.

| | | TWITTER-US | | | |
Authors, method + labels	nr. labels	Acc	Acc@161	mean	median
Han et al. (2014), NB + IGR	378	26%	45%	-	260
Wing and Baldridge (2014), HierLR k-d	"fewer classes"	-	48%	687	191
Rahimi et al. (2017), MLP + k-tree	256	-	55%	581	91
AttCNN + k-d tree	256	27.86%	57.85%	565.64	64.25
AttCNN-N2V + k-d tree	256	28.2%	56.99%	550.77	68.41
AttCNN-M2V + k-d tree	256	29.84%[*]	56.77%	546.97	67.91
AttCNN-M2V-N2V + k-d tree	256	29.12%	56.16%	563.52	77.63
AttCNN + P2C	914	51.22%	61.97%	523.42	0
AttCNN-N2V + P2C	914	51.9%	62.36%	518.34	0
AttCNN-M2V + P2C	914	53.04%[**]	63.64%[**]	483.09[*]	0
AttCNN-M2V-N2V + P2C	914	52.93%[**]	62.91%[**]	510.98[**]	0

Table 1: Model performance and significance levels with respect to text-only models: $^{*} : p \leq 0.05$, $^{**} : p \leq 0.01$

| | | TWITTER-WORLD | | | |
Authors, method + labels	nr. labels	Acc	Acc@161	mean	median
Han et al. (2014), NB + IGR	3135	13%	26%	-	913
Wing and Baldridge (2014), HierLR k-d	"fewer classes"	-	31%	1670	509
Rahimi et al. (2017), MLP + k-tree	930	-	36%	1417	373
AttCNN + k-d tree	930	20.0%	36.39%	1458.63	414.29
AttCNN-N2V + k-d tree	930	22.3%[**]	40.02%[**]	1363.11[**]	330.69[**]
AttCNN-M2V + k-d tree	930	29.26%[**]	46.05%[**]	1155.5[**]	230.17[**]
AttCNN-M2V-N2V + k-d tree	930	28.76%[**]	46.31%[**]	1191.19[**]	223.96[**]
AttCNN + P2C	2818	28.39%	42.5%	1195.92	274.06
AttCNN-N2V + P2C	2818	28.48%	42.18%	1220.02	280.66
AttCNN-M2V + P2C	2818	34.58%[**]	47.91%[**]	1134.08[**]	194.03[**]
AttCNN-M2V-N2V + P2C	2818	33.98%[**]	47.19%[**]	1180.21[**]	208.03[**]

Table 2: Model performance and significance levels with respect to text-only model AttCNN: $^{*} : p \leq 0.05$, $^{**} : p \leq 0.01$

3.5 Multiview Attention-based Convolutional Models

Our models are multi-view neural networks with three input channels: the text view, *node2vec*, and *mentions2vec*. The text view, in turn, contains two channels of convolutional/max pooling layers (with window size 4 and 8) followed by an attention mechanism. Both *node2vec* and *mentions2vec* are fed into a dense layer, followed by an attention mechanism. All the outputs are then concatenated and fed into a fully connected output layer. For a graphical representation, see Figure 1.

We report the performance metrics commonly considered in the literature: accuracy, acc@161 - i.e., the accuracy within 161 km, or 100 miles, from the target point. This allows us to measure the accuracy of predictions within a reasonable distance from the target point. We also report mean and median distance between the predicted and the target points. We evaluate significance via bootstrap sampling, following Søgaard

et al. (2014). The code for the methods described in this paper are available at github.com/Bocconi-NLPLab.

4 Results

Tables 1 and 2 show the performance of our models with and without N2V/M2V, in TWITTER-US and TWITTER-WORLD. Compared to the previous studies using only textual features, our basic model AttCNN shows comparable (TWITTER-WORLD) or better performance (TWITTER-US).

Therefore we consider our base AttCNN model as baseline comparison for the hybrid models AttCNN-N2V, AttCNN-M2V and AttCNN-M2V-N2V. We test two label sets (k-d tree and P2C), and the significance level remarkably changes in these two conditions.

In TWITTER-US, with coarse granularity labels, there is no performance improvement with dense node representations. In contrast, the models with M2V show a significant effect with fine

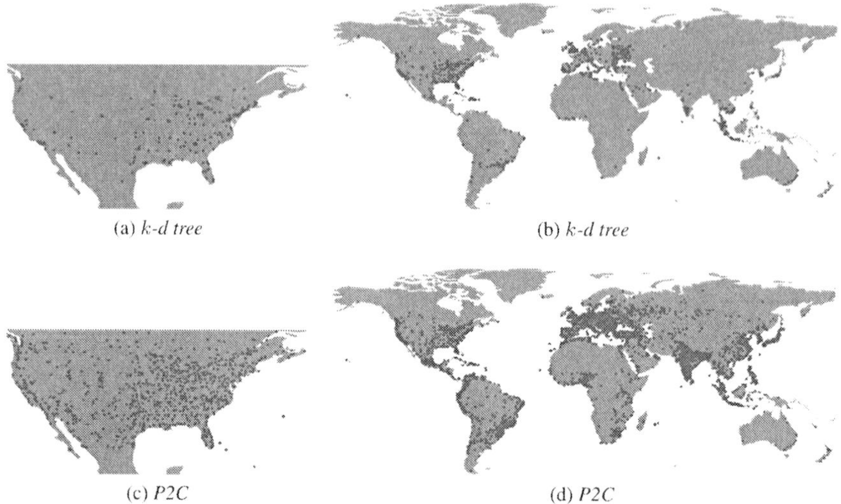

(a) *k-d tree* (b) *k-d tree*

(c) *P2C* (d) *P2C*

Figure 2: Labels' coordinates in TWITTER-USand TWITTER-WORLD

granularity labels. In TWITTER-WORLD, the dense node representations significantly improve the models' performance, with both kind of labels, even though AttCNN-N2V does not show improvements with P2C labels.

5 Discussion

Mentions2vec is a computationally affordable method for dense network representations, designed to capture social interactions. It proves very effective under most experimental conditions. The results suggest that dense users' network representation enhance geolocation performance, in particular when fine-grained labels identify specific geographic areas, rather than when a small number of labels refers to larger areas, where more different social communities can be found. Figure 2 shows the different density of labels identified by k-d tree and P2C. These settings are particularly useful for M2V, which considers the users' linguistic behavior. In contrast, *Node2vec* does not lead to significant improvement in TWITTER-US, presumably because the sampling procedure of *node2vec* does not allow to detect homophily with sufficient clarity. *Mentions2vec*, which does not suffer from this limitation, appears to be more effective in that context. However, in general, the labels' granularity affects the usefulness of the methods. In TWITTER-US, using labels which cover large areas is detrimental for techniques which address geographical homophily, that is,

relatively small cultural/linguistic areas. Even so, it makes sense to use these techniques, as in favourable conditions (for example in TWITTER-WORLD), they lead to remarkable performance improvements.

Acknowledgments

The authors would like to thank the reviewers of the various drafts for their comments. Both authors are members of the Bocconi Institute for Data Science and Analytics (BIDSA) and the Data and Marketing Insights (DMI) unit. This research was supported by a GPU donation from Nvidia, as well as a research grant from CERMES to set up a GPU server, which enabled us to run these experiments.

References

John Adrian Bondy, Uppaluri Siva Ramachandra Murty, et al. 1976. *Graph theory with applications*, volume 290. Citeseer.

Tien Huu Do, Duc Minh Nguyen, Evaggelia Tsiligianni, Bruno Cornelis, and Nikos Deligiannis. 2017. Multiview deep learning for predicting twitter users' location. *arXiv preprint arXiv:1712.08091*.

Tien Huu Do, Duc Minh Nguyen, Evaggelia Tsiligianni, Bruno Cornelis, and Nikos Deligiannis. 2018. Twitter user geolocation using deep multiview learning. In *2018 IEEE International Conference on Acoustics, Speech and Signal Processing (ICASSP)*, pages 6304–6308. IEEE.

Mohammad Ebrahimi, Elaheh ShafieiBavani, Raymond Wong, and Fang Chen. 2017. Exploring celebrities on inferring user geolocation in twitter. In *Pacific-Asia Conference on Knowledge Discovery and Data Mining*, pages 395–406. Springer.

Mohammad Ebrahimi, Elaheh ShafieiBavani, Raymond Wong, and Fang Chen. 2018. A unified neural network model for geolocating twitter users. In *Proceedings of the 22nd Conference on Computational Natural Language Learning*, pages 42–53.

Jacob Eisenstein, Brendan O'Connor, Noah A Smith, and Eric P Xing. 2010. A latent variable model for geographic lexical variation. In *Proceedings of the 2010 conference on empirical methods in natural language processing*, pages 1277–1287. Association for Computational Linguistics.

Tommaso Fornaciari and Dirk Hovy. 2019a. Geolocation with Attention-Based Multitask Learning Models. In *Proceedings of the 5th Workshop on Noisy User-generated Text (WNUT)*.

Tommaso Fornaciari and Dirk Hovy. 2019b. Identifying Linguistic Areas for Geolocation. In *Proceedings of the 5th Workshop on Noisy User-generated Text (WNUT)*.

Aditya Grover and Jure Leskovec. 2016. node2vec: Scalable feature learning for networks. In *Proceedings of the 22nd ACM SIGKDD international conference on Knowledge discovery and data mining*, pages 855–864. ACM.

Bo Han, Paul Cook, and Timothy Baldwin. 2012. Geolocation prediction in social media data by finding location indicative words. *Proceedings of COLING 2012*, pages 1045–1062.

Bo Han, Paul Cook, and Timothy Baldwin. 2014. Text-based twitter user geolocation prediction. *Journal of Artificial Intelligence Research*, 49:451–500.

Bo Han, Afshin Rahimi, Leon Derczynski, and Timothy Baldwin. 2016. Twitter Geolocation Prediction Shared Task of the 2016 Workshop on Noisy User-generated Text. In *Proceedings of the 2nd Workshop on Noisy User-generated Text (WNUT)*, pages 213–217.

Thomas N Kipf and Max Welling. 2017. Semi-supervised classification with graph convolutional networks. In *Proceedings of the International Conference on Learning Representations (ICLR)*.

Quoc Le and Tomas Mikolov. 2014. Distributed representations of sentences and documents. In *International Conference on Machine Learning*, pages 1188–1196.

Tomas Mikolov, Kai Chen, Greg Corrado, and Jeffrey Dean. 2013a. Efficient estimation of word representations in vector space. *arXiv preprint arXiv:1301.3781*.

Tomas Mikolov, Ilya Sutskever, Kai Chen, Greg S Corrado, and Jeff Dean. 2013b. Distributed representations of words and phrases and their compositionality. In *Advances in neural information processing systems*, pages 3111–3119.

Tomas Mikolov, Wen-tau Yih, and Geoffrey Zweig. 2013c. Linguistic regularities in continuous space word representations. In *Proceedings of the 2013 Conference of the North American Chapter of the Association for Computational Linguistics: Human Language Technologies*, pages 746–751.

Yasuhide Miura, Motoki Taniguchi, Tomoki Taniguchi, and Tomoko Ohkuma. 2016. A simple scalable neural networks based model for geolocation prediction in twitter. In *Proceedings of the 2nd Workshop on Noisy User-generated Text (WNUT)*, pages 235–239.

Yasuhide Miura, Motoki Taniguchi, Tomoki Taniguchi, and Tomoko Ohkuma. 2017. Unifying text, metadata, and user network representations with a neural network for geolocation prediction. In *Proceedings of the 55th Annual Meeting of the Association for Computational Linguistics (Volume 1: Long Papers)*, volume 1, pages 1260–1272.

David MW Powers. 1998. Applications and explanations of zipf's law. In *Proceedings of the joint conferences on new methods in language processing and computational natural language learning*, pages 151–160. Association for Computational Linguistics.

Afshin Rahimi, Trevor Cohn, and Tim Baldwin. 2018. Semi-supervised user geolocation via graph convolutional networks. *arXiv preprint arXiv:1804.08049*, pages 2009–2019.

Afshin Rahimi, Trevor Cohn, and Timothy Baldwin. 2015. Twitter user geolocation using a unified text and network prediction model. *arXiv preprint arXiv:1506.08259*.

Afshin Rahimi, Trevor Cohn, and Timothy Baldwin. 2017. A neural model for user geolocation and lexical dialectology. *arXiv preprint arXiv:1704.04008*, pages 209–216.

Stephen Roller, Michael Speriosu, Sarat Rallapalli, Benjamin Wing, and Jason Baldridge. 2012. Supervised text-based geolocation using language models on an adaptive grid. In *Proceedings of the 2012 Joint Conference on Empirical Methods in Natural Language Processing and Computational Natural Language Learning*, pages 1500–1510. Association for Computational Linguistics.

Bahar Salehi, Dirk Hovy, Eduard Hovy, and Anders Søgaard. 2017. Huntsville, hospitals, and hockey teams: Names can reveal your location. In *Proceedings of the 3rd Workshop on Noisy User-generated Text*, pages 116–121.

Anders Søgaard, Anders Johannsen, Barbara Plank, Dirk Hovy, and Héctor Martínez Alonso. 2014. What's in a p-value in nlp? In *Proceedings of the eighteenth conference on computational natural language learning*, pages 1–10.

Haina Tang, Xiangpeng Zhao, and Yongmao Ren. 2019. A multilayer recognition model for twitter user geolocation. *Wireless Networks*, pages 1–6.

Benjamin Wing and Jason Baldridge. 2014. Hierarchical discriminative classification for text-based geolocation. In *Proceedings of the 2014 Conference on Empirical Methods in Natural Language Processing (EMNLP)*, pages 336–348.

Benjamin P Wing and Jason Baldridge. 2011. Simple supervised document geolocation with geodesic grids. In *Proceedings of the 49th annual meeting of the association for computational linguistics: Human language technologies-volume 1*, pages 955–964. Association for Computational Linguistics.

Identifying Linguistic Areas for Geolocation

Tommaso Fornaciari, Dirk Hovy
Bocconi University, Milan, Italy
{fornaciari|dirk.hovy}@unibocconi.it

Abstract

Geolocating social media posts relies on the assumption that language carries sufficient geographic information. However, locations are usually given as continuous latitude/longitude tuples, so we first need to define discrete geographic regions that can serve as labels. Most studies use some form of clustering to discretize the continuous coordinates (Han et al., 2016). However, the resulting regions do not always correspond to existing linguistic areas. Consequently, accuracy at 100 miles tends to be good, but degrades for finer-grained distinctions, when different linguistic regions get lumped together. We describe a new algorithm, Point-to-City (P2C), an iterative k-d tree-based method for clustering geographic coordinates and associating them with towns. We create three sets of labels at different levels of granularity, and compare performance of a state-of-the-art geolocation model trained and tested with P2C labels to one with regular k-d tree labels. Even though P2C results in substantially more labels than the baseline, model accuracy increases significantly over using traditional labels at the fine grained level, while staying comparable at 100 miles. The results suggest that identifying meaningful linguistic areas is crucial for improving geolocation at a fine-grained level.

1 Introduction

Predicting the location of a Social Media post involves first and foremost ways to identify the words that indicate geographic location. Secondly, and perhaps even more fundamentally, though, we also need to determine an effective notion of what a "location" is, i.e., what do our labels represent: a state, a city, a neighborhood, a street? In many NLP tasks, labels are ambiguous and open to interpretation (Plank et al., 2014). In geolocation, the information initially given is an unambiguous latitude/longitude pair, but this format captures a level of detail (precise down to a centimeter) that is both unnecessary and unrealistic for most practical applications. Collapsing coordinates to geographic categories is therefore a common step in geolocation. However, this discretization step is open to interpretation: what method should we choose?

Previous work includes three different approaches to discretizing continuous values into location labels (see also Section 2):

1.) Geodesic grids are the most straightforward, but do not "lead to a natural representation of the administrative, population-based or language boundaries in the region" (Han et al., 2012).

2.) Clustering coordinates prevents the identification of (nearly) empty locations and keeps points which are geographically close together in one location. Unfortunately, in crowded regions, clusters might be too close to each other, and therefore divide cultural/linguistic areas into meaningless groups.

3.) Predefined administrative regions, like cities, can provide homogeneous interpretable areas. However, mapping coordinates to the closest city can be ambiguous. Previous work typically considered cities with a population of at least 100K (Han et al., 2012, 2014). This approach has the opposite problem of clustering: different linguistic areas might be contained within a single administrative region.

Here, we propose Point-To-City (P2C), a new method mapping continuous coordinates to locations. It combines the strengths of the last two approaches, keeping coordinates which appear close to each other in the same location, while also representing them in terms of meaningful administrative regions, with adjustable granularity. We show that these two criteria also result in superior prediction performance for geolocation.

Relying on k-d trees (Maneewongvatana and Mount, 1999), P2C iteratively clusters points

Proceedings of the 2019 EMNLP Workshop W-NUT: The 5th Workshop on Noisy User-generated Text, pages 231–236
Hong Kong, Nov 4, 2019. ©2019 Association for Computational Linguistics

within a specified maximum distance d, and maps them to the coordinates of the closest town with a minimum population size.

We evaluate P2C on two data sets commonly used for geolocation. We create three different conditions by using three different values for d as maximum distance between points, and compare the results to those obtained using k-d tree labels (as used in the W-NUT shared task (Han et al., 2016)). For all four labeling schemes, we train an attention-based convolutional neural network, and evaluate mean and median distance between target and predicted point, and accuracy within 161 km (Acc@161). We also show the standard accuracy score relative to the specific labels, usually much worse than Acc@161, and often not reported in the literature.

Our results show that P2C reliably produces Acc@161 performance which is comparable with state-of-the-art models. For exact accuracy, however, P2C labels always result in substantially better performance than previous methods, in spite of the larger set of classes. This suggests that P2C captures more meaningful location distinctions (backed up by a qualitative analysis), and that previous labels capture only broader, linguistically mixed areas. More generally, our results show that language reflects social and geographical distinctions in the world, and that more meaningful real-world labels help language-based prediction models to perform their task more efficiently.

Contributions The contributions of this paper are the following: 1.) we propose P2C, a k-d tree based procedure to cluster geographic points associated with existing towns within a certain distance between town and cluster centroid. 2.) we show that P2C produces more meaningful, interpretable cultural and linguistic locations 3.) we show that P2C labels substantially improve model performance in exact, fine-grained classification

2   Related work

Geolocation prediction can, in principle, be modeled both as regression and as classification problem. In practice, however, given the difficulty of predicting continuous coordinate values, regression is often carried out in conjunction with the classification (Eisenstein et al., 2010; Lourentzou et al., 2017; Fornaciari and Hovy, 2019b). In general, however, the task is considered a classification problem, which requires solutions for the identification of geographic regions as labels.

Geodesic grids were used for the geolocation of posts on Flickr, Twitter and Wikipedia (Serdyukov et al., 2009; Wing and Baldridge, 2011).

Hulden et al. (2015) noticed that "using smaller grid sizes leads to an immediate sparse data problem since very few features/words are [selectively] observed in each cell".

In order to enhance the expressiveness of the geographic cells, Wing and Baldridge (2014), constructed both flat and hierarchical grids relying on k-d tree, and testing their methods at different levels of granularity. The same labels were used in the study of Rahimi et al. (2018).

Han et al. (2012, 2014), who released TWITTER-WORLD, use the information provided by the Geoname dataset[1] in order to identify a set of cities around the world with at least 100K inhabitants. Then they refer their geo-tagged texts to those cities, creating easily interpretable geographic places. Cha et al. (2015) proposed a voting-based grid selection scheme, with the classification referred to regions/states in US.

Most works use deep learning techniques for classification (Miura et al., 2016). Often, they include multi-view models, considering different sources (Miura et al., 2017; Lau et al., 2017; Ebrahimi et al., 2018; Fornaciari and Hovy, 2019a). In particular, Lau et al. (2017) implemented a multi-channel convolutional network, structurally similar to our model. Rahimi et al. (2018) proposes a Graph-Convolutional neural network, though the text features are represented by a bag-of-words, while we rely on word embeddings.

The ability of the labels to reflect real anthropological areas, however, affects primarily the models which rely on linguistic data. This is the case of the studies of Han et al. (2012) and Han et al. (2014) who based their predictions on the so-called *Location-Indicative Words* (LIW). Recently, neural models have been built with the same purpose (Rahimi et al., 2017; Tang et al., 2019).

3   Methods

Data sets We apply our method to two widely used data sets for geolocation: TWITTER-US (Roller et al., 2012), and TWITTER-WORLD (Han et al., 2012). They are all collections of En-

---

[1] http://www.geonames.org

glish tweets aggregated by author and labeled with geographic coordinates. TWITTER-US and TWITTER-WORLD contain 450K and 1.39M texts, respectively. They are each divided into their own training, development, and test sets. Readers are referred to the respective papers for additional details. We round the coordinates to the second decimal number. A distance of 0.01 degrees corresponds to less than 1.1 km on the longitude axis (the distance is not constant on the latitude axis). Smaller distinctions are not relevant for any common NLP task.

Data set	d	labels	mean	median
Tw.-US	.1	1554	7.07	3.81
	.25	914	9.10	5.64
	.5	418	15.54	12.21
	W-NUT	256	–	–
Tw.-WORLD	.1	3047	0.45	0.00
	.25	2818	1.77	0.00
	.5	2350	3.28	2.39
	W-NUT	930	–	–

Table 1: Number of labels and mean/median distance in km between instances and the cluster town center. For W-NUT, distance can not be computed, as centroids are not close to meaningful places

Point-To-City (P2C)   For the classification, we need to identify labels corresponding to existing cultural/linguistic areas, so that the geographic information conveyed through language can be fully exploited. To this end, P2C iteratively creates clusters of points, and afterwards associates the final clusters with specific towns.

The parameter d controls the maximum spherical distance we allow between points assigned to the same cluster at the initialization step. We run P2C considering three values: 0.1, 0.25, and 0.5 coordinate decimal points, which correspond to 11.12 km (6.91 miles), 27.80 km (17.27 miles), and 55.60 km (34.55 miles) on the longitude axis. We use these values to explore the feasibility of finer (and more challenging) predictions than those usually accepted in the literature.

One of the most popular metrics in previous studies (see Section 2 and 4) is the accuracy of the predictions within 161 km, or 100 mi, from the target point. In contrast, we are interested in the accuracy relative to the precise prediction of the labels, and we want labels representing points aggregated according to a distance much smaller than 161 km/100 mi: even the highest value we

choose for d, 0.5, is about one third the distance of accuracy at 161 km (Acc@161). However, since P2C iteratively creates clusters of clusters, it is possible that the original points belonging to different clusters are further apart than the threshold of d. For this reason, we selected values of d which are about three to fifteen times smaller than 161 km/100 mi.

Given d and a set of coordinate points/instances in the data set, P2C iterates over the following steps until convergence:

1. for each point, apply k-d trees to find clusters of points where each pair has a reciprocal distance less than d;

2. remove redundant clusters by ordering their elements (e.g., (A, B) vs. (B, A));

3. remove subsets of larger clusters (e.g. (A, B) vs. (A, B, C));

4. compute clusters' centroids as the average coordinates of all points belonging to the cluster;

5. assign the points which fall into more than one cluster to the one with the nearest centroid;

6. substitute each instance's coordinates with the centroid coordinates of the corresponding cluster.

The algorithm converges when the final number of points cannot be further reduced, since they all are farther apart from each other than the maximum distance d. After assigning each instance its new coordinates, we follow Han et al. (2012, 2014) in using the GeoNames data set to associate clusters with cities, by substituting the instance coordinates with those of the closest town center. In our case, however, rather than collecting cities with a population of at least 100K, we consider all towns with a population of at least 15K.

This last step further reduces the set of points associated with our instances. Table 1 shows the resulting number of labels, and the mean distance in km between the new instance coordinates and the respective town center.

This choice of 15K inhabitants is coherent with the settings of d: we aim to account for linguistic/social environments more specific than the broad and compound communities of densely populated cities. This is helpful for high resolution

method	model	# labels	Acc	Acc@161	mean	median
TWITTER-US						
Han et al. (2014)	NB + IGR	378	26%	45%	-	260
Wing and Baldridge (2014)	HierLR k-d	"fewer classes"	-	48%	687	191
Rahimi et al. (2017)	MLP + k-d tree	256	-	55%	581	91
	Att-CNN + k-d tree	256	26.17%	55.27%	580.7	93.02
	Att-CNN + P2C .1	1554	44.04%[*]	59.76%[*]	544.35[*]	47.19[*]
	Att-CNN + P2C .25	914	49.08%[*]	60.4%[*]	537.0[*]	39.71[*]
	Att-CNN + P2C .5	418	54.73%[*]	58.56%	537.79[*]	0[*]
TWITTER-WORLD						
Han et al. (2014)	NB + IGR	3135	13%	26%	-	913
Wing and Baldridge (2014)	HierLR k-d	"fewer classes"	-	31%	1670	509
Rahimi et al. (2017)	MLP + k-d tree	930	-	36%	1417	373
	Att-CNN + k-d tree	930	18.35%	33.85%	1506.33	469.48
	Att-CNN + P2C .1	3047	22.57%[*]	39.41%[*]	1372.3[*]	328.42[*]
	Att-CNN + P2C .25	2818	26.68%[*]	39.94%[*]	1269.13[*]	299.04[*]
	Att-CNN + P2C .5	2350	32.64%[*]	41.8%[*]	1257.36[*]	292.09[*]

Table 2: Performance of prior work and of the proposed model with W-NUT and P2C labels. [*] : $p \leq 0.01$.

geolocation both in the case of crowded regions and of areas with low density of inhabitants. However, we found that in spite of qualified information, such as the annual Worlds Cities report of the United Nations, it is actually difficult to set an optimal threshold. In fact, not even that document provides a detailed profile of small towns at a global level. Therefore we rely on the format of the information offered by Geonames.

The code for computing P2C is available at github.com/Bocconi-NLPLab.

Feature selection The two corpora have very different vocabulary sizes. Despite fewer instances, TWITTER-US contains a much richer vocabulary than TWITTER-WORLD: 14 vs. 6.5 millions words. This size is computationally infeasible. In order to maximize discrimination, we filter the vocabulary with several steps.

In order not to waste the possible geographic information carried by the huge amount of low frequency terms, we use replacement tokens as follows: We again take only the training data into account. First, we discard the hapax legomena, that is the words with frequency 1, as there is no evidence that these words could be found elsewhere. Then, we discard words with frequency greater than 1, if they appear in more than one place. We replace low frequency terms which appear uniquely in on place with a replacement token specific for that place, i.e., label. Finally, we substitute these words with their replacement token in the whole corpus, including development and test

set. Since the word distribution follows the Zipf curve (Powers, 1998) we are able to exploit the geographic information of millions of words using only a small number of replacement tokens. The use of this information is fair, as it relies on the information present in the training set only. In terms of performance, however, the effect of the replacement tokens is theoretically not different from that resulting from the direct inclusion of the single words in the vocabulary. The benefit is in terms of noise reduction, for the selective removal of geographically ambiguous words, and computational affordability.

Following Han et al. (2012), we further filter the vocabulary via Information Gain Ratio (IGR), selecting the terms with the highest values until we reach a computationally feasible vocabulary size: here, 750K and 460K for TWITTER-US and TWITTER-WORLD.

Attention-based CNN For classification, we use an attention-based convolutional neural model. We first train our own word embeddings for each corpus, and feed the texts into two convolutional channels (with window size 4 and 8) and max-pooling, followed by an overall attention mechanism, and finally a fully-connected layer with softmax activation for prediction.

For evaluation, as discussed in Section 3, we use the common metrics considered in literature: acc@161, that is the accuracy within 161 km (100 mi) from the target point, and mean and median distance between the predicted and the target points. We are also interested in the exact accuracy. This metric is often not shown in literature, but is important for the geolocation in real case scenarios. We evaluate significance via bootstrap sampling, following Søgaard et al. (2014).

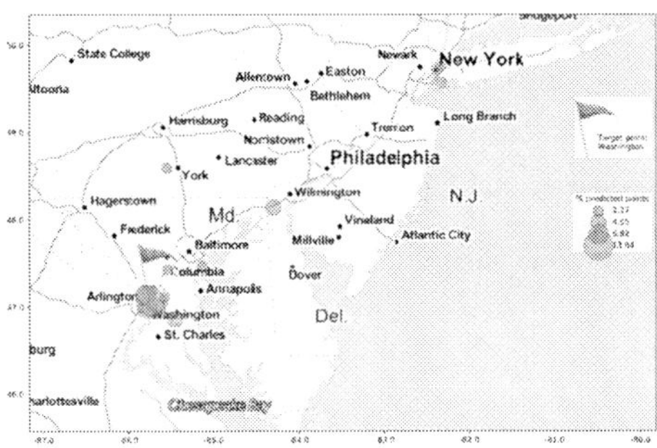

(a) W-NUT labels

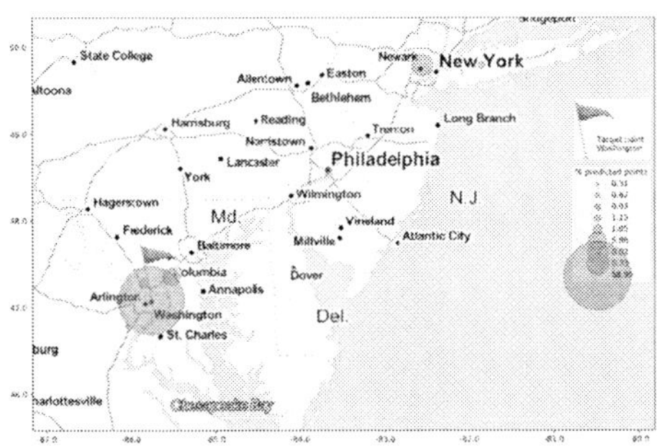

(b) P2C labels

Figure 1: Example of cumulative point accuracy with the two label sets for gold label Washington DC (flag). Circles are predictions, diameter represents percentage of predictions on that point.

4 Results

The model performance is shown in table 2. When applied to the W-NUT labels, our model replicates the results of Rahimi et al. (2017): in TWITTER-US the values correspond perfectly, in TWITTER-WORLD the Att-CNN performance is slightly lower. Compared to the W-NUT labels, the P2C labels are much more granular in every condition and, in spite of their apparent greater difficulty, they help to reach better performance in all metrics, with very high levels of significance. Such differences are surprisingly wide with respect to the accuracy: in TWITTER-US, for P2C with $d = .5$, the performance is more than doubled compared to the same model with the W-NUT k-d

tree labels (54% vs. 26%).

Figure 1 shows the coordinates of the W-NUT (1a) and of the P2C cluster centroids (1b). The diameter of the circles represent the rate correct prediction for those points. As can be seen, P2C identifies a unique linguistic region around Washington, while different W-NUT labels cover more or less the same area. P2C labels also allow a much better concentration of predictions in the same administrative/linguistic area.

5 Conclusion

P2C is a method for geographic labeling that dynamically clusters points and links them to specific towns. The aims are 1) to gather the points belonging to the same linguistic areas; 2) to associate such areas with distinct, existing administrative regions; 3) to improve the models' effectiveness, training them with texts showing consistent linguistic patterns. Compared to the W-NUT k-d tree labels, P2C leads to remarkably higher performance in all metrics, and in particular in the accuracy, even in spite of the higher number of labels identified. This suggests that techniques like P2C might be particularly useful when high performance at high levels of granularity is required.

Acknowledgments

The authors would like to thank the reviewers of the various drafts for their comments. Both authors are members of the Bocconi Institute for Data Science and Analytics (BIDSA) and the Data and Marketing Insights (DMI) unit. This research was supported by a GPU donation from Nvidia, as well as a research grant from CERMES to set up a GPU server, which enabled us to run these experiments.

References

Miriam Cha, Youngjune Gwon, and HT Kung. 2015. Twitter geolocation and regional classification via sparse coding. In *Ninth International AAAI Conference on Web and Social Media*.

Mohammad Ebrahimi, Elaheh ShafieiBavani, Raymond Wong, and Fang Chen. 2018. A unified neural network model for geolocating twitter users. In *Proceedings of the 22nd Conference on Computational Natural Language Learning*, pages 42–53.

Jacob Eisenstein, Brendan O'Connor, Noah A Smith, and Eric P Xing. 2010. A latent variable model for geographic lexical variation. In *Proceedings of the 2010 conference on empirical methods in natural language processing*, pages 1277–1287. Association for Computational Linguistics.

Tommaso Fornaciari and Dirk Hovy. 2019a. Dense Node Representation for Geolocation. In *Proceedings of the 5th Workshop on Noisy User-generated Text (WNUT)*.

Tommaso Fornaciari and Dirk Hovy. 2019b. Geolocation with Attention-Based Multitask Learning Models. In *Proceedings of the 5th Workshop on Noisy User-generated Text (WNUT)*.

Bo Han, Paul Cook, and Timothy Baldwin. 2012. Geolocation prediction in social media data by finding location indicative words. *Proceedings of COLING 2012*, pages 1045–1062.

Bo Han, Paul Cook, and Timothy Baldwin. 2014. Text-based twitter user geolocation prediction. *Journal of Artificial Intelligence Research*, 49:451–500.

Bo Han, Afshin Rahimi, Leon Derczynski, and Timothy Baldwin. 2016. Twitter Geolocation Prediction Shared Task of the 2016 Workshop on Noisy User-generated Text. In *Proceedings of the 2nd Workshop on Noisy User-generated Text (WNUT)*, pages 213–217.

Mans Hulden, Miikka Silfverberg, and Jerid Francom. 2015. Kernel density estimation for text-based geolocation. In *Twenty-Ninth AAAI Conference on Artificial Intelligence*.

Jey Han Lau, Lianhua Chi, Khoi-Nguyen Tran, and Trevor Cohn. 2017. End-to-end network for twitter geolocation prediction and hashing. *arXiv preprint arXiv:1710.04802*, pages 744–753.

Ismini Lourentzou, Alex Morales, and ChengXiang Zhai. 2017. Text-based geolocation prediction of social media users with neural networks. In *2017 IEEE International Conference on Big Data (Big Data)*, pages 696–705. IEEE.

Songrit Maneewongvatana and David M Mount. 1999. It's okay to be skinny, if your friends are fat. In *Center for Geometric Computing 4th Annual Workshop on Computational Geometry*, volume 2, pages 1–8.

Yasuhide Miura, Motoki Taniguchi, Tomoki Taniguchi, and Tomoko Ohkuma. 2016. A simple scalable neural networks based model for geolocation prediction in twitter. In *Proceedings of the 2nd Workshop on Noisy User-generated Text (WNUT)*, pages 235–239.

Yasuhide Miura, Motoki Taniguchi, Tomoki Taniguchi, and Tomoko Ohkuma. 2017. Unifying text, metadata, and user network representations with a neural network for geolocation prediction. In *Proceedings of the 55th Annual Meeting of the Association for Computational Linguistics (Volume 1: Long Papers)*, volume 1, pages 1260–1272.

Barbara Plank, Dirk Hovy, and Anders Søgaard. 2014. Linguistically debatable or just plain wrong? In *Proceedings of the 52nd Annual Meeting of the Association for Computational Linguistics (volume 2: Short Papers)*, pages 507–511.

David MW Powers. 1998. Applications and explanations of zipf's law. In *Proceedings of the joint conferences on new methods in language processing and computational natural language learning*, pages 151–160. Association for Computational Linguistics.

Afshin Rahimi, Trevor Cohn, and Tim Baldwin. 2018. Semi-supervised user geolocation via graph convolutional networks. *arXiv preprint arXiv:1804.08049*, pages 2009–2019.

Afshin Rahimi, Trevor Cohn, and Timothy Baldwin. 2017. A neural model for user geolocation and lexical dialectology. *arXiv preprint arXiv:1704.04008*, pages 209–216.

Stephen Roller, Michael Speriosu, Sarat Rallapalli, Benjamin Wing, and Jason Baldridge. 2012. Supervised text-based geolocation using language models on an adaptive grid. In *Proceedings of the 2012 Joint Conference on Empirical Methods in Natural Language Processing and Computational Natural Language Learning*, pages 1500–1510. Association for Computational Linguistics.

Pavel Serdyukov, Vanessa Murdock, and Roelof Van Zwol. 2009. Placing flickr photos on a map. In *Proceedings of the 32nd international ACM SIGIR conference on Research and development in information retrieval*, pages 484–491. ACM.

Anders Søgaard, Anders Johannsen, Barbara Plank, Dirk Hovy, and Héctor Martínez Alonso. 2014. What's in a p-value in nlp? In *Proceedings of the eighteenth conference on computational natural language learning*, pages 1–10.

Haina Tang, Xiangpeng Zhao, and Yongmao Ren. 2019. A multilayer recognition model for twitter user geolocation. *Wireless Networks*, pages 1–6.

Benjamin Wing and Jason Baldridge. 2014. Hierarchical discriminative classification for text-based geolocation. In *Proceedings of the 2014 Conference on Empirical Methods in Natural Language Processing (EMNLP)*, pages 336–348.

Benjamin P Wing and Jason Baldridge. 2011. Simple supervised document geolocation with geodesic grids. In *Proceedings of the 49th annual meeting of the association for computational linguistics: Human language technologies-volume 1*, pages 955–964. Association for Computational Linguistics.

Robustness to Capitalization Errors in Named Entity Recognition

Sravan Bodapati
Amazon.com
sravanb@amazon.com

Hyokun Yun
Amazon.com
yunhyoku@amazon.com

Yaser Al-Onaizan
Amazon.com
onaizan@amazon.com

Abstract

Robustness to capitalization errors is a highly desirable characteristic of named entity recognizers, yet we find standard models for the task are surprisingly brittle to such noise. Existing methods to improve robustness to the noise completely discard given orthographic information, which significantly degrades their performance on well-formed text. We propose a simple alternative approach based on data augmentation, which allows the model to *learn* to utilize or ignore orthographic information depending on its usefulness in the context. It achieves competitive robustness to capitalization errors while making negligible compromise to its performance on well-formed text and significantly improving generalization power on noisy user-generated text. Our experiments clearly and consistently validate our claim across different types of machine learning models, languages, and dataset sizes.

1 Introduction

In the last two decades, substantial progress has been made on the task of named entity recognition (NER), as it has enjoyed the development of probabilistic modeling (Lafferty et al., 2001; Finkel et al., 2005), methodology (Ratinov and Roth, 2009), deep learning (Collobert et al., 2011; Huang et al., 2015; Lample et al., 2016) as well as semi-supervised learning (Peters et al., 2017, 2018). Evaluation of these developments, however, has been mostly focused on their impact on global average metrics, most notably the micro-averaged F1 score (Chinchor, 1992).

For practical applications of NER, however, there can be other considerations for model evaluation. While standard training data for the task consists mainly of well formed text (Tjong Kim Sang, 2002; Pradhan and Xue, 2009), models trained on such data are often applied on a broad range of domains and genres by users who are not necessarily NLP experts, thanks to the proliferation of toolkits (Manning et al., 2014) and general-purpose machine learning services. Therefore, there is an increasing demand for the strong robustness of models to unexpected noise.

In this paper, we tackle one of the most common types of noise in applications of NER: unreliable capitalization. Noisiness in capitalization is a typical characteristic of user-generated text (Ritter et al., 2011; Baldwin et al., 2015), but it is not uncommon even in formal text. Headings, legal documents, or emphasized sentences are often capitalized. All-lowercased text, on the other hand, can be produced in large scale from upstream machine learning models such as speech recognizers and machine translators (Kubala et al., 1998), or processing steps in the data pipeline which are not fully under the control of the practitioner. Although a text without correct capitalization is perfectly legible for human readers (Cattell, 1886; Rayner, 1975) with only a minor impact on the reading speed (Tinker and Paterson, 1928; Arditi and Cho, 2007), we show that typical NER models are surprisingly brittle to all-uppercasing or all-lowercasing of text. The lack of robustness these models show to such common types of noise makes them unreliable, especially when characteristics of target text are not known a priori.

There are two standard treatments on the problem in the literature. The first is to train a case-agnostic model (Kubala et al., 1998; Robinson et al., 1999), and the second is to explicitly correct the capitalization (Srihari et al., 2003; Lita et al., 2003; Ritter et al., 2011). One of the main contributions of this paper is to empirically evaluate the effectiveness of these techniques across models, languages, and dataset sizes. However, both approaches have clear conceptual limitations. Case-agnostic models discard orthographic infor-

Proceedings of the 2019 EMNLP Workshop W-NUT: The 5th Workshop on Noisy User-generated Text, pages 237–242
Hong Kong, Nov 4, 2019. ©2019 Association for Computational Linguistics

	Annotation	O	O	O	B-ORG	I-ORG	E-ORG
(a)	Original Sentence	I	live	in	New	York	City
(b)	Lower-cased Sentence	i	live	in	new	york	city
(c)	Upper-cased Sentence	I	LIVE	IN	NEW	YORK	CITY

Table 1: Example of Data Augmentation

mation (how the given text was capitalized), which is considered to be highly useful (Robinson et al., 1999); our experimental results also support this. The second approach of correcting the capitalization of the text, on the other hand, requires an access to a high-quality truecasing model, and errors from the truecasing model would cascade to final named entity predictions.

We argue that an ideal approach should take a full advantage of orthographic information when it is correctly present, but rather than assuming the information to be always perfect, the model should be able to *learn* to ignore the orthographic information when it is unreliable. To this end, we propose a novel approach based on data augmentation (Simard et al., 2003). In computer vision, data augmentation is a highly successful standard technique (Krizhevsky et al., 2012), and it has found adoptions in natural language processing tasks such as text classification (Zhang and LeCun, 2015), question-answering (Yu et al., 2018) and low-resource learning (Sahin and Steedman, 2018). Consistently across a wide range of models (linear models, deep learning models to deep contextualized models), languages (English, German, Dutch, and Spanish), and dataset sizes (CoNLL 2003 and OntoNotes 5.0), the proposed method shows strong robustness while making little compromise to the performance on well-formed text.

2 Formulation

Let $\mathbf{x} = (x_1, x_2, \ldots, x_n)$ be a sequence of words in a sentence. We follow the standard approach of formulating NER as a sequence tagging task (Rabiner, 1989; Lafferty et al., 2001; Collins, 2002). That is, we predict a sequence of tags $\mathbf{y} = (y_1, y_2, \ldots, y_n)$ where each y_i identifies the type of the entity the word x_i belongs to, as well as the position of it in the surface form according to IOBES scheme (Uchimoto et al., 2000). See Table 1 (a) for an example annotated sentence. We train probabilistic models under the maximum likelihood principle, which produce a probability score $\mathbb{P}[\mathbf{y} \mid \mathbf{x}]$ for any possible output sequence $\mathbf{y}$.

All-uppercasing and all-lowercasing are common types of capitalization errors. Let $\mathrm{upper}(x_i)$ and $\mathrm{lower}(x_i)$ be functions that lower-cases and upper-cases the word x_i, respectively. Robustness of a probabilistic model to these types of noise can be understood as the quality of scoring function $\mathbb{P}[\mathbf{y} \mid \mathrm{upper}(x_1), \ldots, \mathrm{upper}(x_n)]$ and $\mathbb{P}[\mathbf{y} \mid \mathrm{lower}(x_1), \ldots, \mathrm{lower}(x_n)]$ in predicting the correct annotation $\mathbf{y}$, which can still be quantified with standard evaluation metrics such as the micro-F1 score.

3 Prior Work

There are two common strategies to improve robustness to capitalization errors. The first is to completely ignore orthograhpic information by using case-agnostic models (Kubala et al., 1998; Robinson et al., 1999). For linear models, this can be achieved by restricting the choice of features to case-agnostic ones. On the other hand, deep learning models without hand-curated features (Lample et al., 2016; Chiu and Nichols, 2016) can be easily made case-agnostic by lower-casing every input to the model. The second strategy is to explictly correct the capitalization by using another model trained for this purpose, which is called "truecasing"(Srihari et al., 2003; Lita et al., 2003). Both methods, however, have the common limitation that they discard orthographic information in the target text, which can be correct; this leads to degradation of performance on well-formed text.

4 Data Augmentation

Data augmentation refers to a technique of increasing the size of training data by adding label-preserving transformations of them (Simard et al., 2003). For example, in image classification, an object inside of an image does not change if the image is rotated, translated, or slightly skewed; most people would still recognize the same object they would find in the original image. By training a model on transformed versions of training images, the model becomes invariant to the transformations used (Krizhevsky et al., 2012).

In order to improve the robustness of NER models to capitalization errors, we appeal to the

Model	Method	CoNLL-2003 English			OntoNotes 5.0 English			Transfer to Twitter		
		Original	Lower	Upper	Original	Lower	Upper	Original	Lower	Upper
Linear	Baseline	89.2	57.8	75.2	81.7	37.4	15.1	24.4	6.9	20.2
	Caseless	83.7	83.7	83.7	75.5	75.5	75.5	20.3	20.3	20.3
	Truecasing	83.8	83.8	83.8	76.6	76.6	76.6	24.0	24.0	24.0
	DA	88.2	85.6	86.1	-	-	-	28.2	26.4	27.0
BiLSTM	Baseline	90.8	0.4	52.3	87.6	38.9	15.5	18.1	0.1	7.9
	Caseless	85.7	85.7	85.7	83.2	83.2	83.2	20.3	20.3	20.3
	Truecasing	84.6	84.6	84.6	81.7	81.7	81.7	18.7	18.7	18.7
	DA	90.4	85.3	83.8	87.5	83.2	82.6	21.2	17.7	18.4
ELMo	Baseline	92.0	34.8	71.6	88.7	66.6	48.9	31.6	1.5	19.6
	Caseless	89.1	89.1	89.1	85.3	85.3	85.3	31.8	31.8	31.8
	Truecasing	86.2	86.2	86.2	83.2	83.2	83.2	28.8	28.8	28.8
	DA	91.3	88.7	87.9	88.3	85.8	83.6	34.6	31.7	30.2

Table 2: F1 scores on original, lower-cased, and upper-cased test sets of English Datasets. Stanford Core NLP could not be trained on the augmented dataset even with 512GB of RAM.

same idea. When a sentence is all-lowercased or all-uppercased as in Table 1 (b) and (c), each word would still correspond to the same entity. This implies such transformations are also label-preserving ones: for a sentence $\mathbf{x}$ and its ground-truth annotation $\mathbf{y}$, $\mathbf{y}$ would still be a correct annotation for the all-uppercased sentence $(\mathrm{upper}(x_1), \ldots, \mathrm{upper}(x_n))$ as well as the all-lowercased version $(\mathrm{lower}(x_1), \ldots, \mathrm{lower}(x_n))$. Indeed, all three sentences (a), (b) and (c) in Table 1 would share the same annotation.

5 Experiments

We consider following three models, each of which is state-of-the-art in their respective group: **Linear**: Linear CRF model (Finkel et al., 2005) from Stanford Core NLP (Manning et al., 2014), which is representative of feature engineering approaches. **BiLSTM**: Deep learning model from Lample et al. (2016) which uses bidirectional LSTM for both character-level encoder and word-level encoder with CRF loss. This is the state-of-the-art supervised deep learning approach (Reimers and Gurevych, 2017). **ELMo**: Bidirectional LSTM-CRF model which uses contextualized features from deep bidirectional LSTM language model (Peters et al., 2018). For all models, we used hyperparameters from original papers.

We compare four strategies: **Baseline**: Models are trained on unmodified training data. **Caseless**: We lower-case input data both at the training time and at the test time. **Truecasing**: Models are still trained on unmodified training data, but every input to test data is "truecased" (Lita et al., 2003) using CRF truecasing model from Stanford Core NLP (Manning et al., 2014), which ignores given orthographic information in the text. Due to the lack of access to truecasing models in other languages, this strategy was used only on English. **DA (Data Augmentation)**: We augment the original training set with upper-cased and lower-cased versions of it, as discussed in Section 4.

We evaluate these models and methods on three versions of the test set for each dataset: **Original**: Original test data. **Upper**: All words are upper-cased. **Lower**: All words are lower-cased. Note that both Caseless and Truecasing method perform equally on all three versions because they ignore any original orthographic information in the *test* dataset. We focus on micro-averaged F1 scores.

We use CoNLL-2002 Spanish and Dutch (Tjong Kim Sang, 2002) and CoNLL-2003 English and German (Sang and De Meulder, 2003) to cover four languages, all of which orthographic information is useful in idenfitying named entities, and upper or lower-casing of text is straightforward. We additionally evaluate on OntoNotes 5.0 English (Pradhan and Xue, 2009), which is about five times larger than CoNLL datasets and contains more diverse genres. F1 scores are shown in Table 2 and 3.

Question 1: How robust are NER models to capitalization errors? Models trained with the standard Baseline strategy suffer from significant loss of performance when the test sentence is upper/lower-cased (compare 'Original' column with 'Lower' and 'Upper'). For example, F1 score of BiLSTM on lower-cased CoNLL-2003 English is abysmal 0.4%, completely losing any predictive power. Linear and ELMo are more robust than BiLSTM thanks to smaller capacity and semi supervision respectively, but the degradation is still strong, ranging 20pp to 60pp loss in F1.

Model	Method	CoNLL-2002 Spanish			CoNLL-2002 Dutch			CoNLL-2003 German		
		Original	Lower	Upper	Original	Lower	Upper	Original	Lower	Upper
Linear	Baseline	80.7	1.1	22.1	79.1	9.8	9.7	68.4	11.8	11.3
	Caseless	69.9	69.9	69.9	63.9	63.9	63.9	53.3	53.3	53.3
	DA	77.3	70.9	73.2	74.4	68.5	68.5	61.8	57.8	62.8
BiLSTM	Baseline	85.4	1.0	26.8	87.3	2.0	15.8	79.5	6.5	9.8
	Caseless	77.8	77.8	77.8	77.7	77.7	77.7	69.8	69.8	69.8
	DA	85.3	78.4	76.5	84.8	75.0	75.9	76.8	69.7	69.7

Table 3: F1 scores on original, lower-cased, and upper-cased test sets of Non-English Datasets

Question 2: How effective Caseless, Truecasing, and Data Augmentation approaches are in improving robustness of models? All methods show similar levels of performance on lower-cased or uppercased text. Since Caseless and Data Augmentation strategy do not require additional language-specifc resource as truecasing does, they seem to be superior to the truecasing approach, at least on CoNLL-2003 English and OntoNotes 5.0 datasets with the particular truecasing model used. Across all datasets, the performance of Linear model on lower-cased or upper-cased test set is consistently enhanced with data augmentation, compared with caseless models.

Question 3: How much performance on well-formed text is sacrificed due to robustness? Caseless and Truecasing methods are perfectly robust to capitalization errors, but only at the cost of significant degradation on well-formed text: caseless and truecasing strategy lose 5.1pp and 6.2pp respectively on the original test set of CoNLL-2003 English compared to Baseline strategy, and on non-English datasets the drop is even bigger. On the other hand, data augmentation preserves most of the performance on the original test set: with BiLSTM, its F1 score drops by only 0.4pp and 0.1pp respectively on CoNLL-2003 and OntoNotes 5.0 English. On non-English datasets, the drop is bigger (0.1pp on Spanish but 2.5pp on Dutch and 2.7pp on German) but still data augmentation performs about 7pp higher than Caseless on original well-formed text across languages.

Question 4: How do models trained on well-formed text generalize to noisy user-generated text? The robustness of models is especially important when the characteristics of target text are not known at the training time and can deviate significantly from those of training data. To this end, we trained models on CoNLL 2003-English, and evaluated them on annotations of Twitter data from Fromreide et al. (2014), which exhibits natural errors of capitalization common in user-generated text. 'Transfer to Twitter' column of Table 2 reports results. In this experiment, Data Augmentation approach consistently and significantly improves upon Baseline strategy by 3.8pp, 3.1pp, and 3.0pp with Linear, BiLSTM, and ELMo models respectively on Original test set of Twitter, demonstrating much strengthened generalization power when the test data is noisier than the training data.

In order to understand the results, we examined some samples from the dataset. Indeed, on a sentence like 'OHIO IS STUPID I HATE IT', BiLSTM model trained with Baseline strategy was unable to identify 'OHIO' as a location although the state is mentioned fifteen times in the training dataset of CoNLL 2003-English as 'Ohio'. BiLSTM models trained with all other strategies correctly identified the state. On the other hand, on another sample sentence 'Someone come with me to Raging Waters on Monday', BiLSTM models from Baseline and Data Augmentation strategies were able to correctly identify 'Raging Waters' as a location thanks to the proper capitalization, while the model from Caseless strategy failed on the entity due to its ignorance of orthographic information.

6   Conclusion

We proposed a data augmentation strategy for improving robustness of NER models to capitalization errors. Compared to previous methods, data augmentation provides competitive robustness while not sacrificing its performance on well-formed text, and improving generalization to noisy text. This is consistently observed across models, languages, and dataset sizes. Also, data augmentation does not require additional language-specific resource, and is trivial to implement for many natural languages. Therefore, we recommend to use data augmentation by default for training NER models, especially when characteristics of test data are little known a priori.

References

Aries Arditi and Jianna Cho. 2007. Letter case and text legibility in normal and low vision. *Vision research*, 47(19):2499–2505.

Timothy Baldwin, Marie-Catherine de Marneffe, Bo Han, Young-Bum Kim, Alan Ritter, and Wei Xu. 2015. Shared tasks of the 2015 workshop on noisy user-generated text: Twitter lexical normalization and named entity recognition. In *Proceedings of the Workshop on Noisy User-generated Text*, pages 126–135.

James McKeen Cattell. 1886. The time it takes to see and name objects. *Mind*, 11(41):63–65.

Nancy Chinchor. 1992. Muc-4 evaluation metrics. In *Proceedings of the 4th conference on Message understanding*, pages 22–29. Association for Computational Linguistics.

Jason PC Chiu and Eric Nichols. 2016. Named entity recognition with bidirectional lstm-cnns. *Transactions of the Association for Computational Linguistics*, 4:357–370.

Michael Collins. 2002. Discriminative training methods for hidden markov models: Theory and experiments with perceptron algorithms. In *Proceedings of the ACL-02 conference on Empirical methods in natural language processing-Volume 10*, pages 1–8. Association for Computational Linguistics.

Ronan Collobert, Jason Weston, Léon Bottou, Michael Karlen, Koray Kavukcuoglu, and Pavel Kuksa. 2011. Natural language processing (almost) from scratch. *Journal of machine learning research*, 12(Aug):2493–2537.

Jenny Rose Finkel, Trond Grenager, and Christopher Manning. 2005. Incorporating non-local information into information extraction systems by gibbs sampling. In *Proceedings of the 43rd annual meeting on association for computational linguistics*, pages 363–370. Association for Computational Linguistics.

Hege Fromreide, Dirk Hovy, and Anders Søgaard. 2014. Crowdsourcing and annotating ner for twitter# drift. In *LREC*, pages 2544–2547.

Zhiheng Huang, Wei Xu, and Kai Yu. 2015. Bidirectional lstm-crf models for sequence tagging. *arXiv preprint arXiv:1508.01991*.

Alex Krizhevsky, Ilya Sutskever, and Geoffrey E Hinton. 2012. Imagenet classification with deep convolutional neural networks. In *Advances in neural information processing systems*, pages 1097–1105.

Francis Kubala, Richard Schwartz, Rebecca Stone, and Ralph Weischedel. 1998. Named entity extraction from speech. In *Proceedings of DARPA Broadcast News Transcription and Understanding Workshop*, pages 287–292. Citeseer.

John Lafferty, Andrew McCallum, and Fernando CN Pereira. 2001. Conditional random fields: Probabilistic models for segmenting and labeling sequence data.

Guillaume Lample, Miguel Ballesteros, Sandeep Subramanian, Kazuya Kawakami, and Chris Dyer. 2016. Neural architectures for named entity recognition. *arXiv preprint arXiv:1603.01360*.

Lucian Vlad Lita, Abe Ittycheriah, Salim Roukos, and Nanda Kambhatla. 2003. Truecasing. In *Proceedings of the 41st Annual Meeting on Association for Computational Linguistics-Volume 1*, pages 152–159. Association for Computational Linguistics.

Christopher Manning, Mihai Surdeanu, John Bauer, Jenny Finkel, Steven Bethard, and David McClosky. 2014. The stanford corenlp natural language processing toolkit. In *Proceedings of 52nd annual meeting of the association for computational linguistics: system demonstrations*, pages 55–60.

Matthew E Peters, Waleed Ammar, Chandra Bhagavatula, and Russell Power. 2017. Semi-supervised sequence tagging with bidirectional language models. *arXiv preprint arXiv:1705.00108*.

Matthew E Peters, Mark Neumann, Mohit Iyyer, Matt Gardner, Christopher Clark, Kenton Lee, and Luke Zettlemoyer. 2018. Deep contextualized word representations. *arXiv preprint arXiv:1802.05365*.

Sameer S Pradhan and Nianwen Xue. 2009. Ontonotes: The 90% solution. In *HLT-NAACL (Tutorial Abstracts)*, pages 11–12.

Lawrence R Rabiner. 1989. A tutorial on hidden markov models and selected applications in speech recognition. *Proceedings of the IEEE*, 77(2):257–286.

Lev Ratinov and Dan Roth. 2009. Design challenges and misconceptions in named entity recognition. In *Proceedings of the thirteenth conference on computational natural language learning*, pages 147–155. Association for Computational Linguistics.

Keith Rayner. 1975. The perceptual span and peripheral cues in reading. *Cognitive Psychology*, 7(1):65–81.

Nils Reimers and Iryna Gurevych. 2017. Reporting score distributions makes a difference: Performance study of lstm-networks for sequence tagging. *arXiv preprint arXiv:1707.09861*.

Alan Ritter, Sam Clark, Oren Etzioni, et al. 2011. Named entity recognition in tweets: an experimental study. In *Proceedings of the conference on empirical methods in natural language processing*, pages 1524–1534. Association for Computational Linguistics.

Patricia Robinson, Erica Brown, John Burger, Nancy Chinchor, Aaron Douthat, Lisa Ferro, and Lynette Hirschman. 1999. Overview: Information extraction from broadcast news. In *Proceedings of DARPA Broadcast News Workshop*, pages 27–30.

Gozde Gul Sahin and Mark Steedman. 2018. Data augmentation via dependency tree morphing for low-resource languages. In *Proceedings of the 2018 Conference on Empirical Methods in Natural Language Processing*, pages 5004–5009.

Erik F Sang and Fien De Meulder. 2003. Introduction to the conll-2003 shared task: Language-independent named entity recognition. *arXiv preprint cs/0306050*.

Patrice Y Simard, Dave Steinkraus, and John C Platt. 2003. Best practices for convolutional neural networks applied to visual document analysis. In *null*, page 958. IEEE.

Rohini K Srihari, Cheng Niu, Wei Li, and Jihong Ding. 2003. A case restoration approach to named entity tagging in degraded documents. In *null*, page 720. IEEE.

Miles A Tinker and Donald G Paterson. 1928. Influence of type form on speed of reading. *Journal of Applied Psychology*, 12(4):359.

Erik F. Tjong Kim Sang. 2002. Introduction to the conll-2002 shared task: Language-independent named entity recognition. In *Proceedings of CoNLL-2002*, pages 155–158. Taipei, Taiwan.

Kiyotaka Uchimoto, Qing Ma, Masaki Murata, Hiromi Ozaku, and Hitoshi Isahara. 2000. Named entity extraction based on a maximum entropy model and transformation rules. In *Proceedings of the 38th Annual Meeting on Association for Computational Linguistics*, pages 326–335. Association for Computational Linguistics.

Adams Wei Yu, David Dohan, Minh-Thang Luong, Rui Zhao, Kai Chen, Mohammad Norouzi, and Quoc V Le. 2018. Qanet: Combining local convolution with global self-attention for reading comprehension. *arXiv preprint arXiv:1804.09541*.

Xiang Zhang and Yann LeCun. 2015. Text understanding from scratch. *arXiv preprint arXiv:1502.01710*.

Extending Event Detection to New Types with Learning from Keywords

Viet Dac Lai and **Thien Huu Nguyen**
Department of Computer and Information Science
University of Oregon, OR, USA
{vietl,thien}@cs.uoregon.edu

Abstract

Traditional event detection classifies a word or a phrase in a given sentence for a set of predefined event types. The limitation of such predefined set is that it prevents the adaptation of the event detection models to new event types. We study a novel formulation of event detection that describes types via several keywords to match the contexts in documents. This facilitates the operation of the models to new types. We introduce a novel feature-based attention mechanism for convolutional neural networks for event detection in the new formulation. Our extensive experiments demonstrate the benefits of the new formulation for new type extension for event detection as well as the proposed attention mechanism for this problem.

1 Introduction

Event detection (ED) is a task of information extraction that aims to recognize event instances (event mentions) in text and classify them into specific types of interest. Event mentions are usually associated with an event trigger/anchor in the sentence of the event mentions, functioning as the main word to evoke the event. For instance, in the sentence *"She is going to leave to become chairman of Time Inc."*, an ED system should be able to recognize that the word *"leave"* is triggering an event of type *"End-Position"*.

There have been two major approaches for ED in the literature. The first approach focuses on the development of linguistic features to feed into the statistical models (i.e., MaxEnt) (Ahn, 2006; Ji and Grishman, 2008; Liao and Grishman, 2010; McClosky et al., 2011). The second approach, on the other hand, relies on deep learning (i.e., convolutional neural networks (CNN)) to automatically induce features from data (Chen et al., 2015; Nguyen et al., 2016a; Liu et al., 2017; Lu and Nguyen, 2018), thus significantly improving the performance for ED.

One limitation of the current approaches for ED is the assumption of a predefined set of event types for which data is manually annotated to train the models. For example, the popular benchmark dataset ACE 2005 for ED annotates 8 types and 33 subtypes of events. Once the models have been trained in this way, they are unable to extract instances of new, yet related types (i.e., having zero performance on the new types). To extend the operation of these models into the new types, the common approach is to spend some effort annotating data for the new types to retrain the models. Unfortunately, this is an expensive process as we might need to obtain a large amount of labeled data to adequately represent various new event types in practice. Such expensive annotation has hindered the application of ED systems on new types and calls for a better way to formulate the ED problem to facilitate the extension of the models to new event types.

In this paper, we investigate a novel formulation of ED where the event types are defined via several keywords instead of a large number of examples for event types in the traditional approaches (called the learning-from-keyword formulation (LFK)). These keywords involve the words that can possibly trigger the event types in the contexts. For instance, the event type *End-Position* can be specified by the keywords (*"left"*, *"fired"*, *"resigned"*). Given the keywords to represent event types, the ED problem becomes a binary classification problem whose goal is to predict whether a word in a sentence expresses the event type specified by the keywords or not. This formulation enables the ED models to work with new event types as long as the keywords to describe the new types are provided, thus allowing the ED models to be applicable on a wide range of

Proceedings of the 2019 EMNLP Workshop W-NUT: The 5th Workshop on Noisy User-generated Text, pages 243–248
Hong Kong, Nov 4, 2019. ©2019 Association for Computational Linguistics

new event types and mitigating the needs for large amounts of annotated data for the new types.

The goal of this paper is to evaluate the effectiveness of LFK in the new type extension setting for ED where the models are trained on labeled data from some types but applied to extract instances of unseen types. We would like to promote this problem as a new task for ED for future research. To set the baselines for this problem, we employ the ACE 2005 dataset and recast it into LFK. We examine the performance of the baseline models for ED in the traditional formulation when they are adapted to LFK. The experiments show that with the new formulation, such ED models can actually recognize new event types although their performance should be still further improved in future research. Finally, we demonstrate one possibility to improve the performance of the baseline ED models in LFK by presenting a novel attention mechanism for CNNs based on the feature space to fuse the representations of the keywords and contexts. We achieve the state-of-the-art performance for the new type extension with the proposed attention mechanism.

2 Related work

In the last decade, many machine learning systems have been introduced to solve ED. Before the era of the deep neural networks, these systems are mainly based on supervised learning using extensive feature engineering with the machine learning frameworks (Ahn, 2006; Ji and Grishman, 2008; Hong et al., 2011; Riedel et al., 2009; Riedel and McCallum, 2011a,b; Miwa et al., 2014; Li et al., 2014, 2015). Recently, many advanced deep learning methods were introduced to enhance event detectors such as distributed word embedding (Chen et al., 2015; Nguyen et al., 2016b; Liu et al., 2017; Nguyen and Nguyen, 2019), convolutional neural networks (Chen et al., 2015, 2017; Nguyen and Grishman, 2015; Nguyen et al., 2016b; Nguyen and Grishman, 2018), recurrent neural networks (Nguyen et al., 2016b; Sha et al., 2018), and the attention mechanism (Liu et al., 2017; Nguyen and Nguyen, 2018b; Liu et al., 2018). However, the models proposed in these work cannot extend their operation to new event types.

Regarding the new formulations for ED, previous studies(Bronstein et al., 2015; Peng et al., 2016) also examine keywords to specify event types. However, these studies do not investigate the new type extension setting as we do in this. Recently, zero-shot learning is employed for new types in event extraction(Huang et al., 2018); however, the event types are specified via the possible roles of the arguments participating into the events in this work. It also uses complicated natural language processing toolkits, making it difficult to apply and replicate the settings. Our work emphasizes the simplicity in the setting for new type extension to facilitate future research. Finally, extending ED to the new type is investigated using real examples as new event types (Nguyen et al., 2016c). However, it requires a large number of examples to perform well. Our work instead requires only a few keywords to help the models achieve reasonable performance on new types.

3 Learning-from-Keywords for ED

3.1 Task Definition

In the learning-from-keyword formulation for ED, the inputs include a context (i.e., an n-word sentence $X = \{x_1, x_2, \ldots, x_n\}$ with an anchor word located at position a (the word x_a)) and a set of keywords K. The words in K are the possible trigger words of some event type of interest. The goal is to predict whether the word x_a in S expresses the event type specified by K or not (i.e., a binary classification problem to decide whether the context matches the event keywords or not). An example in LFK thus has the form (X, x_a, K, Y) where Y is either 1 or 0 to indicate the match of X and K.

3.2 Data Generation

To facilitate the evaluation of the ED models in LFK for the new type extension setting, we need to obtain training and test/development datasets so the keyword sets of the examples in the test/development datasets define event types that are different from those specified by the keyword sets in the training datasets. To our best knowledge, there is no existing data following LFK setting, therefore, in this section, we present a process to automatically generate an ED dataset for LFK setting from an existing ED dataset.

We obtain these datasets by leveraging ACE 2005, the popular benchmark datasets for ED. ACE 2005 dataset is annotated for 8 event types $\mathcal{T} = \{t_1, t_2, \ldots, t_8\}$, and 33 event subtypes $\mathcal{S} = \{s_1, s_2, \ldots, s_{33}\}$. There is also a special type/subtype of "*Other*" indicating the non-event instances ($Other \notin \mathcal{S}$) . As each event subtype in ACE 2005 is associated with one event type, let $\mathcal{C}_i$ be the set of subtypes corresponding to the type $t_i \in \mathcal{T}$. Also, let $\mathcal{K}_j$ be the set of trigger words for the event mentions of the subtype $s_j \in \mathcal{S}$. $\mathcal{K}$ is collected from training set of ACE 2005.

To generate the training and test/development datasets, we first split the documents in ACE 2005 into three parts D_{train}, D_{test} and D_{dev} following the previous work on ED (Li et al., 2013). They would contain event mentions for all the possible event types and subtypes in $\mathcal{T}$ and $\mathcal{S}$. Assume that we want to extend the system to a new event type $t_{target} \in \mathcal{T}$, we need a train set without t_{target}. So, we remove every event mention whose subtype belongs to $\mathcal{C}_{target}$ from D_{train}. Whereas, samples with subtypes in $\mathcal{C}_{target} \cup \{Other\}$ are kept in D_{test} and D_{dev}. The results of this removal process are called as D'_{train}, D'_{test} and D'_{dev} (from D_{train}, D_{test} and D_{dev}, respectively). They will be used to generate the actual training/test/development datasets for LFK, respectively.

Specifically, for each of these datasets (i.e., D'_{train}, D'_{test} and D'_{dev}), the goal is to produce the positive and negative examples in corresponding LFK datasets. Algorithm 1 shows the pseudocode to generate the training dataset for LFK from D'_{train}. The same algorithm can be applied for the test and development dastasets of LFK, but replace D'_{train} with D'_{test} and D'_{dev} respectively in line 2, and replace $\mathcal{S} \setminus \mathcal{C}_{target}$ with $\mathcal{C}_{target}$ in line 10.

Since the number of positive examples in D_{test} set is small, we choose two event types (i.e., *Conflict* and *Life*) that have the largest numbers of positive examples in D_{test} as the target types. Applying the data generation procedure above, we generate a dataset in LFK for each of these target types.

4 Model

This section first presents the typical deep learning models in the traditional ED formulation adapted to LFK. We then introduce a novel attention mechanism to improve such models for LFK.

4.1 Baselines

As CNNs have been applied to the traditional formulation of ED since the early day (Chen et al., 2015; Nguyen and Grishman, 2015, 2016), we focus on the CNN-based model in this work and

---

Algorithm 1 Training dataset generation for LFK

1: $D^+_{train}, D^-_{train} \leftarrow \emptyset, \emptyset$ ▷ Positive and negative example sets
2: **for** $(X, x_a, s_j) \in D'_{train}$ **do** ▷ where X : a sentence, $x_a \in X$: the anchor word, $s_j \in \mathcal{S}$: the corresponding subtype
3:     **if** $s_j \neq$ "*Other*" **then**
4:         **for** $u = 1..5$ **do**
5:             $K^u_j \leftarrow$ A subset of $\mathcal{K}_j \setminus \{x_a\}$: $|K^u_j| = 4$
6:             $D^+_{train} \leftarrow D^+_{train} \cup \{(X, x_a, K^u_j, 1)\}$
7:         **end for**
8:     **else** ▷ $s =$ "*Other*"
9:         $s_v \leftarrow$ Some subtype in $\mathcal{S} \setminus \mathcal{C}_{target}$
10:         $K \leftarrow$ A subset of $\mathcal{K}_v$: $|K| = 4$
11:         $D^-_{train} \leftarrow D^-_{train} \cup \{(X, x_a, K, 0)\}$
12:     **end if**
13: **end for**
14: **return** D^+_{train} and D^-_{train}

---

leave the other models for future research.

Encoding Layer: To prepare the sentence S and the anchor x_a for the models, we first convert each word $x_i \in S$ into a concatenated vector $h^0_i = [p_i, q_i]$, in which $p_i \in \mathbb{R}^u$ is the position embedding vector and $q_i \in \mathbb{R}^d$ is the word embedding of x_i. We follow the settings for p_i and q_i described in (Nguyen and Grishman, 2015). This step transforms S into a sequence of vector $H^0 = (h^0_1, h^0_2, \ldots, h^0_n)$.

Convolution Layers: Following (Chen et al., 2015; Nguyen and Grishman, 2015), we apply a convolutional layers with multiple window sizes for the filters W over H_0, resulting in a sequence of hidden vectors $H^1 = (h^1_1, h^1_2, \ldots, h^1_n)$. Note that we pad H^0 with zero vectors to ensure that H^1 still has n vectors. We can essentially run m convolutional layers in this way that would lead to m sequences of hidden vectors $H^1, H^2, \ldots, H^m$.

Keyword Representation: We generate the representation vector V_K for the keyword set K by taking the average of the embeddings of its words.

Given the keyword vectors V_K and the hidden vector sequences from CNNs for S (i.e., $H^1, H^2, \ldots, H^m$), the goal is to produce the final representation $R = G(V_K, H^1, H^2, \ldots, H^m)$, serving as the features to predict the matching between (S, x_a) and K (i.e., R would be fed into a feed-forward neural network with a softmax layer in the end to perform classification). There are two immediate baselines to obtain R adapted from the models for traditional ED:

(i) *Concat*: In this method, we apply the usual max-pooling operation over the hidden vectors for the last CNN layer H^m whose result is concatenated with V_K to produce R (Nguyen and Grishman, 2015; Chen et al., 2015).

(ii) *Attention*: This method applies the popular attention method to aggregate the hidden vectors in H^m using V_K as the query (Bahdanau et al., 2015). The formulas for R are shown below:

$$u_i = \sigma(W_u h_i^m + b_u)$$
$$c = \sigma(W_c[V_K, h_a^m] + b_c)$$
$$\alpha_i = \frac{\exp(c^\top u_i)}{\sum_j \exp(c^\top u_j)}$$
$$R = \sum_i \alpha_i h_i^m$$

4.2 Conditional Feature-wise Attention

The interaction between the keywords and hidden vectors in the baselines is only done in the last layer, letting the intermediate CNN layers to decide the computation themselves without considering the information from the keywords.

To overcome this limitation, we propose to inject supervision signals for each CNN layer in the modeling process. In particular, given the sequence of hidden vectors $H^i = (h_1^i, h_2^i, \ldots, h_n^i)$ obtained by the i-th CNN layer, instead of directly sending H^i to the next layer, we use V_K to generate the representation vectors γ_i and β_i, aiming to reveal the underlying information/constraints from the keywords that the i-th CNN layer should reason about. Such representation vectors condition and bias the hidden vectors in H^i toward the keywords based on the feature-wise affine transformation (Perez et al., 2018). The conditioned hidden vectors from this process (called $\bar{H}^i = (\bar{h}_1^i, \bar{h}_2^i, \ldots, \bar{h}_n^i)$) would be sent to the next CNN layer where the conditional process guided by the keywords continues:

$$\gamma_i = \sigma(W_\gamma^i V_K + b_\gamma^i)$$
$$\beta_i = \sigma(W_\beta^i V_K + b_\beta^i)$$
$$\bar{h}_j^i = \gamma_i * h_j^i + \beta_i$$

where σ is a non-linear function while $W_\gamma^i, b_\gamma^i, W_\beta^i$ and b_β^i are model parameters.

We call the operation described in this section the Conditional Feature-wise Attention (CFA). The application of CFA into the two baselines **Concat** and **Attention** leads to two new methods **Concat-CFA** and **Attention-CFA** respectively.

5 Experiments

We use the datasets generated in Section 3.2 to evaluate the models in this section. Table 1 shows the staticstics of our generated datasets. This dataset will be publicly available to the community.

	Label	Train	Dev	Test
Conflict	+1	14,749	929	509
	-1	177,421	13,130	13,576
Life	+1	17,434	354	154
	-1	177,421	13,130	13,576

Table 1: Numbers of the positive and negative samples of the LFK datasets.

5.1 Parameters

We examine four deep learning models: baselines (i.e., *Concat* and *Attention*) and the proposed models (i.e., *Concat-CFA* and *Attention-CFA*). Following (Nguyen and Grishman, 2015), we employ the `word2vec` word embeddings from (Mikolov et al., 2013) with 300 dimensions for the models in this work. The other parameters for the deep learning models in this work are tuned on the development datasets. In particular, we employ multiple window sizes (i.e., 2, 3, 4 and 5) in the CNN layers, each has 100 filters. We use Adadelta as the optimizer with the learning rate set to 1.0. We apply a dropout with a rate of 0.5 to the final representation vector R. Finally, we optimize the number of CNN layers for each deep learning model.

In addition, we investigate the typical feature-based models with the MaxEnt classifier in the traditional ED formulation for LFK to constitute the baselines for future research. In particular, we examine four feature-based models for ED in LFK:

- **Feature** combines the state-of-the-art feature set for ED designed in (Li et al., 2013) for the input context (S, x_a) with the words in the keyword set K to form its features

- **Word2Vec** utilizes the keyword representation V_K and the average of the embedding of the words in the window size of 5 for x_a in S as the features

Model	Conflict			Life		
	P	R	F1	P	R	F1
Feature	21.7	9.8	13.5	14.4	25.8	18.5
Word2Vec	20.6	72.4	32.1	4.4	61.9	8.2
Feature + Word2vec	27.8	20.2	23.4	15.7	31.6	21.0
Seed	11.9	36.1	17.9	9.5	71.0	16.7
Concat	20.5	57.8	30.0 (4)	10.9	48.3	17.7 (2)
Attention	21.5	59.1	31.4 (4)	12.8	45.0	19.1 (2)
Concat-CFA	25.1	57.1	33.8 (4)	10.6	43.6	16.9 (1)
Attention-CFA	22.5	74.2	**34.1** (1)	18.5	38.7	**25.0** (4)

Table 2: Model performance. The numbers in the brackets indicate the optimized numbers of CNN layers.

- **Feature + word2vec** uses the aggregated features from above models

- **Seed** employs the model with semantic features in (Bronstein et al., 2015).

5.2 Evaluation

Table 2 presents the performance of the models on the test performance for different datasets (i.e., with *Conflict* and *Life* as the target type). Among the features in the feature-based models, the embedding features in *Word2Vec* are very helpful for ED in LFK as the models with these features achieve the best performance (i.e., *Word2Vec* for *Conflict* and *Feature+Word2Vec* for *Life*). Among the deep learning models, the CFA-based models (i.e., *Concat-CFA* and *Attention-CFA*) are significantly better than their corresponding baseline models (i.e., *Concat* and *Attention*) over both *Conflict* and *Life* with *Attention*. This confirms the benefits of CFA for ED in LFK.

Comparing the deep learning and the feature-based models, it is interesting that the feature-based models with average word embedding features can perform better than the deep learning baseline models (i.e., *Concat* and *Attention*) for *Conflict*. However, when the deep learning models are integrated with both attention and CFA (i.e., *Attention-CFA*), it achieves the best performance over both datasets. This helps to testify to the advantage of deep learning and CFA for ED in the new type extension setting with LFK.

Finally, although the models can extract event mentions of the new types, the performance is still limited in general, illustrating the challenge of ED in this setting and leaving many rooms for future research (especially with deep learning) to improve the performance. We hope that the setting in this work presents a new way to evaluate the effectiveness of the ED models.

6 Conclusion

We investigate a new formulation for event detection task that enables the operation of the models to new event types, featuring the use of keywords to specify the event types on the fly for the models. A novel feature-wise attention technique is presented for the CNN models for ED in this formulation. Several models are evaluated to serve as the baselines for future research on this problem.

References

David Ahn. 2006. The stages of event extraction. In *Proceedings of the Workshop on Annotating and Reasoning about Time and Events*, pages 1–8.

Dzmitry Bahdanau, Kyunghyun Cho, and Yoshua Bengio. 2015. Neural machine translation by jointly learning to align and translate. In *ICLR*.

Ofer Bronstein, Ido Dagan, Qi Li, Heng Ji, and Anette Frank. 2015. Seed-based event trigger labeling: How far can event descriptions get us? In *ACL-IJCNLP (Volume 2: Short Papers)*, volume 2, pages 372–376.

Yubo Chen, Shulin Liu, Xiang Zhang, Kang Liu, and Jun Zhao. 2017. Automatically labeled data generation for large scale event extraction. In *ACL*.

Yubo Chen, Liheng Xu, Kang Liu, Daojian Zeng, and Jun Zhao. 2015. Event extraction via dynamic multi-pooling convolutional neural networks. In *ACL-IJCNLP (Volume 1: Long Papers)*, volume 1, pages 167–176.

Yu Hong, Jianfeng Zhang, Bin Ma, Jianmin Yao, Guodong Zhou, and Qiaoming Zhu. 2011. Using cross-entity inference to improve event extraction. In *ACL*.

Lifu Huang, Heng Ji, Kyunghyun Cho, and Clare R Voss. 2018. Zero-shot transfer learning for event extraction. In *ACL*, pages 2160–2170.

Heng Ji and Ralph Grishman. 2008. Refining event extraction through cross-document inference. In *ACL*.

Qi Li, Heng Ji, Yu Hong, and Sujian Li. 2014. Constructing information networks using one single model. In *EMNLP*.

Qi Li, Heng Ji, and Liang Huang. 2013. Joint event extraction via structured prediction with global features. In *ACL*.

Xiang Li, Thien Huu Nguyen, Kai Cao, and Ralph Grishman. 2015. Improving event detection with abstract meaning representation. In *Proceedings of the First Workshop on Computing News Storylines*.

Shasha Liao and Ralph Grishman. 2010. Using document level cross-event inference to improve event extraction. In *ACL*.

Jian Liu, Yubo Chen, Kang Liu, and Jun Zhao. 2018. Event detection via gated multilingual attention mechanism. In *AAAI*.

Shulin Liu, Yubo Chen, Kang Liu, and Jun Zhao. 2017. Exploiting argument information to improve event detection via supervised attention mechanisms. In *ACL*.

Weiyi Lu and Thien Huu Nguyen. 2018. Similar but not the same: Word sense disambiguation improves event detection via neural representation matching. In *EMNLP*.

David McClosky, Mihai Surdeanu, and Christopher Manning. 2011. Event extraction as dependency parsing. In *BioNLP Shared Task Workshop*.

Tomas Mikolov, Ilya Sutskever, Kai Chen, Greg Corrado, and Jeffrey Dean. 2013. Distributed representations of words and phrases and their compositionality. In *NIPS*.

Makoto Miwa, Paul Thompson, Ioannis Korkontzelos, and Sophia Ananiadou. 2014. Comparable study of event extraction in newswire and biomedical domains. In *COLING*.

Minh Nguyen and Thien Huu Nguyen. 2018b. Who is killed by police: Introducing supervised attention for hierarchical lstms. In *COLING*.

Thien Nguyen and Ralph Grishman. 2018. Graph convolutional networks with argument-aware pooling for event detection. In *AAAI*.

Thien Huu Nguyen, , Adam Meyers, and Ralph Grishman. 2016a. New york university 2016 system for kbp event nugget: A deep learning approach. In *TAC*.

Thien Huu Nguyen, Kyunghyun Cho, and Ralph Grishman. 2016b. Joint event extraction via recurrent neural networks. In *NAACL*.

Thien Huu Nguyen, Lisheng Fu, Kyunghyun Cho, and Ralph Grishman. 2016c. A two-stage approach for extending event detection to new types via neural networks. In *Proceedings of the 1st ACL Workshop on Representation Learning for NLP (RepL4NLP)*.

Thien Huu Nguyen and Ralph Grishman. 2015. Event detection and domain adaptation with convolutional neural networks. In *ACL-IJCNLP*.

Thien Huu Nguyen and Ralph Grishman. 2016. Modeling skip-grams for event detection with convolutional neural networks. In *EMNLP*.

Trung Minh Nguyen and Thien Huu Nguyen. 2019. One for all: Neural joint modeling of entities and events. In *AAAI*.

Haoruo Peng, Yangqiu Song, and Dan Roth. 2016. Event detection and co-reference with minimal supervision. In *EMNLP*, pages 392–402.

Ethan Perez, Florian Strub, Harm De Vries, Vincent Dumoulin, and Aaron Courville. 2018. Film: Visual reasoning with a general conditioning layer. In *AAAI*.

Sebastian Riedel, Hong-Woo Chun, Toshihisa Takagi, and Jun'ichi Tsujii. 2009. A markov logic approach to bio-molecular event extraction. In *BioNLP 2009 Workshop*.

Sebastian Riedel and Andrew McCallum. 2011a. Fast and robust joint models for biomedical event extraction. In *EMNLP*.

Sebastian Riedel and Andrew McCallum. 2011b. Robust biomedical event extraction with dual decomposition and minimal domain adaptation. In *BioNLP Shared Task 2011 Workshop*.

Lei Sha, Feng Qian, Baobao Chang, and Zhifang Sui. 2018. Jointly extracting event triggers and arguments by dependency-bridge rnn and tensor-based argument interaction. In *AAAI*.

Distant Supervised Relation Extraction with Separate Head-Tail CNN

Rui Xing, Jie Luo[*]
State Key Laboratory of Software Development Environment
School of Computer Science and Engineering
Beihang University, China
{xingrui, luojie}@nlsde.buaa.edu.cn

Abstract

Distant supervised relation extraction is an efficient and effective strategy to find relations between entities in texts. However, it inevitably suffers from mislabeling problem and the noisy data will hinder the performance. In this paper, we propose the Separate Head-Tail Convolution Neural Network (SHTCNN), a novel neural relation extraction framework to alleviate this issue. In this method, we apply separate convolution and pooling to the head and tail entity respectively for extracting better semantic features of sentences, and coarse-to-fine strategy to filter out instances which do not have actual relations in order to alleviate noisy data issues. Experiments on a widely used dataset show that our model achieves significant and consistent improvements in relation extraction compared to statistical and vanilla CNN-based methods.

1 Introduction

Relation extraction is a fundamental task in information extraction, which aims to extract relations between entities. For example, "Bill Gates is the CEO of Microsoft." holds the relationship **/business/company/founders** between the head entity **Bill Gates** and tail entity **Microsoft**.

Traditional supervised relation extraction systems require a large amount of manually well-labeled relation data (Walker et al., 2005; Doddington et al., 2004; Gábor et al., 2018), which is extremely labor intensive and time-consuming. (Mintz et al., 2009) instead proposes distant supervision which exploits relational facts in knowledge bases. Distant supervision aligns entity mentions in plain texts with those in knowledge base and assumes that if two entities have a relation there, then all sentences containing these two entities will express that relation. If there is no re-

Bag	Sentence	Correct
b_1	**Barack Obama** was born in the **United States**.	True
	Barack Obama was the 44th president of the **United States**.	False
b_2	**Bill Gates** is the CEO of **Microsoft**.	True
	Bill Gates announced that he would be transitioning to a part-time role at **Microsoft** and full-time work in June 2006.	False

Table 1: Examples of relations annotated by distant supervision. Sentences in b_1 are annotated with the *place_of_birth* relation and sentences in b_2 the *business_company_founders* relation.

lation link between a certain entity pair in knowledge base, the sentence will be labeled as a Not A relation (NA) instance. Although distant supervision is an efficient and effective strategy for automatically labeling large-scale training data, it inevitably suffers from mislabeling problems due to its strong assumption. As a result, the dataset created by distant supervision is usually very noisy. According to (Riedel et al., 2010), the precision of using distant supervision aligning Freebase to New York Times corpus is about 70%, an example of labeled sentences in New York Times corpus is shown in Table 1. Therefore, many efforts have been devoted to alleviate noise in distant supervised relation extraction.

With the development of deep learning techniques (LeCun et al., 2015), large amount of work using deep neural networks has been proposed for distant supervised relation extraction (Zeng et al., 2014, 2015; Lin et al., 2016; Liu et al., 2017; Jat et al., 2018; Ji et al., 2017; Han et al., 2018;

---

[*] Corresponding author.

Proceedings of the 2019 EMNLP Workshop W-NUT: The 5th Workshop on Noisy User-generated Text, pages 249–258
Hong Kong, Nov 4, 2019. ©2019 Association for Computational Linguistics

Du et al., 2018; Vashishth et al., 2018; Lei et al., 2018; Qin et al., 2018a,b; Ye and Ling, 2019; Xu and Barbosa, 2019). Various previous work also used well-designed attention mechanism (Lin et al., 2016; Jat et al., 2018; Ji et al., 2017; Su et al., 2018; Du et al., 2018) which have achieved significant results. Besides, knowledge-based methods (Lei et al., 2018; Han et al., 2018; Vashishth et al., 2018; Ren et al., 2018) incorporated external knowledge base information with deep neural network, obtaining impressive performance.

Most of previous work used vanilla Convolution Neural Network (CNN) or Piecewise Convolution Neural Network (PCNN) as sentence encoder. CNN/PCNN adopted the same group of weight-sharing filters to extract semantic feature of sentences. Though effective and efficient, there is still room to improve if we look deeper into properties of relations. We find that semantic properties of relations such as symmetry and asymmetry are often overlooked when using CNN/PCNN. For example, "Bill Gates is the CEO of Microsoft." holds the relationship **/business/company/founders** between the head entity **Bill Gates** and tail entity **Microsoft**. While in the sentence "The most famous man in Microsoft is Bill Gates." where the head entity **Microsoft** and the tail **Bill Gates** do not share that relationship. It indicates that the relation **/business/company/founders** is asymmetric. Most previous work use position embedding specified by entity pairs and piecewise pooling (Zeng et al., 2015; Lin et al., 2016; Liu et al., 2017; Han et al., 2018) to predict relations. However, above examples show that they share similar position embeddings due to their similar position distances to both entities. Vanilla CNN/PCNN is not sufficient to capture such semantic features because it treats the head and tail entities equally. Thus, it tend to "memorize" certain entity pairs and may learn similar context representation when dealing with these noisy asymmetric instances.

In addition to relation properties, we also investigate some noise source in distant supervised relation extraction. NA instances usually account for a large portion in distant supervised datasets, making the data highly imbalanced. Similarly, in objection detection task (Lin et al., 2017), extreme class imbalance greatly hinders the performance.

In this paper, in order to deal with above deficiencies, we propose Separate Head-Tail CNN (SHTCNN) framework, an effective strategy for distant supervised relation extraction. The framework is composed of two ideas. First, we employ separate head-tail convolution and pooling to embed the semantics of sentences targeting head and tail entities respectively. By this means, we can capture better semantic properties of relations in the distant supervised data and further alleviate mislabeling problem. Second, relations are classified from coarse to fine. In order to do this, an extra auxiliary network is adopted for NA/Non-NA binary classification, which is expected to filter as many easy NA instances as possible while maintaining high recall of all non-NA relationships. Instances selected by binary network are treated as non-NA examples for fine-grained multi-class classification. Inspired by Retina (Lin et al., 2017), we make use of focal loss in binary classification. We evaluate our model on a real-world distant supervised dataset. Experimental results show that our model achieves significant and consistent improvements in relation extraction compared to selected baselines.

2 Related Work

Relation extraction is a crucial task and heavily studied area in Natural Language Processing (NLP). Many efforts have been devoted, especially in supervised paradigm. Conventional supervised methods require large amounts of human-annotated data, which is highly expensive and time-consuming. To deal with this issue, (Mintz et al., 2009) proposed distant supervision, which aligned Freebase relational facts with plain texts to automatically generate relation labels for entity pairs. Apparently, such assumption is too strong that inevitably accompanies with mislabeling problem.

Plenty of studies have been done to alleviate such problem. (Riedel et al., 2010; Hoffmann et al., 2011; Surdeanu et al., 2012) introduce multi-instance learning framework to the problem. (Riedel et al., 2010) and (Surdeanu et al., 2012) use a graphical model to select valid sentences in the bag to predict relations. However, the main disadvantage in conventional statistical and graphical methods is that using features explicitly derived from NLP tools will cause error propagation and low precision.

As deep learning techniques (Bengio, 2009; Le-Cun et al., 2015) have been widely used, plenty of work adopt deep neural network for distant su-

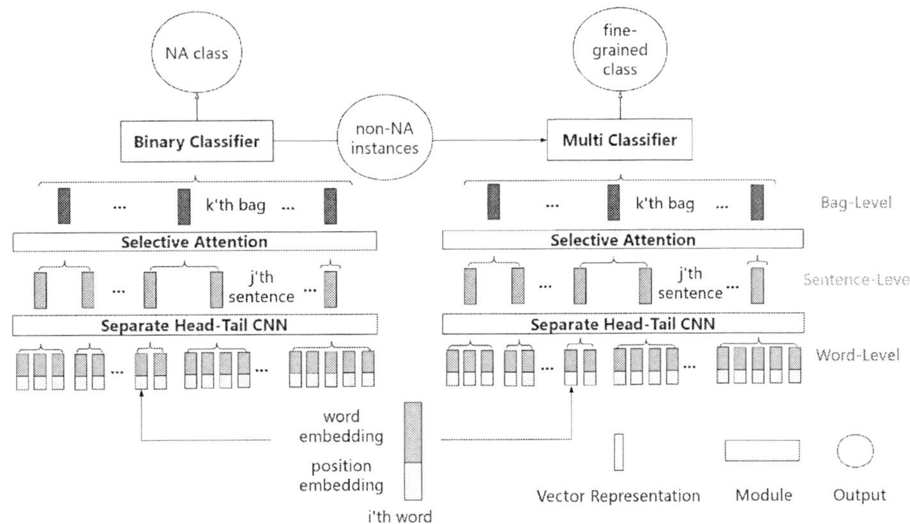

Figure 1: Separate Head-Tail CNN for distant supervised relation extraction

pervised relation extraction. (Zeng et al., 2015) proposed piecewise convolution neural network to model sentence representations under multi instance learning framework while using piecewise pooling based on entity position to capture structural information. (Lin et al., 2016) proposed sentence level attention, which is expected to dynamically reduce the weights of those noisy instances. (Ji et al., 2017) adopted similar attention strategy and combined entity descriptions to calculate weights over sentences. (Liu et al., 2017) proposed a soft-label method to reduce the influence of noisy instances on entity-level. (Jat et al., 2018) used word-level and entity-based attention for efficiently relation extraction. Due to the effectiveness of self-attention mechanism, (Du et al., 2018) proposed a structured word-level self-attention and sentence-level attention mechanism which are both 2-D matrix to learn rich aspects of data. Also, plenty of knowledge based strategies for distant supervised relation extraction have also been proposed. (Ji et al., 2017) uses hierarchical information of relations for relation extraction and achieve significant performance. (Lei et al., 2018) proposed Cooperative Denoising framework, which consists two base networks leveraging text corpus and knowledge graph respectively. (Vashishth et al., 2018) proposed RESIDE, a distantly supervised neural relation extraction method which utilizes additional side information from knowledge bases for improving relation extraction. (Han et al., 2018) aimed to incorporate the hierarchical information of relations for distantly supervised relation extraction. Although these methods achieved significant improvement in relation extraction, they tend to treat entities in sentences equally or rely more or less on knowledge base information which may be unavailable in other domains.

In order to alleviate mislabeling problem and reduce the burden of integrating external knowledge and resource, we propose SHTCNN to provide better sentence representation and reduce the impact of NA instances.

3 Methodology

In this section, we introduce our SHTCNN model. The overall framework is shown in Figure 1. Our model is built under multi-instances learning framework. It splits the training set into multiple n bags $\{\langle h_1, t_1 \rangle, \langle h_2, t_2 \rangle, \cdots, \langle h_n, t_n \rangle\}$, each of which contains m sentences $\{s_1, s_2, \cdots, s_m\}$ mentioning same head entity h_i and tail entity t_i. Note that sentence number m may not be the same in each bag. Each sentence consists of a sequence of k words $\{x_1, x_2, \cdots, x_k\}$. First, sentence representation s_i is acquired using our separate head-tail convolution and pooling on words $\{x_1, x_2, \cdots, x_k\}$. Next, selective attention mechanism is used to dynamically merge sentences to its bag representation $b_i = \langle h_i, t_i \rangle$. On bag level, binary classifier filters out easy NA instances with focal loss, leaving others to multi-class classifier for further fine-grained classification.

3.1 Sentence Encoder

Word Representation

First, the i-th word x_i in sentence is mapped into a d_w-dimensional word embedding e_i. Then, to keep track of head and tail entity position information, two d_p-dimensional position embeddings (Zeng et al., 2014, 2015) are also adopted for each word as p_i^1 and p_i^2 recording the distance to two entities respectively. Thus, the final word representation is the concatenation of these three vectors $w_i = [e_i, p_i^1, p_i^2]$ of $d = d_w + 2p_w$ dimensions.

Separate Head-Tail Convolution and Pooling

Convolution layer are often utilized in relation extraction to capture local features in window form and then perform relation prediction globally. In detail, convolution is an operation between a convolution matrix W and a sequence of vector q_i. We define $q_i \in R^{l \times d}$ of w words in the sentence $s_i = \{w_1, w_2, w_3, \cdots, w_n\}$ with word representations defined above.

$$q_i = w_{i-l+1:i}, \quad \text{where } 1 \leq i \leq m+l-1 \quad (1)$$

Because the window may be out of the sentence boundary when sliding along. We use wide convolution technique by adding special padding tokens on both sides of sentence boundaries. Thus the i-th convolutional filter p_i computes as follows:

$$p_i = [Wq + b]_i, \quad (2)$$

where b is bias vector.

Conventional PCNN uses piecewise pooling for relation extraction which divided convolutional filter p_i into three segments based on positions of head and tail entities. Piecewise pooling is defined as follows:

$$[x]_{ij} = max(p_{ij}), \quad \text{where } 1 \leq j \leq 3 \quad (3)$$

where j indicates position of segments in sentence.

As mentioned in section, traditional methods get representation of each sentence using same group of convolution filters, which focuses on both head entity and tail entity equally and ignores semantic difference between them. We use two separate groups of convolution filters $W_1, W_2 \in R^{d_s \times d}$, where d_s is the sentence embedding size. Also, simply piecewise pooling can not well deal

with examples of which relations are similar but asymmetric. In detail, we utilize two groups of separate head-tail entity convolution W^1, W^2 to represent the sentence s_i as p_i^1, p_i^2.

$$\begin{aligned} p_i^1 &= [Wq + b]_i^1 \\ p_i^2 &= [Wq + b]_i^2 \end{aligned} \quad (4)$$

To exploit such semantic properties of relations expressed by entity pairs, we use separate head-tail entity pooling. Targeting head and tail entities, head-entity pooling and tail-entity pooling are adopted on two convolution results respectively. p_i^1, p_i^2 are further segmented by positions of entity pair for head-tail entity pooling. Head entity pooling is defined as:

$$h_i = [max(p_{i1}^1); max([p_{i2}^1, p_{i3}^1])] \quad (5)$$

Similarly, tail pooling is defined as:

$$t_i = [max([p_{i1}^2, p_{i2}^2]); max(p_{i3}^2)] \quad (6)$$

And i-th sentence vector s_i is the concatenation of h_i and t_i:

$$s_i = [h_i; t_i] \quad (7)$$

Finally, we apply non-linear function such as ReLU as activation on the output.

3.2 Selective Attention

Bags contain sentences sharing the same entity pair. In order to alleviate mislabeling problem on sentence level, we adopted selective attention which is widely used in many works (Lin et al., 2016; Liu et al., 2017; Ji et al., 2017; LeCun et al., 2015; Han et al., 2018; Du et al., 2018). The representation of the bag $b_i = \langle h_i, t_i \rangle$ is the weighted sum of all sentence vectors in that bag.

$$\begin{aligned} b_i &= \sum_i \alpha_i s_i \\ \alpha_i &= \frac{exp(s_i Ar)}{\sum_j exp(s_j Ar)} \end{aligned} \quad (8)$$

where α_i is the weight of sentence representation s_i, A and r are diagonal matrix and relation query.

3.3 Coarse-to-Fine Relation Classification

Traditional methods directly predict relation classes for each bag after obtaining bag representations. However, large amount of NA instances containing mixed semantic information will hinder the performance. To alleviate such impact of

NA instances, we manually utilize a binary classifier to filter out as many NA instances as possible, while leaving hard NA instances for multi-class classification.

Binary classification can also be viewed as an auxiliary task about whether the input sentence hold an NA relation. In this method, NA is treated as negative class while all other non-NA labels are treated as positive class. In this method, we adopted focal loss (Lin et al., 2017) for NA/non-NA classification. Focal loss is designed to address class imbalance problem. When predict class label y for binary task $y \in \{0, 1\}$, we first define the prediction score p_t for positive class:

$$p_t = \begin{cases} p, & \text{if } y = 1, \\ 1 - p, & \text{otherwise} \end{cases} \quad (9)$$

Then traditional weighted cross-entropy loss can be defined as follows:

$$CE(p_t) = -\alpha log(p_t) \quad (10)$$

where α is a hyper-parameter usually set as class ratio.

Focal loss modifies it by changing α to $(1-p_t)^\gamma$ in order to dynamically adjust weights between well-classified easy instances and hard instances as:

$$CE(p_t) = -(1 - p_t)^\gamma log(p_t) \quad (11)$$

For easy instances, prediction score p_t will be high while the loss low and vise versa for hard instances. As a result, focal loss focuses on those hard NA instances. Finally, instances which are predicted as non-NA are selected for multi-class classifier for fine-grained classification. Due to existence of NA instances which are hard to handle, we also add a "NA class" in multi-class classification for further filtering those instances which do not hold an exact relationship.

3.4 Optimization

In this section, we introduce the learning and optimization details for our SHTCNN model. As shown in Figure 1, binary and multi network share only same word representations. We define binary and multi labels as $br \in \{0, 1\}$ and $mr \in \{0, 1, 2, \cdots, n\}$ respectively. Both 0 represent NA class. In binary classification, 1 represents all non-NA classes while in multi-class classification, each non-zero number represents a certain non-NA relation. Besides, we use Θ^1, Θ^2 to denote parameters for binary and multi-class classification

network respectively. The objective function for our model is:

$$\begin{aligned} J(\Theta^1, \Theta^2) = &-\sum_{i=0}^{1} log(br_i|b_i, \Theta^1) \\ &-\sum_{j=0}^{n} log(mr_j|b_i, \Theta^2) \end{aligned} \quad (12)$$

where n is the number of relation classes. All models are optimized using Stochastic Gradient Descent (SGD).

4 Experiments

In this section, we first introduce the dataset and evaluation metrics. Then we list our experimental parameter settings. Afterwards, we compare the performance of our method with feature-based and selected neural-based methods. Besides, case study shows our SHTCNN is an effective method to extract better semantic features.

4.1 Dataset and Evaluation Metrics

We evaluate our model on a widely used dataset New York Times (NYT) released by (Riedel et al., 2010). The dataset was generated by aligning Freebase (Bollacker et al., 2008) relations with New York Times Corpus. Sentences of year 2005 and 2006 are used for training while sentences of 2007 are used as testing. There are 52 actual relations and a special NA which indicates there was no relation between two entities. The training set contains 522,611 sentences, 281,270 entity pairs and 18,152 relational facts. The testing set contains 172,448 sentences, 96,678 entity pairs and 1950 relational facts.

4.2 Comparison with Baseline Methods

Following previous work (Mintz et al., 2009; Lin et al., 2016; Ji et al., 2017; Liu et al., 2017; Han et al., 2018; Du et al., 2018), we evaluate our model in the held-out evaluation. It evaluates models by comparing the relational facts discovered from the test articles with those in Freebase, which provides an approximate measure of precision without requiring expensive human evaluation. We draw precision-recall curves for all models and also report the Precision@N results to further verify the effort of our SHTCNN model.

For fair comparison with sentence encoders, we selected the following baselines:

- **Mintz:** Multi-class logistic regression model used by (Mintz et al., 2009) for distant supervision.

- **MultiR:** Probabilistic graphical model under multi-instance learning framework proposed by (Hoffmann et al., 2011)

- **MIMLRE:** Graphical model jointly models multiple instances and multiple labels proposed by (Surdeanu et al., 2012)

- **PCNN:** CNN based model under multi-instance learning framework for distant relation extracion proposed by (Zeng et al., 2015)

- **PCNN-ATT:** CNN based model which uses additional attention mechanism on sentence level for distant supervision proposed by (Lin et al., 2016)

- **SHTCNN:** Framework proposed in this paper, please refer to Section 3 for more details.

4.3 Experimental Settings

Word and Position Embeddings

Our model use pre-trained word embeddings for NYT corpus. Word embeddings of blank words are initialized with zero while unknown words are initialized with the normal distribution of which the standard deviation is 0.05. Position embeddings are initialized with Xavier initialization for all models. Two parts of our model share the same word and position embeddings as inputs.

Parameter Settings

We use cross-validation to determine the parameters in our model. We also use a grid search to select learning rate λ for SGD among $\{0.5, 0.1, 0.01, 0.001\}$, sliding windows size l among $\{1, 3, 5, 7\}$, sentence embedding size d_s among $\{100, 150, 200, 300, 350, 400\}$ and batch size among $\{64, 128, 256, 512\}$. Other parameters proved to have little effect on results. We show our optimal parameter settings in Table 2.

4.4 Overall Performance

Figure 2 shows the overall performance of our proposed SHTCNN against baselines mentioned above. From results, we can observe that: (1) When recall is smaller than 0.05, all models have reasonable precision. When recall is higher, precision of feature-based models decrease sharply compared to neural-based methods, and the latter

Word Embedding Size	50
Position Embedding Size	5
Sentence Embedding Size	230
Filter Window Size	3
γ in Focal Loss	2
Positive weight in Focal Loss	0.75
Threshold for Selecting non-NA	0.3
Batch Size	128
Learning rate	0.1
Dropout Probability	0.5

Table 2: Parameter Settings

outperform the former over the entire range of recall. It demonstrates that human-designed features are limited and cannot concisely express semantic meaning of sentences in noisy data environment. (2) SHTCNN outperforms PCNN/PCNN-ATT over the entire range of recall, It indicates that SHTCNN is a more powerful sentence encoder which can better capture semantic features of noisy sentences. Further experimental results and case study show the effectiveness of our model.

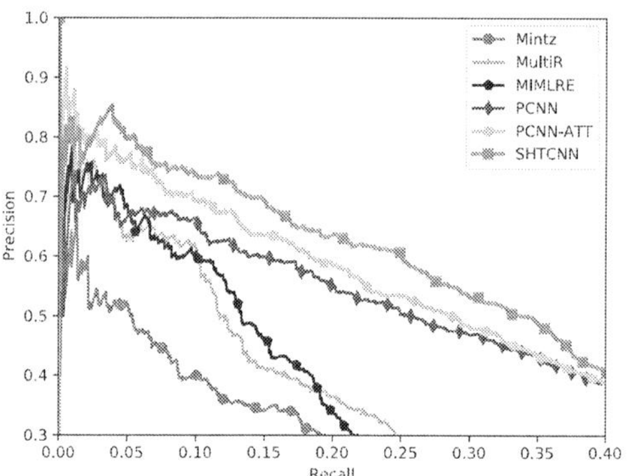

Figure 2: Precision/Recall curves of our model and previous baseline methods.

4.5 Top N Precision

We also conduct Precision@N tests on entity pairs with few instances. In our tests, three settings are used: ONE randomly select an instance in the bag; TWO randomly select two instances for each entity pair; ALL use all bag instances for evaluation. Table 3 shows the results on NYT dataset regarding P@100, P@200, P@300 and the mean of three settings for each model. From the table we can see that: (1) Performance of all methods improves as

Test Settings	ONE				TWO				ALL			
P@N(%)	100	200	300	Mean	100	200	300	Mean	100	200	300	Mean
PCNN+AVE	71.3	63.7	57.8	64.3	73.3	65.2	62.1	66.9	73.3	66.7	62.8	67.6
PCNN+ATT	73.3	69.2	60.8	67.8	77.2	71.6	66.1	71.6	76.2	73.1	67.4	72.2
SHTCNN+AVE	72.3	64.2	60.1	65.5	76.3	71.3	**68.9**	**72.2**	77.2	76.6	71.4	75.1
Coarse-to-Fine	74.3	69.6	63.2	69.0	77.7	74.4	68.2	73.4	78.6	74.3	71.2	74.7
HT+ATT	75.3	74.3	65.1	71.6	79.2	75.6	72.3	75.7	80.4	76.2	74.9	77.2
SHTCNN+ATT	**78.2**	**77.1**	**70.1**	**75.1**	**80.0**	**76.2**	73.2	**76.5**	**86.1**	**79.1**	**75.4**	**80.2**

Table 3: P@N for relation extraction in entity pairs with different number of sentences

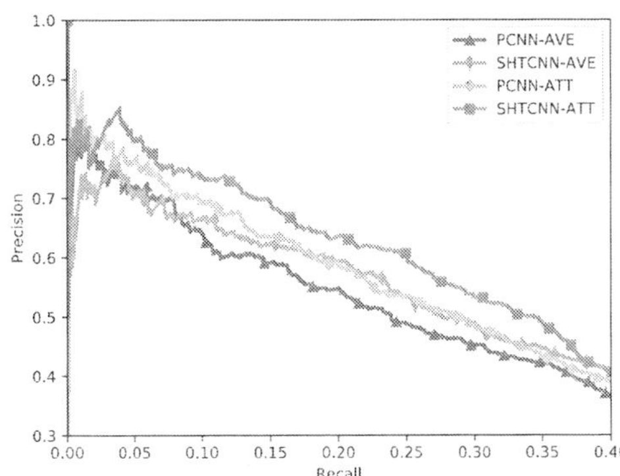

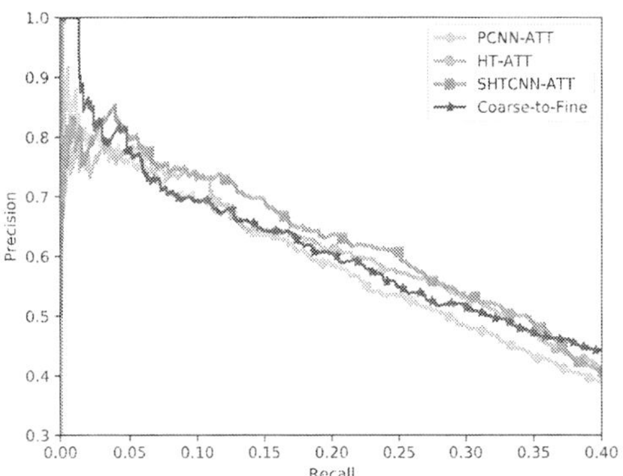

Figure 3: Precision/Recall curves of our model and selected neural based methods. PCNN-AVE and SHTCNN-AVE use Average method (AVE) while PCNN-ATT and SHTCNN-ATT use selective ATTention method (ATT) described in section 3.2 to obtain bag representation from its sentences.

Figure 4: Precision/Recall curves of separate parts of our model. PCNN-ATT is the baseline method introduced in Section 4.2. HT-ATT replaces sentence encoder of PCNN-ATT with separate Head-Tail convolution and pooling (HT) proposed in section 3.1 without using Coarse-to-fine strategy in section 3.3. Coarse-to-Fine solely classifies relation from coarse to fine without using HT. SHTCNN-ATT is our full model combines HT and Coarse-to-Fine relation extraction together.

the instance number increases which shows that more sentences selected in the bag, more information can be utilized. (2) SHTCNN improves precision by over 8% for PCNN, PCNN-AVE and PCNN-ATT model. It indicates that in noisy textual dataset, our SHTCNN is a more powerful sentence encoder to capture better semantic features. (3) Average method improves slowly when instances number increases which indicates that it can not effectively extract relations and be easily distracted by noises in the bag.

4.6 Effectiveness of Separate Head-Tail CNN

To further verify the contribution and effectiveness of two phase of our SHTCNN, we conduct two extra experiments. First, we evaluate the ability of our model to capture better sentence semantic features under different bag representation calculation methods. PCNN-AVE (Average) assumes that all sentences in the bag contribute equally to the representation of the bag, which brings in

more noise from mislabeling sentences. Compared to PCNN-ATT, PCNN-AVE hinders the performance of relation extraction as shown in Table 3. We evaluate our model using Average and Attention respectively. From results in Figure 3, we observe that: (1) Both SHTCNN-AVE and SHTCNN-ATT achieve significant performance than their compared baselines, which proves that SHTCNN offers better sentence semantic features for bag representation with or without selective attention mechanism. (2) SHTCNN-AVE achieves similar performance as PCNN-ATT when recall is between 0.15 and 0.35. (3) When recall is greater than 0.35, SHTCNN-AVE performs even better than PCNN-ATT. It demonstrates that SHTCNN is relatively more robust and stable on dealing with noisier sentences.

Second, we explore the effect of separate head-tail convolution and pooling and contribution of coarse-to-fine relation extraction. From results shown in Figure 4, we can observe that: (1) Both HT-ATT and Coarse-to-Fine improve performance of PCNN-ATT on a wide range of recall, which indicates that separate head-tail convolution and pooling, and coarse-to-fine strategy perform better on predicting relations. (2) Figure 4 and Table 3 both show that separate head-tail convolution and pooling achieve much better results than only using coarse-to-fine strategy, indicating that a better sentence encoder is more important in noisy environment. (3) Our full model SHTCNN improves performance on the entire recall compared to using separate parts (solely separate head-tail convolution and pooling or only coarse-to-fine) of our model which suggests that combining two proposed methods together can achieve better results.

/business/company/founders
That may include the chairman and chief software architect of **Microsoft**, **Bill Gates**, an otherwise infrequent television viewer.
/business/company/founders → **NA**
Bill Gates and Steve Ballmer, for example, were roommates in college, joined forces at **Microsoft** in 1980 and still work together today.
NA → **/business/shopping_center/owner**
Earlier this week, the company said it expected to sell **Madrid Xanad** and its half-interest in two other malls, Vaughan Mills in Ontario and St. Enoch Centre in Glasgow, to **Ivanhoe Cambridge**, a Montreal company that is Mills's partner in the Canadian and Scottish properties .

Table 4: Some examples of Separate Head-Tail CNN corrections compared to PCNN

4.7 Case Study

In Table 4, we show some of our SHTCNN model examples corrections compared to traditional PCNN. Left of the arrow is PCNN predicted class label on the below sentence while the right is our prediction. We can observe that the first sentence is labeled as **/business/company/founders** by both PCNN and SHTCNN since closer entities bring similar position embeddings which benefit both models. However, the second one is similar but does not hold the relationship. PCNN failed to

recognize the relation but SHTCNN corrected the label. Finally, the last sentence is longer and entities are not as close as those in first two sentences. Our model outperformed PCNN by successfully giving correct label to the sentence. It indicates that SHTCNN perform better on modelling relationship in relative long sentences.

5 Conclusion

In this paper, we propose SHTCNN, a novel neural framework using separate head-tail convolution and pooling for sentence encoding and classifies relations from coarse-to-fine. Various experiments conducted show that, in our framework, separate head-tail convolution and pooling can better capture sentence semantic features compared to baseline methods, even in noisier environment. Besides, coarse-to-fine relation extraction strategy can further improve and stabilize the performance of our model.

In the future, we will explore the following directions: (1) We will explore effective separate head-tail convolution and pooling on other sentence encoders like RNN. (2) Coarse-to-fine classification is an experimental method, we plan to further investigate noisy source in distant supervised datasets. (3) It will be promising to incorporate well-designed attention and self-attention mechanisms with two parts of our framework to further improve the performance. All codes and data are available at: `https://bit.ly/ds-shtcnn`.

6 Acknowledgement

This work is supported by National Natural Science Foundation of China (Grant Nos. 61690202). We would like to thank the anonymous reviewers for their insightful comments.

References

Yoshua Bengio. 2009. Learning deep architectures for ai. *Found. Trends Mach. Learn.*, 2(1):1–127.

Kurt Bollacker, Colin Evans, Praveen Paritosh, Tim Sturge, and Jamie Taylor. 2008. Freebase: A collaboratively created graph database for structuring human knowledge. In *Proceedings of the 2008 ACM SIGMOD International Conference on Management of Data*, SIGMOD '08, pages 1247–1250, New York, NY, USA. ACM.

George Doddington, Alexis Mitchell, Mark Przybocki, Lance Ramshaw, Stephanie Strassel, and Ralph

Weischedel. 2004. The automatic content extraction (ACE) program – tasks, data, and evaluation. In *Proceedings of the Fourth International Conference on Language Resources and Evaluation (LREC'04)*, Lisbon, Portugal. European Language Resources Association (ELRA).

Jinhua Du, Jingguang Han, Andy Way, and Dadong Wan. 2018. Multi-level structured self-attentions for distantly supervised relation extraction. In *Proceedings of the 2018 Conference on Empirical Methods in Natural Language Processing*, pages 2216–2225, Brussels, Belgium. Association for Computational Linguistics.

Kata Gábor, Davide Buscaldi, Anne-Kathrin Schumann, Behrang QasemiZadeh, Haïfa Zargayouna, and Thierry Charnois. 2018. SemEval-2018 task 7: Semantic relation extraction and classification in scientific papers. In *Proceedings of The 12th International Workshop on Semantic Evaluation*, pages 679–688, New Orleans, Louisiana. Association for Computational Linguistics.

Xu Han, Pengfei Yu, Zhiyuan Liu, Maosong Sun, and Peng Li. 2018. Hierarchical relation extraction with coarse-to-fine grained attention. In *Proceedings of the 2018 Conference on Empirical Methods in Natural Language Processing*, pages 2236–2245, Brussels, Belgium. Association for Computational Linguistics.

Raphael Hoffmann, Congle Zhang, Xiao Ling, Luke Zettlemoyer, and Daniel S. Weld. 2011. Knowledge-based weak supervision for information extraction of overlapping relations. In *Proceedings of the 49th Annual Meeting of the Association for Computational Linguistics: Human Language Technologies*, pages 541–550, Portland, Oregon, USA. Association for Computational Linguistics.

Sharmistha Jat, Siddhesh Khandelwal, and Partha Talukdar. 2018. Improving Distantly Supervised Relation Extraction using Word and Entity Based Attention. *arXiv e-prints*, page arXiv:1804.06987.

Guoliang Ji, Kang Liu, Shizhu He, and Jun Zhao. 2017. Distant supervision for relation extraction with sentence-level attention and entity descriptions. In *Proceedings of the Thirty-First AAAI Conference on Artificial Intelligence, February 4-9, 2017, San Francisco, California, USA.*, pages 3060–3066.

Yann LeCun, Yoshua Bengio, and Geoffrey E. Hinton. 2015. Deep learning. *Nature*, 521(7553):436–444.

Kai Lei, Daoyuan Chen, Yaliang Li, Nan Du, Min Yang, Wei Fan, and Ying Shen. 2018. Cooperative denoising for distantly supervised relation extraction. In *Proceedings of the 27th International Conference on Computational Linguistics*, pages 426–436, Santa Fe, New Mexico, USA. Association for Computational Linguistics.

Tsung-Yi Lin, Priya Goyal, Ross Girshick, Kaiming He, and Piotr Dollár. 2017. Focal Loss for Dense Object Detection. *arXiv e-prints*, page arXiv:1708.02002.

Yankai Lin, Shiqi Shen, Zhiyuan Liu, Huanbo Luan, and Maosong Sun. 2016. Neural relation extraction with selective attention over instances. In *Proceedings of the 54th Annual Meeting of the Association for Computational Linguistics (Volume 1: Long Papers)*, pages 2124–2133, Berlin, Germany. Association for Computational Linguistics.

Tianyu Liu, Kexiang Wang, Baobao Chang, and Zhifang Sui. 2017. A soft-label method for noise-tolerant distantly supervised relation extraction. In *Proceedings of the 2017 Conference on Empirical Methods in Natural Language Processing*, pages 1790–1795, Copenhagen, Denmark. Association for Computational Linguistics.

Mike Mintz, Steven Bills, Rion Snow, and Dan Jurafsky. 2009. Distant supervision for relation extraction without labeled data. In *Proceedings of the Joint Conference of the 47th Annual Meeting of the ACL and the 4th International Joint Conference on Natural Language Processing of the AFNLP: Volume 2 - Volume 2*, ACL '09, pages 1003–1011, Stroudsburg, PA, USA. Association for Computational Linguistics.

Pengda Qin, Weiran XU, and William Yang Wang. 2018a. DSGAN: Generative adversarial training for distant supervision relation extraction. In *Proceedings of the 56th Annual Meeting of the Association for Computational Linguistics (Volume 1: Long Papers)*, pages 496–505, Melbourne, Australia. Association for Computational Linguistics.

Pengda Qin, Weiran Xu, and William Yang Wang. 2018b. Robust distant supervision relation extraction via deep reinforcement learning. In *Proceedings of the 56th Annual Meeting of the Association for Computational Linguistics (Volume 1: Long Papers)*, pages 2137–2147, Melbourne, Australia. Association for Computational Linguistics.

Feiliang Ren, Di Zhou, Zhihui Liu, Yongcheng Li, Rongsheng Zhao, Yongkang Liu, and Xiaobo Liang. 2018. Neural relation classification with text descriptions. In *Proceedings of the 27th International Conference on Computational Linguistics*, pages 1167–1177, Santa Fe, New Mexico, USA. Association for Computational Linguistics.

Sebastian Riedel, Limin Yao, and Andrew McCallum. 2010. Modeling relations and their mentions without labeled text. In *Proceedings of the 2010 European Conference on Machine Learning and Knowledge Discovery in Databases: Part III*, ECML PKDD'10, pages 148–163, Berlin, Heidelberg. Springer-Verlag.

Sen Su, Ningning Jia, Xiang Cheng, Shuguang Zhu, and Ruiping Li. 2018. Exploring encoder-decoder model for distant supervised relation extraction. In *Proceedings of the Twenty-Seventh International Joint Conference on Artificial Intelligence, IJCAI-18*, pages 4389–4395. International Joint Conferences on Artificial Intelligence Organization.

Mihai Surdeanu, Julie Tibshirani, Ramesh Nallapati, and Christopher D. Manning. 2012. Multi-instance multi-label learning for relation extraction. In *Proceedings of the 2012 Joint Conference on Empirical Methods in Natural Language Processing and Computational Natural Language Learning*, pages 455–465, Jeju Island, Korea. Association for Computational Linguistics.

Shikhar Vashishth, Rishabh Joshi, Sai Suman Prayaga, Chiranjib Bhattacharyya, and Partha Talukdar. 2018. RESIDE: Improving distantly-supervised neural relation extraction using side information. In *Proceedings of the 2018 Conference on Empirical Methods in Natural Language Processing*, pages 1257–1266, Brussels, Belgium. Association for Computational Linguistics.

Christopher Walker, Stephanie Strassel, Julie Medero, and Kazuaki Maeda. 2005. Ace 2005 multilingual training corpus.

Peng Xu and Denilson Barbosa. 2019. Connecting Language and Knowledge with Heterogeneous Representations for Neural Relation Extraction. *arXiv e-prints*, page arXiv:1903.10126.

Zhi-Xiu Ye and Zhen-Hua Ling. 2019. Distant supervision relation extraction with intra-bag and inter-bag attentions. In *Proceedings of the 2019 Conference of the North American Chapter of the Association for Computational Linguistics: Human Language Technologies, Volume 1 (Long and Short Papers)*, pages 2810–2819, Minneapolis, Minnesota. Association for Computational Linguistics.

Daojian Zeng, Kang Liu, Yubo Chen, and Jun Zhao. 2015. Distant supervision for relation extraction via piecewise convolutional neural networks. In *Proceedings of the 2015 Conference on Empirical Methods in Natural Language Processing*, pages 1753–1762, Lisbon, Portugal. Association for Computational Linguistics.

Daojian Zeng, Kang Liu, Siwei Lai, Guangyou Zhou, and Jun Zhao. 2014. Relation classification via convolutional deep neural network. In *Proceedings of COLING 2014, the 25th International Conference on Computational Linguistics: Technical Papers*, pages 2335–2344, Dublin, Ireland. Dublin City University and Association for Computational Linguistics.

Discovering the Functions of Language in Online Forums

Youmna Ismaeil, Oana Balalau, Paramita Mirza
Max Planck Institute for Informatics
{yismaeil, obalalau, paramita}@mpi-inf.mpg.de

Abstract

In this work, we revisit the functions of language proposed by linguist Roman Jakobson and we highlight their potential in analyzing online forum conversations. We investigate the relation between functions and other properties of comments, such as controversiality. We propose and evaluate a semi-supervised framework for predicting the functions of Reddit comments. To accommodate further research, we release a corpus of 165K comments annotated with their functions of language.

1 Introduction

Understanding human conversations has long been an active area of research and has become even more important with the pervasiveness of intelligent assistants in our daily life. A vast amount of work has been dedicated to *speech act* (also referred to as *dialogue act* or *discourse act*) categorization for the purpose of characterizing the discourse of conversations or discussions. Speech acts focus on the addresser's intent in using language and were first introduced by Austin (1975). One of the most influential subsequent work by Searle (1976) focused on the addresser's intent in using language and proposed five categories for speech acts: *representatives*, *directives*, *commissives*, *expressives*, and *declarations*.

With the rise of the internet and online communication, recent works focus on utilizing dialogue acts for analyzing emails, online forums and live chats (Zhang et al., 2017; Joty and Hoque, 2016; Jeong et al., 2009; Forsyth, 2007; Wu et al., 2002).

However, even though they employed sets of dialogue acts based on the Dialogue Act Markup in Several Layers (DAMSL) scheme (Core and Allen, 1997), each work proposed different subsets to annotate the data with, tailored for each specific purpose. Zhang et al. (2017) proposed 9

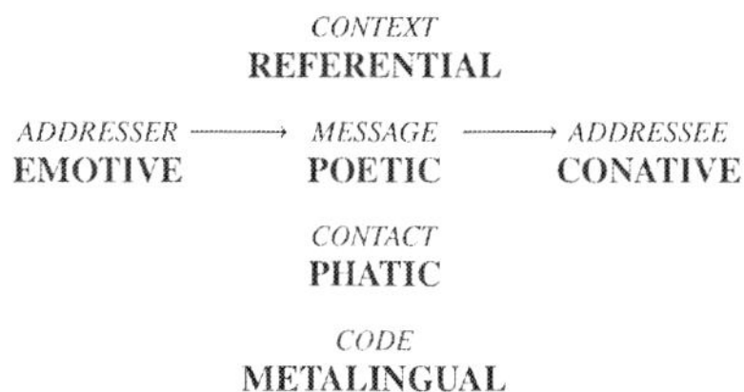

Figure 1: Functions of language (in bold), each focuses on different elements of communication (in italic).

X:	I am so happy, our paper got accepted!	Emotive, Referential
Y:	Seriously?? Congratz.	Emotive, Phatic
X:	Well, the pen is mightier than the sword.	Poetic
Y:	What do you mean?	Metalingual
X:	It's a proverb, meaning to persuade reviewers with words instead of force.	Metalingual
Y:	I see.	Phatic
	Could you send me your paper?	Conative
X:	Sure, it's here: <link>	Referential
Y:	Thanks!	Phatic

Table 1: An example of a discussion where all functions of language are present.

speech acts for characterizing comments in Reddit; Joty and Hoque (2016) utilized 5 coarser classes from 12 acts used in Jeong et al. (2009); while Forsyth (2007) and Wu et al. (2002) defined 15 dialogue acts based on Stolcke et al. (2000). The lack of formalism and the diversity of taxonomies make it difficult to compare different annotated datasets. It is also not clear if the proposed acts cover all kinds of utterances in various conversation types. For instance, Zhang et al. (2017) labelled comments expressing disgust or anger as *negative reaction*, however, the counterpart *positive reaction* is not available as a label. Meanwhile, Joty and Hoque (2016) acknowledge only certain positive reactions labelled as *politeness*.

In this work, we address these issues by adopt-

Proceedings of the 2019 EMNLP Workshop W-NUT: The 5th Workshop on Noisy User-generated Text, pages 259–264
Hong Kong, Nov 4, 2019. ©2019 Association for Computational Linguistics

ing the theory of *language functions* proposed by Jakobson (1960). One key difference between speech acts and language functions is that the former describes the meaning of utterances, while the latter also explains *why* utterances have different meanings, through the dynamic relationship between the elements of communication and their functions. Hence, we argue that the functions of language are a more comprehensive framework for capturing the discourse of human communication. Jakobson's model distinguishes six elements that are *necessary* for communication to occur: a **message** sent by an **addresser** to an **addressee** requires *(i)* a certain **context** to be understood, *(ii)* a common **code**, i.e., common definitions understood by both addresser and addressee, as well as *(iii)* a **contact**, i.e., a physical and psychological connection enabling both addresser and addressee to stay in the communication. Figure 1 illustrates the communicative functions of language in relation to those elements. In Table 1, we present an anecdotal example where all functions are expressed in the conversation.

There is a limited body of work exploring this scheme for content analysis. Bonini and Sellas (2014) use the functions of language to study the behavior of public radio channels on social media. Morrison and Martens (2018) incorporate the phatic function in a dialog system that would follow social norms. We believe we are the first to investigate Jakobson's functions of language for characterizing online forum discussions.

2 Jakobson's Functions of Language

We expand the original definitions of language functions (Jakobson, 1960) with further clarifications from the literature, as well as examples of how each function can be used to characterize messages on online forums.

Referential. The referential function, which is the most frequent one in communication, is marked by a reference to the context of the discussion, which can be a situation, a person, or an object. The message is used to transmit information and the words most often carry literal definitions (denotative). Instances of referential messages include observations, opinions, and factual information.

Examples: factual information (*"Trump won the election"*), opinions (*"He has a shot"*).

Poetic. The poetic function appears when the focus is on the message, marked in conversations by the use of figurative language. Figurative language concerns the use of metaphor, alliteration, onomatopoeia, idioms, irony and oxymorons, among others. Particularly in online forums, users often use slang expressions, which can be considered as poetic as well.

Examples: slang (*"Thanks Obama[1]"*), onomatopoeia (*"ding ding ding"*).

Emotive. The emotive function reflects the attitude or mood of the addresser towards the information being communicated. The message can be perceived as conveying emotion, such as anger, anticipation, joy and sadness. Emotive messages focus more attention on the addresser and less on the information being sent. Despite the absence of emotional tone and nonverbal cues, people can distinguish emotions in a text-based communication (Hancock et al., 2007).

Examples: emotions are often expressed using emojis or slang such as *"lol"* or *"omg"*, as well as words bearing strong sentiment (*"what a horrible human being"*).

Conative. The conative function is marked by a focus on the addressee. A conative message would make the addressee react by performing a verbal act (e.g., answering a question), a psychological act (e.g., changing a conviction), or a physical act (e.g., closing a door). More precisely, messages have a conative function if they represent orders, demands, advice, or wishes, among others.

Examples: demands (*"link please"*,*"Vote for Bernie Sanders"*), warnings (*"don't count on it"*).

Phatic. Sometimes referred to as back-channel or small talk, the phatic function serves the purpose of preserving the physical and psychological contact between speakers. The physical contact is related to the physical environment in which the conversation takes place and in the case of online forums, this will be a reference to the platform, e.g., *"happy cake day![2]"*. The psychological contact refers to the personal relation between speakers and the involvement in the conversation.

Examples: involvement in the conversation (*"I see"*), agreement and disagreement between

---

[1]https://www.urbandictionary.com/define.php?term=Thanks%20Obama

[2]Reddit "Cake Day" is the yearly anniversary of when a user signed up on Reddit.

speakers (*"good point"*, *"I don't think so"*).

Metalingual. The metalingual function corresponds to clarifications regarding the concepts used in the conversation, which can be related to the language used (as the common code) or the system/environment where the communication takes place. The metalingual function is often indicated by linguistic cues such as *"what is a"* or *"what do you mean by"*. The metalingual function appears when we need definitions, as well as ambiguity resolution. *Examples:* clarifying the vocabulary *"what is a noob?"*, or more general concepts *"what does the Supreme Court do?"*.

Relations between Functions. Messages will generally have more than one function of language. Jakobson (1960) highlights the relation between **referential** and **poetic** functions. The author argues that a poetic message will make referential information ambiguous, however, it will not completely discard it. Klinkenberg (2000), on the other hand, justifies the relation between **conative** and **referential** functions. The transfer of information between the addresser and the addressee might determine a change in the behavior of the addressee.

3 Functions of Language on Reddit

3.1 Dataset

In order to have a diverse tone of comments in long discussions, we consider the *Politics*[3] subreddit, a popular forum for political U.S. news. We retrieved $10.6M$ comments on the *Politics* subreddit for the year 2016, the year of the presidential election, using the Reddit API.

In this work, we focus on *short comments*, as they are challenging for existing automatic content analysis tools such as topic models. However, they often carry clear language functions on their own and can be easily distinguished by humans. We consider short comments to be the ones that consist of at most two syntactic phrases or chunks[4], e.g. "I see your point" (NP-VP), obtaining $165K$ comments. After removing punctuation and converting the text to lowercase, we have a final dataset of $4,482$ distinct utterances, which we will refer to as **messages**. Each message might represent several comments and be used in different contexts. Our intuition for removing punctua-

tion and uppercase is that the additional meaning can be added using simple rules. For example, an exclamation mark or text in all caps may suggest surprise or anger.

Manual Annotation. We set aside 920 (420 most frequent and 500 randomly selected) messages from the $4,482$ messages to be manually annotated. Each message was annotated by three human annotators, who are trained with the descriptions and examples of functions of language as have been explained in Section 2. We observed that almost all messages strongly express, and hence, annotated with at most two language functions, as we focus only on short comments. When a message is very ambiguous, the annotators were encouraged to give the label *unclear*. A message receives as a final label a function of language f if that function is assigned by at least two annotators. The Krippendorff's alpha agreement score among annotators is 0.565. We remark that the agreement score which is comparable with results reported for speech act labeling on Reddit (cf. Table 1 in Zhang et al. (2017)). Out of the 920 labelled messages, the annotators disagree on 67 messages, i.e. no label is voted more than once, which we exclude from our final dataset. We also removed 10 messages that are consistently labeled *unclear* by three annotators, leaving 843 labeled messages in our final dataset used for analysis, and later for experiments with automatic methods. The final label distribution is as follows: 352 referential, 288 phatic, 147 emotive, 104 poetic, 71 conative and 16 metalingual.

3.2 Analysis

We now analyze the properties of the annotated messages in relation to the functions of language. For each distinct message, we first retrieve the initial comments containing it. For example, the text *"thank you"* appears in $2,292$ comments, with different letter cases and punctuation. A comment has several properties, including *author, controversiality* and *parent comment*. A comment receives the tag *controversial* when it has a significant amount of votes, and these votes are roughly equally split between upvotes and downvotes. The parent comment is the comment to which the current comment is replying. From the parent child relation of comments, we infer the *number of replies* of a given comment.

---

[3] https://www.reddit.com/r/politics/
[4] We used OSU Twitter NLP by Ritter et al. (2011).

Controversiality. We first investigate which language functions commonly follow controversial comments. Our intuition is that emotive (e.g., expressing surprise or anger) and conative messages (e.g., asking users to behave or to provide evidence) will be written frequently in response to controversial topics or controversial users. The percentage of controversial parent comments per function shown in Table 2 confirms our intuition that conative comments are used to reply to controversial content more often than the other comments. Emotive messages are also written more frequently in reply to controversies, as well as referential messages. For the latter, the user may bring more information about the topic, either to approve or disprove the parent comment.

Function	% controversial parents	% receive reply
referential	**15.87%**	**36.74%**
poetic	12.86%	18.17%
emotive	**16.59%**	15.78%
conative	**20.14%**	**51.03%**
phatic	11.43%	14.61%
metalingual	13.41%	**26.51%**

Table 2: Analysis per language function.

Replies. We also examine which language functions are often followed by at least one reply comment, shown in Table 2. The findings corroborate with the definitions of the language functions, as conative comments, which put the focus on the addressee, often receive replies. Referential and metalingual are the other functions that often receive replies, since they bring more information and naturally prolong the discussion. Meanwhile, the opposite is observed for emotive and phatic comments. Emotive comments such as *"lol"*, *"haha"* representing joy usually require no follow-up in verbal conversations. Poetic comments receive also relatively few replies. Drew and Holt (1998) found that figures of speech are used as transitions between topics or as ending remarks on a topic. This phenomenon may also be present on Reddit. On the subreddit Politics, users initiate discussions via an article or video, hence, phatic messages mostly express involvement (e.g., *"I see"*) or (dis)agreement (e.g., *"good point"*), which require no replies and serve the role of ending the conversation.

Applications. Given the definitions of language functions and the previous observations, we illustrate two use cases for the analysis of language functions in online forums. First, they can be used in combination with other features for the automatic classification of comments or threads as *controversial*, in the absence of sufficient voting activity. Controversial messages require the immediate attention of moderators as they might contain hate speech or false information. Secondly, understanding conversational patterns related to language functions (e.g., a conative message asks for a referential reply, while an emotive message calls for a thoughtful and empathetic response) are beneficial for building smarter chatbots.

3.3 Semi-Supervised Inference of Labels

Annotating posts on social media with functions of language, or any semantic or discourse label in general, is a time-consuming and labor-intensive task. To overcome this challenge, we investigate the utility of a graph-based semi-supervised label propagation framework with the Modified Adsorption (MAD) algorithm (Talukdar and Pereira, 2010), which makes predictions by taking into consideration both labeled and unlabeled data. MAD was shown to perform the best when compared with other semi-supervised frameworks, such as the Label Propagation (LP-ZGL) algorithm and the Adsorption algorithm (Talukdar and Pereira, 2010). MAD computes a soft assignment of labels of the nodes in a graph, allowing multi-label classification. Graph-based semi-supervised learning is widely used by the NLP community, particularly for tasks where acquiring annotated data is expensive, such as semantic parsing (Das and Smith, 2011).

We construct a graph in the following way: the set of $4,482$ messages (e.g., *"thank you"*, *"thanks"*) is considered as the set of nodes and an edge is added between a message and its k-nearest neighbor in the embedding space. Cosine similarity between two messages *embeddings*[5] is assigned as the weight of the edge. We experiment with different values for k and we find that the algorithm performs best for $k = 4$. For evaluation, we used 5-folds cross-validation on the annotated dataset (843 messages) and we report precision, recall, and $F1$-score per function of language in Table 4. Note that we exclude metalingual comments, as they were not sufficient for propagating

---

[5]Pre-trained embeddings from Google's Universal Sentence Encoder (Cer et al., 2018).

referential	phatic	emotive	poetic	conative
she has a credible claim	absolutely agree	shameful	feeltheburn	mind explaining why
what time was that	I'm sorry	barely even human	inverted triple bern	keep fooling yourself
it's all marketing	I upvoted you	epic simply epic	duality of man	dude relax

Table 3: Example of predictions of our semi-supervised approach.

Function	Precision	Recall	F1
referential	0.893	0.888	0.891
phatic	0.905	0.889	0.897
emotive	0.868	0.838	0.853
poetic	0.680	0.798	0.734
conative	0.822	0.890	0.855
Average	**0.834**	**0.861**	**0.847**

Table 4: Precision, recall and $F1$ score per function.

the labels. However, we hypothesize that one sure way to identify metalingual function is by looking at the presence of linguistic cues such as *"what is a"* or *"what do you mean by"*. Apart from metalingual, our approach performs well on all functions yielding around $0.734 - 0.897$ $F1$-scores. The lowest $F1$-score is coined by poetic functions due to the high variation of figurative language. Users can make comparisons, metaphors or puns, among others, making the task at hand challenging and deserving of a focused effort.

Qualitative Analysis. We show in Table 3 examples of the predictions for the unlabelled dataset made by our approach. Even for the difficult task of identifying figurative language, MAD can make good predictions.

4 Conclusion

This paper revisits the functions of language introduced by Jakobson (1960) and investigates their potential in analyzing online forum conversations, specifically political discussions on Reddit. We highlight interesting relations between comments, their properties, and the language functions they express. In addition, we present a graph-based semi-supervised approach for automatic annotation of language functions.

Dataset. For further research in this area, we release a corpus[6] of $165K$ comment IDs labeled with their functions of language.

---

[6]https://github.com/nyxpho/jakobson

References

John Langshaw Austin. 1975. *How to do things with words*. Oxford university press.

Tiziano Bonini and Toni Sellas. 2014. Twitter as a public service medium? A content analysis of the Twitter use made by Radio RAI and RNE. *Communication & Society*, 27(2):125–146.

Daniel Cer, Yinfei Yang, Sheng-yi Kong, Nan Hua, Nicole Limtiaco, Rhomni St John, Noah Constant, Mario Guajardo-Cespedes, Steve Yuan, Chris Tar, et al. 2018. Universal sentence encoder. *arXiv preprint arXiv:1803.11175*.

Mark G Core and James Allen. 1997. Coding dialogs with the DAMSL annotation scheme. In *AAAI fall symposium on communicative action in humans and machines*, volume 56. Boston, MA.

Dipanjan Das and Noah A. Smith. 2011. Semi-supervised frame-semantic parsing for unknown predicates. In *Proceedings of the 49th Annual Meeting of the Association for Computational Linguistics: Human Language Technologies*, pages 1435–1444. Association for Computational Linguistics.

Paul Drew and Elizabeth Holt. 1998. Figures of speech: Figurative expressions and the management of topic transition in conversation. *Language in Society*, 27(04):495–522.

Eric N. Forsyth. 2007. Improving automated lexical and discourse analysis of online chat dialog. In *Masters thesis, Naval Postgraduate School*.

Jeffrey T. Hancock, Christopher Landrigan, and Courtney Silver. 2007. Expressing emotion in text-based communication. page 929.

Roman Jakobson. 1960. Linguistics and poetics. In *Style in language*, pages 350–377. MA: MIT Press.

Minwoo Jeong, Chin-Yew Lin, and Gary Geunbae Lee. 2009. Semi-supervised speech act recognition in emails and forums. In *Proceedings of the 2009 Conference on Empirical Methods in Natural Language Processing*, pages 1250–1259, Singapore. Association for Computational Linguistics.

Shafiq Joty and Enamul Hoque. 2016. Speech Act Modeling of Written Asynchronous Conversations with Task-Specific Embeddings and Conditional Structured Models. *Proceedings of the 54th Annual Meeting of the Association for Computational Linguistics (Volume 1: Long Papers)*, pages 1746–1756.

Jean-Marie Klinkenberg. 2000. *Précis de sémiotique générale*. Le Seuil.

Hannah Morrison and Chris Martens. 2018. "How Was Your Weekend?" A Generative Model of Phatic Conversation. pages 74–79.

Alan Ritter, Sam Clark, Mausam, and Oren Etzioni. 2011. Named entity recognition in tweets: An experimental study. In *Proceedings of the 2011 Conference on Empirical Methods in Natural Language Processing*, pages 1524–1534. Association for Computational Linguistics.

John R Searle. 1976. A classification of illocutionary acts. *Language in society*, 5(1):1–23.

Andreas Stolcke, Noah Coccaro, Rebecca Bates, Paul Taylor, Carol Van Ess-Dykema, Klaus Ries, Elizabeth Shriberg, Daniel Jurafsky, Rachel Martin, and Marie Meteer. 2000. Dialogue act modeling for automatic tagging and recognition of conversational speech. *Computational Linguistics*, 26(3).

Partha Pratim Talukdar and Fernando Pereira. 2010. Experiments in graph-based semi-supervised learning methods for class-instance acquisition. In *Proceedings of the 48th Annual Meeting of the Association for Computational Linguistics*, pages 1473–1481. Association for Computational Linguistics.

Tianhao Wu, Faisal M. Khan, Todd A. Fisher, Lori A. Shuler, and William M. Pottenger. 2002. Posting act tagging using transformation-based learning. In *Foundations of Data Mining and knowledge Discovery*.

Amy Zhang, Bryan Culbertson, and Praveen Paritosh. 2017. Characterizing online discussion using coarse discourse sequences. In *International AAAI Conference on Web and Social Media (ICWSM'17)*.

Incremental processing of noisy user utterances in the spoken language understanding task

Stefan Constantin[*] **Jan Niehues**[+] **Alex Waibel**[*]

[*] Karlsruhe Institute of Technology
Institute for Anthropomatics and Robotic
{stefan.constantin|waibel}@kit.edu

[+] Maastricht University
Department of Data Science and Knowledge Engineering
jan.niehues@maastrichtuniversity.nl

Abstract

The state-of-the-art neural network architectures make it possible to create spoken language understanding systems with high quality and fast processing time. One major challenge for real-world applications is the high latency of these systems caused by triggered actions with high executions times. If an action can be separated into subactions, the reaction time of the systems can be improved through incremental processing of the user utterance and starting subactions while the utterance is still being uttered. In this work, we present a model-agnostic method to achieve high quality in processing incrementally produced partial utterances. Based on clean and noisy versions of the ATIS dataset, we show how to create datasets with our method to create low-latency natural language understanding components. We get improvements of up to 47.91 absolute percentage points in the metric F_1-score.

1 Introduction

Dialog Systems are ubiquitous - they are used in customer hotlines, at home (Amazon Alexa, Apple Siri, Google Home, etc.), in cars, in robots (Asfour et al., 2018), and in smartphones (Apple Siri, Google Assistant, etc.). From a user experience point of view, one of the main challenges of state-of-the-art dialog systems is the slow reaction of the assistants. Usually, these dialog systems wait for the completion of a user utterance and afterwards process the utterance. The processed utterance can trigger a suitable action, e. g. ask for clarification, book a certain flight, or bring an object. Actions can have a high execution time, due to which the dialog systems react slowly. If an action can be separated into subactions, the reaction time of the dialog system can be improved through incremental processing of the user utterance and starting subactions while the utterance is still being uttered. The action still has the same execution time but the action is completed earlier because it was started earlier and therefore the dialog system can react faster. In the domain of airplane travel information, database queries can be finished earlier if the system can execute subqueries before the completion of the user utterance, e. g. the utterance *On next Wednesday flight from Kansas City to Chicago should arrive in Chicago around 7 pm* can be separated in the databases queries *flight from Kansas City to Chicago on next Wednesday* and *use result of the first query to find flights that arrive in Chicago around 7 pm*. In the domain of household robots, e. g. the user goal of the user utterance *Bring me from the kitchen the cup that I like because it reminds me of my unforgettable vacation in the United States* can be fulfilled faster if the robot goes to the kitchen before the user utters what object the robot should bring.

Motivated by this approach to improve the reaction of dialog systems, our main contribution is a low-latency natural language understanding (NLU) component. We use the Transformer architecture (Vaswani et al., 2017) to build this low-latency NLU component, but the ingredient to understand partial utterances and incrementally process user utterances is the model-agnostic training process presented in this work. Secondly, partial utterances are particularly affected by noise. This is due to the short context available in partial utterances and because automatic speech recognition (ASR) systems cannot utilize their complete language model and therefore potentially make more errors when transcribing short utterances. We address the potential noisier inputs by including noisy inputs in the training process. Finally, we present two evaluation schemes for low-latency NLU components.

Proceedings of the 2019 EMNLP Workshop W-NUT: The 5th Workshop on Noisy User-generated Text, pages 265–274
Hong Kong, Nov 4, 2019. ©2019 Association for Computational Linguistics

2 Related Work

Gambino et al. (2018) described time buying strategies to avoid long pauses, e. g. by uttering an acknowledgement or echoing the user input. However, the triggered actions are not finished earlier with this approach, but in cases where long pauses cannot be avoided, even with incremental processing, such time buying strategies can be applied.

The automatically generated backchannel described by Rüde et al. (2017) gives feedback during the uttering of an utterance. However, only acoustic features are used and it does not reduce the latency of actions that can be triggered by the utterances.

Studies have been conducted on incremental NLU. DeVault et al. (2009) used a maximum entropy classificator (Berger et al., 1996) to classify the partial utterances. They optimized the maximum entropy classificator for partial utterances by using an individual classificator for every utterance length. The problem of this classification approach is that it is not suitable for tasks with a lot of different parameter combinations; for such tasks, a slot filling (sequence labeling task) or word by word approach (sequence to sequence task) is more suitable. Such a more suitable approach is described by Niehues et al. (2018) for incrementally updating machine translations. The authors used an attention-based encoder decoder (Bahdanau et al., 2015), which outputs a sequence. We described and evaluated in this work such a more suitable approach for incremental NLU.

Different approaches are available to handle noisy input, such as general-purpose regularization techniques like dropout (Srivastava et al., 2014) and domain-specific regularization techniques e. g. data augmentation by inserting, deleting, and substituting words (Sperber et al., 2017). Our trained models in this work uses the general-purpose techniques and some of our trained models are trained with such augmented data to have a better performance on noisy data.

3 Low-latency NLU component

In this work, we present a model-agnostic method to build an incremental processing low-latency NLU component. The advantages of this model-agnostic method are that we can use state-of-the-art neural network architectures and reuse the method for future state-of-the-art neural network architectures. Our used architecture is described in Section 3.1 and the used data is described in Section 3.2. Our method to include the information necessary to incrementally process user utterances with high quality in the training dataset is described in Section 3.3 and our methods to include noise to process noisy texts with high quality are described in Section 3.4. In Sections 3.5 and 3.6, we present our evaluation metrics and evaluation schemes respectively. The configuration of the used architecture is given in Section 3.7.

3.1 Architecture

We used the Transformer architecture in our experiments to demonstrate the model-agnostic method. The Transformer architecture, with its encoder and decoder, was used as sequence to sequence architecture. The user utterances are the input sequences and their corresponding triggered actions are the output actions (this is described in more details in Section 3.2). We used the Transformer implementation used by Pham et al. (2019) and added the functionality for online translation. The original code[1] and the added code are publicly available[2]. The partial utterances and, in the end, the full utterance were fed successively and completely into the Transformer architecture without using information of the computation of the previous partial utterances. Our proposed method is model-agnostic because of this separate treatment and therefore an arbitrary model that can process sequences can be used to process the partial and full utterances. The method is depicted in Figure 1 for the utterance *Flights to Pittsburgh*.

3.2 Data

For our experiments, we used utterances from the Airline Travel Information System (ATIS) datasets. We used the utterances that are used by Hakkani-Tur et al. (2016) and are publicly available[3]. These utterances were cleaned and every utterance is labeled with its intents and for every token, the corresponding slot is labeled with a tag (in the IOB2 format (Sang and Veenstra, 1999) that is depicted in Figure 2).

We converted the data from the IOB2 format to a sequence to sequence format (Constantin et al., 2019). The source sequence is a user utterance

---

[1] https://github.com/quanpn90/NMTGMinor/tree/DbMajor

[2] https://github.com/msc42/NMTGMinor/tree/DbMajor

[3] https://github.com/yvchen/JointSLU

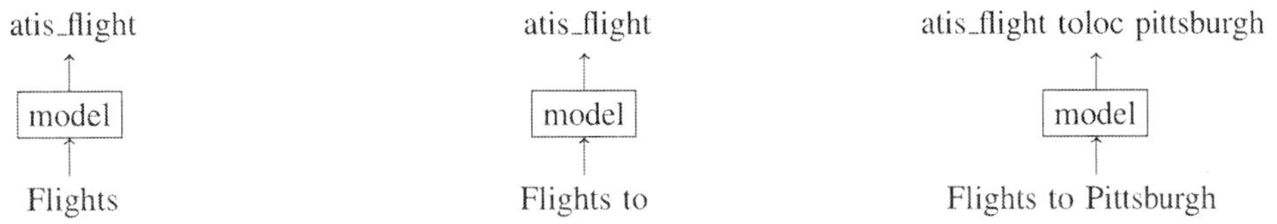

Figure 1: model-agnostic approach

utterance (source sequence)	Which	flights	go	from	New	York	to	Pittsburgh
slots	O	O	O	O	B-fromloc	I-fromloc	O	B-toloc
intents	atis_flight							
target sequence	atis_flight fromloc new york toloc pittsburgh							

Figure 2: joint intents classification and slot filling approach to end-to-end target sequence

and the target sequence consists of the intents followed by the parameters. In this work, the slot tag and the corresponding slot tokens compose an intents parameter. An example of the conversion of the IOB2 format to the sequence to sequence format is depicted in Figure 2. The sequence to sequence format has the advantages that no rules are needed for mapping the slot tokens to an API call or a database query and that this format is more robust against noisy text like *What is restriction ap slash fifty seven*, where the noise word slash is introduced (in the classical IOB2 format, the tokens *ap* and *fifty seven* would not belong to the same chunk).

The publicly available utterances are partitioned in a training and test dataset. The training dataset is partitioned in a training (train-2) and validation (dev-2) dataset. Hereinafter, original training dataset refers to the utterances of the training dataset, training dataset refers to the utterances of the train-2 dataset, and validation dataset refers to the utterances of the dev-2 dataset. We created a file that maps to every utterance in the training dataset the line number of the corresponding utterance in the original training dataset and a file that maps to every utterance in the validation dataset the line number of the corresponding utterance in the original training dataset. We published these two files[4]. The training dataset has 4478 utterances, the validation dataset has 500 utterances, and the test dataset has 893 utterances.

The utterances were taken from the ATIS2 dataset (Linguistic Data Consortium (LDC) catalog number LDC93S5), the ATIS3 training dataset (LDC94S19) and the ATIS3 test dataset (LDC94S26). The audio files of the spoken utterances and the uncleaned human transcribed transcripts are on the corresponding LDC CDs. For the original training dataset and the test dataset, we published[5] in each case a file that maps to every utterance the path of the corresponding audio file and a file that maps to every utterance the path of the corresponding transcript of the corresponding LDC CD. One audio file is missing on the corresponding LDC CD (LDC94S19): atis3/17_2.1/atis3/sp_trn/sri/tx0/2/tx0022ss.wav (corresponding to the training dataset). We used the tool sph2pipe[6] to convert the SPH files (with extension .wav) of the LDC CDs to WAVE files.

The utterances have an average token length of 11.21 - 11.36 in the training dataset, 11.48 in the validation dataset, and 10.30 in the test dataset. We tokenized the utterances with the default English word tokenizer of the Natural Language Toolkit (NLTK)[7] (Bird et al., 2009).

There are 19 unique intents in the ATIS data. In the training dataset, 22 utterances are labeled with 2 intents and 1 utterance is labeled with 3 intents, in the validation dataset, there are 3 utterances with 2 intents and in the test dataset, there are 15 utterances with 2 intents, the rest of the utterances are labeled with 1 intent. The intents are separated by the number sign in the target sequence. The intents are unbalanced (more than 70 % of the utterances have the same intent, more than 90 % of

---

[4] https://github.com/msc42/ATIS-data

[5] see footnote 4

[6] https://www.ldc.upenn.edu/sites/www.ldc.upenn.edu/files/ctools/sph2pipe_v2.5.tar.gz

[7] https://www.nltk.org/

the utterances belong to the 5 most used intents). More information about the intents distribution is given Table 7. There are 83 different parameters that can parameterize the intents. On average, a target has 3.35 (training dataset), 3.46 (validation dataset), and 3.19 (test dataset) parameters.

3.3 Training process to improve incremental processing

We call our dataset, which contains the dataset described in Section 3.2, *cleaned full transcripts*. Our model-agnostic method to achieve good quality for partial utterances works in this manner: We use the dataset with the full utterances and create partial utterances from it. An utterance of the length n is split into n utterances, where the i-th utterance of these utterances has the length i. The target contains all information that can be gotten from the source utterance of the length i. When only a part of a chunk is in the user utterance, only this part is integrated in the target utterances, e. g. *I want a flight from New York to San* has the target *atis_flight fromloc.city_name new york toloc.city_name san*. Such partial information contains information and can accelerate database queries, for example. We created with this method the *cleaned incremental transcripts* dataset. An arbitrary model without modifications, in this work the Transformer architecture, can be trained with this dataset to have an improved incremental processing ability compared to a model trained only with full utterances. Since every partial utterance is regarded as independent utterance, like the full utterances, our approach is model-agnostic. The model-agnostic approach for the utterance *Flights to Pittsburgh* is depicted in Figure 1.

3.4 Training process to improve robustness

In Section 3.3, the training process for improving the incremental processing is described. However, the described process does not consider the fact that the incremental data are noisier. We induced noise in the training by training with artificial noise, human transcribed utterances that contain the noise of spoken utterances, and utterances transcribed by an ASR system.

The dataset *cleaned incremental transcripts with artificial noise* consists of the utterances from the dataset *cleaned incremental transcripts* to these artificial noise were added with the approach described by Sperber et al. (2017). We

published the implementation[8] of this approach. In this approach, random distributions are used to substitute, insert, and delete words. We sampled the words for substitution and insertion based on acoustic similarity to the original input. As vocabulary for the substitutions and insertions, we used the tokens of the utterances of the training dataset of the *cleaned incremental transcripts* dataset and filled the vocabulary with the most frequent tokens not included in the used training dataset occurring in the source utterances of a subset of the Open-Subtitle corpus[9] (Tiedemann, 2009) that is publicly available[10] (Senellart, 2017). We chose the position of the words to be substituted and deleted based on the length. Shorter words are often more exposed to errors in ASR systems and therefore should be substituted and deleted in the artificial noise approach more frequently. Since substitutions are more probable in ASR systems, we reflected this in the artificial noise generating by assigning substitutions a 5-times higher probability than insertions or deletions. For the value of the hyperparameter τ (the induced amount of noise), we used 0.08.

For the dataset *human full transcripts*, we used the human transcribed transcripts given by the LDC CDs. We mapped these utterances to the corresponding targets of the datasets based on the *cleaned full transcripts* dataset. The utterances are not cleaned and have some annotations like noise and repeated words. The dataset *human incremental transcripts*, *human incremental transcripts with artificial noise*, and *human full transcripts with artificial noise* were generated analogous to the described approaches before.

For the dataset *automatic incremental transcripts*, we automatically transcribed the audio files from the LDC CDs with the ASR system Janus Recognition Toolkit (JRTk) (Nguyen et al., 2017, 2018). This ASR system is used as an out-of-domain ASR system - there is no adaption for the ATIS utterances. We used the incremental mode of the JRTk, which means that transcriptions are updated multiple times while transcribing. It is not automatically possible to generate the partial output targets to the partial utterances, because the ASR system makes errors and it is

---

[8]`https://github.com/msc42/NLP-tools/blob/master/noise_adder.py`

[9]based on `http://www.opensubtitles.org/`

[10]`https://s3.amazonaws.com/opennmt-trainingdata/opensub_qa_en.tgz`

impossible to map with 100 % accuracy automatically the wrong transcript *to come up* to the correct transcript *Tacoma*, for example. We used a workaround: We measured the length of a partial transcript, searched the corresponding transcript of the *human incremental transcripts* dataset that has the same length, and used the target of the found transcript. If there were only shorter transcripts, the target of the full transcript was used. This approach punishes insertions and deletions of the ASR system. For the dataset *automatic full transcripts*, we used the last transcript of the incremental transcripts of the ASR system for the user utterance and the full target of the corresponding utterance of the *human full transcripts* dataset. For the mentioned missing audio file, we used the human transcription of the corresponding LDC CD.

An arbitrary model without modifications, in this work the Transformer architecture, is trained with one of the described noisy datasets to have improved robustness compared to a model trained only with clean utterances.

3.5 Evaluation metrics

We evaluated the quality of the models, trained with the different datasets, with the metric F_1-score for which we used an adapted definition for the precision and the recall in this work and the metric intents accuracy.

The adapted definitions for the precision and the recall consider the order of the classes in the target sequence. The intents and the intents parameters are the classes. Intents parameters with the same slot tag are considered as different classes. We call the F_1-score calculated with the adapted definition of the precision and the recall considering order multiple classes F_1-score (CO-MC F_1-score). Order considering means that the predicted parameters have to be in the correct order in the target sequence. In the target sequence

atis_flight fromloc.city_name milwaukee
toloc.city_name orlando depart_date.day_name
wednesday depart_time.period_of_day evening or
or depart_date.day_name thursday
depart_time.period_of_day morning

the order is important. To calculate the true positives, we adapted the Levenshtein distance (Levenshtein, 1966). The entities that are compared in this adapted Levenshtein distance are the classes. The adapted Levenshtein distance is only changed by a match (incremented by one) and the maxi-

mum instead of the minimum function is used to select the best operation. In Figure 3 the recursive definition of the adapted Levenshtein distance (ALD) is depicted. Let r be the reference and h the hypothesis and $|r|$ and $|h|$ the number of classes of the reference or hyptothesis respectively and r_i and h_i the i-th class of the reference or hypothesis respectively. $L_{|h|,|r|}$ is the resultant adapted Levenshtein distance and the number of true positives.

$$ALD_{0,0} = 0$$
$$ALD_{i,0} = i, 1 \leq i \leq |h|$$
$$ALD_{0,j} = j, 1 \leq j \leq |r|$$
$$ALD_{i,j} = max \begin{cases} ALD_{i-1,j-1} + 1, & r_i = h_j \\ ALD_{i-1,j-1}, & r_i \neq h_j \\ ALD_{i-1,j} \\ ALD_{i,j-1} \end{cases}$$
$$1 \leq i \leq |h|, 1 \leq j \leq |r|$$

Figure 3: adapted Levenshtein distance

With this approach, the given example target has 7 instead of 9 true positives if the slot tokens of the intents parameters with the slot tag depart_date.day_name parameter are changed (in this case both parameters are considered as substitutions in the Levenshtein distance). We counted all true positives for the different classes over the evaluated dataset and divided the counted true positives by the reference lengths of all targets for the recall and by the hypothesis lengths for the precision (micro-averaging). The CO-MC F_1-score is more strict than the vanilla F_1-score because of the consideration of the order.

The metric intents accuracy considers all intents as whole. That means the intents accuracy of one target is 100 % if the intents of the reference and the hypothesis are equivalent; otherwise, the intents accuracy is 0 %.

3.6 Evaluation schemes

We used for the evaluation of the models the model version of the epoch with the best CO-MC F_1-score on the following validation datasets with only full utterances: For the models trained with the datasets based on the *cleaned full tran scripts* dataset, we used the validation dataset of the *cleaned full transcripts* dataset, for models trained with the datasets based on the *human full transcripts* dataset, we used the validation dataset of the *human full transcripts* dataset, and for models trained with the datasets based on the *automatic incremental transcripts* dataset, we used the validation dataset of the *automatic full transcribed* dataset.

We evaluated our models with our evaluation metrics in the following manner: First, we evaluated the models with partial utterances that contain the first 100 %, 75 %, 50 %, and 25 % of the tokens of the full utterances. The number of tokens is rounded off to the next integer and this number is called i in the following. For evaluating with the cleaned and the human transcribed utterances, we used the first i tokens of the full utterances. For evaluating with automatically transcribed utterances, we used the first utterance in the *automatic incremental transcripts* dataset of the corresponding utterance that was equal than or greater than i, because the ASR system did not produce partial utterances for all numbers less than the token length of the full utterance. In the following, this evaluation scheme is called *partial utterances processing*.

In addition, we evaluated our models with the metric intents accuracy in the following manner: We predicted the intents incrementally and aborted the incremental processing once a certain confidence for the intents prediction was reached. We used 95 %, 90 %, 85 %, and 80 % as confidence thresholds. When the target confidence was never reached, the full utterance was used to predict the intents, even if the confidence of the full utterance was under the confidence threshold. We used for those experiments the partial utterances successively for the cleaned and human transcribed utterances and the partial utterances successively of the automatically transcribed utterances. In the automatically transcribed utterances, the last transcript is the full utterance. In the following, this evaluation scheme is called *confidence based processing*.

The models trained on the cleaned transcripts cannot be evaluated appropriately on the uncleaned transcripts, because the numbers are written in Arabic numerals in the cleaned transcripts and in words in the uncleaned transcripts. The conversion is often ambiguous. The same applies to the other direction.

3.7   System Setup

We optimized the Transformer architecture for the validation dataset of the *cleaned full transcripts* dataset. The result of this optimization is a Transformer architecture with a model and inner size of 256, 4 layers, 4 heads, Adam (Kingma and Ba, 2015) with the noam learning rate decay scheme (used by Vaswani et al. (2017) as learning rate decay scheme) as optimization algorithm, a dropout of 40 %, an attention, embedding, and residual dropout of each 20 % and a label smoothing of 15 %. We used 64 utterances as batch size. The vocabulary of a trained model contains all words of the training dataset with which it was trained. We trained the models for 100 epochs.

4   Results

4.1   Partial utterances processing

In Tables 1, 3, and 5, the CO-MC F_1-scores and the intents accuracies are depicted for the evaluation scheme *partial hypothesis processing* for the cleaned, human transcribed, and automatically transcribed utterances respectively.

In the following, all percentage differences are absolute percentage differences. The ranges refer to the smallest and biggest improvements on the CO-MC F_1-score. If no artificial noise is explicitly mentioned, the models without artificial noise are meant.

The models that were trained only with full utterances have better results evaluated on the full utterances than models trained with the partial and full utterances (in the range from 1.3 % to 3.24 %). However, the models trained on the partial and full utterances have better results when they are evaluated on the first 75 % and 50 % of the tokens (in the range from 0.81 % to 4.39 %). Evaluated on the utterances of the first 25 % of the tokens, there are even bigger improvements (in the range from 14.44 % to 47.91 %). This means that our proposed training method improves the processing of partial utterances, especially if they are partial utterances produced incrementally at the beginning of the incremental processing of an utterance. For an incremental processing capable NLU component, the best approach is to combine the two models. The model trained on only full utterances is used for the full utterances and the model trained on the partial and full utterances is used for the incrementally produced partial utterances.

With the combination described above, the performance of the models trained with the automatically transcribed utterances decreased less compared to the models trained on the human transcribed utterances, evaluated on the human transcribed utterances (in the range from 0.13 % to 2.01 %) than the models trained with the human transcribed utterances decreased compared to the models trained on the automatically transcribed utterances, evaluated on the automatically transcribed utterances (in the range from 1.22 % to 4 %). In our experiments, the result was consequently that it is better to train on noisier data. This is especially the case on evaluating the full utterances.

We tried to simulate the noise of the automatically transcribed utterances with artificial noise. We used again the same combination described above. The performance of the models trained with the human transcribed utterances with artificial noise decreased less compared to the models trained on the human transcripts, evaluated on the human transcribed utterances (in the range from -1.43 % to 2.5 %) than the models trained with the human transcribed utterances decreased compared to the human transcribed utterances with artificial noise, on the automatically transcribed utterances (in the range from -1.06 % to 5.21 %).

4.2 Confidence based processing

In Tables 2, 4, and 6, the intents accuracies and the needed percentage of tokens on average are depicted for the evaluation scheme *confidence based processing* for the cleaned, human transcribed, and automatically transcribed utterances respectively.

In the following, all percentage differences are absolute percentage differences. The ranges refer to the smallest and biggest improvements on the intents accuracy metric. If no artificial noise is explicitly mentioned, the models without artificial noise are meant.

The following statements apply to the incrementally trained models (the models trained only on the full utterances have only good results if they can use nearly the full utterances and therefore it makes no sense to use them for early predicting of intents). It is better to train on the automatically transcribed utterances. The decreasing is from 1.57 % to 2.58 % if they are evaluated on the human transcribed utterances, but they have an improvement from 2.58 % to 4.25 % if they are eval-

uated on the automatically transcribed utterances compared to the models trained on the human transcribed utterances. The human transcribed utterances with artificial noise decrease by -1.46 % to 2.58 % if they are evaluated on the human transcribed utterances, but they have an improvement from 0.67 % to 3.69 % if they are evaluated on the automatically transcribed utterances compared to the models trained on the human transcribed utterances.

4.3 Computation time

Since the partial utterances are fed successively in the Transformer architecture, the computation must be fast enough for the system to work off all partial utterances without latency. On a notebook with an Intel Core i5-8250U CPU - all computations were done only on the CPU and we limited the usage to one thread (with the app taskset) so other component like the ASR system can run on the same system - it took 310 milliseconds to compute the longest utterance (46 tokens) of the cleaned utterances and 293 milliseconds to compute the utterance (38 tokens) with the longest target sequence (41 tokens - one intent with 17 parameters) of the cleaned utterances. We processed continually both utterances for 15 minutes and selected for both utterances the run with the maximum computation time. The model was the model trained with the cleaned full utterances. This means that it is possible to process an utterance after every word because a normal user needs on average more than these measured times to utter a word or type a word with a keyboard.

5 Conclusions and Further Work

In this work, we report that the best approach for an incremental processing capable NLU component is to mix models. A model trained on partial and full utterances should be used for processing partial utterances and a model trained only on full utterances for processing full utterances. In particular, the improvements are for the first incrementally produced utterances, which contain only a small number of tokens, high if the model is not only trained on full utterances.

Evaluated on the noisy human and even noisier automatically transcribed utterances, we got better results with the models trained with the human transcribed utterances with artificial noise and the models trained with the automatically transcribed

training dataset	first 100 %	first 75 %	first 50 %	first 25 %
cleaned, full	92.90 / 97.09	89.95 / 96.19	88.98 / 90.37	49.36 / 49.05
cleaned, incremental	91.60 / 96.75	94.20 / 94.85	93.37 / 92.05	83.15 / 79.73
cleaned, incremental, art. noise	91.97 / 96.19	94.65 / 94.85	93.22 / 91.83	81.75 / 78.61

Table 1: CO-MC F_1-scores / intents accuracies of the first 100 %, 75 %, 50 %, and 25 % of the tokens of the utterances of the test dataset of the cleaned human transcribed full utterances

training dataset	95 % conf.	90 % conf.	85 % conf.	80 % conf.
cleaned, full	96.98 / 96.36	80.29 / 74.14	72.56 / 30.62	70.66 / 29.93
cleaned, incremental	96.42 / 97.27	95.97 / 92.16	92.83 / 34.74	89.47 / 30.56
cleaned, incremental, art. noise	95.86 / 99.02	95.41 / 92.20	91.71 / 33.12	86.56 / 24.54

Table 2: Intents accuracies / percentages of the used tokens for predicting the intents using the smallest partial utterance of the test dataset of the cleaned human transcribed incremental utterances for which the system has a confidence of more or equal than 95 %, 90 %, 85 %, and 80 %, if the confidence is not reached, the full utterance is used

training dataset	first 100 %	first 75 %	first 50 %	first 25 %
human, full	90.44 / 94.85	87.91 / 94.51	87.75 / 89.14	34.86 / 48.38
human, full, art. noise	87.94 / 95.30	85.77 / 94.74	89.51 / 91.27	67.71 / 68.65
human, incremental	88.57 / 94.40	90.58 / 93.62	91.51 / 90.59	82.77 / 79.06
human, incremental, art. noise	88.24 / 95.41	90.71 / 94.18	92.94 / 91.83	84.14 / 79.17
automatic, full	88.43 / 93.39	86.18 / 93.62	89.24 / 90.37	56.80 / 70.66
automatic, incremental	86.38 / 92.72	89.56 / 93.73	90.05 / 89.03	82.64 / 79.17

Table 3: CO-MC F_1-scores / intents accuracies of the first 100 %, 75 %, 50 %, and 25 % of the tokens of the utterances of the test dataset of the human transcribed full utterances

training dataset	95 % conf.	90 % conf.	85 % conf.	80 % conf.
human, full	94.51 / 96.51	90.82 / 85.59	77.60 / 32.52	76.37 / 30.22
human, full, art. noise	95.41 / 96.33	90.71 / 81.50	77.72 / 30.58	76.04 / 28.13
human, incremental	94.18 / 99.10	93.95 / 89.53	90.59 / 32.83	88.47 / 27.04
human, incremental, art. noise	95.18 / 97.85	95.41 / 92.65	91.60 / 32.78	85.89 / 24.90
automatic, full	88.58 / 91.51	88.35 / 83.19	76.82 / 30.85	75.36 / 28.79
automatic, incremental	92.61 / 99.63	92.16 / 93.38	88.35 / 35.41	85.89 / 30.33

Table 4: Intents accuracies / percentages of the used tokens for predicting the intents using the smallest partial utterance of the test dataset of the human transcribed incremental utterances for which the system has a confidence of more or equal than 95 %, 90 %, 85 %, and 80 %, if the confidence is not reached, the full utterance is used

training dataset	first 100 %	first 75 %	first 50 %	first 25 %
human, full	83.87 / 91.49	80.26 / 91.04	83.13 / 85.78	42.06 / 51.74
human, full, art. noise	81.93 / 91.15	78.94 / 90.71	83.76 / 88.35	74.98 / 68.31
human, incremental	80.63 / 87.91	82.16 / 88.24	85.85 / 85.44	80.49 / 75.93
human, incremental, art. noise	82.93 / 91.04	83.16 / 89.70	88.13 / 88.02	83.75 / 77.27
automatic, full	87.14 / 93.39	82.06 / 92.61	85.15 / 90.03	70.05 / 72.45
automatic, incremental	84.62 / 92.27	84.90 / 91.71	87.07 / 88.35	84.49 / 79.73

Table 5: CO-MC F_1-scores / intents accuracies of the first partial automatically transcribed utterances that have equal or more than the first 100 %, 75 %, 50 %, and 25 % of the tokens of the utterances of the test dataset of the automatically transcribed full utterances

training dataset	95 % conf.	90 % conf.	85 % conf.	80 % conf.
human, full	91.04 / 97.63	87.46 / 88.24	78.84 / 41.52	76.82 / 38.41
human, full, art. noise	90.93 / 96.87	86.79 / 85.60	77.94 / 37.99	76.48 / 34.93
human, incremental	87.68 / 99.18	87.35 / 91.23	86.56 / 42.35	83.99 / 36.96
human, incremental, art. noise	90.59 / 98.29	90.37 / 93.58	88.47 / 40.33	82.98 / 31.53
automatic, full	88.24 / 93.41	87.91 / 86.65	80.40 / 38.74	78.50 / 35.70
automatic, incremental	91.83 / 99.16	91.60 / 94.29	89.14 / 39.67	86.67 / 34.54

Table 6: Intents accuracies / percentages of the used tokens for predicting the intents using the first partial utterance of the test dataset of the automatically transcribed incremental utterances for which the system has a confidence of more or equal than 95 %, 90 %, 85 %, and 80 %, if the confidence is not reached, the full utterance is used

utterances. This is especially the case when evaluating the full utterances. A reason for this could be that the partial utterances can be already considered as noisier utterances.

The short computation time of the processing of an utterance makes it possible to use the incremental processing for spoken and written utterances.

In future work, it has to be evaluated whether our results are also valid for other architectures and other datasets. A balanced version of the ATIS datasets can also be seen as another dataset.

We got better performance with artificial noise. However, the results could be improved by optimizing the hyperparameter of the artificial noise generator.

In this work, we researched the performance using incremental utterances. There should be research on how the results of the incremental processing can be separated into subactions and how much this can accelerate the processing of actions in real-world scenarios.

In future work not only the acceleration, but also other benefits of the incremental processing, like using semantic information for improving the backchannel, could be researched.

Acknowledgement

This work has been conducted in the SecondHands project which has received funding from the European Union's Horizon 2020 Research and Innovation programme (call:H2020- ICT-2014-1, RIA) under grant agreement No 643950.

References

Tamim Asfour, Lukas Kaul, Mirko Wächter, Simon Ottenhaus, Pascal Weiner, Samuel Rader, Raphael Grimm, You Zhou, Markus Grotz, Fabian Paus, Dmitriy Shingarey, and Hans Haubert. 2018. Armar-6: A collaborative humanoid robot for industrial environments. In *IEEE/RAS International Conference on Humanoid Robots (Humanoids)*, pages 447–454.

Dzmitry Bahdanau, Kyunghyun Cho, and Yoshua Bengio. 2015. Neural machine translation by jointly learning to align and translate. In *Proceedings of the Third International Conference on Learning Representations (ICLR)*.

Adam L. Berger, Vincent J. Della Pietra, and Stephen A. Della Pietra. 1996. A maximum entropy approach to natural language processing. *Comput. Linguist.*, 22(1):39–71.

Steven Bird, Ewan Klein, and Edward Loper. 2009. *Natural Language Processing with Python*, 1st edition. O'Reilly Media, Inc.

Stefan Constantin, Jan Niehues, and Alex Waibel. 2019. Multi-task learning to improve natural language understanding. In *Proceedings of the Tenth International Workshop on Spoken Dialogue Systems (IWSDS)*.

David DeVault, Kenji Sagae, and David Traum. 2009. Can I finish? learning when to respond to incremental interpretation results in interactive dialogue. In *Proceedings of the SIGDIAL 2009 Conference*.

Soledad López Gambino, Sina Zarrieß, Casey Kennington, and David Schlangen. 2018. Learning to buy time: A data-driven model for avoiding silence while task-related information cannot yet be presented. In *Proceedings of 22nd Workshop on the Semantics and Pragmatics of Dialogue (Semdial)*.

Dilek Hakkani-Tur, Gokhan Tur, Asli Celikyilmaz, Yun-Nung Chen, Jianfeng Gao, Li Deng, and Ye-Yi Wang. 2016. Multi-domain joint semantic frame parsing using bi-directional rnn-lstm. In *Proceedings of the 17th Annual Meeting of the International Speech Communication Association (Interspeech)*.

Diederik P. Kingma and Jimmy Ba. 2015. Adam : A method for stochastic optimization. In *Proceedings of the Third International Conference on Learning Representations (ICLR)*.

Vladimir I Levenshtein. 1966. Binary codes capable of correcting deletions, insertions, and reversals. *Soviet physics doklady*, 10(8):707–710.

Thai-Son Nguyen, Markus Müller, Matthias Sperber, Thomas Zenkel, Sebastian Stüker, and Alex Waibel. 2017. The 2017 kit iwslt speech-to-text systems for english and german. In *Proceedings of the 14th International Workshop on Spoken Language Translation (IWSLT)*.

Thai Son Nguyen, Matthias Sperber, Sebastian Stüker, and Alex Waibel. 2018. Building real-time speech recognition without cmvn. In *20th International Conference on Speech and Computer (SPECOM)*.

Jan Niehues, Ngoc-Quan Pham, Thanh-Le Ha, Matthias Sperber, and Alex Waibel. 2018. Low-latency neural speech translation. In *Proceedings of the 19th Annual Meeting of the International Speech Communication Association (Interspeech)*.

Ngoc-Quan Pham, Thai-Son Nguyen, Jan Niehues, Markus Müller, and Alex Waibel. 2019. Very deep self-attention networks for end-to-end speech recognition. In *Proceedings of the 20th Annual Meeting of the International Speech Communication Association (Interspeech)*.

Robin Rüde, Markus Müller, Sebastian Stüker, and Alex Waibel. 2017. Enhancing backchannel prediction using word embeddings. In *Proceedings of the 18th Annual Meeting of the International Speech Communication Association (Interspeech)*.

Erik F. Tjong Kim Sang and Jorn Veenstra. 1999. Representing text chunks. In *Proceedings of the Ninth Conference of the European Chapter of the Association for Computational Linguistics (EACL)*.

Jean Senellart. 2017. English chatbot model with opennmt. http://forum.opennmt.net/t/english-chatbot-model-with-opennmt/184.

Matthias Sperber, Jan Niehues, and Alex Waibel. 2017. Toward robust neural machine translation for noisy input sequences. In *Proceedings of the 14th International Workshop on Spoken Language Translation (IWSLT)*.

Nitish Srivastava, Geoffrey E. Hinton, Alex Krizhevsky, Ilya Sutskever, and Ruslan Salakhutdinov. 2014. Dropout: a simple way to prevent neural networks from overfitting. *Journal of Machine Learning Research*, 15(1):1929–1958.

Jörg Tiedemann. 2009. News from OPUS - A collection of multilingual parallel corpora with tools and interfaces. In *Recent Advances in Natural Language Processing*, volume V, pages 237–248. John Benjamins, Amsterdam/Philadelphia.

Ashish Vaswani, Noam Shazeer, Niki Parmar, Jakob Uszkoreit, Llion Jones, Aidan N Gomez, Łukasz Kaiser, and Illia Polosukhin. 2017. Attention is all you need. In *Advances in Neural Information Processing Systems 30*, pages 5998–6008. Curran Associates, Inc.

A Supplemental Material

train	valid	test	intent(s)
73.89	71.4	70.77	atis_flight
8.6	7.6	5.38	atis_airfare
5.14	5.0	4.03	atis_ground_service
3.1	3.6	4.26	atis_airline
2.9	3.4	3.7	atis_abbreviation
1.56	2.2	1.01	atis_aircraft
1.0	1.8	0.11	atis_flight_time
0.92	2.0	0.34	atis_quantity
0.42	0.4	1.34	atis_flight#atis_airfare
0.4	0.2	0.67	atis_city
0.38	0.6	1.12	atis_distance
0.38	0.6	2.02	atis_airport
0.33	0.6	0.78	atis_ground_fare
0.33	0.2	2.35	atis_capacity
0.27	0	8	atis_flight_no
0.13	0	0.67	atis_meal
0.11	0.2	0	atis_restriction
0.04	0	0	atis_airline# atis_flight_no
0.02	0	0	atis_ground_service# atis_ground_fare
0.02	0	0	atis_cheapest
0.02	0	0	atis_aircraft#atis_flight# atis_flight_no
0	0.2	0	atis_airfare# atis_flight_time
0	0	0.22	atis_day_name
0	0	0.11	atis_flight#atis_airline
0	0	0.11	atis_airfare#atis_flight
0	0	0.11	atis_flight_no# atis_airline

Table 7: intents distribution (in percent) of the ATIS utterances used in this work

Benefits of Data Augmentation for NMT-based Text Normalization of User-Generated Content

Claudia Matos Veliz, Orphée De Clercq and Véronique Hoste

LT³, Language and Translation Technology Team - Ghent Univeristy

Groot-Brittanniëlaan 45, 9000, Ghent, Belgium

`Firstname.Lastname@UGent.be`

Abstract

One of the most persistent characteristics of written user-generated content (UGC) is the use of non-standard words. This characteristic contributes to an increased difficulty to automatically process and analyze UGC. Text normalization is the task of transforming lexical variants to their canonical forms and is often used as a pre-processing step for conventional NLP tasks in order to overcome the performance drop that NLP systems experience when applied to UGC. In this work, we follow a Neural Machine Translation approach to text normalization. To train such an encoder-decoder model, large parallel training corpora of sentence pairs are required. However, obtaining large data sets with UGC and their normalized version is not trivial, especially for languages other than English. In this paper, we explore how to overcome this data bottleneck for Dutch, a low-resource language. We start off with a small publicly available parallel Dutch data set comprising three UGC genres and compare two different approaches. The first is to manually normalize and add training data, a money and time-consuming task. The second approach is a set of data augmentation techniques which increase data size by converting existing resources into synthesized non-standard forms. Our results reveal that, while the different approaches yield similar results regarding the normalization issues in the test set, they also introduce a large amount of over-normalizations.

1 Introduction

Social media text are considered important language resources for several NLP tasks (Van Hee et al., 2017; Pinto et al., 2016; Zhu et al., 2014). However, one of their most persistent characteristics is the use non-standard words. Social media texts are considered a type of written user-generated content (UGC) in which several lan-

guage variations can be found as people often tend to write as they speak and/or write as fast as possible (Vandekerckhove and Nobels, 2010). For instance, it is typical to express emotions by the use of symbols or lexical variation. This can be done in the form of the repetition of characters or flooding (*wooooow*), capitalization (*YEY!*), and the productive use of emoticons. In addition, the use of homophonous graphemic variants of a word, abbreviations, spelling mistakes or letter transpositions are also used regularly (Eisenstein et al., 2014).

Since NLP tools have originally been developed for and trained on standard language, these non-standard forms adversely affect their performance. One of the computational approaches which has been suggested to overcome this problem is text normalization (Sproat et al., 2001). This approach envisages transforming the lexical variants to their canonical forms. In this way, standard NLP tools can be applied in a next step after normalization (Aw et al., 2006). Please note that for some NLP applications, e.g. sentiment analysis, it might be beneficial to keep some 'noise' in the data. For example, the use of flooding or capital letters could be a good indicator of the emotion present in the text (Van Hee et al., 2017). However, for applications aiming at information extraction from text, normalization is needed to help to improve the performance of downstream NLP tasks (Schulz et al., 2016). Kobus et al. (2008) introduced three metaphors to refer to these normalization approaches: the spell checking, automatic speech recognition and machine translation metaphors.

In this paper, the focus will be on the machine translation metaphor. One of the most conventional approaches is to use Statistical Machine Translation (SMT) techniques (Kaufmann, 2010; De Clercq et al., 2014; Junczys-Dowmunt and Grundkiewicz, 2016), in particular using

Proceedings of the 2019 EMNLP Workshop W-NUT: The 5th Workshop on Noisy User-generated Text, pages 275–285

Hong Kong, Nov 4, 2019. ©2019 Association for Computational Linguistics

the Moses toolkit (Koehn et al., 2007). However, neural networks have proven to outperform many state-of-the-art systems in several NLP tasks (Young et al., 2018). Especially the encoder-decoder model with an attention mechanism (Bahdanau et al., 2014) for recurrent neural networks (RNN) has lead to a new paradigm in machine translation, i.e., Neural MT (NMT) (Sutskever et al., 2014; Cho et al., 2014; Bahdanau et al., 2014; Luong et al., 2015; Sennrich et al., 2016a).

Many works have adopted and applied these techniques to the normalization task (Ikeda et al., 2016; Mandal and Nanmaran, 2018; Lusetti et al., 2018) some of them outperforming the SMT approach. However, it is well-known that these neural systems require a huge amount of data in order to perform properly (Ikeda et al., 2016; Saito et al., 2017). When it comes to translation these data even have to be parallel and should thus consist of aligned source and target sentences. Unfortunately, when it comes to UGC text normalization there is a lack of parallel corpora in which UGC is considered the source language and its standardized form the target language. Furthermore, the problem even exacerbates when working with low-resourced languages.

In this work, we follow an NMT approach to tackle text normalization of Dutch UGC and explore how to overcome this parallel data bottleneck for Dutch, a low-resource language. We start off with a publicly available tiny parallel Dutch data set comprising three UGC genres and compare two different approaches. The first one is to manually normalize and add training data, a money and time-consuming task. The second approach consists in a set of data augmentation techniques which increase data size by converting existing resources into synthesized non-standard forms. Our results reveal that the different setups resolve most of the normalization issues and that automatic data augmentation mainly helps to reduce the number of over-generalizations produced by the NMT approach.

In the following section, we discuss related work on MT-based text normalization as well as data augmentation techniques. In section 3, we discuss the two approaches to augment the available data: manual annotations of new sentence pairs and augmentation techniques. The data used for our experiments are also explained in detail. Section 4 gives an overview of the experiments and results, whereas section 5 concludes this work and offers prospects for future work.

2 Related Work

Previous research on UGC text normalization has been performed on diverse languages using different techniques ranging from hand-crafted rules (Chua et al., 2018) to deep learning approaches (Ikeda et al., 2016; Sproat and Jaitly, 2016; Lusetti et al., 2018). Three different metaphors were introduced by Kobus et al. (2008) to refer to these normalization approaches. That is the automatic speech recognition (ASR), spell checking, and translation metaphors. The ASR approach exploits the similarity between social media text and spoken language. Several works have followed this methodology, mostly combining it with the others (Beaufort and Roekhaut, 2010; Xue et al., 2011; Han and Baldwin, 2011). In the spell checking approach, corrections from noisy to standard words occurs at the word level. Some approaches have treated the problem by using dictionaries containing standard and non-standard words (Clark and Araki, 2011). However, the success of this kind of systems highly depends on the coverage of the dictionary. Since social media language is highly productive and new terms constantly appear, it is very challenging and expensive to continuously keep such a dictionary up to date.

In this work, we consider the normalization task as a Machine Translation problem and treat noisy UGC text as the source language and its normalized form as the target language. In the past, several works have also used this approach and there are two leading paradigms: Statistical and Neural Machine Translation.

Statistical Machine Translation (SMT) models, especially those trained at the character-level, have proven highly effective for the task because they capture well intra-word transformations (Pennell and Liu, 2011). Besides, they have the advantage of being effective when small training data is provided, thanks to their small vocabulary size. Kaufmann (2010), for example, followed a two step approach for the normalization of English tweets. First, they pre-processed the tweets to remove as much noise as possible, and then they used Moses[1] to convert them into standard English. Moses is a statistical machine translation package which can produce high quality translations from one lan-

---

[1] http://statmt.org/moses/

Source Sentence	Target Sentence	English Translation
iz da muzieksgool vnavnd ? kwt da niemr .	is dat muziekschool vanavond ? ik weet dat niet meer .	is that music school tonight? I don't know that anymore.
wa is je msn k en e nieuwe msn omda k er nie meer op graal . xxx	wat is je msn ik heb een nieuwe msn omdat ik er niet meer op geraak . xx	what is your msn i have a new msn because i can't get it anymore. xx
@renskedemaessc dm me je gsmnummer eens :-)	<user> doormail me je gsmnummer eens <emoji>	<user> mail me your cellphone number once <emoji>

Table 1: Source and target pairs as parallel data for a machine translation approach.

guage into another (Koehn et al., 2007). De Clercq et al. (2013) proposed a phrase-based method to normalize Dutch UGC comprising various genres. In a preprocessing step they handled emoticons, hyperlinks, hashtags and so forth. Then they worked in two steps: first at the word level and then at the character level. This approach revealed good results across various genres of UGC. However, a high number of phonetic alternations remained unresolved.

Recently, neural networks have proven to outperform many state-of-the-art systems in several NLP tasks (Young et al., 2018). The encoder-decoder model for recurrent neural networks (RNN) was developed in order to address the sequence-to-sequence nature of machine translation and obtains good results for this task (Sutskever et al., 2014; Cho et al., 2014; Bahdanau et al., 2014; Luong et al., 2015). The model consist of two neural networks: an encoder and a decoder. The encoder extracts a fixed-length representation from a variable-length input sentence, and the decoder generates a correct translation from this representation. Some works on text normalization have followed the same approach (Lusetti et al., 2018; Cho et al., 2014).

In 2016, Sproat and Jaitly (Sproat and Jaitly, 2016) presented a challenge to the research community: given a large corpus of *written* text aligned to its normalized *spoken* form, train an RNN to learn the correct normalization function. Although their work focuses on the Text to Speech (TTS) use case of text normalization, they compared prior work of text normalization for TTS (Rao et al., 2015; William Chan, 2016) and also discuss the problems that arise when using neural networks for text normalization. They made clear that although RNNs were often capable to produce surprisingly good results and learn some complex mappings, they are prone to make errors like read-

ing the wrong number, or substituting *hours* for *gigabytes*. This makes them risky to apply in a TTS system. Lusetti et al. (2018) performed NMT text normalization over Swiss German WhatsApp messages and compared it to a state-of-the-art SMT system. They revealed that integrating language models into an encoder-decoder framework can outperform the character-level SMT methods for that language.

Although the encoder-decoder model has shown its effectiveness in large datasets, it is much less effective when only a small number of sentence pairs is available (Sennrich et al., 2016b; Zoph et al., 2016). Automatic data augmentation is commonly used in vision and speech and can help train more robust models, particularly when using smaller datasets (Chatfield et al., 2014; Taylor and Nitschke, 2017). Fadaee et al. (2017) present Translation Data Augmentation (TDA), a method to improve the translation quality for low resource pairs (English to German and German to English). Their approach generates new sentence pairs containing rare words in new, synthetically created contexts.

Data augmentation techniques have therefore also been applied to outperform text normalization for low-resourced languages. For example, Ikeda et al. (2016) performed text normalization at the character level for Japanese text and proposed a method for data augmentation using handcrafted rules. Their method transformed existing resources into synthesized non-standard forms using the rules proposed in the work of Sasano et al. (2015). They proved that the use of the synthesized corpus improved the performance of Japanese text normalization. Saito et al. (2017) also proposed two methods for data augmentation in order to improve text normalization. Unlike the previous work, the proposed method did not use prior knowledge to generate synthetic data at the character and morphological level. Instead, they proposed a two-level data augmentation model that converted standard sentences to dialect sentences by using extracted morphological conversion patterns. Their experiments using an encoder-decoder model for Japanese, performed better than SMT with Moses after the data augmentation.

3 Methodology

Our objective is to go from noisy to standard text and we tackle this normalization problem using an NMT approach. Sequence-to-Sequence (seq2seq) models have been used for a variety of NLP tasks including machine translation obtaining state-of-the-art results (Luong et al., 2015; Young et al., 2018). As in general MT, a translation model is trained on parallel data consisting of pairs (x, y) of source sentences/words (= social media text) and their corresponding target equivalents (= standard text). Table 1 lists some examples of the noisy data we are dealing with.

3.1 NMT Approach

In this approach, both input and output sentences are going in and out of the model. As described in the literature overview, the model consist of two neural networks: an encoder and decoder (See Figure 1).

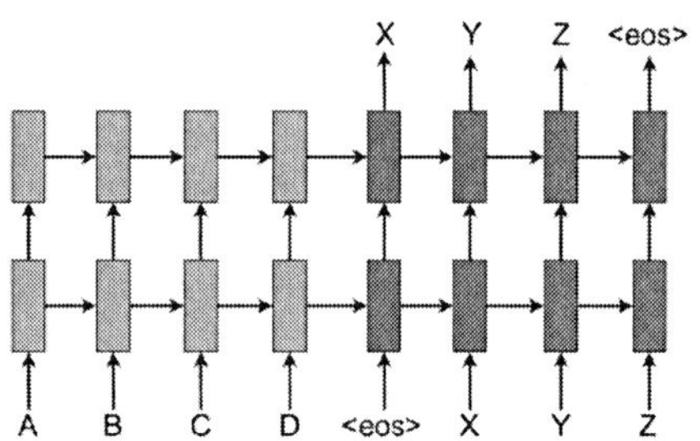

Figure 1: Encoder-decoder architecture. The light-color nodes represent the encoder and the dark-color ones the decoder. Image taken from Luong et al. (2015).

The encoder extracts a fixed-length representation from a variable-length input sentence (*A B C D*), and the decoder generates a correct translation from this representation (*X Y Z*). In the figure, <eos> marks the end of a sentence. The encoder-decoder model is trained on a parallel corpus consisting of source sentences aligned with their normalized form.

We relied on OpenNMT[2] to train our encoder-decoder model. OpenNMT is an open source (MIT) initiative for neural machine translation and neural sequence modeling (Klein et al., 2017). The main system is implemented in the Lua/Torch mathematical framework, and can easily be extended using Torch's internal standard neural network components. We used the version of the system with the basic architecture which consists of an encoder using a simple LSTM recurrent neural network. The decoder applies attention over the source sequence and implements input feeding (Luong et al., 2015).

3.2 Evaluation Metric

To evaluate the results of the normalization, we calculated Word Error Rate (WER) and Character Error Rate (CER) over the three genres. WER is a metric derived from the Levenshtein distance (Levenshtein, 1966), working at the word level. Character Error Rate (CER), instead, works at the character level. These metrics take into account the number of insertions (INS), deletions (DEL) and substitutions (SUBS) that are needed to transform the suggested string into the manually normalized string. The metrics are computed as follows:

$$WER = \frac{INS_w + DEL_w + SUBS_w}{N_w}$$

$$CER = \frac{INS_c + DEL_c + SUBS_c}{N_c}$$

where N_w is the number of words in the reference and N_c represents the number of characters.

The higher the value, the higher the number of normalization operations needed to obtain the target sentence.

3.3 Overcoming Data Sparsity

Since our focus is on Dutch, our starting point is an existing Dutch corpus comprising three UGC genres, which were manually normalized (Schulz et al., 2016). The genres represented in this corpus are the following:

Tweets (TWE), which were randomly selected from the social network.

Message board posts (SNS), which were sampled from the social network Netlog, which was

---

[2]http://opennmt.net

a Belgian social networking website targeted at youngsters.

Text messages (SMS), which were sampled from the Flemish part of the SoNaR corpus (Treurniet et al., 2012).

This corpus is, to our knowledge, the only freely available parallel normalization dataset for Dutch.

Table 2 presents the number of parallel sentences in each genre and the number of words before and after normalization[3]. The WER and CER values computed between the original and target parallel sentence pairs are also shown. These values were calculated per sentence and averaged over the data set. As can be observed, the Dutch tweets (TWE) required hardly any normalization (a WER of 0.09 and a CER of 0.047). This can be explained by the fact that this platform has mainly been mainly adopted by professionals in Belgium who write in a more formal style (Schulz et al., 2016).

Genre	# Sent.	# Words		WER	CER
		Src	Tgt		
TWE	841	12951	12867	0.09	0.047
SNS	770	11670	11913	0.25	0.116
SMS	801	13063	13610	0.27	0.117

Table 2: Dutch parallel corpora data statistics.

On the other hand, we observe that the text messages (SMS) required most normalization (with a WER and CER score of 0.27 and 0.117, respectively). Table 2 also reveals that the corpus amounts to only a few hundred parallel sentences. NMT models often fail when insufficient data is provided (Ikeda et al., 2016; Saito et al., 2017). Because of that, we believe that the mentioned data would not be enough to successfully train a RNN model.

Under these conditions, we decided to experimentally verify which approach works best in order to overcome this data sparsity problem. Our objective is to find out whether annotating more data or using a set of data augmentation techniques is more beneficial and leads to better results.

Collecting More Data

First, we sampled and manually annotated ten thousand additional sentences for each of the three genres. We sampled SMS from the Flemish part of the SoNaR corpus (Treurniet et al., 2012). For

the TWE genre, new data were retrieved by crawling Twitter using the Twiqs software[4], which was specifically designed to crawl Dutch tweets from Twitter. We used emoticons as keyword for the crawling process in order to collect text in which noisy words were present to some extent. For the SNS genre we relied on text collected from the social networking site ASKfm (Van Hee et al., 2018), where users can create profiles and ask or answer questions, with the option of doing so anonymously. ASKfm data typically consists of question-answer pairs published on a user's profile.

For all genres we made sure that there were no duplicates in the texts. Each message was also lowercased and tokenized using the NLTK tokenizer[5] prior to annotation, and the annotators also had to check the tokenization of the sentences. Besides this, hashtags, usernames and emoticons were replaced with a placeholder. All data was then normalized following the procedure described in Schulz et al. (2016). Table 3 shows the size of the newly annotated data in terms of the number of sentences and tokens for each genre. The WER and CER values give an insight into the normalization needed for each of the genres.

Genre	# Sent.	# Words		WER	CER
		Src	Tgt		
TWE	5190	124578	122165	0.10	0.062
SNS	8136	108127	110326	0.23	0.094
SMS	7626	111393	113846	0.15	0.067

Table 3: Parallel corpora data statistics after new annotations.

As can be derived from Table 3, TWE remains the least noisy genre, whereas the SNS genre is now the noisiest one with higher WER and CER values.

Applying Data Augmentation Techniques

A less time-consuming way to overcome data sparsity is to investigate the added value of data augmentation. A rudimentary way to augment the existing data, is to simply add monolingual standard data to both the source and target side of the corpus. This implies providing a large number of standard Dutch sentences from which the model can learn the standard word use. This type of data augmentation, however, is very primitive and, although it could probably provide good training

---

[3]All data was normalized following the procedure described in Schulz et al. (2016)

[4]https://github.com/twinl/crawler
[5]https://www.nltk.org/api/nltk.tokenize.html

data to learn the standard form of sentences, the non-canonical form of the words would be heavily (and even more so than in the beginning) under-represented in the training data.

In order to address this problem, we took our initial parallel data as starting point for the data augmentation. Since we want to obtain more instances of non-canonical words and their corresponding normalized forms, we first relied on pretrained embeddings to replace the standard words by similar ones. These embeddings where trained on Flemish newspapers and magazines data collected from 1999 to 2014 in the Mediargus Archives, which can be accessed through GoPress Academic[6].

	Sentences
Source	jaaa sws *toch* <emoji> *hij is echt leuk*
Target	ja sowieso *toch* <emoji> *hij is echt leuk*
Embed.	jaaa sws **toch** <emoji> **hijzelf** is **wel tof**
	jaaa sws **toch** <emoji> hij **blijft** echt leuk
	jaaa sws **maar** <emoji> hij is **gewoon** leuk
	jaaa sws **dus** <emoji> hij is **inderdaad tof**
English	yes anyway **but/so** <emoji> **he/himself** is **really/just/indeed nice/cool**

Table 4: Data augmentation using pretrained embeddings.

Using this technique, we produced synthesized similar sentences containing the original user-generated text in it. In Table 4, we illustrate this augmentation technique, starting from the user-generated text *jaaa sws toch :) hij is echt leuk* (*yes anyway* <emoji> *he is really nice*). It is important to emphasize that we only replaced words that were already in their standard form in both the source and target side of the corpus. The replacements were made using the most similar words from the embeddings, using a similarity threshold with a value equal or greater than 0.5.

In the upper part of Table 4 the standard words in the source and target sentences are placed in cursive. In the middle and lower part, the bold words show the replacement for the standard words based on the embeddings. Please note that this replacement sometimes caused a (slight) change in the semantics of the sentence, as in *jaaa sws toch* <emoji> *hij blijft echt leuk*. However, since we are only dealing with lexical normalization, we argue that this is not an issue for the task.

In a second step, we applied an additional data augmentation technique which produces new ab-

breviations on the source side of the parallel corpus. We made use of a dictionary of about 350 frequent abbreviations appearing in social media texts, such as *lol* (*laughing out loud*) and *aub* for *alstublieft* (*you are welcome*) (Schulz et al., 2016). We went through every sentence in the newly augmented dataset and duplicated every sentence pair in which a standard word or phrase appeared in the dictionary. In the new source sentence, this standard word was then replaced by its corresponding abbreviation. For those cases in which a standard word had several abbreviation forms, a new original sentence for each of the abbreviation forms was generated.

Table 5 exemplifies this technique. It first lists two examples of newly generated sentences using the embeddings after which the abbreviations step is applied, leading to two additional new sentences.

	Sentences
Source	jaaa sws *toch* <emoji> *hij is echt leuk*
Target	ja sowieso *toch* <emoji> *hij is echt leuk*
Embed.	jaaa sws **maar** <emoji> hij is **gewoon** leuk
	jaaa sws **dus** <emoji> hij is **inderdaad tof**
Abbr.	jaaa sws **maar** <emoji> hij is ***gwn*** leuk
	jaaa sws **dus** <emoji> hij is ***idd* tof**
English	yes anyway **but/so** <emoji> he is **really/just/indeed nice/cool**

Table 5: Data augmentation using dictionary of abbreviations.

3.4 Experimental Setup

To conduct the experiments, both approaches were applied in several steps and combinations.

The first round of experiments (**Setup 0**), which we will consider as the baseline system, consisted in applying the NMT architecture to the original small Dutch parallel corpus, as presented in Table 2. We performed 10-fold cross validation experiments to ensure that each part of the dataset would be used once as training and test set. For the remaining experiments (see Setup 1 to 3 below), this entire small dataset was used as held-out test set in order to find out which approach works best for overcoming data sparsity.

	INS	DEL	SUBS	SUM
TWE	1118	934	355	2407
SNS	2483	2238	1021	5742
SMS	4209	508	758	5475

Table 6: Operations needed at the character level to normalize the test set for each genre.

---

[6]https://bib.kuleuven.be/english/ub/searching/collections/belgian-press-database-gopress-academic

Table 6 shows the number of insertions (INS), deletions (DEL) and substitutions (SUBS) that are needed to transform the source sentences of the test set into manually normalized ones. The last column of the table shows the overall number of operations that would need to be solved by the systems.

The new annotations as presented in Table 3 were used for training **(Setup 1)**. In a next step, we trained the NMT model on the data obtained by first applying the embeddings technique to the newly annotated data **(Setup 2)** and then together with the abbreviation step **(Setup 3)**.

	#Sent.	# Words	
TWE		**Src**	**Tgt**
1	5190	124578	122165
2	697441	20692213	20416466
3	853465	26316110	26002836
SNS		**Src**	**Tgt**
1	8136	108127	110326
2	577281	21120858	21499465
3	835091	70337827	71257870
SMS		**Src**	**Tgt**
1	7626	111393	113846
2	615195	15356594	15669683
3	766946	22066532	22651464

Table 7: Parallel corpora data statistics for each experimental setup.

Table 7 shows the number of parallel training sentences and words in the original and target sides of each setup for each genre.

4 Experiments

As we explained before, the goal of our work is to experimentally verify which approach works best to overcome the data sparsity problem for a low-resourced language such as Dutch UGC: annotating more data or using data augmentation techniques.

Figure 2 presents the WER results for each genre with the different experimental setups and Figure 3 the CER results. As expected, the 10-fold cross validation experiments on the tiny original datasets (Setup 0) leads to bad results. The system's output consisted of sentences of the type $<emoji>$, de , , , . . . $<emoji>$. These are random repetitions of the most represented tokens in the training data like *ik* (*I* in English), punctuation marks or $<emoji>$ labels. The system was thus unable to learn from such a small dataset.

Annotating more data (Setup 1) consistently results in better WER scores, with a more than 50% WER and CER reduction for the SMS genre. The data augmentation techniques (Setup 2 and 3) seem to further affect the normalization results. For the SNS and SMS genre, the WER and CER significantly decreases with the data augmentation technique relying on embeddings. However, when more noise is introduced to the data set (Setup 3) this adversely affects the WER and CER values for all genres.

However, these data augmentation techniques only seem to work when working with similar data. Recall that for the annotation of the new training data, similar data were collected for both the SMS and SNS genre. However, given the lack of noise in the Twitter data, we opted for another strategy to collect the tweets, viz. we used emoticons as keyword to query Twitter. This has resulted in a different style of Twitter corpus which comprises more noisy and longer tweets (see CER in Table 2 vs. Table 3). This difference in training data seems to be amplified during data augmentation. Whereas the use of more training data yields a large WER reduction (from 1.16 to 0.72 WER and 1.37 to 0.74 CER), this effect of adding more data is undone when augmenting the training data with similar data. However, the overall CER and WER results are still better than when just relying on the small original dataset (Setup 0).

When comparing the results of Setups 2 and 3 with the original WER values of our test set (see Table 2) we observe that the normalization task was not solved at all as the WER values are almost always higher. Only for the SMS genre, the results are somewhat similar, with WERs of 0.25 and 0.27 for setups 2 and 3 respectively.

4.1 Error Analysis

Table 8 shows some examples of sentences which were normalized using the proposed NMT approach.

However, the approach still produces a large number of odd normalizations. For example, in the second sentence in Table 8, the system was unable to correctly normalize some of the words. For instance, the word *byyyy* (*there*) was incorrectly normalized as the verb *gedragen* (*behave*). Furthermore, the system also produced odd translations of words that already were in their standard form. For example, the word *tammy*, which is a proper name, is changed into *toevallig* (*accidentally*) and the word *u* (*you*) was duplicated in

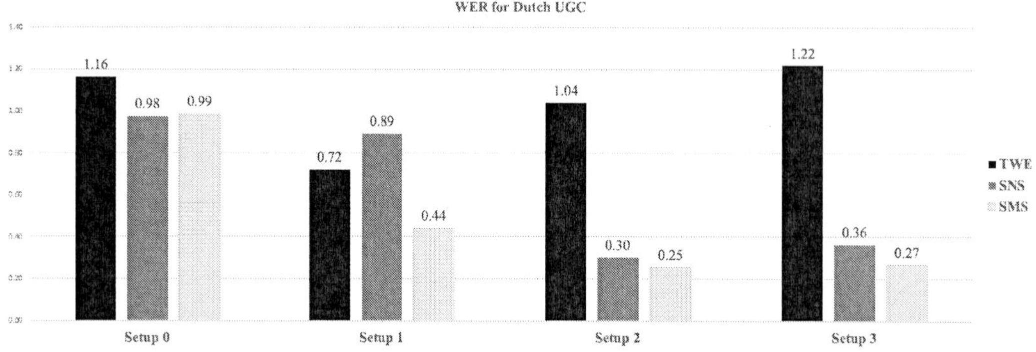

Figure 2: Experimental WER results for each genre using the different setups.

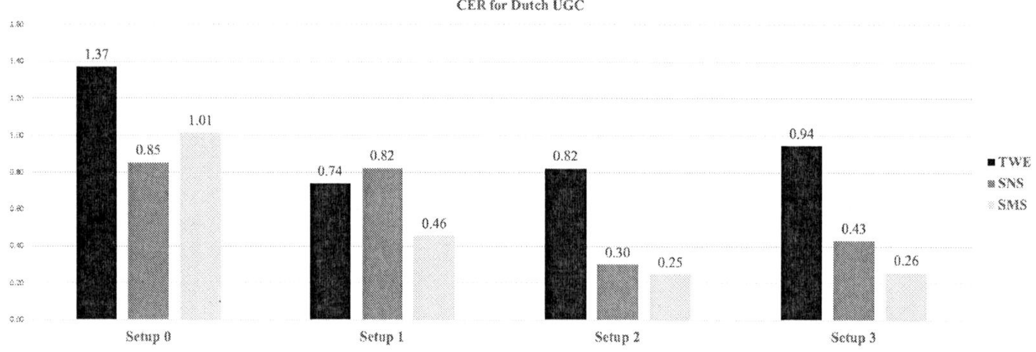

Figure 3: Experimental CER results for each genre using the different setups.

src sent.	haha zekr mdaje n vriend vn matti zyt ! <emoji> x
norm sent.	haha zeker omdat je een vriend van matti zijt ! <emoji> x
tgt sent.	haha zeker omdat je een vriend van matti zijt ! <emoji> x
English	haha certainly because you are a friend of matti !<emoji> x
src sent.	eeh ik sta dr nie byyyy <emoji> I y mis je
norm sent.	he ik sta er niet gedragen <emoji> love you mis je
tgt sent.	he ik sta er niet bij <emoji> love you mis je
English	hey i am not there <emoji> love you miss you
src sent.	jonge tammy , k u
norm sent.	jongen toevallig , ik u u
tgt sent.	jongen tammy , ik u
English	boy tammy, me you

Table 8: Examples of original (src), predicted (norm) and target (tgt) sentences using the NMT approach. An English translation is also provided.

the normalized sentence. So, while the k (I) was correctly normalized, two errors were introduced through normalization. This is a common issue

with encoder-decoder models (Sproat and Jaitly, 2017).

TWE	INS	DEL	SUBS	SUM
Test	1118	934	355	2407
Setup 0	1101	930	351	2382
Setup 1	1099	924	330	2353
Setup 2	1105	917	326	2348
Setup 3	1094	903	325	2322
SNS	**INS**	**DEL**	**SUBS**	**SUM**
Test	2483	2238	1021	5742
Setup 0	2454	2225	992	5671
Setup 1	2468	2220	995	5683
Setup 2	2366	2092	968	5426
Setup 3	2366	2141	971	5478
SMS	**INS**	**DEL**	**SUBS**	**SUM**
Test	4209	508	758	5475
Setup 0	4107	505	727	5339
Setup 1	4094	483	700	5277
Setup 2	4099	470	709	5278
Setup 3	4090	468	710	5268

Table 9: Number of solved operations at the character level after normalization for each genre.

Ideally, the number of operations after normalization should be reduced to zero. As can be derived from the Table 9 many cases where correctly normalized by the systems. However, we can also observe that at the same time a large number of over-normalizations is introduced (Figures 2 and 3). Regarding data augmentation, we conclude that these techniques mainly help to reduce the number of over-normalizations.

5 Conclusions and Future Work

In this article, we have applied text normalization to Dutch written user-generated content from different genres: text messages, message board posts and tweets. We followed a Neural Machine Translation approach to solve the task and investigated different data augmentation techniques to tackle the problem of data sparsity. Results show that for most of the genres, augmenting the data by using pretrained embeddings helped to reduce the errors introduced by the NMT approach. On the other hand, for most of the genres Setup 0, i.e. training the NMT system on the small in-domain data set, solved most of the normalization problems in the test set.

Regarding the quality of the normalization, despite many of the non-standard words being correctly normalized, the system also produced odd translations, which is a common error using encoder-decoder architectures (Sproat and Jaitly, 2016). This is reflected in the number of over-normalizations that are produced by the system. With respect to these errors, we believe that following a modular approach that helps to solve the remaining errors, instead of only using NMT, could lead to a better performance.

References

AiTi Aw, Min Zhang, Juan Xiao, and Jian Su. 2006. A phrase-based statistical model for SMS text normalization. *Proceedings of the COLING/ACL on Main conference poster sessions -*, (July):33–40.

Dzmitry Bahdanau, Kyunghyun Cho, and Yoshua Bengio. 2014. Neural Machine Translation by Jointly Learning to Align and Translate. *arXiv preprint*, pages 1–15.

Richard Beaufort and Sophie Roekhaut. 2010. A hybrid rule/model-based finite-state framework for normalizing SMS messages. *Proceedings of the 48th Annual Meeting of the Association for Computational Linguistics. Association for Computational Linguistics*, 1(July):770–779.

Ken Chatfield, Karen Simonyan, Andrea Vedaldi, and Andrew Zisserman. 2014. Return of the devil in the details: Delving deep into convolutional nets. *BMVC 2014 - Proceedings of the British Machine Vision Conference 2014*, pages 1–11.

Kyunghyun Cho, Bart van Merrienboer, Caglar Gulcehre, Dzmitry Bahdanau, Fethi Bougares, Holger Schwenk, and Yoshua Bengio. 2014. Learning Phrase Representations using RNN Encoder-Decoder for Statistical Machine Translation. *International Conference on Learning Representations ICLR*.

Mason Chua, Daan Van Esch, Noah Coccaro, Eunjoon Cho, Sujeet Bhandari, and Libin Jia. 2018. Text Normalization Infrastructure that Scales to Hundreds of Language Varieties. In *Proceedings of the Eleventh International Conference on Language Resources and Evaluation (LREC)*, pages 1353–1356, Miyazaki, Japan. European Language Resource Association.

Eleanor Clark and Kenji Araki. 2011. Text normalization in social media: Progress, problems and applications for a pre-processing system of casual English. *Procedia - Social and Behavioral Sciences*, 27(Pacling):2–11.

Orphée De Clercq, Sarah Schulz, Bart Desmet, and Véronique Hoste. 2014. Towards Shared Datasets for Normalization Research. *Proceedings of the Ninth International Conference on Language Resources and Evaluation (LREC'14)*, pages 1218–1223.

Orphée De Clercq, Sarah Schulz, Bart Desmet, Els Lefever, and Véronique Hoste. 2013. Normalization of Dutch User-Generated Content. *Proceedings of the 9th International Conference on Recent Advances in Natural Language Processing (RANLP 2013)*, pages 179–188.

Jacob Eisenstein, Brendan O'Connor, Noah A. Smith, and Eric P. Xing. 2014. Diffusion of lexical change in social media. *PLoS ONE*, 9(11):1–13.

Marzieh Fadaee, Arianna Bisazza, and Christof Monz. 2017. Data augmentation for low-Resource neural machine translation. *ACL 2017 - 55th Annual Meeting of the Association for Computational Linguistics, Proceedings of the Conference (Long Papers)*, 2:567–573.

Bo Han and Timothy Baldwin. 2011. Lexical Normalisation of Short Text Messages : Makn Sens a #twitter. *Proceedings of the 49th Annual Meeting of the Association for Computational Linguistics*, pages 368–378.

Taishi Ikeda, Hiroyuki Shindo, and Yuji Matsumoto. 2016. Japanese Text Normalization with Encoder-Decoder Model. *Proceedings of the 2nd Workshop on Noisy User-generated Text (WNUT)*, pages 129–137.

Marcin Junczys-Dowmunt and Roman Grundkiewicz. 2016. Phrase-based Machine Translation is State-of-the-Art for Automatic Grammatical Error Correction. pages 1546–1556.

Max Kaufmann. 2010. Syntactic Normalization of Twitter Messages. *International conference on natural language processing*, 2:1–7.

Guillaume Klein, Yoon Kim, Yuntian Deng, Josep Crego, Jean Senellart, and Alexander M. Rush. 2017. OpenNMT: Open-source Toolkit for Neural Machine Translation. *arXiv preprint*.

Catherine Kobus, Francois Yvon, and Geéraldine Damnati. 2008. Normalizing SMS: are two metaphors better than one? *Proceedings of the 22nd International Conference on Computational Linguistics*, 1(August):441–448.

Philipp Koehn, Hiue Hoang, Alexandra Birch, Chris Callison-Burch, Marcello Federico, Nicola Bertoldi, and Brooke Cowan. 2007. Moses: Open source toolkit for statistical machine translation. *Prague: Proceedings of 45th Annual Meeting of the Association for Computational Linguistics Companion Volume Proceedings of the Demo and Poster Sessions.*, (June):177–180.

Vladimir I. Levenshtein. 1966. Binary codes capable of correcting deletions. *Soviet physics doklady*, 10(8):707–710.

Minh-Thang Luong, Hieu Pham, and Christopher D. Manning. 2015. Effective Approaches to Attention-based Neural Machine Translation. *arXiv preprint*.

Massimo Lusetti, Tatyana Ruzsics, Anne Göhring, Tanja Samardi Samardžic, and Elisabeth Stark. 2018. Encoder-Decoder Methods for Text Normalization. In *Proceedings of the Fifth Workshop on NLP for Similar Languages, Varieties and Dialects (VarDial)*, pages 18–28.

Sounil Mandal and Karthick Nanmaran. 2018. Normalization of Transliterated Words in Code-Mixed Data Using Seq2Seq Model & Levenshtein Distance. In *Proceedings of the 2018 EMNLP Workshop W-NUT: The 4th Workshop on Noisy User-generated Text*, pages 49–53, Brussels, Belgium. Association for Computational Linguistics.

D Pennell and Y Liu. 2011. A Character-Level Machine Translation Approach for Normalization of SMS Abbreviations. *Proceedings of the 5th International Joint Conference on Natural Language Processing*, pages 974–982.

Alexandre Pinto, Hugo Gonalo Oliveira, and Ana Oliveira Alves. 2016. Comparing the performance of different NLP toolkits in formal and social media text. *OpenAccess Series in Informatics*, 51(3):31–316.

Kanishka Rao, Fuchun Peng, Hasim Sak, and Francoise Beaufays. 2015. Grapheme-to-phoneme conversion using Long Short-Term Memory recurrent neural networks. In *2015 IEEE International Conference on Acoustics, Speech and Signal Processing (ICASSP)*, volume 2015-Augus, pages 4225–4229.

Itsumi Saito, Jun Suzuki, Kyosuke Nishida, and Kugatsu Sadamitsu. 2017. Improving Neural Text Normalization with Data Augmentation at Character- and Morphological Levels. *Proceedings of the The 8th International Joint Conference on Natural Language Processing*, pages 257–262.

Ryohei Sasano, Sadao Kurohashi, and Manabu Okumura. 2015. A Simple Approach to Unknown Word Processing in Japanese Morphological Analysis. *Journal of Natural Language Processing*, 21(6):1183–1205.

Sarah Schulz, Guy De Pauw, Orphée De Clercq, Bart Desmet, Véronique Hoste, Walter Daelemans, and Lieve Macken. 2016. Multimodular Text Normalization of Dutch User-Generated Content. *ACM Transactions on Intelligent Systems and Technology*, 7(4):1–22.

Rico Sennrich, Barry Haddow, and Alexandra Birch. 2016a. Improving Neural Machine Translation Models with Monolingual Data. In *Proceedings of the 54th Annual Meeting of the Association for Computational Linguistics*, pages 86–96.

Rico Sennrich, Barry Haddow, and Alexandra Birch. 2016b. Neural machine translation of rare words with subword units. *54th Annual Meeting of the Association for Computational Linguistics, ACL 2016 - Long Papers*, 3:1715–1725.

Richard Sproat, Alan W. Black, Stanley Chen, Shankar Kumar, Mari Ostendorf, and Christopher Richards. 2001. Normalization of non-standard words. *Computer Speech and Language*, 15(3):287–333.

Richard Sproat and Navdeep Jaitly. 2016. RNN Approaches to Text Normalization: A Challenge. *Computing Research Repository (CoRR)*, abs/1611.0.

Richard Sproat and Navdeep Jaitly. 2017. An RNN model of text normalization. *Proceedings of the Annual Conference of the International Speech Communication Association, INTERSPEECH*, 2017-Augus:754–758.

Ilya Sutskever, Oriol Vinyals, and Quoc V. Le. 2014. Sequence to Sequence Learning with Neural Networks. In *Advances in neural information processing systems*, pages 3104–3112.

Luke Taylor and Geoff Nitschke. 2017. Improving Deep Learning using Generic Data Augmentation. *arXiv preprint*.

Maaske Treurniet, Henk van den Heuvel, Nelleke Oostdijk, and Orphée De Clercq. 2012. Collection of a corpus of Dutch SMS. *Proceedings of the Eight*

Conference of International Language Resources and Evaluation., pages 2268–2273.

Cynthia Van Hee, Gilles Jacobs, Chris Emmery, Bart Desmet, Els Lefever, Ben Verhoeven, Guy De Pauw, Walter Daelemans, and Véronique Hoste. 2018. Automatic detection of cyberbullying in social media text. *Plos One*, 13(10):1–21.

Cynthia Van Hee, Marjan Van De Kauter, Orphée De Clercq, Els Lefever, Bart Desmet, and Véronique Hoste. 2017. Noise or music? Investigating the usefulness of normalisation for robust sentiment analysis on social media data. *Revue Traitement Automatique des Langues*, 58(1):63–87.

Reinhild Vandekerckhove and Judith Nobels. 2010. Code eclecticism : Linguistic variation and code alternation in the chat language of Flemish teenagers. *Journal of Sociolinguistics*, 14(5):657–677.

Quoc Le Oriol Vinyals William Chan, Navdeep Jaitly. 2016. Listen, attend and spell: A neural network for large vocabulary conversational speech recognition. *IEEE International Conference on Acoustics, Speech, and Signal Processing (ICASSP) 2016*, pages 4960–4964.

Zhenzhen Xue, Dawei Yin, and Bd Davison. 2011. Normalizing Microtext. *Analyzing Microtext*, pages 74–79.

Tom Young, Devamanyu Hazarika, Soujanya Poria, and Erik Cambria. 2018. Recent trends in deep learning based natural language processing. *ieee Computational intelligenCe magazine*, 13(3):55–75.

Linhong Zhu, Aram Galstyan, James Cheng, and Kristina Lerman. 2014. Tripartite graph clustering for dynamic sentiment analysis on social media. *Proceedings of the ACM SIGMOD International Conference on Management of Data*, pages 1531–1542.

Barret Zoph, Deniz Yuret, Jonathan May, and Kevin Knight. 2016. Transfer Learning for Low-Resource Neural Machine Translation. pages 1568–1575.

Contextual Text Denoising with Masked Language Models

Yifu Sun *
Tencent
yifusun2016@outlook.com

Haoming Jiang
Georgia Tech
jianghm@gatech.edu

Abstract

Recently, with the help of deep learning models, significant advances have been made in different Natural Language Processing (NLP) tasks. Unfortunately, state-of-the-art models are vulnerable to noisy texts. We propose a new contextual text denoising algorithm based on the ready-to-use masked language model. The proposed algorithm does not require retraining of the model and can be integrated into any NLP system without additional training on paired cleaning training data. We evaluate our method under synthetic noise and natural noise and show that the proposed algorithm can use context information to correct noise text and improve the performance of noisy inputs in several downstream tasks.

1 Introduction

Based on our prior knowledge and contextual information in sentences, humans can understand noisy texts like misspelled words without difficulty. However, NLP systems break down for noisy text. For example, Belinkov and Bisk (2017) showed that modern neural machine translation (NMT) system could not even translate texts with moderate noise. An illustrative example of English-to-Chinese translation using Google Translate [1] is presented in Table 1.

Text correction systems are widely used in real-world scenarios to address noisy text inputs problem. Simple rule-based and frequency-based spell-checker are limited to complex language systems. More recently, modern neural Grammatical Error Correction (GEC) systems are developed with the help of deep learning (Zhao et al., 2019; Chollampatt and Ng, 2018). These GEC systems heavily rely on annotated GEC corpora, such as CoNLL-2014 (Ng et al., 2014). The parallel GEC

corpora, however, are expansive, limited, and even unavailable for many languages. Another line of researches focuses on training a robust model that inherently deals with noise. For example, Belinkov and Bisk (2017) train robust character-level NMT models using noisy training datasets, including both synthetic and natural noise. On the other hand, Malykh et al. (2018) consider robust word vectors. These methods require retraining the model based on new word vectors or noise data. Retraining is expensive and will affect the performance of clean text. For example, in Belinkov and Bisk (2017), the robustness scarifies the performance of the clean text by about 7 BLEU score on the EN-FR translation task.

In this paper, we propose a novel text denoising algorithm based on the ready-to-use masked language model (MLM, Devlin et al. (2018)). Notice that we are using English Bert. For other languages, We need to use MLM model pre-trained on that specific language. The design follows the human cognitive process that humans can utilize the context, the spell of the wrong word (Mayall et al., 1997), and even the location of the letters on the keyboard to correct noisy text. The MLM essentially mimics the process that the model predicts the masked words based on their context. There are several benefits of the proposed method:

- Our method can make accurate corrections based on the context and semantic meaning of the whole sentence as Table 1 shows.
- The pre-trained masked language model is ready-to-use (Devlin et al., 2018; Liu et al., 2019). No extra training or data is required.
- Our method makes use of Word Piece embeddings (Wu et al., 2016) to alleviate the out-of-vocabulary problem.

2 Method

Our denoising algorithm cleans the words in the sentence in sequential order. Given a word, the

---

* Work done at Georgia Tech.

[1] https://translate.google.com; Access Date: 08/09/2019

Method	Input Text	Google Translate
Clean Input	there is a fat duck swimming in the lake	湖里 有一只胖鸭子在游泳
Noisy Input	there is a fat dack swimming in the leake	在 leake 里游泳时有一个 胖子
Spell-Checker	there is a fat sack swimming in the leak	在 泄露处 有一个肥胖 袋在游泳
Grammaly[2]	there is a fat dack swimming in the lake	湖里 游泳很胖
Ours	there is a fat duck swimming in the lake	湖里 有一只胖鸭子在游泳

Table 1: Illustrative example of spell-checker and contextual denoising.

algorithm first generates a candidate list using the MLM and then further filter the list to select a candidate from the list. In this section, we first briefly introduce the masked language model, and then describe the proposed denoising algorithm.

2.1 Masked Language Model

Masked language model (MLM) masks some words from a sentence and then predicts the masked words based on the contextual information. Specifically, given a sentence $x = \{x_i\}_{i=1}^{L}$ with L words, a MLM models

$$p(x_j | x_1, ..., x_{j-1}, [MASK], x_{j+1}, ..., x_L),$$

where $[MASK]$ is a masking token over the j-th word. Actually, MLM can recover multiple masks together, here we only present the case with one mask for notation simplicity. In this way, unlike traditional language model that is in left-to-right order (i.e., $p(x_j | x_1, ..., x_{j-1})$), MLM is able to use both the left and right context. As a result, a more accurate prediction can be made by MLM. In the following, we use the pre-trained masked language model, BERT (Devlin et al., 2018). So no training process is involved in developing our algorithm.

2.2 Denoising Algorithm

The algorithm cleans every word in the sentence with left-to-right order except for the punctuation and numbers by masking them in order. For each word, MLM first provide a candidate list using a transformed sentence. Then the cleaned word is selected from the list. The whole process is summarized in Algorithm 1.

Text Masking The first step is to convert the sentence x into a masked form x'. With the use of Word Piece tokens, each word can be represented by several different tokens. Suppose the j-th word (that needs to be cleaned) is represented by the j_s-th token to the j_e-th token, we need to mask them out together. For the same reason, the number of tokens of the expected cleaned word is unknown

So we use different number of masks to create the masked sentence $\{x'_n\}_{n=1}^{N}$, where x'_n denotes the masked sentence with n-gram mask. Specifically, given $x = x_1, ..., x_{j_s}, ..., x_{j_e}, ..., x_L$, the masked form is $x'_n = x_1, ..., [MASK] \times n, ..., x_L$. We mask each word in the noisy sentence by order. The number of masks N can not be too small or too large. The candidate list will fail to capture the right answer with a small N. However, the optimal answer would fit the noisy text perfectly with a large enough N. Empirically, we find out $N = 4$ is sufficiently large to obtain decent performance without too much overfitting.

Text Augmentation Since the wrong word is also informative, so we augment each masked text x'_n by concatenating the original text x. Specifically, the augmented text is $\widetilde{x}_n = x'_n[SEP]x$, where $[SEP]$ is a separation token.[3]

Compared with directly leaving the noisy word in the original sentence, the masking and augmentation strategy are more flexible. It is benefited from that the number of tokens of the expected word does not necessarily equal to the noisy word. Besides, the model pays less attention to the noisy words, which may induce bias to the prediction of the clean word.

Candidate Selection The algorithm then constructs a candidate list using the MLM, which is semantically suitable for the masked position in the sentence. We first construct candidate list V_c^n for each $\widetilde{x}_n$, and then combine them to obtained the final candidate list $V_c = V_c^1 \cup \cdots \cup V_c^N$. Note that we need to handle multiple masks when $n > 1$. So we first find k most possible word pieces for each mask and then enumerate all possible combinations to construct the final candidate list. Specifically,

$$V_c^n = \text{Top-}k\{p([MASK]_1 = w | \widetilde{x}_n)\}_{w \in V}$$
$$\times \cdots \times \text{Top-}k\{p([MASK]_n = w | \widetilde{x}_n)\}_{w \in V},$$

where V is the whole vocabulary and $\times$ means the Cartesian product

---

[2] https://app.grammarly.com; Access Date: 08/09/2019

[3] In BERT convention, the input also needs to be embraced with a $[CLS]$ and a $[SEP]$ token.

There may be multiple words that make sense for the replacement. In this case, the spelling of the wrong word is useful for finding the most likely correct word. We use the edit distance to select the most likely correct word further.

$$w_c = \arg \min_{w \in V_c} E(w, x_j),$$

where $E(w, x_j)$ represent the edit distance between w and the noisy word x_j.

Algorithm 1: Denoising with MLM

Input: Noisy sentence $x = \{x_i\}_{i=1}^{L}$
Output: Denoised sentence $x = \{x_i\}_{i=1}^{L}$
for $i = 1, 2, ..., L$ **do**
  $\{x'_n\}_{n=1}^{N} = \text{Masking}(x)$;
  $\{\tilde{x}_n\}_{n=1}^{N} = \{\text{Augment}(x'_n, x)\}_{n=1}^{N}$;
  for $n = 1, 2, ..., N$ **do**
    $V_c^n = \text{Candidate}(\tilde{x}_n)$;
  end
  $V_c = V_c^1 \cup \cdots \cup V_c^N$;
  $w_c = \arg \min_{w \in V_c} E(w, x_j)$;
  $x_i = w_c$;
end

---

3 Experiment

We test the performance of the proposed text denoising method on three downstream tasks: neural machine translation, natural language inference, and paraphrase detection. All experiments are conducted with NVIDIA Tesla V100 GPUs. We use the pretrained pytorch Bert-large (with whole word masking) as the masked language model [4]. For the denoising algorithm, we use at most $N = 4$ masks for each word, and the detailed configuration of the size of the candidate list is shown in Table 2. We use a large candidate list for one word piece which covers the most cases. For multiple masks, a smaller list would be good enough.

For all tasks, we train the task-specific model on the original clean training set. Then we compare the model performance on the different test sets, including original test data, noise test data, and cleaned noise test data. We use a commercial-level spell-checker api [5] as our baseline method.

In this section, we first introduce how the noise is generated, and then present experimental results of three NLP tasks.

[4] https://github.com/huggingface/ pytorch-pretrained-BERT

[5] https://rapidapi.com/montanaflynn/ api/spellcheck; Access Date: 08/09/2019

No. of $[MASK]$ (n)	Top k	Size
1	3000	3000
2	5	25
3	3	27
4	2	16
Total:		3068

Table 2: Size of the candidate list

3.1 Noise

To control the noise level, we randomly pick words from the testing data to be perturbed with a certain probability. For each selected word, we consider two perturbation setting: artificial noise and natural noise. Under *artificial noise* setting, we separately apply four kinds of noise: Swap, Delete, Replace, Insert with certain probability. Specifically,

- Swap: We swap two letters per word.
- Delete: We randomly delete a letter in the middle of the word.
- Replace: We randomly replace a letter in a word with another.
- Insert: We randomly insert a letter in the middle of the word.

Following the setting in (Belinkov and Bisk, 2017), the first and the last character remains unchanged.

For the *artificial noise*, we follow the experiment of Belinkov and Bisk (2017) that harvest naturally occurring errors (typos, misspellings, etc.) from the edit histories of available corpora. It generates a lookup table of all possible errors for each word. We replace the selected words with the corresponding noise in the lookup table according to their settings.

3.2 Neural Machine Translation

We conduct the English-to-German translation experiments on the TED talks corpus from IWSLT 2014 dataset [6]. The data contains about $160,000$ sentence pairs for training, $6,750$ pairs for testing.

We first evaluate the performance using a 12-layer transformer implemented by fairseq (Ott et al., 2019). For all implementation details, we follow the training recipe given by fairseq [7]. We also evaluate the performance of Google Translate.

[6] https://wit3.fbk.eu/archive/2014-01/ texts/en/de/en-de.tgz

[7] https://github.com/pytorch/fairseq/ tree/master/examples/translation

For the artificial noise setting, we perturb 20% words and apply each noise with probability 25%. For that natural noise setting, we also perturb 20% words. All experiment results is summarized in Table 3, where we use BLEU score (Papineni et al., 2002) to evaluate the translation result.

Text Source	Google	Fairseq
Original	31.49	28.06
Artificial Noise	28.11	22.27
+ Spell-Checker	26.28	21.15
+ Ours	**28.96**	**25.80**
Natural Noise	25.22	17.29
+ Spell-Checker	20.90	15.04
+ Ours	**25.49**	**21.40**

Table 3: BLEU scores of EN-to-DE tranlsation

As can be seen, both fairseq model and Google Translate suffer from a significant performance drop on the noisy texts with both natural and synthetic noise. When using the spell-checker, the performance even drops more. Moreover, our purposed method can alleviate the performance drop.

3.3 Natural Language Inference

We test the algorithm on Natural Language Inference (NLI) task, which is one of the most challenge tasks related to the semantics of sentences. We establish our experiment based on the SNLI (the Stanford Natural Language Inference, Bowman et al. (2015)) corpus. Here we use accuracy as the evaluation metric for SNLI.

Here we use state-of-the-art 400 dimensional Hierarchical BiLSTM with Max Pooling (HBMP) (Talman et al., 2019). The implementation follows the publicly released code [8]. We use the same noise setting as the NMT experiments. All results are presented in Table 4. We observe performance improvement with our method. To see if the denoising algorithm would induce noises to the clean texts, we also apply the algorithm to the original sentence and check if performance will degrade. It can be seen that, unlike the traditional robust model approach, applying a denoising algorithm on a clean sample has little influence on performance.

As shown in the Table4, the accuracy is very close to the original one under the artificial noise. Natural noises contain punctuations and are more complicated than artificial ones. As a result, inference becomes much harder in this way.

[8] https://github.com/Helsinki-NLP/HBMP

Method	Original	Artificial Noise	Natural Noise
HBMP	84.0	75.0	74.0
+Spell-Checker	84.0*	63.0	68.0
+Ours	83.0*	**81.0**	**77.0**

Table 4: SNLI classification accuracy with artificial noise and natural noise. *: Applying denoising algorithm on original texts.

3.4 Paraphrase Detection

We conducted Paraphrase detection experiments on the Microsoft Research Paraphrase Corpus (MRPC, Dolan and Brockett (2005)) consisting of 5800 sentence pairs extracted from news sources on the web. It is manually labelled for presence/absence of semantic equivalence.

We evaluate the performance using the state-of-the-art model: fine-tuned RoBERTa (Liu et al., 2019). For all implemented details follows the publicly released code [9]. All experiment results is summarized in Table 5. We increase the size of the candidate list to $10000 + 25 + 27 + 16 = 10068$ because there are a lot of proper nouns, which are hard to predict.

Method	Original	Artificial Noise	Natural Noise
RoBERTa	84.3	81.9	75.2
+Spell-Checker	82.6	81.3	75.4
+Ours	83.6	**82.7**	**76.4**

Table 5: Classification F1 score on MRPC

4 Conclusion and Future Work

In this paper, we present a novel text denoising algorithm using ready-to-use masked language model. We show that the proposed method can recover the noisy text by the contextual information without any training or data. We further demonstrate the effectiveness of the proposed method on three downstream tasks, where the performance drop is alleviated by our method. A promising future research topic is how to design a better candidate selection rule rather than merely using the edit distance. We can also try to use GEC corpora, such as CoNLL-2014, to further fine-tune the denoising model in a supervised way to improve the performance.

[9] https://github.com/pytorch/fairseq/tree/master/examples/roberta

References

Yonatan Belinkov and Yonatan Bisk. 2017. Synthetic and natural noise both break neural machine translation. *arXiv preprint arXiv:1711.02173*.

Samuel R Bowman, Gabor Angeli, Christopher Potts, and Christopher D Manning. 2015. A large annotated corpus for learning natural language inference. *arXiv preprint arXiv:1508.05326*.

Shamil Chollampatt and Hwee Tou Ng. 2018. Neural quality estimation of grammatical error correction. In *Proceedings of the 2018 Conference on Empirical Methods in Natural Language Processing*, pages 2528–2539.

Jacob Devlin, Ming-Wei Chang, Kenton Lee, and Kristina Toutanova. 2018. Bert: Pre-training of deep bidirectional transformers for language understanding. *arXiv preprint arXiv:1810.04805*.

William B Dolan and Chris Brockett. 2005. Automatically constructing a corpus of sentential paraphrases. In *Proceedings of the Third International Workshop on Paraphrasing (IWP2005)*.

Yinhan Liu, Myle Ott, Naman Goyal, Jingfei Du, Mandar Joshi, Danqi Chen, Omer Levy, Mike Lewis, Luke Zettlemoyer, and Veselin Stoyanov. 2019. Roberta: A robustly optimized bert pretraining approach. *arXiv preprint arXiv:1907.11692*.

Valentin Malykh, Varvara Logacheva, and Taras Khakhulin. 2018. Robust word vectors: Context-informed embeddings for noisy texts. In *Proceedings of the 2018 EMNLP Workshop W-NUT: The 4th Workshop on Noisy User-generated Text*, pages 54–63.

Kate Mayall, Glyn W Humphreys, and Andrew Olson. 1997. Disruption to word or letter processing? the origins of case-mixing effects. *Journal of Experimental Psychology: Learning, Memory, and Cognition*, 23(5):1275.

Hwee Tou Ng, Siew Mei Wu, Ted Briscoe, Christian Hadiwinoto, Raymond Hendy Susanto, and Christopher Bryant. 2014. The conll-2014 shared task on grammatical error correction. In *Proceedings of the Eighteenth Conference on Computational Natural Language Learning: Shared Task*, pages 1–14.

Myle Ott, Sergey Edunov, Alexei Baevski, Angela Fan, Sam Gross, Nathan Ng, David Grangier, and Michael Auli. 2019. fairseq: A fast, extensible toolkit for sequence modeling. In *Proceedings of NAACL-HLT 2019: Demonstrations*.

Kishore Papineni, Salim Roukos, Todd Ward, and Wei-Jing Zhu. 2002. Bleu: a method for automatic evaluation of machine translation. In *Proceedings of the 40th annual meeting on association for computational linguistics*, pages 311–318. Association for Computational Linguistics.

Aarne Talman, Anssi Yli-Jyrä, and Jörg Tiedemann. 2019. Sentence embeddings in nli with iterative refinement encoders. *Natural Language Engineering*, 25(4):467–482.

Yonghui Wu, Mike Schuster, Zhifeng Chen, Quoc V Le, Mohammad Norouzi, Wolfgang Macherey, Maxim Krikun, Yuan Cao, Qin Gao, Klaus Macherey, et al. 2016. Google's neural machine translation system: Bridging the gap between human and machine translation. *arXiv preprint arXiv:1609.08144*.

Wei Zhao, Liang Wang, Kewei Shen, Ruoyu Jia, and Jingming Liu. 2019. Improving grammatical error correction via pre-training a copy-augmented architecture with unlabeled data. *arXiv preprint arXiv:1903.00138*.

Towards Automated Semantic Role Labelling of Hindi-English Code-Mixed Tweets

Riya Pal and **Dipti Misra Sharma**
Kohli Center on Intelligent Systems (KCIS)
International Institute of Information Technology, Hyderabad (IIIT-Hyderabad)
Gachibowli, Hyderabad, Telangana - 500032, India
riya.pal@research.iiit.ac.in
dipti@iiit.ac.in

Abstract

We present a system for automating Semantic Role Labelling of Hindi-English code-mixed tweets. We explore the issues posed by noisy, user generated code-mixed social media data. We also compare the individual effect of various linguistic features used in our system. Our proposed model is a 2-step system for automated labelling which gives an overall accuracy of 84% for Argument Classification, marking a 10% increase over the existing rule-based baseline model. This is the first attempt at building a statistical Semantic Role Labeller for Hindi-English code-mixed data, to the best of our knowledge.

1 Introduction

Semantic Role Labelling (SRL) deals with identifying arguments of a given predicate or verb, in a sentence or utterance, and classifying them into various semantic roles. These labels give us information about the function played by the argument with respect to its predicate in the particular sentence.

With the growing popularity of social media, there is a lot of user generated data available online on forums such as Facebook, Twitter, Reddit, amongst many others. Subsequently, there is an increasing need to develop tools to process this text for its understanding. In multi-lingual communities, code-mixing is a largely observed phenomenon in colloquial usage as well as on social media. Code-mixing is described as *"the embedding of linguistic units such as phrases, words and morphemes of one language into an utterance of another language"* (Myers-Scotton, 1997). Social media data, Code-mixed text in particular, doesn't strictly adhere to the syntax, morphology or structure of any of the involved languages, which results in standard NLP tools not performing well with this data for a lot of

tasks (Solorio and Liu, 2008; Çetinoğlu et al., 2016). T1 is an example from the corpus of Hindi-English code-mixed tweets (The Hindi words are denoted in italics).

T1 : "My life is revolving around '*bhook lagri hai*' and '*zyada kha liya*'"
Translation: My life is revolving around 'I am hungry' and 'I ate too much'

We present a 2-step system for automated Semantic Role Labelling of Hindi-English code-mixed tweets. The first step is to identify the arguments of the predicates in the sentence. The second step is to then classify these identified arguments into various semantic roles. We discuss the effect of 14 linguistic features on our system, of which 6 are derived from literature and rest are specific to Hindi or to the nature of code-mixed text. Semantic Role Labelling will aid in various NLP tasks such as building question-answering systems (Shen and Lapata, 2007), co-reference resolution (Ponzetto and Strube, 2006), document summarization (Khan et al., 2015), information retrieval (Moschitti et al., 2003; Osman et al., 2012) and so on.

The structure of this paper is as follows. We describe our data and the normalisation done for pre-processing of the text for our system in Section 2. The features used and compared are explained in detail in Section 3 along with the architecture of our system. We analyse the experiments and its results in Section 4. In Section 5, we conclude the paper.

2 Data and Pre-Processing

We used a dataset of 1460 Hindi English code mixed tweets comprising of 20,949 tokens labelled with their semantic roles (Pal and Sharma,

Proceedings of the 2019 EMNLP Workshop W-NUT: The 5th Workshop on Noisy User-generated Text, pages 291–296
Hong Kong, Nov 4, 2019. ©2019 Association for Computational Linguistics

2019). This dataset is built on a dependency labelled corpus by Bhat et al. (2018). The tokens are parsed and labelled with Proposition Bank (Prop-Bank) labels shown in table 1, depicting semantic roles of the arguments with respect to the predicates in the sentence (Palmer et al., 2005; Bhatt et al., 2009).

Label	Description
ARGA	Causer
ARG0	Agent or Experiencer or Doer
ARG1	Theme or Patient
ARG2	Benificiary
ARG2_ATTR	Attribute or Quality
ARG2_LOC	Physical Location
ARG2_GOL	Destination or Goal
ARG2_SOU	Source
ARG3	Instrument
ARGM_DIR	Direction
ARGM_LOC	Location
ARGM_MNR	Manner
ARGM_EXT	Extent or Comparison
ARGM_TMP	Temporal
ARGM_REC	Reciprocal
ARGM_PRP	Purpose
ARGM_CAU	Cause or Reason
ARGM_DIS	Discourse
ARGM_ADV	Adverb
ARGM_NEG	Negative
ARGM_PRX	Complex Predicate

Table 1: PropBank Tagset

Social media data doesn't conform to the rules of spelling, grammar or punctuation. These need to be taken into account to maintain uniformity for our system. We incorporated this in our pre-processing steps.

2.1 Misspelling

One of the most widely seen errors in social media data is 'typos', which are errors in spelling, usually slangs or typing errors. These errors can be broadly classified as follows:

- Misspelling leading to another word. For example, "thing"[NN][1] misspelled as "think"[VM].

- Omission of vowels - For example, the token "hr" is a commonly used abbreviation for

the English word 'hour'. In our corpus, it referred to the Hindi word 'har' which is a quantifier and means 'every'.

- Elongation - tokens such as "Loooonng", "Heyyyyy", *"pyaaaar"* and so on.

- Typing errors. For example, "saluet", which should have been 'salute'.

- Non-Uniformity in transliteration of Hindi tokens (usually written in Devanagari script) using the Roman alphabet. For example, the Hindi word for 'no' - *"nahi"* - had a lot of variation in its spelling in the corpus - 'nai', 'naee', 'nahi', 'nahee', 'nhi' etc.

We were able to detect some of the other errors through automated methods, such as elongation and some typing errors. Non-uniformity in transliteration was the most commonly found error in our corpus. These were all normalised and corrected manually to ensure a consistent spelling throughout the corpus.

2.2 Word Sense Disambiguation

A word can have different meanings according to the context in which it is used. T2 is an example from the corpus. The token "dikhny" refers to the Hindi verb *'xeKa'*[2] which means to look. This verb can have different senses according to its context as shown in table 2. From context we know the relevant roleset here would be [xeKa.01]. Available Frame files are used to identify rolesets for the verbs in the corpus (Vaidya et al., 2013; Bonial et al., 2014).

T2: "We are journilist and *hmy sechae dikhny se kiu rok ni skta*"
Translation: We are journalists and no one can stop us from seeing the truth.

Different senses for *xeKa*	
Roleset id	Meaning
xeKa.01	to see something
xeKa.04	to see (without volition)
xeKa.06	to show someone something
xeKa.07	used as a light verb

Table 2: Rolesets and meanings for the Hindi verb *xeKa*.

---

[1] Part of Speech (POS) tag

[2] WX notation

T3: "Shane on you *maine tuje pehle hi* Warne *kiya tha*"

Translation: Shane [NNP] on you, I had Warne [NNP] you before.

Implicit meaning: *Shame* [VM] *on you, I had warned* [VM] *you before.*

T3 is an interesting example from the corpus. The proper nouns 'Shane' and 'Warne' are used as the verbs 'shame' and 'warn' respectively in the sentence, due to their phonetic similarity. The speaker is possibly warning against the famous cricketer Shane Warne, and thus uses his name to convey the same. This sort of word play is not un-common in social media data. These tokens are detected as proper nouns. We added them as pred-icates, according to their context, manually.

3 Semantic Role Labeller

Our Semantic Role Labeller has a 2-step architec-ture. The first step is a binary classification task wherein each token in the tweet is classified as 'Argument' or 'Not an Argument'. This step is called **Argument Identification**. In the second step, the identified arguments from the previous step are classified into the various semantic roles. This is called **Argument Classification**.

We used Support Vector Models (SVM) for bi-nary classification. The identified arguments from this step are then classified into various seman-tic roles mentioned in Table 1. We used the Lin-ear SVC class of SVM (Pedregosa et al., 2011) for one-vs-rest multi-class classification. The data was split in the ratio of 80-20 for training and test-ing respectively. All parameters of the LinearSVC were set to default for training.

3.1 Features used

Hindi and English have very different grammatical rules and vary greatly syntactically as well. We in-corporated linguistic features in our system which may take into account these differences and help the labeller attain higher accuracy in identifying and classifying arguments.

3.1.1 Baseline Features

We used 6 baseline features which have been used extensively for the task of Semantic Role La-belling for English (Gildea and Jurafsky, 2002; Xue and Palmer, 2004). They are as follows:

- Predicate: Identified verb in the sentence

- Headword: Headword of the chunk

- HeadwordPOS: Part of Speech tag of the headword

- Phrasetype: Syntactic category of the phrase (NP, VP, CCP etc.)

- Predicate + Phrasetype

- Predicate + Headword

Semantic Arguments are identified at a phrase or chunk level. Hence we used features such as Headword of the chunk, phrasetype category, as baseline features. We also saw the impact of the part of speech (POS) tag of the Headword.

3.1.2 Features specific to Indian Languages

Previous work on Semantic Role Labelling have used the following features for Hindi specifically (Anwar and Sharma, 2016):

- Dependency(karaka relation): Paninian de-pendency label

- Named Entities

- HeadwordPOS + Phrasetype

- Headword + Phrasetype

We used the same features in our system. Named Entities have previously been seen to be a critical feature for Argument Identification task in English (Pradhan et al., 2004).

Vaidya et al. (2011) showed the strong co-relation between Paninian dependency (karta) la-bels and Propbank labels for Hindi. This feature was also seen to give the best results for Hindi and Urdu monolingual corpus (Anwar and Sharma, 2016). Universal Dependencies (UD) have gained a lot of attention lately for cross-lingual parsing. Tandon et al. (2016) discussed and evaluated UD scheme for Hindi and also compared them to Paninian dependency labels. We evaluated UD part of speech(POS) tags and UD dependency la-bels as features in our system, as mentioned below.

- HeadwordPOS(UD) - UD part of speech tag of the headword

- UD dependency label

3.1.3 Features for code-mixed data

Since we are dealing with code-mixed text, we wanted to see the effect the identified language of a token may have. We thus used the following features:

- Predicate + language: Predicate and its identified language.

- Headword + language: The chunk headword and its identified language.

4 Results and Analysis

We do a thorough analysis of the individual features and their performance for the tasks of Argument identification and Argument Classification separately. Table 3 shows the precision, recall and F1 scores of the features for Argument Identification. Paninian Dependency labels give the highest F1-score of **78**.

Named Entities also give good results for Argument Identification. This is because Named Entities are usually arguments of a predicate. However, they by themselves don't capture much information about the role played by the argument in the sentence. Hence, the score for Argument Classification isn't that high, as can be seen in table 5.

Feature	Argument Identification		
	P	R	f-score
Predicate	33	50	40
Headword (HW)	52	47	49
HeadwordPOS	33	50	40
Phrasetype (PT)	41	34	37
Predicate-PT	42	65	51
Predicate-HW	55	49	51
Dependency	78	78	**78**
Named_Entity	57	50	65
HeadwordPOS-PT	41	34	37
Headword-PT	57	49	53
HeadwordPOS(UD)	32	50	39
UD_dependency	64	65	64
Predicate-language	43	65	52
Headword-language	55	47	51

Table 3: Individual feature performance for Argument Identification.

We also see a significant increase in accuracy when we use the combinational feature of predicate and its language, as compared to using only predicate as a feature (Table 3). T4 is an example from the corpus where the token "ban" is the Hindi verb [bana], 'to become'. This can be confused with the English verb 'ban' (legal prohibition). In such cases, the language of the predicate token can play an important role.

T4: "Dear so called liberals, *kabhi* indian ***ban ke dekho*"
Translation: Dear so called liberals, try being an Indian some time.

Feature	Argument Identification		
	P	R	f-score
Baseline	56	53	55
with predicate-lang	57	54	55
+dependency	81	76	78

Table 4: Accuracy scores for Argument Identification.

Table 4 gives the accuracy scores for the system using baseline features. Here, the score doesn't change much when we use 'predicate-language' as a part of our baseline. We are able to obtain the highest F1-score of 78 for this step by adding dependency label to our baseline features. The rule-based baseline model gives a much higher accuracy of 96.74% (Pal and Sharma, 2019). The baseline model uses the dependency tree structure of the sentence and identifies direct dependents of predicates as their arguments. Auxiliary verbs, post-positions, symbols, amongst others, are not considered as Arguments.

As the Classification step is based on the identified arguments from the first step, we chose to adopt a hybrid approach. We used the rule-based baseline system for Argument Identification, and used statistical approach with SVM for Argument Classification.

The precision, recall and F1 scores of the individual features for Argument Classification are given in Table 5. The best F1-score of 83 is again given by Paninian dependency labels. UD dependency gives a score of 80 which is slightly lower. Paninian dependency labels have performed better for both tasks as seen in Tables 3 and 5. There isn't much variation in performance between 'HeadwordPOS' and 'HeadwordPOS(UD)' for both steps.

The UD tagset is a coarser tagset. The UD POS tagset has only 17 tags, compared to the POS tagset developed for Indian languages which has

32 tags (Bharati et al., 2006). Similarly, in the Paninian dependency scheme, there are in total 82 relations, whereas UD has only 40. From the accuracy scores, we can infer that Paninian depepndency labels capture more semantic information than UD dependency labels.

Feature	Argument Classification		
	P	R	f-score
Predicate	06	09	06
Headword (HW)	18	10	13
HeadwordPOS	05	07	06
Phrasetype (PT)	08	10	08
Predicate-PT	05	08	06
Predicate-HW	05	06	06
Dependency	81	86	**83**
Named_Entity	20	14	16
HeadwordPOS-PT	07	09	08
Headword-PT	12	09	10
HeadwordPOS(UD)	08	11	09
UD_dependency	77	83	80
Predicate-language	06	10	07
Headword-language	18	11	14

Table 5: Individual feature performance for Argument Classification.

Feature	Argument Classification		
	P	R	f-score
Baseline	27	15	19
+dependency	84	84	**84**

Table 6: Accuracy scores for Argument Classification.

Table 6 gives the accuracy scores for Argument Classification while using baseline features, and after incorporating dependency labels. We obtained an F1 score of **84**. This is a significant improvement over the rule-based baseline model (Pal and Sharma, 2019) which gives an overall accuracy of 73.93% for Argument Classification.

5 Conclusion

In this work, we analyse the problems posed by code-mixed social media data. We present a system for automatic Semantic Role Labelling of Hindi-English code-mixed tweets. We used a hybrid approach of rule-based and statistical techniques for Argument Identification and Argument Classification respectively.

References

Maaz Anwar and Dipti Misra Sharma. 2016. Towards building semantic role labeler for indian languages. In *Proceedings of the Tenth International Conference on Language Resources and Evaluation (LREC 2016)*, pages 4588–4595.

Akshar Bharati, Rajeev Sangal, Dipti Misra Sharma, and Lakshmi Bai. 2006. Anncorra: Annotating corpora guidelines for pos and chunk annotation for indian languages. *LTRC-TR31*, pages 1–38.

Irshad Ahmad Bhat, Riyaz Ahmad Bhat, Manish Shrivastava, and Dipti Misra Sharma. 2018. Universal dependency parsing for hindi-english codeswitching. *arXiv preprint arXiv:1804.05868*.

Rajesh Bhatt, Bhuvana Narasimhan, Martha Palmer, Owen Rambow, Dipti Sharma, and Fei Xia. 2009. A multi-representational and multi-layered treebank for hindi/urdu. In *Proceedings of the Third Linguistic Annotation Workshop (LAW III)*, pages 186–189.

Claire Bonial, Julia Bonn, Kathryn Conger, Jena D Hwang, and Martha Palmer. 2014. Propbank: Semantics of new predicate types. In *LREC*, pages 3013–3019.

Özlem Çetinoğlu, Sarah Schulz, and Ngoc Thang Vu. 2016. Challenges of computational processing of code-switching. *arXiv preprint arXiv:1610.02213*.

Daniel Gildea and Daniel Jurafsky. 2002. Automatic labeling of semantic roles. *Computational linguistics*, 28(3):245–288.

Atif Khan, Naomie Salim, and Yogan Jaya Kumar. 2015. A framework for multi-document abstractive summarization based on semantic role labelling. *Applied Soft Computing*, 30:737–747.

Alessandro Moschitti, Paul Morarescu, Sanda M Harabagiu, et al. 2003. Open domain information extraction via automatic semantic labeling. In *FLAIRS conference*, volume 3, pages 397–401.

Carol Myers-Scotton. 1997. *Duelling languages: Grammatical structure in codeswitching*. Oxford University Press.

Ahmed Hamza Osman, Naomie Salim, Mohammed Salem Binwahlan, Rihab Alteeb, and Albaraa Abuobieda. 2012. An improved plagiarism detection scheme based on semantic role labeling. *Applied Soft Computing*, 12(5):1493–1502.

Riya Pal and Dipti Misra Sharma. 2019. A dataset for semantic role labelling of hindi-english code-mixed tweets. In *Proceedings of the 13th Linguistic Annotation Workshop*, pages 178–188.

Martha Palmer, Daniel Gildea, and Paul Kingsbury. 2005. The proposition bank: An annotated corpus of semantic roles. *Computational linguistics*, 31(1):71–106.

Fabian Pedregosa, Gaël Varoquaux, Alexandre Gramfort, Vincent Michel, Bertrand Thirion, Olivier Grisel, Mathieu Blondel, Peter Prettenhofer, Ron Weiss, Vincent Dubourg, et al. 2011. Scikit-learn: Machine learning in python. *Journal of machine learning research*, 12(Oct):2825–2830.

Simone Paolo Ponzetto and Michael Strube. 2006. Exploiting semantic role labeling, wordnet and wikipedia for coreference resolution. In *Proceedings of the Human Language Technology Conference of the NAACL, Main Conference*.

Sameer S Pradhan, Wayne H Ward, Kadri Hacioglu, James H Martin, and Dan Jurafsky. 2004. Shallow semantic parsing using support vector machines. In *Proceedings of the Human Language Technology Conference of the North American Chapter of the Association for Computational Linguistics: HLT-NAACL 2004*, pages 233–240.

Dan Shen and Mirella Lapata. 2007. Using semantic roles to improve question answering. In *Proceedings of the 2007 joint conference on empirical methods in natural language processing and computational natural language learning (EMNLP-CoNLL)*, pages 12–21.

Thamar Solorio and Yang Liu. 2008. Part-of-speech tagging for english-spanish code-switched text. In *Proceedings of the Conference on Empirical Methods in Natural Language Processing*, pages 1051–1060. Association for Computational Linguistics.

Juhi Tandon, Himani Chaudhry, Riyaz Ahmad Bhat, and Dipti Sharma. 2016. Conversion from paninian karakas to universal dependencies for hindi dependency treebank. In *Proceedings of the 10th Linguistic Annotation Workshop held in conjunction with ACL 2016 (LAW-X 2016)*, pages 141–150.

Ashwini Vaidya, Jinho D Choi, Martha Palmer, and Bhuvana Narasimhan. 2011. Analysis of the hindi proposition bank using dependency structure. In *Proceedings of the 5th Linguistic Annotation Workshop*, pages 21–29. Association for Computational Linguistics.

Ashwini Vaidya, Martha Palmer, and Bhuvana Narasimhan. 2013. Semantic roles for nominal predicates: Building a lexical resource. In *Proceedings of the 9th Workshop on Multiword Expressions*, pages 126–131.

Nianwen Xue and Martha Palmer. 2004. Calibrating features for semantic role labeling. In *Proceedings of the 2004 Conference on Empirical Methods in Natural Language Processing*, pages 88–94.

Enhancing BERT for Lexical Normalization

Benjamin Muller   Benoît Sagot   Djamé Seddah
Inria
`firstname.lastname@inria.fr`

Abstract

Language model-based pre-trained representations have become ubiquitous in natural language processing. They have been shown to significantly improve the performance of neural models on a great variety of tasks. However, it remains unclear how useful those general models can be in handling non-canonical text. In this article, focusing on User Generated Content (UGC) in a resource-scarce scenario, we study the ability of BERT (Devlin et al., 2018) to perform lexical normalisation. Our contribution is simple: by framing lexical normalisation as a token prediction task, by enhancing its architecture and by carefully fine-tuning it, we show that BERT can be a competitive lexical normalisation model without the need of any UGC resources aside from 3,000 training sentences. To the best of our knowledge, it is the first work done in adapting and analysing the ability of this model to handle noisy UGC data.[1]

1   Introduction

Pre-trained contextual language models (e.g. ELMo, Peters et al., 2018; BERT, Devlin et al., 2018) have improved the performance of a large number of state-of-the-art models on many Natural Language Processing (NLP) tasks. In this article, we focus on BERT (Bidirectional Encoder Representations from Transformers), the contextual language modelling architecture that recently had the greatest impact.

A major specificity of BERT is that it is trained to jointly predict randomly masked tokens as well as the consecutiveness of two sentences. Moreover, it takes as input *WordPieces* tokens which consists in frequent sub-word units (Schuster and Nakajima, 2012). Finally, available pre-trained models have been trained on the concatenation of the Wikipedia corpus and the BookCorpus, which constitutes a large corpus of canonical (i.e. proper, edited) language.

Putting aside the efficiency of its transformer-based architecture, these three aspects respectively enable BERT to elegantly cope with out-of-vocabulary words and to include contextual information at the token and at the sentence levels, while fully taking advantage of a training corpus containing billions of words.

Without listing all of them, BERT successfully improved the state-of-the-art for a number of tasks such as Name-Entity Recognition, Question Answering (Devlin et al., 2018) and Machine Translation (Lample and Conneau, 2019). Moreover, it has recently been shown to capture a rich set of syntactic information (Hewitt and Manning, 2019; Jawahar et al., 2019), without the added complexity of more complex syntax-based language models.

However, it remains unclear and, to the best of our knowledge, unexplored, how well can BERT be used in handling non-canonical text such as *User-Generated Content* (UGC), especially in a low resource scenario. This question is the focus of this paper.

As described in (Foster, 2010; Seddah et al., 2012; Eisenstein, 2013; Baldwin et al., 2013), UGC is often characterized by the extensive use of abbreviations, slang, internet jargon, emojis, embedded metadata (such as hashtags, URLs or *at* mentions), and non standard syntactic constructions and spelling errors.

This type of non-canonical text, which we characterize as *noisy*, negatively impacts NLP models performances on many tasks as shown in (van der Goot et al., 2017; van der Goot and van Noord, 2018; Moon et al., 2018; Michel and Neubig, 2018) on respectively Part-of-

---

[1] The code is available in the following repository https://gitlab.inria.fr/bemuller/bert_nomalizer

Proceedings of the 2019 EMNLP Workshop W-NUT: The 5th Workshop on Noisy User-generated Text, pages 297–306
Hong Kong, Nov 4, 2019. ©2019 Association for Computational Linguistics

Speech Tagging, Syntactic Parsing, Name-Entity Recognition and Machine Translation.

In this context and as impactful as BERT was shown to be, its ability to handle noisy inputs is still an open question[2]. Indeed, as highlighted above, it was trained on highly edited texts, as expected from Wikipedia and BookCorpus sources, which differ from UGC at many levels of linguistic descriptions, and which, of course, exhibit an important domain gap.

Based on those observations, we take lexical normalisation of UGC as a case study of how BERT can model noisy inputs. Briefly, lexical normalisation is the task of translating non-canonical words into canonical ones. It involves a detection step in assessing if a word is already canonical or not, followed by a normalisation step. All the experiments presented in this paper are carried out on the dataset released by Baldwin et al. (2015), which is the only non-raw resource we use. This is because our goal is to study how well BERT handles noisy UGC by itself, which means that, unlike most previous work (e.g. van der Goot and van Noord, 2017), we cannot make use of external UGC-specific resources such as word embeddings and language models trained on UGC or dedicated lexicons.

Yet, building a lexical normalization model in such a setting is a challenging endeavor. As we will present, blindly fine-tuning BERT on such as task is not possible. It requires architectural and optimization adaptations that constitute the core of our contribution.

In summary, we show that BERT can be adapted to perform lexical normalisation in a low resource setting without external data covering the source UGC domain, aside from 2950 aligned training examples that include only 3928 noisy words. In this purpose, we make three contributions:

- We design a WordPiece tokenizer that enforces alignment between canonical and noisy tokens.
- We enhance the BERT architecture so that the model is able to add extra tokens or remove them when normalisation requires it.
- We fine-tune the overall architecture with a novel noise-specific strategy.

---

[2]The importance of this research question is further confirmed by the very recent pre-publication of the work by (Gopalakrishnan et al., 2018) who study how BERT is affected by synthetic noise

In a few words, our paper is the first attempt to successfully design a domain transfer model based on BERT in a low resource setting.

2 Related Work

There is an extensive literature on normalizing text from UGC.

The first systematic attempt was Han and Baldwin (2011). They released 549 tweets with their normalized word-aligned counterparts and the first result for a normalization system on tweets. Their model was a Support-Vector-Machine for detecting noisy words. Then a lookup and n-gram based system would pick the best candidate among the closest ones in terms of edit and phonetic distances. Following this work, the literature explored different modelling framework to tackle the task, whether it is Statistical Machine Translation (Li and Liu, 2012), purely unsupervised approach (Yang and Eisenstein, 2013), or syllables level model (Xu et al., 2015).

In 2015, on the occasion of the Workshop on Noisy User-Generated Text, a shared task on lexical normalization of English tweets was organized (Baldwin et al., 2015) for which a collection of annotated tweets for training and evaluation was released. We will refer it as the *lexnorm15* dataset. A wide range of approaches competed. The best approach (Supranovich and Patsepnia, 2015) used a UGC feature-based CRF model for detection and normalization.

In 2016, the MoNoise model (van der Goot and van Noord, 2017) significantly improved the State-of-the-art with a feature-based Random Forest. The model ranks candidates provided by modules such as a spelling checker (aspell), a n-gram based language model and word embeddings trained on millions of tweets.

In summary, two aspects of the past literature on UGC normalization are striking. First, all the past work is based on UGC-specific resources such as lexicons or large UGC corpora. Second, most successful models are modular in the sense that they combine several independent modules that capture different aspects of the problem.

3 Lexical Normalisation

3.1 Task

Lexical normalisation is the task of translating non canonical words into canonical ones.. We illustrate it with the following example (Table 1). Given a *noisy* source sentence, our goal is to predict the *gold* canonical sentence.

Noisy	*yea... @beautifulloser8 im abt to type it uuup !!*
Gold	*yeah... @beautifulloser8 i'm about to type it up !*

Table 1: Noisy UGC example and its canonical form (Gold)

We make a few comments on this definition. First, lexical normalisation assumes a certain degree of word level alignment between the non-canonical source text and the canonical one.

Second, language evolves. It varies across domain, communities and time, specifically online (Jurafsky, 2018). There is therefore no universal definition of what is a canonical form and what is not. In the context of NLP, this means that we have to set conventions and define what we consider as canonical. In our case, the task is made less complicated as we are tied to the conventions set by our training data set.

Finally, to grasp the complexity of such a task, we list and illustrate non exhaustively the sort of linguistic phenomenons that lexical normalisation of UGC involves. Lexical normalisation involves handling the following cases :

- spelling errors : *makeing* in *making*
- internet Slang : *lmfao* in *laughing my f.cking ass off* [3]
- contraction : *lil* for *little*
- abbreviation : *2nite* for *tonight*
- phonetics : *dat* for *that*

It also involves detecting that the following should be untouched : *:), @KhalilBrown, #Beyonce, rt*

3.2 Data

We base all our experiments on the WNUT data released by Baldwin et al. (2015). This dataset includes 2950 noisy tweets for training and 1967 for test. Out of the 44,385 training tokens, 3,928 require normalisation leading to an unbalanced data set. Among those 3,928 noisy tokens, 1043 are 1-to-N (i.e. single noisy words that are normalized as several words) and 10 are N-to-1 cases (i.e. several noisy words that are normalized as single canonical words).

As highlighted before, our framework is more challenging than the standard approach to normalisation, illustrated by the 2015 shared task, that usually authorizes external UGC resources. As our goal is to test the ability of BERT, a model trained on canonical data only, we restrain ourselves to only using the training data as examples of normalisation and nothing more.

Our work is therefore to build a domain transfer model in a low resource setting.

4 Normalisation with BERT

4.1 BERT

We start by presenting the components of BERT that are relevant for our normalisation model. All our work is done on the released *base* version.

4.1.1 WordPiece Tokenization

BERT takes as input sub-word units in the form of *WordPiece* tokens originally introduced in Schuster and Nakajima (2012). The WordPiece vocabulary is computed based on the observed frequency of each sequence of characters of the corpus BERT is pre-trained on: Wikipedia and the BookCorpus. It results in a 30 thousand tokens vocabulary. We will refer to the process of getting WordPiece tokens from word tokens simply as *tokenization* for brievety.

Reusing BERT, in any way, requires to use its original WordPiece vocabulary. In the context of handling non canonical data, this is of primary importance. Indeed, frequent tokens in our non canonical data set might not appear in the vocabulary of BERT and therefore will have to be split. For example, the word *lol* appear more than 222 times in the original lexnorm15 dataset (more than the word *like* that appears 187 times). Still, it is not in BERT-base WordPiece vocabulary. For tokenization of WordPieces, we follow the implementation found in the *huggingface pytorch-pretrained-BERT* project [4]. It is implemented as a greedy matching algorithm. We write it in pseudo-code in Algorithm 1.

4.1.2 Masked Language Model

We now present one crucial aspect of BERT architecture. It was trained jointly on two objectives : On *next sentence* prediction on the one hand. On the other hand, it was trained on

---

[3] Normalisation found in the lexnorm 2015 dataset

Algorithm 1: Greedy WordPiece tokenization

```
Vocabulary = Bert WordPiece Vocabulary;
init start=0, string=word,
wordPieceList = list();
while string not empty do
    substring:=string[start:]
    while substring not empty do
        if substring in Vocabulary then
            wordPieceList :=
            wordPieceList U [substring]
            break loop
        else
            substring := substring[:-1]
        end
    end
    start := start + length(substring)
end
Result: wordPieceList
Note : Tokenizing words into wordpiece tokens, by
matching in an iterative way from left to right, the
longest sub-string belonging to the wordpiece
vocabulary
```

Masked Language Model (MLM). As we frame our normalization task very closely to it, we describe MLM briefly.

For each input sequence, 15% of the WordPiece tokens are either replaced with the special token [MASK] (80% of the time), replaced by a random token (10% of the time) or untouched (10% of the time). BERT is trained by predicting this portion of token based on the surrounding context.

4.2 Fine-Tuning BERT for Normalisation

We now present the core of our contribution. How to make BERT a competitive normalisation model? In a nutshell, there are many ways to do lexical normalisation. Neural models have established the state-of-the-art in the related Grammatical Error Correction task using the sequence to sequence paradigm (Sutskever et al., 2014) at the character level. Still, this framework requires a large amount of parallel data. Our preliminary experiments showed that this was unusable for UGC normalisation. Even the use a powerful pre-trained model such as BERT for initializing an encoder-decoder requires the decoder to learn an implicit mapping between noisy words and canonical ones. This is not reachable with only 3000 sentences.

We therefore adapted BERT in a direct way for normalisation. As described in section 4, BERT Masked Language Model ability allows token prediction. Simply feeding the model with noisy tokens on the input and fine-tuning on canonical token labels transforms BERT into a normalisation model. There are two critical points in doing so successfully. The first is that it requires WordPiece alignment (cf. section 4.2.1). The second is that it requires careful fine-tuning (cf. section 4.2.3).

4.2.1 Wordpiece Alignment

We have in a majority of cases, as described in section 3.2, word level alignment between non canonical and canonical text. Still, the dataset also includes words that are not aligned. For 1-to-N cases we simply remove the spaces. As we work at the WordPiece level this does not bring any issue. For N-to-1 cases (only 10 observations), by considering the special token "|" of the lexnorm15 dataset as any other token, we simply handle source multi-words as a single one, and let the wordpiece tokenization splitting them.

We frame normalization as a 1-to-1 WordPiece token mapping. Based on the word level alignment, we present two methods to get WordPiece alignment : an *Independent Alignment* approach and a *Parallel Alignment* one.

Independent Alignment

We tokenize noisy words and non noisy ones independently (cf. algorithm 1). By doing so, for each word we get non-aligned WordPiece tokens. We handle it in three ways :

- If it is the same number of WordPiece tokens, we keep the alignment as such

- If there are more tokens on the target side, we append the special token [MASK] on the source side. This means that at training time, we force the model to predict a token.

- If there are more tokens on the source side, we introduce a new special token [SPACE].

An alignment example extracted from lexnorm15 can be found in table 2. Briefly, we can point some intuitive pros and cons of such an alignment method. On the one hand, applying tokenization that was used in pre-training BERT means that the sequence of tokens observed during training should be modelled properly by BERT. This should help normalisation. On the other-hand, we understand that learning normalisation in this way requires (as potentially many [MASK] will be introduced) abstracting away from the raw tokens in understanding the surrounding context. This should make normalisation harder. We will see in section 5 that despite its simplicity, such

noisy	canonical
ye	yeah
##a	[SPACE]
im	i
[MASK]	'
[MASK]	m
already	already
knowing	knowing
wa	what
##t	[SPACE]

Table 2: Independent Alignment of *yea im already knowing wat u sayin* normalized as *yeah i'm already knowing what you saying*

an alignment allows our model to reach good performances.

Parallel Alignment

We enhance this first approach with a *parallel alignment* method, described in Algorithm 2.

Our goal is to minimize the number of [MASK] and [SPACE] appended into the source and gold sequences. Therefore, for each word, we start by tokenizing in WordPieces the noisy source word. For each WordPiece met, we start the tokenization on the gold side, starting and ending from the same character positions. As soon as we tokenized the entire gold sub-string, we switch to the next noisy sub-string and so on. By doing so, we ensure a closer alignment at the WordPiece level. We illustrate on the same example this enhanced parallel alignment in Table 3.

We highlight two aspects of our alignment techniques. First, introducing the special token [SPACE] induces an architecture change in the MLM head. We detail this in section 4.2.2-(A). Second, appending the extra token [MASK] on the source side based on the gold sequence induces a discrepancy between training and testing. Indeed, at test time, we do not have the information about whether we need to add an extra token or not. We describe in section 4.2.2-(B) how we extend BERT's architecture with the addition of an extra classification module to handle this discrepancy.

4.2.2 Architecture Enhancements

(A) Enhancing BERT MLM with [SPACE]

In order to formalize lexical normalisation as a token prediction we introduced in section 4.2.1 the need for a new special token [SPACE]. We want our normalisation model to predict it. We therefore introduce a new label in our output WordPiece vocabulary as well as a new vector in the last softmax layer. We do so in a straightforward way

---

Algorithm 2: Parallel WordPiece tokenization

```
Vocabulary = Bert WordPiece Vocabulary;
Init start=0; string=canonical word;
string_noisy = noisy word; end_gold=0;
  wordPListNoisy=list(); wordPieceListGold=list();
while string_noisy not empty do
    string_noisy:=string_noisy[start:]
    substr_noisy:=string_noisy
    while substr_noisy not empty do
        breaking:=False
        if substr_noisy in Vocabulary then
            wordPListNoisy :=
            wordPListNoisyU[substr_noisy]
            if start equals length string_noisy then
                end_gold:=length(string)
            else
                end_gold:=
                start+length(substr_noisy)
            end
            while substr_gold not empty do
                substr_gold:=
                string[start:end_gold]
                if substr_gold in Vocabulary then
                    wordPieceListGold:=
                    wordPieceListGold U
                     [substr_gold]
                    break loop
                else
                    end_gold := end_gold -1
                end
            end
        else
            substr_noisy:=substr_noisy[:-1]
        end
        if breaking then
            break loop
        end
    end
    start := start + length(substr_noisy)
end
Result: wordPListNoisy
```

Note : Tokenizing noisy tokens and canonical tokens in wordpieces in parrallel to minimize the number of appended [MASK] and [SPACE]

by appending to the output matrix a vector sampled from a normal distribution[5].

(B) #Next [MASK] predictor

As we have described, alignment requires in some cases the introduction of [MASK] tokens within the source sequence based on the gold sequence. We handle the discrepancy introduced between training and testing in the following way. We add an extra token classification module to BERT architecture. This module takes as input BERT last hidden state of each WordPiece tokens and predict the number of [MASK] to append next

In table 4, we illustrate the training signal of

---

[5] each dimension $v_d \sim \mathcal{N}(mean_i(x_d), \sigma_i^2(x_d))$ (i indexing the WordPiece vocabulary and d the dense dimension of BERT output layer), $mean_i$ (resp. σ_i^2) means mean (resp. variance) along i dimension

Noisy	Canonical
ye	ye
##a	##ah
im	i
[MASK]	'
[MASK]	m
already	already
knowing	knowing
wa	wh
##t	##at

Table 3: Parallel Alignment of *yea im already knowing wat u sayin* normalized as *yeah i'm already knowing what you saying*

Noisy	Gold	#next mask
ye	ye	0
##a	##ah	0
im	i	2
[MASK]	'	-
[MASK]	m	-
already	already	0
knowing	knowing	0
wa	wh	0
##t	##at	0

Table 4: Parallel Alignment of *yea im already knowing wat u sayin* normalized as *yeah i'm already knowing what you saying* with gold number of next masks for each source token

the overall architecture. It takes noisy WordPiece tokens as input. As gold labels, it takes on the one side the gold WordPiece tokens and on the other side the number of [MASK] to append next to each source WordPiece tokens.

At test time, we first predict the number of next masks to introduce in the noisy sequence. We then predict normalized tokens using the full sequence.

This *#next mask* prediction module exceeds the context of normalisation. Indeed, it provides a straightforward way of performing data augmentation on any Masked Language Model architecture. We leave to future work the investigation of its impact beyond lexical normalisation.

4.2.3 Fine-Tuning

We describe here how we fine-tune our architecture for normalisation. Our goal is to learn lexical normalisation in a general manner. To do so, intuitively, our model needs to: on the one hand, preserve its language model ability that will allow generalization. On the other hand, the MLM needs to adjust itself to learn alignment between noisy tokens and canonical tokens.

Based on those intuitions, we performe fine-tuning in the following way:

(i) Our first approach is to back-propagate on all tokens at each iteration. We also dropout 10% of input tokens by replacing them with the [MASK] as done during BERT pre-training. In this setting, all tokens are considered indifferently whether they require normalisation or not .

(ii) The second approach that happens to perform the best is our *Noise-focus* fine-tuning. The intuition is that it should be much easier for the model to learn to predict already normalized tokens than the ones that require normalization. For this reason, we design the following strategy: For a specific portion of batches noted p_{noise} we only back-propagate through noisy tokens. We found that having an increasing number of noise-specific batch while training provides the best results.

Formally we describe our strategy as follows. For each mini-batch, we sample b following the distribution $b \sim \text{Bernoulli}(p_{noise})$, with $p_{noise} = \min\left(\frac{epoch}{n\_epoch}, 0.5\right)$, $epoch$ being the current number of epoch and n_epoch the total number of epochs.

If b equals 1 we back-propagate through noisy tokens, otherwise we back-propagate in the standard way on all the tokens. In other words, while training, for an increasing portion of batches, we train on tokens that require normalization. We found that this dynamic strategy was much more efficient than applying a static p_{noise}. Moreover, we highlight that the portion of noise specific update is capped at 50% (0.5 in the equation). Above this value, we observed that the performances degraded in predicting non-noisy tokens.

4.2.4 Optimization Details

Note that, excluding the fine-tuning strategy and the alignment algorithm, the optimization hyper-parameters are shared to all the experiments we present next. Generally speaking, we found that optimizing BERT for lexical normalisation with WordPiece alignment is extremely sensitive to hyper-parameters. We managed to reach values that work in all our following experiments. For the optimization, we use the Adam algorithm (Kingma and Ba, 2014). We found that 1e-5 provides the most stable and consistent convergence across all experiments as evaluated on validation set. We found that a mini-batch of dimension 4 brings the best performance also across all experiments. Finally, we kept a dropout value of 0.1 within the entire BERT model. We train the model for up to 10 epochs and used performance as measured with the F1-score (detailed in the next section) on the validation set as our early-stopping metric.

5 Experiments

All our experiments are run on the lexnorm15 dataset. We do not use any other resources making our problem falling under a low resource domain transfer framework. As only pre-processing, we lower-case all tokens whether they are on the noisy source side or on the canonical side.

We first present our analysis on the validation set that corresponds to the last 450 sentences of the original training set of lexnorm15.

We define the three evaluation metrics on which we make our analysis. We distinguish between *need_norm* words, words that require to be normalized and *need_no_norm* words that have to be "copied" by the model. We refer the words normalized by our model (i.e our model gave a prediction different from the source word) as *pred_need_norm*. We refer to the number of True Prediction of *need_norm* words as *TP*. We then define recall and precision as:

$$recall = \frac{TP}{\#need\_norm}$$

$$precision = \frac{TP}{\#pred\_need\_norm}$$

Following previous works, we will focus on the F1 score as our main evaluation metric. F1 is simply the harmonic mean of the recall and precision. For more fine grained analysis we also report the recall on sub-sample of the evaluated dataset. Particularly, we distinguish between Out-of-Vocabulary (OOV) and In-Vocabulary words (InV) and report the recall on those subsets. We define it formally as:

$$recall\_sample = \frac{TP \cap sample}{\#need\_norm \cap sample}$$

5.1 Alignment algorithm

Does enforcing alignment in a greedy way as described in Algorithm 2 help normalisation ?

As we compare in figure 1, our parallel alignment method provides a +0.5 F1 improvement

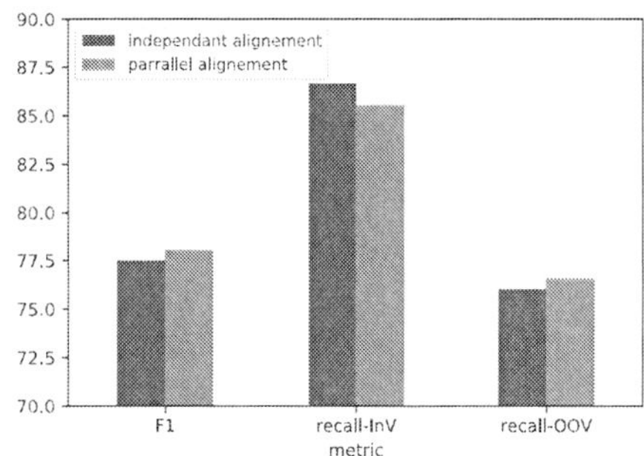

Figure 1: Impact of noisy/canonical alignment method with a focus on generalization by comparing Out-of-Vocabulary (OOV) and In-Vocabulary (InV) performance (development set)

Standard	Noise-focused	Gain
78.1	79.28	+1.18

Table 5: Impact of our noise-specific strategy on the F1 score (development set) reported with best alignment setting

(78.1 vs 77.6 F1). We also compare the performance of our two models on OOV and InV words. Indeed, normalising a seen word is much easier than a word unseen during training. As we observe, the gain coming from our our alignment technique come from a better generalization. We gain +0.6 in recall on OOV thanks to this parallel alignment.

5.2 Fine-Tuning Strategy

As observed in table 5, our fine-tuning strategy focused on noisy tokens improves with a large margin the performance of our system. We interpret it in the following way: lexical normalisation is imbalanced. As seen in 3.2 there are around 9 times more *need_no_norm* than *need_norm* tokens. By specifically training on noisy tokens we successfully manage to alleviate this aspect of the data.

In conclusion, our best model is BERT trained on parallel tokenized data with the noise-focus fine-tuning strategy. We reach 79.28 in F1 score. The following table illustrates how our model performs normalization on a typical example:

Noisy	*@aijaee i hear you u knw hetta to cross mine tho*
Norm	*@aijaee i hear you you know better to cross mine though*

Model	Accuracy
BERT noise-focused	97.5
MoNoise	97.6

Table 6: Comparing our systems to the State-of-the-art system MoNoise (we report on same development dataset reported in MoNoise original paper (last 950 sentences))

Model	F1
Supranovich and Patsepnia, 2015	82.72
Berend and Tasnádi, 2015	80.52
our best model	**79.28**
Beckley, 2015	75.71
GIGO	72.64
Ruiz et al., 2014	53.1

Table 7: Comparing our systems to WNUT 2015 shared task that allowed UGC resources

6 Discussion

We now compare our system to previous works.

As we see in Table 8, our non-UGC system is far from the State-of-the-Art model MoNoise (van der Goot and van Noord, 2017) in terms of F1 score. In order to take into account detection in our metric, we also report the overall accuracy of the system in table 6. We are therefore 6.7 points below in terms of F1 score and 0.2 point below in terms of overall accuracy on lexnorm15 dataset.

However, we emphasize that MoNoise is a feature-based Random Forest based on external modules. Among others, it makes use of a skip-gram model trained on 5 millions tweets, the Aspell tool and a n-gram model trained on more than 700 millions tweets.

In order to have a more balanced comparison, we compare our system to the MoNoise model after removing the feature that has the most impact, according to the original paper: the n-gram module (referred as *MoNoise no n-gram*). In this setting, we significantly outperform the MoNoise model (+1.78 improvement) (Table 8).

Moreover, we based all our work on the lexnorm15 dataset released for the W-NUT 2015 shared task (Baldwin et al., 2015). We compare our model to the competing systems (cf. table 7). Briefly, the second best model (Berend and Tasnádi, 2015) use a n-gram model trained on a English tweet corpus. The best competing system (Supranovich and Patsepnia, 2015) is based on a lexicon extracted from tweets. Still, we see that our model is able to outperform models ranked 3,

Model	F1	UGC resources	speed
MoNoise	86.39	lex15+700Mtweets	57s
our best model	**79.28**	lexnorm15	9.5s
MoNoise NNG	77.5	lex15+5Mtweets	-

Table 8: Comparing our systems to the State-of-the-art system MoNoise on lexnorm15 test. Speed is reported as time to predict 1000 tokens (includes model loading). *MoNoise No-Ngrams* or MoNoise NNG is the score reported in the original paper without the use of UGC-n-grams but with a UGC word2vec

4 and 5 that are all built using UGC resources.

Finally, the state-of-the-art models we presented are modular. They require features from external modules. This makes them extremely slow at test time. We compare it in Table 8, demonstrating another practical interest for our approach. Our model is 6 times faster than MoNoise at prediction time.

Following those observations, we claim that BERT, enhanced to handle token introduction and token removal, fine-tuned in a precise way toward noisy words, is a competitive lexical normalisation model.

This result exceeds the context of lexical normalization of noisy User Generated Content. Indeed, the success of BERT in improving NLP models on a diversity of tasks was, until now, restricted to canonical edited texts. In our work, we showed that it was possible to adapt such a general model to the extreme case of normalising noisy UGC in a low resource setting. We let for future work the adaptation of BERT to other tasks in out-of-domain non canonical context.

7 Conclusion

General pre-trained language model have demonstrated their ability to improve Natural Language Processing systems for most tasks on canonical data. In our work, we demonstrated that they can also be useful in non-canonical noisy text in low resource setting. We hope that this work will pave the way for future research in modelling non-canonical textual data.

Acknowledgments

We thank the reviewers for their valuable feedbacks. This work was funded by the ANR projects ParSiTi (ANR-16-CE33-0021), SoSweet (ANR15-CE38-0011-01) and the French-Israeli PHC Maimonide program.

References

Timothy Baldwin, Paul Cook, Marco Lui, Andrew MacKinlay, and Li Wang. 2013. How noisy social media text, how diffrnt social media sources? In *Proceedings of the Sixth International Joint Conference on Natural Language Processing*, pages 356–364.

Timothy Baldwin, Marie-Catherine de Marneffe, Bo Han, Young-Bum Kim, Alan Ritter, and Wei Xu. 2015. Shared tasks of the 2015 workshop on noisy user-generated text: Twitter lexical normalization and named entity recognition. In *Proceedings of the Workshop on Noisy User-generated Text*, pages 126–135.

Russell Beckley. 2015. Bekli: A simple approach to twitter text normalization. In *Proceedings of the Workshop on Noisy User-generated Text*, pages 82–86.

Gábor Berend and Ervin Tasnádi. 2015. Uszeged: correction type-sensitive normalization of english tweets using efficiently indexed n-gram statistics. In *Proceedings of the Workshop on Noisy User-generated Text*, pages 120–125.

Jacob Devlin, Ming-Wei Chang, Kenton Lee, and Kristina Toutanova. 2018. Bert: Pre-training of deep bidirectional transformers for language understanding. *arXiv preprint arXiv:1810.04805*.

Jacob Eisenstein. 2013. What to do about bad language on the internet. In *HLT-NAACL*, Atlanta, USA.

Jennifer Foster. 2010. "cba to check the spelling": Investigating parser performance on discussion forum posts. In *NAACL*, Los Angeles, California.

Rob van der Goot and Gertjan van Noord. 2017. Monoise: modeling noise using a modular normalization system. *arXiv preprint arXiv:1710.03476*.

Rob van der Goot and Gertjan van Noord. 2018. Modeling input uncertainty in neural network dependency parsing. In *Proceedings of the 2018 Conference on Empirical Methods in Natural Language Processing*, pages 4984–4991.

Rob van der Goot, Barbara Plank, and Malvina Nissim. 2017. To normalize, or not to normalize: The impact of normalization on part-of-speech tagging. *arXiv preprint arXiv:1707.05116*.

Soorya Gopalakrishnan, Zhinus Marzi, Upamanyu Madhow, and Ramtin Pedarsani. 2018. Combating adversarial attacks using sparse representations.

Bo Han and Timothy Baldwin. 2011. Lexical normalisation of short text messages: Makn sens a# twitter. In *Proceedings of the 49th Annual Meeting of the Association for Computational Linguistics: Human Language Technologies-Volume 1*, pages 368–378. Association for Computational Linguistics.

John Hewitt and Christopher D. Manning. 2019. A Structural Probe for Finding Syntax in Word Representations. In *Proceedings of the 2019 Conference of the North American Chapter of the Association for Computational Linguistics: Human Language Technologies*. Association for Computational Linguistics.

Ganesh Jawahar, Benoît Sagot, and Djamé Seddah. 2019. What does BERT learn about the structure of language? In *in proc. of the 57th Annual Meeting of the Association for Computational Linguistics (ACL)*, Florence, Italy.

Dan Jurafsky. 2018. *Speech & language processing*, 3rd edition. Currently in draft.

Diederik P Kingma and Jimmy Ba. 2014. Adam: A method for stochastic optimization. *arXiv preprint arXiv:1412.6980*.

Guillaume Lample and Alexis Conneau. 2019. Cross-lingual language model pretraining. *arXiv preprint arXiv:1901.07291*.

Chen Li and Yang Liu. 2012. Improving text normalization using character-blocks based models and system combination. *Proceedings of COLING 2012*, pages 1587–1602.

Paul Michel and Graham Neubig. 2018. Mtnt: A testbed for machine translation of noisy text. *arXiv preprint arXiv:1809.00388*.

Seungwhan Moon, Leonardo Neves, and Vitor Carvalho. 2018. Multimodal named entity recognition for short social media posts. *arXiv preprint arXiv:1802.07862*.

Matthew E Peters, Mark Neumann, Mohit Iyyer, Matt Gardner, Christopher Clark, Kenton Lee, and Luke Zettlemoyer. 2018. Deep contextualized word representations. *arXiv preprint arXiv:1802.05365*.

Pablo Ruiz, Montse Cuadros, and Thierry Etchegoyhen. 2014. Lexical normalization of spanish tweets with rule-based components and language models. *Procesamiento del Lenguaje Natural*, page 8.

Mike Schuster and Kaisuke Nakajima. 2012. Japanese and korean voice search. In *2012 IEEE International Conference on Acoustics, Speech and Signal Processing (ICASSP)*, pages 5149–5152. IEEE.

Djamé Seddah, Benoît Sagot, Marie Candito, Virginie Mouilleron, and Vanessa Combet. 2012. The French Social Media Bank: a Treebank of Noisy User Generated Content. In *CoLing*, Mumbai, India.

Dmitry Supranovich and Viachaslau Patsepnia. 2015. Ihs_rd: Lexical normalization for english tweets. In *Proceedings of the Workshop on Noisy User-generated Text*, pages 78–81.

Ilya Sutskever, Oriol Vinyals, and Quoc V Le. 2014. Sequence to sequence learning with neural networks. In *Advances in neural information processing systems*, pages 3104–3112.

Ke Xu, Yunqing Xia, and Chin-Hui Lee. 2015. Tweet normalization with syllables. In *Proceedings of the 53rd Annual Meeting of the Association for Computational Linguistics and the 7th International Joint Conference on Natural Language Processing (Volume 1: Long Papers)*, volume 1, pages 920–928.

Yi Yang and Jacob Eisenstein. 2013. A log-linear model for unsupervised text normalization. In *Proceedings of the 2013 Conference on Empirical Methods in Natural Language Processing*, pages 61–72.

No, you're not alone: A better way to find people with similar experiences on Reddit

Zhilin Wang   Elena Rastorgueva   Weizhe Lin   Xiaodong Wu
University of Cambridge, United Kingdom
{zw322, wl356, xw338}@cam.ac.uk,
elenaras@cantab.net

Abstract

We present a probabilistic clustering algorithm that can help Reddit users to find posts that discuss experiences similar to their own. This model is built upon the BERT Next Sentence Prediction model and reduces the time complexity for clustering all posts in a corpus from $O(n^2)$ to $O(n)$ with respect to the number of posts. We demonstrate that such probabilistic clustering can yield a performance better than baseline clustering methods based on Latent Dirichlet Allocation (Blei et al., 2003) and Word2Vec (Mikolov et al., 2013). Furthermore, there is a high degree of coherence between our probabilistic clustering and the exhaustive comparison $O(n^2)$ algorithm in which the similarity between every pair of posts is found. This makes the use of the BERT Next Sentence Prediction model more practical for unsupervised clustering tasks due to the high runtime overhead of each BERT computation.

1 Introduction

On many subreddits within Reddit, such as r/Advice[1], users choose to share highly personal experiences that matter greatly in their lives in order to ask for advice from other users. Relative to other popular social networking sites such as Facebook, Instagram and Twitter, Reddit offers a greater extent of anonymity because there is no requirement for users to register accounts with their real names. Users are therefore often more at ease to reveal their experiences honestly and in full detail because the risk of facing repercussion from their real-life social networks is minimal. An example post is shown in Figure 1. This offers a unique opportunity to use what users posted on these subreddits as a proxy for their real-life experiences,

---

[1] https://www.reddit.com/r/Advice/

Title: "How do I get Vaccinated as a Minor?"
Body: "I am a 16 year old female whose mother became anti-vax a couple of years ago when she got Facebook. I don't think I've gotten a vaccine in 4-6 years at this point.I really want to get vaccinated ..."

Figure 1: An excerpt from a /r/Advice subreddit post.

and what they felt and thought about these experiences. Here, we attempt to cluster similar posts on these subreddits. In this aspect, we are not only interested in the circumstances under which the individuals encountered the experiences, but also how they responded to the various situations in terms of their actions, thoughts and feelings.

To do so, we take advantage of recent improvements in transformer-based mechanisms for transfer learning, most prominently BERT (Devlin et al., 2019). This capacity allows a model to be pre-trained on a large corpus unrelated to our specific task, in order to learn fundamental statistical properties of language relating to syntax and semantics. Specifically, we employ the model of BERT that is pre-trained for the task of Next Sentence Prediction, which seeks to capture semantic congruence between two paragraphs. While this is not entirely similar with finding semantic similarities within Reddit posts (which often contain informal language), we hypothesize that some information encapsulated in the pre-trained model will be transferable to our task. In this way, we can train a model using an extremely limited dataset of around 9000 posts. Currently, we have only trained our model using an English corpus, but given that the BERT model (Devlin et al., 2019) has multi-lingual capabilities, we believe that our findings can apply to languages other than English.

Our key contribution lies in clustering all posts

Proceedings of the 2019 EMNLP Workshop W-NUT: The 5th Workshop on Noisy User-generated Text, pages 307–315
Hong Kong, Nov 4, 2019. ©2019 Association for Computational Linguistics

into groups without needing to calculate the pairwise Next Sentence Prediction likelihood for every pair of posts. This reduces the computational complexity of this process from $O(n^2)$ to $O(nm)$, where n is the number of posts, m is the number of clusters and $n \gg m$. This is an important advancement because an operation on each pair of posts is in itself computationally intensive due to the transformer architecture. Our design can enable such clustering to be more scalable for larger corpora.

2 Related work

2.1 Deductive coding of individual experiences

The first field of related work lies in attempts to create a standard for deductive coding of individual experiences, typically based in the field of psychology. In this approach, trained individuals inspect people's writing of their experience and classify each into a predefined category. The inspection of each individual is then compared to that of others to ensure consistency. Demorest et al. (1999) defined an individual experience in terms of a person's wish, a response from another person and a response from the self in light of the other person's response. At each stage, experiences can be classified into categories such as wanting to be respected, being disliked by others and feeling disappointed because of the rejection. On the other hand, Thorne and McLean (2001) defined experiences in terms of themes. These themes include occasions of life threatening events, relationship-related issues and a sense of mastery. Together, these can provide a basis for identifying the elements within a post that can be used to compare to other posts.

2.2 Computational personality differences

The second field of related work lies in research on how individuals differ in terms of their responses to common life situations and how such differences can be measured by analyzing their writing. The most popular measure is the Myers-Briggs Type Indicator (Myers et al., 1990; Gjurković and Šnajder, 2018), which classifies individuals into 16 types based on their disposition. Another common measure is the Big Five personality traits (Yarkoni, 2010), which gauges people in terms of five dimensions: Openness, Conscientiousness, Extraversion, Agreeableness and Neuroticism. Pennebaker (2011) also investigated how other personality attributes such as a focus on the self (as opposed to others) and differences in status can be predicted based on word choices. All of the above measures seek to group people into distinct categories based on how they write. The relative success of this field in doing so convinced us that it is possible to capture individual differences through a person's writing. However, to help Reddit users find other users with similar experiences, we are interested in not only the general response patterns of an individual but also their specific response to a specific situation. This means that we cannot directly adopt their methodology of performing a supervised classification task. Instead, we decided on unsupervised methodology because it would permit a wider range of situations and responses.

2.3 Analysis of characters and plots in novels and movies

The final field of related work comes from the computational analysis of characters and plots in novels and movies. Bamman et al. (2013, 2014) sought to classify characters into various prototypes in film and novels. Frermann and Szarvas (2017) and Iyyer et al. (2016) went a step further to classify the types of relationships that exist between main characters in a novel, in addition to the prototype of each character in novels. These works inspired this paper on Reddit posts, because events in many novels and movies are relatable to the experiences of real-life individuals. Furthermore, many posts also concern interactions between the author and other people in the author's real-life social networks. However, Reddit posts are much shorter than movies and novels. This means that the recurrent models designed to represent how a character/relationship develops through a novel/movie in literature above is less applicable in our research. Moreover, unlike novels/movies, which often use character names together with personal pronouns, Reddit posts tend to use personal pronouns almost exclusively (in order to preserve anonymity). As a result, a popular coreference resolution framework[2] would not work on Reddit posts. Therefore, most of the methods described in literature above could not be adapted for our research and we had to look elsewhere for a suitable architecture.

---

[2] https://github.com/huggingface/neuralcoref

Algorithm 1

1: **procedure** ONE-PROB-CLUSTERING(posts, m)
2:     unselected_posts $\leftarrow$ posts; clusters $\leftarrow \{\}$
3:     **while** unselected_posts $\neq [\,]$ **do**
4:         selected_post $\leftarrow$ RANDOM-SELECTION(all_unselected_posts) $\triangleright$ Without replacement
5:         **for** query_post in all_unselected_posts **do**
6:             similarity $\leftarrow$ BERT-NEXT-SENTENCE-PREDICTION(selected_post.title, query_post.text)
7:         most_similar $\leftarrow$ most similar $\lfloor n/m \rfloor$ query posts
8:         clusters [selected_post] $\leftarrow$ most_similar
9:         **for** post in most_similar **do**
10:           unselected_posts.remove(post)
11:     **return** clusters

---

3 Probabilistic Clustering

3.1 Data preprocessing

We downloaded 200 days of posts from the r/Advice subreddit[1] using the Pushshift API[3]. After that, we filtered out posts with (i) scores lower than 3 based on the number of upvotes, downvotes and comments they received, which indicated that they might not be pertinent to the users of the subreddit, and (ii) no textual information in the post. This left us with 8865 posts.

3.2 Generating similarities between two posts

We then used the BERT Next Sentence Prediction model[4] to predict the likelihood that the title from post A will be proceeded by the body text of post B. The model had been pre-trained on the BooksCorpus (800M words) (Zhu et al., 2015) and English Wikipedia corpus (2,500M words). During the pre-training process, half of the inputs consist of sentence B being the actual sentence following sentence A (labeled as 'IsNext') while the other half consists of a random sentence from the corpus that does not proceed sentence A (labeled as 'NotNext') (Devlin et al., 2019). We found this to be a feasible method of deciphering the semantic similarity between the title of post A and the body text of post B because in more than 97.7% of our posts, the text is predicted to follow its own title. This is likely because the pre-training task of finding sentences that are likely to follow one another is highly similar to our task of finding text of a post that is likely to be after the title of the same post. While the BERT Next-Sentence-Prediction model was pre-trained on a sentence-

level corpus, this result demonstrates that its effects can translate to a paragraph-level task, which was also noted by Devlin et al. (2019).

Besides using the title of post A and the text of post B, we also experimented with the title of post A and the title of post B as well as the text of post A and the text of post B.

3.3 Clustering based on similarities

Intuitively, clustering can be done by comparing each post with all other posts in the corpus. This would be a $O(n^2)$ operation where n is number of posts. However, due to the large number of weights of the BERT model, each comparison takes a long time to complete. Therefore, even for a small corpus of 8865 posts, it would be infeasible to perform pairwise comparison of every pair. This makes the intuitive algorithm highly unscalable with the number of posts.

To overcome this problem, we invented a probabilistic clustering architecture, described in Algorithm 1.

The computational complexity of this algorithm, ONE-PROBABILISTIC-CLUSTERING can be calculated as follows. Given that the most runtime-intensive step is BERT-NEXT-SENTENCE-PREDICTION, we can choose to solely focus our analysis on this step.

In each while-loop, we have to perform the BERT-NEXT-SENTENCE-PREDICTION process $n_{unselected\,posts}$ times. $n_{unselected\,posts}$ starts from n and decreases by $\lfloor n/m \rfloor$ after each while-loop, where n is the number of posts and m is the number of clusters.

Therefore, S, the total number of times the BERT-NEXT-SENTENCE-PREDICTION process is carried out, follows an arithmetic progres-

---

[3]https://github.com/dmarx/psaw
[4]The uncased small model on https://github.com/huggingface/pytorch-transformers

---

Algorithm 2

1: **procedure** MERGE-MULTIPLE-PROB-CLUSTERING(p, m, posts)
2:     similarity_table ← {}
3:     **for** i ← $0, n - 1$ **do**
4:         similarity_table[i] = [0, 0, ..., 0, 0]   ▷ Initialise with array of size n
5:     **for** i ← $0, p - 1$ **do**
6:         one_probabilistic_clustering = ONE-PROBABILISTIC-CLUSTERING(posts, m)
7:         **for** j in one_probabilistic_clustering.keys() **do**
8:             One_cluster = [j] + [one_probabilistic_clustering[j]]
9:             all_similar_pairs = PERMUTATIONS(one_cluster, 2)
10:             **for** k in all_similar_pairs **do**
11:                 similarity_table[k[0]][k[1]] += 1
12:     **return** similarity_table

Algorithm 3

1: **procedure** GENERATE-CLUSTERS-FROM-SIMILARITY(similarity_table, m, n)
2:     unselected_posts ← posts; clusters ← {}
3:     **while** unselected_posts ≠ [ ] **do**
4:         selected_post = RANDOM-SELECTION(unselected_posts)   ▷ Without replacement
5:         sort similarity_table[selected_post]
6:         most_similar = most similar $\lfloor n/m \rfloor$ posts in unselected_posts
7:         clusters [selected_post] = most_similar
8:         **for** post in most_similar **do** unselected_posts.remove(post)
9:     **return** clusters

---

sion:

$$S = n + (n - \lfloor n/m \rfloor) + (n - 2\lfloor n/m \rfloor) +$$

$$\cdots$$

$$(n - (m - 1) * \lfloor n/m \rfloor) + (n - m * \lfloor n/m \rfloor)$$

$$\leq \frac{n * m}{2} \tag{1}$$

Therefore the time complexity of ONE-PROBABLISTIC-CLUSTERING is $O(nm)$. We chose $m = 30$ because initial experiments using a Gaussian Mixture Model to cluster BERT sentence embedding of Reddit post text (by average-pooling all tokens in the second-to-last layer)[5] suggested that $m = 30$ is the optimal choice because it scored lowest on the Akaike Information Criteria (Akaike, 1973). The absolute computational complexity for ONE-PROBABLISTIC-CLUSTERING, taking into consideration the cost of sorting most_similar is $O(mnlogn)$. When n is small however, the constant factor for BERT-NEXT-SENTENCE-PREDICTION is so great that it dominates the run-time, allowing the run-time to $O(nm)$.

The time complexity for Algorithm 2, MERGE-MULTIPLE-PROB-CLUSTERING, is $O(n^2)$ where n is the number of posts used to generate an n-by-n matrix for the similarity table. However, because the constant factor is so large, when $n = 8865$, it is the time complexity from running ONE-PROBABILISTIC-CLUSTERING that dominates. Therefore, the runtime complexity of MERGE-MULTIPLE-PROB-CLUSTERING is $o(nmp)$, $n = 8865$ where n is the number of posts, m is the number of clusters and p is the number of times that ONE-PROBABILISTIC-CLUSTERING is run. A value of $p = 5$ is chosen because although a more informative similarity table will be constructed when p is higher, it also requires more computational resources.

GENERATE-CLUSTERS-FROM-SIMILARITY has a time complexity $O(mn \log n)$ where n is the number of posts and m is the number of clusters because the while-loop will run for m iterations with each iteration taking $O(n \log n)$ for sorting. In practice however, the runtime is dominated by the previous MERGE-MULTIPLE-PROBALISTIC-CLUSTERING step due to its large constant factor.

---

[5] https://github.com/hanxiao/bert-as-service

3.4 Fine-tuning BERT Next Sentence Prediction

Besides using the pre-trained Next Sentence Prediction model, we also fine-tuned the model using posts from Reddit to better fit the classification to our corpus. We used not only 8865 posts from r/Advice, but also over 300,000 posts from similar subreddits[6]. During the pre-training process, we focused on training the weights for the final BERT pooling layer as well as the classification layer and froze the parameters in all other BERT layers. We made this decision because our corpus was not sufficient for us to retrain the parameters for the layers beneath and doing so might lead to worse performance than using the default pre-trained parameters. Because fine-tuning requires labeled data, we performed fine-tuning based on posts from the same author. In the subreddits that we used, some authors posted multiple times to share about a similar experience. This is likely because they did not receive adequate guidance from the Reddit community after their earlier post(s). Therefore, two posts from the same subreddit and the same author are likely to discuss about similar themes and topics. We used this tendency to generate text-text pairs from the same author with a label 'IsNext' and paired one text with a randomly selected text from another post not from the same author with a label 'NotNext'.

4 Evaluation

4.1 Qualitative Evaluation

Table 1, shows the titles of 3 randomly chosen posts and the five most similar posts to them. There is a high degree of coherence, and the posts are not only similar thematically (in Post 1: pregnant - pregnancy test - dating - hookups), but also emotionally (in Post 2: a sense of succorance) and at a word-level (in Post 3: 'dog').

4.2 Quantitative Evaluation

Baselines

Baseline measurements were done using Latent Dirichlet Allocation (LDA) (Blei et al., 2003) and word2vec (Mikolov et al., 2013). LDA document-topic mappings were performed using

Gensim[7]. Documents were first tokenized, removed of stopwords and lemmatized. A Bag of Words (BoW) corpus was obtained before a term frequency-inverse document frequency (TF-IDF) corpus was derived from it. Topic modeling was then performed on both the BoW corpus (thereafter LDA-BoW) and TF-IDF corpus (thereafter LDA-TFIDF) with the number of topics set to 30, in line with the number of clusters used. The document-topic mapping of each post is then used for computing cosine similarities with all other posts.

Word2Vec embeddings were also used as a benchmark. Specifically, pre-trained word2vec embeddings of dimension 300 (Mikolov et al., 2013) were used to generate two forms of sentence embeddings. The first (thereafter called W2V-Weighted) is calculated by weighing the contribution of each word embedding by the inverse of its relative frequency to the final sentence embedding. In doing so, the contributions of the most common words are minimized. The second (thereafter called W2V-SIF) is calculated by first taking the weighed sentence embedding before removing the first principal component from it. (Arora et al., 2017).

Generating similarities from baselines

Cosine similarities were then calculated between all documents. The resulting cosine similarity matrix was be then entered in the GENERATE-CLUSTERS-FROM-SIMILARITY function (Algorithm 3) with the number of clusters (m) and number of posts (n) kept the same as in the probabilistic clustering model.

Evaluation metrics

To determine if our clustering algorithm is better than baselines, it is imperative to have evaluation metrics. However, because our clustering tasks do not have ground truth labels, we could not find common metrics to evaluate the effectiveness of our algorithm. Therefore, we designed two novel extrinsic metrics for this purpose.

Evaluation Metric 1: Same author score

We designed this metric based on the observation that authors who post multiple times in the r/Advice subreddit tend to post about similar topics. Therefore, a good clustering algorithm might be more effective at clustering posts from the same author in the same cluster. To measure this, we found all pairs of posts with the same author and

---

Randomly chosen post titles
Titles of 5 most similar posts

Post 1: I'm afraid I could be pregnant
1. I bought pregnancy tests bc im paranoidddd
2. What should I think of this convo between my ex and I? I felt guilty...
3. Met an E-guy became really good friends, started 'dating'. We joked sexually and I found it funny.
4. My entire life I skipped school and just didn't really care too much for it.
5. I'm scared of hookups.

Post 2: How do I help support my girlfriend who has been raped?
1. Should this teacher get in trouble for making these comments about male students?
2. How do I help my (severely?) mentally ill daughter?
3. I've been avoiding my family for the past few months, I'm not sure what to do now.
4. How to turn you life around after doing almost nothing for 3-4 years.
5. An old tradition brought me into a rather messed up situation.

Post 3: Neighbor is going nuts and wants to shoot my dog (or my sister, or all of us...)
1. How long do I wait before calling the police for a welfare check?
2. How to help my roommate - crying in his sleep.
3. To dog or not to dog?
4. All day every day my neighbors dog is on a 6-10 ft rope.
5. Dog sitting disaster

Table 1: Each unshaded box shows the titles of a randomly chosen post and the 5 posts most similar to it

counted the proportion of them that are clustered into the same cluster. Finally we account for the likelihood that they were arranged into the same cluster by chance, which is a constant equal to $\frac{1}{m}$. This is described in Eq. 2, where I is the total number of authors and j represents possible combinations of pairs of posts by a single author (hence there are a total of J_i possible combinations for author i). j^0 and j^1 represent the first and second post in the pair, respectively, and e.g. $Cluster(j^0)$ returns the i.d. of the cluster that j^0 has been assigned to.

$$S_{same\ author} = \frac{\sum_{i=1}^{I} \sum_{j=1}^{J_i} \mathbb{1}_{Cluster(j^0)=Cluster(j^1)}}{\sum_{i=1}^{I} \sum_{j=1}^{J} 1} - \frac{1}{m} \tag{2}$$

Evaluation Metric 2: Jaccard score This metric was inspired by the observation that authors who share similar interests tend to post about similar topics on r/Advice. In this case, we measure how similar the interests of the authors are by counting the number of subreddits they have both posted and commented on divided by the number of the union of subreddits they have posted and commented on. In the case that they have both commented and posted in exactly the same set of subreddits, their Jaccard scores will be 1. If they have not posted or commented on any subreddits in common, their Jaccard score will be 0. In our use case, however, the lower bound is strictly higher than 0 because two authors would have both posted in r/Advice. Furthermore, to prevent over-accounting for throwaway accounts, which are only used to post once, we set the Jaccard score of any pair of posts, which consists of at least one that has only posted/commented in one subreddit to 0.

Jaccard scores of all pairs of posts in the same cluster were then added together. The result was then multiplied by the number of clusters to account for the difference in probability that two posts will be put into the same cluster by chance alone, which varies inversely with the number of clusters. Finally, the result is divided by the square of the number of posts because the number of posts in each cluster varies linearly with the total number of posts and therefore the number of combination of two posts in the same category varies linearly to the square of the number of posts.

The metric is described in Eq. 3 where I is the total number of clusters (referred to as m in the rest of this paper) and J_i represents all possible combinations of pairs of posts in the same cluster.

$L_{j^0}^{posted}$ represents the set of subreddits that the author of the first post in the pair has posted to. Likewise j_1 refers to the second author and ^{commented} refers to subreddits the author commented on.

$$S_{Jaccard} = \sum_{i=1}^{I} \sum_{j=1}^{J_i} 0.5 \left(\frac{L_{j^0}^{posted} \cap L_{j^1}^{posted}}{L_{j^0}^{posted} \cup L_{j^1}^{posted}} + \frac{L_{j^0}^{commented} \cap L_{j^1}^{commented}}{L_{j^0}^{commented} \cup L_{j^1}^{commented}} \right) * \frac{n_{clusters}}{n_{posts}^2} \quad (3)$$

4.3 Effectiveness of probabilistic clustering

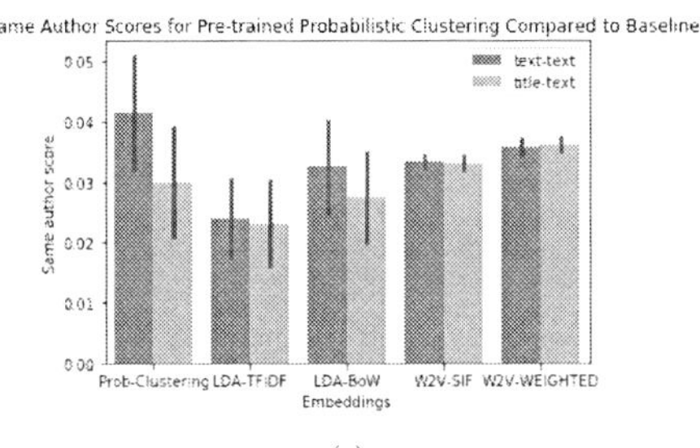

(a)

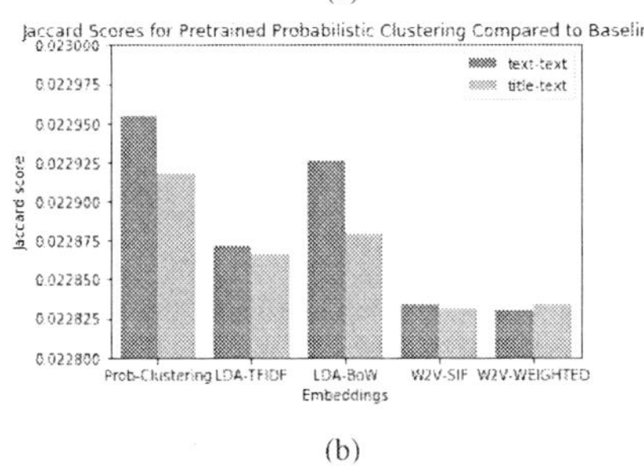

(b)

Figure 2: Same author (a) and Jaccard scores (b) for pre-trained probabilistic clustering compared to baselines. Scores generated by performing 100 iterations and finding the average. Error bars in (a) represent the standard deviation. Error bars are not shown on (b) because standard deviation is insignificant relative to the scale of the figure. Higher is better on both figures.

Figure 2 shows that probabilistic clustering performs better than all baseline embeddings. This is due to the model's capability to learn complex relationships between the two input sentences instead of using cosine distance as the measure of similarity. In nearly all embeddings, using the body text from two posts surpasses the performance of using the title from one post and the body text from the second post, measured in both metrics. This is likely because the body text typically contains more words, which can provide more information for sentence embeddings. A

review of the topic-word mapping for LDA suggests that words were not clearly resolved into distinct topics. Words like "friends", "dating" and "fun" appeared in nearly half of all topics, suggesting that LDA might be inadequate for capturing topics in such Reddit posts. This might be because Reddit posts are mostly informal and uses a limited range of vocabulary with many common words used in different context with highly distinct meanings. Using a transformer-based BERT architecture might be better able to capture such contextual information (Vaswani et al., 2017).

4.4 Fine-tuning

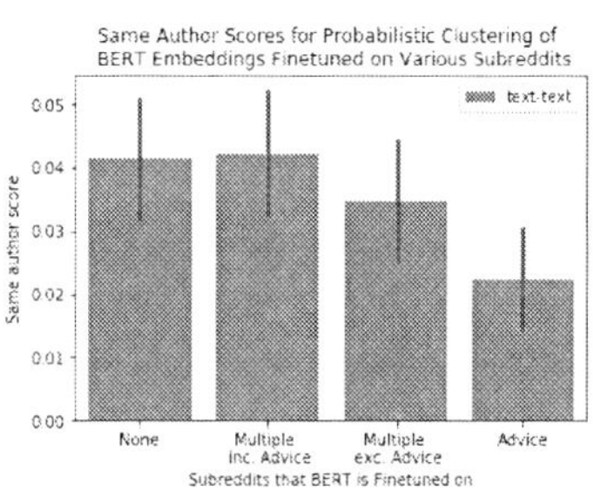

(a)

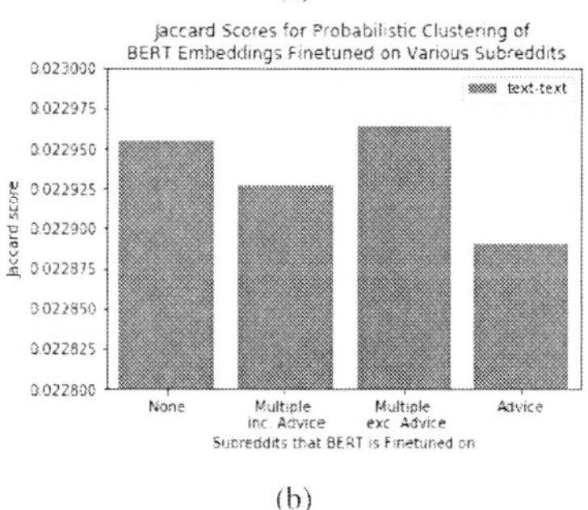

(b)

Figure 3: Same author (a) and Jaccard scores (b) for probabilistic clustering of BERT embeddings fine-tuned on subreddit(s) based on the same author selection criteria. Scores generated by performing 100 iterations and finding the average, with error bars in (a) representing the standard deviation. Error bars not shown on (b) because standard deviation is insignificant relative to the scale of the figure. Higher is better on both figures.

Figure 3b suggests that while some forms of fine-tuning can perform better than the pre-trained model, improvements are usually modest and inconsistent. In both Figures 3a and 3b, the model fine-tuned using only the Advice subreddit performed worst in terms of both metrics suggesting that pre-training on a highly limited corpus should be avoided. Furthermore, its poor performance also supports the hypothesis that the model does not simply memorize the seen corpus because the same set of the corpus was used to train and to test the classifier. On the contrary, pre-training the model with a large corpus, even one that does not contain the testing sample, can lead to some improvement in the Jaccard score, as in Figure 3b. This suggests a lack of over-fitting in our model and correspondingly indicates a high possibility of generalizing our model beyond our corpus.

4.5 Ablation experiments

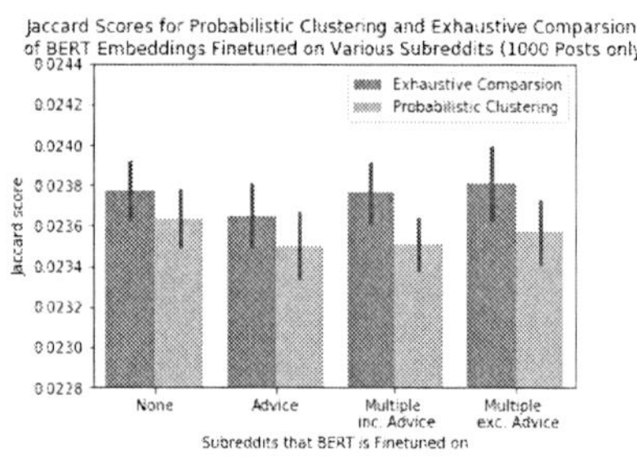

(a)

(b)

Figure 4: (a) Jaccard Scores for the first 1000 posts, obtained from Probabilistic Clustering and Exhaustive Comparison. (b) Similarity scores between Probabilistic clustering and Exhaustive Comparison for the first 1000 posts. Scores generated by performing 50 iterations and finding the average. Error bars represent standard deviation. Higher is better on both figures.[8]

An ablation study was conducted to investigate the contribution of the probabilistic clustering algorithm beyond the value of the BERT Next Sentence Prediction task. In the exhaustive comparison control, the likelihood that the post text of post A will follow the post text of post B was found for all combinations of pairs of posts. This allowed us to construct a complete similarity table that can be used to generate clusters using the procedure GENERATE-CLUSTERS-FROM-SIMILARITY. The same parameters of 1,000 posts and 30 clusters were chosen for both probabilistic

clustering and the exhaustive comparison. Figure 4a suggests that while exhaustive comparison led to higher performance, the difference is typically less than a standard deviation. This means that the reduction in performance is relatively minimal compared to the significant reduction in time complexity, which might make exhaustive comparison increasingly unfeasible as the number of posts increases.

In Figure 4b, Adjusted Rand score (Hubert and Arabie, 1985) and Adjusted Mutual Information (Vinh et al., 2010) were used to measure for coherence between exhaustive comparison and probabilistic clustering. Both scores suggest that the probabilistic clustering of embeddings pre-trained on all corpuses agree with the exhaustive comparison to a degree that is significantly higher than chance would predict (when both scores would be 0). Furthermore, the model pre-trained on the larger corpora of (i) Multiple subreddits inc. Advice and (ii) exc. Advice agree more with the exhaustive comparison. This might be because the models fine-tuned on those corpora are better able to understand the use of language used on Reddit and hence better able to accurately choose the top $\lfloor n/m \rfloor$ similar posts. However, this does not translate to higher Jaccard scores compared to the pre-trained model. This could be due to (i) the Jaccard score metric (measuring the proportion of subreddits that two authors have posted or commented on in common) not being able to fully capture all information that explain the similarity between posts, or (ii) the BERT Next Sentence Prediction model (pre-trained and minimally fine-tuned) being unable to fully capture the relative similarities between posts, even though it is capable of capturing absolute similarities between the title of a post and its post text.

5 Conclusion

In conclusion, we have presented a probabilistic clustering algorithm for clustering similar posts on many subreddits on Reddit such as r/Advice. This algorithm is built on top of the BERT Next Sentence Prediction model and reduces the time complexity of clustering posts from $O(n^2)$ to $O(n)$ with respect to the number of posts. This algorithm can be helpful for users on Reddits to find

---

[8] Only Jaccard scores were used to compare the extrinsic performance of both methods because the low number of pairs of post that share the same author makes the same author score uninformative.

posts similar to those they have written themselves (about their own experiences) or others that they are interested in. To further build on the contribution of this work, we encourage researchers to experiment with alternative fine-tuning methods as well as performing post-processing of similarity tables such as performing post-level normalization to reduce the occurrence of some posts being highly similar to a great number of posts while others being similar to too few. Researchers may also consider incorporating other textual information such as comments on Reddit posts into the model to improve its performance.

References

Hirotugu Akaike. 1973. Information theory and an extension of the maximum likelihood principle. *Czaki, Akademiai Kiado, Budapest*.

Sanjeev Arora, Yingyu Liang, and Tengyu Ma. 2017. A simple but tough-to-beat baseline for sentence embeddings. In *ICLR*.

David Bamman, Brendan O'Connor, and Noah A. Smith. 2013. Learning latent personas of film characters. In *Proceedings of the 51st Annual Meeting of the Association for Computational Linguistics (Volume 1: Long Papers)*, pages 352–361, Sofia, Bulgaria. Association for Computational Linguistics.

David Bamman, Ted Underwood, and Noah A. Smith. 2014. A Bayesian mixed effects model of literary character. In *Proceedings of the 52nd Annual Meeting of the Association for Computational Linguistics (Volume 1: Long Papers)*, pages 370–379, Baltimore, Maryland. Association for Computational Linguistics.

David M. Blei, Andrew Y. Ng, and Michael I. Jordan. 2003. Latent dirichlet allocation. *J. Mach. Learn. Res.*, 3:993–1022.

Amy Demorest, Paul Crits-Christoph, Mary Hatch, and Lester Luborsky. 1999. A comparison of interpersonal scripts in clinically depressed versus nondepressed individuals. *Journal of Research in Personality*, 33(3):265 – 280.

Jacob Devlin, Ming-Wei Chang, Kenton Lee, and Kristina Toutanova. 2019. Bert: Pre-training of deep bidirectional transformers for language understanding. In *NAACL-HLT*.

Lea Frermann and György Szarvas. 2017. Inducing semantic micro-clusters from deep multi-view representations of novels. In *Proceedings of the 2017 Conference on Empirical Methods in Natural Language Processing*, pages 1873–1883, Copenhagen, Denmark. Association for Computational Linguistics.

Matej Gjurković and Jan Šnajder. 2018. Reddit: A gold mine for personality prediction. In *Proceedings of the Second Workshop on Computational Modeling of People's Opinions, Personality, and Emotions in Social Media*, pages 87–97, New Orleans, Louisiana, USA. Association for Computational Linguistics.

Lawrence Hubert and Phipps Arabie. 1985. Comparing partitions. *Journal of classification*, 2(1):193–218.

Mohit Iyyer, Anupam Guha, Snigdha Chaturvedi, Jordan Boyd-Graber, and Hal Daumé III. 2016. Feuding families and former Friends: Unsupervised learning for dynamic fictional relationships. In *Proceedings of the 2016 Conference of the North American Chapter of the Association for Computational Linguistics: Human Language Technologies*, pages 1534–1544, San Diego, California. Association for Computational Linguistics.

Tomas Mikolov, Ilya Sutskever, Kai Chen, Greg S Corrado, and Jeff Dean. 2013. Distributed representations of words and phrases and their compositionality. In C. J. C. Burges, L. Bottou, M. Welling, Z. Ghahramani, and K. Q. Weinberger, editors, *Advances in Neural Information Processing Systems 26*, pages 3111–3119. Curran Associates, Inc.

Isabel Briggs Myers, Mary H.McCaulley, and Allen L. Hammer. 1990. *Introduction to Type: a description of the theory and applications of the Myers-Briggs type indicator*. Consulting Psychologists Press.

James W. Pennebaker. 2011. *The secret life of pronouns: What our words say about us*. Bloomsbury Press, New York, NY.

Avril Thorne and Kate C. McLean. 2001. Manual for coding events in self-defining memories. Unpublished Manuscript.

Ashish Vaswani, Noam Shazeer, Niki Parmar, Jakob Uszkoreit, Llion Jones, Aidan N. Gomez, Lukasz Kaiser, and Illia Polosukhin. 2017. Attention is all you need. In *NIPS*.

Nguyen Xuan Vinh, Julien Epps, and James Bailey. 2010. Information theoretic measures for clusterings comparison: Variants, properties, normalization and correction for chance. *J. Mach. Learn. Res.*, 11:2837–2854.

Tal Yarkoni. 2010. Personality in 100,000 words: A large-scale analysis of personality and word use among bloggers. *Journal of research in personality*, 44(3):363373.

Yukun Zhu, Jamie Ryan Kiros, Richard S. Zemel, Ruslan Salakhutdinov, Raquel Urtasun, Antonio Torralba, and Sanja Fidler. 2015. Aligning books and movies: Towards story-like visual explanations by watching movies and reading books. *2015 IEEE International Conference on Computer Vision (ICCV)*, pages 19–27.

Improving Multi-label Emotion Classification by Integrating both General and Domain Knowledge

Wenhao Ying   **Rong Xiang**   **Qin Lu**

The Hong Kong Polytechnic University, Hong Kong, China

yingwh123@sina.com, {csrxiang, csluqin}@comp.polyu.edu.hk

Abstract

Deep learning based general language models have achieved state-of-the-art results in many popular tasks such as sentiment analysis and QA tasks. Text in domains like social media has its own salient characteristics. Domain knowledge should be helpful in domain relevant tasks. In this work, we devise a simple method to obtain domain knowledge and further propose a method to integrate domain knowledge with general knowledge based on deep language models to improve performance of emotion classification. Experiments on Twitter data show that even though a deep language model fine-tuned by a target domain data has attained comparable results to that of previous state-of-the-art models, this fine-tuned model can still benefit from our extracted domain knowledge to obtain more improvement. This highlights the importance of making use of domain knowledge in domain-specific applications.

1 Introduction

Deep language models (LM) have been very successful in recent years. In pre-training, a deep LM learns to predict unseen words in the context at hand in an unsupervised way, which enables the LM to make use of very large amount of unlabeled data. By using deep structures and large amount of training data, these deep LMs can learn useful linguistic knowledge common to many natural language processing tasks. For example, BERT (Devlin et al., 2019) has the ability to encode grammatical knowledge in context in its representations (Hewitt and Manning, 2019). Deep LMs provide general knowledge of text to benefit downstream tasks. To be adaptive to a target domain, they do need to be fine-tuned by data of the target domain.

Obviously, every domain has its own characteristics which deserve special attention. A typical example is Twitter data. In twitter, people can express their thoughts online in real time. Due to its informal nature, people tend to pick whatever comes to their mind to jot down their opinions even if the writing does not conform to grammar rules. For example, Combinations of characters, such as ":(" and ":-)", are often used to express different emotions. Deliberate irregular spellings also occur in Twitter to indicate authors' attitude. Table 1 shows an example of an irregular expression and how it can be preprocessed at word level, wordpiece level and at domain level. Many of

Snippet	haaapppyyyy birthday best friend!! Love you lots #love
Word	'haaapppyyyy', 'birthday', 'best', 'friend', '!', '!', 'Love', 'you', 'lots', '#', 'love'
Wordpiece	'ha', '##aa', '##pp', '##py', '##y', '##y', '##y', 'birthday', 'best', 'friend', '!', '!', 'Love', 'you', 'lots', '#', 'love'
Domain-specific	'happy', '<elongated>', 'birthday', 'best', 'friend', '!', '<repeated>', 'Love', 'you', 'lots', '</hashtag>', 'love', '<hashtag>'

Table 1: Example of an real-world irregular expression preprocessed by methods at different levels. '##' is a sign of word pieces, and '<>' is a special mark produced by a Twitter-specific preprocessor.

these domain-specific expressions are strong indicators for affective analysis in Twitter, and these characteristics are worthy of special consideration. Simply neglecting them would lose a lot of useful information. Such information can be formulated as domain knowledge by using Twitter preprocessor like (Baziotis et al., 2017). After Twitter-specific preprocessing, these expressions are annotated automatically and we can find informa-

Proceedings of the 2019 EMNLP Workshop W-NUT: The 5th Workshop on Noisy User-generated Text, pages 316–321
Hong Kong, Nov 4, 2019. ©2019 Association for Computational Linguistics

tive token patterns from preprocessed tweets. In the above example, a pattern '[+, <elongated>]' expresses more positive sentiment than a regular positive word. Another pattern '[</hashtag>, *, </hashtag>]' means it is a hashtag and usually has an overall meaning for a tweet.

In this work, we select the popular BERT language model to provide general linguistic knowledge for modelling sentences. As a commonly used deep LM, BERT is not intended to pay attention to domain-specific details in Twitter. BERT actually use sub-word tokens as its inputs for generalization, and a word is first divided into a number of smaller units if necessary before being converted to embeddings. We design a token pattern detector that sifts through preprocessed tweets to obtain domain knowledge, and supplement BERT with extracted domain-specific features. To integrate the domain knowledge with BERT, we first fine-tune BERT to extract general features of Twitter data. Features from the fine-tuned BERT are then integrated with domain-specific features to classify tweets into target emotions. Performance evaluations show that even though BERT was pre-trained on different source domains, the fine-tuned BERT using Twitter data indeed attains comparable results to that of the previous state-of-the-art models. Most importantly, even after BERT is tuned by Twitter data, integration of domain knowledge in our system still makes over one percent improvement on the accuracy of emotion classification compared to the previous state-of-the-art method using BERT only.

2 Related Work

Related works include both deep LMs especially BERT, a representative deep learning based LM and works on Twitter classification.

2.1 Deep Language Models

In contrast to n-gram LMs and early neural models for learning word embeddings, recent LMs have deeper structures. ELMo (Peters et al., 2018) use a stack of bi-directional LSTM to encode word context either from left-to-right or from right-to-left. BERT (Devlin et al., 2019) has a bidirectional structure to learn context from both directions. As a consequence of its bidirectionality, BERT is not trained by predicting words in sequence either from left-to-right or from right-to-left. After masking a part of words in a sentence,

training predicts the masked and unseen words within the remaining context. However, by corrupting inputs with masks, BERT neglects dependency between masked positions. XLNet (Yang et al., 2019) proposes to maximizes the likelihood over all permutations of the factorization order of conditional probability to learn bidirectional context without masking. Recently, RoBERTa (Liu et al., 2019) matches the previous state-of-the-art language models by training BERT on even larger data with optimized hyper-parameters.

In this work, we use BERT as our baseline, a popular deep language model. BERT has a stack of transformer layers (Vaswani et al., 2017). The central part of a transformer is a multi-head attention mechanism to include queries, keys, and values as inputs, which makes scaled dot-product attention among all inputs. Let Q denote a query matrix, K denote a key matrix, V denote a value matrix, and $Q = K = V$ in the case of BERT. The scaled dot-product attention formula is then given as follows:

$$\text{Attention}(Q, K, V) = \text{softmax}(\frac{QK^T}{\sqrt{d_k}})V$$

where d_k is the dimension of queries and keys. For BERT, an input token has a positional embedding and a segment embedding in addition to its regular word embedding. Positional embeddings tell BERT relative positions of two words and segment embeddings help BERT to differentiate two sentences of a pair. In each sentence fed into BERT, a special token [CLS] is inserted at the first place and one uses its corresponding output as the overall representation of this sentence for sentence-level tasks such as entailment or sentiment analysis.

2.2 Twitter Affective Analysis

As a platform to express everyday thoughts, Twitter has huge amount of affect-related text. Thus Twitter is a good source of research study on affective analysis of people towards a topic. N-grams and negative indicators are widely used in affective analysis of Twitter (Mohammad et al., 2013; Miura et al., 2014). Affect-based lexicons are also included to provide general sentiment or emotion information (Hagen et al., 2015). (Go et al.) use :) and :(emoticons as natural labels and collect a pseudo-labeled training data to increase their n-gram classifier. Similarly, Wang et al (Wang et al.,

2012) look for tweets with a target set of hashtags such as #happy and #sad to collect an emotion-linked training data. Due to the abundance of these naturally labeled training data, deep neural networks has proven its dominance in recent competitions by means of the framework of transfer learning (Severyn and Moschitti, 2015; Deriu et al., 2016; Cliche, 2017). They pre-train models on naturally labeled data to get a better starting point and fine-tune their models on the target task.

3 Methodology

The basic idea of our work is to use a Twitter-specific preprocessor to decode Twitter-related expressions. A token pattern detector is then trained to identify affect-bearing token patterns. Finally, a two-step training process is introduced to integrate general knowledge and the detected domain knowledge for emotion classification.

3.1 Domain Specific Information Extraction

Because tweets are informal text with a lot of expression variations, we first use the Twitter preprocessing tool *ekphrasis* (Baziotis et al., 2017) to obtain domain-related information. *ekphrasis* conducts Twitter-specific tokenization, spell checking correction, text normalization and word segmentation. It recognizes many special expressions like emoticons, dates and times with an extensive list of regular expressions. Tokens can also be split further to obtain useful information. A typical example is to split hashtags. After tokenization, expressions with a lot of variations such as user handles and URLs are normalized with designated marks. The result can properly align tokens to their regular forms in the vocabulary without loss of information nor the need to enlarge vocabulary size. Table 2 give a few examples of preprocessed words with annotation, where <*>is a designated annotation mark.

Original	Processed
':)', ':-)'	<happy>
'REAL'	<allcaps>real </allcaps>
'gooooood'	good <elongated>
October 8th	<date>
@jeremy	<user>
#Christmas	<hashtag>Christmas </hashtag>

Table 2: Examples of typical Twitter-specific expressions and their preprocessed versions with annotation marks

3.2 Token Pattern Detector

After Twitter-specific annotation using a preprocessing tool, some input words are annotated and stand out conspicuously. In this step, we identify informative token patterns for emotion classification. A simple convolution network is used to examine tokens within a fixed-length window to detect token patterns. The network structure is a 1D convolution layer followed by temporal max-pooling, similar to that of (Kim, 2014). But we only use a token window of size 3 to simply observe trigrams. The three-token range should cover most of potential token patterns for our work. Given a convolution kernel, it serves as a detector to check whether a particular token pattern appears in a sentence measured by a matching score s_i according to the following formula 1,

$$s_i = w^T[e_i, e_{i+1}, e_{i+2}] + b \qquad (1)$$

where e_i, e_{i+1} and e_{i+2} are word embeddings corresponding to successive tokens at positions $i, i+1, i+2$, w and b are learnable parameters of this kernel. A detector moves through all possible subsequences and produces a list $\{s_1, s_2, \cdots, s_{n-2}\}$. The following temporal max-pooling obtains the maximum value from the list as an indicator suggesting whether a sentence includes a particular token pattern. Hundreds of such detectors are used together to find various types of token patterns. All the outputs of max-pooling for each detector make up the domain-specific representation for a sentence.

3.3 Multi-label Emotion Classification

A two-step training process is designed to integrate general and domain knowledge in multi-label emotion classification. In the first step, we fine-tune BERT on the training data of our target task initialized with pre-trained parameters[1]. The model follows the same input format as pre-training in which a word is divided into several word pieces before they are fed into BERT. Then, we use the output for [CLS] from the last layer as the general feature representation of a sentence. We also train a convolutional detector from scratch on the training data with Twitter-specific annotation and use the output from the last layer as a sentence's domain-specific features. The parameters

---

[1]Pre-trained BERT models are obtained from https://github.com/huggingface/pytorch-transformers

of both models are fixed after this step and therefore the representation produced by each model will not be changed in the next step. In the second step, the two types of representations are concatenated and fed into a linear scoring layer for emotion class predication. For a target emotion i and the representation of a sentence x, its score is computed by $\hat{y}[i] = w^T x$. The layer is tuned on the training data so that general and Twitter-specific features can work collaboratively.

For the gold labels y and prediction scores $\hat{y}$, their loss is given by

$$loss(x, y) = -\frac{1}{C} \sum_i^C (y[i] * \log(\frac{1}{1 + e^{-\hat{y}[i]}})$$
$$+ (1 - y[i]) * \log(\frac{e^{-y[i]}}{1 + e^{-\hat{y}[i]}})) \quad (2)$$

where $\hat{y}[i]$ and $y[i]$ are for the i_{th} emotion class, and C is the number of target emotion classes. If the target emotion class is positive, that is $y[i] = 1$, the loss function requires the corresponding prediction to be as large as possible. When making prediction of a target emotion for a sample, we assign it a positive label if $\hat{y}[i] \geq 0$.

4   Performance Evaluation

Performance evaluation is conducted on multi-label emotion classification of SemEval-2018 Task 1 (Mohammad et al., 2018). Given a tweet, the task requires participants to classify text to zero or more of 11 target emotions.

4.1   Setup

SemEval-2018 dataset was already split into training, development and testing sets by its organizer. We train and tune our models on the training and development sets, and report classification results on the testing set. Word embeddings of our CNN detector are learned from a corpus of 550M unlabeled tweets by word2vec (Mikolov et al., 2013) [2]. Multi-label accuracy, known as Jaccard Index, is used as the evaluation metric, defined as the size of the intersection divided by the size of the union of the true label set and predicted label set. Macro-F1 and Micro-F1 are used as secondary evaluation metrics following the same practice of SemEval-2018 Task 1. In the two-step training, we first train our CNN detector and fine-tune BERT on the

training data 10 times and select the parameters with the best performance on the development set to hopefully provide good representation of both general and domain-specific information. In the second step, the representation for a tweet remains unchanged and only the parameters of a scoring layer is learned.

4.2   Evaluation

Table 3 lists the results of multi-label emotion classification on SemEval-2018. The first blocks are the state-of-the-art models on SemEval-2018 Task 1, where we directly cite the results from their papers. Two BERT models are used as additional baselines including $BERT_{base}$, which has 12 layers of transformers with 768 dimension, and $BERT_{large}$, which has 24 layers of transformers with 1024 dimension. BERT using domain knowledge (DK) proposed by our work are appended with '+DK'. Another baselines include a biLSTM and our CNN detector. To randomize parameter initialization and learning algorithm, we train CNN and BiLSTM from scratch, fine-tune BERT from the given initialized parameters, and learn the weights of scoring layer 10 times, respectively. We report the average performance on the testing set for each model.

Model	acc.	micro F1	macro F1
PlusEmo2Vec (Park et al., 2018)	57.6	69.2	49.7
TCS Research (Meisheri and Dey, 2018)	58.2	69.3	53.0
NTUA-SLA (Baziotis et al., 2018)	58.8	70.1	52.8
CNN Detector	55.8	68.5	50.0
BiLSTM	56.3	68.7	51.0
$BERT_{base}$	58.4	70.4	54.2
$BERT_{large}$	58.8	70.7	55.2
$BERT_{base}$+DK	59.1†‡	71.3†‡	54.9†
$BERT_{large}$+DK	**59.5†‡**	**71.6†‡**	**56.3†**

Table 3: Result of multi-label emotion classification on SemEval-2018. † means the result is statistically significant with $p < 0.01$ in contrast to the state-of-the-art NTUA-SLA. ‡ means the improvement by integrating domain knowledge is statistically significant with $p < 0.01$ compared with its corresponding pure BERT, as $BERT_{base}$ vs $BERT_{base}$+DK. For Macro-F1, the results are statistically significant with $p < 0.05$.

As expected, the CNN detector has the worst

---

[2] We use the pre-trained embeddings from (Baziotis et al., 2018)

Emotion	BERT$_{large}$	+DK	
anger	78.82	79.34	(+0.52)
anticipation	23.60	23.60	(+0.00)
disgust	75.00	76.28	(+1.28)
fear	74.96	76.18	(+1.22)
joy	85.22	86.39	(+1.17)
love	61.52	63.94	(+2.42)
optimism	73.41	73.73	(+0.32)
pessimism	32.05	32.16	(+0.11)
sadness	70.21	71.90	(+1.69)
surprise	22.56	26.24	(+3.68)
trust	9.56	9.03	(-0.53)

Table 4: F1 on binary classification for each emotion class.

performance as this tri-gram model is too simple to learn complex relationships such as long-distance negative relations. The CNN detector is to sift through domain-specific token patterns to supplement the general knowledge of BERT. Both of the fine-tuned pure BERTs are either comparable or slightly better than the performance of the previous state-of-the-art models. With the abundant pre-training data and their deep structure, BERT models obtain a good starting point for a domain-specific task. More importantly, both BERT models benefit from domain knowledge supplied by the CNN detector to obtain performance improvement of 1.20% on major multi-label accuary for both models. Both BERT models with domain knowledge outperform their corresponding pure BERT and the state-of-the-art model statistically significantly with $p < 0.01$ except for Macro-F1 where the results are statistically significant with $p < 0.05$. In the first-step training, the selected CNN, BERT$_{base}$ and BERT$_{large}$ for providing tweet representation has accuracy of 56.7%, 59.0% and 58.9%, respectively. Table 3 shows that BERT integrating with Twitter-specific features outperforms both general and domain-specific component model.

For more detailed investigation of the effect of domain knowledge, Table 4 shows the result of binary classification for each emotion class measured by F1 score. Improvements are obtained in nine out of eleven emotion classes. If excluding 'surprise' and 'trust' which have low percentage of occurrence, salient improvements come mostly from 'disgust', 'fear', 'joy', 'love' and 'sadness'. Abundant domain-specific expressions in Twitter, such as emoticons ':-)' and ':-(' and hashtags like '#offended', are useful affective indicators, which are not used fully by BERT.

5 Conclusion

In this work, we leverage deep language models to provide general sentence representations and integrate them with domain knowledge. We show that integration of both types of knowledge improves multi-label emotion classification of tweets. Evaluation shows that a deep LM like BERT has the capacity to perform well. Yet, its performance can still be further improved by integrating elaborate domain knowledge. Future works may investigate other deep LMs as well as data of other domains.

Acknowledgments

This work was partially supported by a GRF grant from HKUGC (PolyU 152006/16E).

References

Christos Baziotis, Athanasiou Nikolaos, Alexandra Chronopoulou, Athanasia Kolovou, Georgios Paraskevopoulos, Nikolaos Ellinas, Shrikanth Narayanan, and Alexandros Potamianos. 2018. Ntua-slp at semeval-2018 task 1: Predicting affective content in tweets with deep attentive rnns and transfer learning. In *Proceedings of The 12th International Workshop on Semantic Evaluation*, pages 245–255.

Christos Baziotis, Nikos Pelekis, and Christos Doulkeridis. 2017. Datastories at semeval-2017 task 4: Deep lstm with attention for message-level and topic-based sentiment analysis. In *Proceedings of the 11th International Workshop on Semantic Evaluation (SemEval-2017)*, pages 747–754, Vancouver, Canada. Association for Computational Linguistics.

Mathieu Cliche. 2017. Bb_twtr at semeval-2017 task 4: Twitter sentiment analysis with cnns and lstms. In *Proceedings of the 11th International Workshop on Semantic Evaluation (SemEval-2017)*, pages 573–580.

Jan Deriu, Maurice Gonzenbach, Fatih Uzdilli, Aurelien Lucchi, Valeria De Luca, and Martin Jaggi. 2016. Swisscheese at semeval-2016 task 4: Sentiment classification using an ensemble of convolutional neural networks with distant supervision. In *Proceedings of the 10th international workshop on semantic evaluation*, CONF, pages 1124–1128.

Jacob Devlin, Ming-Wei Chang, Kenton Lee, and Kristina Toutanova. 2019. Bert: Pre-training of deep bidirectional transformers for language understanding. In *Proceedings of the 2019 Conference of the North American Chapter of the Association for Computational Linguistics: Human Language Technologies, Volume 1 (Long and Short Papers)*, pages 4171–4186.

Alec Go, Richa Bhayani, and Lei Huang. Twitter sentiment classification using distant supervision.

Matthias Hagen, Martin Potthast, Michel Büchner, and Benno Stein. 2015. Webis: An ensemble for twitter sentiment detection. In *Proceedings of the 9th international workshop on semantic evaluation (SemEval 2015)*, pages 582–589.

John Hewitt and Christopher D Manning. 2019. A structural probe for finding syntax in word representations. In *Proceedings of the 2019 Conference of the North American Chapter of the Association for Computational Linguistics: Human Language Technologies, Volume 1 (Long and Short Papers)*, pages 4129–4138.

Yoon Kim. 2014. Convolutional neural networks for sentence classification. In *Proceedings of the 2014 Conference on Empirical Methods in Natural Language Processing (EMNLP)*, pages 1746–1751.

Yinhan Liu, Myle Ott, Naman Goyal, Jingfei Du, Mandar Joshi, Danqi Chen, Omer Levy, Mike Lewis, Luke Zettlemoyer, and Veselin Stoyanov. 2019. Roberta: A robustly optimized bert pretraining approach. *arXiv preprint arXiv:1907.11692*.

Hardik Meisheri and Lipika Dey. 2018. Tcs research at semeval-2018 task 1: Learning robust representations using multi-attention architecture. In *Proceedings of The 12th International Workshop on Semantic Evaluation*, pages 291–299.

Tomas Mikolov, Ilya Sutskever, Kai Chen, Greg S Corrado, and Jeff Dean. 2013. Distributed representations of words and phrases and their compositionality. In *Advances in neural information processing systems*, pages 3111–3119

Yasuhide Miura, Shigeyuki Sakaki, Keigo Hattori, and Tomoko Ohkuma. 2014. Teamx: A sentiment analyzer with enhanced lexicon mapping and weighting scheme for unbalanced data. In *Proceedings of the 8th International Workshop on Semantic Evaluation (SemEval 2014)*, pages 628–632.

Saif Mohammad, Svetlana Kiritchenko, and Xiaodan Zhu. 2013. Nrc-canada: Building the state-of-the-art in sentiment analysis of tweets. In *Second Joint Conference on Lexical and Computational Semantics (* SEM), Volume 2: Proceedings of the Seventh International Workshop on Semantic Evaluation (SemEval 2013)*, pages 321–327.

Saif M. Mohammad, Felipe Bravo-Marquez, Mohammad Salameh, and Svetlana Kiritchenko. 2018. Semeval-2018 Task 1: Affect in tweets. In *Proceedings of International Workshop on Semantic Evaluation (SemEval-2018)*, New Orleans, LA, USA.

Ji Ho Park, Peng Xu, and Pascale Fung. 2018. Plusemo2vec at semeval-2018 task 1: Exploiting emotion knowledge from emoji and# hashtags. *arXiv preprint arXiv:1804.08280*.

Matthew Peters, Mark Neumann, Mohit Iyyer, Matt Gardner, Christopher Clark, Kenton Lee, and Luke Zettlemoyer. 2018. Deep contextualized word representations. In *Proceedings of the 2018 Conference of the North American Chapter of the Association for Computational Linguistics: Human Language Technologies, Volume 1 (Long Papers)*, pages 2227–2237.

Aliaksei Severyn and Alessandro Moschitti. 2015. Unitn: Training deep convolutional neural network for twitter sentiment classification. In *Proceedings of the 9th international workshop on semantic evaluation (SemEval 2015)*, pages 464–469.

Ashish Vaswani, Noam Shazeer, Niki Parmar, Jakob Uszkoreit, Llion Jones, Aidan N Gomez, Łukasz Kaiser, and Illia Polosukhin. 2017. Attention is all you need. In *Advances in neural information processing systems*, pages 5998–6008.

Wenbo Wang, Lu Chen, Krishnaprasad Thirunarayan, and Amit P Sheth. 2012. Harnessing twitter" big data" for automatic emotion identification. In *2012 International Conference on Privacy, Security, Risk and Trust and 2012 International Confernece on Social Computing*, pages 587–592. IEEE.

Zhilin Yang, Zihang Dai, Yiming Yang, Jaime Carbonell, Ruslan Salakhutdinov, and Quoc V Le. 2019. Xlnet: Generalized autoregressive pretraining for language understanding. *arXiv preprint arXiv:1906.08237*.

Adapting Deep Learning Methods for
Mental Health Prediction on Social Media

Ivan Sekulić and Michael Strube

Heidelberg Institute for Theoretical Studies gGmbH

`{ivan.sekulic,michael.strube}@h-its.org`

Abstract

Mental health poses a significant challenge for an individual's well-being. Text analysis of rich resources, like social media, can contribute to deeper understanding of illnesses and provide means for their early detection. We tackle a challenge of detecting social media users' mental status through deep learning-based models, moving away from traditional approaches to the task. In a binary classification task on predicting if a user suffers from one of nine different disorders, a hierarchical attention network outperforms previously set benchmarks for four of the disorders. Furthermore, we explore the limitations of our model and analyze phrases relevant for classification by inspecting the model's word-level attention weights.

1 Introduction

Mental health is a serious issue of the modern-day world. According to the World Health Organization's 2017 report and Wykes et al. (2015) more than a quarter of Europe's adult population suffers from an episode of a mental disorder in their life. The problem grows bigger with the fact that as much as 35–50% of those affected go undiagnosed and receive no treatment for their illness. In line with WHO's Mental Health Action Plan (Saxena et al., 2013), the natural language processing community helps the gathering of information and evidence on mental conditions, focusing on text analysis of authors affected by mental illnesses.

Researchers can utilize large amounts of text on social media sites to get a deeper understanding of mental health and develop models for early detection of various mental disorders (De Choudhury et al., 2013a; Coppersmith et al., 2014; Gkotsis et al., 2016; Benton et al., 2017; Sekulić et al., 2018; Zomick et al., 2019). In this work, we experiment with the Self-reported Mental Health

Diagnoses (SMHD) dataset (Cohan et al., 2018), consisting of thousands of Reddit users diagnosed with one or more mental illnesses. The contribution of our work is threefold. First, we adapt a deep neural model, proved to be successful in large-scale document classification, for user classification on social media, outperforming previously set benchmarks for four out of nine disorders. In contrast to the majority of preceding studies on mental health prediction in social media, which relied mostly on traditional classifiers, we employ Hierarchical Attention Network (HAN) (Yang et al., 2016). Second, we explore the limitations of the model in terms of data needed for successful classification, specifically, the number of users and number of posts per user. Third, through the attention mechanism of the model, we analyze the most relevant phrases for the classification and compare them to previous work in the field. We find similarities between lexical features and n-grams identified by the attention mechanism, supporting previous analyses.

2 Dataset and the Model

2.1 Self-reported Mental Health Diagnoses Dataset

The SMHD dataset (Cohan et al., 2018) is a large-scale dataset of Reddit posts from users with one or multiple mental health conditions. The users were identified by constructing patterns for discovering self-reported diagnoses of nine different mental disorders. For example, if a user writes *"I was officially diagnosed with depression last year"*, she/he/other would be considered to suffer from depression.

Nine or more control users, which are meant to represent general population, are selected for each diagnosed user by their similarity, i.e., by their number of posts and the subreddits (sub-forums on

Proceedings of the 2019 EMNLP Workshop W-NUT: The 5th Workshop on Noisy User-generated Text, pages 322–327
Hong Kong, Nov 4, 2019. ©2019 Association for Computational Linguistics

	# users	# posts per user
Depression	14,139	162.2 (84.2)
ADHD	10,098	164.7 (83.6)
Anxiety	8,783	159.7 (83.0)
Bipolar	6,434	157.6 (82.4)
PTSD	2,894	160.7 (84.7)
Autism	2,911	168.3 (84.5)
OCD	2,336	158.8 (81.4)
Schizophrenia	1,331	157.3 (80.5)
Eating	598	161.4 (81.0)

Table 1: Number of users in SMHD dataset per condition and the average number of posts per user (with std.).

Reddit) they post in. Diagnosed users' language is normalized by removing posts with specific mental health signals and discussions, in order to analyze the language of general discussions and to be more comparable to the control groups. The nine disorders and the number of users per disorder, as well as average number of posts per user, are shown in Table 1.

For each disorder, Cohan et al. (2018) analyze the differences in language use between diagnosed users and their respective control groups. They also provide benchmark results for the binary classification task of predicting whether the user belongs to the diagnosed or the control group. We reproduce their baseline models for each disorder and compare to our deep learning-based model, explained in Section 2.3.

2.2 Selecting the Control Group

Cohan et al. (2018) select nine or more control users for each diagnosed user and run their experiments with these mappings. With this exact mapping not being available, for each of the nine conditions, we had to select the control group ourselves. For each diagnosed user, we draw exactly nine control users from the pool of 335,952 control users present in SMHD and proceed to train and test our binary classifiers on the newly created sub-datasets.

In order to create a statistically-fair comparison, we run the selection process multiple times, as well as reimplement the benchmark models used in Cohan et al. (2018). Multiple sub-datasets with different control groups not only provide us with unbiased results, but also show how results of a

binary classification can differ depending on the control group.

2.3 Hierarchical Attention Network

We adapt a Hierarchical Attention Network (HAN) (Yang et al., 2016), originally used for document classification, to user classification on social media. A HAN consists of a word sequence encoder, a word-level attention layer, a sentence encoder and a sentence-level attention layer. It employs GRU-based sequence encoders (Cho et al., 2014) on sentence and document level, yielding a document representation in the end. The word sequence encoder produces a representation of a given sentence, which then is forwarded to a sentence sequence encoder that, given a sequence of encoded sentences, returns a document representation. Both, word sequence and sentence sequence encoders, apply attention mechanisms on top to help the encoder more accurately aggregate the representation of given sequence. For details of the architecture we refer the interested readers to Yang et al. (2016).

In this work, we model a user as a document, enabling an intuitive adaptation of the HAN. Just as a document is a sequence of sentences, we propose to model a social media user as a sequence of posts. Similarly, we identify posts as sentences, both being a sequence of tokens. This interpretation enables us to apply the HAN, which had great success in document classification, to user classification on social media.

3 Results

3.1 Experimental Setup

The HAN uses two layers of bidirectional GRU units with hidden size of 150, each of them followed by a 100 dimensional attention mechanism. The first layer encodes posts, while the second one encodes a user as a sequence of encoded posts. The output layer is 50-dimensional fully-connected network, with binary cross entropy as a loss function. We initialize the input layer with 300 dimensional GloVe word embeddings (Pennington et al., 2014). We train the model with Adam (Kingma and Ba, 2014), with an initial learning rate of 10^{-4} and a batch size of 32 for 50 epochs. The model that proves best on the development set is selected.

We implement the baselines as in Cohan et al. (2018). Logistic regression and the linear SVM

	Depression	ADHD	Anxiety	Bipolar	PTSD	Autism	OCD	Schizo	Eating
Logistic Regression	59.00	51.02	62.34	61.87	69.34	**55.57**	**59.49**	56.31	70.71
Linear SVM	58.64	50.08	61.69	61.30	**69.91**	55.35	58.56	**57.43**	**70.91**
Supervised FastText	58.38	48.80	60.17	56.53	61.08	49.52	54.16	46.73	63.73
HAN	**68.28**	**64.27**	**69.24**	**67.42**	68.59	53.09	58.51	53.68	63.94

Table 2: F_1 measure averaged over five runs with different control groups.

were trained on *tf-idf* weighted bag-of-words features, where users' posts are all concatenated and all the tokens lower-cased. Optimal parameters were found on the development set, and models were evaluated on the test set. FastText (Joulin et al., 2016) was trained for 100 epochs, using character n-grams of size 3 to 6, with a 100 dimensional hidden layer. We take diagnosed users from predefined train-dev-test split, and select the control group as described in Subsection 2.2. To ensure unbiased results and fair comparison to the baselines, we repeat the process of selecting the control group five times for each disorder and report the average of the runs.

3.2 Binary Classification per Disorder

We report the F_1 measures per disorder in Table 2, in the task of binary classification of users, with the diagnosed class as a positive one. Our model outperforms the baseline models for *Depression*, *ADHD*, *Anxiety*, and *Bipolar* disorder, while it proves insufficient for *PTSD*, *Autism*, *OCD*, *Schizophrenia*, and *Eating* disorder. We hypothesize that the reason for this are the sizes of particular sub-datasets, which can be seen in Table 1. We observe higher F_1 score for the HAN in disorders with sufficient data, suggesting once again that deep neural models are data-hungry (Sun et al., 2017). Logistic regression and linear SVM achieve higher scores where there is a smaller number of diagnosed users. In contrast to Cohan et al. (2018), supervised FastText yields worse results than tuned linear models.

We further investigate the impact of the size of the dataset on the final results of classification. We limit the number of posts per user available to the model to examine the amount needed for reasonable performance. The results for 50, 100, 150, 200, and 250 posts per user available are presented in Figure 1. Experiments were run three times for each disorder and each number of available posts, every time with a different control group selected. We observe a positive correlation between the data

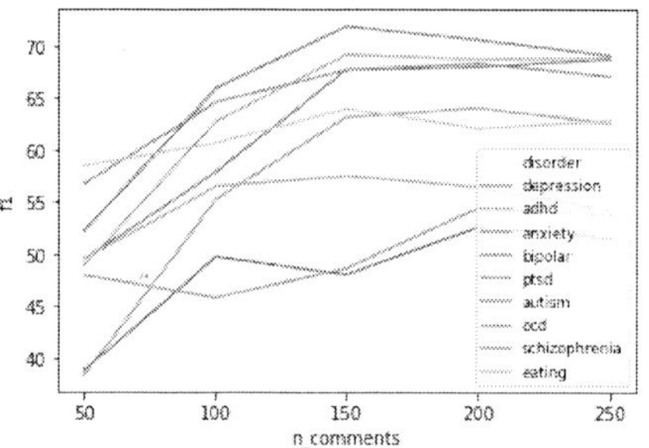

Figure 1: F_1 scores for different number of posts per users made available to HAN, averaged over three runs for different control groups.

provided to the model and the performance, although we find an upper bound to this tendency. As the average number of posts per user is roughly 160 (Table 1), it is reasonable to expect of a model to perform well with similar amounts of data available. However, further analysis is required to see if the model reaches the plateau because a large amount of data is not needed for the task, or due to it not being expressive enough.

3.3 Attention Weights Analysis

The HAN, through attention mechanism, provides a clear way to identify posts, and words or phrases in those posts, relevant for classification. We examine attention weights on a word level and compare the most attended words to prior research on depression. Depression is selected as the most prevalent disorder in the SMHD dataset with a number of studies in the field (Rude et al., 2004; Chung and Pennebaker, 2007; De Choudhury et al., 2013b; Park et al., 2012). For each post, we extracted two words with the highest attention weight as being the most relevant for the classification. If the two words are appearing next to each other in a post we consider them as bigram. Some of the top 100 most common unigrams and bigrams are presented in Table 3, aggregated under the most common LIWC categories.

We observe similar patterns in features shown

	unigrams	bigrams
Pers. pronouns	*I, my, her, your, they*	*I've never, your thoughts*
Affective	*like, nice, love, bad*	*I love*
Social	*friend, boyfriend, girl, guy*	*my dad, my girlfriend, my ex*
Biological	*pain, sex, skin, sleep, porn*	*your pain, a doctor, a therapist*
Informal	*omg, lol, shit, fuck, cool*	*tl dr, holy shit*
Other	*advice, please, reddit*	*thank you, your advice*

Table 3: Unigrams and bigrams most often given the highest weight by attention mechanism in depression classification.

relevant by the HAN and previous research on signals of depression in language. The importance of personal pronouns in distinguishing depressed authors from the control group is supported by multiple studies (Rude et al., 2004; Chung and Pennebaker, 2007; De Choudhury et al., 2013b; Cohan et al., 2018). In the categories *Affective processes*, *Social processes*, and *Biological processes*, Cohan et al. (2018) report significant differences between depressed and control group, similar to some other disorders. Except the above mentioned words and their abbreviations, among most commonly attended are swear words, as well as other forms of informal language. The attention mechanism's weighting suggests that words and phrases proved important in previous studies, using lexical features and linear models, are relevant for the HAN as well.

4   Related Work

In recent years, social media has been a valuable source for psychological research. While most studies use Twitter data (Coppersmith et al., 2015a, 2014; Benton et al., 2017; Coppersmith et al., 2015b), a recent stream turns to Reddit as a richer source of high volume data (De Choudhury and De, 2014; Shen and Rudzicz, 2017; Gjurković and Šnajder, 2018; Cohan et al., 2018; Sekulić et al., 2018; Zirikly et al., 2019). Previous approaches to author's mental health prediction usually relied on linguistic and stylistic features, e.g., Linguistic Inquiry and Word Count (LIWC) (Pennebaker et al., 2001) – a widely used feature extractor for various studies regarding mental health (Rude et al., 2004; Coppersmith et al., 2014; Sekulić et al., 2018; Zomick et al., 2019).

Recently, Song et al. (2018) built a feature attention network for depression detection on Reddit, showing high interpretability, but low improvement in accuracy. Orabi et al. (2018) concatenate all the tweets of a Twitter user in a single document and experiment with various deep neural models for depression detection. Some of the previous studies use deep learning methods on a post level to infer general information about a user (Kshirsagar et al., 2017; Ive et al., 2018; Ruder et al., 2016), or detect different mental health concepts in posts themselves (Rojas-Barahona et al., 2018), while we focus on utilizing all of the users' text. Yates et al. (2017) use a CNN on a post-level to extract features, which are then concatenated to get a user representation used for self-harm and depression assessment. A CNN requires a fixed length of posts, putting constraints on the data available to the model, while a HAN utilizes all of the data from posts of arbitrary lengths.

A social media user can be modeled as collection of their posts, so we look at neural models for large-scale text classification. Liu et al. (2018) split a document into chunks and use a combination of CNNs and RNNs for document classification. While this approach proves to be successful for scientific paper categorization, it is unintuitive to use in social media text due to an unclear way of splitting user's data into equally sized chunks of text. Yang et al. (2016) use a hierarchical attention network for document classification, an approach that we adapt for Reddit. A step further would be adding another hierarchy, similar to Jiang et al. (2019), who use a multi-depth attention-based hierarchical RNN to tackle the problem of long-length document semantic matching.

4.1   Ethical considerations

Acknowledging the social impact of NLP research (Hovy and Spruit, 2016), mental health analysis must be approached carefully as it is an extremely sensitive matter (Šuster et al., 2017). In order to acquire the SMHD dataset, we comply to the Data Usage Agreement, made to protect the users' privacy. We do not attempt to contact the users in the dataset, nor identify or link them with other user information.

5   Conclusion

In this study, we experimented with hierarchical attention networks for the task of predicting mental health status of Reddit users. For the disorders with a fair amount of diagnosed users, a HAN proves to be better than the baselines. However, the results worsen as the data available decreases, suggesting that traditional approaches remain better for smaller datasets. The analysis of attention weights on word level suggested similarities to previous studies of depressed authors. Embedding mental health-specific insights from previous work could benefit the model in general. Future work includes analysis of post-level attention weights, with a goal of finding patterns in the relevance of particular posts, and, through them, time periods when a user is in distress. As some of the disorders share similar symptoms, e.g., depressive episodes in bipolar disorder, exploiting correlations between labels through multi-task or transfer learning techniques might prove useful. In order to improve the classification accuracy, a transformer-based model for encoding users' posts should be tested.

6 Acknowledgments

This work has been funded by the Erasmus+ programme of the European Union and the Klaus Tschira Foundation.

References

Adrian Benton, Margaret Mitchell, and Dirk Hovy. 2017. Multi-task learning for mental health using social media text. *arXiv preprint arXiv:1712.03538*.

Kyunghyun Cho, Bart Van Merriënboer, Dzmitry Bahdanau, and Yoshua Bengio. 2014. On the properties of neural machine translation: Encoder-decoder approaches. *arXiv preprint arXiv:1409.1259*.

Cindy Chung and James W Pennebaker. 2007. The psychological functions of function words. *Social communication*, 1:343–359.

Arman Cohan, Bart Desmet, Andrew Yates, Luca Soldaini, Sean MacAvaney, and Nazli Goharian. 2018. Smhd: a large-scale resource for exploring online language usage for multiple mental health conditions. In *27th International Conference on Computational Linguistics*, pages 1485–1497. ACL.

Glen Coppersmith, Mark Dredze, and Craig Harman. 2014. Quantifying mental health signals in twitter. In *Proceedings of the workshop on computational linguistics and clinical psychology: From linguistic signal to clinical reality*, pages 51–60.

Glen Coppersmith, Mark Dredze, Craig Harman, and Kristy Hollingshead. 2015a. From adhd to sad: Analyzing the language of mental health on twitter through self-reported diagnoses. In *Proceedings of the 2nd Workshop on Computational Linguistics and Clinical Psychology: From Linguistic Signal to Clinical Reality*, pages 1–10.

Glen Coppersmith, Mark Dredze, Craig Harman, Kristy Hollingshead, and Margaret Mitchell. 2015b.

Clpsych 2015 shared task: Depression and ptsd on twitter. In *Proceedings of the 2nd Workshop on Computational Linguistics and Clinical Psychology: From Linguistic Signal to Clinical Reality*, pages 31–39.

Munmun De Choudhury, Scott Counts, and Eric Horvitz. 2013a. Social media as a measurement tool of depression in populations. In *Proceedings of the 5th Annual ACM Web Science Conference*, pages 47–56. ACM.

Munmun De Choudhury and Sushovan De. 2014. Mental health discourse on reddit: Self-disclosure, social support, and anonymity. In *Eighth International AAAI Conference on Weblogs and Social Media*.

Munmun De Choudhury, Michael Gamon, Scott Counts, and Eric Horvitz. 2013b. Predicting depression via social media. In *Seventh international AAAI conference on weblogs and social media*.

Matej Gjurković and Jan Šnajder. 2018. Reddit: A gold mine for personality prediction. In *Proceedings of the Second Workshop on Computational Modeling of Peoples Opinions, Personality, and Emotions in Social Media*, pages 87–97.

George Gkotsis, Anika Oellrich, Tim Hubbard, Richard Dobson, Maria Liakata, Sumithra Velupillai, and Rina Dutta. 2016. The language of mental health problems in social media. In *Proceedings of the Third Workshop on Computational Linguistics and Clinical Psychology*, pages 63–73.

Dirk Hovy and Shannon L Spruit. 2016. The social impact of natural language processing. In *Proceedings of the 54th Annual Meeting of the Association for Computational Linguistics (Volume 2: Short Papers)*, pages 591–598.

Julia Ive, George Gkotsis, Rina Dutta, Robert Stewart, and Sumithra Velupillai. 2018. Hierarchical neural model with attention mechanisms for the classification of social media text related to mental health. In *Proceedings of the Fifth Workshop on Computational Linguistics and Clinical Psychology: From Keyboard to Clinic*, pages 69–77.

Jyun-Yu Jiang, Mingyang Zhang, Cheng Li, Michael Bendersky, Nadav Golbandi, and Marc Najork. 2019. Semantic text matching for long-form documents. In *The World Wide Web Conference*, pages 795–806. ACM.

Armand Joulin, Edouard Grave, Piotr Bojanowski, Matthijs Douze, Hérve Jégou, and Tomas Mikolov. 2016. Fasttext.zip: Compressing text classification models. *arXiv preprint arXiv:1612.03651*.

Diederik P Kingma and Jimmy Ba. 2014. Adam: A method for stochastic optimization. *arXiv preprint arXiv:1412.6980*.

Rohan Kshirsagar, Robert Morris, and Sam Bowman. 2017. Detecting and explaining crisis. *arXiv preprint arXiv:1705.09585.*

Liu Liu, Kaile Liu, Zhenghai Cong, Jiali Zhao, Yefei Ji, and Jun He. 2018. Long length document classification by local convolutional feature aggregation. *Algorithms,* 11(8):109.

Ahmed Husseini Orabi, Prasadith Buddhitha, Mahmoud Husseini Orabi, and Diana Inkpen. 2018. Deep learning for depression detection of twitter users. In *Proceedings of the Fifth Workshop on Computational Linguistics and Clinical Psychology: From Keyboard to Clinic,* pages 88–97.

Minsu Park, Chiyoung Cha, and Meeyoung Cha. 2012. Depressive moods of users portrayed in twitter. In *Proceedings of the ACM SIGKDD Workshop on healthcare informatics (HI-KDD),* volume 2012, pages 1–8.

James W Pennebaker, Martha E Francis, and Roger J Booth. 2001. Linguistic inquiry and word count: Liwc 2001. *Mahway: Lawrence Erlbaum Associates,* 71(2001):2001.

Jeffrey Pennington, Richard Socher, and Christopher Manning. 2014. Glove: Global vectors for word representation. In *Proceedings of the 2014 conference on empirical methods in natural language processing (EMNLP),* pages 1532–1543.

Lina Rojas-Barahona, Bo-Hsiang Tseng, Yinpei Dai, Clare Mansfield, Osman Ramadan, Stefan Ultes, Michael Crawford, and Milica Gasic. 2018. Deep learning for language understanding of mental health concepts derived from cognitive behavioural therapy. *arXiv preprint arXiv:1809.00640.*

Stephanie Rude, Eva-Maria Gortner, and James Pennebaker. 2004. Language use of depressed and depression-vulnerable college students. *Cognition & Emotion,* 18(8):1121–1133.

Sebastian Ruder, Parsa Ghaffari, and John G Breslin. 2016. Character-level and multi-channel convolutional neural networks for large-scale authorship attribution. *arXiv preprint arXiv:1609.06686.*

Shekhar Saxena, Michelle Funk, and Dan Chisholm. 2013. World health assembly adopts comprehensive mental health action plan 2013–2020. *The Lancet,* 381(9882):1970–1971.

Ivan Sekulić, Matej Gjurković, and Jan Šnajder. 2018. Not just depressed: Bipolar disorder prediction on reddit. In *9th Workshop on Computational Approaches to Subjectivity, Sentiment and Social Media Analysis.*

Judy Hanwen Shen and Frank Rudzicz. 2017. Detecting anxiety through reddit. In *Proceedings of the Fourth Workshop on Computational Linguistics and Clinical PsychologyFrom Linguistic Signal to Clinical Reality,* pages 58–65.

Hoyun Song, Jinseon You, Jin-Woo Chung, and Jong C Park. 2018. Feature attention network: Interpretable depression detection from social media. In *Proceedings of the 32nd Pacific Asia Conference on Language, Information and Computation.*

Chen Sun, Abhinav Shrivastava, Saurabh Singh, and Abhinav Gupta. 2017. Revisiting unreasonable effectiveness of data in deep learning era. In *Proceedings of the IEEE international conference on computer vision,* pages 843–852.

Simon Šuster, Stéphan Tulkens, and Walter Daelemans. 2017. A short review of ethical challenges in clinical natural language processing. In *Proceedings of the First ACL Workshop on Ethics in Natural Language Processing/Hovy, Dirk [edit.]; et al.,* pages 80–87.

Til Wykes, Josep Maria Haro, Stefano R Belli, Carla Obradors-Tarragó, Celso Arango, José Luis Ayuso-Mateos, István Bitter, Matthias Brunn, Karine Chevreul, Jacques Demotes-Mainard, et al. 2015. Mental health research priorities for europe. *The Lancet Psychiatry,* 2(11):1036–1042.

Zichao Yang, Diyi Yang, Chris Dyer, Xiaodong He, Alex Smola, and Eduard Hovy. 2016. Hierarchical attention networks for document classification. In *Proceedings of the 2016 conference of the North American chapter of the association for computational linguistics: human language technologies,* pages 1480–1489.

Andrew Yates, Arman Cohan, and Nazli Goharian. 2017. Depression and self-harm risk assessment in online forums. *arXiv preprint arXiv:1709.01848.*

Ayah Zirikly, Philip Resnik, Özlem Uzuner, and Kristy Hollingshead. 2019. CLPsych 2019 shared task: Predicting the degree of suicide risk in Reddit posts. In *Proceedings of the Sixth Workshop on Computational Linguistics and Clinical Psychology,* pages 24–33, Minneapolis, Minnesota. Association for Computational Linguistics.

Jonathan Zomick, Sarah Ita Levitan, and Mark Serper. 2019. Linguistic analysis of schizophrenia in reddit posts. In *Proceedings of the Sixth Workshop on Computational Linguistics and Clinical Psychology,* pages 74–83.

Improving Neural Machine Translation Robustness via Data Augmentation: Beyond Back Translation

Zhenhao Li
Department of Computing
Imperial College London, UK
zhenhao.li18@imperial.ac.uk

Lucia Specia
Department of Computing
Imperial College London, UK
l.specia@imperial.ac.uk

Abstract

Neural Machine Translation (NMT) models have been proved strong when translating clean texts, but they are very sensitive to noise in the input. Improving NMT models robustness can be seen as a form of "domain" adaption to noise. The recently created Machine Translation on Noisy Text task corpus provides noisy-clean parallel data for a few language pairs, but this data is very limited in size and diversity. The state-of-the-art approaches are heavily dependent on large volumes of back-translated data. This paper has two main contributions: Firstly, we propose new data augmentation methods to extend limited noisy data and further improve NMT robustness to noise while keeping the models small. Secondly, we explore the effect of utilizing noise from external data in the form of speech transcripts and show that it could help robustness.

1 Introduction

Neural Machine Translation (NMT) models trained on large, clean parallel corpora have reached impressive performance in translating clean texts following various architectures (Bahdanau et al., 2015; Gehring et al., 2017; Vaswani et al., 2017).

Despite this success, NMT models still lack robustness when applied to noisy sentences. Belinkov and Bisk (2017) show that perturbations in characters could cause a significant decrease in translation quality. They point out that training on noisy data, which can be seen as adversarial training, might help to improve model robustness. Michel and Neubig (2018) propose the Machine Translation on Noisy Text (MTNT) dataset, which contains parallel sentence pairs with comments crawled from Reddit[1] and manual translations. This dataset contains user-generated text

with different kinds of noise, e.g., typos, grammatical errors, emojis, spoken languages, etc. for two language pairs.

In the WMT19 Robustness Task[2] (Li et al., 2019), improving NMT robustness is treated as a domain adaption problem. The MTNT dataset is used as in-domain data, where models are trained with clean data and adapted to noisy data. Domain adaption is conducted in two main methods: fine tuning on in-domain data (Dabre and Sumita, 2019; Post and Duh, 2019) and mixed training with domain tags (Berard et al., 2019; Zheng et al., 2019). The size of the noisy data provided by the shared task is small, with only thousands of noisy sentence pairs on each direction. Hence most approaches participating in the task performed noisy data augmentation using back translation (Berard et al., 2019; Helcl et al., 2019; Zheng et al., 2019), with some approaches also directly adding synthetic noise (Berard et al., 2019). The robustness of an NMT model can be seen as denoising source sentences (e.g. dealing with typos, etc.) while keeping a similar level of informal language in the translations (e.g. keeping emojis/emoticons). Based on this assumption, we believe that back translation of clean texts, although providing a large volume of extra data, is limited since it removes most types of noise from the translations. In addition to adapting models on noisy parallel data, other techniques have been used to improve performance, generally measured according to BLEU (Papineni et al., 2002) against clean references. For example, Berard et al. (2019) apply inline-casing by adding special tokens before each word to represent word casing. In (Murakami et al., 2019), placeholders are used to help to translate sentences with emojis.

In this paper, we also explore data augmenta-

---

[1] www.reddit.com

[2] http://www.statmt.org/wmt19/robustness.html

Proceedings of the 2019 EMNLP Workshop W-NUT: The 5th Workshop on Noisy User-generated Text, pages 328–336
Hong Kong, Nov 4, 2019. ©2019 Association for Computational Linguistics

tion for robustness but focus on techniques other than back translation. We follow the WMT19 Robustness Task and conduct experiments under constrained and unconstrained data settings on Fr↔En as language pairs. Under the constrained setting, we only use datasets provided by the shared task, and propose new data augmentation methods to generate noise from this data. We compare back translation (BT) (Sennrich et al., 2016a) with forward translation (FT) on noisy texts and find that pseudo-parallel data from forward translation can help improve more robustness. We also adapt the idea of fuzzy matches from Bulte and Tezcan (2019) to the MTNT case by finding similar sentences in a parallel corpus to augment the limited noisy data. Results show that the fuzzy match method can extend noisy parallel data and improve model performance on both noisy and clean texts. The proposed techniques substantially outperform the baseline. While they still lag behind the winning submission in the WMT19 shared task, the resulting models are trained on much smaller clean data but augmented noisy data, leading to faster and more efficient training. Under the unconstrained setting, we propose for the first time the use of speech datasets, in two forms: (a) the IWSLT (Cettolo et al., 2012) and MuST-C (Di Gangi et al., 2019) human transcripts as a source of spontaneous, clean speech data, and (b) automatically generated transcripts for the MuST-C dataset as another source of noise. We show that using informal language from spoken language datasets can also help to increase NMT robustness.

This paper is structured as follows: Section 2 introduces the data augmentation methods for noisy texts, including the previously proposed methods and our approaches to data augmentation. Section 3 describes our experimental settings, including the datasets we used, the augmented data and the baseline model. Section 4 shows the results of models built from different training and evaluated on both clean and noisy test sets.

2 Noisy Data Augmentation

2.1 Previous Work

Considering the limited size of noisy parallel data, data augmentation methods are commonly used to generate more noisy training materials.

Previous methods include back translation, injecting synthetic noise, and adversarial attacks. In the WMT19 Robustness Task, back translation

on monolingual data was used to generate noisy parallel sentences (Murakami et al., 2019; Zhou et al., 2019; Berard et al., 2019; Helcl et al., 2019). Zheng et al. (2019) proposed an extension of back translation that generates noisy translations from clean monolingual data. Therefore, after reversing the direction, the noisy translations become the source, which would simulate the noisy source sentences from the MTNT parallel data. Synthetic noise is injected into clean data to form noisy parallel data in Belinkov and Bisk (2017); Karpukhin et al. (2019). However, rule-based synthetic noise injection is limited to certain types of noise. Adversarial methods are proposed to inject random noise into clean training data in Cheng et al. (2018, 2019).

We explore the following new methods as alternative ways to augment noisy parallel data.

2.2 Fuzzy Matches

We adapted the method to augment data from parallel corpus from Bulte and Tezcan (2019). The original method aims to find similar source sentences to those in a parallel corpus (S, T) using a monolingual corpus, and then reuse the translation of the original source sentences as translations for the similar source sentences found. We adapted it to use only on the provided noisy training corpus. For each source sentence $s_i \in S$ in the training set, all other source sentences $s_j \in S(s_i \neq s_j)$ are compared with this sentence by measuring string similarity $Sim(s_i, s_j)$. If the similarity of the two sentences is above a threshold λ, the two sentences are mapped to each other's corresponding target sentence and the two new sentence pairs $(s_i, t_j), (s_j, t_i)$ are added into our augmented training data. The similarity is measured with Levenshtein distance (Levenshtein, 1966) on the token level. The similarity score is calculated as the edit distance divided by the minimum length of the two sentences (Equation 1). In addition to fuzzy matches in the parallel corpus, we experimented with the monolingual corpus by mapping sentence m_i in monolingual corpus to its fuzzy match's target sentence t_j (If $Sim(m_i, s_j) > \lambda$, we add new sentence pair (m_i, t_j) to the training augmented data).

$$Sim(S_i, S_j) = \frac{editdistance(s_i, s_j)}{min(len(s_i), len(s_j))} \quad (1)$$

To boost the speed of finding matches, we followed the approach in Bulte and

Tezcan (2019) and used a Python library `SetSimilaritySearch`[3] to select similar candidates before calculating edit distance. For each source sentence, only the top 10 similar candidates are selected to calculate the edit distance score.

2.3 Forward Translation

Back translation (Sennrich et al., 2016a) is a very popular technique for in-domain data augmentation. In the experiment, we back-translated MTNT monolingual data using a model fine-tuned on MTNT parallel corpus. However, considering that the task of improving robustness is to produce less noisy output, data generated with back translation might have noisy target translations (from monolingual data) and less noisy source texts (from back translation). Since this might increase the noise level of the output texts, we also experimented with forward translation using models fine-tuned on the noisy parallel corpus. Pseudo parallel data generated by forward translation is used for fine tuning models on the same language direction. To avoid overfitting, we merged the noisy parallel data of both language directions to produce noisy forward translations. The pseudo parallel data generated by back translation and forward translation is combined with noisy parallel data and fine-tuned on the baseline model.

2.4 Automatic Speech Recognition

We used ASR systems and transcribed audio files into texts. In this case, we would expect noise to be generated during the process of automatic speech recognition. We selected a dataset with both audio and human transcripts, namely the MuST-C dataset. In this dataset, audio files A, human transcripts S and transcript translated into another language T are provided. We used Google Speech-to-Text API[4] and transcribed the audio files into automatic transcripts S'. The human and ASR transcripts of the audio (S and S') are treated as the source texts while the translations T are target texts. We formed a new set of parallel data (S', T) with ASR generated texts and the corresponding gold translations by humans.

Looking into the ASR transcripts, we found that the ASR system tends to skip some sentences due to the fast speaking speed, therefore we did some filtering based on the length ratio of the human transcripts and the ASR transcripts. We set a ratio threshold λ. For each pair s_i, t_i in the ASR parallel data (S', T), we removed this sentence pair if the length of t_i dividing by s_i is larger than the threshold λ.

3 Experiments

3.1 Corpora

We used all parallel corpora from the WMT19 Robustness Task on Fr↔En. For out-of-domain training, we used the WMT15 Fr↔En News Translation Task data, including Europarl v7, Common Crawl, UN, News Commentary v10, and Gigaword Corpora. In the following sections, we represent the combination of these corpora as "clean data". The MTNT dataset is used as our in-domain data for fine tuning. We also experimented with external corpora, namely the IWSLT2017[5] and MuST-C[6] corpora[7], to explore the effect of informal spoken languages in human transcripts from speech. We also utilized monolingual data in the MTNT dataset. The size of parallel and monolingual data is shown in Table 1.

We used the development set in MTNT and the *newsdiscussdev2015* for validation. Models with best performance on the validation set are evaluated on both noisy (MTNT and MTNT2019) and clean (*newstest2014* and *newsdiscusstest2015*) test sets.

For prepossessing, we first tokenized the data with Moses tokenizer (Koehn et al., 2007) and applied Byte Pair Encoding (BPE) (Sennrich et al., 2016b) to segment words into subwords. We experimented with a large vocabulary to include noisy as well as clean tokens and applied 50k merge operations for BPE. Upon evaluation, we detokenized our hypothesis files with the Moses detokenizer. We used `multi-bleu-detok.perl` to evaluate the BLEU score on the test sets.

---

[3] `https://github.com/ekzhu/SetSimilaritySearch`

[4] `https://cloud.google.com/speech-to-text/`

[5] `https://wit3.fbk.eu/mt.php?release=2017-01-trnted`

[6] `https://ict.fbk.eu/must-c/`

[7] The data from IWSLT has the same sentences in both translation directions, so we reversed the En→Fr data on the Fr→En direction. The MuST-C data is only used on En→Fr direction.

Corpus	Sentences	Words	
		source	target
Gigaword	22.52M	575.67M	672.07M
UN Corpus	12.89M	316.22M	353.92M
Common Crawl	3.24M	70.73M	76.69M
Europarl	2.01M	50.26M	52.35M
News Commentary	200k	4.46M	5.19M
IWSLT	236k	4.16M	4.34M
MuST-C(en-fr)	275k	5.09M	5.30M
MTNT(en-fr)	36k	841k	965k
MTNT(fr-en)	19k	661k	634k
MTNT(en)	81k	3.41M	
MTNT(fr)	26k	1.27M	

Table 1: Size of parallel and monolingual data. Source language represents English unless specified in brackets. The last two rows are noisy monolingual datasets in the MTNT dataset.

3.2 Augmented Data

Fuzzy Match Considering the large size of our clean data, we only looked for noisy matches within the MTNT parallel and monolingual data. The parallel data on both directions was merged to get more combinations. With the similarity threshold setting to 50%, we have 7,290 new sentence pairs in the En→Fr and 7,154 in the Fr→En language directions.

Forward Translation We used noisy monolingual data to produce forward translations. Therefore, the number of parallel samples is the same as the monolingual data in Table 1. Apart from tokenization and BPE, we did not do any other preprocessing to the forward translation.

ASR We filtered the ASR parallel data by different length ratio thresholds (1.5 and 1.2). We measured the noise level of ASR transcripts S' by evaluating Word Error Rate (WER) and Word Recognition Rate (WRR) with `asr_evaluation`[8] library, comparing it to the gold human transcripts S.

Data	WER	WRR
ASR($\lambda = 1.5$)	36.41%	65.38%
ASR($\lambda = 1.2$)	31.70%	70.54%

Table 2: Noise level of ASR generated data filtered with different length ratio thresholds.

[8]https://github.com/belambert/asr-evaluation

3.3 Model

Our baseline model, which only uses clean data for training, is the standard Transformer model (Vaswani et al., 2017) with default hyperparameters. The batch size is 4096 tokens (subwords). Our models are trained with OpenNMT-py (Klein et al., 2017) on a single GTX 1080 Ti for 5 epochs. We experimented with fine tuning on noisy data and mixed training with "domain" tags (Caswell et al., 2019; Kobus et al., 2016) indicating where the sentences are sourced from. We used different tags for clean data, MTNT parallel data, forward translation, back translation, ASR data, and fuzzy match data. Tags are added at the beginning of each source sentences.

During the fine tuning on in-domain data, we continued the learning rate and model parameters. We stop the fine tuning when the perplexity on noisy validation set does not improve after 3 epochs. Best fine-tuned checkpoints are evaluated on the test sets.

The MTNT dataset provides noisy parallel data in specific language pairs. We used models with two fine tuning strategies: Tune-S and Tune-B. The Tune-S model is fine-tuned only with the noisy parallel data in the same direction while the Tune-B model is fine-tuned with the combination of both language directions (Fr→En and En→Fr).

4 Results

We evaluated the models fine-tuned on different datasets in terms of BLEU on both noisy and clean test sets. We note that although both MTNT and MTNT2019 test sets are noisy, the MTNT2019 is less noisy and contains fewer occurrences of noise such as emojis. Similarly, since the *newsdiscuss* test set contains informal language, it is slightly noisier than *newstest* test set. The evaluation results for both directions are shown in Tables 3 and 4.

4.1 Fine Tuning on Noisy Text

It can be seen that for both directions fine tuning on noisy data gives better performance for the noisy test set. Although the size of training data in MTNT is only 19k and 36k sentences, by simply fine tuning on it, the BLEU scores of Tune-S model increase by +5.65 and +6.03 on MTNT test set, +5.44 and +2.68 on MTNT2019 test set (See the second row in the tables). It is also worth noticing that although fine-tuned on noisy data, the

Models	Fine-tune	MTNT	MTNT2019	newstest2014	newsdiscusstest2015
Baseline	None	34.41	36.14	**36.51**	34.43
Constrained	Tune-S	40.16	41.58	35.94	**36.75**
	+BT	37.93	39.19	34.03	34.00
	Tune-B	38.25	40.12	35.36	35.15
	+FM	38.91	40.85	35.62	34.58
	+FT	39.38	41.82	35.56	35.00
	+FT+FM	40.13	**42.80**	35.82	35.88
	+double tune	**40.57**	42.55	36.06	36.53
Unconstrained	IWSLT	34.22	38.28	35.96	32.95
	MTNT+IWSLT	37.52	41.22	36.33	34.07

Table 3: BLEU scores of models fine-tuned on different data in the Fr→En direction. The Tune-B model is fine-tuned with MTNT data merging both Fr→En and En→Fr directions while the Tune-S is fine-tuned only with Fr→En data. BT and FT stand for back and forward translation, respectively. FM means fuzzy matching data. By double tuning we mean we fine-tune the model a second time on the MTNT training data.

Models	Fine-tune	MTNT	MTNT2019	newstest2014	newsdiscusstest2015
Baseline	None	30.12	29.57	35.51	35.93
Constrained	MTNT(Tune-S)	36.15	32.25	36.77	37.16
	+fix punctuation	—	35.49	—	—
	MTNT*(Tune-B)	35.64	31.27	36.67	37.21
	+FM	36.03	31.37	36.58	37.13
	+FT	35.98	31.37	36.30	**37.91**
	+FT+FM	36.21	31.25	36.37	37.76
	+double tune	**36.78**	32.10	36.72	37.84
	+fix punctuation	—	**36.46**	—	—
Unconstrained	IWSLT	33.66	30.58	**36.89**	37.34
	MTNT+IWSLT	35.44	31.24	36.73	37.90
	ASR($\lambda = 1.5$)	30.53	28.66	36.46	35.61
	ASR($\lambda = 1.2$)	31.09	29.48	36.59	35.54
	MuST-C	34.15	31.09	36.27	37.61
Mixed training	None	35.32	31.14	35.5	36.05

Table 4: BLEU scores of models fine-tuned on different data in the En→Fr direction. λ in ASR data represents the filtering threshold, as mentioned in Section 2.4. The mixed-training model combines all data available and adds domain tags in front of each sentence. Other notations are same as in Table 3.

performance on clean test sets increases as well. This shows that noisy parallel data could improve model robustness on both noisy and clean texts.

4.2 Data Augmentation

As it is common in the field, we experimented with back translation (third row in Table 3). We used the target-to-source Tune-S model to back-translate monolingual data in MTNT corpus. The back-translated data is combined with the noisy parallel data and used to fine-tune the baseline model. For Fr→En, by introducing back-translated data, the model performance drops by over 2 BLEU scores compared the simply tuning on parallel data. This would suggest that the back translation data might break the noise level gap between source and target texts, and hence the model fine-tuned on back-translated data tends to output noisier translations and performs worse.

Since the size of the MTNT dataset is too small, we tried merging the data in both language directions, resulting in 55k sentence pairs for fine tuning. For both directions, the models tuned on the merged MTNT data (Tune-B) show worse performance than the models tuned on single direction data (Tune-S). This is due to the introduction of opposite direction data would increase the noise in target texts. We added the forward translation and fuzzy matches data separately and fine-tuned with the merged MTNT data. Results show that the introduction of either forward translation or fuzzy match data would improve model performance on noisy test sets, compared to the Tune-B model. However, with only forward translation or fuzzy match data added, the model still lags behind the Tune-S performance. Therefore, we mix the FT, FM, and merged MTNT data. After we use the mixed data for fine tuning, models in both directions scored better with the augmented data. The Fr→En model with forward translation and fuzzy matches data achieved a performance of 42.80 BLEU score on the MTNT2019 test set, an improvement of +1.32 BLEU points over the Tune-S model. The forward translation data is generated using the Tune-B model, which includes information on the opposite direction, and this might benefit forward translation and prevent the model from overfitting. Compared to back translation, forward translation could keep the noise level difference between the source and target sentences[9].

4.3 Double Fine Tuning

Considering that the opposite direction data from that of the MTNT dataset would harm the model performance, we applied double fine tuning to compensate. We used the model which had already been tuned on the combination of forward translation data, fuzzy match data and merged MTNT data, and fine-tuned it with the MTNT data on the corresponding direction (e.g. Fr→En data for Fr→En model). In this case, the MTNT data in the same language direction would fine-tune the model twice, thus adapting the model to the specific language direction domain. The second fine tuning was able to further improve model robustness to noisy data and keep a similar performance on clean data. In the En→Fr direction, the second fine tuning improves +0.57 and +0.85 BLEU points on MTNT and MTNT2019.

4.4 Punctuation Fixing

The MTNT2019 test set uses a different set of punctuation in French text as the MTNT dataset and clean training data. In the MTNT2019 test set, the French references use apostrophes (’) and angle quotes (« and »), instead of the single quotes (') and double quotes (") used in the MTNT training data (Berard et al., 2019). Therefore, mod-

els fine-tuned with MTNT training data would show an inconsistent performance for punctuation when evaluating on the MTNT2019 test set. We fixed the punctuation in the En→Fr direction as a postprocessing step. This single replacement improves +4.36 BLEU score over the double fine-tuned model. For comparison, we also postprocessed the output from the Tune-S model. The punctuation fix results in an increase of +3.24 BLEU score.

4.5 External Data

To explore the effect of other types of noise, we fine-tuned our baseline model on different external datasets (see the "Unconstrained" rows in Table 3 and 4). We experimented with human transcript and translation in IWSLT dataset. The BLEU score (Fr→En) on MTNT2019 increases by +2.14 over the baseline, while the results on the other three test sets decrease. In the En→Fr direction, fine tuning on IWSLT improves the model performance on all four test sets, and with MTNT data added, the BLEU score on noisy data performs even better than the Tune-B model. The benefit of speech transcripts might come from informal languages such as slang, spoken language, and domain-related words. Apart from this, we also kept the indicating words (e.g. "[laughter]" and "[applause]") in the transcripts, which could also play a role of noise.

When using ASR data generated from the audio files in the MuST-C dataset, we first filtered ASR data by removing sentences where the original transcript length is over 1.5 times that of the ASR transcript. The model fine-tuned on ASR data shows a slight decrease in BLEU scores. We found that the ASR transcript often skips some phrases in a sentence. Therefore, we reduced the length ratio threshold to 1.2, and with that the model achieves similar performance as the baseline model. Evaluated on *newstest*, the ASR-tuned model improves +1.08 BLEU score over the baseline. Finally, we tried with the parallel texts from human transcript and translation in MuST-C corpus, similar to IWSLT, the performance increases on all test data. This suggests that the introduction of external data with different types of noise could improve model robustness, even without the use of in-domain noisy data

Finally, we conducted a domain-sensitive training experiment by adding tags for different data.

---

[9]We experimented with fuzzy matches plus MTNT data (not merged), but it does not improve performance, because without the opposite direction information the model overfits to the tuning data.

We mixed all available data, including the MTNT data (two directions), IWSLT, MuST-C, ASR, forward translation, and fuzzy match data. Tags are added at the beginning of the source sentences. As shown in the last row in Table 4, mixed training could improve the performance over baseline on noisy texts. However, the model does not outperform the models with fine tuning. This might result from the introduction of ASR generated data, which can contain more low quality training samples.

4.6 WMT19 Robustness Leaderboard

We submitted our best constrained systems to WMT19 Robustness Leaderboard[10], as shown in Table 5 and Table 6. In the Fr→En direction, we submitted the model fine-tuned on merged MTNT data, forward translation and fuzzy match data (row 5 in Table 3). In the En→Fr direction, the double-tuned model with punctuation fixed was submitted (row 6 in Table 4).

System	BLEU-uncased
(Berard et al., 2019)	48.8
(Helcl et al., 2019)	45.8
(Zheng et al., 2019)	44.5
Ours	43.8
(Post and Duh, 2019)	41.8
(Zhou et al., 2019)	36.0
(Grozea, 2019)	30.8
MTNT paper baseline	26.2

Table 5: WMT19 Robustness Leaderboard on Fr→En.

System	BLEU-uncased
(Berard et al., 2019)	42.0
(Helcl et al., 2019)	39.1
Ours	37.1
(Zheng et al., 2019)	37.0
(Grozea, 2019)	24.8
MTNT paper baseline	22.5

Table 6: WMT19 Robustness Leaderboard on En→Fr.

Our systems would have achieved the 4th and 3rd place on Fr→En and En→Fr directions. The leading systems use back translation on a large volume of clean monolingual data, therefore could benefit from the size of clean data. Although our system does not utilize clean monolingual data,

we find an alternative way to extend noisy parallel data, which might be more efficient for training. The results show that our systems could achieve a competitive position.

5 Conclusions

In this paper we use data augmentation strategies to improve neural machine translation models robustness. We experiment under the setting of the WMT19 Robustness Task for the Fr↔En language directions. We propose the use of forward translation and fuzzy matches as alternatives to back translation to augment noisy data. Our best models with augmented noisy data could improve +1.32 and +0.97 BLEU scores for Fr→En and En→Fr over models fine-tuned with noisy parallel data. We also explore the effect of external noisy data in the form of speech transcripts and show that models could benefit from data injected with noise through manual transcriptions of spoken language. The ASR generated data does not help improving robustness as it contains low quality training samples that break the sentences, while the human transcripts from speech proved helpful to translate noisy texts, even without in-domain data. Future work might include training a domain-related speech recognition model and generate better ASR parallel data instead of using the off-the-shelf system.

References

Dzmitry Bahdanau, Kyunghyun Cho, and Yoshua Bengio. 2015. Neural machine translation by jointly learning to align and translate. In *3rd International Conference on Learning Representations, ICLR 2015, San Diego, CA, USA, May 7-9, 2015, Conference Track Proceedings*.

Yonatan Belinkov and Yonatan Bisk. 2017. Synthetic and natural noise both break neural machine translation. *ArXiv*, abs/1711.02173.

Alexandre Berard, Ioan Calapodescu, and Claude Roux. 2019. Naver labs europe's systems for the wmt19 machine translation robustness task. In *Proceedings of the Fourth Conference on Machine Translation*, pages 725–731, Florence, Italy. Association for Computational Linguistics.

Bram Bulte and Arda Tezcan. 2019. Neural fuzzy repair: Integrating fuzzy matches into neural machine translation. In *Proceedings of the 57th Annual Meeting of the Association for Computational Linguistics*, pages 1800–1809, Florence, Italy. Association for Computational Linguistics.

Isaac Caswell, Ciprian Chelba, and David Grangier. 2019. Tagged back-translation. In *Proceedings of the Fourth Conference on Machine Translation (Volume 1: Research Papers)*, pages 53–63, Florence, Italy. Association for Computational Linguistics.

Mauro Cettolo, Christian Girardi, and Marcello Federico. 2012. Wit^3: Web inventory of transcribed and translated talks. In *Proceedings of the 16th Conference of the European Association for Machine Translation (EAMT)*, pages 261–268, Trento, Italy.

Yong Cheng, Lu Jiang, and Wolfgang Macherey. 2019. Robust neural machine translation with doubly adversarial inputs. In *Proceedings of the 57th Annual Meeting of the Association for Computational Linguistics*, pages 4324–4333, Florence, Italy. Association for Computational Linguistics.

Yong Cheng, Zhaopeng Tu, Fandong Meng, Junjie Zhai, and Yang Liu. 2018. Towards robust neural machine translation. In *Proceedings of the 56th Annual Meeting of the Association for Computational Linguistics (Volume 1: Long Papers)*, pages 1756–1766, Melbourne, Australia. Association for Computational Linguistics.

Raj Dabre and Eiichiro Sumita. 2019. Nict's supervised neural machine translation systems for the wmt19 translation robustness task. In *Proceedings of the Fourth Conference on Machine Translation*, pages 732–735, Florence, Italy. Association for Computational Linguistics.

Mattia A. Di Gangi, Roldano Cattoni, Luisa Bentivogli, Matteo Negri, and Marco Turchi. 2019. MuST-C: a Multilingual Speech Translation Corpus. In *Proceedings of the 2019 Conference of the North American Chapter of the Association for Computational Linguistics: Human Language Technologies, Volume 1 (Long and Short Papers)*, pages 2012–2017, Minneapolis, Minnesota. Association for Computational Linguistics.

Jonas Gehring, Michael Auli, David Grangier, Denis Yarats, and Yann N Dauphin. 2017. Convolutional sequence to sequence learning. In *Proceedings of the 34th International Conference on Machine Learning-Volume 70*, pages 1243–1252. JMLR. org.

Cristian Grozea. 2019. System description: The submission of fokus to the wmt 19 robustness task. In *Proceedings of the Fourth Conference on Machine Translation (Volume 2: Shared Task Papers, Day 1)*, pages 537–538, Florence, Italy. Association for Computational Linguistics.

Jindřich Helcl, Jindřich Libovický, and Martin Popel. 2019. Cuni system for the wmt19 robustness task. In *Proceedings of the Fourth Conference on Machine Translation*, pages 738–742, Florence, Italy. Association for Computational Linguistics.

Vladimir Karpukhin, Omer Levy, Jacob Eisenstein, and Marjan Ghazvininejad. 2019. Training on synthetic noise improves robustness to natural noise in machine translation. *arXiv preprint arXiv:1902.01509*.

Guillaume Klein, Yoon Kim, Yuntian Deng, Jean Senellart, and Alexander M. Rush. 2017. OpenNMT: Open-source toolkit for neural machine translation. In *Proc. ACL*.

Catherine Kobus, Josep Crego, and Jean Senellart. 2016. Domain control for neural machine translation. *arXiv preprint arXiv:1612.06140*.

Philipp Koehn, Hieu Hoang, Alexandra Birch, Chris Callison-Burch, Marcello Federico, Nicola Bertoldi, Brooke Cowan, Wade Shen, Christine Moran, Richard Zens, Chris Dyer, Ondřej Bojar, Alexandra Constantin, and Evan Herbst. 2007. Moses: Open source toolkit for statistical machine translation. In *Proceedings of the 45th Annual Meeting of the Association for Computational Linguistics Companion Volume Proceedings of the Demo and Poster Sessions*, pages 177–180, Prague, Czech Republic. Association for Computational Linguistics.

Vladimir I Levenshtein. 1966. Binary codes capable of correcting deletions, insertions, and reversals. In *Soviet physics doklady*, volume 10, pages 707–710.

Xian Li, Paul Michel, Antonios Anastasopoulos, Yonatan Belinkov, Nadir Durrani, Orhan Firat, Philipp Koehn, Graham Neubig, Juan Pino, and Hassan Sajjad. 2019. Findings of the first shared task on machine translation robustness. In *Proceedings of the Fourth Conference on Machine Translation*, pages 218–229, Florence, Italy. Association for Computational Linguistics.

Paul Michel and Graham Neubig. 2018. MTNT: A testbed for machine translation of noisy text. In *Proceedings of the 2018 Conference on Empirical Methods in Natural Language Processing*, pages 543–553, Brussels, Belgium. Association for Computational Linguistics.

Soichiro Murakami, Makoto Morishita, Tsutomu Hirao, and Masaaki Nagata. 2019. Ntt's machine translation systems for wmt19 robustness task. In *Proceedings of the Fourth Conference on Machine Translation*, pages 743–750, Florence, Italy. Association for Computational Linguistics.

Kishore Papineni, Salim Roukos, Todd Ward, and Wei-Jing Zhu. 2002. Bleu: a method for automatic evaluation of machine translation. In *Proceedings of the 40th Annual Meeting of the Association for Computational Linguistics*, pages 311–318, Philadelphia, Pennsylvania, USA. Association for Computational Linguistics.

Matt Post and Kevin Duh. 2019. Jhu 2019 robustness task system description. In *Proceedings of the Fourth Conference on Machine Translation*, pages 751–757, Florence, Italy. Association for Computational Linguistics.

Rico Sennrich, Barry Haddow, and Alexandra Birch. 2016a. Improving neural machine translation models with monolingual data. In *Proceedings of the 54th Annual Meeting of the Association for Computational Linguistics (Volume 1: Long Papers)*, pages 86–96, Berlin, Germany. Association for Computational Linguistics.

Rico Sennrich, Barry Haddow, and Alexandra Birch. 2016b. Neural machine translation of rare words with subword units. In *Proceedings of the 54th Annual Meeting of the Association for Computational Linguistics (Volume 1: Long Papers)*, pages 1715–1725, Berlin, Germany. Association for Computational Linguistics.

Ashish Vaswani, Noam Shazeer, Niki Parmar, Jakob Uszkoreit, Llion Jones, Aidan N Gomez, Ł ukasz Kaiser, and Illia Polosukhin. 2017. Attention is all you need. In I. Guyon, U. V. Luxburg, S. Bengio, H. Wallach, R. Fergus, S. Vishwanathan, and R. Garnett, editors, *Advances in Neural Information Processing Systems 30*, pages 5998–6008. Curran Associates, Inc.

Renjie Zheng, Hairong Liu, Mingbo Ma, Baigong Zheng, and Liang Huang. 2019. Robust machine translation with domain sensitive pseudo-sources: Baidu-osu wmt19 mt robustness shared task system report. In *Proceedings of the Fourth Conference on Machine Translation*, pages 758–763, Florence, Italy. Association for Computational Linguistics.

Shuyan Zhou, Xiangkai Zeng, Yingqi Zhou, Antonios Anastasopoulos, and Graham Neubig. 2019. Improving robustness of neural machine translation with multi-task learning. In *Proceedings of the Fourth Conference on Machine Translation (Volume 2: Shared Task Papers, Day 1)*, pages 565–571, Florence, Italy. Association for Computational Linguistics.

Disambiguating Sentiment: An Ensemble of Humour, Sarcasm, and Hate Speech Features for Sentiment Classification

Rohan Badlani [*]
Dept. of Computer Science
Stanford University
rbadlani@stanford.edu

Nishit Asnani [*]
Dept. of Computer Science
Stanford University
nasnani@stanford.edu

Manan Rai [*]
Dept. of Computer Science
Stanford University
mananrai@stanford.edu

Abstract

Due to the nature of online user reviews, sentiment analysis on such data requires a deep semantic understanding of the text. Many online reviews are sarcastic, humorous, or hateful. Signals from such language nuances may reinforce or completely alter the sentiment of a review as predicted by a machine learning model that attempts to detect sentiment alone. Thus, having a model that is explicitly aware of these features should help it perform better on reviews that are characterized by them. We propose a composite two-step model that extracts features pertaining to sarcasm, humour, hate speech, as well as sentiment, in the first step, feeding them in conjunction to inform sentiment classification in the second step. We show that this multi-step approach leads to a better empirical performance for sentiment classification than a model that predicts sentiment alone. A qualitative analysis reveals that the conjunctive approach can better capture the nuances of sentiment as expressed in online reviews.

1 Introduction

Sentiment classification is one of the most widely studied problems in natural language processing, partly since it is a complex problem from a linguistic point of view, and partly since it has huge commercial value for enterprises attempting to understand user behaviour. Online user review datasets have contributed significantly to research in this direction, since they provide large sets of human generated commentary about real products and services, which capture the nuances and complexity of the user-generated text (Zhang et al., 2015) (He and McAuley, 2016).

Traditionally, models developed for sentiment classification have been used to solve other binary or multi-class classification problems in natural language, like intent detection, document tagging, etc. Sentiment classification has also been used as a building block towards more complicated language understanding/generation tasks (Poria et al., 2016) (Hu et al., 2017). Given that sentiment is a complex language attribute influenced by several other features, this paper poses a question more fundamental to the nature of sentiment in human language: can models developed for other tasks, like sarcasm, humor, or hate speech detection, help improve sentiment classification models? Going further, we also attempt to answer if the same model architecture can be used for these tasks, and then be combined to yield higher performance on sentiment classification.

This line of thought is inspired by how humans perceive sentiment in any piece of spoken or written language. Detection of elements of sarcasm help us resolve seemingly contradictory statements ("The restaurant was so clean that I could barely avoid stepping into the puddle!") into their intended sentiment. Similarly, humor (because it can get similarly confusing) and hate speech (since specific offensive words may be the only indicators of sentiment in a review) act as crucial indicators of the intended meaning of phrases in a given utterance.

Since the sentiment model is not optimizing for detecting these language attributes, it is likely to get confused by utterances having them unless it is sufficiently exposed to similar sentences during training. We therefore believe that making sentiment models explicitly aware of these language attributes would help them become more robust to sarcastic, humorous or hateful utterances, and thus get better at classifying sentiment.

Thus, our research hypotheses are as follows:

---

equal contribution

Proceedings of the 2019 EMNLP Workshop W-NUT: The 5th Workshop on Noisy User-generated Text, pages 337–345
Hong Kong, Nov 4, 2019. ©2019 Association for Computational Linguistics

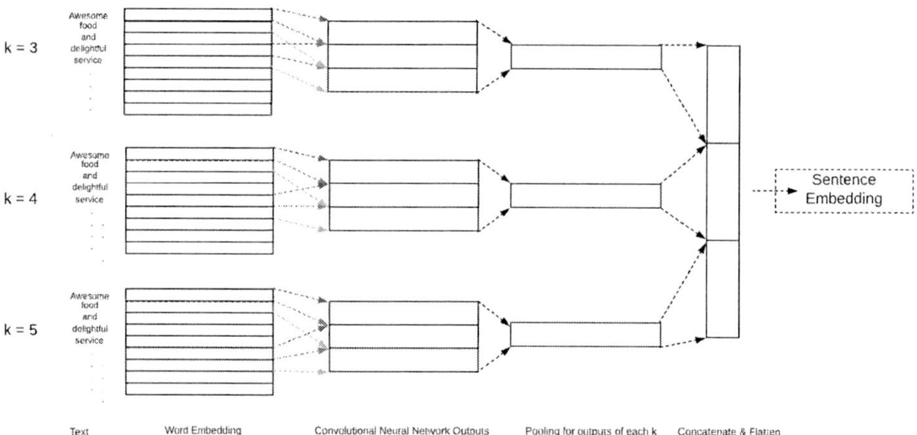

Figure 1: CNN Based Binary Classification Model for embedding generation. We use a stride of 1 in our final CNN model. Different colors in the word embeddings represent different inputs to the convolutional neural network

- **H1**: Models individually learned on sarcasm, humor and hate speech detection, and then used as subroutines to extract features, should boost the performance of a sentiment classification model.

- **H2**: Given that the individual tasks are all binary classification tasks, we believe that a single model architecture should provide reasonable performance on these individual tasks and would make it easier to re-use the same learned models for multiple downstream classification tasks.

2 Related Work

Sentiment classification, sarcasm detection, humor detection and hate speech detection have all seen varying levels of interest from the natural language research community, and have evolved over time as better datasets and modeling techniques have come into the picture.

There has been quite a bit of work on sarcasm detection, especially in the context of Twitter-based self-annotated data and Self-Annotated Reddit Corpus. The seminal work in this area started with (González-Ibáñez et al., 2011) - they used lexical and pragmatic features and found that pragmatic features were more useful in detecting sarcasm. Addition of context-based features along with text-based features in certain subsequent models helped as well in improving perfor-

mance on sarcasm detection. There was a dramatic shift with the introduction of deep learning as feature engineering took a back seat and deep models began to be used for learning task-specific representations. (Hazarika et al., 2018) show that using context, user and text embedding provides state of the art performance, which is challenged by Kolchinski (Kolchinski and Potts, 2018) (West et al., 2014) through a more simplistic user embedding based approach that achieves similar performance without other context (like forum embeddings as used by (Hazarika et al., 2018)).

Hate Speech in natural language research has traditionally been a loosely-defined term, with one cause being the similarity with other categorizations of hateful utterances, such as offensive language. In the context of online reviews, we broadly use hate speech to include any form of offensive language. (Davidson et al., 2017) introduce the seminal dataset in the field, and test a variety of models – Logistic Regression, Naive Bayes, decision trees, random forests, and Support Vector Machines (SVMs), each tested with 5-fold cross validation to find that the Logistic Regression and Linear SVM tend to perform significantly better than other models. Models such as LSTMs and CNNs have also been tried in works such as (Badjatiya et al., 2017) and (de Gibert et al., 2018).

Humour Detection has seen a lot of work, with models being developed on several large-scale public datasets, such as the Pun of the Day, 16000

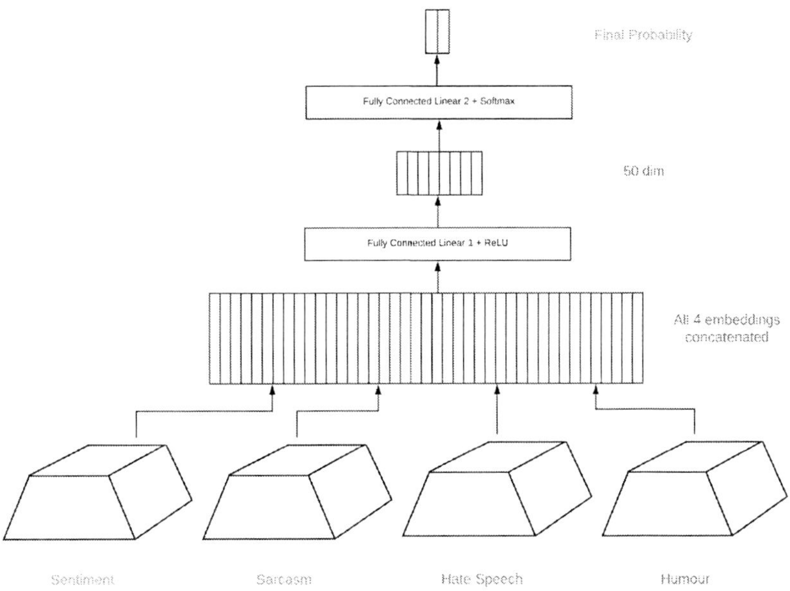

Figure 2: Full Sentiment Classification model with ensemble of features from sarcasm, humour, and hate speech detection models

OneLiners, Short Jokes dataset, and the PTT jokes dataset. (Chen and Soo, 2018) use a Highway Network on top of a CNN on a combination of these datasets. (Kim, 2014) uses CNN for sentence classification, and these models have also been tested on funny-labelled reviews from the Yelp dataset[1].

Recent works have attempted to combine feature extraction models trained on some tasks for a different task. (Poria et al., 2016), for instance, uses knowledge about sentiment, emotion, and personality to better detect sarcasm. This finds a parallel in our attempt here, with the difference that these features include non-linguistic features such as user personality, and we focus only on natural language features to test the transferability of knowledge about certain features to detecting others.

Sentiment classification is a text classification task with the objective to classify text according to the sentimental polarities. This has been a widely researched area (Mäntylä et al., 2016) and recently there has been a lot of success in this area. The current state of the art performance on this task is using transformer (Vaswani et al., 2017) based models like BERT (Devlin et al., 2018) and XL-Net (Yang et al., 2019). These models achieve very high accuracy on the binary classification task of sentiment polarity detection but analyzing the failure modes of these models indicate that these models might fail in cases where there are higher order language concepts like sarcasm, humour and hate speech co-occur in the same utterance. Hence, through this paper, we investigate the performance of sentiment classification when provided with representative features pertaining to these language oriented concepts and at the same time propose a generic approach to compute these feature so as to reuse for multiple downstream tasks.

3 Methods

3.1 Datasets

We experiment with the following datasets corresponding to sentiment, sarcasm, hate speech, and humour to test our hypotheses:

1. **D1 - Sentiment**: The Yelp Review Dataset (Zhang et al., 2015) consists of about 560,000 reviews, with binary sentiment labels. For the purposes of our analysis, we use 100,000 reviews for training and validation and 36,614

---

[1]https://github.com/srishti-1795/Humour-Detection

Review	NLU Aspect Captured
I am a nurse and to characterize this office as nothing but a frustration is a compliment.	Sarcasm
It would have been faster if I would have grown, harvested, and brewed the tea myself.	Sarcasm
If you want to get pastries while being yelled at by the staff and treated like dirt, this is the place for you.	Sarcasm
They are THE RUDEST people I've ever met! The lady with short hair has a crappy attitude, so does the younger guy.	Hate Speech

Table 1: Examples where our combined model is able to predict correct label whereas the baseline sentiment model fails.

reviews for testing.

2. **D2 - Sarcasm**: The SARC (Self-Annotated Reddit Comments) dataset (Khodak et al., 2017) consists of about 1.3 million Reddit comments. These comments have been self annotated using the \s character. The dataset has a balanced set and an unbalanced set. For the purposes of our analysis, we focus on balanced set and take 100,000 comments for training and validation and 20,000 comments for testing.

3. **D3 - Humour**: The Yelp Review Dataset has a field called '*funny*.' We consider a comment to be humorous (i.e positive label) when the comment has a 'funny' score greater than 2.

4. **D4 - Hate Speech**: The hatebase.org Twitter Dataset (Davidson et al., 2017) is a popular hate speech tweet dataset, which consists of 28,000 tweets, each labelled as either having offensive content or not.

3.2 Validating Hypothesis H1

We conduct a quick initial evaluation of hypothesis **H1** using well-performing models for sentiment, sarcasm, humour, and hate speech. These models are discussed below:

1. **M1 - Sentiment**: For sentiment detection, the current state of the art model is BERT Large (Devlin et al., 2018) which provides an accuracy of about 98.11% (Xie et al., 2019). We use the BERT Base model which has a smaller architecture and therefore helps run a quick evaluation (12-layer, 768-hidden, 12-heads, 110M parameters).

2. **M2 - Sarcasm**: The CASCADE model (Hazarika et al., 2018) is the current state of the art on the SARC dataset. This achieves a 77% balanced set accuracy and 79% unbalanced set accuracy. This model computes user-specific embeddings from their comments on other threads, thread embeddings from other user comments on the same thread, and the embeddings of the input text, and uses all of these for sarcasm detection. We use the CASCADE model but without the user and thread embeddings since they were not readily available for this dataset. The CASCADE model modified as above provides reasonable performance for the task of sarcasm detection.

3. **M3 - Humour**: We use an SVM model with bag of words features for humour detection as used in pre-existing implementations[2]. This provides an accuracy of 83% on the yelp reviews dataset.

4. **M4 - Hate Speech**: We use the implementation provided by (Davidson et al., 2017) which is simple Logistic regression model that provides a F1 score of 0.90 on **D4**.

M2, M3, M4 models as described above predict the probability of occurrence of sarcasm, humour and hate speech respectively on a given input text. These probabilities are then fed as features to our BERT-base sentiment classification model as described in **M1** above for the Yelp reviews dataset. We compare our modified model with BERT-base and observe a small improvement in the sentiment detection performance which positively supports our hypothesis **H1**. This motivates us to consider

---

[2]https://github.com/srishti-1795/Humour-Detection

developing embeddings for each of these language specific features instead of using just the probability of their occurrence.

3.3 Validating hypothesis H2

In order to test hypothesis **H2**, we construct a general-purpose feature embedding model E for all the four tasks, along with a classifier C for classification on the combined representation, as discussed below.

3.3.1 Feature Embedding Model

Given a d-word sentence s, we initialize trainable 128-dimensional word embeddings for each word, and create a $d \times 128$ embedding matrix for the sentence. In order to capture n-gram features, we use a word-level Convolutional Neural Network (Kim, 2014) with f filters ($n \times 128$) for $n = 3, 4, 5$. For each n, we compute the $(d-n+1) \times f$ output, and use max pooling to get a f-dimensional vector. We concatenate these vectors for all three values of n and flatten them to get a $3f$-dimensional embedding. With $f = 100$, we get a 300-dimensional embedding for every sentence.

We use one such model for each of Sentiment (**E1**), Sarcasm (**E2**), Hate Speech (**E3**), and Humour (**E4**).

3.3.2 Combination Classifier

Given a d-word sentence s and a set of m feature embedding models ($1 \leq m \leq 4$) $E \subseteq [E1, E2, E3, E4]$, we calculate a set of 300-dimensional embeddings per model, and concatenate them into a single $300 * m$-dimensional feature vector v. This is used as input to a sentiment classifier that predicts $\mathbf{C}(v) \in [0, 1]$ that represents the probability of positive sentiment. This classifier consists of two fully-connected layers with hidden size 50 and ReLU activation. This model is trained and tested separately for several combinations E, and the results from these experiments are discussed in section 4.

4 Experiments and Results

4.1 Results for Hypothesis H1

To test if our hypothesis **H1** holds true, we concatenated predictions from the sarcasm (M2) detection model to the BERT-base model embeddings (M1) used for sentiment classification as described in section 3.2. We used the PyTorch im-

Model	Accuracy (%)
M1	95.13
M1 + M2 (P/L)	**95.22**

Table 2: Testing our hypothesis: M_i refers to the respective model, P and L indicate using predicted probabilities and labels respectively. Both of our augmented models perform better than the sentiment model alone (M1), thus validating our hypothesis.

plementation of BERT Base[3], and our results are tabulated in Table 2. We trained the models for 3 epochs with a learning rate of 2e-5 and a batch size of 32.

This experiment validated our hypothesis that there is tangible sentiment information to be gleaned from a sentence's sarcasm features (and potentially other features as well).

Attribute Combination	Accuracy (%)
Se	95.95
Se + Sc	96.02
Se + Hu	95.93
Se + Ha	95.69
Se + Sc + Hu	96.06
Se + Sc + Hu + Ha	**96.18**

Table 3: Model Performances for various combinations of Sentiment Se (E1), Sarcasm Sc (E2), Humor Hu (E3) and Hate Speech Ha (E4). We find that our combined model performs the best.

4.2 Results for Hypothesis H2

As described in 3.3.1, we used a single model architecture for training separate models on sentiment, sarcasm, humor and hate speech. Due to class imbalance and large dataset sizes, we modified our datasets in the following ways:

- **D1**: We took a subset of the training set for Yelp reviews which amounted to 100k reviews for training and validation combined, and included the entire test set of 36.6k reviews for reporting the performance of our models.

- **D2**: To maintain consistency, we took a sample of 100k comments for training our model on sarcasm detection.

---

[3]https://github.com/huggingface/pytorch-pretrained-BERT

Attribute Combination	Accuracy (%)		
	Run 1	Run 2	Run 3
Se	95.95	95.76	95.85
Se + Sc + Hu + Ha	**96.18**	**96.08**	**96.40**

Table 4: Model performances during several runs of the baseline and the combined (Se + Sc + Hu + Ha) models.

Review	NLU Aspect Missed
...The manager went around and asked the 2 waitresses working all 4/5 tables surrounding us and none of them took responsibility or seemed to want our table. Little did we know this was a blessing in disguise...	Extended story line: the first half of the review is negative, and the model likely misses the turning point towards positive halfway through the review

Table 5: Examples where the combined model goes wrong and the baseline sentiment model predicts the correct sentiment.

Review	NLU Aspect Missed
Say it with me now: Blaaaaaaaaaand	Indicative word missed
This place is closed, and for good reason.	Flip in sentiment

Table 6: Examples where the combined and the baseline sentiment models both fail to predict the correct sentiment.

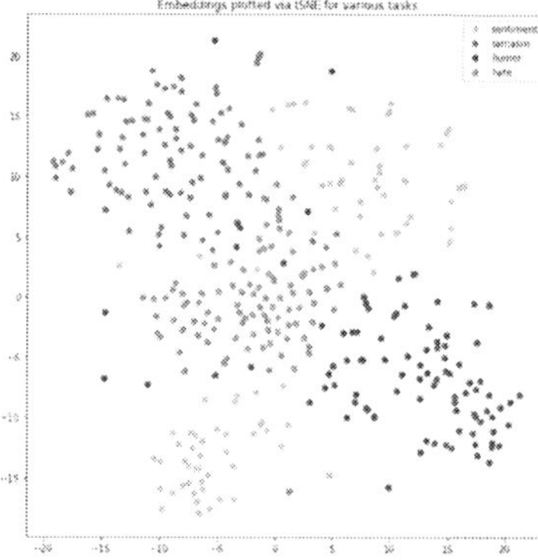

Figure 3: Scatter plot for the various task-specific embeddings (unit normalized) of the first 100 test reviews from the Yelp dataset. It can be seen that sentiment, sarcasm, humor and hate predominantly occupy different regions of the embedding space when reduced to 2D using tSNE.

- **D3**: Since this dataset had a ratio of 19:1 for non-humorous to humorous reviews, we took the entire set of humorous reviews from the original Yelp dataset, and added about twice the amount of randomly sampled non-humorous reviews to maintain a healthy ratio of 2:1. Final number of train/val reviews were 40k and test reviews were 8,661.

- **D4**: The number of hateful tweets in this dataset were 16 times the number of non-hateful tweets. We oversample the non-hateful tweets by 4x, and undersample the hateful tweets by 2x to obtain a ratio of 2:1 in favor of the positive class, for both the training/val and the test datasets. The total number of tweets in train/val are 16,854 and number of test tweets are 3,521.

After training a model each on these datasets following the architecture described in 3.3.1, we obtain the sentiment, sarcasm, humor and hate embeddings for each of the training and testing reviews from **D1**. For this model, we use CNN window sizes of 3, 4 and 5 with 100 kernels each, batch size of 64, learning rate 0.001, and dropout probability 0.5.

Further, we train combined sentiment classifiers (3.3.2) on top of various combinations of subsets of these embeddings for the training set, and then evaluate performance on the test set. The performances of these combinations is reported in Table 3, and results from more runs comparing the baseline against our combined model are shown in 4. In order to test if the improvement of our proposed hybrid model is consistently better than the baseline, we train our the combined and baseline models over fixed training set size multiple times and evaluate the performance on the same held-out test set consisting of 36,614 reviews. Table

4 shows the results of the models on the test set. We observe a consistent improvement using sentiment, sarcasm, humour and hate speech features as compared to just sentiment features.

5 Discussion and Analysis

Our hypothesis **H1** is supported by the experiments in both 4.1 and 4.2, i.e. sarcasm, humor and hate speech are signals that boost the sentiment classification performance on Yelp reviews.

5.1 Different natural language features add mutually exclusive information

As Figure 3 shows, the normalized task-specific embeddings occupy distinct regions of the 2D space (after dimensionality reduction using tSNE). Thus, the three additional models probably assist the sentiment embeddings by combining information from the source review that the sentiment model may not have learned to catch, and that might, in certain cases, help the combined model make better decisions. Since these embeddings have been obtained via a single model architecture trained on different datasets, the increase in performance on sentiment classification validates our hypothesis **H2**. This implies not only that a single architecture might suit multiple natural language problem domains, which models like BERT have already shown, but also that one or more of them can help boost the performance of others, if the reasoning behind such a predicted improvement is linguistically sound.

5.2 Interpretibility of model's success modes

We analyze the contribution of each of the individual models trained for sarcasm, humour and hate speech detection to the performance of sentiment detection by comparing the predicted labels against the ground truth. In each of the matrices in Figure 4, the value in cell (i, j) of category c (which can be TP, TN, FP or FN) denotes the respective fraction of predictions in model i that belong to category c if the predictions of model j are assumed to be the ground truth.

As evident from Figure 4, we find that adding features pertaining to sarcasm, hate speech, and humour to a baseline sentiment classifier increases the number of true positives against the Ground Truth labels (the baseline model predicts 97% of the combined model's positive labels). Since the false positive rate of the combined model (0.02) is also less than that of the sentiment model (0.03) against the ground truth, this shows that the *combined model has a higher precision*. This observation is also consistent with the reasoning that *sarcasm and hate speech are both likely to catch negative reviews which may otherwise sound positive to a naive model*, and thus reduce the false positive rate.

Similarly, looking at the true negatives' matrix shows that the combined (Sentiment + Sarcasm + Humour + Hate Speech) model predicts negative labels better than the (Sentiment + Sarcasm + Humour) model (0.97 against 0.95), which is consistent with the reasoning that *Hate Speech is likely to indicate a negative sentiment*, and that knowledge of Hate Speech helps the model better understand what to look for in a review that is negative because of hateful language.

On looking at some reviews in the test dataset that our combined model (Se + Sc + Hu + Ha) got right and that the baseline sentiment model got wrong, we observe that our model definitively helps with identifying the right sentiment for sarcastic reviews (Table 1) and some hate reviews, although we couldn't find many humorous reviews in this context. Similarly, it seems that the reviews whose sentiment has been classified wrongly by the sentiment-only baseline and that don't have any sarcastic / hate intent don't get classified correctly by our combined model either (Table 6).

5.3 Error Analysis

Tables 5 and 6 present some analysis of the errors made by our model, and how they compare with the baseline Sentiment model. As can be seen, our model doesn't catch the elements of natural language that it was not trained to detect, and while it is quite sensitive to catching negative sentiment, it doesn't do as well when sentiment changes halfway through the review.

6 Conclusions

In this paper we show that features from sarcasm, humor and hate speech help in improving sentiment classification performance on the Yelp reviews dataset. We have also shown that a general-purpose model architecture for binary classification can be trained on each of these natural language tasks individually and that it provides an easy way for end-to-end sentiment classification that combines the strengths of each of these mod-

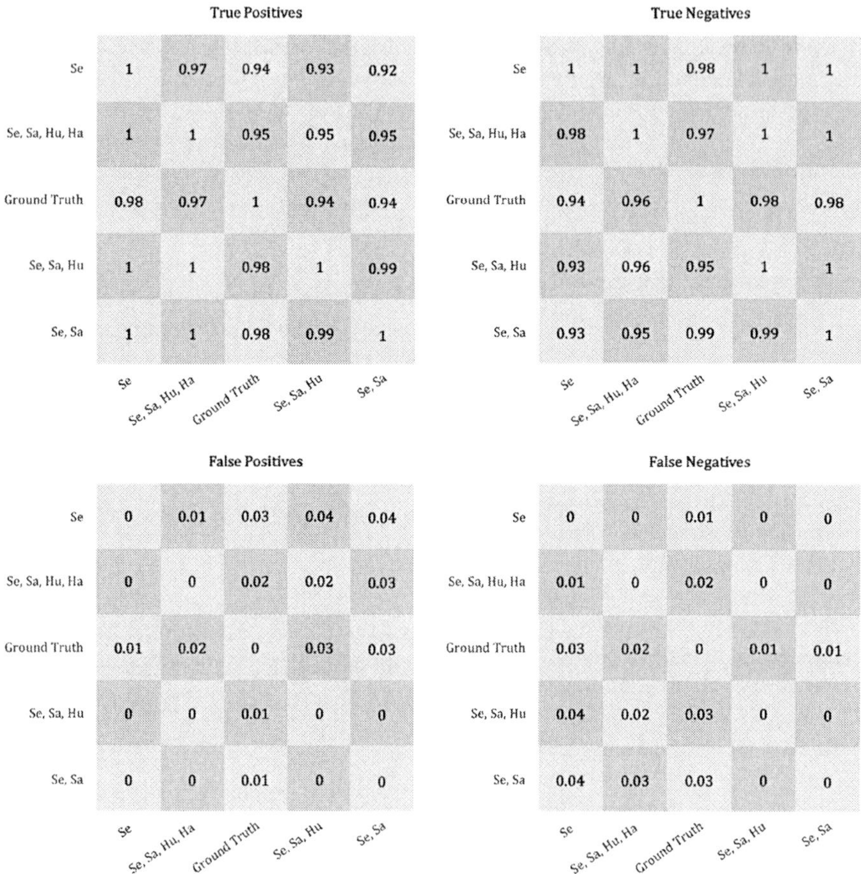

Figure 4: Overlap of model predictions with one another. Adding features from Sarcasm, Hate Speech, and Humour to baseline Sentiment classifier improves its ability to predict True Positives against the Ground Truth labels.

els.

This work shows that natural language understanding problems need not be thought of in isolation of each other. When motivated by human insights on how language is perceived, solutions to nuanced sub-problems might help solve more general problems like sentiment classification.

Future Directions

An interesting future direction is to test the combination of features from sarcasm, humor and hate speech for more fine-grained sentiment classification, as in Yelp (5-way classification) or Stanford Sentiment Treebank (5-way classification). We believe that our formulation would help in this case, by distinguishing between 1-star and 2-star reviews based on offensive language for instance.

It would also be interesting to see if the same generic template achieves state of the art performance on other classification tasks like entailment detection, entity detection, etc.

Acknowledgements

The authors would like to thank Prof Christopher Potts from Stanford NLP Group for valuable suggestions and discussion on experimental evaluation and analysis. The authors would like to thank Min Kim for his suggestions on the experimental setup and the paper writeup. The authors would also like to thank the authors of CNN sentence classification (Kim, 2014) for providing open-source implementations of their models which allowed us to bootstrap our research ideas.

References

Pinkesh Badjatiya, Shashank Gupta, Manish Gupta, and Vasudeva Varma. 2017. Deep learning for hate speech detection in tweets. *CoRR*, abs/1706.00188.

Peng-Yu Chen and Von-Wun Soo. 2018. Humor recognition using deep learning. In *Proceedings of the 2018 Conference of the North American Chapter of the Association for Computational Linguistics: Human Language Technologies, Volume 2 (Short Papers)*, pages 113–117, New Orleans, Louisiana. Association for Computational Linguistics.

Thomas Davidson, Dana Warmsley, Michael Macy, and Ingmar Weber. 2017. Automated hate speech detection and the problem of offensive language. In *Proceedings of the 11th International AAAI Conference on Web and Social Media*, ICWSM '17, pages 512–515.

Jacob Devlin, Ming-Wei Chang, Kenton Lee, and Kristina Toutanova. 2018. BERT: pre-training of deep bidirectional transformers for language understanding. *CoRR*, abs/1810.04805.

Ona de Gibert, Naiara Perez, Aitor García Pablos, and Montse Cuadros. 2018. Hate speech dataset from a white supremacy forum. In *Proceedings of the 2nd Workshop on Abusive Language Online (ALW2)*, pages 11–20, Brussels, Belgium. Association for Computational Linguistics.

Roberto González-Ibáñez, Smaranda Muresan, and Nina Wacholder. 2011. Identifying sarcasm in twitter: A closer look. In *Proceedings of the 49th Annual Meeting of the Association for Computational Linguistics: Human Language Technologies: Short Papers - Volume 2*, HLT '11, pages 581–586, Stroudsburg, PA, USA. Association for Computational Linguistics.

Devamanyu Hazarika, Soujanya Poria, Sruthi Gorantla, Erik Cambria, Roger Zimmermann, and Rada Mihalcea. 2018. CASCADE: Contextual sarcasm detection in online discussion forums. In *Proceedings of the 27th International Conference on Computational Linguistics*, pages 1837–1848, Santa Fe, New Mexico, USA. Association for Computational Linguistics.

Ruining He and Julian McAuley. 2016. Ups and downs: Modeling the visual evolution of fashion trends with one-class collaborative filtering. In *proceedings of the 25th international conference on world wide web*, pages 507–517. International World Wide Web Conferences Steering Committee.

Zhiting Hu, Zichao Yang, Xiaodan Liang, Ruslan Salakhutdinov, and Eric P Xing. 2017. Toward controlled generation of text. In *Proceedings of the 34th International Conference on Machine Learning-Volume 70*, pages 1587–1596. JMLR. org.

Mikhail Khodak, Nikunj Saunshi, and Kiran Vodrahalli. 2017. A large self-annotated corpus for sarcasm. *CoRR*, abs/1704.05579.

Yoon Kim. 2014. Convolutional neural networks for sentence classification. *CoRR*, abs/1408.5882.

Y. Alex Kolchinski and Christopher Potts. 2018. Representing social media users for sarcasm detection. *CoRR*, abs/1808.08470.

Mika Viking Mäntylä, Daniel Graziotin, and Miikka Kuutila. 2016. The evolution of sentiment analysis - A review of research topics, venues, and top cited papers. *CoRR*, abs/1612.01556.

Soujanya Poria, Erik Cambria, Devamanyu Hazarika, and Prateek Vij. 2016. A deeper look into sarcastic tweets using deep convolutional neural networks. *CoRR*, abs/1610.08815.

Ashish Vaswani, Noam Shazeer, Niki Parmar, Jakob Uszkoreit, Llion Jones, Aidan N. Gomez, Lukasz Kaiser, and Illia Polosukhin. 2017. Attention is all you need. *CoRR*, abs/1706.03762.

Robert West, Hristo S. Paskov, Jure Leskovec, and Christopher Potts. 2014. Exploiting social network structure for person-to-person sentiment analysis. *CoRR*, abs/1409.2450.

Qizhe Xie, Zihang Dai, Eduard Hovy, Minh-Thang Luong, and Quoc V Le. 2019. Unsupervised data augmentation. *arXiv preprint arXiv:1904.12848*.

Zhilin Yang, Zihang Dai, Yiming Yang, Jaime G. Carbonell, Ruslan Salakhutdinov, and Quoc V. Le. 2019. Xlnet: Generalized autoregressive pretraining for language understanding. *CoRR*, abs/1906.08237.

Xiang Zhang, Junbo Zhao, and Yann LeCun. 2015. Character-level convolutional networks for text classification. In *Advances in neural information processing systems*, pages 649–657.

Grammatical Error Correction in Low-Resource Scenarios

Jakub Náplava and **Milan Straka**
Charles University,
Faculty of Mathematics and Physics,
Institute of Formal and Applied Linguistics
`{naplava,straka}@ufal.mff.cuni.cz`

Abstract

Grammatical error correction in English is a long studied problem with many existing systems and datasets. However, there has been only a limited research on error correction of other languages. In this paper, we present a new dataset AKCES-GEC on grammatical error correction for Czech. We then make experiments on Czech, German and Russian and show that when utilizing synthetic parallel corpus, Transformer neural machine translation model can reach new state-of-the-art results on these datasets. AKCES-GEC is published under CC BY-NC-SA 4.0 license at `http://hdl.handle.net/11234/1-3057`, and the source code of the GEC model is available at `https://github.com/ufal/low-resource-gec-wnut2019`.

1 Introduction

A great progress has been recently achieved in grammatical error correction (GEC) in English. The performance of systems has since CoNLL 2014 shared task (Ng et al., 2014) increased by more than 60% on its test set (Bryant et al., 2019) and also a variety of new datasets appeared. Both rule-based models, single error-type classifiers and their combinations were due to larger amount of data surpassed by statistical and later by neural machine translation systems. These address GEC as a translation problem from a language of ungrammatical sentences to a grammatically correct ones.

Machine translation systems require large amount of data for training. To cope with this issue, different approaches were explored, from acquiring additional corpora (e.g. from Wikipedia edits) to building a synthetic corpus from clean monolingual data. This was apparent on recent Building Educational Applications (BEA) 2019 Shared Task on GEC (Bryant et al., 2019) when top scoring teams extensively utilized synthetic corpora.

The majority of research has been done in English. Unfortunately, there is a limited progress on other languages. Namely, Boyd (2018) created a dataset and presented a GEC system for German, Rozovskaya and Roth (2019) for Russian, Náplava (2017) for Czech and efforts to create annotated learner corpora were also done for Chinese (Yu et al., 2014), Japanese (Mizumoto et al., 2011) and Arabic (Zaghouani et al., 2015).

Our contributions are as follows:

- We introduce a new Czech dataset for GEC. In comparison to dataset of Šebesta et al. (2017) it contains separated edits together with their type annotations in M2 format (Dahlmeier and Ng, 2012) and also has two times more sentences.
- We extend the GEC model of Náplava and Straka (2019) by utilizing synthetic training data, and evaluate it on Czech, German and Russian, achieving state-of-the-art results.

2 Related Work

There are several main approaches to GEC in *low-resource* scenarios. The first one is based on a noisy channel model and consists of three components: a candidate model to propose (word) alternatives, an error model to score their likelihood and a language model to score both candidate (word) probability and probability of a whole new sentence. Richter et al. (2012) consider for a given word all its small modifications (up to character edit distance 2) present in a morphological dictionary. The error model weights every character edit by a trained weight, and three language models (for word forms, lemmas and POS tags) are used to choose the most probable sequence of corrections. A candidate model of Bryant and Briscoe

Proceedings of the 2019 EMNLP Workshop W-NUT: The 5th Workshop on Noisy User-generated Text, pages 346–356
Hong Kong, Nov 4, 2019. ©2019 Association for Computational Linguistics

(2018) contains for each word spell-checker proposals, its morphological variants (if found in Automatically Generated Inflection Database) and, if the word is either preposition or article, also a set of predefined alternatives. They assign uniform probability to all changes, but use strong language model to re-rank all candidate sentences. Lacroix et al. (2019) also consider single word edits extracted from Wikipedia revisions.

Other popular approach is to extract parallel sentences from Wikipedia revision histories. A great advantage of such an approach is that the resulting corpus is, especially for English, of great size. However, as Wikipedia edits are not human curated specifically for GEC edits, the corpus is extremely noisy. Grundkiewicz and Junczys-Dowmunt (2014) filter this corpus by a set of regular expressions derived from NUCLE training data and report a performance boost in statistical machine translation approach. Grundkiewicz et al. (2019) filter Wikipedia edits by a simple language model trained on BEA 2019 development corpus. Lichtarge et al. (2019), on the other hand, reports that even without any sophisticated filtering, Transformer (Vaswani et al., 2017) can reach surprisingly good results when used iteratively.

The third approach is to create synthetic corpus from a clean monolingual corpus and use it as additional data for training. Noise is typically introduced either by rule-based substitutions or by using a subset of the following operations: token replacement, token deletion, token insertion, multi-token swap and spelling noise introduction. Yuan and Felice (2013) extract edits from NUCLE and apply them on a clean text. Choe et al. (2019) apply edits from W&I+Locness training set and also define manual noising scenarios for preposition, nouns and verbs. Zhao et al. (2019) use an unsupervised approach to synthesize noisy sentences and allow deleting a word, inserting a random word, replacing a word with random word and also shuffling (rather locally). Grundkiewicz et al. (2019) improve this approach and replace a token with one of its spell-checker suggestions. They also introduce additional spelling noise.

3   Data

In this Section, we present existing corpora for GEC, together with newly released corpus for Czech.

3.1   AKCES-GEC

The AKCES (Czech Language Acquisition Corpora; Šebesta, 2010) is an umbrella project comprising of several acquisition resources – CzeSL (learner corpus of Czech as a second language), ROMi (Romani ethnolect of Czech Romani children and teenagers) and SKRIPT and SCHOLA (written and spoken language collected from native Czech pupils, respectively).

We present the AKCES-GEC dataset, which is a grammar error correction corpus for Czech generated from a subset of AKCES resources. Concretely, the AKCES-GEC dataset is based on CzeSL-man corpus (Rosen, 2016) consisting of manually annotated transcripts of essays of non-native speakers of Czech. Apart from the released CzeSL-man, AKCES-GEC further utilizes additional unreleased parts of CzeSL-man and also essays of Romani pupils with Romani ethnolect of Czech as their first language.

The CzeSL-man annotation consists of three Tiers – Tier 0 are transcribed inputs, followed by the level of orthographic and morphemic corrections, where only word forms incorrect in any context are considered (Tier 1). Finally, the rest of errors is annotated at Tier 2. Forms at different Tiers are manually aligned and can be assigned one or more error types (Jelínek et al., 2012). An example of the annotation is presented in Figure 1, and the list of error types used in CzeSL-man annotation is listed in Table 1.

We generated AKCES-GEC dataset using the three Tier annotation of the underlying corpus. We employed Tier 0 as source texts, Tier 2 as corrected texts, and created error edits according to the manual alignments, keeping error annotations where available.[1] Considering that the M2 format (Dahlmeier and Ng, 2012) we wanted to use does not support non-local error edits and therefore cannot efficiently encode word transposition on long distances, we decided to consider word swaps over at most 2 correct words a single edit (with the constant 2 chosen according to the coverage of long-range transpositions in the data). For illustration, see Figure 2.

The AKCES-GEC dataset consists of an explicit train/development/test split, with each set divided into foreigner and Romani students; for de-

---

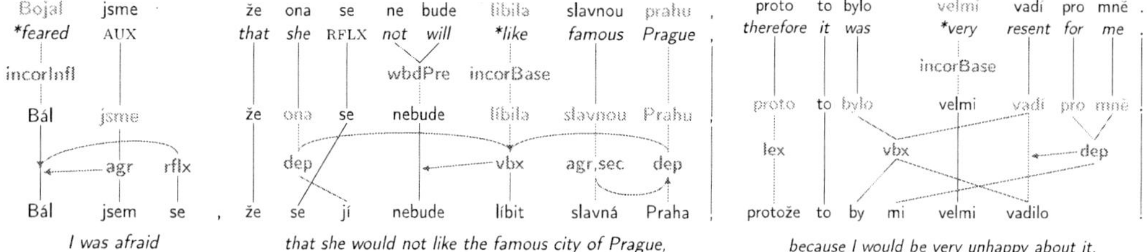

Figure 1: Example of two-level annotation of a sentence in CzeSL corpus, reproduced from (Rosen, 2016).

Figure 2: Word swap over one or two correct words (on the left) is considered a single edit (A B C→ C A B). Word swap over more than two correct words (on the right) is represented as two edits of deleting D and inserting D.

Error type	Description	Example	Occ
incorInfl	incorrect inflection	[**pracovají** → *pracují*] v továrně	8 986
incorBase	incorrect word base	musíš to [**posvětlit** → *posvětit*]	20 334
fwFab	non-emendable, „fabricated" word	pokud nechceš slyšet [**smášky**]	78
fwNC	foreign word	váza je na [**Tisch** → *stole*]	166
flex	supplementary flag used with fwFab and fwNC marking the presence of inflection	jdu do [**shopa** → *obchodu*]	34
wbdPre	prefix separated by a space or preposition w/o space	musím to [**při pravit** → *připravit*]	817
wbdComp	wrongly separated compound	[**český anglický** → *česko-anglický*] slovník	92
wbdOther	other word boundary error	[**mocdobře** → *moc dobře*]; [**atak** → *a tak*]	1326
stylColl	colloquial form	[**dobrej** → *dobrý*] film	3 533
stylOther	bookish, dialectal, slang, hyper-correct form	holka s [**hnědými očimi** → *hnědýma očima*]	156
agr	violated agreement rules	to jsou [**hezké** → *hezcí*] chlapci; Jana [**čtu** → *čte*]	5 162
dep	error in valency	bojí se [**pes** → *psa*]; otázka [**čas** → *času*]	6 733
ref	error in pronominal reference	dal jsem to jemu i [**jejího** → *jeho*] bratrovi	344
vbx	error in analytical verb form or compound predicate	musíš [**přijdeš** → *přijít*]; kluci [**jsou**] běhali	864
rflx	error in reflexive expression	dívá [∅ → *se*] na televizi; Pavel [**si** → *se*] raduje	915
neg	error in negation	[**půjdu ne** → *nepůjdu*] do školy	111
lex	error in lexicon or phraseology	dopadlo to [**přírodně** → *přirozeně*]	3 967
use	error in the use of a grammar category	pošta je [**nejvíc blízko** → *nejblíže*]	1 458
sec	secondary error (supplementary flag)	stará se o [**našich holčičkách** → *naše holčičky*]	866
stylColl	colloquial expression	viděli jsme [**hezký** → *hezké*] holky	3 533
stylOther	bookish, dialectal, slang, hyper-correct expression	rozbil se mi [**hadr**]	156
stylMark	redundant discourse marker	[**no**]; [**teda**]; [**jo**]	15
disr	disrupted construction	známe [**hodné spoustu** → *spoustu hodných*] lidí	64
problem	supplementary label for problematic cases		175
unspec	unspecified error type		69 123

Table 1: Error types used in CzeSL corpus taken from (Jelínek et al., 2012), including number of occurrences in the dataset being released. Tier 1 errors are in the upper part of the table, Tier 2 errors are in the lower part. The *stylColl* and *stylOther* are annotated on both Tiers, but we do not distinguish on which one in the AKCES-GEC.

velopment and test sets, the foreigners are further split into Slavic and non-Slavic speakers. Furthermore, the development and test sets were annotated by two annotators, so we provide two references if the annotators utilized the same sentence segmentation and produced different annotations.

The detailed statistics of the dataset are presented in Table 2. The AKCES-GEC dataset is released under the CC BY-NC-SA 4.0 license at

```
http://hdl.handle.net/11234/1-3057.
```

We note that there already exists a CzeSL-GEC dataset (Šebesta et al., 2017). However, it consists only of a subset of data and does not contain error types nor M2 files with individual edits.

3.2 English

Probably the largest corpus for English GEC is the Lang-8 Corpus of Learner English (Mizumoto

		Train				Dev				Test		
		Doc	Sent	Word	Error r.	Doc	Sent	Word	Error r.	Doc	Sent	Word	Error r.
Foreign.	Slavic	1 816	27 242	289 439	22.2 %	70	1 161	14 243	21.8 %	69	1 255	14 984	18.8 %
	Other					45	804	8 331	23.8 %	45	879	9 624	20.5 %
Romani		1 937	14 968	157 342	20.4 %	80	520	5 481	21.0 %	74	542	5 831	17.8 %
Total		3 753	42 210	446 781	21.5 %	195	2 485	28 055	22.2 %	188	2 676	30 439	19.1 %

Table 2: Statistics of the AKCES-GEC dataset – number of documents, sentences, words and error rates.

et al., 2011; Tajiri et al., 2012). It comes from an online language learning website, where users are able to post texts in language they are learning. These texts then appear to native speakers for correction. The corpus has over 100 000 raw English entries comprising of more than 1M sentences. Due to the fact that texts are corrected by online users, this corpus is also quite noisy.

Other corpora are corrected by trained annotators making them much cleaner but also significantly smaller. NUCLE (Dahlmeier et al., 2013) has 57 151 sentences originating from 1 400 essays written by mainly Asian undergraduate students at the National University of Singapore. FCE (Yannakoudakis et al., 2011) is a subset of the Cambridge Learner Corpus (CLC) and has 33 236 sentences from 1 244 written answers to FCE exam questions. Recent Write & Improve (W&I) and LOCNESS v2.1 (Bryant et al., 2019; Granger, 1998) datasets were annotated for different English proficiency levels and a part of them also comes from texts written by native English speakers. Altogether, it has 43 169 sentences.

To evaluate system performance, CoNLL-2014 test set is most commonly used. It comprises of 1 312 sentences written by 25 South-East Asian undergraduates. The gold annotations are matched against system hypothesis using MaxMatch scorer outputting $F_{0.5}$ score. The other frequently used dataset is JFLEG (Napoles et al., 2017; Heilman et al., 2014), which also tests systems for how fluent they sound by utilizing the GLEU metric (Napoles et al., 2015). Finally, recent W&I and LOCNESS v2.1 test set allows to evaluate systems on different levels of proficiency and also against different error types (utilizing ERRANT scorer).

3.3 German

Boyd (2018) created GEC corpus for German from two German learner corpora: Falko and MERLIN (Boyd et al., 2014). The resulting dataset comprises of 24 077 sentences divided into training, development and test set in the ratio of 80:10:10. To evaluate system performance, MaxMatch scorer is used.

Apart from creating the dataset, Boyd (2018) also extended ERRANT for German. She defined 21 error types (15 based on POS tags) and extended spaCy[2] pipeline to classify them.

3.4 Russian

Rozovskaya and Roth (2019) introduced RULEC-GEC dataset for Russian GEC. To create this dataset, a subset of RULEC corpus with foreign and heritage speakers was corrected. The final dataset has 12 480 sentences annotated with 23 error tags. The training, development and test sets contain 4 980, 2 500 and 5 000 sentence pairs, respectively.

3.5 Corpora Statistics

Table 3 indicates that there is a variety of English datasets for GEC. As Náplava and Straka (2019) show, training Transformer solely using these annotated data gives solid results. On the other hand, there is only limited number of data for Czech, German and Russian and also the existing systems perform substantially worse. This motivates our research in these low-resource languages.

Table 3 also presents an average error rate of each corpus. It is computed using maximum alignment of original and annotated sentences as a ratio of non-matching alignment edges (insertion, deletion, and replacement). The highest error rate of 21.4 % is on Czech dataset. This implies that circa every fifth word contains an error. German is also quite noisy with an error rate of 16.8 %. The average error rate on English ranges from 6.6 % to 14.1 % and, finally, the Russian corpus contains the least errors with an average error rate of 6.4%.

---

[2] https://spacy.io/

Language	Corpus	Sentences	Err. r.
English	Lang-8	1 147 451	14.1%
	NUCLE	57 151	6.6%
	FCE	33 236	11.5%
	W&I+LOCNESS	43 169	11.8%
Czech	AKCES-GEC	42 210	21.4%
German	Falko-MERLIN	24 077	16.8%
Russian	RULEC-GEC	12 480	6.4%

Table 3: Statistics of available corpora for Grammatical Error Correction.

3.6 Tokenization

The most popular metric for benchmarking systems are MaxMatch scorer (Dahlmeier and Ng, 2012) and ERRANT scorer (Bryant et al., 2017). They both require data to be tokenized; therefore, most of the GEC datasets are tokenized.

To tokenize monolingual English and German data, we use spaCy v1.9.0 tokenizer utilizing *en_core_web_sm-1.2.0* and *de* model. We use custom tokenizers for Czech[3] and Russian[4].

4 System Overview

We use neural machine translation approach to GEC. Specifically, we utilize Transformer model (Vaswani et al., 2017) to translate ungrammatical sentences to grammatically correct ones. We further follow Náplava and Straka (2019) and employ source and target word dropouts, edit-weighted MLE and checkpoint averaging. We do not use iterative decoding in this work, because it substantially slows down decoding. Our models are implemented in Tensor2Tensor framework version 1.12.0.[5]

4.1 Pretraining on Synthetic Dataset

Due to the limited number of annotated data in Czech, German and Russian we decided to create a corpus of synthetic parallel sentences. We were also motivated by the fact that such approach was shown to improve performance even in English with substantially more annotated training data.

We follow Grundkiewicz et al. (2019), who use an unsupervised approach to create noisy input sentences. Given a clean sentence, they sample a probability p_{err_word} from a normal distribution with a predefined mean and a standard de-

viation. After multiplying p_{err_word} by a number of words in the sentence, as many sentence words are selected for modification. For each chosen word, one of the following operations is performed with a predefined probability: substituting the word with one of its ASpell[6] proposals, deleting it, swapping it with its right-adjacent neighbour or inserting a random word from dictionary after the current word. To make the system more robust to spelling errors, same operations are also used on individual characters with p_{err_char} sampled from a normal distribution with a different mean and standard deviation than p_{err_word} and (potentially) different probabilities of character operations.

When we inspected the results of a model trained on such dataset in Czech, we observed that the model often fails to correct casing errors and sometimes also errors in diacritics. Therefore, we extend word-level operations to also contain operation to change casing of a word. If a word is chosen for modification, it is with 50% probability whole converted to lower-case, or several individual characters are chosen and their casing is inverted. To increase the number of errors in diacritics, we add a new character-level noising operation, which for a selected character either generates one of its possible diacritized variants or removes diacritics. Note that this operation is performed only in Czech.

We generate synthetic corpus for each language from WMT News Crawl monolingual training data (Bojar et al., 2017). We set p_{err_word} to 0.15, p_{err_char} to 0.02 and estimate error distributions of individual operations from development sets of each language. The constants used are presented in Table 4. We limited amount of synthetic sentences to 10M in each language.

4.2 Finetuning

A model is (pre-)trained on a synthetic dataset until convergence. Afterwards, we finetune the model on a mix of original language training data and synthetic data. When finetuning the model, we preserve all hyperparameters (e.g., learning rate and optimizer moments). In other words, the training continues and only the data are replaced.

When finetuning, we found that it is crucial to preserve some portion of synthetic data in the training corpus. Finetuning with original training

---

[3] A slight modification of MorphoDiTa tokenizer.
[4] https://github.com/aatimofeev/spacy_russian_tokenizer
[5] https://github.com/tensorflow/tensor2tensor

[6] http://aspell.net/

Language	Token-level operations					Character-level operations				
	sub	ins	del	swap	recase	sub	ins	del	recase	toggle diacritics
English	0.6	0.2	0.1	0.05	0.05	0.25	0.25	0.25	0.25	0
Czech	0.7	0.1	0.05	0.1	0.05	0.2	0.2	0.2	0.2	0.2
German	0.64	0.2	0.1	0.01	0.05	0.25	0.25	0.25	0.25	0
Russian	0.65	0.1	0.1	0.1	0.05	0.25	0.25	0.25	0.25	0

Table 4: Language specific constants for token- and character-level noising operations.

data leads to fast overfitting with worse results on all of Czech, German and Russian. We also found out that it also slightly helps on English.

We ran a small grid-search to estimate the ratio of synthetic versus original sentences in the finetuning phase. Although the ratio of 1:2 (5M original oversampled training pairs and 10M synthetic pairs) still overfits, we found it to work best for English, Czech and German, and stop training when the performance on the development set starts deteriorating. For Russian, the ratio of 1:20 (0.5M oversampled training pairs and 10M synthetic pairs) works the best.

The original sentences for English finetuning are concatenated sentences from Lang-8 Corpus of Learner English, FCE, NUCLE and W&I and LOCNESS. To better match domain of test data, we oversampled training set by adding W&I training data 10 times, FCE data 5 times and NUCLE corpus 5 times to the training set. The original sentences in Czech, German and Russian are the training data of the corresponding languages.

4.3 Implementation Details

When running grid search for hyperparameter tuning, we use *transformer_base_single_gpu* configuration, which uses only 1 GPU to train *Transformer Base* model. After we select all hyperparameter, we train *Transformer Big* architecture on 4 GPUs. Hyperparameters described in following paragraphs belong to both architectures.

We use Adafactor optimizer (Shazeer and Stern, 2018), linearly increasing the learning rate from 0 to 0.011 over the first 8000 steps, then decrease it proportionally to the number of steps after that (using the `rsqrt_decay` schedule). Note that this only applies to the pre-training phase.

All systems are trained on Nvidia P5000 GPUs. The vocabulary consists of approximately 32k most common word-pieces, the batch size is 2000 word-pieces per each GPU and all sentences with more than 150 word-pieces are discarded during training. Model checkpoints are saved every hour.

At evaluation time, we decode using a beam size of 4. Beam-search length-balance decoding hyperparameter alpha is set to 0.6.

5 Results

We present results of our model when trained on English, Czech, German and Russian in this Section. As we are aware of only one system in German, Czech and Russian to compare with, we start with English model discussion. We show that our model is on par or even slightly better than current state-of-the-art systems in English when no ensembles are allowed. We then discuss our results on other languages, where our system exceeds all existing systems by a large margin.

In all experiments, we report results of three systems: *synthetic pretrain*, which is based on Transformer Big and is trained using synthetic data only, and *finetuned* and *finetuned base single GPU*, which are based on Transformer Big and Base, respectively, and are both pretrained and finetuned. Note that even if the *finetuned base* system has 3 times less parameters than *finetuned*, its results on some languages are nearly identical.

We also tried training the system using annotated data only. With our model architecture, all but English experiments (which contain substantially more data) starts overfitting quickly, yielding poor performance. The overfitting problem could be possibly addressed as proposed by Sennrich and Zhang (2019). Nevertheless, given that our best system on English is by circa 10 points in $F_{0.5}$ score better than the system trained solely on annotated data, we focused primarily on the synthetic data experiments.

Apart from the W&I+L development and test sets, which are evaluated using ERRANT scorer, we use MaxMatch scorer in all experiments.

System	W&I+L test	W&I+L dev	CoNLL 14 test	
			No W&I+L	With W&I+L
including ensembles				
Lichtarge et al. (2019)	–	–	60.40	–
Zhao et al. (2019)	–	–	61.15	–
Xu et al. (2019)	67.21	55.37	–	63.20
Choe et al. (2019)	69.06	52.79	57.50	–
Grundkiewicz et al. (2019)	**69.47**	53.00	**61.30**	**64.16**
no ensembles				
Lichtarge et al. (2019)	–	–	**56.80**	–
Xu et al. (2019)	**63.94**	52.29	–	60.90
Choe et al. (2019)	63.05	47.75	–	–
Grundkiewicz et al. (2019)	–	50.01	–	–
no ensembles				
Our work – synthetic pretrain	51.16	32.76	41.85	44.12
Our work – finetuned base single GPU	67.18	52.80	59.87	–
Our work – finetuned	69.00	53.30	60.76	63.40

Table 5: Comparison of systems on two English GEC datasets. CoNLL 2014 Test Set is divided into two system groups (columns): those who do not train on W&I+L training data and those who do.

System	P	R	$F_{0.5}$
Boyd (2018)	51.99	29.73	45.22
Our work – synthetic pretrain	67.45	26.35	51.41
Our work – finetuned base single GPU	78.11	59.13	73.40
Our work – finetuned	78.21	59.94	73.71

Table 6: Results on on Falko-Merlin Test Set (German).

5.1 English

We provide comparison between our model and existing systems on W&I+L test and development sets and on CoNLL 14 test set in Table 5. Even if the results on the W&I+L development set are only partially indicative of system performance, we report them due to the W&I+L test set being blind. All mentioned papers do not train their systems on the development set, but use it only for model selection. Also note that we split the results on CoNLL 14 test set into two groups: those who do not use the W&I+L data for training, and those who do. This is to allow a fair comparison, given that the W&I+L data were not available before the BEA 2019 Shared Task on GEC.

The best performing systems are utilizing ensembles. Table 5 shows an evident performance boost (3.27-6.01 points) when combining multiple models into an ensemble. The best performing system on English is an ensemble system of Grundkiewicz et al. (2019).

The aim of this paper is to concentrate on low-resource languages rather than on English. Therefore, we report results of our single model. Despite that our best system reaches 69.0 $F_{0.5}$ score, which is comparable to the performance of best systems that employ ensembles. Although Grundkiewicz et al. (2019) do not report their single system score, we can hypothesise that given development set scores, our system is on par with theirs or even performs slightly better.

Note that there is a significant difference between results reported on W&I+L dev and W&I+L test sets. This is caused by the fact that each sentence in the W&I+L test set was annotated by 10 annotators, while there is only a single annotator for each sentence in the development set.

5.2 German

Boyd (2018) developed a GEC system for German based on multilayer convolutional encoder-decoder neural network (Chollampatt and Ng, 2018). To account for the lack of annotated

System	Test Subset	P	R	$F_{0.5}$
Richter et al. (2012)	All	68.72	36.75	58.54
Our work – synthetic pretrain	All	80.32	39.55	66.59
Our work – finetuned base single GPU	All	84.21	66.67	80.00
Our work – finetuned	Foreigners – Slavic	84.34	71.55	81.43
	Foreigners – Other	81.03	62.36	76.45
	Romani	86.61	71.13	83.00
	All	83.75	68.48	80.17

Table 7: Results on on AKCES-GEC Test Set (Czech).

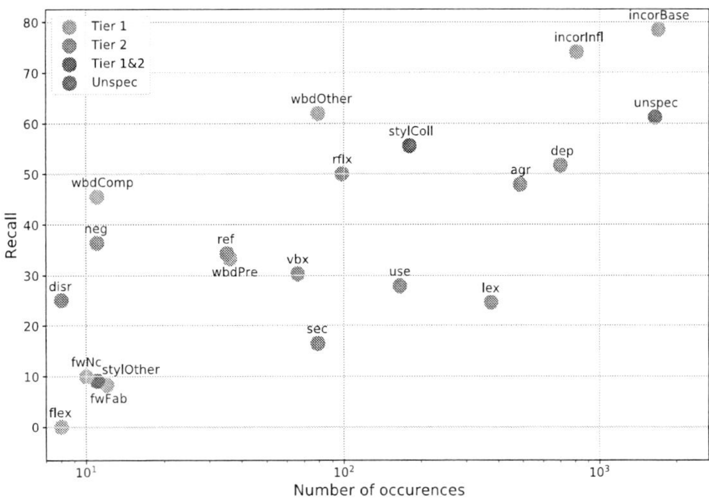

Figure 3: Recall for each error type in the test set of AKCES-GEC, computed using the first annotator (ID 0).

data, she generated additional training data from Wikipedia edits, which she filtered to match the distribution of the original error types. As Table 6 shows, her best system reaches 45.22 $F_{0.5}$ score on Falko-Merlin test set. All our three systems outperform it.

Compared to Boyd (2018), our system trained solely on synthetic data has lower recall, but substantially higher precision. The main reason behind the lower recall is the unsupervised approach to synthetic data generation. Both our finetuned models outperform Boyd (2018) system by a large margin.

5.3 Czech

We compare our system with Richter et al. (2012), who developed a statistical spelling corrector for Czech. Although their system can only make local changes (e.g., cannot insert a new word or swap two nearby words), it achieves surprisingly solid results. Nevertheless, all our three system perform

better in both precision, recall and $F_{0.5}$ score. Possibly due to already quite high precision of the pretrained model, the finetuning stage improves mainly model recall.

We also evaluate performance of our best system on three subsets of the AKCES-GEC test set: Foreigners–Slavic, Foreigners–Other and Romani. As the name suggests, the first of them is a part of AKCES-GEC collected from essays of non-Czech Slavic people, the second from essays of non-Czech non-Slavic people and finally Romani comes from essays of Romani pupils with Romani ethnolect of Czech as their first language. The best result is reached on Romani subset, while on Foreigners–Other the $F_{0.5}$ score is by more than 6 points lower. We hypothesize this effect is caused by the fact, that Czech is the primary language of Romani pupils. Furthermore, we presume that foreigners with Slavic background should learn Czech faster than non-Slavic foreigners, because of the similarity between their mother tongue and

System	P	R	$F_{0.5}$
Rozovskaya and Roth (2019)	38.0	7.5	21.0
Our work – synthetic pretrain	47.76	26.08	40.96
Our work – finetuned base single GPU	59.13	26.05	47.15
Our work – finetuned	63.26	27.50	50.20

Table 8: Results on on RULEC-GEC Test Set (Russian).

Czech. This fact is supported by Table 2, which shows that the average error rate of Romani development set is 21.0%, Foreigners–Slavic 21.8% and the Foreigners–Other 23.8%.

Finally, we report recall of the best system on each error type annotated by the first annotator (ID 0) in Figure 3. Generally, our system performs better on errors annotated on Tier 1 than on errors annotated on Tier 2. Furthermore, a natural hypothesis is that the more occurrences there are for an error type, the better the recall of the system on the particular error type. Figure 3 suggests that this hypothesis seems plausible on Tier 1 errors, but its validity is unclear on Tier 2.

5.4 Russian

As Table 8 indicates, GEC in Russian currently seems to be the most challenging task. Although our system outperforms the system of Rozovskaya and Roth (2019) by more than 100% in $F_{0.5}$ score, its performance is still quite poor when compared to all previously described languages. Because the result of our system trained solely on synthetic data is comparable with the similar system for English, we hypothesise that the main reason behind these poor results is the small amount of annotated training data – while Czech has 42 210 and German 19 237 training sentence pairs, there are only 4 980 sentences in the Russian training set. To validate this hypothesis, we extended the original training set by 2 000 sentences from the development set, resulting in an increase of 3 percent points in $F_{0.5}$ score.

6 Conclusion

We presented a new dataset for grammatical error correction in Czech. It contains almost twice as much sentences as existing German dataset and more than three times as RULEC-GEC for Russian. The dataset is published in M2 format containing both separated edits and their error types.

Furthermore, we performed experiments on three low-resource languages: German, Russian and Czech. For each language, we pretrained Transformer model on synthetic data and finetuned it with a mixture of synthetic and authentic data. On all three languages, the performance of our system is substantially higher than results of the existing reported systems. Moreover, all our models supersede reported systems even if only pretrained on unsupervised synthetic data.

The performance of our system could be even higher if we trained multiple models and combined them into an ensemble. We plan to do that in future work. We also plan to extend our synthetic corpora with data modified by supervisedly extracted rules. We hope that this could help especially in case of Russian, which has the lowest amount of training data.

Acknowledgments

The work described herein has been supported by OP VVV VI LINDAT/CLARIN project (CZ.02.1.01/0.0/0.0/16_013/0001781) and it has been supported and has been using language resources developed by the LINDAT/CLARIN project (LM2015071) of the Ministry of Education, Youth and Sports of the Czech Republic. This research was also partially supported by SVV project number 260 453, GAUK 578218 of the Charles University and FP7-ICT-2010-6-257528 (MŠMT 7E11042).

References

Ondřej Bojar, Chatterjee Rajen, Christian Federmann, Yvette Graham, Barry Haddow, Huck Matthias, Koehn Philipp, Liu Qun, Logacheva Varvara, Monz Christof, et al. 2017. Findings of the 2017 conference on machine translation (wmt17). In *Second Conference onMachine Translation*, pages 169–214. The Association for Computational Linguistics.

Adriane Boyd. 2018. Using wikipedia edits in low resource grammatical error correction. In *Proceedings of the 2018 EMNLP Workshop W-NUT: The 4th Workshop on Noisy User-generated Text*, pages 79–84.

Adriane Boyd, Jirka Hana, Lionel Nicolas, Detmar Meurers, Katrin Wisniewski, Andrea Abel, Karin Schöne, Barbora Stindlová, and Chiara Vettori. 2014. The merlin corpus: Learner language and the cefr. In *LREC*, pages 1281–1288.

Christopher Bryant and Ted Briscoe. 2018. Language model based grammatical error correction without annotated training data. In *Proceedings of the Thirteenth Workshop on Innovative Use of NLP for Building Educational Applications*, pages 247–253.

Christopher Bryant, Mariano Felice, Øistein E Andersen, and Ted Briscoe. 2019. The bea-2019 shared task on grammatical error correction. In *Proceedings of the Fourteenth Workshop on Innovative Use of NLP for Building Educational Applications*, pages 52–75.

Christopher Bryant, Mariano Felice, and Edward John Briscoe. 2017. Automatic annotation and evaluation of error types for grammatical error correction. Association for Computational Linguistics.

Yo Joong Choe, Jiyeon Ham, Kyubyong Park, and Yeoil Yoon. 2019. A neural grammatical error correction system built on better pre-training and sequential transfer learning. *arXiv preprint arXiv:1907.01256*.

Shamil Chollampatt and Hwee Tou Ng. 2018. A multi-layer convolutional encoder-decoder neural network for grammatical error correction. In *Proceedings of the Thirty-Second AAAI Conference on Artificial Intelligence*.

Daniel Dahlmeier and Hwee Tou Ng. 2012. Better evaluation for grammatical error correction. In *Proceedings of the 2012 Conference of the North American Chapter of the Association for Computational Linguistics: Human Language Technologies*, pages 568–572. Association for Computational Linguistics.

Daniel Dahlmeier, Hwee Tou Ng, and Siew Mei Wu. 2013. Building a large annotated corpus of learner english: The nus corpus of learner english. In *Proceedings of the eighth workshop on innovative use of NLP for building educational applications*, pages 22–31.

Sylviane Granger. 1998. The computer learner corpus: A versatile new source of data for SLA research. In Sylviane Granger, editor, *Learner English on Computer*, pages 3–18. Addison Wesley Longman, London and New York.

Roman Grundkiewicz and Marcin Junczys-Dowmunt. 2014. The wiked error corpus: A corpus of corrective wikipedia edits and its application to grammatical error correction. In *International Conference on Natural Language Processing*, pages 478–490. Springer.

Roman Grundkiewicz, Marcin Junczys-Dowmunt, and Kenneth Heafield. 2019. Neural grammatical error correction systems with unsupervised pre-training on synthetic data. In *Proceedings of the Fourteenth Workshop on Innovative Use of NLP for Building Educational Applications*, pages 252–263.

Michael Heilman, Aoife Cahill, Nitin Madnani, Melissa Lopez, Matthew Mulholland, and Joel Tetreault. 2014. Predicting grammaticality on an ordinal scale. In *Proceedings of the 52nd Annual Meeting of the Association for Computational Linguistics (Volume 2: Short Papers)*, pages 174–180, Baltimore, Maryland. Association for Computational Linguistics.

Tomáš Jelínek, Barbora Štindlová, Alexandr Rosen, and Jirka Hana. 2012. Combining manual and automatic annotation of a learner corpus. In *Text, Speech and Dialogue*, pages 127–134, Berlin, Heidelberg. Springer Berlin Heidelberg.

Ophélie Lacroix, Simon Flachs, and Anders Søgaard. 2019. Noisy channel for low resource grammatical error correction. In *Proceedings of the Fourteenth Workshop on Innovative Use of NLP for Building Educational Applications*, pages 191–196.

Jared Lichtarge, Chris Alberti, Shankar Kumar, Noam Shazeer, Niki Parmar, and Simon Tong. 2019. Corpora generation for grammatical error correction. *arXiv preprint arXiv:1904.05780*.

Tomoya Mizumoto, Mamoru Komachi, Masaaki Nagata, and Yuji Matsumoto. 2011. Mining revision log of language learning sns for automated japanese error correction of second language learners. In *Proceedings of 5th International Joint Conference on Natural Language Processing*, pages 147–155.

Jakub Náplava. 2017. Natural language correction. Diploma thesis, Univerzita Karlova, Matematicko-fyzikální fakulta.

Jakub Náplava and Milan Straka. 2019. Cuni system for the building educational applications 2019 shared task: Grammatical error correction. In *Proceedings of the Fourteenth Workshop on Innovative Use of NLP for Building Educational Applications*, pages 183–190.

Courtney Napoles, Keisuke Sakaguchi, Matt Post, and Joel Tetreault. 2015. Ground truth for grammatical error correction metrics. In *Proceedings of the 53rd Annual Meeting of the Association for Computational Linguistics and the 7th International Joint Conference on Natural Language Processing (Volume 2: Short Papers)*, pages 588–593.

Courtney Napoles, Keisuke Sakaguchi, and Joel Tetreault. 2017. Jfleg: A fluency corpus and benchmark for grammatical error correction. In *Proceedings of the 15th Conference of the European Chapter of the Association for Computational Linguistics: Volume 2, Short Papers*, pages 229–234, Valencia, Spain. Association for Computational Linguistics.

Hwee Tou Ng, Siew Mei Wu, Ted Briscoe, Christian Hadiwinoto, Raymond Hendy Susanto, and Christopher Bryant. 2014. The conll-2014 shared task on grammatical error correction. In *Proceedings of the Eighteenth Conference on Computational Natural Language Learning: Shared Task*, pages 1–14.

Michal Richter, Pavel Straňák, and Alexandr Rosen. 2012. Korektor–a system for contextual spell-checking and diacritics completion. In *Proceedings of COLING 2012: Posters*, pages 1019–1028.

Alexandr Rosen. 2016. Building and using corpora of non-native Czech. In *Proceedings of the 16th ITAT: Slovenskočeský NLP workshop (SloNLP 2016)*, volume 1649 of *CEUR Workshop Proceedings*, pages 80–87, Bratislava, Slovakia. Comenius University in Bratislava, Faculty of Mathematics, Physics and Informatics, CreateSpace Independent Publishing Platform.

Alla Rozovskaya and Dan Roth. 2019. Grammar error correction in morphologically rich languages: The case of russian. *Transactions of the Association for Computational Linguistics*, 7:1–17.

Karel Šebesta, Zuzanna Bedřichová, Kateřina Šormová, Barbora Štindlová, Milan Hrdlička, Tereza Hrdličková, Jiří Hana, Vladimír Petkevič, Tomáš Jelínek, Svatava Škodová, Petr Janeš, Kateřina Lundáková, Hana Skoumalová, Šimon Sládek, Piotr Pierscieniak, Dagmar Toufarová, Milan Straka, Alexandr Rosen, Jakub Náplava, and Marie Poláčková. 2017. CzeSL grammatical error correction dataset (CzeSL-GEC). http://hdl.handle.net/11234/1-2143 LINDAT/CLARIN digital library at the Institute of Formal and Applied Linguistics (ÚFAL), Faculty of Mathematics and Physics, Charles University.

Rico Sennrich and Biao Zhang. 2019. Revisiting low-resource neural machine translation: A case study. *arXiv preprint arXiv:1905.11901*.

Noam Shazeer and Mitchell Stern. 2018. Adafactor: Adaptive learning rates with sublinear memory cost. *arXiv preprint arXiv:1804.04235*.

Toshikazu Tajiri, Mamoru Komachi, and Yuji Matsumoto. 2012. Tense and aspect error correction for esl learners using global context. In *Proceedings of the 50th Annual Meeting of the Association for Computational Linguistics: Short Papers-Volume 2*, pages 198–202. Association for Computational Linguistics.

Ashish Vaswani, Noam Shazeer, Niki Parmar, Jakob Uszkoreit, Llion Jones, Aidan N Gomez, Łukasz Kaiser, and Illia Polosukhin. 2017. Attention is all you need. In *Advances in neural information processing systems*, pages 5998–6008.

Karel Šebesta. 2010. Korpusy češtiny a osvojování jazyka [Corpora of Czech and language acquisition]. In *Studie z aplikované lingvistiky [Studies in Applied Linguistics]*, volume 2010(2), pages 11–33.

Shuyao Xu, Jiehao Zhang, Jin Chen, and Long Qin. 2019. Erroneous data generation for grammatical error correction. In *Proceedings of the Fourteenth Workshop on Innovative Use of NLP for Building Educational Applications*, pages 149–158.

Helen Yannakoudakis, Ted Briscoe, and Ben Medlock. 2011. A new dataset and method for automatically grading esol texts. In *Proceedings of the 49th Annual Meeting of the Association for Computational Linguistics: Human Language Technologies-Volume 1*, pages 180–189. Association for Computational Linguistics.

Liang-Chih Yu, Lung-Hao Lee, and Li-Ping Chang. 2014. Overview of grammatical error diagnosis for learning chinese as a foreign language. In *Proceedings of the 1st Workshop on Natural Language Processing Techniques for Educational Applications*, pages 42–47.

Zheng Yuan and Mariano Felice. 2013. Constrained grammatical error correction using statistical machine translation. In *Proceedings of the Seventeenth Conference on Computational Natural Language Learning: Shared Task*, pages 52–61.

Wajdi Zaghouani, Behrang Mohit, Nizar Habash, Ossama Obeid, Nadi Tomeh, Alla Rozovskaya, Noura Farra, Sarah Alkuhlani, and Kemal Oflazer. 2015. Large scale arabic error annotation: Guidelines and framework.

Wei Zhao, Liang Wang, Kewei Shen, Ruoyu Jia, and Jingming Liu. 2019. Improving grammatical error correction via pre-training a copy-augmented architecture with unlabeled data. *arXiv preprint arXiv:1903.00138*.

Minimally-Augmented Grammatical Error Correction

Roman Grundkiewicz[†‡] and **Marcin Junczys-Dowmunt**[‡]
† University of Edinburgh, Edinburgh EH8 9AB, UK
‡ Microsoft, Redmond, WA 98052, USA
`rgrundki@inf.ed.ac.uk, marcinjd@microsoft.com`

Abstract

There has been an increased interest in low-resource approaches to automatic grammatical error correction. We introduce Minimally-Augmented Grammatical Error Correction (MAGEC) that does not require any error-labelled data. Our unsupervised approach is based on a simple but effective synthetic error generation method based on confusion sets from inverted spell-checkers. In low-resource settings, we outperform the current state-of-the-art results for German and Russian GEC tasks by a large margin without using any real error-annotated training data. When combined with labelled data, our method can serve as an efficient pre-training technique.

1 Introduction

Most neural approaches to automatic grammatical error correction (GEC) require error-labelled training data to achieve their best performance. Unfortunately, such resources are not easily available, particularly for languages other than English. This has lead to an increased interest in unsupervised and low-resource GEC (Rozovskaya et al., 2017; Bryant and Briscoe, 2018; Boyd, 2018; Rozovskaya and Roth, 2019), which recently culminated in the low-resource track of the Building Educational Application (BEA) shared task (Bryant et al., 2019).[1]

We present Minimally-Augmented Grammatical Error Correction (MAGEC), a simple but effective approach to unsupervised and low-resource GEC which does not require any authentic error-labelled training data. A neural sequence-to-sequence model is trained on clean and synthetically noised sentences alone. The noise is automatically created from confusion sets. Additionally, if labelled data

is available for fine-tuning (Hinton and Salakhutdinov, 2006), MAGEC can also serve as an efficient pre-training technique.

The proposed unsupervised synthetic error generation method does not require a seed corpus with example errors as most other methods based on statistical error injection (Felice and Yuan, 2014) or back-translation models (Rei et al., 2017; Kasewa et al., 2018; Htut and Tetreault, 2019). It also outperforms noising techniques that rely on random word replacements (Xie et al., 2018; Zhao et al., 2019). Contrary to Ge et al. (2018) or Lichtarge et al. (2018), our approach can be easily used for effective pre-training of full encoder-decoder models as it is model-independent and only requires clean monolingual data and potentially an available spell-checker dictionary.[2] In comparison to pre-training with BERT (Devlin et al., 2019), synthetic errors provide more task-specific training examples than masking. As an unsupervised approach, MAGEC is an alternative to recently proposed language model (LM) based approaches (Bryant and Briscoe, 2018; Stahlberg et al., 2019), but it does not require any amount of annotated sentences for tuning.

2 Minimally-augmented grammatical error correction

Our minimally-augmented GEC approach uses synthetic noise as its primary source of training data. We generate erroneous sentences from monolingual texts via random word perturbations selected from automatically created confusion sets. These are traditionally defined as sets of frequently confused words (Rozovskaya and Roth, 2010).

We experiment with three unsupervised methods for generating confusion sets:

---

[1] `https://www.cl.cam.ac.uk/research/nl/bea2019st`

[2] GNU Aspell supports more than 160 languages: `http://aspell.net/man-html/Supported.html`

Proceedings of the 2019 EMNLP Workshop W-NUT: The 5th Workshop on Noisy User-generated Text, pages 357–363
Hong Kong, Nov 4, 2019. ©2019 Association for Computational Linguistics

Word	Confusion set
had	hard head hand gad has ha ad hat
night	knight naught nought nights bight might nightie
then	them the hen ten than thin thee thew
haben	habend halben gaben habe habet haken
Nacht	Nachts Nascht Macht Naht Acht Nach Jacht Pacht
dann	sann dank denn dünn kann wann bannen kannst
имел	им ел им-ел имела имели имело мел умел
ночь	ночью ночи дочь мочь ноль новь точь
затем	за тем за-тем затеем затеям зятем затеями

Table 1: Examples of spell-broken confusion sets for English, German and Russian.

Edit distance Confusion sets consist of words with the shortest Levenshtein distance (Levenshtein, 1966) to the selected confused word.

Word embeddings Confusion sets contain the most similar words to the confused word based on the cosine similarity of their word embedding vectors (Mikolov et al., 2013).

Spell-breaking Confusion sets are composed of suggestions from a spell-checker; a suggestion list is extracted for the confused word regardless of its actual correctness.

These methods can be used to build confusion sets for any alphabetic language.[3] We find that confusion sets constructed via spell-breaking perform best (Section 4). Most context-free spell-checkers combine a weighted edit distance and phonetic algorithms to order suggestions, which produces reliable confusion sets (Table 1).

We synthesize erroneous sentences as follows: given a confusion set $C_i = \{c_1^i, c_2^i, c_3^i, ...\}$, and the vocabulary V, we sample word $w_j \in V$ from the input sentence with a probability approximated with a normal distribution $\mathcal{N}(p_{\mathrm{WER}}, 0.2)$, and perform one of the following operations: (1) substitution of w_j with a random word c_k^j from its confusion set with probability p_{sub}, (2) deletion of w_j with p_{del}, (3) insertion of a random word $w_k \in V$ at $j + 1$ with p_{ins}, and (4) swapping w_j and w_{j+1} with p_{swp}. When making a substitution, words within confusion sets are sampled uniformly.

To improve the model's capability of correcting spelling errors, inspired by Lichtarge et al. (2018); Xie et al. (2018), we randomly perturb 10% of characters using the same edit operations as above.

---

[3] For languages with logosylabic writing system like Chinese, the edit distance can be calculated on transcribed text, while word embeddings can be generated after word-segmentation.

Lang.	Corpus	Dev	Test	Train
EN	W&I+LOCNESS	4,384	4,477	34,308
DE	Falco+MERLIN	2,503	2,337	18,754[4]
RU	RULEC-GEC	2,500	5,000	4,980

Table 2: Sizes of labelled corpora in no. of sentences.

Character-level noise is introduced on top of the synthetic errors generated via confusion sets.

A MAGEC model is trained solely on the synthetically noised data and then ensembled with a language model. Being limited only by the amount of clean monolingual data, this large-scale unsupervised approach can perform better than training on small authentic error corpora. A large amount of training examples increases the chance that synthetic errors resemble real error patterns and results in better language modelling properties.

If any small amount of error-annotated learner data is available, it can be used to fine-tune the pre-trained model and further boost its performance. Pre-training of decoders of GEC models from language models has been introduced by Junczys-Dowmunt et al. (2018b), we pretrain the full encoder-decoder models instead, as proposed by Grundkiewicz et al. (2019).

3 Experiments

Data and evaluation Our approach requires a large amount of monolingual data that is used for generating synthetic training pairs. We use the publicly available News crawl data[5] released for the WMT shared tasks (Bojar et al., 2018). For English and German, we limit the size of the data to 100 million sentences; for Russian, we use all the available 80.5 million sentences.

As primary development and test data, we use the following learner corpora (Table 2):

- English: the new W&I+LOCNESS corpus (Bryant et al., 2019; Granger, 1998) released for the BEA 2019 shared task and representing a diverse cross-section of English language;

- German: the Falko-MERLIN GEC corpus (Boyd, 2018) that combines two German learner corpora of all proficiency levels;

---

[4] The original training part of Falco+MERLIN consists of 19,237 sentences, but is contaminated with some test sentences. We have removed training examples if their target sentences occur in the development or test set.

[5] http://data.statmt.org/news-crawl

System	P	R	$F_{0.5}$
Random	32.8	6.7	18.49
Edit distance	39.9	9.5	24.27
Word embeddings	39.7	9.0	23.56
Spell-breaking	43.1	10.6	26.66
+ OOV + Case	**44.9**	10.9	27.70
$\rightarrow$ WER $= 0.25$	43.3	11.8	27.50
$\rightarrow$ Edit-weighted $\Lambda = 2$	43.0	**12.6**	**28.99**

Table 3: Performance for different confusion sets and edit weighting techniques on W&I+LOCNESS Dev.

- Russian: the recently introduced RULEC-GEC dataset (Alsufieva et al., 2012; Rozovskaya and Roth, 2019) containing Russian texts from foreign and heritage speakers.

Unless explicitly stated, we do not use the training parts of those datasets. For each language we follow the originally proposed preprocessing and evaluation settings. English and German data are tokenized with Spacy[6], while Russian is preprocessed with Mystem (Segalovich, 2003). We additionally normalise punctuation in monolingual data using Moses scripts (Koehn et al., 2007). During training, we limit the vocabulary size to 32,000 subwords computed with SentencePiece using the unigram method (Kudo and Richardson, 2018).

English models are evaluated with ERRANT (Bryant et al., 2017) using $F_{0.5}$; for German and Russian, the M2Scorer with the MaxMatch metric (Dahlmeier and Ng, 2012) is used.

Synthetic data Confusion sets are created for each language for $V = 96,000$ most frequent lexical word forms from monolingual data. We use the Levenshtein distance to generate edit distance based confusion sets. The maximum considered distance is 2. Word embeddings are computed with *word2vec*[7] from monolingual data. To generate spell-broken confusion sets we use Enchant[8] with Aspell dictionaries.[9] The size of confusion sets is limited to top 20 words.

Synthetic errors are introduced into monolingual texts to mimic word error rate (WER) of about 15%, i.e. $p_{\text{WER}} = 0.15$, which resembles error frequency in common ESL error corpora. When confusing a word, the probability p_{sub} is set to 0.7, other probabilities are set to 0.1.

System	Dev	P	R	$F_{0.5}$
Top BEA19 (Low-res.)	44.95	70.2	48.0	64.24
Top BEA19 (Restricted)	53.00	72.3	60.1	69.47
Spell-checker	10.04	23.7	7.4	16.45
Spell-checker w/ LM	12.00	41.5	6.8	20.52
MAGEC w/o LM	28.99	53.4	26.2	44.22
MAGEC	31.87	49.1	37.5	46.22
MAGEC Ens.	33.32	53.0	34.5	47.89
Fine-tuned (Real)	44.29	61.2	54.1	59.62
Fine-tuned (Real+Synth.)	49.49	66.0	58.8	64.45

(a) English (W&I+LOCNESS)

System	Dev	P	R	$M^2_{0.5}$
Boyd (2018) (Unsup.)	—	30.0	14.0	24.37
Boyd (2018)	—	52.0	29.8	45.22
Spell-checker	20.97	33.0	9.5	22.06
Spell-checker w/ LM	24.14	43.6	8.6	24.27
MAGEC w/o LM	49.25	58.1	27.2	47.30
MAGEC	52.06	57.9	34.7	51.10
MAGEC Ens.	53.61	58.3	36.9	**52.22**
Fine-tuned (Real)	68.13	72.2	54.0	67.67
Fine-tuned (Real+Synth.)	70.51	73.0	61.0	70.24

(b) German (Falko-MERLIN)

System	Dev	P	R	$M^2_{0.5}$
Rozovskaya and Roth (2019)	—	38.0	7.5	21.0
Spell-checker	18.32	19.2	7.2	14.39
Spell-checker w/ LM	22.01	30.7	7.5	18.99
MAGEC w/o LM	24.82	30.1	20.4	27.47
MAGEC	27.13	32.3	29.5	31.71
MAGEC Ens.	27.87	33.3	29.4	**32.41**
Fine-tuned (Real)	30.28	35.4	31.1	34.45
Fine-tuned (Real+Synth.)	30.64	36.3	28.7	34.46

(c) Russian (RULEC-GEC)

Table 4: Unsupervised and fine-tuned MAGEC systems for English, German and Russian, contrasted with systems from related work and spell-checking baselines.

Training settings We adapt the recent state-of-the-art GEC system by Junczys-Dowmunt et al. (2018b), an ensemble of sequence-to-sequence Transformer models (Vaswani et al., 2017) and a neural language model.[10]

We use the training setting proposed by the authors[11], but introduce stronger regularization: we increase dropout probabilities of source words to 0.3, add dropout on transformer self-attention and filter layers of 0.1, and use larger mini-batches with

---

~2,500 sentences. We do not pre-train the decoder parameters with a language model and train directly on the synthetic data. We increase the size of language model used for ensembling to match the Transformer-big configuration (Vaswani et al., 2017) with 16-head self-attention, embeddings size of 1024 and feed-forward filter size size of 4096. In experiments with fine-tuning, the training hyper-parameters remain unchanged.

All models are trained with Marian (Junczys-Dowmunt et al., 2018a). The training is continued for at most 5 epochs or until early-stopping is triggered after 5 stalled validation steps. We found that using 10,000 synthetic sentences as validation sets, i.e. a fully unsupervised approach, is as effective as using the development parts of error corpora and does not decrease the final performance.

4   Results and analysis

Confusion sets   On English data, all proposed confusion set generation methods perform better than random word substitution (Table 3).Confusion sets based on word embeddings are the least effective, while spell-broken sets perform best at 26.66 $F_{0.5}$. We observe further gains of +1.04 from keeping out-of-vocabulary spell-checker suggestions (OOV) and preserving consistent letter casing within confusion sets (Case).

The word error rate of error corpora is an useful statistic that can be used to balance precision/recall ratios (Rozovskaya and Roth, 2010; Junczys-Dowmunt et al., 2018b; Hotate et al., 2019). Increasing WER in the synthetic data from 15% to 25% increases recall at the expense of precision, but no overall improvement is observed. A noticeable recall gain that transfers to a higher F-score of 28.99 is achieved by increasing the importance of edited fragments with the edit-weighted MLE objective from Junczys-Dowmunt et al. (2018b) with $\Lambda = 2$. We use this setting for the rest of our experiments.

Main results   We first compare the GEC systems with simple baselines using a greedy and context spell-checking (Table 4); the latter selects the best correction suggestion based on the sentence perplexity from a Transformer language model. All systems outperform the spell-checker baselines.

On German and Russian test sets, single MAGEC models without ensembling with a language model already achieve better performance than reported by Boyd (2018) and Rozovskaya and

System	CoNLL	JFLEG
Bryant and Briscoe (2018) ⋆	34.09	48.75
Stahlberg et al. (2019) ⋆	44.43	52.61
Stahlberg et al. (2019) (659K real data)	58.40	58.63
MAGEC Ens. ⋆	44.23	56.18
MAGEC Fine-tuned (34K real data)	56.54	60.01

Table 5: Comparison with LM-based GEC on the CoNLL (M^2) and JFLEG (GLEU) test sets for unsupervised (⋆) and supervised systems trained or fine-tuned on different amounts of labelled data.

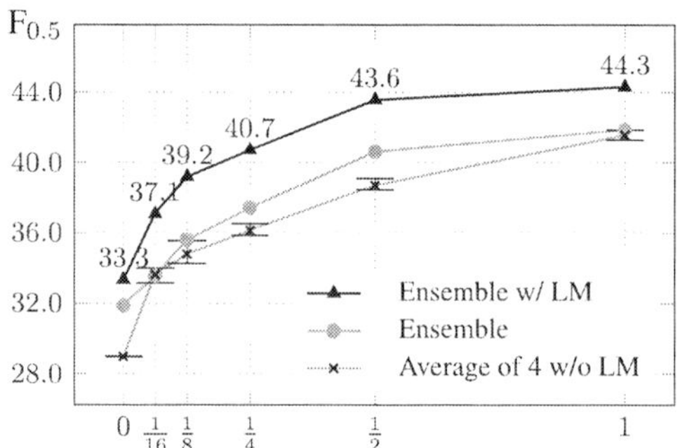

Figure 1: Improvements from fine-tuning on subsets of W&I+LOCNESS Train. The smallest $\frac{1}{16}$ part of the dataset contains 2,145 sentences. Averaged F-scores over 4 runs trained on different subsets of the data.

Roth (2019) for their systems that use authentic error-annotated data for training (Table 4b and 4c). Our best unsupervised ensemble systems that combine three Transformer models and a LM[12] outperform the state-of-the-art results for these languages by +7.0 and +11.4 $F_{0.5}$.

Our English models do not compete with the top systems (Grundkiewicz et al., 2019) from the BEA shared task trained on publicly available error-annotated corpora (Table 4a). It is difficult to compare with the top low-resource system from the shared task, because it uses additional parallel data from Wikipedia (Grundkiewicz and Junczys-Dowmunt, 2014), larger ensemble, and n-best list re-ranking with right-to-left models, which can be also implemented in this work.

MAGEC systems are generally on par with the results achieved by a recent unsupervised contribution based on finite state transducers by Stahlberg et al. (2019) on the CoNLL-2014 (Dahlmeier et al., 2013) and JFLEG test sets (Napoles et al., 2017) (Table 5).

---

[12]The weight of the language model is grid-searched on the development set.

Lang.	Spell.+punc.			Other errors		
	P	R	$F_{0.5}$	P	R	$F_{0.5}$
EN	28.8	24.1	27.68	33.5	16.8	27.93
DE	54.8	71.4	57.43	63.6	55.8	61.83
RU	26.7	75.0	**30.70**	14.6	19.7	**15.37**

Table 6: Performance of single MAGEC w/ LM models on two groups of errors on respective development sets.

All unsupervised systems benefit from domain-adaptation via fine-tuning on authentic labelled data (Miceli Barone et al., 2017). The more authentic high-quality and in-domain training data is used, the greater the improvement, but even as few as ~2,000 sentences are helpful (Fig. 1). We found that fine-tuning on a 2:1 mixture of synthetic and oversampled authentic data prevents the model from over-fitting. This is particularly visible for English which has the largest fine-tuning set (34K sentences), and the difference of 5.2 $F_{0.5}$ between fine-tuning with and without synthetic data is largest.

Spelling and punctuation errors The GEC task involves detection and correction of all types of error in written texts, including grammatical, lexical and orthographical errors. Spelling and punctuation errors are among the most frequent error types and also the easiest to synthesize.

To counter the argument that – mostly due to the introduced character-level noise and strong language modelling – MAGEC can only correct these "simple" errors, we evaluate it against test sets that contain either spelling and punctuation errors or all other error types; with the complement errors corrected (Table 6). Our systems indeed perform best on misspellings and punctuation errors, but are capable of correcting various error types. The disparity for Russian can be explained by the fact that it is a morphologically-rich language and we suffer from generally lower performance.

5   Conclusions and future work

We have presented Minimally-Augmented Grammatical Error Correction (MAGEC), which can be effectively used in both unsupervised and low-resource scenarios. The method is model independent, requires easily available resources, and can be used for creating reliable baselines for supervised techniques or as an efficient pre-training method for neural GEC models with labelled data. We have demonstrated the effectiveness of our method and outperformed state-of-the-art results for German

and Russian benchmarks, trained with labelled data, by a large margin.

For future work, we plan to evaluate MAGEC on more languages and experiment with more diversified confusion sets created with additional unsupervised generation methods.

References

Anna Alsufieva, Olesya Kisselev, and Sandra Freels. 2012. Results 2012: Using flagship data to develop a Russian learner corpus of academic writing. *Russian Language Journal*, 62:79–105.

Ondřej Bojar, Christian Federmann, Mark Fishel, Yvette Graham, Barry Haddow, Philipp Koehn, and Christof Monz. 2018. Findings of the 2018 conference on machine translation (WMT18). In *Proceedings of the Third Conference on Machine Translation: Shared Task Papers*, pages 272–303, Belgium, Brussels. Association for Computational Linguistics.

Adriane Boyd. 2018. Using Wikipedia edits in low resource grammatical error correction. In *Proceedings of the 2018 EMNLP Workshop W-NUT: The 4th Workshop on Noisy User-generated Text*, pages 79–84, Brussels, Belgium. Association for Computational Linguistics.

Christopher Bryant and Ted Briscoe. 2018. Language model based grammatical error correction without annotated training data. In *Proceedings of the Thirteenth Workshop on Innovative Use of NLP for Building Educational Applications*, pages 247–253, New Orleans, Louisiana. Association for Computational Linguistics.

Christopher Bryant, Mariano Felice, Øistein E. Andersen, and Ted Briscoe. 2019. The BEA-2019 shared task on grammatical error correction. In *Proceedings of the Fourteenth Workshop on Innovative Use of NLP for Building Educational Applications*, pages 52–75, Florence, Italy. Association for Computational Linguistics.

Christopher Bryant, Mariano Felice, and Ted Briscoe. 2017. Automatic annotation and evaluation of error types for grammatical error correction. In *Proceedings of the 55th Annual Meeting of the Association for Computational Linguistics (Volume 1: Long Papers)*, pages 793–805, Vancouver, Canada. Association for Computational Linguistics.

Daniel Dahlmeier and Hwee Tou Ng. 2012. Better evaluation for grammatical error correction. In *Proceedings of the 2012 Conference of the North American Chapter of the Association for Computational Linguistics: Human Language Technologies*, pages 568–572, Montréal, Canada. Association for Computational Linguistics.

Daniel Dahlmeier, Hwee Tou Ng, and Siew Mei Wu. 2013. Building a large annotated corpus of learner English: The NUS corpus of learner English. In *Proceedings of the Eighth Workshop on Innovative Use of NLP for Building Educational Applications*, pages 22–31.

Jacob Devlin, Ming-Wei Chang, Kenton Lee, and Kristina Toutanova. 2019. BERT: Pre-training of deep bidirectional transformers for language understanding. pages 4171–4186.

Mariano Felice and Zheng Yuan. 2014. Generating artificial errors for grammatical error correction. In *Proceedings of the Student Research Workshop at the 14th Conference of the European Chapter of the Association for Computational Linguistics*, pages 116–126, Gothenburg, Sweden. Association for Computational Linguistics.

Tao Ge, Furu Wei, and Ming Zhou. 2018. Fluency boost learning and inference for neural grammatical error correction. In *Proceedings of the 56th Annual Meeting of the Association for Computational Linguistics (Volume 1: Long Papers)*, pages 1055–1065, Melbourne, Australia. Association for Computational Linguistics.

Sylviane Granger. 1998. The computer learner corpus: A versatile new source of data for SLA research. In Sylviane Granger, editor, *Learner English on Computer*, pages 3–18. Addison Wesley Longman, London and New York.

Roman Grundkiewicz and Marcin Junczys-Dowmunt. 2014. The WikEd error corpus: A corpus of corrective Wikipedia edits and its application to grammatical error correction. In *Advances in Natural Language Processing — Lecture Notes in Computer Science*, volume 8686, pages 478–490. Springer.

Roman Grundkiewicz, Marcin Junczys-Dowmunt, and Kenneth Heafield. 2019. Neural grammatical error correction systems with unsupervised pre-training on synthetic data. In *Proceedings of the Fourteenth Workshop on Innovative Use of NLP for Building Educational Applications*, pages 252–263, Florence, Italy. Association for Computational Linguistics.

Geoffrey E Hinton and Ruslan R Salakhutdinov. 2006. Reducing the dimensionality of data with neural networks. *science*, 313(5786):504–507.

Kengo Hotate, Masahiro Kaneko, Satoru Katsumata, and Mamoru Komachi. 2019. Controlling grammatical error correction using word edit rate. In *Proceedings of the 57th Annual Meeting of the Association for Computational Linguistics: Student Research Workshop*, pages 149–154. Association for Computational Linguistics.

Phu Mon Htut and Joel Tetreault. 2019. The unbearable weight of generating artificial errors for grammatical error correction. In *Proceedings of the Fourteenth Workshop on Innovative Use of NLP for Build-*

ing Educational Applications, pages 478–483, Florence, Italy. Association for Computational Linguistics.

Marcin Junczys-Dowmunt, Roman Grundkiewicz, Tomasz Dwojak, Hieu Hoang, Kenneth Heafield, Tom Neckermann, Frank Seide, Ulrich Germann, Alham Fikri Aji, Nikolay Bogoychev, André F. T. Martins, and Alexandra Birch. 2018a. Marian: Fast neural machine translation in C++. In *Proceedings of ACL 2018, System Demonstrations*, pages 116–121, Melbourne, Australia. Association for Computational Linguistics.

Marcin Junczys-Dowmunt, Roman Grundkiewicz, Shubha Guha, and Kenneth Heafield. 2018b. Approaching neural grammatical error correction as a low-resource machine translation task. In *Proceedings of the 2018 Conference of the North American Chapter of the Association for Computational Linguistics: Human Language Technologies, Volume 1 (Long Papers)*, pages 595–606, New Orleans, Louisiana. Association for Computational Linguistics.

Sudhanshu Kasewa, Pontus Stenetorp, and Sebastian Riedel. 2018. Wronging a right: Generating better errors to improve grammatical error detection. In *Proceedings of the 2018 Conference on Empirical Methods in Natural Language Processing*, pages 4977–4983, Brussels, Belgium. Association for Computational Linguistics.

Philipp Koehn, Hieu Hoang, Alexandra Birch, Chris Callison-Burch, Marcello Federico, Nicola Bertoldi, Brooke Cowan, Wade Shen, Christine Moran, Richard Zens, Chris Dyer, Ondrej Bojar, Alexandra Constantin, and Evan Herbst. 2007. Moses: Open source toolkit for statistical machine translation. In *Annual Meeting of the Association for Computational Linguistics*. The Association for Computer Linguistics.

Taku Kudo and John Richardson. 2018. SentencePiece: A simple and language independent subword tokenizer and detokenizer for neural text processing. In *Proceedings of the 2018 Conference on Empirical Methods in Natural Language Processing: System Demonstrations*, pages 66–71, Brussels, Belgium. Association for Computational Linguistics.

Vladimir I Levenshtein. 1966. Binary codes capable of correcting deletions, insertions, and reversals. In *Soviet physics doklady*, volume 10, pages 707–710.

Jared Lichtarge, Christopher Alberti, Shankar Kumar, Noam Shazeer, and Niki Parmar. 2018. Weakly supervised grammatical error correction using iterative decoding. *CoRR*, abs/1811.01710.

Antonio Valerio Miceli Barone, Barry Haddow, Ulrich Germann, and Rico Sennrich. 2017. Regularization techniques for fine-tuning in neural machine translation. In *Proceedings of the 2017 Conference on Empirical Methods in Natural Language Processing*, pages 1489–1494, Copenhagen, Denmark. Association for Computational Linguistics.

Tomas Mikolov, Ilya Sutskever, Kai Chen, Greg S Corrado, and Jeff Dean. 2013. Distributed representations of words and phrases and their compositionality. In C. J. C. Burges, L. Bottou, M. Welling, Z. Ghahramani, and K. Q. Weinberger, editors, *Advances in Neural Information Processing Systems 26*, pages 3111–3119. Curran Associates, Inc.

Courtney Napoles, Keisuke Sakaguchi, and Joel Tetreault. 2017. JFLEG: A fluency corpus and benchmark for grammatical error correction. In *Proceedings of the 2017 Conference of the European Chapter of the Association for Computational Linguistics*, Valencia, Spain. Association for Computational Linguistics.

Marek Rei, Mariano Felice, Zheng Yuan, and Ted Briscoe. 2017. Artificial error generation with machine translation and syntactic patterns. In *Proceedings of the 12th Workshop on Innovative Use of NLP for Building Educational Applications*, pages 287–292, Copenhagen, Denmark. Association for Computational Linguistics.

Alla Rozovskaya and Dan Roth. 2010. Generating confusion sets for context-sensitive error correction. In *Proceedings of the 2010 Conference on Empirical Methods in Natural Language Processing*, pages 961–970, Cambridge, MA. Association for Computational Linguistics.

Alla Rozovskaya and Dan Roth. 2019. Grammar error correction in morphologically-rich languages: The case of Russian. *Transactions of the Association for Computational Linguistics*, 7:1–17.

Alla Rozovskaya, Dan Roth, and Mark Sammons. 2017. Adapting to learner errors with minimal supervision. *Comput. Linguist.*, 43(4):723–760.

Ilya Segalovich. 2003. A fast morphological algorithm with unknown word guessing induced by a dictio nary for a web search engine. In *MLMTA*, pages 273–280. CSREA Press.

Felix Stahlberg, Christopher Bryant, and Bill Byrne. 2019. Neural grammatical error correction with finite state transducers. In *Proceedings of the 2018 Conference of the North American Chapter of the Association for Computational Linguistics: Human Language Technologies*, Minneapolis, USA. Association for Computational Linguistics.

Ashish Vaswani, Noam Shazeer, Niki Parmar, Jakob Uszkoreit, Llion Jones, Aidan N Gomez, Łukasz Kaiser, and Illia Polosukhin. 2017. Attention is all you need. In *Advances in Neural Information Processing Systems 30*, pages 5998–6008. Curran Associates, Inc.

Ziang Xie, Guillaume Genthial, Stanley Xie, Andrew Ng, and Dan Jurafsky. 2018. Noising and denoising natural language: Diverse backtranslation for grammar correction. In *Proceedings of the 2018 Conference of the North American Chapter of the Association for Computational Linguistics: Human Language Technologies, Volume 1 (Long Papers)*, pages 619–628, New Orleans, Louisiana. Association for Computational Linguistics.

Wei Zhao, Liang Wang, Kewei Shen, Ruoyu Jia, and Jingming Liu. 2019. Improving grammatical error correction via pre-training a copy-augmented architecture with unlabeled data. *CoRR*, abs/1903.00138.

A Social Opinion Gold Standard for the Malta Government Budget 2018

Keith Cortis
Maynooth University, Maynooth, Ireland
Malta Information Technology Agency, Malta
`keith.cortis.2019@mumail.ie`

Brian Davis
ADAPT Centre,
Dublin City University,
Glasnevin, Dublin 9, Ireland
`brian.davis@adaptcentre.ie`

Abstract

We present a gold standard of annotated social opinion for the Malta Government Budget 2018. It consists of over 500 online posts in English and/or the Maltese less-resourced language, gathered from social media platforms, specifically, social networking services and newswires, which have been annotated with information about opinions expressed by the general public and other entities, in terms of sentiment polarity, emotion, sarcasm/irony, and negation. This dataset is a resource for opinion mining based on social data, within the context of politics. It is the first opinion annotated social dataset from Malta, which has very limited language resources available.

1 Introduction

European usage trends show that Malta is the second highest user of social media, with around 90% of the adult population being online and active on social media (Eurostat, 2017), whereas around 80% of users read news online (Caruana, 2018). In terms of social media, this is not only used by individuals, but is also increasingly being used by enterprises (Eurostat, 2018). In fact, governments and businesses are spreading their news via social media and moving away from newswires (Grech, 2019). This has increased the importance of social opinions and the need to refine data mining techniques that are able to identify and classify opinions related to a particular aspect, e.g., entity or topic, which can be beneficial.

This paper presents a dataset of opinion-annotated social online posts targeting the Malta Government Budget for 2018[1] presented on 9th October 2017 by the Honourable Minister for Finance, Edward Scicluna. It contains the opinions and reactions (in terms of sentiment, emotions,

[1] https://mfin.gov.mt/en/The-Budget/Pages/The-Budget-2018.aspx

etc.) of the public and professionals towards the mentioned budget as expressed over various social channels, specifically, social networking services and newswires, during and after the event. In addition, it has the potential of identifying commendations, regrets and other reactions concerning any presented measure, such as tax matters, industry specific initiatives, strategic initiatives and social measures. This dataset can support government initiatives for the development of opinion mining tools to better capture the public perception towards an upcoming/current/past budget presented to the House of Representatives. Such valuable insights can be taken in consideration within the upcoming budgets and/or any bills presented and discussed in Parliament.

2 Related Work

The Politics domain is one of the most popular application areas in the social media-based opinion mining domain, with such techniques being applied on election, debate, referendum and other political events' (such as uprisings and protests) datasets. However, applying such techniques on government budgets is not common.

Kalampokis et al. (2011) proposed a method that integrates government and social data (from social media platforms, such as Twitter and Facebook) to enable decision makers to understand public opinion and be able to predict public reactions on certain decisions. The methodology discussed by Hubert et al. (2018), uses emotion analysis to study government-citizen interactions on Twitter for five Latin American countries that have a mature e-Participation, namely Mexico, Colombia, Chile, Uruguay and Argentina. Similarly, the city of Washington D.C. in the United States, uses sentiment analysis to interpret and examine the comments posted by citizens and businesses over

Proceedings of the 2019 EMNLP Workshop W-NUT: The 5th Workshop on Noisy User-generated Text, pages 364–369
Hong Kong, Nov 4, 2019. ©2019 Association for Computational Linguistics

social media platforms and other public websites (Eggers et al., 2019).

The economic content of government budgets is made publicly available for various countries. The Global Open Data Index[2] provides public open datasets about national government budgets of various countries, but lacks open budget social and transactional data. The OpenBudgets[3] Horizon 2020 project provided an overview of public budget and spending data and tools, in order to support various entities (Musyaffa et al., 2018). However, this project targeted public budget and spending data and not the yearly budgets presented by governments. Moreover, it did not use any data from social media platforms and apply any text mining tasks, such as opinion mining.

To the best of our knowledge, the gold standard presented is the first annotated dataset from a social aspect at a European and national level and in the context of Maltese politics.

3 Method

A variety of Web social media data covering the local Maltese political domain was taken in consideration for this study, namely traditional media published by newswires, and social media published through social networking services.

3.1 Data Collection

The following data sources were selected to collect the dataset: i) Newswires (News): Times of Malta[4], MaltaToday[5], The Malta Independent[6]; and ii) Social networking services (SNS): Facebook[7], Twitter[8]. The selection of the data sources were based on their popularity and usage with the Maltese citizens. In fact, Facebook and Twitter are two social media platforms that are highly accessed (TMI, 2018), with the Times of Malta, MaltaToday and The Malta Independent being amongst the top news portals accessed in Malta[9] for both reading and social interaction purposes. Table 1 presents details about the social dataset collected on the Malta Budget 2018.

Three different kinds of online news articles –in

Source Type & Name	Query strings/ Articles	Online Posts
SNS - Twitter	1	38
SNS - Facebook	1	28
SNS - Twitter-The Malta Independent	1	12
News - Times of Malta	4	249
News - MaltaToday	4	175
News - The Malta Independent	4	45

Table 1: Data sources used for the consolidated dataset

terms of content published– were selected for each newswire mentioned:

- Overview of the upcoming budget, published on the budget day;

- Near to real-time live updates in commentary format, on the budget measures being presented for the upcoming year;

- Overview of the presented budget, published after the budget finishes, on the same day and/or the following day.

The aforementioned news articles above allow users to post social comments, which in nature are similar to online posts published on social networking services. These comments were extracted for our dataset, given that the annotation of opinions from user-generated social data is the main objective of this work. In addition, for diversity purposes, four online articles for each newswire were chosen to gather as much online posts as possible from the general public. This ensures that the different opinions expressed throughout on both the budget at large and specific budget topics, are captured.

With regards to the online posts from social networking services, a small sample was extracted, specifically the ones that contained the "malta budget 2018" search terms (as keywords and/or hashtags) that were posted on 9th and 10th October 2017. The criteria for the chosen keywords were based on the manual identification of common keywords associated with content relevant to the Malta Budget. The necessary filters were applied to exclude any spam and irrelevant content, whereas any references to non-political people were anonymised.

3.2 Annotation

A total of 555 online posts were presented to **two** raters. Both were proficient in Malta's two official

---

[2]https://index.okfn.org/dataset/budget/

[3]http://openbudgets.eu/

[4]https://www.timesofmalta.com/

[5]https://www.maltatoday.com.mt/

[6]http://www.independent.com.mt/

[7]https://www.facebook.com/

[8]https://twitter.com/

[9]https://www.alexa.com/topsites/countries/MT

languages - Maltese (Malti) –a Semitic language written in the Latin script that is the national language of Malta– and English, which are equally important[10]. Moreover, the raters worked in the technology domain, were given a lecture about opinion mining and provided with relevant reading material and terminology for reference purposes. The following metatdata and annotation types (#6-13) were created for each online post:

1. **Online Post Identifier:** unique numerical identifier for the online post;

2. **Related Online Post Identifier**: numerical identifier for the parent online post (if any);

3. **Source Identifier**: numerical identifier referring to the actual data source (e.g., website) of the online post;

4. **Source Name**: origin of the online post (e.g., Twitter, MaltaToday);

5. **Online Post**: textual string of the online post;

6. **Sentiment Polarity**: a categorical value (3-levels) for the sentiment polarity of the online post (negative, neutral, positive);

7. **Sentiment Polarity Intensity**: a categorical value (5-levels) for the sentiment polarity intensity of the online post (very negative, negative, neutral, positive, very positive);

8. **Emotion (6-levels)**: a categorical value for the emotion of the online post based on Ekman's (Ekman, 1992) six basic emotions (anger, disgust, fear, happiness, sadness, surprise);

9. **Emotion (8-levels)**: a categorical value for the emotion of the online post based on Plutchik's (Plutchik, 1980) eight primary emotions (joy, sadness, fear, anger, anticipation, surprise, disgust, trust);

10. **Sarcasm/Irony**: binary value, with 1 referring to sarcasm and irony in online posts[11];

11. **Negation**: binary value, with 1 referring to negated online posts[12];

12. **Off-topic**: binary value, with 1 referring to off-topic online posts that are political but not related to the budget;

13. **Maltese**: binary value, with 1 referring to online posts (full text or majority of text) in Maltese, and 0 referring to posts in English.

The raters were advised to follow any web links present in their online posts, for example "Budget 2018: #Highlights and #Opportunities can be accessed here - *https://lnkd.in/eQxeM7G* #MaltaBudget18 #KPMG", when required to reach a decision, especially for determining the sentiment polarity, sentiment polarity intensity and/or emotion.

The online post with textual content *"Tallinja Card b'xejn għal dawk bejn 16 u 20 sena. #maltabudget2018"* (English translation: "free transport card for people aged between 16-20 years") provides an example of the annotation types created for each collected post:

- **Sentiment Polarity**: Positive;

- **Sentiment Polarity Intensity**: Positive;

- **Emotion (6-levels)**: Happiness;

- **Emotion (8-levels)**: Joy;

- **Sarcasm/Irony**: 0;

- **Negation**: 0;

- **Off-topic**: 0;

- **Maltese**: 1.

3.3 Reliability and Consolidation

Inter-rater reliability, that is, the level of agreement between the raters' annotations was determined. The percent agreement (basic measure) was primarily calculated on the annotations performed by the two raters. This was followed by the Cohen's Kappa (Cohen, 1960), a statistical measure that takes chance agreement into consideration, which is commonly used for categorical variables. Moreover, this statistic is calculated when two raters perform annotations on the same categorical values and dataset. Table 2, shows the inter-rater reliability agreement scores for each annotation type.

A fair Kappa agreement was achieved for the sentiment polarity, sentiment polarity intensity and emotion (6-levels) annotations, with a slight

---

[10]In Malta both languages are used by the general public, especially English or a mix for transcription purposes, hence why it is important to collect online posts in both

[11]These are treated as one class for this study

[12]A negated post refers to the opposite of what is conveyed due to certain grammatical operations such as 'not'

agreement obtained for the emotion (8-levels) annotation[13]. The percent agreement highlights the challenges behind these annotation tasks, especially when an annotation type such as emotion, has several categorical values to choose from and can convey multiple ones, e.g., anger and surprise. These annotation tasks are not trivial, where detecting emotion in text can be difficult for humans due to the personal context of individuals which can influence emotion interpretation, thus resulting in a low level of inter-rater agreement (Canales Zaragoza, 2018). Moreover, words used in different senses can lead to different emotions, hence making emotion annotation more challenging (Mohammad and Turney, 2013). This claim is also supported by Devillers et al. in (Devillers et al., 2005), who mention that categorisation and annotation of real-life emotions is a big challenge given that they are context-dependent and also highly person-dependent, whereas unambiguous emotions are only possible in a small portion of any real corpus. Therefore, the nature of relevant emotion data is too infrequent to provide adequate support for consistent annotation and modelling through fine-grained emotion labels.

Furthermore, a moderate agreement was achieved for sarcasm/irony detection, whereas negation obtained a chance agreement, which underlines how challenging such a task can be. Off-topic annotations achieved a fair level of agreement, whereas detection of Maltese online posts resulted in a near perfect agreement.

Annotation Type	% Agreement	Cohen's Kappa
Sentiment Polarity	0.6015	0.3703
Sentiment Polarity Intensity	0.4132	0.2182
Emotion (6-levels)	0.3985	0.2394
Emotion (8-levels)	0.2669	0.119
Sarcasm/Irony	0.7843	0.5027
Negation	0.8940	0.0581
Off-topic	0.7148	0.3494
Maltese	0.9854	0.9669

Table 2: Inter-rater reliability measures for each annotation type

A third expert in the domain consolidated the annotations to create a final dataset. In cases where both raters agreed on the annotation this was selected, whereas in cases of non-agreement,

the third expert selected the most appropriate one to the best of their knowledge.

4 Dataset

The gold standard obtained through the method described in Section 3 consists of 547 online posts. This number was achieved after discarding irrelevant posts and ones that consisted of images only. Moreover, some online posts that were originally collected after the budget, were deleted from the original data source at the time of rating, in which case they were also removed. The distribution of the dataset annotations are represented as follows: sentiment polarity in Table 3, sentiment polarity intensity in Table 4 and emotion in Tables 5 and 6, respectively.

Polarity	Online Posts	Percentage
Positive	122	22.3%
Neutral	145	26.5%
Negative	280	51.2%

Table 3: Distribution of sentiment polarity annotations

Polarity Intensity	Online Posts	Percentage
Very Positive	37	6.8%
Positive	85	15.5%
Neutral	145	26.5%
Negative	193	35.3%
Very Negative	87	15.9%

Table 4: Distribution of sentiment polarity intensity annotations

Emotion	Online Posts	Percentage
Anger	131	23.9%
Disgust	159	29.1%
Fear	10	1.8%
Happiness	132	24.1%
Sadness	26	4.8%
Surprise	89	16.3%

Table 5: Distribution of emotion (6-levels) annotations

Emotion	Online Posts	Percentage
Anger	121	22.1%
Anticipation	95	17.4%
Disgust	154	28.2%
Fear	5	0.9%
Joy	50	9.1%
Sadness	23	4.2%
Surprise	39	7.1%
Trust	60	11%

Table 6: Distribution of emotion (8-levels) annotations

The dataset annotation results displayed do not fully reflect the opinions portrayed by the writers,

---

[13]Ekman's 6-levels (Ekman, 1992) and Plutchik's 8-levels (Plutchik, 1980) emotion categories were chosen due to them being the most popular for Emotion Analysis

since a large amount of online posts were off-topic to the budget (34.2%). These are still very relevant for filtering out noisy user-generated posts, which are very common in Malta for such kind of public feedback, especially in newswire comments. Examples of such posts are the ones discussing the topic of smoking and how easy/difficult it is to stop smoking and on the contraband of cigarettes. These emerged as a result of no budget measure being taken towards increasing cigarette prices.

Moreover, certain sentiment polarities, polarity intensities and/or emotions were not targeted at budget measures, but to some previously submitted online post/set of posts. In such cases, the context of the online posts should be considered when determining the opinion, including any related posts[14]. This is a task for aspect-based opinion mining (Hu and Liu, 2004), which classifies a particular opinion type, such as sentiment polarity and/or emotion, for a given entity/aspect, such as a political party or budget measure.

Table 7 presents the distribution of sarcasm/irony, negation, off-topic and Maltese annotations. With regards to the latter, several online posts contained text with Maltese and English terminology. The ones that contained only one term/phrase in a particular language were not considered when annotating the language. The sarcasm and irony annotation was merged given that they convey similar characteristics in the content meaning the opposite of what is being said, where the former has a malicious intention towards the target i.e. person, whereas the latter does not.

Annotation	Online Posts	Percentage
Sarcasm/Irony	126	23.0%
Negation	39	7.1%
Off-topic	187	34.2%
Maltese	177	32.4%

Table 7: Distribution of the sarcasm/irony, negation, off-topic and Maltese language annotations

The dataset has been published[15] for general use under the Creative Commons Attribution-NonCommercial-ShareAlike 4.0 International (CC BY-NC-SA 4.0) license[16].

---

[14]346 online posts were related to at least one another post
[15]https://github.com/kcortis/malta-budget-social-opinion/
[16]https://creativecommons.org/licenses/by-nc-sa/4.0/

5 Benefits

The following are the benefits of this dataset for the Natural Language Processing community:

- Contains online posts in Malta's two official languages, Maltese and English;

- Hand-crafted rules using linguistic intuition can be built based on the given data, i.e., a knowledge-based approach, which can be a good start if a rule-based social opinion mining approach is primarily used before evolving towards a hybrid approach (rule and machine learning/deep learning-based) once more data is collected and annotated. The VADER lexicon and rule-based sentiment analysis tool is one such example of a high performing knowledge-based system that implements grammatical and syntactical rules (Hutto and Gilbert, 2014);

- Can be used to bootstrap a semi-automatic annotation process for large-scale machine learning i.e., deep learning models;

- Can encourage more researchers/people working in this domain to add to this dataset which is available for public use;

- Is a representative corpus for computational corpus linguistic analysis for social scientists.

6 Conclusions

We have described a novel dataset of social opinions for the Malta Government Budget 2018 which is a valuable resource for developing opinion mining tools that gather political and socio-economic insights from user-generated social data in Malta's two official languages, Maltese and English. Therefore, it has potential of being used for initiatives by the Maltese Government, such as building intelligence on the Maltese Economy. The novelty of including Maltese and English online posts in this dataset, makes it a valuable resource for Maltese Human Language Technology and for testing Opinion Mining applications in general.

Moreover, it has been annotated with several forms of opinions in sentiment, emotion, sarcasm and irony, making it highly beneficial and a first contribution of its kind for Malta. Finally, this dataset is a work in progress and its volume will be increased per annual budget.

References

2018. Social media usage trends in malta in 2018. The Malta Independent.

Lea Canales Zaragoza. 2018. Tackling the challenge of emotion annotation in text.

Claire Caruana. 2018. Just 10 per cent of maltese are not on social media. Times of Malta.

Jacob Cohen. 1960. A coefficient of agreement for nominal scales. *Educational and psychological measurement*, 20(1):37–46.

Laurence Devillers, Laurence Vidrascu, and Lori Lamel. 2005. Challenges in real-life emotion annotation and machine learning based detection. *Neural Networks*, 18(4):407–422.

William D. Eggers, Neha Malik, and Matt Gracie. 2019. Using ai to unleash the power of unstructured government data. Deloitte Insights.

Paul Ekman. 1992. An argument for basic emotions. *Cognition & emotion*, 6(3-4):169–200.

Eurostat. 2017. Living online: what the internet is used for.

Eurostat. 2018. Almost 75 % of enterprises in malta use social media.

Herman Grech. 2019. Here's the bad news. Times of Malta.

Minqing Hu and Bing Liu. 2004. Mining and summarizing customer reviews. In *Proceedings of the tenth ACM SIGKDD international conference on Knowledge discovery and data mining*, pages 168–177. ACM.

Rocío B Hubert, Elsa Estevez, Ana Maguitman, and Tomasz Janowski. 2018. Examining government-citizen interactions on twitter using visual and sentiment analysis. In *Proceedings of the 19th Annual International Conference on Digital Government Research: Governance in the Data Age*, page 55. ACM.

Clayton J Hutto and Eric Gilbert. 2014. Vader: A parsimonious rule-based model for sentiment analysis of social media text. In *Eighth international AAAI conference on weblogs and social media*.

Evangelos Kalampokis, Michael Hausenblas, and Konstantinos Tarabanis. 2011. Combining social and government open data for participatory decision-making. In *International Conference on Electronic Participation*, pages 36–47. Springer.

Saif M Mohammad and Peter D Turney. 2013. Crowdsourcing a word–emotion association lexicon. *Computational Intelligence*, 29(3):436–465.

Fathoni A Musyaffa, Lavdim Halilaj, Yakun Li, Fabrizio Orlandi, Hajira Jabeen, Sören Auer, and Maria-Esther Vidal. 2018. Openbudgets. eu: A platform for semantically representing and analyzing open fiscal data. In *International Conference on Web Engineering*, pages 433–447. Springer.

Robert Plutchik. 1980. Chapter 1 - a general psycho-evolutionary theory of emotion. In Robert Plutchik and Henry Kellerman, editors, *Theories of Emotion*, pages 3 – 33. Academic Press.

The Fallacy of Echo Chambers: Analyzing the Political Slants of User-Generated News Comments in Korean Media

Jiyoung Han[1], Youngin Lee[1], Junbum Lee[2], Meeyoung Cha[3][1]
[1]Korea Advanced Institute of Science and Technology (KAIST), Daejeon, Korea
[2]Seoul National Univ. of Education, Seoul, Korea
[3]Institute for Basic Science (IBS), Daejeon, Korea
jiyoung.hann@gmail.com, antagonist@kaist.ac.kr,
jun@beomi.net, meeyoung.cha@gmail.com

Abstract

This study analyzes the political slants of user comments on Korean partisan media. We built a BERT-based classifier to detect political leaning of short comments via the use of semi-unsupervised deep learning methods that produced an F1 score of 0.83. As a result of classifying 21.6K comments, we found the high presence of conservative bias on both conservative and liberal news outlets. Moreover, this study discloses an asymmetry across the partisan spectrum in that more liberals (48.0%) than conservatives (23.6%) comment not only on news stories resonating with their political perspectives but also on those challenging their viewpoints. These findings advance the current understanding of online echo chambers.

1 Introduction

User-generated news comments manifest the interactive and participatory nature of online journalism. Unlike letters to the editor, the comments section allows readers to express their thoughts and feelings in response to news stories they read more publicly and instantaneously. Moreover, comments themselves generate subsequent user reactions from others. For example, in South Korea, news portals wherein the vast majority consume news online displays the list of "most commented" articles along with the "most viewed" news stories. This aggregation of user responses is a major contributing factor toward news selection (KPF, 2018). As such, real-time user reactions, rather than the cover stories of newspapers, now tell people what to read and think about, signifying the shift of the traditional direction of agenda-setting (Lee and Tandoc, 2017).

On a related note, about 63% of South Koreans getting news online reported they regularly read the comments section (DMCReport, 2013) and consider them as a valid, direct cue to public opinion (Lee and Tandoc, 2017). Much research has corroborated the role of comments on the formation of public opinion (Springer, Engelmann, and Pfaffinger, 2015; Waddell, 2018). Nonetheless, diverging from the massive scholarly attention paid to the role of hyper-partisan news media, little research has analyzed political biases of news comments. This study aims to fill this void in current literature by examining political slants of news comments as well as the overlap of commenters across the partisan spectrum. These examinations will contribute to advancing the current understanding of the presence of echo chambers in the realm of online news comment sections.

To analyze comments on a million scale, we took two different approaches. First, we trained a BERT model based on news stories published by both liberal and conservative news outlets. Second, we expanded the seed data of human-labeled news comments with the use of user information and built a comment-specific classifier. Next, based on the best performing model, the political slants of 21.6K news comments were analyzed. This allows us to examine the composition of the political diversity of commenters within each liberal and conservative news outlet. For the identified liberal- or conservative-leaning commenters, we also tracked whether they leave comments on news stories resonating with their own political preferences or do so to news stories challenging their political viewpoints.

2 Related Work

2.1 Partisan Media and Echo Chambers

The proliferation of partisan media has invited much scholarly concern about the rise of echo chambers (Sunstein, 2009). As more people tune into news outlets congenial to their political viewpoints, their existing preferences reinforce and, in turn, opinion polarization and social ex-

Proceedings of the 2019 EMNLP Workshop W-NUT: The 5th Workshop on Noisy User-generated Text, pages 370–374
Hong Kong, Nov 4, 2019. ©2019 Association for Computational Linguistics

tremism become prevalent (Iyengar and Hahn, 2009; Stroud, 2010). The recent employment of web tracking technologies, however, rebuts the echo chamber hypothesis with the observational data showing accidental or purposeful crosscutting news exposure (Gentzkow and Shapiro, 2011; Flaxman, Goel, and Rao, 2016).

However, in the realms of online discussion forums including online news commenting sections, to date there is no evidence opposing the extant findings such that people are more likely to leave comments in alignment with the other posts, thus leaving user commenting sections homogeneous (Lee and Jang, 2010; Hsueh, Yogeeswaran, and Malinen, 2015). Interestingly, whereas user comments posted on news websites exerted considerable power in the perceptions of individuals' inference about public opinion (Lee and Jang, 2010, 2010), no such effect emerged when it comes to user comments posted on news outlets' Facebook pages (Winter, Brückner, and Krämer, 2015).

2.2 Neural Network for Text Classification

User-contributed news comments are, by nature, informal, irregular, and erratic. To reduce the noise of the dataset as such, many studies have adopted various data cleaning methods. However, user generated text is difficult to sanitize and the results could be misleading if we apply a naive statistic method. Recent NLP (natural language processing) research has shown that neural network approaches outperform conventional statistical models. For instance, TextCNN (Kim, 2014) gained performance in text classification tasks via introducing convolutional layers and BERT (Devlin, Chang, Lee, and Toutanova, 2018) shows state-of-the-art results via its bidirectional transformer network, and it shows Modern text classification methods utilize pretrained models like BERT by fine-tuning them on the target NLP domain.

3 Data Collection

Using "minimum wage" as a keyword, we crawled news stories and their associated user comments on NAVER, the top news portal site in South Korea. The platform offers its own user commenting section and ten times more Internet users are known to read news on NAVER compared to individual news websites. From January to July of 2019, 1534 articles from three conservative news outlets–*Chosun Ilbo, Joongang Ilbo,*

and *Donga Ilbo*–and 765 from thee progressive ones–*Hankyoreh, Kyunghyang Shinmun,* and *OhMyNews*–were collected, with a total of 2299 news stories.

We collected press releases of the two major political parties in South Korea–the liberal Democratic Party of Korea and the conservative Liberty Korea Party–containing the phrase "minimum wage." This data serves as the basis for learning partisan framing and for filtering out irrelevant topics that might create noise in determining the political stance of news comments. We performed part-of-speech tagging on the press releases and analyzed the frequency of nouns and bigrams. From the list of nouns and bigrams appearing more than a hundred times, the authors carefully examined and selected phrases that were relevant. In this way, the list of related keywords (i.e., nouns and bigrams) on the minimum wage was compiled for the liberal and conservative parties, respectively. This list includes a wide range of phrases relevant to politics in general, such as inter-Korean summit, denuclearization, corruption, flexible working hours, labor union, and unemployment rates.

Online news comments were also collected from NAVER's top "most commented" stories on each of seven major news sections including national, politics, economy, culture, world, and lifestyle, resulting in a total of 210 most commented news stories per day. These news stories received around 38 million news comments by 1.8 million unique users. This data contains text content as well as user identifiers.

4 Language Models

4.1 Classification from News Articles

We first built a classifier trained on news articles in order to observe how well news articles could proxy comments in the task of political bias classification. To compensate for the relatively small news article dataset, we spliced the news articles into individual sentences and then filtered in sentences that included at least one of the identified partisan-specific keywords. Two hundred conservative and liberal articles (100 each) were set aside for validation tests. The remaining 2,099 articles were spliced sentences, resulting in 49.8K sentences. Each sentence was labeled as either conservative or liberal based on the political leaning of the news outlets. The completed dataset consists of 20.3K liberal and 29.5K conservative sentences.

Using the BERT-based pre-trained model for the Korean language, KorBERT[1], we trained a classifier for binary classification task of news sentences. Test data composed of the 200 news articles mentioned above (i.e., 100 each from liberal and conservative news outlets). Test sets were further prepared in two different manners: (1) the HEADLINE representation includes headlines only of the labeled data and (2) the BODY-TEXT representation includes only sentences containing partisan-specific keywords in the news body text. The former representation was considered since political slant are known to be more apparent in news headlines.

4.2 Classification from News Comments

We also built another language model that is trained on the slants of news comments directly. To obtain labels, we randomly sampled 4,827 user comments that had been posted to stories on the minimum wage and employed three coders. These coders labeled each comment as liberal, conservative, or other (including nuetral). After a series of training sessions, coders could achieve an acceptable inter-coder reliability (Krippendorff's alpha = .7015). Coders next independently labeled the rest. This human-labeled dataset consisted of 1,345 liberal (27.6%), 1,597 conservative (32.8%), and 1,930 other (39.6%) comments.

To ensure sufficient training data, we expanded the comment labels by a semi-unsupervised method. All online users who had authored at least two comments in the human-labeled dataset were identified. The bias of each user was computed as the mean of their comment labels, where scores are -1 for a liberal comment and +1 for a conservative. We selected those users whose mean bias score was below -0.8 or above 0.8 and identified 250 such users, whose political leaning could be recognized. We then collected all comments authored by the 250 users from the entire news corpus of 6 months. Under the assumption that the political stance of these users would be constant during this time period, we labeled these comments with the author's computed political bias. The final dataset contained a total of 93,565 comments, out of which 17,535 were liberal and 76,030 were conservative.

The expanded comment labels were used to train two NLP models: TextCNN and BERT. We undersampled 17,535 conservative comments to balance the labels, resulting in a total of 35,070 labels. We set aside 10% of labels as the test set, then split the remainder into 10% of the validation set and 90% of the train set to train the models.

The TextCNN-based model employed padding up to 300 characters, which is the maximum length of comments on NAVER. Comments were tokenized on character level and fed into an embedding layer of 300 dimensions. The model used a single-dimensional CNN with the channels of sizes 5, 10, 15, and 20, respectively. Then the data were fed into the max-pooling layer with a dropout ratio of 0.5 and classified through a linear layer. We used Adam optimizer with the default learning rate (1e-3) and trained six epochs, as validation loss did not converge. For the second model, we again utilized the pretrained BERT model for the Korean language, KorBERT. Comments were tokenized by words and padded to a size of 70. The model converged after two epochs with a higher learning rate (1e-3), with the lowest loss.

5 Results

5.1 Bias Classification

After training the BERT classifier on news sentence labels, we evaluated the model by classifying political slants of the HEADLINE and BODY-TEXT representations into liberal and conservative labels. The performance of the classifiers was measured in terms of Matthew's correlation coefficient, accuracy, and F1-scores. Table 1 summarizes the results, which shows the BODY-TEXT representation of the validation set showed the best result. The slant detection model trained on news article data, however, was not effective in detecting slant of user-contributed comments, indicated by the low F1 score of 0.3571.

Test set	Matthew's	Accuracy	F1
HEADLINE	0.7825	0.8900	0.8942
BODY-TEXT	0.8202	0.9100	0.9109
Comments	-0.0844	0.4600	0.3571

Table 1: Performance of Article Bias Classifier

When comment labels were utilized for training, existing language models could successfully detect the slant of news comments, as dis-

[1]http://aiopen.etri.re.kr/

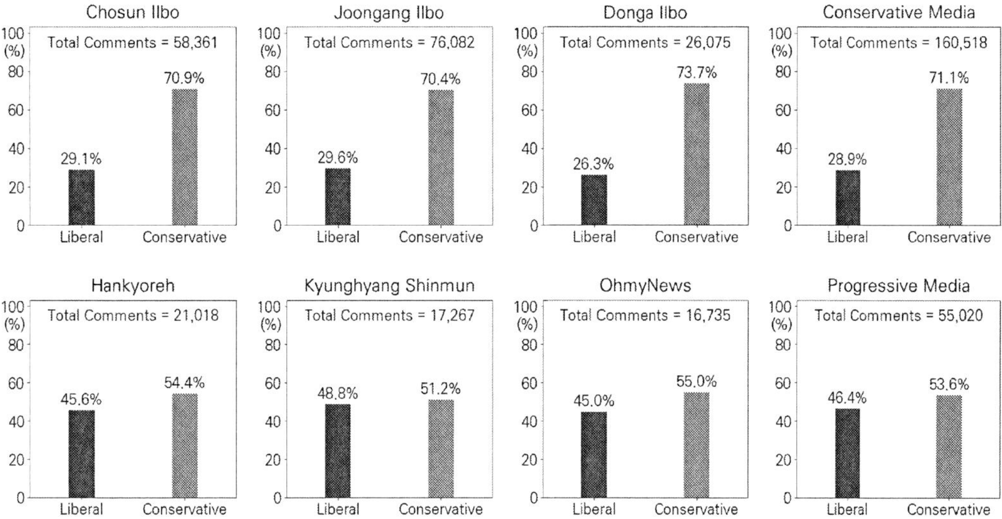

Figure 1: The proportion of liberal and conservative news comments within the progressive and conservative media's comment sections

played in Table 2. BERT-based model outperformed TextCNN model in this domain-specific learning task.

Models	Matthew's	Accuracy	F1
TextCNN	0.5087	0.7516	0.7684
BERT	0.6644	0.8322	0.8322

Table 2: Performance of Comment Bias Classifier

5.2 Bias Distribution in User Comments

We analyzed the distribution of political slants in the comment sections. From the set of news articles on minimum wage, we inferred political bias labels for the comments of all articles published by the aforementioned major outlets with the best-performing model (i.e., BERT-based model trained on comment labels) and used it to derive a statistic on bias distribution.

Fig 1 shows the percentage of liberal and conservative comments for each news outlet based on the labels inferred. The figure demonstrates a clear presence of conservative bias in user comments across all partisan news media; Even for the bottom three liberal outlets, more news comments are conservative-leaning, as opposed to the widely accepted echo chamber conjecture in digital media.

6 Discussion & Conclusion

The slant classifier trained on news articles related to the minimum wage issue performed well on similar news articles. However, the same model performed poorly in the comments section. This may be due to the unstructured nature of the user-generated data that is very different from editorialized news content. The slant classifiers trained on the labeled comment data, however, showed promising performance on classifying the political bias of crowd-generated comments.

The analysis in this paper revealed that the majority of user comments are pro-conservatives in Korean news outlets, although conservative partisan media attracted more congenial comments (71.1% conservative *versus* 28.9% liberal) than liberal ones (46.4% liberal *versus* 53.6% conservative). This finding may suggest the fallacy of online echo chambers in Korean news media.

We do not, however, argue that the prominent crossover, of news commenters in both liberal and conservative news stories, represents that online users in South Korea have established a more balanced news reading habits nor have disrupted the "filter bubble." Notably, because a recent study indicated that being exposed to opposing views can sometimes backfire and further increase polarization (Bail et al., 2018).

Moreover, the auxiliary analyses tracking user IDs further showed that less than half of liberals

(48.0%) and conservatives (23.6%) commented on both congenial and uncongenial partisan news outlets. This finding provides imperative insights to the current understanding of online political discussions in the era of partisan media.

This work bares several limitations that can be improved. First, the expanded comments dataset that was built from human-labeled news comments could be validated further. While we assumed people's slant remains consistent over a half a year, there is a chance that the political slant of commenters could differ by news topics. Second, while this paper utilized data from contributors who post news comments frequently, future methods could also consider data from one-time commenters. Such methods could reveal the political slant map of comments more comprehensively.

References

Bail, C. A., Argyle, L. P., Brown, T. W., Bumpus, J. P., Chen, H., Hunzaker, M. B. F., ... Volfovsky, A. (2018). Exposure to opposing views on social media can increase political polarization. *Proceedings of the National Academy of Sciences*.

Devlin, J., Chang, M.-W., Lee, K., & Toutanova, K. (2018). Bert: Pre-training of deep bidirectional transformers for language understanding. *arXiv preprint arXiv:1810.04805*.

DMCReport. (2013). Online news consumption in korea. *DMC report 2013*.

Flaxman, S., Goel, S., & Rao, J. M. (2016). Filter bubbles, echo chambers, and online news consumption. *Public opinion quarterly*, *80*(S1), 298–320.

Gentzkow, M. & Shapiro, J. M. (2011). Ideological segregation online and offline. *The Quarterly Journal of Economics*, *126*(4), 1799–1839.

Hsueh, M., Yogeeswaran, K., & Malinen, S. (2015). "leave your comment below": Can biased online comments influence our own prejudicial attitudes and behaviors? *Human Communication Research*, *41*(4), 557–576.

Iyengar, S. & Hahn, K. S. (2009). Red media, blue media: Evidence of ideological selectivity in media use. *Journal of Communication*, *59*(1), 19–39.

Kim, Y. (2014). Convolutional neural networks for sentence classification. *arXiv preprint arXiv:1408.5882*.

KPF. (2018). *2018 news consumer report*. Seoul: Korea Press Foundation.

Lee, E.-J. & Jang, Y. J. (2010). What do others' reactions to news on internet portal sites tell us? effects of presentation format and readers' need for cognition on reality perception. *Communication Research*, *37*(6), 825–846.

Lee, E.-J. & Tandoc, E. C. (2017). When news meets the audience: How audience feedback online affects news production and consumption. *Human Communication Research*, *43*(4), 436–449.

Springer, N., Engelmann, I., & Pfaffinger, C. (2015). User comments: Motives and inhibitors to write and read. *Information, Communication & Society*, *18*(7), 798–815.

Stroud, N. J. (2010). Polarization and partisan selective exposure. *Journal of communication*, *60*(3), 556–576.

Sunstein, C. R. (2009). *Going to extremes: How like minds unite and divide*. Oxford University Press.

Waddell, T. F. (2018). What does the crowd think? how online comments and popularity metrics affect news credibility and issue importance. *New Media & Society*, *20*(8), 3068–3083.

Winter, S., Brückner, C., & Krämer, N. C. (2015). They came, they liked, they commented: Social influence on Facebook news channels. *Cyberpsychology, Behavior, and Social Networking*, *18*(8), 431–436.

Gabriel Stanovsky
University of Washington
Allen Institute for Artificial Intelligence
gabis@allenai.org

Ronen Tamari[*]
Hebrew University of Jerusalem
ronent@cs.huji.ac.il

Y'all should read this!

Identifying Plurality in Second-Person Personal Pronouns in English Texts

Abstract

Distinguishing between singular and plural "you" in English is a challenging task which has potential for downstream applications, such as machine translation or coreference resolution. While formal written English does not distinguish between these cases, other languages (such as Spanish), as well as other dialects of English (via phrases such as "y'all"), do make this distinction. We make use of this to obtain distantly-supervised labels for the task on a large-scale in two domains. Following, we train a model to distinguish between the single/plural 'you', finding that although in-domain training achieves reasonable accuracy ($\geq 77\%$), there is still a lot of room for improvement, especially in the domain-transfer scenario, which proves extremely challenging. Our code and data are publicly available.[1]

1 Introduction

The second-person personal pronoun (e.g., "you" in English) is used by a speaker when referring to active participants in a dialog or an event. Various languages, such as Spanish, Hebrew, or French, have different words to distinguish between singular "you" (referring to a single participant) and plural "you" (for multiple participants). Traditionally, English has made this distinction as well. The now archaic "thou" indicated singular second-person, while "you" was reserved for plural uses. The last several hundred years, however, have seen modern formal written English largely abandoning this distinction, conflating both meanings into an ambiguous "all-purpose you" (Maynor, 2000).

In this work, we are interested in the following

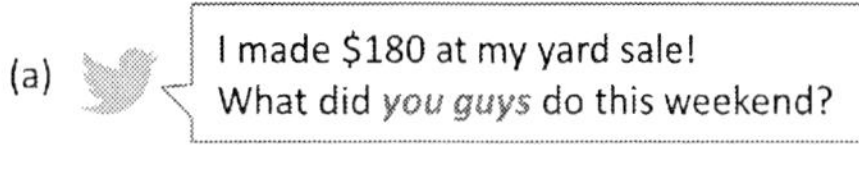

Figure 1: We use two sources for distant-supervision for singular (marked in purple) versus plural (marked in blue) second person pronouns: (a) we find colloquial uses on Twitter, and (b) through alignment with Spanish, which formally distinguishes between the cases.

research question: *How can we automatically disambiguate between singular and plural "you"?*

While this topic has received much attention in linguistic literature (Jochnowitz, 1983; Tillery and Bailey, 1998; Maynor, 2000; Haspelmath, 2013; Molina, 2016), it has been largely unexplored in the context of computational linguistics, despite its potential benefits for downstream natural language processing (NLP) tasks. For example, distinguishing between singular and plural "you" can serve as additional signal when translating between English and a language which formally makes this distinction. See Figure 2 where an error in interpreting a plural "you" in the source English text results in a non-grammatical Hebrew translation. This example can be amended by replacing "you" with the informal "you guys".

To tackle this task, we create two large-scale corpora annotated with distantly-supervised binary labels distinguishing between singular and plural "you" in two different domains (see Figure 1). First, we regard Twitter as a noisy corpus for informal English and automatically identify speakers who make use of an informal form of the English plural "you", such as "y'all" or "you

---

[*] Work done during an internship at the Allen Institute for Artificial Intelligence.

[1] https://github.com/gabrielStanovsky/yall

Proceedings of the 2019 EMNLP Workshop W-NUT: The 5th Workshop on Noisy User-generated Text, pages 375–380
Hong Kong, Nov 4, 2019. ©2019 Association for Computational Linguistics

Figure 2: An example translation from English to Hebrew (Google Translate, Aug. 21, 2019). The first sentence depicts wrong interpretation of "you" resulting in a non-grammatical Hebrew translation, due to wrong inflections of pronoun and verb (marked in red). Both issues are fixed when changing "you" to "you guys" in English in the second example (marked in green).

Domain	Example	Plurality
Twitter	# goodnight #twittersphere <3 I love **y'all**! Including @anonimized. Even if she hates me. <3	*Plural*
(masked)	# goodnight #twittersphere <3 I love **you**! Including @anonimized. Even if she hates me. <3	
Twitter	! @anonimized, Happy anniversary of entering the world! Look how much **you** have done!	*Singular*
Europarl	I am terribly sorry, Mr Hansch and Mr Cox. I did not see **you** asking to speak.	*Plural*
Europarl	I should be very grateful, Mrs Schroedter, if **you** would actually include this proposed amendment in the part relating to subsidiarity in your positive deliberations.	*Singular*

Table 1: Examples from our two domains. Twitter is informal, includes hashtags, mentions (anonymized here), and plural "you" (e.g., "y'all" in the first example), which we mask as a generic "you" as shown in the second row. In contrast, Europarl is formal and "you" is used for plural (third example), as well as singular uses (last example).

guys", which are common in American English speaking communities (Katz, 2016). We record a *plurality* binary label, and mask the tweet by replacing these with the generic "you". Second, we use the Europarl English-Spanish parallel corpus (Koehn, 2005), and identify cases where the formal plural Spanish second-person pronoun aligns with "you" in the English text.

Finally, we fine-tune BERT (Devlin et al., 2018) on each of these corpora. We find that contextual cues indeed allow our model to recover the correct intended use in more than 77% of the instances, when tested in-domain. Out-of-domain performance drops significantly, doing only slightly better than a random coin toss. This could indicate that models are learning surface cues which are highly domain-dependent and do not generalize well.

Future work can make use of our corpus and techniques to collect more data for this task, as well as incorporating similar predictors in down-stream tasks.

2 Task Definition

Given the word "you" marked in an input text, the task of *plurality identification* is to make a binary decision whether this utterance refers to:

- A single entity, such as the examples in rows 2 or 4 in Table 1.

- Multiple participants, such as those referred to in the third line in Table 1.

In the following sections we collect data for this task and develop models for its automatic prediction.

3 Distant Supervision: The *y'all* Corpus

Manually collecting data for this task on a large-scale is an expensive and involved process. Instead, we employ different techniques to obtain distantly supervised labels in two domains, as

	Twitter	Europarl
Train	58963	11249
Dev	7370	1405
Test	7370	1405
Total	**73703**	**14059**

Table 2: Number of instances in our two corpora. Each of the partitions (train, dev, test) is equally split between plural and singular second-person personal pronouns.

elaborated below. These are then randomly split between train (80% of the data), development, and test (10% each). See Table 2 for details about each of these datasets, which we make publicly available.

3.1 The Twitter Domain

As mentioned in the Introduction, English speaking communities tend to maintain the singular versus plural "you" distinction by introducing idiosyncratic phrases which specifically indicate a plural pronoun, while reserving "you" for the singular use-case. We operationalize this observation on a large Twitter corpus (Cheng et al., 2010) in the following manner:

- First, we identify speakers who use an informal plural "you" at least once in any of their tweets.[2]

- Following, we assume that these users speak an English dialect which distinguishes between singular and plural second-person pronouns, interpreting their "you" as a singular pronoun. See the first two tweets in Table 1, for an example of these two uses by the same user.

- Finally, we mask out the plural pronoun in each of their tweets by replacing it with a generic "you" (see the second row in Table 1). This allows us to test whether models can subsequently rely on contextual cues to recover the original intention.

This process yields about 36K plural instances, which we augment with 36K singular instances from the same users, to obtain a corpus which is balanced between the two classes.

<hr>

[2]We use a fixed list of informal plural "you", including *you guys*, *y'all* and *youse*. See `https://en.wikipedia.org/wiki/You#Informal_plural_forms` for the complete list.

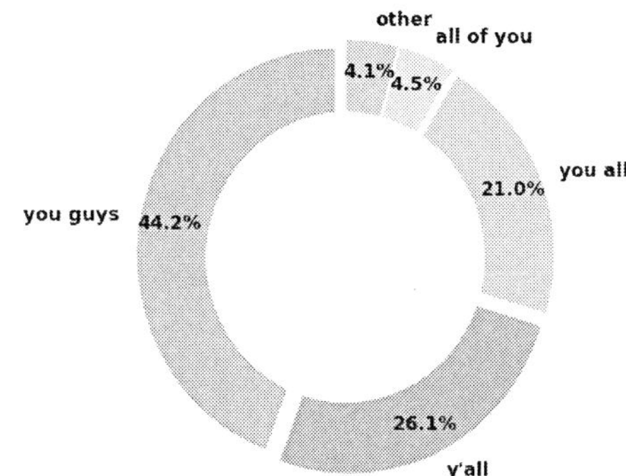

Figure 3: Histogram distribution of informal plural "you" forms in the development partition of our Twitter corpus.

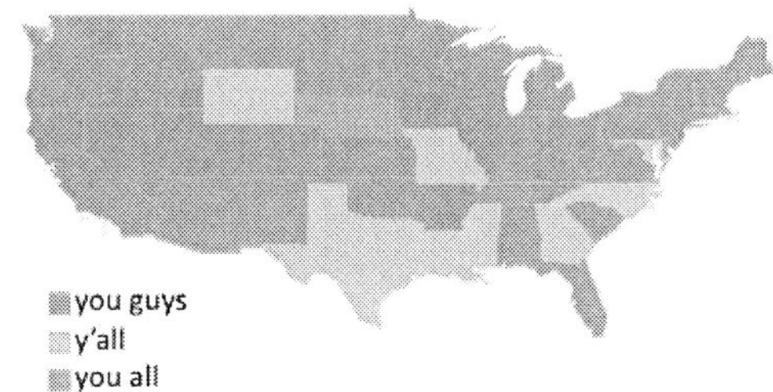

Figure 4: Variation in the most common phrase used for plural "you" in our Twitter corpus across states in the continental United States.

Data analysis Our Twitter corpus was composed of U.S. based users, and included geo-locations for 36.8K of the plural tweets. This allows for several interesting observations. First, Figure 3 shows the distribution of informal plural "you" phrases in our corpus (before masking). Second, using the tweets geo-location, we can plot the geographical variation in usage. Figure 4 shows the most common term for plural "you" in each state in the continental United States. While most of the U.S. prefers "you guys", southern states (such as Texas or Louisiana) prefer "y'all". Katz (2016) reached similar conclusions through a large-scale online survey. Interestingly, our survey of Twitter usage differs from theirs for several Midwestern states, such as Wyoming or Nebraska.

Quality estimation. We evaluate the assumption we made above (i.e., that users reserve "you" for the singular case) by asking an English native-speaker to annotate a sample of 100 singular "you" instances from our Twitter corpus. In 70% of the instances, the annotator agreed that these indeed represent a singular "you", leaving the other 30% to either ambiguous or inconsistent usage (i.e., sometimes "you" *is* used for a plural use-case). Overall, while there is a non-negligible amount of noise in the Twitter domain, in Section 5 we show that the signal is strong enough for models to pick up on and achieve good accuracy.

3.2 The Europarl Domain

Another method to obtain distant supervision for this task is through an alignment with a language which distinguishes between the two usages of the pronoun. To that end, we use the Spanish and English parallel texts available as part of Europarl (Koehn, 2005), a large corpus containing aligned sentences from meeting transcripts of the European parliament.

As these texts originate from a formal setting, we expect to find much less colloquial phrases. Indeed, the term "y'all" does not appear at all, while "you guys" appears only twice in about 2 million sentences. Instead, we rely on the gold alignment with Spanish sentences, which have a formal plural "you" - *ustedes* or *vosotros*. We find Spanish sentences which have exactly one plural "you" and which aligns with an English sentence containing exactly one "you". This process yields about 7K sentences which we mark with a "plural" label. Similarly to the Twitter domain, we augment these with the same amount of singular "you", found in the same manner; by tracing a Spanish singular "you" to a single English "you". This process yields a balanced binary corpus.

Quality estimation We sampled 100 instances from the Europarl domain to estimate the quality of our binary labels. Unlike the Twitter domain, in Europarl we rely on gold alignments and cleaner text. As a result, we found that about 90% of the labels agree with a human annotator, while the remaining 10% were ambiguous.

3.3 Discussion

The distinction between plural and singular "you" in English is an instance of a more general phenomenon. Namely, semantic features are expressed in varying degrees of lexical or grammatical explicitness across different languages.

For instance, languages vary in grammatical tense-marking (Wolfram, 1985), from languages with no morphological tense, such as Mandarin (Wang and Sun, 2015), to languages

test → train ↓	Europarl	Twitter
Europarl	77.1	56.8
Twitter	56.3	**83.1**
Joint	**77.5**	82.8

Table 3: Accuracy (percent of correct predictions) of our fine-tuned BERT model, tested both in- and out-of-domain. Rows indicate train corpus, columns indicate test corpus. Bold numbers indicate best performance on test corpus.

with 9 different tense-marking morphological inflections (Comrie, 1985). Similarly, languages vary in gender-marking in pronouns, from genderless Turkish, to languages with six genders or more (Awde and Galaev, 1997).

The two data collection methods we presented here, finding colloquial explicit utterances on social media, and alignment with another language, may also be applicable to some of these phenomena and present an interesting avenue for future work.

4 Model

We fine-tune the BERT-large pretrained embeddings (Devlin et al., 2018)[3] on the training partition of each of our domains (Twitter and Europarl), as well as on a concatenation of both domains (Joint). We then classify based on the [CLS] token in each of these instances. We use a fixed learning rate of $2e - 5$ and a batch size of 24. Training for 10 Epochs on a Titan X GPU took about 3 hours for the Twitter domain, 2 hours for the Europarl domain and roughly 5 hours for the Joint model.

5 Evaluation

We test models trained both in and out of domain for both parts of our dataset (Twitter and Europarl) as well as a joint model, trained on both parts of the dataset. We use accuracy (percent of correct predictions), as our dataset is binary and both classes are symmetric and evenly distributed. Our main findings are shown in Table 3. Following, several observations can be made.

---

[3]Using Hugging Face's implementation: https://github.com/huggingface/pytorch-transformers

In-domain performance does significantly better than chance. For both domains, BERT achieves more than 77% accuracy. Indicating that the contextual cues in both domains are meaningful enough to capture correlations with plural and singular uses.

Out-of-domain performance is significantly degraded. We see significant drop in performance when testing either model on the other part of the dataset. Both models do only slightly better than chance. This may indicate that the cues for plurality are vastly different between the two domains, probably due to differences in vocabulary, tone, or formality.

Training jointly on the two domains maintains good performance, but does not improve upon it. A model trained on both the Twitter and Europarl domains achieves the in-domain performance of each of the individual in-domain models, but does not improve over them. This may indicate that while BERT is expressive enough to model both domains, it only picks up on surface cues in each and does not generalize across domains. As a result, robustness is questionable for out-of-domain instances.

6   Related Work

Several previous works have touched on related topics. A few works developed models for understanding the second-person pronoun within coreference resolution frameworks (Purver et al., 2009; Zhou and Choi, 2018). Perhaps most related to our work is Gupta et al. (2007), who have tackled the orthogonal problem of disambiguation between generic (or editorial) "you" and referential "you".

To the best of our knowledge, we are the first to deal with plurality identification in second-person personal pronouns in English.

7   Conclusion and Future Work

We presented the first corpus for the identification of plurality in second-person personal pronouns in English texts. Labels were collected on a large scale from two domains (Twitter and Europarl) using different distant-supervision techniques.

Following, a BERT model was fine-tuned on the labeled data, showing that while models achieve reasonable in-domain performance, they significantly suffer from domain transfer, degrading performance close to random chance. Interesting avenues for future work may be to extend this data to new domains, develop more complex models for the task (which may achieve better cross-domain performance), and integrating plurality models in downstream tasks, such as machine translation or coreference resolution.

Acknowledgements

We thank the anonymous reviewers for their many helpful comments and suggestions.

References

Nicholas Awde and Muhammad Galaev. 1997. *Chechen-English English-Chechen: Dictionary and Phrasebook*. Hippocrene Books.

Zhiyuan Cheng, James Caverlee, and Kyumin Lee. 2010. You are where you tweet: a content-based approach to geo-locating twitter users. In *CIKM*.

Bernard Comrie. 1985. *Tense*, volume 17. Cambridge university press.

Jacob Devlin, Ming-Wei Chang, Kenton Lee, and Kristina Toutanova. 2018. BERT: Pre-training of deep bidirectional transformers for language understanding. In *NAACL-HLT*.

Surabhi Gupta, Matthew Purver, and Dan Jurafsky. 2007. Disambiguating between generic and referential you in dialog. In *Proceedings of the 45th Annual Meeting of the Association for Computational Linguistics Companion Volume Proceedings of the Demo and Poster Sessions*, pages 105–108.

Martin Haspelmath. 2013. Politeness distinctions in second-person pronouns. In *The Atlas of Pidgin and Creole Language Structures*, pages 68–71. Oxford Univ. Pr.

George Jochnowitz. 1983. Another view of you guys. *American Speech*, 58(1):68–70.

Josh Katz. 2016. *Speaking American: How Y'all, Youse, and You Guys Talk: A Visual Guide*. Houghton Mifflin Harcourt.

Philipp Koehn. 2005. Europarl: A parallel corpus for statistical machine translation.

Natalie Maynor. 2000. Battle of the pronouns: Y'all versus you-guys. *American speech*, 75(4):416–418.

Ralph Molina. 2016. *Y'all, This Paper Is Crazy Interesting: A Study of Variation in US English*. Ph.D. thesis.

Matthew Purver, Raquel Fernández, Matthew Frampton, and Stanley Peters. 2009. Cascaded lexicalised classifiers for second-person reference resolution.

In *Proceedings of the SIGDIAL 2009 Conference: The 10th Annual Meeting of the Special Interest Group on Discourse and Dialogue*, pages 306–309. Association for Computational Linguistics.

Jan Tillery and Guy Bailey. 1998. Yall in oklahoma.

William SY Wang and Chaofen Sun. 2015. *The Oxford handbook of Chinese linguistics*. Oxford University Press.

Walt Wolfram. 1985. Variability in tense marking: A case for the obvious. *Language Learning*, 35(2):229–253.

Ethan Zhou and Jinho D Choi. 2018. They exist! introducing plural mentions to coreference resolution and entity linking. In *Proceedings of the 27th International Conference on Computational Linguistics*, pages 24–34.

An Edit-centric Approach for Wikipedia Article Quality Assessment

Edison Marrese-Taylor[1], Pablo Loyola[2], Yutaka Matsuo[1]
Graduate School of Engineering, The University of Tokyo, Japan[1]
{emarrese, matsuo}@weblab.t-utokyo.ac.jp
IBM Research, Tokyo, Japan[2]
e57095@jp.ibm.com

Abstract

We propose an edit-centric approach to assess Wikipedia article quality as a complementary alternative to current full document-based techniques. Our model consists of a main classifier equipped with an auxiliary generative module which, for a given edit, jointly provides an estimation of its quality and generates a description in natural language. We performed an empirical study to assess the feasibility of the proposed model and its cost-effectiveness in terms of data and quality requirements.

1 Introduction

Wikipedia is arguably the world's most famous example of crowd-sourcing involving natural language. Given its open-edit nature, article often end up containing passages that can be regarded as noisy. These may be the indirect result of benign edits that do not meet certain standards, or a more direct consequence of vandalism attacks. In this context, assessing the quality of the large and heterogeneous stream of contributions is critical for maintaining Wikipedia's reputation and credibility. To that end, the WikiMedia Foundation has deployed a tool named ORES (Halfaker and Taraborelli, 2015) to help monitor article quality, which treats quality assessment as a supervised multi-class classification problem. This tool is static, works at the document-level, and is based on a set of predefined hand-crafted features (Warncke-Wang et al., 2015).

While the ORES approach seems to work effectively, considering the whole document could have negative repercussions. As seen on Figure 1, article length naturally increases over time (see Appendix A.1 for additional examples), which could lead to scalability issues and harm predictive performance, as compressing a large amount

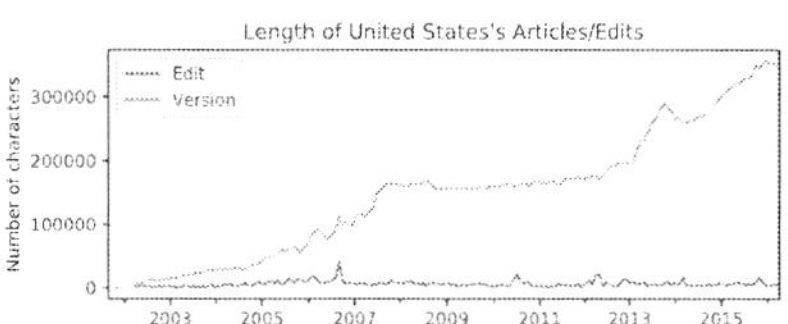

Figure 1: Monthly average of the article/edits length (in number of characters) for the United States article.

of content into hand crafted features could diminish their discriminative power. We conducted an exploratory analysis using a state-of-the-art (Dang and Ignat, 2016) document-level approach, finding that there is a clear negative relationship between document length and model accuracy (see details on Appendix A.2).

In light of this, we are interested in exploring a complementary alternative for assessing article quality in Wikipedia. We propose a model that receives as input only the edit, computed as the difference between two consecutive article versions associated to a contribution, and returns a measure of article quality. As seen on Figure 1, edit lengths exhibit a more stable distribution over time.

Moreover, as edits are usually accompanied by a short description which clarifies their purpose and helps with the reviewing process (Guzman et al., 2014), we explore whether this information could help improve quality assessment by also proposing a model that jointly predicts the quality of a given edit and generates a description of it in natural language. Our hypothesis is that while both tasks may not be completely aligned, the quality aspect could be benefited by accounting for the dual nature of the edit representation.

We performed an empirical study on a set of Wikipedia pages and their edit history, evaluating the feasibility of the approach. Our results show that our edit-level model offers competitive re-

Proceedings of the 2019 EMNLP Workshop W-NUT: The 5th Workshop on Noisy User-generated Text, pages 381–386
Hong Kong, Nov 4, 2019. ©2019 Association for Computational Linguistics

sults, benefiting from the proposed auxiliary task. In addition to requiring less content as input, we believe our model offers a more natural approach by focusing on the actual parts of the documents that were modified, ultimately allowing us to transition from a static, document-based approach, to an edit-based approach for quality assessment. Our code and data are available on GitHub[1].

2 Related Work

In terms of quality assessment, the pioneer work of Hu et al. (2007) used the interaction between articles and their editors to estimate quality, proposed as a classification task. Later, Kittur and Kraut (2008) studied how the number of editors and their coordination affects article quality, while Blumenstock (2008) proposed to use word count for measuring article quality.

Warncke-Wang et al. (2013, 2015) took the classification approach and characterized an article version with several hand-crafted features, training a SVM-based model whose updated version was deployed into the ORES system. More recent work has experimented with models based on representation learning, such as Dang and Ignat (2016) who used a doc2vec-based approach, and Shen et al. (2017) who trained an RNN to encode the article content. While all these models are inherently static, as they model the content of a version, the work of Zhang et al. (2018) is, to the best of our knowledge, the only one to propose a history-based approach.

On the other hand, Su and Liu (2015) tackled the quality problem by using a psycho-lexical resource, while Kiesel et al. (2017) aimed at automatically detecting vandalism utilizing change information as a primary input. Gandon et al. (2016) also validated the importance of the editing history of Wikipedia pages as a source of information.

In addition to quality assessment, our work is also related to generative modeling on Wikipedia. Recent work includes approaches based on autoencoders, such as Chisholm et al. (2017), who generate short biographies, and Yin et al. (2019) who directly learn diff representations. Other works include the approach by Zhang et al. (2017) which summarizes the discussion surrounding a change in the content, and by Boyd (2018) who utilizes Wikipedia edits to augment a small dataset for grammatical error correction in German.

3 Proposed Approach

Our goal is to model the quality assessment task on Wikipedia articles from a dynamic perspective. Let $v_1, \ldots, v_T$ be the sequence of the time-sorted T revisions of a given article in Wikipedia. Given a pair of consecutive revisions (v_{t-1}, v_t), an *edit* $e_t = \Delta_{t-1}^t(v)$ is the result of applying the Unix *diff* tool over the *wikitext*[2] contents of the revision pair, allowing us to recover the added and deleted lines on each edition.

Due to the line-based approach of the Unix *diff* tool, small changes in *wikitext* may lead to big chunks (or hunks) of differences in the resulting *diff* file. Moreover, as changes usually occur at the sentence level, these chunks can contain a considerable amount of duplicated information. To more accurately isolate the introduced change, we segment the added and removed lines on each hunk into sentences, and eliminate the ones appearing both in the added and removed lines. Whenever multiple sentences have been modified, we use string matching techniques to identify the before-after pairs. After this process, e_t can be characterized with a set of before-after sentence pairs (s_{ti}^-, s_{ti}^+), where s_{ti}^+ is an empty string in case of full deletion, and vice-versa.

Similarly to Yin et al. (2019), to obtain a fine-grained characterization of the *edit*, we tokenize each sentence and then use a standard *diff* algorithm to compare each sequence pair. We thus obtain an alignment for each sentence pair, which in turn allows us to identify the tokens that have been added, removed, or remained unchanged. For each case, we build an *edit-sentence* based on the alignment, containing added, deleted and unchanged tokens, where the nature of each is characterized with the token-level labels $+$, $-$ and $=$, respectively.

For a given *edit* e_t we generate an *edit* representation based on the contents of the associated *diff*, and then use it to predict the quality of the article in that time. We follow previous work and treat quality assessment as a multi-class classification task, with labels Stub $\leq$ Start $\leq$ C $\leq$ B $\leq$ GA $\leq$ FA. We consider a training corpus with T edits e_t, $1 \leq t \leq T$.

Our quality assessment model encodes the input *edit-sentence* using a BiLSTM. Concretely, we use a token embedding matrix E_T to represent the input tokens, and another embedding matrix E_L

---

to represent the token-level labels. For a given embedded token sequence X_t and embedded label sequence L_t, we concatenate the vectors for each position and feed them into the BiLSTM to capture context. We later use a max pooling layer to obtain a fixed-length edit representation, which is fed to the classifier module.

3.1 Incorporating Edit Message Information

When a user submits an *edit*, she can add a short message describing or summarizing it. We are interested in studying how these messages can be used as an additional source to support quality assessment task. A natural, straightforward way to incorporate the message into our proposal is to encode it into a feature vector using another BiLSTM with pooling, and combine this with the features learned from the *edit*.

Furthermore, we note that the availability of an edit message actually converts an *edit* into a dual-nature entity. In that sense, we would like to study whether the messages are representative constructs of the actual *edits*, and how this relation, if it exists, could impact the quality assessment task. One way to achieve this is by learning a mapping between *edits* and their messages.

Therefore, we propose to incorporate the edit messages by adding an auxiliary task that consists of generating a natural language description of a given *edit*. The idea is to jointly train the classification and the auxiliary task to see if the performance on quality assessment improves. Our hypothesis is that while both tasks are not naturally aligned, the quality aspect could benefit by accounting for the dual nature of the *edit* representation.

Our proposed generative auxiliary task is modeled using a sequence-to-sequence (Sutskever et al., 2014; Cho et al., 2014) with global attention (Bahdanau et al., 2015; Luong et al., 2015) approach, sharing the encoder with the classifier. During inference, we use beam search and let the decoder run for a fixed maximum number of steps, or until the special end-of-sentence token is generated. This task is combined with our main classification task using a linear combination of their losses, where parameter λ weights the importance of the classification loss. Figure 2 shows how the model with the auxiliary task looks like.

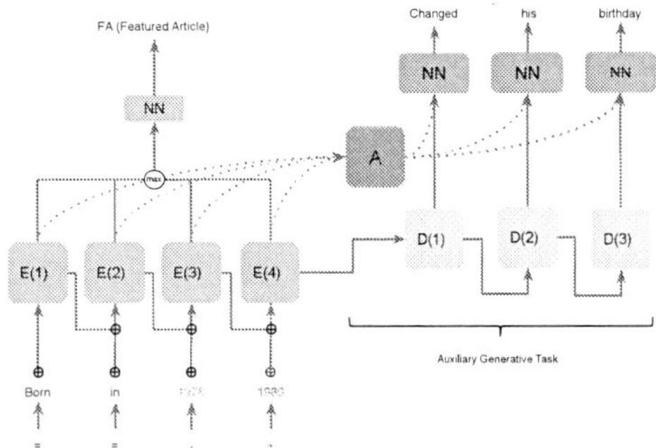

Figure 2: Proposed model with the addition of the module for the auxiliary generative task.

4 Empirical Study

We collected historical dumps from Wikipedia, choosing some of the most edited articles for both the English and German languages. Wikipedia dumps contain every version of a given page in *wikitext*, along with metadata for every *edit*. To obtain the content associated to each $\Delta_{t-1}^t(v)$, we sorted the extracted *edits* chronologically and computed the *diff* of each pair of consecutive versions using the Unix diff tool. We ignore *edits* with no accompanying message. For English sentence splitting we used the automatic approach by Kiss and Strunk (2006), and Somajo (Proisl and Uhrig, 2016) for German. The quality labels are obtained using the ORES API, the official platform of the WikiMedia Foundation to perform quality assessment. This platform is built upon a random forest classifier with 100 trees (Warncke-Wang et al., 2015), which when trained on a small corpus of 2,272 random articles obtained an F1-Score of 0.425. The API gives us a probability distribution over the quality labels for each revision, which in this work we use as a silver standard. We randomize and then split each dataset using a 70/10/20 ratio.

For comparison, we also consider the *Wikiclass* dataset built by Warncke-Wang et al. (2015), which consists of 30K revisions of random Wikipedia articles paired with their manually-annotated quality classes. To use this dataset with our models, we identified and downloaded the page revision immediately preceding each example using the Wikipedia API, to later apply the Unix *diff* tool and obtain the *edits*. We use the train/test splits provided and 20% of the training set as a validation. Other similar datasets are not suitable for us as they do not include the revision ids which we require in order to obtain the edits.

4.1 Experimental Setting

On our collected datasets, the classification models are trained using the Kullback-Leibler divergence as the loss function —which in our preliminary experiments worked better than using the derived hard labels with cross entropy— while for the *Wikiclass* dataset we used the cross entropy with the gold standard. In both cases we used accuracy on the validation set for hyper-parameter tuning and evaluation, and also measured macro-averaged F1-Score. For the models with the auxiliary task, we also evaluate our generated descriptions with sentence-level BLEU-4 (Papineni et al., 2002). All our models are trained with a maximum input/output length of 300 tokens, a batch size of 64 and a learning rate of 0.001 with Adam.

4.2 Results

We firstly conducted an ablation study to identify the model components that have greater impact on the performance. We compare our *edit-sentence* encoder with a regular encoding mechanism, where the tokens from s_{ti}^{-} and s_{ti}^{+} are concatenated (separated with a special marker token), and with a version that ignores the token-level label embeddings.

Model	F1	Acc	BLEU
Regular	0.47	0.74	-
+ *edit-sentence*	0.56	**0.80**	-
+ *diff* tags	0.62	0.78	-
+ Generation $\lambda = 0.2$	0.28	0.61	0.25
+ Generation $\lambda = 0.5$	0.33	0.68	0.24
+ Generation $\lambda = 0.8$	0.41	0.77	0.25
+ Generation $\lambda = 0.9$	**0.65**	0.77	0.22
Only Generation ($\lambda = 0$)	-	-	0.23

Table 1: Impact of the parameters on validation performance for the WWII article history.

As seen on Table 1, when compared against the regular encoder, utilizing our *edit-sentence* approach with token-level labels leads to a higher F1-Score and accuracy, showing the effectiveness of our proposed *edit* encoder. These results also shed some light on the trade-off between tasks for different values of λ. We see that although a higher value tends to give better classification performance both in terms of F1-Score and accuracy, it is also possible to see that there is a sweet-spot that allows the classification to benefit from learning an *edit*-message mapping, supporting our hypothesis. Moreover, this comes at a negligible variation in terms of BLEU scores, as seen when we compare against a pure message-generation task (Only Generation on the table).

On the other hand, when we tested the alternative mechanism to combine the edit and message information simply combining their representations and feeding them to the classifier, we obtained no performance improvements. This again supports our choice to model the *edit*-message mapping for the benefit of quality assessment.

Since we discarded *edits* that were not accompanied by messages during pre-processing, it is difficult to assess the impact that the absence of these messages may have on quality assessment. In those cases, we believe our model with the auxiliary generative task could be used as a drop-in replacement and thus help content reviewers.

Dataset Model		Validation			Test		
		F1	Acc	BL	F1	Acc	BL
Barack	C	0.50	0.92	-	0.62	**0.91**	-
Obama	C+G	0.57	0.89	0.21	**0.66**	0.88	0.20
Donald	C	0.69	0.79	-	**0.47**	**0.78**	-
Trump	C+G	0.69	0.76	0.22	**0.47**	0.77	0.20
Guns n'	C	0.28	0.86	-	0.18	**0.84**	-
Roses	C+G	0.31	0.79	0.23	**0.30**	0.81	
Xbox 360	C	0.22	0.60	-	0.30	0.61	-
	C+G	0.37	0.62	0.34	**0.32**	**0.63**	0.31
Chicago	C	0.36	0.71	-	0.38	**0.72**	-
	C+G	0.44	0.70	0.30	**0.39**	0.71	0.29
Pink	C	0.43	0.79	-	0.35	0.80	-
Floyd	C+G	0.46	0.80	0.34	**0.37**	**0.80**	0.35
Manchester	C	0.15	0.24	-	0.17	0.72	-
United F.	C+G	0.29	0.79	0.43	**0.39**	**0.77**	0.43
Deutschland	C	0.19	0.31	-	0.12	0.31	-
	C+G	0.22	0.38	0.31	**0.17**	**0.33**	0.36
Zweiter	C	0.26	0.29	-	0.15	**0.30**	-
Weltkrieg	C+G	0.29	0.32	0.35	**0.18**	**0.30**	0.28

Table 2: Summary of our results. C indicates models that only perform classification, and C+G models with the auxiliary generative task. BL is short for BLEU-4.

Table 2 summarizes our best results on each selected article. We see how the addition of the generative task can improve the classification performance for both considered languages. In terms of the task trade-off, controlled with parameter λ, we empirically found that higher values tend to work better for datasets with more examples.

Regarding the *Wikiclass* dataset, we compared our model against a state-of-the-art document-level approach (Dang and Ignat, 2016; Shen et al., 2017) based on on doc2vec (Le and Mikolov, 2014). In this scenario, our model obtains an accuracy of 0.40 on the test set, while the document level approach reaches 0.42. While the document level approach performed slightly better, our model is able to obtain a reasonable performance in a more efficient manner as it requires an input that averages only 2K characters (the edits), which contrasts to the average 12K characters in the documents. It is worth mentioning that the performance of the document-level approach reported by Dang and Ignat (2016) significantly differs from the value reported here. By looking at their implementation[3] we note that this value is obtained when also using the test documents to train.

5 Conclusion and Future work

In this work we proposed a new perspective to the problem of quality assessment in Wikipedia articles, taking as central element the dynamic nature of the *edits*. Our results support our hypothesis and show the feasibly of the approach. We believe the temporal view on the problem that the proposed approach provides could open the door to incorporating behavioral aspects into the quality estimation, such as user traces and reverting activity, which are also critical to limit the amount of noise and ensure the reliability of Wikipedia.

We think our results could represent a concrete contribution in improving our understanding of the evolution knowledge bases, in terms of of both software and scientific documentation, from a linguistic perspective. We envision this as a tool that could be useful for supporting documentation and quality-related tasks in collaborative environments, where human supervision is insufficient or not always available.

References

Dzmitry Bahdanau, Kyunghyun Cho, and Yoshua Bengio. 2015. Neural machine translation by jointly learning to align and translate. In *Proceedings of the 2015 International Conference on Learning Representations*, San Diego, California.

Joshua E Blumenstock. 2008. Size matters: word count as a measure of quality on wikipedia. In *Proceedings of the 17th international conference on World Wide Web*, pages 1095–1096. ACM.

Adriane Boyd. 2018. Using Wikipedia Edits in Low Resource Grammatical Error Correction. In *Proceedings of the 2018 EMNLP Workshop W-NUT:*

The 4th Workshop on Noisy User-generated Text*, pages 79–84, Brussels, Belgium. Association for Computational Linguistics.

Andrew Chisholm, Will Radford, and Ben Hachey. 2017. Learning to generate one-sentence biographies from wikidata. In *Proceedings of the 15th Conference of the European Chapter of the Association for Computational Linguistics: Volume 1, Long Papers*, pages 633–642, Valencia, Spain. Association for Computational Linguistics.

Kyunghyun Cho, Bart van Merrienboer, Caglar Gulcehre, Dzmitry Bahdanau, Fethi Bougares, Holger Schwenk, and Yoshua Bengio. 2014. Learning Phrase Representations using RNN EncoderDecoder for Statistical Machine Translation. In *Proceedings of the 2014 Conference on Empirical Methods in Natural Language Processing (EMNLP)*, pages 1724–1734, Doha, Qatar. Association for Computational Linguistics.

Q. Dang and C. Ignat. 2016. Quality assessment of Wikipedia articles without feature engineering. In *2016 IEEE/ACM Joint Conference on Digital Libraries (JCDL)*, pages 27–30.

F. Gandon, R. Boyer, O. Corby, and A. Monnin. 2016. Wikipedia editing history in dbpedia: Extracting and publishing the encyclopedia editing activity as linked data. In *2016 IEEE/WIC/ACM International Conference on Web Intelligence (WI)*, pages 479–482.

Emitza Guzman, David Azócar, and Yang Li. 2014. Sentiment analysis of commit comments in github: An empirical study. In *Proceedings of the 11th Working Conference on Mining Software Repositories*, MSR 2014, pages 352–355, New York, NY, USA. ACM.

Aaron Halfaker and Dario Taraborelli. 2015. Artificial intelligence service ores gives wikipedians x-ray specs to see through bad edits.

Meiqun Hu, Ee-Peng Lim, Aixin Sun, Hady Wirawan Lauw, and Ba-Quy Vuong. 2007. Measuring article quality in wikipedia: models and evaluation. In *Proceedings of the sixteenth ACM conference on Conference on information and knowledge management*, pages 243–252. ACM.

Johannes Kiesel, Martin Potthast, Matthias Hagen, and Benno Stein. 2017. Spatio-temporal analysis of reverted wikipedia edits.

Tibor Kiss and Jan Strunk. 2006. Unsupervised multilingual sentence boundary detection. *Comput. Linguist.*, 32(4):485–525.

Aniket Kittur and Robert E Kraut. 2008. Harnessing the wisdom of crowds in wikipedia: quality through coordination. In *Proceedings of the 2008 ACM conference on Computer supported cooperative work*, pages 37–46. ACM.

---

[3]github.com/vinhqdang/doc2vec_dnn_wikipedia

Quoc Le and Tomas Mikolov. 2014. Distributed representations of sentences and documents. In *International Conference on Machine Learning*, pages 1188–1196.

Thang Luong, Hieu Pham, and Christopher D. Manning. 2015. Effective approaches to attention-based neural machine translation. In *Proceedings of the 2015 Conference on Empirical Methods in Natural Language Processing*, pages 1412–1421, Lisbon, Portugal. Association for Computational Linguistics.

Kishore Papineni, Salim Roukos, Todd Ward, and Wei-Jing Zhu. 2002. Bleu: a method for automatic evaluation of machine translation. In *Proceedings of 40th Annual Meeting of the Association for Computational Linguistics*, pages 311–318, Philadelphia, Pennsylvania, USA. Association for Computational Linguistics.

Thomas Proisl and Peter Uhrig. 2016. Somajo: State-of-the-art tokenization for german web and social media texts. In *Proceedings of the 9th Web as Corpus Workshop (WaC-X) and the EmpiriST Shared Task*, pages 57–62, Berlin, Germany. Association for Computational Linguistics.

Aili Shen, Jianzhong Qi, and Timothy Baldwin. 2017. A Hybrid Model for Quality Assessment of Wikipedia Articles. In *Proceedings of the Australasian Language Technology Association Workshop 2017*, pages 43–52. Event-place: Brisbane, Australia.

Q. Su and P. Liu. 2015. A psycho-lexical approach to the assessment of information quality on wikipedia. In *2015 IEEE/WIC/ACM International Conference on Web Intelligence and Intelligent Agent Technology (WI-IAT)*, volume 3, pages 184–187.

Ilya Sutskever, Oriol Vinyals, and Quoc V Le. 2014. Sequence to sequence learning with neural networks. In *Advances in neural information processing systems*, pages 3104–3112.

Morten Warncke-Wang, Vladislav R. Ayukaev, Brent Hecht, and Loren G. Terveen. 2015. The Success and Failure of Quality Improvement Projects in Peer Production Communities. In *Proceedings of the 18th ACM Conference on Computer Supported Cooperative Work & Social Computing*, CSCW '15, pages 743–756, New York, NY, USA. ACM.

Morten Warncke-Wang, Dan Cosley, and John Riedl. 2013. Tell Me More: An Actionable Quality Model for Wikipedia. In *Proceedings of the 9th International Symposium on Open Collaboration*, WikiSym '13, pages 8:1–8:10, New York, NY, USA. ACM.

Pengcheng Yin, Graham Neubig, Miltiadis Allamanis, Marc Brockschmidt, and Alexander L Gaunt. 2019. Learning to represent edits. In *Proceedings of the 2019 International Conference on Learning Representations*.

Amy X. Zhang, Lea Verou, and David Karger. 2017. Wikum: Bridging discussion forums and wikis using recursive summarization. pages 2082–2096.

S. Zhang, Z. Hu, C. Zhang, and K. Yu. 2018. History-Based Article Quality Assessment on Wikipedia. In *2018 IEEE International Conference on Big Data and Smart Computing (BigComp)*, pages 1–8.

Additive Compositionality of Word Vectors

Yeon Seonwoo, **Sungjoon Park**, **Dongkwan Kim**, and **Alice Oh**
School of Computing, KAIST, Republic of Korea
{yeon.seonwoo, sungjoon.park, dongkwan.kim}@kaist.ac.kr,
alice.oh@kaist.edu

Abstract

Additive compositionality of word embedding models has been studied from empirical and theoretical perspectives. Existing research on justifying additive compositionality of existing word embedding models requires a rather strong assumption of uniform word distribution. In this paper, we relax that assumption and propose more realistic conditions for proving additive compositionality, and we develop a novel word and sub-word embedding model that satisfies additive compositionality under those conditions. We then empirically show our model's improved semantic representation performance on word similarity and noisy sentence similarity.

1 Introduction

Previous word embedding studies have empirically shown linguistic regularities represented as linear translation in the word vector space, but they do not explain these empirical results mathematically (Mikolov et al., 2013b; Pennington et al., 2014; Bojanowski et al., 2017).

Recent studies present theoretical advances to interpret these word embedding models. Levy and Goldberg (2014b) show that the global optimum of SGNS (Skip-Gram with Negative Sampling) is the shifted PMI (PMI$(i, j) - k$). Arora et al. (2016) propose a generative model to explain PMI-based distributional models and presents a mathematical explanation of the linguistic regularity in Skip-Gram (Mikolov et al., 2013a). Gittens et al. (2017) provide a theoretical justification of the additive compositionality of Skip-Gram and shows that the linguistic regularity of Skip-Gram is explained by additive compositionality of Skip-Gram (Mikolov et al., 2013a). One property of the word vectors that equates to satisfying additive compositionality is the following:

$$\vec{u}_c = \sum_{i=1}^{n} \vec{u}_{c_i}$$

where word c is the paraphrase word of the set of words $\{c_1, ..., c_n\}$, and $\vec{u}$ is the vector representation of a word. We explain additive compositionality in more detail in section 3.3.

In this paper, we provide a more sound mathematical explanation of linguistic regularity to overcome the limitations of previous theoretical explanations. For instance, Levy and Goldberg (2014b) do not provide a connection between shifted-PMI and linguistic regularity, and Arora et al. (2016) and Gittens et al. (2017) require strong assumptions in their mathematical explanation about linguistic regularity. Arora et al. (2016) assume isotropy, a uniformly distributed word vector space, and Gittens et al. (2017) assume a uniform word frequency distribution within a corpus, $p(w) = 1/|V|$.

We propose a novel word/sub-word embedding model which we call OLIVE that satisfies exact additive compositionality. The objective function of OLIVE consists of two parts. One is a global co-occurrence term to capture the semantic similarity of words. The other is a regularization term to constrain the size of the inner product of co-occurring word pairs. We show that the global optimum point of OLIVE is the exact PMI matrix under certain condition unlike SGNS whose optimum approximates PMI due to the sampling process in training (Levy and Goldberg, 2014b). The source code and pre-trained word vectors of OLIVE are publicly available [1]. By being a more theoretically sound word embedding model OLIVE shows improved empirical performance for semantic representation of word vectors, and by eliminating sampling process in SGNS, OLIVE shows robustness on the size of the vocabulary

---

[1] https://github.com/yeonsw/OLIVE

Proceedings of the 2019 EMNLP Workshop W-NUT: The 5th Workshop on Noisy User-generated Text, pages 387–396
Hong Kong, Nov 4, 2019. ©2019 Association for Computational Linguistics

and sentence representation performance on various noisy settings. We evaluate the semantic representation performance with the word similarity task, and we show the robustness of our model by conducting word similarity task on various vocabulary size and sentence similarity task on various noisy settings.

The contributions of our research are as follows:

- We present a novel mathematical explanation of additive compositionality of SGNS.

- We propose a word/sub-word embedding model that theoretically satisfies additive compositionality. We provide the code for this model for reproducibility.

- In addition to theoretical justification, we show the empirical performance of our model and its robustness.

2 Related Work

Learning word co-occurrence distribution is known as an effective method to capture the semantics of words (Baroni and Lenci, 2010; Harris, 1954; Miller and Charles, 1991; Bullinaria and Levy, 2007).

Based on this word co-occurrence distribution, two major types of word embedding research have been conducted. One is to use the local context of words in a corpus to train a neural network (Mikolov et al., 2013a,b; Bojanowski et al., 2017; Xu et al., 2018; Khodak et al., 2018). The other is to use the global statistics (Huang et al., 2012; Pennington et al., 2014). Aside from the general purpose embedding, some approaches are specific to a domain (Shi et al., 2018) or use extra human labeled information (Wang et al., 2018). In this paper, we focus on the general purpose word embedding.

Among those, SGNS (Skip-Gram with Negative Sampling) (Mikolov et al., 2013b) and FastText (Bojanowski et al., 2017) are widely-used neural network based word and sub-word embedding models that use negative sampling (Gutmann and Hyvärinen, 2012; Mnih and Kavukcuoglu, 2013). With the argument that global co-occurrence statistics, overlooked in SGNS and FastText, are important in capturing the word semantics, Pennington et al. (2014) propose GloVe.

There were empirical studies of linguistic regularity in word embedding vector space (Levy and

Goldberg, 2014a; Socher et al., 2012; Botha and Blunsom, 2014; Mikolov et al., 2013c; Socher et al., 2013).

Although Skip-Gram and GloVe seem to capture the linguistic regularity sufficiently, from the theoretical perspective of additive compositionality of word vectors, both models are lacking because they require extra and strong assumptions (Gittens et al., 2017; Arora et al., 2016).

Recently, (Allen and Hospedales, 2019) claim strong assumptions in the previous word embedding studies (Gittens et al., 2017; Arora et al., 2016) and propose theoretical explanation about linguistic regularity in SGNS based on paraphrase definition in (Gittens et al., 2017). Although their theory explains linguistic regularity in SGNS, there are remaining mathematical properties in SGNS: uniqueness of the paraphrase vector, and the meaning of the negative sampling parameter.

In this paper, we recognize the importance of additive compositionality of word vectors which connects word vectors, and their linguistic regularity and we provide a novel mathematical explanation of SGNS's additive compositionality and uniqueness property in additive compositionality. Further, we propose a novel word/sub-word embedding model that satisfies additive compositionality based on our theory and show its capabilities in capturing the semantics of words.

3 Preliminaries

In this section, we describe three important concepts about word vectors and how they are used in existing word embedding models. First, we describe the PMI matrix which is an approximated global optimum point of SGNS (Skip-Gram with Negative Sampling) (Levy and Goldberg, 2014b) and known to capture the semantic meaning of words in vector space (Arora et al., 2016). Second, we describe sub-sampling, a word frequency balancing method to increase word embedding performance. Third, we describe additive compositionality, the notion that a paraphrase word vector is a vector sum of its context word set (Gittens et al., 2017).

3.1 Objective Function

There are two major types of objective functions used in word embedding models. One is used in SGNS and is based on the PMI; and the other is used in GloVe, based on the joint probability distribution of word pairs, $p(w_1, w_2)$.

3.1.1 Skip-Gram with Negative Sampling

SGNS iteratively trains word vectors for each co-occurring word pair in the same local context window (Mikolov et al., 2013b). The objective function for each word pair is as follows,

$$
\begin{aligned}
L_{\text{SG}}(i, j) = {} & \log \sigma(\vec{u}_i^T \vec{v}_j) \\
& + \sum_{i=1}^{k} \mathbb{E}_{n \sim p(w)}[\log \sigma(-\vec{u}_i^T \vec{v}_n)].
\end{aligned}
\tag{1}
$$

By minimizing (1), we get the global optimum point of SGNS as follows, Levy and Goldberg (2014b)

$$
\vec{u}_i^T \vec{v}_j = PMI(i, j) - \log k,
$$

where k is the number of negative samples.

One problem of SGNS which trains word vectors for each independent context window is that it cannot utilize the global statistics of a corpus (Pennington et al., 2014).

3.1.2 GloVe

To capture the global co-occurrence statistics of word pairs, Pennington et al. (2014) propose GloVe with the following objective function,

$$
L_{\text{GloVe}} = \sum_{i,j \in D} f(i, j)(\vec{u}_i^T \vec{v}_j + \tilde{b}_i + \tilde{b}_j - \log X_{ij})^2,
$$

which learns the word vectors that capture the global co-occurrences of word pairs (X_{ij}). Note that this model does not result in the optimum being the PMI statistic, which is the condition for additive compositionality described in section 4.

3.2 Sub-sampling

Word embedding models such as SGNS, Fast-Text, and GloVe use various balancing methods that reduce the frequencies of very frequent words. These balancing methods are known to improve the semantic structure learned by a word embedding model. GloVe uses a clipping method to their weighting function that has an upper bound on the number of co-occurrences of word pairs. SGNS and FastText use a sub-sampling method that probabilistically discards frequent words during the learning procedure with the discard probability of word i as follows (Mikolov et al., 2013b),

$$
p_s(i) = 1 - \left(\sqrt{\frac{s}{p(i)}} + \frac{s}{p(i)} \right).
\tag{2}
$$

Here, $p(i)$ is word frequency of word i in a corpus. s is a sub-sampling parameter. In this paper, we propose a statistical sub-sampling method that is based on sub-sampling method in SGNS. Our proposed method can be applied to a model that uses global statistics.

3.3 Additive Compositionality of Gittens et al. (2017)

Gittens et al. (2017) provide a mathematical definition of additive compositionality and a theoretical framework to justify the additive compositionality of Skip-Gram. They define additive compositionality by formulating a link between a paraphrase word and its context words, where the definition of paraphrase words is,

$$
c = \arg\min_{w \in V} D_{KL}(p(\cdot|C) | p(\cdot|w)).
\tag{3}
$$

Here, c is a word and $C = \{c_1, ..., c_n\}$ is a set of words. So, if a word c minimizes (3) for given set of words C, then we say the word c is a paraphrase of the word set, C. If paraphrase vector $\vec{u}_c$ is captured by vector addition of words $\{c_1, ..., c_n\}$, we call the word vectors, $\vec{u}$ satisfy additive compositionality. Gittens et al. (2017) introduce two conditions of a paraphrase word vector c to be vector sum of a set C, $\vec{u}_c = \sum_{i=1}^{n} \vec{u}_{c_i}$.

- Given context word c, the probability that word w occurs within the same window can be calculated as follows,

$$
p(w|c) = \frac{1}{Z_c} \exp(\vec{u}_w^T \vec{v}_c).
\tag{4}
$$

- Given the set of words C, the probability distribution of word w can be calculated as follows,

$$
p(w|C) = \frac{p(w)^{1-m}}{Z_C} \prod_{i=1}^{m} p(w|c_i)
\tag{5}
$$

where Z_c and Z_C are normalization variables ($Z_c = \sum_{w \in V} \exp(\vec{u}_w^T \vec{v}_c)$, $Z_C = \sum_{w \in V} p(w)^{1-m} \prod_{i=1}^{m} p(w|c_i)$).

We are inspired by this mathematical definition of additive compositionality, and our work is based on their problem definition.

4 Additive Compositionality

To prove additive compositionality of word vectors, i.e., (4) and (5) are satisfied, Gittens et al.

(2017) assume uniform word frequency distribution, $p(w) = 1/|V|$. We know from Zipf's law that this assumption is not realistic, so we propose to replace (4) with the following such that the word embedding model satisfies additive compositionality without the uniform distribution assumption:

$$p(w|c) = \frac{p(w)}{Z_c} \exp\left(\vec{u}_w^T \vec{v}_c\right) \qquad (6)$$

where $Z_c = \sum_{w \in V} p(w) \exp\left(\vec{u}_w^T \vec{v}_c\right)$.

Theorem 1. *If a word embedding model satisfies (5) and (6), then the embedding vector of a paraphrase word, $\vec{u}_c$ can be represented by the vector sum of its context word set, $c_1, ..., c_m$, $\vec{u}_c = \sum_{i=1}^{m} \vec{u}_{c_i}$.*

Proof. The KL divergence (3) between (5) and (6) is computed as follows,

$$\mathrm{D_{KL}} = -\sum_{w \in V} p(w) \exp(\vec{u}_C^T \vec{v}_w)\left\{ (\vec{u}_c - \vec{u}_C)^T \vec{v}_w \right.$$
$$\left. - \log\left(\sum_{w' \in V} p(w') \exp(\vec{u}_c^T \vec{v}_{w'})\right) + \log Z \right\}\frac{1}{Z}. \qquad (7)$$

Here, $Z = Z_C \prod_{i=1}^{m} z_{c_i}$. $\vec{u}_C = \sum_{i=1}^{m} \vec{u}_{c_i}$. Differentiating (7) by $\vec{u}_c$, we get

$$\frac{\partial \mathrm{D_{KL}}}{\partial \vec{u}_c} = -\frac{1}{Z}\sum_{w \in V} p(w) \exp(\vec{v}_w^T \vec{u}_C)\vec{v}_w$$
$$+ \frac{1}{Z}\sum_{w \in V} p(w) \exp(\vec{v}_w^T \vec{u}_c)\vec{v}_w \qquad (8)$$
$$\times \frac{\sum_{w \in V} p(w) \exp(\vec{v}_w^T \vec{u}_C)}{\sum_{w \in V} p(w) \exp(\vec{v}_w^T \vec{u}_c)}$$

Since (7) is convex and (8) becomes 0 when $\vec{u}_c = \vec{u}_C$, a paraphrase word vector can be represented by the vector sum of its context words set, C. We explain the details of the proof about convexity of (7) in the Appendix. □

From (4) and (6), we can show that SGNS approximately satisfies additive compositionality without the uniform word frequency distribution assumption.

Theorem 2. *SGNS (Skip-Gram with Negative Sampling) approximately satisfies additive compositionality.*

Proof. The approximated global optimum point of SGNS is shifted-PMI (Levy and Goldberg,

Symbol	Description
V	Vocabulary
$\mathcal{G}_i$	Set of sub-words in word i
i, j	Index of a word in vocabulary
D	Set of co-occurring word pairs
σ	Sigmoid function
$\vec{u}_i, \vec{v}_j$	Embedding vector of word i, j
$\vec{g}_i, \vec{h}_j$	Embedding vector of sub-word i, j
k	Regularization parameter
s	Statistic sub-sampling parameter
S_{ij}	Regularization coefficient of word pair (i, j)

Table 1: Summary of the symbols

2014b). We can rewrite the approximated global optimum point as follows,

$$p(i|j) = \frac{p(i)}{k^{-1}} \exp(\vec{u}_i^T \vec{v}_j). \qquad (9)$$

Since (9) is the same as (6) and we can prove (5) with Bayes' theorem, we prove that SGNS approximately satisfies additive compositionality. □

5 Model

In this section, we describe our word embedding model OLIVE which satisfies additive compositionality described in section 4. We first describe our word level embedding model and its properties, then we expand the model to the sub-word level.

5.1 Word Level Embedding

5.1.1 Loss Function

The loss function in OLIVE consists of two parts: 1) a global co-occurrence term to capture the semantic similarity of co-occurring word pairs, and 2) a regularization term with sigmoid function and a different coefficient value for each word pair. Here, we use the regularization term to control the global optimal point of our model. Our proposed loss function is

$$L_{\mathrm{OLIVE}} =$$
$$-\sum_{ij \in D} p(i, j) \log \sigma(\vec{u}_i^T \vec{v}_j) + \sum_{ij \in D} S_{ij}\sigma(\vec{u}_i^T \vec{v}_j). \qquad (10)$$

Here, D is the set of co-occurring word pairs, $p(i, j)$ is the probability that the words (i, j) occur in the same context window, $\vec{u}, \vec{v}$ are the word embedding vectors, and S_{ij} is the regularization coefficient for word pair (i, j). The notations used in our model are summarized in Table 1. By minimizing this loss function, we get the word embedding vectors $\vec{u}$ and $\vec{v}$.

5.1.2 Properties

The global optimum of (10) depends on the value S_{ij}. When S_{ij} is $p(i,j)+p(i)p(j)k$, our model has a single local optimum – the global optimum point which is the shifted PMI. Also, OLIVE satisfies additive compositionality when $S_{ij} = p(i,j) + p(i)p(j)k$. We describe the theorem and the proof below.

Theorem 3. *If $S_{ij} = p(i,j) + p(i)p(j)k$ and the dimension of word embedding vector $\vec{u}, \vec{v}$ is sufficiently large to get global optimum point of L_{OLIVE}, then L_{OLIVE} has a unique local optimum with respect to $\vec{u}_i^T \vec{v}_j$, and $\vec{u}_i^T \vec{v}_j$ becomes $PMI(i,j) - \log k$ at the local optimum.*

Proof. Let $r = \vec{u}_i^T \vec{v}_j$. First derivative of (10) is as follows,

$$\frac{\partial L_{\text{OLIVE}}}{\partial r}$$
$$= p(i)p(j)k\sigma(-r)\sigma(r)e^{-r} \times (e^r - \frac{p(i,j)}{p(i)p(j)k}) \tag{11}$$

Since $p(i)p(j)k\sigma(-r)\sigma(r)e^{-r}$ is always positive, $\frac{\partial L_{\text{OLIVE}}}{\partial r}$ is positive when r satisfies the following condition:

$$r \in (\log \frac{p(i,j)}{p(i)p(j)k}, \infty). \tag{12}$$

Second derivative of L_{OLIVE} is as follows,

$$\frac{\partial L_{\text{OLIVE}}}{\partial r^2} = - p(i)p(j)k\sigma(-r)\sigma(r)^2 e^{-r}$$
$$\times (e^r - (2\frac{p(i,j)}{p(i)p(j)k} + 1)) \tag{13}$$

Since $p(i)p(j)k\sigma(-r)\sigma(r)^2 e^{-r}$ is always positive, $\frac{\partial L_{\text{OLIVE}}}{\partial r^2}$ is positive when r satisfies following condition:

$$r \in (-\infty, \log(\frac{2p(i,j)}{p(i)p(j)k} + 1)) \tag{14}$$

which leads to the following properties:

(a) $\frac{\partial L_{\text{OLIVE}}}{\partial r^2} > 0$ if $r \in (-\infty, \log(\frac{2p(i,j)}{p(i)p(j)k} + 1))$

(b) $\frac{\partial L_{\text{OLIVE}}}{\partial r} > 0$ if $r \in (\log(\frac{p(i,j)}{p(i)p(j)k}), \infty)$

Since $\log(\frac{2p(i,j)}{p(i)p(j)k} + 1) > \log(\frac{p(i,j)}{p(i)p(j)k})$, L_{OLIVE} has a unique local optimum with respect to $\vec{u}_i^T \vec{v}_j$. By simply finding r that makes (11) 0, we can show that the global optimum is $\text{PMI}(i,j) - \log k$. $\square$

Theorem 4. *If $S_{ij} = p(i,j) + p(i)p(j)k$, then L_{OLIVE} satisfies additive compositionality.*

Proof. From Theorem 1, we can prove Theorem 4 by showing that L_{OLIVE} satisfies (5) and (6).

(a) We can simply prove (5) with Bayes' theorem.

(b) From Theorem 3, we can rewrite the global optimum of our model as

$$p(i|j) = \frac{p(i)}{k-1} \exp(\vec{u}_i^T \vec{v}_j). \tag{15}$$

Since (15) is the same as (6), we prove that our model satisfies (6).

$\square$

5.2 Sub-word Level Embedding

We can expand (10) to a sub-word level embedding model without losing the properties in section 5.1.2. Let $\vec{u}_i = \sum_{x \in \mathcal{G}_i} \vec{g}_x/|\mathcal{G}_i|$ and $\vec{v}_j = \sum_{y \in \mathcal{G}_j} \vec{h}_y/|\mathcal{G}_j|$. Then, the expanded sub-word level model can be defined by the loss funtion

$$L_{sub} =$$
$$- \sum_{ij \in D} p(i,j) \log \sigma((\frac{1}{|\mathcal{G}_i|} \sum_{x \in \mathcal{G}_i} \vec{g}_x)^T (\frac{1}{|\mathcal{G}_j|} \sum_{y \in \mathcal{G}_j} \vec{h}_y))$$
$$+ \sum_{ij \in D} S_{ij}\sigma((\frac{1}{|\mathcal{G}_i|} \sum_{x \in \mathcal{G}_i} \vec{g}_x)^T (\frac{1}{|\mathcal{G}_j|} \sum_{y \in \mathcal{G}_j} \vec{h}_y)), \tag{16}$$

where x, y are sub-word indicators in words i, j. $\vec{g}, \vec{h}$ are sub-word embedding vectors, and $\mathcal{G}_i$ is the set of sub-words in word i.

5.3 Statistical Sub-sampling

Similar to SGNS and FastText, we apply sub-sampling to improve word embedding performance, but because SGNS sub-samples words in each iteration of the learning process, we cannot directly apply it to OLIVE which uses the global statistics. Instead we propose a statistical sub-sampling based on the same discard probability form as (2) but considering for each word whether it needs to be sub-sampled, as follows:

$$p_s(i) = \begin{cases} \sqrt{\frac{s}{p(i)}} + \frac{s}{p(i)} & \text{if } p(i) > s \cdot (\frac{\sqrt{5}+1}{2})^2 \\ 1 & \text{otherwise} \end{cases} \quad (17)$$

Here, s is the sub-sampling parameter. By multiplying the above probability to the frequency of the word, we can get the sub-sampled global statistic of a word. The statistics can be calculated by

$$N_i^s = N_i \cdot p_s(i), \quad N_{i,j}^s = N_{i,j} \cdot p_s(i) \cdot p_s(j) \quad (18)$$

where N_i is the frequency of word i and $N_{i,j}$ is the co-occurrence frequency of word pair (i, j).

5.4 Updating Rule

In the learning process of (10) and (16), the word vectors are updated by gradient descent, where the gradient of a word vector $\vec{u}_i$ in (10) is

$$\frac{\partial L}{\partial \vec{u}_i} = \sum_{j \in D_i} p(i)p(j)k\vec{v}_j\sigma(-\vec{u}_i^T \vec{v}_j)\sigma(\vec{u}_i^T \vec{v}_j)$$
$$- \sum_{j \in D_i} p(i,j)\sigma(-\vec{u}_i^T \vec{v}_j)^2 \vec{v}_j.$$
$$(19)$$

In (16), the gradient of the sub-word vector $\vec{g}_x$ and $\vec{h}_y$ can be simply calculated by (19) as

$$\frac{\partial L}{\partial \vec{g}_x} = \sum_{\{i|x \in \mathcal{G}_i\}} \frac{\partial L}{\partial \vec{u}_i}, \quad \frac{\partial L}{\partial \vec{h}_y} = \sum_{\{j|y \in \mathcal{G}_j\}} \frac{\partial L}{\partial \vec{v}_j}. \quad (20)$$

We update the word vectors with the normalized gradient of the word vector. The updating rule is

$$\vec{u}_i := \vec{u}_i - \eta \cdot \frac{\partial L}{\partial \vec{u}_i} \cdot \left| \frac{\partial L}{\partial \vec{u}_i} \right|^{-1} \quad (21)$$

where η is the learning rate.

6 Experiment

In this section, we conduct three experiments to show the empirical effects of theoretical improvement on OLIVE. First, we conduct an experiment on the word similarity task to verify the semantic representation performance of OLIVE. Second, we report the word similarity performance of OLIVE on various vocabulary sizes and noisy sentence representation performance to show the robustness of OLIVE.

6.1 Training Settings

We train our model and baseline models with the Wikipedia English corpus with 4 billion tokens. We preprocess the corpus with Matt Mahoney's perl script [2]. We use Skip-Gram, FastText, GloVe, and Probabilistic-FastText (Athiwaratkun et al., 2018) as baseline models. For all word and sub-word experiments, we set dimension $= 300$ and windowsize $= 5$. To train our word/sub-word model, we set $s = 10^{-5}$, $k = 50$, the number of iterations to 500, and the initial learning rate, η_0 to 0.5. For every iteration, we decrease the learning rate by the following formula:

$$\eta_t = \eta_0 \times \frac{1}{(t + 1)^{0.25}} \quad (22)$$

In Skip-Gram and FastText, we set the number of negative samples to 5, the sub-sampling parameter to 10^{-5} and the initial learning rate to 0.025. In GloVe, we set the parameter x_max to 100 following their paper (Pennington et al., 2014). In Prob-FastText (Athiwaratkun et al., 2018), we set the parameters to the default settings in their code [3]. In the sub-word experiment, we extract sub-words whose length is in the range $[2, 7]$.

6.2 Word Similarity

We evaluate our word embedding performance with the word similarity task using three word similarity datasets: MTurk-(287, 771) (Radinsky et al., 2011), and SL-999 (Hill et al., 2015). We compare our model with four models: Skip-Gram, FastText, GloVe, and Probabilistic-FastText, a multisense sub-word embedding model (Athiwaratkun et al., 2018).

Table 3 shows the results of the word similarity experiment with words that occur two or more times in the corpus for a vocabulary size of 6.2 million words. Table 2 shows the results for the same experiment but with words that occur five or more times in the corpus for a vocabulary size of 2.8 million words. With both of these tables, we can see that OLIVE outperforms all four comparison models.

6.2.1 Effect of Vocabulary Size

When we compare tables 2 and 3 we see significant performance decreases in FastText, Skip-Gram, and Prob-FastText for the larger vocab-

---

[2] http://mattmahoney.net/dc/textdata
[3] https://github.com/benathi/multisense-prob-fasttext

	FastText	Skip-Gram	GloVe	Prob-FastText	OLIVE-sub	OLIVE-word
MTurk-287	64.73	66.30	60.62	66.49	65.69	**66.54**
MTurk-771	63.92	65.32	62.30	65.81	65.43	**66.31**
SL-999	35.09	36.01	32.53	**36.54**	34.86	36.18

Table 2: Spearman's rank correlation coefficient of word similarity task on 2.8×10^6 vocabulary size.

	FastText	Skip-Gram	GloVe	Prob-FastText	OLIVE-sub	OLIVE-word
MTurk-287	62.46	63.38	60.77	63.17	64.33	**67.22**
MTurk-771	59.60	61.67	61.91	64.56	65.32	**66.66**
SL-999	33.04	34.20	31.98	33.83	34.99	**35.81**

Table 3: Spearman's rank correlation coefficient of word similarity task on 6.2×10^6 vocabulary size.

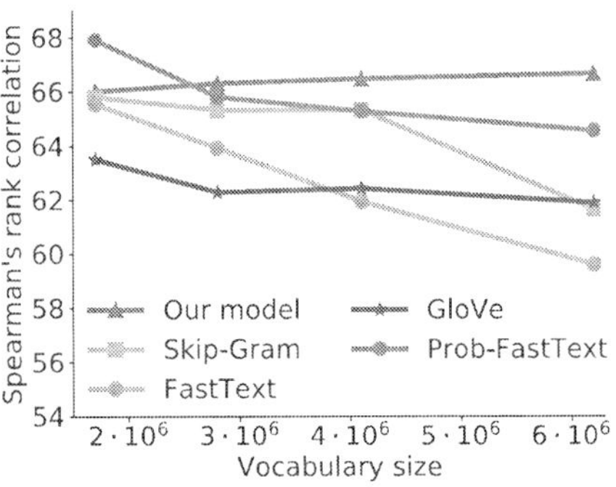

Figure 1: Spearman correlation of our model, Skip-Gram, and FastText on various vocabulary size in MTurk-771 testset.

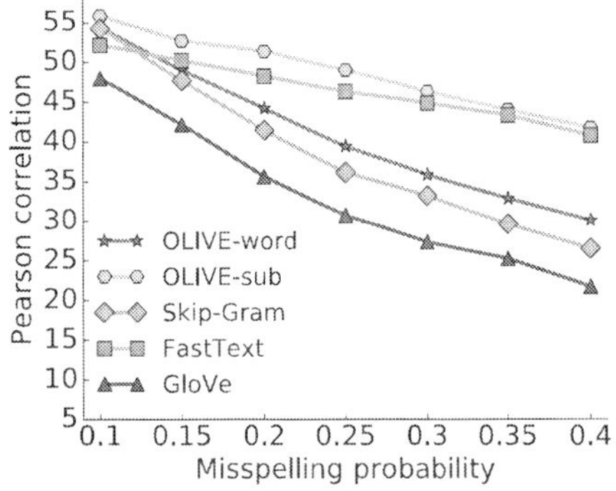

Figure 2: Pearson correlation of OLIVE, SGNS, GloVe, and FastText on SICK-dataset. We misspell words with probability between $[0.1, 0.4]$.

ulary size. On the other hand, our model and GloVe show consistent performance, and we interpret that as a result of using the global word co-occurrence statistics. To visualize that more clearly, we plot in Figure 1 the word similarity scores for the MTurk 771 dataset on various vocabulary sizes for the different models. This figure clearly shows the robustness of our model with respect to the vocabulary size.

6.3 Noisy Sentence Representation

In sections 4 and 5.1.2, we have shown that our model satisfies additive compositionality and SGNS's approximated additive compositionality. Theorem 1 implies equality between finding paraphrase vector of context words and finding sentence vector, which makes the sentence vector that minimizes the KL divergence (7) to $\vec{u}_{\text{sentence}} = \sum_{w \in \text{sentence}} \vec{u}_w$. To see robustness on additive compositionality of OLIVE that comes from removing the approximation in SGNS, we measure sentence similarity on various noise settings with

the sentence vectors calculated by the sum of word vectors in the sentence.

We use SICK dataset (Marelli et al., 2014) and all the STS-English dataset (Cer et al., 2017): STS-train, STS-dev, and STS-test. These datasets contain sentence pairs and human-annotated similarity scores for each sentence pair. To make noise in a sentence, we use two types of noise settings: typo and omitted-word. We use misspelling generation method proposed in Piktus et al. (2019) to make typos in a sentence with probability p. Piktus et al. (2019) use query logs of a search engine to build probabilistic distribution of misspelled words of a word, $p(\text{misspelled word}|\text{word})$. In omitted-word setting, we randomly discard words in each sentence with probability p. In both typo/omitted-word settings, we measure sentence similarity on various noise probability settings, $p \in [0.1, 0.15, 0.2, 0.25, 0.3, 0.35, 0.4]$.

To compute the similarity of a pair of sentences, we first calculate the sentence vector and take the cosine similarity of the sentence vector pair. Then

		Word Vector Model			Sub-word Vector Model	
		SGNS	GloVe	OLIVE-word	FastText	OLIVE-sub
Typo	STS-Train	**55.80/58.45**	44.68/44.18	54.95/58.00	**52.77/55.58**	52.03/**57.45**
	STS-Dev	56.79/54.27	44.59/38.53	**58.80/57.82**	57.85/54.87	**65.05/65.16**
	STS-Test	**46.21/48.07**	34.88/34.65	42.22/45.21	52.30/52.89	**54.35/57.10**
	SICK	42.15/47.70	39.75/42.19	**44.56/48.99**	43.58/50.21	**45.05/52.70**
Omit	STS-Train	**52.63**/53.53	43.06/41.93	52.40/**54.49**	45.73/45.34	**46.44/50.72**
	STS-Dev	55.92/49.09	45.00/34.72	**57.19/54.98**	49.82/44.13	**59.37/59.42**
	STS-Test	**42.57/42.20**	31.65/31.23	39.14/40.89	44.83/42.05	**47.28/49.35**
	SICK	48.22/53.98	44.44/46.51	**49.92/55.14**	38.63/41.38	42.15/48.48

Table 4: Spearman/Pearson correlation of sentence similarity on typo/omitted-word setting. We misspell/discard words with probability 0.15. The left is Spearman correlation and the right is Pearson correlation.

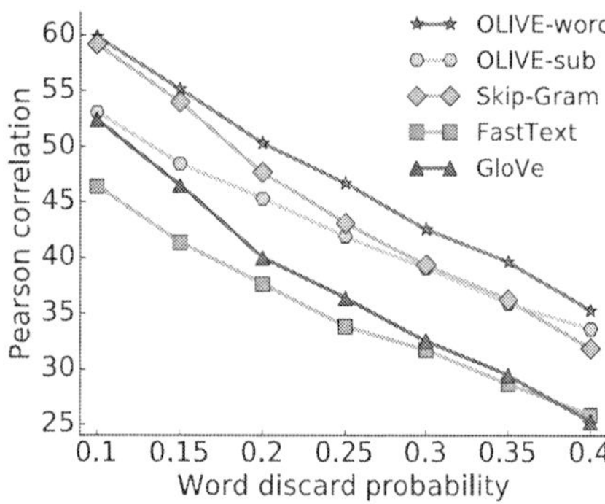

Figure 3: Pearson correlation of OLIVE, SGNS, GloVe, and FastText on SICK-dataset. We discard words with probability between [0.1, 0.4].

we calculate the Spearman and Pearson correlations between the human-annotated similarity and the cosine similarity of the sentence vector pair. We report results on various typo/omitted-word setting in figure 2, 3 and results of typo/omit-word setting on 0.15 noise probability in table 4.

Table 4 show that OLIVE outperforms in each sub-word and word embedding group on both typo/omitted-word settings. When we compare the performance of GloVe, Skip-Gram, and OLIVE in table 4, we get an empirical evidence of approximate and exact additive compositionality in (2) and (4). Since GloVe does not theoretically satisfy additive compositionality, the correlation of GloVe is lower than Skip-Gram. Overall, we establish that our model captures noisy sentence representation better than Skip-Gram, GloVe, and FastText.

Since OLIVE-sub and FastText are character n-gram embedding models, $\vec{u}_i = \frac{1}{|\mathcal{G}_i|} \sum_{x \in \mathcal{G}_i} \vec{g}_x$, misspelling in a word tends to affect vector rep-

resentation of a word insignificantly. In figure 2, we empirically show significant performance difference between sub-word embedding models and word embedding models on typo setting. Also, figure 2 and 3 show that OLIVE outperforms in each sub-word and word embedding group on both typo/omit-word settings with various noise settings.

7 Conclusion

In this paper, we proposed 1) novel theoretical conditions of additive compositional word embedding model and 2) novel word/sub-word embedding model which we call OLIVE that satisfies additive compositionality. The loss function of OLIVE consists of a term for learning semantic similarity and a regularization term. From the loss function, we derived three properties of OLIVE: additive compositionality, uniqueness of local optimum, and shifted-PMI as the global optimum. Through several experiments, we showed OLIVE outperforms other existing embedding models on various word similarity task and showed robustness with respect to the size of the vocabulary. With sentence similarity task on various noisy settings, we showed robustness on additive compositionality of OLIVE.

Acknowledgments

This work was partly supported by NAVER Corp. and Institute for Information & communications Technology Planning & Evaluation(IITP) grant funded by the Korea government(MSIT) (No.2017-0-01780, The technology development for event recognition/relational reasoning and learning knowledge based system for video understanding).

References

Carl Allen and Timothy Hospedales. 2019. Analogies explained: Towards understanding word embeddings. In *ICML*.

Sanjeev Arora, Yuanzhi Li, Yingyu Liang, Tengyu Ma, and Andrej Risteski. 2016. A latent variable model approach to pmi-based word embeddings. *Transactions of the Association for Computational Linguistics*, 4:385–399.

Ben Athiwaratkun, Andrew Wilson, and Anima Anandkumar. 2018. Probabilistic fasttext for multisense word embeddings. In *ACL*.

Marco Baroni and Alessandro Lenci. 2010. Distributional memory: A general framework for corpus-based semantics. *Computational Linguistics*, 36(4):673–721.

Piotr Bojanowski, Edouard Grave, Armand Joulin, and Tomas Mikolov. 2017. Enriching word vectors with subword information. *Transactions of the Association of Computational Linguistics*, 5(1):135–146.

Jan Botha and Phil Blunsom. 2014. Compositional morphology for word representations and language modelling. In *ICML*.

John A Bullinaria and Joseph P Levy. 2007. Extracting semantic representations from word co-occurrence statistics: A computational study. *Behavior research methods*, 39(3):510–526.

Daniel Cer, Mona Diab, Eneko Agirre, Inigo Lopez-Gazpio, and Lucia Specia. 2017. Semeval-2017 task 1: Semantic textual similarity multilingual and crosslingual focused evaluation. In *SemEval*.

Alex Gittens, Dimitris Achlioptas, and Michael W Mahoney. 2017. Skip-gram-zipf+ uniform= vector additivity. In *ACL*.

Michael U Gutmann and Aapo Hyvärinen. 2012. Noise-contrastive estimation of unnormalized statistical models, with applications to natural image statistics. *Journal of Machine Learning Research*, 13(Feb):307–361.

Zellig S Harris. 1954. Distributional structure. *Word*, 10(2-3):146–162.

Felix Hill, Roi Reichart, and Anna Korhonen. 2015. Simlex-999: Evaluating semantic models with (genuine) similarity estimation. *Computational Linguistics*, 41(4):665–695.

Eric H Huang, Richard Socher, Christopher D Manning, and Andrew Y Ng. 2012. Improving word representations via global context and multiple word prototypes. In *ACL*.

Mikhail Khodak, Nikunj Saunshi, Yingyu Liang, Tengyu Ma, Brandon Stewart, and Sanjeev Arora. 2018. A la carte embedding: Cheap but effective induction of semantic feature vectors. In *ACL*.

Omer Levy and Yoav Goldberg. 2014a. Linguistic regularities in sparse and explicit word representations. In *CoNLL*.

Omer Levy and Yoav Goldberg. 2014b. Neural word embedding as implicit matrix factorization. In *NIPS*.

Marco Marelli, Luisa Bentivogli, Marco Baroni, Raffaella Bernardi, Stefano Menini, and Roberto Zamparelli. 2014. Semeval-2014 task 1: Evaluation of compositional distributional semantic models on full sentences through semantic relatedness and textual entailment. In *SemEval*.

Tomas Mikolov, Kai Chen, Greg Corrado, and Jeffrey Dean. 2013a. Efficient estimation of word representations in vector space. *arXiv*.

Tomas Mikolov, Ilya Sutskever, Kai Chen, Greg S Corrado, and Jeff Dean. 2013b. Distributed representations of words and phrases and their compositionality. In *NIPS*.

Tomas Mikolov, Wen-tau Yih, and Geoffrey Zweig. 2013c. Linguistic regularities in continuous space word representations. In *NAACL-HLT*.

George A Miller and Walter G Charles. 1991. Contextual correlates of semantic similarity. *Language and cognitive processes*, 6(1):1–28.

Andriy Mnih and Koray Kavukcuoglu. 2013. Learning word embeddings efficiently with noise-contrastive estimation. In *NIPS*.

Jeffrey Pennington, Richard Socher, and Christopher Manning. 2014. Glove: Global vectors for word representation. In *EMNLP*.

Aleksandra Piktus, Necati Bora Edizel, Piotr Bojanowski, Edouard Grave, Rui Ferreira, and Fabrizio Silvestri. 2019. Misspelling oblivious word embeddings. In *NAACL*.

Kira Radinsky, Eugene Agichtein, Evgeniy Gabrilovich, and Shaul Markovitch. 2011. A word at a time: computing word relatedness using temporal semantic analysis. In *WWW*.

Bei Shi, Zihao Fu, Lidong Bing, and Wai Lam. 2018. Learning domain-sensitive and sentiment-aware word embeddings. In *ACL*.

Richard Socher, John Bauer, Christopher D Manning, et al. 2013. Parsing with compositional vector grammars. In *ACL*.

Richard Socher, Brody Huval, Christopher D Manning, and Andrew Y Ng. 2012. Semantic compositionality through recursive matrix-vector spaces. In *EMNLP-CoNLL*.

Guoyin Wang, Chunyuan Li, Wenlin Wang, Yizhe Zhang, Dinghan Shen, Xinyuan Zhang, Ricardo Henao, and Lawrence Carin. 2018. Joint embedding of words and labels for text classification. In *ACL*.

Yang Xu, Jiawei Liu, Wei Yang, and Liusheng Huang. 2018. Incorporating latent meanings of morphological compositions to enhance word embeddings. In *ACL*.

for all non-zero vector $\vec{x}$. So, the Hessian of D_{KL} is positive definite matrix which leads to convexity of the D_{KL}.

A   Convexity of (7)

The second derivative of D_{KL} is as follows,

$$\frac{\partial^2 D_{KL}}{\partial \vec{u}_c \partial \vec{u}_c^T}$$

$$= K \frac{\partial}{\partial \vec{u}_c} \frac{\sum_{w \in V} p(w) \exp(\vec{v}_w^T \vec{u}_c) \vec{v}_w}{\sum_{w \in V} p(w) \exp(\vec{v}_w^T \vec{u}_c)}$$

$$= K \frac{\sum_{w \in V} p(w) \exp(\vec{v}_w^T \vec{u}_c) \vec{v}_w \vec{v}_w^T}{\sum_{w \in V} p(w) \exp(\vec{v}_w^T \vec{u}_c)}$$

$$- K \frac{\sum_{w \in V} p(w) \exp(\vec{v}_w^T \vec{u}_c) \vec{v}_w}{\sum_{w \in V} p(w) \exp(\vec{v}_w^T \vec{u}_c)}$$

$$\times \frac{\sum_{w \in V} p(w) \exp(\vec{v}_w^T \vec{u}_c) \vec{v}_w^T}{\sum_{w \in V} p(w) \exp(\vec{v}_w^T \vec{u}_c)},$$

where K is $\frac{1}{Z} \sum_{w \in V} p(w) \exp(\vec{v}_w^T (\sum_{i=1}^m \vec{u}_{c_i}))$.

To prove the second derivative of D_{KL} is positive definite matrix, we multiply non-zero vector $\vec{x}$ to the Hessian matrix $(\frac{\partial^2 D_{KL}}{\partial \vec{u}_c \partial \vec{u}_c^T})$.

$$\vec{x}^T \frac{\partial^2 D_{KL}}{\partial \vec{u}_c \partial \vec{u}_c^T} \vec{x}$$

$$= K \frac{\sum_{w \in V} p(w) \exp(\vec{v}_w^T \vec{u}_c) \vec{x}^T \vec{v}_w \vec{v}_w^T \vec{x}}{\sum_{w \in V} p(w) \exp(\vec{v}_w^T \vec{u}_c)}$$

$$- K \frac{\sum_{w \in V} p(w) \exp(\vec{v}_w^T \vec{u}_c) \vec{x}^T \vec{v}_w}{\sum_{w \in V} p(w) \exp(\vec{v}_w^T \vec{u}_c)}$$

$$\times \frac{\sum_{w \in V} p(w) \exp(\vec{v}_w^T \vec{u}_c) \vec{v}_w^T \vec{x}}{\sum_{w \in V} p(w) \exp(\vec{v}_w^T \vec{u}_c)}$$

$$= K \sum_{w \in V} r_w q_w^2 - K (\sum_{w \in V} r_w q_w)^2$$

$$\tag{23}$$

Where,

$$r_w = \frac{p(w) \exp(\vec{v}_w^T \vec{u}_c)}{\sum_{w \in V} p(w) \exp(\vec{v}_w^T \vec{u}_c)}, \quad q_w = \vec{x}^T \vec{v}_w.$$

By Jensen's inequality,

$$K \sum_{w \in V} r_w q_w^2 > K (\sum_{w \in V} r_w q_w)^2.$$

Now, we get

$$\vec{x}^T \frac{\partial^2 D_{KL}}{\partial \vec{u}_c \partial \vec{u}_c^T} \vec{x} > 0$$

Contextualized *context2vec*

Kazuki Ashihara
Osaka University
ashihara.kazuki@ist.osaka-u.ac.jp

Tomoyuki Kajiwara
Osaka University
kajiwara@ids.osaka-u.ac.jp

Yuki Arase
Osaka University
arase@ist.osaka-u.ac.jp

Satoru Uchida
Kyushu University
uchida@flc.kyushu-u.ac.jp

Abstract

Lexical substitution ranks substitution candidates from the viewpoint of paraphrasability for a target word in a given sentence. There are two major approaches for lexical substitution: (1) generating contextualized word embeddings by assigning multiple embeddings to one word and (2) generating context embeddings using the sentence. Herein we propose a method that combines these two approaches to contextualize word embeddings for lexical substitution. Experiments demonstrate that our method outperforms the current state-of-the-art method. We also create CEFR-LP, a new evaluation dataset for the lexical substitution task. It has a wider coverage of substitution candidates than previous datasets and assigns English proficiency levels to all target words and substitution candidates.

1 Introduction

Lexical substitution (McCarthy and Navigli, 2007) is the finest-level paraphrase problem. It determines if a word in a sentence can be replaced by other words while preserving the same meaning. It is important not only as a fundamental paraphrase problem but also as a practical application for language learning support such as lexical simplification (Paetzold and Specia, 2017) and acquisition (McCarthy, 2002). Table 1 shows an example of the lexical substitution task with a sentence,[1] the target word to replace, and words of substitution candidates. The numbers in parentheses represent the paraphrasability of each candidate, where a larger value means the corresponding word is more appropriate to substitute the target word. The lexical substitution task ranks these candidates according to assigning

context	... explain the basic concept and purpose and get it **going** with minimal briefing .
target	go
candidate	start (4), proceed (1), move (1) ...

Table 1: Example of the lexical substitution tasks

weights. The key technology to solve lexical substitution tasks is to precisely capture word senses in a context.

There are mainly two approaches for lexical substitution: (1) generating contextualized word embeddings by assigning multiple embeddings to one word and (2) generating context embeddings using the sentence. The former realizes static embeddings as it pre-computes word embeddings. One example of the first approach is *DMSE* (Dependency-based Multi-Sense Embedding), which was proposed by Ashihara et al. (2018) to contextualize word embeddings using words with dependency relations as a clue to distinguish senses. As an example of the second approach, *context2vec* (Melamud et al., 2016) generates a context embedding by inputting the sentence into bidirectional recurrent neural networks. It combines context embedding and a simple word embedding to generate a dynamic embedding. These two methods are current state-of-the-arts among methods of each approach.

We focus on the fact that these two methods have a complementary nature. *DMSE* considers only a single word as context, while *context2vec* uses a simple word embedding. Herein we combine *DMSE* and *context2vec* to take advantages of both contextualized word embeddings and context embeddings. Specifically, we apply a contextualized word embedding generated by *DMSE* to replace the word embedding used in *context2vec*.

---

[1] In this paper, the terms *context* and *sentence* are used interchangeably wherever the context for the target refers to the sentence.

Proceedings of the 2019 EMNLP Workshop W-NUT: The 5th Workshop on Noisy User-generated Text, pages 397–406
Hong Kong, Nov 4, 2019. ©2019 Association for Computational Linguistics

In addition, we create a new evaluation dataset for lexical substitution, named CEFR-LP. It is an extension of CEFR-LS (Uchida et al., 2018) and is created for lexical simplification to support substitution tasks. The benefits of CEFR-LP are that it expands the coverage of substitution candidates and provides English proficiency levels. These features are unavailable in previous evaluation datasets such as LS-SE (McCarthy and Navigli, 2007) and LS-CIC (Kremer et al., 2014).

The evaluation results on CEFR-LP, LS-SE, and LS-CIC confirm that our method effectively strengthens *DMSE* and *context2vec*. Additionally, our proposed method outperforms the current state-of-the-art methods. The contributions of this paper are twofold:

- A method that takes advantages of contextualized word embedding and dynamic embedding generation from contexts is proposed. This method achieves a state-of-the-art performance on lexical substitution tasks.

- Creation and release[2] of CEFR-LP, which is a new evaluation dataset for lexical substitution with an expanded coverage of substitution candidates and English proficiency levels.

2   Related Work

There are two major approaches to lexical substitution. One approach generates contextualized word embeddings by assigning multiple embeddings to one word. Paetzold and Specia (2016) generated word embeddings per part-of-speech of the same word assuming that words with the same surface have different senses for different part-of-speech. Fadaee et al. (2017) also generated multiple word embeddings per topic represented in a sentence. For example, the word `soft` may have embeddings for topics of food when used like `soft cheese` and that for music when used like `soft voice`. To adequately distinguish these word senses, both methods assign embeddings that are too coarse. For example, the phrases `soft cheese` and `soft drink` both use `soft` as an adjective and are related to the food topic. The former has the sense of `tender` while the latter represents the sense of `non-alcoholic`. To solve this problem, *DMSE* generates finer-grained word

embeddings because it generates embeddings for words with dependency relations based on the CBOW algorithm of word2vec (Mikolov et al., 2013). It concatenates words with dependent relations within a specific window, which is a hyper-parameter in CBOW. Hence considered context in *DMSE* is bounded by the window size. *DMSE* achieves the highest performance for lexical substitution tasks among the methods categorized into the first approach.

The other approach dynamically generates contextualized embeddings considering a sentence. *Context2vec* generates a context embedding using bidirectional long short-term memory (biLSTM) networks (Schuster and Paliwal, 1997). Then it combines the context embedding with a simple word embedding. *Context2vec* is the current state-of-the-art method for representative lexical substitution tasks. Its advantage is that it can consider the entire sentence as the context, while *DMSE* is bounded by a window size. However, *DMSE* can use contextualized word embeddings, whereas *context2vec* just uses a simple word embedding for each word. The complementary nature of these two methods inspired us to combine them. More recently, *ELMo* (Peters et al., 2018) showed a language modeling using biLSTM networks produces contextualized word embeddings, which are effective for various NLP tasks such as named entity recognition. *Context2vec* differs from *ELMo* when explicitly considering word embeddings of substitution targets. Our experiments empirically confirm that *context2vec* outperforms *ELMo* in Section 6.

3   Proposed Method

We combine *DMSE* and *context2vec* to take advantage of both fine-grained contextualized word embeddings and context embeddings.

3.1   Overview

DMSE is designed to train its word embeddings using CBOW, which we replaced with biLSTM networks in *context2vec*. *DMSE* contextualizes a word using words with dependency relations (both head and dependents) in a given sentence. Hereafter, words with dependency relations are referred to as *dependency-words*.[3]

There are numerous number of combinations

---

[2]`http://www-bigdata.ist.osaka-u.ac.jp/arase/pj/CEFR-LP.zip`

[3]These are called as *context-words* in Ashihara et al. (2018).

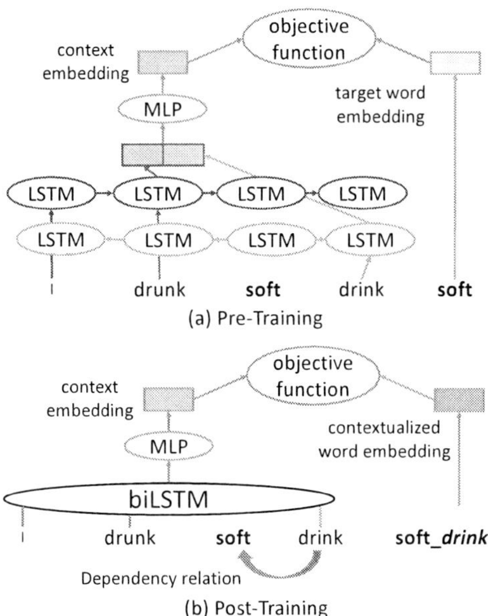

Figure 1: Design of the proposed method where `soft` is the target to generate embedding.

of words and *dependency-words*. Similar to Ashihara et al. (2018), we implement a two-stage training: pre-training and post-training for computational efficiency. In the pre-training, simple word embeddings (one embedding per word) and parameters of biLSTM networks are trained by *context2vec*. In the post-training, only contextualized word embeddings are trained starting from the pre-trained word embeddings.

3.2 Pre-Training

Figure 1 (a) overviews pre-training, which corresponds to the training of *context2vec*. Word embeddings and parameters of biLSTM networks are set.

First, the entire sentence is inputted into the biLSTM networks. At time step k, the forward network encodes words from the beginning to the k-th word. The backward network does the same except in the opposite direction. Therefore, the outputs of each LSTM network before and after a target word represent the preceding and following contexts surrounding the target word, respectively. These outputs are concatenated and inputted into a multi-layer perceptron to generate a unified context embedding for the target word. On the other hand, the target word is represented by a word embedding that has the same dimensions as the con-

text embedding.

The objective function is the negative sampling proposed by Mikolov et al. (2013). A positive example is the target word and its context, whereas negative examples are random words. Note that word embeddings, forward LSTM network, and the backward LSTM network each have their own parameters.

3.3 Post-Training

Figure 1 (b) outlines post-training. Multiple word embeddings are generated for words with the same surface but with different *dependency-words* as contextualized word embeddings.

First, the sentence is parsed to obtain *dependency-words* of the target. For each *dependency-word* and target pair, its word embedding is trained. The process is simple. These words are concatenated with an under-bar (_) and treated as a single word, whose embedding is used as a contextualized word embedding of the target word. The contextualized word embeddings are trained in the same manner with pre-training.

The contextualized embeddings are initialized by assigning the pre-trained word embeddings in Section 3.2. The pre-trained word embeddings and biLSTM networks are fixed, and only the contextualized word embeddings are updated during post-training. This setting allows the contextualized embeddings to be trained in parallel.

3.4 Application to Lexical Substitution Task

This section describes how to tackle the lexical substitution task using both contextualized word embeddings and context embeddings obtained by the proposed method.

Ranking Method As shown in Table 1, lexical substitution ranks substitution candidates of the target word based on their paraphrasabilities under a given context. We use the same ranking method with *context2vec*, which assumes not only that a good substitution candidate is semantically similar to the target word but also is suitable for a given context. This assumption is commonly used in recent lexical substitution models (Melamud et al., 2015; Roller and Erk, 2016).

Here we have target word t and its *dependency-word* d. The contextualized word embedding of t is noted as v_t^d and the word embedding of a substitution candidate s contextualized by d is v_s^d. Finally, the context embedding is denoted as v_c. The following scores are calculated for each substitution candidate and ranked them in descending order.

$$S(\boldsymbol{v}_s^d|\boldsymbol{v}_t^d, \boldsymbol{v}_c)$$
$$= (\cos{(\boldsymbol{v}_t^d, \boldsymbol{v}_s^d)} + 1)(\cos{(\boldsymbol{v}_s^d, \boldsymbol{v}_c)} + 1). \quad (1)$$

Here, $\cos(\cdot, \cdot)$ calculates the cosine similarity between two vectors. If the word embedding does not exist in the vocabulary, the word embedding of $\langle \text{unk} \rangle$ is used.

Dependency-word Selection When there are multiple *dependency-words* to contextualize a word embedding, the most appropriate one must be selected to characterize the sense of the target word in a given context. Ashihara et al. (2018) proposed the following *dependency-word* selection method for the *DMSE* model.

$$S_{\text{maxc}} : d = \arg\max_{d \in D} S(\boldsymbol{v}_s^d|\boldsymbol{v}_t^d, \boldsymbol{v}_c),$$

where D is a set of *dependency-words* of the target word in the context. If the contextualized word embedding $\boldsymbol{v}_s^d$ or $\boldsymbol{v}_t^d$ does not exist in the vocabulary, the corresponding simple word embeddings ($\boldsymbol{v}_s$ or $\boldsymbol{v}_t$) pre-trained for *context2vec* are used.

S_{maxc} uses the *dependency-word* that maximizes the paraphrasability score, but there is no guarantee that this *dependency-word* best characterizes the sense of the word in the given context. Therefore, we propose the following *dependency-word* selection methods based on the similarity between the target word or candidate words and the context.

$$S_{\text{tar}} : d = \arg\max_{d \in D} \cos(\boldsymbol{v}_t^d, \boldsymbol{v}_c),$$
$$S_{\text{can}} : d = \arg\max_{d \in D} \cos(\boldsymbol{v}_s^d, \boldsymbol{v}_c).$$

These methods should select more appropriate *dependency-word* using both contextualized word embeddings and context embeddings.

4 CEFR-LP: New Evaluation Dataset

In addition to proposing a method for lexical substitution, we created CEFR-LP, which mitigates limitations of previous evaluation datasets.

4.1 Principle of CEFR-LP

LS-SE (McCarthy and Navigli, 2007) and LS-CIC (Kremer et al., 2014) are the standard evaluation datasets for lexical substitution. However, they have limited annotation coverage because the annotators provide substitution candidates manually. Specifically, each annotator provides up to three substitution candidates for LS-SE and up to five substitution candidates for LS-CIC. These candidates are regarded as appropriate candidates for a target under a specific context. During an evaluation, these candidates are combined for the same targets with different contexts. This leads to two limitations. First, annotators may not derive all the appropriate candidates for the target. Second, some appropriate candidates for a target among the combined ones are regarded as inappropriate because they were missed by the anasnotators when annotating the target under the given context.

To mitigate these limitations, CEFR-LS (Uchida et al., 2018) was constructed to improve the coverage. However, the target is lexical simplification rather than substitution. Herein we extend CEFR-LS and build a new evaluation dataset called CEFR-LP for lexical substitution tasks that:

1. Define the substitution candidates

2. Determine the paraphrasability label

3. Evaluate the number of annotators

The first extension adapts to lexical substitution. CEFR-LS only includes substitutions from complex words to simpler ones because it is specifically intended for simplification. On the other hand, CEFR-LP includes not only complex to simple substitutions but also simple to complex substitutions and substitutions between equivalent complexities. The substitution candidates are a synonym set of target words extracted from a dictionary.[4] The second extension generates fine-grained judgments for paraphrasability. CEFR-LS is annotated with binary labels, while CEFR-LP is annotated with continuous values representing paraphrasability. This extension allows automatic evaluation via the Generalized Average Precision (GAP) score (Kishida, 2005; Thater et al., 2009), which is common in recent lexical substitution studies. The last extension reduces potential annotation biases. While CEFR-LS was annotated by one expert, CEFR-LP employs more than five annotators per target to reduce bias due to annotator subjectivity. Following CEFR-LS,

---

[4] http://www.thesaurus.com/

context	..., and to create elixirs to cure disease and extend life . From alchemy came the historical **progressions** that led to modern chemistry : the isolation of drugs from natural sources , metallurgy , and the dye industry . Today , chemistry continues to deepen our understanding ...
target	progressions [C1]
candidate	block [B1] (0), development [B1] (6), advancement [B2] (8), break [A2] (1), ...
context	... Competition would ensure that prices remained low and faulty goods disappeared from the market . In this way , businesses would reap profits , consumers would have their needs satisfied , and society as a whole would **prosper** . Smith discussed these ideas, ...
target	prosper [B2]
candidate	thrive [C1] (8), blossom [B2] (6), yield [B2] (1), bear [A2] (0), flourish [C2] (8), ...
context	... That is , a member of the population may be chosen only once . Most samples are taken from **large** populations and the sample tends to be small in comparison to the population . Since this is the case , sampling without replacement is approximately ...
target	large [A1]
candidate	substantial [B1] (8), giant [B1] (6), extravagant [C2] (0), wide [A2] (1), ...

Table 2: Examples of CEFR-LP. "Context" shows context sentences where the target word is presented in **bold**. "Target" shows the target and "candidate" lists the substitution candidates. Square brackets indicate CEFR levels of targets and candidates. Round brackets indicate the weights of candidates.

CEFR-LP also provides CEFR (the Common European Framework of Reference for Languages) levels (A1 (lowest), A2, B1, B2, C1, and C2 (highest)) for the target and candidates as English proficiency levels.

4.2 Annotation

Following CEFR-LS, we use sentences extracted from textbooks publicly available at the OpenStax website[5] initiated by Rice University. We hired annotators on Amazon Mechanical Turk,[6] who (1) possessed a degree from an accredited university in the United States and (2) held the Mechanical Turk Masters qualification or a past acceptance rate above 98%.

Annotators were given a target word, its context, and a list of synonyms. They annotated each substitution candidate in the synonym list with paraphrasability labels ("sure", "maybe", and "not possible") considering the given context. As the context, a sentence on which the target word appeared as well as two more sentences before and after it were provided. To avoid overloading the annotator, target words with more than 30 synonyms were excluded.

Following CEFR-LS, we used the following annotation criteria:

Grammatical Reformation Stage When paraphrasing the target word into the substitution candidate, grammatical accuracy such as the part-of-speech and the connection to the preposition must be maintained. The morphology of the target word such as past tense and third person singular are automatically corrected.

Definition Stage The target word and the substitution candidate have the same meaning.

Context Stage The candidate should retain the nuance of the target word in a given context and not affect the meaning of the sentence.

If all of the above conditions were met, a label of "sure" is assigned. If either condition was not met, a label of "not possible" was assigned. If the judgment was difficult, a label of "maybe" was assigned.

Each annotation set was assigned to at least five annotators. To improve the reliability of annotation labels, we discarded the result from the annotator who had the lowest agreement with the others. Consequently, each set had four annotators and the average Fleiss' kappa was 0.33.

To use CEFR-LP for a lexical substitution task, the assigned labels were consolidated as a weight. For example, LS-SE and LS-CIC were set such that a weight to the number of annotators produced

[5] https://cnx.org/
[6] https://www.mturk.com/

	CEFR-LP	LS-SE	LS-CIC
number of target words	863	2,010	15,344
number of substitution candidates	14,259	34,600	601,257
average number of substitution candidates per target	16.5	17.2	39.2
average number of paraphrasable candidates per target	10.0	3.48	6.65

Table 3: Basic statistics in CEFR-LP compared to LS-SE and LS-CIC

CEFR level	target	candidate
all	863	14,259
A1	300	2,090
A2	190	2,856
B1	110	4,513
B2	186	3,201
C1	30	648
C2	47	951

Table 4: Distribution of CEFR levels in CEFR-LP

context embedding units	300
LSTM hidden/output units	600
MLP input units	1200
MLP hidden units	1200
sentential context units	600
target word units	600
number of negative samples	10
negative sampling rate	0.75
number of epochs	10

Table 5: *Context2vec* hyper-parameters that show the best performance in (Melamud et al., 2016).

a certain candidate. A "sure", "maybe", and "not possible" label were assigned values of 2, 1, and 0 points, respectively. These values were summed to give the weight of the candidate. Because each substitution candidate has four annotation labels, the weight ranged from 0 to 8. The larger the value, the higher the paraphrase possibility.

Table 2 shows examples sampled from CEFR-LP. "Context" gives sentences, including a target word. "Target" is the target word with its CEFR level in a square bracket, which is represented by a bold style in the context sentences. "Candidate" lists substitution candidates with their CEFR levels in square brackets and weights computed based on annotated labels in round brackets.

4.3 Analysis of CEFR-LP

Table 3 shows the basic statistics for CEFR-LP compared to those in LS-SE and LS-CIC. CEFR-LP provides 14,259 substitution candidates for 863 target words. The average number of paraphrasable candidates per word is 10.0, which is larger than 3.48 of LS-SE and 6.65 of LS-CIC. Here, a paraphrasable candidate means substitution candidates with a weight of 1 or more (*i.e.*, at least one annotator judged it can paraphrase the target in a given context). Compared to LS-SE and LS-CIC, CEFR-LP has an enhanced coverage of substitution candidates.

Table 4 shows the distribution of CEFR levels

in CEFR-LP. Words at the C1 and C2 levels are naturally less frequent than others in general documents. The distribution reflects this tendency. We believe that these CEFR levels are useful when applying lexical substitution technologies to educational applications.

5 Evaluation Settings

This section describes the evaluation settings used to investigate the performance of our method on lexical substitution tasks.

5.1 Training of Our Method

To train contextualized word embeddings by using our method, we used 61.6M sentences[7] extracted from the main contents of English Wikipedia[8] articles. We lemmatized each word using the Stanford Parser (Manning et al., 2014) and replaced words less than or equal to ten frequency to $\langle unk \rangle$ tag to reduce the size of the vocabulary.

Pre-training used the same hyper-parameter settings of *context2vec* (Table 5). These settings achieved the best performance on lexical substitution tasks in Melamud et al. (2016).

---

[7]To speed-up the training of *context2vec*, all sentences consisting of more than 25 words are discarded.

[8]https://dumps.wikimedia.org/enwiki/
20170601/

For post-training, dependency relations were derived using the Stanford Parser. To avoid the data sparseness problem, *dependency-words* were limited to nouns, verbs, adjectives, and adverbs. The number of training epochs in the post-training was set to one because our post-training aims to contextualize word embeddings that have been pre-trained. Hence, a long-time training does not have to be assumed. In the future, we plan to investigate the effects of the number of training epochs in post-training.

5.2 Evaluation Dataset

We used the following datasets in the evaluation.

LS-SE

This is an official evaluation dataset in the lexical substitution task of SemEval-2007. For each target word, five annotators suggested up to three different substitutions. As the context, a sentence where a target word appears is provided. Every target has ten context sentences. The number of targets is 201 (types). Consequently, there are $2,010$ sets of target, candidates, and context sentences are available.

LS-CIC

This is a large-scale dataset for a lexical substitution task. For $15,629$ target words, six annotators suggested up to five different substitutions under a context. Unlike LS-SE, three sentences are provided as context: a sentence containing the target word, its preceding sentence, and its following sentences.

CEFR-LP

Our new dataset for lexical substitution, which is described in Section 4.

5.3 Evaluation Metrics

We used GAP (Kishida, 2005; Thater et al., 2009) as an evaluation metric. GAP is a commonly used metric to evaluate lexical substitution tasks. GAP calculates the ranking accuracy by considering the weight of correct examples:

$$p_i = \frac{\sum_{k=1}^{i} x_k}{i},$$

$$GAP = \frac{100 \sum_{i=1}^{n} I(x_i)p_i}{\sum_{i=1}^{n} I(y_i)\overline{y_i}},$$

where x_i and y_i represent the weight of the i-th substitution candidate ranked by an automatic

method and by the ideal ranking, respectively. n represents the number of substitution candidates. $I(x)$ ($x \in \mathbb{N}$) is a binary function that returns 1 if $x \geq 1$. Otherwise, it returns 0. In this experiment, we regarded the number of annotators suggesting a substitution candidate under a given context as the weight of the candidate for LS-SE and LS-CIC. For CEFR-LP, we used the weight of the candidate that was computed based on the annotated labels as described in Section 4.2.

5.4 Baseline Method

We used the following baselines for comparison.

DMSE (S_{maxc})

For *dependency-word* selection, S_{maxc} showing the highest performance is used herein. This is the best-performing model among the methods that generate contextualized word embeddings.

Context2vec

This is the current state-of-the-art method among those proposed for lexical substitution. Note that this corresponds to the pre-trained model of our method.

ELMo

We concatenate embeddings generated from three hidden layers in *ELMo* as contextualized word embeddings.[9]

DMSE and *ELMo* were trained using the same Wikipedia corpus as our method. These methods rank the substitution candidates in descending order of the cosine similarity between embeddings of the target and substitution candidate. For *context2vec*, the candidates are ranked in the same manner using our method based on Equation (1).

5.5 Ideal Selection of *Dependency-words*

The performance of our method depends on how *dependency-words* are selected. We simulate the performance when our method selects ideal *dependency-words* that maximize the GAP score. This selection method of *dependency-words* is denoted as S_{best}.

---

[9] As a preliminary experiment, we compared methods to generate contextualized word embeddings. One used one of three layers of embeddings, one summed these embeddings, and one concatenated these embeddings. The results confirmed that concatenation performed best.

Model	LS-SE	LS-CIC	CEFR-LP
DMSE (S_{maxc})	49.3	46.5	71.1
ELMo	47.6	48.1	74.9
context2vec	51.1	50.0	75.3
context2vec + DMSE (S_{maxc})	52.2	50.9	75.5
context2vec + DMSE (S_{tar})	**52.3**	50.9	**75.6**
context2vec + DMSE (S_{can})	**52.3**	**51.0**	**75.6**
context2vec + DMSE (S_{best})	55.6	52.9	77.2

Table 6: GAP scores on LS-SE, LS-CIC and CEFR-LP datasets, where **bold** denotes the highest scores.

	A1	A2	B1	B2	C1 / C2
DMSE (S_{maxc})	67.9	75.2	65.7	74.9	72.7
context2vec	75.2	78.5	69.4	75.7	75.2
context2vec+DMSE (S_{can})	**75.3**	**78.9**	**69.9**	**76.2**	**75.9**

Table 7: GAP scores on different CEFR levels of target words in CEFR-LP

6 Results

Table 6 shows the GAP scores for LS-SE, LS-CIC and CEFR-LS datasets. Our method is denoted as *context2vec + DMSE* where the *dependency-word* selection method is represented in parenthesis as S_{maxc}, S_{tar}, or S_{can}.

When using S_{can} for *dependency-word* selection, *context2vec + DMSE* outperformed *DMSE* by 3.0 points, 4.5 points, and 4.5 points for LS-SE, LS-CIC, and CEFR-LP, respectively. It even outperformed *context2vec*, the current state-of-the-art method, by 1.2 points, 1.0 points, and 0.3 points on these datasets, respectively. These results confirm the effectiveness of our method, which combines contextualized word embeddings and context embeddings to complement each other.

All *dependency-word* selection methods show fairly competitive performances, but S_{can} consistently achieved the highest GAP scores. Context embedding may be effective to select *dependency-words* rather than comparing contextualized word embeddings. The last row of Table 6 shows the performance of our method with S_{best} (*i.e.*, when the ideal *dependency-word* was selected). This best selection method outperformed 1.6 - 3.3 points higher than our method with S_{can}, demonstrating the importance of *dependency-word* selection. In the future, we will improve the selection method.

CEFR-LP analyzes performances from the perspective of the CEFR levels of target words. Table 7 shows the GAP score of *DMSE (S_{maxc})*, *context2vec*, and *context2vec+DMSE (S_{can})*. Note that scores are *not* comparable across levels because the number of appropriate substitution candidates varies. Our method consistently outperforms *DMSE (S_{maxc})* and *context2vec*. Such an analysis is important when applying lexical substitution to educational applications.

Table 8 lists the results where each row shows a ranking of substitution candidates by compared methods. The annotated weights of each candidate are presented in parentheses. Here, the outputs of *context2vec+DMSE (S_{maxc})* to use the same *dependency-words* with *DMSE (S_{maxc})*.

Inputs (1) and (2) show the cases where the meanings of polysemous target words (`go` and `tender`) are successfully captured by our method. It ranks `start` and `soft` first for each target, respectively. On the other hand, *DMSE (S_{maxc})* failed to rank correct candidates higher although it referred to the same *dependency-words*. *Context2vec* also failed, but it used context embeddings. These results demonstrate that contextualized word embeddings and context embeddings complement each other. On Input (3), both *DMSE (S_{maxc})* and our method failed while *context2vec* successfully rank the correct candidate (`grasp`) on top. This is caused by incorrect *dependency-word* selection. In Input (3), there are two major *dependency-words*, `sat` and `hands`. In this context, `hands` should be useful as a clue to iden-

Input (1)	To make these techniques work well , explain the basic concept and purpose and *get* it **going** with minimal briefing .
DMSE (S_maxc)	try (0), move (1), proceed (1), leave (0), ...
context2vec	proceed (1), run (0), start (4), move (1), ...
context2vec+DMSE (S_maxc)	start (4), proceed (1), move (1), run (0), ...
Input (2)	Rabbits often feed on young , **tender** perennial *growth* as it emerges in spring , or on young transplants .
DMSE (S_maxc)	immature (0), young (0), great (1), soft (4), ...
context2vec	delicate (1), immature (0), soft (4), painful (0), ...
context2vec+DMSE (S_maxc)	soft (4), delicate (1), immature (0), young (0), ...
Input (3)	A doctor *sat* in front of me and **held** my *hands* .
DMSE (S_maxc)	put (0), lift (1), grasp (3), carry (0), ...
context2vec	grasp (3), carry (0), take (1), keep (0), ...
context2vec+DMSE (S_maxc)	take (1), carry (0), keep (0), lift (1), ...

Table 8: Example outputs of each method. Target words in the input sentences are presented in **bold** and all of their *dependency-words* are presented in *italic*. Outputs are ranked lists of candidates, where the numbers in parentheses show candidates' weights. Our method ranks the appropriate candidates on top for the first two examples, but it failed on the last example due to incorrect *dependency-word* selection.

tify target word's sense but `sat` was mistakenly selected as the *dependency-word*. This result suggests that dependency types matter when selecting *dependency-words*, which we will tackle in the future.

7   Conclusion

Herein we proposed a method that combines *DMSE* and *context2vec* to simultaneously take advantage of contextualized word embeddings and context embeddings. The evaluation results on lexical substitution tasks confirm the effectiveness of our method, which outperforms the current state-of-the-art method. We also create a new evaluation set for lexical substitution tasks called CEFR-LP.

In the future, we will consider the dependency types in contextualized word embeddings for further improvements. Additionally, we plan to extend CEFR-LP to cover phrasal substitutions.

Acknowledgments

We thank Professor Christopher G. Haswell for his valuable comments and discussions. We also thank the anonymous reviewers for their valuable comments. This research was supported by the KDDI Foundation.

References

Kazuki Ashihara, Tomoyuki Kajiwara, Yuki Arase, and Satoru Uchida. 2018. Contextualized Word Representations for Multi-Sense Embedding. In *Proceedings of the Pacific Asia Conference on Language, Information and Computation*, pages 28–36.

Marzieh Fadaee, Arianna Bisazza, and Christof Monz. 2017. Learning Topic-Sensitive Word Representations. In *Proceedings of the Annual Meeting of the Association for Computational Linguistics*, pages 441–447.

Kazuaki Kishida. 2005. Property of Average Precision and its Generalization: An Examination of Evaluation Indicator for Information Retrieval Experiments. *National Institute of Informatics Technical Reports*, pages 1–19.

Gerhard Kremer, Katrin Erk, Sebastian Padó, and Stefan Thater. 2014. What Substitutes Tell Us - Analysis of an "All-Words" Lexical Substitution Corpus. In *Proceedings of the Conference of the European Chapter of the Association for Computational Linguistics*, pages 540–549.

Christopher Manning, Mihai Surdeanu, John Bauer, Jenny Finkel, Steven Bethard, and David McClosky. 2014. The Stanford CoreNLP Natural Language Processing Toolkit. In *Proceedings of the Annual Meeting of the Association for Computational Linguistics*, pages 55–60.

Diana McCarthy. 2002. Lexical Substitution as a Task for WSD Evaluation. In *Proceedings of the ACL Workshop on Word Sense Disambiguation*, pages 109–115.

Diana McCarthy and Roberto Navigli. 2007. SemEval-2007 Task 10: English Lexical Substitution Task. In *Proceedings of the International Workshop on Semantic Evaluations*, pages 48–53.

Oren Melamud, Ido Dagan, and Jacob Goldberger. 2015. Modeling Word Meaning in Context with Substitute Vectors. In *Proceedings of the Conference of the North American Chapter of the Association for Computational Linguistics*, pages 472–482.

Oren Melamud, Jacob Goldberger, and Ido Dagan. 2016. context2vec: Learning Generic Context Embedding with Bidirectional LSTM. In *Proceedings of the SIGNLL Conference on Computational Natural Language Learning*, pages 51–61.

Tomas Mikolov, Kai Chen, Greg Corrado, and Jeffrey Dean. 2013. Efficient Estimation of Word Representations in Vector Space. In *Proceeding of the International Conference on Learning Representations*, pages 1–12.

Gustavo Henrique Paetzold and Lucia Specia. 2016. Unsupervised Lexical Simplification for Non-Native Speakers. In *Proceedings of the Association for the Advancement of Artificial Intelligence*, pages 3761–3767.

Gustavo Henrique Paetzold and Lucia Specia. 2017. A survey on lexical simplification. *Journal of Artificial Intelligence Research*, pages 549–593.

Matthew E. Peters, Mark Neumann, Mohit Iyyer, Matt Gardner, Christopher Clark, Kenton Lee, and Luke Zettlemoyer. 2018. Deep Contextualized Word Representations. In *Proceedings of the Annual Conference of the North American Chapter of the Association for Computational Linguistics*, pages 2227–2237.

Stephen Roller and Katrin Erk. 2016. PIC a Different Word: A Simple Model for Lexical Substitution in Context. In *Proceedings of the Annual Conference of the North American Chapter of the Association for Computational Linguistics*, pages 1121–1126.

Mike Schuster and Kuldip K. Paliwal. 1997. Bidirectional Recurrent Neural Networks. *IEEE Transactions on Signal Processing*, pages 2673–2681.

Stefan Thater, Universität Saarlandes, Georgiana Dinu, Universität Saarlandes, Manfred Pinkal, and Universität Saarlandes. 2009. Ranking Paraphrases in Context. In *Proceedings of the Workshop on Applied Textual Inference*, pages 44–47.

Satoru Uchida, Shohei Takada, and Yuki Arase. 2018. CEFR-based Lexical Simplification Dataset. *Proceedings of the International Conference on Language Resources and Evaluation*, pages 3254–3258.

Phonetic Normalization
for Machine Translation of User Generated Content

José Carlos Rosales Núñez[1,2,3]   **Djamé Seddah**[3]   **Guillaume Wisniewski**[1,2,4]

[1]Université Paris Sud, LIMSI
[2] Université Paris Saclay
[3] INRIA Paris
[4] Université de Paris, LLF, CNRS

`jose.rosales@limsi.fr   djame.seddah@inria.fr`
`guillaume.wisniewski@univ-paris-diderot.fr`

Abstract

We present an approach to correct noisy User Generated Content (UGC) in French aiming to produce a pre-processing pipeline to improve Machine Translation for this kind of non-canonical corpora. Our approach leverages the fact that some errors are due to confusion induced by words with similar pronunciation which can be corrected using a phonetic look-up table to produce normalization candidates. We rely on a character-based neural model phonetizer to produce IPA pronunciations of words and a similarity metric based on the IPA representation of words that allow us to identify words with similar pronunciation. These potential corrections are then encoded in a lattice and ranked using a language model to output the most probable corrected phrase. Compared to other phonetizers, our method boosts a `Transformer`-based machine translation system on UGC.

1 Introduction

In this work we aim to improve the translation quality of User-Generated Content (UGC). This kind of content generally contains many characters repetitions, typographic errors, contractions, jargon or non-canonical syntactic constructions, resulting in a typically high number of Out-of-Vocabulary words (OOVs), which, in turn, significantly decreases MT quality and can introduce noisy artefacts in the output due to rare tokens. Hereby, we propose a normalization pipeline that leverages on the existence of UGC specific noise due to the misuse of words or OOV contractions that have a similar pronunciation to those of the expected correct tokens. This method works without any supervision on noisy UGC corpora, but exploits phonetic similarity to propose normalization token candidates. To explore the capacities of our system, we first assess the performance of our normalizer and then

conduct a series of MT experiments to determine if our method improves the translation quality of some Phrase-Based Statistical Machine Translation (`PBSMT`) and Neural Machine Translation (NMT) baselines. Our results show that including a phonetization step in conjunction with a `Transformer` architecture (Vaswani et al., 2017) can improve machine translation over UGC with a minimum impact on in-domain translations. This suggests that phonetic normalization can be a promising research avenue for MT and automatic correction of UGC.

Our contribution in this paper is threefold:

- we propose a pre-processing pipeline to normalize UGC and improve MT quality;

- by quantifying the corrections made by our normalizer in our UGC corpora, we assess the presence of noise due to phonetic writing and demonstrate that this knowledge can be potentially exploited to produce corrections of UGC without any annotated data;

- we explore the performance improvement that can be achieved in machine translation by using a phonetic similarity heuristic to propose different normalization candidates.

2 Related Work

Several works have focused on using lattices to model uncertain inputs or potential processing errors that occur in the early stage of the pipeline. For instance, Su et al. (2017) proposed `lat2seq`, an extension of `seq2seq` models (Sutskever et al., 2014) able to encode several possible input possibilities by conditioning their GRU output to several predecessors' paths. The main issue with this model is that it is unable to predict the score of choosing a certain path by using future scores, i.e, by considering words that come after the current

Proceedings of the 2019 EMNLP Workshop W-NUT: The 5th Workshop on Noisy User-generated Text, pages 407–416
Hong Kong, Nov 4, 2019. ©2019 Association for Computational Linguistics

token to be potentially normalized. Sperber et al. (2017) introduced a model based on `Tree-LSTMs` (Tai et al., 2015), to correct outputs of an Automatic Speech Recognition (ASR) system. On the other hand, Le et al. (2008) use lattices composed of written subword units to improve recognition rate on ASR.

However, none of the aforementioned works have focused on processing noisy UGC corpora and they do not consider our main hypotheses of using phonetizers to recover correct tokens. They aim to correct known tokens such that a neural language model chooses the best output when an uncertain input is present (typically words with similar pronunciation from an ASR output). Instead, our approach calculates the phonetization of the source token and candidates are proposed based on their phonetic similarity to it, where this original observation can be a potential OOV.

On the same trend, (Qin et al., 2012) combined several ASR systems to improve detection of OOVs. More recently, van der Goot and van Noord (2018) achieved state-of-the-art performance on dependency parsing of UGC using lattices.

Closely related to our work, Baranes (2015) explored several normalization techniques on French UGC. In particular, to recover from typographical errors, they considered a rule-based system, SxPipe (Sagot and Boullier, 2008), that produced lattices encoding OOVs alternative spelling and used a language model to select the best correction.

Several works have explored different approaches to normalize noisy UGC in various languages. For instance, Stymne (2011) use Approximate String Matching, an algorithm based on a weighted Levenshtein edit distance to generate lattices containing alternative spelling of OOVs. Wang and Ng (2013) employ a Conditional Random Field and a beam-search decoding approach to address missing punctuation and words in Chinese and English social media text. More recently, Watson et al. (2018) proposed a neural sequence-to-sequence embedding enhancing `FastText` (Bojanowski et al., 2017) representations with word-level information, which achieved state-of-the-art on the QALB Arabic normalization task (Mohit et al., 2014).

3 Phonetic Correction Model

To automatically process phonetic writing and map UGC to their correct spelling, we propose a simple model based on finding, for each token of the sentence, words with similar pronunciations and selecting the best spelling alternative, using a language model. More precisely, we propose a four-step process:

1. for each word of the input sentence, we automatically generate its pronunciation. We consider all words in the input sentence as misspelled tokens are not necessarily OOVs (e.g. "*j'ai manger*" — literally "*I have eat*" — which must be corrected to "*j'ai mangé*" — "*I have eaten*", the French words "manger" and "mangé" having both the same pronunciation /mã.ge/);

2. using these phonetic representations, we look, for each word w of the input sentence, to every word in the training vocabulary with a pronunciation "similar" to w according to an ad-hoc metric we discuss below;

3. we represent each input sentence by a lattice of $n + 1$ nodes (where n is the number of words in the sentence) in which the edge between the i-th and $(i + 1)$-th nodes is labeled with the i-th word of the sentence. Alternative spellings can then be encoded by adding an edge between the i-th and $(i + 1)$-th nodes labeled by a possible correction of the i-th word. Figure 1 gives an example of such a lattice. In these lattices, a path between the initial and final nodes represents a (possible) normalization of the input sentence.

4. using a language model, we compute the probability to observe each alternative spelling of the sentence (note that, by construction, the input sentence is also contained in the lattice) and find the most probable path (and therefore potential normalization) of the input sentence. Note that finding the most probable path in a lattice can be done with a complexity proportional to the size of the sentence even if the lattice encodes a number of paths that grows exponentially with the sentence size (Mohri, 2002). In our experiments we used the `OpenGRM` (Roark et al., 2012) and `OpenFST` (Allauzen et al., 2007) frameworks that provide a very efficient implementation to score a lattice with a language model.

This process can be seen as a naive spellchecker, in which we only consider a reduced set of variations,

tailored to the specificities of UGC texts. We will
now detail the first two steps discussed above.

**Generating the pronunciation of the input
words** To predict the pronunciation of an input word, i.e. its representation in the International Phonetic Alphabet (IPA), we use the
`gtp-seq2seq` python library[1] to implement a
grapheme-to-phoneme conversion tool that relies
on a `Transformer` model (Vaswani et al., 2017).
We use a 3 layers model with 256 hidden units
that is trained on a pronunciation dictionary automatically extracted from `Wiktionary` (see Section 4.1 for a description of our datasets). This
vanilla model achieves a word-level accuracy of
94.6%, that is to say it is able to find the exact correct phonetization of almost 95% of the words of
our test set.

We also consider, as a baseline, the pronunciation generated by the `Espeak` program.[2] that uses
a formant synthesis method to produce phonetiza-
tions based on acoustic parameters.

Finding words with similar pronunciation In
order to generate alternatives spelling for each input word, we look, in our pronunciation dictionary,[3] for alternate candidates based on phonetic
similarity. We define the phonetic similarity of
two words as the edit distance between their IPA
representations, all edit operations being weighted
depending on the articulatory features of the sounds
involved. To compute the phonetic similarity we
used the implementation (and weights) provided
by the `PanPhon` library (Mortensen et al., 2016).

To avoid an explosion of the number of alternatives we consider, we have applied a threshold
on the phonetic distance and consider only homophones, i.e. alternatives that have the exact same
pronunciation as the original word.[4]

To account for peculiarities of French orthography we also systematically consider alternative
spellings in which diacritics (acute, grave and cir-
cumflex accents) for the letter *"e"* (which is the
only one that changes the pronunciation for different accentuation in French) were added wherever

possible. Indeed, users often tend to 'forget' diacritics when writing online and this kind of spelling
error results in phonetic distances that can be large
(e.g. the pronunciation of *bebe* and *bébé* is very
different).

We ultimately only keep as candidates those that
are present in the train corpus of Section 4.3 to
filter out OOV, and nonexistent words.

4 Datasets

In this section, we present the different corpora
used in this work. We will first describe the dataset
used to train our phonetic normalizer; then, in §4.2,
the UGC corpora used both to measure the performance of our normalization step and evaluate the
impact of phonetic spelling on machine translation.
Finally, in § 4.3 we introduce the (canonical) parallel corpora we used to train our MT system. All our
experiments are made on French UGC corpora.[5]
Some statistics describing these corpora are listed
in Table 1.

4.1 Pronunciation Dictionary

To train our Grapheme-to-Phoneme model we use
a dictionary mapping words to their pronunciation (given by their IPA representation). To the
best of our knowledge, there is no free pronunciation dictionary for French. In our experiments,
we have considered a pronunciation dictionary automatically extracted from `Wiktionary` dumps
building on the fact that, at least for French, pronunciation information are identified using special
templates, which makes their extraction straightforward (Pécheux et al., 2016).[6]

The dictionary extracted from the French
`Wiktionary` contains 1,571,090 words. We
trained our G2P phonetizer on 1,200,000 examples, leaving the rest to evaluate its performance.
When looking for words with similar pronunciation (§3), we consider only the word that appear
in our parallel training data (described in §4.3) to
speed up the search. After filtering, our dictionary
contained pronunciation information for roughly
82K French words.

4.2 UGC Corpora

The Parallel `Cr#pbank` corpus The Parallel
`Cr#pbank`, introduced in (Rosales Núñez et al.,

---

[1]`https://github.com/cmusphinx/
g2p-seq2seq`

[2]`espeak.sourceforge.net`

[3]see § 4.1 for the description of the data we used

[4]We have explored using several values for this parameter
but in this work only the most conservative distance (0) is
used since higher values add too much candidates and rapidly
decreases performance due to the number of ambiguities.

[5]Applying our work to other languages is straightforward
and left to future work.

[6]Our French pronunciation dictionary will be made available upon publication.

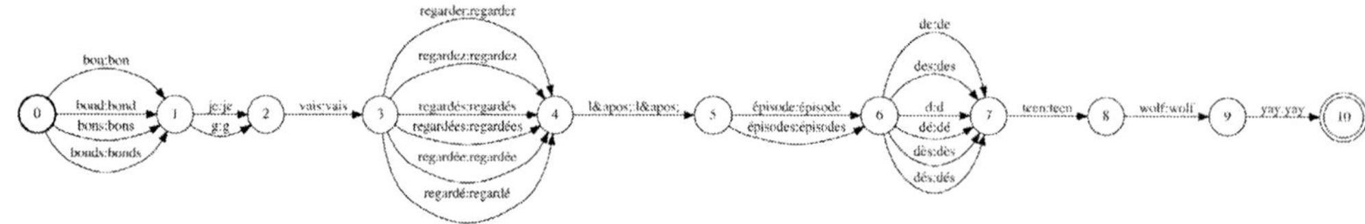

Figure 1: Example of lattice for a segment of a `Cr#pbank` UGC sample.

Corpus	#sentences	#tokens	ASL	TTR	Corpus	#sentences	#tokens	ASL	TTR
train set					*UGC test set*				
WMT	2.2M	64.2M	29.7	0.20	`Cr#pbank`	777	13,680	17.60	0.32
Small	9.2M	57.7M	6.73	0.18	MTNT	1,022	20,169	19.70	0.34
Large	34M	1.19B	6.86	0.25					
test set					*UGC blind test set*				
`OpenSubTest`	11,000	66,148	6.01	0.23	`Cr#pbank`	777	12,808	16.48	0.37
`NeswTest`	3,003	68,155	22.70	0.23	MTNT	599	8,176	13.62	0.38

Table 1: Statistics on the French side of the corpora used in our experiments. *TTR stands for Type-to-Token Ratio, ASL for average sentence length.*

2019), consists of 1,554 comments in French, translated from an extension of the French Social Media Bank (Seddah et al., 2012) annotated with the following linguistic information: Part-of-Speech tags, surface syntactic representations, as well as a normalized form whenever necessary. Comments have been translated from French to English by a native French speaker with near-native English speaker capabilities. Typographic and grammar error were corrected in the gold translations but some of the specificities of UGC were kept. For instance, idiomatic expressions were mapped directly to the corresponding ones in English (e.g. "mdr" (*mort de rire,* litt. *dying of laughter*) has been translated to "lol" and letter repetitions were also kept (e.g. "ouiii" has been translated to "yesss"). For our experiments, we have divided the `Cr#pbank` into two sets (test and blind) containing 777 comments each. This corpus can be freely downloaded at `https://gitlab.inria.fr/seddah/parsiti`.

The MTNT corpus We also consider in our experiments, the MTNT corpus (Michel and Neubig, 2018), a multilingual dataset that contains French sentences collected on `Reddit` and translated into English by professional translators. We used their designated test set and added a blind test set of 599 sentences we sampled from the MTNT validation set. The `Cr#pbank` and MTNT corpora both differ in the domain they consider, their collection date, and in the way sentences were filtered to ensure they are sufficiently different from canonical data.

4.3 Canonical Parallel Corpora

To train our MT systems, we use the 'standard' parallel data, namely the `Europarl` and `NewsCommentaries` corpora that are used in the WMT evaluation campaign (Bojar et al., 2016) and the `OpenSubtitles` corpus (Lison et al., 2018). We will discuss the different training data configurations for the MT experiments more in detail in Section 5.

We also use the totality of the French part of these corpora to train a 5-gram language model with Knesser-Ney smoothing (Ney et al., 1994) that is used to score possible rewritings of the input sentence and find the best normalization, as we have discussed in Section 3.

5 Machine Translation Experiments

To evaluate whether our approach improve the translation quality of UGC, we have processed all of our test sets, both UGC and canonical ones with our phonetic normalization pipeline (Section 3). The corrected input sentences are then translated by a phrase-based and NMT systems.[7] We evaluate translation quality using SACREBLEU (Post, 2018).

The MT baselines models were trained using the parallel corpora described in Section 4.3. We use 3 training data configurations in our experiments: WMT, `Small` `OpenTest` and `Large`

---

[7] In our experiments we used `Moses` (Koehn et al., 2007) and `OpenNMT` (Klein et al., 2018).

	PBSMT				Transformer			
	Crap	MTNT	News	Open	Crap	MTNT	News	Open
WMT	20.5	21.2	**22.5**†	13.3	15.4	21.2	27.4†	16.3
Small	28.9	27.3	20.4	26.1†	**27.5**	**28.3**	**26.7**	31.4†
Large	**30.0**	**28.6**	22.3	**27.4**†	26.9	28.3	26.6	**31.5**†

Table 2: BLEU score results for our two benchmark models for the different train-test combinations. None of the test sets are normalized. The best result for each test set is marked in bold, in-domain scores with a dag. *Crap, News and Open respectively stand for the* Cr#pbank, NeswTest *and* OpenSubTest.

	PBSMT				Transformer			
	Crap	MTNT	News	Open	Crap	MTNT	News	Open
WMT	20.4	20.2	**21.9**†	13.4	15.0	20.4	**26.7**†	16.2
Small	28.4	26.2	19.9	26.1†	**29.0**	28.3	25.7	31.4†
Large	**29.0**	27.6	21.8	**27.4**†	28.5	28.2	25.9	**31.5**†

(a) (**G2P**) phonetizer.

	PBSMT				Transformer			
	Crap	MTNT	News	Open	Crap	MTNT	News	Open
WMT	20.4	20.4	21.7†	13.4	14.6	20.7	26.5†	16.1
Small	28.0	26.3	19.8	26.2†	28.5	**28.8**	25.6	31.4†
Large	28.3	**27.7**	21.6	**27.4**†	27.5	28.6	25.8	**31.5**†

(b) (**Espeak**) phonetizer.

Table 3: BLEU score results for our three benchmark models on normalized test sets. The best result for each test set is marked in bold, in-domain scores with a dag.

OpenTest, for which Table 1 reports some statistics. We will denote Small and Large the two OpenSubtitles training sets used in the MT experiments. For every model, we tokenize the training data using byte-pair encoding (Sennrich et al., 2016) with a 16K vocabulary size.

BLEU scores for our normalized test sets are reported in Table 3a and Table 3b, for the G2P and Espeak phonetizers. Results of the unprocessed test sets are reported in Table 2. We present some UGC examples of positive and negative results along with their normalization and translation in Table 6.

6 Results Discussion

We noticed significant improvement in results for the UGC test corpora when using the Transformer architecture trained with the Small OpenTest training set. Specifically, a BLEU score improvement for the Cr#pbank and MTNT test corpora in Tables 3a and 3b, compared to the baseline translation in Table 2. Interestingly, these improvements only hold for the Transformer model, whereas we consistently obtain a slight decrease of BLEU scores when the normalized text is translated using the PBSMT model. Moreover, our trained G2P phonetizer achieved the best improvement over the Cr#pbank corpus, attaining +1.5 BLEU points compared to the baseline. On the other hand, the Espeak phonetizer produces the highest translation improvement on the MTNT corpus (+0.5 BLEU).

Regarding the performance decrease on our non-UGC test corpora, newstest'14 and OpenSubtitles, we observe that there is usually a considerable under-performance on the latter (-0.65 BLEU averaging over our 6 model and training set configurations), that is not as noticeable in the former (-0.1 BLEU in the worst case). This could be explained by the substantially longer sentences in newstest'14 compared to OpenSubtitles, which have roughly 6 times more words in average according to Table 1. When sentences are longer, the number of possible lattices paths grow exponentially, thus adding confusion to our language model decisions that will ultimately produce the most probable normalization. Such observation strongly suggests that our normalizing method performances is somewhat dependent

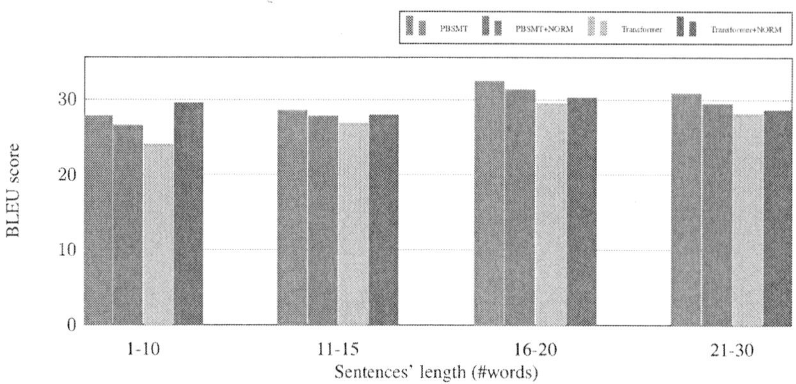

Figure 2: Bar plot of the BLEU score for the `Cr#pbank` test set translation divided in sentences' length groups.

on the length of the target sentence that are to be normalized.

In addition, we display the number of replacements performed by our normalizer over the `Cr#pbank` test set for several values of the phonetic distance threshold in Figure 3. We can notice that the higher this threshold is, the higher the number of replacements. In our experience, the normalization candidates proposed by our method do not share a close pronunciation for threshold values above 0.2, thus adding a substantial quantity of spurious ambiguities.

We have also calculated and proceed to display the BLEU score of the `Cr#pbank` corpus by groups of sentences length in Figure 2 in order to further investigate why our method enhances the `Transformer` MT systems output, whereas this is not the case for the `PBSMT` models, as seen in Table 3. In this way, in Figure 2, we can notice that the highest improvement caused by our phonetic normalization pipeline is present in short sentences (between 1 and 10 words). It is worth noting that this is the only case where the `Transformer` outperforms `PBSMT` in this Figure. Hence, the higher overall `Transformer` BLEU score over `PBSMT` is certainly due to a relatively high successful normalization over the shortest sentences of the `Cr#pbank` test set. This agrees with the documented fact that NMT is consistently better than `PBSMT` on short sentences (Bentivogli et al., 2016) and, in this concrete example, it seems that the `Transformer` can take advantage of this when we apply our normalization pipeline. Additionally, these results could be regarded as evidence supporting that our proposed method performs generally

better for short sentences, as observed in Table 3 results' discussion.

System	Blind Tests	
	MTNT	Cr#pbank
`Large` – PBSMT Raw	**29.3**	**30.5**
`Large` – PBSMT Phon. Norm	26.7	26.9
`Small` – Transformer Raw	**25.0**	**19.0**
`Small` – Transformer Phon. Norm	24.5	18.3
`M&N18` Raw	19.3	13.3
`M&N18` UNK rep. Raw	21.9	15.4

Table 4: BLEU score results comparison on the MTNT and `Cr#pbank` blind test sets. The G2P phonetizer has been used for normalization. *M&N18 stands for (Michel and Neubig, 2018)'s baseline system.*

Furthermore, we have applied our method over a blind test set of the UGC corpora MTNT and `Cr#pbank`. These results are displayed in Table 4, we also show the performance of the (Michel and Neubig, 2018)'s baseline system on such test sets. The translation system is selected as the best for each of the UGC sets from Table 3. For such test corpus, we noticed a 0.5 and a 3 BLEU points decrease for `Transformer` and `PBSMT` systems, respectively, when our normalizer is used over the MTNT blind test. On the other hand, we obtained a 0.7 BLUE point loss for the `Transformer` and a 3.6 point drop for `PBSMT`, both on the `Cr#pbank` blind test. These results suggest that, when we do not tune looking for the best translation system, and for certain UGC, our approach introduces too much noise and MT performance can therefore be detrimentally impacted.

Normalization	a→à	sa→ça	et→est	la→là	à→a	tous→tout	des→de	regarder→regardé	ils→il	prend→prends
Number of app.	87	16	15	13	12	11	8	7	6	6

Table 5: Most frequent normalization replacements on the `Cr#pbank` test corpus.

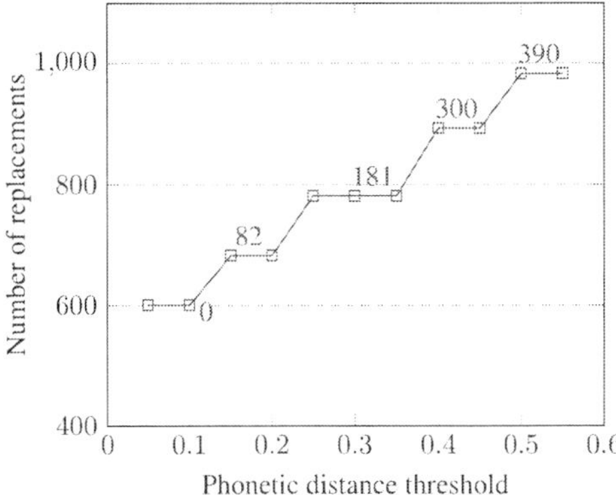

Figure 3: Number of replacement operations of our normalizer over the `Cr#pbank` test set. The quantity of non-homophones normalizations are displayed as point labels.

7 Qualitative Analysis

We display the most frequent normalization changes in the `Cr#pbank` test set, along with their phonetic distance in Table 5. We notice that the 20 most frequent normalization changes are homophones, i.e. they have a 0.0 phonetic distance even when the threshold is set to 0.2.[8] Replacements with a phonetic distance of 0.1 to 0.2, appear at most twice in this test set, except for *"apres"* → *"après"* and *"tt"* → *"td"* that appear, respectively, 6 and 4 times.

Table 6 reports some examples of the output of our method along with their translation before and after correction.

For Example 6.1, we can notice that our normalizer enables the MT system to produce the first part of the translation (*"When I get to the taff"*). This is a result of correctly changing the French homophones *"arriver"* → *"arrivé"*, i.e. from the infinitive to the past form. It is very interesting to notice that the robustness of the Transformer using subword units seems to be good enough to correctly translate the typographical error *"ce met a battre"*, thus, the correct proposed normalization (*"se met à battre"*) does not impact the MT result but it certainly does impact the correctness of the

French phrase.

Regarding Example 6.2, we can notice that our normalized proposition significantly improves MT translation, producing an output closer to the reference translation, when compared to the raw MT output. The key normalization change is the misused French token *"faite"* (pronounced /fɛt/) — *"does"* in English — by its correct homophone *"fête"* — *"celebrates"* in English —. It is worth noting that the MT system robustness is once again capable of correctly translating a phonetic contraction *"c"* as the two correct tokens *"c'est"*.

Example 6.3 shows how semantically different can be a misused French word due to homophones confusion. We can observe that the normalization replacement *"nez"* ("nose" in English) → *"né"* ("born" in English), which are French homophones, drastically changes the meaning of the output translation. Additionally, the correction *"marqué"* → *"marquer"*[9] (changing to correct verb tense) also causes the translation to be closer to the reference.

Finally, in Example 6 we display some inconveniences for our method, where the correct original plural *"Cartes bancaires ... restrouvés"* was changed to the singular form *"Carte bancaire ... retrouvé"*. This is due to the homophonic property of most French singular and plural pronunciations. Whenever there is no discriminant token with different pronunciation, such as an irregular verb, the language model has trouble choosing the correct final normalized phrase since both plural and singular propositions are proposed as candidates and can be indistinctly kept as final normalization since both forms are correct and theoretically very similar in their perplexity measure.

8 Conclusions

In this work, we have proposed a pre-processing method that relies on phonetic similarity to normalize UGC. Our method is able to improve the translation quality of UGC of a state-of-the-art NMT system. Conversely, we have performed error analysis showing that the MT system achieves to correctly translate phonetic-related errors with its increased robustness. However, it must be noted that

---

[8]This is the highest value for which we consider a related pronunciation, according to our preliminary trials.

[9]*marked* vs *mark*-INFINITIVE in English.

①	src	**arriver au taff, des que j'ouvre le magasin** je commence **a** avoir le vertige mon coeur **ce met a battre a 200** et je sens que je vais faire un malaise,
	ref	**once at work, as soon as I open the store** I'm starting to feel dizzy my heart **starts racing at 200** and I feel I'm gonna faint,
	raw MT	I start to get dizzy. My heart starts to beat at 200 and I feel like I'm going to faint.
	norm	**arrivé au taff, dès que j'ouvre le magasin** je commence **à** avoir le vertige mon coeur **se met à battre à 200** et je sens que je vais faire un malaise,
	norm MT	**When I get to the taff, as soon as I open the store**, I start to get dizzy. My heart starts pounding at 200 and I feel like I'm gonna get dizzy.
②	src	c un peu plus que mon ami qui **faite son annif**,
	ref	it's a bit more than a friend to me who **celebrate his birthday**,
	raw MT	It's a little more than my friend **doing his birthday**,
	norm	c un peu plus que mon amie qui **fête son annif**
	norm MT	It's a little more than my friend **celebrating her birthday**,
③	src	zlatan est **nez** pour **marqué**
	ref	Zlatan was **born** to **score**
	raw MT	Zlatan's **nose** is for **marking**
	norm	zlatan est **né** pour **marquer**
	norm MT	Zlatan was **born** to **score**
④	src	**Cartes bancaires** de Zlatan retrouvés dans un taxi... On en parle ou pas WWW44
	ref	Zlatan's **bank cards** found in a cab... we talk about it or not WW44
	raw MT	Zlatan's **bank cards** found in a cab... we talk about it or not WW44
	norm	**Carte bancaire** de Zlatan retrouvé dans un taxi... On en parle ou pas WWW44
	norm MT	Zlatan **bank card** found in a taxi... we talk about it or not WWW44

Table 6: Examples from our noisy UGC corpus.

we obtained negative results on a blind test evaluation, suggesting that the phonetic normalization approach introduced more noise than useful corrections on totally unseen data. This highlights the importance of holding out data so that the real efficiency of an MT system can be verified. In addition, we have applied our normalizer to clean canonical test data and have shown that it slightly hurts MT quality. Further study is needed to assess whether our proposed normalization pipeline can correct phonetic-related errors on UGC for other languages and other difficult UGC scenarios, such as video-games chat logs (Martínez Alonso et al., 2016) while maintaining the level of the performance on cleanly edited text steady.

Acknowledgments

We thank our anonymous reviewers for providing insightful comments and suggestions. This work was funded by the ANR projects ParSiTi (ANR-16-CE33-0021).

References

Cyril Allauzen, Michael Riley, Johan Schalkwyk, Wojciech Skut, and Mehryar Mohri. 2007. Openfst: A general and efficient weighted finite-state transducer library. In *Proceedings of the 12th International Conference on Implementation and Application of Automata*, CIAA'07, pages 11–23, Berlin, Heidelberg. Springer-Verlag.

Marion Baranes. 2015. *Spelling Normalisation of Noisy Text*. Theses, Université Paris-Diderot - Paris VII.

Luisa Bentivogli, Arianna Bisazza, Mauro Cettolo, and Marcello Federico. 2016. Neural versus phrase-based machine translation quality: a case study. In *EMNLP*.

Piotr Bojanowski, Edouard Grave, Armand Joulin, and Tomas Mikolov. 2017. Enriching word vectors with subword information. *TACL*, 5:135–146.

Ondrej Bojar, Rajen Chatterjee, Christian Federmann, Yvette Graham, Barry Haddow, Matthias Huck, Antonio Jimeno-Yepes, Philipp Koehn, Varvara Logacheva, Christof Monz, Matteo Negri, Aurélie Névéol, Mariana L. Neves, Martin Popel, Matt Post, Raphael Rubino, Carolina Scarton, Lucia Specia, Marco Turchi, Karin M. Verspoor, and Marcos Zampieri. 2016. Findings of the 2016 conference on machine translation. In *Proceedings of the First Conference on Machine Translation, WMT 2016, colocated with ACL 2016, August 11-12, Berlin, Germany*, pages 131–198.

Rob van der Goot and Gertjan van Noord. 2018. Modeling input uncertainty in neural network dependency parsing. In *Proceedings of the 2018 Conference on Empirical Methods in Natural Language Processing, Brussels, Belgium, October 31 - November 4, 2018*, pages 4984–4991.

Guillaume Klein, Yoon Kim, Yuntian Deng, Vincent Nguyen, Jean Senellart, and Alexander M. Rush.

2018. Opennmt: Neural machine translation toolkit. In *Proceedings of the 13th Conference of the Association for Machine Translation in the Americas, AMTA 2018, Boston, MA, USA, March 17-21, 2018 - Volume 1: Research Papers*, pages 177–184.

Philipp Koehn, Hieu Hoang, Alexandra Birch, Chris Callison-Burch, Marcello Federico, Nicola Bertoldi, Brooke Cowan, Wade Shen, Christine Moran, Richard Zens, Chris Dyer, Ondrej Bojar, Alexandra Constantin, and Evan Herbst. 2007. Moses: Open source toolkit for statistical machine translation. In *ACL 2007, Proceedings of the 45th Annual Meeting of the Association for Computational Linguistics, June 23-30, 2007, Prague, Czech Republic*.

Viet Bac Le, Sopheap Seng, Laurent Besacier, and Brigitte Bigi. 2008. Word/sub-word lattices decomposition and combination for speech recognition. In *Proceedings of the IEEE International Conference on Acoustics, Speech, and Signal Processing, ICASSP 2008, March 30 - April 4, 2008, Caesars Palace, Las Vegas, Nevada, USA*, pages 4321–4324.

Pierre Lison, Jörg Tiedemann, and Milen Kouylekov. 2018. Opensubtitles2018: Statistical rescoring of sentence alignments in large, noisy parallel corpora. In *Proceedings of the Eleventh International Conference on Language Resources and Evaluation, LREC 2018, Miyazaki, Japan, May 7-12, 2018*.

Héctor Martínez Alonso, Djamé Seddah, and Benoît Sagot. 2016. From noisy questions to Minecraft texts: Annotation challenges in extreme syntax scenario. In *Proceedings of the 2nd Workshop on Noisy User-generated Text (WNUT)*, pages 13–23, Osaka, Japan. The COLING 2016 Organizing Committee.

Paul Michel and Graham Neubig. 2018. MTNT: A testbed for machine translation of noisy text. In *Proceedings of the 2018 Conference on Empirical Methods in Natural Language Processing, Brussels, Belgium, October 31 - November 4, 2018*, pages 543–553

Behrang Mohit, Alla Rozovskaya, Nizar Habash, Wajdi Zaghouani, and Ossama Obeid. 2014. The first QALB shared task on automatic text correction for arabic. In *Proceedings of the EMNLP 2014 Workshop on Arabic Natural Language Processing, ANLP@EMNLP 20104, Doha, Qatar, October 25, 2014*, pages 39–47.

Mehryar Mohri. 2002. Semiring frameworks and algorithms for shortest-distance problems. *Journal of Automata, Languages and Combinatorics*, 7(3):321–350.

David R. Mortensen, Patrick Littell, Akash Bharadwaj, Kartik Goyal, Chris Dyer, and Lori S. Levin. 2016. Panphon: A resource for mapping IPA segments to articulatory feature vectors. In *Proceedings of COLING 2016, the 26th International Conference on Computational Linguistics: Technical Papers*, pages 3475–3484. ACL.

Hermann Ney, Ute Essen, and Reinhard Kneser. 1994. On structuring probabilistic dependences in stochastic language modelling. *Computer Speech & Language*, 8(1):1–38.

Nicolas Pécheux, Guillaume Wisniewski, and François Yvon. 2016. Reassessing the value of resources for cross-lingual transfer of pos tagging models. *Language Resources and Evaluation*, pages 1–34.

Matt Post. 2018. A call for clarity in reporting BLEU scores. In *Proceedings of the Third Conference on Machine Translation: Research Papers, WMT 2018, Belgium, Brussels, October 31 - November 1, 2018*, pages 186–191.

Long Qin, Ming Sun, and Alexander I. Rudnicky. 2012. System combination for out-of-vocabulary word detection. In *2012 IEEE International Conference on Acoustics, Speech and Signal Processing, ICASSP 2012, Kyoto, Japan, March 25-30, 2012*, pages 4817–4820.

Brian Roark, Richard Sproat, Cyril Allauzen, Michael Riley, Jeffrey Sorensen, and Terry Tai. 2012. The OpenGrm open-source finite-state grammar software libraries. In *Proceedings of the ACL 2012 System Demonstrations*, pages 61–66, Jeju Island, Korea. Association for Computational Linguistics.

José Carlos Rosales Núñez, Djamé Seddah, and Guillaume Wisniewski. 2019. Comparison between NMT and PBSMT performance for translating noisy user-generated content. In *Proceedings of the 22nd Nordic Conference on Computational Linguistics*, pages 2–14, Turku, Finland. Linköping University Electronic Press.

Benoît Sagot and Pierre Boullier. 2008. SxPipe 2: architecture pour le traitement pré-syntaxique de corpus bruts. *Traitement Automatique des Langues*, 49(2):155–188.

Djamé Seddah, Benoît Sagot, Marie Candito, Virginie Mouilleron, and Vanessa Combet. 2012. The french social media bank: a treebank of noisy user generated content. In *COLING 2012, 24th International Conference on Computational Linguistics, Proceedings of the Conference: Technical Papers, 8-15 December 2012, Mumbai, India*, pages 2441–2458.

Rico Sennrich, Barry Haddow, and Alexandra Birch. 2016. Neural machine translation of rare words with subword units. In *Proceedings of the 54th Annual Meeting of the Association for Computational Linguistics, ACL 2016, August 7-12, 2016, Berlin, Germany, Volume 1: Long Papers*.

Matthias Sperber, Graham Neubig, Jan Niehues, and Alex Waibel. 2017. Neural lattice-to-sequence models for uncertain inputs. In *Proceedings of the 2017 Conference on Empirical Methods in Natural Language Processing, EMNLP 2017, Copenhagen, Denmark, September 9-11, 2017*, pages 1380–1389.

Sara Stymne. 2011. Spell checking techniques for replacement of unknown words and data cleaning for
haitian creole SMS translation. In *Proceedings of
the Sixth Workshop on Statistical Machine Translation, WMT@EMNLP 2011, Edinburgh, Scotland,
UK, July 30-31, 2011*, pages 470–477.

Jinsong Su, Zhixing Tan, Deyi Xiong, Rongrong Ji, Xiaodong Shi, and Yang Liu. 2017. Lattice-based recurrent neural network encoders for neural machine
translation. In *Proceedings of the Thirty-First AAAI
Conference on Artificial Intelligence, February 4-9,
2017, San Francisco, California, USA.*, pages 3302–
3308.

Ilya Sutskever, Oriol Vinyals, and Quoc V. Le. 2014.
Sequence to sequence learning with neural networks.
In *Advances in Neural Information Processing Sys-
tems 27: Annual Conference on Neural Informa-
tion Processing Systems 2014, December 8-13 2014,
Montreal, Quebec, Canada*, pages 3104–3112.

Kai Sheng Tai, Richard Socher, and Christopher D.
Manning. 2015. Improved semantic representations
from tree-structured long short-term memory networks. In *Proceedings of the 53rd Annual Meeting of the Association for Computational Linguistics
and the 7th International Joint Conference on Natural Language Processing of the Asian Federation of
Natural Language Processing, ACL 2015, July 26-
31, 2015, Beijing, China, Volume 1: Long Papers*,
pages 1556–1566.

Ashish Vaswani, Noam Shazeer, Niki Parmar, Jakob
Uszkoreit, Llion Jones, Aidan N Gomez, Ł ukasz
Kaiser, and Illia Polosukhin. 2017. Attention is all
you need. In I. Guyon, U. V. Luxburg, S. Bengio,
H. Wallach, R. Fergus, S. Vishwanathan, and R. Garnett, editors, *Advances in Neural Information Processing Systems 30*, pages 5998–6008. Curran Associates, Inc.

Pidong Wang and Hwee Tou Ng. 2013. A beam-search
decoder for normalization of social media text with
application to machine translation. In *Human Language Technologies: Conference of the North American Chapter of the Association of Computational
Linguistics, Proceedings, June 9-14, 2013, Westin
Peachtree Plaza Hotel, Atlanta, Georgia, USA*,
pages 471–481.

Daniel Watson, Nasser Zalmout, and Nizar Habash.
2018. Utilizing character and word embeddings for
text normalization with sequence-to-sequence models. In *Proceedings of the 2018 Conference on Empirical Methods in Natural Language Processing,
Brussels, Belgium, October 31 - November 4, 2018*,
pages 837–843.

Normalization of Indonesian-English Code-Mixed Twitter Data

Anab Maulana Barik, Rahmad Mahendra, Mirna Adriani
Faculty of Computer Science, Universitas Indonesia
Depok, Indonesia
maulanaanab@gmail.com, {rahmad.mahendra, mirna}@cs.ui.ac.id

Abstract

Twitter is an excellent source of data for NLP researches as it offers a tremendous amount of textual data. However, processing tweet to extract meaningful information is very challenging, at least for two reasons: (i) using non-standard words as well as informal writing manner, and (ii) code-mixing issues, which is combining multiple languages in single tweet conversation. Most of the previous works have addressed both issues in isolated different task. In this study, we work on normalization task in code-mixed Twitter data, more specifically in Indonesian-English language. We propose a pipeline that consists of four modules, i.e tokenization, language identification, lexical normalization, and translation. Another contribution is to provide a gold standard of Indonesian-English code-mixed data for each module.

1 Introduction

Twitter has gained interest from Natural Language Processing (NLP) researchers over the last decade because it offers various textual data, such as public opinions, conversation, and breaking news, in a huge number. However, tweets are mostly noisy texts as they contain a lot of typos, slang terms, and non-standard abbreviations. This noisy data results dropping in the accuracy of the past NLP systems (Liu et al., 2011).

Another common phenomenon found in social media, including Twitter, is that people tend to alternate between multiple languages in one utterance. The embedding of linguistic units such as phrases, words, and morphemes of one language into the usage of other different languages is known as code-mixing (Myers-Scotton, 1993). The phenomenon of code-switching causing grief for NLP systems due to the grammar and spelling variations.

Indonesia, the most fourth populous country in the world, is bilingual[1]. While Bahasa Indonesia is the only official language, English is also used in formal education and business. Nowadays, the Indonesian young generation gets used to mix both languages in daily life. Code-mixing is frequently found in social media conversation in Indonesia.

In this paper, we design standardization system for Indonesian-English code-mixed Twitter data. Our solution is a pipeline of 4 modules, i.e. tokenization, language identification, lexical normalization, and translation.

1. **Tokenization**: The tweet is tokenized into several tokens. Each token may represent a word, an idiom, an interjection (e.g. haha, hehe, wkwkw), numbers, emoticon, punctuation marks, and tweet entity (i.e link, hashtag, mention). In this study, the name of entities i.e movies, people, etc. is considered as one single token.

2. **Language Identification**: Every token within tweet is labeled with corresponding language tag. The label 'en' is assigned for English token, 'id' for Indonesian token, and 'rest' for the token that not clearly belongs to either English or Indonesian (e.g. proper name, number).

3. **Normalization**: Tokens with label 'id' or 'en' are normalized into standard form. To reduce the number of token variations in the data set, we reduce character repetition to be not more than two (e.g. the interjection token "*heheeee*" is standardized into "*hehee*"). The tokens with label "rest" are left as they are

---

[1] https://blog.swiftkey.com/celebrating-international-mother-language-day/

Proceedings of the 2019 EMNLP Workshop W-NUT: The 5th Workshop on Noisy User-generated Text, pages 417–424
Hong Kong, Nov 4, 2019. ©2019 Association for Computational Linguistics

4. **Translation**: We merge the sequence of normalized tokens back into complete tweet, and translate the tweet into Indonesian, with the exception of the name entities that are kept in original language (i.e term "The Lion King" is not translated into "Raja Singa").

To our knowledge, this is the first attempt to normalize Indonesian-English code-mixed language. For our experiment, we build the data set consisting of 825 tweets.

2 Related Work

Text normalization has been studied for Twitter data using a variety of supervised or unsupervised methods. Liu et al. (2011) modelled lexical normalization as a sequence labelling problem, by generating letter-level alignment from standard words into nonstandard variant words, using Conditional Random Field (CRF).

Beckley (2015) performed English lexical normalization task in three steps. First, compiled a substitution list of nonstandard into standard words, then built a rule-based components for -ing and duplication rule as it is often found in the data set. Last, applied sentence-level re-ranker using bigram Viterbi algorithm to select the best candidate among all the candidates generated from first and second steps.

Sridhar (2015) proposed an unsupervised approach for lexical normalization by training a word embedding model from large English corpora. The model is used to create a mapping between non-standard into standard words. Hanafiah et al. (2017) approached lexical normalization for Indonesian language using the rule-based method with the help of a dictionary and a list of slang words. If the token is OOV, then they create a candidate list based on the consonant skeleton from the dictionary.

For code-mixed data, Singh et al. (2018) created clusters of words based on embedding model (pre-trained on large corpora) for the semantic features and Levenshtein distance for lexical features. Then, one word is picked to become the parent candidate for each cluster, and other words in each cluster are normalized into the parent candidate.

Mave et al. (2018) worked a language identification task on code-mixed data. The experiment shown that Conditional Random Field (CRF) model outperformed Bidirectional LSTM.

Types	Count
Number of tweets	825
Number of tokens	22.736
Number of 'id' tokens	11.204
Number of 'en' tokens	5.613
Number of 'rest' tokens	5.919

Table 1: Data Set Detail

Dhar et al. (2018) augmented existing machine translation by using Matrix Language-Frame Model proposed by Myers-Scotton (1997) to increase the performance of the machine translations apply on code-mixed data.

Bhat et al. (2018) presented a universal dependency parsing with the Hindi-English dataset using a pipeline comprised of several modules such as language identification, back-transliteration, normalization using encoder-decoder framework and dependency parsing using neural stacking. It is found that normalization improves the performance of POS tagging and parsing models.

3 Data Set

We utilize three kinds of Twitter corpora in this study i.e. English, Indonesian, and Indonesian-English code-mixed corpus. We obtain 1.6M English tweets collection from 'Sentimen40' (Go et al., 2009) and 900K Indonesian tweets from Adikara (2015). We collect 49K Indonesian-English code-mixed tweets by scrapping them using Twitter API. To harvest those tweets, first we take 100 English and Indonesian stopwords from wiktionary[2]. To fetch code-mixed tweets, we use the stopwords as query term and set the language filter as the opposite of the stopword one (e.g. Indonesian tweets are collected using a English stopword as a query, vice versa).

We select 825 tweets randomly from code-mixed corpus for the experiment. The data is labeled by two annotators. The gold standard is constructed for four individual tasks.

The inter-annotator agreement has 97,92% for language identification and 99,23% for normalization. Our data has a code-mixing index (Das and Gambäck, 2014) of 33.37, means that the level of mixing between languages in the data is quite high (see Table 1 for detail)

---

[2] https://en.wiktionary.org/wiki/Wiktionary:Frequency lists

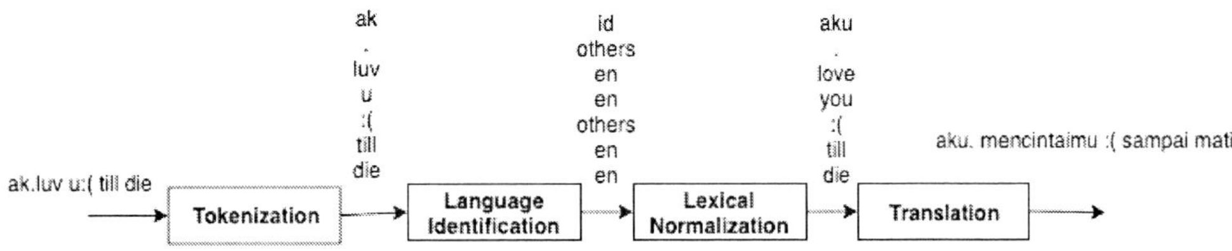

Figure 1: An Input-Output Example of Pipeline Model

4 Methods

The main objective of this study is to standardize the lexical form of code-mixed tweets. To achieve this, we propose a pipeline which is composed of four modules, tokenization, language identification, lexical normalization, and translation. The pipeline takes the code-mixed Indonesian-English tweet as the input, runs each module sequentially, and produces tweet in well-formed Indonesian language as output. Figure 1 depicts the pipeline model with an example of input and output.

4.1 Tokenization

The tokenization module takes a single tweet as input, and produces a sequence of tokens (one token can be a multiword expression) as output. Default delimiter in tokenization, i.e. whitespace, does not work well for social media domain due to non-standard writing style, for example, space disappearance (*of course not..absolutely not*) and space excesses (*E N D*). More specific problem found in the Indonesian is writing inaccuracy of morphological affix "di" as a preposition, and vice versa. While whitespace is needed to separate preposition "di" and the next word (e.g. *"di kelas"*, in English. *"at class"*); this does not apply for affixation case (e.g. *"dimakan"*, in English: *"eaten"*).

We approach this task as a sequence labeling at the character level with inside/outside chunk representation, as introduced by Ramshaw and Marcus (1999). We use three different tags: **B** represents the beginning of a new chunk, **I** means that the current token is inside the chunk, and **O** indicates that the current token is outside of any chunks. For instance, a sentence *"this car"* will be encoded into *"BIIIOBII"*.

The features set used in tokenization comprises of morphological information of the character i.e current character, is alphabet, is digit, is uppercase, and n-window character (n = 5). Sequence labeling model is trained using Conditional Random Field.

4.2 Language Identification

This module takes a sequence of tokens outputted from the tokenization module as an input, and identifies the language for each token. The language tag is one of these labels: 'en', 'id', 'rest'.

The features set for language identification consist of the current token in which the language to be determined, morphological information of current token, n-neighbor tokens, and n-gram character of the current token (n = 5). For morphological information, we use the binary features such as is alphabet, is digit, is capital, contains alphabet, contains digit, and has apostrophes. We do not include Part-Of-Speech (POS) information in our selected features, as recommended by Mave et al. (2018). The model is trained using Conditional Random Field.

4.3 Lexical Normalization

This module takes a sequence of tokens along with their language tags as input, and normalize the token one by one independently by substituting out-of-vocabulary (OOV) tokens into their standard equivalents that exist in the vocabulary. We identify nine common types of OOV token within code-mixed data, as details in Table 2.

Our approach is unsupervised. We create a mapping between OOV tokens into their standard forms using word distribution. However, some types are specific to a language, and cannot be solved with the word distribution information only. Thus, we combine the distributional approach with the rule-based method. Our method is outlined as follows.

1. OOV types which are encountered at both languages is tackled using translation dictionary built from word distribution approaches.

2. For "reduplication with 2" problem, we removes character 2, apply the reduplication, and insert the hyphen in the text.

Types	Language	Example / Explanation
Non-standard spelling/typo	'en', 'id'	*lvie* or *youuuu*
Informal Abbreviations	'en', 'id'	"lht" for "lihat" (in English: "see"), "ppl" for "people"
Slang words	'en', 'id'	"epic" or "gue" for "saya" (in English: "I")
Spelled phonetically	'en', 'id'	"plis" for "please", "kalo" for "kalau" (in English: "if")
Reduplication with 2	'id'	In Indonesian, plural form of noun is written with a hyphen, e.g. "orang-orang" (in English: "people"). However, informal writing style often use the number "2" to indicate this (e.g. "orang2")
Hyphenless reduplication	'id'	On the other hand, the hyphen is sometimes not written (e.g. "orang orang")
Contracted words	'en'	"im" for "i am"
Combining English word with Indonesian prefix (nge-)	'en'	Indonesian people tend to use an informal prefix (nge-) before the words to stress that the word is a verb. For instance, the word "vote" is written as "ngevote"
Combining English word with Indonesian suffix (-nya)	'en'	Suffix "-nya" in Indonesian means the possessive pronoun (e.g. "miliknya" similar to "hers" or "his"). Suffix "-nya" can also refers to the definite article (in English: "the"). Informally, the suffix is used to follow English word usage in Indonesian conversation, e.g. "jobnya" (in English: "the job")

Table 2: Type of OOV Tokens

3. For "reduplication without hyphen" problem, we check whether the token consists of multiple words, then replace the space delimiter with "-" if it is a reduplication case.

4. For "contracted words" problem, we normalize them by utilizing the list provided by Kooten [3].

5. For problem of "combining English word with Indonesian prefix (nge-)", we remove the prefix (-nge) from the word.

6. For problem of "combining English word with Indonesian suffix (-nya)", we remove the suffix (-nya) and add the word "the" before the word.

There are two sub tasks in lexical normalization module. First, create mapping between OOV tokens to their standard forms. Then, build the system to incorporate the rule-based method with the distributional semantics.

4.3.1 Build OOV and normal word mapping

Word embedding can be used to cluster words because it can model word relatedness, both syntactically and semantically. We use embedding model to construct mapping between OOV and its normal form. The word embedding model is trained by using skip-gram architecture (Mikolov et al., 2013). The procedure is described as follows:

1. Collect Indonesian and English vocabulary from Kateglo[4] and Project Gutebnberg[5].

2. For each word $normal\_word$ in the vocabulary, get 100 most similar words from social media corpus by using embedding model.

3. For each most similar words w_i to $normal\_word$

   - If w_i exists in the dictionary, it means that w_i is already normalized.
   - otherwise, w_i is OOV, then add a mapping instance between OOV word w_i into $normal\_word$.

[3] https://github.com/kootenpv/contractions

[4] http://kateglo.com/
[5] http://www.gutenberg.org/ebooks/3201

4. If an OOV w_j is mapped into several *normal_word* entries, choose one which has the highest lexical similarity with w_j.

We use the lexical similarity function (Hassan and Menezes, 2013). The function is based on the Longest Common Subsequence Ration (LCSR), which is the ratio of the length of the Longest Common Subsequence (LCS) and the length of the longer token (Melamed, 1999). The lexical similarity function defined as:

$$lex\_sim(s_1, s_2) = \frac{LCSR(s_1, s_2)}{ED(s_1, s_2)} \quad (1)$$

$$LCSR(s_1, s_2) = \frac{LCS(s_1, s_2)}{MaxLength(s_1, s_2)} \quad (2)$$

We apply static mapping as our mapping mechanism instead of finding the replacement online because of the execution time and memory performance. It is much faster to look up at the mapping rather than calculate it from the word embedding model. Furthermore, the memory needed to store the mapping is much smaller than the word embedding model.

4.3.2 Combine rules with mapping list

Normalization system employs combination of hand-crafted rules and mapping of words as follows.

1. Skip this procedure when the input is not a word (e.g hastag, mention, link, emoticon).

2. If the token is a multiword (there are more than one single word that is separated by white space), split the token into the list of single words. Try to normalize each word independently by applying the rules, and merge them back into one token. For instance, put the hyphen for reduplication case.

3. If the input is a word, then transform it into lowercase format. Reduce character repetition to at most two and consider any possible transformation. For instance, word *"Pleasssseee"* is transformed into *"pleassee"*, *"pleasee"*, *"pleasse"*, and *"please"*. Check whether one of generated transformed word is a normal form. If not, apply rule-based strategy. Last, use the mapping list created by utilizing word embedding.

4.4 Translation

This module aims to merge the list of tokens processed in previous modules back into one tweet and translates the tweet into Indonesian grammatical language. The module needs the Machine Translation (MT) system which is specific to the Indonesian-English code-mixed text domain. However, such MT system is not available at this moment. Dhar et al. (2018) found similar problem and tackled this by augmenting Matrix Language-Frame (MLF) model on top of the existing state-of-the-art MT system.

In the MLF model proposed by Myers-Scotton (1997), the code-mixed sentence can be splitted into the dominant language (the matrix language) and the embedded language. The matrix language grammar sets the morphosyntactic structure for the code-mixed sentence, while the embedded language borrows words from its vocabulary.

Thus, in this module, first, we merge the list of tokens into one tweet. Then, we separate the tweet into several sentences using sentence delimiter such as period (.), comma (,), the question mark (?), the exclamation mark (!), etc. For each sentence, we decide the language of the sentence (English or Indonesian sentence). To do that, we count how many words are English and how many words are Indonesian. The language which has a bigger frequency is the dominant language and also the language of the sentence, and the language which has a smaller frequency is the embedded language. After we decide the language of the sentence, we translate all the words into the language of the sentence. Last, if the language of the sentence in English, we translate the whole sentence into Indonesian. We use Microsoft Machine Translation[6] as the MT system. Figure 2 shows an example of input and output of translation module.

5 Experiments and Evaluation

We evaluate the performance of our implementation for each module and the pipeline model as whole process. First two modules (tokenization and language identification) are evaluated in supervised way using 4-fold cross validation setting.

Tokenization is evaluated at both character-level and token-level. The character-tagging achieves **98.70** for F1-score, while token identification obtains **95.15** for F1-score.

---

[6] https://www.microsoft.com/en-us/translator/business/machine-translation/

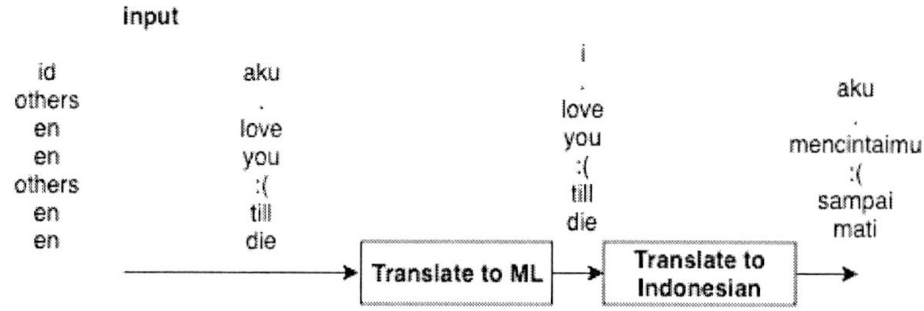

Figure 2: An Input-Output Example of Translation Module

The performance of our tokenization module excels NLTK *TweetTokenizer* tool, which scores F1 of 90.98 on evaluating token identification.

Language Identification module gets **89.58** F1-score and **90.11** accuracy. F1-score for label 'en', 'id', and 'rest' are respectively 87.07, 91.99, and 89.44 (the detail is in Table 3)

Language	prec	recall	F1-score
en	89.90	84.42	87.07
id	88.13	96.22	91.99
rest	94.99	83.96	89.14

Table 3: Language Identification Experiment Result

For evaluation of **lexical normalization**, we conduct a number of scenario. We test the difference of corpus source for building embedding model, i.e. combined corpora vs separated corpora. In first scenario, we only build single embedding model from merging of Indonesian and English corpus. While, in later, two distinct models are learned respective from each monolingual corpus. We also examine the contribution of rule-based strategy to enhance the word normalizer.

F1-score and accuracy are used as metric for evaluation. Those are measured across all the unique OOV words. If an OOV appears several times in the corpus, it is counted once. False positive is defined as a word that is actually a normalized form, but the system detects it as OOV word and normalizes the word incorrectly. On the contrary, false negative is a word that is OOV, but the system fails to detect it or fails to normalize the word into its standard form.

The best result is 81.31 for F1-score and 68.50 for accuracy, achieved when the mapping list of OOV and normal form is provided for separated language. A set of rules double the performance of normalization system. See Table 4) for detail.

Type	F1-score	Accuracy
Combined Corpora	47.49	31.14
Separated Corpora	48.34	31.87
Combined Corpora + Rule-based	80.96	68.01
Separated Corpora + Rule-based	81.31	68.50

Table 4: Lexical Normalization Experimental Result

Moreover, we investigate the errors by drawing sample of misclassified cases. False positive mostly happens in affixed words. In this case, affixed word is forced to transform into stem form. False negative occurs with words that supposed to be slang words, but they do exist in the vocabulary. For example, the word "aja" is commonly slang form of word "saja" (in English: "only"), but "aja" is found in Indonesia dictionary with different meanings.

When evaluating **translation** module, we test the effect of augmenting Matrix Language-Frame (MLF) Model into MT system. Incorporating MT system with MLF Model achieves better performance, **71.54** for BLEU and **19.50** for WER, as presented in Table 6.

Type	BLEU	WER
Without MLF	66.69	21.45
With MLF	71.54	19.50

Table 5: Translation Experimental Result
(BLEU: higher is better, WER: lower is better)

As integration of aforementioned modules, we evaluate the pipeline model by conducting four experiments, 1) comparing raw tweets with final tweets, 2) comparing raw tweets which have been translated (without MLF model) into Indonesian with final tweets, 3) comparing raw tweets which have been translated (with MLF Model) into Indonesian with final tweets, and 4) comparing raw tweets which have been normalized and translated (with MLF Model) into Indonesian with final tweets. From the experiments, our final pipeline obtains **54.07** for BLEU and **31.89** for WER. From Table 6, we can see that each module affects positively toward the performance of the pipeline. The pipeline model increases BLEU score for 8 points, and WER for 14 points compared to the baseline (raw tweets).

Pipeline	BLEU	WER
Raw Tweets	46.07	45.75
Raw Tweets + Translation (1 + 4 Module)	51.02	34.37
Raw Tweets + Translation with MLF Model (1 + 2 + 4 Modules)	51.75	34.39
Raw Tweets + Normalization + Translation with MLF Model (Full pipeline)	54.07	31.89

Table 6: Pipeline Experiment Result
(BLEU: higher is better, WER: lower is better)

6 Conclusion and Future Work

In this paper, we have proposed a pipeline model comprising of four modules, i.e. tokenization, language identification, lexical normalization, and translation. In addition, we also have prepared gold standard data consisting of 825 Indonesian-English code-mixed tweets for four different tasks corresponding to the modules. The data set is freely available online for research purpose only.[7] We experiments with Indonesian-English code-mixed Twitter data and the evaluation shows that our model works satisfactorily. Overall, the pipeline yields 54.07 scores for BLEU and 31.89 scores for WER.

However, the final result is not as high as the performance at the translation module because the final result uses the output from previous modules as inputs. The error from each module will propagate to the next modules. At the normalization module, using vector representations from word embedding for Indonesian-English code-mixed data quite good and applying the rule-based

approach for each language improve the performance significantly. At the translation module, there are some errors caused by the MT system, but we could not do much about it since we use the existing MT system.

Moving forward, we would like to augment more data and enhance technique in order to improve performance of the model. Currently, lexical normalization module is much dependent of handcrafted rules. While the rule-based approach can increase the performance, it still not a robust solution seen from how language evolved.

Acknowledgments

The authors acknowledge the support of Universitas Indonesia through Hibah PITTA B 2019 Pengolahan Teks dan Musik pada Sistem Community Question Answering dan Temporal Information Retrieval.

References

Putra Pandu Adikara. 2015. Normalisasi kata pada pesan/status singkat berbahasa indonesia. Master's thesis, Universitas Indonesia, Depok.

Russell Beckley. 2015. Bekli: A simple approach to twitter text normalization. In *Proceedings of the Workshop on Noisy User-generated Text*, pages 82–86.

Irshad Ahmad Bhat, Riyaz Ahmad Bhat, Manish Shrivastava, and Dipti Misra Sharma. 2018. Universal dependency parsing for hindi-english code-switching. *arXiv preprint arXiv:1804.05868*.

Amitava Das and Björn Gambäck. 2014. Identifying languages at the word level in code-mixed indian social media text. In *Proceedings of the 11th International Conference on Natural Language Processing*, pages 378–387.

Mrinal Dhar, Vaibhav Kumar, and Manish Shrivastava. 2018. Enabling code-mixed translation: Parallel corpus creation and mt augmentation approach. In *Proceedings of the First Workshop on Linguistic Resources for Natural Language Processing*, pages 131–140.

Alec Go, Richa Bhayani, and Lei Huang. 2009. Twitter sentiment classification using distant supervision. *CS224N Project Report, Stanford*, 1(12):2009.

Novita Hanafiah, Alexander Kevin, Charles Sutanto, Yulyani Arifin, Jaka Hartanto, et al. 2017. Text normalization algorithm on twitter in complaint category. *Procedia computer science*, 116:20–26.

---

[7]https://github.com/seelenbrecher/code-mixed-normalization

Hany Hassan and Arul Menezes. 2013. Social text normalization using contextual graph random walks. In *Proceedings of the 51st Annual Meeting of the Association for Computational Linguistics (Volume 1: Long Papers)*, pages 1577–1586.

Fei Liu, Fuliang Weng, Bingqing Wang, and Yang Liu. 2011. Insertion, deletion, or substitution?: normalizing text messages without pre-categorization nor supervision. In *Proceedings of the 49th Annual Meeting of the Association for Computational Linguistics: Human Language Technologies: short papers-Volume 2*, pages 71–76. Association for Computational Linguistics.

Deepthi Mave, Suraj Maharjan, and Thamar Solorio. 2018. Language identification and analysis of codeswitched social media text. In *Proceedings of the Third Workshop on Computational Approaches to Linguistic Code-Switching*, pages 51–61.

I Dan Melamed. 1999. Bitext maps and alignment via pattern recognition. *Computational Linguistics*, 25(1):107–130.

Tomas Mikolov, Ilya Sutskever, Kai Chen, Greg S Corrado, and Jeff Dean. 2013. Distributed representations of words and phrases and their compositionality. In *Advances in neural information processing systems*, pages 3111–3119.

Carol Myers-Scotton. 1993. Common and uncommon ground: Social and structural factors in codeswitching. *Language in society*, 22(4):475–503.

Carol Myers-Scotton. 1997. *Duelling languages: Grammatical structure in codeswitching*. Oxford University Press.

Lance A Ramshaw and Mitchell P Marcus. 1999. Text chunking using transformation-based learning. In *Natural language processing using very large corpora*, pages 157–176. Springer.

Rajat Singh, Nurendra Choudhary, and Manish Shrivastava. 2018. Automatic normalization of word variations in code-mixed social media text. *arXiv preprint arXiv:1804.00804*.

Vivek Kumar Rangarajan Sridhar. 2015. Unsupervised text normalization using distributed representations of words and phrases. In *Proceedings of the 1st Workshop on Vector Space Modeling for Natural Language Processing*, pages 8–16.

Unsupervised Neologism Normalization Using Embedding Space Mapping

Nasser Zalmout,⋆ Aasish Pappu† and Kapil Thadani‡
⋆Computational Approaches to Modeling Language Lab
New York University Abu Dhabi, UAE
†Spotify Research, New York, USA
‡Yahoo Research, New York, USA
nasser.zalmout@nyu.edu, aasishp@spotify.com, thadani@verizonmedia.com

Abstract

This paper presents an approach for detecting and normalizing neologisms in social media content. Neologisms refer to recent expressions that are specific to certain entities or events and are being increasingly used by the public, but have not yet been accepted in mainstream language. Automated methods for handling neologisms are important for natural language understanding and normalization, especially for informal genres with user generated content. We present an unsupervised approach for detecting neologisms and then normalizing them to canonical words without relying on parallel training data. Our approach builds on the text normalization literature and introduces adaptations to fit the specificities of this task, including phonetic and etymological considerations. We evaluate the proposed techniques on a dataset of Reddit comments, with detected neologisms and corresponding normalizations.

1 Introduction

Linguistic evolution and word coinage are naturally occurring phenomena in languages. However, the proliferation of social media in recent years may expedite these processes by enabling the rapid spread of informal textual content. One aspect of this change is the increasing use of neologisms. Neologisms are relatively recent terms that are used widely and may be in the process of entering common use, but have not yet been fully accepted into mainstream language. Neologisms are rarely found in traditional dictionaries or language lexica, and they usually have lexical, phonetic or semantic connections to some relevant canonical words. They are also often, but not necessarily, generated by combining two different words into a single blend word. Examples include the word *burkini*, which is coined from the words *burka* and *bikini*. The burkini has its own individual meaning that cannot be entailed by a burka or bikini alone.

The goal of neologism normalization is not to generate a perfect replacement for the original text but rather to assist both humans and automated systems in understanding informal text. Inexact normalizations may nevertheless be useful hints to human readers who are unfamiliar with the new words. Normalizations can also substitute for out-of-vocabulary words in downstream NLP applications in order to compensate for data sparsity.

In this paper, we present an unsupervised approach for normalization, based on the hypothesis that neologisms—and non-standard words (NSWs) in general—are likely to share contexts with related canonical words. For instance, NSWs may be expected to lie near their canonical forms in a suitable embedding space. We develop measures to relate words more accurately using both orthography and distributed representations. We also enhance the embedding space with multi-word phrases and subword units, which induces a clustering of compound words with shared etymology, phrases with overlapping words, and entities with common names, thereby capturing novel puns, nicknames, etc.

2 Related Work

Prior work on automatic neologism handling, whether for detection or normalization, is relatively scarce. Most existing neologism detection approaches rely on exclusions lists of canonical or accepted words to filter plausible neologisms (de Yzaguirre, Lluis, 1995; Renouf, 1993). Other contributions based on the same architecture utilize additional filters like eliminating words with spelling errors or named entities to further reduce the set of detected plausible neologisms (Kerremans et al., 2012; Gérard et al., 2014; Cartier, 2016, 2017). There are also several machine learning based approaches, but with limited performance (Falk et al., 2014; Stenetorp, 2010).

In the broader text normalization literature, several supervised approaches have been proposed

Proceedings of the 2019 EMNLP Workshop W-NUT: The 5th Workshop on Noisy User-generated Text, pages 425–430
Hong Kong, Nov 4, 2019. ©2019 Association for Computational Linguistics

(Mays et al., 1991; Church and Gale, 1991; Brill and Moore, 2000; Aw et al., 2006; Sproat and Jaitly, 2016), all of which require relatively large datasets. Several unsupervised normalization models have also been presented. Li and Liu (2014); Rangarajan Sridhar (2015) use distributed word embeddings, where the embeddings are used to capture the notion of contextual similarity between canonical and noisy words, along with other measures. Rangarajan Sridhar (2015) further builds on this approach with phrase-based modeling using existing phrase corpora. Hassan and Menezes (2013) use a random-walk based algorithm to calculate contextual similarity, along with edit distance metrics, to obtain normalization candidates. In this paper, we extend the distributed word representation approach (Rangarajan Sridhar, 2015) for unsupervised neologism normalization through several adaptations.

3   Neologism Detection

We first present our neologism and NSW detection approach for Reddit comments. The resulting list of plausible neologisms is then used to analyze neologism etymology and coinage patterns, and later to produce normalization candidates in the normalization model.

Owing to the noisy domain of user-generated text and to the fact that neologisms must exclude names, domain jargon and typos, corpus frequency alone is not reliable for identifying neologisms. Exclusion lists prove effective at recovering a high-precision set of neologisms for this task when combined with frequency-based filters and adaptations to increase coverage. Our pipeline for neologism detection includes the following steps:

- Tokenization: We split on whitespace and handle many Reddit-specific issues, including URLs and specific punctuation patterns.

- Named entity removal: We use the SpaCy NLP toolkit[1] to identify named entities in context and eliminate them from the plausible neologisms list.

- English exclusion lists: We use several corpora of English content as exclusion lists.

- Non-English content removal: We use the Langdetect library[2] to identify and eliminate non-English content.

- Social media jargon removal: We use the social media word clusters from the work by

Owoputi et al. (2013) along with the Reddit glossary[3] as additional exclusion lists.

We apply exclusion list filtering on the stem level to further reduce the sparsity of the analysis and reduce the vocabulary. We use NLTK's Snowball stemmer.[4]

4   Neologism Normalization

Our approach is based on the hypothesis that neologisms and NSWs are likely to have similar contexts as their plausible canonical equivalents. We model this using distributed word representations derived from word2vec (Mikolov et al., 2013) via Gensim (Řehůřek and Sojka, 2010). We use these embeddings to learn normalization lexicons and use these lexicons to obtain plausible candidates for normalizing each neologism. We then select among these candidates using a language model and lattice-based Viterbi decoding.

4.1   Lexicon and Lattice Decoding

We use a list of canonical word forms as normalization candidates. This list of canonical forms can be obtained from traditional English language lexica like the Gigaword corpus. For each canonical candidate, we get the N nearest neighbors from the embedding space. This effectively functions as a reversed normalization lexicon, where the canonical candidates are mapped to the potential neologisms. We score the canonical forms using several similarity metrics. We then reverse this mapping to get the list of scored canonical candidates for each neologism.

Neologisms are expected to share semantic, lexical, and phonetic similarity with their canonical counterparts. We capture these different aspects using multiple measures of similarity:

Semantic similarity using the cosine distance over embeddings R_i corresponding to strings S_i.

$$\text{Cos}(S_1, S_2) = \frac{R_1 \cdot R_2}{||R_1|| \times ||R_2||} \tag{1}$$

Lexical similarity based on the formula presented by Hassan and Menezes (2013) and used by Rangarajan Sridhar (2015)

$$\text{Lex}(S_1, S_2) = \frac{LCSR(S_1, S_2)}{ED(S_1, S_2)} \tag{2}$$

---

[1]Version 2.0.0: https://spacy.io

[2]Version 1.0.7: https://pypi.python.org/pypi/langdetect

[3]https://www.reddit.com/r/TheoryOfReddit/wiki/glossary

[4]Version 3.2.4: http://www.nltk.org/api/nltk.stem.html

where ED is the edit distance and LCSR refers to the longest common subsequence ratio

$$\text{LCSR}(S_1, S_2) = \frac{LCS(S_1, S_2)}{\max(|S_1|, |S_2|)} \qquad (3)$$

where LCS is the longest common subsequence in the two strings of length $|S_1|$ and $|S_2|$.

Phonetic similarity through the Metaphone phonetic representation algorithm (Philips, 1990), which is used for indexing words by their English pronunciation. We calculate the normalized edit distance for the Metaphone representation of S_1 and S_2 and use this score to reflect the phonetic similarity between the strings.

$$\text{PHON}(S_1, S_2) = 1 - \frac{ED(mP(S_1), mP(S_2))}{\max(|S_1|, |S_2|)} \qquad (4)$$

where $mP(S_i)$ is a Metaphone representation.

Next, a language model is used to further control the fluency of the normalized output in context. We use SRILM (Stolcke, 2002) to build the model. To decode the optimal path given the similarity scores and the language model probabilities, we encode the sentence, along with the various normalization candidates, in the HTK format. We then use SRILM's lattice-tool toolkit to decode the space of potential paths using Viterbi decoding.

4.2 Phrases and Subword Units

The system so far is primarily targeted to word-level normalization, without explicitly handling multi-word phrases in the canonical form or recognizing shared etymology in the embeddings for plausible neologisms. This limits the normalization space for neologisms as the blending of two or more words is a common neologism pattern.

Multi-word phrases: We use a data-driven approach for identifying common phrases within the given corpus (Mikolov et al., 2013). Phrase candidates with scores above a certain threshold have their constituent words joined by a delimiter and are considered as a single word-like token for subsequent analysis. We ensure that the detected phrases do not contain punctuation sequences or URLs, which are common in Reddit data.

Subword units: Traditional morphology-based analysis falls short of detecting proper subword entities in neologisms, where the form and etymology of the neologisms are not fixed. Moreover, n-gram character sequences are also not optimal here given the intractability of the analysis. Instead we segment words based on the *byte pair encoding*

(BPE) algorithm (Gage, 1994), which was adapted for use in neural machine translation (NMT) by Sennrich et al. (2016).

We add the detected phrases to the list of canonical candidates as potential normalization targets and add the subwords to the neologism lists.

4.3 Combining Word Representations

An important aspect to consider when combining word, phrase and subword representations is to maintain the distributional properties of the text. We combine these representations by having the choice to switch to a certain representation for each word dictated through a uniformly distributed random variable. That is, for a given sentence T in a corpus, and for each word $w_i \in T$, the resulting representation w_i' based on the distribution $q(w_i'|w_i)$ is managed by the control variable $c = rand(\alpha)$, where $\alpha \in \{0, 1, 2\}$ indicates the choice of word/phrase/subword representations. We repeat this process for all the words of each sentence k different times, so we end up with k different copies of the sentence, each having a randomly selected representation for all of its words. k is tunable and we set $k = 5$ for our experiments. A somewhat similar approach is used by Wick et al. (2016) to learn multilingual word embeddings.

5 Experimental Setup and Results

5.1 Dataset

We use a dataset of Reddit comments from June 2016 to June 2017 for the normalization experiments in this paper, collected with the Reddit Big-Query API.[5] We focus on five popular subreddit groups: *worldnews, news, politics, sports,* and *movies.* This dataset contains about 51M comments, 2B tokens (words), and 6M unique words.

A dataset of 2034 comments annotated with neologisms and their normalizations was used for tuning[6] and evaluating the normalization model. These comments were selected from comments identified as containing unique plausible neologisms using the neologism detection pipeline described in Section 3. Normalization annotations were obtained using Amazon Mechanical Turk using three judgments per comment. Annotators were asked to provide up to five normalization candidates for each neologism; candidates that at

---

[5]https://bigquery.cloud.google.com/
dataset/fh-bigquery:reddit_comments

[6]Parameters were tuned using a held-out validation set drawn from the manual neologism annotations. This also applies to the tuning of weights for the linear combination of the different similarity metrics.

	Sample of detected neologisms
politics	pizzagate, drumpf, trumpster, shillary, killary
news	antifa, brexit, drumpf, Libruls, redpilling, neonazi
worldnews	burkini, brexit, pizzagate, edgelord, petrodollar
sports	deflategate, handegg, ballboy, skurfing, playstyle
movies	plothole, stuckmannized, jumpscare, MetaHuman
gaming	playerbase, pokestop, jumpscare, hitscan

Table 1: Subreddit-level detected neologisms

	Accuracy	BLEU
Baseline	55.3	81.3
This work	64.2	87.7

Table 2: Evaluation of the normalization systems

	Sentence
Raw	republicans who don't want drumpf are voting for hilldawg
Best system	republicans who don't want trump are voting for hillary
Reference	republicans who don't want trump are voting for hillary
Raw	this is one of the biggest clickbate news outlets
Best system	this is one of the biggest click bait news outlets
Reference	this is one of the biggest click bait news outlets
Raw	the hillbots have gone full insanity
Best system	the hill bots have gone full insanity
Reference	the hillary bots have gone full insanity

Table 3: Normalization examples

least two of the three annotators agree upon were selected as normalizations.[7]

5.2 Neologism Detection

We apply the detection pipeline we discussed earlier on the Reddit dataset. We use the most frequent 64K words in the Gigaword corpus as an exclusion list for proper English words along with NLTK's Words and Wordnet corpora. We further eliminated the terms that had a frequency lower than 10 as potential spelling errors.

Table 1 shows samples of the top detected neologisms for each subreddit. We took a random sample of 500 Reddit comments to inspect manually. Based on our observations, 5% of the comments contained neologisms, and 82% of these neologisms are present in our list of plausible neologisms, which suggests the recall of the proposed detection pipeline.

5.3 Normalization

We trained the word2vec model using the Reddit dataset using the skip-gram algorithm, a window of 5 words, and an embedding size of 250. For phrase learning, we used a threshold score of 10 and minimum count of 5. For lattice decoding, we used a trigram language model with Kneser-Ney discounting trained on LDC's Gigaword Fourth Edition corpus (LDC2009T13) (Parker et al., 2009).

As a baseline, we use the model of Rangarajan Sridhar (2015), which does not consider subwords and phonological similarity. They use language models and lattices, similar to our work, but targeted for text normalization. Our work extends these ideas to normalize a wide variety of neologisms including phrases, nicknames and compound words.

For evaluation metrics, we use the accuracy of the normalization on the word level (the

neologisms/canonical-equivalents level) along with using BLEU score (Papineni et al., 2002). BLEU is an algorithm for evaluating text quality based on human references and is commonly used in the machine translation literature. Using BLEU is relevant here due to the potentially multi-word output of the system with phrases and subwords. Evaluation scores are calculated with some relaxed matching, namely considering the occurrences of plurals, lower/upper case, hyphenation and punctuation, among others. So we treat terms like *trump* and *Trumps* as equivalent, same for *posting* and *postings*.

Table 2 shows the results. The system with phrases and subwords clearly outperforms the baseline, for both accuracy and BLEU scores. BLEU scores are relatively high for both systems since most of the sentences are preserved with only modifications for the plausible neologisms. The rest of the sentence should be an exact match to the reference.

Table 3 presents three normalization examples, with the raw, gold reference, and the output of our system. The examples show a promising behavior, but as can be seen at the third example, there is still a room for improvement in normalizing the individual phrase components. A potential future direction here would be to improve embedding space mappings for the subword entities.

6 Conclusion

We presented an approach to detect and normalize neologisms in social media content. We leveraged the fact that the neologisms and their canonical equivalents are likely to share the same contexts and hence have relatively close distributional representations. We also presented some techniques for handling phrases and subwords in the plausible neologisms, which is important given the etymology behind most neologisms. Our approach also makes use of the phonetic representation of the words, to capture coinage patterns that involve phonetic-based modification. Our results show that the model is effective in both detection and

---

normalization. Future work includes more explicit generation models, utilizing natural language generation techniques, along with expanding and enhancing the coverage of the annotated data.

References

AiTi Aw, Min Zhang, Juan Xiao, and Jian Su. 2006. A phrase-based statistical model for sms text normalization. In *Proceedings of the COLING/ACL on Main Conference Poster Sessions*, COLING-ACL '06, pages 33–40, Stroudsburg, PA, USA. Association for Computational Linguistics.

Eric Brill and Robert C. Moore. 2000. An improved error model for noisy channel spelling correction. In *Proceedings of the 38th Annual Meeting on Association for Computational Linguistics*, ACL '00, pages 286–293, Stroudsburg, PA, USA. Association for Computational Linguistics.

Emmanuel Cartier. 2016. Neoveille, système de repérage et de suivi des néologismes en sept langues. *Neologica : revue internationale de la néologie*, (10).

Emmanuel Cartier. 2017. Neoveille, a web platform for neologism tracking. In *Proceedings of the Software Demonstrations of the 15th Conference of the European Chapter of the Association for Computational Linguistics*, pages 95–98, Valencia, Spain. Association for Computational Linguistics.

Kenneth W. Church and William A. Gale. 1991. Probability scoring for spelling correction. *Statistics and Computing*, 1(2):93–103.

CabrÃl', Maria ; de Yzaguirre, Lluis. 1995. StratÃl'gie pour la dÃl'tection semi-automatique des nÃl'ologismes de presse. *TTR*, 8(2):89–100.

Ingrid Falk, Delphine Bernhard, and Christophe Gérard. 2014. From non word to new word: Automatically identifying neologisms in french newspapers. In *Proceedings of the Ninth International Conference on Language Resources and Evaluation (LREC'14)*, Reykjavik, Iceland. European Language Resources Association (ELRA). ACL Anthology Identifier: L14-1260.

Philip Gage. 1994. A new algorithm for data compression. *C Users J.*, 12(2):23–38.

Christophe Gérard, Ingrid Falk, and Delphine Bernhard. 2014. Traitement automatisé de la néologie: pourquoi et comment intégrer l'analyse thématique? In *SHS Web of Conferences*, volume 8, pages 2627–2646. EDP Sciences.

Hany Hassan and Arul Menezes. 2013. Social text normalization using contextual graph random walks. In *Proceedings of the 51st Annual Meeting of the Association for Computational Linguistics (Volume 1: Long Papers)*, pages 1577–1586, Sofia, Bulgaria. Association for Computational Linguistics.

Daphné Kerremans, Susanne Stegmayr, and Hans-Jörg Schmid. 2012. The neocrawler: identifying and retrieving neologisms from the internet and monitoring on-going change. *Current methods in historical semantics*, 73:59.

Chen Li and Yang Liu. 2014. Improving text normalization via unsupervised model and discriminative reranking. In *Proceedings of the ACL 2014 Student Research Workshop*, pages 86–93, Baltimore, Maryland, USA. Association for Computational Linguistics.

Eric Mays, Fred J. Damerau, and Robert L. Mercer. 1991. Context based spelling correction. *Information Processing & Management*, 27(5):517 – 522.

Tomas Mikolov, Ilya Sutskever, Kai Chen, Greg S Corrado, and Jeff Dean. 2013. Distributed representations of words and phrases and their compositionality. In C. J. C. Burges, L. Bottou, M. Welling, Z. Ghahramani, and K. Q. Weinberger, editors, *Advances in Neural Information Processing Systems 26*, pages 3111–3119. Curran Associates, Inc.

Olutobi Owoputi, Brendan O'Connor, Chris Dyer, Kevin Gimpel, Nathan Schneider, and Noah A. Smith. 2013. Improved part-of-speech tagging for online conversational text with word clusters. In *Proceedings of the 2013 Conference of the North American Chapter of the Association for Computational Linguistics: Human Language Technologies*, pages 380–390, Atlanta, Georgia. Association for Computational Linguistics.

Kishore Papineni, Salim Roukos, Todd Ward, and Wei-Jing Zhu. 2002. Bleu: A method for automatic evaluation of machine translation. In *Proceedings of the 40th Annual Meeting on Association for Computational Linguistics*, ACL '02, pages 311–318, Stroudsburg, PA, USA. Association for Computational Linguistics.

Robert Parker, David Graff, Junbo Kong, Ke Chen, and Kazuaki Maeda. 2009. English gigaword fourth edition ldc2009t13. *Linguistic Data Consortium, Philadelphia*.

Lawrence Philips. 1990. Hanging on the Metaphone. *Computer Language*, 7(12 (December)).

Vivek Kumar Rangarajan Sridhar. 2015. Unsupervised text normalization using distributed representations of words and phrases. In *Proceedings of the 1st Workshop on Vector Space Modeling for Natural Language Processing*, pages 8–16, Denver, Colorado. Association for Computational Linguistics.

Radim Řehůřek and Petr Sojka. 2010. Software Framework for Topic Modelling with Large Corpora. In *Proceedings of the LREC 2010 Workshop on New Challenges for NLP Frameworks*, pages 45–50, Valletta, Malta. ELRA. http://is.muni.cz/publication/884893/en.

Antoinette Renouf. 1993. Sticking to the text: a corpus linguistâĂŹs view of language. *ASLIB*, 45(5):131–136.

Rico Sennrich, Barry Haddow, and Alexandra Birch. 2016. Neural machine translation of rare words with subword units. In *Proceedings of the 54th Annual Meeting of the Association for Computational*

Linguistics (Volume 1: Long Papers), pages 1715–1725, Berlin, Germany. Association for Computational Linguistics.

Richard Sproat and Navdeep Jaitly. 2016. RNN approaches to text normalization: A challenge. *CoRR*, abs/1611.00068.

Pontus Stenetorp. 2010. *Automated extraction of swedish neologisms using a temporally annotated corpus*. MasterâĂŹs thesis, Royal Institute of Technology(KTH), Stockholm, Sweden.

Andreas Stolcke. 2002. Srilm – an extensible language modeling toolkit. In *In Proceedings of the 7th International Conference on Spoken Language Processing (ICSLP 2002*, pages 901–904.

Michael Wick, Pallika Kanani, and Adam Pocock. 2016. Minimally-constrained multilingual embeddings via artificial code-switching. In *Proceedings of the Thirtieth AAAI Conference on Artificial Intelligence*, AAAI'16, pages 2849–2855. AAAI Press.

Lexical Features Are More Vulnerable,
Syntactic Features Have More Predictive Power

Jekaterina Novikova[1], **Aparna Balagopalan**[1], **Ksenia Shkaruta**[2] and **Frank Rudzicz**[1,3]

[1]Winterlight Labs, {jekaterina, aparna}@winterlightlabs.com
[2]Georgia Tech, ksenia.shkaruta@gatech.edu
[3]University of Toronto; Vector Institute for Artificial Intelligence, frank@cs.toronto.edu

Abstract

Understanding the vulnerability of linguistic features extracted from noisy text is important for both developing better health text classification models and for interpreting vulnerabilities of natural language models. In this paper, we investigate how generic language characteristics, such as syntax or the lexicon, are impacted by artificial text alterations. The vulnerability of features is analysed from two perspectives: (1) the level of feature value change, and (2) the level of change of feature predictive power as a result of text modifications. We show that lexical features are more sensitive to text modifications than syntactic ones. However, we also demonstrate that these smaller changes of syntactic features have a stronger influence on classification performance downstream, compared to the impact of changes to lexical features. Results are validated across three datasets representing different text-classification tasks, with different levels of lexical and syntactic complexity of both conversational and written language.

1 Introduction

It is important to understand the vulnerability of linguistic features to text alteration because (1) pre-defined linguistic features are still frequently used in health text classification, e.g., detecting Alzheimers disease (AD) (Masrani et al., 2017; Zhu et al., 2018; Balagopalan et al., 2018), aphasia (Fraser et al., 2015), or sentiment from language (Maas et al., 2011); and (2) understanding the importance of syntactic and lexical information separately as well as interactively is still an open research area in linguistics (Lester et al., 2017; Blaszczak, 2019).

Lexical richness and complexity relate to nuances and the intricacy of meaning in language. Numerous metrics to quantify lexical diversity, such as type-token ratio (TTR) (Richards, 1987)

and MLTD (McCarthy, 2005), have been proposed. These metrics capture various dimensions of meaning, quantity and quality of words, such as variability, volume, and rarity. Several of these have been identified to be important for a variety of tasks in applied linguistics (Daller et al., 2003). For example, metrics related to vocabulary size, such as TTR and word-frequencies, have proven to help with early detection of mild cognitive impairment (MCI) (Aramaki et al., 2016), hence are important for early dementia diagnosis. Discourse informativeness, measured via propositional idea density, is also shown to be significantly affected in speakers with aphasia (Bryant et al., 2013). Furthermore, lexicon-based methods have proved to be successful in sentiment analysis (Taboada et al., 2011; Tang et al., 2014).

Syntactic complexity is evident in language production in terms of syntactic variation and sophistication or, in other words, the range and degree of sophistication of the syntactic structures that are produced (Lu, 2011; Ortega, 2003). This construct has attracted attention in a variety of language-related research areas. For example, researchers have examined the developmental trends of child syntactic acquisition (e.g., (Ramer, 1977)), the role of syntactic complexity in treating syntactic deficits in agrammatical aphasia (e.g., (Melnick and Conture, 2000; Thompson et al., 2003)), the relationship between syntactic complexity in early life to symptoms of Alzheimers disease in old age (e.g., (Kemper et al., 2001; Snowdon et al., 1996)), and the effectiveness of syntactic complexity as a predictor of adolescent writing quality (e.g., (Beers and Nagy, 2009)).

Indefrey et al. (2001) reported data on brain activation during syntactic processing and demonstrated that syntactic processing in the human brain happens independently of the processing of lexical meaning. These results were supported

Proceedings of the 2019 EMNLP Workshop W-NUT: The 5th Workshop on Noisy User-generated Text, pages 431–443
Hong Kong, Nov 4, 2019. ©2019 Association for Computational Linguistics

by the more recent studies showing that different brain regions support distinct mechanisms in the mapping from a linguistic form onto meaning, thereby separating syntactic agrammaticality from linguistic complexity(Ullman et al., 2005; Friederici et al., 2006). This motivates us to explore the importance of lexical and syntactic features separately.

To our knowledge, there is no previous research in medical text classification area exploring the individual value of lexical and syntactic features with regards to their vulnerability and importance for ML models. Syntactic and lexical feature groups are often used together without specifying their individual value. For example, recent work in text classification for AD detection revealed that a combination of lexical and syntactic features works well (Fraser et al., 2016; Noorian et al., 2017); the same is true for other cognitive disease or language impairment detection (Meteyard and Patterson, 2009; Fraser et al., 2014), as well as sentiment detection in healthy speech and language (Negi and Buitelaar, 2014; Marchand et al., 2013; Pang et al., 2002).

In this paper, we focus on individual value of lexical and syntactic feature groups, as studied across medical text classification tasks, types of language, datasets and domains. As such, the main contributions of this paper are:

- Inspired by the results of neuroscience studies (Indefrey et al., 2001), we explore selective performance of lexical and syntactic feature groups separately.

- We demonstrate, using multiple analysis methods, that there is a clear difference in how lexical features endure text alterations in comparison to the syntactic ones as well as how the latter impact classification.

- We report results on three different datasets and four different classifiers, which allows us to draw more general conclusions.

- We conduct an example-based analysis that explains the results obtained during the analysis.

2 Related Work

Prior research reports the utility of different modalities of speech – lexical and syntactic (Bucks et al., 2000; Fraser et al., 2016; Noo-

rian et al., 2017; Zhu et al.) – in detecting dementia. Bucks et al. (2000) obtained a cross-validated accuracy of 87.5% among a sample of 24 participants in detecting AD using eight linguistic features, including part-of-speech (POS) tag frequencies and measures of lexical diversity. A similar feature set was employed by Meilán et al. (2014) in a larger sample, where measures of lexical richness were less useful than features indicative of word finding difficulty (such as pauses and repetitions). Orimaye et al. (2014) obtained F-measure scores up to 0.74 using a combination of lexical and syntactic features on transcripts from a large dataset of AD and controls speech, DementiaBank (see Section 3.1)

Similarly, varying feature sets have been used for detecting aphasia from speech. Researchers have studied the importance of syntactic complexity indicators such as Yngve-depth and length of various syntactic representations for detecting aphasia (Roark et al., 2011), as well as lexical characteristics such as average frequency and the imageability of words used (Bird et al., 2000). Patterns in production of nouns and verbs are also particularly important in aphasia detection (Wilson et al., 2010; Meteyard and Patterson, 2009). Fraser et al. (2014) used a combination of syntactic and lexical features with ASR-transcription for the diagnosis of primary progressive aphasia with a cross-validated accuracy of 100% within a dataset of 30 English-speakers. More recently, Le et al. (2017) proposed methods to detect paraphasia, a type of language output error commonly associated with aphasia, in aphasic speech using phone-level features.

Sentiment analysis methodologies often use lexicon-based features (Taboada et al., 2011; Tang et al., 2014). Syntactic characteristics of text such as proportions of verbs and adjectives, nature of specific clauses in sentences are also salient in sentiment detection (Chesley et al., 2006; Meena and Prabhakar, 2007). Additionally, systems using both syntactic and lexical features have been proposed in prior work (Negi and Buitelaar, 2014; Marchand et al., 2013). For example, Marchand et al. (2013) trained ML models on patterns in syntactic parse-trees and occurrences of words from a sentiment lexicon to detect underlying sentiments from tweets while Negi and Buitelaar (2014) employed syntactic and lexical features for sentence level aspect based sentiment analysis. Pang et al.

		Datasets		
		DemB	IMDBs	AphB
Task nature	Structured	X	X	
	Partially structured			X
Language type	Verbal	X		X
	Written		X	
Lexics	Complex			X
	Medium		X	
	Simple	X		
Syntax	Complex		X	
	Medium	X		
	Simple			X

Table 1: Comparison of the datasets in terms of task nature, type of language used to collect the data, lexical and syntactic complexity.

(2002) showed that unigrams, bigrams and frequencies of parts-of-speech tags such as verbs and adjectives are important for an ML-based sentiment classifier.

3 Method

3.1 Datasets

In the following section, we provide context on each of three similarly-sized datasets that we investigate that differ in the following ways (see also Section 4):

1. Binary text classification task (AD detection, sentiment classification, aphasia detection).

2. Type of language

3. Level of lexical and syntactic complexity.

3.1.1 DementiaBank (DemB)

DementiaBank[1] is the largest publicly available dataset for detecting cognitive impairments, and is a part of the TalkBank corpus (MacWhinney, 2007). It consists of audio recordings of verbal descriptions and associated transcripts of the Cookie Theft picture description task from the Boston Diagnostic Aphasia Examination (Becker et al., 1994) from 210 participants aged between 45 to 90. Of these participants, 117 have a clinical diagnosis of AD ($N = 180$ speech recordings), while 93 ($N = 229$ speech recordings) are cognitively healthy. Many participants repeat the task within an interval of a year.

3.1.2 AphasiaBank (AphB)

AphasiaBank[2] (MacWhinney, 2007) is another dataset of pathological speech that consists of

[1]https://dementia.talkbank.org
[2]https://aphasia.talkbank.org

aphasic and healthy control speakers performing a set of standard clinical speech-based tasks. The dataset includes audio samples of speech and associated transcripts. All participants perform multiple tasks, such as describing pictures, storytelling, free speech, and discourse with a fixed protocol. Aphasic speakers have various sub-types of aphasia (fluent, non-fluent, etc.). In total, there are 674 samples, from 192 healthy ($N = 246$ speech samples) and 301 ($N = 428$ speech samples) aphasic speakers.

3.1.3 IMDB Sentiment Extract (IMDBs)

The IMDB Sentiment (Maas et al., 2011) dataset is a standard corpus for sentiment detection that contains typewritten reviews of movies from the IMDB database along with the review-associated binary sentiment polarity labels (positive and negative). This dataset is used in order to extend the range of 'healthy' language and test generalizability of our findings. The core dataset consists of 50,000 reviews split evenly into train and test sets (with equal classes in both train and test). To maintain a comparable dataset size to DemB and AphB, we randomly choose 250 samples from the train sets of each polarity, totalling 500 labeled samples.

All the three datasets cover a breadth of transcripts in terms of presence or absence of impairment, as well as a spectrum of 'healthy' speech.

3.2 Feature Extraction

Following multiple previous works on text classification, we extract two groups of linguistic features – lexical and syntactic.

Lexical features: Features of lexical domain have been recognized as an important construct in a number of research areas, including stylistics, text readability analysis, language assessment, first and second language acquisition, and cognitive disease detection. In order to measure various dimensions of lexical richness in the datasets under comparison, we compute statistics on token/unigram, bigram, and trigram counts. Additionally, we use the Lexical Complexity Analyser (Ai and Lu, 2010) to measure various dimensions of lexical richness, such as lexical density, sophistication, and variation.

Following Oraby et al. (2018), Dušek et al. (2019), and Jagfeld et al. (2018), we also use Shannon entropy (Manning and Schtze, 2000,

p. 61ff.) as a measure of lexical diversity in the texts:

$$H(\text{text}) = - \sum_{x \in \text{text}} \frac{\text{freq}(x)}{\text{len(text)}} \log_2 \left(\frac{\text{freq}(x)}{\text{len(text)}} \right) \tag{1}$$

Here, x stands for all unique tokens/n-grams, *freq* stands for the number of occurrences in the text, and *len* for the total number of tokens/n-grams in the text. We compute entropy over tokens (unigrams), bigrams, and trigrams.

We further complement Shannon text entropy with n-gram conditional entropy for next-word prediction (Manning and Schtze, 2000, p. 63ff.), given one previous word (bigram) or two previous words (trigram):

$$H_{cond}(\text{text}) = - \sum_{(c,w) \in \text{text}} \frac{\text{freq}(c,w)}{\text{len(text)}} \log_2 \left(\frac{\text{freq}(c,w)}{\text{freq}(c)} \right) \tag{2}$$

Here, (c, w) stands for all unique n-grams in the text, composed of c (context, all tokens but the last one) and w (the last token). Conditional next-word entropy gives an additional, novel measure of diversity and repetitiveness: the more diverse text is, the less predictable is the next word given the previous word(s) is; on the other hand, the more repetitive the text, the more predictable is the next word given the previous word(s).

Syntactic Features: We used the D-Level Analyser (Lu, 2009) to evaluate syntactic variation and complexity of human references using the revised D-Level Scale (Lu, 2014).

We use the L2 Syntactic Complexity Analyzer (Lu, 2010) to extract 14 features of syntactic complexity that represent the length of production units, sentence complexity, the amount of subordination and coordination, and the frequency of particular syntactic structures. The full list of lexical and syntactic features is provided in Appendix A.

3.3 Classification Models

We benchmark four different machine learning models on each dataset with 10-fold cross-validation. In cases of multiple samples per participant, we stratify by subject so that samples of the same participant do not occur in both the train and test sets in each fold. This is repeated for each text alteration level. The minority class is oversampled in the training set using SMOTE (Chawla et al., 2002) to deal with class imbalance.

Feature subgroup	Feature	DemB	IMDBs	AphB
Lexical richness	distinct tokens occuring once, %	0.58	**0.64**	0.32
	distinct bigrams occuring once, %	0.89	**0.95**	0.83
	distinct trigrams occuring once, %	0.96	**0.99**	0.92
Lexical complexity	unigram entropy	5.42	6.53	**6.70**
	bigram entropy	6.4	7.46	**8.68**
	trigram entropy	6.55	7.54	**9.19**
	bigram conditional entropy	1.01	0.95	**1.99**
	trigram conditional entropy	0.16	0.09	**0.51**
	lexicon complexity	1.33	**1.47**	1.32
Length of production unit	Mean length of clause	7.45	**9.24**	5.42
	Mean length of sentence	8.77	**21.42**	6.01
	Mean length of T-unit	11.85	**18.99**	6.15
Sentence complexity	Clauses per sentence	1.21	**2.35**	1.08
	D-level 0	0.63	0.26	**0.74**
	D-level 1-4	**0.23**	0.21	0.14
	D-level 5-7	0.14	**0.52**	0.11
Amount of subordination	Clauses per T-unit	1.62	**2.07**	1.12
	Complex T-units per T-unit	0.19	**0.55**	0.14
	Dependent clauses per T-unit	0.68	**1.00**	0.19
Amount of coordination	Coordinate phrases per clause	0.11	**0.22**	0.10
	Coordinate phrases per T-unit	0.17	**0.44**	0.11
	T-units per sentence	0.77	**1.13**	0.95
Particular structures	Complex nominals per clause	0.64	1.09	0.33
	Complex nominals per T-unit	1.03	**2.28**	0.38
	Verb phrases per T-unit	1.93	**2.64**	1.19

Table 2: Lexical complexity and richness, and syntactic complexity of the three datasets. Counts for n-grams appearing only once are shown as proportions of the total number of respective n-grams. Highest values on each line are typeset in bold.

We consider Gaussian naive Bayes (with equal priors), random forest (with 100 estimators and maximum depth 5), support vector Machine (with RBF kernel, penalty $C = 1$), and a 2-hidden layer neural network (with 10 units in each layer, ReLU activation, 200 epochs and Adam optimizer) (Pedregosa et al., 2011). Since the datasets have imbalanced classes, we identify F1 score with macro averaging as the primary performance metric.

3.4 Altering Text Samples

There can be three types of language perturbations at the word level: insertions, deletions, and substitutions on words. (Balagopalan et al., 2019) showed that deletions are more affected (significantly) than insertions and substitutions, so we likewise focus on deletions. Following Balagopalan et al. (2019), we artificially add deletion errors to original individual text samples at predefined levels of 20%, 40%, 60%, and 80%. To add the errors, we simply delete random words from original texts and transcripts at a specified rate.

3.5 Evaluating Change of Feature Values

In order to evaluate the change of feature values for different levels of text alterations, z-scores are used. We calculate z-scores of each individual feature in the transcripts with each level of alteration, with relation to the value of that feature in the original unaltered transcript.

$$Z^x_{feat} = (feat^x - \mu_{no-alteration})/\sigma_{no-alteration}, \quad (3)$$

where $feat^x$ refers to a given syntactic or lexical feature extracted from a transcript with an alteration level of $x = 20..80$, μ and σ are computed over the entire original unaltered dataset.

Then, we average the individual z-scores across all the features within each feature group (syntactic and lexical) to get a z-score per feature group.

$$Z^x_{syntactic} = \frac{1}{N_{syn}} \sum_{i=1}^{N_{syn}} Z^x_{feat_i} \quad (4)$$

$$Z^x_{lexical} = \frac{1}{N_{lex}} \sum_{i=1}^{N_{lex}} Z^x_{feat_i}, \quad (5)$$

where N_{syn} and N_{lex} refer to the total number of syntactic and lexical features, respectively.

3.6 Evaluating change of feature predictive power

We extract $\Delta F1_x$, or change in classification F1 macro score, with $x\%$ alteration with respect to no alteration, for $x = 20, 40, 60, 80$, i.e,

$$\Delta F1_x = F1_{x\% alteration} - F1_{no-alteration}. \quad (6)$$

To identify the relative importance of syntactic or lexical features on classification performance, we estimate coefficients of effect for syntactic and lexical features. These coefficients are obtained by regressing to F1 deltas using the syntactic and lexical feature z scores described in Section 3.5 for each alteration level. Thus, the regression equation can be expressed as:

$$\Delta F1 = \alpha Z_{syntactic} + \beta Z_{lexical}. \quad (7)$$

The training set for estimating α and β consists of $\Delta F1_x; (Z^x_{syntactic}, Z^x_{lexical})$ for $x = 20, 40, 60, 80$.

4 Comparing datasets

Three datasets used in our exploration represent different dimensions of lexical and syntactic complexity, and are unique in the nature of the tasks they involve and their type of language, as shown in Tab.1. AphB is the only dataset that includes speech samples of unstructured speech, while

Dataset	Level (%) of alterations	Lexical features (z-score)	Syntactic features (z-score)
DemB	20	**0.35**	0.30
	40	**0.75**	0.62
	60	**1.21**	0.94
	80	**1.85**	1.31
AphB	20	0.10	**0.15**
	40	**0.26**	0.26
	60	**0.51**	0.37
	80	**0.93**	0.51
IMDBs	20	**0.29**	0.13
	40	**0.61**	0.25
	60	**1.00**	0.35
	80	**1.61**	0.31

Table 3: Change of feature values, per dataset and per level of text alterations.

IMDBs is unique as it contains samples of written language, rather than transcripts of verbal speech.

In terms of lexical and syntactic complexity, it is interesting to note that AphB contains samples that are most lexically complex, while at the same time it is the most simple from the syntactic point of view. We associate this with the fact that AphB data come from partially unstructured tasks, where free speech increases the use of a more complex and more diverse vocabulary. IMDB is the most lexically rich dataset (see Table 2), with the highest ratio of uni-, bi-, and trigrams occuring only once.

IMDB is the most complex according to various measures of syntactic complexity: it has the highest scores with metrics associated with length of production unit, amount of subordination, coordination, and particular structures, and it also has the highest amount of complex sentences (sentences of D-level 5-7, as shown in Table 2). This may be explained by the fact it is the only dataset based on typewritten language. AphB has the lowest level of syntactic complexity, containing the highest amount of the simplest sentences (D-level 0), and lowest scores in other subgroups of syntactic features (see Table 2).

Next, we analyse if these variously distinct datasets have any common trend with regards to the vulnerability and robustness of lexical and syntactic feature groups.

5 Results and discussion

5.1 Feature vulnerability

Following the method described in Section 3.5, we analyse if any of the feature groups (lexical or syntactic) is influenced more by text alter-

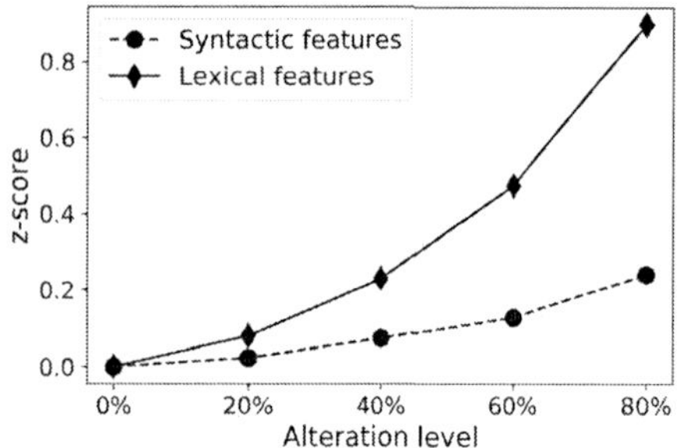 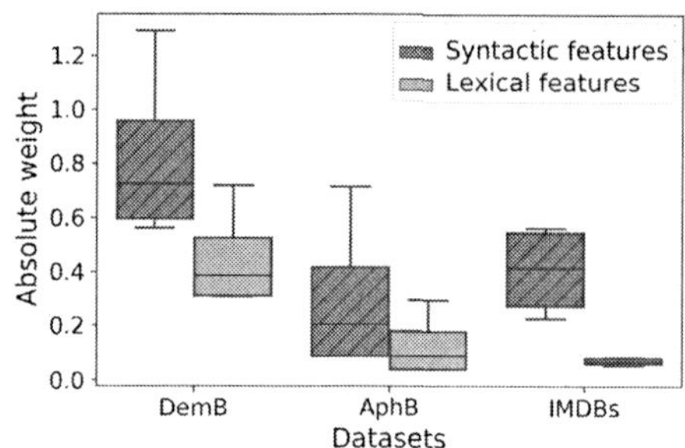

Figure 1: Left: Change of syntactic and lexical feature values at different alteration levels, averaged across three datasets. Right: Impact of syntactic and lexical features on classification for DementiaBank, AphasiaBank and IMDBsentiment datasets, averaged across fours classifiers.

ations. As shown in Figure 1, the values of lexical features are, on average, influenced significantly more than syntactic ones (Kruskal-Wallis test, $p < 0.05$). Such a difference is observed in all three datasets individually (see Table 3).

The differences of z-scores between lexical and syntactic feature groups are higher for the IMDBs dataset, which suggests that the difference is most visible either in healthy or in written language.

These results suggest that lexical features are more vulnerable to simple text alterations, such as introduced deletion errors, while syntax-related features are more robust to these modifications. However, stronger changes of raw feature values do not necessarily mean that the resulting modified features become more or less important for classifiers. This leads us to inspect the impact of text alteration on feature predictive power.

5.2 Feature significance and the impact of alterations on feature predictive power

A simple method to understand the potential predictability of a feature is by looking at how different the feature value is between classes and whether this difference is statistically significant. This method was previously used in studies assessing automatic speech recognition for Alzheimer's (Zhou et al., 2016) and aphasia detection (Fraser et al., 2013).

We rank the p-values obtained, in each condition, from a two tailed non-parametric Kruskal-Wallis test performed on each feature between the two classes (healthy vs unhealthy in the DB and AphB datasets, and positive vs negative in IMDBs) and assign rank to each feature. It is interesting to note that lexical features occupy the overwhelming majority of first places across all

Dataset	Classifiers			
	NN	SVM	RF	NB
DemB	1.82	1.83	1.98	1.80
IMDBs	5.22	6.39	7.15	3.74
AphB	2.22	2.44	2.28	2.17

Table 4: Ratio of coefficients, calculated as $Importance_{syntactic}/Importance_{lexical}$. Ratio higher than one indicates that syntactic features are more important for a classifier than lexical ones.

datasets, showing that lexical features are significantly different between classes. We further analyse, following (Brunato et al., 2018), how the rank of each feature changes when different levels of text alterations are introduced. The maximum rank increase is higher on average for lexical features than for syntactic (see Figure 2 for details of rank changes in DemB dataset) across all datasets. The ratio of features that become insignificant after text alteration is also higher for lexical features rather than in syntactic on average across all datasets. As Figure 2 shows, the features with increased rank are those that were not initially significantly different between classes. The combination of these results suggest that not so important lexical features become more and more important with addition of text alterations, which may decrease the performance of classification.

The above method of calculating p-values is analogous to feature selection performed as a preprocessing step before classification. Although this step may provide some initial insights into feature significance, it does not guarantee the most significant features will be those having the most predictive power in classification.

Lexical features	Level of alterations				Syntactic features	Level of alterations			
	20%	40%	60%	80%		20%	40%	60%	80%
slextypes	-14	-45	-31	-24	T/S	-33	-22	-36	-57
swordtypes	-21	-37	-29	-26	C/S	-34	-27	-24	-42
rttr	-14		-35	-20	C		-52	-58	-56
cttr	-12		-33	-18	CT		-42	-45	-46
lextypes		-20	-4	0	T			-49	-49
slextokens		-23	-15	-14	MLS	-6	-1	-1	-1
wordtypes		-16	-6	-1	CP	-20			
ndw		-16	-6	-1	CN		-40	-36	-29
distinct_bigrams		-28	-15	-7	VP		-32	-34	-35
distinct_tokens		-10	-1	4	CT/T		-34	-35	-37
ls2	0	-31	-43	-45	C/T	-22	-11	-17	-30
swordtokens		-24	-27	-28	DC		-16	-26	-26
uber	8	-14	-37		S				-46
entropy_2gram		-8	4	7	CP/T	-21	-45	-51	-55
entropy_1gram		-16	-8	4	CP/C	-14	-35	-46	-50
lextokens		4	12	13	MLT	-8	-5	-2	-2
distinct_trigrams		-11	-3	2	CN/T		-44	-43	-36
bigrams		-8	0	6	DC/T	-24	-17	-28	-32
entropy_3gram		4	14	15	CN/C	-25		-47	-44
trigrams		1	4	7	DC/C		-21	-30	-33
ndwerz			-19	4	MLC	-18	-18	-19	-27
ls1	10	-19	-30		VP/T	0	0	2	-4

Figure 2: Change of lexical (left) and syntactic (right) feature rank when text alterations of different levels are introduced. Negative numbers denote decrease in rank, and positive numbers are an increase of rank. Blue cell colours denote the highest increase in rank, red (the highest decrease) and yellow (a smaller level of increase or decrease). Features are ranked based on p-values with the lowest p-value at the top. White cells show that features were not significantly different between classes in the original text samples, based on DemB dataset.

We use the method described in Section 3.6 to evaluate the impact of text alteration on the features predictive power. The results in Table 4 show that syntactic features have more predictive power than lexical features. The lowest ratio is observed with DemB, and the AphB results are very close, suggesting that syntactic features are approximately twice as important than lexical features in predicting pathological speech. In healthy written language, the difference is even higher and reaches 7.15 for the random forest classifier.

In summary, the predictive power of syntactic features is much stronger than that of lexical features across three datasets and four main classifiers, which suggest the results can be generalizable across several different tasks and domains.

5.3 Example-based Analysis

As shown in previous sections, values of lexical features are on average more influenced by text alterations but this change does not affect classification as much as smaller value changes in syntactic features. Table 5 provides examples of two features, one lexical and one syntactic, their value changes when text samples are modified, and the associated change of the classifier's predictions.

The value of lexical feature *cond_entropy_3gram*, showing conditional entropy calculated for trigrams, decreases by more than 50% when the text sample is modified by only 20%. This change is much higher than the associated absolute change of the syntactic feature *C/S* (that shows the number of clauses per sentence) that increases by 11% only on the same level of alteration. The prediction made by a classifier in the case of the lexical feature, however, is the same as the prediction of original transcript. Only when the general level of alteration reaches 60% and the value of the lexical feature decreases by more than 85%, the prediction becomes incorrect. In the case of syntactic features, the prediction already changes to incorrect with the general level of alteration of 20%, although the feature value is still quite close to the original one.

Consider this sentence in the original transcript:

Alteration level	Text sample	Feature	Feature value / Δ	Prediction	Dataset
original	&uh the boy is reaching into the cookie jar. he's falling off the stool. the little girl is reaching for a cookie. mother is drying the dishes. the sink is running over. mother's getting her feet wet. they all have shoes on. there's a cup two cups and a saucer on the sink. the window has draw withdrawn drapes. you look out on the driveway. there's kitchen cabinets. oh what's happening. mother is looking out the window. the girl is touching her lips. the boy is standing on his right foot. his left foot is sort of up in the air. mother's right foot is flat on the floor and her left she's on her left toe. &uh she's holding the dish cloth in her right hand and the plate she is drying in her left. I think I've run out of. yeah.	lexical (cond_entropy_3gram)	0.24 / -	Correct (healthy)	DemB
20%	&uh the boy reaching the cookie jar. he's falling off the stool. the little girl is reaching for cookie. mother is the dishes. the sink is over. mother's getting her feet. all have shoes. there's cup two cups a saucer on sink. window has draw withdrawn drapes. you look out on driveway. there's kitchen cabinets. oh what's happening. mother out the window. the girl is lips. the boy standing on. his left foot is sort of up in the air. mother's right foot is flat on the floor and left she's on her left toe. &uh she's holding the cloth in right hand the plate she drying in her left. think I've run out of.	lexical (cond_entropy_3gram)	0.11 / 0.48	Correct (healthy)	DemB
40%	&uh reaching the jar. he's falling the stool. the little is reaching a cookie. mother drying the dishes. the sink is running over. mother's her wet. all have shoes on. a two and a sink. the. you look driveway. there's kitchen. oh what's happening. mother out the window. the is her. is his foot. his left foot is sort of up air. foot is flat floor and she's her toe. &uh she's holding the dish cloth in right the she is drying in left. I think of.	lexical (cond_entropy_3gram)	0.07 / 0.28	Correct (healthy)	DemB
60%	&uh is cookie. falling stool. for cookie. the dishes. the. mother's feet wet. they have. a two cups a sink. the has withdrawn drapes. the. there's. oh. mother the window. the lips. the boy right. is sort of. right foot is flat on floor on her left. &uh cloth right hand and the she is in her left. yeah.	lexical (cond_entropy_3gram)	0.03 / 0.14	Incorrect (AD)	DemB
original	okay. well in the first place the the mother forgot to turn off the water and the water's running out the sink. and she's standing there. it's falling on the floor. the child is got a stool and reaching up into the cookie jar. and the stool is tipping over. and he's sorta put down the plates. and she's reaching up to get it but I don't see anything wrong with her though. yeah that's it. I can't see anything.	syntactic (C/S)	1.1 / -	Correct (healthy)	DemB
20%	well the first the the mother forgot to turn off the water the water's out the sink. and standing there. it's falling floor. is got a stool and into the cookie jar. and the stool is tipping. and he's sorta down the plates. and she's reaching to get it but I don't see anything wrong with her though. that's it. I can't see anything.	syntactic (C/S)	1.22 / 1.11	Incorrect (AD)	DemB
40%	okay. well in the forgot the water the water's out the sink. and she's standing there. it's on the. the is got a stool and reaching up the. the is tipping. and he's sorta the. and she's reaching up to get but I her. yeah that's. I can't.	syntactic (C/S)	1.0 / 0.91	Incorrect (AD)	DemB
60%	okay. in water's out the sink. falling. the got stool the cookie jar. and the stool is over. and he's down the plates. and she's up but don't wrong. can't see anything.	syntactic (C/S)	1.0 / 0.91	Incorrect (AD)	DemB

Table 5: Examples of two features, *cond_entropy_3gram* and *C/S*, their value change when text samples are modified on the level of 20%, 40% and 60%, and associated classifier's predictions. Examples are provided using the DemB transcript samples and feature values.

She's holding the dish cloth in her right hand and the plate she is drying in her left.

With 20% of errors it is converted to the following:

She's holding the cloth in right hand the plate she drying in her left.

It is clear that lexical features based on the frequency of uni-, bi- and trigrams are affected by this change, because quite a few words disappear in the second variant. In terms of syntactic structures, however, the sentence is not damaged much, as we still can see the same number of clauses, coordinate units, or verb phrases. Such an example helps explain the results in the previous sections.

6 Conclusions and Future Research

This paper shows that linguistic features of text, associated with syntactic and lexical complexity, are not equal in their vulnerability levels, nor in their predictive power. We study selective performance of these two feature aggregations on three distinct datasets to verify the generalizability of observations.

We demonstrate that values of lexical features are easily affected by even slight changes in text, by analysing z-scores at multiple alteration levels. Syntactic features, however, are more robust to such modifications. On the other hand, lower changes of syntactic features result in stronger effects on classification performance. Note that these patterns are consistently observed across different datasets with different levels of lexical and syntactic complexity, and for typewritten text and transcribed speech.

Several methods to detect and correct syntactic (Ma and McKeown, 2012) and lexical errors (Klebesits and Grechenig, 1994) as a postprocessing step for output from machine translation or ASR systems have been proposed in prior work. Since our analysis indicates that error-affected syntactic features have a stronger effect on classification performance, we suggest imposing higher penalties on detecting and correcting syntactic errors than lexical errors in medical texts. A limitation in our study is that we focused on text alterations of a specific type, and the results were only tested on relatively small datasets. In future work, we will extend the analysis to other simple text alterations such as substitutions as well as adversarial text attacks (Alzantot et al., 2018). In addition, we will extend the current work to see how state-of-the-art neural network models, such as Bert, can handle text alterations as they capture lexical, syntactic and semantic features of the input text in different layers. Finally, note that the datasets considered in this study are fairly small (between 500 and 856 samples per domain). Efforts to release larger and more diverse data sets through multiple channels (such as challenges) in such domains as Alzheimer's or aphasia detection, and depression detection (Valstar et al., 2016; MacWhinney, 2007; Mozilla, 2019) need to be reinforced.

References

Haiyang Ai and Xiaofei Lu. 2010. A web-based system for automatic measurement of lexical complexity. In *27th Annual Symposium of the Computer-Assisted Language Instruction Consortium. Amherst, MA.*

Moustafa Alzantot, Yash Sharma, Ahmed Elgohary, Bo-Jhang Ho, Mani Srivastava, and Kai-Wei Chang. 2018. Generating natural language adversarial examples. In *Proceedings of the 2018 Conference on Empirical Methods in Natural Language Processing*, pages 2890–2896.

Eiji Aramaki, Shuko Shikata, Mai Miyabe, and Ayae Kinoshita. 2016. Vocabulary size in speech may be an early indicator of cognitive impairment. *PloS one*, 11(5):e0155195.

Aparna Balagopalan, Jekaterina Novikova, Frank Rudzicz, and Marzyeh Ghassemi. 2018. The Effect of Heterogeneous Data for Alzheimer's Disease Detection from Speech. In *Proceedings of the Machine Learning for Health (ML4H) Workshop at NeurIPS 2018.*

Aparna Balagopalan, Ksenia Shkaruta, and Jekaterina Novikova. 2019. Impact of ASR on Alzheimer's Disease Detection: All Errors are Equal, but Deletions are More Equal than Others. *arXiv:1904.01684.*

James T Becker, François Boiler, Oscar L Lopez, Judith Saxton, and Karen L McGonigle. 1994. The natural history of alzheimer's disease: description of study cohort and accuracy of diagnosis. *Archives of Neurology*, 51(6):585–594.

Scott F Beers and William E Nagy. 2009. Syntactic complexity as a predictor of adolescent writing quality: Which measures? which genre? *Reading and Writing*, 22(2):185–200.

Helen Bird, Matthew A Lambon Ralph, Karalyn Patterson, and John R Hodges. 2000. The rise and fall of frequency and imageability: Noun and verb production in semantic dementia. *Brain and language*, 73(1):17–49.

Joanna Blaszczak. 2019. *Investigation into the Interaction between the Indefinites and Negation*, volume 51. Walter de Gruyter GmbH & Co KG.

Dominique Brunato, Lorenzo De Mattei, Felice DellOrletta, Benedetta Iavarone, and Giulia Venturi. 2018. Is this sentence difficult? do you agree? In *Proceedings of the 2018 Conference on Empirical Methods in Natural Language Processing*, pages 2690–2699.

Lucy Bryant, Elizabeth Spencer, Alison Ferguson, Hugh Craig, Kim Colyvas, and Linda Worrall. 2013. Propositional idea density in aphasic discourse. *Aphasiology*, 27(8):992–1009.

Romola S Bucks, Sameer Singh, Joanne M Cuerden, and Gordon K Wilcock. 2000. Analysis of spontaneous, conversational speech in dementia of alzheimer type: Evaluation of an objective technique for analysing lexical performance. *Aphasiology*, 14(1):71–91.

Nitesh V Chawla, Kevin W Bowyer, Lawrence O Hall, and W Philip Kegelmeyer. 2002. Smote: synthetic minority over-sampling technique. *Journal of artificial intelligence research*, 16:321–357.

Paula Chesley, Bruce Vincent, Li Xu, and Rohini K Srihari. 2006. Using verbs and adjectives to automatically classify blog sentiment. *Training*, 580(263):233.

Helmut Daller, Roeland Van Hout, and Jeanine Treffers-Daller. 2003. Lexical richness in the spontaneous speech of bilinguals. *Applied linguistics*, 24(2):197–222.

Ondřej Dušek, Jekaterina Novikova, and Verena Rieser. 2019. Evaluating the State-of-the-Art of End-to-End Natural Language Generation: The E2E NLG Challenge. *Journal of Computer Speech & Language*, 59:123–156.

Kathleen Fraser, Frank Rudzicz, Naida Graham, and Elizabeth Rochon. 2013. Automatic speech recognition in the diagnosis of primary progressive aphasia. In *Proceedings of the fourth workshop on speech and language processing for assistive technologies*, pages 47–54.

Kathleen C Fraser, Naama Ben-David, Graeme Hirst, Naida Graham, and Elizabeth Rochon. 2015. Sentence segmentation of aphasic speech. In *Proceedings of the 2015 Conference of the North American Chapter of the Association for Computational Linguistics: Human Language Technologies*, pages 862–871.

Kathleen C Fraser, Jed A Meltzer, Naida L Graham, Carol Leonard, Graeme Hirst, Sandra E Black, and Elizabeth Rochon. 2014. Automated classification of primary progressive aphasia subtypes from narrative speech transcripts. *cortex*, 55:43–60.

Kathleen C Fraser, Frank Rudzicz, and Graeme Hirst. 2016. Detecting late-life depression in alzheimers disease through analysis of speech and language. In *Proceedings of the Third Workshop on Computational Linguistics and Clinical Psychology*, pages 1–11.

Angela D Friederici, Christian J Fiebach, Matthias Schlesewsky, Ina D Bornkessel, and D Yves Von Cramon. 2006. Processing linguistic complexity and grammaticality in the left frontal cortex. *Cerebral Cortex*, 16(12):1709–1717.

Peter Indefrey, Peter Hagoort, Hans Herzog, Rüdiger J Seitz, and Colin M Brown. 2001. Syntactic processing in left prefrontal cortex is independent of lexical meaning. *Neuroimage*, 14(3):546–555.

Glorianna Jagfeld, Sabrina Jenne, and Ngoc Thang Vu. 2018. Sequence-to-Sequence Models for Data-to-Text Natural Language Generation: Word- vs. Character-based Processing and Output Diversity. In *Proceedings of the 11th International Conference on Natural Language Generation*, Tilburg, The Netherlands. ArXiv: 1810.04864.

Susan Kemper, Marilyn Thompson, and Janet Marquis. 2001. Longitudinal change in language production: effects of aging and dementia on grammatical complexity and propositional content. *Psychology and aging*, 16(4):600.

K Klebesits and Th Grechenig. 1994. Lexical error correction using contextual linguistic expectations. In *Computer Science 2*, pages 337–345. Springer.

Duc Le, Keli Licata, and Emily Mower Provost. 2017. Automatic paraphasia detection from aphasic speech: A preliminary study. In *Interspeech*, pages 294–298.

Nicholas Lester, Laurie Feldman, and Fermín Moscoso del Prado Martín. 2017. You can take a noun out of syntax...: Syntactic similarity effects in lexical priming.

Xiaofei Lu. 2009. Automatic measurement of syntactic complexity in child language acquisition. *International Journal of Corpus Linguistics*, 14(1):3–28.

Xiaofei Lu. 2010. Automatic analysis of syntactic complexity in second language writing. *International journal of corpus linguistics*, 15(4):474–496.

Xiaofei Lu. 2011. A corpus-based evaluation of syntactic complexity measures as indices of college-level esl writers' language development. *Tesol Quarterly*, 45(1):36–62.

Xiaofei Lu. 2014. *Computational methods for corpus annotation and analysis*. Springer.

Wei-Yun Ma and Kathleen McKeown. 2012. Detecting and correcting syntactic errors in machine translation using feature-based lexicalized tree adjoining grammars. *International Journal of Computational Linguistics & Chinese Language Processing, Volume 17, Number 4, December 2012-Special Issue on Selected Papers from ROCLING XXIV*, 17(4).

Andrew L Maas, Raymond E Daly, Peter T Pham, Dan Huang, Andrew Y Ng, and Christopher Potts. 2011. Learning word vectors for sentiment analysis. In *Proceedings of the 49th annual meeting of the association for computational linguistics: Human language technologies-volume 1*, pages 142–150. Association for Computational Linguistics.

Brian MacWhinney. 2007. The talkbank project. In *Creating and digitizing language corpora*, pages 163–180. Springer.

Christopher D. Manning and Hinrich Schtze. 2000. *Foundations of statistical natural language processing*, 2nd printing edition. MIT Press, Cambridge, MA, USA.

Morgane Marchand, Alexandru Ginsca, Romaric Besançon, and Olivier Mesnard. 2013. [lvic-limsi]: Using syntactic features and multi-polarity words for sentiment analysis in twitter. In *Second Joint Conference on Lexical and Computational Semantics (* SEM), Volume 2: Proceedings of the Seventh International Workshop on Semantic Evaluation (SemEval 2013)*, volume 2, pages 418–424.

Vaden Masrani, Gabriel Murray, Thalia Field, and Giuseppe Carenini. 2017. Detecting dementia through retrospective analysis of routine blog posts by bloggers with dementia. In *BioNLP 2017*, pages 232–237, Vancouver, Canada,. Association for Computational Linguistics.

Philip M McCarthy. 2005. *An assessment of the range and usefulness of lexical diversity measures and the potential of the measure of textual, lexical diversity (MTLD)*. Ph.D. thesis, The University of Memphis.

Arun Meena and TV Prabhakar. 2007. Sentence level sentiment analysis in the presence of conjuncts using linguistic analysis. In *European Conference on Information Retrieval*, pages 573–580. Springer.

Juan José G Meilán, Francisco Martínez-Sánchez, Juan Carro, Dolores E López, Lymarie Millian-Morell, and José M Arana. 2014. Speech in alzheimer's disease: Can temporal and acoustic parameters discriminate dementia? *Dementia and Geriatric Cognitive Disorders*, 37(5-6):327–334.

Kenneth S Melnick and Edward G Conture. 2000. Relationship of length and grammatical complexity to the systematic and nonsystematic speech errors and stuttering of children who stutter. *Journal of Fluency Disorders*, 25(1):21–45.

Lotte Meteyard and Karalyn Patterson. 2009. The relation between content and structure in language production: An analysis of speech errors in semantic dementia. *Brain and language*, 110(3):121–134.

Mozilla. 2019. Common Voice dataset.

Sapna Negi and Paul Buitelaar. 2014. Insight galway: syntactic and lexical features for aspect based sentiment analysis. In *Proceedings of the 8th International Workshop on Semantic Evaluation (SemEval 2014)*, pages 346–350.

Zeinab Noorian, Chloé Pou-Prom, and Frank Rudzicz. 2017. On the importance of normative data in speech-based assessment. *arXiv preprint arXiv:1712.00069*.

Shereen Oraby, Lena Reed, and Shubhangi Tandon. 2018. Controlling Personality-Based Stylistic Variation with Neural Natural Language Generators. In *Proceedings of the 19th Annual SIGdial Meeting on Discourse and Dialogue*, Melbourne, Australia.

Sylvester Olubolu Orimaye, Jojo Sze-Meng Wong, and Karen Jennifer Golden. 2014. Learning predictive linguistic features for alzheimers disease and related dementias using verbal utterances. In *Proceedings of the Workshop on Computational Linguistics and Clinical Psychology: From Linguistic Signal to Clinical Reality*, pages 78–87.

Lourdes Ortega. 2003. Syntactic complexity measures and their relationship to l2 proficiency: A research synthesis of college-level l2 writing. *Applied linguistics*, 24(4):492–518.

Bo Pang, Lillian Lee, and Shivakumar Vaithyanathan. 2002. Thumbs up?: sentiment classification using machine learning techniques. In *Proceedings of the ACL-02 conference on Empirical methods in natural language processing-Volume 10*, pages 79–86. Association for Computational Linguistics.

Fabian Pedregosa, Gaël Varoquaux, Alexandre Gramfort, Vincent Michel, Bertrand Thirion, Olivier Grisel, Mathieu Blondel, Peter Prettenhofer, Ron Weiss, Vincent Dubourg, et al. 2011. Scikit-learn: Machine learning in python. *Journal of machine learning research*, 12(Oct):2825–2830.

Andrya LH Ramer. 1977. The development of syntactic complexity. *Journal of Psycholinguistic Research*, 6(2):145–161.

Brian Richards. 1987. Type/token ratios: What do they really tell us? *Journal of child language*, 14(2):201–209.

Brian Roark, Margaret Mitchell, John-Paul Hosom, Kristy Hollingshead, and Jeffrey Kaye. 2011. Spoken language derived measures for detecting mild cognitive impairment. *IEEE transactions on audio, speech, and language processing*, 19(7):2081–2090.

David A Snowdon, Susan J Kemper, James A Mortimer, Lydia H Greiner, David R Wekstein, and William R Markesbery. 1996. Linguistic ability in early life and cognitive function and alzheimer's disease in late life: Findings from the nun study. *Jama*, 275(7):528–532.

Maite Taboada, Julian Brooke, Milan Tofiloski, Kimberly Voll, and Manfred Stede. 2011. Lexicon-based methods for sentiment analysis. *Computational linguistics*, 37(2):267–307.

Duyu Tang, Furu Wei, Nan Yang, Ming Zhou, Ting Liu, and Bing Qin. 2014. Learning sentiment-specific word embedding for twitter sentiment classification. In *Proceedings of the 52nd Annual Meeting of the Association for Computational Linguistics (Volume 1: Long Papers)*, volume 1, pages 1555–1565.

Cynthia K Thompson, Lewis P Shapiro, Swathi Kiran, and Jana Sobecks. 2003. The role of syntactic complexity in treatment of sentence deficits in agrammatic aphasia. *Journal of Speech, Language, and Hearing Research*.

Michael T Ullman, Roumyana Pancheva, Tracy Love, Eiling Yee, David Swinney, and Gregory Hickok. 2005. Neural correlates of lexicon and grammar: Evidence from the production, reading, and judgment of inflection in aphasia. *Brain and Language*, 93(2):185–238.

Michel Valstar, Jonathan Gratch, Björn Schuller, Fabien Ringeval, Denis Lalanne, Mercedes Torres Torres, Stefan Scherer, Giota Stratou, Roddy Cowie, and Maja Pantic. 2016. Avec 2016: Depression, mood, and emotion recognition workshop and challenge. In *Proceedings of the 6th international workshop on audio/visual emotion challenge*, pages 3–10. ACM.

Stephen M Wilson, Maya L Henry, Max Besbris, Jennifer M Ogar, Nina F Dronkers, William Jarrold, Bruce L Miller, and Maria Luisa Gorno-Tempini. 2010. Connected speech production in three variants of primary progressive aphasia. *Brain*, 133(7):2069–2088.

Luke Zhou, Kathleen C Fraser, and Frank Rudzicz. 2016. Speech recognition in alzheimer's disease and in its assessment. In *INTERSPEECH*, pages 1948–1952.

Zining Zhu, Jekaterina Novikova, and Frank Rudzicz. Detecting cognitive impairments by agreeing on interpretations of linguistic features. In *Proceedings of the 2019 Annual Conference of the North American Chapter of the Association for Computational Linguistics, NAACL*, pages 1431–1441.

Zining Zhu, Jekaterina Novikova, and Frank Rudzicz. 2018. Deconfounding age effects with fair representation learning when assessing dementia. *arXiv:1807.07217*.

A   List of Linguistic Features

Lexical Feature	Description
distinct_tokens	Number of distinct tokens
distinct_tokens_ratio	Number of distinct tokens occuring once
bigrams	Number of distinct bigrams
distinct_bigrams	Number of distinct bigrams occuring once
distinct_bigrams_ratio	Ratio of distinct bigrams occuring once
trigrams	Number of distinct trigrams
distinct_trigrams	Number of distinct trigrams occuring once
distinct_trigrams_ratio	Ratio of distinct trigrams occuring once
entropy_1gram	Unigram entropy
entropy_2gram	Bigram entropy
entropy_3gram	Trigram entropy
cond_entropy_2gram	Conditional bigram entropy
cond_entropy_3gram	Conditional trigram entropy
wordtypes	Number of word types
swordtypes	Number of sophisticated word types
lextypes	Number of lexical types
slextypes	Number of sophisticated lexical word types
wordtokens	Number of word tokens
swordtokens	Number of sophisticated word tokens
lextokens	Number of lexical tokens
slextokens	Number of sophisticated lexical tokens
ld	Lexical density
ls1	Lexical sophistication I
ls2	Lexical sophistication II
vs1	Verb sophistication I
vs2	Verb sophistication II
cvs1	Corrected VS1
ndw	Number of different words
ndwz	NDW (first 50 words)
ndwerz	NDW (expected random 50)
ndwesz	NDW (expected sequence 50)
ttr	Type / token ratio
msttr	Mean segmental ttr (50)
cttr	Corrected ttr
rttr	Root ttr
logttr	Bilogarithmic ttr
uber	Uber coefficient

Syntactic Feature	Description
S	Number of sentences
VP	Number of verb phrases
C	Number of clauses
T	Number of T-units[3]
DC	Number of dependent clauses
CT	Number of complex T-units
CP	Number of coordinate phrases
CN	Number of complex nominals
MLS	Mean length of sentence
MLT	Mean length of T-units
MLC	Mean length of clause
C/S	Clauses per sentence
VP/T	Verb phrases per T-unit
C/T	Clauses per T-unit
DC/C	Dependent clauses per clause
DC/T	Dependent clauses per T-unit
T/S	T-units per sentence
CT/T	Complex T-units per T-unit
CP/T	Coordinate phrases per T-unit
CP/C	Coordinate phrases per clause
CN/T	Complex nominals per T-units
CN/C	Complex nominals per clause

---

[3]Here, T-unit is defined as the shortest grammatically al
lowable sentences into which writing can be split or minimally terminable unit. Often, but not always, a T-unit is a
sentence.

Towards Actual (Not Operational) Textual Style Transfer Auto-Evaluation

Richard Yuanzhe Pang [§]

New York University, New York, NY 10011, USA

yzpang@nyu.edu

There are advances on developing methods that do not require parallel corpora, but issues remain with automatic evaluation metrics. Current works (Pang and Gimpel, 2018; Mir et al., 2019) agree on the following three evaluation aspects. (1) Style accuracy of transferred sentences (measured by a pretrained classifier). (2) Semantic similarity between the original and transferred sentences. (3) Naturalness or fluency: researchers use perplexity of transferred sentences, using the language model pretrained on the original corpora.

Problem 1: Style Transfer Tasks. If we think about the practical use cases of style transfer (writing assistance, dialogue, author obfuscation or anonymity, adjusting reading difficulty in education, artistic creations such as works involving literature), we would find that the two would-be-collected non-parallel corpora have different vocabularies, *and* it is hard to differentiate style-related words from content-related words. For example, when transferring Dickens' to modern style literature (Pang and Gimpel, 2018), the former may contain "English farm", "horses"; the latter may contain "vampire", "pop music." But these words should stay the same, as they are content-related but not style-related. On the other hand, Dickens' literature may contain "devil-may-care" and "flummox", but these words *are* style-related and should be changed. Recent works, however, mostly deal with the **operational** style where corpus-specific content words are changed. The operational style transfer models work well on Yelp sentiment transfer which almost all researches focus on, but it does not inspire systems in practical use cases.

Problem 2: Metrics. Consider: *Oliver deemed the gathering in York a great success.* The ex-pected transfer from Dickens to modern literature style should be similar to "Oliver thought the gathering was successful" (**actual** style transfer). However, the most likely transfer (if we use most existing models) will be "Karl enjoyed the party in LA" (**operational** style transfer). In evaluating semantic similarity, Mir et al. (2019) masked style keywords determined by a classifier. In this case, all corpus-specific content words (as well as style words) will be masked, and evaluation will fail. However, we can create the list of style keywords with outside knowledge. We can also consider keeping the words as they are without masking. Similar problems exist for the other two metrics.

Problem 3: Trade-off and Aggregation. Aggregation of metrics is especially helpful as there are tradeoffs (Pang and Gimpel, 2018; Mir et al., 2019), and we need to tune and select models systematically. Use A, B, C to represent the three metrics. For sentence s, define $G_{t_1,t_2,t_3,t_4}(s) = \left([A-t_1]_+ \cdot [B-t_2]_+ \cdot \min\{[t_3-C]_+, [C-t_4]_+\}\right)^{\frac{1}{3}}$ where t_i's are the parameters to be learned.[1] (Small and large C's are both bad.) The current research strives for a universal metric. We can randomly sample a few hundred pairs of *transferred* sentences from a range of style transfer outputs (from different models—good ones and bad ones) from a range of style transfer tasks, and ask annotators which of the two transferred sentences (from the same original sentence) is better. We can then train the parameters based on pairwise comparison. To make G more convincing, we may design more complicated functions $G = f(A, B, C)$. If we do not need a universal evaluator, then we can repeat the above procedure by only sampling pairs of transferred sentences from the dataset of interest, which is more accurate for the particular task.

[§] Abstract written while the author was a student at the University of Chicago.

[1] Inspired by geometric mean.

Proceedings of the 2019 EMNLP Workshop W-NUT: The 5th Workshop on Noisy User-generated Text, pages 444–445
Hong Kong, Nov 4, 2019. ©2019 Association for Computational Linguistics

References

Remi Mir, Bjarke Felbo, Nick Obradovich, and Iyad Rahwan. 2019. Evaluating style transfer for text. *arXiv preprint arXiv:1904.02295.*

Yuanzhe Pang and Kevin Gimpel. 2018. Learning criteria and evaluation metrics for textual transfer between non-parallel corpora. *arXiv preprint arXiv:1810.11878.*

CodeSwitch-Reddit: Exploration of Written Multilingual Discourse in Online Discussion Forums[*]

Ella Rabinovich   **Masih Sultani**   **Suzanne Stevenson**

Dept. of Computer Science, University of Toronto, Canada

`{ella,masih,suzanne}@cs.toronto.edu`

Multilingual communities adopt various communicative strategies that navigate among multiple languages. One of the most notable of such strategies is *code-switching* (CS) – when a bilingual mixes two or more languages within a discourse, or even within a single utterance.

The sociolinguistic underpinnings of code-switching as an *oral* conversational strategy have been investigated extensively for many decades. By contrast, the analysis of *written* code-switching has only recently enjoyed a surge of interest, and remains seriously under-studied. Written text often differs greatly from conversation in its levels of both spontaneity and formality, and findings thus far have differed in their conclusions regarding the extent to which various genres of written text reflect the same communicative functions of CS as observed in oral conversation.

The growing popularity of social media and online discussion platforms poses both opportunities and new research questions regarding written code-switching. Global online forums, in which English is a lingua franca, not only draw on but create wide-reaching multilingual communities. The resulting communications lead to a wealth of data that potentially includes a large amount of code-switching across multiple language pairs. Moreover, communication on discussion platforms often resembles a hybrid between speech and more formal writing. These differing characteristics lead to new research questions regarding the extent to which findings from oral CS carry over to these online interactions.

Research is only just beginning to grapple with these issues. Computational work on code-switching in online venues has largely focused on the practical challenges that multiple interleaved languages pose to the application of standard NLP tools, rather than on the communicative purposes of CS. More broadly, computational investigation of the sociolinguistic aspects of written CS is dominated by studies conducted with a limited number of language-pairs and/or authors, thereby constraining the nature of questions that can be addressed with this data. Our work here seeks to address these gaps in the study of code-switching in online interactions. We begin by introducing the *CodeSwitch-Reddit* corpus: a novel, large, and diverse dataset of written code-switched productions, carefully curated from topical threads of multiple (including understudied) bilingual communities on the Reddit discussion platform. The corpus comprises over 135K CS messages by over 20K unique authors, spanning five language-pairs, with average post length of 75 tokens.

The uniform nature of our data (written communication from a single online discussion platform), as well as its ample size, pose novel opportunities for large-scale empirical investigation of research questions on code-switching – questions that have thus far been mainly addressed in the context of oral language. As a first study, here we explore fundamental questions about both the content and style of code-switched posts, as well as about the English proficiency level of authors who frequently code-switch.

The contribution of this work is twofold: First, we construct a novel code-switching corpus, whose size, number of language pairs, and diversity of content (consisting of posts of unrestricted length in a variety of topics) make it a desirable testbed for a range of research questions on CS in online discussion forums. Second, we demonstrate the usefulness of this dataset through an empirical investigation that sheds new light on postulated universals of CS – involving linguistic proficiency, style, and content – when inspected through the lens of online communication.

---

[*] Accepted for publication at EMNLP2019

Proceedings of the 2019 EMNLP Workshop W-NUT: The 5th Workshop on Noisy User-generated Text, page 446
Hong Kong, Nov 4, 2019. ©2019 Association for Computational Linguistics

Author Index

Association for Computational Linguistics
209 N. Eighth Street
Stroudsburg, Pennsylvania 18360

ISBN 978-1-7138-0088-0